REMEMBERING FOR THE FUTURE:

THE HOLOCAUST IN AN AGE OF GENOCIDE

REMEMBERING
FOR THE
FUTURE

The Holocaust in an Age of Genocide

Editors in Chief
John K. Roth and Elisabeth Maxwell

Editor
Margot Levy

Managing Editor
Wendy Whitworth

Volume 2
Ethics and Religion

palgrave

First published 2001 by
PALGRAVE
Houndmills, Basingstoke, Hampshire RG21 6XS and
175 Fifth Avenue, New York, N.Y. 10010
Companies and representatives throughout the world

PALGRAVE is the new global academic imprint of St. Martin's Press LLC
Scholarly and Reference Division and Palgrave Publishers Ltd (formerly
Macmillan Press Ltd).

ISBN 0–333–80486–4

This book is printed on paper suitable for recycling and
made from fully managed and sustained forest sources.

A catalogue record for this book is available
from the British Library.

Library of Congress Cataloging-in-Publication Data
is available from the Library of Congress.

10   9   8   7   6   5   4   3   2   1
10   09   08   07   06   05   04   03   02   01

Printed in Great Britain by
Antony Rowe Ltd., Chippenham

REMEMBERING FOR THE FUTURE:
THE HOLOCAUST IN AN AGE OF GENOCIDE

VOLUME ONE: HISTORY

VOLUME TWO: ETHICS AND RELIGION

VOLUME THREE: MEMORY

CONTENTS

VOLUME TWO: ETHICS AND RELIGION

A list of the contents of all three volumes will be found in Volume 1

PLENARY ADDRESSES

What happened to ethics? Where was religion? The Holocaust and genocide raise those questions, for whenever mass murder takes place ethics and religion are found wanting. As a consequence, what ethics and religion ought to be after Auschwitz, what they should become in an age of genocide, looms large as well. Echoing all the plenary addresses that introduce this Remembering for the Future volume on ethics and religion, the ethicist John T. Pawlikowski keynotes the articles that follow when he observes that 'I am obliged to probe the implications of Nazi ideology for contemporary human self-understanding.'

INTERFAITH DIALOGUE:

A Message from His Eminence Professor Dr Damaskinos Papandreou, Metropolitan of Switzerland, Director of the Orthodox Centre of the Ecumenical Patriarchate (Chambésy-Geneva)

THE YEAR 2000 is for all of us a privileged moment to reconsider the future with hope. The dawn of a millennium always bears a promise. However, as it is clearly stated in the title of the Conference, the goal is not to dream of a 'glorious' future, but rather to draw the conclusions from a painful past in order to build a better future, without hatred, without genocide. In order to achieve this you have called upon historical science, religion, ethics and also education and culture. The past shows us that science alone cannot guarantee peace and love of one's neighbour; neither can ethics or religion, or even culture, for they all can be enlisted into the service of fanaticism or hatred.

By inviting us to address this message, you have invited us to a dialogue. As you know, this dialogue between Jews and Christians for many years has been close to our hearts. Since 1976 we have not ceased to take all possible steps to see this dialogue develop and gradually overcome prejudices which nourish distrust and intolerance. For this reason we have twice organized meetings between the World Jewish Congress and the Orthodox Centre of the Ecumenical Patriarchate, in 1977 in Luzern in Switzerland and in 1979 in Bucharest in Romania. A third international academic meeting on the theme 'Continuity and Renewal' between Judaism and Orthodoxy took place in Athens in 1993. We met again in Israel in 1998 over the question of 'The Encounter of Christian Orthodoxy and Judaism with Modernity'.

Interfaith dialogue is necessary to confront violence in the future.

By its very nature and spiritual mission in the world, religion is and 'should be' the mirror of heavenly peace on earth. In this sense, religion is 'and should be' the most important factor for peaceful coexistence among peoples, regardless of their religious convictions. However, religion is incarnate in human society and society receives the spiritual message of religion without abandoning its own specific cultural heritage and without being emancipated from the inevitable tensions of the world. Moreover, religion does not abolish man's relations with the world, but it should be in harmony with its teaching regarding man's relations with God.

Thus religion takes care of numerous needs of earthly life for its believers, but should never dissociate them from the spiritual content of its teaching relating to the balance of man's relations to God and to the world. In this context, religion alone cannot impose peace or prevent war between peoples, given that its spiritual message cannot always curb the tensions of the world. But through its teaching, it can ceaselessly enlighten man about peace, social justice and sincere cooperation in relations between peoples.

It is this educational mission that religions should jointly pursue in the future. For memory is not only recollection; it is also fidelity, that is to say, promise. To remember the Holocaust and the genocides which have darkened this 20th century – of which we are so proud in other respects for discoveries in the material realm – is therefore first of all to show how man can go astray when he breaks the sacred links which unite him to God his Creator, whatever his faith may be. But it is also to encourage him to rediscover the value of these links for the creation of peace.

Peoples of all religions have lived through the tragic experience of war, but have never ceased to aspire to peace in liberty and justice. The three monotheistic religions – Judaism, Christianity and Islam – certainly contain within their teaching all the necessary founding elements of their responsibility, both for the peaceful coexistence of their faithful in the same world and for an absolute respect of the religious freedom of believers of other religions, although this common precept has not always been respected in the course of the historical tensions which have sometimes disrupted even social relations.

Historical confrontations between the religions usually had a polemical or apologetic character, aiming to establish the superiority of one tradition in regard to another or to justify their particular elements; at the same time, religions also attested their close spiritual relations through their indisputable reference to God's plan for the salvation of man. If this rapprochement was facilitated in the course of the 18th century by intensified metaphysical anguish concerning God confronted with common problems deriving from the questioning of religious faith, it is certain that contemporary anguish concerning the sacred character of the human being and the integrity of the creation constitutes an even more pressing demand for the rapprochement and collaboration of religions.

God and man are the two irremovable poles of the divine plan and the spiritual history of humanity. This dialectic dismisses the confining of God to his metaphysical transcendence and his ideological disappearance behind the models of anthropocentric indifferentism or anti-theism proper to our age. Both of these extreme attitudes disfigure man's relations with God or with the world and at the same time change the authentic content of the common religious faith concerning the unity and fraternity of the human race according to the reason for divine creation.

The consequences of these hermeneutical aberrations were in fact grievous both for the history of Judaism and Christianity. In contemporary societies in which antagonism and emulation are necessary conditions for survival through the latest socio-political developments which have brought peoples closer together, we should all insist on what unites us, and respect and understand what separates us. That can only take place through dynamic and creative education, broadening man's mind and liberating him from the patterns and prejudices of the past.

When we succeed in subjugating our individual interest to the common interest and in making our own the problems of others; when the powerful understand that it is their duty (or rather their interest) to help towards the parallel development of peoples and countries, which today face insurmountable problems as a result of the imperfections of their social organization, economy and educational system, then we shall be sure that no holocaust will ever happen again. For alongside the holocaust of human lives, there is also the holocaust of ideas and minds, the holocaust of values, of the environment, of the quality of life.

Interfaith dialogues aim to remove the dangerous confusion between religion and other national or political objectives. All religions, even if they have different approaches, are aware that liberty, peace and justice are gifts of God to man, whilst war is contrary to

God's will. All religions are aware that they alone have never been able in the past, and are still today unable, to provoke a war between peoples. Yet constantly contemporary armed conflicts are deemed to be religious conflicts, when we know perfectly well that for the most part these are political manipulations.

It is evident that today, perhaps more than in the past, interfaith dialogues represent an inner need of religions to reveal their true awareness of themselves, and also a supreme duty with regard to modern man, who suffers and feels the tragic absurdity of the current crisis.

It was as a response to this pressing need that the Foundation for Interreligious and Intercultural Research and Dialogue was founded in Geneva in 1999, by eminent representatives of the three religions of the Book. Its mandate is specifically to determine the most authentic message that the three monotheistic religions, Judaism, Christianity and Islam, can address to the world of today in view of the 21st century. Its aim is to be an instrument of peace in the service of humanity. To achieve rapprochement between the three monotheistic religions through dialogue, the Foundation has judged it necessary to begin by 'purifying the memory'; that is to ensure that the misunderstandings and dramas of the past should be overcome, and with them the prejudices rooted in inadequate, even truncated, information. This exercise should also concern the institutions of the three religions and the people who work within them, so that the latter learn to know and respect each other.

To purify the memory is to allow the future to be constituted on a sound basis; it is also to go back to the sources. To show its willingness to return to these three holy sources, the Foundation publishes, on the threshold of the new millennium, the original text of the Books of the three religious monotheistic traditions in a single set, thus offering everyone the opportunity to draw therefrom. But the Foundation also works in the longer-term towards religious and cultural rapprochement, through research and dialogue, by raising media awareness and through education. It also intends to add its contribution to the joint edifice: this arduous task which constitutes the construction of the future on the basis of a past which is remembered, but reconciled in the present.

QUO VADIS, HUMANITY?
THE HOLOCAUST AS CONTINUING CHALLENGE
FOR RELIGION AND ETHICS

John T. Pawlikowski

Plenary Address, Oxford, 18 July 2000

W E H A V E witnessed a remarkable upsurge of Holocaust research and educational programmes since the initial Remembering for the Future Conference here in Oxford in 1988. But the concern that I have is that, despite all the important research, there remains a real question whether the Holocaust will yet leave a permanent and decisive impact on how we conceive humanity's role in the future. We now know so much more about the details of the Holocaust than we did when we met in 1988. But has all that knowledge helped us to better understand our role as human agents responsible for the survival of humanity and the rest of creation? So far I do not believe we have successfully transferred the religious and ethical implications of the Holocaust to society at large.

As a scholar in ethics committed to a particular religious tradition, I am obliged to probe the implications of Nazi ideology for contemporary human self-understanding. I do so conscious of the need always to remember its specific victims, for as Elie Wiesel has so ably put it, 'to forget the victims is indeed to kill them a second time.' I do so conscious as well of the need to connect my reflection to the 'details' of the Holocaust so well uncovered by my colleagues in historical studies. But I remain convinced that acts of Holocaust memory and in-depth studies of the Holocaust, as crucial as they may remain, will leave us bereft of the understanding we desperately require today if the human community and the creation with which we are intertwined are to survive the challenges that lie before us.

I was recently struck by two interconnected realities. The first was the unveiling of Sue, the most intact dinosaur remains, at the Field Museum in Chicago. The other was a film I viewed on a recent flight to London on the total destruction of the great Mayan civilization in the Americas. Both brought to light the disappearance of powerful forces in creation. Both reminded me that brute strength and power are no guarantee of future survival. The Mayan example, in particular, impressed upon me the very real possibility of great civilizations totally vanishing.

I raise these examples because the Nazi ideology as I see it was perhaps the strongest assertion of power and control that we have experienced in the history of humanity. It involved the meshing of powerful military force and theological assertions of unlimited human power to shape the future of humanity. It claimed that religion was dead as an effective counterforce to the assertion of human power. Steven Katz is absolutely correct in his contention that Nazi ideology cannot be forced into traditional categories of evil. It represented a new phase in human self-understanding, one that carried within it the seeds of creational destruction on a global scale. In my judgment the religious community has so far failed to respond to the challenge that Nazi ideology poses for human responsibility. Only a few scholars such as Irving Greenberg and Richard Rubenstein have addressed the challenge in its very depth. Too many have simply tried to return to 'religion as usual' after the Holocaust, reasserting traditional covenenantal religion. One example is David Hartman, whom I greatly admire in many areas, but who I believe has done us a great disservice by insisting that we only mourn the victims of the Holocaust and not try to reinterpret religion today in light of its profound ideological challenge. If religion is to produce a deep ethical counterforce to the ideology of the Holocaust, it cannot do so by merely reasserting biblical religious notions. While not ignoring biblical tradition, it must seek to build a new understanding of the human responsibility for the survival of creation, an understanding that will refashion significantly the respective roles of human and divine agency in the exercise of this responsibility. Irving Greenberg may have gone too far in asserting an almost total role reversal in human and divine responsibility after the Holocaust, but I applaud him for his boldness in raising a question that far too many have simply ignored.

Back in the early seventies two futurists introduced us to a fundamentally new reality with which religious ethics has yet adequately to grapple. Victor Ferkiss, a political scientist out of the Catholic tradition, and Hans Jonas, a social philosopher of Jewish background, served warning that humankind had reached a new threshold in its evolutionary journey. The human community now faced a situation whose potential for destruction was equal to its possibilities for new levels of human creativity and dignity. What path humanity would follow was a decision that rested with the next several generations. Neither divine intervention nor the arbitrary forces of nature would determine the choice in the end. And the decision would have lasting impact, well beyond the lifespan of those who are destined to make it. It would, in fact, determine what forms of life, if any, will continue to survive on this planet.

Ferkiss's 1974 volume *The Future of Technological Civilization* put the late 20th-century challenge to humankind in these words: 'Man has...achieved virtually godlike powers over himself, his society, and his physical environment. As a result of his scientific and technological achievements, he has the power to alter or destroy the human race and its physical habitat.'

Hans Jonas, in a groundbreaking speech in Los Angeles in 1972 at a gathering of learned societies of religion and subsequently in published writings, conveyed essentially the same message as Ferkiss. Ours is the very first generation to have to face the question of basic creational survival. In the past, there was no human destructive behaviour from which we could not recover. But today, we have reached the point through technological advancement where this principal no longer obtains. Humankind now seems increasingly capable of actions which inflict terminal damage on the whole of creation and raise serious questions about the future of human life itself. Buckminister Fuller did not exaggerate the profundity of the choice before us when he asserted that contemporary humanity now stands on a threshold between utopia and oblivion.

For me, the Holocaust represents the clearest contemporary example of the fundamental challenge now facing humanity as described by Ferkiss, Jonas and Fuller. I have emphasized in a number of published essays that in the final analysis I view the Holocaust as inaugurating a new era in human self-awareness and human possibility, an era capable of producing unprecedented destruction or unparalleled hope. With the rise of Nazism the mass extermination of human life in a guiltless fashion became thinkable and technologically feasible. The door was now ajar for dispassionate torture and the murder of millions not out of xenophobic fear, but through a calculated effort to reshape history supported by intellectual argumentation from the best and brightest minds in the society. It was an attempt, Emil Fackenheim has argued, to wipe out the 'divine image' in history. 'The murder camp,' Fackenheim has insisted, 'was not an accidental by-product of the Nazi empire. It was its essence.'

The basic challenge of the Holocaust lies in our changed perception of the relationship between God and humanity and its implications for the basis of moral behaviour. What emerges as a central reality from the study of the Holocaust is the Nazis' sense of a new Aryan humanity, freed from the moral restraints previously imposed by religious beliefs and capable of exerting virtually unlimited power in the shaping of the world and its inhabitants. In a somewhat indirect, though still powerful, way, the Nazis had proclaimed the death of God as a governing force in the universe. In pursuit of their objectives, the Nazis became convinced that all the 'dregs of humanity,' first and foremost the Jews, but also Poles, Gypsies, Gays and the disabled, had to be eliminated or at least their influence on culture and human development significantly curtailed.

The late Uriel Tal captured as well as anyone the basic theological challenge presented by the Holocaust. In his understanding, the so-called 'Final Solution' had as its ultimate objective the total transformation of human values. Its stated intent was liberating humanity from all previous moral ideals and codes. When the liberating process was complete, humanity would be rescued once and all from subjection to God-belief and its related notions of moral responsibility, redemption, sin and revelation. Nazi ideology sought to transform theological ideas into exclusively anthropological and political concepts. In Tal's perspective, the Nazis can be said to have adopted a kind of 'incarnational' theology, but not in the New Testament sense of the term. Rather, for the Nazis, 'God becomes man in a political sense as a member of the aryan race whose highest representative on earth is the Führer.'

If we accept this interpretation of the ultimate implication of Nazism, as I basically do, we are confronted with a major theological challenge. How does the human community properly appropriate the genuine sense of human liberation that was at the core of Nazi ideology without surrendering its soul to massive evil? However horrendous their legacy, the Nazis were perceptive in at least one respect. They correctly understood that some basic changes were under way in human consciousness. The impact of the new science and technology, with its underlying assumption of freedom, was beginning to provide humankind on a mass scale with a Promethean-type experience of escape from prior moral chains. People were starting to perceive, however dimly, an enhanced sense of dignity and autonomy that went well beyond what Christian theology had traditionally conceded.

Traditional theological concepts that had shaped much of the Christian moral perspective, notions such as divine punishment, hell, divine wrath and providence were losing some of the hold they had exercised over moral decision making since biblical times. Christian theology had tended to accentuate the omnipotence of God which in turn intensified the impotence of the human person and the rather inconsequential role played by the human community in maintaining the sustainability of creation. The Nazis totally rejected this previous relationship. In fact, they were literally trying to turn it upside down.

In this era of postmodernity the issue of the responsible use of human freedom is coupled with an alarming decrease in a sense of social commitment. How do we instill in people a renewed sense of human commitment that so marked the rescuers during the Holocaust? Is this to be only a rare occurrence? We saw what the absence of such commitment meant during the Nazi era. Its marginalization in the 20th century could prove disastrous for the very survival of the planet. And how do we make social commitment a widespread reality in a world where global social systems are continuing to erode possibilities of direct human responsibility.

The historian Peter Hayes of Northwestern University has done some of the most important work in recent years on the erosion of personal responsibility within Nazi culture, particularly among German businessmen. His studies have served as a warning with regard to a similar situation taking place in society today in the name of globalization. 'What else can I do?' has in fact become a stock phrase in the vocabulary of global capitalism. The dynamics of the marketplace must reign supreme no matter what the cost in human terms, no matter that, as a recent European Union report has shown, some 250 million children around the world are used to support this system, living in conditions in many instances of virtual slavery. Pope John Paul II, in what may prove in the end to be his most prophetic statement, has warned that the global ideology of the market, which has tended to replace the competing Cold War ideologies in recent years, cannot ensure the preservation of human dignity. 'The rapid advance toward the globalization of economic and financial systems also illustrates the urgent need to establish who is responsible for guaranteeing the global common good and the exercise of economic and social rights.' In an address to a Vatican meeting of scholars and political leaders convened by Pope John Paul II at Castel Gandolfo in August 1998 former American national security advisor Zbigniew Brzezinski argued along much the same lines as the Pope himself, calling for an increasing sensitivity to social respons-ibility. 'That sensitivity,' he maintained, 'has to be as important a consideration as efficiency and performance in the determination of economic decisions and guiding economic development.'

The so-called 'Nazi ethic' has opened up what unquestionably is the most decisive moral question of this new millennium. How can the human community maintain a sense of human responsibility in a global system of human organization? The Holocaust has shown us how destructive a failure to address this question head-on can be for human and creational survival.

Ethicians and religious scholars will also have to grapple with two other major issues in light of the Holocaust. The first is the ever-increasing enhancement of human power. Soon after the Holocaust the Catholic philosopher Romano Guardini spoke words in this regard that remain as prophetic as when they were first uttered: 'In the coming epoch, the essential problem will no longer be that of increasing power – though power will continue to increase at an even swifter tempo – but of curbing it. The core of the new epoch's intellectual task will be to integrate power into life in such a way that man can employ power without forfeiting his humanity, or to surrender his humanity to power and perish.'

We shall also have to confront the vitalistic side of humanity. The regeneration of the vitalistic side of humanity, albeit in a high destructive direction, stood at the heart of the Nazi enterprise. The historian J.L. Talmon once described Nazi ideology as the denial of any 'final station of redemption in history' which gave birth to a cult of power and vitality as needs in themselves. No scholar has made this point as clearly as the late George Mosse, who spent considerable time examining the impact of Nazi public liturgies during his scholarly career. While it verges on the obscene to give the Nazis credit for anything, Mosse's writings demonstrate that the Nazi leadership was extremely perceptive in recognizing the influence of symbolism in human life. We need to develop what the psychologist Robert Moore has termed 'ritual containment' in human society. In light of the Holocaust we can no longer afford to give scant attention to the vitalistic dimension of humanity, to reduce it simply to the realm of popular cultural expression, if we hope to develop the sense of human responsibility to which the Holocaust summons us.

As I close, let me repeat my initial assertion. Studying the details of the Holocaust and continuing to memorialize its victims remains a sacred task. But we shall ultimately fail the victims of the Nazis if we do not choose life over death, as Deuteronomy instructs us, by wrestling with the ultimate ideological implication of Nazism for our time. In the Slovak Pavilion at Expo 2000 in Hanover, Germany, there is a powerful film that is in part based on the Holocaust. The film's title asks a question that remains our question after the Holocaust, *Quo vadis humanity?*

RELIGION AND THE UNIQUENESS OF THE HOLOCAUST

Richard L. Rubenstein

Plenary Address, Oxford, 18 July 2000

F EW EVENTS of the 20th century have been the object of as much continuing popular interest as the Holocaust. When the United States Holocaust Memorial Museum opened its doors in April 1993, museum officials estimated that one million people would visit the museum during its first year. In reality, approximately two million people visited the museum during that period, two-thirds of whom were non-Jews. As of 1 June 2000, a total of 14.2 million people had visited the museum. It is difficult to account for this interest simply in terms of the number of Holocaust victims or the fact that the *Shoah* was perpetrated by the government of one of the best educated and technologically proficient nations in the world, although that fact cannot be discounted. There have been many other large-scale, demographic catastrophes perpetrated by human beings in the 20th century. Nevertheless, it is unlikely that a museum devoted to Stalin's murders, the Armenian genocide of 1915 or the massacres in former Yugoslavia or Rwanda would consistently draw so large a number of visitors as Washington's Holocaust Memorial Museum.

What then accounts for the persistence of interest in the Holocaust more than half a century after the end of World War II? It is, I believe, the fact that, more than any other 20th-century disaster, the Holocaust resonates with the religio-mythic traditions of biblical religion, the dominant religious inheritance of western civilization. Put differently, the response to the Holocaust reflects the pervasiveness in the Judaeo-Christian west of what Stephen R. Haynes has called the 'witness people myth', the belief that whatever happens to the Jews, for good or ill, is an expression of God's providential justice and, as such, is a sign 'for God's church.'[1] According to Haynes, the witness-people myth is 'a deep structure in the Christian imagination ... a complex of ideas and symbols that, often pre-critically and unconsciously, informs ideas about Jews among persons who share a cultural heritage.' The myth has its roots in the biblical doctrine that God has chosen Israel as his people by bestowing upon them a covenant stipulating that Israel's fidelity would be rewarded by divine protection, as surely as infidelity would be harshly punished. As we know, in the aftermath of the Fall of Jerusalem in 70 C.E., the rabbis interpreted that event as God's punishment of a sinful Israel for failing to keep the commandments ordained in Scripture. Christian thinkers of the same period agreed that the Fall of Jerusalem was divine punishment, but they argued that the rejection of Jesus as Lord and Messiah was God's motive for laying waste to Jerusalem and the Holy Temple. According to the Christian interpretation, the Jews could only regain God's favour by truly accepting baptism. As long as they refused, God would condemn them to the suffering, humiliation and indignity of exile. The suffering of the 'witness people' was thus understood as a confirmation of Christian faith in which the Jews were seen as *justly* paying a bitter price for their refusal to accept the truth as understood by Christianity.

Given the enormous weight both Judaism and Christianity have traditionally placed on the interpretation of Jewish disaster as an expression of God's justice and providence, it was inevitable that both Jews and Christians would respond to the Holocaust in accordance with their respective traditions. It is, for example, possible for believing Christians to view the Armenian genocide or the Pol Pot massacres in Kampuchea as purely secular events without raising the question of whether they possess some transcendent religious meaning. Not so, the Holocaust. The Holocaust almost inevitably elicits some form of religious interpretation at every level of intellectual sophistication. This phenomenon is evident in such questions as 'How could a good God permit . . . ?' and 'Can we believe in God after Auschwitz?' It can also be seen in the rise of Holocaust theology as a distinctive discipline among a large number of post-World War II Jewish theologians and a smaller but influential group of Christian thinkers. The latter include John Pawlikowski, Paul van Buren, Franklin Littell, Alice and Roy Eckardt and John K. Roth. Never before in Jewish history had there been a catastrophe of such magnitude and if one believes, as do most Jews and Christians, in a God who is the ultimate Author of the drama of history, then the question of divine involvement in the Holocaust is bound to arise.

No matter how the question of God's involvement is resolved, neither academically trained theologians nor ordinary laypersons can entirely ignore it. For some, the Holocaust is *ipso facto* proof that a sinful Israel had been justly punished by a righteous God. Many others – both Jewish and Christian – are unable either to abandon some semblance of faith in the biblical God-who-acts-in-history or to assert that the Holocaust was in any sense God's righteous judgement. Unable to abandon either position, they are impaled on the horns of a dilemma, made more painful by their respective liturgical traditions, both of which stress the righteous and saving acts of the Lord.

Most academically trained historians argue that events like the Holocaust can be adequately explained in terms of the political, social and material interests of the perpetrators. Undoubtedly, much can be learned from a socio-economic reading of history. Nevertheless, such a reading underestimates the power of religion and myth to define cultural reality. The overwhelming majority of human beings understand the world in terms of the way their religion and culture define reality for them. Moreover, a given society's religio-mythic inheritance is normally opaque to critical scrutiny by its members because that same inheritance is a very important part of the interpretive matrix by which the same individuals are able to comprehend reality.

Even in a relatively secular age, the power of religion to define reality largely determines the experiences available to Jew and Christian alike, at least in relation to each other. According to Haynes, most Christians can be said to *dwell within the witness people myth* and to comprehend Jewish history and experience in and through it.[2] That is why the deicide accusation has been so potent a force throughout the ages. That is also why the image of Judas has played so important a role in determining the way Jews have been perceived by Christians, especially in times of stress.[3]

Thus, the fate of the Jews as a distinctive people is too closely connected with the religio-mythic inheritance of both Judaism and Christianity for the Holocaust to have lacked profound religious significance for either believing Jews or Christians, especially at the level of unreflective, pre-theoretical consciousness. The Holocaust is linked to the Fall of Jerusalem in 586 B.C.E. to the Babylonians and in 70 C.E. to the Romans. More than any other event in modern history, it is also linked to the response those events elicited from the prophets, the rabbis, the authors of the New Testament and the Church Fathers.

No other instance of genocide or attempted genocide in modern times elicits associations so directly linked to the Bible and its worldview as does the Holocaust. Other peoples have depicted themselves as the 'Christ among the nations' and have interpreted their suffering as an assault on God's people, but in no other instance did the event occur to those who were directly linked to the biblical drama of God's involvement in history as the Jews. More people died under Stalin than in the Holocaust, albeit a lesser proportion of the peoples of the Soviet Union perished than was the case with Europe's Jewish population. 'Ethnic cleansing' in former Yugoslavia, and the recent massacres in Rwanda are horrendous examples of mass slaughter and inhumanity. Nevertheless, these events do not have the same religio-mythic overtones for Jews and Christians as does the Holocaust.

My conviction that the religious dimension is responsible for the uniqueness of the Holocaust has been strengthened by frequent visits to Asia. Starting in the late 1970s, I have visited Japan and Korea more than fifteen times. As I came to know Japanese, Chinese and Korean scholars, it became apparent that, except for the Christians among them, the Holocaust had very little meaning for Asians. It did not happen on their continent and, terrible as it was, it was perceived as simply one of the many bloody chapters in human history of no distinctive importance in and of itself. The scholars were by no means indifferent to human suffering. Nevertheless, except for Asian Christians, the Holocaust was seen as a purely western secular event.

Most Asians do not respond to Jews, either positively or negatively, in as emotionally complex a manner as do westerners. For example, even Japanese anti-Semites were largely incapable of the kind of visceral anti-Jewish hatred that pervaded much of Europe in the years leading up to and including World War II.[4] Japanese anti-Semitism first became a significant force in the aftermath of the Bolshevik Revolution when the 75,000 man Japanese Expeditionary Force and its White Russian allies were defeated by the Bolsheviks in Eastern Siberia and forced to retreat to Manchuria. The Japanese found credible the White Russian explanation of the Bolshevik Revolution. According to the defeated White Russian officers who fought alongside of the Japanese, the Bolshevik Revolution was allegedly the result of a secret Jewish conspiracy for world domination. As 'proof', they offered the infamous forgery, *The Protocols of the Elders of Zion*, which was speedily translated into Japanese. In addition to finding the Bolshevik system repugnant, with their profound reverence for the Emperor the Japanese were horrified at the murder of Tsar Nicholas II and his family by the Bolsheviks. Convinced that the Jews were deeply implicated in the Russian Revolution, a group of Japanese officers and ultra-nationalists began to study Jews and Judaism in the 1920s. They concluded that many of the disorders brought about by modernity were deliberate elements in a grandiose Jewish plot. Although the Japanese group saw the Jews as a potential danger to Japan, in the 1930s they decided on a radically different strategy in dealing with them than that of the National Socialists: if the Jews were as powerful and as potentially dangerous as the *Protocols* alleged, they were to be dealt with with great care in order to turn their alleged abilities and influence into an advantage for Japan.

In the 1920s and 30s Captain Norihigo Yasue and Naval Lieutenant Koreshige Inuzuka were regarded as among Japan's leading 'experts' on Jews and Judaism. Both had been attached to the White Russian military command during the unsuccessful campaign against the Bolsheviks in the Russian Far East. It was Yasue who translated the *Protocols* into Japanese. He was also the author of several tracts warning of a Jewish conspiracy to take over the world. In 1927 the Foreign Ministry borrowed Yasue from the Army and sent him to Europe and the Middle East where he met with Zionist leaders such as David Ben Gurion, Chaim Weizman and Menahem Ussishkin as well as rabbis and ordinary Jews. He was impressed by the kibbutzim which he believed the Jews would use to colonize the countries they would eventually conquer. Nevertheless, he reported honestly to his superiors that he heard no hint of any conspiracy for world domination while among Palestine's Jews.[5]

Like Yasue, Naval Lieutenant Inuzuka was as convinced of a Jewish world conspiracy as any hard-core Nazi, but he and his fellow Japanese 'experts' reacted very differently. In a report to the Naval General Staff on 18 January 1939 Inuzuka spelled out the difference: '[The Jews are] just like a *fugu* (blowfish) dish. It is very delicious but unless one knows well how to cook it, it may prove fatal to his life.'[6] The *fugu* fish is regarded by the Japanese as a great delicacy when properly prepared. There is, however, no margin for error. An improperly prepared *fugu* can result in almost instantaneous death. Nevertheless, the 'experts' were convinced that they knew how to prepare this particular *fugu*.

Yasue was also a key figure in protecting the 17,000 Jews residing in Shanghai during the war. In July 1942 Colonel Joseph Meisinger, the Gestapo chief for Japan, China and Manchukuo who had served in conquered Warsaw in 1939, and two other German officials met with local authorities in Shanghai to demand that the Japanese exterminate their Jewish charges 'like garbage' on Rosh Hashanah.[7] Shanghai's Japanese authorities were inclined at first to accede to Meisinger's demands, but Vice Consul Mitsugi Shibata found both Meisinger and his proposals revolting. He took the highly unusual step of warning the leaders of the Shanghai Jewish community of their peril. He urged them to use their contacts in the Japanese government to thwart Meisinger.[8] The Shanghai Jews got word to Dr. Abraham Kaufman, a leading Jew in Harbin, Manchuria, who enjoyed the favour of some of Japan's most important leaders. When Kaufman used his contacts to apprise Foreign Minister Matsuoka and Colonel Norihiro Yasue of the impending danger, the Japanese government rejected Meisinger's proposals.[9] To appease its German ally, the government decreed on 18 February 1943 that 'stateless refugees' would be confined to a ghetto in the Hongkew section of Shanghai, one of the poorest sections of the metropolis. Nevertheless, within Hongkew, the Jews were not harmed.

In spite of persistent German efforts to bring Japan's policy into line with National Socialism on the Jewish question, more than 20,000 Jews found a safe haven during the war in Japanese-occupied Shanghai, several other Chinese cities controlled by Japan and the puppet-state of Manchukuo (Manchuria). With a few exceptions some of Japan's leading anti-Semites were among the most effective protectors of the Jewish refugees. Protecting Jews under their own names, they followed a consistent pattern of writing and translating anti-Semitic tracts under pseudonyms.

There have been periods when Japan has been flooded with anti-Semitic literature.[10] World War II was such a period. In the late 1980s and 90s, there was another upsurge in the dissemination of anti-Semitic literature. Nevertheless, Japanese anti-Jewish feeling has never had the emotionally-overladen impact that has characterized European anti-Semitism. The reason is fairly obvious: The emotions engendered by the Judaeo-Christian rivalry are largely absent among the Japanese. The overwhelming majority of Japanese are not Christians influenced by the witness-people myth. Hence, they do not perceive the Jews as deicides or Jewish history as the continuing record of divine chastisement for failure to accept Christ as Lord.

The Holocaust is not a unique event for the Japanese or for most other Asians. The same cannot be said of the western world where it is difficult to extricate the Holocaust from the matrix of meanings concerning Jews and Judaism to be found in the biblical religions. To repeat, as a catastrophic event in Jewish history, the Holocaust can only be compared to the Fall of Jerusalem in ancient times. Inevitably, it elicits a religious response as did that earlier catastrophe. This is especially true in the United States with its pervasive biblical tradition. For a very large number of Americans, by no means all of them Fundamentalists or Dispensationalists, the Bible is a living document and contemporary events tend to be comprehended in its terms. Moreover, far more Christians than care to say so in public regard the Holocaust 'as a sign of God's providence', as did the early Christians at the time of the Fall of Jerusalem to the Romans. Some see the event as a precursor of Christ's Second Coming; others, as noted, see the *Shoah* as God's punishment for Israel's continuing refusal to accept faith in Christ.

In spite of National Socialism's unremittingly racist anti-Semitism, the motives of many Europeans for either seeking or passively approving the elimination of the Jews from their midst were as much religious as racial. Apart from the Jews, in Europe's formative centuries all those who rejected baptism were either expelled or exterminated.[11] For example, in 1995 Norway celebrated a millenium of adherence to Christian religion. It is instructive, however, to remember how Christianity won the day in that country: According to the Norse sagas, in 995 King Olaf I Tryggvason returned from Dublin to give Norwegians a stark choice: death or baptism.[12]

Put differently, the king was offering his subjects the choice of death or becoming Europeans. For the king and for Europe's princes and prelates in the centuries that followed, the price of admission to full participation in European civilization was membership in the Christian Church. Moreover, today, no less than yesterday, few aspects of European civilization – art, literature, music, philosophy, religion, politics, its universities, its status hierarchies – can be entirely divorced from its Christian roots. Even European secularism is an unintended consequence of Europe's Christian culture, as the German social theorist Max Weber and others have recognized.[13]

To this day, genuine religious diversity is by no means highly valued in many European countries. Whenever a group or a movement arose that was perceived as constituting a serious challenge to the primacy of Christianity in Europe, whether it was the external challenge of Islam or the internal challenge of the heretical Cathar movement in 13th-century Southern France, the response of European Christendom was to drive away or eliminate the non-believers. Before the Enlightenment and the French Revolution, Jews were tolerated in parts of Europe as long as they were perceived as materially useful but lacking serious political or cultural influence. After the French Revolution, that perception no longer held and it was only a question of time before they were eliminated by expulsion or worse.

Admittedly, the motives for initiating the Holocaust were by no means entirely religious. Nevertheless, the event did achieve an important goal for most conservative European Christians, the elimination for all practical purposes of the Jewish demographic presence and Jewish religio-cultural influence within European Christendom. In vast areas of Central and Eastern Europe the surviving Jews constitute little more than a living museum, to be exhibited or suppressed as suits the momentary political objectives of the governing elite.

NOTES

1 See Stephen R. Haynes, *Jews and the Christian Imagination: Reluctant Witness* (Louisville: Westminster/John Knox Press, 1995), Introduction, pp.8ff.

2 Haynes, *op. cit.*, p.9.

3 On the influence of Judas on Christian perceptions of Jews, see Richard L. Rubenstein, *After Auschwitz: History, Theology and Contemporary Judaism*, 2nd ed. (Baltimore: Johns Hopkins University Press, 1992), pp.21–22, 45, 50–51.

4 For an examination of Japanese attitudes towards Jews during World War II, see See David Kranzler, *Japanese, Nazis and Jews: The Jewish Refugee Community of Shanghai, 1935–1945* (Hoboken: KTAV, 1988)

5 Marvin Tokayer and Mary Swartz, *The Fugu Plan: The Untold Story of the Japanese and the Jews During World War II* (New York: Paddington Press, 1979), p.49.

6 Cited by Kranzler, *op. cit.*, p.169.

7 Tokayer and Swartz, *op. cit.*, pp.222–26.

8 Shibata was imprisoned and dismissed from the Consular Service when his activities became known to local Japanese authorities. See Kranzler, *op. cit.*, pp.478–79.

9 The sources disagree concerning Col. Yasue's first name. Kranzler, *op. cit.*, lists the name as 'Senko.' Tetsu Kohno lists the name as 'Norihigo.' I have accepted the latter. See Tetsu Kohno, 'The Jewish Question in Japan, 'The Jewish Question in Japan', in *The Jewish Journal of Sociology*, vol. XXIX, no.1, June 1987.

10 See See David G. Goodman, 'Japanese Anti-Semitism', *The World and I*, November 1987.

11 On this point, see Robert Bartlett, *The Making of Europe: Conquest, Colonization and Cultural Change 950–1350* (Princeton: Princeton University Press, 1993).

12 'Norway Celebrates a Millenium of Christianity Despite Fires', *New York Times*, 4 June 1995.

13 For a brief discussion of the Christian roots of secularization, see Peter Berger, *The Sacred Canopy: Elements of a Sociological Theory of Religion* (Garden City: Anchor Books, 1969) pp.105–26.

ETHICAL CHOICES

Apart from human choices, genocide would not exist and there would have been no Holocaust. Where human self-understanding is concerned, arguably nothing is more important than knowing – and acting upon – the difference between choices that are ethical and those that are not. Drawing on history and philosophy, politics, culture and religion, the articles in this section help us, in the words of the philosopher Leonard Grob, to 'rethink the relationship between morality and power'.

Articles on related themes will also be found in the next section, on Rescue.

THE MASK OF ADMINISTRATIVE EVIL:
REMEMBERING THE PAST, FORGETTING THE PRESENT

Guy B. Adams and Danny L. Balfour

How we remember our collective past is a crucial element in present and future behaviour. Because memory consists largely of a reconstruction of events, we are, to an extent, able to choose how and what we remember. Our memories are constructed by the salience of powerful images and the desire to forget that which disturbs or challenges our collective identity. During the 20th century, modern civilizations have been reluctant to remember past involvement in genocide and other dehumanizing events. More specifically, we choose how to remember genocide, often in a relatively narrow and self-serving way.[1]

As the following cases illustrate, this tendency toward selective remembering is reinforced by the masked nature of administrative evil, which has been part and parcel of most crimes against humanity in the last century. Administrative evil thrives on attenuated memory, on limited historical consciousness. A future without still more genocide, without greater violations of human rights, depends, in part, on our ability to recognize administrative evil, and more broadly, to remember in a way that does not escape taking responsibility for both the intended and unintended consequences of administrative action.

WHAT IS ADMINISTRATIVE EVIL?

We begin with the premise that evil is inherent in the human condition. As one examines human history, clearly there have been many great and good deeds and achievements, and real progress in the quality of at least many human's lives. We also see century after century of mind-numbing, human-initiated violence, betrayal and tragedy. Those instances when humans inflict pain and suffering on other human beings, we call *evil*.

Evil is defined in the *Oxford English Dictionary* as the antithesis of good in all its principal senses. A more practical definition of evil has been provided by Katz:

> ...behavior that deprives innocent people of their humanity, from small scale assaults on a person's dignity to outright murder...[this definition] focuses on how people behave toward one another – where the behavior of one person, or an aggregate of persons is destructive to others.[2]

This behavioural definition suggests a continuum, with horrible, mass eruptions of evil, such as the Holocaust and other instances of mass murder, at one extreme, and the 'small' white lie, which is somewhat hurtful, at the other.[3] Both ends of the continuum are important to recognize, because the road to great evil often begins with small, first steps. Evil, in many cases, is enmeshed in cunning and seductive processes that can lead ordinary people in ordinary times down the proverbial slippery slope.

The modern age, especially the 20th century, has had as its hallmark what we call *technical rationality*. Technical rationality is a way of thinking and living (a culture) that emphasizes the scientific–analytic mindset and faith in technological progress. For our purposes here, the culture of technical rationality has also introduced a new form of evil that we call administrative evil. What is different about administrative evil is that its appearance is masked within the ethos of technical rationality. Ordinary people may simply be acting appropriately in their organizational role, just doing what is expected of them while participating in what a critical observer, usually well after the fact, would call evil. And, under conditions of what we call *moral inversion*, ordinary people can engage in acts of administrative evil while believing that what they are doing is not only proced-urally correct but, in fact, good. Because administrative evil wears a mask, no one has to accept an overt invitation to commit an evil act, because such overt invitations are very rarely issued. Rather, the 'invitation' may come in the form of an expert or technical role, couched in appropriate language, or even packaged as a good and worthy project.

People have always been able to delude themselves into thinking that their evil acts are not really so bad, and we have certainly had moral inversions in times past, but there are three very important differences in administrative evil. One is our modern inclination to un-name evil, an old concept that does not resonate with the technical-rational mindset. The second difference stems from the modern, complex organization, which diffuses individual responsibility and requires the compartmentalized accomplishment of role expectations to perform work on a daily basis. The third difference is found in how the culture of technical rationality has analytically narrowed the processes by which public policy is formulated and implemented, so that moral inversions become more likely.[4]

Thus evil also occurs along another continuum: from acts that are committed in relative ignorance to those that are knowing and deliberate acts of evil, or what we would characterize as masked and unmasked. Plato maintained that no one would knowingly commit an evil act. The fact that someone did evil indicates his ignorance. Individuals and groups can engage in evil acts without recognizing the consequences of their behaviour, or when convinced their actions are justified or serving the greater good. Administrative evil falls within this range of the continuum, where people engage in or contribute to acts of evil without recognizing that they are doing anything wrong.

Lang argues that in the case of genocide, it is difficult to maintain that evil occurs without the knowledge of the actor.[5] Genocide is a deliberate act; mass murderers know that they are doing evil. Katz recounts several instances in which deliberate acts of evil have occurred in bureaucratic settings (such as those based on the testimonies of the commandants of Auschwitz and Sobibor). However, the direct act of mass murder, even when facilitated by bureaucratic organizations, is not what we call administrative evil, or at least represents its most extreme, and unmasked, manifestation. Before and surrounding such overt acts of evil, there are many more and much less obviously evil administrative activities that lead to and support the worst forms of human behaviour. Moreover, without these instances of masked evil, the more overt and unmasked acts are less likely to occur.

If administrative evil means that people inflict pain and suffering on others, but do so *not* knowingly or deliberately, can they be held responsible for their actions? When ordinary people inflict pain and suffering on others in the course of performing their 'normal' organizational or policy role, they usually justify their actions by saying that they were just following orders and doing their job. This reflects the difficulty of identifying administrative evil, and the possibility of missing it altogether, or perhaps worse, calling mistakes or misjudgments evil. We maintain that identifying administrative evil is most difficult within one's own culture and historical time period.

The opaque nature of administrative evil, however, should not lead us to conclude that it cannot be recognized, and that administrative entities are inherently evil or that evil cannot be prevented from developing into its worst manifestations. The Holocaust is an example of the latter, where evil ran unchecked, both masked and unmasked, towards its most extreme manifestations. We remember it now as an instance of administrative evil, but only after several decades of denial and suppressed memories. Other examples, two of which we recount below, show how what we remember is often not as important as what remains unseen or forgotten beneath the mask of administrative evil.

FROM DORA TO NASA

Here we tell the story of the von Braun team of German rocket scientists and engineers who were brought to the U.S. after World War II. They became the elite rocket development team in this country, and designed and built the Saturn rockets that propelled Apollo to the moon. Of the 118 members of the von Braun team who came to the U.S. in 1945, about half had been members of the Nazi party. Most were 'nominal members', and therefore not barred from entering the U.S. But at least a handful, including Werner von Braun, had been actively engaged in the decision to use, and in using, SS-provided slave labour in weapons production, an act that led directly to the conviction for war crimes of Albert Speer, Hitler's Minister of Armaments. In the end, we are left with the reality that some of America's most competent and successful public managers in the government agency that was lionized in the 1960s – and again in the 1990s – as the paradigmatic high-performing organization, had been either 'committed Nazis' or had themselves directly engaged in actions for which others were convicted of war crimes. This story begins at Mittelbau-Dora, where administrative evil wore no mask.

MITTELBAU-DORA

Although Mittelbau-Dora was not one of the most notorious Nazi concentration camps, it does merit a special place in the history of the 20th century. Dora was not a death camp, like Treblinka and Auschwitz, but a slave labour camp. Even in this it was far from unique, for German corporations invested heavily in concentration camp industry, for example IG Farben at Auschwitz. Dora was unique for other reasons. It was the site of the huge underground Mittelwerk factory that built the V-2 rockets for the Reich. It was the last SS concentration camp to be formally established, and was the only camp exclusively formed for weapons production. It was one of the first camps liberated by advancing American troops, who found corpses stacked like cordwood and ranks of emaciated survivors. Mittelwerk produced just about 6,000 rockets and 20,000 deaths in its less than two years of operation.[6] For two periods of its short life, it was arguably among the worst of the living hells produced by the SS concentration camps.

Dora was initially a minor appendage of the Buchenwald concentration camp. Only in 1943, when Hitler decided to make V-2 rocket production the top armament priority, did Dora mushroom. In August 1943, after the extensive British air raid on Peenemunde, the Nazi rocket development facility on the Baltic Ocean, V-2 production had to be moved to a place as secure from air attack as possible. An underground location had become the preferred choice for all German armament and industrial production. Mittelwerk had two huge tunnels, each wide enough for two rail lines apiece and each about a mile in length. These two main tunnels were connected at regular intervals by 46 smaller tunnels of 500 feet apiece. Mittelwerk incorporated about 35 million cubic feet of space. At Mittelwerk's peak, 10,000 slave labourers lived and toiled in this massive complex.

Unfortunately for those who would work and perish there, SS General Hans Kammler was placed in charge of the construction of Mittelwerk. He had previously directed the construction of the F-1 production facility at Peenemunde. Kammler's resumé included the razing of the Warsaw ghetto and the construction of the death camps at Maidenek and Belzec, plus the later phases of the Auschwitz death camp. He had a well-earned reputation as among the most vicious and inhuman officers in the entire SS.[7]

During the early phase at Mittelwerk, prisoners were housed in several of the cross tunnels, which were immediately adjacent to the final mining operations in Tunnel A. This meant that after working twelve-hour shifts, prisoners were crammed into bunks (sometimes two at a time) where they could get little or no sleep because of continuous mining noise, including explosives. Deplorable conditions led to a remarkable death rate: 18 in October 1943; 172 in November; 670 in December; 719 in January 1944; 536 in February, and in March, 767. Until a crematorium could be built at Dora, corpses were stacked at the railhead for shipment to the crematorium at Buchenwald. Dora quickly developed a considerable reputation at Buchenwald. There were also transports of the seriously ill or otherwise 'useless' prisoners to other camps such as Bergen-Belsen. The death toll at Dora during this construction phase was estimated at 6,000 in six months.[8] As Kammler knew only too well, there was a virtually inexhaustible supply of slave labour available to the SS.

By the end of 1944 and the first two months of 1945, the inmate population began to grow, and conditions deteriorated quickly. As the Russians advanced from the east, the concentration camps located in Poland began to be overrun, and the SS instituted the practice of shipping the remaining inmates to other camps and then attempting to destroy the camps – and with them, the evidence of their horrors. Large numbers of Jews from Auschwitz in particular, but also from Gross Rosen and Mauthausen, were shipped to Mittelbau-Dora, with the overall prisoner population reaching a peak of over 40,000 and Dora itself housing nearly 20,000.

Of the 60,000 prisoners who came to Mittelbau-Dora, approximately 20,000 perished – more than three for every rocket. About ten thousand of those died directly from work on the V-2. The V-2 was thus a highly unusual weapon:

> More people died producing it than died from being hit by it. In round numbers, 5,000 people were killed by the 3,200 V-2s that the Germans fired at English and Continental targets. By that measure, at least two-thirds of all Allied victims of the ballistic missile came from the people who produced it, rather than from those who endured its descent.[9]

This result was not what the German rocket scientists and engineers, who worked diligently during the war years at a weapons development and production facility on the Baltic coast, had in mind.

PEENEMUNDE

The origins of the German rocket programme were in the early 1930s. Although the Luftwaffe would also become interested in rockets, it was an army ordnance officer, Walter Dornberger, who discovered the young Wernher von Braun, who became one of the world's pioneers of rocket science. In 1937, the new rocket development facility, *Heeresversuchsstelle* (Army Research Station) Peenemunde opened, and the entire team moved north to the Baltic coast. It was here that the design and testing of the V-1 cruise missile and V-2 rocket were accomplished. Dornberger, who was to become a Major General by the end of the war, commanded the facility, and von Braun was the technical director. The group of engineers and scientists, later to be known as the von Braun team and who would follow von Braun to the United States, was first assembled at Peenemunde.

Throughout German industry from 1941 onwards there were increasingly severe labour shortages. The Russian front demanded more and more manpower for the German army. In such difficult circumstances, the use of prisoner-of-war forced labour, although lamentable, seems predictable enough. This was the initial choice at Peenemunde for rocket production. The use of slave labour was an entirely different issue. These were concentration camp prisoners (*Häftlinge*) under the control of the SS. Werner von Braun was fully aware of the use of SS-provided slave labour in the production of rockets; indeed, the management team led by Dornberger and von Braun explicitly discussed and adopted as policy the use of SS-provided slave labour in rocket production (Neufeld, 1996: 187).

Slave labour had been investigated, promoted and then requisitioned by Arthur Rudolph, who headed the Development and Fabrication Laboratory.[10] On 2 June 1943, Rudolph formally requested 1,400 slave labourers from the SS. The first 200 members of this group arrived on 17 June. Later, after V-2 production was shifted to Mittelwerk, Dornberger, Rudolph and von Braun were all present at a meeting in May 1944 when the use of additional slave labor was discussed and agreed. Von Braun travelled a number of times from Peenemunde to Mittelwerk, as did Dornberger and other members of the von Braun team. Arthur Rudolph was among a number of personnel who moved full time to Mittelwerk where he became the chief production engineer, with an office on one of the main tunnels. Another dozen members of the von Braun team who eventually came to the U.S. also staffed Mittelwerk. No one could have any illusions about a factory whose production mode during most of its existence was quite simply to work its labour force to death, although their roles may not have involved some of them directly in decisions about *Häftlinge*, or relationships with them. Von Braun's substantial involvement, however, is quite clear.[11] The coming end of the war brought disaster to Mittelbau-Dora, but it marked a new beginning for the von Braun team of rocket scientists and engineers.

OPERATIONS OVERCAST AND PAPERCLIP
The von Braun team was brought to the U.S. as a part of Operations Overcast and Paperclip. How this happened has two rather distinct story lines. Werner von Braun clearly relished telling one version of this story, a version which appears in several publications, most of them sanctioned by NASA. This 'official story' has only some tenuous connections to what actually happened, and is much like virtually all of the von Braun team's disingenuous and self-serving accounts of their wartime experiences.

The most credible account of what occurred begins with an SS order from General Hans Kammler directing von Braun and his team to move nearly all Peenemunde operations – personnel and records – to the Mittelwerk. Here, von Braun and his team spent nearly three months. Mittelwerk was still in full production at this time, and conditions were deteriorating. The thousands of Peenemunde personnel did not all move at once, but over a period of about a month. Of over 4,000, about three quarters relocated to the Mittelwerk. The Peenemunde records were deliberately hidden in a deserted mine shaft in the area, for use as a bargaining counter with the Americans. As it happened, the rocketeers had no need for such bargaining.

In April 1945, Kammler issued another evacuation order. This time the von Braun team was ordered to move to Oberammagau, a small village in the Bavarian mountains of

southern Germany. Of the 3,000 who had moved to the Mittelwerk, only 400 went to
Bavaria. One can speculate that von Braun and the others may have welcomed this order,
since it had the effect of putting a considerable distance between the von Braun team and
the Mittelwerk and Dora Camp. Within a week of von Braun's departure, Mittelbau-
Dora and the Mittelwerk were liberated by the U.S. Third Army. The von Braun team
made contact with the Americans on 2 May 1945. The unconditional surrender of
Germany came five days later.

POST-WAR CHAOS
The summer of 1945 was traumatic and chaotic in post-war Germany. Living conditions for
ordinary Germans were very difficult. A number of Displaced Persons (DP) camps had
been established for Holocaust survivors and many others who had been imprisoned or
otherwise displaced by the Nazis. Conditions in these camps, though an infinite improvement over concentration camps, were also difficult. As the war was winding down, a large
number of technical teams were formed under the auspices of the Combined Intelligence
Objectives Committee (CIOS); these teams had a three-part mission:

> First, they were to find out what the Germans knew about weapons, radar, synthetic rubber,
> torpedoes, rockets, jet engines, infrared, communications, and other such things...
> Secondly, they were to gather information that could help shorten the war against
> Japan...Finally, the CIOS teams were to locate and detain – even intern – German
> scientists and technicians to interrogate them for information...and to prevent them from
> slipping away to seek safe haven in another country and continue their wartime research and
> development programs and projects.[12]

These CIOS technical teams represented a developing U.S. policy toward German
scientific and technical knowledge in the postwar world. This emerging policy was
handled under the jurisdiction of the U.S. military, in particular, the Joint Chiefs of
Staff. Several principles were being advocated, some in at least partial conflict with
others. One was not to repeat the mistake of leaving the German nation with the
scientific and technical capacity to rearm, as was done after World War I. This principle
was given added weight by the demonstrated Nazi superiority in several areas, including
rocketry. Another principle was to prevent any intact groups of scientists or technicians
from escaping to another country and simply continuing their research

DENAZIFICATION
At the same time, we also had a policy of denazification, and of bringing Nazi war
criminals to justice.[13] Denazification was carried out first by the military government
until May 1946, and then under the German Law for Liberation from National Socialism
and Militarism.[14] The earliest definition of a 'committed Nazi' (that is, more than a
'nominal Nazi') came in 1944, and included anyone who joined the Nazi Party before
Hitler came to power in 1933. A later, July 1947 policy listed 136 mandatory removal and
exclusion categories, and indicated that Nazi Party membership prior to May 1937 was
cause for mandatory removal and exclusion. The centrepiece for denazification policy
was a questionnaire, *Fragebogen*, which was quite widely distributed. Later, when
denazification had been turned over to the German authorities, a new questionnaire
(*Meldebogen*) was used, and officials utilized five categories for respondents: major
offenders; offenders; lesser offenders; followers or nominal Nazis; and persons exonerated. Denazification policy under the Germans became progressively weaker, and after
1948, only the more obvious cases were pursued.

One of the more revealing juxtapositions of these competing U.S. policies became evident in and around Mittelwerk and Dora. While two of the CIOS technical teams were rounding up all of the V-2 components from the Mittelwerk and interviewing people to find the rocket scientists and engineers, other teams were interviewing Dora survivors and others for the coming War Crimes trials and as part of the larger effort at denazification. In a number of instances, these teams were directed to the same people. In August, 1945, the U.S. initiated Operation Overcast, the aim of which was to bring selected Germans over to participate in the production of German-inspired weapons, including V-2s, against the Japanese. Overcast was given final approval in August 1945, but the Japanese surrendered later that month. Operation Overcast explicitly included an assurance that any committed Nazis unintentionally brought to the U.S. would be returned to Europe for trial.

In September 1945, von Braun and 118 members of his team came to the U.S. under Operation Overcast, which was revised and renamed as Operation Paperclip in March 1946. Under Overcast, early permission was obtained to bring over this key group of rocket scientists and engineers. Their first stop was Fort Bliss, Texas, and the nearby proving grounds in White Sands, New Mexico. Here, they supervised a large number of V-2 launches. By the end of the 1940s they had moved on to the Redstone Arsenal at Huntsville, Alabama, which later became the Marshall Space Flight Center.

By this time, the real difficulty was that the original Overcast group could not easily be allowed to leave the U.S. because they already were privy to top-secret knowledge about the projects they had been working on. Eventually, the practical goals of obtaining as much scientific and technical personnel and information as possible for national security purposes simply superseded other considerations, including legal and ethical ones. The eventual shift of emphasis away from whether denazification procedures had been followed to the satisfaction of two new criteria: whether the individual's entry was in the national interest, and whether the individual was likely to become a security threat to the U.S. in the future, eventually resolved the fundamental contradiction within the Operation Paperclip policy.

THE VON BRAUN TEAM

Within a few years of the end of World War II, the uncomfortable moments for the von Braun team had largely passed. The Army clearly had a vested interest in them, and had shielded some of them from testifying at the Mittelbau-Dora war crimes trial, held at Dachau in 1947. Von Braun himself and other members of the team successfully maintained the fiction that the use of slave labour had been the exclusive province of the SS, and that they were rocket scientists interested in space flight who had been forced to take a temporary detour into wartime weapons development. They enjoyed a better than half-hearted acceptance, after a time, from their adopted community of Huntsville, Alabama and their colleagues within NASA. Still later, they were rewarded for their great achievements in the Apollo Program. Huntsville now has a Werner von Braun civic centre, and several of the Germans, including Arthur Rudolph, received NASA's highest civilian honour, the Distinguished Service Award.

It was only after most of the team had left government service in the early 1970s that the facts about their past began to emerge. Survivors of the French resistance who had been imprisoned at Dora knew and spoke the truth all along.[15] Americans have been much slower to recognize the unsavoury past of some of these Germans, and the recent celebration of the thirtieth anniversary of the Apollo moon landing ignored the topic altogether.

Nevertheless, based on the information we now have, it would be equally mistaken to issue a blanket condemnation of all of the Germans who came over with von Braun. Of the 118 who originally joined him, between half and three quarters had been members of the Nazi party. Certainly, most of these were only nominal members. Most also had no direct involvement with slave labour and the policy decision to use it. Only four were known to have joined the SS, although there may have been more. Von Braun himself was one of these, receiving his commission in 1941, although this is not an early membership which ordinarily would mark a 'committed Nazi'. He is reported to have worn his SS uniform only once; however, it was clearly to his advantage to do so on the day that Heinrich Himmler, the head of the SS, visited Peenemunde to see for himself how rocket development was going. Himmler rewarded von Braun with a promotion to major. In this action and in many others, von Braun appears as more an opportunist than a Nazi. Another SS member was Kurt Debus, although he was an earlier adherent and apparently more committed. Debus reportedly wore his SS uniform regularly at Peenemunde. and at one point denounced a colleague to the Gestapo as an anti-Nazi.[16] Debus, after working for some time with von Braun in Huntsville, became the first Director of the Kennedy Space Flight Center in Florida. Arthur Rudolph was a seriously committed Nazi, who joined the party in June 1931 and had other early Nazi affiliations as well.

SATURN AND APOLLO

In the 1960s NASA was widely regarded as the paradigmatic example of the successful, high-performing organization, and especially so for a public sector organization.[17] The Apollo programme and its great success, punctuated by the moon landing, was clearly the principal reason. The von Braun team at the Marshall Space Flight Center was an integral part of this success since it was their Saturn rockets that boosted all of the crews into orbit and on to the moon.

The Project Manager in charge of the Saturn V Program Office was none other than Arthur Rudolph. Much as Werner von Braun established himself as an outstanding manager and leader in the U.S., Arthur Rudolph demonstrated outstanding management with the Saturn Program Office. He developed the concept of the 'Program Control Center', which essentially gathered relevant information about all the Saturn subsystems in one large conference room and made them visually accessible. The Saturn Program Office was typically portrayed as a premier example of the matrix and project forms of management for which NASA was nationally famous during this period.

A look at the organization chart from the Marshall Space Flight Center from 1960 shows that about three-quarters of the management and laboratory director positions were held by former Peenemunders. This remained the case during the entire ten-year tenure of von Braun at Marshall. The von Braun team was obviously a very tightly knit group, if for no other reason than they came as a group to a new country. They also shared a past, part of which needed to be kept secret. While most of them had been nominal Nazis, and had not engaged directly in utilizing slave labour, their leader and several of the other key members of the team had a past that needed to be hidden – or, at a minimum, whitewashed – for the group to be successful in their new country. Keeping this secret, which required widespread collusion, was clearly another factor in the Germans' insularity.

The von Braun team at Marshall developed a kind of siege mentality, together with a feeling that they had to do better work than anyone else in order to overcome what they perceived as unfair treatment. They knew that President Eisenhower had chosen the Navy rocket programme to launch America's first satellite, and they knew it was because the Army missile programme was run by 'a bunch of Germans'. The von Braun team felt misunderstood, slighted and even attacked, and, quite naturally, they fostered a kind of 'fortress Marshall' mentality over the years. Even in the glory years of Apollo, they never felt they received the degree of credit they were due, and all because they were Germans. The organizational culture developed first at Redstone and then at Marshall was thus a defensive one.

Later, as Apollo began to wind down after 1970, the von Braun team began to retire. Some were forced out by the reductions-in-force which swept NASA during this time. The Germans of course did not enjoy the veterans' preference, and some retired or left rather than take a reduction in rank leading to a reduced role. Even at the end, the von Braun team felt victimized, referring to this period at Marshall as the 'Great Massacre'. There was probably no intent to refer to the experience of about a dozen members of the von Braun Team at Mittelbau-Dora, but the irony is striking.

Arthur Rudolph, an outstanding public manager in the most successful American public organization in modern times and earlier at the Mittelwerk in the Third Reich, retired from NASA with its highest civilian award. He was living in retirement in San Jose, California, collecting his government pension, when he was confronted in the early 1980s by the Office of Special Investigations, the Justice Department unit created by Congress in 1979 for the express purpose of pursuing Nazi war criminals living in the United States. Unsurprisingly, surviving members of the von Braun team were an early subject of OSI investigations; some still were as of 1997.

In 1984 Rudolph renounced his U.S. citizenship voluntarily and left the country, after signing an admission that he could not contest the OSI charges in court; in effect admitting his guilt. He did not lose his federal pension, however. Werner von Braun died in 1977, so he never had to face a war crimes investigation by OSI. However, in 1985, a fortieth anniversary reunion and celebration of the von Braun team's arrival in the U.S. was held in Huntsville. Rudolph was invited back, and attempts were made to obtain a temporary visa for him. These efforts failed. Rudolph died on 1 January 1996 in Hamburg, Germany, at the age of 89.

In the Holocaust, administrative evil went unmasked for all to see, and certainly evil went unmasked at Mittelbau-Dora, where Arthur Rudolph completed the first leg of his highly successful career as a manager. However, it was American public policy and our own public servants who placed the mask on this administrative evil, under Operations Overcast and Paperclip, and brought it to the U.S. in the form of some of the members of the von Braun team. The CIOS technical teams may or may not have been truly aware of the evil that was Dora, but what is clear is that their single-minded pursuit of their narrow technical goal blinded them to larger issues that mattered a great deal, at a minimum to Dora's survivors. Or perhaps they simply failed to notice at all. In essence, they made a Faustian bargain with administrative evil, only to find that evil sullying our nation's greatest technical achievement, the moon landing.

THE EVACUATION AND RELOCATION OF 'ALL PERSONS OF JAPANESE ANCESTRY'

Between March 1942 and December 1945, about 120,000 Japanese-Americans and Japanese citizens in the U.S. were subjected to a process of evacuation and relocation, in which they were removed from their homes and businesses in the western United States and placed in a number of 'Relocation Centers'.[18] About 35,000 were successfully 'resettled' outside the military exclusion zone (roughly, east of the Rocky Mountains).

This episode has been widely castigated as among the most dismal in all of American history, with frequent references to 'America's concentration camps'.[19]

The evacuation and relocation of Japanese Americans was a deeply flawed policy, and certainly qualifies as an example of administrative evil.[20] While in no way attempting to defend a policy and programme that are fundamentally indefensible, this episode is nonetheless instructive for the way it differs from Operations Overcast and Paperclip, a policy and programme that arose within the same administrations (both overlapped the Roosevelt and Truman administrations) but has been remembered very differently. It also serves as an interesting contrast with similar processes in the Holocaust that led to far different results.

'THE DECISION NOBODY MADE'

While the Japanese attack on Pearl Harbour on 7 December 1941 was certainly the immediate precipitant of the Relocation, the context requires a look at events both before and after that event. For most of the 20th century, there was growing American anxiety about Japanese aggression and militarism. The western United States in particular was characterized by racism toward all Asian-Americans, but perhaps most notably toward Japanese. The Immigration Act of 1924 has excluded Japanese as 'aliens ineligible to citizenship'. Feelings ran sufficiently high that in the fall of 1941, well before Pearl Harbour, President Sproul of the University of California initiated the Northern California Committee for Fair Play for Citizens and Aliens of Japanese Ancestry, a group that was widely subscribed to by academics and other community leaders.

The attack on Pearl Harbour escalated existing anxieties exponentially. It was followed in short order by successful attacks on Guam and Wake Island. Hong Kong fell by Christmas, and on 2 January 1942 Manila in the Philippines was overrun. Americans on the west coast were genuinely fearful of an imminent Japanese invasion. With hindsight, we know this fear was unwarranted, but it was widely shared across military and civilian boundaries. Even the most responsible and cautious elements were honestly concerned. Thus we can probably safely say in hindsight that the relocation policy was justified by a perceived military necessity that arguably never existed in reality. But it most certainly existed in perception at the time. Other factors, such as racism and deep cultural differences between Americans and Japanese doubtless made their contribution as well.

One author calls the relocation of Japanese Americans the 'decision nobody made' and this characterization is apt.[21] The sequence of events resembles quite closely a functionalist interpretation of the Holocaust, as well as the evolution of Operations Overcast and Paperclip. As we have observed, no one sets out to do administrative evil. There was certainly a debate within the Roosevelt administration concerning this policy. As often happens, the War Department had a quite different perspective on this issue from the Justice Department. Attorney General Francis Biddle, of the 'blue blood' Philadelphia family, was initially very resistant to the notion of evacuation:

> War threatens all civil rights and although we have fought wars before, and our personal freedoms have survived, there have been periods of gross abuse, when hysteria and hate and fear ran high, and when minorities were unlawfully and cruelly abused . . . If we care about democracy, we must care about it as a reality for others, for Germans, for Italians, for Japanese, for those who are with us as those who are against us. For the Bill of Rights protects not only American citizens but all human beings who live on our American soil, under our American flag . . . all are alike under the law. And this we must remember and sustain – that is if we really love justice, and really hate the bayonet and the whip and the gun, and the whole Gestapo method as a way of handling human beings.[22]

President Roosevelt responded in a similar manner:

> It is one thing to safeguard American industry, and particularly the defense industry, against sabotage; but it is very much another to throw out of work honest and loyal people who, except for the accident of birth, are sincerely patriotic . . . Remember the Nazi technique: 'Pit race against race, religion against religion, prejudice against prejudice. Divide and Conquer.' We must not let that happen here. We must not forget what we are defending: Liberty, decency, justice . . . [23]

Church organizations, the governor of California and the California Attorney General, Earl Warren, echoed these sentiments. With this level and quality of opposition, how could the policy of evacuation and relocation have carried the day?

THE MILITARY TRUMP CARD IN WARTIME

John DeWitt, by all accounts a rather undistinguished and punctilious 61-year-old general, was commanding officer of the Western Defense Command, and was thus charged with defending American soil on the west coast from potential – and widely feared – Japanese invasion. The rapid succession of Japanese military victories following hard on the heels of Pearl Harbour, along with sporadic incidents such as a Japanese submarine shelling a shore installation in Oregon, escalated tensions. West coast cities were under a blackout at night, and there were occasions of sporadic anti-aircraft fire, even if there were never any actual Japanese planes. There was widespread concern that those of Japanese ancestry, some of whom happened to live in close proximity to sensitive military installations, would use shortwave radios or other signals to guide a Japanese attack to its target.

Quite apart from the military issues, concern grew about the safety of both Japanese aliens and Japanese-American citizens when both they and their property were subject to increasing levels of harassment and violent attacks. This concern was shared to some extent within the various Japanese communities. Thus, part of the momentum for evacuation came from genuine concern for the safety of those in Japanese communities.

General DeWitt was at first rebuffed when he sought the evacuation of the Japanese. His initial response was to request mass raids without warrants in Japanese communities which were close to the most sensitive defence and military areas; his primary objective was uncovering and confiscating shortwave radios, but he also wanted to identify and remove those who genuinely posed a national security threat. Attorney General Biddle stonewalled this initiative. Ironically, if these mass raids had gone forward, it is possible that the momentum for a total evacuation might have slowed or even stopped.

Gradually, the momentum for at least some form of exclusion grew. Biddle asked three prominent New Deal attorneys for an opinion about the legality of exclusion. Their reply was: 'So long as a classification of persons is reasonably related to a genuine war need and does not under the guise of national defense discriminate against any class of citizens for a purpose unrelated to the national defense, no constitutional guarantee is infringed.'[24] Symbolic of the change in climate was a Walter Lippmann column, entitled 'The Fifth Column on the Coast' in which he warned of the west coast being in imminent danger of attack from both within and without.[25] Lippmann opined that the entire west coast should be treated as a war zone under special rules.

As the climate continued to change, Attorney General Biddle essentially ceded authority for any evacuation to the War Department, and it was Secretary of War, Henry Stimson, who proposed to President Roosevelt that the most sensitive military areas be evacuated, and was told to go ahead but to 'be as reasonable as you can', a response that would have been somewhat surprising in wartime only if it had been otherwise.[26] On 19 February 1942, a little over two months after Pearl Harbour, Executive Order 9066 initiated the official policy of evacuation of Japanese aliens and of Japanese-American citizens from certain military exclusion zones. The words 'concentration' and 'internment' were deliberately dropped from usage; instead the initial collection points, run by the military, were euphemistically called 'Assembly Centers', and were most typically at racetracks and fairgrounds. The eventual destinations, which had to be built hurriedly, were called 'Relocation Centers' and, as it turned out, they had some significant differences from both internment and concentration camps.

IMPLEMENTATION

The initial evacuation from military exclusion zones was voluntary; this was an unmitigated disaster.[27] Those in the Japanese communities were in a horrible dilemma as to whether or when they should leave, and the obvious opportunities for exploitation by outsiders were rapidly and chillingly taken advantage of. 'Fire sales' of personal and real property, for pennies on the dollar, were rampant.[28] The movement to forced evacuation, in this context, was in many ways positive, in that it meant a 'controlled' evacuation, under government protection and with at least some certainty of expectation.

Perhaps not so surprising, given the centrality of property rights in our culture, immediate attention was given to protecting the property of those who were evacuated. Interestingly, the Federal Reserve Bank was initially given responsibility for recording and storing evacuees' property through a hastily created 'Evacuee Property Department'. So far as we know, virtually all property that entered this system – about $200,000,000 worth – was eventually restored to its owners. The policy, which remained intact when responsibility was passed to the newly created War Relocation Authority, was to ship property free of charge to the Relocation Centers, if requested. Alternatively, property was held until evacuees returned to their old – or new – homes, and then shipped to that location free of charge. It is important to note that the property of most evacuees did not enter this federal system, and thus was not as well safeguarded, or was lost altogether. Much property was entrusted to friends, to churches, and others. Still more was sold off at pennies on the dollar. The substantial losses of property and income, possibly $100,000,000 or more, were clearly among the worst outcomes of this unfortunate policy.

Overall authority for the evacuation and relocation was transferred from the Wartime Civil Control Administration to the War Relocation Authority (WRA) created by Executive Order 9102 in March 1942. The WRA developed into a very interesting agency. Its first director, Milton Eisenhower (Dwight's youngest brother), described its mission as:

> (1) aiding the army in carrying out the evacuation of military areas, (2) developing and supervising a planned, orderly program of relocation for evacuees, (3) providing evacuees with work opportunities so that they may contribute to their own maintenance and to the national production program, and (4) protecting evacuees from harm in the areas where they are relocated. The first specific task of the authority is to relocate some 100,000 alien and American-born Japanese from the military areas of the far Western states.[29]

The agency drew its personnel largely from the Department of Agriculture (including both of its directors, Milton Eisenhower and later, Dillon Myer) and it developed its own culture as a New Deal agency that was going to create communities (the relocation centres) that were 'schools of democracy', overtly contrasted with the concentration camps of the Germans.[30]

By June 1942 Military Area 1 (coastal California, Oregon and Washington) was evacuated, and Military Area 2 (most of the rest of the Western Defense Command) by August 1942. The initial destinations were the Assembly Centers. Church organizations were present and visible at all of the Assembly Centers, organized primarily by the Protestant Church Commission for Japanese Service.[31] They assisted in a variety of ways, one way being to act as an informal watchdog for mistreatment. There were fourteen Assembly Centers, in California, Oregon, Washington and Arizona. Their populations peaked in May and June of 1942 and by mid-November, 1942, the last Assembly Center closed down (Manzanar in California and Poston in Arizona began as Assembly Centers and were converted to Relocation Centers).

Milton Eisenhower, who idolized Woodrow Wilson, was determined to put a human face on the Relocation policy. He met and consulted regularly with an advisory council made up of members of the Japanese-American Citizens League (JACL), which was headed by the able Mike Masaoka. While quite capable of representing the evacuees, Masaoka was only 24 years of age, a very young man, which was insulting to the Issei, the Japanese nationals who were older men, and thus in positions of greater respect in Japanese culture.[32] This kind of cultural misunderstanding was rampant during the entire episode. Equally evident was the genuine attempt to implement this policy in a uniquely American, democratic and humane manner. Eisenhower went into a meeting with the inter-mountain Governors, looking for cooperation with the WRA's primary policy initiative of resettling evacuees into new homes and jobs outside the exclusion areas. With the exception of the Governor of Colorado, the governors excoriated Eisenhower for attempting to dump the nation's enemies into their towns and cities. Eventually, resettlement was most successful in midwestern and eastern metropolitan areas.

Eisenhower left the WRA after only three months, and sent a final memorandum to President Roosevelt, which ran in part:

> ...I cannot help expressing the hope that the American people will grow toward a broader appreciation of the essential Americanism of a great majority of the evacuees and the difficult sacrifice they are making. Only when the prevailing attitudes of unreasoning bitterness have been replaced by tolerance and understanding will it be possible to carry forward a genuinely successful relocation program and to plan intelligently for re-assimilation of the evacuees into American life when the war is over. I wish to give you my considered judgment that fully 80 to 85 percent of the Nisei are loyal to the United States, perhaps 50 percent of the Issei are passively loyal; but a large portion of the Kibei (American citizens educated in Japan and about 9,000 in number) have a strong cultural attachment to Japan.[33]

Eisenhower's hopes were largely not realized, although arguably Japanese-Americans are today well assimilated into American culture.

Dillon Myer, who succeeded Eisenhower as Director of WRA, shared most of his aspirations.[34] He fully supported the notion of making the Relocation Centers into 'little democracies', largely self-governing, with their own community councils. Here again, cultural misunderstandings were an obstacle, as the Issei were initially excluded from the councils; this policy was rescinded in April 1943. While the Relocation Centers may indeed have superficially resembled concentration camps, surrounded as they were by barbed wire fences and with the military presence of guards, there were important differences.[35] Both the fencing and the guards were largely symbolic; each Center had a detachment of about three officers and 125 troops to 'guard' communities of between eight and twelve thousand inhabitants. Many residents came and went freely from the Centers, and increasingly large numbers came to be 'on leave' from the Centers. The leave policy included short-term, work and indefinite leave. Indefinite leave was granted for those who were successfully resettled, and while this policy never succeeded as planned, about 35,000 individuals and families were eventually resettled. Ironically, many residents initially denounced the leave programme and resettlement more generally, as an abdication of the government's responsibility to care for them.[36]

In yet another irony, the Battle of Midway in June 1942 effectively cancelled out the whole premise of the evacuation. The Japanese defeat at Midway eliminated any realistic chance of a Japanese invasion of the west coast of the U.S. This occurred before very many of the evacuees had left the Assembly Centers for the Relocation Centers. It was probably too much to hope for any sort of rapid about-face in policy. The population of the Relocation Centers peaked in January 1943 at 110,240, and had dropped through resettlement by July 1943 to 103,282 and went on to decline further at a rate of about 10,000 per month.[37] As mentioned, eventually some 35,000 Japanese-American citizens were resettled.

DENOUEMENT

By mid-1944 the threat of Japanese invasion had long since passed and a consensus in the government had formed that the Centers could be closed. However, there was concern in the administration that if Centers were closed before the Presidential election the electoral votes of California could be jeopardized. The decision to terminate the Centers was finally taken in December 1944, and all the Centers, with the exception of the special case of Tule Lake in California, were closed by December 1945.[38] As evacuees successfully returned to old and new homes in the former exclusion zones, initial resistance to leaving the Centers abated, and people left more readily.

The population dynamics of the Japanese communities were quite different after the return.[39] Nearly 45,000 of just over 50,000 resettled to the east of the exclusionary areas remained in their new homes. Chicago, Denver, Salt Lake City, Detroit and New York were the metropolitan areas that became the new homes of thousands of Japanese-Americans. California had about 93,000 Japanese and Japanese-Americans before the relocation; as of March 1946, about 49,000 returned. Only about thirty percent of Washington State's Japanese community returned, about 4,000. For good reason, those who returned were much more likely to settle in urban than in rural areas. The WRA had centres in the large urban areas, and these provided assistance to returning evacuees. Church organizations, an important source of support and aid throughout the process, were also more likely to have a presence in the cities. Likewise, law enforcement agencies in urban centres were more likely to treat Japanese and Japanese-Americans equitably.

It is worth noting that over 25,000 Japanese-Americans served in the U.S. armed forces between 1940 and 1945. About twenty percent of the total number became casualties (killed, wounded or missing in action). The Japanese Americans from the mainland formed the 442nd Combat Team and served with great distinction in the European theatre. In fact, the Nisei 442nd became the most decorated unit in the U.S. Army.[40] In an ironic turn of events, part of the 442nd, soldiers of the 622nd Field Artillery Battalion, were among the Allied troops that liberated Dachau. The heroic exploits of the all-Nisei 442nd were widely reported in the press, and played a part in turning public opinion toward closing the Relocation Centers.

In perhaps the final irony of a tragic episode that had many such paradoxes, the Japanese American Citizens League held a dinner in Dillon Myer's honour at a New York hotel in May 1946. At the dinner, Myer was presented with a scroll that commended him as a 'champion of human rights and common decency whose courageous and inspired leadership ... aided materially in restoring faith and conviction in the American way to ... Americans of Japanese ancestry and their resident alien parents'.[41]

CONCLUSION

These two episodes provide insight into the processes that lead to administrative evil. While not extreme cases, both are examples of '(administrative) behaviour that deprives innocent people of their humanity, where the behaviour of one person, or an aggregate of persons, is destructive to others.'[42] Both cases involve moral inversion, where administrators set out believing that what they were doing was in the best interests of the country. Despite these similarities, the two episodes have been remembered very differently.

With hindsight, it has been easier to discern administrative evil at work in the case of the internment of Japanese-Americans due to the spectre of barb-wired internment camps and thousands of citizens deprived of their rights. And the implementation of the internment camp policy resembled Nazi concentration camps in more subtle ways. The policy evolved gradually, from 'reasonable' wartime concern about the loyalty and safety of Japanese-Americans, to 'voluntary' relocation, then to forced relocation to internment camps and a policy that continued well beyond any practical justification for its existence. Further, each step was cloaked with euphemism and legalities and buttressed by the long-standing prejudice against Asian immigrants to the U.S. Administrators in multiple agencies and levels of government helped to implement the policy without ever believing that they were doing anything wrong, and, in fact, believing that they were doing good. These images are imprinted on our memories.

But there is another key reason why we remember the internment camp case. It is now seen as safely in the past, an unfortunate wartime incident. The organizations responsible for the internment camps are gone or renamed, the principal actors dead. It is now part of another time and place, firmly distanced from our contemporary moral universe. This was not always so. The camps were not talked about for years after the fact, although they were in no way a secret. Only decades later did the nation confront its past and offer small reparations, which allowed the nation to demonstrate its 'moral advancement' since those darker times.

The willingness to at least acknowledge the evil of the internment camps might be laudable if not for the utter blindness to the administrative evil of the von Braun case. By contrast, decades after the fact there is still no recognition of the sad background of the space programme. Unlike the internment camps, the space programme is not just in the past, but is very much a part of the present. National pride and identity are wrapped up in the space programme. Images of technical accomplishment and organizational excellence take center stage and obscure the moral compromises on which they were built.

The von Braun case thus illustrates the power of technical rationality as a mask of administrative evil. We shall probably never know the extent to which those who crafted Operation Paperclip knew of the slave labour and mass murder at Dora when they initiated the U.S. space programme's reliance on von Braun and his compatriots. Regardless of what they knew, once the programme was under way, administrative processes and technical achievements progressively placed layer after layer of masking on the wartime activities of von Braun, Rudolf and others, thereby obscuring the effect of their values (or lack of them) and the concerns about their past on the organizational culture at Marshall, and later at NASA.

The perceived need to use the German (and former Nazi) rocket scientists to achieve technical superiority, and their subsequent successes, led NASA's leaders to build our space programme on a tainted legacy by placing technical advancement over respect for the humanity of those who were exploited and killed under the Nazi regime. This case shows how administrative evil became a hidden yet pervasive part of the organizations built on the foundation of Operation Paperclip.[43] For the most part, its influence remains largely unacknowledged as America continues to celebrate the achievements of the space programme and the triumph of technical rationality.

Despite procedural resemblance to the Holocaust, the internment camp policy did not progress to the extremes of exploitation and extermination found at Mittelbau-Dora. The key difference is the extent to which victims of the Holocaust, including those forced to build the V-2 rockets, were treated as a 'surplus population' by the Nazis and their collaborators. They became subject to dehumanization and extermination when they ceased to belong to a polity and lost all rights and connections to a protective community.[44] The Nazis had no intention of returning these concentration camp inmates to society. They did not fit into the Nazi vision of a community and country, and essentially ceased to exist once they entered the camps.

In the case of Japanese-American internment, key administrators such as Dillon Myer managed to view the internees as citizens and kept in mind their eventual return to society. While this may provide little solace to the victims of the policy or justify the violations of their rights, it is worth noting that administrators were able to curtail administrative evil and avoid its worst consequences. For the most part, government officials were able to recognize the internees as belonging to the polity and deserving of protection, a fact worth remembering. This was not the case in Operation Paperclip, where the victims of the Mittelbau-Dora were not considered in the process of building the U.S. space programme, and still are not recognized 50 years later as we celebrate the achievements to which they unwillingly contributed with their lives.

NOTES

1 Herbert Hirsch, *Genocide and the Politics of Memory* (Chapel Hill and London: University of North Carolina Press, 1995).
2 Fred. E. Katz. *Ordinary People and Extraordinary Evil: A report on the beguilings of evil* (Albany: State University of New York Press, 1993), p.5.
3 Sisela Bok, *Lying: Moral Choice in Public and Private Life* (New York: Vintage, 1978).
4 Guy B. Adams and Danny L. Balfour, *Unmasking Administrative Evil* (Thousand Oaks, CA: Sage Publications, 1998).
5 Berel Lang, *Act and Idea in the Nazi Genocide* (Chicago: University of Chicago Press, 1990).
6 Michael. J. Neufeld, *The Rocket and the Reich* (Cambridge, MA: Harvard University Press, 1996).
7 Raul Hilberg, 'The Bureaucracy of Annihilation', in F. Furet (ed.), *Unanswered Questions: Nazi Germany and the Genocide of the Jews* (New York: Schoken, 1989), pp.119–133.
8 Dennis Piskiewicz, *The Nazi Rocketeers: Dreams of Space and Crimes of War* (Westport, CT: Praeger, 1995), p.135.
9 Neufeld, p.264.
10 Piskiewicz, pp.96–97.
11 Neufeld, p.228.
12 J. Gimbel, 'U.S. policy and German scientists: the early Cold War', *Political and Science Quarterly* 101 (1986): 433–451.

13 M. Lippman, *The End of the Republican Era* (Norman, OK: University of Oklahoma Press, 1955).

14 Gimbel, p.443.

15 Jean Michel, *Dora*. (London: Weidenfeld & Nicholson, 1979).

16 Piskiewicz, p.237.

17 Howard McCurdy, *Inside NASA: High Technology and Organizational Change in the U.S. Space Program*. (Baltimore: Johns Hopkins University Press, 1993). See also, H.J. Anna, *Task Groups and Linkages in Complex Organizations: A Case Study of NASA* (Beverly Hill, CA: Sage Publications, 1976); A.L. Delbecq and A. Filley, *Program and Project Management in a Matrix Organization: A Case Study* (Madison, WI: Bureau of Business Research and Service, University of Wisconsin-Madison, 1974; and A.S. Levine, *Managing NASA in the Apollo Era* (Washington, D.C.: National Aeronautics and Space Administration, 1982).

18 Page Smith, *Democracy on Trial: The Japanese American Evacuation and Relocation in World War II* (New York: Simon and Schuster, 1995).

19 Morton Grodzins, *Americans Betrayed: Politics and the Japanese Evacuation* (Chicago: University of Chicago Press, 1949).

20 Commission on Wartime Relocation and Internment of Civilians, *Report: Personal Justice Denied* (Washington, DC: Government Printing Office, 1982).

21 Smith, p.88.

22 *ibid.*, p.99.

23 *ibid.*, p.100.

24 *ibid.*, p.119.

25 *ibid.*, p.117.

26 *ibid.*, p.122.

27 U.S. Department of War, *Japanese Evacuation from the West Coast, 194: General John DeWitt's Final Report* (Washington, DC: War Department, 1943).

28 U.S. House of Representatives, Select Committee (Tolan) Investigating National Defense Migration, *Preliminary Report and Recommendations on Problem of Evacuation of Citizens and Aliens from Military Areas*, 77th Congress, second session (Washington, DC: House of Representatives, 1942).

29 Milton Eisenhower, *The President is Calling* (Garden City, NY: Doubleday, 1974).

30 Alexander Leighton, *The Governing of Men: General Principles and Recommendations Based on Experience at a Japanese Relocation Camp* (Princeton, NJ: Princeton University Press, 1945).

31 Lester Suzuki, *Ministry in the Assembly and Relocation Centers of World War II* (Berkeley: Yardbird Press, 1979).

32 Diasuke Kitigawa, *Issei and Nisei: The Internment Years* (New York: Simon & Schuster, 1967).

33 Eisenhower, p.145.

34 Dillon S. Myer, *Uprooted Americans* (Tucson AZ: University of Arizona Press, 1971).

35 Edward H. Spicer et al., *Impounded People: Japanese-Americans in the Relocation Centers* (Tucson: University of Arizona Press, 1969).

36 John Tateishi, *And Justice for All: An Oral History of the Japanese American Detention Camps* (New York: Random House. 1984).

37 Smith, *op.cit.*

38 Jeanne W. Houston and James Houston, *Farewell to Manzanar* (New York: Bantam, 1966).

39 Roger Daniels, Sandra C. Taylor, and Harry H.L. Kitano, *Japanese Americans: From Relocation to Redress* (Salt Lake City: University of Utah Press, 1986).

40 Orville C. Shirey, *The Story of the 442nd Combat Team* (Washington, DC: The Infantry Journal, 1946).

41 Smith, p.420.

42 Katz, *op.cit.*

43 Adams and Balfour, *op.cit.*

44 Richard L. Rubenstein, *The Cunning of History* (New York: Harper & Row, 1975).

GEMILAT CHESED AND MORAL BEHAVIOUR AT WESTERBORK:
LESSONS FROM THE PAST TO REMEMBER FOR THE FUTURE

Ellen Ben-Sefer

These are the precepts that have no prescribed measure, the corner of a field (which must be left for the poor) the first fruit offering, the pilgrimage, acts of kindness and Torah study

(*Mishnah peah*, 1:1).

These are the precepts whose fruits a person enjoys in This World but whose principal remains intact for him in the World to Come. They are: the honour due to father an mother, acts of kindness, early attendance at the house of study morning and evening, hospitality to guests, visiting the sick, providing for a bride, escorting the dead, absorption in prayer, bringing peace between man and his fellow – and the study of Torah is equivalent to them all

(Talmud, *Shabbos*, 127a).

Notation to text: though one is rewarded for these mitzvot in This World, his reward in the World to Come is not diminished.

(*The Art Scroll*, Siddur, 16)

GEMILAT CHESED AND JUDAISM

IN ORDER to appreciate the meaning of *gemilat chesed* (acts of kindness) through the framework of Westerbork and, in particular, their application through the delivery of nursing care, it is essential that the concepts and principles, as well as the sources of such acts, are clarified. The principles and concepts supporting *gemilat chesed* are central to Jewish life and have been long established within the religion as well as the culture.

Leininger (1988) defined culture as learned and shared values and beliefs. These values and beliefs, furthermore, are transmitted as lifeway practices of a particular group. These practices and beliefs guide the thinking processes, decision making, and actions of specific groups of people in a highly patterned way of behaving.

Culture, for the purposes of this discussion, includes those Jews who are not halachically, that is, strictly observant in day-to-day life. That is, it includes those who do not practice stringent adherence to the performance of daily prayers, kashrut observance and Sabbath observance, but who have absorbed key principles that are essential to cultural survival in areas such as communal responsibility. The concept of 'loving one's neighbour as oneself', or community responsibility, is without doubt an extension of *gemilat chesed* commandments. While the same principle exists within Christian theology, there are essential differences between Jewish and Christian values. Judaism is grounded by the commandments, rather than theology, and *gemilat chesed* an essential one of those commandments.

Trepp (1966) commented that while many Jews are not strictly observant or involved in daily prayer, they nevertheless have been faithful to the *mitzvoth* in a wider sense with particular respect to tsedakah (charity) and *gemilat chesed* through their work in social justice. They have remained champions of movements such as the civil rights movement of the United States. Their adherence to Jewish thought and tradition may be construed as an adherence to the spirit rather than the letter of the law. Social action, then, is a universal function of all human beings.

This important acknowledgment of communal responsibility is highlighted in the *Pirkei Avot* (Ethics of the Fathers) in which one is enjoined to refrain from separating oneself from the community. In other words, the individual is held to a principle of collective responsibility to and for the community.

According to Donin (1972), the very concept of *chesed*, or kindness, includes all such services that may be performed for another person. Talmudic interpretation refers to numerous citations including Hillel that prescribe the necessity of exercising humanity and acts that indicate one's love of one's fellow mortals. These acts are interpreted to include visiting the sick, providing hospitality, provision of funds for orphans, and visiting and comforting those in mourning.

Arguably, the most important verses in the Old Testament are those which state that man is created in the image of G–d, and that man is to love one's neighbour as oneself. Being created in the image of G–d does not necessarily refer to physical appearance; rather, it refers to the spiritual resemblance and the consequent behaviours that are associated with such an image.

Loving one's neighbour as oneself includes the difficult task of 'loving' those who have done harm to others under certain circumstances. In Chapter 23 of Deuteronomy, a call is made to avoid rejection of Egyptians despite their enslavement of the Hebrews. This is meant as a specific reminder that despite enslavement in Egypt, Egypt provided both food and shelter to Jacob and his family when they sought shelter. This is a powerful recognition for the years in which the Hebrews dwelt in Egypt peacefully during famine throughout the known world.

Gemilat chesed has no ulterior motive. True kindness, the greatest act of kindness according to Scherman (1993, *Art Scroll Chumash*, p.23), is that which cannot be returned. This is considered '*chesed shel emet*', literally, the 'kindness of truth', and is composed of those acts that are performed for the deceased. Obviously, the deceased have no way of reciprocating any act of kindness, so the deed is performed without thought of remuneration.

Interestingly, no blessing is required before performing any act of kindness, despite the fact that it is a commandment and, as such, would ordinarily require a blessing to be made. Two important reasons are linked with this extraordinary distinction in this specific commandment. First, there is an acknowledgment that an opportunity to perform such an act should never be missed through time lost seeking the appropriate blessing. In other words, the act is of paramount importance, and nothing should stand in the way of its performance. Second, the performance of kind acts is not time bound as other commandments are, such as kindling Sabbath lights. They can and should be performed whenever and wherever possible. In addition, *gemilat chesed* is neither gender bound, as is daily prayer, nor age restricted, as are other commandments.

GEMILAT CHESED AND TSEDAKAH

Acts of kindness should be clearly differentiated from the laws of charity (*tsedakah*), which are also incumbent on all Jews. Every individual is required to give according to one's individual means. Even those persons who are recipients of charity must give a sum of money, if only a little. However the distinction between tzedakah and *gemilat chesed* should be specified.

Without doubt, the most notable differentiation between *gemilat chesed* and *tsedakah* is that no quantitative value is placed on *gemilat chesed*. Rather succinctly, donation in monetary terms carries a value. Consequently, while the wealthy person can give more than one with less means, *gemilat chesed* rests on the performance of some act of kindness. It follows that those with lesser means have just as great an opportunity to perform such an act the wealthy person.

Furthermore, it is rather significant that the Torah does not prescribe how much is involved in the performance of these specific mitzvot. That is, a quantitative guideline is not expressed or formulated in terms of the amounts of time of funds involved in meeting the required act, as opposed to suggestions regarding dispersal of funds for charitable reasons.

Donin explained that the concept of kindness includes all forms of benevolence shown by a person whenever he exerts himself on behalf of another. According to Steinsaltz (1982), the mitzvah (commandment) of *gemilat chesed* can be performed in many ways and have multiple levels of potential fulfillment. Help for the individual may include provisions of loans, visiting the sick, healing rifts between individuals, and similar helping actions. Steinsaltz reiterated that the pursuit of justice and kindness has equal importance for the giver and the recipient. It involves the capacity to see the recipient as a 'brother,' rather than a stranger. The ability to see beyond oneself aids the individual in his own spiritual development. The essential ingredient in the relationship between the two is the donor's capacity to appreciate the other's need and move beyond oneself. That is, it is incumbent on the donor to have a strong sense of empathy, an understanding from the inside rather than simple sympathy, a perspective from the outside of the donor.

Tsedakah, on the other hand, which is most often translated as charity, more correctly refers to righteousness from the Hebrew word. It implies rather powerfully that giving to another is the correct and just thing to do. Here, one must to distinguish between *gemilat chesed, tsedakah* and simple charity. Charity, derived from Latin, means 'from the heart'.

For the Jew, *gemilat chesed* and *tsedakah* are commandments, which classifies them as acts that one must do. It is important to distinguish these acts from those which involve choice and over which one may exercise a decision. That is, for Jews it is a commandment, which makes the act something one must do, not what one might like to do or in which one may exercise a choice. The recipient, then, is entitled by right to receive these benefits; thus, emphasis is placed equally on donor and recipient. Charity, while recognizably important, has a different perspective. The donor will 'feel good' because of doing one's duty or behaving in a benevolent manner. The recipient may also live in hope that such actions will improve one's standing in the 'next world,' a vague, elusive concept in Judaism. Judaism primarily provides the commandments to ensure a practical guide to one's life in the here and now, rather than promises or hopes of betterment in another life.

The religious significance of *gemilat chesed*, according to Steinsaltz (1957), is that Judaism, while recognizing the existence of evil in the world, aims to replace it with a better perfected world. As such, Jewish understanding of the world points to a co-partnership with the Almighty. In the 'Alenu' daily prayers, the concept of *Tikun Olam*, that is, 'to repair the world,' is clearly stated, which leads one to conclude that it is a primary responsibility of each individual and is central to Jewish thinking. 'Alenu' points to the day when all humanity worships a Universal G–d, not necessarily as Jews, but in the acknowledgment of His sovereignty along with the ethical duties that flow from that acknowledgment (Donin, 1980).

Thus, acts of kindness are a vital factor in the move forward in this ethical structure of creating a more caring society and a culture that values care and caring practices. Education from a young age is an essential component of achieving that perfection. The reform begins with the internal spiritual betterment out of which the larger social improvement can grow and attain a lasting existence. Furthermore, social science theory suggests that role-modelling behaviour is a powerful means of determining the behaviour that children will adopt (Bandura, 1971).

Perhaps equally significant to note is that the reminder concerning *gemilat chesed* appears twice in the morning prayers, denoting its importance within the context of Jewish daily life. Furthermore, the reward that one receives has been interpreted as one that shall be obtained both in this world and the elusive spiritual world that has never been clearly defined in Judaism. Finally, these are practices, as much of Judaism is practiced, within the home and family context, rather than ritual practices in a syn-agogue. In the author's experience, individuals often commiserate that they come from homes in which little Jewish education was given. Their statement is based on lack of rituals, rather than an absence of behaviours and practices that often are associated with families irrespective of their observance of Jewish rituals.

In summary one may interpret these statements to mean that acts of kindness are not only inherent within Jewish life and practice, but also are deemed to be vitally important. There are no distinctions within the community concerning this commandments such as males requirements of prayer or women's responsibility regarding the kindling of Sabbath lights. They are incumbent upon all Jews, both adults and children, men and women equally, and vitally central to the way of life within Jewish communities.

GEMILAT CHESED AND THE TORAH

An example from the Torah that carries particular relevance to the subject of nursing is found in the opening chapters of the Book of Exodus. Two midwives are called before the Pharaoh and ordered to kill all boys born to the Hebrews. Despite the inherent threat in refusing to obey the order, the two, Shifrah and Puah, refuse, and the central character of Exodus, Moses, is subsequently born, eventually leading to the freedom of the Hebrew slaves. Interestingly, little is known about the two aside from their names, giving rise to speculation among commentators, some of whom theorise that the two women are Hebrew midwives, while others put forth the view that they are midwives to the Hebrew population, but not necessarily Hebrew themselves. Other commentary suggests that they are pseudonyms for Jochebed and Miriam, mother and sister to Moses (Scherman, 1993; *Art Scroll Chumash; Softah*, 11b). Clearly, there has been considerable speculation over the identity of these two midwives; however, the deed overshadows the identity in this case.

Without the specific refusal by these two relatively unknown women to disobey the Pharoh, the greatest figure in Jewish thought and development of moral codes of behaviour, Moses, would not have survived. This holds true both in traditional and reformed streams of Judaism. Furthermore, the Ten Commandments, a cornerstone of Western thought and behaviour, would not have been granted after the exodus. Yet, these two midwives are not heroes or even central to the story; they are superseded by others such as Aaron, Miriam, and even Jethro and Tsiporah. Nevertheless, the contribution and actions of these two women had a vital impact on world history and Jewish thought.

In summary, the concept of providing for charities as well as performing acts of kindness have a vital central role in Jewish religion and practice mandated by commandment rather than choice. Westerbork, as a geographic entity, was populated almost exclusively by Jewish inmates; it follows that *gemilat chesed* is an important concept in terms of providing some understanding of events that occurred in Westerbork.

THE NATURE OF CARE AND CARING RELATIONSHIPS

Acts of kindness imply that a caring relationship must exist between the donor and the recipient. According to Oliner and Oliner, care is the assumption of personal responsibility for the welfare of other individuals. Caring relationships, then, include a specific attaching process that must take place which enables care and caring to occur. These include processes such as bonding and empathizing with others. Bonding is described as the formation of positive connections between two or more individuals. Empathizing is a way of understanding the feelings of others from their perspective, rather than from the perspective the carer.

It is vital to understand that a great difference exists between the feelings of sympathy and the feelings of empathy. Sympathy includes commiseration with others, that is, looking at the situation from one's own perspective and from a distance. Empathy, on the other hand, refers to a sense of feeling along with the individual and responding to the situation from the individual's terms. Sympathizers, then, act from their own needs, and their help often is perceived as being condescending and often patronizing. Empathizers act on the basis of others' needs and thoughts, and respond more appropriately to those who need their help; as a result, the cared for respond with much more appreciation. Effective help, then, requires those who provide aid to encounter the crisis from an internal knowledge of the recipient's needs.

The issue of care and caring continues to permeate nursing literature. Research, scholarly debate, and discussion continue into this very elusive essence of nursing practice. A considerable body of literature has been put forth in recent years that concerns itself with the meaning of care in nursing practice. According to MacDonald (1993), this is a reasonable phenomenon worthy of attention, because the imperative that underlines this work is that all nurses must care. However, this still gives rise to different interpretations of the meaning of care or caring within that professional context. Benner and Wrubel (1989) considered care to be the essential element in any relationship between the nurse and a patient. Furthermore, that ability to make emotional contact with the patient represents the empathic relationship essential to the profession.

Benner and Wrubel implied that in a caring relationship, a condition exists in which someone who is outside the individual matters and a situation thereby exists in which personal concerns must be created. Consequently, the process of caring determines what is of importance to an individual and provides a marker for those situations or events that also may be stressful. The very act of caring provides multiple possibilities and, with meaningful distinction, that provides a strong sources of motivation for the carer, as a direction for those who will serve as carers.

Practicing care and assuming personal responsibility presume the participation of the carer in caring practices and developing a personal sense of obligation towards such practices. Examples of such caring practices, according to Benner and Wrubel, involve activities in our culture that include parenting, child care, and education, nursing, counselling and community service.

Other researchers have identified specific behaviours that have been associated with perceptions of caring. Knowlden (1988) concluded that the extension of hope, listening, touching, laughter, and building self-esteem are integral aspects of the caring relationship between nurse and patient. Kim (1997) found eight therapeutic means of effective caring in study of mentally ill patients in South Korea. These include noticing, participating, sharing, active listening, companioning, complementing, comforting and hoping.

There appears to be a considerable diversity in discerning the meaning of caring, even within the 'caring' professions. While some authors speak of dedication, others speak of compassion and empathy. The critical element in all of these definitions, however, appears to be the concept of an intricate relationship, in this case, between nurse and patient, that has great intimacy (Kuhse, 1997). Despite the diversity of thought and areas of nursing practice, there are clearly key areas that link theory and practice within the context of nursing irrespective of culture. Perhaps the significant connection between these theorists and researchers is that specific aspects of a caring process and behaviour are identified by all of them irrespective of the culture or setting. These practices and the way in which they are delivered form a link between the cultural understanding of acts of chesed and the practice of nursing in Westerbork in which these caring norms will be described through the individual recollections of several nurses.

Practitioners in different professional fields are bound by a code of moral obligations that are applicable to their professional practice. An example that is most well known is the Hippocratic oath taken by physicians, which reflects a specific theory of moral obligation. Ethical theories of practice assume that the agent, in this instance the nurse, has a specific capacity for action because of special types of skills. Knowledge of moral value and obligation is essential nursing practice and helps the nurse to provide care and develop a caring ethic as a code of behaviour that ensures that the approach to each individual client as a person with special value and worth (Nicholl, 1992).

Caring or kind behaviour is simply, then, an act that involves two individuals, without justification, without ideology, without asking whether or not the recipient is worthy of the act, but a powerful interaction between the two for the benefit of the recipient. Despite its seeming simplicity, its everyday character, it is this interaction that defines caring behaviour. The act of kindness and caring for another person is, according to Todorov (1996), the essence of a human being. It is this characteristic and the behaviour and practices engendered within the concept that will endure as long as the human race exists.

In a society that has become increasingly autonomous and independent, celebrating the process and concept of caring is culturally embarrassing and the antithesis of individualistic view of self. Cultural icons from Schwarzenegger to pop stars are the heroes for contemporary society, highlighting physical strength, violence, and physical responses. Cartoon characters from Superman to Wonder Woman celebrate the dominance of strength and physical force as attributes for the young to emulate. Spiritual strength and emotional strength pale in comparison to the physical in popular culture. Caring is the antithesis of such physical behaviours, because it highlights the importance of interdependence between individuals and acknowledges the fragile nature of human life and the reality that human beings essentially depend on one another. To care, then, and experience the phenomenon of caring, elevates the individual a well as a society and culture (Heidegger, 1962, cited in Benner and Wrubel, 1989).

To learn any skills, including caring practices, one must be able to observe them in action, much as one learns music, art, or any craft, from an advanced or master practitioner of the skill (Sacks, 1997). Such practices can be encouraged in schools and in homes. Caring, like any other skill mastery, requires practice. While professional, social, and ideological factors influence the behaviour of individuals, including the notion of caring practices, ultimately, a culture, such as the culture of caring in which these practices hold value, strongly encourages the individual to continue to exhibit such behaviours and practices, irrespective of the circumstances.

While there has been some evidence that girls tend to be more generous and helpful than boys, it has also been noted that girls received more affection from parents and more explanations for the consequences of their actions. Age itself may be a factor in the development of altruistic responses. Altruistic children tend to be more able to put himself or herself in another person's place and to be more advanced in mental reasoning.

Parents of altruistic children promote empathy with others by encouraging children to appreciate how others would feel over specific incidents. Often empathetic, caring children are held to high standards of behaviour and conduct and are given responsibility at home. Prosocial behaviour that is embedded within the entire culture, such as the kibbutz movement in Israel, enables such conduct to flourish, leading to the development of caring rules and values.

In the author's experience, it is noteworthy that some schools will foster values through homework projects such as searching for newspaper articles that may be about chesed for primary school children or keeping a chesed chart for preschool and younger children. Such concrete assignments and evidence help to expose young children to the importance of chesed and imprint the value of such acts upon them.

In summary, the issue and puzzle of care, caring practices, and their expression continue to permeate nursing literature as better understanding of the phenomena associated with these concepts is sought. The ideas and understanding of *gemilat chesed*, that is, acts of kindness, have demonstrable parallels with care and caring as noted in the practices associated with caring in the nursing literature.

NURSING IN KAMP WESTERBORK

Westerbork, the main transit camp for Dutch Jewry, provides a framework for relating accounts of care and caring within a nursing discipline. The camp itself had a large hospital and an extensive, highly qualified staff of health care professionals who delivered care to inmates in the camp itself. Nursing care is defined here as a caring practice, and it is often construed from individual experiences.

Westerbork provides an opportunity to examine the roles of such nurses due to several particular factors. However, in order to appreciate the reasons for that perspective, it is essential to briefly consider the purpose of Westerbork. Westerbork was the main transit camp in the Netherlands, initially conceived by the Dutch government as a temporary solution for refugee German Jews who had no entry visa for other countries. During the Nazi occupation of the Netherlands, the camp became a transit camp to which Dutch Jews could be conveniently sent for subsequent deportation to the east.

On 9 October 1939, the first German Jewish refugees arrived in Westerbork. By May 1940, they numbered 750 people. While the camp changed jurisdiction, falling under the various titles of 'central camp for refugees' and 'police transit camp'; on 1 July 1942, the German authorities declared Westerbork to be a transit camp. The Wannsee conference of 20 January 1943 inevitably changed the purpose and character of Westerbork. Until that time, the camp could logically be considered a home for stateless people or refugees. According to Moore (1997), the first Dutch Jews did not arrive in Westerbork until the summer of 1942. This may be presumed to be due directly to the decisions regarding the 'Final Solution' of European Jewry at Wannsee earlier that year. After that time, the camp became a holding pen for the Dutch Jews who were rounded up, beginning in 1942, from which they could be sent east to Poland. Westerbork was perceived then as a funnel through which Jews would pass, never to return.

Isolated from the surrounding Dutch population, the inmates awaited transport to the east and the death camps. As a transit camp, Westerbork was not an extermination centre; brutality such as that which existed in the infamous camps of Germany and the occupied countries of Eastern Europe was a relatively rare occurrence. According to Presser (1969), all those who entered Westerbork were struck by the highly organized manner in which the camp was run. This organization of camp life was primarily the achievement of the initial inmates, that is, the German Jews who had already been there for several years.

In a peculiar parallel to normal life, Westerbork presented a facade to the newcomer and bore a resemblance to a town with its school, police force, cabaret, and recreational facilities as well as being the largest hospital in the Netherlands. It contained 1,725 beds, an outpatient clinic, a pharmacy, and a dental clinic,[1] and was operated by a highly qualified staff of over a thousand (Thomas and Witts, 1974).

By all accounts from both patients and staff, the hospital provided a high quality level of care to its patients and had reasonable supplies of medications available. Wards such as paediatrics, men and women's surgical and medical, infectious diseases, and maternity existed in the hospital. Surgery was carried out in an operating theatre within the camp. Without doubt, this hospital was a part of the cruel design of the Nazis to create an illusion that would lull prisoners into a false sense of security and hope that the camps in the east would not be much worse than Westerbork.

While Westerbork had a succession of commandants, the one most closely associated with the deportations was Albert Konrad Gemmeker. Gemmeker remarked in a letter sent to The Hague that the nursing care in Westerbork was better in 1943 than it had been in general anywhere in 1939 (Doc 806 Inv. NR. 8512–12 (Herinneringscentrum Kamp Westerbork-original held at Nederlands Instituut voor Oorlogsdocumentarie). Gemmeker most certainly had his own ulterior reasons for such claims; nevertheless, the letter evidences that the care at Westerbork, was indeed excellent, from the point of view of staff, patients and the Nazi overseers.

A brief account of the survivors' recollections may shed some light on the caring environment in Westerbork. The following, then, is based in part on literature, but primarily on interviews with these survivors conducted as a portion of a research project conducted by the author.

The Nurses
Seventy-five percent of the Dutch Jewish population, 105,000 people, perished in the Shoah. Consequently, very few nurses who worked in the Westerbork hospital survived. The few who did survive to relate events that took place in and around the hospital in Westerbork paint a picture of nurses who cared deeply about their patients, were devoted to helping them, and did their utmost to ease pain and suffering despite their own fragile existences. The nurses interviewed for this project were themselves divided in their opinions as to whether their positions as nurses protected them from deportation. While several thought their positions afforded some protection, others vehemently disagreed

with this viewpoint. The five nurses interviewed for this project all met different fates on their departures from Westerbork. Two were sent to Bergen-Belsen where they continued nursing, one to Theresienstadt, one to Auschwitz, and one escaped through the efforts of the resistance.

Bob Cahen

One of the first to arrive in Westerbork was Bob Cahen. Bob was arrested on 2 August 1942 in one of the first national *razzia* (round-ups of Jews), along with his mother and brother in The Hague. From there they were sent to Amersfoort and subsequently to Westerbork. On 18 January 1944, Bob was sent to Theresienstadt and subsequently to Auschwitz.

Bob accompanied patients from the hospital in Westerbork to the Groningen hospital when outside treatment was necessary. During these trips, he smuggled out letters from the camp, others as well as his own, at considerable risk. Bob's letters survived the war, and in one, he described the roundup of 17,000 Jews in October 1942, thrown into a camp that had places for only 10,000. Bob kept his word, as written in one of his letters, vowing to return at the end of the war. He resides in The Hague today and is active in youth education accompanying young pupils on educational excursions to Westerbork.

> ...the barracks became still more crowded. People lay or sat outside. During the night they slept in or under wheelbarrows in the open air. There was not enough food. Sometimes there was hot food one in three days and even then insufficient. Babies did have not milk, there was nothing else. The pumping machine for the water supply worked under tension. Could not cope with the situation and did not purify the water sufficiently, with the result that people had to drink unpurified water – with all the consequences of this.
>
> Barracks, which in normal times housed 400 people, were now crowded with 1000 lying on the floor and everywhere. Lavatories were insufficient and clogged. Men and women lay in one ward, it was chaos. In this chaos we had to work, take away the patients and nurse them. Our hospital was full, was extended with an enormous barrack. 5 wards extra. New staff engaged. Hurry up. One day after this full again. A large barrack was fitted with an emergency hospital – Nursing itself no material, pots and urinals were lacking, plates to eat were absent, there was no hot water, sheets blankets were not present (Cahen, 1988, pp.9–10).

Bob addressed the anguish, moral and ethical dilemmas being faced by himself and his colleagues and his attempts to convey those feelings to family and friends still outside the camp. He went on to describe with great feeling the death of an observant Jew whose wife presented Bob with his *tefillin* (phylacteries) as a token of thanks for his care. Bob clearly expressed the feelings of desperation felt by the nursing and medical staff trying frantically to provide aid to their fellow Jews. He further described his finding of one man, who had attempted suicide by slashing his throat, whom he carried to the hospital and helped to save. To his great anguish, his efforts resulted in the man eventually being sent on transport.

Bob also was assigned 'train duty' during which he was required to attend those who were to be sent on transport at the actual rail siding. He was required to calm those who became unmanageable at the train loading, if necessary with an injection of a sedative (J.B. Cahen, personal communication, 8 July 1998).

The expression of compassion, empathy and commiseration with the victims is apparent from Bob's recollections of these events. A sense of sharing and participating with the victims, compassionate care and a deep sense of commitment to them is clearly reflected in his account.

Trudel van Reemst de Vries

Trudel van Reemst de Vries was born in Frankfurt-am-Main in 1914 into a middle-class Jewish family. As a child, she recollected a number of childhood anti-semitic incidents. At the age of 11 years, her family moved to The Netherlands, where they lived in both Eindhoven and The Hague. Trudel's family was associated with the Zionist movement and she joined a Zionist youth group. She worked in the Jewish hospital in Rotterdam, eventually becoming a nurse. In 1937, she went to Spain to help during the Civil War; she met her husband there. When the war broke out she served in the resistance. In 1942 she was arrested and sent to Westerbork where she remained for six months.

Trudel was assigned to the maternity ward of the hospital. There she cared for new mothers and babies. In her account of that time, she recalled that the quality of care delivered was very high (Lindwer, 1990). She recollected a number of poignant incidents including the death of a number of infants due to a diphtheria epidemic. Nursing mothers were released from transport at that time. Consequently, mothers whose infants had died nursed other babies in order to be released from transport. One can only speculate on the feelings of the women nursing other babies as a desperate means of saving their lives while knowing that their own infants had died.

Without doubt, Trudel's most vivid memory is of Michael, a tiny infant born in Vught concentration camp after the women had been forced to stand at appel for a considerable number of hours, which resulted in a premature birth. As the women were forced into cattle cars, the other women wrapped the infant in whatever they could find to keep him warm. At Westerbork, because the mother was unable to nurse the infant, she was deemed 'worthless' and sent on transport. Trudel and another nurse were assigned to care for the child. According to Trudel's recollections, Gemmeker took a 'special interest' in the care of the child, ordering an incubator for him, a special paediatric consult, and arrangements for special feeding by nasogastric tubes. Both Trudel and the other nurse assigned to care for the infant poured their hearts into their fight for the life for this child. The nurses interpreted this behaviour as positive. The child evolved into a symbol of hope, since Gemmeker would allow the child to live. Their hopes were dashed when Michael attained the weight of six pounds and was sent on 'transport to labour'. Another nurse noted this recollection of Gemmeker's 'special interest' in various activities in the hospital. It will be discussed at a later point.

More than 50 years after this event, Trudel remained devastated by its recollection. It supplied evidence to refute the myth that Gemmeker 'adored children and took a special interest in them'. Whatever special interest he may have had, it did not prevent the transport of thousands of children under his command to the death camps of Eastern Europe. Trudel provided further evidence to Gemmeker's attempts to delude pregnant women on transport by sending midwives to accompany them on the journey.

Despite this tragic event, Trudel stated her belief that the most important care that she gave to people in Westerbork was to try to instill a feeling of hope in them and to spend time listening carefully to what her patients needed to express. In her own words, to be a nurse in Westerbork 'was to have solidarity with other human beings. To give and receive solidarity is to be a nurse under those circumstances.' She related that one personal result of her incarceration in Westerbork was her inability to say goodbye to anyone at a train station.

In spite of these experiences, Trudel has steadfastly maintained a belief in social justice and remained an optimist who clearly relishes life. By her description of her nursing care and involvement with her patients, she illustrated some of the specific practices identified by researchers previously cited. These include the provision of hope, which she explicitly stated herself, as well as a clear involvement with patients through participation and sharing. She lives today in Amsterdam and has contributed to various historians and filmmakers in developing an understanding of the Shoah and its impact on the Dutch Jewish community.

Sara Jacobs

Sara Jacobs was only 14 years old when she arrived at Westerbork. She was born and raised in Rotterdam, where she attended school until Jewish children were forcibly removed from Dutch schools. After that time, a Jewish teacher organized admission of Jewish girls to a domestic science school. In a parallel to Anne Frank and her family, whom she later met in Bergen-Belsen, her family had planned to go into hiding and had been betrayed. Adolescence in Westerbork was a very tenuous age indeed. While a school existed in Westerbork, not all adolescents were able to attend. Many were assigned to jobs, and, according to Moskin (1972), adolescents above the age of 16 years could be transported without their families. Sara had received some training in the care of children. As a result, she was assigned to look after children ranging in age from young infants to the age of three years. She worked extensively with the paediatrician Dr. Wolf. Sara recollected assisting with minor surgical treatment, fighting off her own revulsion, in order to aid the children. Sara provided care that included regular measurement of height and weight such as carried out today in early childhood centres in many parts of the world. She also made time to play with the children. When asked during a recent interview what she thought was the most important care she provided to the children Sara replied, 'I made sure that each child going on transport had a toy to take along.' The children were so young that very little was told to them about the transport; they could not understand, and so they were simply told that they were going to another place.

Sara lives today in The Hague. For many years, she was active in the Jewish community of Delft, prior to her retirement. As is common to many other survivors, wartime recollections, particularly the years spent in Westerbork and Bergen-Belsen, continue to haunt Sara and remain painful and difficult experiences to recall. This was more apparent with Sara than the others. As the youngest of the group, she was still within her adolescent and formative years. Despite the emotional upheaval that recalling her history inevitably causes, she remained committed to the idea of telling about her experiences for the benefit of others and to provide understanding for today's generation (S. Jacobs, personal communication, 8 July 1998).

Jeanne van den Berg van Cleeff

Jeanne was born and raised in The Netherlands. She studied in Utrecht, and went on to live in Rotterdam. Jeanne and her parents were picked up by the Germans and taken to Westerbork where she remained from September 1942 to September 1944. During those two years, she worked in the hospital, particularly as a circulating nurse in the operating theatre. Similar to Trudel's recollection, Jeanne had frequent contact with Gemmeker. She recalled that the operating theatre was a particular hobby of the commandant, and Gemmeker often came in to observe operations (personal communication, December 1997).

In her own words, Jeanne stated her belief that the most important thing that she was able to do for her patients was to provide a sense of hope. In an interview with the author on 28 June 1998, Jeanne stated that hope was 'something we had ourselves, so we gave it to other people.' This belief was also supported by open-ended questions to patients which included eliciting their ambitions and plans for after the war. Such questions provided the subtle implication that they would indeed survive.

During the interview Jeanne commented that 'it sounds silly, I know but whenever I meet with other survivors that I knew in the camps one of the first things we say is, 'Do you remember laughing about . . . ?' (personal communication, 28 June 1998).

Jeanne again provided distinct models of behaviours associated with caring practices. She never lost the ability to laugh or her sense of humour, a factor that has been more recently examined by Shoah researchers as a factor in survival. Furthermore, she understood the importance of giving people hope when it was so powerful within her.

Curiously, Jeanne specifically recalled in both interviews and letters Gemmeker's frequent visits to the operating theatre. He often watched surgical procedures, and it was not considered unusual for the commandant to be in attendance in the operating theatre. Other nurses, interviewed for this project, denied seeing Gemmeker in their area of the hospital. While it appears that the commandant had 'pet' areas of interest, as described by Trudel and Jeanne, this did not extend to the entire hospital complex.

Jeanne was sent to Bergen-Belsen, where she continued nursing others, even without the benefit of anything other than water as a medicine; this again reinforces the concepts of caring behaviours as essential to nursing practice. Jeanne's parents were murdered in Sobibor.

Jeanne lives today in Maarsen, a short distance north of Amsterdam. Like many others, Jeanne still finds it difficult to discuss some aspects of her war experiences, especially with her own children and grandchildren.

Kitty Nystad-de Wijze
Kitty Nystad-de Wijze suffered the loss of her parents and her first husband, whom she married in Westerbork. A compassionate, gracious woman, she recalled that when all else failed, she was able to commiserate with patients and cry with them if they were to be transported. She believed that it was important to be gentle with people, talk to family who were visiting patients, and remain interested in her patients. In her own words, she felt strongly that she had to remain 'human' (personal communication, 7 July 1998). Kitty clearly understood the importance of sharing with patients their concerns, their worries and anxieties. She cheerfully stated that if patients wanted her to sing, she would gladly do so to please them.

Kitty most certainly had an empathetic point of view. Her descriptions of her caring practices illustrate the delivery of empathetic care that was the result of active listening, participating, sharing, and companioning when necessary to her patients. Kitty and her husband live in The Netherlands with their family nearby.

MORAL BEHAVIOUR
Barbarism in any form, including that conducted during the Shoa, provides graphic evidence of the evil that can be unleashed when people determine that they can make up their own rules of morality or immorality, leading to a bankruptcy in moral and ethical values. Jewish tradition and practice are primarily considered to be based on a compilation of laws and their various interpretations. The practices and guidelines provide one with a framework for these beliefs and values, practical applications, and an understanding of how one should comport oneself. This includes *gemilat chesed* as a way in which to live. Irrespective of their stringent attention to religious observance, many Jews

clearly may be observing the spirit of the law rather than the letter of the law. Consequently, the scale of values is that which one lives by rather than what one preaches or professes.

Despite profession of positive values, those who behave in a barbarous manner provide their own evidence, despite what they may preach, simply through the demonstration of the values by which they have chosen to live.

The Shoah has provided a modern example of what can and does happen when human beings separate themselves from a sense of morality, as well as examples of those who chose the opposite. Furthermore, according to Aiken (1996), it has also evidenced the inability and inadequacy of the human conscience to determine adequate moral values and rules through its own self-serving nature. A rejection of moral laws and values allows people to do anything, as is so clearly apparent from The Shoah and the horrors engendered within that time period. Indeed, the Nazi extermination camp system established 'new world' norms of de-humanization that led one to believe that moral behaviour and values had disappeared from this world.

Interestingly, Todorov (1996) argued that moral behaviour did not, in fact, disappear during the Shoah, but certain acts were reinterpreted under such condition. He illustrated this view with the example of murder committed to prevent assassins from carrying out further cruel and vicious deeds. This was also illustrated, paradoxically, by Moses, the greatest figure in Jewish thought and possibly in Western civilization. In Exodus, it is clearly related that Moses killed an Egyptian taskmaster, who was beating a Hebrew slave, to prevent further harm. Nevertheless, he remained an unconvicted killer himself, never punished for the crime.

All too many times, the question has been raised as to why the Shoah happened. While no answer can even satisfy that question, the essence of a moral reply is that one must make every attempt to lead a meaningful life. The behaviour, then, of these five nurses at Westerbork clearly illustrates the distinction between Todorov's definitions of vital and moral values. Vital values, according to Todorov (1991), are those which recognize the importance of one's own life as sacred. Moral values, however, recognize that the life of others is paramount.

This, itself, was the moral reply of the nurses previously discussed. This is hardly surprising, considering the finding of two researchers concerning with moral development. Kohlberg's theory of moral development suggests that moral reasoning evolves and continues during adolescence and adulthood (Colby and Kohlberg, 1987). His work was conducted primarily with males, who were found to have a decidedly different orientation than females. Men were more concerned with rules, laws, and justice. Gilligan (1982), however, found that a distinct difference exists between men and women. While women have a justice perspective in moral reasoning, a care and caring perspective is the primary orientation of women's moral reasoning. This caring perspective is centred on the ethics of care and interpersonal relationships with others. Considering these findings, it is hardly surprising that nursing continues to be a female-dominated profession, despite the entry of males into nursing. Indeed, Bob Cahen provides evidence of the caring phenomenon within the male context in Westerbork. Nevertheless, nursing was and continues to be dominated by women.

Despite their circumstances, these nurses, both men and women, made a moral choice to provide meaningful care, to provide acts of kindness whether large or small to their fellow inmates. Perhaps equally important, The Shoah has also provided a clear cut understanding that morality itself cannot and does not allow for neutrality for human beings (Aiken, 1996). Rather, each individual must decided to live his or her own life attempting to live in truth despite over-riding factors. Under such circumstances, even to make the effort to survive is a statement of moral fortitude. According to Telushkin, (1996), Rabbi Milton Steinberg said, 'When I was young, I admired clever people. Now that I am older, I admire kind people' (p. 126). The significance of this statement is that the rabbi understood that, ultimately, being kind is of considerable more importance than being clever.

The Talmud strongly suggests that despite the best of intentions, everyone will behave in morally negative reprehensible ways at least some of the time. The issue is not whether one does so or not, but whether or not one chooses to make oneself better and attempts to influence others to do better despite the conclusion that neither will achieve complete perfection. The principle of 'Tshuvah', that is, repentance, implicitly accepts that all human beings can be wrong and do wrong, but that one has been given a chance to right the wrong behaviour. Western civilisation accepts that the Ten Commandments form a cornerstone for moral behaviour that has existed from ancient times until the present. While the first five commandments are linked to man's relationship with G-d, the second five deal specifically with man's relationship to his fellow man.

In his discussion of heroic behaviour and heroes, Todorov (1996) commented that a hero is an individual who fights against the odds and by some remarkable way bends destiny to his own ends. The hero does not accept fate, but prefers to view life as a revolutionary. This individual is differentiated from others who are carers. Caring, in his terms is an ordinary virtue undertaken for the sake of an individual, not a heroic virtue.

CONCLUSION

Despite nursing's considerable articulation of the process of care and caring, there is still some criticism that the profession's views of the phenomenon, and caring practices in general, are inadequate and still incomplete (Johnstone, 1989). To some degree, the concept of care may never be definable; however, care and caring practices take place in the real world and in very real circumstances of life for all humans. Identification of practices historically associated with care and caring make the very concept and practice of care considerably more visible as a principle of moral behaviour as well as a cardinal principle of practice. The historical examples provided by these nurses serve to illustrate that the issues, concept, and perceptions of care have not changed despite advances in technology in nursing practice. Indeed, care remains the one constant, despite advances in technology, and therefore merits consideration as the one force that unites all areas of nursing. It also retains the ability to provide a moral fibre for society as a whole.

The experience of the Shoah seems to bolster Aiken's contention that everything that an individual may hold dear or value, whether it be a home, car, material possessions or loved ones, can disappear unexpectedly. The generation that survived The Shoah can readily identify with such a stance (Aiken, 1996). However, Aiken did add that the one thing that cannot be taken from the individual is his or her reputation. Whether one chooses to be remembered as a caring or non-caring individual rests in the will of that individual. Those who withstood the pressures to detach themselves from their charges and maintain a professional stance as non-carers made the choice to care, consequently leaving a reputation as caring individuals.

In the concrete situations faced by individuals in the camps of terror and dehumanization, caring behaviours and practices, as illustrated by the group of nurses interviewed for this project, flourished despite the circumstances. Their behaviours, attitudes, and strategies all strongly suggest a particular response shared by the entire group. The group confirmed these were practices learned within Jewish homes and provided by Jewish nurses to Jewish patients.

While the nurses interviewed for this project may have had different sociological and educational backgrounds and were different ages at the time they were in Westerbork, the common denominator was their Jewish background. Despite differences in adherence to religious practice, all of them responded in the same manner to the questions concerning why they chose to behave in caring ways. Their responses all suggested that they could not conceive of any other way of behaving under the circumstances. Indeed, they responded that they were raised to behave in such a manner and never considered behaving differently. This contention, then, supports the belief that lack of ritual Jewish practice does not constitute a lack of Jewish education in the home, but rather the values of *gemilat chesed* that are instilled become paramount in one's conduct.

In hindsight, one may conclude that the hospital in Camp Westerbork was merely a sinister deception intentionally used by Gemmeker and the Nazi system to encourage people to build false hope about the quality of life in the East. In the context of that time, the hospital provided excellent care; a hospital stay would be extended if transport could be avoided through a longer stay, irrespective of the health of the patient. Neither the doctors nor nurses could have known that they were providing care to heal people only to send them to their deaths. Nevertheless, this is irrelevant to the issue of caring for other humans.

From the stories of the nurses and letters that survived the war, it is apparent that they were involved with their patients and provided whatever care and comfort that they were to able to provide under their circumstances. They placed a high priority on communication; in spending time listening to their patients and they recognized the importance of meeting needs beyond their physical care. The importance of seeing their patients through a holistic perspective, rather than as physical entities to be treated with medications or dressings was apparent as well as their appreciation for the importance of involvement and communication with patients.

It is quite evident from the stories of the Westerbork nurses that they were deeply involved in the caring process as exemplified by the incidents that were related. They made time to talk not only with their patients, but also their families. They were able to empathize and open themselves to their patients in their objective of delivering loving and gentle care to their patients. Indeed, they continue that very practice by relating their stories to contemporary nurses through the sharing of their experience, ideas, and knowledge of the past. Watson (1979) claimed that the caring attitude has existed in every society. That attitude, however, is transmitted through a culture that that views caring as a unique process and form of coping. The recounting of these events by these nurses is that transmission through the culture of nursing.

In her letters, Etty Hillesum (1987) described the overwhelming anxiety, fear, and sadness permeating the hospital on the night that the transport lists are announced. Despite the anxiety and misery, the nurses did their best to support their patients, even in these horrific circumstances soothing them, helping them organize their few belongings, and to dress properly for their journey into the unknown. The nurses would not have known for certain until that announcement if their names or the names of family and close friends were included on the dreaded transport list until the announcement; even so, they immediately went to work, thereby making the needs of others paramount under these extraordinary, horrific circumstances.

Contemporary health care often places great reliance on medical technology, which can inadvertently create a distance between health care practitioners and their patients. It is

of particular import to acknowledge that these nurses, while utilising whatever technology may have been available, appreciated the concept of holistic practice long before it
became a common term in nursing. Their approach to their patients is as relevant a
lesson to today's practitioners in health care as it was over 50 years ago and serves as an
example of professional conduct under disastrous circumstances and the provision of care
under those circumstances.

Todorov (1996) remarked that memory cannot be relied upon to completely rebuild
events of the past, but, rather, it can be used to reconstruct a portion of those elements
that are most meaningful and relevant to our society. This reconstruction is essential to
the process of justice. Justice is constructed from the act of mingling truth and knowledge to bring it to light; not only the meting of punishment. It is then the responsibility
of all of us to recognize the small and often unacknowledged acts of human dignity,
caring, and kindness as a means of affirming their importance. Furthermore, such
recognition stimulates us and others to value such acts, to encourage them more, and
to recognize that every individual is capable of achieving such acts at many different
levels.

Heroes, according to Todorov, fight against odds. In that context, so too did the
nurses in Westerbork. According to Cohen (1988), most prisoners in camps underwent
three distinct phases. The first phase was a period of initial reaction during which
the prisoner began to understand what might happen, eventually progressing into
adaptation. During this adaptive phase, Cohen claimed that the prisoner's ultimate
survival chances would be determined. During this critical phase, the prisoner would
adapt to circumstances and difficult conditions with accompanying loss of compassion for
others. Prisoners finally descended into a stage of resignation of the fate that awaited
them.

Ritvo and Plotkin (1998) argued that most doctors and nurses fell into the third
category; however, this fails to acknowledge that while some many have indeed entered
that third phase of adaptation, the expected loss of compassion associated with that phase
never took place, as indicated by the stories from Westerbork. Instead, these stories are
permeated with examples of compassion, caring, and acts of kindness. Whether or not,
these nurses were halachically observant, they chose a particular route to follow. The
route they chose to emulate was that of Abraham, patriarch of the Jewish people.
Abraham, it should be noted, was called 'HaIvri', one who was to the side. Despite
living in a world and civilisation of idolators, Abraham made a clear choice to stand on
the other side, even if that meant standing alone. Despite the evil and barbarism
surrounding them, the nurses discussed in this paper made active choices not to descend
to such a level of behaviour, practicing caring, delivering kindness and positive values to
those in their charge. They chose to continue the heroic tradition inherent in Jewish
values much like their mysterious predecessors, the enigmatic Shifrah and Puah. In every
sense, then, they too are heroes, who fought against the temptation and odds that so
many succumbed too during those dark times. In every sense, too, they were true to the
spirit of *gemilat chesed*. In the final analysis, *gemilat chesed*, acts of loving kindness are the
supreme achievement of humankind.

NOTES

Interviews and personal communications
The following personal communications took place between the author and individuals during her
research:

J. Bob Cahen, personal interview with the author, The Hague, 8 July 1998; Sara Jacobs, personal interview with the author, The Hague, 8 July 1998; Kitty Nystad-de Wijze, personal interview with the author, Lochem, The Netherlands, July 1998; Jeanne Van den Berg van Cleeff, personal interviews and correspondence with the author, Amsterdam, December 1997 and 28 June 1998; Trudel Van Reemst de Vries, personal interview with the author, Amsterdam, 24 June 1998.

REFERENCES

L. Aiken, *Why me, G-d?* (Northvale, NJ: Aronson, 1996).

A. Bandura, 'Analysis of modeling processes', in A. Bandura (ed.), *Psychological Modeling* (Atherton: Chicago. 1971).

P. Benner and J. Wrubel, *Primacy of Caring: Stress and Coping in Health and Illness* (Menlo Park: Addison Wesley, 1989).

J. Boas, *Boulevard des Miseres* (Hamden, CT: Archon Books, 1985).

J.B. Cahen, *Somewhere in the Netherlands: A letter from Kamp Westerbork, Nov. 1, 1942* (Remembrance Centrum Kamp Westerbork, 1988), pp.9–10.

E. Cohen, *Human Behaviour in the Concentration Camp* (London: Free Association Books, 1998).

A. Colby and L. Kohlberg, *The measurement of moral development* (Cambridge: Cambridge University Press, 1987).

H. Donin, *To Be Jew* (New York: Basic Books, 1972).

H. Donin, *To Pray As A Jew* (New York: Basic Books, 1980).

A.K. Gemmerker, Letter of 1943, Doc 806 Inv. NR. 8512-12, Herinneringscentrum Kamp Westerbork; original held at NIOD Nederlands Instituut voor Oorlogsdocumentarie.

L. Gething, D. Papalia and S. Olds, *Lifespan Development*, 2nd Australasian edn (Sydney: McGraw Hill. 1995).

C. Gilligan, *In a Different Voice: Psychological Theory and Women's Development* (Cambridge: Harvard University Press. 1982).

Etty Hillesum, *Letters from Westerbork* (London: Grafton Books. 1988).

M. Johnstone, *Bioethics: A Nursing Perspective* (Sydney: W.B. Saunders, 1989).

S. Kim, 'Out of darkness' *Reflections*, 24/3 (1998): 8–13.

V. Knowlden, 'Nurse caring as constructed knowledge', in R. M. Neil and R. Watts (eds.), *Caring and Nursing: Explorations in Feminist Perspectives* (New York: National League for Nursing, 1991).

H. Kuhse, *Caring: Nurses, Women and Ethics* (New York: Blackwell, 1997).

M. Leininger, *Culture, Care, Diversity and Universality: A Theory of Nursing* (New York: National League for Nursing Press, 1991).

W. Lindwer, *Kamp van Hoop en Wanhoop* (Amsterdam: Balans, 1990).

J. MacDonald, 'The Caring Imperative: A Must?', *Australian Journal of Advanced Nursing* 11/1 (1993): 26–30.

A. Marriner-Tomey, *Nursing Theorists and their Work*, 2nd edn, (St. Louis, MO: C.V. Mosby, 1989).

B. Moore, *Victims and Wurvivors: The Nazi Persecution of the Jews in the Netherlands 1940–1945* (New York: St. Martin's Press, 1997).

M. Moskin, *I am Rosemarie* (New York: Scholastic, 1972).

L. Nicholl (ed.), *Perspectives on Nursing Theory*, 2nd edn (Philadelphia: J.B. Lippincott, 1992).

N. Noddings, *Caring: A Feminine Approach to Ethics and Moral Education* (Berkeley: University of California Press, 1984).

P. Oliner and S. Oliner, *Towards a Caring Society ideas into Action* (Westport, CT: Praeger Publishers, 1995).

J. Presser, *The Destruction of the Dutch Jews: A Definitive Account of the Holocaust in the Netherlands* (New York: E. P. Dutton, 1969).

R. Ritvo and D. Plotkin, *Sisters in Sorrow* (College Station: Texas A&M Press, 1998).

J. Sacks, *The Politics of Hope* (London: Jonathan Cape, 1997).

S. Samson, *Between Darkness and Light* (Jerusalem: Rubin Mass Ltd, 1990).

N. Scherman, *The Art Scroll Machzo* (Brooklyn: Menorah Publications, 1984).

N. Scherman, *The Torah: Haftaros and Five Megillos with a Commentary Anthologized from the Rabbinic Writing* (Brooklyn: Menorah Publications, 1993).

A. Steinsaltz, *Letaken Olam Bemalhut Shaddai* (1957). Available at http://www.judaica.ru/english/articles/letaken.

A. Steinsaltz, *Teshuvah: A Guide for the Newly Observant Jew*. (Jerusalem: Domino Press, 1982).

J. Telushkin, *Words that Hurt, Words that Heal* (New York: Quiet William, 1996).

G. Thomas, and M. Witts, *Voyage of the Damned*. (New York: Stein and Day, 1974).

T. Todorov, *Facing Extreme Moral Behaviour in the Concentration Camps* (New York: Henry Holt and Co., 1996).

S. Toperoff, *Avot: A Comprehensive Commentary on the Ethics of the Fathers* (Northvale, NJ: Aronson, 1997).

L. Trepp, *Judaism: Development and Life* (Belmont, CA: Dickenson, 1966).

J. Watson, *They Shall Not Hurt* (Colorado: Colorado Associated University Press, 1989).

HUMANITARIAN CONCERN VERSUS ZYKLON B

Florent Brayard

That the clear distinction between good and evil becomes partially blurred, that the Resistance fighter could sometimes seem to be very close to the executioner: such is the inescapable consequence of the human condition in a totalitarian system.

—Saul Friedländer[1]

I N 1986, forty years after Auschwitz, Primo Levi considered afresh, and doubtless in still greater depth than in *If This is a Man*, certain aspects of the complex of facts which have the extermination of the Jews and the system of concentration-camps at its centre. One of the chapters of the new book, *The Drowned and the Saved*, was entitled 'Useless Violence', and the author described some of the abuses which seemed, both from the observer's and the victim's point of view, to be cruel. He then tried to find out what had motivated these abuses: overcrowding and lack of hygiene or food in the deportation convoys; violation of modesty by enforced nakedness; the two daily roll-calls; tattooing. Finally, Levi's careful analysis distinguished between the concept of simple cruelty, i.e. the 'deliberate creation of suffering as an end in itself',[2] and an instrumental concept of violence, where it is exercised precisely not as an end in itself but is conditioned by another end from which violence proceeds incidentally, or which uses violence as a way of achieving its purpose.

The title of Levi's chapter seemed to echo that of an article by Emmanuel Lévinas published some years earlier, in 1982, in the *Giornale di Metafisica*. That article, 'Useless Suffering', is fundamentally no less complex or less analytical than Primo Levi's chapter, most probably because uselessness or pointlessness, which is a very different thing from chance, is a concept hard to grasp. Lévinas began by establishing a clear distinction between suffering endured by the thinking subject who may be capable of profiting by it, and suffering affecting other people for which no meaning can be found. Lévinas then asked, without actually saying so explicitly, what lessons Auschwitz compelled us to learn. He noted the impossibility of inscribing this phenomenon within any sort of theodicy, the failure of ancestral modes of explaining the 'scandal' of suffering. Thus his twofold line of thought could not be related to any continuity, for the continuity had been broken; it had to start afresh from the break. From a religious point of view, for the Jewish people, the Holocaust meant the duty of renewed fidelity to their origins, so that the work of destruction would not be total. From a moral point of view, the Holocaust, together with other catastrophes of the tragic twentieth century, engendered the need for a new philosophy – the term is too weak – a new order of things. This order, an 'inter-human' one, would have to be based on '*my* responsibility for the other, without looking for any return', or, still more clearly, on 'the asymmetry in the relation of *one* to *another*'.[3]

It is in the light of these considerations by Lévinas and Levi, both on intentions and the relationship to the other, that we are now going to focus on the problem of the utilization of Zyklon B for the extermination of the Jews.

*　　　*　　　*

As is well known, the concept of humanitarian concern – *Humanität* – having been progressively devalued from the end of the 19th century onwards,[4] was ferociously rejected by Nazi ideology, which considered it to be the exact opposite of all the values prized by the new regime[5]. Thus, the entry for '*Humanität*' in the 1938 edition of *Meyers Lexikon* gives a list of several redundant definitions, the very length of which, plus the fact that they were redundant, pointed to this violent rejection[6]. Humanitarian concern was a 'predilection for what is weak, ill, very often for what is criminal, with an accompanying mistrust of what is specific, strong, heroic and creative'; it was also a 'denial of all racial and national [*völkisch*] differences, accompanied by the adoration of undifferentiated humanity [*Menschheit*]; it was, finally, in Rosenberg's own words, the attitude 'which pities every criminal individually but nevertheless forgets about the State, the people, and in short the category'.[7]

However, although the condemnation of the concept of '*Humanität*' was univocal and seemed final, it was not accompanied by the systematic banishing of the adjective '*human*', humane, which was used in various contexts, including those dealing with the Jewish genocide. Retrospectively, this use poses problems. Was the use of the adjective '*human*' leading up to a covert reintroduction of the 'humanitarian concern' which was officially condemned by the regime? Or else was it based on an older meaning of the term, one of whose synonyms could be '*rücksichtsvoll*' – full of delicacy or consideration?[8] For the sake of argument, to begin with I will not focus on this possible plurality of meanings, but enquire more simply what was put at stake by the use of the adjective '*human*'.

*　　　*　　　*

Thus we see that Hitler in his political testament, drawn up when he was on the very point of committing suicide, recalled his promise that the death of millions of Germans would not happen without the people who were really guilty of that massacre, i.e. the Jews, being punished for it, even though, as he stated, the means employed to carry out this expiation would be more humane ('*humanere Mittel*'); the implication being that it was more humane than the bombings.[9] Hitler, then, was boasting both about having carried out the genocide and, at the same time, of having done it in a relatively humane way – which may here mean with an absence of cruelty.

Himmler was basically saying the same thing when he stated, in October 1943, that the genocide of the Jews constituted 'a glorious page in our history' which was carried out without the executioners losing their 'human honesty',[10] even though there were some exceptions. Whatever the case, we are facing retrospective discourses, and, no doubt, unacknowledged attempts to alleviate the sense of guilt.

*　　　*　　　*

Sometimes it was in the actual course of events, in the very movement of the action, that the adjective '*human*' was introduced. The report sent by Höppner, who was in charge of the SD at Posen, to Eichmann on 16 July 1941 is well known in this regard. Höppner envisaged the construction of a work-camp for 300,000 Jews in Warthegau (the occupied Polish territory annexed by the German Reich), proposed the sterilization of the women, and addressed the question of the fate of Jews who were unfit for work. As there would probably not be sufficient supplies to feed them during the winter, 'it would be a good idea to consider seriously whether the most humane solution ("*humanste Lösung*") would not be that of liquidating Jews incapable of work, by some rapid means. In any case that would be more acceptable than leaving them to starve to death.'[11] Höppner, who, as no one can doubt for a moment, wished to get rid of the greatest possible number of Jews from Warthegau, was in the midst of a process of negotiation with the central authorities, in the course of which he put forward proposals and arguments. He used two arguments to justify the rapid and deliberate putting to death of Jews who were unfit to work. First, that the proposed solution was more humane in comparison with the cruelty of the alternative – and the point at issue here is not so much whether or not he was sincere in this plea for humaneness (no matter how it should best be understood), as the fact that he believed this argument would carry some weight with the person to whom it was addressed, namely Eichmann. Moreover, this argument was backed up by another: that his proposed solution was 'more acceptable'. It is quite clear that this second argument was still more powerful, to Höppner's mind, than the first, and that it was not the victims he was thinking of but the executioners – it was to them that a rapid death would be 'more acceptable'.

There is another example of this shift in the usage of the notion of humanitarian concern, introduced by the adjective '*human*', occurring at the same time as the above one. In the middle of August 1941 Himmler was present at the shooting of about a hundred prisoners at Minsk and, according to the testimony of Erich von dem Bach-Zelewski, was extremely shocked by it. It seems that he then ordered Nebe, chief of the *Einsatzgruppe* B and head of Office 5 of the RSHA, to find a 'more humane' means of execution[12] – thus giving a decisive impulse to the development of gas-lorries, which in turn would lead to the development of the gas-chambers themselves. Once again, the notion of humanitarian concern was used, and once again in a corrupted and perverted sense. It was not the victims who were the cause for concern but the executioners, who could be 'disturbed' by their task of killing, rendered 'useless for the rest of their lives', becoming 'neurotic and brutal', in Bach-Zelewski's own words.[13]

The change from mass executions by firing-squad, as practised by the *Einsatzgruppen*, to execution by gas in extermination camps, was thus dictated by a humanitarian concern understood in a restricted and completely selfish sense. It obviously entailed an asymmetry in the relation of self to the other, but in exactly the opposite sense to that which Lévinas was crying out for. Violence and cruelty were reprehensible because of the effect they had on the people who became their instruments, because they corrupted them without their being aware of it. Still violence and cruelty were unimportant with regard to the suffering they inflicted on the victims. Rudolf Höss said the same in his autobiography, when he spoke of the progress which extermination using Zyklon B represented, by comparison with either firing-squads or lorry exhaust-gas. For both the latter methods, he explained, the *Einsatz-Kommandos* needed 'worrying quantities [*unheimliche Mengen*] of alcohol' in order to complete their work.[14] At Auschwitz this was not the case, he seemed to be saying; the division of labour had been taken to such an extreme that these tasks did not weigh so heavily on those employed on them.

*   *   *

Sometimes, however, it seems that the suffering of the victim *was* taken into account. Werner Kichert, for example, a subordinate of Grawitz, the *Reichsführer SS und Polizei*, was involved in autumn 1939 in the completely new operation of exterminating mentally ill people, at a time when the choice of gas to be used was not yet established. Several possibilities were envisaged, foremost among which was prussic acid. At one point, Kichert was asked to give his opinion on the use of Zyklon B. He rejected this option in favour of industrial carbon monoxide, contained in iron bottles, which, he said, was 'the most humane way of putting people to death [*humanstes Tötungsmittel*]'.[15] As is well known, it was in fact this gas rather than Zyklon B which was used in 'Aktion T4', though it is impossible to determine whether Kichert's expertise was a deciding factor in the choice.

This is an episode which deserves careful study. We have to recognize that our knowledge of its existence rests on the testimony of just one person (as is often the case in these matters), that of Kichert himself. But its probability is strengthened by other testimonies on early proposals for the use of prussic acid[16]. The least one can say is that a choice had been made and that Kichert was trying to take the credit for it by attributing the choice, rightly or wrongly, to himself.

The other point to examine is whether this choice was more 'humane'. There can be no doubt that carbon monoxide poisoning caused rapid loss of consciousness which prevented both physical pain and awareness of what was being done. After all, an expert did estimate in the course of a trial of Aktion T4 members in 1967, that this procedure was 'one of the most humane ways of putting people to death [*eine der humansten Tötungsarten*]'.[17] What is of interest here is rather the issues involved in this choice. Let us accept provisionally, for the sake of argument, the fact that the choice was guided by humanitarian concern – i.e., in this case, the desire to reduce the suffering of the victims in so far as it was possible. What was the consequence of this, not for the victim but for the executioner? The choice between one gas or another, in itself, made no fundamental difference. The question of psychological harm done to the executioners was not yet being asked, and the question whether prussic acid or carbon monoxide was easier to use, seems never to have been raised.

As far as the perpetrator was concerned, it was a zero-sum game. It is in this very absence of stakes, that at that precise moment, for one particular agent, the question of pointless violence and suffering could arise.

                   *   *   *

Exceptionally, it also happened that a certain *acteur* – I am using the word here in the sense of 'perpetrator', or the German *Täter* – reasoned in humanitarian terms, but in a situation which was not only not indifferent, but actually implying not inconsiderable risk. Before going on to consider this case, one which is both well and badly known, I think it appropriate to set out some of the characteristics of Zyklon B, the gas in question.

Zyklon B is an industrial derivative of prussic acid which was developed in the 1920s by Degesch, a Frankfurt firm.[18] Used for destroying vermin in warehouses, flats and clothes, and for exterminating rats in mills and ships, it worked so efficiently that it was dangerous for people using it. Accordingly, to the prussic acid, which normally has a sweetish smell, a warning element (*Warnstoff*) was added: an irritant, so that if anyone inadvertently entered a room being treated with Zyklon B, the immediate reaction was to get out as fast as one could.[19] The use of this gas for vermin control was, moreover, surrounded with all sorts of legal and practical safeguards to prevent any accidents.

Similar precautions were taken when Zyklon B began to be used for the purposes of genocide. The Zyklon B operators received special training, and furthermore at Auschwitz a doctor had to be present at the gassing of prisoners in case of any accidents.[20] It is unquestionably because the Operation Reinhard camps (Belzec, Sobibor and Treblinka) did not have any permanent medical staff, that the use of Zyklon B was not adopted in them, despite at least one attempt, to which I shall return later. This is as much as to say that Zyklon B was chosen for Auschwitz and Majdanek because of its efficiency, and in spite of the danger it entailed.

In the spring of 1943 Rolf Günther, Eichmann's assistant, ordered Kurt Gerstein, head of the 'Sanitary Techniques' office of the Waffen SS Hygiene Institute, to transmit to Degesch a series of orders for a monthly delivery of about 400 kg. of Zyklon B.[21] There can be no doubt that these consignments were intended to be used for homicide, because both Kurt Gerstein and another witness have testified to this. However, it remains unclear precisely who the intended victims were to be. Gerstein stated, in a series of written testimonies, that it could have been for concentration camp inmates, or members of the intelligentsia, or foreign workers who had been requisitioned for work in Germany.[22] It is also quite possible that the order formed part of the extermination of the Jews and that Gerstein, for one reason or another, wished to conceal this fact. Whatever the case, two things are clear: the deliveries did actually take place on a monthly basis for the space of a year, half going to Auschwitz and half to Oranienburg; and secondly, it has never been clearly established that these particular consignments of Zyklon B were in fact used for killing people.[23]

Concerning the first part of this story we only have Gerstein's testimony. The second is only known to us through the interrogations of Gerhard Peters, the manager of Degesch, to whom Gerstein had transmitted the order. What Peters said he knew or did not know about the group of people who were condemned to die does not make much difference to our understanding of the facts; what does matter here is that this series of orders were very singular in one respect: they were for Zyklon B deliberately produced without the irritant. Peters declared:

> [Gerstein] told me, 'We need to eliminate a collection of worthless people [minderwertige Leute], idiots and sick people. It is to be done with prussic acid. That's torture.' He wanted to reduce the torture. He said, 'Above all I want to prevent the torture caused by the irritant (...) That's atrocious,' he said. 'We have to prevent that sort of torture. Help me to develop some procedure which takes effect quickly, instantaneously.' All I could suggest was that he should use prussic acid without irritant, and that was it. I never saw him again after that.[24]

Thus a man who was a member of the Waffen SS could not endure the thought of the suffering of people being gassed with Zyklon B. He found such suffering reprehensible for its inhumanity and, moreover, pointless, since a way could be found of avoiding it. The solution, however, brought its own problems: by leaving out the warning irritant, the victims' sufferings were indeed reduced, but the gas was also rendered (almost) undetectable for the executioners. Here we are confronted with a situation in which humanitarian concern for the victims entailed greater danger for the executioners. And it was a real danger, though it should not be overestimated. In the summer of 1942 an SS man had been poisoned at Auschwitz by Zyklon B, presumably containing too little irritant.[25] At the beginning of the summer of 1944 Degesch issued stocks of Zyklon B without irritant, because of a shortage caused by the bombing of the Dessau factory.[26] This gave rise to some degree of concern on the part of firms using it, as to the danger caused by the absence of the irritant,[27] and a few weeks later an article appeared in a professional journal to clarify the matter.[28]

This fact has the indirect consequence of leading us to question the truthfulness of Peters's statements. He was manager of both Degesch and one of its distribution subsidiaries, Heli, and also head of two government-sponsored commissions on disinfection. He was thus the person principally responsible for all questions concerning Zyklon B in the Reich and the conquered territories. Is it possible that a man in his position could have accepted and indeed suggested a solution which was in such direct breach of the policy of maximum safety for the users which he had been promoting for so many years? Several sources attest that an event took place in the course of summer 1942 which belies Peter's version. To cut a long story short, he was mistaken or lying either about the actual content of his conversation with Gerstein, or about the date on which it took place.

*   *   *

This sequence of events is also well known. On 8 June 1942, a year before the conversation described above took place, Günther appeared in Gerstein's office in civilian clothes. He said that a certain quantity of Zyklon B was to be conveyed to the Belzec camp, for the Operation Reinhard camps were going to change from using exhaust-gas, a method which was judged to be too inefficient owing to frequent breakdowns, to using Zyklon B. The mission was undertaken in mid-August, and was a failure. Gerstein managed to make people believe that the Zyklon B he had brought was decomposed and in a dangerous state, and he buried it – this fact is born out by evidence.[29] Christian Wirth, the camp commandant, was himself quite satisfied and even proud of the way his installations worked, though he no doubt exaggerated the results. Gerstein's lack of good will and Wirth's refusal together resulted in the project to modernize the gas installations being abandoned. According to all the available testimonies this mission was a complete waste of time.

Among these testimonies, as well as the Gerstein reports, there are the various interrogations of Wilhelm Pfannenstiel, one of Grawitz's close advisers, who had taken part in the mission either by chance or acting on orders. Through Pfannenstiel, we are in a position to reconstruct the discourse developed by Gerstein during the journey.

> [Gerstein] explained to me that in his eyes, being killed by exhaust gas was too slow and that, if one could speak of humanitarianism in such a context, it had to be done in a more humane way [*humanere Art*], by using prussic acid which acts immediately. I do not know if it was his idea. In any case, I could see that something that killed more quickly would be preferable to exhaust gas, which took a certain time.[30]

The similarity between the accounts of Peters and Pfannenstiel is striking, even though in 1943 the improvement suggested by Gerstein to Peters was leaving the irritant out of the Zyklon B, while what Gerstein proposed in his conversation with Pfannenstiel in 1942 was simply a change from exhaust gas to Zyklon B. However, it is probable that Pfannenstiel's recollections were imprecise, because he gave one additional detail which is of great importance: the Zyklon B which Gerstein took delivery of at the Kolin factory near Prague consisted of prussic acid in liquid form, contained in iron bottles[31] – and as such much more dangerous. It even seems very probable that between Prague and Lublin one of the bottles ceased to be leakproof,[32] and Gerstein took a great risk in burying it.[33] Pfannenstiel's account finds corroboration in the text of an interrogation conducted on Gerstein in Paris, in July 1945.[34]

What, then, was the intention behind this dangerous choice of liquid prussic acid, when industrial Zyklon B, adsorbed on granules and far easier to use, had already been in use for several months at Auschwitz? The intention was simple: the liquid prussic acid was a raw material which did not yet have the addition of the irritant which would convert it into Zyklon B. In other words, the concern to avoid the suffering provoked by the irritant was already present in 1942, even if Pfannenstiel did not remember it.

The question then of the truthfulness of Peters' testimony arises again. If the conversation had taken place in the spring of 1943, it is obvious that Gerstein knew exactly what he wanted: Zyklon B without the irritant, the same product he had taken to Belzec the summer before. Peters, in that case, had merely been obeying an order, which he then twisted in his testimony into a 'humanitarian' suggestion, hoping to gain something by it as an attenuating circumstance. But there exists another hypothesis, hardly more improbable: that the conversation between Peters and Gerstein actually took place at the beginning of the summer of 1942 – in which case it is clear that the people of less value ('*minderwertige Leute*') whom Peters spoke of had been Jews, and that he had known this.

*   *   *

Gerstein's humanitarian concern cannot be doubted. We possess declarations by Peters and Pfannenstiel, but also numerous testimonies from his friends or people whom he had only met once. What is more, Gerstein had repeatedly tried to warn the religious authorities and the Allies about the genocide which was under way, not altogether without success.[35] This concern, however, also poses a number of problems.

Gerstein himself explained his ideas on the question of humanitarian concern, in one of the versions of his report. 'Overall, people took no more trouble than that to carry out the killings in a "humane" sort of way ("*irgendwie human*") – if that word can ever be used at all in this context! And this was undoubtedly less out of sadism than out of a total indifference and inertia towards these things.'[36] This comment by a witness who was himself implicated in the events, undoubtedly ties in with some of Levi's analyses on useless violence; and his very hesitation about using the word 'humane' in such a context dispels the ambiguity we have hitherto encountered: Gerstein's understanding of it in 1945 is beyond doubt the same as ours today. Moreover the fact that Gerstein was himself implicated might be considered, in some respect, as an illustration of the 'responsibility for the other, without looking for any return', the 'asymmetry in the relation of *one* to *another*' Lévinas spoke of. Gerstein made his choices knowing that his personal, selfish gain would be zero in any case, while the personal risk he was incurring would be all the greater. And his choices were made for the sole benefit of the other, the victim, the Jew in the gas chamber.

However, although this behaviour certainly manifests humanitarian concern, it was still within an overall context of absolute inhumanity, to which it accommodated in some degree. We are in fact compelled to recognize that neither Gerstein, nor Peters, nor Pfannenstiel, nor so many others, ever entertained the notion of reasoning outside the inhumane, criminal framework within which they were working or which was imposed upon them. The improvement proposed by Gerstein was clearly marginal to the project of which it nevertheless formed part – it aimed to kill the Jews without making them suffer, but to kill them all the same. This is an issue for Levi and Lévinas, the survivor haunted by the question of ethics and the philosopher, who may answer with authority: is a relative good at the heart of an absolute evil still good? Personally speaking, however, I will state here that it seems to me that the answer is no.

This answer, nevertheless, is not the limit to our examination. Once the concern for humaneness has been brought into the open, together with the moral framework in which it is set, we still need to consider further about its deep meaning and the way in which it was or was not reflected in deeds.

In this frame of mind, a first aspect is that of evaluating one's own power to influence things. To be specific, the aim of making the project of genocide more humane, even marginally, was conceived by Gerstein in order to redeem his own part in that same project. The question of whether that redemption was complete inevitably takes us back to the moral problem we have just raised. But what becomes of this problem if the attempt at making the project more humane turned out to be only an illusion? Let us return to the discussion between Peters and Gerstein on the question of leaving out the irritant. What guarantee could Gerstein have had that Peters would really have some Zyklon B produced without the irritant? Peters could equally well have just stamped '*Ohne Reizstoff*' ['without irritant'] on some of the standard product. And if he had, it would have been no more than half a lie, because the shortages caused by the war had brought about a modification in the composition of Zyklon B entailing a drastic reduction in the amount of irritant added (the proportion had gone down from 5% to 0.5%).[37] The distinction between almost none and none at all is difficult to establish,[38] and perhaps would have been impossible to check up on for Gerstein, who probably knew nothing about this state of affairs.

This modification in the composition of Zyklon B in the course of the war reveals the second aspect of the possibly illusory nature of Gerstein's humanitarian efforts. If the Zyklon B used to exterminate the Jews in the gas-chambers at Auschwitz contained little or extremely little irritant, what was the real advantage for the victims in omitting it completely?

*   *   *

The problem of the agent's mastery over his action, his power, his omnipotence, needs to be evoked from another angle in the case of Gerstein. We have established here, for the first time, that both the consignment of Zyklon B for Belzec and that ordered for Auschwitz and Oranienburg were Zyklon B without the irritant. We must also note that Gerstein always remained absolutely silent about this particular feature of the orders he had transmitted; it is our own deduction from the nature of the containers in the first case, and Peters (and archive documents) in the second, that supply this information. To understand the reasons for his silence we need to measure what exactly was the singular nature of these orders for the person who transmitted them, at the moment when he transmitted them.

The story given to us by Gerstein, through the different versions of his report, through his correspondence, and the testimony of his friends, is that of a man to whose lot it fell to order some Zyklon B for the purpose of putting people to death, and who accepted that task in order to destroy the entire quantity of this potentially lethal chemical by burying it or making sure it was only used for disinfection purposes. The story which Peters and Pfannenstiel now give us is that of a man who contented himself with introducing a humanitarian concern at the margin of the machinery of genocide. The two images are far from being incompatible. We can easily imagine that Gerstein always intended to destroy the Zyklon B and was sure he would manage to do it, and at the same time took certain precautions in the unlikely event of failure; the precautions here consisting of making sure that the Zyklon B in question would kill, if such were the case, without causing excessive suffering.

But this co-existence within one man's line of thought, of the certainty of success and the allowance for possible failure, gives a much more mixed image of Gerstein's personality, one less obviously heroic than the one Gerstein himself wanted to leave us with. By removing from his account all references to the singular character of the Zyklon B he had ordered, Gerstein was retrospectively denying that he had ever considered the possibility of failure. Besides, he said, he had succeeded.

However, this equilibrium between the conviction of success and the realisation of the danger is only the fruit of subsequent reconstruction. Who knows what conviction the agent held, how much he may have weighed his chances of success or failure, and which thought took precedence over which, at the moment when the action had not yet begun? Gerstein said, or thought, 'The Zyklon B which I have delivered will be used to exterminate Jews. At least they will not suffer. But I am going to try and ensure, in addition, that it is never used.' Or else he said or thought, 'I'm going to destroy this Zyklon B. If I do not succeed, at least the victims will not suffer.' A winning gamble made in the knowledge that it might be lost, but which did in fact win; a losing gamble made in the hope of winning nevertheless, which won in the end; or even a gamble that lost: who knows?

*   *   *

But won or lost for whom? Let us look back for a moment. We have seen that the notion of humanitarian concern could be reintroduced into their discourse by the Nazis with the use of the adjective '*human*', and that this usage was not merely ambiguous but also perverted, since it was only humanitarian concern for the executioner which was taken into account. We have then seen that this notion of humane concern might be employed, if need be, towards the victims, but in a situation where its application made no difference from the perpetrators' point of view. Then we described the case of Kurt Gerstein, for whom humanitarian concern towards the victims entailed real danger for the perpetrator, even though that danger, as also the actual benefit to the victims, might have been overestimated through his being misinformed, and might in any case have made only a very small difference. We then moved up to the level of the intention behind it, in order to try understanding, if that is ever possible, how humanitarian concern was transformed into action. The time has now come to re-examine this case from the inverse point of view, that of what was achieved.

We find that Gerstein, in regard to the two series of orders in which he was personally concerned, took credit to himself for having prevented the Zyklon B from being used for killing people. This was Gerstein's basic message in a solemn, almost testamentary letter to his father, after having evoked obliquely the Nazi policy of genocide: 'I never turned my hand to all that. When I received orders of that kind I never carried them out, or I prevented them from being carried out. I myself have emerged from the affair with clean hands and my conscience perfectly at peace.'[39]

Gerstein's singular personality can certainly be seen as an example of aspiring towards purity – as was witnessed in the 1930s by his writings on religion or sexual education. His paradoxical destiny could itself be summed up as the confrontation between that aspiration and the most abominable impurities, crimes and temptations of the century. From that confrontation Gerstein always wanted to emerge victorious, untouched.

But if that victory ever came, if Gerstein told the exact truth to those close to him, if he did in fact manage to destroy the Zyklon B without the irritant which he had ordered, the victory had a reverse side. When gains and losses are summed up, the result is a gain for Gerstein, because he had preserved what at heart he himself prized more than anything else, his purity; and loss for the victims, because while very few people were concerned about their sufferings, nobody at all transformed the humanitarian concern into reality.

To put things in another way, in the reasoning process which Gerstein had established and if concern for the other would have been the highest value, as Lévinas exhorts us to accept after Auschwitz, then it was necessary to have the use of Zyklon B without the irritant, conceived of as a more humane way of putting people to death, imposed everywhere – accepting *ipso facto* the defilement of one's own soul by participating in crime. Gerstein made another choice. But what modern Faust, with his back against a gas-chamber, would have agreed to throw away his soul purely out of concern for the other?

NOTES

Translation from the French by Helena Scott, University of Westminster, London

1 Saul Friedländer, *Kurt Gerstein ou l'ambiguïté du bien* (Paris: Casterman, 1967), p.191.

2 Primo Levi, *The Drowned and the Saved. Forty years after Auschwitz* (London: Michael Joseph, 1988 [Italian edition 1986]), p.87.

3 Emmanuel Lévinas, 'La violence inutile', in *Entre nous. Essai sur le penser-à-autre* (Paris: Grasset, 1991), p.112. English translation: *Entre nous: on thinking of the other*, translated from the French by Michael B. Smith and Barbara Harshav (New York: Columbia University Press, 1998).

4 I am very grateful to Carlo Ginzburg for having drawn my attention to the important question of the semantic shift in the German words '*Humanität*' and '*human*'. On the evolution of the concept of '*Humanität*', see *Geschichtliche Grundbegriffe. Historisches Lexikon zur politisch-sozialen Sprache in Deutschland*, ed. Otto Brunner, Werner Conze and Reinhard Koselleck, (Stuttgart: Ernst Klee Verlag, 1982); entry for *Menschheit* by Hans Erich Bödeker, Vol.3, p.1127.

5 Cf. Karl-Heinz Brackmann and Renate Birkenhauer, *NS-Deutsch. 'Selbstverständliche' Begriffe und Schlagwörter aus der Zeit des Nationalsozialismus* (Straelen: Straelener Manuskprite Verlag, 1988), entry *Humanität*, p.100.

6 8th edition, '*in völlig neuer Bearbeitung*', of *Meyers Lexikon*, Leipzig, Bibliographisches Institut, 1938. It should be noted that in this entry Jews and Freemansons are associated with the spreading of the concept.

7 This quotation is taken from *Le Mythe du XXème siècle*. Rosenberg was lamenting – which should not surprise us – the fact that in the name of humanity or humanitarian concern, people 'tried to block the process of natural selection'.

8 '*rücksichtsvoll*' is the last synonym given, after '*menschlich*', '*menschenfreundlich*' and '*wohlwollend*' in the sixth edition of *Meyers Grosses Konversations-Lexikon* (Leipzig and Vienna: Bibliographisches Institut, 1908).

9 Raul Hilberg, *La Destruction des Juifs d'Europe* (Paris: Fayard, 1988), p.855.

10 *Ibid.*, p.871.

11 Peter Longerich, *Politik der Vernichtung. Eine Gesamtdarstellung der nationalsozialistischen Judenverfolgung*, Munich, Piper, 1998, p.425.

12 Volker Riess, *Die Anfänge de Vernichtung 'lebensunwerten Lebens' in den Reichsgauen Dantzig-Westpreussen und Wartheland 1939/40* (Frankfurt am Main: Peter Lang, 1995), pp.273 ff.

13 Raul Hilberg, *La Destruction...*, *op.cit.*, p.869.

14 Martin Broszat (ed.), *Kommandant in Auschwitz. Autobiographische Aufzeichnungen des Rudolf Höss* (Munich: DTV, 1998 [1958]), p.191.

15 Volker Riess, *Die Anfänge der Vernichtung...*, *op.cit.*, p.302.

16 *Ibid.*, & ff.

17 Quoted in Ernst Klee, *Was sie Taten – was sie wurden. Ärzte, Juristen und andere Beteiligte am Kranken-oder Judenmord* (Frankfurt am Main: Fischer Taschenbuch Verlag, 1986), p.215.

18 Jürgen Kalthoff and Martin Werner, *Die Händler des Zyklon B. Tesch & Stabenow. Eine Firmengeschichte zwischen Hamburg und Auschwitz* (Hamburg: VSV, 1998) is a good introduction to all these matters.

19 Testimony of Herbert Rauscher dated 13 April 1948 (Federal Archives of Weisbaden, 461/36342–8).

20 Steven Paskuly (ed.), *Death Dealer. The Memoirs of the SS Kommandant at Auschwitz* (Buffalo, NY: Prometheus Books, 1992), p.30 and p.223.

21 On Kurt Gerstein's character, see Saul Friedländer, *Kurt Gerstein ou l'ambiguïté du bien, op.cit.* For this series of orders, see pp.156 ff. Note also that as well as Pierre Joffroy's 30-year-old biography (Pierre Joffroy, *L'Espion de Dieu. La passion de Kurt Gerstein*, Paris: Grasset, 1969), there is a new biography by Jürgen Schäffer, *Kurt Gerstein – Zeuge des Holocaust, Ein Leben zwischen Bibelkreisen und SS* (Bielefeld: Luther Verlag, 1999).

22 Report by Kurt Gerstein in German dated 6 May 1945, Nuremberg documentation 2170-PS.

23 See especially the investigations carried out with reference to the various enquiries held on Gerhard Peters. The different judgements have been published in the collection of Irene Sagel-Grande, H.H. Fuchs and C.F. Rüter, *Justiz und NS-Verbrechen. Sammlung deutscher Strafurteile wegen nationalsozialistischer Tötungsverbrechen*, Band 13 (Amsterdam: University Press Amsterdam, 1975), Lfd 415.

24 Interrogation of Gerhard Peters dated 26 October 1947 (Yad Vashem 0.2/977).

25 The event is cited by Jean-Claude Pressac, *Les Crématoires d'Auschwitz. La machinerie du meurtre de masse* (Paris: Editions du CNRS, 1993), p.46. The note by Höss dated 12 August 1942 attributes the accident to a low proportion of irritant.

26 Note from Dr. Heinrich to Mr. Amend dated 21 June 1944, NI-12110.

27 The archives still show traces of a request for information from one of these firms, namely Testa, which asked about the effects this modification might have on the conservation of the product (correspondence from Testa to Degesch, dated 6 June 1944, Wiesbaden, 461/3398/Testa 3).

28 This article appeared in August 1944 in the corporation's journal, 'Journal of insecticides and parasite control' (quoted by Jacques Brillot, 'L'argent sans mémoire: Degussa-Degesch', *Le Monde Juif*, NS-151, May–August 1994).

29 Besides the declarations by Pfannenstiel to this effect, it is worth noting that the bottles in question appear to have been excavated at Belzec in 1971, if we are to believe the summary of a paper given by Zdzislaw Spaczynski, '*Elementy genezy i topografia obozu was Belzcu: Belzec, Sobibor, Treblinka*', at a University of Lublin Conference, 25–27 August 1987.

30 Interrogation of Wilhelm Pfannenstiel dated 30 October 1947 (Institut für Zeitgeschichte, Munich, Pfannenstiel I/ZS 1922).

31 *Ibid.* Moreover, an employee at the Kolin factory remembered having issued prussic acid in liquid form (interrogation of Victor Graf dated 12 March 1946, NI-11950).

32 According to the testimony of Pfannenstiel, dated 6 June 1950 (Institut für Zeitgeschichte, Munich, Pfannenstiel I / ZS 1922).

33 According to the belated testimony of Gerstein's wife Elfriede, dated 5 September 1976 (Landeskirchliches Archiv Bilefeld, Bestand Gerstein, no.54).

34 Interrogation of Kurt Gerstein dated 19 July 1945, published in the article by George Wellers, 'Encore sur le "témoignage Gerstein"', *Le monde juif*, 1980, no.97. In the course of this interrogation, Gerstein stated that it was he himself who had decided on his own initiative the quantity of Zyklon to be conveyed, which demonstrates Gerstein's opinion of Günther's ignorance on technical matters, and at the same time considerably strengthens the hypothesis now to be developed, that the choice of Zyklon without irritant should be imputed to Gerstein.

35 Saul Friedländer has already dealt with these aspects. It should be noted that a report by the Dutch Resistance, drawn up on the basis of Gerstein's accounts, reached London at the beginning of summer 1943 – though without provoking any reaction (Jim van der Hoeven, 'De Nederlandse regering in ballingschap wist at heel vroeg van de "Endlösung"', *Vrii Nederland*, 2 May 1992); see also my paper on this document in *Bulletin du Centre historique français de Jérusalem*, Spring 2000, with French and English translations of the Dutch report.

36 Kurt Gerstein's report in German dated 6 May 1945, quoted above.

37 Interrogation of Gerhard Peters dated 26 October 1947, quoted above. Among other testimonies on this state of affairs, see that of Heinrich Sossenheimer dated 23 April 1948 (Wiesbaden, 461/36342–8).

38 The problem is complicated still further by the fact that the stabilizing element added to prussic acid also had irritant qualities, so that the Zyklon B produced 'without irritant' by Dessau, did

nevertheless contain an irritant of sorts. And the person in charge of production at Dessau, Alfred Gülleman, affirmed that Zyklon B had never been produced without the stabilizer (Interrogation dated 14 July 1948, Wiesbaden, 461/36342–8).

39 Letter from Gerstein to his father, most probably written in Autumn 1944, quoted here from the translation of Saul Friedländer, *Kurt Gerstein, op.cit.*, p.176.

TIKKUN OLAM AND CHRISTIAN ETHICS
AFTER THE HOLOCAUST

Robert A. Everett

THE JEWISH concept of *Tikkun Olam* was first brought to my attention while reading the works of Gershom Scholem and Emil Fackenheim.[1] As a Christian, I have found this theme to be extremely useful for theological reflection. *Tikkun Olam* conjures up a powerful image of the world torn apart by injustice, hatred and violence being knit back together through the acts of men and women seeking to restore the image of God in the faces of their brothers and sisters, as well as restoring creation to its divinely sanctioned holiness and wholeness. Fackenheim's image of a *Tikkun* mending up a rupture in history is one of the most important theological concepts produced in contemporary religious thought. In considering the quest for social justice in relation to the doctrine of creation, I believe this Jewish theme needs to be borrowed by Christians in order to broaden their search for a viable social ethic, which avoids both an excessive privatization of faith and moral quietism and the danger of confusing ideology with the essentials of faith. In this sense, both conservative and liberal Christians would be well served by the concept of *Tikkun Olam*. This paper is a preliminary meditation on how this concept can be appropriated by Christians for their own theological reflection.

The idea of *Tikkun Olam* found in the writings of kabbalists like Isaac Luria of Safed was developed against the historical backdrop of the expulsion of Jews from Spain in 1492. The expulsion had a profound impact on Jewry, and this historical event brought forth new thinking about creation and evil, history and human responsibility for the world. Emil Fackenheim employs this theme of *Tikkun* in his reflections on Jewish existence, 'Christianity and Philosophy after the Holocaust'. He draws upon this Lurianic Kabbalist tradition to grapple with the Holocaust, which he rightly claims has ruptured all human history in a way previously unimagined. This rupture affects not just Jewish history, but all of human history. Thus, the theme *Tikkun* must always be read as *Tikkun Olam* – the mending of the world.

Fackenheim argues that after the Holocaust a *Tikkun* becomes the 'impossible necessity', a concept which echoes the idea of Reinhold Niebuhr that the Christian law of self-giving love is an 'impossible possibility'. This is an apt comparison, I believe, because both paradoxical concepts point in the same direction concerning the use of these concepts for the quest for social justice. Just as Niebuhr warned against thinking that love will be easily achieved in human history and can be simply applied to ethical problems, Fackenheim sees no simple way for a *Tikkun* to take place in light of the unique rupture caused by the Holocaust within human history. He says instead that 'in our search for a post-Holocaust *Tikkun* we must accept from the start that, at most, only a fragmentary *Tikkun* is possible.'[2]

As a Christian whose theology has been forever altered by its encounter with the Holocaust, I find some comfort in Fackenheim's 'fragmentary *Tikkun*'. The reality of the Death Camps of Nazi Europe loom on the gloomy horizon of human history, constantly impinging on the landscape of my theological imagination, and they always remind me of the depth of evil which is still active in creation. There is no escaping their reality, and their presence makes contemporary theological language and post-Holocaust faith diffi-cult. The triumphalistic language traditionally used by Christian theology, which seems to reduce the question of redemption in history to an achieved reality in the death and resurrection of Jesus Christ, rings hollow, at best, when asked the question, 'But what about Auschwitz?'. The dangers of making history a meaningless experience after the Christ event is ever present when Christians attempt to interpret the human condition through the eyes of faith. It is a real temptation to allow ourselves to think that the problem of evil has been overcome, that the victory over death is complete, and that historical events after Jesus no longer effect our faith. The privatization of faith and a christology divorced from the reality of human existence leads to serious social con-sequences, which tend to emaculate Christian ethics. Arthur Cohen stated the problem well:

> It would not be to press the matter too strongly to suggest that indeed the Christian turn toward interiority and privatism – that insistence that the relationship between the Christian and the Christ is settled by the mysterious lines of personal faith and divine race, instructed, but not reordered by the demands of the public weal or the moral exigencies of history – has at least as one of its outcomes the prospect of a final solution of the Jewish question, virtually unopposed and unresisted by faithful Christians and Christian Churches. What is the line of privatism and piety, which stretches back through history to those accommoda-tions by which the realms of Caesar and Christ were settled and distinguished? The early adjudication and separation of realms of temporal state and spiritual salvation, although antinomic principalities in themselves, were both placed under the authority of the Church, an authority so easily compromised and suborned, when the interests of power rose against the ministrations of love.[3]

Cohen's admonition need be well heeded by Christians. The separation of human existence into two realms, sacred and profane, occurs repeatedly in Christian thought with Luther's doctrine of the Two Kingdoms being an obvious example.

It would be too much of an exaggeration, however, to say that all Christian theology falls prey to this sort of dichotomy, but the Christian stress on personal piety often produces a dualistic impulse which works to hinder serious Christian concern for the world, history and creation. The theme of personal salvation is very easily divorced from any serious concern for the problem of justice in the world. The world is often seen as merely an evil place one hopes to escape at death in order to dwell peacefully in heaven. The influence of Platonic/Neo-Platonic thinking on Christian theology manifested itself in a radical separation between body and soul, flesh and spirit, and this sort of dichotomy has grave implications for any quest for social justice, which takes seriously the problems of the body as well as the soul.

This problem has been aggravated by the Church's tendency to read the epistles of Paul as supporting this sort of split between flesh and spirit, grace and works. Some modern commentators on Paul have offered alternative readings of the Epistles,[4] but the fact remains that the traditional reading of Paul's letters continues to influence in large measure how the Church understands the relationship of faith and works. This point is clearly seen when one compares the influence of Paul with that of the book of James, which offers a position on faith and works entirely the opposite of Paul's understanding.

It was no accident that Luther wanted to remove James from the canon. The stress on grace over works in the Christian tradition has been a contributing factor to this problem. As the Church seeks to find a viable social ethic in post-Holocaust time, this will be an emphasis, which must be seriously rethought.

This is a particularly serious problem for Protestants who have been so greatly influenced by Paul, Augustine and Luther.[5] The Reformers may have been correct in challenging the Medieval Synthesis of Roman Catholicism, which all too often confused faith and politics, but the Reformers' solution to the problem merely created more problems. In fact, the Catholic position actually may have contained a greater promise for a viable social ethic. The reformers' stress on sin and human depravity was a profound description of the human condition up to a point, but it seems unable to then find anything worthy of redemption in human beings or creation. The worth and dignity of human beings as children of God is seemingly destroyed by virtue of the Fall. But the whole concept of redemption makes sense only if one thinks that redemption is possible. According to Herbert Richardson:

> The Reformation idea of the total corruption of man without corresponding emphasis on his dignity undercuts ways it intended to support; Man's sense that he needs a redeemer.... The world all agrees that all men are sinners, but it does not see that the redemption of sinners is worth caring about. The relative failures of Christianity to be an effective redemptive force in the world arises in large part from this failure to affirm clearly the spiritual dignity of human life.... The power of Judaism to survive in the face of constant enmity and disadvantage arises from its firm sense of being a 'holy people' and from its recurring celebration of the Sabbath sacrament.[6]

Acknowledging the worth and dignity of human beings requires that human existence in this world and its rootedness in history can be seen as important and meaningful. Their creation has meaning only if the creation they dwell in has meaning. The meaning of that creation is to be found in the Creator. Christians, by virtue of sharing the Tanak with Jews, know that Creator to be the God of Israel. No amount of supersessionist theology, which attempts to divorce Christianity from its Jewish roots, can ever alter this simple fact. The problem with Christian theology and its doctrine of creation lies with its constant flirtation with the ideas of the heretic, Marcion, whose theology was built precisely around the idea of separating Christianity from the creator God of Israel.

Marcion believed that creation was an evil place, and the that the world was 'stupid and bad, crawling with vermin, a miserable hole, and object of scorn.'[7] That Marcion was appalled at the suffering and evil in the world is understandable, but his solution to the problem undercut any meaning creation could have for human existence. His insistence on making the creator God of Israel a *Demiurge*, whom he considered to be 'the author of evils, to take delight in war, to be infirm in his purpose and even to be contrary to himself, ignorant, cruel, inconsistent, mutable, and wicked',[8] introduced a radical cleavage between Creator/Creation and human existence. He postulated a good God who would undo the work of the creator by sending Jesus to redeem the race of man enslaved by the *Demiurge*. Marcion believed himself to be a true follower of the Apostle Paul, but unlike Paul, Marcion wanted to eradicate any trace of Judaism from Christianity, including the Hebrew Bible. Marcion's most famous modern admirer, Adolf Harnack, agreed with him on this point. According to Harnack,

> The rejection of the Old Testament in the second century was a mistake which the Great Church rightly refused to make; the retention of it in the sixteenth century was a fatal legacy which the Reformation could not yet avoid; but for Protestantism since the nineteenth

century to treasure it as a canonical document is the result of paralysis which effects religion and the Church. To make a clean sweep and to pay homage to the truth in confession and instruction is he heroic action demanded of Protestantism today – and it is almost too late.[9]

Harnack is right. It is almost too late, but not for the reasons he thought. It is almost too late because the Church has allowed a heretic to colour its view of creation much more than it realizes. More often than not, the Christian doctrine of Creation verges close to a Marcionist position, which accepts a dichotomy between the God of the 'Old Testament' (Creator) and God of the New Testament (Redeemer), such that the two are seen as being in radical opposition to one another. I dread to think how many sermons are preached each Sunday which contrasts the 'Old Testament' God of wrath with the New Testament God of love. Underneath such a dichotomy lies the influence of Marcion.

Christian theology does not exactly reject creation, but it tends to give the doctrine a certain twist, which continues to hint at a 'dark God of creation'. Turning to Arthur Cohen again, he writes:

> It is not simply that the Church holds on to the God of creation disclosed in the Hebrew Bible, refusing the efforts of Marcion to polarize the histories of both communities and the divinities that he believed to have inspired them, the reconciliation adopted by the Church installs a theological dualism whose ambivalent resonation remains within the Church to the present day. Indeed, the God of Abraham, Isaac and Jacob is the God of Christians and the God of creation is the God of Christians, and the God of Deutero-Isaiah is the God of Jesus Christ. But even there – in the very assertion that the Bible continues – is underscored the apologetic insistence that what begins in one is consummated in the other, what starts on the one is fulfilled in the other, and the darkly perceived and imperfect God of the Jews is transfigured and illuminated by the God of Christian grace and love. Marcionism was repudiated as having indited an absolute theological *caesura*, but the Marcionist suspicion and loathing for the dark God of creation and the Jews is preserved as the teaching of the humiliation of Israel.[10]

If the Church is to take creation seriously, it must resist this Marcionist temptation to set creation and redemption over and against one another. There seems to be a very great temptation among Christians to believe that redemption is from creation rather than for creation. A 'Marcionist' suspicion and loathing of creation colours the Christian understanding of the doctrine of redemption in such a way that release from this worldly 'vale of tears' becomes the ultimate goal of human existence. The brokenness of creation merely confirms the desire to escape it rather than being seen as a rupture, which needs mending.

If the Church seriously wishes to engage in social justice and perform a *Tikkun*, it must break the Marcionist sway of so much of its theology. The most effective way to do this is by engaging in a hermeneutics of suspicion, which seriously re-examines its texts and doctrines to see whether or not they properly teach that the God which is trusted in as redeemer is known to be the God of Israel, maker of heaven and earth, creator of the world.[11] 'The Church's doctrine of Creation, therefore, can only confirm Israel's confession, echoing the great Yes of the Creator with the feeble Yes of its response: In the beginning God created the heavens and earth. That is the God of whom Israel, and therefore also, the Church speaks.'[12] Clearly, the lesson that the Church must begin to relearn at the feet of Israel is that the redemption wrought by God is to be trusted in precisely because it is the God of creation whom we discover to be the Creator. God's work as Redeemer only makes sense when it is viewed as God's effort to secure and guarantee the ultimate goals of human existence sought within creation itself. The goal of *Tikkun Olam* only makes sense if creation is seen as being essentially good and worthy of redemption. Human life must be included in this view of creation. All of creation must be mended. Two Biblical texts point us in this direction.

The creation story of Genesis is the most obvious. The creation story has man and woman being created on the sixth day. They are created like all other parts of creation. But creation does not end on the sixth day. It is on the seventh day that the Sabbath is created, and it is the Sabbath, which is the chief end of God and creation. It is the crown of God's creation. The Sabbath does not come into being because God is tired. It comes into being because this is what God intended for all of creation – the Shalom of the Sabbath. The goal of restoring *imagio dei* in human beings may be based on the sixth day, but it is not the ultimate goal of creation. The ultimate goal is for creation to dwell in God's Sabbath. Herbert Richardson has written profoundly on this subject:

> But why is it the case that Christ's work in restoring or actualizing the *imagio dei* is less than God's chief end in the creation of the world? The answer is that this pertains to God's intention for the sixth day (when He created man in His own image) rather than to the Sabbath Day, the chief end of God. Unless the work of Christ fulfills God's Sabbath intention, then it is less than the work of God in creating the world. Not only has Western theology failed to recognize this problem, but it has heightened it by setting the sixth day in opposition to the seventh day. How often have we heard that Jesus Christ abolishes the Sabbath so that men may be truly free? But this suggestion is sheer theological nonsense. The work of Christ cannot contradict the purpose for which God created the world, to assert such a contradiction by implicitly opposing the Sabbath is to reiterate the old Gnostic claim that the God of the Old Testament and the God of the New Testament are two different 'Gods'.[13]

Richardson has raised the Marcionist problem once again. *Contra* Marcion, Christianity must place its doctrine of the Incarnation within the doctrine of creation. The chief work of Jesus Christ is not redemption, but the sanctification of creation. According to Richardson, this will help to provide Christianity with a proper understanding of the Incarnation. He writes:

> The incarnation is not a rescue operation decided upon only after sin had entered the world. Rather, the coming of Christ fulfills the purpose of God in creating the world. Sanctification, not redemption is the chief work of Jesus Christ – 'God with us' rather than 'God for us'. For this reason, to know only the benefits of Christ is not to know Christ. To know Christ only with gratitude because of what He has done or will do for us is not to know Christ. Rather to know Christ is to enjoy he presence of His person, to take delight in His nearness, to love Him as a friend 'being with' who is its own sufficient reason. Only after we first know Jesus as 'God with us' can we truly know him as 'God for us'. Only after we know Him as a friend can we know Him as a Redeemer. The western concentration upon sin and its redemption has pushed this correct understanding of the Incarnation into the background.[14]

Richardson goes on to make a very important point in our attempt to understand the *Tikkun Olam* from a Christian perspective. He writes that, 'Unless we insist that the sanctification of the world by His mere Sabbath presence is the primary reason Jesus Christ is here, we lack the presupposition that makes his redemptive work worthwhile. For it is clear that unless human life has worth and dignity, here is no necessary reason why anyone should care whether it is redeemed or not.'[15] Richardson's imaginative interpretation of the sixth day of creation provides us, I believe, with an important counter to the Marcionist tendencies so destructive to the Church.

There is a problem, however, in limiting our ideas about creation to the Genesis account. A certain *fait accompli* runs through the text, which appears to betray the realities of human history, particularly the reality of chaos in creation obvious to all. Jon Levenson argues that the theme of God's constant struggle with the forces of chaos in creation is a theme, which is more prominent in the Tanak than is usually admitted:

> Although it is now generally recognized that creation *ex nihilo*, the doctrine that God produced the physical world out of nothing, is not an adequate characterization of creation in the Hebrew Bible, the legacy of this dogmatic or prepositional understanding lives on and continues to distort the perceptions of scholars and laypersons alike. In particular, a false finality or definitiveness is ascribed to God's act of creation, and consequently, the fragility of the created order and its vulnerability to chaos tend to be played down. Or, to put the point differently, the formidability and resilience of the forces counteracting creation are usually not given their due, so that the drama of God's exercise of omnipotence is lost, and a static idea of creation then becomes the cornerstone of an overly optimistic understanding of the theology of the Hebrew Bible.[16]

The problem of accounting for chaos in creation leads us to our second text from Genesis, the story of the Flood and the covenant with Noah. The story of Noah's covenant with God marks a point where creation and covenant are brought together in such a way that, as Levenson says, 'creation has become a corollary covenant'[17].

The Flood story dramatizes the fragility of creation and its vulnerability to chaos. Far from being safe and secure, creation is actually unsafe and full of danger. Chaos is always threatening to overwhelm creation, always lurking and waiting for the opportunity to destroy creation. The Noachide covenant makes creation's stability and endurance dependent upon God's willingness to preserve creation against chaos. God's pledge to preserve creation relates closely to the human anxiety over creation's ability to survive. The static picture of creation gives way to a more confused and uncertain picture of creation. 'Creation through chaos' is how Levenson terms it. He points to Psalm 74: 12–17, Isaiah 51: 9–11, Psalm 104: 6–9, and Job 38: 8–11 as Biblical references to this understanding of the doctrine of creation.

Faith in God's redemptive powers in the world is linked directly here to His primordial victories over chaos in the past. His convenantal promises to preserve creation became the foundation of the belief in His ability to redeem His covenanted people Israel, but that redemption is never seen to be outside the context of the redemption of all creation. The risks and dangers of creation are clearly acknowledged, nevertheless, God the Redeemer is trusted precisely because God is first known as God the Creator, dedicated to preserving creation. Levenson's comments on Psalm 74 are useful here:

> The composition of Psalm 74 expresses a theology that is reluctant to accept the hymnic language of primordial creation as a given, but instead honestly and courageously draws attention to the painful and yawning gap between the liturgical affirmation of God's absolute sovereignty and the empirical reality of evil triumphant and unchecked. The psalmist refuses to deny the evidence of his senses in the name of faith, to pretend that there is some higher or inner world in which these horrific events are unknown. But he refuses to abandon the affirmation of God's world-ordering mastery, his power to defeat even the primeval personifications of chaos and to fashion the world as he sees fit. In short, the author or redactor of Psalm 74 acknowledges the reality of militant, triumphant, and persistent evil, but he steadfastly and resolutely refuses to accept this reality as final and absolute. Instead he challenges YHWH to act like the hero of old, and conform to his magisterial nature: 'Rise, O God, champion your cause; be mindful that You are blasphemed by base men all day long' (v. 22).[18]

The theme of *Tikkun Olam* is closely related to the creation vs. chaos motif in Scripture. Two expressions from Genesis actually remind us of this fact: 'In the beginning' (V.1), and 'God saw everything that He had made, and behold, it was good' (V.31). The implication being that creation is beginning, but it is in no way complete. That creation is good is obvious from the text, but there is nothing to lead us to assume that it is perfect. *Tikkun Olam* is a concept, which follows directly from these verses. In *The Torah: A Modern Commentary*, the commentator writes on Genesis 1, 'Six times the Bible says that God found His creation "good"; after man was created He found it "very good": Being is better than nothingness, order superior to chaos, and man's existence – with all its difficulties – a blessing. But creation is never called perfect; it will in fact be man's task to assist the Creator in perfecting His creation, to become His co-worker' (p.22).

The task of being God's co-worker in helping to perfect creation reveals the moral seriousness of human life. It is also clear that our work with God takes place within the realm of human history. Roy Eckardt writes:

> Persons of faith are historical beings with historical obligations. But yet it is in the very avowal of overarching religious truth that the integrity of history is asserted – through, primarily, the doctrine that divine creation is good. The very declaration of the integrity of history presupposes a transcending reality that affords history its meaning. Transcendence and historicity are linked by abiding tension and interpretation.[19]

The meaning of history is intimately connected to creation. Its meaning comes from the human action to help perfect creation, but its ultimate consummation lies beyond the tragedies of history.

The fact remains, however, that the very creatures charged with this task are also the ones who pose the greatest danger to creation. The moral fabric of creation, which undergirds both the individual and society, lies in the hands of human beings who have the freedom to either work with God or against God in the battle against chaos and evil. If God's covenant with creation involves His willingness to struggle against the forces of chaos, the human acceptance of the covenant – symbolized by both Sinai and Calvary – involves the acceptance of responsibility to help sustain creation by obedience to the moral direction of God's will and to seek to mend the world within the dramas of history whenever a rupture occurs. The human acceptance of the covenant is made freely without coercion, but it is made in the face of a keen awareness of the dangers of chaos. Commenting on Genesis 1: 2 (The earth was without form and void, and darkness was upon the face of the deep), Gerhard Van Rad remarks that 'man has always suspected that behind all creation lies the abyss of formlessness, that the chaos, therefore, signifies the threat to everything created; and this suspicion has been a constant temptation for his faith.'[20]

Anxiety about one's life in the face of chaos in creation marks the point where human beings can turn from being co-workers for creation to co-conspirators against creation. This 'temptation for his faith' seduces a human being to seek after a security and completeness in creation, which is not historically available. Reinhold Niebuhr wrote that the saying of Jesus, '"Therefore I say to you be not anxious", contains the whole genius of the Biblical view of the relation of finiteness to sin in men ... It is not finiteness dependence and weakness, but his anxiety about it which tempts him to sin.'[21] An honest appraisal of human experience in history reveals the tension between God's sovereignty and the reality of evil. The fragility of human existence, its struggle for meaning and purpose, and its threatened historical condition all raise questions, which tempt faith. Questions which make human beings unsure about God's covenant to preserve and protect creation. 'Mortality, insecurity and dependence are not in themselves evil', writes

Niebuhr, but become the occasion of evil when man seeks in his pride to hide his mortality, to overcome his insecurity by his own power and to establish his independence.'[22] It is important to note here that it is not human creaturliness which makes one sinful, but the refusal to accept this aspect of existence and to work on behalf of creation within the limits of his finitude. 'The distinctive Christian doctrine of sin has its source not in morality but in man's willful refusal to acknowledge the finite and determinate character of his existence.'[23]

Contra Marcion, sin is not in the essence of creation *qua* creation, but in the refusal of human beings to accept creation for what is and their place in creation. Eckardt says of sin: 'It is the power that fabricates destructive discontinuities between faith and the world – not in the sense of "good spirit" versus "evil matter", but the very opposite of this: the corruption of a good material world by the exercise of spiritual idolatry.'[24]

From this discussion, we begin to see a paradox for a *Tikkun Olam* is made necessary by the rupturing of creation caused by misuse of human freedom; it is made possible by the willingness of human beings to use their freedom within the limits of their creaturliness to help to perfect creation, albeit in a most fragmentary way. The cause of the rupture in creation can become the source of its mending.

The theme of *Tikkun Olam* offers profound insights into human existence with its understanding of the dialectic between human sin and human goodness. The very reason *Tikkun Olam* functions so well as a metaphor for the religious meaning of life lies precisely in its dialectic between faith and realism. *Tikkun Olam* reaffirms the goodness of creation and the value of trying to mend it, while recognizing the dangers and evils in creation, which cannot be ignored or trivialized by a false utopianism. The fact that the task of *Tikkun Olam* has fallen into human hands reinforces the importance of human history; for it is here that the mending of he world must take place. The understanding that the world is good, but still incomplete and imperfect, gives to *Tikkun Olam* its moral imperative. Van Buren offers this observation:

> God's creation is good, but it can be otherwise. If the Biblical authors and the Rabbis after them lacked the theological sense of the Greeks, they made up for this with their sense of the moral seriousness of the world. Because their witness is to the centrality of moral choice, they can confront us with a world that may not become what God intended... The consequences of seeing the world as incomplete, with human decisions contributing positively and negatively to its course, are the realization that history counts in the story of reality. Such is surely the basic import of the rabbinical saying that all is in the hands of heaven except the fear of heaven. It was just this that worried the Rabbis: it was little comfort that all was in the hands of heaven if heaven's hands were tied by Israel's failure to live by the Torah.[25]

A Christian gloss on this commentary can be found in First John 2: 4–6:

> He who says: 'I know him', but disobeys his commandments are a liar, and the truth is not in him; but whoever keeps his word, in him truly love of God is perfected. By this we may be sure that we are in him; he who says he abides in him ought to walk in the same way, which he walked.

Human responsibility for the state of creation cannot be relieved by an escape into an otherworldly-oriented theology. Faith in the ultimate consummation of history by the power of God can only be trusted in by those who know Him as the creator of this world in which they live and where their responsibilities lie. Living between faith and realism, pessimism and optimism marks the reality of the human condition. 'In the Jewish–Christian tradition', writes Niebuhr, 'this problem of pessimism and optimism is solved by faith in a transcendent God who is at once the creator of the world (source of meaning) and the judge of the world (i.e. the goal of its perfection).'[26] One aspect of the divine character is logically linked to the other aspect.

Regarding the character of God, *Tikkun Olam* as a concept includes an idea about the limitations of God's power. That idea is embodied in the doctrine of *Tsimtsum* found in Lurianic Kabbalist thought which stated, according to Scholem, 'that the existence of the universe is made possible by a process of shrinkage of God.'[27] Creation comes at a painful cost to God, but it also comes with a great responsibility to those who acknowledge God as Creator. The task of reconstructing God's presence in the world though Tikkun Olam belongs to them. Scholem comments:

> The process in which God conceives, brings forth, and develops Himself does not reach its final conclusion in God. Certain parts of the process of restitution are allotted to man. Not all the lights which are held in captivity by the powers of darkness are set free by their own efforts; it is man who adds the final touch to the divine countenance; it is he who completes the enthronement of God, the King and the mystical creator of all things in his own Kingdom of Heaven; it is he who perfects the Maker of all things! In certain spheres of existence of being, divine and human existence is interwined. The intrinsic extra-mundane *Tikkun* symbolically described as the birth of God's personality corresponds to the process and the innermost soul, the religious act of the Jew, prepare the way for the final restitution of all the scattered lights and sparks . . . Every act of man is related to this final task, which God has set for His creation.[28]

Tikkun Olam is the great process of redemption in the world, a process that struggles against the evil and chaos which seeks to keep God from being wholly one with creation and therefore Holy. The whole idea seriously challenges the traditional notion of Divine omnipotence and the view that history has, at some point in the past, found its ultimate meaning.

The reality of human evil in this world has always challenged a simplistic notion of divine omnipotence, a Greek philosophic idea of an impassable Absolute which has trouble reconciling itself to the more dynamic image of God found in Scripture.[29] Surely, honesty requires us to either re-think divine omnipotence or to accuse God of immoral behaviour on the grounds of divine righteousness.[30] 30 We are on terrifying ground here. The whole idea of *Tikkun Olam* is meaningless if God is omnipotent, but God's omnipotence is challenged by the reality of evil and by our awareness that *Tikkun Olam* is both a meaningful task and the ground of human existence and morality in the world. Given that the events of the Holocaust mandate that we reconsider the whole idea of divine omnipotence if our theological language is to have any meaning at all, the doctrine of *Tikkun Olam* is a good place to begin that re-examination.[31]

Tikkun Olam points us in the proper direction away from a false sense of divine omnipotence to a more worthy idea of human-divine separation in the world. Judaism makes no attempt to hide her eyes from the reality of evil and the limits of God's powers. Christianity, with its symbol of the Cross, would seem to be a faith, which also knows that the struggles for victory over the powers of evil is by no means complete. 'The Cross shows', writes Van Buren, 'that history runs without guarantees. It can even include defeats and death.'[32] The cross is not a victory in history, but a symbol of God's struggle in history with the forces of evil in co-operation with those who abide by the covenant He made with Israel, in this case, the Jew Jesus. The cross of Jesus is the symbol of the struggle of creation to be restored and renewed. As Paul wrote; 'We know that the whole creation has been groaning in travail together until now; and not only the creation, but we ourselves, who have the first fruits of the Spirit, groan inwardly as we wait for adoption as sons, the redemption of our bodies' (Romans 8: 22–23).

The Cross can be seen then as *Tikkun*. It is not a final one, as some Christian tradition would have it be, but a *Tikkun* by which Gentiles are invited into the covenant of Israel to join in the struggle to mend the world created by the God of Israel. The doctrine of the Resurrection may function proleptically as a sign for the future of news creation, but to read it as an accomplished feat complete with triumphalistic language is to ignore its ambiguity and it eschatological meaning for history.

Auschwitz, the symbol of the Shoah, profoundly questions any Christian attempt to resolve the problems of evil and death too quickly. If death has been conquered, how do we explain the Death Camps of Nazi Europe? The belief that the death of one Jew on a cross is the most significant and final act of meaning in history is challenged on moral grounds by the death of nearly one million Jewish children, many burned alive in open pits, and whose deaths continue to haunt modern memory. Their little ghosts continually remind us to take care when we speak theologically. Hence the profoundly disturbing statement of Irving Greenberg: 'No statement, theological or otherwise, should be made that would not be credible in the presence of burning children – those thrown into the ovens alive to save less than one fiftieth of the German mark that would have cost to provide gas for a slightly less agonizing death.'[33] In like manner, we read Johannes Metz's comment:

> What Christian theologians can do for the murdered of Auschwitz and thereby for Christian–Jewish ecumenism is, in every case this; Never again to do theology in such a way that its construction remains unaffected, or could remain unaffected, by Auschwitz. In this sense, I make available for my students an apparently very simple, but, in fact, extremely demanding criterion for evaluating the theological scene: Ask yourselves if the theology you are learning is such that it could remain unchanged before and after Auschwitz. If this is the case, be on your guard.[34]

Indeed, Christians must be on their guard when making theological statements about Christ and redemption, particularly if they wish to make statements, which try to explain away the realities of human history and the evils found therein. The Catholic theologian, David Tracy, has suggested that a 'hermeneutics of suspicion' be applied to Christian theological tradition. Such a hermeneutics may discover that 'later historical events can demand reinterpretations of the founding events. Indeed, later historical events can even challenge not the founding event but the authoritative response to the event.'[35] Certainly, the idea that the Christ-event is a once and for all event which makes all history after it meaningless and unable to affect our faith needs to be re-thought in terms of an already/ not yet theology of redemption.[36] Van Buren writes:

> Perhaps the greatest question that Auschwitz raises for the tradition of Christian teaching about the cross is whether we can continue to say with Hebrews (and perhaps with Paul in Romans 6: 10) that it happened 'once and for all'. The price of doing so is to set God's authorization of Jesus on a radically different plain for his authorization of the Jewish people. This is of course precisely what the orthodox tradition has done with the doctrine of the Incarnation. The result was the introduction of a profound discontinuity in the conception of God's dealing with Israel. That this stands opposed to Paul's insistence that all God's promises (i.e. to Israel and the world through Israel) are affirmed and confirmed through Christ (2 Cor.1: 20) does not appear to have bothered that tradition. It must, however, bother a church that has declared its conviction that God's covenant with Israel, the Jewish people, is eternal. A Church that affirms the Jewish people as the continuing Israel of God cannot coherently define the authorization of Jesus so as to undercut God's authorization of the people Israel. In a world that has known Auschwitz, consequently, the cross can only be presented as a world-redeeming event in more qualified terms than those of 'once and for all'.[37]

By seeing the Cross within the history of God's struggle with the forces opposing the restoration of creation, the Church can free itself from a triumphalistic theology which has tended to historicize the eschatological, and return once again into history.[38] The Church is forced to reconsider its ideas of an omnipotent God and the dangers of theological quietism, which leaves all in the hands of God and stresses faith over works. In thinking about this problem, Van Buren offers an alternative view of God that fits closely to the doctrine of *Tikkun Olam*:

> It is also possible to conclude that God did not come to the rescue of his child Jesus or His many children in the Holocaust because He did not choose to do so, for reasons of which we cannot be sure. Could it be that God prefers to suffer with his chosen ones rather than to solve their problems for them? Could it be that God wants his creatures to take far more responsibility for the future of God's creation than those who trust in God have generally dared to assume? Could it be that God wants such trust in him that his creatures acknowledge and understand that God has entrusted his cause to human hands and hearts, so that if evils seen in Roman tyranny or Nazi bestiality are to be overcome, God's creatures must address themselves to the task.[39]

These are unsettling ideas, but they do drive us closer to a position, which faces history in an honest fashion without losing the dimension of faith so essential to the human condition. Theology must be done, however, within this tension between faith and realism.

If Christianity is to humbly appropriate the Jewish theme of *Tikkun Olam* it must do so with a clear awareness of the moral responsibility it brings with it. The task of mending creation requires a commitment to social justice, peace and love. This is the way in which the Creator God wished his creation to be ordered. The prophets of Israel were constantly reminding the people of this in their pronouncements. The task of the people was to live according to the covenant and Torah, to obey the commandments, and to do justice. The Christian tradition has had the unfortunate habit of reading the Prophets in an inappropriate fashion which ignores the deep-seated connection between the Torah and justice found in the Prophets, and have substituted, instead, a universalism that tends to ignore covenanted life. Perhaps the habit of reading the Prophets allegorically in order to defend the Church's christological claims has blinded the Church to this connection between Torah – covenant – justice. As Isaiah says, 'But the Lord of hosts shall be exalted in justice, the Holy One of Israel sanctified in righteousness' (5: 16). And this Holy One is none other than the God of Israel, creator of Heaven and Earth. The quest for social justice is not based on philosophical moral principles, but on the living response of men and women of faith in the Creator/ Redeemer God who underlies the foundations of creation making all human endeavours meaningful. That is the promise of the covenant, and according to Abraham Heschel, the Prophets believed that 'justice contributes to the covenant'.[40]

Justice is to be sought in human history for it is here that human beings are charged with God's mission. Justice is that which defines righteousness in human life. Heschel writes that 'righteousness is not just a value; it is God's part in human life, God's stake in human history. Perhaps it is because the suffering of man is a blot upon God's conscience; because it is in relations between man and man that God is at stake. Or is it simply because the infamy of a wicked act is infinitely greater than we are able to imagine? People act as they please, doing what is vile, abusing the weak, not realizing that they are fighting God, affronting the divine, or that the oppression of men is the humiliation of God.'[41] The Prophet, as spokesmen of God, called the people to attention about this fact in the name of the Creator of the World with whom a covenant had been struck. Any attempt to break off the quest for social justice from the theme of creation cannot sustain itself Biblically. Here we see why Marcionist ideas are so very dangerous to the Christian moral enterprise.

The idea that social justice can be easily achieved in history is put to rest by a proper understanding of creation and *Tikkun Olam*. We have already argued for a position, which finds the source of sin in human anxiety about the stability of creation. The romantic notion, so common in certain Christian circles, that self-sacrificing love will cure the ills of the world ignores this fact. As Reinhold Niebuhr wrote, 'The good news of the gospel is not the law that we ought to love one another. The good news of the gospel is that there is a resource of divine mercy which is able to overcome contradiction within our souls, which we cannot ourselves overcome.'[42]

Tikkun Olam reminds us of the ongoing need for human beings to be constantly attempting to mend the world. At their most profound, both Judaism and Christianity reject false optimism and romantic utopianism and opt instead for a realistic view of man as sinner seeking to live righteously in the world. Justice is seen as something very difficult to achieve, and it is always understood as being tenuous and fragile. Quite often justice precludes peace, hence the two different terms. Justice is linked to sin in the sense that sin makes living and acting simply according to the law of love the 'impossible possibility'. 'The refusal to recognize that sin', writes Niebuhr, 'introduces an element of conflict into the world and invariably means that a morally perverse preference is given to tyranny over anarchy (war). If we are told that tyranny would destroy itself, if only we would not challenge it, the obvious answer is that tyranny continues to grow if it is not resisted. If it is to be resisted, the risk of overt conflict must be taken.'[43] The struggle for social justice requires the use of power that can easily be misused, but settling too quickly for peace can actually lead to greater injustice.

Justice also precludes 'moral even-handedness', an odd concept of justice found in some liberal Protestant circles. Power and force are often necessary for justice to prevail. Modern history should have taught us lessons about the immorality of powerlessness and the morality of power, in addition to the lessons about the inherent dangers of power falling prey to human pretensions and abuse.[44] Justice is quite often the balancing of power between groups, and it can seldom be free of conflict. I take a decidedly Niebuhrian view of social justice, and I continue to find his ideas about the relationship between love and justice the most useful guide in the quest for social justice. Concerning love, justice and power, he writes,

A balance of power is something different from and inferior to, the harmony of love. It is a basic condition of justice, given the sinfulness of man. Such a balance of power does not exclude love. In fact, without love the frictions and tensions of a balance of power would be intolerable. But without the balance of power even the most loving relations may degenerate into unjust relations, and love may become the screen, which hides the injustice.[45]

Such a notion of justice as a balance of power tempered by a recognition that the law of love judges it less than perfect recognizes the fragmentary condition of any *Tikkun*, but it also makes the effort of seeking a *Tikkun* possible. The idea of *Tikkun* rejects the notion of moral perfectionism by recognition of the power of evil and chaos to rupture creation and produce sin through human anxiety and pretension, but it also rejects moral cynicism, which regards any act of *Tikkun* as a meaningless exercise of naïve romanticism. *Tikkun* makes our quest for justice possible even as it reminds us of a realistic perspective concerning our need to act in a discriminatory and fragmentary way: Niebuhr writes:

A simple Christian moralism is senseless and confusing. It is senseless when, as in the World War, it seeks uncritically to identify the cause of Christ with the cause of democracy without a religious reservation. It is just as senseless when it seeks to purge itself of this error by an uncritical refusal to make any distinction between relative values in history. The fact is that we might as well dispense with the Christian faith entirely if it is our conviction that we cannot act in history only if we are guiltless. This means that we must either prove our guiltlessness in order to act; or refuse to act because we cannot achieve guiltlessness. Self-righteousness or inaction are only alternatives of secular moralism. If they are also the only alternatives of Christian moralism, one rightly suspects that Christian faith has become diluted with secular perspectives.[46]

In an age in which Christianity seems polarized in its thinking about moral and political issues regarding justice by either quietism produced by overwhelming evil or the seduction of the utopian ideology of Marxism's 'realized kingdom of God on earth', Niebuhr's dialectic is most useful. His may no longer be such a popular position, but a commitment to *Tikkun Olam* requires that we struggle against hopelessness and reject false utopianisms. On this point Niebuhr helps to lead the way.

Tikkun Olam calls us to the task of mending the world when it is ruptured by evil and injustice. Its fragmentary nature does not excuse us from struggling to achieve it. For the person of faith, this task only makes sense within the context of faith in the Creator God known as the God of Israel on whom the final redemption of the world depends. But those called into covenant life, either through Sinai or Calvary, are called to the task of trying to perfect the creation to the best of their ability. The task requires a willingness to approximate our goals, to accept human finitude without excuse and to see beyond the tragedies of life. It is a task, which reminds us of our connection to all of life. (And I mention in passing here the whole issue of Animal Rights: A question that should be put on the contemporary theological agenda.[47]) We must take seriously a human condition marked by moments of faith and doubts, meaning and meaninglessness. As Niebuhr wrote:

> Let man stand at any point in history, even in a society which has realized his present dreams of justice, or if he surveys the human problem profoundly he will see that every perfection which he has achieved points beyond itself to a greater perfection, and this greater perfection throws light upon his sins and imperfections. He will feel in that tension between what is and what ought to be the very glory of life, and will come to know that the perfection, which eludes him, is not only a human possibility and impossibility, but also a divine fact.[48]

I have suggested in this paper that the mystical doctrine of the Lurianic Kabbalists, *Tikkun Olam*, is a useful doctrine for Christians to appropriate in a non-triumphalistic manner. I believe it helps Christians to re-think the doctrine of creation, the meaning of the Atonement, the meaning of history after the Easter event, and human responsibility in the moral life of society. As with any paper on theology, I repeat Karl Barth's comment, 'That the angels will laugh when they read my theology.' I can only hope that they do not laugh too hard. I do think that *Tikkun Olam* is a very important theological theme, and this paper is only the beginning of my reflections on it. Its significance for Christian thought remains to be tested, but the following statement of Paul Van Buren seems an appropriate ending to my meditation.

> To understand the death of Christ as a significant moment within the continuing history of God's covenantal relationship with creation excludes any understanding of the atonement as a divine transaction carried out 'over our heads' without our participation. God's involvement in the death of Jesus was rather his engagement against sin and for us, calling us to

engage for God and against sin. The transaction, in short, is still going on, and God's history with his creatures and their history with him is not over. In history, in our history now, is where God's unfinished, continuing, transaction of reconciling the world to him is happening.[49]

Tikkun Olam helps to make that reconciling activity part of our daily life and faith for both Jews and Christians.

NOTES

 1 Gershom Sholem, *Major Trends in Jewish Mysticism* (New York: Schocken Press, 1971), pp.244–286; Emil Fackenheim, *To Mend the World: Foundations for Future Jewish Thought* (New York: Schocken Press, 1982).
 2 Fackenheim, *To Mend the World*, p.254.
 3 Arthur A. Cohen, 'The Holocaust and Christian Theology: An Interpretation of the Problem', in *Judaism and Christianity under the Impact of National-Socialism (1919–1945)* (Jerusalem: The Historical Society of Israel, 1982), p.427.
 4 Reinhold Niebuhr, *The Nature and Destiny of Man, Vol.1* (New York: Charles Scribner's Sons, 1964) pp.175–176. See also E.P. Sanders, *Paul and Palestinian Judaism and Paul, the Law and the Jewish People*; Lloyd Gaston, *Paul and the Torah*; Paul Van Buren, *A Christian Theology of the People Israel*, pp.277–284; A. Roy Eckardt, *For Righteousness' Sake*, pp.36–50.
 5 Van Buren, *ibid.*, p.105.
 6 Herbert Richardson, *Toward an American Theology* (New York: Harper and Row, 1967), p.132.
 7 Quoted in Abraham Heschel, *The Prophets*, vol.2 (New York: Harper Torchback, 1962), p.79.
 8 *ibid.*, p.80.
 9 *ibid.*, p.85.
10 Cohen, *op. cit.*, p.424.
11 David Tracy, '*Religious Values after the Holocaust*' in *Christians and Jews After the Holocaust* (Philadelphia: Fortress Press, 1982), pp.87–107.
12 Van Buren, *op. cit.*, p.58.
13 Richardson, *op. cit.*, p.130.
14 *ibid.*, p.131.
15 *ibid.*, p.13.
16 Jon Levenson, *Creation and the Persistence of Evil* (San Francisco: Harper and Row, 1987), p.xiv.
17 *ibid.*, p.15.
18 *ibid.*, p.18.
19 A. Roy Eckardt, *op. cit.*, p.246.
20 Quoted in Bernard Anderson, *Creation versus Chaos: A Reinterpretation of Mythical Symbolism in the Bible* (New York: Association Press, 1967), p.172.
21 Neibuhr, *op. cit.*, p.168.
22 *ibid.*, p.174.
23 *ibid.*, p.175.
24 Eckardt, *op. cit.*, p.136.
25 Van Buren, *op. cit.*, p.100.
26 Reinhold Niebuhr, *Christianity and Power Politics* (Hamden, CT.: Archon Books, 1969), p.180.
27 Scholem, *op. cit.*, pp.260ff; also Van Buren, *op. cit.*, pp.63ff.
28 *ibid.*, p.274.
29 See Heschel's discussion of the pathos of God in *The Prophets*.
30 Eckardt, *op. cit.*, pp.13–33 and pp.301–326.
31 Paul Van Buren, *A Theology of the Jewish-Christian Reality: Christ in Context, Part 3* (San Francisco: Harper and Row, 1988), pp.164–67.
32 *ibid.*, p.187.
33 Irving Greenberg, 'Judaism and Christianity after the Holocaust', *Journal of Ecumenical Studies* (Fall 1975), p.533.
34 Quoted in Cohen, *op. cit.*, p.433.

35   *ibid.*, p.436.
36   David Tracy, *The Analogical Imagination: Christian Theology and the Culture of Pluralism* (New York: Crossroads, 1987), pp.429–438.
37   Van Buren, *Christ in Context*, p.165.
38   38 Eckardt, *op. cit.*, pp.225–264.
39   Van Buren, *Christ in Context*, p.166.
40   Heschel, *op. cit.*, p.209.
41   *ibid.*, p.198.
42   Niebuhr, *Christianity and Power Politics*, p.1.
43   *ibid.*, p.15.
44   Alice Eckardt, *'Power and Powerlessness: The Jewish Experience'* in *Toward an Understanding and Prevention of Genocide* (Boulder, CO.: Westview Press, 1984) pp.183–196.
45   Niebuhr, *Christianity and Power Politics*, pp.26–27.
46   *ibid.*, p.29.
47   *Eckardt, op. cit.*, pp.326–329.
48   Niebuhr, *Christianity and Power Politics*, p.201.
49   Van Buren, *Christ in Context*, p.102.

ETHICS WITHOUT CHOICE:
LESSONS LEARNED FROM RESCUERS AND PERPETRATORS

Darrell J. Fasching

A TESTIMONY:

'I had no choice, I was in this web – this network of authority... They would say, "Don't disturb the Organization"' (from an interview by Robert Jay Lifton with a Nazi physician who selected Jews for death in the gas chambers).[1]

A SECOND TESTIMONY:

'How can you call us "good"? We were doing what had to be done. Who else could help them?... Things had to be done, that's all, and we happened to be there to do them' (from an interview with Magda Trocme, wife of Pastor André Trocme. Together they led the citizens of Le Chambon sur Lignon in the rescue of over five thousand Jews during the Holocaust).[2]

ARE PERPETRATORS AND RESCUERS MORAL EQUIVALENTS?
Peter Haas's Moral Equavalency Argument
In 1988, Peter Haas published his important book *Morality After Auschwitz*.[3] This is not a book analysing abstract philosophical theories but a detailed analysis of how a society adopts a new ethic – one capable of redefining the moral life so that what had been identified as evil becomes good and vice versa. Using a sociology of knowledge approach, the book provides a detailed historical analysis of how the Nazi ethic became embodied in the institutions and practices of German society. Haas traces the Nazi ethic from its sectarian base in a small political party (the National Socialist Worker's Party) to its growth into a transcultural ethic covering most of Europe under Nazi rule. He follows the development of this new ethic in the transformation of political, legal and technical bureaucracies. As a consequence, everything that was done by the Nazis was, within this new frame of reference, both legal and ethical. In the end, Haas argues, we must conclude that the Holocaust was 'not the result of absolute evil but of an ethic that conceives good and evil in different terms... That is why the horrors of Auschwitz could be carried on by otherwise good, solid, caring human beings.'[4]

Looking at human behaviour from a sociological perspective, Haas argues:

Like any ethic, the Nazi ethic produced its few fanatic and self-righteous adherents, its mass of unreflective supporters, and a subclass of dedicated and deviant opponents. In this,

Nazism was no different from any other ethical code. Each person would, over a lifetime, establish a certain relationship to the regnant ethic, a relationship that grew not out of philosophical analysis but out of that person's personality, character, and social situation. In other words, conformity or opposition to an ethic is rarely, if ever, a matter of philosophical analysis. It is almost always a matter of accident, of where one happens to find oneself along the way. That means that it is wrong to judge people as evil simply because they conformed to the Nazi ethic, or as saints simply because they ended up opponents or rescuers. Their activities, one way or the other, were generally the result of mixed and unreflective motives.[5]

In making this claim, Haas goes on to argue for the moral equivalency of the actions of perpetrators and rescuers. So, for instance, he suggests that a bureaucrat in the German Foreign office by the name of (ironically) Martin Luther, who advocated mass executions of Jews, belongs to the same moral category as André Trocme, who led the French village of Le Chambon in rescuing some five thousand Jews.

Luther sought to advance his career by currying favour with the SS. He suggested a solution to the problem of Jewish emigration – mass executions by firing squads. Trocme, his family and his parishioners, on the other hand, willingly risked their own lives in the rescue of Jews from the Nazis. Yet in Haas's view, Trocme is no saint and Luther is not an evil man. The actions of each simply reflect the random statistical variation in behaviour one can expect in relation to any societal ethic. That is, every society will produce some fanatic adherents seeking to advance themselves by advancing the cause of that society, whatever it is. And every society produces some social deviants, alienated from the system, who will protest its norms and therefore such actions represent no great moral virtue.

Indeed, we are told, it is only by hindsight that we label one a hero and the other a villain. Both, he says, operated out of impulses that we all have and the truth is that neither could conceive of acting differently than they did because each did what their character, shaped by their social context, required them to do. Hence the perpetrators of the Holocaust 'were not unintelligent, amoral, or insensitive. They acted consciously, conscientiously, and in good faith in pursuit of what they understood to be the good.'[6] Now Haas says that he would like to argue that not everything that a society embodies in its ethic is moral, including the Nazi ethic. And yet he recognizes that on the sociological premises of his own argument such judgments are utterly relative. I can only call the actions of the other evil within my frame of reference, while clearly within the other's frame of reference the actions are praiseworthy. What we have, he seems to argue, is the clash of two arbitrary societal worldviews – a clash of what Alasdair MacIntyre would call, 'incommensurate first principles'.[7]

Ethics and the Limits of Social Conditioning
The strength of Haas's book lies in the challenge it presents by forcing us to understand that ethical behaviour is deeply affected by institutional contexts and societal trends. He is right, I believe, in suggesting that ethical behaviour is seldom the outgrowth of philosophical reflection. And yet if all behaviour is to be explained purely in terms of social and institutional forces, and described in terms of random statistical variation, we are tied to a perspective of sociological determinism and ethical relativism that renders moral praise and blame for human actions irrelevant, and moral reflection useless.

In my view, to reduce ethical protest to social deviance as a statistically random phenomenon (i.e., just one more accident of social conditioning and a mere reflection of the time and place one happens find oneself in) is to engage in a mystification of language that obscures the very evidence needed to engage in ethical reflection. The lesson to be learned from the rescuers is not that they were no better than the perpetrators but rather that they had the courage to act counter to their environment, to rise above their conditioning, assume responsibility and act with a courage and a compassion that bears no resemblance to the actions of the perpetrators.

This does not mean that they were not influenced by their environments but it does mean that their actions cannot be reduced to those influences. To account for their actions purely in terms of statistical random variation is to violate their dignity and demean their moral courage. Just as to account for the actions of the perpetrators in this way too quickly absolves them of their moral failure. The final consequence of such accounts is to render ethical reflection useless and promote the kind of acquiescence to social trends that made the Holocaust possible in the first place. What is missing from Haas's explanation is any account of the limits of social scientific explanation. For this kind of sociological analysis ignores the fundamental observation of the social sciences that no society has ever succeeded in totally socializing even one of its members.

The limits of socialization suggests that while its power is tremendous, socialization cannot be equated with determinism. We are all to some degree social deviants who are capable of calling into question 'the way things are'. Therein lies our capacity for ethics. In raising such questions we assume responsibility for our actions in defiance of the social and cultural currents that are shaping our behaviour. Having said this, however, I am compelled to deal with the serious objection that can be raised by noting that both rescuers and perpetrators have often explained why they did what they did by saying they had 'no choice'.

In the pages that follow, I shall examine this claim on the part of both perpetrators and rescuers in order to show: (1) that their respective understandings of this phrase are radically opposite in ethical significance; (2) that neither claim can be taken literally but rather both reflect the power of the ethical imagination, as an expression of our character, to render some options 'unimaginable'; (3) that it is the shift from the language of ethics to the modern subjectivist language of values that gives a false plausibility to the moral equivalency thesis and (4) that the Holocaust forces a radical transformation of our understanding of the role of religion in ethics, but one that has deep affinities with the biblical tradition of hospitality to the stranger.

PERPETRATORS AND RESCUERS: THE PARADOX OF ETHICS WITHOUT CHOICE
People Who Act Don't Agonize
In 1988 Pierre Sauvage did a documentary entitled *Weapons of the Spirit*[8] on the community of French peasant villagers of Le Chambon-sur-Lignon. These villagers saved over five thousand Jewish lives during World War II and did so non-violently (see also Philip Hallie's *Lest Innocent Blood be Shed*). Sauvage wanted to know how they went about making the decision to risk their lives for total strangers. In an interview with Bill Moyers, he commented that he had always envisioned such individuals as spending long sleepless nights weighing the consequences of helping or not helping others and then after totalling up the pros and cons, finally making a decision, to act or not act, with fear and trembling. What he discovered, however, was that among these villagers just the opposite was the case. They saw a stranger in danger, they identified with the plight of that person and they acted spontaneously to help that person, virtually without thinking about it. Therefore, he argued: 'I have come to realize people who agonize don't act and people who act don't agonize' (quoted from an interview with Bill Moyers for Public Broadcasting).

When asked why they did what they did, these villagers said they felt they had 'no choice'. In fact in survey after survey of those who rescued Jews during the Holocaust, this is a fairly typical answer.[9] Paradoxically, not only the rescuers but also the perpetrators of the Holocaust frequently give this answer. The psychiatrist Robert Jay Lifton, in his book *The Nazi Doctors*,[10] asked these physicians how they were able to reconcile their oath to be healers with their role as those who selected Jews and others for death in the gas chambers. They too responded by saying they had 'no choice'. And yet their actions were totally at odds with those of the rescuers. Does this mean that Peter Haas is right? Is it the case that both are recognizing that what they did was purely the result of the social circumstances in which they found themselves? To answer that question, we need to look more closely at the meaning of these statements of both the perpetrators and the rescuers.

The Nazi Doctors: The Excuse of 'No Choice'

How is it that ostensibly quite ordinary men and women, well educated persons, medical professionals dedicated to healing and giving life, could one day reverse course and become the key figures in the selections for the gas chambers? The answer, Robert Jay Lifton's work suggests, is twofold – (1) a narrative that allowed them to interpret killing as an act of healing and (2) a psychological process of doubling that allowed them to compartmentalize their actions, separating their 'true self' from their 'professional self'.

First, the doctors were deeply influenced by a bio-medical narrative that allowed them to think of killing as an act of healing. The Jews were vermin infecting the healthy body of the pure Aryan race. Or, the Jews were a cancer on the body of the German Volk. In order to restore that body to health the vermin had to be destroyed or the cancer had to be cut out. Hence, one had to kill in order to heal. The Nazis insisted that only physicians do the selecting for the gas chambers, Lifton argues, because it lent credibility to the view that exterminating the Jews was a public health measure. The scientific and medical stature of the physicians gave plausibility to such an interpretation.

Second, the doctors compartmentalized their identity so as to shield their personal identity from the behaviour they believed they had to engage in as professionals. Lifton called this process 'doubling'. Alongside their pre-death-camp identity as healers, the physicians developed a new 'professional' identity that allowed them to engage in killing. This doubling originates when the self is placed in an environment radically discontinuous with its previous environment in its values and practices, such that one's previous self becomes dysfunctional. In doubling, one self denies any real relation to what the other self does. The individual doctor was aware of what he was doing. What is repudiated is not the action itself but the meaning of the action. The Nazi doctor knew that he selected, but did not interpret selections as murder.

Lifton's analysis of doubling offers an account on the individual level of precisely the process that Haas is studying on a macro-social level – the transformation of an ethic. Doubling is a kind of migration into a new world in which what would be immoral within the first world is perfectly moral and rational within the second. The new self exists within a new cosmos (a new institutionally embodied narrative) and that cosmos has built into it its own ethical norms to which the self is expected to conform as long as it exists in that cosmos.

In doubling, the new 'killing self' parasitically draws upon the virtuous aspects of the prior self for its own self image while disavowing the second self as not being who one *really* is. This process is deeply rooted in the modern distinction between private and public life. Using this distinction the physicians could argue as follows: 'In my community, among family and friends I am a devoted husband, father and citizen, kind and compassionate. In that social and institutional situation I am acting for myself and am a "good" person. But when I go to work, I am not acting for myself but for my company or my country. In such public and professional contexts my obligation is to repress my personal inclinations and act as a professional and a soldier (as members of the SS, the Nazi physicians were both). It is not "I" that is acting but the institution that is acting through me. Therefore, I am not personally responsible. It is not my job to question but to obey and live up to my public duty. It's a dirty job but someone has got to do it. My personal virtue is not tainted by what I have to do. Indeed, one could say that it is morally praiseworthy to sacrifice one's personal concern about virtue for the good of the community to which one belongs.'

This way of thinking reflects the power of bureaucratic organization to neutralize our capacity to be ethical. In our personal life we choose both the ends and the means (both what we are going to do and how we are going to do it) when we act and therefore we feel the connection between them and may have some sense of personal responsibility. But in a bureaucracy ends and means are separated. Someone higher up is thought to have a larger perspective and therefore is best suited to choose the ends. As a professional or technical expert lower down in the hierarchy, one's job is to provide the means whereby the pre-declared ends can be realized. One's task is purely technical. It has no place for ethical considerations. Ethical consciousness is neutralized. One does not see oneself as being in a position to question either the ends or the means.

Bureaucratic social organizations therefore inherently require doubling. Thus when the Nazi doctors say they had no choice and were not personally responsible for what they did, they see themselves as impotent before the massive bureaucracy and victims of their social situation. As one physician reported: 'One couldn't ... really be against it ... That is, mass killing was the unyielding *fact of life* to which everyone was expected to adapt.'[11] Individual refusal to obey orders was not considered to be viable option. First, because of the possible dire consequences of such a refusal. Second, because the doctors thought of themselves as interchangeable cogs in a massive machine. If they refused they simply risked their own life and career without affecting any real change. Someone else would do the selecting in their place and the killing would go on. Therefore, they reasoned, they had no choice.

When a physician raised the question of how these things could be done, a process of *reality therapy* would set in. Under the conditions of war, it was argued, physicians have a duty to 'select.' Why should the physicians' responsibilities be any less demanding than those at the battle front? One must not shirk one's duty, no matter how unpleasant. In fact, the more unpleasant, the more morally praiseworthy it was to have the 'courage' to perform it. Indeed, the Nazi doctors might seem to be a perfect example of Haas's claim that people's actions are the result of social determinants and therefore beyond praise and blame. Or is it the case that their claim to have 'no choice' is simply a pathetic excuse used to deny responsibility for their moral failure?

The Rescuers of Le Chambon: The Paradox of 'No Choice'
It is possible, as Peter Haas claims, that the behaviour of the rescuers is also the product of social determinants which should likewise be the object of neither praise or blame. That would be one explanation for why rescuers also frequently say they had 'no choice.' I am inclined to contest this interpretation, even as I do for the behaviour of the perpetrators. But then I am faced with a paradox: Am I going to say that the rescuers' appeal to explanations of 'no choice' are also attempts to evade responsibility? One can

understand why one would want to evade responsibility for misdeeds, but why so for good deeds? These considerations invite us to look more closely at the deeds and explanations of rescuers to see if we can solve this puzzle.

The story of Le Chambon is as extraordinary as it is untypical of Christians, during the Holocaust. Over a four-year period in World War II, while France was under Nazi control, this village of some three thousand citizens saved over five thousand Jewish lives and did so non-violently.[12] A vast informal network of villagers and farmers took in Jewish families, provided them with false papers, fed them, educated them and hid them from the Nazis.

Much of the rescue work was done under the leadership of the French Protestant (Huguenot) Pastor, André Trocme. An inner circle of thirteen parish leaders met with Trocme twice a month and then weekly with other small groups, orchestrating rescue activities as needed. These villagers risked their lives and the lives of their families to help strangers. And some, like Daniel Trocme (a nephew of the Pastor), died in the concentration camps. Among the villagers the code word for 'Jews' was 'Old Testament'. When two or three showed up in need of shelter, the word would go out that some 'Old Testaments' had arrived, asking who could take them.

What is striking about these villagers is that, on the face of it, they seem to offer an explanation for their activities that sounds very similar to that of the Nazi doctors interviewed by Robert Jay Lifton – they tend to say they had 'no choice'. Yet, closer scrutiny of this answer will show that very different meanings are involved. What the doctors meant when they said they had 'no choice' was that they feared for their lives if they didn't follow orders. They also felt they were merely cogs in a larger bureaucratic machine. Hence they did not feel personally responsible for their actions. They were just following orders. The doctors' decisions seemed to be ruled entirely by external circumstances with a view to their own self-preservation.

The villagers of Le Chambon and other rescuers, by contrast, meant something quite different when they said they had 'no choice.' Where the Nazi doctors were motivated take care of themselves and 'doubled' to distance themselves emotionally from their own actions and their impact on other human beings, the villagers seemed to be incapable of doubling and unable to make self-preservation their first priority. Whatever 'no choice' meant for them, it was clearly the opposite of what the Nazi doctors meant. For they acted despite fearing for their lives and well being, and in spite of the overwhelming power of the omnipresent Nazi bureaucracy. They refused to be intimidated in any way.

THE RESCUERS, ETHICS AND SOCIAL CONVENTION
Kohlberg and Gilligan on Conventional and Post-Conventional Ethics

In order to makes sense of the rescuer's claims of 'no choice' it will be helpful to look at the study of rescuers done by Samuel and Pearl Oliner. The Oliners interviewed almost 700 persons (406 rescuers, 126 non-rescuers and 150 survivors) in an attempt to identify what, if any, factors could explain the behaviour of the rescuers. In their book *The Altruistic Personality*, the Oliners use the ethical theories of Lawrence Kohlberg and Carol Gilligan to try to identify the motivations of different types of rescuers.[13] Therefore it will be useful to briefly review Kohlberg and Gilligan's theories first, before turning to a review of the Oliners' work.

In Kohlberg's theory, moral development proceeds through three progressive levels: pre-conventional, conventional and post-conventional. Children begin at the *pre-conventional* level where their moral decisions are egocentrically based on self-advantage, especially fear of punishment and hope for reward. As children mature they begin to develop a social contract which brings them into the *conventional* level where their goal is to be a good person as that is defined by their community. Here they seek the approval of others in the reference group with which they identify and learn to sacrifice for the good of the group as a whole. Finally, as the children grow into mature persons, they arrive at the *post-conventional* level where moral judgements are made through the use of autonomous and logical abstract reasoning based on universal principles with respect to equality and reciprocity. At this level individuals are capable of asking not only what does society approve of, but whether what it approves of is just and fair. When the responses of men and women are compared as to how they would solve a moral problem, Kohlberg noted, men will typically operate at the third level, women at the second level.

Kohlberg tends to rate female ways of thinking ethically as less mature and developed than that of male's because women seem to be stuck at the conventional level of social relationships and have not yet arrived at the third level of abstract autonomous reasoning based on principles. Gilligan, however, suggests that what is going on in these diverse responses is a conflict of alternative frames of reference for approaching ethics. Men tend to see the world as a world of autonomous, separate individuals who must balance their rights and duties. Women tend to see the world as a world of relationships and the responsibilities they entail. Men think in terms of rational choices, women in terms of the obligations that come with relationships. Men think in terms of the hierarchy of principles and of social order, women in terms of the web of life, interdependence and equality. *Men think in terms of justice and fairness, women in terms of relationships and care.*

From Gilligan's perspective the ethics of care is not motivated primarily by the approval of significant others but by compassion for others encountered in the web of relationships that sustain our lives. As such the ethics of care is just as much an example of post-conventional ethics as is the ethics of justice. These two views (the male ethic of justice and human rights and the female ethic of relationality and care), she argues, are complementary. Each has something the other needs. Men need to discover that their self only occurs in interdependence with other selves and women need to discover that interdependence requires them to have a self. Not all self-regard is selfishness. If justice demands that all selves have dignity and rights, then the moral agent herself must be included in ethical reflection.

The Ethics of Rescuers: Conventional or Post-Conventional?

In *The Altruistic Personality*, Samuel and Pearl Oliner attempt to identify what, if any, factors could explain the behaviour of the rescuers. The 406 rescuers were identified using the criteria developed by Yad Vashem to recognize 'Righteous Gentiles': (1) motivated by humanitarian considerations only (2) they risked their own life and (3) they received no remuneration of any kind.[14]

The Oliners' findings can help us to better assess Peter Haas's claims about the moral equivalence of rescuers and perpetrators. The Oliners' use the theories of Kohlberg and Gilligan to try to identify the motivations of three primary types of rescuers. Drawing on Kohlberg they identified some rescuers who acted out of a conventional ethic in order to get the approval of their reference group. These they called *normocentric* rescuers. They identified others as *principled* rescuers who acted on universal principles. And using Gilligan, they identified still other rescuers who were motivated by *empathic*-relational identification with the other. The result is a three-pronged typology:

> Rescuers who were *empathically* oriented responded to an external event that aroused or
> heightened their empathy. Rescuers who were characteristically *normocentrically* oriented

responded to an external event which they interpreted as a normative demand of a highly valued social group. Rescuers who characteristically behaved according to their own over-arching *principles*, in the main autonomously derived, were moved to respond by an external event which they interpreted as violating these principles.[15]

Normocentric rescuers typically did not respond directly to the needs of victims but rather acted out of 'a feeling of obligation to a social reference group with whom the actor identifies and whose explicit and implicit rules he feels obliged to obey.'[16] They did not initiate rescue actions but 'went along' with actions initiated by others whom they respected. They tended to rescue because it furthered the goals of an organization or movement they belonged to (e.g., resistance organizations seeking to obstruct the Nazis, etc.) or because someone in authority (e.g., a political or religious leader) asked them to do so.

The actions of principled rescuers, like normocentric rescuers, were only indirectly tied to the needs of particular victims. However, they acted because of their convictions that rationally derived universal norms were being violated. Interestingly, the Oliners note that not all principled rescuers fit Kohlberg's model, for some principled rescuers acted not in response to rational principles of justice (e.g., 'the right of innocent people to be free from persecution') but rational principles of care (e.g., 'the obligation to help the needy'). In both of these types, the rescuers were prepared to respond 'in principle' to anyone (of any race, religion, etc.) who fell into such categories. The third type, empathic rescuers, by contrast, focused on the needs of others not as a group but as individuals. They rescued out of compassion for the plight of particular individuals whom they encountered. This type of rescuer tended to act spontaneously, with little or no deliberation, because he or she identified with the suffering of the particular victim. The analysis of the responses from the questionnaires given to rescuers showed that the largest number, 52%, were normocentrically motivated. They were followed by the empathically motivated, 37%, with principled motivation accounting for 11%.

The fact that just over half of the rescuers were normocentrically motivated lends considerable weight to Haas's theory about the socially conditioned nature of human ethical action. And yet the Oliners' research also indicates that just under half the rescuers were motivated by either empathy or principles rather than group norms. These motivations are allowed no independent legitimacy in Haas's account. Moreover, the Oliners note that those normocentric rescuers who engaged in repeated acts of rescue typically moved beyond normocentric motivations, embracing empathic motivations after their first rescue experience. The same is true for principled rescuers.[17]

The Oliners specifically raise the question of whether the rescuers simply acted in response to circumstances or if their actions involved some type of post-conventional ethic. Their answer has direct bearing on our inquiry. 'Rescuers did not happen on opportunities for rescue; they actively created, sought, or recognized them where others did not. Their participation was not determined by circumstances but their own personal qualities.'[18] Nechama Tec's study of Polish rescuers, *When Light Pierced the Darkness*, likewise led her to conclude that rescuers 'were propelled by moral standards and values not necessarily shared by others, standards that did not depend on the support and approval of others but rather on self-approval.'[19]

Both the rescuers and bystanders (i.e., those who did not get involved) that the Oliners questioned were hostile to the Nazis. However, bystanders were 'overcome with fear, hopelessness and uncertainty' leading to self-centred concern for their own well being and emotional distancing from the plight of others.[20] In contrast, while rescuers did not differ from non-rescuers with regard to overall capacity for emotional empathy (i.e., identification with the general moods of others such as elation, disappointment, etc.), they were more likely than perpetrators and bystanders to respond to the pain of others. And they stood apart in their tendency to see others as similar to themselves, while non-rescuers emphasized their differences. Moreover, rather than being fearful and seeing themselves as helpless and hopeless, they 'felt they could control events and shape their own destinies and were more willing to risk failure' and accept the consequences.[21]

Finally, the Oliners note that the actions of rescuers were 'not the consequence of objective external events but rather of the subjective meanings rescuers conferred on them. Rescuers and nonrescuers interpreted the demands on themselves differently. Faced with the same knowledge, observation of needs or requests [as bystanders], only rescuers felt compelled to help.'[22] The Oliners' point needs to be underscored. The crucial mistake of all deterministic/behaviouristic interpretations of human action is the failure to take into account the symbolic/interpretive nature of human experience. The same influences that impinge on human behaviour can yield different responses from different people in significant part because different *meanings* are attached to the same stimuli. Our capacity for ethical reflection and behaviour is rooted in this fact. While social conditioning does clearly play a role in the behaviour of rescuers, especially in the normocentric group, the data collected by the Oliners (and also Nechama Tec) clearly demonstrates that rescuers were able to go beyond such conditioning.

The Ethical Imagination and the Limits of Choice
What the Oliners' study suggests is that while many rescuers began with normocentric motivations, repeat rescuers demonstrated the ability to transcend conventional morality and call into question and defy the social determinants in their environment, either through principled action or, more likely, through empathically motivated action.

The villagers of Le Chambon and other rescuers, meant something quite different from the perpetrators when they said they had 'no choice'. Where the Nazi doctors doubled to distance themselves emotionally from their own actions and their impact on other human beings in order to take care of themselves, the villagers so powerfully identified with the suffering of the stranger that they were incapable of doubling and unable to make self-preservation their first priority, despite the obvious dangers.

When the rescuers of Le Chambon, for instance, said they had 'no choice' they meant that given who they were, they could not imagine turning their back on a stranger in need, even if it meant risking their own lives and the lives of their families. One could argue, quite rightly, that they too were shaped by an institutional context, but a very different one – the long history of a persecuted Protestant minority in Catholic domin-ated France. For these villagers were mostly Huguenots, French Calvinists, who had suffered a long history of discrimination and persecution by Catholics in France from the time of the Reformation. This history was part of their story, passed on from generation to generation.

In addition, being shaped by the Calvinist tradition, they were predisposed to see the Jews as God's 'chosen people.' For, unlike the Lutheran branch of the Reformation, which saw the Old Testament as a book of law which stood in opposition to the grace of the Gospel, the Calvinists saw God's law as a form of grace and of 'good news' (i.e., gospel) from the very first page of Genesis. While this was not enough to make most Calvinists elsewhere in Europe into rescuers, combined with their own history of persecution, it seems to have enabled the villagers of Le Chambon to strongly identify with the Jews. Thus, unlike most Christians in World War II Europe, they were able to identify with the plight of the Jews.

Their actions demonstrate the power of their story and community to shape their character and school them in the virtues characteristic of compassionate human beings, especially the virtue of hospitality to the stranger. Because of their experience as 'outsiders' in their own society they knew what it was like to be a stranger and to be persecuted. Thus when these villagers encountered Jews running from the Nazis, they immediately identified with them and took them in. They seemed to have experienced deep and immediate emotional empathy. This response was a matter of character and identity for these villagers. What these villagers meant when they said they 'had no choice' was that they simply could not imagine turning these strangers away. In order not to respond to the need of the stranger they would have had to abandon their very identity and they simply could not imagine doing that – even if it meant death, not only for themselves but their families.

The morality of risking the lives of one's own spouse and children deserves further consideration in a separate paper. Here we can only suggest that these rescuers clearly believed that some things were more important than survival. They not only could not imagine not rescuing those in need, they could not imagine raising their families to disregard the suffering of others.

What does all of this teach us about ethics? The lesson is, I think, that the ethical response is not primarily a rationalistic process of weighing costs and benefits in order to solve dilemmas. 'People who act don't agonize' argues Pierre Sauvage. While this is clearly an overstatement, in that some rescuers did agonize, especially when it came to risking the lives of their family, still it is remarkably true for empathic rescuers. For most of the villagers of Le Chambon there was no dilemma. *They simply did what they had to do.* Their response was rooted in their identity and character, the kind of people they were because of their own experiences and their own story, which led them to identify with the stranger in similar circumstances.

There is a sense in which one could argue that the villagers of Le Chambon embody an ethic that is simultaneously, normocentric, principled and empathic. For they clearly acted out of group cohesion as well as the principled conviction that all strangers are to be welcomed and, most importantly, out of empathic identification with the particular strangers at their doorstep. But if this is so, it only illustrates the tremendous difference between normocentric behaviour governed by authority and oriented toward taking care of one's own and normocentric behaviour governed by empathy and expressed in what the biblical tradition calls 'hospitality to the stranger.' To acknowledge this would be to acknowledge that normocentric behaviour can reinforce not only conventional but also post-conventional ethics. Too much behaviour during the Holocaust exemplified the 'conspiracy of evil' whereby people 'went along' with the perpetrators, but at Le Chambon, evidence suggests the opposite is also possible – 'a conspiracy of goodness'.

Peter Haas could argue that I have demonstrated that both the Nazi doctors and the citizens of Le Chambon did what they did because of their historical and institutional context; they were both the products of their specific social environments even though these were different social environments. Are perpetrators and rescuers both examples of conventional ethics, or can we say that the rescuers are really models of a post-conventional morality that exercises independent judgment over what society defines as good and evil?

In light of the Oliners' study, I would argue that the behaviour of perpetrators, such as the Nazi doctors, reflects conventional ethics, while the behaviour of the principled and empathic rescuers reflects a post-conventional ethic. Even the normocentric rescuers frequently stand apart in being governed by post-conventional norms generated by other rescuers whom they respected. Many rescuers at Le Chambon, for instance, were influenced by their community and tradition, but precisely in such a way as to enable them to challenge social conditions and conventions. They stood apart from the bystanders and perpetrators who were motivated by self-preservation and fear. Their actions were governed by ideals of principled compassion and by empathy or identification with the stranger in need.

Despite their testimony, both groups really had a choice. Their response of having 'no choice' is a testimony to the power of the imagination over the ethical life. When the perpetrators and bystanders said they had no choice they meant they were motivated by considerations of self-preservation which made any other choice unimaginable. When the *rescuers* said they had no choice they meant that they were motivated by their empathic identification with the other in their need and could not imagine turning them away. The first reflects self-centred moral cowardice, the second selfless moral courage. The first reflects moral failure, the second models the ideal of the ethical life – hospitality to the stranger. It is utterly beyond comprehension to treat the two as moral equivalents.

BEYOND VALUES: FROM ALIENATION TO ETHICS
Beyond Values and 'Moral Equivalency'

One has to ask: Why would anyone suggest that these totally opposite motivations and behaviours be conceived as moral equivalents? What frame of reference would make such a claim seem plausible? The moral equivalency argument, I believe, depends on a conception of ethics as being about 'values' and sees all values as culturally relative. This leads to the view that the rightness or wrongness of actions are decided by the social context that determines them and that therefore, one can concede that even the Nazis were well-meaning people who did what was good as they understood it.

I would argue that the very appeal to 'values' as the main subject of ethics undermines our ability to think ethically. The language of 'values' is relatively new in the history of ethics. This language was born out of the historical and comparative study of civilizations. It first appeared in the nineteenth century with the emergence of the social sciences. Before then, ethicists talked about subjects like the good and the common good, honour and duty, obligation, character and virtue.

The comparative consciousness of the social sciences led theorists to look for a new language to express the diversity of human social worlds. For this purpose a term 'value' which had primarily an economic meaning (as in 'x is a good value' – that is, 'a good buy') gradually came to take on a new meaning – expressing the collective preferences of each civilization (and its individual members) in contrast with every other. That is, 'value' became a term to express the new consciousness of cultural and ethical relativism. What cultures 'valued' were often different. Why one *valued* 'x' and another 'y' seemed subjective and arbitrary. No reasons, it seemed, could be given for one preference over another that were not circular (i.e., appealing to the 'preferences' of that society) whether one reflected on the behaviour of cultures as a whole or on the behaviour of the individual members of a culture. Values were therefore understood as subjective, privatized personal judgments concerning contingent and arbitrary objects of desire, which one person or culture preferred and another did not.

By the late 19th century, all of this seemed so obvious to the philosopher Nietzsche, that he rewrote the history of ethics as a *Geneology of Morals*[23] or history of values, in which he showed that values are arbitrary constructions which are not really about what is 'good' at all but about the 'will to power.' The language of values, he argued, has been, in every age simply a mask behind which those with power and those without power express their conflicting tastes along with their approval of their own and their disapproval of all others. The future, Nietzsche argued, belonged to those who had the courage to transform the values of their culture in accordance with their own taste. He called this 'transvaluing all values.' Ethics was reduced to aesthetics – having the courage to set the standards of good taste, standards that would rise above common values of the herd (i.e., the common man) and allow one to be a creative and unique being.

This language of 'values' not only distorts the nature of ethics by privatizing and subjectivizing ethical reflection but also by technologizing it. When we think that ethics is about values and values are treated as objects which we subjectively choose then our relationship to values becomes not only arbitrary but also technological. That is, we think of values as objects which we can change and transform according to our desires the way we transform raw materials into finished products to satisfy our desires. Nietzsche's dubious accomplishment was to preside over the death of ethics by dismantling the language of ethics and replacing it with the language of values – the 'transvaluing' all values.

What is missing from this picture? Fundamentally, I would argue, it is the fact that ethics is not private and subjective but relational and objective. It is about our relationship to other human beings. It is about the obligations we experience toward the humanity of other human beings. It is about seeing our own actions from the point of view of the other to whom we are related, whether this is a relationship of choice or chance.

A little reflection on our actual experience should tell us that there is something seriously wrong with 'transvaluation' as a model for ethics. For example, if a friend turns to me in his hour of need and I am not there for him because I can't be bothered, I have not 'transvalued' friendship. I am simply a failure as a friend. I have demonstrated a significant ethical flaw in my character.[24]

If you want the good that comes from having friends you have to acknowledge the objectivity and validity of the moral claims the lives of others make upon you. Recognizing the obligations that come with the desire to pursue this good is to acquiesce to neither authoritarian 'values' imposed by others nor libertarian 'values' invented by oneself, but rather to accept and embrace the ethical obligations that come with friendship and are internal to the very structure of such relationships.

We do not 'transvalue friendship' rather the obligations of friendship, if acknowledged, transform us into better human beings. To admit this is to understand the difference between the language of ethics and the language of values. The former has none of the privatistic, subjective and technologizing qualities of the latter. Relationships to family, friends and even strangers make objective claims upon us. In the ethically mature person they evoke a sense of inner compulsion that enables a person to transcend preoccupation with personal well-being and survival, with the knowledge that engaging in certain actions (such as the betrayal of one's friends) would be self-destructive. To do so would be to preserve my life at the cost of losing my identity. I would be acting 'out of character' as a friend and would cease to be who I say I am.

Only a society in which ethical language has been reduced to value language would treat as morally equivalent the behaviour of the perpetrators and the rescuers – that, for instance, of the Nazi doctors with that of the rescuers of Le Chambon. To treat the self-preoccupation of the Nazi doctors with their own well being as morally equivalent with the willingness of the rescuers of Le Chambon to risk their lives for the well-being of strangers, is to be so confused and disoriented by modern values consciousness as to be utterly incapable of ethical reflection. That is the pathway of an ethical relativism that can only pave the way to yet future Holocausts.

The Ethics of Hospitality: 'Remember, You Too Were Strangers in the Land of Egypt'
Where does religion factor into all of this? One cannot help but be struck by the research of the Oliners and others that overwhelmingly suggests that religion was not a decisive factor in the motivation of rescuers. 'In fact, several studies suggest an inverse relationship: More intense religiosity is frequently associated with greater prejudice.'[25] Indeed, while approximately ninety percent of both rescuers and non-rescuers cited religious affiliations while growing up, only fifteen percent of rescuers cited religion as a motivation for rescue, although some twenty-six percent of those rescued believed their rescuers to be religiously motivated.[26] (Those rescuers who did cite religion, stood apart from others in emphasizing teachings concerning the common humanity of all people.) Clearly religious affiliation by itself does not tell us much. Qualitative distinctions have to be made between different ways of being religious, even within the same tradition.

What is troubling is that, at first glance and given the history of Christian anti-Judaism in Europe, religion seems to have had a more prominent role among the perpetrators and bystanders than among the rescuers. I believe that one of the lessons of the Holocaust is that the critical dividing line of the ethical life has to be drawn not between religious and non-religious but between two different types of ethical imagination and social organization that deeply influence the behaviour of all persons in a way that cuts across traditional categories of religious and non-religious. Indeed this has been the central thesis of my last three books: *Narrative Theology After Auschwitz: From Alienation to Ethics* (Fortress, 1992), *The Ethical Challenge of Auschwitz and Hiroshima* (SUNY, 1993) and *The Coming of the Millennium* (Trinity Press International, 1996).

The French sociologist and theologian Jacques Ellul has argued that religion is only one rendition of the sacred.[27] The sacred also manifests itself in political, economic and other forms. Thus if religion is only about God or gods then it is not relevant to much of human behaviour but if it is about what people hold sacred, it is pervasive. It has been said that the Nazi death camps demonstrated that the modern world has become so secular that nothing is any longer sacred, not even human life. However, from a broader perspective of 'the sacred' that view is mistaken. Nazi Germany, like every society known to history, was very religious. Around the globe what people typically hold most sacred is their way of life. It is what they are willing to die for, and more tellingly, what they are willing to kill for.

The problem was not that human life was no longer viewed as sacred but rather that life was not viewed as human unless that life belonged to a member of their sacred society. In a sacred society, all who are the same, fitting the description of an ideal type (like *pure Aryan*), are considered human and all who are different, all who are aliens and strangers, are taken to be less than human. The Nazis called such persons *untermensch* or sub-humans. A sacred society creates an ethnocentric morality that obliges its citizens only to take care of their own. This sacred morality has no place for the stranger who is considered less than human and therefore beyond the pale of ethical obligation. But justice requires more than just 'taking care of our own.' The measure of justice, and therefore of all morality, is how we treat the stranger.

Jacques Ellul, in his book *The New Demons*, made the interesting move of treating the terms 'sacred' and 'holy' as antonyms rather than synonyms. Following his lead, I would identify a holy community as founded on a hospitality to the very strangers that a sacred society rejects. The core message of the biblical tradition, through many of its stories, is hospitality to strangers. The command to welcome the stranger occurs in the Torah thirty-six times – more than any other commandment. It plays a similar role in the New Testament. The one who welcomes the stranger is said to welcome either God (Genesis 18:1–5), God's messiah (Matthew 25:35) or God's messengers/angels (Hebrews 13:2). The people Israel were reminded to welcome the stranger and love the stranger, for they knew what it was to be a stranger, having been so in the land of Egypt (Exodus 23:9).

We could think of a sacred society as a circle whose centre is within itself – that centre being an ideal identity held in common by all those who are alike. All those within the sacred circle who share this identity are considered human; all beyond its circumference (all who are different) are viewed as less than human. If, according to the biblical tradition, to welcome the stranger is to welcome God, or the messiah or at least God's messengers (angels), and God is the centre of a holy community, then we must say that in contrast to a sacred society, a holy community has its centre outside its boundaries in the stranger. A holy community has no sacred centre but remains always a community of strangers to the world around it precisely because its centre and sense of identity lies outside itself in the stranger, that is, in difference rather than similarity. Like God, the stranger is one whose thoughts are not our thoughts and ways are not our ways (Isaiah 55:8–9). The stranger, like God, enters our world from the outside, and by his or her very presence as one who is alien, calls into question our sacred ethnocentric, religio-centric and ego-centric identities.

A corollary of Ellul's insight that religion is only one rendition of the sacred is, in a parallel fashion, religion is only one rendition of the holy. After the Holocaust, Jewish scholars such as Irving Greenberg, Elie Wiesel and Emil Fackenheim have concluded, the traditional line between the religious and non-religious has been dissolved.

Who is the true person of faith?, Greenberg asks, the atheist Jean Paul Sartre, who fought anti-Semitism or the Pope Paul VI who failed to publicly to protest it? During the 1967 war against Israel, it was Sartre, the atheist, who spoke out against potential genocide and Pope Paul VI who was silent. After Auschwitz, Greenberg concludes, we must say that it is Sartre, not the Pope, who has shown himself to be a person of faith, *one who has experienced the reality of God and God's image in every human being.*[28] Or again, he argues that in Israel today, it is the secular Israelis who represent authentic faith and not the Ultra-Orthodox Jews. For it is the secular Israelis who insist on the admission of all Jews to Israel and not orthodox Jews, who even after the Holocaust, would turn their backs on some Jews who do not meet their 'religious' standards.

Hospitality to the stranger is the measure of holiness, whether it manifests in a religious or a secular guise. I would argue that all human behaviour, whether it appears religious or secular, is deeply shaped by an ethical imagination governed by either a sense of the sacred or the holy. The sacral imagination is incapable of identifying with anyone other than 'one's own' and so can never be anything but 'conventional' and 'normo-centric' in its focus on self-preservation. The sanctified imagination, by contrast, identifies precisely with the stranger and so calls into question the sacred order of 'one's own'. This is the critical difference between the self-serving morality of the perpetrators and the bystanders, and the ethical audacity of the rescuers.

If were are willing to restructure our terminology so as to call these orientations (i.e., sacred vs holy) that encompass the behaviour of both believers and unbelievers by the name 'religious', then both represent 'religious' orientations but only one offers the possibility of the ethical life. Only one leads to the ethical life and an authentic life of faith, whether one is a 'believer' or not. If it is true that to welcome the stranger is to welcome God then it is not institutional affiliation but a spiritual orientation of hospitality to the stranger that separates the rescuers (whether institutionally affiliated with 'religion' or not) from the perpetrators and bystanders and makes them models not only of the ethical life but also the life of faith.

The root of the sanctified life is the capacity for empathy. It is the heart of biblical ethics (and, indeed, of all ethics) – love the stranger and welcome the stranger for you too were once strangers. Nechama Tec's study of Polish rescuers came to the conclusion that the only thing virtually all Polish rescuers had in common was a sense of marginality, of being different combined with a sense of adventurousness or risk-taking; what we might call a sense of audacity.[29] Their marginality was not necessarily social marginality, for some individuals it might have a psychological source. One might be from the social mainstream and yet feel alien because one was the least favoured child in a large family, or some other such personal factor.

Whatever the reason, however, such persons experienced themselves as aliens and strangers in their own world. Indeed, Tec draws an analogy between the Polish rescuers and those of Le Chambon and rescuers elsewhere, whom she insists shared this common characteristic.[30] Therefore, when they were confronted by a stranger in need, they impulsively identified with and sought to help them, for they remembered what it is like to be a stranger. Moreover, such individuals typically had a life history of such actions of compassion. So that when they encountered a stranger in need it would have been *out of character* for them not to respond. 'Such aid began either as an automatic, impulsive reaction or in a gradual but unpremeditated way. In none of the cases was it a conscious decision in which its possible implications were systematically considered.'[31] In short, they had no choice.

The overwhelming fact to emerge concerning the rescuers in the Oliners' study, is the inclusiveness of the rescuers – their hospitality toward the stranger. The rescuers were three times more likely than bystanders to emphasize the inclusiveness of moral obligations toward all human beings.[32] In the end, it was not normocentric conformity but principles of care and empathy for actual persons in need that moved most repeat rescuers to action. More than half of all rescuers had no previous relationship with the Jews they helped and the overwhelming majority (90%) helped at least one Jew who was a complete stranger.

The overwhelming majority of rescuers (76%) used the language of compassion to describe what they did. The Oliners describe their decisions to rescue as an 'inner compulsion' to rescue.[33] Indeed, the overwhelming majority (70%) indicated they acted to rescue within minutes of being presented with the need of another and 80% consulted no one. That is, 'to a large extent, then, helping Jews was less a decision made at a critical juncture than a choice prefigured by an established character and way of life ... "at crucial moments of choice most of the business of choosing is already over." Many rescuers themselves reflected this view, saying that they "had no choice".'[34]

Of course, both perpetrators and rescuers did make choices but the critical choices were made long before the moment of testing. It was the incremental and repeated choices of a life time that gave them their character as 'rescuers' or 'bystanders' or 'perpetrators'. These were choices about what kind of persons they would be. For the perpetrators and bystanders it was the choice to take care of one's own. It was a choice defined by a sacral spirituality. For the rescuers it was the choice to welcome the stranger. It was a choice defined by a sanctified spirituality of hospitality. To make such a choices again and again over the course of their lives led them to be unable to choose otherwise in the moment of testing, for by then they were ruled by compulsion and unable to imagine having a choice other than to be who one is. For the perpetrators and bystanders it was an external compulsion to take care of their own, for the rescuers it was an internal compulsion to identify with the stranger. To say that they are morally equivalent is to say that it is a matter of indifference what kind of world we live in – that it is a matter of indifference whether we live in a world that welcomes strangers or in a world that sends all strangers to death camps. Since I believe it does matter, I am unwilling to treat these two orientations as morally equivalent.

NOTES

1 Robert Jay Lifton, *The Nazi Doctors*, (New York: Basic Books, 1986), p.106.
2 Philip P. Hallie, *Lest Innocent Blood Be Shed* (New York: HarperCollins, 1979), pp.20–21.
3 Peter Haas, *Morality After Auschwitz* (Philadelphia: Fortress Press, 1988).
4 *ibid.*, p.170.
5 *ibid.*, p.181.
6 *ibid.*, p.233.
7 Alasdair MacIntyre, *After Virtue*, 2nd edition (Notre Dame, University of Notre Dame Press, 1981, 1984).
8 Sauvage, Pierre *Weapons of the Spirit* [Film]. (Los Angeles: Pierre Sauvage Production and Friends of le Chambon Inc., 1988).
9 My main focus is on Samuel P. and Pearl M. Oliners, *The Altruistic Personality: Rescuers of Jews in Nazi Europe* (New York: Macmillan, Free Press, 1988) [henceforth Oliners]. See also such studies as: Philip P. Hallie, *Lest Innocent Blood Be Shed* (New York: HarperCollins, 1979); Nechama Tec, *When Light Pierced the Darkness: Christian Rescue of Jews in Nazi-Occupied Poland* (New York: Oxford University Press, 1986); Eva Fogelman, *Conscience and Courage: Rescuers of Jews During the Holocaust* (New York: Anchor Books, Doubleday, 1994); David P. Gushee, *The Righteous Gentiles of the Holocaust: A Christian Interpretation* (Minneapolis: Fortress Press, 1994).
10 Robert Jay Lifton, *The Nazi Doctors*, (New York: Basic Books, 1986).
11 Lifton, p.196.
12 Philip P. Hallie, p.3.
13 Samuel P. and Pearl M. Oliner, *The Altruistic Personality: Rescuers of Jews in Nazi Europe* (New York: Macmillan, Free Press, 1988) For a discussion of Gilligan's dispute with Kohlberg see, Carol Gilligan's *In a Different Voice* (Cambridge, MA: Harvard University Press, 1982).
14 Oliner and Oliner, p.2.
15 *ibid.*, p.188.
16 *ibid.*, p.199.
17 *ibid.*, p.221.
18 *ibid.*, p.142.
19 Nechama Tec, *When Light Pierced the Darkness* (Oxford: Oxford University Press, 1986), p.164.
20 Oliner and Oliner, p.146.
21 *ibid.*, p.177.
22 *ibid.*, p.188.
23 Friedrich Nietzsche, *The Birth of Tragedy* and *The Geneology of Morals*, tr. Francis Golffing, (New York: Doubleday Anchor Books, 1956).
24 A parallel example may lend plausibility to this account. If I am a graduate student engaged in biological experiments under the guidance of my advisor, it makes no sense to tell one's advisor that he or she is trying to impose his or her values on me, in trying to teach me not to 'fudge the data' to fit my preconceived conclusions. Honest and integrity in following the questions wherever they lead are not subjective values but objective requirements of doing science. They are internal to the very structure of the activity. I am not free to 'transvalue' science. On the contrary doing science makes demands upon me and transforms me.
25 Oliner and Oliner, p.155, quoting C. Glock and R. Stark, *Christian Beliefs and Anti-Semitism* (New York: Harper & Row, 1966).
26 Oliner and Oliner, p.155.

27 Jacques Ellul, *The New Demons*, (New York: Seabury Press, 1973 & 1975), p.48.
28 Greenberg, 'Cloud of Smoke, Pillar of Fire: Judaism, Christianity an Modernity after the Holocaust', in Eva Fleischner (ed.), *Auschwitz: Beginning of a New Era?* (New York: KTAV, 1977), p.47.
29 Tec, see especially chapters 10 and 11.
30 *ibid.*, p.153.
31 *ibid.*, p.189.
32 Oliner and Oliner, pp.163–169.
33 *ibid.*, p.81.
34 *ibid.*, p.222.

CONSCIENCE, CONSCIENCE, CONSCIOUSNESS:
EMMANUEL LEVINAS, THE HOLOCAUST AND THE LOGIC OF WITNESS

Sandor Goodhart

CONSCIENCE n. f. Faculté qu'a l'homme de connaître sa propre réalité et de la juger; cette connaissance. I. *Conscience psychologique*. 1. Connaissance immédiate de sa propre activité psychique...*Conscience de soi*...II. (*Conscience morale*) 1. Faculté ou fait de porter des jugements de valeur morale sur ses actes...*Avoir de la conscience*.

Le Petit Robert

La conscience de soi se surprend inévitablement au sein d'une conscience morale. Celle-ci ne s'ajoute pas à celle-là, mais en est le mode élémentaire. Etre pour soi, c'est déjà savoir ma faute commise à l'égard d'autrui. Mais le fait que je ne m'interroge pas sur le droit de l'autre indique paradoxalement qu'autrui n'est pas une *réédition du moi*; en sa qualité d'autrui, il se situe dans une dimension de hauteur, de l'idéal, du divin et, par ma relation avec autrui, je suis en rapport avec Dieu.

La relation morale réunit donc à la fois la conscience de soi et la conscience de Dieu. L'éthique n'est pas le corollaire de la vision de Dieu, elle est cette vision même. L'éthique est une optique. De sorte que tout ce que je sais de Dieu et tout ce que je peux entendre de Sa parole et Lui dire raisonnablement, doit trouver une expression éthique.

Levinas, 'Une religion d'adultes'[1]

Dieu qui se voile la face...c'est l'heure où l'individu juste...ne peut triompher que dans sa conscience, c'est-à-dire nécessairement dans la souffrance....La souffrance de juste pour une justice sans triomphe est vécue concrètement comme judaïsme.

Levinas, 'Aimer la Thora plus que Dieu'[2]

What is the difference between consciousness and conscience? The first, we say, is a matter of perception or awareness. In philosophy, for example, I am a subject of consciousness before an object of knowledge. The second is a matter of moral authority, the degree to which I am constrained or governed by a voice which speaks to me of what I should or should not do. In Freudian language (as opposed to Kantian language), the first would correspond to the scheme conscious, pre-conscious, unconscious, the second to the scheme id, ego, and supergo, where conscience would translate superego. In French, the same word, *conscience*, designates both.

Could their conjunction be more than an accident of language? In the final pages of his introduction to Ellen Fine's book on Elie Wiesel, Terrence Des Pres speaks of a 'kind of consciousness identical with conscience' which would be necessary if we are to encompass the 'enormity' of the 'capacity for destruction' that the event of the Holocaust brings with it.[3] A 'French' consciousness we might say then, an awareness in which what we should or should not do is coextant (and coterminous) with awareness itself, an awareness, that is to say, in which it is no longer possible to separate ethical questions from perceptual ones, in which both the detached observer and the isolated voice of moral authority are historical, psychological, or metaphysical fictions.

An awareness in which the ethical results of my behaviour, the suffering or injury they may cause, are known in advance, calculated into the very possibility of my behaviour. An ethics that is also an optics. A testimonial or prophetic understanding, therefore, as opposed to a representational one, a factoring in of my responsibility for the origins and consequences of that behaviour, for myself, and for others, an owning of the continuity of myself with those others from whom I would most want to detach or isolate my observation or my morality. In short, Judaism, as Emmanuel Levinas understands it.

Is such a post-Holocaust perspective, such a *conscience*, or consciousness, or 'conscience-ness', possible?

In the paper that follows, I will explore this notion of such a Levinasian conscience-ness, an ethics that is also an optics, in three different registers. I will turn first to the work of Zvi Kolitz, a Lithuanian-born Jewish writer, theatre (and film) producer and political activist who writes a short story about the Holocaust shortly after the war that strangely takes on, as he describes it, a 'life of its own.' Secondly, I will turn to the work of Jesuit Father Frans Jozef van Beeck. Father van Beeck is interested in Jewish-Christian relations and in particular in Martin Buber and happens upon the work of Emmanuel Levinas in this context, and through Levinas, upon the work of Zvi Kolitz as the author of one of the texts upon which Emmanuel Levinas comments. Van Beeck puts the two of them, Emmanuel Levinas and Zvi Kolitz, side by side in a way that only complicates and compounds the problem he is trying to resolve, both when he tries to correct what he sees as a misunderstanding in the reception of Kolitz's text, and when he tries to translate Levinas for a Christian audience. Finally, I will turn to the work of Levinas, who has written the text about Judaism and about the Holocaust that van Beeck finds so powerful, and which turns out to concern the Zvi Kolitz story (a fact apparently unknown to Levinas), and I will suggest some of the ways in which Levinas's interpretations of Zvi Kolitz's story (and through it of Judaism and the Holocaust) help us to develop insights about his subject matter that also enable us to read the gestures and the fortunes of these two other writers.

PART I   POSSESSION

Is a perspective that unites conscience with consciousness possible after the Holocaust? Zvi Kolitz's story, 'Yossel Rakover Speaks to God', offers us an occasion for asking this question in some detail. In the summer of 1946, Zvi Kolitz travelled to Argentina to attend a meeting of the World Zionist Congress.[4] Sitting in his hotel room in Buenos Aires (the City Hotel, we are told), he penned in Yiddish a short story to which he assigned the title 'Yossel Rakovers Vendung Tsu G-ot' ['Yossel Rakover's Appeal to God'].[5] Later that fall, the story appeared (on Tuesday 25 September 1946) in *Di Yiddische Tsaytung*, a Yiddish-language daily whose editor had in fact first requisitioned the piece.[6] The following year, back at home in New York City, Zvi Kolitz had the story translated into English (by Sh'muel Katz so the story goes) in an abbreviated form under the title 'Yossel Rakover's Appeal to God' and he included it in a collection of short fictions he published with Creative Age Press, which he entitled (borrowing a phrase of Ury Zvi Greenberg), *The Tiger Beneath the Skin: Stories and Parables of the Years of Death.*[7]

The story seems to have been a smashing success. It was reprinted in a somewhat abbreviated form in 1968 by Albert Friedlander in *Out of the Whirlwind: A Reader of Holocaust Literature*.[8] Friedlander notes in a brief introduction that it was circulated among students in typescript form during the High Holiday liturgy at Yale University.[9] Zvi Kolitz himself revised and reprinted the piece in a new collection entitled *Survival For What?*[10]

The story also attracted a wide audience in Europe, and even in Israel. It was translated into French and drew the attention of Emmanuel Levinas, Jewish philosopher and teacher. In 1955 Levinas made it the centrepiece of a radio broadcast, 'Écoute Israël', which he included later in a collection of his essays on Judaism, *Difficile liberté*.[11] It was translated into German in the 1950s by Anna Maria Jokl and attracted the attention of a number of writers, among them Rudolf Krämer-Badoni, Sebastian Müller, and perhaps most famously, Thomas Mann. The story was translated into Hebrew and included in a volume entitled *Ani Mamin [I Believe]*, and a version of it sparked discussion of the piece in Israeli journals.[12]

What is the nature of the story that garnered so much attention? The story assumes the form of a document, the last will and testament of a survivor of the Warsaw ghetto uprising (a pious Hasidic Jew), written on the night before the final onslaught. The narrator describes the death of his children and other family members under conditions of atrocity, as well as the death of his eleven comrades, and he offers us his final thoughts upon the fate that has befallen himself and his people.

What are those thoughts? A modern-day commentary on the Rabbinical theme 'though He slay me, I will love Him.' In the face of the *hester panim*, the hiding of God's face, as Deuteronomy describes it, 'I will love You all the more. No matter what You do to me, no matter how difficult You make it for me to accept You, I will repudiate your attempts to dissuade me and I will accept You that much more fully. I am proud to remain among the ranks of the Jewish people. One thinks of the midrash about Rabbi Akiba, who was flayed and burned alive for teaching Torah, and who is said to have remarked, as his flesh was being combed from his body, 'All my life I have said the words of the Shema ["Thou shalt love the LORD thy God with all thy heart, with all thy soul, and with all thy might," Deut. 6] and been troubled by the words "with all thy soul." Now, at last, I shall have the opportunity to really fulfill them.' He is said to have died pronouncing the word *echad* ('one').[13]

Zvi Kolitz could hardly have known, of course, that his little story about a pious Polish Jew, written by a secular Lithuanian-born Jew (living in Palestine during the war and America afterwards), would have such a strange itinerary. For after the Yiddish-language version appeared in the fall of 1946, another version surfaced in 1954, this one submitted to Abraham Sutzkever, editor of the Yiddish language publication *Di Goldene Keyt*. Slightly truncated and attenuated, this version did in fact generate something of an odd history – either deliberately or inadvertently. For this version failed to include one salient detail: the name of the author, Zvi Kolitz. It was passed off as itself a document, a last will and testament, found in the manner of so many other documents among the ruins of the Warsaw ghetto. In this form it was translated into French by Arnold Mandel for the Zionist French periodical *Le Temps retrouvé* (where it drew the attention of Levinas – who later called his essay, 'Aimer la Thora plus que Dieu' ['To Love the Torah More Than God'] – and it was in this form, without authorial attribution, that it drew the attention of the German writers I mentioned previously. Krämer-Badoni wrote a posthumous and effusive open letter to 'Yosl Rackower', Sebastian Müller wrote a similar piece, and Thomas Mann's comment, given shortly before his death, has become legendary.[14]

On the surface, at least, it is not hard to see how such a text, such a fictional construction, may give way to misunderstanding. In form, the text may not appear significantly different from other texts that have been found (one thinks of Adam Czerniakow's diaries upon which Raul Hilberg has commented, or of the diaries of Emmanuel Ringelblum). One would think that a simple notification by the verifiable author of the fictional status of the text would be sufficient to set matters straight.

But here is where the story begins to take an unexpected turn. As early as the 1950s Zvi Kolitz learned of the double history of the text and attempted to clear up the misunderstanding. To no avail, as it turns out. His attempts to claim authorship were met either with silence, or more interestingly, with the counter charge that he was attempting to usurp the rights of another, to claim authorship for a text that was not really his own and that in fact the text belonged to Yossel Rakover.

An incident in the 1970s reflects this strange process. In 1972, Zvi Kolitz writes to the magazine *Shedemoth* the following letter.

> Dear Friends: A few months ago, my brother Haim Kolitz, who lives in Jerusalem, sent me issue No.43 of *Shedemoth*, which contained a quotation from a story entitled *Yosl Rakover Argues With His God*, which the writer of the article uses as an authentic testament, allegedly found in the Warsaw ghetto. Now I want to draw your attention to the fact that this Yosl Rakover is not a will which was discovered in the ruins of the ghetto, but an original story which I wrote and published about twenty years ago in New York [...].
>
> My attention has also been called to the fact that in a book, *I Believe* [...], to which the author of the article in *Shedemoth* was probably referring, this story of mine was published as a will. This error has apparently been repeated again and again, as has become known to me after the fact, ever since, in 1953, a great Yiddish poet, Avram Sutzkever, was misled by a Jew from Argentina, who had read the story in Yiddish and passed it on to Sutzkever as a 'document.' Mr. Sutzkever published it as such in *Die Goldene Kait* [...].
>
> Meanwhile the origin of this error has become clear, but errors like these have a life of their own. The refusal of this particular error to die, and the fact that many persons, and capable ones to boot, like Mr. Sutzkever, who were in the ghetto (which is not the case with me), saw *Yosl Rakover* as something that gives an authentic expression to the spiritual turmoil of a believing Jew in the last hours of the Warsaw ghetto – all of this is certainly a source of satisfaction to me. But there is a further testimony here. It is the testimony of my own spiritual turmoil, which did not subside with my giving it a fictional (and, I hope, artistic) expression; it went to the depth of the pain of a people that has the awesome right to take God to court.[15]

There is a great deal to comment upon in Kolitz's letter. The 'further testimony' about which he speaks, the fact that 'errors like these have a life of their own' – these ideas are not entirely contained by the context on which they appear. It is as if the very attempt to manage these matters through language only makes them worse, even more in need of management, and as if that unmanageability is somehow at the very heart of the problem. Before pursuing these issues, let us continue sketching the curious double history of this text. For the story does not end at this point.

Enter Frans Jozef van Beeck. In the middle 1970s, Jesuit Father Frans Jozef van Beeck, who had studied philosophy and theology for several years in Europe, and who happened to be interested in Martin Buber's work (and in particular *I and Thou*) as a way of engaging Jewish-Christian dialogue, is given a copy of Emmanuel Levinas's text on the Zvi Kolitz story. The text challenges his Christian faith. He decides that he needs to confront Levinas's work if he is to maintain his Christian belief intact. He also discovers that the story upon which Levinas comments in French is well known in the United States as the fictional composition of Zvi Kolitz (through the Friedlander anthology). He does a little research, finds the 1954 Yiddish version of the story published by Sutzkever, assumes it is an 'expansion' of the English original of 1947, and decides to publish a translated hybrid of the two (the discrepancies of the 1954 version added to the 1947 text) in English, with authorial attribution, along with Emmanuel Levinas's commentary (which he also translates into English), his own account of the implications of Levinas's Jewish thought for a Christian audience, and an account of the circumstances surrounding Kolitz's text and its double history. In 1989, he publishes *Loving the Torah More Than God? A Catholic Appreciation of Judaism*.[16]

Van Beeck's attempt to set matters straight is no more successful at first than Zvi Kolitz's, though for very different reasons. As theology, Father van Beeck's book is a wonderful volume for opening a serious discussion of the relationship between Judaism and Christianity and the possible implications of Levinas for Catholicism, and Eugene's Borowitz's introduction is particularly helpful in that regard. But unfortunately, von Beeck gets the story of Kolitz wrong. Von Beeck assumes the original was the English language version of 1947 and that the Yiddish version of 1954 was 'pirated' from Kolitz's original, 'expanded' by an anonymous Yiddish speaker, and submitted in that form to Sutzkever to be published in South America. He makes this assumption, he reports later, on the basis of Kolitz's statement in the above letter to *Shedemoth* where Kolitz writes '. . . this Yosl Rakover is not a will which was discovered in the ruins of the ghetto, but an original story which I wrote and published about twenty years ago in New York.'

Some time after publishing his book in 1989, van Beeck has contact with Paul Badde, a journalist who had just interviewed Zvi Kolitz for a feature article in *Frankfurter Allgemeine Zeitung*. Badde informs him of his error, and the fact that the original was indeed Yiddish, and in particular the text Kolitz wrote in 1946 for *Di Yiddische Tsaytung* which appeared on Tuesday September 25, 1946. With effusive apologies to Kolitz, and with the help of a young colleague and Yiddishist at Loyola University of Chicago, Jeffrey Mallow, van Beeck now publishes a second version of the story in *Cross Currents*, this one based on the Yiddish original of 1946. Billing this text as the 'first complete English language version' of Kolitz's story, he follows it with an 'Afterword' in which he explains the intervening events and in particular his error.

The story is not over. Some time before 1993, the text had attracted the interest of German journalist Paul Badde (mentioned above), who had read in German an earlier account of the story by Anna Maria Jokl – who had herself already published the story several times previously.[17] Badde now flies to New York, conducts an interview with Zvi Kolitz, obtains a copy of the Yiddish original from the documentation centre in Buenos Aires (the Asociación Mutualista Israelita Argentina, miraculously, from the same Oscar Lateur who a few days earlier could not find it), speaks with van Beeck about it, and publishes a feature article on the story and the man in the *Frankfurter Allgemeine Zeitung* in April of 1993.[18] In 1995, the text is reprinted once more (a fourth time) by Zvi Kolitz himself (who was still alive in New York City) in a volume entitled *Yossel Rakover Speaks to God. Holocaust Challenges to Religious Faith*. This volume includes a new English translation of the Yiddish original of 1946, the Levinas text translated by van Beeck, a new essay (his third) by van Beeck on the circumstances of the double tradition and his misunderstanding of it, and the dossier of other essays (including those by Badde, Müller, and Krämer-Badoni) that were published in Germany, Israel, and elsewhere on the text. As a kind of coda, Kolitz adds another text of his own, 'Requiem for a Jealous Boy', concerning two boys named Mosheh and Akiba.[19]

A final addendum. In 1995, there is a terrorist bombing of the Jewish documentation centre in Argentina housing the original document (from which Paul Badde obtained a copy), and the building along with its contents is severely damaged. An e-mail note I received from the head of YIVO in New York (who had somehow learned about my intention to speak publicly about this text) informs me that some of the 'furniture' from the centre survived. 'Who knows,' the writer of my note quips, 'perhaps among the ashes we may still find Zvi Kolitz's original manuscript.'

PART 2   DISPOSSESSION

What is an author? Michael Foucault's question from the 1970s resonates in this new context in a powerful and unexpected way.[20] His response – that the author is a function, an effect, the product of a set of social determinants – was an important correlative to the Anglo-American literary critical tradition in which an author is the set of intentional, rhetorical, and commercial relations a writer maintains with his or her text.[21] But in the present context, other aspects of authorial attribution become clear.

For although there may be more revelations to come (and there have been a number of twists and turns along the way I have not mentioned), a pattern is already emerging.[22] A manifest confusion gives way to an attempted rectification but that rectification in turn, rather than put an end to the difficulty, serves only to compound it and lead to more confusion.

Zvi Kolitz writes and publishes his piece in 1946 on a trip to South America. An anonymous individual gives the piece without authorial attribution to Sutzkever in 1954 who is struck by its power and publishes it in his journal, and thus begins the double tradition. Kolitz tries to clear up the matter, and is rebuffed either by silence or with the claim that he is usurping the text of 'Yossel Rakover' who is his fictional character.

The pattern is not limited to these kinds of exchanges and recurs on other levels. Father van Beeck spots the problem of the two traditions and, trying to be helpful, compounds the difficulty. He writes a book in which he explains the anonymous transmission and assigns originality to the abbreviated English New York 1947 translation rather than the 1946 Yiddish version. The nature of the accident has shifted from omission to misunderstanding but the effect is the same.

In a similar vein, Albert Friedlander, who anthologizes Zvi Kolitz's text again in the sixties, and who is aware that the text has been circulated without authorial attribution, writes that although 'there is no actual document written by Yossel Rakover . . . there was a Yossel Rakover who died in the flames,' a claim that according to Paul Badde is also a fabrication ('None of this is true,' Badde writes).[23] And as if history itself were collaborating with the confusion, the terrorist bombing puts an end – presumably forever – to the question of the original newspaper publication since henceforth all versions will be copies.

What is going on? The motives of the participants are not to be impugned. Those who respond as if they are reading an actual will – Rudolf Krämer-Badoni or Sebastian Müller or Thomas Mann, for example – feel (and express) a heartfelt connection to this lonely figure in the Warsaw ghetto writing on the last night of his life. Kolitz has written a fiction which is part of a lifelong political and artistic activism in which he has served in the Irgun, and helped produce Hochhuth's *The Deputy* (also an historical fiction) and other theatre and film projects dedicated to exposing the horrors of the war years, and it is not unreasonable for him to claim credit for the story he has written (in addition to being flattered that it has been considered by its readers so authentically). Van Beeck is doing his utmost to bring the confusion to the light of day and clear it up, a gesture perhaps not unrelated to his furthering of better Jewish-Christian relations.

But it remains curious nonetheless that accidents and confusions proliferate around this story, and that despite all the good intentions a pattern emerges that has an uneasy familiarity to it. Kolitz is charged with theft, with usurping intellectual property that is not his own. The copy transmitted to Sutzkever is said to be 'pirated' by an anonymous 'Jew' and 'expansions' are said to have been added to a smaller English language version – charges of dispossession, in other words, that align themselves with traditional negative stereotypes of Jews and Judaism.

The case of Father van Beeck is particularly interesting this regard. Father van Beeck's unimpeachable intentions are marked by a kind of hapless misfortune. He is confident that his Christian belief is intact and then he encounters Emmanuel Levinas. He thinks he has Levinas under control and realizes the 'document' Levinas is working on is a fiction. He thinks he has the fiction/document issue resolved, and then he gets the account of the history of that confusion wrong.

Does he at last get things right in his translation? He republishes the Levinas text in the Kolitz book – as he had published it in his own book – but he gets one more thing wrong: he mistranslates Levinas's use of the word *conscience* for conscience, which might not be so bad if the word 'conscience' in English were not precisely a Christian characterization of Judaism over the past two centuries (as the 'conscience' of Europe).

Van Beeck translates the Levinas text in which he encounters Zvi Kolitz's narrative, in other words, in a way that *cannot have occurred*, that is decidedly Christian, and that curiously reproduces the very structures of exclusion he is trying to undo in the process of trying to undo them. He makes interpretive choices that can only come from a misunderstanding, even though such misunderstanding is precisely the one he trying to avoid.

Here is the French original French of Levinas.

> Dieu qui se voile la face n'est pas, pensons-nous, une abstraction de théologien ni une image du poète. C'est l'heure où l'individu juste ne trouve aucun recours extérieur, où aucune institution ne le protège, où la consolation de la présence divine dans le sentiment religieux enfantin se refuse elle aussi, où l'individu ne peut triompher que dans sa conscience, c'est-à-dire nécessairement dans la souffrance. Sens spécifiquement juif de la souffrance qui ne prend à aucun moment la valeur d'une expiation mystiques pour les péchés du monde. La position des victimes dans un monde en désordre, c'est-à-dire dans un monde où le bien n'arrive pas à triompher, est souffrance. Elle révèle un Dieu qui, renonçant à toute manifestation secourable, en appelle à la pleine maturité de l'homme responsable intégralement.
>
> Mais aussitôt ce Dieu qui se voile la face et abondonne le juste à sa justice sans triomphe – ce Dieu lointain – vient du dedans. Intimité qui coïncide, pour la conscience, avec la fierté d'être juif, d'appartenir concrètement, historiquement, tout bêtement au peuple juif. 'Être juif, cela signifie ... nager éternellement contre le crasseux et criminel courant humain ... Je suis heureux d'appartenir au peuple le plus malheureux de tous les peuples de la terre, au peuple dont la Thora représente ce qu'il y a de plus élevé et de plus beau dans les lois et les morales.'[24]

Here is Frans Jozef van Beeck's translation of these two paragraphs.

> God veiling His countenance: I think this is neither a theologian's abstraction nor a poetic image. It is the hour when the just person has nowhere to go in the outside world; when no institution affords him protection; when even the comforting sense of the divine presence,

experienced in a childlike person's piety, is withdrawn; when the only victory available to the individual lies in his conscience, which necessarily means, in suffering. This is the specifically Jewish meaning of suffering – one that never takes on the quality of a mystical expiation for the sins of the world. The condition in which victims find themselves in a disordered world, that is to say, in a world where goodness does not succeed in being victorious, is suffering. This reveals a God who, whiles refusing to manifest Himself in any way as a help, directs His appeal to the full maturity of the integrally responsible person.

But by the same token this God who veils His countenance and abandons the just person, unvictorious, to his own justice – this faraway God – comes from inside. That is the intimacy that coincides, in one's conscience, with the pride of being Jewish, of being concretely, historically, altogether mindlessly, a part of the Jewish people. 'To be a Jew means . . . to be an everlasting swimmer against the turbulent, criminal human current . . . I am happy to belong to the unhappiest people in the world, to the people whose Torah represents the loftiest and most beautiful of all laws and moralities.'

Many of van Beeck's renderings are quite helpful. He avoids all jargon and his style is exceedingly clear. But he misses the mark on a crucial point: he translates Levinas's use of the word *conscience* as 'conscience' rather than as 'consciousness'.

Now, the French language is supple, and certainly the French word *conscience* can be translated as 'conscience' in certain circumstances. The primary definition given for the word in *Le Robert* is 'faculté qu'a l'homme de connaître sa propre réalité et de la juger; cette connaissance,' a faculty which is then divided into 'connaissance immédiate' and 'connaissance intérieure'. When the second usage is introduced, it often appears as *la conscience morale* to distinguish it from *la conscience de soi* which is its first meaning, although sometimes, it is true, the word *conscience* can be used to mean conscience alone.

But Emmanuel Levinas almost never uses it in this fashion. And since he is working within phenomenological philosophic tradition specifically, 'consciousness' would be his primary interest. And in those rare instances where Levinas does use *conscience* to mean 'conscience,' he spells that out specifically, as he does, for example, in 'Religion of Adults,' excerpted above, in an essay that we can be sure van Beeck knows about since he quotes it.[25]

Why is this matter important? Is it possible van Beeck is simply making a minor translational error?

The matter is important because 'conscience' differs from 'consciousness' along precisely the lines argued against in Emmanuel Levinas's essay. In representing Levinas as saying 'conscience', he represents him as arguing a different position with the effect that at least in English van Beeck can profit from that alteration.

For what is conscience? We customarily think of conscience (as we suggest above) as a kind of inner voice guiding our moral decision-making, or perhaps our memory of such past decision-making. It is an important word for Christian theology – as the work of a 19th-century Italian theologian, Antonio Rosmini, who writes a full-length treatise on *Conscience*, suggests.[26]

But in Judaism, as Levinas argues, the entirety of consciousness is ethical. The Christian notion of a consciousness which identifies one part of consciousness as moral, namely, conscience, presupposes that there is another part which is not, which is free of its moral obligation to the other, and which can function as a 'detached observer' to objective experience. The whole of Levinas's argument is against such limitations. For Levinas, we are never finished with our ethical obligations to the other individual (*autrui*). As Buber argues (whom van Beeck has certainly read), there is no 'detached observer' and to act as if there is one is to suppress the ethical from which human decision-making begins. Rather than argue against Levinas, van Beeck suppresses Levinas's text so that Levinas already says what van Beeck would have him say. He rewrites Levinas in order to approve him – which of course is another form of rejecting what he does say.

Moreover, Levinas makes his case for limitlessness of our ethical obligation to the other individual among other places in this very essay. If the narrator of the story feels so alone, it is in order to feel on his shoulders all the responsibilities of God, responsibilities such that I can never reach a point where I can say that my obligations have been completed, and responsibilities that only I alone can fulfill (which is how I am elected by this obligation and how paradoxically this infinite obligation determines my freedom). No one other than me can fulfill these obligations anymore than another can die in my place.

Translating Levinas, van Beeck misses its import, even though he appears to appreciate Levinas's work on many other levels. At the level of translation, he misses the forest for the trees. He is like the game player described by Dupin in Poe's short story who cannot see the word Europe on the map before him because it is written too large.

Why is van Beeck's misrendering of conscience important in this context in which Zvi Kolitz's text is misunderstood? Because the issue of conscience is not unrelated to readers who would like to think of Zvi Kolitz's text as a document and of their reply to it as an act of conscience. To render Levinas as saying that suffering is a matter of conscience rather than consciousness is to put on the very 'spectacle of the Passion' and render suffering 'expiatory' in a way that Levinas explicitly refuses, and as such to participate in the very suppression of Judaism that van Beeck is trying so hard in other ways to dismantle.[27]

To bring these matters together, let us turn to Levinas's own account of Zvi Kolitz's text, where he raises larger questions about Judaism and the Holocaust and Jewish-Christian relations, questions that are not unrelated to the dispossession of Zvi Kolitz's text, or to van Beeck's attempt to set matters straight, actions which issue only in factual and translational mishaps that we might justly characterize as a 'further testimony.'

PART 3 THEODICY AND USELESS SUFFERING

Emmanuel Levinas has presumably no idea that the narrative before him upon which he comments in his radio broadcast in 1955 is written by Zvi Kolitz, although he raises the possibility that the text is fiction with an almost uncanny awareness.[28] Whether fiction or non-fiction, however, it is in his view testimony and its testimonial or witness status is primary. It offers we may say a 'further testimony' to the spiritual turmoil in which both its narrator and its author are immersed. Within it, Levinas notes, 'each one of us who are survivors may dizzily recognize his own life.'

> I have just read a text that is both beautiful and true, true as only fiction can be. Published in an Israeli journal by an anonymous author, and translated under the title of 'Yossel, son of Yossel Rakover of Tarnopol, speaks to God' for *La Terre retrouvée* – a Parisian Zionist periodical – by Arnold Mandel, it . . . translates an experience of spiritual life that is at once profound and authentic.
>
> *The text presents itself to us as a document*, written during the final hours of the Resistance of the Warsaw Ghetto. The narrator would have been witness to all the horrors; he would have lost his young children under conditions of atrocity. As the last survivor of his family and with only a few moments left, he bequeaths to us his ultimate thoughts. This is literary

fiction, of course; but fiction in which each one of us who are survivors may dizzily recognize his own life.[29]

What is the theme of this turmoil? The impossibility once and for all of a God of children and the necessity of a God (and a religion) of adults. The abrogation of a Supreme Being and of a universe in which an all-powerful and all-knowing God punishes the bad and rewards the good, and the assumption rather of a God that is otherwise than being, and of human responsibility for human behaviour, of infinite responsibility or obligation for the other individual. In short, the end of theodicy and the beginning of witness.

> What is the meaning of this suffering of the innocent? Does it not bear witness to a world that is without God, to a land where man alone measures Good and Evil? The simplest and most common response to this question would lead to atheism. This is no doubt also the sanest reaction for all those for whom up until a moment ago a God, conceived a bit primitively, distributed prizes, inflicted sanctions, or pardoned faults, and in His kindness treated human beings as eternal children. But with what narrow-minded demon, with what strange magician did you thus populate your sky, you who now declare it to be deserted? And why under such an empty sky do you continue to seek a world that is meaningful and good?
>
> Yossel ben Yossel reveals to us the certitude of God with a new force under an empty sky. For if he exists so alone, it is in order to feel upon his shoulders all the responsibilities of God. On the path that leads to the unique God there is a relay point that is without God. True monotheism must respond to the legitimate exigencies of atheism. The God of adults manifests Himself precisely through (*par*) the emptiness of the sky of a child. This is a moment when God withdraws from the world and conceals His face (according to Yossel ben Yossel) ...
>
> A God who conceals His face is not, I think, a theological abstraction or a poetic image. It is a way of talking about the hour when the just individual no longer finds any external recourse, when no institution protects him, when the consolation of divine presence in childish religious sentiment is similarly of no avail, when the individual can no longer triumph except in his own consciousness (*conscience*), which is to say, necessarily in suffering; a specifically Jewish sense of suffering, which never at any moment assumes the value of a mystical expiation for the sins of the world. The condition of being a victim (*la position des victimes*) in a world in disorder, which is to say, in a world where the good does not triumph, *is* suffering. Suffering reveals a God who, renouncing all helpful manifestation, appeals to the full maturity of the integrally responsible man ... The suffering of the just for a justice that is without triumph is lived concretely *as* Judaism. Israel – historic and carnal – has become once again a religious category.[30] (italics in final paragraph added)

In the wake of the Holocaust, the idea that God has died or that God never existed at all might well seem the most natural (perhaps even the most reasonable) conclusion to reach. But we reach that conclusion only if we have held up until this moment a particularly childlike conception of God – of one who inflicts injury and awards prizes, a God, that is to say, of eternal children.

On the other hand, if we expand our conceptualization of transcendence, alternative possibilities appear. God's very absence may be taken, for example, less as a sign of our abandonment than an index of our own responsibility for (and implication in) human behaviour. It may lead to the recognition that suffering is not an interruption of human experience from the outside (as if a condition independent of suffering were achievable under the right circumstances) nor an experience to which may be attached any symbolic value whatsoever (as if, for example, it were redemptive) but a given in consciousness, an inevitable extension of that consciousness in a disordered world where the good and the just do not triumph.

Moreover, that in the face of such ineluctable suffering, what we *can* do is respond, trace the path of our own implication in the fortunes of the neighbour, the other individual, whose absolute alterity from us I have attempted to objectify and master. Discovering the suffering of the other individual, we discover the origin of our own subjectivity and the fact that Judaism has never been any other but the living of that discovery. 'The suffering of the just for a justice that is without triumph is lived concretely *as* Judaism' (italics added).

In another essay, 'Useless Suffering,' Levinas makes the point even more directly.[31] Suffering, he says there, is 'unassumable' and 'unassumability,' the collapse of the ability to appropriate. Suffering is 'dans la conscience, une *donnée*,' a 'given in consciousness, like the lived experience of colour, of sound, of contact, like any sensation.' As such, it has no inherent meaning, no use; it is 'intrinsically meaningless' and therefore when it occurs it is 'precisely an evil.' Suffering is 'pure undergoing,' a passivity 'more passive than experience,' more passive than the opposite of active.

On the other hand, since suffering is 'pure undergoing,' it can open the possibility of a bond within the 'inter-human,' the 'between human beings' as Buber called it, *das Zwischenmenschliche*.

> In this perspective a radical difference develops between *suffering in the Other* (*la souffrance en autrui*), which for *me* is unpardonable and solicits me and calls me, and suffering *in me*, my own adventure of suffering whose constitutional or congenital uselessness can take on a meaning, the only meaning to which suffering is susceptible, in becoming a suffering for the suffering – be it inexorable – of someone else.[32]

Useless and of no value in itself, and unforgivable when it occurs in the other individual, suffering can acquire meaning in my own case as a suffering for the other individual, as an act of my 'non-indifference' and 'dis-inter-ested-ness' (the removal of myself from among others with whom I maintain an ontological identity). As such, it becomes a modality of my responsibility for the other individual and can provide an ethical foundation across human groups.

> It is this attention to the [suffering of the] Other [individual] which, across the cruelties of our century – despite these cruelties, because of these cruelties – can be affirmed as the very bond of human subjectivity, even to the point of being raised to a supreme ethical principle – the only one which it is not possible to contest – a principle which can go so far as to command the hopes and practical discipline of vast human groups.[33]

In this context, to wait 'for the saving actions of an all-powerful God' is a form of 'degradation' (*déchoir*). The Holocaust in this context is the paradigm of unmitigated and useless human suffering not because it is transcendental or transhistorical but because it is transhuman. 'À la mémoire,' reads the French dedication (in contrast to the Hebrew) to *Autrement qu'être, ou au délà de l' essence* (the second of Levinas's major philosophic treatises), 'des êtres les plus proches parmi les millions d'assassinés par les nationaux socialistes, à coté des millions et des millions d'humains de toutes confessions et de toutes nations, victimes de la même haine de l'autre homme, du même antisémitisme.'[34]

Auschwitz, in other words, for Levinas, is an event in the history of the human. After the Holocaust, a *conscience* which unites consciousness and conscience, in which perceptual consciousness rediscovers itself at the heart of a moral consciousness, is not only possible but necessary. It has never in fact not been necessary. But after such a demonstration, the alternatives are unthinkable. To go on as if nothing has changed is monstrous. But is is equally monstrous to go on in such a way that claims to acknowledge Auschwitz and implicitly represses its evidentiary signs, a repression that in effect secures its perpetuation.

How does Levinas escape such monstrosity? By recognizing, I suggest, the commentary and the witness implicit in the text before him, whether or not the text itself acknowledges such commentary or such witness. Levinas uncovers the anti-theodicial potential of Kolitz's text whether or not the story's narrator or Zvi Kolitz himself acknowledges that potential, and whether or not readers of the story such as Rudolf Krämer-Badoni, Sebastian Müller, or Frans van Beeck acknowledge or enact it. In fact, one of the reasons van Beeck may be so attracted to Levinas's work is that Levinas manages to express the difficulty he finds with a Christian approach in a way that offers Christians a way out, a way to save face, a way to make oneself more fully Christian rather than less.

The Holocaust, Levinas tells us, is the end of theodicy. Theodicy as a word entered the language as the title of a book by Leibnitz at the beginning of the eighteenth century. But as an idea, and in particular as the 'vindication of divine justice in the face of the existence of evil,' it may be as old as Judaism.[35] We find echoes of it in the Book of Ezra, for example, where the collapse of the Temple is justified as a divine punishment for the sins of the people. Theodicy is the continuation of mythic thinking into revealed religious thinking.

Theodicy, in other words, was never a fact of life. But if we ever thought it was and needed a demonstration of its insufficiency, the Holocaust was such a demonstration with a vengeance. The Holocaust as an event for Levinas aligns itself with the deepest order of human catastrophe. It is the return of the moment of the exile, the beginning of the first diaspora. All responsibility is in our hands, not because there is no God, or because God has concealed or veiled His Face but because, he tells us, there never was such a God to begin with, because the dream of such a God is the dream of children who would deflect human responsibility onto the divine. To become adult for Levinas is to assume a full responsibility for human behaviour that is not the product of my freedom but ironically its condition, that is given in the created fabric of the world. And to become such an adult – infinitely responsible for the other individual (and here is really the second part of it) – is clearly in fact to engage God in relationship, a God who is otherwise than being, a God who demands of us nothing less than shouldering God's own responsibility for others, for their lives, for their responsibility, even for their deaths.

> how does Judaism conceive of humanity?...by experiencing the presence of God through one's relation to man.... The way that leads to God therefore leads *ipso facto* – and not in addition – to man.... The fact that the relationship with the Divine crosses the relationship with men and coincides with social justice...epitomizes the entire spirit of the Jewish Bible.[36]

The truth of testimony, for Levinas, is not the truth of representation. The inability of Zvi Kolitz's readers to recognize themselves in Zvi Kolitz's narrative itself bears witness to the truth of its claims, as Levinas reads them. The struggle to separate what is true from what is fictive about it continues the circumstances already internal to it and generates the problem to anew. Yossel Rakover finds himself in a circumstance in which the unthinkable has happened in the Warsaw ghetto and to deal with it he relies upon the traditional Rabbinic theme of *hester panim*. Zvi Kolitz in 1946 finds himself in a situation in which the unthinkable has occurred in Europe and responds by invoking a traditional literary theme. He writes a short story about it in which heroism triumphs over adversity. Reading Zvi Kolitz's text from 1946 to 1995, van Beeck finds both the circumstances internal to the narrative and the circumstances involving its transmission intolerable and responds by invoking a traditional rationalist theological schema to set things straight: whether the text is a 'real document' or 'only a fiction,' Zvi Kolitz deserves credit for having written it and Emmanuel Levinas deserves credit for having noticed its testimonial potential.

The subject matter of the unthinkable changes. In one case, it is the behaviour of the Nazis and the world surrounding them. In another, it is the experience of a secular Yiddish writer living after the war in America reflecting upon his past. In still another, it is the experience of a writer living after the war in Germany, or a Lithuanian Jewish philosopher working after the war in France, or a Dutch Jesuit theologian doing work after the war on Jewish-Christian relations reflecting upon their own memories. But in each case the insupportability of the reality they encounter is noted and a traditional response engaged, and in that fashion the 'same' situation continues. The internal narrative and the external narrative bear witness, finally, not to the heroism of Yossel Rakover or of Zvi Kolitz or of Krämer-Badoni or of Frans Jozef van Beeck (or for that matter of Emmanuel Levinas) but to the circumstances in which such judgement is rendered, circumstances in which a structure of possession and dispossession has the potential to unleash accusation, suffering, and theodicy – mythic, anthropomorphic, interpretative, sacrificial consequences that engender only more suffering and more evil.

CONCLUSION

We continue to live in the shadow of Auschwitz – all the more fully as we attempt to evade or deny that shadow. And we are likely to do so – Geoffrey Hartman observes – for some time to come.[37] The literature of our age bears witness to that shadow whether we would present it or conceal it. We may act out that shadow in our fictions, in our literary criticism, in our theologies, in our philosophies, or in our day-to-day behaviour. Or we may work through it, a working through that does not necessarily avoid acting it out (and may even require it), but that attempts at least to take stock of it, and in doing so binds us to a tradition of scriptural exegesis which has also never not been thinking and acting along the same paths, a traditional Jewish Talmudic interpretative mode which, far from having ended in the second century of the common era (as is sometimes said) continues in this fashion in writers like Emmanuel Levinas as an ongoing available prophetic creative thoughful possibility.

On the eve of the 21st century, it might be more helpful for us to register the critical testimonial prophetic status of our most powerful writing and reading rather than try to determine what is true or untrue about it, fictional or non-fictional, decidable or (as much of avant-garde critical theorizing is wont to say), undecidable. Our most powerful writing, like our most powerful reading, is both/and, and neither/nor, already entirely otherwise than the being within which we would struggle to discover and confine it.

WORKS CITED

Badde, Paul, 'Zvi Kolitz.' In Kolitz (1995), 1–12.
Booth, Wayne, *Rhetoric of Fiction* (Chicago: University of Chicago Press, 1983).
Bouchard, Donald F. (ed.), *Language, Counter-memory, Practice: Selected Essays and Interviews with Michel Foucault*. Translated from the French by Donald F. Bouchard and Sherry Simon (Ithaca, N.Y.: Cornell University Press, 1977).

Bernasconi, Robert and Wood, David, *The Provocation of Levinas* (London and New York: Routledge and Kegan Paul, 1988).

Eliav, Mordecai, *Ani Mamin [I Believe]* (Jerusalem: Mosad Harav Kook, 1965).

Fine, Ellen S. *Legacy of Night. The Literary Universe of Elie Wiesel* (Albany: State University of New York Press, 1982).

Foucault, Michel. 'What is an Author?' See Bouchard 1977.

Friedlander, Albert, (ed.), *Out of the Whirlwind: A Reader of Holocaust Literature* (New York: Schocken Books, 1976).

Friedlander, Albert, (ed.), *Out of the Whirlwind: A Reader in Holocaust Literature* (New York: Union of American Hebrew Congregations, 1968).

Goodhart, Sandor, *Sacrificing Commentary. Reading the End of Literature* (Baltimore: Johns Hopkins University Press, 1996).

Hartman, Geoffrey, (ed.), *Bitburg in Moral and Political Perspective* (Bloomington: Indiana University Press, 1986).

Hilberg, Raul, Stanislaw Staron, and Josef Kermisz, (eds.) *The Warsaw Diary of Adam Czerniakow: Prelude to Doom*, translated by Stanislaw Staron and the staff of Yad Vashem (New York: Stein and Day, 1979).

Kolitz, Zvi, 'Yosl Rakover Ret tsu G-t,' *Di Goldene Keyt* 18 (1954), 102–110.

Kolitz, Zvi, *Yossel Rakover Speaks to God. Holocaust Challenges to Religious Faith* (Hoboken, New Jersey: Ktav Publishing House, Inc., 1995).

Kolitz, Zvi, 'Yossel Rakover Speaks to God.' In Kolitz (1995), 13–26.

Kolitz, Zvi, 'Yossel Rakover's Appeal to God.' In Kolitz (1947), 81–95.

Kolitz, Zvi, 'Yossel Rakover's Appeal to God.' In Friedlander (1976), 390–399.

Kolitz, Zvi, 'Yossel Rakover's Appeal to God. A New Translation with Afterword by Jeffrey V. Mallow and Frans Jozef van Beeck,' *Cross Currents* 44 (1994a): 362–77.

Kolitz, Zvi, 'Yossel Rakovers Vendung Tsu G-t,' *Di Yiddische Tsaytung*, Tuesday 25 September, 1946.

Kolitz, Zvi, *Jossel Rackower spricht zu Gott*, unter Mithilfe von David Kohan aus dem Jiddischen übersetzt von Anna Maria Jokl (Neu-Isenburg: Verlag Tiessen, 1985).

Kolitz, Zvi, *Jossel Rakover's Wendung zu Gott*, translated from the Yiddish and edited by Paul Badde (Möhlin and Villingen: Raureif Verlag, 1994).

Kolitz, Zvi, *Survival For What?* (New York: Philosophical Library, 1969).

Kolitz, Zvi, *The Tiger Beneath the Skin: Stories and Parables of the Years of Death* (New York: Creative Age Press, 1947).

Levinas, Emmanuel, *Autrement qu'être ou au-delà de l'essence* (The Hague: Martinus Nijhoff, 1974).

Levinas, Emmanuel, *Difficult Freedom*, translated by Seán Hand (Baltimore: Johns Hopkins University Press, 1990).

Levinas, Emmanuel, *Difficile liberté* (Paris: Albin Michel, 1983). See Levinas (1990).

Levinas, Emmanuel, *Entre nous. Essais sur le penser-a-l'autre* (Paris: Grasset) (1991).

Levinas, Emmanuel, 'Useless Suffering.' Translated by Richard Cohen. In Bernasconi and Wood (1988), 156–167.

Morris, William, (ed.), *The American Heritage Dictionary* (New York: Houghton Mifflin Company, 1975).

Rosmini, Antonio, *Conscience*, translated by D. Cleary and D. Watson (Durham, UK: Rosmini House, 1989).

van Beeck, S.J., Frans Jozef, *Loving the Torah More Than God? Toward a Catholic Appreciation of Judaism*, (Chicago: Loyola University Press, 1989).

van Beeck, S.J., Frans Jozef, 'My Encounter with Yossel Rakover', in Kolitz (1995), 41–63.

van Beeck, S.J., Frans Jozef and Jeffrey V. Mallow, 'Afterword,' in Kolitz (1994a), 373–377.

NOTES

1 'Self-consciousness inevitably surprises itself at the heart of a moral consciousness. The latter cannot be added to the former, but it provides its basic mode. To be for oneself is already to know the fault I have committed with regard to the other individual. But the fact that I do not question myself about the rights of the other paradoxically indicates that the other individual is not a *new edition of myself*, as

another individual he is situated in a dimension of height, of the ideal, of the divine, and through my relation with the other individual, I am in touch with God.

The moral relation therefore reunites both self-consciousness and consciousness of God. Ethics is not the corollary of the vision of God, it is that very vision. Ethics is an optic, such that everything I know of God and everything I can hear of His word and reasonably say to Him must find an ethical expression.' See Levinas (1983), 33 and 1990, 17. I have modified Seán Hand's translation slightly.

2 'A God who conceals his face . . . is a way of talking about the hour when the just individual . . . can no longer triumph except in his own consciousness (*conscience*), which is to say, necessarily in suffering . . . The suffering of the just for a justice that is without triumph is lived concretely as Judaism.' Levinas 1983, 191. My translation.

3 For the remark by Des Pres, see Fine (1982), xi.

4 Van Beeck and Mallow (1994a), 373.

5 *ibid.*; Badde (1995), 12.

6 *ibid.*, Badde says the piece was requisitioned by a Señor Mordechai Stoliar (Kolitz 1995), 5.

7 See Kolitz (1947), vii. The quote from Greenberg reads: '. . . For we are tired of bearing our sadness alone/And the secrets of tigers under the skin of a lamb.'

8 Friedlander (1968).

9 Friedlander (1976), 390.

10 Kolitz (1969).

11 Levinas (1983) and Levinas (1990).

12 See Eliav (1965) and van Beeck (1989).

13 The opening six words of the shema are *Sh'ma 'yisrael Adonai eloheiynu Adonai echad* ('Listen, Israel, the LORD our God, the LORD is one'). The extension of the pronunciation of the initial *ayin* (concluding the word *sh'ma*) and the final *daled* (concluding the word *echad*) are gestures suggested by the Rabbis to produce in hearing the Hebrew word for witness, *'eid*.

14 According to Badde, Mann 'praised it as a holy text, a "shattering human and religious document"' (Kolitz 1995), 7–8.

15 See van Beeck (1989), 86–7.

16 See Van Beeck (1989).

17 According to Badde (Kolitz 1995, 7), the '"discovered document" is broadcast in the German language version of Anna Maria Jokl by Radio Free Berlin' in January 1955. In October 1955, the text was broadcast again, this time 'with the author's full and correct name' (Kolitz) 1995, 8. Jokl reports and comments on it later that year in the *Tagesspiegel* and again the following year in the *Neue Deutsche Hefte*. In 1985, Jokl publishes the text in a book with Kolitz's name. See Jokl (1985).

18 Kolitz gives the date of Badde's story and article as 'April 1, 1993' although van Beeck gives it as 'April 23, 1993.' See Kolitz (1995), xviii and 51.

19 Kolitz (1995).

20 For the Foucault essay, see Bouchard (1977).

21 On the intentional and implied author, see Booth (1983).

22 For example, in Kolitz (1995), xviii, Kolitz notes that Paul Badde 'wrote his comprehensive article, which was published in the magazine of the Sunday edition of the *Frankfurter Allgemeine Zeitung* on April 1, 1993.' In the same volume (Kolitz 1995, 51), Father van Beeck writes that the first three pages sent by Oscar Lateur to Paul Badde were 'sufficient to enable Paul Badde, a few weeks later, In [sic] the *Frankfurter Allgemeine Magazin* of 23 April, 1993, to publish an almost complete German translation of the story based on the Yiddish, along with a moving feature article on Zvi Kolitz' ('April 23, 1993' is the same date van Beeck gives in his second article in van Beeck (1994), 375). Is the article to which van Beeck refers another article by Badde on Kolitz written three weeks later? Has Kolitz gotten the date wrong? Has van Beeck gotten the date wrong? Again?

23 Friedlander (1976), 390. For Badde, see Kolitz (1995), 8.

24 Levinas (1983), 189–91.

25 See epigraph.

26 Rosmini (1989).

27 'Nous nous refusons à offrir en spectacle la Passion des Passions et à tirer un quelconque gloriole d'auteur ou de metteur en scènes de ces cris inhumain' (Levinas (1983), 189). [We refuse the option of offering as a spectacle the Passion of all Passions and of deriving any glory whatsoever as an author or director from these inhuman cries.'] Levinas may be referring to the responses of Krämer-Badoni and Müller to Anna Maria Jokl's broadcast of the story in German (on Radio Free Berlin) two months earlier, both of whom became effusive and saw the document as a call to conscience.

28 Jokl broadcast the story in German without authorial attribution in January of 1955. Levinas delivered his radio talk in April of the same year. Jokl rebroadcast the narrative with Kolitz's name attached in October of 1955. Levinas published his essay, 'Aimer la Thora plus que Dieu' in 1963. He may not have known initially that it was a text by Kolitz, but upon learning in October of the same year that it was a literary fiction, he may have decided to add some remarks when he came to publish it later, and thereby generate the text we have now. What is important for him in any event is not whether it is a literary fiction or a document but its 'further testimony,' its capacity to 'translate an experience of spiritual life that is at once profound and authentic.'

29 Goodhart (1996), 236.

30 Goodhart (1996), 237.

31 Levinas (1991), 100–12.

32 Levinas (1988), 159.

33 Levinas (1988), 159.

34 'To the memory of beings who were the closest to me among the six million assassinated by the National Socialists, alongside millions upon millions of other human beings of all faiths and all nations, victims of the same hate of the other man, of the same antisemitism.'

35 Morris (1975), 1334.

36 Levinas (1990), 16.

37 See Hartman (1986).

POST-HOLOCAUST ETHICS:
THE MORALITY OF THE USE OF POWER

Leonard Grob

I F, AS has often been argued, the Holocaust constitutes a 'watershed' event in human history, then it follows that our Western tradition of ethics must come under severe scrutiny. How can it be, we must ask, that at the heart of modern Western civilization, our ethico-religious legacies failed to provide a safeguard against unprecedented genocidal behaviour? Is it possible, we might ask, that these traditions not only proved incapable of averting the catastrophe that was the Holocaust, but were also, in some measure, implicated in its very coming-to-be? Did these traditions not merely fail to successfully address the 'problem', but were themselves, in some respect, *part* of it?

These questions, I will argue, require, in particular, that a post-Holocaust world rethink the relationship between morality and power. Given the vulnerability of traditional moral checks on the unbridled use of power during the Holocaust, must we not ask what might constitute *moral* uses of power in the world after Auschwitz? According to Richard Rubenstein, 'there are absolutely no limits to the degradation and assault the managers and technicians of violence can inflict upon men and women who lack the power of effective resistance.'[1] Rubenstein adds that in the post-1945 world, we must come to the realization that '... human rights and dignity depend on the *power* of one's community to grant or withhold them from its members.'[2] What are the implications for a post-Holocaust ethics of this implied call for state power to counter the power of those bent on genocidal action? How do we envision a relationship between morality and power after Auschwitz?

Drawing on the work of two 20th-century philosophers, Emmanuel Levinas and Martin Buber, I will endeavour, in this paper, to sketch the beginnings of some responses to these critical questions. With Levinas, I will contend that pre-Holocaust ethical traditions in the West have been articulated within the framework of Western thought most often understood as *ontology*, the endeavour to grasp the nature of being itself. Our tradition of thought, in other words, has been characterized, at bottom, as the attempt to com-prehend, i.e., to take together or unify all that is within a conceptual order. Our word 'universe' is itself an allusion to that unifying activity of the human subject which makes the world intelligible *qua* world. For Levinas, this subject – or ego, as some have called it – becomes the fundamental atom, the 'building block' of being: In its endeavour to make sense of its world, the 'I' is seen in Western thought as appropriating all that exists; as such, the 'I' can be termed nothing short of 'regal', 'unconditioned' and 'sovereign'. Alluding to the powers of the meaning-making subject, Levinas concludes that 'In the last analysis ... everything is at my disposal, even the stars if I but reckon them.'[3] In other words, everything becomes subject to my knowing grasp: If I do not know it, it is not because it is unknowable *on principle*, but rather because it is not-yet-known, because I have not *as yet* subsumed it under my totalizing grasp. World, as Levinas understands its meaning within the Western philosophical tradition, is always, in some substantial sense, world-for-me.

Within an historical frame of reference in which Western thought has thus been conceived of as an 'egology', ethical thinkers have been bound to take as their point of departure what, in Levinas's term, is the 'imperialist' vocation of the self. And here ethics confronts what Levinas sees to be an insuperable problem: The other person, in the ontological schema, is, like any other being, able on principle to-be-encompassed within the categorizing activities of the mind. As the *object* of the schemas of my cognitive processes, the other can never be, for me, a *co-subject*. The other is inevitably, 'for-me', and thus can never be free of the meaning I grant her/him. I must always see the other person as bound by the categorizations I inevitably attribute to him or her. For Levinas, philosophy can never see the Other[4] as an independent being, unaffected by the objectifying forces of my consciousness – and thus a truly *other* being to whom I can have *ethical* duties. An ethics based in Western-thought-as-ontology can never articulate a set of authentic obligations toward an other, simply because that other is never other-enough. It is always an other-for-me: in short, my object. In a subject-object schema, ethics, like any other branch of thought, can never free itself of the taint of egoism, the suspicion that what I (seemingly) *must* do for an Other is always, in some fundamental sense, something that I am (ultimately) doing *for-me*. Traditional moral thought, for Levinas, can thus certainly never articulate a set of ethical obligations which would be adequate to the challenges hurled at it by the threat of genocidal action.

Furthermore, as I have indicated above, traditional ethical systems have not merely failed to prevent the Holocaust; such systems may indeed have played some role in contributing to a mode of thinking which has helped make the Holocaust possible. Traditional Western thought, as we have seen, is linked to the activity of grasping, of appropriating. Such thinking, in Levinas's words, is an 'activity...independent...of any finality exterior to it...philosophical activity paves the way for instrumentalist thinking.'[5] The means-end mental processes referred to by Levinas may have played a role in generating a climate of thought in which that massive bureaucratization and industrialization of killing that was the Holocaust could more easily take shape.

What, then, is an alternative model of ethical thinking? What might a post-Holocaust ethics look like? Such an ethics would first and foremost be required to root itself in a critique of the totalizing ambitions of the objectifying ego of traditional ontology. In other words, a notion of obligation-which-is-truly-obligation would have to be articulated. For Levinas, traditional ego-centred ontology must be replaced by a mode of thinking that grants primacy to the primordial encounter of an 'I' with an other who is truly an independent being, and thus someone who can challenge my hegemony over all that exists.

Who is it who can thus encounter me at the core of my being? Who can authentically confront the imperial 'I', what Levinas refers to as a 'totalizing' being? As we have seen, this being cannot be the other as traditionally understood; this other, like all else in my world, would be subject to my appropriate, objectifying acts. Even if he or she seemingly confronts me – indeed, even succeeds in objectifying me – it is only the flip side of my acts of objectifying her or him. It is simply a matter of egos taking turns becoming first subject, and then object![6] Nothing fundamental has occurred to produce what Levinas calls a 'rupture' in being, a break with the 'sameness' of being, which would allow for truly ethical behavior to be born. To be truly other, that Other would have to exist on another level of being, and thus stand outside the mainstream of Western thought in which being is being-to-be-comprehended.[7]

The Other who can offer a critique of my being as appropriative cannot be someone who combats my power with a power akin to my own – an alter ego – but rather one who quits being as a field of combat between competing egos altogether. My encounter with this Other is a primordial, originary event: 'Since the Other looks at me, I am responsible for him without even having taken on responsibilities in his regard.'[8] I cannot become responsible if I begin with an understanding of being in which the 'I' is the fundamental atom of existence: 'Responsibility,' Levinas insists, 'is the essential, primary and fundamental structure of subjectivity.... Responsibility in fact is not a simple attribute of subjectivity, as if the latter already existed in itself, before the ethical relationship.'[9] In other words, the structure of human existence *qua* human is to be responsible to the Other. I enter the world in a non-appropriative relationship to the Other; I do not first exist, in any authentic sense of that word, and then, as a discreet ego, proceed to attempt to build a relationship of responsibility. If the solitary self is deemed the basic building block of existence, I will never be able to relate to another in any fashion but as other-for-me. For Levinas, authentic ethics can come to be only if I am born-toward-responsibility, if the fundamental structure of being is relationship with an other who is truly Other?

But how am I thus called to responsibility? It cannot be the case, as we have observed, that my egoist ambitions are merely crushed by a power greater than my own. What must be contested in an authentic call to responsibility is not the *extent* of my power but rather my desire to exercise it, my very *right* to do so. One who is truly Other contests me, calling me to account for myself at the core of my being, and thus allows my basic humanity to emerge. He or she *requires* me to respond, to be responsible. My response, however, is not something coerced: The encounter with what Levinas calls the 'face' of the Other is both a contestation *and a plea*. The Other summons me to responsibility without the force of arms, but rather by dis-arming me. Using terms from the Bible, Levinas speaks of the Other as both my master, in the sense of calling me to account for myself, and also as the widow or orphan, appealing to me – without employing power – to renounce the power-play of an egoist existence. Moving toward this Other is, in Levinas's more traditionally religious writings, a moving toward God.

Prior to the meeting with the Other just described, there can be, for Levinas, no authentic ethics: 'Morality begins when freedom, instead of being justified by itself, feels itself to be arbitrary and violent.'[10] In other words, within Levinas's imagery system – borrowed from the Bible – what I hear from the Other is 'Thou shalt not kill.' The Other is the occasion of my coming to take responsibility for the conduct of my being.

The significance of Levinasian thought for a rethinking of ethics in the post-Holocaust age cannot be emphasized strongly enough. For Levinas, the totalizing activity of traditional ontology can be likened to war. Within the terms of war, all aspects of human conduct take on a new cast of meaning: Killing, lying, betraying – all assume new and different meanings. In Levinas's words, 'War is not only one of the ordeals – the greatest – of which morality lives; it renders morality derisory.'[11] By analogy, all beings, as ontologists have traditionally understood them, are creatures of the schematizing, appropriative mind which sees them, ultimately, as mere ciphers – morally speaking – within the totality in which they are placed. If all of us are to find our meaning solely within the confines of this whole, then a totalizing thinking – seemingly so innocent – can turn *totalitarian*. And, yes, victims of Nazi oppression were stripped of their humanity precisely by being viewed in terms of racial categories applied to them *as a whole*. Western philosophy-as-egology has contributed to a climate of thinking within which the racist ideologies of the Nazi leadership could more easily come to the fore.

If Levinas's responsible self replaces the ego-as-locus-of-power at the core of our existence, what lessons are thus to be learned about how to live our lives in the post-Holocaust world? What, in particular, are we to make of that alleged lesson of the Holocaust, alluded to by Rubenstein, concerning a need to counter power with power? How are we to reconcile Levinas's philosophical vision, celebrating responsibility-to-the-Other as the fundamental structure of our humanity, with the contention of Rubenstein and others that in a post-Holocaust world we have learned the hard lesson that 'rights do not belong to men by nature.'[12] As we have seen, Rubenstein contends that rights are only conferred upon individuals by the *polis*, and, he reminds us, 'there is no polis or Christian commonwealth of nations.'[13] Without belonging to a state, one is ultimately powerless. Indeed, we know that the endeavour to effect the 'final solution to the Jewish problem' was nearly fully successful, leading to the murder of two-thirds of European Jewry. This fact certainly supports the claim that stateless people are at the mercy of those with the power to kill them. For Rubenstein, 'The power to injure remains the most credible deterrent to a would-be aggressor's violence,'[14] How do we reconcile Levinas's implied directive to keep before us the face of the Other who commands 'Thou shalt not kill' with the claim, implied in Rubenstein's work, that we had better seek shelter in the power of the state to counter the power of those who might view us as mere 'surplus people?'

Yet more needs to be said. Rubenstein does not end his warnings about the need to counter power with power with his reflections on statelessness: In his words, '...if Auschwitz has taught us the hazards of statelessness, it can also teach us that membership in a political community is no longer a guarantee of the most elemental human rights. With the collapse of every credible religious and moral restraint on the state...the state's sovereignty can achieve an ultimacy unimpeded by any contending claim.'[15] Even *within* Germany Jews were subject to forms of persecution – and to murder itself – deemed lawful. Even *within* the state, the Freudian conception of '*homo homini lupus*', man is a wolf to man, rules the day. How are we to square the argument that 'all that men possess by nature is the necessity to participate in the incessant life and death struggle for existence of any animal,'[16] with the Levinassian vision of a *pacific* relationship with the Other as the ground of being?

First of all, it must be admitted that for Levinas *hearing* the command of the Other, 'Thou shalt not kill,' is not the same as *obeying* this same command. The other cannot coerce me to behave responsibly. I can indeed behave unethically, even to the extent of murdering another. In so doing, however, I am only (!) killing others, not the Other, who remains inviolable. The Other survives any refusal on my part to heed its call, incessantly re-calling me – even as murderer – to my authentic humanity as one who *must not kill*.

Yet, in the face of the challenges posed above by Rubenstein, it is little comfort to posit a seemingly abstract Other who remains, as it were, 'above the fray'. How are we to grasp Levinas's claim that the Other survives the murder of others in such a way as to create an understanding which would be – as Irving Greenberg reminds us – 'credible in the presence of burning children'?

Levinas would contend that the inviolable Other is no mere philosophical abstraction taking its place among the parade of abstractions which constitute the history of philosophy-as-ontology; it is, indeed, just this history which Levinas has devoted his life to calling into question. Levinas warns us against turning his words into dogma within which the lived encounter with the Other would be reified. No, the encounter with the Other is not *posited*, but rather witnessed, attended to as call or command. More vocative than indicative in its structure, the relationship with the Other is no tenet of a philosophical system, but rather a summons to be heard. In the process of avoiding dogmatism of all sorts – in the process of continually endeavouring to 'unsay the said'[17] – Levinas reminds us of that encounter to which we can bear witness within the *Lebenswelt*.

When all this has been said, however, there remains an uneasiness with regard to the pointed questions raised above by Rubenstein. It is certainly the case that Levinas would reject any understanding of 'Never Again!' as merely an injunction never to allow power to be exercised against oneself with impunity. And yet the question remains: How are we to confront the threat (or actuality) of violence on the part of those who would wish to subject us to their control in the present or future? In the face of ongoing genocide in the second half of the current century, and in the face of the threat of new genocides in centuries to come, what might Levinas have to say about the nature of a *moral* response to the challenge of power which may be exercised against us? How are we to stand, as moral agents, in the face of a future clearly fraught with potential for new genocides? What guidance in these critical matters is to be given us from a philosopher who celebrates, as a primordial event, a fundamentally pacific encounter with the Other?

It should be noted that Levinas's work constitutes no body of rights or obligations as such. Levinas posits no specific ethical tenet or set of tenets. His concern, as we have seen, is to found all of what has hitherto been called 'ethical' in the moment of the encounter of an I with that Other who commands me not to kill. Levinas cannot point us toward a set of concrete moral directives which would address threats of genocide in the post-Holocaust world. What he *has* done is remind us that without keeping before us the face of the Other who challenges our egoist hegemony, no moral directive will find its proper ground. Unless we continually endeavour to see the face of the Other before us, we run the risk of de-facing, dehumanizing our world through actions – whether traditionally called moral or immoral – which are ultimately rooted in self-interest. Although Levinas provides us with no guide, no handbook for acting in the face of portents of genocide, he succeeds in giving us a framework of thought within which we can build an ethics on its proper foundation: the calling into question by the Other of my *right* to exercise power.

A crucial question remains: Does the Levinasian founding of ethics upon this critique of the hegemonic powers of the ego preclude outright the use of power to counter power – 'power' understood here, in terms familiar to social scientists, as the exercise of control or domination over another?[18] If power, as the ability to compel obedience, is most often linked to the threat or actual use of violence, are we then to be led, inevitably, in the direction of a philosophy of non-violence? In the face of contemporary instances of genocidal violence, how are we to conduct ourselves toward the perpetrators? Are we to renounce violence, as such, as a response to genocidal violence in the 'incessant life and death struggle for existence' which, for Rubenstein, constitutes our natural legacy as humans? With regard to these queries, the philosophy of Emmanuel Levinas fails to give us concrete guidance.

It is to the thought of a second contemporary religious existentialist thinker, the philosopher Martin Buber, that we can turn for help in responding to the questions articulated above. Writing, for the most part, a few decades earlier in the century than Levinas, Buber expounds a political philosophy which locates itself within the spirit of much of Levinas's basic ethical vision. In turning to Buber, however, it becomes clear that we will not receive – here either – a set of tenets within which to locate a moral use of power in the post-Holocaust world. While failing to give us concrete directives, Buber nonetheless *does* provide additional sound guidance in the struggle to articulate the morality of the use of power after Auschwitz.

For Buber, as for Levinas, 'In the beginning is the relation.'[19] That is to say, for both thinkers, the relationship of an I to and Other (in Buber's terms, a 'Thou') constitutes the point of departure for all that is, i.e., a structural (rather than temporal) beginning. Like the Levinassian 'face-to-face' encounter, the Buberian I-Thou relationship grounds all of being; only 'later', structurally speaking, do the component parts of Buberian dialogue emerge as separate. These kindred thinkers, however, depart from one another with regard to the issue, among others, of whether the relationship between the I and the Other/Thou is fundamentally symmetrical or asymmetrical. For Buber, there is reciprocity, mutuality in the dialogical relationship. For Levinas, as we have seen, there is a fundamental asymmetry in the face-to-face encounter; only a radical alterity can constitute the Levinassian Other. However, for both thinkers, the quality of being-responsible-to-the-other is not something added on to the attributes of a solitary ego. Buber's understanding of the 'innate' Thou as a being-already-present parallels Levinas's depiction of the Other as a 'structure of subjectivity.'

For Buber, as for Levinas, philosophical systems are, at bottom, suspect. Buber refuses to stand 'on the broad upland of a system', preferring, instead a stance on a 'narrow rocky ridge between the gulfs'.[20] When challenged by Mahatma Gandhi to employ *satyagraha* or truth-force against Nazi military might, Buber counters by exclaiming that 'We have not proclaimed, as you did and did Jesus, the son of our people, the teaching of non-violence. We believe a man must sometimes use force to save himself or even more his children.'[21] Buber concludes, in an open letter to Gandhi, that there may be instances which demand the use of force 'if there is not any other way of preventing the evil destroying the good.'[22] Buber, in other words, refuses dogma of any sort, even – as he believes is the case with Gandhi's concept – *satyagraha*-as-dogma.

But if we must 'sometimes' use force to counter force, how are we to tell when it is that these times arise? On what basis are we to judge when to counter the use of violent power with violent power and when *not* to do so? For Buber – and here there is another link to Levinas's emphasis upon *witnessing* in place of *positing* – no idea-qua-idea can qualify to fulfill this role of fixed criterion for ethical judgment. In the political arena, all rules or principles stand the risk of congealing into system or dogma. To the notion of any abstract principle allowing me to make such a decision, Buber contrasts the notion of a 'living idea', an idea first formed and then continually reformed in existential encounter with what constitutes the situation at hand.

Buber's political thought is thus characterized by a refusal to adhere to any fixed teaching regarding the use of violence, whether it be the utopian teaching of pacifism or the dogma of realism-become-Realpolitik. This is not to say that for Buber both pacifism and political realism have nothing to contribute to a dialogue concerning the morality of the use of power: 'In each of them,' Buber reminds us, 'there is a moral component: In the former, there is the potential for prophetic vision, in the latter a potential attention to our enrootedness in the here-and-now.[23] Both potentials, however, become fully actualized only – and here, again, we hear the echo of Levinas – insofar as each demands of a moral agent that he or she take a stance in the fullness of responsibility – the ability-to-respond – to the political demands of the hour. In Buber's words: 'You stand before a political decision... You are drawn by a command of justice and, your heart stirred by it... You make present to yourself, as strongly as you possibly can all... You do not spare yourself, you let the cruel reality of both sides inflict itself on you without reducing it.'[24]

Buber warns us that he is not here talking about what is often been termed 'conscience.' For Buber, what comes into play in the decision of whether or not to employ power against power – indeed, what comes into play in *any authentic* political decision – is the need to discover what he calls a deeper 'unknown conscience in the ground of being.'[25] In more traditionally religious language, what Buber alludes to is the need to respond to 'what is demanded by God', something that cannot be known before the moment in which it is so demanded. What Buber asks us to bring to every political situation is nothing short of an openness before the 'Face of God.'[26] Buber seeks, in other words, to find a dimension of transcendence in my response to a given political dilemma. Just as Levinas enjoins us to stand before an Other – often identified with the Divine – so Buber calls upon us to encounter God's face.

This goal of living in response to a demand for encounters manifesting a dimension of transcendence is a goal which has been termed nothing short of Buber's most important contribution to political philosophy.[27] This norm for the ethical use of power differs from other alleged norms in that it fails to provide a fixed point for reference; instead, Buber offers what could be construed to be a merely abstract, even nebulous goal: the goal of serving God 'as much as one can.' In his words, '...there is no once-for-all: in each situation that demands decision, the demarcation line between service and service must be drawn anew – not necessarily with fear, but necessarily with that trembling of the soul which precedes every genuine decision...'[28] What Buber suggests is that I extract from every political decision I make the maximum amount of divinity that I can.

How does this Buberian teaching bear more specifically on the question of the use of power against power embraced by Rubenstein? In a 1929 speech, Buber argues that the moral agent – in this instance, a revolutionary – when confronted with the decision of whether or not to use force in the face of evil, assumes the responsibility for determining a 'line of demarcation'. 'The watchword of his spirit,' Buber tells us, 'is "Up to here" and for that "Up to here" there is no fast rule, each moment presenting it with a new face.'[29] The issue, for Buber, should not be framed as 'I must here use force, but I do not want to do so,'[30] but rather I must confront both the ideal of pacifism and the teachings of political realism within the context of the present moment. In doing so, I realize that I am involved in an encounter which may run the full length of a continuum between absolute non-violence and a knee-jerk exercise of a violence which kills. As Buber concludes, 'I have taken it upon myself to use as much force as is necessary...but alas for me and for [the revolution] if more force is used than is necessary.'[31]

To illustrate his 'point' – if it is the case that a demand requiring us to bear witness to a dimension of transcendence constitutes a 'point' – Buber recalls the exchange of letters with Gandhi, alluded to above. Buber, as we have seen, admonishes Gandhi for applying *satyagraha* in so sweeping fashion as to include the allegedly moral responses of Hindus in South Africa and of Jews in Germany: 'And do you think perhaps a Jew in Germany could pronounce in public one single sentence of a speech such as yours without being knocked down?... a diabolical steamroller cannot so be withstood.'[32] Gandhi, in Buber's terms, has succumbed to the temptation of adhering to an ideology. He has failed to encounter the moment with the fullness of his being; he has failed to address the question of the morality of the use of power in 'holy insecurity'.

Buber goes to great lengths to emphasize that we should proceed – in the decision of whether or not to counter violence (or the threat of violence) with violence – to serve God '*quantum satis*', as much as one can?[33] Here we must be careful not to trivialize Buber by interpreting his '*quantum satis*' in terms of what in common parlance might be understood as 'doing the best we can.' For Buber, we must bear witness with all of our being to the 'truth' of a dialogical encounter. In this encounter I am not merely weighing the pros and cons of contrasting ideologies; I am not responding in merely affective terms to the givens of what confronts me; nor, finally, am I merely 'trying to do my best.' Rather, the whole of me is attempting to respond to the call of the 'Thou' in the situation at hand. Buber demands of us, in other words, that in response to competing claims of the exercise of non-violence and that of violence, we wring from each situation the maximum amount of divinity which it will permit. For Buber, engaging in such an encounter constitutes the 'hallowing of the everyday' in which we become nothing other than God's partner in creating a moral universe.[34]

But is not Buber's so-called 'guidance' to us who are attempting to understand what might constitute a moral use of power – is not this guidance just as elusive as was that offered by Levinas? What, concretely, has Buber added to our discussion of a moral use of power? Buber, I contend, would endeavour to refute any charge of 'elusiveness' by claiming that his task – like that of Levinas – is to provide a grounding vision within which concrete moral judgments can emerge. In sum, in the endeavour to explore the morality of the use of power in the post-Holocaust world, two Jewish existential thinkers – their own lives deeply affected by Nazi oppression – have spoken their word. The word of neither one is ultimately satisfying – if by 'satisfying' is meant the articulation of specific moral directives in response to Rubenstein's warning that, after Auschwitz, we must be sure to employ the 'power of effective resistance' against those who would deem us 'surplus.'

It is certainly the case, as Rubenstein strongly suggests, that the Holocaust teaches us the need to resist those who would control our destiny through the force of arms – both those arms which are the literal weapons of war and those which take the form of the bureaucratization of society in the service of mindless obedience to racist authority. Yet I would argue that this lesson is but *one* of the infinite number of lessons that have to be learned from the Holocaust.[35] I wish to emphasize, along with Levinas and Buber, that to protect ourselves from the danger of co-opting – however minimally – the means employed by Nazi oppressors in their oppression, all 'resistance' must be grounded in an ethical vision which subtends each and every concrete act on our part. Underlying all alleged 'lessons' of how to relate morality to the use of power is the injunction to heed the encounter with the Other who casts in doubt my hegemonic powers. Any moral directive, in other words, must avoid placing itself within a closed system of allegedly fixed 'truths'; it must find its foundation in that openness to critique which prevents it from becoming reified, from becoming sheer dogma. Such openness to critique is a constant reminder of the unjustified ambitions of a solitary ego. Such openness recalls us to the 'fact' that *relationship* is the primary given, the building block of human existence. Such openness protects ethics after Auschwitz against that depersonalization which characterized so-called Nazi 'ethics' and, indeed, the alleged 'ethics' of any totalizing-cum-totalitarian force. Such openness provides a ground upon which a post-Holocaust ethics can be built.

NOTES

1 Richard L. Rubenstein, *The Cunning of History: The Holocaust and the American Future* (New York: Harper Torchbooks, 1987), p.90.

2 Rubenstein, *The Cunning of History*, p.91. Emphasis is mine.

3 Emmanuel Levinas, *Totality and Infinity: An Essay on Exteriority*, tr. Alphonso Lingis (Pittsburgh: Duquesne University Press, 1969), p.37.

4 Following Levinas, I have adopted the convention of capitalizing 'other' when what is meant is that being who stands outside the totality of being, incapable of being appropriated by the powers of my ego.

5 Emmanuel Levinas, 'Ethics as First Philosophy', in *The Levinas Reader*, ed. Sean Hand (Oxford: Basil Blackwell, 1989), pp.76–77.

6 Here I am indebted to the work of Jean-Paul Sartre. For Sartre, the struggle between me and the other is a matter of my attempting to free myself from the hold that the other wishe to place on me at the same time as he or she tries to free her/himself from the hold with which I wish to enslave him or her. See *Being and Nothingness*, tr. Hazel Barnes (New York: Pocket Books, 1956), especially pp.474–475.

7 It should be noted that Levinas admits that Western ethical thought, from Plato onward, does give hints, allusions to this Other who would be truly Other – an Other beyond the plane of being. But these adumbrations of an Other who could truly contest my egoism fail to occupy a central space in Western thought; often these Others hinted at are quickly reabsorbed into a mainstream of totalizing: The name of God, for example, is, for Levinas, 'subject to abuse'.

8 Emmanuel Levinas, *Ethics and Infinity: Conversations with Philippe Nemo*, tr. Richard A. Cohen (Pittsburgh: Duquesne University Press, 1965), p.96.

9 *Ibid.*

10 Levinas, *Totality and Infinity*, p.84.

11 *Ibid.*, pp.21–22.

12 Rubenstein, *The Cunning of History*, p.89.

13 *Ibid.*

14 *Ibid.*

15 *Ibid.*, p.87.

16 Ibid., p.89.

17 Levinas, *Totality and Infinity*, p.30.

18 Nancy Hartsock, 'Political change: Two Perspectives on Power', in Charlotte Bunch and others, ed. *Building Feminist Theory* (New York: Longman, 1981), pp.3–4.

19 Martin Buber, *I and Thou*, tr. Ronald G. Smith (New York: Collier Books, 1987), p.18.

20 Martin Buber, 'What is Man', in *Between Man and Man*, tr. Ronald Gregor Smith (New York: Macmillian, 1965), p.184.

21 Buber, 'Two Letters to Gandhi from Martin Buber and J.L. Magnes, *Pamphlets on the 'Bond'* (Jerusalem: Ruben Mass, April 1939), p.19.

22 *Ibid.*, p.21.

23 Buber, 'Warum muss der aufbau Palastinas ein Sozialistischer sein', in *Der Jude und sein Judentum*, 338. Cited and translated in Bernard Susser, *Existence and Utopia: The Social and Political Thought of Martin Buber* (Rutherford, NJ: Fairleigh Dickinson University Press, 1981), p.114.

24 Buber, 'Replies to My Critics', in *The Philosophy of Martin Buber*, ed. Paul Schilpp and Maurice Friedman, The Library of Living Philosophers, vol.13 (La Salle, Ill.: Open Court), pp.722–723.

25 Buber, 'The Question to the Single One', in *Between Man and Man*, p.69.

26 *Ibid.*, p.68.

27 Robert Weltsch, 'Buber's Political Philosophy', in *The Philosophy of Martin Buber*, p.442.

28 Buber, 'The Validity and Limitation of the Political Principle', in *Pointing the Way*, tr. Maurice S. Friedman (New York: Harper & Row, 1963), p.217.

29 Buber, 'Recollections of a Death', in *Pointing the Way*, p.118.

30 *Ibid.*, p.117.

31 *Ibid.*

32 Buber, 'Two Letters to Gandhi from Martin Buber and J.L. Magnes', pp.5–6.

33 Buber, 'The Validity and Limitation of the Political Principle', in *Pointing the Way*, p.217.

34 Buber, 'And If Not Now, When?' in *Israel and the World: Essays in a Time of Crisis* (New York: Schocken Books, 1948), p.239.

35 It should be noted here that this contention is something with which I believe Rubenstein would certainly agree.

REFLECTIONS ON 'ETHICS', 'MORALITY' AND 'RESPONSIBILITY' AFTER THE HOLOCAUST

Herbert Hirsch

IN A marvellous film, *Breaker Morrant*, the lead character, Harry Morrant, on trial for following orders to execute Boer prisoners during the Boer War in South Africa (1899–1902), notes, as he is on his way to the firing squad: 'these days it is so very easy to be on the wrong side.' Harry phrased, concisely and eloquently, a central moral question: How does one choose, or even know, the 'right' side when so many choices appear morally repugnant?

When confronted with seemingly ambiguous alternatives, all clamouring for allegiance, deciding which choices are the moral ones may appear eminently difficult in an era when any action appears to threaten the innocent. Choices that in hindsight might seem very clear, are, in the heat of the moment, not always so easily discernible.

For example, the recent NATO bombing of Yugoslavia was viewed by some as an inhumane and disproportionate response to the Serbian attempt to ethnically cleanse the Kosovar Albanians. Others argued that it was a much too limited response which should have included the use of ground forces to fully stop the atrocities. The choice may have appeared ambiguous, but in this confusing modern era, most choices will remain ambiguous and one must often choose the lesser of two evils. In the real world the ideal choice rarely presents itself.

Looking back on the Holocaust from this perspective, it seemed as though it would be easy to pick the right side. Since the Holocaust was the first public genocide, the first genocide about which large numbers of people had any knowledge, it has become the paradigmatic genocide, the one we all use to talk about crimes against humanity – it is our ruler, our measuring rod, our basis of comparison. It also marks the symbolic and real decline of the somewhat naive view of the enlightenment that the thin veneer of western civilization could control the baser impulses of humans to kill each other in large numbers. With this perceptual chasm bridged, the defeat of Nazi Germany signalled to the victors that they should try to put the genie back into the bottle. Thus, they hoped, perhaps optimistically and naively, to establish moral and ethical guidelines which they devoutly wished would keep such events from being repeated. To accomplish this it was decided that it was necessary to punish those who committed the most egregious crimes and demonstrate to the world that certain actions would not be tolerated by what ultimately turned out to be an illusory 'international community of nations'. Hence, the defeat of Nazi Germany and Japan led to war crimes trials and the incorporation into international law of the Nuremberg Principles.[1]

The victorious coalition put on trial the high-ranking German and Japanese officials thought to be responsible for laying waste to a large portion of the planet. The result of the trials made individual responsibility a part of international law and set precedents that have, in spite of their incorporation into international law, not been followed in subsequent instances of genocide. In the post-Holocaust period perpetrators have, for the most part, gotten away with genocide and, when trials have occurred, they focused on apprehending lower level officials instead of those most responsible. This created a situation in which notions of morality and responsibility have been re-defined so that the lessons of the Holocaust have been, if not lost, then applied in a different fashion.

The implication, of course, is that any definition of morality which could be used to hold perpetrators responsible for their behaviour has become murky. How does one talk about ethics, morality and responsibility within this context? In order to attempt to structure such a discussion it is necessary to begin by attempting to define that about which we are speaking. What do these terms mean in the new century?

ETHICS AND MORALITY AFTER THE HOLOCAUST

There are numerous ways to define the key concepts in the terminology of moral discourse. I want to begin this discussion by narrowing the boundaries and proposing to accept some stipulative definitions. First, it is necessary to draw a distinction between law and ethics.

The use of international law as a mechanism to punish the perpetrators raises important issues of meaning. Hence, it is important to note that ethics are not laws. Even though ethical judgements often use words similar to those used in courts of law, they are different. Law, as Philip Hallie notes, 'moves and lives in public institutions; life-and-death ethics (which is the area of ethics closest to criminal law) moves and lives in individuals.'[2] Laws are made and enforced by public institutions, ethical judgements are personal and there are no mechanisms of enforcement. There are times when law and ethics may be in harmony, but usually, the needs of the state are placed before those of the ethical conscience of the individual.

This is an important distinction and it was so for Harry Morrant. Given orders to execute Boer prisoners he did as he was told by the representatives of the authority of the of the British army. When it became inconvenient for Britain to admit the practice, when they needed scapegoats to appease the German government in their attempt to get out of the war, Harry and his fellow Australian troopers, who were by the definition of the times, 'good soldiers', became victims of the perceived needs of the state. Or, as stated in the film, they became 'scapegoats for the empire'.

So that is the very dilemma faced by all who wish to see ethical principles as part of state law. In fact, if Harry and his fellows had not followed orders they would have been court martialled or shot, which they eventually were anyway. So, what does one do when confronted with this dilemma? The easy solution is to counsel those in such a situation to follow their own conscience. But this is the luxury of academics in warm offices writing about the real world. In that world of ambiguity it is not often as clear as it appears in hindsight. So the issue phrased by Harry goes to the heart of the distinction between law and ethics.

In order to address this ethics must be situated in public spaces. Ethics are not, and cannot, be only private. They have to be communal and based on some concept of community.[3] Ethics and law, when applied in a nation with ethical principles, of which there are very few if any, would, theoretically, have the same common goal – to restrain the destructive power of humans.

Law and ethics, in this case, would both rest on fundamental principles – beliefs that are accepted by a society or group. A principle such as 'Innocent until proven guilty,' is, for example, a presumption of United States criminal law, while the 'presumption at the foundation of life-and-death ethics is that all human life is precious.'[4]

Law and ethics also have codes which make demands upon individuals to learn to control certain 'passions.' The difference is that while law threatens punishment from without, by the state, ethics 'is inwardly experienced self control. When the moral law within you rules your passions, you are good. When your inward government is in chaos, in anarchy, you are bad.'[5] In short, ethics are a matter of human character and are based in a community. They cannot be divorced from history or from action since they must concern themselves with how human beings behave, but, generally, when we talk about ethics we mean some internal restraint on behaviour resulting from standards or norms which have arisen within a community – however defined. As we shall see, a community might mean a small contiguous group or a larger international setting in which there may or may not be general agreement upon ethical ideas.

Missing from this type of discussion, however, is an important dimension of critical reflection. Given the ambiguity of reality, questions of right and wrong, of ethics and morality must, as all others, be the subject of critical evaluation. So, even though the terms 'ethics' and 'morality' are often used interchangeably, a distinction is helpful. 'Morality' may be defined, following McCollough, as referring to 'commonly accepted rules of conduct, patterns of behaviour approved by a social group, values and standards shared by the group. It consists of beliefs about what is good and right held by a community with a shared history.'[6]

'Ethics', on the other hand, is the critical analysis of morality. 'It is a reflection on morality with the purpose of analysis, criticism, interpretation and justification of the rules, roles, and relations of a society.' In this sense, ethics 'is concerned with the meaning of moral terms, the conditions in which moral decision making takes place, and the justification of the principles brought to bear in resolving conflicts of values and of moral rules.' In other words, ethics involves a reflection and critical analysis of 'what we say, what we do, and what we are.'[7]

Those of us who examine the Holocaust and genocide are, therefore, engaged in ethical reflection on morality, and what we are trying to do is to incorporate these into laws that will impose some sense of responsibility and ultimately be used to punish those who commit genocide. The key to understanding the ethical implications of the moral principles derived from examining the Holocaust, therefore, may very well be centred in the idea of responsibility.

RESPONSIBILITY AFTER THE HOLOCAUST

If attempts to regulate the worst aspects of human behaviour are to have any major impact there must be some way to assign responsibility – to assure that individuals are held accountable for the acts they commit. This becomes difficult in an era which has witnessed a perversion of language unmatched in any period of history. While politicians and self-proclaimed moralists propound and preach about the lack of responsibility, the meaning of the term remains ambiguous. There is no reason for this confusion since Stanley Milgram clarified the idea of responsibility many years ago.[8]

While Milgram's work has been controversial, it remains the foundation for all later examinations of obedience and responsibility. In fact, in spite of repeated attempts to elaborate Milgram's essential interpretations, they remain the clearest conceptualization of the perversion of the idea of responsibility in the modern era.[9]

For Milgram, 'responsibility' no longer meant what it had in a previous time. In the modern era, he argued, responsibility now referred to the single-minded pursuit of selfishness – to get what you can for yourself and the hell with anyone else – especially if they get in your way or you perceive them as standing in your way. In short, any notion of responsibility is thought to be divorced from any idea of the public good or community. In the contemporary era it is tied to what Milgram referred to as the 'agentic state'. If there is any responsibility it is to authority, to obey orders, to be the agent of others and to do what you are told, do not cause trouble and, least of all, be responsible for the consequences of your actions because if you do something unethical or immoral it is not your fault since you did it in the name of obedience. Hence, you are able to convince yourself that your actions are actually the responsible thing to do, you obeyed and did not cause trouble. It is, after all, the troublemakers, the questioners who are irresponsible. This, it turns out, is a very 'Nazi'-like notion of 'responsibility'.

It is also a new notion of responsibility. It is responsibility without compassion, without caring, without concern for others. Since there is no notion of the public good, of community, because responsibility is defined individualistically, we are unable to hold others responsible and we find it difficult to decide, as Harry Morrant noted, which is the wrong side. In fact, one has to wonder if there is any clear way to decide which side is 'right' and which is 'wrong'? There certainly does not seem to be any consensus among nations or groups as they appear reluctant to accept a moral-ethical code which defines responsibility? There are, of course, at least two excellent reasons to raise these issues. First, there are numerous impediments to a general acceptance of any moral ideas which cut across cultural and national boundaries. Second, the prescriptions offered by scholars are, most generally, based upon suppositions which ignore some of the unpleasant realities of the real world of politics and human behaviour.

IMPEDIMENTS TO CHOOSING THE 'RIGHT SIDE'

Culture and Nationalism.   All observers do not agree that there are universal humanitarian standards. Some argue that even the idea of codes such as individual human rights are culture bound and tied to Western ideology. Proponents of cultural relativism, and those who hesitate to apply human rights principles to their own situation because of their use of power to abuse individual rights, do not accept human rights standards as universal. In fact, some argue that 'indigenous-aboriginal peoples, have achieved both dignity and, equally important, a harmony with nature without the conception of rights.'[10] There are nation states which go even farther and argue that rights such as freedom of religion and freedom from sexual discrimination violate their cultural traditions and are not appropriate for a multi cultural world. In short, it is their right to engage in activities such as cutting off a person's hand for stealing or stoning a woman to death for committing adultery without outside interference in their affairs. Ideas of human justice and equality are, according to these perspectives, culture bound and tied to imperialistic notions of the west. These ideas are tied not only to culture, but also to the nation state which claims, according to the doctrine of sovereignty, the right to be free from outside interference in its treatment of its citizens. The rise of the nation state left the individual without intervening institutions and the state repeatedly killed and dominated ever larger numbers of people in the last century. Culture and nationalism, therefore, remain major impediments to a more generally acceptable morality.

Scholarly Wishful Thinking and the Appeal of Violence. Among the many recent attempts to outline a more universal morality two, in my view, stand out. Lifton and Markusen's effort to develop what they call a 'species mentality',[11] and Kelman and Hamilton's concern with ways to break the habit of obedience and create a 'global perspective'.[12]

Lifton and Markusen argue that what they call the species mentality is an alternative that is life enhancing rather than life destroying. They define this as 'full consciousness of ourselves as members of the human species'...

> Species consciousness contributes to a sense of self that identifies with the entire human species. But the self cannot live, so to speak, on the human species alone. Its traditional forms of immediate identification – other people, family, work, play, religion, ethnic groups and nation – give substance to the species identification and are necessary to it.[13]

This is, of course, nothing other than the old notion of the importance of community. Since it is really a re-expression of some of the oldest traditions it is not a startling insight. Nor is their prescription concerning how to achieve this goal.

To achieve this, they argue, the human self has to re-align elements of the self so that concern and caring are now extended from the immediate self and family to the species as a whole. While they do not specifically discuss the politics involved in transforming the present mentality into the species mentality, they do identify several traditions of species consciousness. Here they point out that 'Species consciousness has been advocated over the centuries by spiritual traditions of moral and intellectual power.'[14] Their list of advocates includes Gandhi; Martin Luther King; religious traditions including Hindu, Moslem and Jewish; Marx; and the reaction of the world to Nazi atrocities after World War II, among others. In the long run, their concern, like that of most students of genocide, is to stop the murder. To accomplish this they call for all people to 'join in a vast project – political, ethical, psychological – on behalf of perpetuating and nurturing our humanity...We become healers, not killers, of our species.'[15]

Kelman and Hamilton are likewise interested in psychological mechanisms to deter obedience and the creation of a general purpose morality. Their view, I surmise, is that if the habit of obedience is broken, the next step will be to move to the creation of the species mentality, except that in their case they call it a 'global perspective.' Kelman and Hamilton offer a more detailed analysis of the concrete problem of obedience. Specifically, they explore how the habit of obedience might be broken by changing social structures, increasing political participation and changing the socialization process, and creating 'collective support systems that are needed to develop a more responsible citizenry – a citizenry prepared to apply human values and moral principles in evaluating the political authorities' policies and demands.'[16]

According to Kelman and Hamilton, individuals are bound to authority systems, in a manner originally identified by Milgram, by role definitions, chain of command, and the general bureaucratic hierarchy. Potential victims are dehumanized or neutralized and individuals respond differently to authority situations according to their conceptions of responsibility and their political orientations. The important thing is to promote personal responsibility, and Kelman and Hamilton recommend two means to reduce what they call rule and role oriented behaviour and induce or encourage value oriented behaviour.

First, by reducing the impact of forces that bind the individual to an authority system by reducing the 'individual citizen's distance from authority, so that they will be more familiar with it and feel more capable of judging its demands.'[17] It is also necessary, they argue, to change the social structure, the education experiences, and the group support structure so that individual citizens will be empowered and begin to feel a renewed sense of personal efficacy. According to their formulation:

Empowerment means having the opportunity and the right to make decisions about one's own life and to participate in decision making on public issues. Efficacy means possessing the skills, the knowledge, the material resources, and the social supports that enhance people's ability to determine their own fate and to influence public policy.[18]

They are related, and the way to enhance them is to disperse authority by increasing decentralization of political and economic institutions. Decentralizing authority is a key idea in Kelman and Hamilton's theory and they believe that it will have a 'liberating effect' because those who experience having some authority are less likely to abuse that authority and less likely to obey other authority figures.

But this neglects a sad and repetitious reality. It is not necessarily the case that dispersing authority makes it more humane. Lt. Calley, one of their primary examples, was clearly in a position of authority, as were Himmler and Eichmann. The simple fact of dispersing authority will make little difference if there are more fundamental problems facing the creation of a more humanitarian ethic.

They then argue that education promotes empowerment and enhances efficacy.[19] Education may enhance empowerment and efficacy, but empowerment and efficacy do not necessarily enhance morality. Einsatzgruppen were composed of highly educated individuals who were wiling to obey and kill. Education, even at the highest levels, does not necessarily mean that people will not obey. Heidigger went along with, and at first celebrated the Nazi rise to power,[20] as did numerous professors, lawyers, physicians and other highly educated citizens of the Third Reich. To offset this potential criticism Kelman and Hamilton reason that exposing people to different perspectives and changing the structure of decision making groups by breaking down the boundaries and emphasizing dissent as an obligation of citizenship are also necessary. The ideal of citizenship, they argue, should promote dissent and the citizen should have allegiance to multiple authorities.[21]

Generally, they sum up their analysis of authority by noting that individuals have to re-acquire a sense of personal responsibility – perceive themselves as personally causing harmful outcomes. Their proposed corrective involves, education directed toward individualizing potential victims so that they no longer would be seen as 'anonymous members of stereotyped categories',[22] While this is similar to Lifton and Markusen's idea of a species mentality neither examines the political and psychological reality of a world which does not always operate in the fashion they would like.

REFLECTIONS

Of course it is difficult to find fault with such resolve to stop the epidemic of mass death. Indeed, my quarrel is not with that resolve, but with what is missing. Suppose we begin our quest with the opposite assumptions. That is, suppose humans really do not wish to get along with each other? Suppose, instead, there is something in all of us that moves us toward the very darkest part of our nature. Suppose we, in some deep recess of our psyche, like to hurt our fellow humans and view this as a legitimate means to achieve our own goals. This means that the creation of the species mentality or a global perspective, or any other alternative morality, will be much more difficult than simply stating it on a piece of paper. In fact, of course, the history of the species appears to substantiate the power of violence to draw us in ways we do not like to admit.

Without acknowledging the power and appeal of violence, without acknowledging that there may be something within all of us that appeals to our darker nature, without acknowledging that we too may be capable of the most horrendous acts, it is unlikely that the genocidal mentality will undergo the miraculous change so desired by so many observers. As with most attempts to suggest alternative world views, they neglect to discuss, in convincing fashion, how to get from where we are to where they would like to see us go.

While these ideas about what a more humane perspective would resemble are important and necessary, they are not sufficient since they neglect certain sad ironies and realities. Both Storr[23] and Milgram point out that some of the very themes of moral behaviour that they wish to incorporate into their new moralities may, in fact, cause violence. As I pointed out above, there is no general agreement on the desired morality which is to guide behaviour. According to different cultural and national circumstances individuals may very well believe that your 'right side', is their 'wrong side'. Consequently, we are back to Harry's observation.

What is defined in one religion, culture or nation as conscientious behaviour, might very well be in another immoral. In fact, Baum[24] notes that 'conscientiousness can take the place of conscience very easily.' A person may be very conscientious about their behaviour and perform with complete moral indifference. He argues that moral indifference is the opposite of moral responsibility which involves concern about the consequences of our actions. But this is not true either. Moral indifference in one culture or one nation may not be the same in another. All cultures and states have constructed elaborate justifications, guidelines for how they wish their subjects to behave. The reason it is easy to carry out what might be considered immoral acts even under the guidelines of Lifton and Markusen and Kelman and Hamilton is because they are justified in terms of a higher good. The great irony is that in the name of good, evil is committed, and as Kren argues,

> the primary source of violence is found in the willingness of individuals to be self sacrificing for an ideal, ideology, or cause. When individuals speak of a willingness to die for a cause, they also mean a willingness to kill. 'Give me liberty or give me death' is soon followed by 'give me liberty or I will give you death.'[25]

The human desire to change the world to bring about their own particular vision of a 'better' society, to change the world from what it is to what it should be, may also be a source of destructive behaviour. Just as Christianity led to the Crusades and the Inquisition, visions of an ideal democracy and the city on the hill and manifest destiny lead Anglo-Americans to exterminate and steal the land of Native Americans.

The conditions created within a group or society as a means to move toward some particular vision creates the environment within which certain kinds of behaviour are rewarded and others discouraged. What happens is that force and violence win out and become the consensual tools to achieve success. In international politics genocide becomes a tool of success as Bosnians are killed by Serbs and their land is confiscated while the world watches and does nothing. Power triumphs. What is most important are the sets of behaviours receiving the institutionalized rewards of a society, national or global, and the kinds of models that are created. If one recognizes rewards for violence, for war and aggression, that is the form of behaviour most likely to be displayed. If, on the other hand, one sees violence and aggression punished, and peaceful negotiation rewarded that will be the form of desired behaviour. One does not need to be a very perceptive observer to note what is now rewarded and celebrated.

So, now we come to Harry's dilemma. In a world which rewards an ethic of violence, counter-violence is necessary to protect people from the aggression. As Storr points out, while we would all like to 'rid ourselves of our proclivities for violence', if we did we 'might find that we could no longer stand up for ourselves or assert our separate identities. Aggression seems closely linked with self-preservation, self-assertion, and self-affirmation. An aggressive attack upon another individual involving the use of physical force is a crude, extreme example of self-assertion at the expense of the other.'[26] The paradox is that if one is not willing to die for a cause and use violence to stop, in the case of our discussion, genocidal violence, then it will continue. The matter, therefore, of replacing one morality with another, or of imposing one set of community standards as opposed to another, is not necessarily a solution to the problem of genocidal violence.

SUMMING UP
The longer I study violence and human behaviour the more suspicious and perhaps cynical I become about academic prescriptions to halt the violence or to replace one morality with another. No religion has been free of murder, no nation state has failed to kill to achieve the goals leaders wish to pursue. To be able to make Harry's judgment, to be able to ascertain which is the 'wrong side', is more complicated than simply putting forth some definitions.

Our contemporary world is not homogenous and there are major disagreements over what once might have appeared to be fundamental, agreed upon ideas of how humans were to behave toward each other – although they clearly never did act in that fashion. The old rules of the major ethical and religious traditions have given way to justifications for virtually any form of behaviour humans may wish to pursue. While there are movements afoot to return to the older ethical traditions, these meet with controversy and there is little agreement over what tradition would best serve as the guideline for behaviour.

So perhaps the optimal solution is unlikely and there are always unforeseen consequences from any action. Often artists and writers capture these age-old questions, such as that posed by Harry Morrant at the outset of this paper concerning how to make the right choice, in a morally ambiguous world, in a more direct, honest and concise fashion than historians or social scientists. In an intriguing novel about the conflict between police and criminals in the city of Montreal, John Farrow sums up the ethical dilemma with which I have just been wrestling:

> Our enemies instinctively will exploit our ethics as a weakness. Do we tolerate that? Do we
> let the bastards win? Do we say, we're ethical, we're within the law? The country, the
> society, the Western world may be destroyed but at least we will choose the honorable
> course, now that barbarians must answer to God. Is that our plan? Or do we meet the bad
> guys on the streets, or on their country estates, and treat them for what they are – enemies,
> warriors to be fought and brought down with firepower? Do we behave as they do?[27]

And he concludes by describing a brilliant sunny day in summer, where winter has fled and where the sky is blue and where the 'world was wholly at peace with itself.' And ends: 'This was a day like that, dreamlike and fleeting.'[28]

The implication is obvious, as summer gives way to winter with the return of snow and cold, so the periods of success in controlling genocidal violence will give way to new outbreaks. We are dealing, unfortunately, with a world in which morality and responsibility are secondary to ambition and power and are not unambiguous. Sorry, Harry, it is still so very easy to find oneself on the wrong side.

NOTES

I should like to express my appreciation to The Earhart Foundation for the support which allowed me to complete this project.

1 These principles are found in Falk (1971), pp.106–7.

   The Nuremberg Principles of 1946

   1. Principles of International Law Recognized in Charter of the Nuremberg Tribunal and in the Judgment of the Tribunal

   2. As formulated by the International Law Commission, June–July 1950.

   Principle I

     Any person who commits an act which constitutes a crime under international law is responsible therefor and liable to punishment.

   Principle II

     The fact that internal law does not impose a penalty for an act which constitutes a crime under international law does not relive a person who committed the act from responsibility under international law.

   Principle III

     The fact that a person who committed an act which constitutes a crime under international law acted as Head of State or responsible government official does not relieve him from responsibility under international law.

   Principle IV

     The fact that a person acted pursuant to order of his Government or of a superior does not relieve him from responsibility under international law, provided a moral choice was in fact possible to him.

   Principle V

     Any person charged with a crime under international law has the right to a fair trial on the facts and law.

   Principle VI

   The crimes hereinafter set out are punishable as crimes under international law:

     a. Crimes against peace:

     (i) Planning, preparation, initiation or waging of a war of aggression or a war in violation of international treaties, agreements or assurances.

     (ii) Participation in a common plan or conspiracy for the accomplishment of any of the acts mentioned under (i).

     b. War crimes:

     Violations of the laws or customs of war which include, but are not limited to, murder, ill-treatment or deportation to slave-labour or for any other purpose of civilian populations of or in occupied territory, murder or ill-treatment of prisoners of war or persons on the seas, killing of hostages, plunder of public or private property, wanton destruction of cities, towns, or villages, or devastation not justified by military necessity.

     c. Crimes against humanity:

     Murder, extermination, enslavement, deportation and other inhuman acts done against any civilian population, or persecutions on political, racial or religious grounds, when such acts are done or such persecutions are carried on in execution of or in connexion with any crime against peace or any war crime.

   Principle VII

     Complicity in the commission of a crime against peace, a war crime, or a crime against humanity as set forth in Principle VI is a crime under international law.

2 Philip Hallie, *Lest Innocent Blood Be Shed* (New York: Harper and Row, 1979), p.270.

3 *ibid.*, p.271.

4 *ibid.*, p.273.

5 *ibid.*, p.278.

6 Thomas E. McCollough, *The Moral Imagination and Public Life: Raising the Ethical Question* (Chatham, New Jersey: Chatham House Publishers, Inc., 1991), pp.6–7.

7   *ibid.*, p.7.
8   Stanley Milgram, *Obedience to Authority* (New York: Harper and Row, 1974). Milgram made some further elaborations in a later work, *The Individual in a Social World* (Reading, Mass.: Addison-Wesley, 1977).
9   See, for example: David R. Blumenthal, *The Banality of Good and Evil: Moral Lessons From The Shoah and Jewish Tradition* (Washington, D.C.: Georgetown University Press, 1999) and Herbert C. Kelman and V. Lee Hamilton, *Crimes of Obedience: Toward a Social Psychology of Authority and Responsibility* (New Haven: Yale University Press, 1989).
10 David P. Forsythe, *The Internationalization of Human Rights* (Lexington, Mass.: Lexington Books, 1991), p.3.
11 Robert Jay Lifton and Erik Markusen, *The Genocidal Mentality: Nazi Holocaust and Nuclear Threat* New York: Basic Books, 1990).
12 Kelman and Hamilton, *op.cit.*, pp.307–338.
13 Lifton and Markusen, *op.cit.*, p.258.
14 *ibid.*, p.263.
15 *ibid.*, p.279.
16 Kelman and Hamilton, *op.cit.*, p.308.
17 *ibid.*, p.322.
18 *ibid.*, p.323.
19 *ibid.*, p.325.
20 Victor Farias, *Heidegger and Nazism* (Philadelphia: Temple University Press, 1989).
21 Kelman and Hamilton, *op.cit.*, p.330.
22 *Ibid.*, p.337.
23 Anthony Storr, *Human Destructiveness* (New York: Ballantine Books, 1991).
24 Rainer Baum, 'Holocaust: Moral Indifference as *the* Form of Modern Evil,' in *Echoes from the Holocaust* edited by Alan Rosenberg and Gerald E. Myers (Philadelphia: Temple University Press, 1988), p.56.
25 George M. Kren, 'The Holocaust: Moral Theory and Immoral Acts,' in Rosenberg and Myers, *op.cit.*, p.255.
26 Storr, *op.cit.*, p.7.
27 John Farrow, *City of Ice* (New York: Random House, 1999), p.402.
28 *ibid.*, p.403.

ETHICS, HUMAN GENETICS AND THE HOLOCAUST

Hans-Peter Kröner

T HE TERM 'human genetics' for the scientific investigation of human heredity was not commonly used in Germany until after the Second World War.[1] The disciplines dealing with the hereditary variability of humankind in the broadest sense were called physical anthropology, human heredity, hereditary pathology, eugenics or racial hygiene according to the aspect of human hereditary qualities being primarily investigated by the corresponding scientist and which areas of application were opening up. The Cologne geneticist Benno Müller-Hill was one of the first scientists to point to the part investigators of human heredity played in 'the selection of Jews, gipsies and the mentally ill from 1933–1945', that being the subtitle of his book *Murderous Science*, published in 1984.[2]

VALUE AND VARIABILITY: GENETICISTS, ANTHROPOLOGISTS AND THE 'THIRD REICH'

Although National Socialism never drew up a closed ideological system, all its separate ideological statements are based on a biologistic conception of the world. This biologism held that a value-laden, biologically or hereditarily founded inequality determines success or failure in each individual's life. Thus, achievement, social position etc. were based on the genes, and social change could operate through a biological policy, i.e. through positive or negative selection. Translated into the language of National Socialism, there were people with valuable genes and people with valueless genes, the former being the source of all social achievement, thus constituting, so to speak, the nation's biological capital. Their unhindered and prolific reproduction was to be supported in every way. The latter caused only social cost, reducing the resources available for the 'valuable ones'. They were therefore undesirable and their reproduction, later increasingly their lives, had to be curtailed.

The biological valuation was continued on a collective level: races could be typified by the common possession of certain genes, on which depended not only their specific outward appearance but, above all, their cultural capacity. Hence there was a hierarchy of races according to their supposed capability of adopting or developing a certain culture. At the top ranked the 'nordic' or 'aryan' race, to which all cultural achievements of European history were ascribed. Its opposite incarnation was an alleged 'Jewish race', which was not only incapable of culture but was described in pathological terms as a race of 'parasites' destructive to the culture of the 'host nation'. Just as the indiscriminate mixing of a hereditarily ill with a hereditarily healthy individual had to be avoided as it purportedly produced 'less valuable' offspring, so the mixing of differently valued races was supposed to be detrimental to the further development of the higher-ranking race and its culture.

Like other ideologies in the 20th century, National Socialism made use of science to justify its basic tenets. Since the Enlightenment, scientific racism had replaced religiously founded racism, its function being above all the justification of slavery and colonial exploitation.[3] Anthropographical taxonomies, particularly when linked to cultural evaluations, had, it is true, passed their scientific peak by the 1930s but were not yet considered to be obsolete or, to use a modern term, politically incorrect.[4] Nevertheless, theories of racial value had always been no more than hypotheses, which as a rule argued with historical evidence of the alleged superiority of the 'white man' in the course of history. That applied above all to the doctrine of the harmfulness of racial miscegenation. Hybridization experiments with plants and animals had yielded no trace of a disadvantage of racial mixing; on the contrary, there were indications that in some cases the filial generations were superior to the parental generations in terms of vitality (longevity) and efficiency (fertility). In these cases, too, history had to be called upon to 'prove' that racial mixing inevitably led to cultural downfall.[5] Finally, there was not common agreement on what should be regarded as taxonomic unity in the different anthropographies. The anthropologists agreed only in regard to the 'major races'.[6] In regard to the 'subraces', almost every anthropologist built up his own system, using stereotypes that seldom corresponded to what was found in the real world. The motley variety of 'nordic', 'falic', 'dinaric', 'weddid' and even 'Jewish' races stemmed rather from a projective construction of the anthropologists than from really existing sub-unities of the species *Homo sapiens*.[7] As a result, the National Socialists waived the idea of relating the quality of 'being Jewish' to 'objective racial' criteria and, in the Nuremberg Race Laws, tied it to the religious creed of the grandparents.

The 'hereditary health policy', which was based on the concept of eugenics and, along with National Socialist 'race policy', constituted the National Socialist 'race hygiene', proved similarly problematic. The race hygienist and human geneticist Otmar von Verschuer defined in 1934 'the new task of national medicine' as 'care for the body of the nation by preserving and promoting good stock, by eliminating ill genes and by conserving the racial characteristics of our nation, that is by eugenics and by racial care'.[8] Eugenic measures, even forced measures like sterilization, were an aspect of national policy in other industrial countries in the Thirties, but the National Socialists exceeded all comparable nations in the radicality of their sterilization policy, which by 1939 or even earlier had come to sanction the murder of those considered eugenically or racially undesirable. As early as 1932 the Prussian Health Council had discussed a draft sterilization law which was to serve the National Socialists as a pattern for their *Gesetz zur Verhütung erbkranken Nachwuchses* (Law for the Prevention of Genetically Diseased Offspring). The Prussian draft provided only for voluntary sterilization, thus taking into account the scientific uncertainties relating to eugenic measures, since knowledge of the hereditary basis of individual diseases was not yet so certain that it could justify deep interventions into a person's rights: that was at least the opinion of the experts in 1932. In addition, calculations of population genetics had shown that the frequency of recessive genes could be reduced by sterilization only over a very long space of time, of hundreds of years, as long as it was not possible to keep the phenotypically healthy heterozygous carriers from reproducing. For the same reason, the threatened degeneration of the population so often conjured up by the National Socialists was no immediate danger, as populations were known to develop gene balances that remained stable over long periods of time.

The German race hygienists knew about those uncertainties; they knew the hypothetical character of the doctrine of race mixing and had only expressed very cautious opinions on these matters before 1933. Given the radical nature of the Nazi measures, of the thousands and thousands of interventions into the bodily integrity of so-called hereditarily diseased people, of the deliberate social identification, exclusion, expulsion and finally annihilation of ethnic and social minorities, it would have been a duty of scientific honesty to point to the vague and disputed scientific basis of National Socialist policies on heredity and race, represented by the National Socialists as long-proven scientific facts. The race hygienists, however, confirmed the Nazis' claim to the scientific character of their ideology; they made their experience available for drafting and commenting on Nazi race legislation, defended this legislation with their scientific authority in Germany as well as abroad, and offered themselves to the newly-founded health courts and courts of justice to give expert opinions on matters of hereditary health or race. The 'euthanasia' of the mentally ill and the annihilation of the Jews were two sides of an ideology aiming at the biological 'cleansing' of the body of the nation from internal threats (the mentally ill) and external ones (the Jews, Gipsies etc.), who were often compared to parasites or pathological germs. The technology of mass annihilation was developed in the psychiatric institutions and then later exported to the death camps. The exploitation of the victims 'in the name of science', their being transformed into slide preparations, anatomical specimens or human guinea pigs in concentration camp experimentation further demonstrates the fundamental connection between euthanasia and the Holocaust. Here, too, human geneticists participated to a formidable extent. Josef Mengele, the notorious 'physician of Auschwitz', was an anthropologist and geneticist, a disciple of Otmar von Verschuer, director of the renowned Kaiser-Wilhelm Institute for Anthropology, Human Heredity and Eugenics in Berlin. Mengele carried out part of his experimentation on behalf of his Berlin mentor and funded by the Deutsche Forschungsgemeinschaft (German Research Association).[9] The American historian Sheila F. Weiss draws the following conclusion in regard to the relation between eugenics and the Holocaust:

> Although the extermination of millions of European Jews cannot really be viewed as a measure designed to boost national efficiency, the interpretation of the Jews as an unfit, surplus, and disposable group is not unrelated to the emphasis implicit in German race hygiene regarding 'valuable' and 'valueless' people.[10]

'IN THE SERVICE OF PURE SCIENCE': THE REESTABLISHMENT OF NAZI RACE-HYGIENISTS

None of the Nazi race hygienists or geneticists was called to account after 1945. Nor was there a discussion of Nazi 'health and race politics' let alone a confession of guilt from them to be perceived. The race hygienists had not condescended to 'dirty their own hands' after all, but, as they never tired of maintaining, had only served pure science. Other countries, they argued, had also carried out a eugenically oriented policy. So it is small wonder that Fritz Lenz, one of the Third Reich's leading race hygienists, was appointed to the Göttingen 'Chair of Human Heredity' as early as 1946. Günther Just, race hygienist at the Reich's 'Health Office', a department of the Ministry of Interior, could resume his teaching obligations at the Institute of Anthropology of Tübingen University in 1948. Mengele's mentor von Verschuer had to wait a little longer as his involvement in the Auschwitz experiments weighed heavier, but even he, having failed in Frankfurt and Tübingen, could take over a chair for human genetics at Münster University in 1951.[11] Leading Nazi anthropologists like Hans Weinert, Johannes Schaeuble, Egon von Eickstedt or the former SS-member Wilhelm Gieseler also held academic positions after 1945.

In 1997, the American geneticist and Nobel prize-winner James Watson castigated the German physicians of molecular medicine, gathered for a conference in Berlin, for what he saw as their hesitant and reserved attitude towards the Human Genome Project. The reason for their hesitation, according to Watson, was the 'original sin of eugenics', that is, the participation of leading human geneticists in 'the elimination of the mentally ill, Jews and Gipsies by means of scientific selection'. By having reinstated two of the leading Nazi race hygienists, Otmar von Verschuer, former director of the Kaiser-Wilhelm Institute of Anthropology, Human Hereditary and Eugenics, and Fritz Lenz, chief of the department of eugenics at the same institute and chair-holder of race hygiene at the university of Berlin, the 'filth of Nazi genetics' had tainted the German academic system up to the late Sixties. Adolf Butenandt, Nobel prizewinner and later president of the Max-Planck Society, had played a decisive part in the 'white-washing' of von Verschuer. So in Germany neither genetics nor geneticists had the 'odour of integrity' when new possibilities of human genetic manipulation opened up in the Seventies. Watson called upon the molecular physicians collectively 'to at last come to terms with the Nazi past of genetics'.[12]

Watson maintained that the reinstatement of the Nazi race hygienists had checked progress in genetics in Germany ever since. That is certainly true for the early years of the Federal Republic, but Watson's judgement that reinstating the race hygienists had created the sensitivity within German society towards the issue of manipulation of human genes seems to me problematic. He probably overrates the importance of human genetics in public perception. In the first 15–20 years of the Federal Republic, human genetics played no important scientific nor, as an applied science rendering services, social role. Its minimal importance was reflected by the low degree of institutionalization of human genetics in the Fifties. Certainly one reason for this was the 'political burden' weighing on the discipline and on the majority of its exponents, which led also to the international isolation of those scientists. An additional factor was that there was no urgent social need of human genetics; during the initial period of reconstruction there were more important problems than the reinstatement of a politically incriminated science whose applications, apart from the discredited practice of radical eugenics, tended towards zero. This situation changed only after 1955, when a new social need for human genetic research arose through the creation of Germany's nuclear power programme.[13] It took until the middle of the Sixties, however, for this new need to be reflected in a higher level of institutionalization.

Watson's line of reasoning is a classical example of the way the Holocaust is utilized in Germany for political or ideological purposes. What was new was that one of the founders and advocates of the new genetics based his arguments on that history. Usually, it is opponents of molecular genetics who use Nazi race hygiene and the Holocaust as an analogy for a slippery slope which modern human genetics could also risk if there were no ethically founded limits to its research. It is also true that ethical concerns in Germany and a sceptical public have led to more restrictive legislation on human genetic research than in comparable western countries. But it is certainly not the case that these concerns and the resistance to genetics can be attributed to the reinstatement of Nazi race hygienists and the resulting failure of the public in general and geneticists in particular to deal sufficiently with that history. The accusation of dealing inadequately with history touched a sore spot in the German consciousness. For the reinstatement of Nazi race hygienists had indeed caused their disciples too to neglect the issue of Nazi race hygiene, as mentioning it would have meant, according to Helmut Baitsch, a human geneticist free of any taint of Nazi affiliations, 'to touch a subject, the discussion of which would have inevitably led to an argument about men of rank and name'.[14] But that applied to any discipline in Germany in the Fifties. There too, the majority of chairs were held by professors who had already flourished under National Socialism. That was to change only at the end of the Sixties through the revolt of the protest generation, which in Germany had also been a revolt against the Nazi fathers and teachers.

NO MORE UTOPIAS: COMING TO TERMS WITH THE PAST
In 1969, German human geneticists at a conference in Marburg dealt for the first time with the social implications of their discipline and with its incriminated past.[15] Particularly in regard to the Nazi past, the human geneticists rejected all new utopias of human breeding such as those discussed since the Ciba Symposium in London 1961. At a second conference in Bremen in 1981, which was dedicated to the relation between human genetics and society, the human geneticist Helmut Baitsch from Ulm talked about 'the responsibility of human geneticists', referring directly to 'the German past between World War One and Two'.[16] Human geneticists and medical historians in Bonn, Freiburg, Göttingen, Lübeck, Münster and elsewhere have cooperated in joint teaching programmes on the Nazi past of German genetics. Peter Becker, disciple of Fritz Lenz and successor to his Chair of Human Genetics in Göttingen, has written two authoritative books on the Nazi history of human genetics and anthropology.[17] The German Society of Human Genetics acknowledged its historical heritage still in 1996 by declaring:

> The specific history of human genetics in Germany has shown that human genetics can be at risk of losing the respect for the dignity of man, of being abused and of finally actively supporting that abuse. This happened in the age of National Socialism when the fundamental principles of scientific and medical behaviour were damaged. The principles of equality and autonomy of man were subordinated to national and political interests which led to the violation, or even to the complete disregard for and cancellation of fundamental human rights. Through this, great suffering was inflicted upon many people and their families. Human geneticists are aware of their responsibility to work against the repetition of such developments.[18]

The historical discussion of National Socialist medicine had increased in Germany from the beginning of the Eighties. Whereas the contemporary historical preoccupation with National Socialism belonged to the founding agreements of the Federal Republic, the history of science of that period had remained under a taboo for a long time. Just like the myths about the part played by nuclear physicists in the Third Reich, the medical history of National Socialism had also been either anathema – in the official medical historiography for instance – or an object of belittlement by representatives of the German Medical Association. Medical historiography had never progressed beyond Alexander Mitscherlich's documentation of the Nuremberg Doctors' Trial. That documentation, furthermore, had never been accepted by the medical profession but had only been utilized as a proof that the German doctors had 'come to terms' with their past. Since then, the medical representatives had taken the view that the German medical profession, in the overwhelming majority, had demonstrated irreproachable professional conduct under National Socialism. The medical crimes of the National Socialists, 'euthanasia' and human experimentation in the concentration camps, had only been the work of a few 'degenerate' and brutish individual perpetrators.[19] It was only at the 'Gesundheitstag' [Health Conference] in Berlin in 1980, a 'counter event' to the official 'Ärztetag' [Doctors' Conference] of the Medical Association and arranged by doctors, nurses and other medical professionals who were dissatisfied with the politics of their official representatives, that National Socialist medicine was discussed in a broad frame and predominantly by historical laymen. Victims of Nazi medicine, sterilized persons, survivors of concentration camps and exiled Jewish doctors also received a hearing there. In the aftermath, a medical-historical 'grassroot' movement came into being, against which the official medical historiography within universities could no longer close ranks. Today, the number of publications on the subject is almost too numerous to survey. Finally, at the official 'Doctors' Conference' in Berlin in 1989, the professor of medical history Richard Toellner publicly confessed to the medical profession's guilt of the crimes committed under National Socialism.[20]

The controversy on the medical crimes at the Nuremberg Doctors' Trial had resulted in the formulation of the 'Nuremberg Code'. The Code gives ethical guidelines for human experimentation in medical research and has laid the foundation for other codes such as the Helsinki Declaration of the World Medical Association.[21] In Germany, Nazi medicine had at first only little influence on medical ethics. There was a short and vehement discussion directly after the war and under the impression of the Doctors' Trial, which was soon followed by a return to the classical paternalistic themes of German medical ethics.[22] National Socialism remained an a-historical catchword, predominantly used to avoid a discussion, as shown, for instance, in the abortion debate and the coining of the word 'fetocide', in analogy to 'genocide'. The word 'euthanasia' is so politically incriminated that it is understood in Germany only in terms of 'National Socialist murder of the mentally ill'. It is because of the long shadow of Nazi euthanasia that other forms of help for the dying have been discussed in Germany only with reservation and very belatedly.[23]

Alongside the preoccupation with Nazi medicine, there was a discussion of problems resulting from the new possibilities of human genetic manipulation. That discussion was of course influenced by the 'new' knowledge about Nazi medicine. What was new in that knowledge was the realization that Nazi race hygiene and 'euthanasia' had a long history before 1933, that National Socialism had found widespread support among doctors, and that university medicine and medical research were deeply involved in the identification, selection, 'medical' killing and exploitation of the victims of National Socialist 'race and health politics'. No critical publication on reproductive medicine or genetic engineering failed to point out the dangers of eugenic abuse as practised by the National Socialists.[24] Political spokesmen, whether they were opponents or followers of the new technologies, alluded in their statements on genetic engineering to Nazi history and emphasized the special responsibility of Germany just because of that history, as did the former Minister of Justice Leutheuser-Schnarrenberger when she rejected the Bioethics Convention of the European Council.[25] The legal prohibition of germ line manipulation had been discussed early in the Federal Republic and had found its way into German legislation as the Law for the Protection of Embryos of 1991.[26]

Thus the discussion on the advantages and risks of genetic engineering was at first left to journalists or politicians or was led by a critical public especially sensitive to the endangering of humane and ecological issues, especially within the environment of the Peace- or No-Nukes-Movement and parts of the Green Party. Philosophers and moral theologians in Germany, however, abstained for a long time from discussing normative issues in the field of medicine and biotechnology. Consequently there was a belated response and institutionalization of Anglo-American bioethics, which began in the Federal Republic only in the late 1980s and has still not reached a state equivalent to that in comparable western countries. One of the reasons for that belated reception was undoubtedly the Kantian, Hegelian, Aristotelian tradition of German philosophical ethics. Another reason, however, was the history of medicine under National Socialism, which had led to a deep distrust of philosophical standpoints trying to handle and operationalize problems of human existence, specifically of the beginning and end of life as existence, and also of the human essence, of what might be considered part of the *conditio humana*. This distrust tended to see in bioethics an ethics of justification, an apology to do what could be done, comparable to the part race hygienists and followers of a Social Darwinist ethics of evolution had played in the Third Reich.

GENETICS AND THE HOLOCAUST: A LESSON TO LEARN?

The conflict between followers of a 'deontologically guided culture of the sanctity of life' and of a 'consequentialistically guided culture based on interests' clashed for the first time – according to the Swiss bioethicist Anton Leist – in the so-called 'Singer affair'.[27] The Australian philosopher Peter Singer, an advocate of utilitarianism, holds among other things that the killing of a badly handicapped new born infant could be ethically justified under certain conditions.[28] Singer had been invited to a conference in Marburg in 1989 sponsored by, among other organizations, Lebenshilfe [Help for Living], the main organization in Germany for parents with mentally handicapped children. Singer had also accepted an invitation from Christoph Anstötz to give a lecture at the University of Dortmund on the question 'Have the most severely handicapped new born infants a right to live?' Just before Singer's arrival, the organizers of the Marburg conference cancelled his invitation on the grounds that his acceptance of the Dortmund invitation could give the impression that Lebenshilfe was helping to propagate Singer's ideas of euthanasia in Germany. What followed was a vehement discussion in the media on whether there was an unlimited right of free speech. The autonomous organizations (NGOs) of handicapped people in particular held that views rejecting the right to life of whole groups of handicapped people had no claim to public propagation and therefore did not fall within the right of free speech or academic freedom. At the universities, lectures on Singer's 'Practical Ethics' were disturbed or even cancelled. The 1991 Wittgenstein Symposium in Austria on applied ethics had to be cancelled after a number of groups exerted pressure on the organizers to cancel the invitations to Singer and other bioethicists.[29] Singer's views were compared to Nazi euthanasia and defamed as being fascist.[30] But there was also a counter movement which stood up for the right of free speech without necessarily sharing Singer's views, condemning the disruption of lectures or disciplinary actions against lecturers. A group of German philosophers emphasized in a 'Declaration on the so-called Singer affair' that a rational discussion of issues dealing with human life and death belonged to the tasks of practical philosophy, and expressed their apprehension that such a discussion when touching on Singer's theses could be prevented or hampered by certain circles. But the philosophers also declared:

> Our knowledge of the criminal National Socialist 'euthanasia' practice imposes a special duty of conscientiousness on any discussion of this whole range of themes. We acknowledge emphatically this special obligation.[31]

No German newspaper or magazine was willing to publish the declaration, not even *Die Zeit*, which had previously stood up for at least discussing Singer's theses and had thus incurred the hostility of organizations of handicapped people. A declaration of Berlin philosophers, however, condemning the prevention of a discussion of Singer's arguments as 'scandalous', was published in two German daily newspapers, the Berlin *Tageszeitung* and the *Frankfurter Rundschau*, both newspapers more or less closely connected to the Green Party and the Social Democrats. Usually bioethicists located the opponents of a public discussion among the political left, among neo-marxists, anti-nuclear campaigners and feminists. Schöne-Seifert and Rippe, for instance, insinuated that these groups fundamentally question the future of industrial society. Accordingly, the movement against genetic engineering was said to have replaced the No-Nukes-Movement which had also had an 'anticapitalistic thrust'.[32] This analogy remains incomprehensible, as the authors had previously emphasized that nuclear technology once set out to solve the world energy problem, expectations that had given way to an ambivalent attitude even among their proponents. But it had been the very contradiction between technological promise and the unsolved and belittled problems of reactor security and disposal of nuclear waste which had kindled resistance against the use of nuclear energy. This resistance had primarily been a resistance of people personally affected because they lived in the environs of an atomic power plant. The opponents of genetic engineering, and only so far the analogy holds true, like to point to the experience with nuclear technology and demand therefore a broad social discussion of the new biotechnology before again factors were created serving as inherent necessities, as had been the case with nuclear energy.

Hence, the 'antibioethic movement' which had formed after the 'Singer affair' cannot be politically classified according to a simplistic right-left-pattern and particularly not when such patterns are often used as in Germany to defame an opponent as ideologically pigheaded and therefore not worth discussion. To be sure, an antibioethics attitude as such, identifying bioethics as agent and apologist of concerted scientific and commercial interests, is to be found only with a minority of the broader movement which takes a sceptical stand towards genetic engineering and its promise of happiness. In that broader movement there are both conservative, christian followers of a doctrine of the 'sanctity of life' and representatives of a consequentialistical attitude, wishing to discuss first of all the potential social consequences of the new technology. This broad social scepticism, which is reflected by a restrictive legislation and is sometimes rash in prohibiting procedures such as germ line therapy, which are still far from being realisable in the near future, is certainly based on the historical burden of the Holocaust. That heritage does not so much consist of a lack of political liberality and tolerance towards different moral attitudes in a pluralistic society, as some bioethicists maintain, but in a historical experience only incompletely expressed in terms of lack or want. There is certainly a traditional weakness of political liberalism in Germany which contributed to the catastrophe of National Socialism. That weakness is therefore rather a cause than a consequence of the Holocaust. In certain circles, particularly in East Germany due to the continuation of dictatorship after 1945, this illiberality has possibly survived the catastrophe. But if there is political liberalism in Germany today, then it is the result of a change in attitudes, a new orientation which has been brought about above all by the historical experience of the Holocaust.

Hence it is not a lack of information on what is going on in clinics, intensive wards and genetic laboratories which has led to the widespread scepticism in Germany, as Anton Leist for instance has claimed.[33] The activists in particular, as in the earlier Anti-Nuclear movement, are familiar with the technical and ethical problems of the new technology. It is rather specific knowledge from which this scepticism springs. This knowledge is the result of the development of historiography in the 1970s and 80s, its turning away from political history and history of events towards social history, towards the history of everyday life, a history seen above all from regional or local aspects. This has made many people familiar with National Socialism in an almost unbearable way. National Socialism is no longer something 'completely different' from which it was easy to disassociate oneself. The history of National Socialism teaches how evil comes stealthily. It tells us something about the *conditio humana*, about the thin line between bourgeois respect-ability and unchained lust for murder, about the temptability of man believing to act in the service of a higher mission, about the reduction of persons to objects of social techniques. It is in that sense, as anthropological potential and not as a concrete historical repetition, that National Socialism is present in Germany. And it is from that knowledge and not from an obscure anti-technological attitude that the fears and scepticism facing the new genetics spring.

Naturally, such fears can be abused by people who only jump on the band-wagon because they have an axe to grind, who draw up unbroken lines of continuity between Nazi race hygiene and modern medicine or human genetics.[34] How much more problem-atical it must therefore be that one of the leading molecular geneticists utilizes the Holocaust, even if with reversed premises, to influence public opinion in favour of the Human Genome Project in a both trite and unbearable way and at a time when the 'hysteria' of the Singer affair' was beginning to calm down in Germany and bioethics, here mostly called medical ethics or ethics of medicine, was being more and more institutionalized. The way Watson proceeded only confirmed the reservation towards the new genetics in wide sections of the population. First he criticized the German reserve regarding the Human Genome Project as economically disadvantageous as Germany was thereby renouncing the possibility of applying for patents. The reason for this reserve is, according to Watson, the bad image of genetics still identified with Nazi race hygiene in Germany. In a classical black and white drawing, Nazi race hygiene is pictured as the 'completely different', exercised by criminals who unfortunately were allowed to continue their evil-doing after 1945 which led to the historical repression of any discussion of Nazi race hygiene and its advocates. I have tried to show that this view is only partly true and has been outstripped by the development of historiography in Germany for a long time.

As a counter-example, Watson then invokes the American geneticists who also had 'skeletons in their closets'. In the US too, there had been forced eugenic sterilization, eugenically-based racism and a scientific cooperation between leading American eugenic-ists and Nazi race hygienists. Unfortunately Watson does not say which lesson the American geneticists learnt from that history. I dare doubt, however, that this history, particularly in regard to the Nazi cooperation, is known by American geneticists, let alone by the population. The historian of American eugenics, Daniel Kevles, remains silent on that cooperation.[35] It is above all the merit of the German historian Stefan Kühn to have pointed to the international connections of Nazi race hygiene.[36] It is only recently that American historians have started to deal with that aspect of the history of eugenics.[37] Watson called upon the German geneticists to come to terms with their past – a call that will be grist to the mill of those demanding an end to the discussion of National Socialism in Germany. For Watson's appeal reeks too much of a call for a final line, for one last discussion, connected perhaps to a confession of guilt or at least of being ashamed, in order then to let bygones be bygones and allow geneticists to be able to dedicate themselves to the business of the day.

The representative of the German Ministry of Science received a taste of Watson's anger after she said Germany's entry into the Human Genome Project was based on economic considerations and that only research leading to patents would be funded. That, Watson said, had given him the unmistakable impression 'that Germany had entered the genome game only to help itself and not to help the world as a whole'. Now he understood 'why Germany did not join the unselfish release of data which

American and British scientists had agreed upon one year previously: namely to publish data on the World Wide Web the day they were available'.[38] Watson gave the impression that the Human Genome Project was the work of pure idealists inspired only by the desire 'to fight the destructive effects of genetic diseases' and accompanied by a pro- gramme analysing the ethical, legal, and social consequences of genetic research for which five percent of the budget had been reserved and which was, moreover, utterly committed to international transparency. What he did not mention was the international atmosphere of a 'gold rush' connected to the Genome Project in regard to potential patents; he did not mention that the release of data to the World Wide Web was by no means 'unselfish', a 'help for the world', but that the criterium of cost efficiency was behind the agreement. It was the fear of an expensive repetition of the repetitive and widely automatic work of charting and sequencing which had led to an international coordination of the research work. 'Cooperation and information-sharing reduce the costs and speed up the procedures,' writes the English moral theologian Julie Clague.[39] And the American theologian Lisa Sowle Cahill admits that social considerations would gradually enter the discussion on genetic engineering but that 'even on those fields [issues of patenting, genetic screening, gene therapy, health insurance, *H.-P. K.*] politics is still decisively determined by market considerations.'[40]

What now lurks behind Watson's intervention, which was certainly not coincidentally published in the renowned *Frankfurter Allgemeine Zeitung*, a conservative daily news- paper which has no reputation for being hostile to trade and industry? For some time, German trade and industry have been complaining at the restrictions on genetic research in Germany. The majority of German geneticists and genetic researchers have joined in the complaint as they see both their freedom of research and their freedom to exploit the results being infringed. Almost daily the media report on Germany's role as a major centre of commerce and research being at stake, on the emigration of qualified scientists abroad. If, however, German scepticism of genetic engineering is a consequence of the Holocaust, then it belongs to the constituent elements of the Federal Republic, and that is, of Germany as a centre of commerce and research as well. Such historical facts are not simply disposable, as Watson insinuates. Thus far he has done a disservice to the proponents of reducing the number of restrictions on genetic research. All critics of unrestricted genetic research light up their warning lamps when a famous geneticist in a high moral tone and without the slightest shadow of doubt paints a picture of unselfish genetics, in the service only of fighting human suffering, when he gives a politician, who only honestly voiced what everybody thinks and does, a dressing-down in a self- righteous and arrogant way. The National Socialist race hygienists, too, were fascinated by the utopia of a world free from disease and suffering; they, too, were carried away by the belief in their mission, in the high moral content of their task and they despised the politicians and their narrow-minded limitation to the trivialities of daily politics, which does not mean, however, that they did not know how to make use of the advantages the Nazi regime offered to them. It is true that the widespread scepticism of genetic engineering in Germany has economic and scientific disadvantages. We cannot, however, step out of history or voluntarily draw a final line. What we can do, is accept the Holocaust as part of our history. Perhaps what seemed like a disadvantage in the economical field then proves an advantage in another one. In regard to genetic engineer- ing and human genetics, this could mean that the protracted introduction of new genetic procedures and the reserve in certain fields of research such as research on human embryos, could yield more social, legal, and ethical security. In regard to the victims murdered in the name of race hygiene, that would be more fitting for the Federal

Republic of Germany rather than once more indiscriminately to become addicted to genetic utopias.

NOTES

1 It was Otmar von Verschuer of all people, one of the leading racial hygienists in the Third Reich, who called his new institute, founded in Münster in 1951, Institute für Humangenetik, which can also be read in German as 'humane genetics', the German word 'human' meaning both 'human' and 'humane'.

2 Benno Müller-Hill, *Tödliche Wissenschaft. Die Aussonderung von Juden, Zigeunern und Geisteskranken 1933–1945* (Reinbek: Rowohlt Taschenbuchverlag, 1984).

3 Before the development of racial anthropological systems in the 18th century there had been only a very rough concept of race equating the major races with the descendants of Noah's sons. Black Africans were believed to be descendants of Noah's cursed son Ham ('Hamites').

4 Elazar Barkan, *The Retreat of Scientific Racism. Changing Concepts of race in Britain and the United States between the World Wars* (Cambridge: Cambridge University Press, 1991).

5 A favourite example was the downfall of the Roman Empire: the Romans, degenerated by indiscriminate racial miscegenation as it was believed, could finally not resist the assault of the 'pure-bred' Germanic peoples.

6 Since the 18th century the following races were described as major races: Caucasian (or European), African, Mongolian race. Besides there was a discussion whether an American and an Australian 'major' race existed or whether they were subdivisions of the Mongolian and African races.

7 Niels C Lösch, *Rasse als Konstrukt. Leben und Werk Eugen Fischers* (Frankfurt Berlin: Peter Lang, 1997).

8 Otmar von Verschuer, *Erbpathologie. Ein Lehrbuch für Ärzte* (Dresden Leipzig: Theodor Steinkopff, 1934), p.2.

9 As to the relationship between Verschuer/Mengele, see Benno Müller-Hill, *Tödliche Wissenschaft. Die Aussonderung von Juden, Zigeunern und Geisteskranken 1933–1945* (Reinbek: Rowohlt Taschenbuchverlag, 1984). Paul Weindling, *Health, Race and German Politics between National Unification and Nazism, 1870–1945* (Cambridge: University Press, 1989). Lucette Matalon Lagnado and Sheila Cohn Dekel, *Children of the Flames. Dr. Joseph Mengele and the untold story of the twins of Auschwitz* (New York: William Morrow and Company, 1991). Hans-Peter Kröner, *Von der Rassenhygiene zur Humangenetik: Das Kaiser-Wilhelm-Institut für Anthropologie, menschliche Erblehre und Eugenik nach dem Kriege* (Stuttgart Jena Lübeck Ulm: Gustav Fischer, 1998).

10 Sheila F. Weiss, 'The Race Hygiene Movement in Germany, 1904–1945', in Mark B. Adams (ed.), *The Wellborn Science. Eugenics in Germany, France, Brazil, and Russia* (Oxford: Oxford University Press, 1990), pp.8–68, here p.49.

11 Verschuer's first attempts to find a new position had failed because the Americans in their zone applied higher standards to the political integrity of scientists than the British did. Göttingen where Lenz taught and Verschuer's later place of activity Münster were both situated in the British Zone.

12 James D. Watson, 'Leichte Schatten über Berlin. Die Deutschen und ihre Genetiker: Anmerkungen eines amerikanischen Nobelpreisträgers', *Frankfurter Allgemeine Zeitung* 19 July 1997: 165.

13 Hans-Peter Kröner, 'Förderung der Genetik und Humangenetik in der Bundesrepublik durch das Ministerium für Atomfragen in den fünfziger Jahren', in Karin Weisemann, Hans-Peter Kröner, Richard Toellner (eds.), *Wissenschaft und Politik. Humangenetik in der DDR 1949–1989* (Münster Hamburg: LIT Verlag, 1997), pp.69–82.

14 Helmut Baitsch, 'Verantwortung des Humangenetikers in Forschung und Praxis', in Werner Schloot, *Möglichkeiten und Grenzen der Humangenetik* (Frankfurt New York: Campus Verlag, 1984), S.279.

15 Gerhard Wendt (ed.), *Genetik und Gesellschaft* (Stuttgart: Marburger Forum Philippinum, 1970).

16 Helmut Baitsch, Verantwortung des Humangenetikers', *op. cit.*

17 Peter Emil Becker, *Zur Geschichte der Rassenhygiene. Wege ins Dritte Reich* (Stuttgart/New York: Georg Thieme, 1988). Peter Emil Becker, *Sozialdarwinismus, Rassismus, Antisemitismus und Völkischer Gedanke* (= Wege ins Dritte Reich part II) (Stuttgart New York: Georg Thieme, 1990).

18   Kommission für Öffentlichkeitsarbeit und ethische Fragen der Gesellschaft für Humangenetik e.V.,
     Positionspapier, Medizinische Genetik 8, 1996: 125–131. Quoted according to Marcus in Düwell,
     Dietmar Mieth (eds.), *Ethik in der Humangenetik. Die neueren Entwicklungen der genetischen Frühdiag-
     nostik aus ethischer Perspektive* (Tübingen Basel: Francke Verlag, 1998), p.461.

19   That was for example the stand which the 'Arbeitsgemeinschaft deutscher Landesärztekammern' took
     in regard to Mitscherlichs documentation. Alexander Mitscherlich and Fred Mielke, *Medizin ohne
     Menschlichkeit* (Frankfurt: Fischer Taschenbuch Verlag, 1978), p.15.

20   Richard Toellner, 'Ärzte im Dritten Reich', in Johanna Bleker and Norbert Jachertz (eds.), *Medizin
     im 'Dritten Reich'* (Köln: Deutscher Ärzte-Verlag, 1993), pp.11–24.

21   George Annas, Michael A Grodin (eds.), The Nazi Doctors and the Nuremberg Code. Human
     Rights in Human Experimentation (New York Oxford: University Press, 1992).

22   Hans-Peter Kröner, 'Die Bedeutung der NS-Geschichte für die medizinische Ethik', in Richard
     Toellner and Urban Wiesing (eds.), *Geschichte und Ethik in der Medizin* (= Medizin-Ethik vol.10)
     (Stuttgart Jena Lübeck Ulm: Gustav Fischer, 1997), pp.155–172.

23   The German word 'Sterbehilfe' [help for the dying] can mean both an active 'help to die' as being
     practiced in the Netherlands and a 'care for the dying' without deliberately shortening life as being
     practised by the hospice movement.

24   Early examples were for instance: Jost Herbig, *Der Bio-Boom. Geschäfte mit dem Leben* (Hamburg:
     Stern Buch, 1982). Wolfgang Daele, *Mensch nach Mass. Ethische Probleme der Genmanipulation und
     Gentherapie* (München: Verlag C. H. Beck, 1985). More recent examples are: Ursel Fuchs, *Gentechnik
     – der Griff nach dem Erbgut. Eine kritische Bestandsaufnahme* (Bergisch Gladbach: Bastei-Lübbe
     Taschenbuch, 1996). Michael Wunder and Therese Neuer-Miesbach (eds.), *Bio-Ethik und die
     Zukunft der Medizin* (Bonn: Psychiatrie-Verlag, 1998).

25   Quoted according to Urban Wiesing, 'Genetics in Germany – History and Hysteria', in Ruth
     Chadwick et al. (eds.), *The Ethics of Genetic Screening* (Dordrecht: Kluwer Academic Publishers,
     1999), pp.147–156. See also: Enquete-Kommission des Deutschen Bundestages (ed.), *Chancen und
     Risiken der Gentechnologie. Dokumentation des Berichts an den Deutschen Bundestag* (= Gentechnologie
     – Chancen und Risiken vol. 12) (Frankfurt München: J. Schweitzer Verlag, 1987). Helmut Kohl, Wir
     wollen humanen Fortschritt: Chancen und Grenzen der Gentechnologie, in: Heinz Seeing (ed.),
     Technologischer Fortschritt und menschliches Leben part 2: Gentechnik am Menschen (Frankfurt
     München: J. Schweitzer Verlag, 1988), S.3–6.

26   § 5 des Gesetzes zum Schutz von Embryonen vom 13. Dezember 1990, Bundesgesetzblatt I,
     p.2746. For former discussions see: Bundesminister für Forschung und Technologie (ed.), In-
     vitro-Fertilisation, Genomanalyse und Gentherapie (= Gentechnologie – Chancen und Risiken
     vol.6, Bericht der Benda-Kommission) (Frankfurt München: J. Schweitzer Verlag, 1985). Enquete-
     Kommission des Deutschen Bundestages (ed.), Chancen und Risiken der Gentechnologie. Doku-
     mentation des Berichts an den Deutschen Bundestag (= Gentechnologie – Chancen und Risiken
     vol.12, (Frankfurt München: J. Schweitzer Verlag, 1987). Richtlinien zur Gentherapie beim
     Menschen der Deutschen Bundesärztekammer, Deutsches Ärzteblatt 86, 1989: A-2957–2962.

27   Anton Leist, 'Bioethics in a Low Key: A Report from Germany', *Bioethics* 7 (1993): 272–279, here
     p.273.

28   Peter Singer, *Praktische Ethik* (Stuttgart: Philipp Reclam[2] 1994 [*Practical Ethics* (Cambridge:
     Cambridge University Press,[4] 1993)]; Helga Kuhse and Peter Singer, *Should the Baby Live?* (Oxford:
     Oxford University Press, 1985).

29   See: 'Wie man in Deutschland mundtot gemacht wird'. Anhang zu: Peter Singer, *Praktische Ethik*,
     Stuttgart: Philipp Reclam,[2] 1994), pp.425–451. First published as: Peter Singer, 'On Being Silenced
     in Germany', *The New York Review of Books*, 15 August 1991.

30   Singer is the son of Austrian Jewish refugees from the Third Reich. Three of his grandparents died in
     concentration camps.

31   'Erklärung deutscher Philosophen zur sog. "Singer-Affäre".' Reprinted in Rainer Hegselmann and
     Reinhard Merkel (eds.), *Zur Debatte über Euthanasie* (Frankfurt: Suhrkamp Taschenbuch, 1991), p.328.

32   Bettina Schöne-Seiffert and Klaus-Peter Rippe, *Silencing the Singer. Antibioethics in Germany*, Hast-
     ings Center Report, November–December 1991: 20–27, here p.21. See also Urban Wiesing, 'Genetics

in Germany – History and Hysteria', in Ruth Chadwick et al. (eds.), *The Ethics of Genetic Screening* (Dordrecht: Kluwer Academic Publishers, 1999), p.147–156, here p.150.

33 Anton Leist, 'Bioethics in a Low Key: A Report from Germany', *Bioethics* 7 (1993): 272–279, here p.273

34 E.g. see: Udo Sierck and Nati Radtke,. *Die Wohltäter-Mafia. Vom Erbgesundheitsgericht zur Human-genetischen Beratung* (Hamburg: Selbstverlag, 1984). Bettina Rainer, *Euthanasie – Zu den Folgen eines harmoniesüchtigen Weltbildes* (Wien: Wiener Frauenverlag, 1995). Peter-Ferdinand Koch, *Menschen-versuche. Die tödlichen Experimente deutscher Ärzte* (München Zürich: Piper 1996).

35 Daniel J Kevles, *In the Name of Eugenics. Genetics and the Uses of Human Heredity* (New York: Alfred A. Knopf, 1985).

36 Stefan Kühl, *The Nazi Connection. Eugenics, American Racism and German National Socialism* (New York Oxford: University Press, 1994). Stefan Kühl, *Die Internationale der Rassisten. Aufstieg und Niedergang der internationalen Bewegung für Eugenik und Rassenhygiene im 20. Jahrhundert* (Frankfurt New York: Campus, 1997).

37 Diane B Paul, *Controlling Human Heredity, 1865 to the Present* (Atlantic Highlands: Humanities Press, 1995). Garland E Allen, 'The Social and Economic Origins of Genetic Determinism: a Case History of the American Eugenics Movement, 1900–1940 and its Lesson for Today', *Genetica* 99 (1997): 77–88.

38 James D. Watson, 'Leichte Schatten über Berlin. Die Deutschen und ihre Genetiker: Anmerkungen eines amerikanischen Nobelpreisträgers', *Frankfurter Allgemeine Zeitung*, 19 July 1997: 165

39 Julie Clague, 'Genetisches Wissen als Ware. Das Genomprojekt, Märkte und Konsumenten', *Concilium* 34 (1998): 120–129, here p.124.

40 Lisa Sowle Cahill, 'Genetik, Ethik und Sozialpolitik: Stand der Debatte', *Concilium* 34 (1998): 113–119, here p.117.

HUMAN RESPONSIBILITY:
CONTEMPORARY REFLECTIONS IN LIGHT OF NAZI IDEOLOGY

John T. Pawlikowski

BACK IN the early seventies two futurists introduced us to a fundamentally new reality with which religious ethics has yet adequately to grapple. Victor Ferkiss, a political scientist out of the Catholic tradition, and Hans Jonas, a social philosopher of Jewish background who escaped the Nazis, served warning that humankind had reached a new threshold in its evolutionary journey. Humanity was now standing on a threshold between utopia and oblivion, as Buckminster Fuller has put it. The human community now faced a situation whose potential for destruction equalled its capacity for reaching new levels of creativity and human dignity. What path humanity would follow was a decision that rested with the next several generations. Neither direct divine intervention nor the arbitrary forces of nature would determine the ultimate outcome. Human choice was now more critical than ever in the past for creational survival. And the decision would have lasting impact, well beyond the lifespan of those who are destined to make it. It would, in fact, determine what forms of life will experience continued viability.

Ferkiss's 1974 volume, *The Future of Technological Civilization*, put the late 20th-century challenge to humankind in these words: 'Man has...achieved virtually godlike powers over himself, his society, and his physical environment. As a result of his scientific and technological achievements, he has the power to alter or destroy both the human race and its physical habitat.'[1]

Hans Jonas, in a groundbreaking speech in Los Angeles in 1972 at a gathering of learned societies of religion and subsequently in published writings, conveyed essentially the same message as Ferkiss. Ours is the very first generation to have to face the question of basic creational survival. In the past, there was no human destructive behaviour from which we could not recover. But today, we have reached the point through technological advancement where this principle no longer holds. Humankind now seems increasingly capable of actions that inflict terminal damage on the whole of creation and raise serious questions about the future of humanity itself.[2]

For me, the Holocaust represents perhaps the clearest 20th-century example of the fundamental challenge now facing humanity as described by Ferkiss and Jonas. I have emphasized in a number of published essays[3] that in the final analysis I view the Holocaust as inaugurating a new era in human self-awareness and human possibility, an era capable of producing unprecedented destruction or unparalleled hope. With the rise of Nazism the mass extermination of human life in a guiltless fashion became thinkable and technologically feasible. The door was now ajar for the dispassionate torture and the murder of millions not out of xenophobic fear, but through a calculated effort to reshape history supported by intellectual argumentation from the best and brightest minds in the society. It was an attempt, Emil Fackenheim has argued, to wipe out the 'divine image' in history. 'The murder camp', Fackenheim insists, 'was not an accidental by-product of the Nazi empire. It was its essence.'[4]

The basic challenge of the Holocaust lies in the need to alter significantly our perception of the relationship between God and humanity. Such a change carries with it profound implications for human moral responsibility. What emerges as a central reality from the study of the Holocaust is the Nazis' sense of a new Aryan humanity freed from the moral restraints previously imposed by religious beliefs and capable of exerting virtually unlimited power in the shaping of the world and its inhabitants. In a somewhat indirect, though still powerful way the Nazis had proclaimed the death of God as a governing force in the universe. In pursuit of their objective, the Nazis became convinced that all the so-called 'dregs of humanity', first and foremost the Jews but also Poles, Gypsies, Gays and the disabled, had to be eliminated or at least their influence on culture and human development significantly curtailed.[5]

The late Uriel Tal captured as well as anyone the basic theological challenge presented by the Holocaust. In his understanding, the so-called 'Final Solution' had as its ultimate objective the total transformation of human values. Its stated intent was liberating humanity from all previous moral ideals and codes. When the liberating process was complete, humanity would be rescued once and for all from subjection to God-belief and its related notions of moral responsibility, redemption, sin and revelation. Nazi ideology sought to transform theological ideas into exclusively anthropological and political concepts. In Tal's perspective, the Nazis can be said to have adopted a kind of 'incarnational' ideology, but not in the New Testament sense of the term. Rather, for the Nazis, 'God becomes a man in a political sense as a member of the Aryan race whose highest representative on earth is the Führer.'[6]

If we accept this interpretation of the ultimate implications of Nazism, we are confronted with a major theological challenge. How does the human community properly appropriate the genuine sense of human liberation that was at the core of Nazi ideology without surrendering its soul to massive evil? However horrendous their legacy, the Nazis were correct in at least one respect. They rightly perceived that some basic changes were underway in human consciousness. The impact of the new science and technology, with its underlying assumption of freedom, was beginning to provide humankind on a mass scale with a Promethean type experience of escape from prior moral chains. People were starting to perceive, however dimly, an enhanced sense of dignity and autonomy that went well beyond what Western Christian theology was prepared to concede.

Traditional theological concepts that had shaped much of the Christian moral perspective, notions such as divine punishment, hell, divine wrath and providence were losing some of the hold they had exercised over moral decision making since biblical times. Christian theology had tended to accentuate the omnipotence of God which in turn intensified the impotence of the human person and the rather inconsequential role played by the human community in maintaining the sustainability of creation. The Nazis totally rejected this previous relationship. In fact, they were trying to turn it upside down.

Numerous Jewish writers have attempted to respond to the fundamental implications of the Holocaust in terms of human and divine responsibility. Emil Fackenheim, David Hartman, Richard Rubenstein, Elie Wiesel, Arthur Cohen, David Blumenthal and Zygmunt Bauman are authors who have made significant contributions to the post-Holocaust discussion. One of the responses I still find particularly intriguing in both its theological and practical dimensions has come from Irving Greenberg.

For Greenberg the Holocaust has destroyed all further possibility of a 'commanded' dimension to our understanding of the God-human community relationship. 'Covenant-ally speaking,' he has said, 'one cannot order another person to step forward to die.'[7] Any meaningful understanding of a covenantal relationship between God and humanity must now be understood as voluntary. The voluntary nature of the post-Holocaust covenantal relationship unquestionably heightens human responsibility in the eyes of Greenberg: 'If after the Temple's destruction, Israel moved from junior partner to true partner in the covenant, then after the Holocaust, the Jewish people is called upon to become the senior partner in action. In effect, God was saying to humans: you stop the Holocaust. You bring the redemption. You act to ensure that it will never again occur. I will be with you totally in whatever happens, but you must do it.'[8] Based on this theological reversal in divine-human responsibility after the Holocaust, Greenberg strongly argues for the assumption of power on the part of the human community that is unprecedented. For Greenberg it would be morally irresponsible to abandon the quest for power today, as some in the religious community have urged. The only option in the post-Holocaust world that will enable us to avoid repetitions of human degradation and evil akin to what surfaced during the Nazi era is for the human community to combine the assumption of new power over creation with what Greenberg terms the development of 'better mechanisms of self-criticism, correction and repentance'. Only in this way will humankind utilize power 'without being the unwitting slave of bloodshed or an explo-itative status quo'.[9]

Though Greenberg wrote these words some years ago, I still find them a compelling interpretation of the new challenge to human responsibility in light of the Holocaust. I especially concur with Greenberg's insistence on the human community's assumption of power. For that reason I find myself at odds as a social ethicist with those of my colleagues who espouse an unqualified pacifist position or what is known as the 'deep' ecological perspective which tends to submerge humanity within creation as such, destroying awareness of the enhanced dimensions of human responsibility in our day. But I do feel that Greenberg has carried the theological role reversal too far. Viewing God as the 'junior partner' renders God overly impotent in terms of creational respons-ibility. I would opt for a more co-equal relationship, though with a redefined under-standing of divine responsibility.

The language of co-creatorship, developed mostly in Christian theological literature, even in official Catholic documents coming from Pope John Paul II and various conferences of bishops,[10] but also present in some Jewish writings,[11] represents the most promising paradigm after the Holocaust. While this notion of co-creatorship has roots in the biblical tradition,[12] its full magnitude has become apparent only in light of such events as the Holocaust and, as theologian Philip Hefner has emphasized, with our enhanced appreciation of the vast evolutionary process in which the role of human responsibility emerges as absolutely decisive.[13]

There have been critics of the notion of human co-creatorship among biblical scholars and within ethical circles where a scholar such as Stanley Hauerwas has strongly criticized Pope John Paul II's appropriation of 'co-creatorship' in his encyclical *Laborem exercens*[14] on the grounds that it would lead to a Nazi-like mentality within the human community. Some ecological activists also reject the notion out of hand on the grounds that it would open the door to creational destruction by intensifying the already existing hierarchical model of society. Surely any affirmation of human co-creatorship must be tempered by the notion that the Creator God retains a central role in the process of caring for and preserving creation. Hence my rejection of any 'junior status' role for God along the lines suggested by Greenberg. And Hauerwas' call for 'humility' in the use of human power in light of the Holocaust sounds an important cautionary note for any co-creatorship paradigm. But to enshrine 'humility' as the prevailing motif for understanding the human/divine responsibility problematic would likely prevent humankind from assuming full governance of creation, a failure that might well entail economic, ecological and even nuclear disaster on a global scale.

Unless we recognize that human responsibility has been raised to a new level in consequence of the Holocaust and through our improved understanding of the evolutionary dynamic the human community will likely refrain from taking those decisive steps that will ensure the continuity of life at all levels of creation. To follow Hauerwas or the deep ecologists in terms of envisioning humankind's role in creational governance may well result in people of faith becoming bystanders rather than central actors in human history. To ensure that the notion of co-creatorship does not wind up elevating human power to a new destructive level, we need to reaffirm the role of divine responsibility, but in a refined sense. The paradigm of an all-powerful God who will intervene to halt human and creational destruction is simply dead after the Holocaust and in light of our contemporary evolutionary consciousness. On this point the Nazi ideologues were perceptive. Where their vision was fatally flawed, and so humanly destructive, was in responding to the 'death' of the interventionist God with an assertion, as Michael Ryan once put it, of all-pervasive power for themselves.[15]

If we are successfully to curb the excessive use of human power within a paradigm of co-creatorship we must reintroduce into human consciousness, especially in our now highly secularized societies parented by the Enlightenment and its revolutionary heritage, a deep sense of what I have called a 'compelling' God. This compelling God whom we must come to experience through symbolic encounter that is both personal and cultural will result in a healing, a strengthening, an affirming that will bury any need to assert our humanity, to try to 'overpower' the Creator God, through the destructive, even deadly use of human power. This sense of a compelling parent God who has gifted humanity, whose vulnerability for the Christian has been shown in the Cross (as Jurgen Moltmann has well articulated in *The Crucified God*)[16] is the indispensable foundation for any adequate paradigm of co-creatorship today.

I remain convinced that the notion of a compelling God, a God to whom we are drawn rather than a God who simply imposes upon us, must be sustained both in our personal consciousness and in our societal consciousness. This latter point is especially challenging for those of us who subscribe to the vision of church-state separation enshrined in Western democracies and which, for Catholicism, was raised to a level of theological principle at the II Vatican Council in its Declaration on Religious Liberty.[17] Nonetheless we also need to take very seriously Vatican II's Declaration on the Church in the Modern World which strongly emphasized the centrality of culture in shaping morality both public and personal. Unless a sense of a compelling God is integrated into Western communal consciousness, not in a fundamentalistic or exclusivistic way but as a true moral barometer, I fear that personal consciousness of a compelling God by itself will prove ineffective in guarding against the abuse of human co-creatorship. It could easily lead, as the church historian Clyde Manschreck warned some years ago, to 'naked state sovereignty'.[18]

To sum up my first major point, the Holocaust and our contemporary evolutionary consciousness force upon us a major reformulation of divine and human responsibility. It will have to be a reformulation that takes into account the prophetic words uttered by Catholic philosopher Romano Guardini soon after the Holocaust: 'In the coming epoch, the essential problem will no longer be that of increasing power – though power will continue to increase at an even swifter tempo – but of curbing it. The core of the new epoch's intellectual task will be to integrate power into life in such a way that man can employ power without forfeiting his humanity, or to surrender his humanity to power and perish.'[19] Neither a return to religious fundamentalism nor a paradigm of 'junior level' divine agency will respond adequately to this challenge. Only a vision of human co-creatorship anchored in a personal and communal sense of a 'compelling' God has the possibility of meeting that challenge.

THE NEED FOR STRUCTURAL JUSTICE

If the human community is truly to confront its heightened sense of responsibility in this new millennium we will also need to deal with several other issues beyond the funda-mental perception of the divine-human relationship. These include the significance of structural justice for maintaining a sense of co-creatorship, the basic importance of a commitment to human rights and, finally, an understanding of the role of the vitalistic in sustaining moral commitment and in what some have termed the 'ritual containment' of evil in society.

In recent years two leading ethicists centrally involved about the moral implications of the Holocaust, Peter Haas of Vanderbilt and Didier Pollefeyt of the Catholic University of Leuven (Belgium) have debated the issue of structural morality during the Nazi era. Haas launched this discussion with the publication of his volume *Morality After Ausch-witz: The Radical Challenge of the Nazi Ethic* in 1988.[20] In that book Haas asked the question why the Nazis failed to recognize evil as evil and, as a consequence, why they made no effort to distance themselves from it. His response given in *Morality After Auschwitz* and in subsequent writings takes the following direction. The Nazi ideologues created what appeared to many as a scientifically valid ethic. 'The problem,' he says, 'is that a moral system that is thought out and elaborated along "scientific" lines, that is through the application of a strict logic, hardens such facts into universal givens.' This results, according to Haas, in a loss of any sense of the difference between murder and killing. 'Morality' becomes much more a matter of acting in a way that 'fits' the pre-established system. For Haas, the scientific system removes from my consciousness any notion of myself as having personal morality responsibility for my actions: 'I then lose sight of my own moral agency, of my own power to create not only the acts through my observation of them, but also to create the text that gives the act its moral value. I at that moment stop being a moral agent and become instead a passive actor in someone else's drama.'[21] Haas goes on to say that ultimately what went awry with what Haas terms 'the Nazi ethic' was that it pre-defined morality for people under its sway. It proclaimed not only what was right and what was wrong from a scientific perspective, and therefore unquestionable, but also what actions fell into each category: 'The result was,' Haas insists, 'that people did atrocious things because they took them to be morally mandated. The Nazi morality pre-defined what was acceptable to such an extent, and in such an authoritative, scientific way, that many people, especially intellectuals, simply fell into line. The living relationship between the human as moral agent on the one hand, and the moral act on the other was lost.'[22] He concludes by affirming the need to maintain a moral foundation for ethics today that is rooted in the dynamics of human relationship, cooperation, openness to the other and compassion for the other.

Didier Pollefeyt takes issue with Haas on several points, including whether we can speak of a 'Nazi ethic'. He prefers to speak of Nazism as having 'perverted' authentic morality. But he does in the end recognize the systematic nature of the Nazi approach to human acts. For him, it is better to view Nazism as espousing a 'totalitarian ethic'. But, just as Haas, Pollefeyt emphasizes that such an ethic generates 'moral sameness' by removing any personal sense of responsibility from the response framework. He agrees with Haas that the Nazi ideologues created a closed ethic in which any response that did not fit into the preconceived pattern was eliminated. Such an ethic, Pollefeyt also underlines, eliminates any sense of mercy and compassion. It removes God as a moral barometer of any sort. Instead 'God' is used to legitimate the closed and murderous social order.

For Pollefeyt Nazism became a politics without a true ethical framework. It had no room for alterity and demanded the eradication of anything that was not in conformity with 'the system'. 'As such,' he argues, 'Nazism was an idolatrous effort that radicalised itself and eliminated everything that did not conform.... This is for us the primary lesson of the Nazi genocide, but also of other forms of racism and discrimination, such as nationalism, sexism or religious fundamentalism.'[23]

In my judgement both Haas and Pollefeyt have uncovered a crucial dimension of Nazism that remains critical for understanding the moral challenge before us today. In highlighting the importance of the Nazi framework for human response, whether one decides to call it an ethic or not, they have shown that a central characteristic of modernity (and one might argue post-modernity as well) is the determination of morality by political and cultural structures. Nazism was the first modern political system to 'programme' human societal responses in a systematic fashion.

Historian Peter Hayes of Northwestern University has further illuminated this dimension of Nazism in his continuing research on business leaders in the period of the Third Reich.[24] Hayes concludes that in the end German big business were willing 'to walk over corpses'. There were many factors internal to Germany that contributed to this process of moral numbing. But, above all, says Hayes, was the fact that 'the Third Reich constructed a framework of economic policy in which the effective pursuit of corporate survival or success had to serve, at least outwardly, the goals and ideological requirements of the regime.'[25] The indifference of German businessmen during the Third Reich, Hayes continues, reveals the all-too-common penchant in the modern world to hide behind so-called professional responsibilities in the face of a deep moral challenge. 'The obligation to achieve the best possible return for the firm and those who own or work for it to secure their long term prospects, which in decent contexts can be a guarantee against personal corruption or frivolous management, became an excuse for participating in cruel, eventually murderous acts, indeed a mandate to do so.'[26] Most alarming about this development was not even the complicity in murder, but a sense of innocence about such complicity on the part of very many of the businessmen. They were able to subdue any moral hesitations they may have experienced with the response, 'What else can I do?' losing sight of the far more important question, according to Hayes, 'What must I never do?'[27]

Hayes' studies provide solid data for the position of Haas and Pollyfeyt about the erosion of a sense of personal responsibility within Nazi culture. They also serve as a warning for a similar situation that is taking hold in society today in the name of globalization. 'What else can I do?' has in fact increasingly become a stock phrase in the vocabulary of global capitalism. The dynamics of the market must reign supreme no matter what the cost in human terms, no matter that, as a recent European Union report has shown, some 250 million children around the world are used to support this system, living in conditions in many instances of virtual slavery. Pope John Paul II, in what may prove in the end to be his most prophetic concern, has warned that the global ideology of the market, which has tended to replace the competing Cold War ideologies in recent years, cannot ensure the preservation of human dignity. 'The rapid advance toward the globalization of economic and financial systems also illustrates the urgent need to establish who is responsible for guaranteeing the global common good and the exercise of economic and social rights. The free market by itself cannot do this, because in fact there are many human needs which have no place in the market.'[28] In an address to a Vatican meeting of scholars and political leaders convened by Pope John Paul II at Castel Gandolfo in August 1998 former American national security adviser Zbigniew Brzezinski argued along much the same lines as the Pope himself, calling for an increasing sensitivity to social responsibility within our global economic system. 'That sensitivity,' he maintained, 'has to be as important a consideration as efficiency and performance in the determination of economic decisions and guiding economic development.'[29]

The so-called 'Nazi ethic' has opened up what unquestionably is the most decisive moral question of the last century and into the next millennium. How can the human community maintain a sense of human responsibility in a global system of human organization? The Holocaust has shown us how destructive a failure to address this question head-on can be for human and creational survival.

THE HOLOCAUST AND HUMAN RIGHTS

In this section I would like to speak specifically as a Catholic. It is my conviction that the absence of a human rights tradition contributed significantly to moral failures on the part of Catholics during the Third Reich.

Modernity, especially the Enlightenment with its creation of new pluralistic societies rooted in individual equality and human rights, posed a real dilemma for classical Catholic thought. In many instances Catholics were not above appealing for protection under the laws of the new democratic, secular societies. But their theology had not yet freed itself from the ideal of Catholic domination of the state where that could be achieved nor the principle that human liberties were ultimately dependent on adherence to the authentic faith tradition possessed by Catholicism.[30]

In the United States the appropriating of the liberal tradition of the Enlightenment was not predicated on hostility towards religion as it was in Europe. American revolutionary leaders never placed the goddess of reason on the high altar and some of them, such as Jefferson and Franklin, proposed a national seal for the United States depicting Moses crossing the Red Sea – something totally unthinkable to their French compatriots. While U.S. Catholics generally continued to hold to the classical theology of Church dominance over the state despite their rather enthusiastic practical embrace of American pluralism, the American liberal ethos eventually generated new thinking on the theological level as well. The most prominent name in this regard was, of course, Fr. John Courtney Murray, S.J., who eventually would become a primary contributor to Vatican II's *Declaration On Religious Liberty*. Clearly American Catholicism was a decisive conduit for the eventual acceptance of the liberal tradition and its core commitment to human rights by global Catholicism at Vatican II.

When we come to the question of Catholicism and the Holocaust, we still are very much in a pre-Vatican II mindset in terms of the Church's attitude towards the public order. Here it is critical to stress the profound differences between liberalism in America and liberalism in Europe which, unlike its American counterpart, displayed profound hostility toward all forms of Christianity. A virtual state of war existed between the liberals of Europe, especially in the form of freemasonry, and the Catholic leadership in particular. Even Catholic liberals who claimed a Christian basis for democratic principles were castigated by Catholic authorities with some leaving the Church.[31] The liberals were identified with a deliberate attempt to overthrow the prevailing social order and, in the case of Italy, to undermine Rome's sovereignty over the Papal States. In 1832 Pope Gregory XVI issued an encyclical *Mirari vos* against the 'errors' and 'evils' of those 'shameless lovers of liberty' and those Catholic reformers who maintained the idea that 'liberty of conscience must be maintained for everyone.'

Gregory XVI's successor as Pope, Pius IX, was first thought somewhat more sympathetic to liberal ideas because of political reforms he introduced at the outset of his Pontificate. But as the challenge to Vatican sovereignty over the Papal States grew strong, Pius IX became more vocal in his opposition to liberalism. In 1864 he issued the famous *Syllabus of Errors* which condemned liberalism as an 'absurd principle' which argued that the state should treat all religions alike without distinction. In Italy he forbade Catholics to serve in the government or even vote in general elections. For the clergy trained in this era and who established the tone in the Catholic Church for the coming decades, liberalism was the political programme of Freemasons who oppressed Christianity and opposed its values.

The accession of Leo XIII to the Papacy in 1878 brought a bit of moderation to the Catholic war against liberalism. Leo encouraged French Catholics to abandon their notion of restoring a Catholic monarchy and instead urged them to utilize their constitutional liberties for the good of the Church. But on the theological level he described any notion of Church-state separation as a 'fatal error'. While he was open to a measure of toleration in the public order, he refused to recognize that unconditional rights to freedom of speech, worship, etc. could ever become part of Catholic teaching. In the Italian context he was especially condemnatory of the Freemasons and their liberal ideas. He described them as part of the kingdom of Satan which was at war with God in their struggle against the Church and Christendom. He spoke of a conspiracy at work that was endangering the very fabric of Christian civilization.

The thirties were a time of great anxiety among Catholic leaders in Germany, France and elsewhere that the Weimar Republic's liberal governmental model, which in part was now associated with the Jews, would cause the final collapse of the classical Christian notion of the social order. Many Protestant leaders shared this apprehension. Pope Pius XI, in his social encyclical *Quadragesimo anno* (1931) hoped that the experiences of the stock market crash in 1929 and the harsh realities of the Russian revolution would turn people away from liberalism and socialism. He proposed an organic notion of society heavily rooted in the medieval Catholic social vision. Liberalism again was soundly denounced as opposed to the Catholic social vision in this encyclical.

My point is therefore that the two Popes of the Holocaust era, Pius XI and Pius XII, worked within the framework of a century-long crusade against liberalism. They were not enamoured with fascism. Pius XI in his anti-Nazi encyclical (with which Cardinal Pacelli, the future Pius XII, was closely associated in his role as Papal Secretary of State) soundly denounced Nazism. But when the Church faced the hard choice of a coalition partner, liberalism (and socialism) were ruled out as realistic possibilities because of the priority of defending the Catholic social order. Fascism, and even Nazism, despite their severe limitations as ideologies, became the preferred options for protecting Catholic institutional interests. Historians such as Michael Marrus are quite correct in arguing that the primary goal of Vatican policy during the Nazi era was 'the safeguarding of the institutional interests of the Church in a perilous political world'.[32] Marrus does not find in Vatican documents any clear indication of pro-Nazi sympathies or the supremacy of opposition to the USSR. These documents clearly demonstrate that neither simple hostility nor indifference explains Rome's posture during this critical period. What the documents do establish with reasonable certainty is the dominance of a policy of 'reserve and conciliation' under Pius XII, a policy that shaped not only his personal approach but strongly influenced the basic tenor of the Church's diplomatic corps as well. Marrus puts it this way: 'The goal was to limit the global conflict where possible, and above all to protect the influence and standing of the Church as an independent voice.... Fearful ... of threats from the outside, the Pope dared not confront the Nazis or the Italian Fascists directly.'[33]

Within such an ecclesiastical framework the human rights of Jews, and even of basically Catholic victims of the Nazis such as the Poles and the Roma (Gypsies), had little or no priority. Viewed in the context of a fundamental commitment to ecclesiastical preservation for the sake of a moral public order and ultimately for the sake of human salvation, Jews, Poles, Gypsies and other victim groups became, to use the language of Nora Levin,[34] 'unfortunate expendables'. Polish American historian Richard Lukas[35] and Catholic historian John Morley[36] have both noted, for example, strong Polish criticism of Pius XII within Poland itself and from the Polish government-in-exile in London. The fact that human rights was a centrepiece of the discredited liberal tradition (expressed in part in the popular culture generated during the 'liberal' Weimar Republic) associated with the Masonic conspiracy against Christianity only enhanced the Catholic Church's capacity to push concern for individual victims to the periphery of, or even beyond the edge, of moral concern.

The lack of a human rights perspective thus significantly curtailed the Catholic institutional response to Nazism. Now that we are coming to see that at the level of institutional Christianity fear of liberalism and concern for the loss of the Church's influence over the public order were in fact stronger motives for acquiescence or even collaboration with Nazism and Fascism than classical Christian antisemitism itself, we are in a position to ask seriously whether the Church's response would have been different if those Christian voices who advocated incorporation of dimensions of the liberal vision into Christianity, including its human rights vision, had been heeded. And what if Church leaders had made a concerted effort to establish a working relationship with the liberal opposition to Nazism despite that opposition's widespread hostility to religious belief? I recognize hindsight can never reproduce the difficulty of the actual challenge in this regard. But my suspicion is that if Catholicism had earlier embraced aspects of the liberal vision prior to the rise of Nazism, rather than adopting the position of fierce opposition that I summarized earlier on in this essay, such a coalition would have proven far more feasible. Whether it would have resulted in the survival of many more Jews, Poles and Roma is an open question. Some prominent historians such as Michael Marrus and Gunther Lewy believe it would not have made much difference. But on the level of protecting the Church's basic moral integrity, it might have proven quite significant.

The reality is that as we move towards the latter years of the Nazi era we see some profound changes beginning, even within the mind set of Pius XII. In his Christmas radio addresses to Europe in 1940, 1941 and 1942, Pius XII began to speak of the need for an entirely new global order. What one detects here is a decisive turn by the Vatican leadership away from its linkage with Nazism and Fascism and its support of the old monarchial order. No longer is liberalism denounced in the manner of the social encyclicals of 1891 and 1931. Pius was beginning to see that World War II had rendered the classical Catholic social vision barren. Something new was needed. Pius XII was not himself to provide this new vision. But it is interesting to note, for example, some definite increase in activity on his part in terms of the Jewish community during this period. Can we prove cause and effect? Not exactly. But I suspect that there might have been some connection between the changing political vision and the increase in human-itarian efforts on behalf of Jews.

In bringing these observations on human rights and the Holocaust to a close, let me say that while it is important to ask what might have been during the Holocaust had the Catholic Church headed the calls of important Catholic thinkers such as Felicite de Lamennais and Henri Lacordaire for Catholicism to integrate some of the good aspects of liberal thought (including liberalism's emphasis on human rights) into its own perspective,[37] it is even more vital to reflect on what the Church's posture should be as a Christian community today. We cannot change the record of the World War II Church, though, as the late Cardinal Joseph Bernardin insisted,[38] we should confront it as honestly as possible. But we are in a position to shape the response of the Church in this new millennium.

In the first place, we need to take very seriously the point made by Professor Donald Dietrich in his volume *God and Humanity: Jewish–Christian Relations and Sanctioned Murder*. Dietrich argues that 'the Holocaust has reemphasized the need to highlight the person as THE central factor in the social order to counterbalance state power.'[39] Put another way, any authentic notion of ecclesiology after the experience of the Holocaust must make human rights a central component. The vision of the Church that must direct post-Holocaust Christian thinking is one that sees the survival of all persons as integral to the authentic survival of the Church itself. Jews, Poles, the Roma, gays and the disabled should not have been viewed as 'unfortunate expendables' during the Nazi period. There is no place for any similar classification today. There is no way for Christianity, or for any other religious tradition, to survive meaningfully if it allows the death or suffering of other people to become a byproduct of its efforts at self-preservation. Surely for Christians a communal sense of ethics must accompany the commitment to personal human rights. But no communal ethical vision can ever remove personal human rights from the centre of its concern.

There definitely appears to be some understanding of the shift in ecclesiological vision demanded by the experience of the Holocaust. I can cite several examples such as the stance of many of the churches in South Africa in the face of apartheid, the strong support given by local church leaders to the revolution that brought down the Marcos regime in the Philippines and the courageous stance taken by the Catholic bishops of Malawi when the late Dr. Hastings Banda threatened the human rights of many of the country's citizens. The last situation is especially relevant because the bishops were willing to risk institutional Church survival when President Banda made a serious threat to murder them and their catechists if they continued in their protest on behalf of people who, in most instances, were not Catholic or even Christian.

But the picture is not all positive. In the Philippines and in South Africa Catholic bishops had to go against the papal representatives who urged caution and even support for the incumbent regimes. The situations in such countries as Haiti and Argentina clearly show a Catholic leadership that had learned little or nothing from the experience of the Holocaust.

My second concluding observation follows upon the perspective comment of Professor Gordon Zahn, author of the first major scholarly study on Catholic attitudes towards Nazism.[40] Zahn maintained that the overriding lesson for religious communities emerging from an analysis of the Holocaust is that they can ill afford to become so enmeshed in a particular socio-political experiment that they lose their potential for constructive dissent and disobedience. He writes that

> ...the Church must recognize that it has a stake in maintaining a separation of Church and state as that separation is defined from its own perspective. It is a serious mistake to see that separation... only in terms of protecting the purity and independence of the secular order from unwarranted intrusions or domination by the spiritual. The problem as it developed in Germany... is also one of preserving the purity and independence of the spiritual community and its teaching from domination by the national state, with its definitions of situational needs and priorities.[41]

Only with such a separation will the Church have the freedom to pursue its prophetic mission of standing up for the human rights of all.

Clearly, then, I hope that I have demonstrated that the Holocaust was and remains a major challenge for reflection on the central issue of human rights in our day. This is true for Catholicism, for religious communities in general, and for society at large. Pastor Martin Niemoller remains as prophetic as ever: If we try to preserve ourselves by denying or ignoring the human rights of others, in the end we will all perish.

SUSTAINING HUMAN RESPONSIBILITY THROUGH RITUAL

My interest in the topic of ritual and the Holocaust has been instigated by the writings of three scholars in particular. They are the Catholic liturgist David Power, the ethicist Reinhold Niebuhr and the historian George Mosse. In addition, my colleague in the Hyde Park Cluster of Theological Schools, the psychologist Robert Moore, has provoked my thinking with his emphasis on what he calls 'ritual containment' if society is to develop a sensitivity to justice and human rights along the lines underlined earlier in this essay. What all these scholars have shown is that human reason by itself cannot guarantee human responsibility because the human person is an intricate blend of reason and what Niebuhr termed the 'vitalistic'. Any adequate social morality must recognize that good and evil emerge from both human faculties. Yet, as I have shown in other writings,[42] there has been a strong tendency in Western thinking, including Western ethical thought, to downplay the role of the vitalistic.

The regeneration of the vitalistic side of humanity, albeit in highly destructive directions, stood at the heart of the Nazi enterprise. The historian J.L. Talmon once described Nazi ideology as the denial of any 'final station of redemption in history' which gave birth to a cult of power and vitality as needs in themselves.[43] The Nazis became aware of the tremendous power of this vitalistic dimension. No scholar has made this point as clearly as George Mosse who spent considerable time examining the impact of the Nazi public liturgies during his scholarly career. While it verges on the obscene to give the Nazis credit for anything, Mosse's writings demonstrate that the Nazi leadership was extremely perceptive in recognizing the influence of symbolism in human life.[44] The contemporary Holocaust scholar Irving Greenberg has also acknowledged the significance of this aspect of Nazism. Reflecting on the failure of Enlightenment-based liberalism to provide an effective moral counterweight to the Nazi manipulation of human vitalism shows the inadequacy of any exclusively rational-based morality after the Holocaust. Greenberg makes this point quite strongly:

> How naive the nineteenth-century polemic with religion appears to be in retrospect: how simple Feuerbach, Nietzsche, and many others. The entire structure of autonomous logic

and sovereign human reason now takes on a sinister character... For Germany was one of the most 'advanced' Western countries – at the heart of the academic, scientific, and technological enterprise. All the talk about 'atavism' cannot obscure the way in which such behaviour is the outgrowth of democratic and modem values, as well as pagan gods.[45]

One of the convictions that has continued to deepen within me as I have studied the Holocaust these many years under the tutelage of colleagues such as Mosse and Greenberg and within a framework of reflection provided by the likes of liturgist David Power and ethicist Reinhold Niebuhr is that moral sensitivity remains an indispensable prelude to moral reasoning. We ethicists can provide the necessary clarifications of human response mandated by such sensitivity. Such clarifications are absolutely essential if religious experience is not to degenerate into religious fanaticism. But, as an ethicist, I cannot create the sensitivity itself. Mere appeals to reason, authority, and/or natural law will prove ineffective by themselves. Such sensitivity will reemerge only through a new awareness of God's intimate link with humankind, in suffering and joy, through symbolic experience. Nothing short of this will suffice in light of the Holocaust.

I see an urgent need to counter the growing one-dimensionality in Western society in the midst of a growing awareness of human power and freedom through the development of a new moral sensitivity. This moral sensitivity must be engendered by a symbolic encounter with the Creator God who speaks to us in a new compelling way, along the lines I outlined in the first part of this essay. Strange as it may seem, the Holocaust provides us with some help in this regard. For if the Holocaust reveals one permanent quality of human life, it is the enduring presence of, the ongoing need for, symbolic communication. Mothers often sang to their children in the camps up till the door of the gas chambers. Camp music and camp songs were vital to survival for the inmates as well as a source of defiance to the evil all around them.[46] But we must be clear. The experience of the vitalistic in our life is no guarantee of goodness. As Didier Pollefeyt has observed, 'Creativity... does not automatically generate goodness. Sometimes aesthetics and crimes coincide. Some Nazis, for example, read poetry after their duty.'[47] And clearly public ritual played a central role in the implementation of Nazi ideology. That is why the text and structure of liturgy become so significant.

Many experiences of prayer and meditation may be vitalistically energizing. But they remain neutral in terms of human responsibility in the social arena because there are no directional texts connected with them. Regrettably, in the West, ritual has often been relegated almost exclusively to the realm of play and recreation. Yet it is the power inherent in this vitalistic side of humanity that ritual has the greatest potential for channelling into an intensification of human responsibility.

In light of the Holocaust we can no longer afford to give scant attention to the vitalistic dimension of humanity, to reduce it simply to the realm of play and recreation, if we hope to develop the sense of human responsibility to which the Holocaust summons us. The development of moral reasoning remains crucial; but it is no substitute for the healing of the destructive tendencies in humanity's vitalistic side with required symbolic encounter with a loving God. Without ritual containment of the vitalistic dimension of human life human responsibility cannot grow.

CONCLUDING REFLECTIONS

My reflections in this essay have primarily focused on the more overarching moral implications of the Holocaust, implications that require continued addressing as we begin a new millennium. But I would be remiss if I completely overlooked the significance of Holocaust as a central moment in the long, generally conflictual history of the Christian–Jewish relationship. Emphasizing the more general moral implications of the Holocaust can never allow us to overlook its more specific moral dimensions. While the churches and some church leaders and members did respond to the Jewish catastrophe, far too many stood on the sidelines and some even actively collaborated with the effort. If the churches are to press the general moral implications of the Holocaust I have outlined above, they can only do so with credibility in the world community if they first confront their pronounced failure during this critical era. While I would affirm the argument made by important scholars that the Nazi attack on the Jews represented a quantum leap beyond classical Christian antisemitism, there is no denying that a significant link existed between the two forms of antisemitism. Historically the Christian church tried to marginalize the Jews and render them perpetually miserable as a punishment for their supposed killing of Christ and as a warning of what will happen to those who stray from the Christian path. The Nazis' goal was total annihilation of the world Jewish community. We cannot lose sight of the difference. But on the popular level especially traditional Christian antisemitism provided an indispensable seed bed for the considerable success achieved by the Nazis in pursuit of the goal.

The Vatican document *We Remember* goes a long way in moving Catholicism towards a confrontation with its role during the Holocaust. It may yet make a profound difference if its call for Holocaust education throughout the Catholic world is heeded. But one of its significant failures is to connect complicity in the Holocaust on the part of Catholic individuals with the tradition of Christian antisemitism. The 'wayward brothers and sisters' in terms of antisemitism indicted in this document went astray not because of some marginal teachers but because degradation of the Jews was commonplace in the preaching, catechesis and church art which was the ordinary fare of their life in the church. This is not clearly enough recognized in *We Remember*, though Cardinal Cassidy, principal author of the document, in a subsequent commentary on the text does do better in making the direct linkage.[48]

The churches must be prepared to take direct responsibility for an important role in forming the prevailing negative image of Jews and Judaism over the centuries in Western society, an image that directly contributed to popular acquiescence and even outright support for Nazism despite the fact that the roots of Nazi ideology lay elsewhere. It is insufficient for the churches merely to point to the difference between Christian antisemitism and the Nazi variety. If they are to restore their moral integrity and become strong supporters of the new depth of human responsibility to which the experience of the Holocaust calls humankind in the 21st century, they must first come to grips with their general failure in moral responsibility towards Hitler's victims, particularly the Jews. Nothing else will suffice. Anything short of this will make appeals for enhanced general moral responsibility ring hollow.

NOTES

1 Victor Ferkiss, *The Future of Technological Civilization* (New York: George Braziller, 1974), p.88.
2 Hans Jonas, *The Imperative of Responsibility* (Chicago: University of Chicago Press, 1984). Jonas has also reflected on the ethical implications of the Holocaust, but regrettably has never integrated these separate reflections. See Hans Jonas, *Mortality and Morality: A Search for the Good After Auschwitz* (Evanston, IL: Northwestern University Press, 1996), and Hans Jonas, 'The concept of God after Auschwitz: a Jewish voice', *Journal of Religion*, January 1987: 143–157.

3 See John T. Pawlikowski, OSM, *The Challenge of the Holocaust for Christian Theology* (New York: Anti-Defamation League, 1982); John T. Pawlikowski, 'Christian Theological Concerns After the Holocaust', in Eugene J. Fisher (ed.), *Visions of the Other: Jewish and Christian Theologians Assess the Dialogue* (New York/Mahwah: Paulist 1994), p.285; and John T. Pawlikowski, 'Christian Ethics and the Holocaust: A Dialogue with Post-Auschwitz Judaism', *Theological Studies* (December 1988): 649–669.

4 Emil Fackenheim, *The Jewish Return Into History* (New York: Schocken Books, 1978), p.246.

5 See John T. Pawlikowski, 'Uniqueness and Universality in the Holocaust: Some Ethical Reflections', in Linda Bennett Elder, David L. Barr and Elizabeth Struthers Malbon (eds.), *Biblical and Human, A Festschrift for John F. Priest* (Atlanta: Scholars Press, 1996), pp.275–289.

6 Uriel Tal, 'Forms of Pseudo-Religion in the German Kulturbereich Prior to the Holocaust', *Imannual* 3 (1973–74): 69; and Uriel Tal, *Christians and Jews in Germany: Religion, Politics and Ideology in the Second Reich, 1870–1914* (Ithaca: Cornell University Press, 1975).

7 Irving Greenberg, 'The Voluntary Covenant', *Perspectives* #3 (New York: National Jewish Resource Center, 1982), p.15.

8 *ibid.*, pp.17–18.

9 Irving Greenberg, 'The Third Great Cycle in Jewish History', *Perspectives* #1 (New York: National Jewish Resource Center, 1981), pp.24–25.

10 For the texts of Pope John Paul 11's Encyclical *Laborem Exercens* (On Human Work) and the U.S. Catholic Bishops Pastoral Letter on the Economy, see David J. O'Brien and Thomas A. Shannon (eds.), *Catholic Social thought: The Documentary Heritage* (Maryknoll. NY: Orbis Books, 1992), pp.350–392; 572–680. For the text of the U.S. Bishops' statement on the energy see Hugh J. Nolan (ed.), *Pastoral Letters of the United States Catholic Bishops, Vol.IV (1975–1983)* (Washington: National Conference of Catholic Bishops/United States Catholic Conference, 1983), pp.438–463. For the text of the Canadian Bishops' statement on the Canadian economy, see David M. Byers (ed.), General Introduction and Document Introductions by John T. Pawlikowski, OSM, *Justice In the Marketplace: Collected Statement of the Vatican and the United States Catholic Bishops on Economic Policy, 1891–1984* (Washington: United States Catholic Conference, 1985), pp.480–491.

11 David Hartman, *A Living Covenant: The Innovative Spirit in Traditional Judaism* (New York: Free Press, and London: Collier Macmillan Publishers, 1985).

12 John T. Pawlikowski, 'Co-Creators with a Compelling God', *Ecumenism* (June 1999): 8–11.

13 Philip J. Heffier, *The Human Factor: Evolution, Culture and Religion* (Minneapolis: Fortress, 1993); also see John T. Pawlikowski, OSM, 'Theological Dimensions of an Ecological Ethic', in Richard N. Fragomeni and John T. Pawlikowski (eds.), *The Ecological Challenge: Ethical, Liturgical and Spiritual Responses* (Collegeville, MN: Liturgical Press, 1994), pp.39–51.

14 Stanley Hauerwas, 'Jews and Christians Among the Nations', *Cross Currents* (Spring 1981): 34.

15 Michael Ryan, 'Hitler's Challenge to the Churches: A Theological – Political Analysis of *Mein Kampf*', in Franklin Littell and Hubert G. Locke (eds.), *The German Church Struggle and the Holocaust* (Detroit: Wayne State University Press, 1974), pp.160–161.

16 Jurgen Moltmann, *The Crucified God* (New York: Harper & Row, 1974).

17 See John T. Pawlikowski, OSM, 'Catholicism and the Public Church: Recent U.S. Developments', in D.M. Yeager (ed.), *The Annual of the Society of Christian Ethics 1989*, pp.147–165; and 'Walking With and Beyond John Courtney Murray', *New Theology Review*, August 1996, pp.20–40.

18 Clyde L. Manschreck, 'Chruch-State Relations – A Question of Sovereignty', in Clyde L. Manschreck and Barbara Brown Zikmund (eds.), *The American Religious Experiment: Piety and Practicality* (Chicago: Exploration Press, 1976), p.121.

19 Romano Guardini, *Power and Responsibility* (Chicago: Henry Regnery, 1961), p.xiii.

20 Peter J. Haas, *Morality After Auschwitz: The Radical Challenge* (Philadelphia: Fortress, 1988); also 'The Morality of Auschwitz: Moral Language and the Nazi Ethic', in Franklin Littell and others (eds.), *Remembering For The Future*, Vol.2 (Oxford: Pergamon, 1989), pp.1893–1902.

21 See Peter J. Haas, 'Fare etica in un'eta di scienza', in Emilio Baccarini and Lucy Thorson (eds.), *Il Bene e Il Male Dopo Auschwitz: Implicazioni Etico-Theologiche per L'oggi* (Milano: Paoline, 1998), p.176. An English version of this volume will appear soon from KTAV.

22 Peter Haas, 'Fare etica un un'eta di scienza', pp.176–177.

23 Didier Pollefeyt, 'Ma Moralita di Auschwitz? Confronto critico con l'interpretazione etica dell'Olocausto di Peter J. Haas', in Emilio Baccarini and Lucy Thorson (eds.), *Il Bene e Il Male Dopo Auschwitz*, p.204.

24 See Peter Hayes, *Industry and Ideology: I.G. Farben in the Nazi Era* (Cambridge: Cambridge University Press, 1988).

25 Peter Hayes, 'Conscience, Knowledge, and "Secondary Ethics"; German Corporate Executives from "Aryanization" to the Holocaust', Paper presented to the 1999 Bernardin Center Catholic-Jewish Studies Conference, Catholic Theological Union, Chicago, May 4, 1999, 25. This paper will be published as part of the conference proceedings by Sheed & Ward.

26 Peter Hayes, 'Conscience, Knowledge, and "Secondary Ethics"', p.25.

27 *ibid.*, p.26.

28 Pope John Paul II, 'Respect for Human Rights: The Secret of True Peace', 1999 World Day of Peace Message, *Origins* (24 December 1998): 491.

29 Zbigniew Brzezinski, 'Global Dilemmas Democracy Faces', *Origins* (3 September 1998): 210.

30 For more on the Catholic human rights tradition, See my articles 'Human Rights in the Roman Catholic Tradition', in Max Stackhouse (ed.) *Selected Papers: The American Society of Christian Ethics 1979*, 145–166 and 'Liberal Democracy, Human Rights, and the Holocaust: The Political and Historical Context of Pope Pius XII', *Catholic International*, October 1998, 454–458.

31 There were some individual Catholic leaders who did call for some reconciliation between Catholicism and the emerging liberal tradition. They generally were marginalized in the Catholic Church and in some cases left the Church entirely. See Thomas Bokenkotter, *Church and Revolution: Catholics in the Struggle for Democracy and Social Justice* (New York: Doubleday, An Image Book, 1998).

32 See Michael R. Marrus, 'The Vatican and the Holocaust', *Congress Monthly*, January 1988, 6.

33 Michael R. Marrus, 'The Vatican and the Holocaust', 7.

34 Nora Levin, *The Holocaust* (New York: Schocken, 1973), p.693.

35 Richard Lukas, *Forgotten Holocaust: The Poles Under German Occupation 1939–1944* (Lexington: University Press of Kentucky, 1986), p.16.

36 John Morley, *Vatican Diplomacy and the Jews During the Holocaust: 1939–1943*.

37 See Thomas Bokenkotter, *Church and Revolution*, chapters 1–4.

38 Cardinal Joseph L. Bernardin, *A Blessing To Each Other* (Chicago: Liturgy Training Publications, 1996), p.132.

39 Donald Dietrich, *God and Humanity In Auschwitz: Jewish–Christian Relations and Sanctioned Murder* (New Brunswick, NJ and London: Transaction, 1995), p.269.

40 See Gordon Zahn, *German Catholics and Hitler's Wars: A Study In Social Control* (New York: Sheed & Ward, 1962).

41 Gordon Zahn, 'Catholic Resistance? A Yes and a No', in Franklin H. Littell and Hubert G. Locke (eds.), *The German Church Struggle and The Holocaust* (Detroit: Wayne State University Press, 1974), pp.234–235.

42 See my 'Liturgy and the Holocaust: How do we Worship in an Age of Genocide', paper presented to a conference on Holocaust and Genocide, Boston College, 17 September 1999, to appear in the conference proceedings to be published by Syracuse University Press.

43 See J.L. Talmon, 'European History Seedbed of the Holocaust', *Midstream* (May 1973): 22–24.

44 See George Mosse, *The Nationalization of the Masses: Political Symbolism and Mass Movements In Germany From the Napoleonic Wars Through the Third Reich* (New York: New American Library, 1977).

45 Irving Greenberg, 'Cloud of Smoke, Pillar of Fire: Judaism, Christianity and Modernity after the Holocaust', in Eva Fleischner (ed.), *Auschwitz: Beginning of A New Era?* (New York: KATV, 1977), p.17.

46 See David H. Hirsch, 'Camp Music and Camp Songs: Szymon Laks and Aleksander Kulisiewicz', in G. Jan Colijn and Marcia Sachs Littell (eds.), *Confronting the Holocaust: A Mandate For The 21st Century* (Lanham/New York/Oxford: University Press of America, 1997), pp.157–168.

47 Didier Pollefeyt, 'Auschwitz or How Good People Can Do Evil: An Ethical Interpretation of the Perpetrators and Victims of the Holocaust in Light of the French Thinker Tzvetan Todorov', in G. Jan Colijn and Marcia Sachs Littell (eds.), *Confronting the Holocaust*, p.108.
48 See my essay, 'The Vatican and the Holocaust: Putting We Remember In Context', *Dimensions* 12:2, 11–16; also see Secretarist for Ecumenical and Interreligious Relations, *Catholics Remember The Holocaust* (Washington: United States Catholic Conference, 1998).

GERMAN-JEWISH PHILOSOPHERS FACING THE SHOAH

Julius Simon

'This is how one pictures the angel of history. His face is turned toward the past.
Where we perceive a chain of events, he sees one single catastrophe
which keeps piling wreckage upon wreckage and hurls it in front of his feet.
The angel would like to stay, awaken the dead, and make whole what has been smashed.
But a storm is blowing from Paradise;
it has got caught in his wings with such violence that the angel can no longer close them.
This storm irresistibly propels him into the future to which his back is turned,
while the pile of debris before him grows skyward.
This storm is what we call progress.'

—Walter Benjamin

A S WE face the past in considering the events of the 20th century, we tend to
continue to describe armed conflicts as *theatres of war*, our backs to the future.
Such descriptions presuppose that we are capable of speaking about how the
actions are staged and performed and that the experience of such events is not only
presentable but also capable of representation. As we look back through the debris, we
also notice another tendency, i.e., that genocides frequently have been associated with
actions of modern war and rationalized and justified as necessary extensions of violent
struggles for survival. This has been no less the case in, most recently, the Balkans, than
during the 1970s in Rwanda or Cambodia and from 1939–45 in Nazi Germany. Speaking
of genocide as a kind of 'theatre', however, seems even more absurd than referring to the
performative acts of war in terms of protagonistic and antagonistic actors, directors,
spectators, and impartial critics of the whole process. But what other choice do we have
than to deal with the terms of absurdity? Are we not constrained in our engagements
with others to *act* in one way or another through exercising simulation or dissimulation,
revealing or concealing our intentions or desires behind the masks which we daily don?
Are we not forced to admit and confront what are considered human aberrations from
our stipulations of *normal* human behaviour? Are we not also then constrained to
engage again and again in the difficult tasks of expression and interpretation of
signs and gestures? Given that constraint, in the intermingling of our roles as actor,
spectator and critic, then, we present and perceive public faces which are marked and
masked with lines and traces of our ethical relations. Both the wonder and the tragedy of
being human occurs in the faces we encounter and in how we inscribe our lives in facing
or turning our backs away from the other, a face animated in play between the

possibilities and realizations of joy and suffering, of honesty and deceit. The question then becomes: when confronted with the other's face do I respond to their sensual call or do I reduce that other to an object of instrumental calculation, processed through material utilization – a mere object of my self-extension? Do I allow myself to be reduced?

Mistrusting historical realism, critical of the abuse of attempts to systematically represent to each other in writing, or any other form of signification, adequate accounts of events which have occurred – such as the Shoah – Theodor W. Adorno and Max Horkheimer constructed what they called a *dialectic of enlightenment* presented in their jointly authored text by the same name.[1] That prefaced Adorno's relatively well-known utterance, post-Shoah, that 'after Auschwitz, it is no longer possibly to poeticize.'[2] But if it is the case that humans communicate through aesthetic expression and that nonetheless it is no longer possible to poeticize after Auschwitz, how do we respond at all to past events, especially one that has affected so many so deeply and so tragically? Given that each and every communiqué presupposes some form of aesthetic, how do we continue – faced with such abysmal tragedy and therefore condemned by the judgement of meaningless speech – to build thoughtful social relations, given that which Adorno and others claim challenges the very possibility of meaningful communicative relations? To help respond to such questions, I have cast a small gathering of German-Jewish intellectuals whose performances on just these issues, I maintain, typifies important trends in German-Jewish philosophy.

WALTER BENJAMIN

The historian is not merely a medium of transmission but installs herself in events as an 'eyewitness' of the events and carries forward the work of naming and speaking in the name of the dead others. She herself can be said to 'give off' aura in a chain of transmission.

—Edith Wyschogrod[3]

Conflating aesthetic and social theory, Walter Benjamin asserts that socio-political criticism depends upon our ability to read the evidential material of cultural inscriptions and legends, essays and translations – the embedded material of current communities. As he aphoristically points out in *One Way Street*, 'The most meaningful literary effectiveness can only originate in the strict [*streng*] changes arising from acting and writing; it has to develop the less apparent forms which better correspond to influencing active communities,' rather than the more demanding universal forms like books.[4] Hence, he critically validates newspaper and journal articles, pamphlets and brochures – the new organs of mass media – for the way they use active and direct language to address and inform a broad spectrum of the masses quickly and effectively, the first necessary step in transforming the world into a literary and, therefore, ethically responsive presence. This is not to say that Benjamin uncritically accepts mass media or unloads the ongoing significance of canonical literature; on the contrary, his critique leads to a revaluation of just what is salvageable and redemptive in great books and scripts such as the Bible or Hölderlin's poems, despite and because of the current degeneration of human communicative relations. Others have argued that Benjamin can only be understood as precisely determining and dealing with what is salvageable in canonical literature.[5] I will suggest that Benjamin can be consulted for pointing us in the direction of what may be salvageable out of the fragments of the various traditions thrown into question in our modern era, an era scarred by genocides and by validations of human elimination supported through the abuse of aesthetic media.

In addition to his seminal influence on the Institute for Social Research in general and on Adorno in particular, as well as his ties to other Jewish intellectuals through Gershom Scholem, Franz Rosenzweig and the *Lehrhaus* in Frankfurt,[6] Benjamin is important on biographical grounds alone, since his fate was directly and tragically determined by the Nazi attempt to annihilate European Jews. His suicide may well have been precipitated by his despair at being unable to escape Nazi pursuit and his perception that his life's work, his treasured library in Paris, had been destroyed by the Nazis. Anecdotal reports of his death include rumours that his corpse was removed from its grave and thrown into a communal grave where other common folk from the previous five decades had been cast, consigned to oblivion.[7] Benjamin, of course, has not been consigned to oblivion, but instead has become one of the most written-about and written-from intellectuals of the 20th century, important for his early influence on literary and critical theory and for having inspired recent developments in interpretive strategies for the history of culture, philosophy, the philosophy of history and the history of philosophy.[8]

Drawing on Benjamin's early philosophical texts, which deal with philosophy of speech and politics, among them 'Critique of Force', 'Fate and Character', 'The Life of the Students', 'The Destructive Character', and 'The Task of the Translator',[9] Derrida argues that by 1921 Benjamin had already anticipated the Nazi *'Endlösung'*. In response, Burkhardt Lindner aggressively denies that Benjamin could have had any inkling of the impending attempt to destroy systematically all of European Jewry.[10] Lindner rightly criticizes Derrida's questionable association of 'blood-thinking' in both Benjamin and Rosenzweig as propadeutic, for connecting the 'unbloody destruction' of the gas-chambers and the burning ovens. Lindner points out that Benjamin does comment on the threat of how a 'gas-war' promised to give the 'face' of any future imperialist war – and here Benjamin would mean the destruction of others for more living space (as he argues in 'The Destructive Character') – a destructive capability which is indefensible. According to Benjamin, the limits of such a gas-war were incalculable, evidenced by the erasure of the distinction between civilian and combatant in the First World War.

Turning aside from that important debate, I contend on other grounds that Benjamin does forecast the impending Shoah, indications of which can be gathered from his later writings on art and history. What can be asked of Benjamin is: in what way does he bring to light changes in cultural relations which were indeed preparatory for the destruction of the European Jews and which continue to allow other genocides to be performed?

Benjamin concludes his short essay 'What is Epic Theater?' by reflecting on how the aims of epic theatre may be more easily defined by observing changes in stage construction than in changes in the content of the dramatic action. Benjamin notes that this perspective

> may be called the filling in of the orchestra pit. The abyss which separates the players from the audience as it does the dead from the living; the abyss whose silence in a play heightens the sublimity, whose resonance in an opera heightens the intoxication-this abyss, of all elements of the theater the one that bears the most indelible traces of its ritual origin, has steadily decreased in significance. The stage is still raised, but it no longer rises from an unfathomable depth; it has become a dais. The didactic play and the epic theater are attempts to sit down on a dais.[11]

Benjamin composed this essay as a reflected fragment from the evolution of a specific art form, a specific activity of how humans, with certain signs and gestures, meaningfully communicate with each other. In this case, the change in communication consists of noting the differences between the form of theatre called dramatic tragedy – the critique of which arguably constitutes Benjamin's most significant major work,[12] and the kind of art and theatre of communal solidarity initiated by Brecht et al. This image is essential to an excursus on German-Jewish philosophers and the Shoah because of Benjamin's depiction of the separation and the erasure of the separation of players from an audience, that is, his observation that in epic contemporary theatre not only is the audience one with the actors, but so is the commenting critic.

That solidarity of community is one extreme which consumed Benjamin along with his interest in alienation as the other extreme of human relational activity, extremes resulting from the technologically determined social forces of modernity, forces effect-ively coopted in the 1930s by the Nazis and other fascists. Because so many failed to come to terms with how modern culture conditions the forms of our communication, because so many failed to read the developmental signs of the processes of historical oppression as the process of losing the sense of the auratic uniqueness of our very being, the stage was set for the genocidal catastrophe(s) of modernity.[13] Benjamin's work reveals that the ongoing degeneration of aura is part of that process of the ongoing effects of how we create and produce art and which is indicative of our decreasing abilities to communicate the originality and irreplaceability of each other. The abyss that once separated players from audiences, an ethical distancing enacted and re-enacted throughout human history as ritual and then as theatre, has been replaced by the unutterable abyss of mass human destruction and suffering, precipitated by the loss of ethical distance.

Those very inabilities have to do with the tensions of solidarity and alienation, of community and isolation, which haunt Benjamin's work and which led Benjamin to explore diverse stories of the changing faces of humanity. Benjamin's preoccupation with his own and others' experiences of homelessness and exile constitute much of his later work, especially his analyses of Kafka, Baudelaire, Proust, the architecture of Paris and his last unfinished work, 'Theses on the Philosophy of History'. In all of these works, Benjamin explores various facets related to the themes of exile, homelessness and the nature of the distance between humans.[14] One of his chief concerns is to create his own ethical stance by probing the role of the author *vis à vis* the collapse of predictable social conditions. Reflecting on the 'Technik' of the author in *One Way Street*, Benjamin writes: 'Nur der Kritiker richtet im Angesicht des Autors' ('Only the critic judges (or directs) in the face of the author').[15] The ethical critic judges, enters into ethical war with the social conditions, via dialectical confrontation, via breaking the bounds of aesethetic categories, by presenting an 'other' perspective. The ethical critic is able to provide such a different perspective because s/he is not content with simple commentary, and there-fore does not remain merely with the stuff [*Sache*] at hand. Rather, the critic remains concerned with the former place of the 'abyss', with the loss of critical distance, with the active or inactive roles played by witnesses, perpetrators and victims – by the play of the players and the audience.

ERICH FROMM[16]

Composed just two years after the Nazi forces had rolled into Poland, *Escape From Freedom* includes all of the major themes which Fromm, acting as an 'ethical entity', would elaborate during the next several decades, namely, the various psychological analyses of what he called the 'character structure of modern man'.[17] It is also the work where Fromm deals with the destructive forces that lead to the attempt, in the guise of Fascism, to eliminate the Jews of Europe.

Rejecting the generalities of previous attempts to understand the roots of Fascism, Fromm contends that the dominant trends of an individual's 'character structure' determine their activity and that that determination was directly related to choices of freely resisting or submitting to the claims of totalitarianism:

> We have been compelled to recognize that millions in Germany were as eager to surrender their freedom as their fathers were to fight for it; that instead of wanting freedom, they sought for ways to escape from it; that other millions were indifferent and did not believe the defense of freedom worth fighting for.[18]

Fromm claims there is both negative and positive freedom in the nature of being human and that Fascism arose because of psychological factors moulded by socio-economic factors determining those freedoms. Only an analysis which takes into account the powerful drives of humans resulting from our need for solidarity and spontaneous expression of unique individuality – through the spontaneity of love and innovative, productive work – can begin to account for the hold which Nazism had on the masses.

Fromm argues that all humans emerge as individuals from their primary ties with the natural world which was especially true during the Middle Ages. There was no individual as such, since humans achieved identity through their respective places in the structures of their community. However, as capitalism emerged with its impetus in individual initiative and competition, centralization weakened and individualism arose, and along with it the eventual destruction of traditional ties and the protections of the feudal church and state. That process resulted in both: (1) a striving for freedom and independence and (2) feelings of aloneness and powerlessness in the face of natural and social forces which can easily overwhelm the individual. The two possible responses to these forces are either to choose between 'negative freedom' or 'positive freedom'. We choose freedom negatively by submitting to a greater external force or authority, that is, through submitting to a force which we perceive to be greater than ourselves which can protect us and provide us with a feeling of belonging. Through such submission, symbolically returning to the womb of the mother or the protective lap of the father, the psychic anxiety and aloneness of the individual are apparently satisfied. In fact, though, the contradiction is never resolved since what it means to be human is to strive for greater independence and spontaneous expression free from coercion while submission results in ongoing dependence and the loss of strength and integrity of the self.

Fromm's thesis is that the Renaissance represented the beginning of modern individualism, with the development of commercial and industrial capitalism by a small aristocratic class who then provided a financial base for the artists and philosophers to express the ideas of this culture. But the Reformation represented the actual beginning of modern capitalism since it was a movement of the urban lower middle class. Drawing on Weber's theses about Protestantism and the roots of capitalism,[19] Fromm points out that 'Protestantism and Calvinism, while giving expression to a new feeling of freedom, at the same time constituted an escape from the burden of freedom.'[20]

In medieval society, the individual labourer could count on his place in the social order and enjoy the protection of the guild for his economic security. But with the move to increasing monopolization, the independence of journeymen, the emergence of industrial capital – which resulted in an elite non-labouring class and a large class of labourers who sold their labour as a commodity, the conditions of the peasant working class rapidly deteriorated. A consequence of these changes in the work environment led to psychological changes where time was reevaluated according to standards of utilitarian efficiency – time was too valuable to be wasted in anything but commerce. As Fromm points out, the 'increasing role of *capital*, of the *market*, and of *competition*, changed their personal situation into one of insecurity, isolation and anxiety.'[21] Where before a man was judged by his good works in an ethical structure which regulated labour expectations, the hostile market day increasingly became the day of final judgement for the individually estranged worker.

This growth in individual freedom which resulted in the isolation and uprootedness of the majority of the lower classes, became fertile ground for the doctrines of Lutheranism and Calvinism. Frightened and alone in their new freedom from external restraints and faced with unbearable insecurity, members of the lower middle class fled to the new structures of religion which promised an authority to which the anxious individual could submit and escape. Luther was a typical representative of the 'authoritarian character' who as a leader was capable of directing this new mass of people, likewise susceptible to the authoritarian character, and each needing the other in a symbiotic interdependency to work out their respective character structures. Luther's emphasis on the fundamental evilness and powerlessness of humans led to his solution that the only way to be 'saved' was by complete, humiliating submission to a higher authority, God, and God's servants on earth, the princes of the German states; and the masses responded.

For Luther, salvation can only be attained through a faith which entails accepting one's powerlessness and absolute insignificance of one's works, through acts of total self-effacement and complete submission. Luther himself, while in awe of authority, hated and despised the rabble and the powerless masses, especially in their revolutionary tendencies, an ambivalence which is nonetheless typical of the 'authoritarian character.'

> At this point it is important to understand that Luther's attitude towards secular authority was closely related to his religious teachings. In making the individual feel worthless and insignificant as far as his own merits are concerned, in making him feel like a powerless tool in the hands of God, he deprived man of the self-confidence and of the feeling of human dignity which is the premise for a firm stand against oppressing secular authorities.[22]

Fromm further notes that Luther advocated a traditional role in the economic order, but that his doctrines had the direct result of paving the way not only for members of the lower classes to unquestioningly submit to secular authorities but to subordinate one's life to the higher, external powers of economic achievements. As a result, 'this trend . . . reached a peak in the Fascist emphasis that it is the aim of life to be sacrificed for 'higher' powers, for the leader or the racial community',[23] and that 'Arbeit macht frei'.

For Fromm, while Luther's teachings disastrously affected the Germanic countries, Calvin's teachings corrupted the Anglo-Saxon ones, thus effectively spreading Protestant poison throughout Europe. Insidiously, Fromm claims, Calvinist predestination 'found its most vigorous revival in Nazi ideology: the principle of the basic inequality of men.'[24] In fact, the most powerful equalizer of human solidarity, fate, is also denied in the Calvinist teaching of the chosen and the damned. Such teachings of election reveal a deep contempt and hatred for other human beings and such a God, in stark contrast to the claims of the adherents, must be absolutely unjust and tyrannical because absolutely arbitrary. Again, Fromm points out the insidiousness: 'The doctrine that men are basically unequal according to their racial background is confirmation of the same principle with a different rationalization.'[25]

Just as damaging, Calvinism with its doctrine of predestination created 'compulsive neurotics' with a drive for relentless work to prove one's elective status but fuelled by unconscious hostility and resentment.

Luther and Calvin portray this all-pervading hostility. Not only in the sense that these two men, personally, belonged to the ranks of the greatest haters among the leading figures of history, certainly among religious leaders; but, which is more important, in the sense that their doctrines were colored by this hostility and could only appeal to a group itself driven by an intense, repressed hostility.[26]

The teachings of conscience and duty by Luther and Calvin emphasized the intense hatred towards oneself and others which, for Fromm, could only be rooted in the unconscious forces resulting from the new freedoms of modernity. Thus, Protestantism taught humans to despise themselves and others and to submit more readily to exploitation. In this way of submission, a new character structure was formed: 'compulsion to work, passion for thrift, the readiness to make one's life a tool for the purposes of an extra personal power, asceticism, and a compulsive sense of duty'[27] – as productive grounds for a new social order ready to be adapted to new ideologies promising stability.

Essential for his thesis is Fromm's psychological analysis of what he calls 'mechanisms of escape', used to analyse the psychological significance of Fascism and the structures of authoritarian systems in current democracies. These mechanisms result from insecurities and powerlessness which are the isolating consequences of religious and economic conditions of the modern human. Fromm contends that all humans strive to overcome their isolation by becoming 'one again with man, nature, and himself, without giving up the independence and integrity of his individual self', which he characterizes as positive freedom, or by eliminating the distance between oneself and the world through somehow re-merging oneself in a kind of primal unity. This latter scenario is only possible in a kind of negative freedom accomplished via either of two forms of escape: authoritarianism and automaton conformity. While the first is associated with modern Fascism and the second with modern democracy, both result in submission to social forces and the unconscious sacrifice of freedom as ways to escape the unbearable situations and/or the responsibility of freedom.

Drawing on the research of Freud, Adler, Reich, Horney and himself, Fromm reconstructs a profile of the sado-masochistic symbiotic relationship to typify the authoritarian character structure. The sado-masochistic type of authoritarian character results from changes in modern social structures already alluded to above which play out in cultural manifestations:

> If the individual finds cultural patterns that satisfy these masochistic strivings (like the submission under the 'leader' in Fascist ideology), he gains some security by finding himself united with millions of others who share these feelings.[28]

Masochistic individuals attempt to overcome their feelings of powerlessness and insecurity by becoming

> part of a bigger and more powerful whole outside of oneself, to submerge and participate in it. This power can be a person, an institution, God, the nation, conscience, or a psychic compulsion. By becoming part of a power which is felt as unshakably strong, eternal, and glamorous, one participates in its strength and glory. One surrenders one's own self and renounces all strength and pride connected with it, one loses one's integrity as an individual and surrenders freedom: but one gains a new security and a new pride in the participation in the power in which one submerges.[29]

Moreover, the sadist demonstrates similar feelings of powerlessness and isolation and stands in a symbiotic relationship with the masochist, that character structure 'to which Nazi ideology had its strongest appeal'.[30] What is important in this type is dominance, never solidarity, and differences in sex or race are only understood in terms of superiority or inferiority. However, Fromm carefully distinguishes this kind of character structure from what he calls the destructive character structure.

Although commonly combined with sado-masochism, the destructive character structure is actually intent on elimination versus incorporation and continued dependence. Also, as opposed to how Freud situates the destructive drive within the biological constitution of an individual, Fromm traces the social grounds for destructive tendencies. These range from experiences of escape from powerlessness by dominating the external world to removal of the external object or world which threatens one's security. Even more suggestive is his thesis that the amount of resorting to destructiveness increases in proportion to the extent that an individual's spontaneity and expansiveness are curtailed:

> Life has an inner dynamism of its own; it tends to grow, to be expressed, to be lived. It seems that if this tendency is thwarted the energy directed toward life undergoes a process of decomposition and changes into energies directed toward destruction. In other words: the drive for life and the drive for destruction are not mutually independent factors but are in a reverse interdependence.[31]

Destructiveness is not an isolated phenomenon, but is the 'outcome of an unlived life'[32] and the suppression of life and the enjoyment of life from a harsh and unrelenting perversion of religious and economic asceticism, leads to a vast reservoir of hostile tendencies directed towards both oneself and one's neighbour.

Fromm concludes 'Mechanisms of Escape' by discussing how the substitution of pseudo acts for original acts of thinking, willing and feeling leads to the unconscious replacement of the original self by a pseudo self:

> The pseudo self is only an agent who actually represents the role a person is supposed to play but who does so under the name of the self. It is true that a person can play many roles and subjectively be convinced that he is 'he' in each role. Actually he is in all these roles what he believes he is expected to be, and for many people, if not most, the original self is completely suffocated by the pseudo self.[33]

His point is that this unconscious replacement of the 'original self' by the 'pseudo self' is the result of the convergence of powerful structural changes in economics and religion from the Middle Ages to Modernity which especially affected the character structure of individuals of the lower middle class and most disastrously manifested itself in the psychological character structure, both individual and social, of Germans under the influence of the Nazis.

But Nazism can only be understood as a phenomenon resulting from both political/ economic factors *and* psychological factors, which Fromm develops in the 'Psychology of Nazism.' His thesis is that individuals who suffer from inner psychological maladies lack the requisite inner resistance or energy to consciously oppose even an obviously sado-masochistic *and* destructive authoritarian system of government. Ample empirical support is available, including correspondences between the political and social factors of Germany during the first decades of the 20th century and into the period of the Weimar Republic, the social character structure already developed, and the peculiarities of Hitler's biography, an individual character structure.

Fromm contends that two major groups constituted the overwhelming support for the Nazis in Germany following the first Great War. While the working class and the liberal and Catholic bourgeosie demonstrated relative passive resistance to the Nazis, they eventually resigned themselves to Nazi domination because of an 'inner tiredness' from economic conditions, disbelief and disenchantment in liberal political leaders and a loss of hope in socialist solutions to social problems. Once the Nazis were in power, this group readily identified with the totalitarian policies of the Nazis because they were the only route to any German identity at all, and most persons chose to be identified with the larger group rather than being isolated and alone. In fact, their identification became so strong that they were blind to the very political propaganda within which they increasingly became immersed, defending Germany against all attacks regardless of the ethical consequences. The ethical distance had been erased. Drawing on his own Jewish ethical roots, Fromm claims that the only alternative to manipulative propaganda is to adhere to a trans-national community of those who hold to a circumscribed set of ethical principles which would cultivate genuine individuality, supportive solidarity and possibilities of spontaneous love and creative, cooperative work.

Meanwhile, however, those conditions were not present in Germany in the 1920s and early 1930s and so the Nazi ideology was enthusiastically welcomed by the lower middle class, that is, the small shopkeepers, artisans, and white-collar workers. Members of this class became the most active supporters of the Nazis, the older generation providing mass support while the younger generation, including the Nazi Youth, became the most aggressive fighters:

> For them the Nazi ideology – its spirit of blind obedience to a leader and of hatred against racial and political minorities, its craving for conquest and domination, its exaltation of the German people and the 'Nordic Race' – had a tremendous emotional appeal, and it was this appeal which won them over and made them into ardent believers in and fighters for the Nazi cause.[34]

Fromm identifies this group according to the tendencies which he identifies in their social character as opposed to that of the working class, the upper strata of the middle class or members of the aristocratics and upper classes. The lower middle class distinguished themselves by:

> their love of the strong, hatred of the weak, their pettiness, hostility, thriftiness with feelings as well as with money, and essentially their asceticism. Their outlook on life was narrow, they suspected and hated the strange, and they were curious and envious of their acquaintances, rationalizing their envy as moral indignation; their whole life was based on the principle of scarcity – economically as well as psychologically.[35]

These traits were also present in the other classes as well, especially, for example, the working class, but that they were most evident *and typical* in the lower middle class. The result of this preponderance of traits was that with the emergence of the Nazis, the more negative aspects of the social structure of this class intensified and emerged to become identified with that which most clearly characterized the Nazi ideology, namely, 'its craving for submission and its lust for power'.[36] But with the harsh economic conditions of the late 1920s their faith in the state to protect their economic security was shattered. Add the embarrassment of the lower middle class at having to assume responsibility for Germany's defeat in the First Great War, the demise of the monarchy, a loss of faith in traditional institutions – including family, and the powerlessness resulting from monopolistic capitalism, and we have a populace so socially frustrated, alienated and insecure that they readily became an abundant and submissive source to mobilize the ranks of the National Socialists.

Fromm's other pole in his analysis of the psychological-social structure of the Nazis is, of course, Hitler, a leader who could appeal so strongly to the lower middle class because he represented an extreme version of the same authoritarian character structure as that class. According to *Mein Kampf*, Hitler was well aware of the longing for submission in the tired masses, destructively despising and loving those masses at the same time.

Quoting Hitler: the masses 'neither realize the impudence with which they are spiritually terrorized, nor the outrageous curtailment of their human liberties for in no way does the delusion of this doctrine dawn on them.'[37] Hitler took every opportunity to break the will of his audience, playing on their tiredness, the time of meeting, the numbers of the crowd which would encourage adherence through mass suggestion – revealing his cynical and sadistic contempt for their gullibility and belief in their masochistic pliability. Hitler compulsively loved the powerful and hated the powerless, typical of the sado-masochistic character structure. Moreover, Hitler and other Nazi leaders counselled the masochistic rank and file to accept their own 'personal insignificance, dissolve [themselves] in a higher power, and then feel proud in participating in the strength and glory of this higher power.'[38] The aim of education had to be restructured to 'teach the individual not to assert his self', to be obedient and to bear injustice in silence.[39]

As I have pointed out, Fromm develops two character types, the automaton and the authoritarian character as a basis for analysing the psychology of Nazism and the ongoing challenges of modern democracy. If the social and political conditions of any society do not provide for the possibilities of solidarity, then the individual will feel isolated and powerless and freedom will become an unbearable burden. That unbearable burden serves as the source of his analysis of the psychology of Nazism which itself is the condition for his analysis of the social character of modern democracies and for those formative forces which enable a people to not only actively promote fascist policies but also to meekly submit to totalitarian dictators. Fromm concludes that even in our post-Nazi era there are fertile grounds for the atrocities of genocidal acts to be committed. The only alternative to resolve the newly unbearable responsibility of freedom is for each human to cultivate 'active solidarity with all men and his spontaneous activity; love and work, which unite him again with the world, not by primary ties but as a free and independent individual.'[40]

ARENDT

Unquestionably, Hannah Arendt counts as one of the most significant and philosophically critical intellectuals who have been involved in discourse on the Shoah during the course of the 20th century.[41] From her comprehensive and sweeping analyses of anti-semitism in *The Origins of Totalitariansim* and her role as critical provocateur in coining the phrase, 'banality of evil', and in assigning roles of responsibility to both oppressor and victim in *Eichmann in Jerusalem*, Arendt worked tirelessly to ensure that her day on the stage would be memorable, as tirelessly as she worked for the 'dead others.' Often misunderstood and unfairly maligned, her original and independent ideas about the Shoah and antisemitism may be better appreciated if situated within the montage of her other, more philosophical, works.

Although trained in the rigorous discipline of German academic philosophy in the 1930s, Arendt resisted identifying herself as a philosopher throughout her entire life. In fact, she introduced her last major work, *The Life of the Mind* by asserting: 'I have neither claim nor ambition to be a "philosopher" or be numbered among what Kant, not without irony, called *Denker von Gewerbe* (professional thinkers).'[42] What attracts readers to Arendt is that, her protest notwithstanding, by presenting to the public her 'preoccupation with mental activities' she provides not only some of the most original philosophical activity of the twentieth century but also an important alternative to the 'banality of evil.'

Worth considering are her critical breaks with various traditions in order to affirm the worth, dignity and freedom of human particularity in a pluralistic world. Tradition is signified for her publicly by political and institutional structures as well as by various systematic frameworks – academic, social, military, ethnic and religious communities as well as established feminist groupings. To locate the source of this sense of alienated particularity, her intellectual and social choices should be traced by focusing on her defiant independence as it is rooted in her German-Jewess identity. That identity began with her early education in Germany and her initial desire to both study philosophy and to make sense of her place in an antisemitic and anti-feminist society. That 'making sense' occurs in her first significant and overlooked work, *Rahel Varnhagen: The Life of a Jewess*.

> Since Rahel in spite of all her efforts could form no social ties, since her inclinations toward assimilation remained entirely suspended in an unpeopled vacuum, she was unable to become one human being among others.[43]

Arendt does not situate well within traditional feminist groupings and resisted inclusion in the emergent discipline of feminist Jewish philosophy.[44] Nevertheless, she should be cast in such a role among others. In an outstanding introduction to the new edition of *Rahel Varnhagen: The Life of a Jewess*,[45] Liliane Weissberg analyses Arendt's sense of being a Jewish woman intellectual and how that identity played out in her ideas about antisemitism, Jewish assimilation and Zionism. She also observes that Arendt denied philosophy because of her belief that philosophers were removed from actively engaging life and that Arendt chose political science because speech-acts in politics become historically effective, since Arendt wished most of all to live an effective life as a Jewish intellectual woman. Although that choice was denied her in Germany because of her Jewish heritage it was precisely through a legal argument in connection with reparations from the German government after the war that Arendt officially entered the discipline of philosophy through a public act based on a political decision.[46] In other words, what Arendt said needs to be measured by what she effectively and in fact did, complicating simple categories of identification.

Assembling the montage of Arendt's work is like viewing what Ingebord Nordman calls 'a topography of differences...which in themselves become ever-more differentiated.'[47] Some of the prominent elements of that montage are: (1) her early work on *Rahel Varnhagen: The Life of a Jewess*; (2) the work of her middle phase, including *The Origins of Totalitarianism*, *Eichmann in Jerusalem*, and *The Human Condition*; and (3) her later work, especially *Men in Dark Times* and *Life of the Mind*. Tracing her choices in how she developed that montage leads to the realization that she resisted commitments to fixity of place and, instead, presents narrative accounts of individual lives exploring social forces which formed identities and how they affected greater historical developments. The process of focusing on reconstructing individual narratives and their exemplary status presents us with her philosophy of history as well as illuminates the creative process of her own personal history. An ongoing parameter for her choices has to do precisely with her enduring engagement or 'preoccupation with mental activities' in order to counteract the blind obedience of thoughtless cultural habits in favour of critical independent thought, in favour of con-science (acting with-thinking). That preoccupation was conditioned by her own status as a pariah and her clear and constant awareness of the thoughtless extermination of Jewish lives in the Shoah. Through her essays into individual performances she presents the alternative of her own mental activity which entails the public performance of demonstrating a hope for humanity revealed in her depictions of individual portraits, i.e., of human faces, and thus revealing the face of humanity. In so doing she actively fights her own sense of the fragmented nature of the modern history of human relations which results in the human proclivity to dissemble and mask intentions and desires.

Not only her speech-acts and writing, but her political decisions reveal the extent of her resistance to traditional philosophies and institutions as well as every kind of ideology by how she distanced herself from belonging to any kind of political identity. If anything, she identified herself with a People – German, Jewish or Woman – but not with a State, rejecting the identities of nation, society, and career. One of the claims which Arendt makes is that she rejected the academic life of philosophy because of her conviction that the life of the philosopher was one of obedience and subservience to the political status quo. Accordingly, her choice for the political was a choice for a life of action that *would* make and *did* make a difference in the world. Committed to changing the world, she had to do so via the political acts of her writing and by not accepting the political status quo. She acted by forming her own original response to what she referred to as an abyss (*Abgrund*) of thought and history, an abyss which she identified as the attempt to exterminate the Jews during the Shoah and which she defined as an outgrowth of historical antisemitism.

It is not coincidental that Arendt began *Rahel* while still under the strong psychological and intellectual influence of Heidegger. Within that text one clearly makes out her attempts to come to terms not only with the antisemitism of the early 19th century, but also with the retarding affects of Heidegger's influence on the process of her identity formation in the 20th century and how insidiously his antisemitism pervaded the very roots of her struggle with social acceptance and intellectual/emotional growth. On the other hand, she learned to love philosophy from her two primary mentors, Heidegger and Jaspers, and, especially through Heidegger, learned to draw upon both Ancient Greek philosophy and poetry for solace from an oppressive intellectual climate and for inspiration to explore foreign worlds, while also learning the languages of homelessness.

What is especially clear in *Rahel,* though, is her knowledge of the formative roots of German Idealism in the socio-political culture of early 19th-century Europe, evidenced through her performing the movements which played out between the social scenes created by the storm and stress of German political and intellectual history. In that text, the most evident philosophical voice is Fichte's, heard through his 'Addresses to the German Nation', which, under the mask of a philosophy of history nonetheless affected and was affected by political attitudes towards Jews and women replayed in the scenes Arendt reconstructs of Berlin salon society.

According to Fichte, as quoted by Rahel and applied to her own situation, 'Belonging, in fact, was promised precisely to the person who had "annihilated" himself as a "sensuous individual",[48] in his sensuous specificity, with a particular origin and a particular situation in the world. The historical community of the future would be determined not by individuals, but by 'us as a commonality in which the individual person is absorbed by the concept of the whole, is absolutely forgotten in a unity of thought.' For Rahel, this determination of commonality showed the priority of the human mind 'since after all it is through the mind alone that we understand everything' and that, therefore, 'the *outsider* can understand history and the world without benefit of tradition, and without the natural self-assurance of social status.' She learned from Fichte the 'pariah's arrogant conceit in exceptionally profound experiences and emotions'[49] and that in order to fully assimilate one needed to give up one's particularity and Jewess specificity. But Arendt also points out that for Fichte, as for other German intellectuals, nobles and merchants, at least up until the war of 1813 when Germans needed Jewish money, being patriotic also meant being antisemitic. So in order to fully assimilate, to become a complete patriot, one also needed to adopt the reactionary antisemitism of the dominant conservative classes.

Arendt wrote the last two chapters of *Rahel* in homeless exile in Paris, those which deal with the concept of 'pariah', a term which she uses to denote that individual who stands on the borders of society, and is discriminated against and excluded from the social, economic and political realms of society. She identifies just such a situation with the historical phenomenon of antisemitism, but adds that, since the Jew is not accepted by society, the Jew therefore does not have to accept the rules of that society and is able, then, to sharpen her independent powers of judgment. Moreover, the pariah is one who, precisely because of her lack of fixity in a social structure, enjoys a view of the whole and is able, thereby, to be critical of hardened truths. In fact, in the hands of Arendt, the problem of the Jewish pariah is transformed into a problem-structure which presents itself to anyone who would battle against conformity and banality.

While Arendt associates the Jew with being the outsider, and therefore with that one who is able to distance herself from socio-political forms, including intellectual and cultural movements such as the Enlightenment and Romanticism, she does not take the further step of creating the other or outsider as one who is aesthetically desirable. Rather, *differenz* is depicted as precisely that human experience of an individual characterized by heartbreak because of subordination, uncertainty, transitoriness and involuntary homelessness. For Arendt, Rahel – with her reconstructed acceptance of her Jewess particularity – serves as a place-marker for all displaced humans as Arendt gives her a human face and through her reconstruction works against her reduction to merely a fragment of a broken social order. In other words, in the role as quintessential *other* the Jewess shares the destiny of all oppressed whose suppression is justified by myriad systems of totality; including the closed worlds of politics, civil service, the general social order and thinking itself.

In *Rahel*, Arendt replays the life of a Jewess in order to give a particular exemplar a human face and in order to wed the narrative of storytelling with the analysis and critical voice of philosophy, moving from the personal to the political. In her next text, *The Origins of Totalitarianism*, she uses Rahel as a placeholder for how individuals composed individual movements which effected and were affected by socio-political developments. Even within the Jewish-sponsored salons of Berlin in the early 1800s, it was chic to be antisemitic and, in fact, as noted earlier, adopting antisemitism was the official entry ticket to full assimilation. Finally, Arendt's thoughtful reconstruction of the individuality of Rahel's life enables Arendt to accentuate possible objectifications of life itself through Rahel's exemplary capacity to illustrate active engagement in the social conditions of her time. More importantly, though, narrating Rahel's story enables Arendt to overcome the subjectivity of Arendt's own experience of life, exposing thereby not only the historical conditions of a past life, but of a present life as well. In doing so, Arendt provides an exposition for determining meaning in life.

That meaning has to do with how we are presented with the determination of Rahel's/ Arendt's humanity: '... another trait equally characteristic of the pariah was what Rahel called "too much consideration for a human face".' For Rahel,

> this sensitivity is an emotionally exaggerated understanding of the dignity of every human being, a passionate comprehension unknown to the privileged. In a society based upon privilege, pride of birth and arrogance of title, the pariah instinctively discovers human dignity in general long before Reason has made it the foundation of morality.[50]

It is the very nature of being an outcast or exile which provides the Jewess with the possibility to effect critical distance: the pariah, precisely because he is an outcast, can see life as a whole, and the very road upon which the pariah can attain to her '*great* love for free existence'[51] enables her to see how everything in life is related and that that critical vision and love of freedom are what constitute a meaningful life.

Arendt's accentuation of the role that alienation has for constituting human difference can be traced in her later works, especially in its foundational application in *The Human Condition* but also in her controversial *Eichmann in Jerusalem*, her collection of individual portraits in *Men in Dark Times* and in her specifically philosophical *The Life of the Mind*. For example, in *The Human Condition* the only other philosopher who merits as many references as either Plato or Aristotle is Marx and it is Marx's theory of alienation which serves as a critical fulcrum for her development of the reversal which takes place from the *vita contemplativa* to the *vita activa*.

While I would like to consider the application of her Jewess roots to the development of her philosophical perspective as a whole or at least to those works which she did immediately after *Rahel*,[52] I will concentrate on only a few references from *The Human Condition* tracing the effects of her German-Jewess experience via the categories of pariah, exile and alienation. This particular work, like most of the others, was written episodically and on the occasion of a public performance. Delivered as a series of lectures at the University of Chicago in April 1956, in *The Human Condition* Arendt turns from direct attention on the Shoah and explores the nature of human activity, traversing in turn the antinomies of the public and private realms of experience, philosophy as the love of wisdom and religion as the love of goodness, and the nature of human contemplation versus human activity.

The consequences for the limitations of modern science for Arendt are clearly spelled out as a distancing of the human from nature, but also as a kind of self-discovery: 'Instead of objective qualities, in other words, we find instruments, and instead of nature or the universe – in the words of Heisenberg – man encounters only himself.'[53] In other words, she proposes the now ubiquitous conclusion that in the world of contemporary astrophysics, the observed object has no independent existence apart from the observing object. At the time, her conclusion was striking, however, and emerges from the vantage point she gained earlier of which only the pariah is capable. Based on our contemporary activity in physics (atomic accelerators, etc.), she argues,

> ... we always handle nature from a point in the universe outside the earth. Without actually standing where Archimedes wished to stand (*dos moi pou stō*) still bound to the earth through the human condition, we have found a way to act on the earth and within terrestrial nature as though we dispose of it from outside, from the Archimedean point. And even at the risk of endangering the natural life process we expose the earth to universal, cosmic forces alien to nature's household.[54]

She explores this vantage point and presents a post-modern consequence: 'It means that we no longer feel bound even to the sun, that we move freely in the universe, choosing our point of reference wherever it may be convenient for a specific purpose.'[55] We range freely because, in fact, the scientific move from the geocentric universe to the helio-centric one results in 'a universe without a fixed center' which only now has created us as 'universal' beings. This is a peculiar kind of universality, however, which she develops along the lines of Einstein's theory of relativity, a theory which supports the 'implied denial that Being which appears in time and place possesses an absolute reality.'[56] She argues that this denial was presaged by 16th-century theories of science which were really 'an indication of the astounding human capacity to think in terms of the universe while remaining on the earth, and the perhaps even more astounding human ability to use cosmic law as guiding principles for terrestrial action.'[57]

In short, what determined the course and development of modern society was, and is, a thoughtful kind of *world alienation*, which corresponds to her affirmation of alienated Jewess experience, as the ground for her claim that neither the astronomer's desire for mathematical simplicity or the Renaissance renewal of love for the earth were instrumental for determining the modern human ethos. World alienation determined modern society while earth alienation determined modern science. For example, the move from geometry to algebra, from measuring the earth to the powers of cognition and non-spatial symbolic logic of mathematical symbols is a move from extending human ability through physical instruments, such as the telescope, to extending human ability through the exercise of mental instruments.[58] Hence, natural phenomena were placed under the conditions of the human mind, from a universal, cosmic standpoint outside of nature itself, which is why mathematics became the leading science of the modern age.[59] It is no longer the science of Being which holds but the science of the structure of the human mind which determines the meaning of human existence.[60]

This leads to her theme which echoes that of the earlier homelessness of the pariah, namely, that, in modernity, 'man had lost his home as well as his privileged position in creation, and ourselves, who still and probably forever are earth-bound creatures, dependent upon metabolism with a terrestrial nature, and who have found the means to bring about processes of cosmic origin and possibly cosmic dimension.'[61] The technological consequences of such a homeless distancing from the earth are, on the one hand, that we are now able to more easily and efficiently destroy the earth and each other, but also, on the other hand, we are able to create new elements never before found in nature, to transform mass into energy, to place artificial heavenly bodies around the earth, and to even begin to 'create or re-create the miracle of life', an act that was previously restricted to the prerogative of divine action.

NOTES

1 Max Horkheimer and Theodor W. Adorno, *Dialectic of Enlightenment*, originally published by Social Studies Association, Inc., New York, 1944; then by S. Fischer Verlag GmbH, Frankfurt am Main, 1969; and most recently by The Continuum Publishing Company, New York, 1999.

2 Adorno retracts his unrelenting assertion later by claiming that, 'darum mag falsch gewesn sein, nach Auschwitz ließe kein Gedicht mehr schreiben.' But qualifies the retraction with: 'Nicht falsch aber ist die minder kulturelle Frage, ob nach Auschwitz noch sich leben lasse...' See Theodor W. Adorno, *Negative Dialektik* (Frankfurt am Main: Suhrkamp, 1966), 355.

3 Edith Wyschogrod, *An Ethics of Remembering: History, Heterology, and the Nameless Others* (Chicago: The University of Chicago Press, 1998), 76.

4 Walter Benjamin, *Einbahnstraße*, (Frankfurt am Main: Suhrkamp, 1955), 7.

5 'For Walter Benjamin, all significant knowledge lies in the depths of canonical literature.' Norbert Bolz and Willem van Reijen, *Walter Benjamin*, trans. Laimdota Mazzarins (Atlantic Highlands: Humanities Press International, 1996; orig. Frankfurt am Main: Campus Verlag GmbH, 1991), 1.

6 For a thorough tracing of Benjamin's influence by Rosenzweig, especially for the influence of Rosenzweig's idea of Messianic Redemption on Benjamin's ideas of progress and Redemption as the revolution towards political utopia, see Stéphan Moses, 'Walter Benjamin and Franz Rosenzweig', in *Benjamin*, ed. Gary Smith (Chicago: University of Chicago Press, 1983), 228–246. Arendt claims Adorno was Benjamin's 'first and only disciple', despite Adorno's criticisms of Benjamin. Cf. Hannah Arendt, *Men in Dark Times*, (Orlando: Harcourt Brace and Co., 1968), 154, 163.

7 *Walter Benjamin: 1892–1940*, special issue of the *Marbacher Magazin*, 55/1990 (Deutsche Schiller-gesellschaft, 1990), 352. This catalogue of a photo exhibition includes material, images and text which help to illustrate Benjamin's biography.

8 'Walter Benjamin, who never found a political, religious, or academic home anywhere, is regarded today as the leading authority on historical materialism, negative theology, and even literary decon-structivism.' Norbert Bolz and Willem van Reijen, *Walter Benjamin*, (Frankfurt am Main: Campus Verlag, 1991), trans. By Laimdota Mazzarins (Princeton, NJ [**please confirm place of publication**]: Humanities Press, 1996), 1.

9 Most of these essays are readily available in *Illuminations: Walter Benjamin: Essays and Reflections*, ed. and intro. by Hannah Arendt, (New York: Schocken, 1969).

10 Cf. Jacques Derrida, 'Gesetzeskraft. Der "mystische Grund der Autorität",' in *Cardozo Law Review* 11, Nr. 5/6 (1990), 919ff. and for the response: Burkhardt Lindner, 'Derrida. Benjamin. Holocaust. – Zur politischen Problematik der "Kritik der Gewalt", in *Zeitschrift für kritsche Theorie*, Heft 5/1997, (Lüneberg: zu Klampen), 65–100.

11 Walter Benjamin, *Illuminations: Essays and Reflections*, ed. and intro. by Hannah Arendt, (New York: Schocken Books, 1968), 154.

12 His dissertation on German tragic drama of the baroque period, *Der Begriff der Kunstkritik in der deutschen Romantik* (*The Concept of Art Criticism in German Romanticism*) was his first extended treatment of a theme which would continue to command his attention, namely, the theme of the role of criticality in a textually ordered world. For Benjamin, the burning of books by the Nazis could only be second as an unreconcilable abyss of tragedy to the destruction of Benjamin's carefully collected library by those same hands.

13 While Benjamin began his *Der Ursprung des deutschen Truerspiels* (*The Origin of German Tragic Drama*) in 1923 with the intention of presenting it for his *Habilitation* requirements, that desire remained unrequited and led Benjamin to change course from an academic path to one of journalism, literary criticism, philosophical critique and radio broadcasting. That work was eventually published by Rowohlt in 1928.

14 Cf. Chryssoula Kambas, *Walter Benjamin in Exil: Zum Verhältnis von Literatutr-politik und Ästhetik* (Tübingen: Max Niemeyer Verlag, 1983).

15 *Einbahnstrasse*, 52.

16 Fromm's theses about the general involvement of German masses in Nazi ideology, and therefore by extension in the destruction of European Jews, appears to share similar empirical fallacies as Gold-hagen's claims about the universality of antisemitism in Germany prior to and during the Holocaust, but the similarities are only apparent. Goldhagen's claims are that not only were Germans almost universally united in their need and desire to eliminate the Jews, but that Jewish anti-Semitism was the amalgamating core of their eliminationist ideology. However, he supports his argument for quantitative universality on what even he confesses to be a deficient data base. Cf. Daniel Jonah Goldhagen, *Hitler's Willing Executioners* (Random House, New York, 1997), 47–48. Fromm, on the other hand, is quite clear that his analysis of psychological and social character is meant to elucidate trends in the spheres of psychological and social dynamisms of modern Europeans and Americans and is therefore much less pretentious.

17 Cf. Erich Fromm, *Escape from Freedom*, Henry Holt and Company, New York, 1969; first edition, 1941), xvii: 'I have tried to do some of this work [of elaboration] myself...In the *Sane Society* I amplified and deepened the analysis of contemporary society; in *Man for Himself* I developed the theme of ethical norms based on our knowledge of man, rather than on authority and revelation; in the *Art of Loving* I analyzed the various aspects of love; in *The Heart of Man* I followed up the roots of destructiveness and hate; in *Beyond the Chains of Illusion* I analyzed the relationship between the thoughts of the two great theorists of a dynamic science of man: Marx and Freud.'

18 *ibid.*, 3.

19 Max Weber, *The Protestant Ethic and the Spirit of Capitalism*, Charles Scribner's Sons, New York, 1930.

20 Fromm, 50.

21 *ibid.*, 60.

22 *ibid.*, 83.
23 *ibid.*, 84.
24 *ibid.*, 89.
25 *ibid.*, 90.
26 *ibid.*, 95.
27 *ibid.*, 102.
28 *ibid.*, 152.
29 *ibid.*, 154.
30 *ibid.*, 162.
31 *ibid.*, 182.
32 *ibid.*, 190.
33 *ibid.*, 202.
34 *ibid.*, 209.
35 *ibid.*, 210.
36 *ibid.*, 211.
37 In Fromm 220; Adolf Hitler, *Mein Kampf* (New York: Reynal & Hitchcock, 1940), 53.
38 *Escape from Freedom*, 231.
39 *ibid.*, 232; Also, Martin Heidegger, perhaps the most notable educator who counted himself a loyal Nazi, presents the clearest answer to Hitler's claims in his Rectoral Address of 1933, 'The Self-Assertion of the German University', where he argues for systematic change in the German University system to bring it in line with the principles of the Nazi party, significantly, the cohesion and collusion of: education service, with military service and labor service. Martin Heidegger, 'The Self-Assertion of the German University', in *The Heidegger Controversy*, ed. Richard Wolin, (MIT Press, Cambridge, 1993), 29–39.
40 *Escape from Freedom*, 35.
41 An earlier version of the material in this section on Arendt was presented March 1999 to the West Texas-New Mexico Philosophical Society.
42 Hannah Arendt, *Life of the Mind* (New York: Harcourt Brace, 1971), 3.
43 Hannah Arendt, *Rahel Varnhagen: The Life of a Jewess.* Ed. and with an introduction by Liliane Weissberg (Baltimore: The John's Hopkins University Press, 1997), 185.
44 Heidi M. Raaven. 'Observations on Jewish Philosophy and feminist thought', *Judaism: A Quarterly Journal of Jewish Life & Thought*, 46/4 (Fall 1997), 422–439.
45 *Rahel*, 23–41.
46 For having lost the possibility of a career in philosophy in Germany because she had to flee the Nazis, *Rahel* became her *Habilitation* work, which she needed for promotion and which was judged as 'excellent' even though unfinished by her former mentor Jaspers; and thus *Rahel* entered twentieth century philosophical discourse on Jaspers' response to the book and Arendt's reply. See *Correspondence: Hannah Arendt and Karl Jaspers*, ed. and introd. Lotte Kohler and Hans Saner; trans. Robert and Rita Kimber (New York: Harcourt Brace Jovanovich, 1992), 192–210. This particular exchange of letters is also where Arendt acknowledges that Benjamin and her husband Heinrich Blucher 'kept pestering me about' finishing *Rahel* until she did so in the summer of 1938.
47 Ingebord Nordman, *Hannah Arendt*. Frankfurt: Campus Verlag, 1994.
48 *Rahel*, 183.
49 *ibid.*
50 *ibid.*, 248.
51 *ibid.*
52 Upon her emigration to the United States, Arendt produced three remarkable texts in a very short period of her life: *The Origins of Totalitarianism* (New York: Harcourt Brace & Company, 1951–66), *The Human Condition* (Chicago: The University of Chicago Press, 1958) and *Eichmann in Jerusalem* (New York: Viking Press, 1963).
53 *The Human Condition*,
54 *ibid.*, 261.
55 *ibid.*, 262.

56 *ibid.*
57 *ibid.*, 264.
58 This line of thinking eventually leads to her dealing with Kant in her final text, *The Life of the Mind*, New York: Harcourt Brace & Co., 1978, especially in the unfinished segment on 'judging' which she was working on when she suddenly died.
59 Which has nothing to do with Plato and his predilection for the Ideal forms or eternal being of geometry purified of human sensuality. Arendt proposes an 'unsafe' sensual embodied philosophy.
60 As Heidegger develops in a different context.
61 *The Human Condition*, 268.

CHRISTANITY, THE OTHER, AND THE HOLOCAUST

Michael R. Steele

Violence is not only what we do to the Other. It is prior to that. Violence is the very construction of the Other.

— Regina M. Schwartz, *The Curse of Cain: The Violent Legacy of Monotheism*

THIS STUDY, part of a much more detailed but unfinished project, involves the use of culture studies and discourse theory to investigate the ways in which Christianity has been involved in the social relationships of the phenomenon of power over the Other, how that power expresses and perpetuates itself, and how it manifested itself during the Holocaust. Such a study is of crucial importance because Christianity has, for many centuries, constituted a culture, or a major determinant of Western culture, by which hundreds of millions of believing Christians have had their most deeply-held beliefs formulated. Scripture, scripture commentary, papal bulls, the arts, and countless sermons, pamphlets and books constitute the discourse within which those millions have lived. The tentative hope is that this analysis will reveal the underlying cultural substrata that helped empower those who either actively perpetrated or passively acquiesced in the Holocaust.

What is common to my concern with the Other and the Holocaust is Christianity. In all the cases to be examined here, Christianity largely defined the terms by which people were perceived to be either within or outside the circle of moral obligation, the latter being the Other. This could be done in a variety of ways: by demonising a group, otherwise anathematising them, or perceiving them as sub-human (without eternal souls), or as infidels or heretics. Regina Schwartz's study of monotheism and violence finds that 'Monotheism is a myth that grounds particular identity in universal transcendence...a myth that forges identity antithetically – against the Other'.[1] Her study cites examples of this myth both before the Common Era and after. That being the case, the trajectory of violence nevertheless strikes me as increasing dramatically in the Common Era. For one thing, Israel was unable to operate as a military power after Rome achieved full prominence, subjecting the Jews in the process. Once allied with the power of Imperial Rome, the Christian religion, eventually becoming a cultural institution affecting virtually all other institutions in Western Europe, served to create and reward attitudes and behaviours that led to a long series of violent, repressive, and emiserating responses by Christians and Christianity practised against the Other – those who stand outside the Christian confession, either by geographical accident, race, religious tradition or chosen belief, or some other demarcating factor. This approach does not explain the Shoah as a specifically Christian event, but analyses it as one that had its sanctioning and conditioning in historical antecedents that go far to account for the (a) apathy of bystanders, insofar as Christianity devised a 'moral universe' both excluding non-Christians and others deemed to be beyond the pale, while also targeting them for a variety of sanctions, and (b) a pre-existing moral framework supporting and empowering the willing executioners in the myriad details of their chosen work. My work will thus examine key examples in which a Christian-influenced culture led to both structural and outright violence practised against the Other, in a series of preludes to the Holocaust.

Daniel Goldhagen's controversial 1996 book, *Hitler's Willing Executioners*, details the process by which German antisemitism evolved from what he terms an 'eliminationist mind-set' to an 'exterminationist one'.[2] Not surprisingly, as a political scientist, Goldhagen declares that 'the state would have to be the primary agent of change' from one mind-set to the other[3] – a charge this study contests to the degree that culture has been left out of the analysis. His work is quite specific in declaring Germans to be the only national group capable of perpetrating the Holocaust, an assertion that has drawn the sharp criticism of many scholars, who point out that German planning and perpetration often received the support of many auxiliaries from other countries.

To the contrary of the view that the Holocaust was a German-specific event in terms of its perpetration, Peter Weiss, author of the 1966 play *The Investigation*, has argued that any group of people, including even the victims, could have functioned as Holocaust perpetrators. Having based his play on the 1964 Frankfurt trial of Auschwitz personnel, and his own anguished visit to the camp, he claims: 'I see Auschwitz as a scientific instrument that could have been used by anyone to exterminate anyone. For that matter, given a different deal, the Jews could have been on the side of the Nazis. They, too, could have been the exterminators.'[4] In the play, the Third Witness articulates Weiss's position:

> Many of those who were destined
> to play the part of prisoners
> had grown up with the same ideas
> the same way of looking at things
> as those
> who found themselves acting as guards
>
> . . .
>
> And if they had not been designated prisoners
> they could equally well have been guards.[5]

Such assertions, not surprisingly, proved to be as controversial in certain quarters as Goldhagen's approach thirty years later.

Goldhagen's background as a political scientist surely conditions his explanations in his book. Peter Weiss approaches Auschwitz from a socialist perspective, focusing on an economic critique. Having said that, however, Weiss has a better grasp, in my view, of the cultural factors involved, although he uses other concepts: for him, the perpetrators' 'acts flowed inevitably from the nature of the society in which they lived'.[6] Although Weiss accuses capitalism specifically, he concludes that it is 'indeed the whole Western way of life . . . that is on trial' in his play.[7] (I do not agree with Weiss that the victims could have been perpetrators, not as long as they were the Other. Weiss does not delve into the matter of culture with enough rigour.)

These two approaches may not, taken in isolation, be very fruitful; there may be no compromise between them either. This study's approach, however, emphasises that

murderous attitudes and behaviours are not unknown in the history and culture of the
Christian West. Looking back from the Holocaust, one perceives clear antecedents,
virtually unmistakable warning signs – if anyone had cared to note them or their
implications. Moving forward from the beginning of the Common Era, there are key
points that would seem to be necessary developments for the eventual outcome known as
the Holocaust. My argument takes a third approach to those taken by Goldhagen and
Weiss, one that does not blame Germans alone, one that does not generalise the
perpetration of the event potentially to all humans. In this latter regard, for instance, it
is very difficult envisioning Native Americans conceiving and implementing an Auschwitz based on their history, cultural values and practices. They lack the foundational
documents, the religious animosities, twenty centuries of antisemitism, the ability to
project legal and military power over extensive territories and populations, and the
universalist, triumphalist attitudes found in the Christian West that seem to be key
aspects of the crucial background needed for an Auschwitz to occur.

We may understand culture to be 'a whole way of life, material, intellectual, and
spiritual'.[8] Clifford Geertz writes of the 'traffic...in significant symbols...anything
...used to impose meaning upon experience...to orient [oneself] within "the ongoing
course of experienced things"', quoting John Dewey.[9] Geertz argues that human beings
experience a vacuum between what their bodies tell them is needed and what they need
'to know in order to function...' People fill this vacuum themselves, but with 'information (or misinformation) provided by our culture'. Thus, he argues, people 'are cultural
artifacts'.[10] This is a crucial observation – that humans are, to a considerable degree,
formulated by the culture in which they are born or find themselves; as Graeme Turner
notes, 'we are the subjects, not the authors, of cultural processes.'[11] That is, the culture
perpetuates itself through humans by virtue of 'living' within them, replicating itself in
the course of human activity. Humans thus serve as the hosts through which the culture
is transmitted from one generation to the next.

With regards to religion, Geertz asserts that the 'holy bears within it everywhere a sense
of intrinsic obligation: it not only encourages devotion, it demands it; it not only induces
intellectual assent, it enforces emotional commitment'.[12] In Christian Europe, Suzanne
Langer notes, 'the Church brought men daily (in some orders even hourly) to their knees, to
enact if not to contemplate their assent to the ultimate concepts.'[13] Following from these
points, the culture spoken of in this study is that which encompasses the myriad details of
life as commonly lived – the views and attitudes deriving from the dominant religion, to be
sure, but made operative in the countless decisions and choices comprising a human life.
For the Other to be identified, defined, targeted, ignored, or acted upon legally, socially,
militarily, economically, and so forth, involves a complex array of human beings in various
social structures in order to execute these tactics. As Rubenstein and Roth assert in
Approaches to Auschwitz, virtually all levels and components of German society were
involved in the perpetration of the Holocaust.[14] This would include, to name a few, all
those needed to implement a massive programme and all those on the margins, but
necessary nonetheless, to such a project: lawyers, judges, police, bureaucrats, military
personnel, engineers, civil servants, railway workers, construction personnel, journalists,
educators, industrialists and their workers, neighbours, and families of all of the above. This
study contends that similar levels of active and passive support, enabled by a certain
ideology and culture, were required in the following cases: starting with Christianity in
the late Roman Empire, the Crusades, the Inquisition, church actions against heretics,
contact with indigenous people in the Americas, and slavery there. This paper will focus on
the early centuries of Christianity's rise to imperial eminence and the early stages of

European contact with Native Americans. The cultural processes under investigation will be seen in both cases.

There is little doubt that the moral, ontological and eschatological claims of a religion constitute some of the most compelling life directives that human beings encounter in their cultures. In the Christian world view, the experience of religion involves truth claims about one's soul and its status for virtually all of eternity. There is the promise of the possibility of a direct relationship for the true believer with his or her God, or identification with a powerful, universal corporate entity such as the Roman Catholic Church, or both. Early Christian apologists found that the Bible has 'all truth . . . contained in it, and all truth is Christian truth'.[15] Adherence to certain normative beliefs, in thought and deed and in both public and private spheres, helps the believer achieve the promised ends. Given the process by which Christianity emerged from its parent religion, Judaism, and the consequent rejection of that parent religion (involving what Rubenstein and Roth have termed 'religiously legitimated incitement to homicidal violence'),[16] the practise of various aspects of that rejection of Judaism became incumbent upon Christian believers over the centuries.

Furthermore, this practise involved not only the ultimate truth claims of Christianity (the presence of the Messiah in human history, the role of Judaism in God's plan, etc.) but also enactment of the religion's system of eternal rewards and punishments. One should not underestimate the power of Christianity's system for rewards and sanctions in motivating its believers – but it is also important to keep in mind, for the purposes of this study, that this motivation involved what John Gager has identified as 'ideological nihilation and conceptual liquidation'[17] of Judaism's basic tenets. (Gager is speaking of the origins of antisemitism, but those attitudes have persisted. Sadly, we have come to learn that religious belief is no guarantee against genocidal acts. Indeed, greater 'religiosity is frequently associated with greater prejudice'[18]). The Servite priest John T. Powlikowski refers to the 'very serious distortion of Judaism central to Christian theology'.[19] This surely amounts to the cultural 'misinformation' to which Geertz refers.

Such cultural misinformation, originally expressed in theological disputations during the period of Christianity's break from Judaism, eventually manifested in the Middle Ages as a wide variety of superstitious claims concerning Jews,[20] and continues in this century's treatment of Judaism as seen, for instance, in the clerical education most prospective pastors encounter, in mass consumed entertainment,[21] and in increased hate crimes in the U.S. as recorded by the FBI.[22] Father Edward H. Flannery writes of 'pathological anti-Semitism' (one wonders if this is similar to Goldhagen's 'eliminationist anti-Semitism'), and notes its presence 'in society as a source of infection that can contaminate the normal in times of stress'.[23] If there is, as Robert E. Willis suggests, an evil essence to Christianity,[24] which surely contributes to the cultural misinformation Geertz mentions, the wonder is that any goodness ever derived from it. Yet it strikes me that much goodness has, indeed, been provided by the religion and its adherents throughout its existence in terms of consolation, social amelioration, and demands for justice. But even this must be considered in light of the theological strings often attached and, certainly, of the simple fact that whatever goodness has come about is necessarily alloyed with centuries of the most troubling attitudes and behaviours as well as countless repulsive deeds.

In *Modernity and the Holocaust*, Zygmunt Bauman makes the case that modern genocide, indeed, modern culture and the work of the modern state, is little else than a 'gardening' operation[25]: 'viewing the society it rules as an object of designing, cultivating and weed poisoning';[26] 'separating and setting apart useful elements destined to live and thrive, from harmful and morbid ones, which ought to be exterminated'.[27] This is a useful observation, although I shall argue that there are clear antecedents to those manifested by the modern state and in modern culture. Alan Davies, however, has inverted the gardening image in *Infected Christianity: A Study of Modern Racism*, observing that 'Once the Jewishness of Jesus has been diluted . . . Christianity is easily captured by nationalism and racism and, once captured, is not so easily rescued from their snares, for the roots of these alien weeds are deeply embedded in the soil of Western civilization, where eradication is not an easy task.'[28] Perhaps the weeds he speaks of, once having taken root, virtually become the garden, protected from eradication by the removal of competing entities. Gardening, as performed in Bauman's sense of the word, has been practised for many centuries, from the theologically inspired 'gardening' from the Roman era until today.

Certainly one of the most significant turning points in the world's history took place in the 4th century CE, when Christianity became aligned with Imperial Rome under Constantine. This convergence of the twain would prove to have disastrous consequences for non-Christians in later centuries, not the least being the Jews in Europe in the 20th century. The alignment of the emerging religion and its truth claims (which had previously eschewed violence in general as well as service in the Roman military) with the power and structure of the Roman state apparatus proved to be a potent cultural and ideological mix, beginning a train of events that would see an aggressive, absolutist church united with a variety of political entities to have its way when it saw fit. Prior to Constantine, Christianity sought religious toleration instead of persecution; within fifty years after ascending to the status of imperial state religion, it became 'the persecutor of every other form of religious expression'.[29] Several factors contributed to this: on the one hand, Christianity made universal claims regarding its message and function; regarded its truth claims as the only valid truth claims, replacing those of the parent religion; and interpreted the will of its God partially through historical events – some of which it initiated and controlled. David Olster observes that the alliance of Christianity with the Roman Empire provided the religion with 'a religio-political rhetoric called triumphalism' that was rooted in three themes: 'victory demonstrated divine power . . . divine favor guaranteed victory, and . . . the emperor [was] the empire's mediator for, and personal recipient of, divine favor'.[30] Matters of religious doctrine became questions of 'power within the framework of Roman imperial government'.[31] Averil Cameron, with reference to Foucault and Michael Mann, notes that Christianity thus operates as a 'totalizing discourse' with 'transcendent ideological power in human history'.[32] (For our purposes a useful definition of discourse is 'socially produced groups of ideas or ways of thinking that can be tracked in individual texts or groups of texts').[33]

A good example of the results of such totalizing discourse is found in 4th-century Spain: after a long period of tolerance and acceptance of local religious customs, an imperial decree declared the confiscation of all lands used – even unwittingly – for 'prohibited worship'. The decree would have been read, with appropriate fanfare and solemnity, in the most crowded of public places. Ramsay MacMullen's study of *Christianizing the Roman Empire* lists the kind of state-sponsored language regarding prohibited religious activity to which the citizens hearing this would have been exposed: 'madness, contamination, poison, perfidy, monstrousness, polluted contagion . . .'. More to the point for my concerns is MacMullen's awareness of how the perspective of the state's approved religion could circulate among the people far removed from the centre of imperial splendour:

> What items of experience were people talking about and passing on to their neighbors? What impinged on a person's settled universe of ideas, disturbing it and preparing him to question his previous beliefs and even abandon them? What made news? The most likely

items on the religious page concerned Christian holy men, miracles, exorcisms, healings, wonderful things. They concerned the emperor's laws read aloud in the town center, declaring all but Christian views to be entirely intolerable. They were oratorical displays in cathedrals for both everyday folk and the upper classes. For the latter alone, new publication of any ideologically aggressive sort likely to attract attention was Christian. The prevailing close social and economic relations did not allow non-Christian people to shut out this noise of Christian exuberance, this din of defeat.[34]

Rome, for its part, thus obviously provided a platform for Christianity to use to broadcast its message, one based on the twin pillars of Roman law and military organiza- tion, strength, and presence throughout the Empire – that is, the ability to project Roman power and law across much of Europe, northern Africa and eastern Asia. This change of fortune provided Christianity a quantum leap in its ability either to persuade or coerce non-Christians to convert and to execute punitive measures against Jews and Judaism – and, later, other infidels and heretics. It is highly instructive to consider the legislative specifics that impacted the lives of Jews either in the Empire or, later, under the influence and control of Christianity:

Christianity created ghettos; prohibited mixed marriages; prohibited Jews from serving as judges . . .[35]

Rome barred intermarriage; removed Jews from the army; prohibited construction of new synagogues; barred Jews from serving in administrative and municipal positions; rewarded conversion to Christianity; forbade Jewish parents to disinherit children who converted; decreed the death penalty for those who attacked Jewish apostates; decreed the death penalty for intermarriage (also loss of property or exile); forced Jews to obey Roman law instead of Jewish law; disallowed synagogues taxation rights of Jews; forbade circumcision unless of one's son; denied the study of the Mishna in synagogues.[36]

Both before and after the demise of the Roman empire, Orthodox and Catholic Church councils continued the pressures against the Jews:

Christians not to eat unleavened bread sent to them by Jews; not be friendly with Jews; not to use medicines prescribed by Jews; not to bathe with Jews; no Jews to own Christian slaves; no Christian to rest on Saturday – but work; Christians not to accept gifts from Jews, nor celebrate holidays with them.

The Catholic Synod in Elvira in 306 CE declared no intermarriage; Jews not to bless a field owned by a Christian.

The 465 CE Synod in Vennes, France, mandated clergy not to eat with Jews (extended to laymen in 517).

The Narbonne Synod in France did not allow Christians to stay in a house with a Jew.

The Synod of Macon in 581 CE prohibited Jews from being in the streets during Holy Week; mandated that Jews must pay attention to the wishes of Christian clerics; Jews must not sit in the presence of such clerics unless permitted; Jews could not be judges or tax collectors over Christians; could not own Christian slaves (greatly diminishing Jewish access to farming).

The 633 CE Synod in Toledo kept converted Jews from having any dealings with Jews (even relatives).

The 681 CE Synod of Toledo led to the Visigothic code of law: old laws were renewed: Jews not to insult the trinity; Jews not to withdraw themselves, sons, or male servants from baptism or conversion; Jews not to celebrate Passover in their traditional manner, nor celebrate their Sabbath or festivals; Jews must stay away from work on Sunday; Jews not permitted to make distinctions among foods; Jews not to advise relatives; Jews not to attack Christianity nor defend their sect; Jews not to emigrate to apostate again; Jews not to read books rejected by Christianity; their slaves freed if converted to Christianity; no Jewish landlord allowed over Christian serfs; Jews new to a country had to identify themselves to the bishop – who could require them to appear before him on certain days.

The 694 Synod of Toledo added that the king could make Jews into slaves; their children could be removed after seventh year and married to Christians.[37]

The Synod of Toulouse in 883 ruled and 'the emperor confirmed that on every Christmas, Good Friday and Ascension Day a Jew was to be given a powerful slap in the face in front of the church door' – the slapped Jew to 'shout three times: "It is just that Jews must bend their neck under the beatings of Christians, as they are unwilling to submit to Christ."'[38]

The 1209 Synod of Avignon forced Jews to work on Sunday, prohibited their eating meat on Christian holidays, prohibited the taking of usurious interest and to return it to those from whom they had received it.

The Fourth Lateran Council of 1215 declared that Jews had to wear different clothes from Christians (to give a clear sign to avoid sexual intercourse).[39]

This overview reveals that, once allied with the state apparatus, Christianity did not tarry in making life as difficult as possible for the Jews in its midst. These laws, rescripts and edicts – some executed locally, others across the Empire – impacted and invaded the most intimate details and functions of life and constructed obstacles that made normal human relations with and for Jews virtually impossible. The structure and complexity of Roman governance meant that the promulgation of these laws involved a wide array of officials as they moved the paperwork along: those involved included the emperor, possibly a complainant, the praefecti praetorio, departmental heads at court such as 'the Master of Offices . . . the Comes of the sacred Largesses . . . the Comes of the Private Property . . . the Comes and the Master of the Two Services . . . the "Comes of the East" to name a few'.[40] Laws were edited, recorded in a register and, later, deposited in archives after codification and manuscript transmission.[41]

This brief account offers a clear sense of the large number of government personnel involved, prefiguring the legislative and bureaucratic precision of Germany some 1,500 years later. Such restrictions on the activities and lives of Jews echo down throughout the centuries, resonating in Luther's lifetime, in Spain during the Inquisition, and into the Third Reich, among other lamentable episodes. Thus an implicit ideology emerged, one lacking overt reference to theological rationales, but one that nevertheless came to be experienced as the norm by Christians. Newly empowered in the secular sphere, Christianity in Roman times thus set out on a course that would alter the lives of virtually every human being who would ever come under its sway in the centuries ahead – although it may be argued that it did not do this without seriously compromising its message of love and charity for all, a harsh price to pay for making universal proclamations and condemnations of the Other.

In this latter regard, one of the most significant vestiges of the Roman-Christian past is the change in practice allowing Christian males to serve in the Roman army. In the first two centuries of the Common Era, the church's theology and practice was pacifistic.[42] With Constantine's triumph over Maxentius, according to Adolf Harnack, the Christian God was revealed to be the 'God of war and victory';[43] accordingly, pacifism was eventually lost as one of the options for the 'lay person's expression of Christian ethical life'.[44] Indeed, after 313 CE, Christians could be excommunicated if they attempted to *leave* the military. At the end of the 4th century, St. Basil had mandated that a soldier 'with unclean hands abstain from communion for three years'.[45] By the time of Theodosius II, in 416 CE, *only* Christians could serve in the Roman military,[46] a development signifying a stunning reversal of Church teaching and practice within the passing of a single century. For Augustine, only the clergy could practice pacifism; for others, killing could be done out of duty, not malice.[47] This brief overview of developments involving Christianity's gradual embrace of military roles and values reveals what Jean-Michel Hornus sees as the triumph of the Empire over Christianity, the infection of the emerging religion with reasons of state.[48]

Aside from these changes for Christians, the example of John Chrysostom is a particular case in point of the emerging dominant culture for his numerous attacks on Jews and Judaisers. Marcel Simon finds him to be an extreme case but by no means a unique case in the first few centuries after Christ. His attitudes were reflected every-where in early Church writings. Reading Chrysostom's venomous attacks today is a shocking experience.[49] At the time, however, his sermons were very public events, delivered in a setting in which his pulpit was located in the centre of the nave, with his listeners pressing close upon him, 'like crowds around a soap-box orator ...'. Christians of the 4th century CE were accustomed to dramatic performances in church services rivalling what they liked in theatre.[50] Simon makes the important point that virulent attitudes like Chrysostom's were not isolated to the hierarchy of the Church, nor were the Church's august figures the only source of information for believers. He finds anti-Judaism prominently displayed in the liturgy, although he believes that its anti-Jewish sentiments were not uniformly spread throughout the liturgical year, clustering instead around certain holy observances.

Contrary to Simon's sense of the issue is the perspective that 'Anti-Jewish polemic ... was thus driven into the minds of the believers and shaped their entire way of thinking. Being thus reinforced day by day, anti-Jewish sentiments hardened' in the minds of Christian believers.[51] Michael Mann, a sociologist, confirms this view:

> The tentacles of this institution reached into the life of every court, every manor, every village, every town of Europe ... Indeed, this was the only authoritative interaction network that spread so extensively while also penetrating 'intensively into everyday life'.[52]

By the 7th century, David M. Olster argues, religion was 'far better integrated into the political culture than many might expect',[53] replacing classical Roman ideology with a culture well-rooted in a 'unitary Christian world view'.[54] Hermann Doerris sees the resulting intolerance going much deeper than any intolerance practised by pre-Constantinian heathens. Given the nature of its claims, believers in Christianity had to dedicate their whole personal life to their god because the 'jurisdiction of the state extended to souls and consciences. For that reason the intolerance of the Christian faith was more incisive and far-reaching'.[55] Doerris makes the ominous note that there was a reaction among believers to this intolerance without which 'the outcome would have resembled the modern totalitarian state'.[56] Christianity in the process assumed certain functions of Imperial Rome. In the estimation of Alan Davies, this 'conviction led both to crusades against the children of darkness, and, in due course, to colonial expansion as a kind of final crusade'.[57] This observation keeps before us the matter of the chronological continuity of Christianity's impact on historical events.

I I

'The Anglo-Europeans who came here had one goal: destruction of life... one of the best
ways I know to discover purpose is to examine outcome.'

Paula Gunn Allen, *Spider Woman's Granddaughters*

Before the ships carrying Columbus and his crews were first seen by the indigenous people
of the Americas, the destinies of the natives had already been declared in a variety of texts,
words written in a dead language they could not have known, inscribing concepts that were
perhaps even more alien. A 1302 papal bull, *Unam Sanctum*, of Boniface VIII asserted the
pontiff's right to dominion: 'that to be submitted to the Roman pontiff is for any creature a
necessity for salvation'.[58] Pope Nicolas V issued a papal bull, *Romanus Pontifex*, in 1454 that
seemed to reach the logical extension of the 1302 position: in it, Nicolas denies non-
Christians the right to their own possessions; gives to the Portuguese the right to invade
and conquer the lands of non-Christians, force their expulsion, vanquish them, enslave
them, and 'expropriate their possessions'. In the case of failed attempts to convert non-
Christians on *terra nullius*, colonizers could kill the natives as 'an act of faith and a religious
duty...'.[59] The grounds for this treatment derived from the medieval interpretation that
there was no legitimate secular power aside from the Church and that after Christ, 'all
legitimate secular power was transferred to the Christian faithful'.[60] Given this theological
and cultural orientation to the Other, it is not surprising that the first European-built
structure in the New World was a fort, or that Columbus would plant a cross in the soil of
the new lands he was claiming on behalf of Christianity.[61]

In 1502, A Dominican friar named Bartolomé de Las Casas is recorded as having
arrived in Spain's new possession, Hispaniola. His father had been involved in the
earliest Spanish contact with the indigenous people a few years earlier. The younger
Las Casas recalled seeing some of the Native Americans taken to Spain by Columbus
after that initial contact.[62] The life of Las Casas was changed permanently in 1511 when
he heard a passionate sermon preached by the Dominican Fr. Antonio de Montesinos in
which he insisted on the basic humanity of the native people.[63]

Subsequently, Las Casas came to devote much of his long remaining life to the matter
of bringing to the Spanish Crown's attention his view that violent Spanish practices
against the natives in the New World were unworthy of his sense of the most basic
Christian principles. His persistence in this matter resulted in a 'debate' in 1550 with Fr.
Juan Ginés de Sepulveda, the crown's chaplain and chronicler,[64] who argued in support
of the inhumane Spanish policies as the best means of bringing the natives to the
Church. Las Casas, however, prevailed and eventual changes in practices were mandated
by the Crown, although Native Americans never enjoyed any complete respite from
European-inspired depredations.

(Las Casas had his limitations. He supported both the Inquisition and the sending of
Africans to the New World to be enslaved.[65] In this, his life recalls the tortured existence
of one Kurt Gerstein, German nationalist, Nazi protester, SS man, potential war crimes
witness, man of conscience – but a man trapped nevertheless by the unperceived
limitations of his commitment to a certain world view, a failure to grasp the depths of
the evil he was attempting to destroy. Taken together, Las Casas and Gerstein perhaps
reveal the extreme difficulties encountered when people must attempt to reinterpret
events of atrocity going on around them in order 'to be able to integrate it into [their]
own vision'.[66])

In his report to the Crown, *The Devastation of the Indies: A Brief Account*, Las Casas recorded an unbelievable litany of atrocities inflicted by the Spanish conquerors upon the nearly helpless natives. After detailing yet another in a long register of mass slaughters, one particular atrocity stands out:

> Now, in God's name, you who read this, consider . . . whether it is accurate to call such Christians devils. . . . I am going to tell of another action the Spanish engage in . . . and it still goes on at the present time . . . the Spaniards train their fierce dogs to attack, kill and tear to pieces the Indians. It is doubtful whether anyone, whether Christian or not, has ever heard of such a thing as this. The Spaniards keep alive their dogs' appetite for human beings in this way . . . And the Spaniards have butcher shops where the corpses of Indians are hung up, and someone will come in and say, more or less, 'Give me a quarter of that rascal hanging there, to feed my dogs until I can kill another one for them.' As if buying a quarter of a hog or other meat.[67]

This butcher shop selling body parts of human beings for dog food is perhaps only the most vivid example of many such instances, attitudes and behaviours that are this study's concern. The chronicle of Las Casas is filled with similar examples: dismembering people like animals in a slaughterhouse . . . killing infants in front of their mothers . . . - cutting off hands . . . roasting natives on fire grids . . . feeding burned humans to dogs . . . practising 100:1 reprisals . . . burning people in their straw huts[68] . . . torturing people to death . . . burning people at the stake . . . disfiguring children's faces with swords.[69]

These atrocities were perpetrated by Spanish soldiers who felt, according to Las Casas, that they had the God-given right to do so or were following the orders of their superiors.[70] The practice of invoking the Christian God as the ultimate warrant for such violent acts enjoyed a plethora of scriptural or theological sources. As in the case of the complex support services needed to keep the death camps fully operational, we may suspect that a butcher shop featuring a variety of choice human selections for dogs would also require a degree of complexity in the supporting personnel. First, such a shop requires the conquerors to see the natives as non-human or sub-human, mere objects to exploit[71] (reflected in the debates within the Church as to whether or not the natives possessed souls) – and no one of conscience on the scene to contest the matter. One could argue that such a shop would be unknown at that time on the European mainland. It was sited, after all, thousands of miles from the mother country, with a vast ocean separating it from the homeland. Having said that, however, such a location also presupposes a Crown charter or the like, all the support services needed for a significant maritime venture, church involvement, military personnel, various adventurers, those with capital interests, a variety of general labourers, supervisors, accountants, government represent- atives, and so forth. Of course, all of these people would also have access to others – their families back home, friends, and neighbours. How far did the outrage of Las Casas permeate his society, the supporting personnel behind the effort?

Encountering the indigenous people of the New World proved to be an experience that 'didn't fit within Christianity's explanation of the moral universe'.[72] We may justifiably ask, however, if those who witnessed this butcher shop (or the other atrocities detailed by Las Casas) were so hardened that they never felt the need to make comment to those close to them? Or, if they did, in what terms and attitudes were the descriptions couched? How would the information have been received? Were the clergy assigned to the colony, other than Las Casas and Montesinos, so immured within the cultural mandates regarding the Other that these scenes did not cause them to shudder in revulsion or reconsider the theological underpinnings? (Would the clergy have noticed the Spanish conquerors' habit of executing Native Americans in groups of thirteen – 'in honour and reverence for our Redeemer and the twelve Apostles'?[73]) That they did not feel the need to make comment speaks volumes of the strength of the culture's assumptions and beliefs about the Other.

Indeed, the revelations of Las Casas led eventually to the controversy known as The Black Legend, based essentially on an unwillingness to believe the particulars, or downplaying their significance. This argument may be indicative of the Western culture's difficulty in fully coming to terms with the implications of atrocities like those practiced in the Americas, and genocides such as the Holocaust (not to mention what Holocaust revisionism reveals), especially with regard to the cultural core values that did much to contribute to these events. The ubiquitous, incessant claims of universality, transcendence, and triumphalism – allied with the obvious historical significance that material prosperity represents – make it difficult for those fully invested in those claims to see anything else, to see fully and clearly the brutal impact Western culture has had on hundreds of millions of innocent people. Indeed, Christianity provided a 'triadic formal model' – composed of [1] Christians, [2] infidels (Muslims, Jews), and [3] idolators (pagans)[74] – that provided believers with a schema they could rely upon for making decisions about moral obligations. (A contemporary example of the cultural mandates pressing against the Other is found in the action of the Southern Baptist International Mission Board in publishing a 'prayer guide' recently distributed in 40,000 U.S. churches. The prayer guide was published to coincide with Rosh Hashanah in order to convince Jews to convert to Christianity.[75] Just as Europeans sought new lands and peoples to find new converts, many such large-scale efforts continue today 'to invade the most sacred inner precincts of another man's being'.[76])

Sylvia Wynter contends that the 'truths' people live by 'once put into place, must necessarily be not only "impervious to philosophical attack" but impervious also to empirical counterevidence'.[77] Luis Villoro strikes the crucial note:

> If the meaning of history is the final triumph of Christianity, if its development is governed by the design of Providence, that which is irreducible to Christianity can only be that which contradicts that design. And the one who contradicts it has, in our cultural tradition, a name: Satan. The other's culture, insofar as it cannot be translated to ours, cannot be but devilish. This is the most common interpretation amongst the missionaries and chroniclers. Their basic belief of the world holds that there can only be one truth and one destiny for man. . . . If some other culture intends to have another truth or destiny, it denies our picture of the world . . . The other is the obscure and occult, that which says 'no' to the world, the Satanic. Then, by definition, it is what cannot be integrated into our world, that which is open to destruction.[78]

The cultural expectations and truths that sustained Europeans in their treatment of the indigenous peoples of the New World are still operating today. Sylvia Wynter identifies 'the deep-seated belief in the *genetic* nonhomogeneity of the human species' as the 'belief system . . . responsible not only for innumerable atrocities that were to climax in Auschwitz, but also for a sociosystematically produced series of savage inequalities'.[79] That savagery has been a feature of the belief system that perceives the saved apart from the damned, or those with souls and those without, or the white good and the dark evil, the Christian and the non-Christian.

This disturbing example of the butcher shop Las Casas witnessed has a horrifying but revealing counterpart from the Holocaust (surely one of countless such). As recounted by Regina Landau, we learn that the Gestapo used Jewish children to discover more adult Jews being sought in a follow-up sweep after a massacre of Jews in the town of Lanzut, Poland. The children were tortured by the Gestapo, but the children did not reveal what they knew. According to Landau, the Gestapo ended the affair this way: 'As the children were led to the cemetery they were urged not to cry, for they would "go to heaven, and meet their mother, father and aunts." After the children had been shot the Gestapo took their bodies to the circus performing in Lanzut, to be eaten by the beasts.'[80]

This enormity engenders concerns similar to those articulated in the case of the Spanish butcher shop. Revealed, obviously, is the Gestapo's ability to dehumanise the Other totally, to see Jewish children as unworthy of life. But we should note in particular the willingness to use a reference to a heaven and an afterlife as a means of 'consoling' the children. The usual values associated with a heaven are here completely perverted – the Gestapo persecutors were making the job easier for themselves, attempting to create fully compliant victims, not primarily offering 'comfort' to the doomed children. The utter emptiness of their gesture is underscored by the subsequent use of the children's bodies to feed circus animals. As in the Spanish case, the stark facts of humans consciously being used by their tormentors as food for animals is not isolated to the perpetrators: the horror extends to the larger surrounding social context. In this case, a circus – a place for family enjoyment, entertainment, frivolity... indeed, a place for children to indulge themselves and live out their innocent fantasies – becomes a site of their ultimate degradation, but also a site where the larger culture expresses itself. Furthermore, the prelude to that degradation involved an awareness of the accepted cultural religious context – albeit one used in a cruel, calculated manner.

Both the Spanish butcher shop and the German use of Jewish children to feed circus animals take place within the larger culture and are based on attitudes inculcated within that culture. Both derive from Christian perspectives – one that devalued the so-called 'heathen' or pagans, giving dominion over all non-Christians, and then the age-old disconfirming Other of Christianity. These values assisted the perpetrators in their work but also provided the bystanders with the kind of supporting rationale required for them to do nothing, to see nothing amiss, nothing worth resisting or protesting. Altruism is normally practised towards those humans one can identify with; but more to the point under consideration here is that altruism is all too rarely manifested towards the Other.[81]

III

'In the beginning there was the Holocaust. We must therefore start all over again.'
– Elie Wiesel[82]

Robert Jay Lifton, in *Nazi Doctors*, theorizes that German physicians involved in the death factories practiced what Lifton calls 'doubling' and 'derealisation' in order to function with minimal psychological distress,[83] which Lifton sees as part of the 'universal proclivity toward constructing good motives while participating in evil behavior'.[84] Lifton defines doubling as the partition of the self into 'two functioning wholes', with one of the partial selves serving as the whole self.[85] Thus, physicians having sworn the Hippocratic Oath could throw themselves into the daily tasks involving mass death found at Auschwitz. Derealization, according to Lifton, divests the self 'from the actuality of what one is part of, not experiencing it as "real"'.[86] Added to this is a feeling of powerlessness, that one is merely a very small part of a much larger functioning unit.[87] Taken together, these make the perpetrator's assignment more easily rendered; the gardening operation spoken of by Zygmunt Bauman becomes an easier task, if not altogether enjoyable in every case. The inaction of bystanders, likewise, is facilitated by doubling. Although Lifton's work is not without its critics, it strikes me that his points may be applied to those who seemingly are not so morally compromised (in terms of a professional oath prescribing one's behaviour) as were the Nazi doctors. The Nazi doctors were faced with making their circle of moral and professional obligation slightly smaller, rejecting Jews. This is not quite what many other people in the Christian West faced because their world view had in many ways already excluded Jews. We see that this cultural apparatus functioning over the centuries to anathematise Jews lent itself readily to reactions against different Others when encountered – Muslims, indigenous people in the New World, Africans, heretics, gays, witches, and others.

Contrary to Lifton's 'divided-self' notion of perpetrating evil is James E. Waller's insightful 'unitary-self' concept. For Waller, 'the primary, and only, self or psychological constellation *is* fundamentally altered as a result of the power of potent social forces generated by the situation or organization'.[88] Waller cites several studies dealing with 'the foot-in-the-door' phenomenon – 'the tendency for people who have first agreed to a small request to comply later with a larger request'.[89] Waller concludes that harming 'victims can become "normal" behaviour'.[90]

Both theories offer relevant possibilities, although from the perspective of this study, Lifton's argument clearly gives a degree of personal choice to the individual in a situation involving atrocity. Waller's account, which is closer to the approach taken in this paper, in my view more accurately reveals the impact on the individual, the self, of much larger forces. (Indeed, 'impact' may miss the point – culture actually does much to create and inform the self that operates in a social setting.) Waller's unitary-self theory sees the individual as in essence neither inherently good nor evil: 'we become that to which we are exposed'.[91] If that larger entity is itself evil, the devastating human results should not be surprising. The culture of Western Europe and Christianity did seek compliance from believers regarding its views of the Other, but more than mere compliance happens when acted out. It may help to recall the famous line about a village by the U.S. Marine officer in Vietnam: 'We had to destroy it to save it'. A transcendent hierarchy of values privileges the soul and eternal afterlife over the body, the life lived on earth – an especially powerful concept when the believer operates against the Other with the strong, if not absolute, assurance of one's own righteousness and salvation. The cultural discourse of Christianity both mandated and empowered believers to 'save' the Other – through either conversion or destruction (as seen in the Inquisition).

The issues raised here necessarily involve the implications of what it means to be involved in a culture – that is, what does it mean to give one's assent to a belief system, an ideology? This is, generally, not a conscious decision, but it entails virtually any thought the believer may have, any attitude, any behaviour. In the focus of this study – a dominant religion operating across twenty centuries – individuals are not readily able to ascertain whether that institution or its culture is morally compromised, or evil in its essence and many functions, and not inclined to perform the ideological critique that could determine such. There is much evidence available to the believer that his or her involvement is benign, producing positive, good, moral results. Perpetrating evil acts, or bystanding, will have a rationalized support system. In a private communication with Dr. Johnathan Shay, a specialist in combat-induced post-traumatic stress disorder,[92] the author asked why German Holocaust perpetrators did not seem to suffer PTSD as did

American veterans of the Vietnam conflict. His response was that German perpetrators enjoyed the benefit of a strong supporting social system – a culture, in the terms of this study. That is, there was, for them, in the Holocaust no trauma over which to suffer stress. This would seem to hold true for bystanders as well.

Unresolved at this point is the matter of resistance. As asserted by Elie Wiesel, it is time to start over. Is there some way by which people can avoid entrapment in a culture serving inhumane, destructive purposes, even though these are presented as normal and right in the legal system, one's education, the arts, and worship? The enculturation process would not seem to include those methods designed to call into doubt foundational documents and truth claims. Yet we have ample and instructive evidence that some individuals are able to see beyond the limited perspectives and moral obligations inculcated for and lived out by the majority of people.[93]

Most scholars see the Holocaust as a terrible rupture in western culture and civilization, an event that shattered all previously known moral categories. With the greatest of respect for these scholars and their work, but to the contrary, my work seeks to reveal that the Holocaust, with its distinguishing features, is the culminating point of a process covering at least seventeen centuries. That is to say, Western Christianity's civilization and culture did not really 'fail' – indeed, they operated as they had been designed to do for centuries, achieving an unparalleled peak of efficiency in the death camps. (During those centuries, all available technologies had been brought to bear against the Other; the Holocaust continued that pattern.)

Continuity marks the depredations practised against the various groups constituting the Other from the early centuries of Christianity until today. We see violent words and violent actions aimed at Jews in the 4th century CE, continued pressures against them through the next several centuries under various synods, full-scale warfare against Muslims and Jews in the Crusades, an entire bureaucratic apparatus of violence created for the Inquisition, military and theological coercion activated against the indigenous peoples of the New World, and scriptural, social, and legal terror directed against Africans to enslave them. All of these are complicated events, discourses and processes, but there remain crucial, uniform cultural elements central to all of them.

Joshua Trachtenberg observed that in the Middle Ages, 'vilification' against Jews became 'actuality in the mind of the uncritical'. For those people, Satan and the Jews had battled against not only Christ in his lifetime, but also 'in the contemporaneous war against the Church and its civilization'. Christianity's response then was a summons to a 'holy war of extermination' against Satan, in the person of the Jews.[94]

One would be hard pressed to detect the differences in the antisemitic rhetoric of Chrysostom, Luther, German sermons and periodicals, and Hitler's fulminations. Holocaust survivor Walter Zwi Bacharach has traced the vilifications against the Jews found in German Catholic sermons. In one instance, the priest called for 'the annihilation of these impudent desecrators of Divine law'.[95] Other sermons included the following charges against Jews: they are 'murderers, criminals, evil ones, sinners, enraged, inhuman, despicable, corrupt, desecrators, impudent, cunning serpents, poisonous, enemies of God ... garbage'.[96] Sermons designed for the edification of children were little different.[97]

Bacharach's study focuses primarily on the delivery of such views to a wide, popular audience, including the rural areas. Robert P. Ericksen concentrates on three of the elite figures in Germany's theological circles in the Hitler era – Gerhard Kittel, Paul Althaus, and Emmanuel Hirsch – representative of the majority of their colleagues in German universities and the churches,[98] and all three badly compromised by their respective positions during the Nazi years. Gerhard Kittel's defence of his behaviour in those years included two points that are central to the concerns of this study. Ericksen notes that Kittel asked: 'Could it not be believed that [his] position towards the Jewish question was imposed upon him by God?' Then, the 'final question is "whether in the Christian cultural world it counts as a crime which must be prevented through legal punishment, that one represents a position on the Jewish question based upon the instruction of Jesus and the Apostles?"'[99]

Kittel's anguished questions ring with poignancy and urgency down through twenty centuries of Christian existence and seventeen centuries of Christian domination. We should note his sense of a lack of autonomy – God imposed his position upon him. Strictly speaking, to fail to execute a divine wish could be construed as sinful. Certainly, Kittel's scholarship had revealed for him massive textual and cultural substantiation for his position. That he was even dimly aware of the possible criminal implications of his past reveals a conscience not entirely devoid of sensitivity – but the key point is that he is also able to connect his personal past with the 'instruction' of Jesus and the Apostles. For Kittel, there is a personal continuum of perspectives from these figures to his own life. The Christian conscience, under those circumstances, is nullified into passivity – or activated into evil. Ericksen also makes the acute observation regarding the difficulty 'of distinguishing the insane from the believers'[100] – a problem that takes on awesome dimensions from the perspective of the Other.

All of the seemingly countless small steps taken toward dehumanising the Other over the centuries left not a chasm to be crossed, but just another small, incremental step to take. The Germans, and their helpers, proved to be fully capable of taking that step. They had, after all, abundant examples to model themselves upon. In this sense, then, the Holocaust was implicit in the trajectory of development of Western culture and history, once the culture set out in a certain way, without developing a restraining ideological critique. As stated earlier, the process continues even after the Holocaust – witness the 1948 Darmstadt Declaration (the German Lutherans' blaming of the Jewish victims for their fate), and the 1999 Southern Baptists' concerted effort to convert Jews during Rosh Hashanah. The Holocaust seems not to have presented any insurmountable difficulties for the Christians involved in these efforts. The theological and cultural mandate to continue implementing the destructive patterns from the past against the Other proved to be powerful indeed in these instances.

One of the driving features of a Christian culture and civilisation is that it relies upon or seeks 'transcendent' answers to the difficult, baffling problems of life. This kind of reliance often displaces more mundane considerations and explanations. Transcendent explanations are usually keyed to the overarching designs of God. Under these circumstances, it is difficult for the members of a culture to perceive or acknowledge the evil components of its presence in history – as seen in the case of Gerhard Kittel. As an ideology making all-encompassing, transcendent claims, Christianity provides 'a mode of interpretation in which the intrinsic sense of the dominant idea is applied in all possible directions until everything in history and human experience is subsumed under its logic',[101] hence operating as a key component of the larger culture. Alan Davies has noted that 'individualistic illusions' fostered by Protestantism, in particular, causes believers to 'underestimate the depth of' problems such as racism[102]. If this is true, as a principle it might be extended to similar concerns in this study, the failure to realize, for instance, what Robert E. Willis sees as the evil essence of Christianity.

There is virtual unanimity among such scholars that the Holocaust cannot be equated with or usefully compared to any other historical events involving wholesale slaughters or genocides. I understand and sympathize with these positions, but wish to urge that we stand to gain much by becoming more aware of and examining crucial patterns of behaviour within our cultural discourse that contributed in large measure, over many centuries, to laying the groundwork for the acts of the perpetrators and the bystanders against the victims of the Holocaust and the Other – and have done so for many centuries.

N O T E S
1   Regina M. Schwartz, *The Curse of Cain: The Violent Legacy of Monotheism* (Chicago: The University of Chicago Press, 1997), p.16.
2   Daniel Jonah Goldhagen, *Hitler's Willing Executioners* (New York: Alfred A. Knopf, 1996), p.71.
3   *ibid.*, p.75.
4   Oliver Clausen, 'Weiss/Propagandist – Weiss/Playwright', *New York Times Magazine*, 2 October 1966, p.132.
5   Peter Weiss, *The Investigation* (New York: Atheneum, 1966), p.108.
6   *ibid.*, p.132.
7   *ibid.*, p.134.
8   Raymond Williams, *Keywords* (London: Fontana, 1976), p.16.
9   Clifford Geertz, *The Interpretation of Cultures* (New York: Basic Books, 1973), p.45.
10 *ibid.*, pp.50–51.
11 Graeme Turner, *British Cultural Studies: An Introduction* (London: Routledge, 2nd ed., 1996), p.26.
12 Geertz, p.126.
13 Suzanne Langer, *Philosophy in a New Key* (Cambridge, Mass.: Pub, 4th. ed., 1960), p.287.
14 Richard Rubenstein and John K. Roth, *Approaches to Auschwitz: The Holocaust and Its Legacy* (Atlanta: John Knox Press, 1987), p.139.
15 Marcel Simon, *Verus Israel: A Study of the Relations Between Christians and Jews in the Roman Empire (135–425)*, trans. H. McKeating, (New York: Oxford University Press, 1986), p.146.
16 Rubenstein and Roth, p.59.
17 John Gager, *The Origins of Anti-Semitism* (New York: Oxford University Press, 1985), p.22.
18 Samuel P. and Pearl M. Oliner, *The Altruistic Personality: Rescuers of Jews in Nazi Europe* (New York: The Free Press, 1988), p.155. See also n.8 on p.373.
19 John T. Powlikowski, 'The Teaching of Contempt: Judaism in Christian Education and Liturgy', in Eva Fleischner, ed., *Auschwitz, Beginning of a New Era? Reflections on the Holocaust* (New York: KTAV Publishing House Inc., 1977), p.155.
20 Too numerous to detail in this short study; see Joshua Trachtenberg, *The Devil and the Jews: The Medieval Conception of the Jew and Its Relation to Modern Anti-Semitism* (Philadelphia: The Jewish Publication Society of America, 1943) and Léon Poliakov, *The History of Anti-Semitism*, tr. Richard Howard (New York: Schocken Books, 1974).
21 Powlikowski, pp.162–165.
22 Michael R. Steele, *Christianity, Tragedy, and Holocaust Literature* (Westport, Ct.: Greenwood Press, 1995), p.118.
23 Edward H. Flannery, 'Anti-Zionism and the Christian Psyche', in Harry James Cargas, *When God and Man Failed: Non-Jewish Views of the Holocaust* (New York: Macmillan Publishing Co., Inc., 1981), pp.109–110.
24 Robert E. Willis, 'Auschwitz and the Nurturing of Conscience', in Cargas, p.149.
25 Zygmunt Bauman, *Modernity and the Holocaust* (Ithaca: Cornell University Press, 1991), p.92.
26 *ibid.*, p.13.
27 *ibid.*, p.70.
28 Alan Davies, *Infected Christianity: A Study of Modern Racism* (Kingston: McGill – Queen's University Press, 1988), p.120.
29 Rosemary Reuther, 'Judaism and Christianity: two fourth-century religions', *Studies in Religion*, 2, 1972, p.6.
30 David M. Olster, *Roman Defeat, Christian Response, and the Literary Construction of the Jew* (Philadelphia: University of Pennsylvania Press, 1994), p.30.

31 Reuther, p.5.
32 Averil Cameron, *Christianity and the Rhetoric of Empire* (Berkeley: University of California Press, 1991), pp.2–3.
33 Turner, p.30.
34 Ramsay MacMullen, *Christianizing the Roman Empire (A.D. 100–400)* (New Haven: Yale University Press, 1984), pp.66–67.
35 Simon, p.106.
36 Gerhard Falk, *The Jew in Christian Theology* (Jefferson, NC: McFarland & Company, Inc., Publishers, 1992), pp.21–28. See also Amnon Linder, *The Jews in Roman Imperial Legislation* (Detroit: Wayne State University Press, 1987) and James Parkes, *The Conflict of the Church and the Synagogue: A Study in the Origins of Antisemitism* (New York: Atheneum, 1974).
37 Falk, pp.28–35.
38 *ibid.*, pp.35–36.
39 *ibid.*, p.36.
40 Linder, pp.22–23.
41 Linder, for further details, see pp.25–40.
42 John Friesen, 'War and Peace in the Patristic Age', in Willard Swartley, ed., *Essays on War and Peace: Bible and Early Church* (Elkhart, In.: Institute of Mennonite Studies, 1986), p.130.
43 Adolf Harnack, *Militia Christi*, tr. David McInnes Gracie (Philadelphia: Fortress Press, 1981), p.99.
44 Friesen, p.144.
45 Jean-Michel Hornus, *It is Not Lawful For Me to Fight: Early Christian Attitudes Toward War, Violence, and the State*, tr. Alan Krieder (Scottsdale, Pa.: Herald Press, 1980), p.171.
46 *ibid.*, p.181.
47 Friesen, pp.150–151.
48 Hornus, pp.198, 186.
49 See his rhetoric in *Saint John Chrysostom: Discourses Against Judaizing Christians*, trans. Paul W. Harkins (Washington, D.C.: The Catholic University of America Press, 1979).
50 Robert L. Wilken, *John Chrysostom and the Jews: Rhetoric and Reality in the Late 4th Century* (Berkeley: University of California Press, 1983), pp.105 and 116.
51 Simon, p.222.
52 Michael Mann, *The Sources of Social Power* (Cambridge: Cambridge University Press, 1986), p.380.
53 Olster, p.183.
54 Olster, quoting Averil Cameron's *Procopius*, p.9.
55 Hermann Doerris, *Constantine and Religious Liberty*, tr. Roland H. Bainton (New Haven: Yale University Press, 1960), pp.54–55.
56 *ibid.*, p.55.
57 Davies, p.8.
58 Valentin Y. Mudimbe, '*Romanus Pontifex* and the Expansion of Europe,' *Race, Discourse, and the Origins of the Americas*, ed. Vera Lawrence Hyatt and Rex Nettleford (Washington: Smithsonian Institution Press, 1995), p.60.
59 Mudimbe, pp.60–61.
60 Kenneth J. Pennington, Jr., 'Bartolome de las Casas and the Tradition of Medieval Law', *Church History*, 39, 1970, p.152.
61 Kirkpatrick Sale, *The Conquest of Paradise: Christopher Columbus and the Columbian Legacy* (New York: Penguin Books), pp.93 and 117.
62 Bartolomé de Las Casas, *The Devastation of the Indies: A Brief Account*, tr. Herma Briffault (New York: The Seabury Press, 1974), p.43.
63 Beatriz Pastor Bodmer, *The Armature of Conquest: Spanish Accounts of the Discovery of America, 1492–1589*, tr. Lydia Longstreth Hunt (Stanford: Stanford University Press, 1992), p.212.
64 Anthony Pagden, *The Fall of Natural Man: The American Indian and the origins of comparative ethnology* (Cambridge: Cambridge University Press, 1982), p.109.
65 Juan Friede and Benjamin Keen, *Bartolomé de Las Casas in History: Toward an Understanding of the Man and His Work* (DeKalb, Il.: Northern Illinois University Press, 1971), pp.290–291.

66 Luis Villoro, 'Sahagún, or the Limits of the Discovery of the Other', 1992 Lecture Series, University of Maryland Department of Spanish and Portugese, p.12.

67 Las Casas, p.137.

68 *ibid.*, pp.43–49.

69 *ibid.*, pp.58, 70, 91.

70 *ibid.*, pp.87–88, 104.

71 Sylvia Wynter, '1492: A New World View', in Hyatt and Nettleford, p.17.

72 James Louwen, 'Columbus in High School', in *Confronting Columbus*, John Yewell, Chris Dodge, Jan DeSirey eds. (Jefferon, NC: McFarland & Company, Inc., Publishers, 1992), p.98.

73 Sale, p.157.

74 Wynter, p.29.

75 Hanna Rosin, 'Southern Baptist campaign aims to convert Jews to Christianity', *The Oregonian*, 9 September 1999, p.A3.

76 Daniel S. Matson and Bernard L. Fontana, quoted in Timothy J. O'Keefe, ed., *Columbus, Confrontation, Christianity: The European–American Encounter Revisited* (Los Gatos, Ca.: Forbes Mill Press, 1994), p.145.

77 Wynter, p.31.

78 Villoro, p.5.

79 Wynter, p.40.

80 Jacob Glatstein, Israel Knox, Samuel Margoshes, eds., *Anthology of Holocaust Literature* (Philadelphia: Jewish Publication Society, 1969), p.117.

81 Wynter, p.32.

82 Elie Wiesel, 'Jewish Values in the Post-Holocaust Future', *Judaism*, 16, 1967, p.285.

83 Robert Jay Lifton, *Nazi Doctors* (New York: Basic Books, 1986), pp.418, 422.

84 *ibid.*, p.458.

85 *ibid.*, p.418.

86 *ibid.*, p.442.

87 *ibid.*, p.458.

88 James E. Waller, 'Perpetrators of the Holocaust: Divided and Unitary Self Conceptions of Evildoing, *Holocaust and Genocide Studies*, 10, 1, Spring 1996, p.16.

89 Waller, p.20; see n.50, p.31.

90 *ibid.*, p.28.

91 *ibid.*, p.27.

92 See Johnathan Shay, *Achilles in Vietnam: Combat Trauma and the Undoing of Character* (New York: Simon & Schuster, 1995). Private correspondence, January, 1998.

93 See, for instance, Philip Hallie, *Lest Innocent Blood be Shed* (New York: Harper and Row, 1979) and Samuel P. and Pearl M. Oliner, *The Altruistic Personality: Rescuers of Jews in Nazi Europe*.

94 Trachtenberg, pp.21–22.

95 Walter Zwi Bacharach, *Anti-Jewish Prejudices in German-Catholic Sermons*, tr. Chaya Galai (Lewiston, NY: Edwin Mellen Press, 1993), p.59.

96 *ibid.*, p.60.

97 *ibid.*, p.70.

98 Robert P. Ericksen, *Theologians Under Hitler* (New Haven: Yale University Press, 1985), p.199.

99 *ibid.*, p.41.

100 *ibid.*, p.17.

101 Davies, p.15.

102 *ibid.*, p.xi.

THE SHIFT TOWARDS DEATH:
A COMPARISON OF THE NAZI EUTHANASIA PROGRAMME AND CONTEMPORARY DEBATES ON EUTHANASIA AND PHYSICIAN-ASSISTED SUICIDE

Amy C. Zaro

EUTHANASIA, THE notion of having a good death, is an idea that originated in ancient Greece. Greek discussions about euthanasia illustrate that the human fear of a slow death and the subsequent loss of quality of life are not new issues and have in fact been a major aspect of moral debates throughout the history of Western civilization. Under the Nazi regime, however, euthanasia became a biological solution to a political problem rather than simply a moral debate about 'a good death'. It grew into a legalized method for mass murder that introduced a certain rhetoric and instituted a tragic softening of conscience that culminated in the Final Solution. Perhaps the most startling aspect of the euthanasia policies of the Third Reich is that some of the rhetoric and reasoning used then are still present in contemporary physician–assisted suicide and euthanasia debates. These contemporary debates tackle the problematic issue of when it is medically, socially, and legally permissible to terminate life. While there are many crucial differences between the euthanasia programme in Nazi Germany and current debates, there are certain continuities which should be explored. These continuities include the pressures of social responsibility, of maintaining of quality of life, and of limits on personal autonomy. This paper will seek to offer background on both the euthanasia programme under the Nazis and the contemporary debates on legalizing physician-assisted suicide and euthanasia. This background will be followed by a discussion of how the past horrors of the Nazi regime should be integrated into our current collective conscience in determining the norms of life and death.

THE NAZI EUTHANASIA PROGRAMME

In 1933, with the Nazi seizure of power, essentially each aspect of German life underwent the process of *Gleichshaltung*, a widespread coordination and Nazification process. Many in the medical and scientific communities who had been espousing notions of racial purity in the eugenic debates saw the Nazi Party as the political machine to implement their ideas.[1] Notions of racial hygiene became dominant as physicians and scientists embraced Nazism as well as the political and career opportunities it afforded. These communities were strong supporters of the Nazi regime and this support can be seen in a memo dated 23 May 1933 from Professor M. Planck to Hitler stating:

> The members of the Kaiser Wilhelm Society for the Advancement of the Sciences, gathered at their 22nd General Assembly, have the honor of sending their respectful greeting to the Chancellor of the Reich. They solemnly vow that German science is ready to make every

possible effort to collaborate in the reconstruction of the new national state, which, in turn, has declared itself to be our protector and our patron.[2]

Ultimately more physicians joined the Nazi party than did any other profession. Thus, the scientific and medical communities were easily coordinated into the Nazi regime while any opposition within these communities to this synchronization was quickly forced out.

Much of the scientific reasoning used to justify the Nazi euthanasia programme originated in the rhetoric of the eugenics movement. Eugenics was largely the social adaptation of Darwinist theories of biological determinism. It was a movement that flourished throughout the western world in the first few decades of the 20th century. In Weimar Germany, the eugenics movement began to grow racially oriented under the guidance of such scientists as Fritz Lenz who spoke of Nordic supremacy. This racial element led to much controversy within the movement and drew heavy criticism from outside circles. It also, however, appealed to many Germans as a rational solution to widespread social problems. To compound this increase in the racial aspect of eugenics, there were also increasing efforts to popularize the science. These efforts included offering more eugenic courses at universities and the establishment of various research institutes including The German Research Institute for Psychiatry, founded in 1918 in Munich.[3] In 1920 the prominent German scholars Karl Binding and Alfred Hoche wrote *Die Freigabe der Vernichtung lebensunwerten Lebens* (Authorization for the Destruction of Life Unworthy of Life). Binding and Hoche argued for the legalization of euthanasia and used the example of a terminal cancer patient. This notion was extended to include *lebensunwerten Lebens* or lives determined unworthy of living[4] One can begin to see the transformation of the movement from a relatively banal ideological social science into a potentially dangerous and exploitable ideology. As the eugenics movement became increasingly widespread and publicly recognized, Germany simultaneously faced the strains of severe economic depression and post-war discontent that created an atmosphere of panic.

With the smooth alignment of the medical and scientific communities into the Nazi regime, new government agencies and policies were quickly established to accommodate the now unified goals of the Nazi and eugenic communities. In 1933, shortly after the Nazi seizure of power, Interior Minister Wilhelm Frick gave a speech to the new Expert Committee for Population and Racial Policy and stated: 'In order to raise the number of genetically healthy progeny, we must first lower the money spent on asocial individuals, the unfit and the hopelessly, hereditarily diseased, and we must prevent the procreation of severely, hereditarily defective people.'[5] Thus, the exclusion of the hereditarily diseased was made a priority from the start as was the economic rationale used by the Nazis. This same year a Sterilization Law, based largely on a 1932 proposal in the Weimar government, was passed by the state. This law enacted compulsory sterilization for those individuals diagnosed with a variety of hereditary diseases including congenital feeblemindedness, hereditary blindness and even severe alcoholism. These categories were extremely vague and could be stretched to include people with the most minor of inflictions. Consequently, the Sterilization Law quickly became another form of terror and social control that swept through Germany and led to a general passivity among the populace. Sterilization began the process of exclusion and stigmatization of certain groups from the national community, and it became a testing ground for the methods and rhetoric used in subsequent euthanasia policies.[6]

The vast majority of sterilizations were involuntary and made possible by applications sent in by physicians and guardians from all over Germany. These applications were reviewed by specially established hereditary health courts that were attached under the general appellate courts. These health courts, comprised of a judge and two physicians, became crucial in establishing a notion of legality, which added to the authority of the sterilization measures.[7] In 1934 there were 84,604 applications for sterilization; only seven percent were rejected.[8] The legal and administrative bureaucracy needed for the more complex euthanasia measures was being put into action.

While independent acts of euthanasia had become quite common in Nazi Germany, Nazi officials observed a desire on the part of the medical community to have these actions legitimized. By signing an authorization, Hitler empowered Philip Bouhler, head of the Chancellery of the Fuher (KdF) and his escorting physician Karl Brandt to implement a programme to kill mentally or physically handicapped children. This authorization was backdated to September 1939, as the start of World War II provided the perfect context for the euthanasia measures to be enacted. Involuntary euthanasia was economically justified as a 'preemptive triage.[9] This aspect of the Nazi euthanasia programme illustrates the dramatic effects of legalization on the nature of euthanasia. With Hitler's authorization, physicians were able to abandon any lingering moral doubts or sense of responsibility.

The organization of the Nazi euthanasia programme was top secret and highly intricate. The KdF, Bouhler's charge, was Hitler's independent chancellory and thus was not a direct part of the government. This helped programme leaders to effectively avoid the huge number of government officials, civil servants and a twisting bureaucratic path. As the programme was to be highly confidential, the planners founded a front organization, the Reich Committee for the Scientific Registration of Serious Hereditarily and Congenitally Based Diseases, to cover up the involvement of the KdF. This committee, known as the Reich Committee, was completely fictitious and all official decrees came from the RMdI.[10] On 18 August 1939, the RMdI issued a decree called the 'Requirement to Report Deformed, etc. Newborns'. This decree mandated that all physicians and midwives were to report any births where the infant had a specific medical condition. By October of 1939 the killing had begun.[11] Several other decrees were issued by the RMdI throughout the programme, each one riddled with misinformation and a vague stated purpose of furthering scientific investigation.

The first killing ward was established at Brandenburg-Gorden and was soon followed by the establishment of similar killing centres throughout Germany. The programme evolved into an intricate 'killing system that involved physicians, parents, and bureaucrats' and required the cooperation of various sectors of the state, the Reich Committee and local authorities.[12] It is estimated that about 5,000 children were killed during this initial phase of the euthanasia programme. The physician 'specialists' at the killing centres most often killed their patients through various combinations of starvation and overdosing on common medications. These children were killed because they did not fit into a predetermined Germany and because the physicians saw these children as a way to further science or even their own careers.[13] These physicians proved even more eager to expand the programme to include adults.

In order to convince physicians that they could not be prosecuted for the killings, Bouhler and Brack drafted a document for Hitler to sign that authorized the 'mercy killings'. With this authorization, Bouhler and Brack easily brought together a team of willing physicians who were motivated by a 'missionary zeal' and an awe of 'leading academic psychiatrists in the KdF who could in turn rely on their status and authority as "gods in white coats".' The majority of these doctors truly believed that their actions would strengthen the Nazi state, thus rationalizing any feelings of conscience.[14]

The role of the doctor in the euthanasia programme was particularly complex as there arose a variety of motivations which compelled doctors to participate in the murders. One such motivation was a perverted scientific idealism expressed by many doctors who believed that they were not only strengthening the state, but that they were also helping their patients by rescuing them from their existences.[15] Other doctors were motivated by more racial ideals, as Dr. Fritz Klein reasoned: 'Of course I am a doctor and I want to preserve life. And out of respect for human life, I would remove a gangrenous appendix from a diseased body. The Jew is the gangrenous appendix in the body of mankind.'[16] This pervasive theme of strengthening the community at the cost of selected individuals shaped much of physician involvement. Many other doctors simply focused on the more practical side of things. For example, the doctor who discovered the rare congenital brain disease, Hallervorden-Spatz disease, requested hundreds of brains from euthanasia victims for his studies, claiming that 'there was wonderful material among these brains, beautiful mental defectives, malformations, and early infantile disease. I accepted these brains of course. Where they came from and how they came to me, was really none of my business.'[17] This scientific indifference provided the euthanasia programme with many enthusiastic physicians to implement the killings.

The headquarters for the euthanasia programme was moved to a confiscated Jewish villa in Berlin at Tiergartenstrasse 4, giving the programme its subsequent name, Operation T4. Local governments were requested by the RMdI to 'provide by 15 October 1939 a complete listing of institutions in their geographic area holding mental patients, epileptics, and the feebleminded. The listing was to included public, charitable, religious, and private institutions, and it was to specify the institution's name, address, affiliation, and patient capacity.'[18] Questionnaires were sent to each of these institutions and the completed questionnaires were forwarded to T4 to be reviewed by the resident 'experts'. The 'experts' who reviewed these forms were most often young psychiatrists, some without basic certification, and they quickly processed forms determining who would die and who would live. Sometimes decisions were accidents, sometimes they were made to cover up mistakes; in one instance a 'child whose legs and lower body were paralyzed was killed. Surgical neurological intervention could have cured this condition, but the so-called specialists at the children's ward failed to recognize this possibility.'[19] The illogical disorganization of such methods embody the nature of the programme. One cannot dismiss the potential for similar oversights and mistakes today, since the inevitable bureaucratic tangle resulting from legalized euthanasia would create ample opportunity for such errors.

The killing methods used to murder the children, starvation and overdosing of common medications, proved too slow and ineffective for the larger numbers of adult victims. Therefore, the killing centres experimented with the most effective method of mass murder and gassing proved to be it. Hadamar became one of the most notorious of the euthanasia killing centres and as one observer recalls: 'In the chamber there were patients, naked people, some semi-collapsed, others with mouths terribly wide open, their chests heaving. I saw that, I have never seen anything more gruesome. I turned away, went up the steps, upstairs was a toilet. I vomited everything I had eaten.'[20] These horrific descriptions are tragic examples of the unspeakable atrocities at work and a complete breakdown of ethics and basic human compassion. The abstract rhetoric of Nazi ideology and its perverted implementation by the physicians and scientists of the Third Reich are examples of the possibilities in a world gone mad.

After the gassings, the victims were examined for plausible causes of death to report to the relatives. There was a detailed list of potential causes of death, ailments that would be sudden in appearance and quick to kill. Attempts were made to avoid infamous mistakes such as the reporting of acute appendicitis for a patient who had his appendix removed 10 years earlier. The relatives were sent short form condolence letters with notice that the body had been cremated to prevent any epidemics. There was a web of paperwork and bureaucracy to muddle the system and make it harder for relatives to find out valid information. The incredible methods used to cover up the killing include the story of Mr. Merkle who worked at Hadamar and was careful to space out the reported dates of death so as to report a steady number. He, however, alphabetized these deaths so that one day A's and B's died and the next C's and D's. Large killing centre staffs were required to implement these murders and to create the layers of misinformation.[21] In the course of Operation T4 over 80,000 innocent victims were murdered.

On 24 August 1941 Hitler issued a stop order to the T4 phase of euthanasia. It is most likely that this stop order was issued because the 'secret' operation was not too secret and was drawing sharp criticism from both the German and international public. Attempts to conceal the programme were futile and the public soon grew suspicious of the many deaths. Mass murder on such a large scale could not be hidden when performed in Germany and the 'attack on the handicapped did not strike at an isolated ethnic minority but instead a group of fellow citizens still connected to family and neighbors.'[22] The handicapped of Germany had not been excluded enough for the public to remain silent. Moreover, to have these murders occur on German soil was literally too close to home. As the handicapped were still integral parts of the community, there was not the easier path to murder that was present for the excluded Jewish community that had been deported to Poland. From the technology of the gas chambers to measuring the tolerance of the community, Operation T4 became a crucial model in the development of the Final Solution.

Ultimately, the stop order did not stop the killings. Instead what followed was the next phase in the programme known as 'wild' euthanasia. This new phase in the killings was unsystematic and arbitrary and seemed closer to the practices occurring in the concentration camps.[23] The euthanasia programme grew increasingly radicalized and the lack of an overall plan became more problematic. Whereas the first phase was more ideologically based – the removal of *lebensunwerten Lebens*, a temporary alleviation of visible ills – the second phase was to empty hospital beds for more 'necessary patients'.[24] For the public's sake, everything seemed to return to acceptable practices. The hospital Hadamar, for instance, appeared to return to normal, but thousands were still killed through such methods as lethal medications.[25] Moreover, in an operation known as 14f13, thousands of prisoners from concentration camps such as Dachau and Sachsenhausen were sent to different euthanasia centres to be killed. At the camps, SS physicians selected a potential group of victims and then visiting T4 physicians quickly chose final victims with the efficiency acquired in the euthanasia programme.[26] Historian Henry Friedlander estimates that about 20,000 prisoners were ultimately killed in this operation and he notes the significance of the link between Operation 14f13 and the Final Solution.[27]

What began as an idealized intellectual, political, and social movement towards creating a healthier and stronger society became dramatically escalated. The Nazis sought to strengthen the community through killing as many today seek to strengthen the individual through a 'right to die.' No matter the goal, no matter the motivation, to sanction killing is to unleash a culture of death. The euthanasia programme under the Nazi regime, which began with the murder of children and ended with a sophisticated model for mass murder, is a prime example of the destructive disorderly power of the Nazi regime. Individual ambition, perverted ideology and greed weakened the morality of ordinary men until their reasoning lost all sensitivity to human dignity. It is also a model of how unremarkable the path towards mass murder is. With certain individuals focusing on the potential good and ignoring the innate destruction of moral standards, death prevailed. The Nazi euthanasia programme further demonstrates how abstract social ideals can evolve into a policy of death. This policy eroded traditional norms and allowed the dark side of human nature to emerge. The compounding abuses and compromises that shaped the Nazi euthanasia programme illustrate the horrific potential of sanctioning death.

EUTHANASIA IN THE MODERN WORLD

In the modern context, arguments in favour of legalizing euthanasia tend to regard the Nazi euthanasia programme as something that occurred in a different time and place. Physicians today answer to legitimate government organizations, not front agencies for the Nazi regime. Any contemporary euthanasia policies or arguments offer guidelines that reflect concerns about potential abuses and provide boundaries for the physician to adhere to. The Nazi euthanasia programme offered no such guidelines and the main concern appeared to be public reaction to the killings. Also, the goal of the Nazi euthanasia programme was to eradicate unwanted elements from society, whereas the goal of contemporary policies and arguments are to protect the individual from the prolonged agony of a terminal illness. On the surface, these differences indicate that the Nazi euthanasia programme would not influence modern debates and policies as the particulars of the Nazi programme do not reflect the realties of our world. I would, however, argue that the Nazi euthanasia programme is in fact a crucial model of the reaches of any euthanasia programme. The tragedy of the Nazi euthanasia programme was not an isolated event that occurred in a foreign and unrelated climate. Rather, it was a tangible progression towards a culture of death and acceptance. This culture grew out of a human weakness, not merely a Nazi one. It is such universals in human nature that one should appreciate. The vulnerability of policies, individuals and institutions being coerced by shifting norms and attitudes is as real today as it was in Nazi Germany.

American society today is by no means analogous to Nazi society; it is not a moral vacuum dominated by fear and tyranny. Contemporary American society generally embraces diversity, places individual rights above those of the community, and does not support the extremes of greed and ambition seen in Nazi Germany. There are however tremendous anxieties about exploding health care costs, the limits of science and medicine, and questions about quality of life. Traditional moral norms maintained by the medical profession, the legal community and the general population are being challenged by those anxieties. As the lessons of the Nazi past fade for some, it becomes compelling to wonder what shifts could occur in our society before that fragile moral fibre is torn. An analysis of the contemporary euthanasia and physician-assisted suicide debates can illuminate where these shifts might occur.

Tremendous medical advancements have empowered contemporary physicians to sustain life to unprecedented levels. With this development, the issue of where to draw the line has emerged. From cessation of extraordinary life sustaining treatment to active euthanasia, there is a wide range of points in between. Physician-assisted suicide is when a patient asks a doctor for help in ending life. Usually the term refers to a patient who is terminally ill and involves the physician providing lethal medications for the patient to use. Euthanasia is when the physician actually performs the killing, for example, by actively injecting the patient with a lethal dose of morphine. Euthanasia is generally considered much more problematic than physician-assisted suicide. Within the concept of euthanasia itself, there are significant distinctions. Passive euthanasia, on the one hand, is regarded as letting the patient die. In removing such life sustaining treatment as a respirator, it is the ailment and not the physician that kills the patient. Similarly, proscribing palliative care that could potentially hasten death is regarded as passive, because the aim is to lessen pain, not to kill. Passive euthanasia is generally accepted in today's medical community as illustrated by a proliferation in living wills and Do Not Resuscitate orders. Active euthanasia, on the other hand, is when the physician intentionally kills a patient by administering lethal medications. There are also the further distinctions of voluntary or involuntary. Voluntary euthanasia is when the patient asks the physician to be killed. In most contemporary debates it is physician-assisted suicide and active voluntary euthanasia that are advocated for legalization. Involuntary euthanasia is the killing of a patient without his or her consent and describes the euthanasia that occurred in Nazi Germany. In most contemporary debates, the idea of involuntary euthanasia is considered morally abhorrent. However, as will be discussed later, the shift from voluntary to involuntary is not as dramatic as one would assume.

The implications of a potential shift towards involuntary euthanasia sheds tremendous light on the horrific dangers of any sanctioning of active euthanasia or physician-assisted suicide. Moreover, while the general trend in contemporary debates focuses on physician-assisted suicide and active voluntary euthanasia being the most pure forms of patient autonomy and thus a beneficent goal, the eugenics debate began with similarly idealistic origins. Eugenics began with the genuine ideal of strengthening and improving the human condition through science and medicine. Eugenics then began to argue that there were less valuable genetic characteristics, which grew into less valuable lives. Proponents then argued that sterilization would help eradicate unwanted characteristics. Then it became argued that perhaps we could help these less valuable lives by ending them and the spiral intensified. Today physician-assisted suicide and euthanasia are seen as tools to ensure the highest level of self-determination, thus improving levels of patient autonomy. The potential shift from an abstract social ideal into a sliding uncontrollable reality, however, is as pressing today as it was in the 1920s and 1930s.

Within the last few generations, medical and scientific advancements have altered the nature of dying in our society. Dramatic improvements have led to death becoming a less natural and less inevitable event in our lives. With this massive shift, traditional aspects of death such as dying at home in the presence of family members and a priest have moved to hospital. According to the ethicist John Robinson this 'revolution involved the displacement of the family and the priest by the doctor as the basic minister to the person suffering from some potentially lethal condition.'[28] Robinson further reflects that this shift has led to a certain nostalgia for more traditional deaths and the development of a deep hostility to the medicalized deaths of today. Moreover, physician-assisted suicide and euthanasia debates are emerging amidst a tremendous health care crisis where resource allocation and care of the terminally ill are critical issues.[29] Legalization in such volatile times would heighten the risks of abuse. Social conditions often shape the application of public policy and this leads to considerable societal consequences.[30] These consequences include an increased risk to the medically indigent, a possible correlation between insurance costs and the withholding of treatment, and an opportunity to avoid dealing with the financial and ethical crisis plaguing the health care industry. It is in such a climate that passionate debates on one's 'right to die' have emerged.

From Dr. Quill prescribing a lethal dosage of barbiturates to his terminally ill cancer patient in 1988 to recent Oregon legislation allowing physician-assisted suicide in certain circumstances, the debate over death and dying issues in the United States has been fierce.[31] Medical ethicist M. Cathleen Kaveny asserts that this debate has hardened into legalistic and abstract terms. According to Kaveny, 'No longer at the forefront of the discussion is the question when, if ever, it is *morally right* for dying or seriously ill individuals to intentionally take their own lives. Instead, the issue occupying the centre stage is whether they should have a *legal right* to do so, and if necessary to enlist the aid of a physician willing to prescribe the lethal dose.'[32] The shift from an emphasis on morality to individual rights is similar in nature to the shift that occurred in Germany in the 1930s. In Germany, the intrinsic value of any human life became buried under arguments for the good of the community. Today, ironically, the intrinsic value of life is buried under discussions of autonomy. Whether it is for the good of the community or the individual, the value of life is still reduced. Traditional norms and value orientations are bogged down by other issues and their importance is lost. As the medical ethicist Daniel Callahan warns,

> [W]e should not deceive ourselves into thinking of euthanasia or assisted suicide as merely personal acts, just a slight extension of the already established right to control our bodies and to have medical treatment terminated . . . (it) is a radical move into an entirely different realm a morality: that of the killing of one person by another.[33]

One of the key arguments in favour of physician-assisted suicide and euthanasia is that choosing when to die is the ultimate expression of one's personal autonomy. However, many opponents of legalization have also argued that euthanasia and physician-assisted suicide in fact strike at the heart of true autonomy. Callahan points out:

> If we really believe in self-determination, then any competent person should have a right to be killed by a doctor for any reason that suits him. If we believe in relief of suffering, then it seems cruel and capricious to deny it to the incompetent. There is, in short, no reasonable or logical stopping point once the turn has been made down the road to euthanasia.[34]

To define the limits of self-determination to a set of preconditions, seems to undermine the essence of individual integrity. Many agree that physician-assisted suicide and euthanasia are the clearest exercises of self-determination and personal autonomy, yet these same people want to limit this right to a very small and very specific group of people, namely the terminally ill. The inherent nature of the autonomy argument destroys any notion of limitations. To afford a certain right to one person, and then to deny it to another is a serious offence that strikes at the heart of autonomy. To use personal autonomy to eradicate life, is acting against the very foundation of autonomy and this is where the autonomy argument falls apart.[35] To recognize personal autonomy is to recognize the value and dignity of human life. To have this life terminated is the grossest perversion of autonomy.

In addition to issues surrounding personal autonomy, one must consider the impact of legalizing physician-assisted suicide and euthanasia on the medical profession and society as a whole. As Callahan argues, physicians should not be given the right to judge which lives are worth living and which are not. To do so would challenge the traditionally accepted belief that medicine's purpose is to preserve and maintain health.[36] Moreover, physicians must resist the temptation of modern medicine to heal the human condition, not merely to preserve health.[37] The medical profession is a moral community that holds a sacred moral responsibility to patients and to society to protect the sanctity of life. To legalize physician-assisted suicide and euthanasia would put unrealistic burdens on the medical community and on physicians.

Beyond undermining the integrity of physician as healer is the undermining of the value of life for certain vulnerable sectors of society. We live in a heterogeneous society that faces tremendous economic and social problems, not unlike Germany of the 1920s. Legalized physician-assisted suicide and euthanasia would create a tremendous risk for certain vulnerable populations. These groups already have their autonomy compromised by poverty or association with a stigmatized social group.[38] These groups could become the victims of not only involuntary abuses, but subtle pressures to request euthanasia because of being economic and social burdens on their families and society.[39] Some may feel it is their medical duty to acquiesce to 'a good death'. The claim to such risks are not unfounded, as one looks to the extreme process of dehumanization and marginalization that was present during Nazi Germany.

The very nature of death in our society would be further altered by the legalization of physician-assisted suicide and euthanasia. It would radically alter our conception of human life and would introduce into our legal system a category of lives not worth living.[40] To alter traditional views of human life in such a manner would shift us from a society valuing life to a society valuing death. Such a shift is even more compelling when one considers that it would originate with the state. As Alexander Capron notes:

> By directly involving an official body, appointed under state procedures, it would seem to sanction the taking of life, a result that opens the door to abuses by the state and at the very least makes every act of euthanasia a collectively imposed sentence of death on innocent patients, some of whom would never have actually requested euthanasia.[41]

Such a development would be tragic and would bring our society closer to the abuses of the Nazi regime.

One of the most well-known arguments against the legalization of physician-assisted suicide and euthanasia is the slippery slope argument. Essentially this argument reasons that once physician-assisted suicide or euthanasia are accepted, society will slide down a 'slippery slope' towards a tragic end with no means to turn back. This argument is often disregarded as being overly simplistic and making unsubstantiated claims for the future, but it can be a useful tool in illustrating the compounding effects of accepting euthanasia and physician-assisted suicide. The slippery slope argument most often refers to the continuously expanding limits of acceptable cases for physician-assisted suicide and euthanasia. This dynamic embodies a general apprehension that any form of euthanasia would sooner or later be extended to the handicapped and patients with long term disabilities. The underlying fear of the slippery slope argument is that the 'right to die' will evolve into the 'duty to die'. Such a development would categorize some people as expendable and make them helpless targets for cost-cutting.[42] Such an expansion and an acceptance of any person as 'expendable' is a development that is possible and has tremendous implications. As John Paris reflects, these 'potential difficulties are engendered in a society grown indifferent to the taking of life. That indifference would be compounded if the very segment of society committed to saving life were commissioned to destroy it.'[43] It is such effects, the mere potential of a slippery slope and a dangerous shift in the value of human life that demonstrate the crucial necessity of not accepting physician-assisted suicide and euthanasia on any terms. History has shown us the danger of reducing the value of any life. Abstract German ideals of a healthy community blinded people to the implications of the sanctioning of death. When these implications were realized, the downward spiral had begun. Today abstract ideals of personal autonomy have once again blinded many to the realities of human nature.

Many of the above arguments rely on speculation of what would unfold if euthanasia or physician-assisted suicide were legalized. Recent developments in Dutch euthanasia practices offer a concrete example of the realities of what occurs when a contemporary society accepts euthanasia. The Dutch are renowned for a deep toleration which is reflected in their liberal policies towards drugs, prostitution, and now euthanasia. The Netherlands is a prosperous western European social democracy that emphasizes certain collective ideals and a strong influence of the state. The Dutch population is relatively homogeneous with minimal unemployment or homelessness. Its medical system is one of the most highly developed in the world with advanced technology, abundant resources and universal health care coverage. This coverage includes extensive long term and home care privileges, making current abuses in Dutch euthanasia practices all the more profound. The retired American cardiologist Richard Fenigsen observes that Holland has one of the best health care systems in the world. It is an advanced system that provides comprehensive care for its older population and its disabled population. Nevertheless, a significant number of lives are being terminated, some without consent or request.[44] Compared to the United States' current social climate that is wrought with discrimination, limited resources, tremendous financial concerns, and an unprecedented current health care crisis – it is alarming to consider what abuses could occur here.

Even while euthanasia and physician-assisted suicide were not legal in the Netherlands, if certain state regulations for performing euthanasia were followed the physician would not be prosecuted. Euthanasia is generally accepted among the Dutch legal and medical communities and the public, making it a relatively normal action. In the 1970s the Royal Dutch Medical Association (KNMG) issued a statement suggesting that euthanasia for terminally ill patients should be an option. This statement became widely accepted throughout Dutch society and seriously altered the nature of medicine and of dying in the Netherlands.

Despite this popular acceptance, a physician was prosecuted for performing euthanasia on a terminally ill patient in 1984. The physician subsequently appealed this decision and the Dutch Supreme Court ultimately supported the physician. This decision became another step towards the acceptance of euthanasia. It is even more remarkable because the decision seemed to encourage the supreme role of the physician in determining when it is appropriate to kill.[45] Another significant outcome of this decision was that it prompted the KNMG to establish five requirements for acceptable cases of euthanasia. These requirements are: (1) voluntary request; (2) competent request; (3) durable wish for death; (4) unacceptable suffering; (5) physician consultation with colleague who is in agreement.[46] Many observers regard these requirements as extremely vague, precluding their effectiveness and placing the role of the decision solely in the hands of the physician.[47] In light of the subsequent abuses, such concerns about the vagueness of these requirements are warranted. In the years following 1984, additional regulations were instated. These regulations include mandating a physician to report the euthanasia case to the local District Attorney and requiring that the second opinion be from a colleague who is not an acquaintance of the primary physician. In 1994, the Dutch Supreme Court did not prosecute a physician who helped kill a depressed but otherwise healthy woman. Ultimately, the Court equated physical and psychological pain, adding another category for acceptable euthanasia.[48] Such a huge shift in such a short time is chilling. To include psychological depression – a condition that is treatable – as a source of unbearable suffering worthy of death is a significant broadening of who can be considered for euthanasia.

Another remarkable development in the acceptance of euthanasia in the Netherlands also occurred in 1994 when the Chief Inspector of Public Health, Dr. J. Verhof declared that if a physician were to refuse a patient's request for euthanasia and then not recommend the patient to a more willing physician, that doctor would be guilty of malpractice and subject to prosecution.[49] Ultimately, the nature of euthanasia compromises even the autonomy of the physician and indicates the downward spiral predicted by so many. That concerns about such developments abound in the Netherlands is reflected in a letter written by a group of severely disabled adults from Amersfoort to officials at the Parliamentary Committees for Health Care and Justice. This group wrote: ' "We feel our lives threatened. We realize that we cost the community a lot . . . many people think we are useless . . . Often we notice that we are being talked into desiring death." A study conducted among the hospital patients showed that some fear their own families because these are the people who decide upon euthanasia or pressure them to request it.'[50] Such insights are tragic and illustrate how little patient autonomy is involved in euthanasia and now the push for euthanasia reduces the dignity of their lives more than any illness could. They also provide a link between the barbaric abuses of the Nazi euthanasia programme and the reality of contemporary Dutch practices.

In order to better understand the practice of euthanasia in the Netherlands, the government organized the Remmelink Committee to conduct a study. In 1990, the committee asked P.J. van der Maas, Professor of Public Health and Social Medicine at Erasmus University, to design and conduct this study. In his study, van der Maas consulted over 405 physicians, including general practitioners, specialists, and nursing home directors, about their involvement with euthanasia. These surveys were done both retrospectively and prospectively to provide a thorough sense of the attitudes and practices that are prevalent in Dutch healthcare. In addition, van der Maas surveyed over 8,500 death certificates to complement these surveys. According to the study euthanasia was defined as 'the intentional action to terminate a person's life, performed by somebody other than the involved person upon the latter's request.' With such a definition, van der Maas concluded that out of the 129,000 Dutch deaths in 1990, 2300 or 1.8% were due to euthanasia.[51]

Proponents of Dutch euthanasia saw this study as a great success as it ultimately reflected the relatively small impact of euthanasia on death in the Netherlands. Despite such optimistic interpretations of the Remmelink study, it is in fact an important source of the terrifying abuses present in the Dutch system. First of all, 1.8% of any nation's deaths is not an insignificant number. As John Paris reflects:

> The Dutch apologists for the practice suggest that the euthanasia accounts for two to three percent at most, of all deaths in the Netherlands. In a country with a published mortality rate of 120,000, this would imply from 2,400 to 3,600 cases of euthanasia a year. In the United States with a rate of approximately two million deaths a year, this would translate into some 40,000 to 60,000 people killed each year by their physician.[52]

Such numbers become more startling when one considers the observation by John Keown that the study is more a matter of personal definition, not evaluation.[53] Ultimately the narrow definition used by the Remmelink committee drastically impacted the final numbers. By including such practices as increasing palliative care dosages or withholding treatment, both with the explicit or partial purpose of shortening life, the number of deaths would jump to approximately 26,350. As Keown concludes, this means that one in twelve of all Dutch deaths in 1990 were intentionally accelerated by a physician.[54] These are remarkable numbers and when one uses Paris's American estimates this would mean 160,000 similar deaths in the United States. Other startling statistics to emerge from the study include: 57% of physicians who performed euthanasia list their primary motivation being to preserve the loss of dignity, 98% of nursing home physicians have withheld or stopped nonfutile life-sustaining treatment without the consent of the patient, and 72% of responding physicians who preformed euthanasia reported the patients death as 'natural causes.'[55]

The most controversial aspect of the Remmelink report, however, was the number of involuntary euthanasia cases it reported. An estimated .8% or 1000 deaths were described as involuntary euthanasia. According to Weile: 'The researchers explained that this is not amazing since physicians are more often guided by their own impressions of the patients unspoken but probable wishes, than by explicit oral or written patient requests. One may wonder whether such "impressions" are always correct. At any rate, a paradox emerges between this kind of reasoning and the very opposite reasoning by a number of courts and legislators that suffering is purely subjective phenomenon and that, consequently, only the patient can decided whether his or her suffering has become unbearable.'[56] It is such contradictions and the mere existence of involuntary euthanasia that has fuelled a heated debate.

This debate inspired several Dutch medical ethicists to conduct a study on Life-terminating Acts Without Explicit Request of Patient (LAWER). This group surveyed 405 stratified physicians and compiled the following data: 25% of the physicians had performed LAWER, 35% would and 41% would never do so. Of the 25% who had, 70% spoke about it with a colleague, 83% spoke with the family and 2% spoke with no one. Also, 56% of their patients had expressed an earlier interest in euthanasia before becoming incompetent, 41% had never spoken of it.[57] Such numbers do not lead one to consider involuntary euthanasia or LAWER to be an insignificant occurrence. Despite this, the group concluded that such numbers do not confirm a slippery slope, but rather they open the way for more discussion. According to the group:

> There are two ways to describe LAWER – that is a physician killing a person who has become defenceless, or that it is a response to the injustice that a person unable to make an explicit request has to suffer to the end even when his or her doctor, who may have been responsible for this patient for a long time, and perhaps the relatives also feel confident that the patient's wishes would have been for life to be ended.[58]

Such excuses are problematic and John Keown notes how striking the numbers of euthanasia cases performed without explicit request are. He further contends that by including intentional termination by omission of treatment, the numbers 'indicate that nonvoluntary euthanasia is in fact more common than voluntary euthanasia.'[59] Such realizations not only support the slippery slope theory, but they make such theories a chilling reality.

The above reflections indicate serious problems in the Dutch euthanasia practices. These problems become particularly significant when one applies them to what would happen if similar policies were adopted in the United States. It should be remembered that the Netherlands is a relatively homogenous society with a population that not only enjoys universal health care, but is much more receptive to government intervention and regulations. As John Paris notes:

> The Dutch experience show that to construct the argument for euthanasia in terms of autonomy is to misconstrue the reality of what happens to those who cannot truly be

autonomous. If this is true in a nation with universal health care coverage, how much greater the danger in a society in which 37% of the population is uninsured and concern for rising cost dominates the health care agenda.[60]

Paul van der Maas, who conducted the Remmelink study and is a tremendous supporter of euthanasia in the Netherlands, has stated that without universal health care coverage he would oppose the acceptance of euthanasia. Van der Maas claims that he fears that economic pressure would inspire doctors to save money rather than treat patients.[61] Withholding the impact of this financial variable present in the United States, Hendin makes a chilling observation: 'If voluntary euthanasia, with competent patients alone, were to take place in the United States at the same frequency as it does in the Netherlands, at the most conservative estimate it would lead to seventy five thousand such deaths a year – more than the current number of suicides and homicides combined.'[62] Such reflections and conclusions provide concrete evidence as to why any legalization of physician-assisted suicide and euthanasia would be a tragic error.

Dutch ethicist D.J. Bakker argues:

> The reasons for not wishing to live anymore can be many: pain and the fear for future pain, solitude, fear of death without dignity, oppression or fear of it, and many others. Not recognizing, in the request for euthanasia, the request for help and then exploring this question together with the patient is a grave mistake.[63]

Bakker further contends that most patients requesting euthanasia are actually hoping for reassurance that their lives are still valued and that the dependent nature of any illness precludes any true voluntariness.[64] Herbert Hendin notes that the Dutch experience shows that the legalization of physician-assisted suicide and euthanasia is not the answer, as every guideline established by the Dutch to regulate euthanasia has been violated. Hendin concludes:

> Dutch euthanasia advocates have been seduced by death. They have come to see suicide as a cure for disease and a way of appropriating death's power over the human capacity for control. They have detoured what could be a constructive effort to manage the final phase of life in more varied and individualistic ways onto a dangerous road to nowhere.[65]

As the Nazi and Dutch euthanasia models clearly illustrate, there are tremendous dangers in any sanctioning of physician assisted suicide or euthanasia. Contemporary American debates focus on patient autonomy and the implicit right of each individual to determine the time and manner of his or her death. As Bakker further argues,

> The assumed possibility of a voluntary request is based upon the concept of an individual, who by his reasoning can decide about his norms or values and can independently make decisions for his own life. No individual is ever completely free from his surroundings and fellow human beings, not even when he is healthy and apparently capable of taking care of himself. There is always some kind of dependency on something or somebody.[66]

It is this very dependency that restricts the autonomy of any physician-assisted suicide or euthanasia argument. Such a restriction inspires the search for a method to best protect both the interests of society and the interests of patient autonomy.

Modern medical technology, an aging population, and crumbling traditional social bonds have altered the nature of dying in our culture. Dying has become lonelier, longer and more clinical. To have the words of loved ones and priests largely replaced by the humming of machines is traumatic. To be kept alive indefinitely is terrifying. It is these development that make arguments in favour of physician-assisted suicide and active voluntary euthanasia compelling. These factors, however, do not make physician-assisted suicide and euthanasia the answer. The answer lies in removing some of the agitation and depression surrounding the uncertainties of death. This can largely be done by advances in palliative and hospice care. While improved pain management is central to this, equally important is improved psychological and spiritual management. To better train physicians and health care workers in the relief of suffering and to educate the public on the right to refuse life-sustaining treatment will increase patient autonomy and quality of life far more than physician-assisted suicide or euthanasia. The Nazi euthanasia experience illustrates the horrific dehumanization when any culture absolutizes community interests. However, the Dutch model demonstrates the similar danger in absolutizing personal autonomy. The concerns surrounding death and dying are real and must be dealt with. The answer lies in balancing the best interests of the individual and of society. This balance can in fact be very complementary. To cherish the implicit value of life and to reintroduce death as a natural event, not an imposed action or prolonged agony, advances both the good of society and the good of the individual.

NOTES

1 For additional information on the German scientific and medical communities during the Nazi seizure of power, see: Christian Pross, 'Nazi Doctors, German Medicine, and Historical Truth', *The Nazi Doctors and the Nuremberg Code*, eds. George J. Annas and Michael A. Grodin (Oxford: Oxford University Press, 1992); Robert Proctor 'Nazi Doctors, Racial Medicine, and Human Experimentation', *The Nazi Doctors and the Nuremberg Code*, eds. George J. Annas and Michael A. Grodin (Oxford: Oxford University Press, 1992); Paul Weindling, *Health, Race, and German Politics Between National Unification and Nazism, 1870–1945* (Cambridge: Cambridge University Press, 1989), chapter 8; Henry Friedlander, *The Origins of Nazi Genocide* (Chapel Hill, NC: University of North Carolina Press, 1995).

2 Qtd. in Benno Muller Hill, *Murderous Science: Elimination by Scientific Selection of Jews, Gypsies, and Others in Germany, 1933–1945* (Oxford: Oxford University Press, 1988): 25.

3 Sheila Faith Weiss, 'The Racial Hygiene Movement in Germany, 1904–1945', *The Wellborn Science: Eugenics in Germany, France, Brazil, and Russia*, ed. Mark B. Adams (Oxford: Oxford University Press, 1990): 36.

4 Friedlander, 15.

5 Weiss, 'The Racial Hygiene', 43.

6 For additional background on the Sterilization Law, see: Robert Jay Lifton, *The Nazi Doctors: Medical Killing and the Psychology of Genocide* (New York: Basic Books, Inc., 1986), chapter 1; Daniel Nadav, 'Sterilization, Euthanasia, and the Holocaust – the Brutal Chain', *Medicine, Ethics and the Third Reich: Historical and Contemporary Issues*, ed. John Michalczyk (Kansas City, MO: Sheed and Ward, 1994); Robert Proctor, *Racial Hygiene: Medicine under the Nazis*, chapter 4; Weindling, chapters 7 and 8.

7 Lifton, 15.

8 Friedlander, 26.

9 Proctor, 24.

10 Michael Burleigh, 'Racism as Social Policy: The Nazi "Euthanasia" Program, 1939–1945', *Ethnic and Racial Studies* 14 (1991): 455.

11 Friedlander, 45.

12 *ibid.*, 48.

13 *ibid.*, 58.

14 Nadav, 'Sterilization, "Euthanasia", and the Holocaust', 47.

15 Lifton, 54.

16 *ibid.*, 15.

17 Christian Pross, 'Nazi Doctors', 37.

18 Friedlander, 75.

19 *ibid.*, 169.

20 Michael Burleigh and Wolfgang Wipperman, *The Racial State: Germany, 1933–1945* (Cambridge: Cambridge University Press, 1991): 159.

21 Hugh Gallagher, *By Trust Betrayed: Patients, Physicians, and the License to Kill in the Third Reich* (Arlington, VA: Vandamere Press, 1995): 8.

22 Friedlander, 112.

23 *ibid.*, 152.

24 Aly, 82.

25 Friedlander, 159.

26 *ibid.*, 144.

27 *ibid.*, 150.

28 John H. Robinson, 'Physician-Assisted Suicide: Its Challenge to the Prevailing Constitutional Paradigm', *Notre Dame Journal of Law, Ethics and Public Policy* 9 (1995): 3477.

29 David Schanker, 'Of Suicide Machines, Euthanasia Legislation, and the Health Care Crisis', *Indiana Law Journal* 68 (1993): 980.

30 *ibid.*, 1004.

31 For background information on the American movement for legalized euthanasia and physician-assisted suicide, see: Lisa Sowle Cahill, 'Bioethical Decisions to End Life', *Theological Studies* 52 (1991): 107–121; E. J. Emmanuel, 'The History of the Euthanasia Debates in the United States and Britain', *Annals of Internal Medicine* 121 (1994): 793–802; 'It's Over, Debbie', *JAMA* 2759 (1988): 272; George Lundberg, 'It's Over, Debbie' and the Euthanasia Debate', *JAMA* 259 (1988): 2142; Willard Gayland, Leon Kass, Edmund Pellegrino and Mark Siegler, 'Doctors Must Not Kill', *JAMA* 259 (1988): 24–45, Timothy Quill, 'Death and Dignity: A Case of Individualized Decision Making', *New England Journal of Medicine* 324 (1991): 691–94; *Quill v. Vacco*, 80F.3d 716 (Second Circuit, 1996).

32 M. Cathleen Kaveny, 'Assisted Suicide, Euthanasia, and the Law', *Theological Studies* 58 (1997): 125.

33 Qtd. in John Paris, 'Active Euthanasia', *Theological Studies*, 53 (1992): 121.

34 Qtd. in Franklin G. Miller and John C. Fletcher, 'Physician-Assisted Suicide and Active Euthanasia', *Physician-Assisted Death*, eds. James M. Humber, Robert F. Almeder, and Gregg A. Kasting (Totowa, New Jersey: Humana Press, 1994), 80.

35 Edmund Pellegrino, 'Doctors Must Not Kill', *Euthanasia: The Good of Patient, the Good of Society*, ed. Robert Misbin (Frederick Maryland: University Publishing Group, 1992), 30.

36 Daniel Callahan, 'When Self-Determination Runs Amok', *Hastings Center Report* (March–April 1992): 52

37 *ibid.*, 55.

38 Kaveny, 134.

39 Diane E. Meier, 'Doctors' Attitudes and Experiences with Physician-Assisted Death:: A Review of the Literature', *Physician Assisted Death*, eds. James M. Humber, Robert F. Almeder, and Gregg A. Kasting (Totowa, New Jersey: Human Press, 1993): 8.

40 Luke Gormally, ed. *Euthanasia, Clinical Practice, and the Law* (London: Linacre Centre for Health Care Ethics, 1994): 30.

41 Franklin G. Miller and John C. Fletcher, 'Physician Assisted Suicide and Active Euthanasia', *Physician-Assisted Death*, eds. James M. Humber, Robert F. Almeder, and Gregg A. Kasting (Totowa, New Jersey: Human Press, 1993): 90.

42 'To Cease Upon the Midnight', *The Economist* (September 17, 1994): 22.

43 Paris, 119.

44 Richard Fenigsen, 'Physician-Assisted Death in the Netherlands: Impact on Long Term Care', *Issues in Law and Medicine* 3 (1995): 283.

45 John Keown, 'Euthanasia in the Netherlands: Sliding down the Slippery Slope?' *Euthanasia Examines: Ethical, Clinical and Legal Perspective*, ed. John Keown (Cambridge: Cambridge University Press, 1995): 263.

46 Pieter Admiraal, 'Voluntary Euthanasia: The Dutch Way', *Death, Dying, and the Law*, ed. Sheila A.M. McLean (Aldershot: Dartmouth, 1996): 114.

47 Keown, 265.

48 Alison Hall, 'To Die with Dignity: Comparing Physician-Assisted Suicide in the United State, Japan and the Netherlands', *Washington University Law Quarterly* 74 (1996): 827.
49 Herbert Hendin, *Seduced by Death: Doctors, Patients, and the Dutch Cure* (New York: W.W. Norton and Company, 1997, 141.
50 Fenigsen, 291.
51 Keown, 270.
52 Paris, 125.
53 Keown, 274.
54 *ibid.*, 270–273.
55 *ibid.*, 282.
56 Weile, 425.
57 Loes Pinjenborg, Paul van der Maas, Johannes J.M. van Delden, Casper W.N. Looman, 'Life-Terminating Acts Without Explicit Request of Patient.' *The Lancet* 341 (May 8, 1993): 1197.
58 *ibid.*, 1198.
59 Keown, 278.
60 Paris, 125.
61 Paul van der Maas Qtd. In Ezekiel Emmanuel, 'Whose Right to Die?' *The Atlantic Monthly* (March 1997): 78.
62 Hendin, *Seduced by Death*, 165.
63 D.J. Bakker, 'Active Euthanasia: Is Mercy Killing the Killing of Mercy?' *Euthanasia: The Good of the Patients, the Good of Society*, ed. Robert I. Misbin (Frederick, MD: University publishing Group, 1992): 88.
64 Quoted in Hendin, *Seduced By Death*, 107
65 Hendin, *Seduced By Death*, 224.
66 Bakker, 92.

RESCUE

Ethical and religious reflection about the Holocaust and genocide must study the perpetrators who provoked mass killing and the bystanders who permitted the perpetrators to do their worst. But no less important for ethics and religion are the people who risked everything to rescue those in need. Why did these ordinary people do such extraordinary things to remove children, women, and men from harm's way? How could those extraordinary deeds be made more ordinary so that the 21st century does not become another age of genocide? Such questions govern the following articles on rescue.

Articles on related themes will also be found in the section on Survivors in Volume 3.

PERPETRATOR/RESCUER:
THE TWO KEY FACTORS

David Blumenthal

T HERE ARE two questions that haunt the second and third generations after the shoah[1]: Where was God? And, where was humanity? Put differently: How could a good God have permitted the shoah to happen, especially to people chosen by God? And, how could so many people have been turned into passive and active participants in the shoah? I have given a forthright, if not popular, answer to the first question and have also proposed an answer to the second.[2] It is with one aspect of the question about humanity that I will deal here.

There are two sides to this coin: What enabled perpetrators and bystanders to do significant evil and not feel guilty about it? And, what enabled rescuers, of varying degrees, to do significant good in the face of enormous pressures? The question, generically put, is: What are the factors which facilitate the doing of good and the doing of evil? Interestingly, while there has been social-psychological research and historical study of the problems of obedience and altruism, and of perpetrators and rescuers, these topics have not been considered together in any systematic way.[3] The question must, however, be studied and the evidence from the disciplines of both psychology and of history must be considered. There are, it seems to me, two key factors which facilitate the doing of good and the doing of evil: (1) insertion into a hierarchy which does, or which tolerates, good or evil and (2) patterns of childhood discipline.

INSERTION INTO A HIERARCHY THAT DOES, OR TOLERATES, EVIL
The overwhelming evidence for the proposition that insertion into a hierarchy which does, or which tolerates, evil facilitates the doing of evil comes from social psychology, though the evidence from history is equally compelling.

The Milgram experiments. Milgram's[4] famous experiments required subjects to administer what they believed were painful and / or lethal electric shocks to innocent people simply on the basis of the assertion of the authority of the experimenter. Quite contrary to expectations, 50–65% of the subjects followed instructions into the lethal range of shocks (pp.35, 60–61). The percentage reached 85% in Germany (p.171) and among young people (p.173). No difference was registered for women (pp.62–3). With unrelenting clarity, Milgram notes that these results are not a function of class, religious affiliation, gender, location, educational background, ideology, and general culture (pp.62–3, p. 170). Nor are they a result of character or psychopathology (p.187). The results derive solely from the assertion of hierarchy-authority in the form of the experimenter.

Milgram concludes that hierarchy and authority are inherent in any society (p.152); that this hierarchy and authority are internalized and serve as the basis for obedience to legitimate authority (p.141); and that conscience, which regulates impulsive aggressive action, is diminished at the point of entering a hierarchical structure (p.132) such that the person enters an 'agentic state' in contrast to the usual 'autonomous state' (pp.132–4). In the agentic state, morality becomes obedience to authority; that is, that which is good is obedience to the authority (pp.145–6); the superego is shifted from independent evaluation of the morality of action to the judgment of how well one has functioned in the hierarchical-authoritative setting (p.146). The move to the agentic state, then, minimizes the damage to the ego and self-image, though a certain amount of strain is observable during the transition from, and in the ongoing tension between, the agentic and the autonomous states (pp.154–7).

The brown-eyed/ blue-eyed children experiments.   The same results in a not-strictly experimental setting were obtained in Riceville, Iowa, where a teacher, Mrs. Jane Elliot, in an attempt to teach her third-grade class about the nature of discrimination, set the blue-eyed children against the brown-eyed children.[5] The bigotry shown by the class, which actually affected the learning curves of the students, was surfaced solely by the authority of the teacher, which is all the more remarkable since she reversed the hierarchy of blue-eyed and brown-eyed children on the second day simply by saying that she had been wrong on the previous day. The teacher's authority extended so far that the parents did not object to the bigotry shown in class. Later work by Mrs. Elliot showed that this 'experiment' works in prisons and elsewhere, that is, among adults, because they too accept, and act upon, the authority of someone legitimately placed in the social hierarchy.[6]

My Lai and its aftermath.   In a long and deep study of the trial of Lt. Calley for his part in the massacre at My Lai during the Vietnam war and of the aftermath of the trial, Kelman and Hamilton[7] explored the question of legitimate authority with great thoroughness. After devoting a chapter to the events of 16 March 1968, the authors spend a chapter discussing the problem of 'legal crimes', putting it very succinctly: 'When subordinates receive orders from duly constituted authorities operating in an apparent legal framework, they may well assume that the orders themselves are legal' (p.47, quoting Arendt). Kelman and Hamilton, then, devote chapters 3–6 to the problem of legitimate authority. They point to the 'habit of obedience' (p.57) and to the fact that legitimate authority demands, it does not persuade; its demands, thus, have an obligatory character which is linked to the roles of the hierarchy (pp.89–91). They also point to the temporary surrender of the right to choose which allows the influence of authority to be felt, thereby creating obedience (p.91).

To maintain its legitimacy, an authority must focus individuals on rule-, role-, and value-oriented decisions; not on decisions based on personal, subjective preference. It must also be able to claim legitimate access to power, remain within the cultural norms, abide by the implicit rules for the use of power, and be generally accountable. If this is done, then, even if there is doubt, most persons will insert themselves into the hierarchy and obey legitimate authority (pp.122–5).

Surveying reactions to the events at My Lai and later to the trial of Lt. Calley, Kelman and Hamilton develop other typologies which generate the corroborative result that, if the authority is legitimate and if the subordinates and superiors stay within their assigned roles then, if a legal crime is committed, most people feel that there should be no punishment because role-within-legitimate-authority takes precedence over independent moral judgement of the act itself (p.206), though there is some variation depending upon one's place in the hierarchy (pp.207–8).

The SS. Historians studying the shoah have reached much the same conclusion as the social psychologists. Hannah Arendt,[8] observing the trial of Eichmann, pointed out that he was not a fanatic or a monster. On the contrary, he was terrifyingly normal; he felt he did no wrong; and he would not have felt the slightest remorse had the Nazis won and had he been able to carry out the final solution (pp.146, 276, 288).[9] For Eichmann, the 'führer's wish' and word were law and, when that law contradicted orders from superiors – as when Himmler ordered him to stop the deportation of the Jews to extermination camps – it was the law that he needed to, and did, follow; not the orders (pp.137–46). It was, therefore, precisely his conscience that motivated Eichmann (pp.146–7); his conscience was the law (p.293). Eichmann was so obedient that the Israeli judges got more information from him than either set of lawyers, precisely because they were higher in the authority hierarchy (p.223). From this, Arendt reasoned that anyone could have filled Eichmann's place in the hierarchy (p.278) and that evil was banal[10] precisely because insertion into a social hierarchy made it normal.

More than thirty years after the war, Klee and his colleagues interviewed former SS officers.[11] Again, the thesis of insertion into hierarchy appears very strong:

> 'I am however convinced that very many men of lower rank under the then authoritarian regime and under such strict and tough commanders as Stahldecker never even entertained the thought of giving expression to their inner conflict, fearing privately that a refusal to take part in a shooting would have had very serious consequences. In my experience, amongst the lower ranks there was not so much an objective necessity to obey orders, more of a subjective one . . .' (p.85, quoting).

And again:

> 'We had been drilled in such a way that we viewed all orders issued by the head of state as lawful and correct. We police went by the phrase, "Whatever serves the state is right, whatever harms the state is wrong." I would also like to say that it never even entered my head that these orders could be wrong. Although I am aware that it is the duty of the police to protect the innocent I was however at that time convinced that the Jewish people were not innocent but guilty. . . . I followed these orders because they came from the highest leaders of the state and not because I was in any way afraid' (pp.220–21, quoting).[12]

Ordinary Germans. With the invasion of Russia, the crack troops of the German army and the SS divisions moved out of Poland to form the fighting units and the Einsatz-gruppen. However, there were still almost 3,000,000 Jews left in Poland who, according to the final solution, needed to be exterminated. Who was minding the store? Who would carry out this 'project'? In a stunning book, Christopher Browning[13] follows the history of Police Battalion 101, a group of men who weren't fit for the fighting units, whose job it became to carry out the final solution in Poland. Sometimes, this meant shooting everyone, person by person; at other times, it included shooting the sick, the weak, the elderly, and the infants while forcibly deporting the rest. The transformation of this remarkably undistinguished group of men, only 25–30% of whom were members of the nazi party (p.48), into mass murderers is one of the most horrifying stories of the shoah.

Browning carefully reconstructs the actions of Police Battalion 101, taking into account all the appropriate problems of dealing with such historical sources, and concludes that 80–90% of the men continued to kill Jews while only 10–20% of the men refused, asked to be excused, or simply evaded the killing tasks (pp.74, 160). Of those who continued to kill, a small percentage became hardened killers who enjoyed their work and volunteered for killing missions; the greatest number 'did everything that was asked of them and never risked confronting authority.'[14] Browning also points out that the work of this group of men who, by November 1942 had executed 6500 Jews and deported 42,000 more (p.121), was not an episode but an ongoing, relentless task that required sustained attention (132). It was, thus, not a battle frenzy as in My Lai but 'atrocity by policy' (pp.160–61). Furthermore, this was not depersonalized action but hands-on killing with high salience to the victims (p.162). Nor were these men specially selected, nor was the majority self-selected (pp.165–9). There was no special coercion[15] and no 'putative duress' (pp.170–71). Revulsion, when it occurred, was physical; not ethical (p.74).

In an attempt to wonder why and how, Browning admits the effect of brutalization and numbing, of the context of racial war, of psychological splitting, and of ideology. However, he maintains that these factors were contributory, subsidiary (pp.161, 163, 182, 184). The main mechanism that enabled these ordinary men to become 'grass roots' killers was insertion into the hierarchy of army command. Their officers only needed to invoke the authority of their hierarchy to obtain obedience, even though it was sometimes accompanied by anger and upset (pp.69, 74, 151, 171–75). Peer pressure – not to be 'weak' but to be 'tough' (pp.150, 183) – reinforced authority; it did not create it (p.175).

In another study of ordinary Germans done in the 1950s, Milton Mayer[16] went to a small village in Germany and, hiding his Jewish identity, interviewed the local people about life under nazism. The motif of insertion into a hierarchy which does, or tolerates, evil was very strong:

> When 'big men,' Hindenbergs, Neuraths, Schachts, and even Hohenzollerns, accepted Nazism, little men had good and sufficient reason to accept it. '*Wenn die "Ja" sagen*'', said Herr Simon, the bill-collector, '*dann sagen wir auch "Ja*." ' What was good enough for *them* was certainly good enough for us.... My friends were little men – like the Führer himself' (pp.44–5).

And again:

> This immense hierarchicalism, based upon blind servility in which the man on the third rung would never dare to imagine that the man on the second would order him to do something wrong, since, after all, the man on the second had to answer to the man on the first, nourished the buck-passing instinct to fantastic proportions.... The only objection is that men who always do what they are told do not know what to do when they're not. Without the thoughtful habit of decision, they decide... thoughtlessly. If they are forbidden to beat Jews, they learn how not to want to, something a free man who wants to beat Jews never learns....' (pp.162–3).

And again:

> 'The new National Socialist faith believed in God but not in the divinity of Christ. That's the simplest way to put it.... We little people didn't know whether or not to believe it. "Is it right, or isn't it?" we asked ourselves... One believed one way, one another. It wasn't ever decided. Perhaps, if the war had been won, it would have been decided finally.' 'By whom?' 'By the men on top. But they didn't seem to have decided yet themselves. A man didn't know what to think' (pp.232–3).

The story of the German judiciary is another example of the agentic shift which allowed normal German jurists to excel at the doing of evil.[17]

INSERTION INTO A HIERARCHY THAT DOES, OR TOLERATES, GOOD
As insertion into a hierarchy works to facilitate evil, so it works to facilitate the doing of good. Here, too, the evidence from social psychology and from history is probative.

The Princeton experiment. In a well-known experiment, Darley and Batson[18] took a group of 67 Princeton Theological Seminary students and administered to them a series of personality and religiosity psychometric tests. They, then, gave the students the parable of the Good Samaritan (Luke 10: 29–37) to read, and assigned half of them to deliver a homily on the parable and half of them to prepare a brief talk on alternate ministry. The testing and reading were done in one building and the homily or talk was done in another. Each group was, then, divided into three sub-groups: one was 'high-hurry,' that is, they were told to hurry to the second location to complete the assignment; one was 'intermediate-hurry,' that is, they were told to hurry to the second location to complete the assignment; one was 'intermediate-hurry,' that is, they were told to go directly to the second location; and one was 'low-hurry,' that is, they were told they had ample time to get to the second location. A suffering victim, who was actually a confederate in the experiment, was placed on the way to the second location.

The purpose of the experiment was to see how many theology students, who had just read the parable of the Good Samaritan and were preparing either to give a short homily on the subject or to talk about ministry, would stop to aid this experimental victim – as the Good Samaritan had stopped to aid a victim by the wayside – and to determine what kind of help they would offer. Sixty percent, that is, more than half, did not stop to offer help to the victim on the wayside. Of the 40% who did stop, 10% were in the 'high-hurry' group, 45% in the 'intermediate-hurry' group, and 63% in the 'low-hurry' group. The conclusions were quite clear:

> A person not in a hurry may stop and offer help to a person in distress. A person in a hurry is likely to keep going. Ironically, he is likely to keep going even if he is hurrying to speak on the parable of the Good Samaritan, thus inadvertently confirming the point of the parable. (Indeed, on several occasions, a seminary student going to give his talk on the parable of the Good Samaritan literally stepped over the victim as he hurried on his way!) . . . It is hard to think of a context in which norms concerning helping those in distress are more salient than for a person thinking about the Good Samaritan, and yet it did not significantly increase helping behavior (p.107, parentheses original).

Darley and Batson, then, speculated on the cause of this phenomenon:

> Why were the seminarians in a hurry? Because the experimenter, *whom the subject was helping*, was depending on him to get to a particular place quickly. In other words, he was in conflict between stopping to help the victim and continuing on his way to help the experimenter . . . . Conflict, rather than callousness, can explain their failure to stop (p.108, emphasis original).

The helping distressed persons experiments. In an equally dramatic series of experiments, Staub[19] took groups of various ages, assigned them an irrelevant task, and then gave them one of three sets of instructions: one group was given permission to leave the task room if necessary; one group was given no instructions on leaving the task room; and one group was prohibited from leaving the room. Then, from an adjacent room, cries of distress were simulated. The purpose of the experiment was to test resistance to authority in a situation evoking helping behaviour as a response to the distress stimulus. The experiment showed that, when permission was given, a 'high frequency of helping behavior' resulted and, conversely, when prohibition was the instruction, it 'substantially reduced active attempts to help.' In the case of no information, adults tended to help while children tended to refrain from helping (pp.323–4). Staub summarizes the results dramatically: 'Almost all subjects in the *permission* condition actively helped' (p.313, emphasis original).

These experiments confirm the insights of the previous section on obedience; to wit, that insertion into a hierarchy of authority is very important in determining a person's willingness to act – except that the inescapable result of this experiment is that *authority can permit ethically correct behaviour; that is, that authority can function, as authority, to justify and permit prosocial behaviour.*

In a study of the influence of television on prosocial and antisocial behavior, Eron and Huesmann[20] showed that

> [E]xposure to prosocial content [programs such as 'Mr. Rogers,' 'Lassie,' and 'Father Knows Best'] led to increased prosocial behavior, whereas exposure to aggressive content led to increased aggressive behavior.... Those boys who watch violent television and identify with aggressive television characters are predictably more aggressive two years later regardless of their initial level of aggressiveness' (pp.293, 304).

Here, again, an authority – in this case, the cultural authority of television[21] – acts as an authority to sanction *both* prosocial and aggressive behaviour.

Revisiting the obedience experiments.   A closer look at Milgram's obedience experiments also reveals the power of authority and obedience to sanction prosocial behaviour. One of the subjects was a professor of Old Testament. The subject discontinued the experiment after reaching 150 volts saying, 'If he [the learner/victim] doesn't want to continue, I'm taking orders from him.' In the post-experiment discussion, the professor said, 'If one had as one's ultimate authority God, then it trivializes human authority' (pp.47–9). Authority and obedience to that authority – in this case, the victim and then God – sanctioned prosocial action. In yet another set of experiments, two experimenters were brought into the room, one who advocated continuing the experiment and one who advocated discontinuing it (pp.105–7). In this case of split authority, '[N]ot a single subject "took advantage" of the instructions to go on; in no instance did individual aggressive motives latch on to the authoritative sanction provided by the malevolent authority. Rather, action was stopped dead in its tracks' (p.107). Milgram maintained that this was because of a 'contamination' of the hierarchical system, noting that some subjects tried to ascertain which experimenter was the higher authority (*ibid*). The possibility also exists that, at least in some cases, the presence of two authorities, one sanctioning antisocial action and the other sanctioning prosocial action, allowed or permitted the subjects to follow the impulse to do good precisely because they had a choice of which authority to follow.

Rescuers invoke authority.   The evidence from the historians confirms this view. Baron[22] notes that Dutch Calvinists rescued Jews: because they believed the Jewish people was the people of God and hence Christians were obligated to rescue them, because they had a ministry to the persecuted, or because they were predestined to rescue (pp.318–19). Sauvage[23] cites the same testimony from Hugenot France, and Fogelman[24] quotes one Christian as asking, 'What would Jesus do?' (p.177) and another as saying, 'I have to save these people, as many as I can. If am disobeying orders, I'd rather die with God and against men than with men and against God' (p.201). She also observes: 'Indeed, this conviction among religious rescuers – that they were accountable to a higher and more fearsome authority – was the most salient aspect of their rescuer self. It overcame antisemitism, transcended fear, and impelled them to action' (pp.176–77). Kurek-Lesik[25] cites the following:

> 'I come from nationalist circles, often charged with anti-Semitism. Why did I save Jewish children? Because they were children, because they were people. I would save any man [sic]

in danger of death, and a child – every child – is particularly dear to me. This is what my Catholic religion *orders* me to do.' . . . A persecuted Jew somehow stopped being a Jew and became simply a man, woman, or child in need of help. The Polish nuns were motivated by a Christian *duty* towards others and by their fidelity to the ideal that they were pledged to do so in a special way by their vows. . . . This is why saving Jews and Jewish children should first of all be seen in the broader context of monastic service to humanity (pp.330–32, emphasis added).

Sometimes, the authority invoked was not religion but national resistance. Thus, Baron notes that 42% of the Dutch rescuers were also in the resistance and, hence, saving Jews was sanctioned by the political authority of the resistance even if one had no particular religious or social feeling for Jews (pp.312–13).

The evidence, then, is quite consistent: people who do prosocial acts often invoke a higher authority to sanction their actions. The implications of this for building a better society are substantial.

Peer support as an appeal to authority.   Peer support is another form of authority and it, too, sanctions prosocial action. In one part of the Milgram experiments, subjects had peers, who were actually confederates in the experiment, who objected to continuing the experiment (pp. 116–21). The results were noteworthy: 'In this group setting, 36 of the 40 subjects defy the experimenter (while the corresponding number in the absence of group pressure is 14). The effects of peer rebellion are very impressive in undercutting the experimenter's authority' (p. 118). The peer 'provides social confirmation for the subject's suspicion that it is wrong to punish a man against his will, even in the context of a psychological experiment. . . . dispersion of responsibility . . . every failure of authority to exact compliance with its commands weakens the perceived power of the authority' (pp. 120–21).[26]

Staub[27] observed the same phenomenon. First, he cited well-known experiments by Latané and Darley showing that increase in the number of passive bystanders leads to decreased bystander action (p. 296). Then, on a variant of the adjacent-room distress experiments, Staub had confederates generate 'positive verbal definition' of the situation ('That sounds bad. Maybe we should do something.'); 'negative verbal definition' ('That sounds like a tape recording. Maybe they are trying to test us.'); 'indirect help definition' ('I'll go try to find the experimenter.'); 'prohibition definition' ('I'll go try to find the experimenter. Don't go in there. I don't think we're supposed to.'); and 'maximum positive influence definition' ('I'll go try to find the experimenter. You go in and see what happened.'). The results were very clear: 'The behavior of the confederate greatly affected the frequency of active help . . . *Maximum positive influence* produced the greatest helping behavior – all subjects helped' (p. 318, emphasis original).[28]

Data from the historians supports this thesis too. The Oliners[29] write about the importance of networks which, however, under conditions of terror must perforce be kept small and discrete (pp. 102–8). And Fogelman notes the 'channel factors', a term drawn from Kurt Lewin, which were necessary prerequisites of rescue. They include the availability of a hiding place and a network to supply identity cards, ration cards, escape route, warning in case of impending raid, etc. (pp. 60–61). Furthermore, the Oliners point out that only one-third of the rescuers began helping Jews on their own initiative; the rest – fully two-thirds – of the rescuers undertook rescue activity only after being asked by a potential victim, a parent or other relative, a religious functionary or representative of the resistance, a teacher, or an acquaintance or a friend (pp. 312–17).

The conclusion to be drawn is clear: *Legitimate social authority – hierarchical or peer authority – facilitates both antisocial and prosocial behaviour.* Legitimate social authority creates the agentic shift, thus allowing the individual to invoke authority to do either good or evil.[30]

The implications of this realization for moral education are enormous, the clearest being: *Authority figures must be taught to stigmatize the doing of evil but, more important, they must be taught to actively give permission for the doing of good and to diligently structure their hierarchies and institutions to demand prosocial attitudes and behaviours.*[31]

PATTERNS OF ANTISOCIAL CHILDHOOD DISCIPLINE

Listening to Hitler's speeches and watching him speak in films such as *Triumph of the Will*, one is impressed with his screaming. Everything he seemed to have said was screamed, especially in his public appearances. The same phenomenon of continuous screaming was also noticed in the camps. Survivors report the yelling, the screamed commands, no matter what the task at hand. To Americans the screaming was a puzzle, even comical as in Charlie Chaplin's *The Great Dictator*; to Germans it was not.

Alice Miller,[32] in her profound study of German culture, looks into the personal-developmental history of Germans using the tools of both cultural history and thera-peutic case-history. The case of Hitler's screaming serves as a paradigm for Miller's general theory of the origin of social evil: authoritarian culture permits a father to abuse his children – verbally, emotionally, and physically. Furthermore, she notes, this culture and these phenomena allow the adult abused child to do evil with one aspect of the self, to be 'normal' with the other, and to sustain both 'selves' in a tense but workable coexistence.

In a similarly famous study of prejudice, Adorno[33] also concluded that the authoritar-ian personality can be characterized as one which grew up in, and perpetuates, an atmosphere of harsh discipline: 'Prejudiced subjects tend to report a relatively harsh and more threatening type of home discipline which was experienced as arbitrary by the child. Related to this is a tendency apparent in families of prejudiced subjects to base interrelationships on rather clearly defined roles of dominance and submission in contra-distinction to equalitarian policies. In consequence, the images of parents seem to acquire for the child a forbidding or at least a distant quality. Family relationships are character-ized by fearful subservience to the demands of the parents and by an early suppression of impulses not acceptable to them' (pp. 256–7).

The Oliners have put it well:

> . . . punishment implies the need to curb some intrinsic wildness or evil intent. Routine gratuitous punishment implies that powerful persons have the right to exert their will arbitrarily. . . . Having had little influence over their parents' behavior, [such children] are more inclined to feel a sense of helplessness in influencing others generally. . . . Human relationships are construed in power terms, superordination and subordination viewed as the inherent social condition of humankind. The best one can do in the face of power is to succumb (*Altruistic Personality*, pp. 182–3).

The more abusive the environment, then, the more the child is subject to the whim of the abusive parent. Punishment becomes more and more erratic, unpredictable, and capricious as well as more and more invasive and violent. This is both physically harmful as well as psychologically destabilizing.[34]

In its exteme form, harsh discipline can turn very ugly. Miller notes that authoritarian, child-abusive culture generates great inner rage which is turned inward by repression and, then, outward by projection. Indeed, Germans felt a sense of relief upon reading *Mein Kampf* and learning that it was permissible to hate the Jews because this meant that all their anger at their own abused and despised selves – the product of abusive child-hood discipline – could be projected onto the Jews. This, in turn, led to the cruelty toward, and extermination of, the Jews (pp. 166, 187–8):

> [They] led a million children, whom they regarded as the bearers of the feared portions of their own psyche, into the gas chambers. One can even imagine that by shouting at them, beating them, or photographing them, they were finally able to release the hatred going back to early childhood. From the start, it had been the aim of their upbringing to stifle their childish, playful, and life-affirming side. The cruelty inflicted on them, the psychic murder of the child they once were, had to be passed on in the same way: each time they sent another Jewish child to the gas ovens, they were in essence murdering the child within themselves (pp. 86–7).[35]

Or, as F. Katz has commented:[36]

> Evil can be, and sometimes has been, *developed into a culture of cruelty*, a distinctive culture in its own right. As such it is systematically organized to reward individuals for their acts of cruelty: for being creative at inventing cruelties and for establishing a personal reputation for their particular version of cruelty. Here cruelty can be a macabre art-form... here, too, cruelty can be a distinctive 'economy,' where one's credit rating depends on one's level of cruelty – the more cruel, the higher one's standing. By contrast, acts of kindness can lead to publicly declared bankruptcy, and in some situations the punishment for this bankruptcy is a death sentence (31, emphasis original)... we must admit that, *under some circumstances, individuals will deliberately choose to do evil.* For example, a culture of cruelty can be highly attractive. It can offer an individual the opportunity to live creatively, and creative living touches on a profound human yearning. At times individuals may discover that acting cruelty is a way, perhaps the only way, they can be creative. They are then likely to embrace a culture of cruelty when some facilitating conditions exist in their immediate context (127, emphasis original).

One can conclude, then, that early childhood discipline which is excessive and erratic – that is, abusive in its broad sense – helps to create the authoritarian personality, thereby facilitating the doing of evil. Excessive and erratic discipline does this by instilling an attitude of obedience, by bullying and frightening the child into submission. Excessive and erratic discipline also creates a deep anger in the abused self. This anger, indeed rage, must be suppressed because the child cannot retaliate against the parent; however, it is very likely to surface in later hostile acts which will be directed against a helpless, socially stigmatized other. Antisocial childrearing cultivates the xenophobic, rigid, submissive, and totalitarian personality, creating thereby the possibility for the doing of evil.

PATTERNS OF PROSOCIAL CHILDHOOD DISCIPLINE

The key factor uniting rescuers of Jews during the shoah was not economic status, religious or political conviction, hatred of the nazis, or even a special relationship to Jews. Rather, it was, as the Oliners have shown, a commitment to caring for other human beings which was deeply rooted in childhood attitudes toward authority and punishment. A disciplinary milieu characterized by reason and proportion is central:

> ... significantly fewer rescuers recalled any controls imposed on them by the most intimate persons in their early lives.... parents of rescuers depended significantly less on physical punishment and significantly more on reasoning.... Thus, it is in their reliance on reasoning, explanations, suggestions of ways to remedy the harm done, persuasion, and advice that parents of rescuers differed most from nonrescuers (*Altruistic Personality*, pp. 179–81).

It [parental punishment] includes a heavy dose of reasoning – explanations of why behaviors are inappropriate, often with reference to their consequences for others. Physical punishment is rare: when used, it tends to be a singular event rather than routine. Gratuitous punishment – punishment that serves as a cathartic release of aggression for the parent or is unrelated to the child's behavior – almost never occurs (*Altruistic Personality*, p. 249).

Fogelman, too, notes that studies of anti-nazi German men show their homes to have been 'more accepting and less rigid' while studies of rescuers show that they experienced 'a loving and trusting relationship with an affectionate mother [and] had a communicative and nonauthoritarian father.' These studies supported her own findings of parents of rescuers 'who explained rules and used inductive reasoning' (pp. 255–7).

The Oliners account for the connection between prosocial behavior and prosocial childhood discipline as follows:

Reasoning communicates a message of respect for and trust in children that allows them to feel a sense of personal efficacy and warmth toward others. It is based on a presumption of error rather than a presumption of evil intent. It implies that had children but known better or understood more, they would not have acted in an inappropriate way. It is a mark of esteem for the listener; an indication of faith in his or her ability to comprehend, develop and improve (*Altruistic Personality*, p. 182).

Parents have power over children; they are not only physically stronger but also have access to material resources they can bestow or withhold. Societal norms generally support their superior position.... When adults voluntarily abdicate the use of power in favor of explanation, they are modeling appropriate behavior toward the weak on the part of the powerful. Faced with powerless others, children so raised in turn have at their disposal an internal 'script' – a store of recollections, dialogues, and activities ready to be activated. They need not depend on innovation or improvisation but rather simply retrieve what is already imprinted on their memories (*Altruistic Personality*, p. 183).

The social scientific evidence independent of the shoah also supports the conclusion that caring authority in childhood is crucial in the formation of prosocial attitudes.

Parents whose disciplinary techniques are benevolent, particularly those who rely on reasoning, are more likely to have kind and generous children... Induction focuses children's attention on the consequences of their behaviors for others, drawing attention to others' feelings, thoughts, and welfare... more inclined to develop empathy toward others.[37]
A great deal of laboratory and socialization research shows that prosocial behavior is influenced by a combination of (1) parental warmth and nurturance, (2) *induction*, pointing out to children the consequences of their behavior on other people, and (3) firm control by parents, so that children actually behave in accordance with important values and rules.... The more parents and socializers in other settings, such as schools, particularly in the early school years, use such a pattern, the more we can expect prosocial orientation, empathic responsiveness, and behavioral tendencies for increased altruism and less aggression in children.... While reasonable parental control is important, it is also important that parents respond to the child's own reasoning and be willing to consider the child's point of view.[38]

The conclusion to be drawn is clear: Patterns of antisocial childhood discipline, ranging from unnecessarily strict to outright abusive, create an authoritarian personality which will conform to the demands of authority and may even be drawn into a culture of cruelty. Patterns of prosocial childhood discipline, in which authority acts with measured and reasoned behaviour and allows itself to be challenged, create an altruistic personality which will question the demands of authority and is likely to be drawn into a culture of care.

SUMMARY

To summarize: The two key factors that facilitate the doing of good and the doing of evil are: (1) insertion into a hierarchy which does, or tolerates, the doing of good or evil and (2) patterns of childhood discipline. The lessons to be drawn from this are: (1) social authorities must be taught to stigmatize the doing of evil but must be also be taught to actively give permission for the doing of good and to diligently structure their hierarchies and institutions to demand prosocial attitudes and behaviours. And (2), social authorities in the family, school, and society must be taught to administer childhood discipline in a manner which is measured and reasoned, and which allows, even encourages, the challenging of authority. By observing these two precepts, we may be able to approach the time when ours will be more fully a culture of care and true justice.

NOTES

1 For many years I used the word 'holocaust' to designate the destruction of European Jewry during the second world war. I have since been persuaded that 'holocaust' should not be used for two reasons: First, it bears the additional meaning of 'a whole burnt offering', which is certainly not the theological overtone to be sounded in this context. And second, the destruction of European Jewry happened to Jews and, hence, it is they who should have the sad honour of naming this event with a Hebrew term. The word 'shoah' has been used for a long time in Hebrew to denote the catastrophe to Jewry during World War II and has even been adopted by many non-Jews as the proper designation. I now adopt this usage and acknowledge my debt to Professor Jean Halpérin of Geneva and Fribourg for the insight.

It is my practice to capitalize only nouns referring to God, together with nouns usually capitalized in English. This is a theological-grammatical commitment to the sovereignty of God. Thus, I spell 'messiah', 'temple', etc. Furthermore, to infuse literature with ethics, I especially do not capitalize 'nazi', 'führer', 'fatherland', 'third reich', 'national socialist', 'final solution', etc. except in quotations. I am indebted to Hana Goldman, a plucky ten year old, who defied her teachers by refusing to capitalize 'nazi', thereby setting an example for all of us. The word 'shoah' falls in this category and, therefore, I consistently do not capitalize it.

2 For the question about God, see my *Facing the Abusing God: A Theology of Protest* (Louisville, KY, Westminster / John Knox: 1993). For the question about humanity, see my *The Banality of Good and Evil: Moral Lessons from the Shoah and Jewish Tradition* (Washington, DC, Georgetown University Press: 1999).

3 The exception is E. Staub, *The Roots of Evil: The Origins of Genocide and Other Group Violence* (Cambridge, Cambridge University Press: 1989).

4 S. Milgram, *Obedience to Authority: An Experimental View* (New York, Harper and Row: 1974); also available as a film.

5 Film, 'In the Eye of the Storm' and later in a film, 'A Class Divided'; the latter appeared as a book by W. Peters, *A Class Divided Then and Now* (New Heaven: Yale University Press: 1987).

6 This is clear from 'A Class Divided'. My students tell me that Mrs. Elliot appeared on the Oprah Winfrey show with great success.

7 H.C. Kelman and V.L. Hamilton, *Crimes of Obedience* (New Haven, CT: Yale University Press: 1989).

8 H. Arendt, *Eichmann in Jerusalem: A Report on the Banality of Evil* (New York: Viking Press: 1963).

9 This is confirmed by the analysis of the Rorschach data for the Nuremberg accused. No psycho-pathology was found (G. Borofsky and D. Brand, 'Personality Organization and Psychological Functioning of the Nuremberg War Criminals: The Rorschach Data', in J. Dimsdale, *Survivors, Victims, and Perpetrators: Essays on the Nazi Holocaust* [New York: Hemisphere Publishing Co.: 1980], 359–403).

10 The concept of 'the banality of evil' is a very powerful analytic tool. Used originally by Hannah Arendt, the term has been construed to mean three things: (1) evil which is normal, prosaic, or matter-of-fact; (2) evil which is rationalized as good because it is obedient or because it serves a larger

purpose; and (3) evil which is trite, hackneyed, or stale. The last implies that evil is not immoral or grossly wrong. Arendt never meant to imply that nazi evil was trite and hence not immoral. Rather, Arendt meant to say that nazi evil was 'banal' both in being matter-of-fact and in being so because it was rationalized as good. I follow Arendt in this usage. In this sense, even abusiveness can be 'banal', that is, normal, prosaic, matter-of-fact, and rationalized as a greater good. Indeed, as Alice Miller has pointed out, Hitler was a role model for abusiveness precisely because his actions were very close to the everyday reality of middle-European family life.

11 E. Klee et al., '*The Good Old Days*', transl. D. Burnstone (New York: Free Press, 1988, 1991).

12 The issue of 'putative duress' seems to be very complicated. Browning (p.171) implies that there was none at all, at least not for his subjects since they were specifically given the opportunity not to participate by their commanding officer in Jósefow. The first quotation from Klee indicates that there was a distinct subjective, though not objective, putative duress; the second sets the issue in the context of willing obedience.

13 C. Browning, *Ordinary Men: Reserve Police Battalion 101 and the Final Solution in Poland* (New York: Harper Collins, 1992). See also *idem.*, 'Ordinary Germans or Ordinary Men', *Address and Response at the Inauguration of the Dorot Chair of Modern Jewish and Holocaust Studies*, ed. D. Blumenthal (Atlanta, GA: Emory University, 1994) pp.7–14.

14 'Ordinary Germans or Ordinary Men', p.11; see also page 9 where he calls these men 'grass roots' killers.

15 It is now well-known that there is not one single case of a person put to death for refusing to kill Jews. See Browning, p.170; Klee, pp.75–86, with p.80 and p.82 for Himmler's verbal and written orders on the subject; and D. Kitterman, 'Those Who Said, "No!": Germans Who Refused to Execute Civilians during World War II', *German Studies Review* 9:2 (May 1988): 241–54. See Browning, p.103, that those who resisted were yelled at but not disciplined.

16 M. Mayer, *They Thought They Were Free: The Germans 1933–1945* (Chicago: University of Chicago Press, 1955, 1966).

17 I. Müller, *Hitler's Justice: The Courts of the Third Reich*, transl. D.L. Schneider (Cambridge, MA: Harvard University Press, 1991) – reviewed by me in *Modern Judaism* 13 (1993): 95–106.

18 J. M. Darley and C.D. Batson, 'From Jerusalem to Jericho: A Study of Situational and Dispositional Variables in Helping Behavior', *Journal of Personality and Social Psychology* 27:1 (1973): 100–8.

19 E. Staub, 'Helping a Distressed Person', L. Berkowitz, *Advances in Experimental Social Psychology* 7 (New York: Academic Press, 1974): 293–341.

20 L. Eron and L. Huesmann, 'The Role of Television in the Development of Prosocial and Antisocial Behavior', D. Olweus et al., *Development of Antisocial and Prosocial Behavior* (New York: Academic Press, 1986), pp.285–314.

21 Called by the authors 'observational learning' (p.309).

22 L. Baron, 'The Dutchness of Dutch Rescuers: The National Dimension of Altruism', P. Oliner et al., *Embracing the Other: Philosophical, Psychological, and Historical Perspectives* (New York: New York University Press, 1992), pp.306–27 – reviewed by me in *Pastoral Psychology* 46:2 (1997): 131–34.

23 In the film *Weapons of the Spirit*. One of the most moving moments in the film occurs when the visiting nazi finishes his speech and shouts 'Heil Hitler'. He is greeted by silence and, in that silence, one person shouts, 'Long live Jesus Christ.'

24 E. Fogelman, *Conscience and Courage: Rescuers of Jews during the Holocaust* (New York: Anchor Books, 1994) – reviewed by me in *Journal of Psychology and Theology* 23 (1995): 62–63.

25 E. Kurek-Lesik, 'The Role of Polist Nuns in the Rescue of Jews, 1939–1945', in Oliner, *Embracing*, pp.328–34.

26 The Milgram experiments probably could not be conducted today because of stricter rules on experimentation with human subjects but, if one were to redo these experiments, one would need to redesign this part to test more fully the role of peer support in defying authority. More importantly, the Stanford Prison experiment (P.G. Zimbardo, et al. 'The Psychology of Imprisonment: Privation, Power and Pathology', *Doing Unto Others*, ed. Z. Rubin (Englewood Cliffs, NJ: Prentice-Hall, 1974); available in slide presentation and, later, in a film, *Quiet Rage;* see *New York Times Magazine*, 8 April 1973) would have to be completely redesigned to test for resistance to add,

for example: a resisting confederate among the guards, the prisoners, and the parents; or, a series of humanizing moments such as joint meals between prisoners and guards, a built-in reminder of the experimental framework; etc.

27 Staub, 'Helping', pp.316–21.

28 Interestingly, prohibition did not seem to inhibit helping. Further, subjects alone also helped at very high levels because, consistent with Latané and Darley's work, subjects alone feel more responsibility.

29 S. and P. Oliner, *The Altruistic Personality: Rescuers of Jews in Nazi Europe* (New York: Free Press, 1988).

30 See also C.D. Batson, *The Altruism Question: Toward a Social-Psychological Answer* (Hillsdale, NJ: Laurence Erlbaum Associates: 1991), p.160, that low-empathy persons need feedback on their helping activities.

31 For three attempts to provide direct, clear guidance see my 'The Banality of Good and Evil: Antisocial Behavior, Prosocial Behavior, and Jewish Religious Teaching' in *Good and Evil After Auschwitz: Ethical Implications for Today* (Rome: SIDIC, 1998), English version not yet available; 'What to Do' (paper delivered at a conference at Notre Dame entitled, *Humanity at the Limit: The Impact of the Holocaust on Jews and Christians*, to be published by them); and chapter 8 of *The Banality of Good and Evil*, entitled 'Do This.'

32 A. Miller, *For Your Own Good*, transl. H. and H. Hannum (New York: Farrar, Straus, Giroux, 1983).

33 T. W. Adorno et al., *The Authoritarian Personality*, abridged edition (New York: W. W. Norton and Co.: 1950, 1982).

34 All first-year psychology students are familiar with the experiments in which rats who are subjected to erratic and excessive electric shocks are driven 'insane'.

35 In the psychobiographical section on Hitler (pp.142–97), Miller gives evidence that Hitler's father was abusive and also that Hitler had a personality that was split and seriously repressed, that he idealized and identified with his father, and that he projected his idealized father into the image of the führer while he projected the part of his childhood that needed to be repressed and extinguished onto the Jews (pp.156ff., 176–80).

36 *Ordinary People and Extraordinary Evil*, (Albany, NY: SUNY Press, 1993).

37 Hoffman and others, cited in *Altruistic Personality*, pp.178–79.

38 E. Staub, 'A Conception of the Determinants and Development of Altruism and Aggression: Motives, the Self, and the Environment', in C. Zahn-Waxler, et al., *Altruism and Aggression: Biological and Social Origins* (Cambridge, Cambridge University Press: 1986), 150–52 (emphasis original), citing many sources. Cf. also J.A. Piliavin and H. W. Charng, 'Altruism: A Review of Recent Theory and Research', *American Review of Sociology*, 16 (1990): 41.

SIX FROM LEIPZIG:
KINDERTRANSPORT AND THE CAMBRIDGE REFUGEE CHILDREN'S COMMITTEE

Gertrude W. Dubrovsky

I N THE tally of victims, not counted are those who fled the madness and escaped with their lives. Though they did not go up in smoke, they lost their homes, their families, and their place in society. Among those were children who were shipped out from Germany, Austria, Czechoslovakia and Poland just before Germany marched into Poland and England was drawn into the war. To save their children, parents sent them to Holland, France, Denmark, Sweden, Switzerland, Portugal – in fact, to any country that permitted them to enter. The largest number, 10,000, were sent to England where they survived; most never saw their parents after their last goodbye.

Almost immediately after Hitler assumed power in March 1933, English community leaders anticipated refugees needing help. By May 1933, the Central British Fund, a fund-raising agency for Jewish relief work, was in place and citizen groups started mobilizing on behalf of refugee families and unaccompanied refugee children. The care of the children came under the supervision of a voluntary organization eventually known as the Refugee Children's Movement [RCM]. The RCM incorporated under its umbrella as many as 100 local groups who were divided into twelve regional offices, coinciding with the map of an air raid warning system, already in place.

This paper deals with the work of the Cambridge Refugee Children's Committee [CRCC], which started as a small local group and soon became the head office of Region IV. It is also about six young cousins, child refugees from Leipzig, who came under the administrative arm and watchful eyes of the CRCC. The six provide a microcosm of sorts, through whose experiences we can appreciate the difficulties and rewards of helping foreign children in their struggle to live and become productive members of society.

The Leipzig children arrived in England on four different transports. One was on the first *Kindertransport* [children's transport] to arrive in England; three [the youngest, aged six, three, and seven months] were on the last. In common with the other refugee children of the time, these six were separated from their parents without fully under-standing why, taken to a country whose language they did not know, cared for by people they had never seen, and soon were regarded as enemy aliens. And like others, they did not know what had happened to their parents until long after the war ended. Eventually, they all ended up in Cambridge or Cambridgeshire – six of the two thousand refugee children under the wings of the Cambridge committee.

Vera Ribetsky was one of the children who arrived at Dovercourt on that first *Kindertransport*. Not quite thirteen, and the only child of the widowed Yetta Ribetzky, she was accompanied to the train station in Leipzig, a short walk from her home, by the entire extended family – grandmother, aunts, uncles, cousins. Her strongest memory of the farewell is that nobody cried. In telling the story, Vera twice repeats, 'Nobody cried', and tears run silently down her cheeks. She only remembers clearly her mother telling her that soon the whole family would be together in England. Everything else is a blur. What remains with her is the unkept promise and the pain of the separation from her mother.

Now a woman of seventy-four with children and grandchildren of her own, she cannot put the pain behind her. Nor can any of the fifty-plus adults I interviewed who had been on transports. In common with them, Vera knows very little about how the transports were organized or what agencies were involved in the mechanism of identifying the endangered children of Leipzig and getting them ready to leave.

The Refugee Children's Movement dates its history back to 1936, when the Inter-Aid Committee [IAC] was established to rescue 'from Germany children who were already suffering because of the political views of their parents'.[2] But, European children – both Christian and Jewish – were arriving alone in England from the early Thirties, sent from their homes to schools or universities. Between May 1936 and July 1937, the IAC found schools and hospitality for 124 children; by November 1938, the number of children for whom the committee assumed the same responsibility more than tripled to 471. According to the RCM's First Annual Report,[3] the early arriving children were equally divided with respect to religion: 45% Christian; 55% Jewish (p.1). However, later reports, about which there is little disagreement, reflect different statistics. Of the approximately 10,000 children who arrived in England on Kindertransports, 90% were registered as Jewish; 10% were Catholics and Protestants.[4]

The RCM evolved from the IAC as an administrative agency charged with supervising the placement, care and education of the children. Eventually, it encompassed over one hundred local groups divided into twelve regions. Each region had its own central office with its own administrator who reported to the RCM.

The Cambridge Refugee Committee [CRC] organized as a small local group in 1935 in anticipation of refugees.[5] Its mission was to help refugee families and single adults, including a fair number of displaced academics, emigrate. The Cambridge Refugee Children's Committee, an offshoot of the CRC, had a similar goal but focused on helping the refugee children emigrate. It then assumed an ongoing responsibility of assisting the children in the difficult transition to a new country, and the painful acceptance of a new reality. As a local group, it was one of a hundred that spontaneously sprung up all over England with a similar mission.

In 1938, Cambridge assumed for the RCM the administrative responsibility for Region IV, a very large district which included all of Cambridgeshire, the whole of East Anglia, and Letchworth. The two Cambridge committees worked in a deliberate way on the agenda they had set themselves, until *Kristallnacht* dramatically changed everything.

Following the events of *Kristallnacht*, the British Council for German Jewry sought to promote the transport of children from Germany on a larger scale and worked actively with the IAC towards that end. Together, they petitioned for and received the support of the government for help. Immediately, the Home Office made arrangements to stream-line the procedure by which foreign children could be admitted to Great Britain. Passports were dispensed with and replaced instead by a simple card which contained a photograph of the child entering and a few particulars, including names and address of parents, and age of the child. These cards were issued by the RCM on their guarantee that the children would not become a public charge. The plan was that they would be re-emigrated before they reached the age of 18 or when their training in England was completed. However, the rapidly changing political situation caused these conditions to be repeatedly renegotiated. According to Greta Burkill, 'Kristallnacht sent a shock wave through all of England. We knew we had to step up the pace of our work if we were to save the children.'[6]

On 28 November 1938, the RCM issued an appeal for financial and in-kind support which was broadcast by the English press. Money and offers of hospitality and help came from all parts of the British Isles, and were dealt with by a staff consisting mainly of volunteers working staggered hours and days. It was necessary to establish a department or sub-committee to investigate the suitability of the homes offered and to ascertain if those who offered could afford to maintain an arriving child. The process slowed down the pace at which transports arrived, and the RCM endured much criticism for the resulting delays. But the RCM had pledged to the government that no child would require public funds for maintenance, and it had to establish its credibility on this account. Local Guardian Committees were set up all over the country to help with the search for homes and to look after the children once they settled down.

The major problem which the English committees had to confront, aside from the on-going problem of funding, was how to choose the most urgent cases from among the 60,000 children on the continent identified as being in danger. These included Jewish children (the greatest number), non-Aryan Christians with one Jewish parent; and Christian children whose parents subscribed to a political ideology inimical to the Nazis.

The RCM needed cooperation from committees or groups on the continent in order to rescue a maximum number of children. Quakers and other Christian denominations and churches established contacts with their counterparts in Europe. But the racist policies of the Nazis forced Jewish social agencies to keep a low profile in their rescue efforts and much remains purposely undocumented.[7] Thus it is difficult to determine authoritatively the interchange between committees in England and those on the Continent helping to organize the transports.

The First Annual Report of the RCM, issued in 1940 for the year November 1938 to December 1939, identifies the committees in Germany and Austria as 'large central organizations to look after the interest of the Jewish communities and to facilitate emigration'.[8] They are identified as *Reichsvertretung der Juden in Deutschland* [Reich Representation of the Jews in Germany]; and the *Israelitische Kultus Gemeinde* [Jewish Synagogue Association] in Austria. The First Annual Report notes that 95% of the Jews in Austria lived in Vienna, making the identification of Jewish children needing assistance easier.

On 12 March 1938, eight months before *Kristallnacht*, the Nazis took over the office of the *Israelitische Kultus Gemeinde* in Vienna. Less than a week later, Adolf Eichmann, director of the Department of Jewish Affairs in the Reich Security Office, took charge of Jewish emigration. He called the Jews in, stripped them of their livelihood and property rights, and issued passports good for two weeks with a letter J stamped on them. If the Jews could not find a country willing to issue them a visa within that time, they were subject to imprisonment. The organization of the Jewish community was in total disarray. Eventually, the *Kultus Gemeinde*, with the help of an emissary from the West London Synagogue, secured permission from the Gestapo to restore their services. Two British citizens, Captain B.M. Woolf, secretary of the West London Synagogue, and Ruth Fellner, a Jewish Refugee Committee staff member, helped restore some of its communal activities.[9] They provided a necessary link with English groups and facilitated some parts of the emigration plan. As far as the *Reichsvertretung* in Berlin, it had been disbanded immediately after *Kristallnacht*.

In 1935, the leaders of the German Jewish community voluntarily established the *Reichsvertretung der deutschen Juden* (National Representation of Jews in Germany) with no interference by the Nazi authorities.[10] During the first years of its existence, it was a kind of forum or federation whose limited powers were limited by the needs and desires of its members. Although the *Reichsvertretung* had no legal standing in the Reich, the Jewish communities of Germany were functioning as democratic bodies within a totalitarian dictatorship until 10 November 1938. After *Kristallnacht*, the offices of all the Jewish communities and organizations were closed. They were reopened at the command of the Gestapo.[11] Towards the end of November 1938,[12] the Gestapo set up the *Reichsvereinigung fur judische Auswanderungsforsorge* [National Union in charge of the Migration of the Jews].

A copy of a letter dated 17 November 1938 by Quaker Hilda Sturge in the file of the Cambridge Refugee Children's Committee states: 'We are now receiving excellent co-operation from the *Selbsthilfe Deutscher Ausgewanderter* (Jewish self-help) and they are now helping us with the case of a Ph.D. in Cambridge.' However, what Sturge understands to be a Jewish self-help organization was actually established by the Nazis to promote emigration.[13] On 4 July 1939, the *Reichsvereinigung der Juden in Deutschland* [National Association of the Jews of Germany] replaced the *Reichsvertretung*, but kept the same staff. It was conceived as the general organization for all Jews of the German Reich.

Historian Yehuda Reshef[14] identifies the *Reichsvereinigung* as a 'compulsory organization of all Jews in Nazi Germany (excepting Austria and the Protectorate of Bohemia-Moravia).' He summarizes its function and duties:

> The [*Reichsvereinigung*] was established by Nazi law and not by consensus of the Jewish organizations...Its duties, as fixed by law, were to promote Jewish emigration from Germany and to support the Jewish school system and Jewish welfare. A special provision empowered the minister of the interior to assign additional tasks to [it]. *The main advantage* [was that the Nazis could deal with] *a single Jewish organization subject to* [the Nazis'] *supervision. The existence of the Reichsvereinigung enabled the Nazis to implement many of their deadliest orders without much publicity and to play off the Jewish leadership against the Jewish population who naturally blamed their own leaders.* [emphasis added]...Rabbi Leo Baeck, Otto Hirsch, Paul Epstein, and their colleagues continued at their posts until their arrest and deportation....The local activities of the *Reichsvereinigung* were executed by the Jewish communities, compulsorily called Judische *Kultusvereinigung* (Jewish synagogue association)....The [*Kultusvereinigung*] dealt with small communities or with single Jewish families. In the course of time the Jewish communities were dissolved and their property transferred to the Reichsvereinigung. All Jewish publications were suspended and only the publication of the bulletin of the Reichsvereinigung, *Judisches Nachrichtenblatt*, was permitted. It served as a channel for the Gestapo to inform the Jews of new restrictions and confiscations without stirring up too much dissent from the outside....Only two...leaders [of the *Reichsvereinigung*], Leo Baeck and Moritz Henschel, survived the Holocaust.[15]

In that the *Reichsvereinigung* employed Jews to accomplish and carry out plans seriously affecting the Jewish community, it served very much as the Judenrat did in the far flung cities and villages of Poland and the Ukraine.

The *Kindertransports* to England out of Germany, Austria, Czechoslovakia, and Poland depended upon coordination between English committees and German organizations. By its own admission, the RCM saw its most difficult task to be determining how to choose the limited number of children from the tens of thousands of children in Austria and Germany anxious to find refuge and safety in Great Britain.[16] Thousands of letters begging for help were received by the RCM; enclosed were photographs and particulars.

The dilemma posed by the letters to the volunteers is reflected in the First Annual Report:

> Many were so touchingly written that it required a hard heart to consign them to files and indexes; yet, how were we to know which children to choose since we could not take all? We obviously could not adopt the principle of 'first write, first come,' and how were we to be sure that all the details in the letters were absolutely correct?[17]

Unable to choose the most urgent cases, the English Movement decided to rely entirely on the judgment of the committees in Germany and Austria, except in the case of those children for whom guarantees had been signed in England, generally by relatives or close acquaintances. In other words, the Movement left it up to the Germans.

It appears that in 1938 and 1939, the Germans were willing to let the children leave; the limitations on the numbers emigrating were placed by the countries which allowed them entry. Presumably, the staff of the *Reichsvereinigung* prepared the lists of children for the Germans. The situation was one ripe for bribery and/or other kinds of pay offs by desperate parents anxious about their children. The First Annual Report of the RCM notes that from every list given them, the Germans withheld some names:

> A foreign central organisation [sic]…submitted the permits to the German police for permission to emigrate the children [on the lists]. From each batch of Permits the police withheld certain cases for reasons best known to themselves; the remainder of the permit cards were handed to the leaders of the transport of children to show to the immigration authorities on arrival in England.[18]

Greta Burkill, one of the leading members of the Cambridge Refugee Children's Committee, describes in a memoir the urgency members felt as they worked:

> On we worked, finding homes and jobs until November 1938 [when] Kristallnacht made the goal of the Nazis unmistakably clear.…The Nazis ran amok, killing, destroying and rounding people up for Concentration Camps.…The urgency piled up, the whole of Great Britain was aghast – the horror of it all went like an electric current through every town and village. The feeling was 'we must save the children.'[19]

In order to save as many children as possible, numerous tasks were undertaken simultaneously: members needed to identify those who would guarantee to assume the child's expenses [guarantors], to find jobs for women and men, and above all, to work quickly. The CRCC energetically pursued job opportunities for refugees hoping to emigrate to England. They urged the women or men who qualified for the jobs to include on their visa applications the names of all their infant children. The CRCC promised to take care of the children once the families arrived, so that the parents could fulfill their commitment to work.[20] The parent Cambridge Refugee Committee tried to handle, as efficiently as possible, the complicated problems of middle-class German women (and their children) emigrating as domestics in Cambridge homes.[21] In this way, the CRCC, locally and regionally, were instrumental in helping 500 women leave Germany for such positions. For the unaccompanied refugee children and for children of displaced academics who were in Cambridge or the surrounding neighbourhood, the Committee acted *in loco parentis*. Often, an entire family needed help and the committee members provided it. In short, volunteer Committee members worked in all directions at one and the same time.

The community of Cambridge, as a whole participated in the efforts to help the children. Two refugees, a doctor and a dentist, attended free to their medical and dental needs; the local committee assumed the financial responsibility for school fees and were successful in getting the Perse Girl's School, Cambridge, to reduce its fees and accept pupils as soon as they arrived in the country. The Committee were gratified to find that the children, arriving with no English language skills, learned quickly.

A strong priority of the committee was to find as many 'guarantors' as possible. While there was no limit placed on children for whom sponsors agreed to assume the cost for their care, the Home Office imposed a cap of 1,000 per month of unguaranteed children – those without sponsors. Thus, the more guarantors the Committee could identify, the more unguaranteed children could be rescued. By knocking on doors and showing people on the streets pictures of charming children, the local Cambridge committee secured guarantees and homes from Cambridge residents for some 70–80 refugee children.

On 21 November 1938, a diverse group of representatives met with the British Home Secretary, Sir Samuel Hoare, who joined them in recognizing the claims of the endangered children on the humanity of all decent people. He immediately made arrangements with the Home Office for simplified procedures by which children could be admitted speedily to England.

Private homes were sought for the refugee children as the best substitute for family left behind. About 7,500 children were placed in foster homes, 5,000 of whom were Jewish. While the Movement's policy was to place children in a home with the same religion, not enough Jewish families stepped forward to offer homes to the children. Thus, most of the Jewish children were with Christian foster parents. Often, older children were sent to group farms, such as Whittingham in Northumberland, or religion-based group homes. Hostels or group homes, originally feared to be onerous, turned out to be a good experience; the children living in them became a quasi-family for each other. The CRCC established a hostel, Parkside, in Cambridge for children with particular needs and problems.[22]

Many of the older children who arrived alone in Great Britain immediately started searching for ways to help their parents. In a reversal of traditional roles, children became instant adults as they acted on behalf of their parents, now vulnerable and helpless as children in Europe. But most young refugees trying to manage the complicated application process did not have sufficient maturity or language skills. Nor were they able to easily identify the appropriate committees to whom they had to press petitions. They did not know the geography of the country, or have any kind of mastery of the transportation systems so they could get from one place to another, even assuming they had the money to buy bus or train tickets. In addition, those fourteen and over were past the age of mandatory schooling and were required to work. And on top of it all, they had their own complex feelings of guilt and trauma with which they had to live.

Refugee children carried into their adult lives guilt over the relief they felt to have escaped and guilt over the excitement they experienced for the adventure of travelling to a new place. The guilt added to and intensified their remorse and dread concerning the fate of their parents and families left behind, about whom they had little information. Many did not know the whereabouts of their siblings who were on the same transport. Nor did they know what their host families expected of them.

In September of 1939, England was at war and the rescue operations all but ceased.[23] The bombing of London triggered the speedy enactment of a plan that already was in place for the evacuation of children to safer places. A mass evacuation to the countryside was promptly enacted. Whole institutions of various kinds moved from London to Cambridge.

The RCM committees were given the charge of supervising the placements of the children – both British and recently arrived refugee children. They had to know at all times where the children were. The refugee children who had been placed in the town of Cambridge were easier to track than the evacuated children spread out all over the region. The complexity of the job with which the women of the CRCC were faced can barely be appreciated today, in our age of computerized data banks and lists. In 1939, during the evacuation of the children from London to Cambridge and Cambridgeshire, women had to sort dossiers of 800 children, get to know about them, and find out where they were placed. They had to do this overnight.

By law, everyone with an extra room in their homes had to take children. For most of the children, the evacuation was traumatic. For the recently arrived refugee children, it was devastating. Burkill of the CRCC empathizes with their anguish:

> They had left their homeland, where their life had been abused, where they could no more go to their schools, where their parents, from being honest, hard-working citizens, had to use any subterfuge to keep alive and to eke out enough to support themselves and their children, never knowing when the fated knock would come to their door. From this experience and this insecurity they were transplanted to a country with a different language, completely different mores, and frequently placed with people who did not share their religion, who did not light candles on Friday night, and for whom Saturday was a working day.[24]

Five of the six cousins from Leipzig were among the thousands of British school children evacuated to safety in the English countryside. The three youngest of the cousins, Harold, Sigmar and Zilla, had only just arrived at the crowded and tense home of relatives in London. Given the chaotic situation in London, their removal to Cambridge turned out to be a blessing, a silver lining in a very dark cloud of uncertainty and trauma.

Entire schools from London landed in the vicinity of Cambridge under the supervision of the CRCC. The Jewish Free School for Boys and Jewish Free School for Girls were evacuated to Ely, a famous cathedral city in the Cambridge area where most of the local people had never seen a Jew. Because of their special religious needs, Orthodox children could not easily be accommodated in British homes. The billeting officer, who happened to be the vicar's wife, commandeered a large country house for the two Jewish Free Schools and the CRCC hired cooks from London who understood and observed Jewish dietary laws and made sure that general standards of Kashrut and cleanliness were maintained.

The Jewish Free School in England was under the direction of Rabbi Solomon Schonfeld, the future son-in-law of Chief Rabbi Hertz. Schonfeld's close ties with the ultra orthodox Agudah was reflected in the orientation of the Jewish Free Schools' curriculum. However, when the schools were evacuated to Ely, they came under the administrative charge of the CRCC. Both the CRCC and the Movement shared a strong belief that whatever else the refugee students learned, they had to learn English language skills so that they would be employable. Thus, the Jewish Free School programme in Ely provided a range of subjects which included Hebrew and English language instruction, Biblical literature and secular subjects such as art, science and extra-curricular activities. A story in the January 1942 issue of the Hereward Hall Gazette, edited by Ely Jewish Boy's School headmaster Dr. E. Bernstein, and printed at the Evacuation Headquarters of the Jewish Free Boy's School Press, spoke of a new pottery kiln installed in the school, and the value of art in the lives of the boys. (Issue No.21) In July 1942, the lead article of the news sheet concerned a boys' programme of building model planes which a resident, Mr. W.M. Lane, supervised (Issue No.23). The popular programme met at the school two evenings a week and was attended by interested students and non-Jewish local boys who participated in the craft work.[25] Differences in looks and speech among the young boys disappeared as they were mutually engaged in building their airplanes and working out the math and physics as they applied to certain parts of the models. The program appeared to be popular, effective, and enriching.

Yet, the presence of religious refugee students in Ely produced a nervous reaction from a segment of the Jewish community, stemming in part from an editorial in the *Jewish Chronicle* (10 November 1939, the first anniversary of *Kristallnacht*). The editorial warned that the evacuation presented a thorny problem for the nation, but serious and special difficulties for Jews – religious, educational, and social problems. The writer argues that Jewish evacuees are different in experience, attitude, and even in looks. Expected to live among people who never saw a Jew, the children presented 'a first-class risk of mutual misunderstanding.' The editorial asks for adequate measures to be taken, lest the children become the harbinger of new waves of anti-semitism. 'The situation cannot be permitted to continue,' the editorial cautions. 'Further delay means asking for trouble and getting it.'

Chief Rabbi Hertz and the Board of Deputies launched a major fund raising drive for Jewish religion classes to be provided to evacuated Jewish children. In the spring of 1941, full page advertisements appeared in the *Jewish Chronicle* with large-type headlines blaring out challenging questions to readers while announcing a new appeal for funds: WHO WILL BE RESPONSIBLE IF THEY GROW UP WITHOUT RELIGION? THE ANSWER IS YOU – UNLESS YOU HONOUR YOUR OBLIGATION TOWARDS THEM BY CONTRIBUTING TO THE BOARD OF DEPUTIES APPEAL.

Jewish historian Richard Bolchover explains the anxiety as the 'politics of fear'. He writes: 'Implicit [in the behaviour of the community] was the fear of a retributive anti-semitism,' which led British Jewry to dread appearing as anything but a religious community.[26] Given what was happening on the continent, the anxiety is understandable. At the same time, the concern for the education of evacuated children is in sharp contrast to the initial silence of Rabbi Hertz and the Board of Deputies when foreign refugee children arrived and were placed in British Christian homes.

From November of 1938 on, the Chief Rabbi Hertz was well aware of the imminent arrival of the refugee children and of their need for homes. But, he was publicly quiet on the subject. Nowhere in the weekly column he published in the *Jewish Chronicle* does he address his readers with a plea for them to step forward and offer hospitality to Jewish children. Nor does he remind them that the Jewish community had a special obligation to look after these most vulnerable of all Jewish refugees. Nowhere does he talk about the interrupted Jewish education and the seriously disrupted Jewish lives of the refugee children. It was a point not lost upon some of the members of the Board of Deputies at whose meetings the issue was heatedly debated. Everyone knew that the refugee children were placed in the homes of those who offered hospitality. By and large, they were not Jewish people. The children therefore had no Jewish contacts and no Jewish friends. No effort had been made over the years to give them religious education.

S. Gestetner, a member of the board of the Movement and on the Board of Deputies, reminded the community that parents who separated from their children did so in order to save them. Gestetner suggests that Jews owe thanks to Christians who took the children into their homes. He writes:

All parents who consented to separate from their children had only one wish at heart, to save them from further Nazi persecution. Thanks to the open-heartedness of people in this country, we were able to bring this large number of children over in such a short time. The response of Anglo-Jewry was not as great as we anticipated, and we were more than thankful for the hospitality of those true Christians who felt it their duty to save these persecuted Jewish children.[27]

While the discussions and arguments were going on, Rabbi Schonfeld, determined to get boys out of Ely by any means he could, took matters into his own hands. Years later, a man who had been a student in the Jewish Free School for Boys commented on Schonfeld's commitment: 'If he didn't trust the education a child was getting, he would remove the child by any means, fair or foul.'[28]

Reacting to what he understood to be a religious emergency, Rabbi Schonfeld, son-in-law of Chief Rabbi Hertz, obtained the agreement of Rabbi Hertz to form a new committee, the Chief Rabbi's Religious Emergency Committee [CRREC] which Schonfeld chaired and was its only member.[29] Apparently with the Chief Rabbi's agreement, Schonfeld decided to remove some of the orthodox Jewish boys from the Jewish Free School in Ely. His office sent questionnaires to selected boys at Ely from whom he solicited information concerning their ritual practices and sought names of other orthodox boys in the town.[30] It appears that Schonfeld used this information to secure the cooperation of Yeshiva boys to lure the Ely students to London. They wrote to Ely students, sending instructions to them with details as to how they should leave their school surreptitiously and proceed to London. Even worse, the letters contained money and a promise of more as soon as the boy arrived at one of three yeshivas. Five boys, all under fourteen years of age, were thus seduced away from their placement, without the permission or knowledge of the people in charge of them.[31]

Greta Burkill, responsible for these children, took action immediately. She sent a detailed report to W. Seaborne Davies, a Member of Parliament from Bournemouth, informing him what was happening in Ely. She writes that the 'enticing' was detrimental to all refugees and to 'the happiness of the children involved.'[32] Burkill minces no words in laying out the problems the Cambridge Committee were experiencing in Ely as a result of unauthorized and illegal acts of what amounted to 'kidnapping'.

The end result of Burkill's report was an extended battle, lasting for five years, over the issue of guardianship for the refugee children. Ultimately, Parliament ruled that the legal Guardianship of the children would be vested with the head of the Refugee Children's Movement, and specifically with Lord Gorell who had been acting in that capacity during the course of the battle. He was given a mandate by the Guardianship Act to take 'any steps necessary to safeguard the child's religious education and, moreover, will have a legal duty to take such steps'.[33]

Rabbis Hertz and Schonfeld initially tried to block the passage of the Children's Refugee Guardianship Act. Failing that, they wanted to have the guardianship assigned to Chief Rabbi Hertz. In an effort to mobilize support for the Chief Rabbi, Rabbi Schonfeld published a pamphlet, widely distributed in the synagogues, 'The Child Estranging Movement: An Exposé on the Alienation of Jewish Refugee Children in Great Britain from Judaism.' In it, Schonfeld accuses the Movement for the Care of Children of being remiss in its duty to see that its charges were brought up in the faith of their parents. Although, says the writer, the Refugee Children's Movement was formed with capital donated by Anglo-Jewry, 'there has been a persistent though veiled tendency throughout to direct the education of the children away from orthodoxy ... away from orthodox Judaism.' He accuses the RCM of using the children by sending them 'as ambassadors into the homes of Christian foster-parents where they could assimilate and create Christian-Jewish good-will'. Schonfeld stops just short of saying it would have been better not to have saved the children in the first place.

In his pamphlet, Schonfeld cites as sample cases a dozen children who, by his account, are suffering grave injustices because of the intransigence of the Refugee Children's Movement in placing children in Christian homes. Among the children listed are the three youngest of the Leipzig six: Harold, Sigmar, and Zilla Koppold. Harold had by then been in a very Jewish home for three years and belonged to a serious Zionist youth group; Sigmar was with the Mansfields in Cambridge, a Christian family with whom the child was strongly bonded. With their encouragement, he was going to Hebrew school, and studying for his forthcoming *Bar Mitzvah*. The youngest child, Zilla, was living in the Parkside Hostel in Cambridge with her cousins Paula and Edith, the three girls forming a family unit. The hostel was very close to where Zilla's brothers lived and to the home of Ann Sofier where the children spent every Shabbat and most Jewish holidays.

In January of 1944, on the eve of a vote on the Guardianship Bill, Chief Rabbi Hertz admitted, in a letter to the *Chronicle*, the failure of the Jewish community, although he does not accept personal responsibility. He writes:

> A way has been found for removing genuine Orthodox children from non-Orthodox environments. But not *every* Jewish child; and five years after Anglo-Jewry failed to answer the challenge of the refugee children reaching our shores, it seems almost impossible to achieve more.[34]

On 31 December 1943, a letter to the *Chronicle* from Dayan I. Grunfeld urges the Jewish community to provide homes for Jewish refugee children. He is five years too late.

While the experience in Ely was, for the Cambridge Refugee Children's Committee, 'a cross to bear,' in the words of Greta Burkill, she also recognized the positive side. In one of her memoirs, she says that the influx of so many uncomprehending children during that difficult time had a beneficial effect on British attitudes, particularly among the untutored citizens. Although the English villagers knew little of the complex happenings in Central Europe, they understood the refugee children had no parents and therefore needed more 'cosseting' than the British children. In Burkill's words, ordinary British middle-class, or working-class people showed great kindness even though 'sometimes the child was by no means easy.' She writes:

> Certainly, in Region 4, the people who gave a home to these lost children were very rarely Jewish...One must be conscious that these young children who came to Great Britain were already psychologically disturbed before they ever arrived and the different way of life here...must have been very difficult.[35]

SIX FROM LEIPZIG

In all, 10,000 unaccompanied children arrived in Great Britain in the ten-month period between *Kristallnacht* and the declaration of war on 3 September 1939. The existing CRCC files list 2000 children who came through the office of Region IV, though the constant number for whom the Committee was immediately responsible was eight hundred. Among those under the watchful eye and administrative arm of the CRCC were the six cousins from Leipzig, children of three sisters. They are the only survivors of a large extended family who lived a respectable life in Poland and Germany before the Nazis put an end to both respectability and life.

Their grandparents had relocated the family from Warsaw to Berlin in 1900 and then to Leipzig in 1905 when the grandfather became the cantor of the Broder Synagogue. In leaving Warsaw for Germany, the grandparents anticipated better opportunities for their children; Germany had opened their schools to Jewish children. In fact, the family did move up the economic ladder to attain a comfortable middle-class life style in Leipzig.

Their uncle Leo Shmulovitz worked for a Jewish agency in Leipzig and knew in the summer of 1938 that committees in England were working on the logistics of organizing transports so that children in Germany, Austria, and Czechoslovakia could be sent out of harm's way. His office was busy contacting members of Leipzig's Jewish community, urging them to register their children to go to England. Leo understood all too well the necessity for the children to leave as soon as possible. On the application forms given to parents, they were asked to indicate religious preferences for their children's foster homes.[36] Although the entire Shmulovitz family was Orthodox, Leo must have encouraged his sisters to state no religious preference. The Jewish population of Great Britain was very small and Leo knew it would take longer to identify English Jews who were both ritually observant and willing to accept the responsibility of foster children in their homes.

He and his wife did not have any children, but he had five nieces and nephews, and another due to arrive in January of 1939. He entered all their names on the waiting lists for departure. After the baby was born, he added her name. The whole family knew that if the children were safely out of the country, the parents would have more flexibility in their movements and more options to save themselves. Further, it was reasoned that once a child was in London, it might be easier for the others to follow. Older children might identify or secure in England job offers for the parents who could then receive visas. In the worldwide economic crisis of the 1930s, the only jobs available in England for foreigners without money were as farm workers and domestics. Many well-educated and cultured middle-class women worked as maids or cooks while the men accepted jobs as field and farm labourers.

Vera, an only child, was on the first transport, arriving at Dovercourt on 1 December 1938. Her transport was composed primarily of children twelve to seventeen who were vulnerable to arrest and detention in work camps. Older boys and orphans were given priority on the first transport; Vera, without a father, was eligible. It was hoped that she would be the family representative and advocate in England, paving the way for the others to leave. The three Koppold children were on one of the last transports, arriving on 1 September 1939, less than eight months after the baby was born. The transports virtually halted after the war started. Of his whole extended family then living in Poland and in Germany, only the six nieces and nephews Leo Shmulovitz registered for the transport survived. They survived in England, their care monitored by the Cambridge Refugee Children's Committee and the Refugee Children's Movement.

Vera. Vera Ribetsky, still a child and not yet five feet tall, traumatized by her reluctant departure from her family, was hardly up to the tasks a sturdier person might have taken on. An only child whose father had died when she was scarcely two years old, Vera was tightly bonded with her mother. 'My mother was everything; my whole emotional stability,' she says. Before her daughter boarded the train, Vera's mother reassured her that in approximately five weeks they would see each other again. Vera clung to that promise.

Today, Vera's memories of her parting are too painful for words. She cannot recall many of the details. But she does remember the children crying on the train and the Nazis walking in the aisles, laughing. Like all events remembered sixty years after the fact, they may or may not be accurate in the details. The train stopped in Berlin; the children were taken off and escorted by Jewish personnel to something like a YMHA where cots had been set up for them to sleep. In the morning, more children boarded the train. When they crossed the border into Holland, the transport had five hundred children on it. She remembers the Dutch women boarding the train in Holland and distributing hot chocolate and cookies.

At the Hook of Holland, the children boarded a boat for Dovercourt, an adult summer holiday camp on the southeastern shore of England. All Vera could think of was how lonely she was, and how cold it was in December. She and another child were assigned to a small two-bed unheated bungalow and were given hot-water bottles. Neither of the children knew what to do with them; Vera opened her bottle and was scalded. Trying to cope with her pain and confusion, she was hardly aware that the hopes for survival of the whole family left behind were invested in her.

Vera spent a week in Dovercourt while volunteers from all over England were there to help settle the children. Prospective foster parents arrived daily to pick out children they would take home with them. Vera's foster mother was among a small group of people from Norwich (northeast of London) who had come to claim children. Vera describes what she remembers:

> Every evening in Dovercourt, people [responding to advertisements in the papers] came around . . . to take . . . foster children back home with them. One night, a woman stopped at my table, and said, 'May I take this child?' I couldn't understand her, I couldn't speak English. But the counsellors who were helping told me in German that 'this lady wants to take you to her house.' I thought I was being sold, I was very frightened. I was homesick and scared. The woman counsellor said, 'No. She is not buying you. You are just supposed to go there till your mother picks you up.' I said, 'Okay. But could I stay just one more day?' Because the next day they were going to show *Snow White and the Seven Dwarfs*. They were opening the local cinema just for the children. The counsellor said, 'Yes.' I took a train the next day.[37]

Vera joined the family of Bertha Staff [Jewish], her husband Arthur [not Jewish] and their two children: a daughter, Lottie, twelve years old; and a sixteen-year-old son. By Vera's admission, the family was very kind, yet she could do nothing but cry and her foster mother cried with her. Finally, Arthur Staff told his wife that if she could not stop weeping, they would have to send Vera away. Woman and child stopped crying and Vera remained with the family for eight years. She says they were wonderful to her; they all bonded as a family. But she never stopped mourning. She recalls her first months with the Staffs:

> I couldn't speak any English. I was so nervous, I would break dishes all the time. They asked me to help dry dishes. Due to my nervousness, I would drop everything. And I was afraid to tell them because I thought I would be out on the street. I had my suitcase under the bed and I would wrap up all the broken pieces and put them into my suitcase. This poor lady didn't know what was happening to her dishes. They were just disappearing. (transcript, page 7)

Vera claims to have survived emotionally because of the Orthodox religious background she carried within her. She never lost faith, although the Messiah she avidly hoped for did not come.

> I had terrible nightmares. . . . I was a child. I needed my mother. . . . But I grew up. You know, you cry and you cry and you gradually stop. I got a few communications from my mother and then the war broke out. She knew where I was. My mother was sent back to

Poland from Germany, because all the Poles were sent back. And she got caught in the bombing. And then she went back to Germany after Poland was captured by Germany. She was with her mother and her sister. And then they all went to a camp. My cousin Paula said it was Terezin. I don't know. I'm not sure. Nobody ever confirmed it. But they all died.[38] (transcript, page 8)

Vera's foster mother, a patient and compassionate woman, never filled the void. But Vera understood that Bertha Staff wanted to do that which Vera's mother would approve. She taught Vera English by using objects – an apple, a teapot, a spoon, etc. As Vera became more fluent in English, she was less comfortable in German. She began to worry that when she and her mother would meet again, they would not be able to communicate, a frightening thought. With tears, she says, 'I didn't have to worry. I never saw anyone again.' Today, she still understands simple German, but she speaks it like a 'foreigner'.

Vera found Norwich a charming and delightful town. Its Jewish community, always small, dates back to the 12th century. Early in its history, the Jews of Norwich enjoyed special protection from the king. Perhaps their special status was responsible for the slanderous blood libel which plagued Jews for centuries. Popularized by Chaucer's 'Prioress' Tale', the myth accused the Norwich Jews of killing a Christian child so they could drink his blood on Passover. No doubt the small Jewish community never lost the sense of otherness and insecurity engendered by such ancient and calumnious stories.

Bertha Staff, Vera's foster mother, grew up in Norwich and was aware of its latent anti-semitism. Perhaps that was behind her insistence that Vera go to the synagogue every Saturday, accompanied by Lottie, her foster sister. In fact, Bertha Staff instructed Vera to stand up for herself: 'If anyone calls you a bloody Jew, spit right into their face. You don't have to take any garbage from anyone. It's a free country.' Nevertheless, in the school Vera attended, the day started with a prayer and Vera always left the room because, in her words, 'I was raised far too Orthodox to accept anything else.'

England was obligated to educate all children only until age fourteen. Vera had no illusions about getting higher education. She attended a secretarial school so that she might be able to work, but when war broke out, she was considered an enemy alien and no longer had the same privileges as others. As it was difficult for her to find work, she helped the Staffs in their general store. Eventually, she worked a switchboard in an iron factory for five years, until age twenty-one.

Vera believes that the local Norwich Refugee Children's Committee [part of Region IV under the jurisdiction of the Cambridge Committee] was composed primarily of Jewish people and presumes that only Jews went to Dovercourt to take children home with them. But that seems highly unlikely, given that, by her own estimate, Norwich's Jewish population included only about twenty-five Jewish families.[39]

Not only was Bertha Staff a foster mother to Vera; she eventually became a foster aunt to Vera's cousin Paula, who arrived in England about nine months after Vera. Paula frequently visited Vera at the Staff home, and eventually Paula lived with Bertha's sister Florry in London. When rockets exploded in London, Florry's home was destroyed and everyone had to find other shelter.

Paula and Edith.   Paula, the oldest of the six children, remembers life in Leipzig as being pleasant and orderly. Her father was modern Orthodox and an active Zionist. The whole family accepted Judaic rituals and obligations, and spoke Yiddish and Hebrew. However, the parents insisted that the children learn and speak correct German.

When Hitler came to power, Paula was nine years old. By the time she was a teenager, she could not go to the park or the pool because there were continually increasing restrictions on attendance. Eventually, Paula had to be transferred from the school she attended to a Jewish school. The family – indeed, all the Jews – had to register their movements with the police. After *Kristallnacht*, Paula learned about the camps the hard way. Germans confiscated her father's business and sent him to a slave labour camp (transcript, Spielberg interview, p.4).

On June 30, 1939, seven months after Vera left Leipzig for England, her cousin, fourteen-year-old Paula Grunbaum, arrived in Southampton. She went directly to the home of their grandmother's niece, Dora Binki, in the East End of London. Five days later, Paula's seven year old sister Edith arrived. Paula met her at the boat, and escorted her to the Binki family in London.

Paula and her sister were 'guaranteed' by the Binki family, who provided assurance that the children would not become the responsibility of the government. She believes the Binki family gave guarantees for at least five of the six children. Yet, in spite of the guarantees, Paula feels they did become a burden. Their parents sent money for them with friends, but the friends did not deliver the money to the children or their sponsors.

Almost as soon as she arrived in London, Paula tried to get to the office of the Jewish Refugee Committee in Bloomsbury House, Russell Square. She needed to start a process for the emigration of her parents. Today, she still blames herself for not succeeding: 'Lots of things I failed in. I failed my parents.' (transcript, Spielberg interview, p.6)

Like Vera, Paula received assurances from her parents before she left that the family would soon be together, reunited after a temporary separation. 'They made it seem as if I were going on a vacation' (Spielberg, p.6). The family's resolve to show the children a positive face apparently broke down when they parted with Paula's sister, Edith. On her arrival in England, five days after Paula, Edith reported that she never saw her father cry so much as he did when they said goodbye.

Although Edith endured much stress with the Binki family, Paula remains grateful for all the Binkis did for her family: 'These were not easy times for anybody, not even the Jewish people in England. At least we had someplace to go to. Dora opened the door for me and Edith and then accepted Harold, Sigmar, and Zilla' (Dubrovsky interview, p.4). But Paula is not comfortable talking about Edith's experience at the Binkis. The little girl apparently had a hard time adjusting. Nor could the Binkis, living in an already crowded apartment, cope very well with an unhappy and perhaps rebellious child. Soon after she arrived, Edith went to the home of Rose Jacobs, Dora Binki's daughter. Shortly thereafter, Rose Jacobs took Edith to the office of the Jewish Refugee Committee and left her there. That experience was repeated when a second family, with whom the child was placed, also returned her to the Committee.

Paula does not wish to talk about what had happened. She says, 'The Binkis [relatives] led a different life. They were in hard times. Their business went bankrupt. They couldn't speak proper English. It was an adjustment.' In addition, the home of the London relatives was crowded with other relatives from the continent who had moved in with them, and there was great tension and strain between husband and wife.

Paula did not have an appropriate place for Edith, nor could she take the time to look for one. Indeed, she hardly could think of anything but her parents who needed to have help leaving Germany. Because she was the oldest, all letters begging for assistance were directed to her. Paula's aunt Clara Koppold implored her in a letter to keep tabs on the three Koppold children who would shortly arrive.[40] Paula's mother wrote urgent letters, hoping Paula would secure for her and her husband the necessary papers they needed to leave Germany. Her mother also depended on Paula to take care of Edith. She writes to Paula, urging her to stay close to the child: 'Above all, stick together like two loaves. Do not worry too much. Everything will be all right, and everything will have been like a bad dream. Has my Paula made the right inquiries?'

In another letter, dated 23 August 1939, Paula's mother writes from Poland, where she was forced to go after being declared stateless in Germany. Her parents sent items and money for the children with people they knew who were emigrating. Much of the correspondence is an effort to confirm if the children received what was sent for them. Paula says today she did not get anything, but was reluctant, in 1939, to give her mother this distressing news.

Paula felt a keen responsibility to keep informed as to her cousins' and her sister's whereabouts and to ensure that they received the best care they could get. At the same time, she also was desperately trying to find jobs for her uncle Leo and his wife, for her parents, and her other relatives. In the letters they wrote to her, they asked her to see if she could get visas or find sponsors in England for them. From long distance, Paula's mother tries to coach her in what must be done:

> You have to look for a position for me, but you must not forget that in my papers my age is over and beyond the limit. And I have heard that after 35, one cannot get such work any more. That's why, dear Paula, make thorough enquiries as we don't want to run into any difficulties.

The mother also asks her daughter to help her grandmother. She advises Paula to write to her uncle Leo explaining what papers are necessary and where he should send them. Her mother's anguish and despair is evident in short almost whispered phrases. She writes: 'I want you to start to get things in motion and don't waste time. Leave everything else alone and just attend to that.' And, almost as an afterthought, she adds: 'We have to emigrate, we are not permitted to stay here any longer ... Paula, you have the information. I hope that you will be able to take care of everything.' (letter #5)[41]

Paula went from agency to agency, trying to accomplish something on behalf of her parents and her aunt and uncle, but with no success. She was always aware of her lack of communication skills. She wanted to study English but could not go to school because she was over fourteen. Without language skills, few employers could help her. She worked as a sewing machine operator in a mattress factory, and then sewed buttons in a coat factory. When the Enemy Alien Registration Act was enacted, it became even harder for Paula. Like other German and Austrian born people, she was considered an enemy alien, and had to stand up at a tribunal and convince a panel of judges that she meant no harm to England. She simply needed to work and earn. Having been given instructions to 'keep an eye on the children', Paula spent all her spare money and time in England travelling from place to place to keep tabs on the dispersed children. Meanwhile, her young sister, expelled from one home after another, felt abandoned and neglected.

Paula's cousins, the three Koppold children arrived on 1 September 1939, just two days before England was at war. Paula met them at Southampton and took them to the Binkis.

Soon after the declaration of war, all children living on the eastern coast of England were evacuated inland. This included the newly arrived refugee children. For all the children, the move was stressful; for the refugee children, life was chaotic and frightening in the extreme. For the six from Leipzig, the silver lining of the traumatic September 1939 events was that all the children in London were evacuated to Cambridge. Vera, remaining in Norwich, East Anglia, and was connected to the others through the agency of the CRCC. The five in London were sent, together with Dora Binki, to a hostel in Cambridge and were boarded in two rooms. Perhaps thinking that bombs in London would be less stressful to her than five children in two rooms in Cambridge, Dora returned to London as soon as she could, leaving Paula to look after four small children, one of whom was an infant. Paula was able to find a family in Devon for Edith, and Harold Koppold, six years old, returned to his placement in Peterborough. Paula was then left with Sigmar, three years old, and his sister Zilla, a seven-month-old infant. During this time, Paula received a heart breaking letter from her aunt Clara, the mother of the three Koppold children, in which the distraught woman implored: 'I am sending you my life. Please take care of them [the children], always keep an eye on them.'

Paula accepted all the responsibility almost as a sacred obligation from which she says she gained a great deal. She says:

> I didn't know how to handle a baby. The baby was teething and crying and I was walking around with her at night. And Siggy started crying. [Paula pauses in her recounting the events of the time.] But you know, we made it. We did. [Another pause.] By doing this I really gained. Because it gave me strength. It kept me on the straight and narrow. And I have a relationship to this day with my cousins. During those years, it was my life. All of them.

In April of 1940, seven or eight months after the three had settled in the Cambridge hostel, representatives of the CRCC appeared for an unexpected visit and wanted to speak to Dora Binki. When Paula informed them that Mrs. Binki had returned to London, the Committee told her she could not stay alone with the two children and took them away from her.

While Paula was trying the best she could, the family in Leipzig continued to desperately seek help from relatives living in different parts of the world. But communication was difficult and visas almost impossible to obtain. They were declared stateless because most of them were born in Poland. And their perilous situation changed daily. Up until May 1940, letters got through to England. Then they stopped. In 1946, the surviving children heard from a prewar friend of the family how the family spent its last few months – running, existing on very little, worried always about their children but relieved that the children were not with them. In September 1948, Paula received a letter from the American Red Cross, Detroit Chapter, reporting that her father died in Dachau on 23 April 1945. He was political prisoner number 140.147. The Red Cross had no information concerning the fate of her mother.

The Koppold Children: Harold. On 28 August 1939, Clara Koppold took her three children to a photographer in Berlin to have passport pictures taken. The two little boys each sat for a photograph; the baby could not sit alone. Her mother put her infant daughter on her lap, and the photographer recorded the moment. The picture outlived the mother and remains as a witness of the time. The young mother, a thin woman with haunting, sorrowful eyes holds the baby and looks directly into the camera. Her eyes speak to the world, long after they could no longer see. Two days later, the mother, the children, and a young Christian woman boarded a train bound for Holland. The mother carried with her food for everyone. In suitcases marked for each child were new clothes which their father, a dressmaker and tailor, made for them: warm coats for the three, new suits for the boys, dresses for the baby. Before the train crosses the border to Holland, the mother will have to leave and the Christian woman will be responsible for the delivery of this precious cargo to London. Clara Koppold will kiss the children for the very last time and will leave quickly to return to Leipzig. If she did not return as she promised, her relatives would be made accountable. After delivering the children to Paula at the station, the young woman who brought them to England will return to Leipzig. Only the oldest child, Harold, six years old then, remembers anything about life in Leipzig before the journey to London. One memory is seared in his mind.

Sometime in 1939, he was sitting in his father's tailor shop, playing on the floor with a box of buttons. An SS soldier appeared, his black boots directly in line with the child's eyes. The soldier told his father that he was doing an inventory of the merchandise in his shop. When the inventory was completed, the soldier asked Adolf Koppold if there were anything else, to which Adolf responded, 'No, just what you see in the shop.' Harold, sitting on the floor, then spoke: 'But Papa, you forgot the merchandise in the basement next door.' The black boots moved towards his father, and two pairs of feet left the room. When his father returned from the police station, he was considerably bruised. Harold is haunted by the memory and carries it with him everywhere, every day.

I first heard of Harold, who changed his name in Israel to Tsvi, when I visited Ann Sofier in London. During my search to interview a foster parent of a refugee child, her name had been recommended to me. Harold Koppold had come to her attention through her only son, Norman, several years older than the refugee boy. Harold had already had two placements when Norman became aware of him in the small synagogue on Thompson Lane in Cambridge. To Norman, an only child, Harold seemed a sad and lonely boy, but bright.

At the time of our interview, Ann lived in an assisted living facility. When I called to ask if she would speak to me, she immediately asked me to come for lunch. She spoke about her foster parenting as one of the most exciting and rewarding experiences she had had in her life, second only to raising her own son. 'I got much more out of it than I gave,' she said. She very much wanted me to meet Tsvi, the name he took in Israel where he lived since leaving England. She said I needed to hear his reactions first-hand. Ann knew I was going to Israel to attend the 50th reunion of Kindertransport, and she had prepared a small box of chocolates for me to deliver to Tsvi. He lives, she told me, on a kibbutz near the Gaza border. But perhaps, she offered, he would come to see me in Jerusalem.

Tsvi did come to visit me in Jerusalem, twice. At each encounter, I had difficulty getting him to speak more than a few words at a time. The first meeting was at Yad Vashem where a memorial plaque is placed on a wall dedicated to righteous Christians. Tsvi identified me before I even knew he was there. He said he came for the ceremony but had to visit his son in a town nearby. He agreed to return the next day to speak to me. In the glitzy Renaissance Hotel, where the meeting was held, he seemed ill at ease. I thought he might have a speech problem, then I thought he might be retarded, and finally, I thought I had lost my interviewing skills. I gave up and invited Tsvi to join me for dinner, a rather stiff affair in the hotel dining room. Clearly, he was uncomfortable. As he was about to leave, he said, 'I would like you to come to my kibbutz to see my sculptures.' It was the longest sentence he had spoken and it was delivered very clearly. I knew immediately that I had to go, no matter how far and how difficult the journey might be. I made arrangements for a cab driver to take me to his kibbutz. When I called Tsvi to give him my arrival time, he suggested I stay overnight, which I was happy to do.

On his own territory, Tsvi had no difficulty communicating. But what really amazed me were his sculptures. In fact, I was speechless. His sculptures are all over the small settlement, adding grace and beauty to a forlorn outpost near very hostile neighbours.

Many are abstractions, some are realistic, most are clearly related to his saying goodbye to his home and his parents. A figure of a child sits on the shoulders of an adult and waves; a baby suckles at the breast of an abandoned looking figure. The emotional content make the stone figures seem alive, and I wept for the pain I saw in them. In the evening, sitting on the floor of his and his wife's cottage, he told me of how he betrayed his father. I remind him that he was six years old, and was only speaking the truth. 'But those boots marched my father out,' he responds. Intellectually, he knows he cannot be held accountable. But emotional truth has nothing to do with rationality.

His memory of going to the train is sketchy. He says his mother was not crying, but she was pale and upset. She accompanied the children to the border of Holland, and at the last station she returned to Leipzig alone. He did not understand what was happening. 'I did not quite catch on because I was too young,' he explains. He remembers his mother packing clothes for each of them before they left. His father worked at home, and he knows he made two coats for him, but for the others, he does not know.

He showed me photographs taken in Berlin for their transit pass before he, his brother, and his sister boarded the train. The mother's dark grieving eyes staring at the camera continue to haunt me – the sweet innocence of the child on her lap is in stark contrast to the mother's prescient truth. Tsvi promised to send me copies of letters sent by a neighbour to his cousins Paula and Vera after the war was ended, detailing what his family had to endure before they were taken away. His cousin Paula had translated them. As promised, he sent copies of the letters and thoughtfully added a few genealogical notes for my benefit, identifying family relationships. The letters themselves were in a plastic binder secured with pink ribbon. Again, I wept at his thoughtfulness, and the tender and graceful treatment of the scraps that remain of the family he loved and lost.

Before I had left England for Israel, I sent him a letter asking if we could meet so that I could speak with him. His answer follows:

> I am quite willing to talk to you about my experiences, in fact, I am more than eager to do so. I can hardly explain myself, but I understand that this is a common phenomena [sic], although perhaps, in my case, it has taken an unusually long time. I am sure that you realize that as much as I have to tell, mine are the memories of a small child (at the outbreak of war I was six years old), some merely trivial, such are the memories of children. But then, of course, the history of the kindertransport is very much the story of pain and frustration of the helpless and I am glad that you intend to look at that. I must say that [your work] is not an intrusion into private life. It cannot be forgotten, if we wish it or not.

Sigmar and Zilla.   Youngest cousins of the Leipzig six, Sigmar and Zilla, siblings, were respectively thirty months and seven months when they came to England. Their memories of Leipzig consist of overheard stories acquired in later years. Sigmar appears to have had at once better and worse experiences than others. Better, in that two of his placements were exemplary; worse because he was 'untimely ripped' from the womb of his foster family with whom he had developed a very strong bond.

After the CRCC took him away from Paula at the Parkside Hostel, Sigmar was placed with the family of John Longland and his wife. A member of the Cambridge Refugee Children's Committee was a sister to Longland, then assistant superintendent of the Hertfordshire schools and later superintendent of a school district.[42] Longland's wife was pregnant with her second child when he was called for military service and they reluctantly had to notify the Cambridge Committee that they could no longer care for Sigmar. He had been with the family for approximately two years. During that time, he attended a nursery school in Welwyn Garden City, and had his tonsils and adenoids removed in a hospital. In a letter to Sigmar, thirty years after the fact, Longland confesses that he is not sure they did the right thing by sending the child back to the Cambridge Committee. He hopes that Sigmar can understand why they did it, and forgive them if it caused him pain.

Sigmar's next placement was, in his words, 'at the opposite end of the social scale,' the cottage home of Len and Elsie Mansfield, brother and sister. Len Mansfield was a butler at one of the colleges of Cambridge University. His sister was, in Sigmar's words, 'a spinster, a charwoman' who had lost her fiancé in World War I. He describes their home:

> They had a little row house on Eden Street, around the corner from Orchard Street where the Sofiers and my brother lived and not far from the Parkside Hostel where Paula and Edith lived .... Being a butler at a college in Cambridge meant that he had access to the buttery or the pantry and meant that during the war I [Sigmar] would once in a while get a special treat of an orange or some ice cream, which was rare indeed. In the middle of Cambridge, we kept nine chickens, which was just below the legal limit, and we had eggs.[43]

With the Mansfields, also lived an orphaned cousin, Gladys. She was about ten years older than Sigmar, who was five when he arrived there. Sigmar became part of a family group who gave him stability and much tender loving care. In addition, the Mansfields lived very near to both the Parkside Hostel where Paula, Edith, and later Zilla lived, and close to the Sofiers, where his brother lived. In a way, he had the best of all possible worlds: he was surrounded by people whom he trusted and who cared for him.

Ann Sofier knew Sigmar and the Mansfields from that time. Indeed, her home, especially at the Jewish holidays, was the place where five of the Leipzig six regularly congregated, and where Vera, living in Norwich, often visited. Ann fondly recalls that time as full of people and warmth. She says, 'They all ended up with me a lot. I ended up having so many.' And she smiled with pleasure at the warm memory.

Sigmar visited his brother, Harold, and Ann's son, Norman, every Saturday. To Ann Sofier, he seemed very happy in his home and healthier than he was when he first arrived at the Mansfields. She said when he first came there, Sigmar seemed weak and delicate. Ann's observation is confirmed in the record book of the Cambridge Refugee Children's Committee, where frequent references are made both to Sigmar and Zilla, the two babies of Clara and Adolf Koppel.[44] The children needed medical attention and specialists were called in to supervise their care. Ann Sofier said Elsie Mansfield responded to Sigmar's delicate condition, 'He was five when he came to the Mansfields. Elsie Mansfield was afraid to let him walk any distance. She pushed him in a pram to school and back, because she did not want him to overtax his energies.'

A bright student who loved to read, Sigmar did well on his eleven-plus exams and won a scholarship to one of the best schools.[45] In addition, Ms Mansfield saw to it that he went to Hebrew school and the synagogue. When he was approaching his twelfth birthday, she talked to Ann Sofier about preparing him for a Bar Mitzvah.

Then conditions changed dramatically and drastically, both for the Mansfields and Sigmar. Word arrived from America, whence his cousins had already emigrated, that Sigmar was adopted by a family in New Jersey. He was literally taken away, kicking and screaming, and put on a boat to America in the care of a couple contacted by the CRCC.[46] Ann Sofier explains:

> When the girls were sixteen, they discovered an uncle in America ... a whole family in America. That family then took the children over there, including Sigmar who lived with a wonderful woman, Ms Mansfield. He did not want to go, and they dragged him away from her. She was very upset. ... I thought he should stay with Ms Mansfield who was wonderful

to him. It was terrible. But his family, Paula and the cousins, thought he should be in a Jewish home. Ms Mansfield was rather old; at least she looked old to them. . . . I was against his going. They wanted to take Harold as well, but he wouldn't go, he refused to go. Absolutely refused. Very rich people adopted Sigmar. They had never had a child. He was very unhappy at first. He tried to run away, I think. Ms Mansfield loved him as any mother would love a child. More, I think. And he loved her.[47]

Today, Sigmar reflects on his leaving the home he had with the Mansfields. He says:

My leaving the Mansfield household was a major wrench. I lived there from age five through age 11. It was the most stable situation I had known or was to know. The middle-class household that I later moved into was no comparison with that other household. I never did attach to Bessie Silber the way I did to Elsie Mansfield, even though Meyer and Bessie formally adopted me.

The Silbers gave Sigmar every advantage. He had the Bar Mitzvah, originally planned by Elsie Mansfield, in a large synagogue in Patterson, New Jersey; he did very well in school; and attended the Massachusetts Institute of Technology. But he became ill at MIT, was hospitalized, and left school. He married quite young, at age twenty-one, because, he says, 'I wanted my own family to replace what I lost.' He finished his undergraduate education at night. Indeed, he completed a master's degree and a law degree by attending school for ten years at night. He has a successful law practice and three children, all married, all committed Jews. He and his wife expect to have ten grandchildren by the turn of the century.

The memory of his forced removal from the Mansfields continues to pain him. In a way, it is the same pain that Vera feels for the loss of her mother. Although he is satisfied with his life and his family, he regrets leaving Cambridge. He thinks if he had stayed he would have attended Cambridge University.

Mrs. Burkill tried to intercede on Sigmar's behalf before he left Cambridge. In a letter to Vera in America, Greta Burkill pleads that she be in touch with Miss Mansfield who was very pained over the loss of her dearly loved foster child. Burkill reminds Vera that the children have been the responsibility of the CRCC since September of 1939 and she wants 'to be very sure indeed that they will grow up into happy and contented human beings with a good future. I know you want the same, but I must have all the assurances possible that no mistakes are made.'[48]

In America, Sigmar often visited Zilla and her adoptive family. After all, she was the only sibling living close enough to him to visit. Zilla reports that her brother's relationship with his new family was 'terrible, terrible. They were too old to adopt him. They tried to be kind and sweet, but they were too old. He had a lot of trouble with them, and he used to come to my father often to talk about it.'

Now, Sigmar and Zilla hardly speak to each other. Zilla says she simply cannot communicate with him; she just does not understand him. They see each other infrequently at family celebrations. If they know the source of conflict between them, they do not reveal it.

Zilla. The youngest child known to have come to England on a transport, Zilla has no memory of her parents, knows only sketchy items about the events that led to her ending up first in England and then at the home of the Schnalls in New York state. Like her cousins before her, she arrived at the home of the Binkis. But she and her brothers were there for scarcely a week or ten days before they were all evacuated to Cambridge, and there the Koppold children lived until after the war. Her memories of Cambridge are essentially happy, although her first placement in Cambridge left much to be desired.

Zilla was placed with a family named Singer. The wife, a spiritualist, controlled Zilla by threatening to call her father or mother from the grave to come take care of her if she was not good. Sometimes, she, a baby, was put into a room or a closet by herself. But Zilla does not dwell on these negative experiences. She may not even remember them. Paula complained to the Cambridge committee and eventually Zilla was put back under Paula's care. Paula and Edith were her real family, she says. Edith was then in school; the housekeeper of the Parkside Hostel watched Zilla while Paula worked as a photographer's assistant. Every once in a while, she and her brother Sigmar, two and a half years older than she, played together. Sometimes, especially on Jewish holidays, all the cousins got together at the Sofiers. Life seemed normal and happy for the child.

Zilla has no gruesome Holocaust memories to haunt her. In fact, she has sparse information about her family. For example, she did not know she had an uncle, Leo, her mother's brother, who was the principal force behind the children's rescue. But then, she was an infant when she left home, and a young child when she was received into a new family in America. And that family knew little about the background of the Shmulovitz and/or Koppold families in Leipzig.

Zilla left for America with Paula and Edith. The new country seems to have fatally fractured her relationship with her natural brothers. She hardly ever speaks to Sigmar. Although she claims to feel close to her brother Tsvi, she has seen him only three times since she came to America. Several times Zilla said that Paula, Edith and she were a family in Cambridge, but she appears to have little interaction with them or with Vera. She visited Edith in Michigan for a week when she was sixteen and has seen her only sporadically since then. She says Edith is very easy for her to talk to, and she can call her up at any time and immediately they have a meaningful conversation. She volunteered that Vera and Paula are displeased when she does not come to family functions.

Vera's uncle in America appears to have been the agent for locating homes for both Sigmar and Zilla. At least that is how Zilla understands it. She says, 'Mr. Ribetsky was in the clothing manufacturing business; so was Sigmar's father and my father. They all knew each other.' Ribetsky showed pictures of Sigmar and Zilla to people he interacted with in the trade. On the basis of the picture, a childless couple wanted to adopt Zilla upon condition that she break all ties with her family of origin.

When Ribetsky's friend, Charles Schnall, heard this, he reported it to his wife. She insisted it was cruel and suggested to her husband that they take Zilla into their family. The Schnalls already had three children; Zilla became their fourth child. Ironically, Jean Schnall later requested that Paula reduce her visits to Zilla, causing Paula considerable pain. After all, Paula was Zilla's surrogate mother under the most difficult and stressful conditions. Asked why her mother did not wish Paula to visit, Zilla offers that Paula was trying to tell Jean Schnall what to do, and her mother, with the experience of raising three other children, resented the intrusion.

Zilla, now past sixty and a mother and grandmother, is grateful for the family she acquired and considers her own. She feels quite fortunate to be a part of it. 'A family is a treasure. It is the most important thing in life,' she says. But, with her own family of origin, or the surrogate family of Paula and Edith from her Cambridge days, there are strains.

*   *   *

I have tried to piece the story together as best I could from available documentary sources. It takes years to understand, if complete understanding is ever possible, what drove the decisions of historic times. The questions remain; the answers elude us. Whatever was done fell short of what might have been done. Those rescued were a minuscule number of those murdered. Had people acted differently, the outcome might have been different. But even hindsight cannot give us any kind of assurance. All we can do is try to understand and hope that we can forgive the lapses in judgement, the unexpected prejudice, the very human foibles that both inspire and plague us.

N O T E S

1 The cover page of the First Annual Report of the Movement for the Care of Children From Germany (November 1938 – December 1939) gives a capsule summary of its evolution. We learn that this new organization incorporated within it the previous Inter-Aid Committee for Children; and that it is associated with the Children's Section of the British Committee for Refugees from Czecho-Slovakia. Its office is Bloomsbury House, Bloomsbury Street, London, WC 1. It has a branch office: The Grange, Hindhead, Surrey. Its executive committee includes: Chairman, Lord Gorell; Deputy Chair, the Marchioness of Reading; Treasurer, Reverend R.S. Lewis. Other members of the Execut-ive Committee include: Mrs. Norman Laski, the Very Rev. Cannon G.L. Craven, the Rev. W.W. Simpson, Sigmund Gestetner, Esq. and the General Secretary: Sir Charles Stead. It is certainly a distinguished list of British citizens, including clergy and Jews.

   By the second annual report for the year 1940, we learn that the 'Movement for the Care of Children from Germany' has abbreviated its title and at the same time enlarged its possible scope. Its new title is the Refugee Children's Movement, Ltd.

2 First Annual Report of the Movement for the Care of Children, p.3.

3 First Annual Report, Movement for the Care of Children from Germany,. p.1.

4 Refugee Children's Movement, Second Annual Report, 1940. p.6. See also Amy Gottlieb, *Men of Vision: Anglo-Jewry's Aid to Victims of the Nazi Regime, 1933–1945* (London: Weidenfeld & Nicolson, 1998), pp.79–80.

5 Some of the information in this section comes from a recorded interview with Greta Burkill, 1980. Sound Archive, Imperial War Museum, London.

6 M.G. Burkill, Memoir [typescript}, Manuscript Room, Cambridge University Library.

7 As of this writing, I have not yet found the German records I need to review, although records of committees working in England are, to some degree, accessible. Many of the records of Jewish agencies were destroyed or lost.

8 Movement for the Care of Children from Germany, Ltd., First Annual Report, November 1938–December 1939 (Churchill College Archives, Cambridge, England), p.5.

9 See Amy Zahl Gottlieb, *Men of Vision*, pp.79–80.

10 Frederick Brodnitz claims that the Reichsvertretung der deutschen Juden started in 1933; see Frederick Brodnitz, 'Memories of the Reichsvertretung: A Personal Report', *Leo Baeck Institute Yearbook* 21 (1986). Yehuda Reshef (*Jewish Encyclopedia*) says the plan was first proposed in 1933, but it was not realized as an organization until 1935. A Jewish organization for social services in Germany was originally proposed by the Germans in April of 1933, to be called specifically *Judenrat*. The main function envisioned for this organization was to implement the directives and orders of the Nazi regime, as was, in fact, later done.

11 As reported by Shaul Esh, 'The Establishment of the "Reichsvereinigung der Juden in Deutschland" and its Main Activities', *Yad Vashem Studies on the European Jewish Catastrophe and Resistance* (Jewish Agency, Yearbook, Vol.7, 1957), p.24.

12 It was at this time that the RCM's Annual Report says there was much interaction between it and what must have been the phantom Reichsvertretung. It is likely that the RCM had no knowledge of the change within the structure of the so-called Jewish communal organization. The staff of the two organizations were essentially the same.

13 See Burkill Collection, Cambridge University Library, Manuscript Room, Letter 17. November 1938. In return for helping the Cambridge Refugee Committee with 'the case of a Ph.D. in Cam-bridge,' the German organization cited in the letter wanted information concerning what has been termed 'urgent cases,' and sent a list of four people. Sturge asks the addressee, a Miss Banyard, to make enquiries in the House of Commons of Dr. Kenneth Pickthorne. The names on the list are not children, but the mechanism of identifying urgent cases seems to be laid out here.

14 'Reichsvereinigung' in *Encyclopaedia Judaica*, Vol.14, pp.50–51.
15 *ibid*. Apparently, at this particular time, the Nazis were willing to look at ways in which to help the Jews leave, provided they left their property behind. However, the countries of the world, almost uniformly, did not open their gates, especially to Jews stripped of everything but their lives.
16 First Annual Report, Movement for the Care of Children from Germany, November 1938–December 1939, p.4.
17 *ibid*.
18 First Annual Report, Movement for the Care of Children from Germany, pp.4–5.
19 The Refugee Children's Movement Ltd. 1938–1945. Ms, August 1978, Burkill Collection, Cambridge University Library
20 Undated memoir, M.E. Burkill, Cambridge University Library.
21 England, needing laborers for certain occupations, granted visas to people willing to work in them, i.e.: domestics, farmers, certain types of factory jobs, and the more highly skilled professionals.
22 To fit severely traumatized children into suitable homes or institutions was sometimes impossible. The younger ones did not understand why their parents abandoned them on a train, the older ones had no common language with the complete strangers who were their hosts.
23 Some few refugees managed to find their way to England following a route through neutral countries, an aspect of rescue and relief efforts not yet adequately researched.
24 Undated memoir, Cambridge University Library
25 *Hereward Hall Gazette: Incorporating the Evacuation News Sheet of the Jews' Free Boys School*, Ely, January 1942 and July 1942. Available at the Cambridge City Library, Cambridgeshire Collection, C457.
26 Richard Bolchover, *British Jewry and the Holocaust* (Cambridge: Cambridge University Press, 1993), p.103.
27 *Jewish Chronicle*, 13 June 1941, p.24.
28 Conversation with G. Dubrovsky at 55th Reunion of Kinder, Jerusalem.
29 He used the authority of the agency of the Chief Rabbi to approach government officials to obtain their cooperation for programs he wanted established. See, for example: David Kranzler and Gertrude Hirschler, *Solomon Schonfeld: His Page in History* (New York: Judaica Press, 1982).
30 Copies in Schonfeld file, Parkes Archive, Southampton University. England.
31 The entire correspondence between the boys is at the Imperial War Museum, Burkill File.
32 Burkill File, Imperial War Museum, London.
33 Hansard, Proceedings of the House of Commons 1943–44, 'Guardianship (Refugee Children) [Lords]', 1576–1582.
34 *Jewish Chronicle*, 24 December 1943, p.5.
35 *op.cit.*, pp.2–4.
36 Some copies of questionnaires parents were required to complete prior to sending their children to England can be found among the Schonfeld Papers, Parkes Archive, Southampton University Library.
37 Transcript of interview by Gertrude Dubrovsky, p.4.
38 In a book listing people on various transports, I found that Vera's aunt, Clara Koppold, and her grandmother, Rosa Asman Shmulovitz, were deported together to Auschwitz. I could not find other names of the family. Deportation Buch, 1942–1945. Bundes Archiv, Berlin.
39 The *Jewish Encyclopedia* indicates a Jewish population in 1948 of about 200 people. I have not been able to find a breakdown of the number of volunteers in each local district, nor would they necessarily be identified as Jewish. In Cambridge, which also had a small Jewish population, a smaller number of Jews participated in refugee work. However, if one were to compare percentages of the population of each ethnic group who volunteered for work on the Committees helping refugees, the percentage of Jews in Cambridge participating might be larger than the corresponding percentage of non-Jews.
40 The letters Vera and Paula received and kept are heartbreaking to read today. How the children were able to deal with them is a matter of wonder.

41 The originals of the letters received by the cousins have been deposited in the Holocaust Museum, Washington, D.C.

42 Longland was knighted in 1970, after years of service as Director of Education in Derbyshire; see *Who's Who* (New York, 1990), p.1111.

43 Interview with Sigmar Silber by Dubrovsky, 28 November 1994.

44 Burkill Collection, Manuscript Room, Cambridge University Library. Members of the committee weekly discussed cases of children that needed to be watched. It is noted that Sigmar had stomach problems, Zilla had what was referred to in the report as 'a pigeon chest'. Zilla also appeared to have frequent bouts of colic. She is described as crying a great deal and her appearance was totally sad, both looking and acting.

45 Transcript of interview with Ann Sofier, 1994; private collection of Gertrude Dubrovsky

46 Greta Burkill, aware of the excellent parenting that Sigmar was getting, tried to convince Vera and Paula, then in America, to consider what the consequences might be for the Mansfields and for Sigmar. See Bertha Leverton and Shmuel Lowensohn (eds.), *I Came Alone: The Stories of the Kindertransports* (London: The Book Guild Ltd, 1991), p.319.

47 Ann Sofier interview transcript. *op.cit.*

48 *I Came Alone*, p.319.

SOCIAL DIMENSIONS OF RESCUE IN THE HOLOCAUST

Mary J. Gallant

A S SOCIO-HISTORIANS review the Holocaust, it is the silence of the bystanders that is considered the most prevalent social response, not rescue. But in the last twenty years scholars have increasingly taken inspiration from the ideal of rescue as a critical aspect of the picture of humanity to be entered into the record along with the saga of torture, carnage and wanton destruction representing the 20th century. Witnessing the condemnation of innocents of all ages during the Holocaust, individuals involved in rescue risked their own lives so that those in danger might be saved (see Rubenstein and Roth, 1987:363; Fogelman and Wiener, 1985). Examples of rescue in the Holocaust usually contain some reference to a wider context in community life, less visible, less publicized perhaps than other elements of the heroic tale, and in which social factors appear to have some salience. Acts of rescue during the Holocaust were accomplished within networks of resistance in various nations, as for instance the *Kindertransport* into Britain in 1938–39, the various efforts of the World Jewish Congress to arrange for the rescue of children, as well as the contribution of the fishermen of Denmark, Holland and Sweden, who kept a flow of refugees streaming out of occupied Europe and into safe haven in Britain throughout much of the Nazi occupation. Rescue is also associated with the effort in Le Chambon sur Lignon in the French Alps. What we see in Holocaust rescue narratives are strong characters active within a wider field of community as the action unfolds.

Rescue has both normative and heroic expressions as well as emergent and situational aspects; it can be found in orderly or chaotic contexts. While rescue has been documented across time, its occurrence in the past was sporadic and associated with the altruism of an individual or a community.[1] In modern urban North American society, by contrast, rescue has become normative, that is, part of the historical unfolding of its cultural foundations. In our times, rescue has transformed itself into more than a passion but an institutionally organized societal expression where personal bravery is normalized in many fields of endeavour, especially those related to the helping professions.

Ironically, the rescuer ideal has emerged in an age of individualism, when threats to humanity and humanism have increased. We may assume that the act of rescue occurred throughout human history, but it received relatively little attention in societies of the past where rescue was not sufficiently problematic to become a predominant cultural theme. By contrast, rescue today is a major concern, a focus for art, cinema, television, literature and journalism. The heroic ideal, whether played out in normative or altruistic action, involves doing something to help the helpless. In the past, rescue reached only members of a community imperilled in some crisis. Today we have moved to a time when the heroic rescue of the destitute and of those beyond the pale of acceptability in any community is expected, and rescuers may be lionized.[2]

To whatever extent rescue has been with us across the centuries, and however varied its expression when it occurred, the act of rescue is a form of altruism and a necessary component of what we understand as society. The capacity to act for the good of the whole even at the sacrifice of one's own life is part of the individual commitment that Durkheim (1895; 1897; see also Bellah 1973) identified with social integration. However, the particular structure of society in dynamic interrelation with historical and situational forces affects the way interpersonal acts are played out in community. In the homogeneous village society of the past, the identification of the individual with dominating hegemonies was not problematic; altruism was expressed in terms of unquestioningly expressing group boundary maintenance functions. Any acts of heroic risk-taking that occurred would not be in contradistinction to the whole but rather in synchrony with it. In the community of the past, organized as it was upon the principle of homogeneity, the voice of conscience was expressed as an act of conformity rather than critique. In our times, with community based upon the principle of interdependence among diverse parts, altruism is associated with complex, modern, organic solidarities spanning a great diversity of characteristics and orientations among its member units. Organizations as well as individuals are legitimated by principled orientation toward any of the innocent in need regardless of background.

The shift in standards of interaction from closed to inclusive kinds of communal orientation, parallels a wider and more profound change in Western society, increasingly moving us toward a kind of social structure better able to support the complexity of modern urban life.[3] As this fortuitous association of elements unfolded, humanism has been adopted as a favoured standard and the expectation of help, saving or rescue has come to be taken for granted. It may be false to superimpose our present expectation of rescue upon the past as a criterion of humanism. While we recognize the silence of the bystanders as an outgrowth of ethnic hatred and religious rivalry, the counter-trend symbolized by rescue surfaces as a normative practice as society takes on increasing levels of structural complexity and diffuse heterogeneity. Rescue in the Holocaust taking this social analytic approach was of the heroic or altruistic rather than the normative type.

HEROIC RESCUERS: THE INDIVIDUAL AND THE BEHEMOTH

Whatever the nature of the act of rescue, it is important to remember it as we honour the suffering of the victims of the Holocaust, and the darkness of the human countenance in these past times, for if we do not recall the precious points of light by which we turned from the brink of unsurpassable catastrophe, we would be ill prepared to build a welcoming future.[4]

Heroism has and will always be a personal act that may or may not be well thought out, and may or may not be supported by others. While the social actor is privileged to express heroism, the costs associated with fulfilling its directives are often prohibitive. Rescue occurs at interruptions in the established order when the individual must search out ways to create structures that articulate values missing in the current situation. Heroism transcends cultures and regional histories without being oblivious to them; it emerges from the individual's being called on by the failure of a given historical moment to reflect overarching values, such as humanism, that lie unexplored in the intricacies of the social structures in place.

Looking at the actual instances of rescue during the Holocaust, Nora Levin (1990: 117–125), analyses a long list of nations, agencies, religions and industrial organizations that failed to rescue or help Jews. In many cases they aided the perpetrators instead. However, the actions of individual officials representing nations, agencies, religions and industries paint a different picture. Levin (1990; see also Gutman 1990) notes that in the 1940s the Orthodox Patriarch of Constantinople wrote all his bishops in the Balkans and Central Europe urging them to help Jews and reminding parishioners that to conceal Jews was their sacred duty. Monseigneur Angelo Roncalli, later to become Pope John XXIII, then serving as apostolic delegate to Turkey, used false baptismal certificates to rescue Jews in the Balkans. In fact, Yad Vashem honours at least three thousand individuals, men and women from all the countries of Nazi-occupied Europe who adopted, hid, fed, provided false papers for or helped smuggle across borders Jews brought to them seeking refuge.

Names that stand out among the many – too numerous to mention here – who were connected with the rescue of Jews came from a wide diversity of religions and ethnicities: Raoul Wallenberg and Hannah Szenes, Joseph Andre and Wladyslowa Choms, Marie Benoit the monk and Elizabeth Abegg the Quaker, Edouard and Mildred Thies together with André and Magda Trocme of Le Chambon and their Huguenot congregation, Anna Barkowska and Petras Baublys, Bernadotte Folke and Mala Zimetbaum, Lodewijk Ernst Wisser and Hanna Van Der Voort, Gabor Sztehlo and Irena Sendler, Aristides de Sousa Mendes and Joop Westerweel. From ambassadors and military officers to peasants and concentration camp inmates, each was responsible for rescuing one or more people, either single handedly or with underground organizations. The 'heroes' were people leading ordinary lives, committed to their professions and their careers, clergy and laity, the politically inclined and the apolitical, romantics and conservatives.

Looking at a few of the less famous among these names we can get a sense of what they did and the risks they took. Anna Borowksa, a Dominican nun and mother superior of a small cloister near Vilna, Lithuania, helped smuggle weapons into the Vilna ghetto. She had heard of the massacre of Jews at Ponary, a space in the forest where Jews were brought to be shot during the summer months of 1941. She concealed seventeen members of the Jewish Zionist group and instructed the now famous Abba Kovner of the Vilna ghetto uprising in the proper use of grenades. She was arrested in 1943, the convent closed and the sisters dispersed. André Joseph, a Belgian abbot, helped rescue hundreds of Jewish children. He joined with the Jewish underground and helped coordinate rescue activities through his parish office which just happened to be located near the German military headquarters at Namur. Travelling from place to place, he implored individuals at monasteries, convents and private homes to take Jewish children under their protection. Eventually he was forced to go into hiding but he continued his efforts to help the children. After the war he returned the children he had rescued to their parents. Wladyslawa Choms was a Polish rescuer who headed the Lvov branch of the Polish Council for Aid to Jews (Zegota), a Polish organization based in Warsaw.[5] Lodewijk Ernst Visser was a Dutch jurist who was suspended as a supreme court judge by the Nazis in May 1940. He argued for the rights of Jews in Holland and demanded the Dutch administration uphold its constitutional obligation to protect Jewish citizens. When he learned that Dutch Jewish children were deported to Mauthausen in retaliation for a conflict between Dutch Jews and Dutch Nazis, he passionately addressed the secretaries general of the Dutch government, calling on them to resist the order to send people to the concentration camps. He continued to protest the deportation of Jews in Holland and finally, three days after receiving a warning to desist or be deported to a concentration camp, died of a heart attack. Hanna van der Voort was a Dutch rescuer who found hiding places for 123 Jewish children, becoming associated with the Dutch

Underground in order to do this. She was eventually arrested and tortured, suffering permanent damage to her health.

RESCUE DURING THE HOLOCAUST

Rescue during the Holocaust, was both a tribute to humanity and a personal act, an intimate gift.[6] It required of the rescuer the investment of imagination, conscience, trust and fellow-feeling. Structurally it pertained to situations not governed by formal and legitimated social processes. It was punished rather than rewarded by the authoritarian governments in place under the Nazis.[7] As an ideal type of human action, rescue in the Holocaust was a response to crisis, interruption and cruel repression. In practice, rescue represented at the situational and individual level a complex unfolding of purpose (see also Fogelman 1995), commitment to higher principle, talent and luck. At the time, rescue implicitly appealed to principles of ethics and conscience, taking the side of the innocent violated by official regimes so that they did not stand alone when their lives were in danger.

Survivor testimony has provided us with a literature in which the rescuer is variously portrayed, ranging from capable opportunist to heroic altruist. Those who write on rescue in the Holocaust deal with it less as a public cause than as a turning of the heart toward virtue (see also Flender 1963; Friedman 1978; Hallie 1979). Rescue was seen as a voluntary act that an individual might accept or reject without any direct gain or loss of community standing but which put the rescuer's life in grave danger. If caught, the rescuer would not only be condemned as a traitor, but was likely to be killed and perhaps tortured. The strength of conviction required was often daunting but with great modesty rescuers interviewed in the postwar years saw it only as very natural.

Heroic rescue during the Holocaust – standing against what we now collectively recognize as the greatest corruption of human morality in history – was associated with reason, justice, individualism and personal strength. Rescue was an act of altruism. Witnessing the condemnation of the persecuted and helpless, rescuers risked their own lives to help. It is not surprising that many scholars have concerned themselves with what determined the personal characteristics of rescuers. Samuel P. Oliner, for instance, in *The Roots of Heroism: Rescue Behavior in Nazi-Occupied Europe* (1986), identified the characteristics of the rescuer as including: (1) holding deeply internalized values of helpfulness, responsibility, fairness, justice, compassion and friendship; (2) having friends in groups outside their own family circle or immediate community; (3) being tolerant of differences and feeling responsible for many kinds of people; (4) having high levels of self-confidence and self-esteem and being willing to take calculated risks; (5) having the approval of their families in their rescue efforts, that is, having a supportive emotional network. Any or all of these were part of the social processes in which individuals undertook rescue. Nechama Tec (1986: 154; see also 1995) listed a similar set of characteristics for her sample of rescuers, stating as important: individuality, marginality, self-reliance, and cherishing the helping role. Tec's rescuers saw what they did as a duty, and the rescue they were part of was generally unplanned. With much of the intuitive and spontaneous about it, rescue demanded flexibility and synthetic imagination as likely facilitating attributes.

Celebration of rescue involves a direct acknowledgment of the nobility of the human spirit. But can we gather anything about the nature of the human community from which such acts emerge? Can we conceptualize rescue beyond the descriptions of the individual events in which they occurred? Can we find more than individual level phenomena at work in situations of rescue? Stone's (1977) concept of 'personal act' which contributes to a better understanding of the self in everyday life, also lends important facets to the interpretation of rescue and heroism while not forsaking the notion of community. Rescuers had 'just decided' to help when the opportunity arose – they were upholding their sense of community. Some identified with Jewish victims and anti-Nazi sentiments; others did not. In fact there may not be any necessary individual attributes for rescue to occur. Rhetorics related to helping and protecting the innocent may have been invoked to support a risky decision, but were a second line of affirmation after practical concerns about being able to do it had come into play. Nebulous strands of values unique to the rescuer's biography in community life constituted the first line of affirmation supporting their initiative.

Rubenstein and Roth (1987: 363; see also Kenneally 1982), mention Oskar Schindler's taking to heart the Talmudic verse quoted to him by Yitzhak Stern in 1939: 'He who saves the life of one man saves the entire world.' The verse speaks of the sanctity of humanity, a voice in the wilderness under Nazi domination. Schindler encompasses the contradictions in the role-person conflict associated with rescuing. He was known as a pleasure-seeking profiteer, a Nazi speculator who set out to capitalize on cheap labour in the ghettos. He eventually came to save more than a thousand Jews in his enamelware/ armaments factories, spending a fortune in bribes. Schindler seems to have been a person who could both adapt with the times and consider people as individuals. He was flexible enough from the start to parlay compromise into gain and, for different reasons, give as much credibility to an Amon Goeth as a Yitzak Stern or a Mila Pfefferberg. He seemed to have the capacity to enjoy people, to understand them, and use this talent to shape and further his goals His motives changed over the course of the six years from 1939 to 1945, as he changed from being the rational financier making effective use of human capital to a man with the goal of keeping the hundreds of workers in his care alive and giving them a future.

In the corrupt and greedy Nazi system, what turned his motives toward the heroic? It might be facile to assume he had become a different personality entirely by 1944–45. He seemed from the outset to be more attuned to the tastes and habits of postmodern times than the authoritarian patterns of the Nazi era. He found repression and its overlords repugnant, their personal greed pathetic. Given his close-up view of the SS who were in charge of operations in Poland, would it be unreasonable to assume that altruism might have seemed a redeeming way of setting his life apart from the naked greed and corruption which the Nazi elite had come to represent? Schindler was in a position to see Nazi villainy. His marginal position in community life meant that he could choose to identify instead with those who represented valued ideals, that is, the workers, epitom-ized in his colleague Yitzak Stern. Also, given that the victims might so abundantly be valorized over their persecutors, might a Schindler not find it worthy to take risks on their behalf? In short, within the situational and personal dispositions of the time, Schindler was a most believable character. Unlike many of those enveloped within the mechanical solidarity of institutional structures based on tradition,[8] his marginality allowed him to choose aspects of his life others were predisposed by circumstance to reject.

RESCUE AS AN INTERPERSONAL ORCHESTRATION
If rescue may be seen as choosing to act, it can also be viewed as an interpersonal accomplishment. Rescue is the partnership of two elements of social life, one represented by the rescuer, the other the rescued. As such it is a jointly constructed act in which witting or unwitting participants have pre-existing commitments on opposite sides of a

historical exigency. While there is no particular setting for it, rescue involves (1) recognizing a situation as being potentially dangerous for certain targeted individuals; (2) finding the knowledge and social resources to transcend the danger; (3) locating the rhetorical devices to construct alternative supporting identity structures to shore up the structures displaced in the rescuing stance; (4) having a reasonable set of strategies for getting out of the situation of danger; and (5) having the means to resume the taken-for-granted aspects of life without inviting reproof.

As a social process, rescue complicated the simple constancies of the rescuers' relatively ordered lives with risky and innovative practices. Though many tried to live their lives normally in the wake of their decision to rescue others, the decision constituted a turning point for them, as in the case of Trocme/Le Chambon (Hallie 1994) or Joop Westerweel (Gutman 1990; see also Tec 1986: 154). So much of what rescuers did represented a single-handed effort to carve their own path out of a reality that socialization had not directly anticipated. When we think, then, of rescue in the Holocaust as something good that happened in a very bad time, it may instead have been a response, unheralded and unforseen, within a series of events, all unusual and unwanted, in which acts that became part of 'rescue' appeared as the more constructive choice. It involved not just negotiating reality but manipulating illusion, lifting or suspending some of the situational expectations of others so as to bring off an act that looked familiar but yet accomplished ends unanticipated by formal community – invisible, or masked by what people wanted to see. Considered in this way, the rescuer in the Holocaust is one who is discursively aware of differing perspectives, offering compassion to others across social boundaries. The rescuer had the symbolic means to conceptualize reality from a perspectival approach to truth and morality, with sound anchorage in principle being a considerable support. It merely needs to be added that rescue, however meanly it transpired, was ineluctably an act of the highest moral stance.

Rescue as a social process may be further explored if we examine the case of 'Louise', a survivor who is part of my study of the Holocaust. Louise's narrative allows us to focus on the processual and unfolding nature of rescue while it exemplifies the reciprocal nature of the roles of rescuer and rescued in achieving an bringing a goal to fruition. At the same time it illustrates Arendt's conceptualization of goodness,[9] that stumbling confluence of fortuitous events and well intended deeds that creates the sublime in the daily trammel.

LOUISE

Louise Stein was the youngest of two daughters born to an affluent Jewish family living in Rotterdam in the 1930s. Though her maternal grandparents were observant, her parents were not. Her father had moved to Holland from Vienna after the First World War. He started out in the stock market and then went on to form his own business as a furrier. The family lived with Louise's maternal grandparents when they all moved to Amsterdam before the War broke out. Louise's father was by birth a Berliner who had served in World War I. She remembered him as being very sensitive to the Nazi danger in the times:

> I would overhear my father listening to the radio and Hitler's speeches. My father had a very high awareness of what was going on. He was instrumental in getting his mother, his sister, his brother-in-law ... he brought them to Holland unfortunately. He helped some of

his nephews to go to Israel and one nephew went to South America. He's the only one who I still have contact with.

So he was very aware of the impending threat and consequently I was aware. There were the discussions at home and he made the decision to emigrate. This was about 1939 after the actual... The Germans didn't invade the Netherlands till May 1940. In September '39 they invaded Poland. The minute they invaded Poland and the Second World War officially started, he made a decision to leave.

After the German invasion of Holland in 1940, but before conditions became very repressive he shifted his assets to New York through a business contact there and then tried to get immigration visas for himself and his family. His efforts were thwarted by a variety of factors, among them the impending death of his wife's mother from breast cancer. A web of circumstances slowed their progress so that when the family were able to go, they were stopped literally at the docks.

Anyway, so, here we were. But after my grandmother died, the family was free to leave. So my father tried to book passage on a ship to Curacao and it was filled. That's where luck and fate play a role because that ship was called the *Simon Bolivar*. It was torpedoed and everybody drowned. So... [pause]. He booked passage on the next ship which would sail three weeks after the Simon Bolivar on the third week of May. The Germans invaded the tenth of May. So we never got out.

While the Dutch army tried to hold back the Nazis at Rotterdam, the liners still scheduled to sail filled quickly and even small fishing boats were being chartered to ferry people to England. Among those trying to get away there was a sense of desperation and looming tragedy. Louise was a child of seven thinking only of leaving the dog at home with the maid as the family tried their luck.

I still remember us driving out of our driveway and we drove to the harbor outside of Amsterdam. That was just around the time of the capitulation. I don't know whether it was the same night or the next day... it must have been the same night. We were in a hotel and there were the families of my parents closest friends... several families, and I remember everybody starting to cry and falling into each other's arms.

They were trying to charter fishing boats to sail over to England and some people did. Some made it and some were shot down and drowned. But we never even got the fishing boat. We just went back along with some of the other families.

Wretched with anxiety and disappointment, the family nevertheless settled back to life with the compromises they knew were inevitable. Observing what had happened to Jews in Austria and Poland, they began to prepare for confiscation of property, possible 'resettlement' to some other part of the city, and rationing. The refugees in Holland were the first to be trapped.

Many of these refugees were probably not like ourselves, not even able to travel further, thinking they'd be safe in Holland, and what happened was that [pause] whatever laws ... whatever laws the Germans enacted, they were directed at those German refugees first. So, in the beginning we always knew what was up ahead because we knew what happened to them was going to happen to us.

Rescue and resistance in Holland were obstructed by a combination of Nazi lies and the protectionist orientations of the occupation government. Those most likely to seek rescue had the social resources to underwrite it once they found help. Louise felt that the contacts and information that her family were able to mobilize directly related to their prestigious class standing.

Working class Jewish population in Amsterdam, being in very clearly defined neighbour-hoods and clearly defined industries, didn't have anywhere near the means to go in hiding or leave that the more affluent people with connections of various sorts would have. There were some very courageous Underground people and some very dedicated people who would help [all] Jews, and I am not saying any ... casting any aspersions on those people. It was just the reality of the situation.

As they waited, conditions worsened for them all. Louise remembered the Gestapo going to affluent homes in the suburbs confiscating property in the name of the State. Typically, someone would enter their house 'to take inventory'. The family developed a form of humour to deal with such ironies and with it their own style of 'resistance'.

Oh there were endless jokes, endless jokes, you know. There were all kinds of nicknames for these people [Nazis]. But I can remember how my parents would hand over stacks and stacks of dinnerware across the fence to the non-Jewish neighbors. Some of the neighbors were very helpful and we would give all kinds of things that would be around to those near to us. People had started to horde food, too, you know – bags of rice and flour and so on. That, too. Gave it all to the next door neighbours.

We had a chesterfield suite that had cushions that were filled with eiderdown which was considered very precious and – it [the story] has its own tragicomical angles to it. They ... well, in those days you had specific people that you would deal with. This was an upholsterer ... that they had done work with before. He [father] had them pick up all the pillows and took out the eiderdown and filled those pillows with the worse kind of filth and dust that you could ever imagine and everybody would laugh at the idea of how some German housewife in Berlin would forever try to clean those pillows when she got the furniture! Never to be able to clean them, you see!!

In this way the family established an exchange network with neighbours that celebrated their shared anti-Nazi sentiments. There were other signs of tacit allegiance coming forward daily. This changed things little in the course of events but it did lend to hopefulness and a delicate optimism. By April of 1942 anti-Jewish laws were well in effect. Louise remembered all Jews had to wear a yellow star. All Jewish families had to register and receive identification papers, those with jobs in the civil service were dismissed, professionals were not allowed to practise outside the Jewish community and most of their equipment was confiscated. Food had to be bought from Jewish grocers who never received an adequate stock of rations. Islands of reprieve in this deepening nightmare came from individuals making spontaneous gestures of good faith to one another.

I remember the first day I went out – we had blocked off streets and we would roller skate in the ... And I would go out on my roller skates with my star on. The first person I encountered was an older man who lived somewhere down the street who would normally not even pay attention to me. And he saw me with this star and the first thing he did was he took off his hat and he bowed very deeply [illustrates] for me. And that made a very deep impression on me.

Eventually they were 'resettled' to a poor, inner city area. Her family were processed through a quarantine area, stripped, searched for lice and venereal disease, then packed off to a set of rooms where a small stove provided for heat and cooking needs. Their business was confiscated. In the gloom, family solidarity was a strong bulwark against the disheartening conditions.

Gestapo raids in their new ghetto neighborhood were timed to occur during the mayhem surrounding Allied bombing runs. All anyone could do was watch as people were taken away. Everyone was kept perpetually off guard and in constant fear. By late

1942, their kin remaining in Rotterdam were captured and deported to Sobibor. They were gassed. The idea of hiding had surfaced in family conversation at the start of the trouble, but as long as the precautions they had already taken seemed to be working, they put the notion aside. Louise's father was against doing anything extreme. Louise's mother, however, was determined to 'not be lugged away like a sheep'. Louise said, 'In the end, she won the argument. She won the argument the day my father discovered that some of his colleagues were deported, despite the fact that their identifications were stamped as "purveyor to the German army".'

Once the decision to hide was taken a myriad of details were involved in each step of the process. The decision to go into hiding required coming to a consensus within the family, but accomplishing even the smallest task required a wide network of contacts. Their own staying power as difficulties and contradictions mounted had to be constantly nurtured, backed up by endless vigilance, ample resources and a capacity for detail. The resistance effort was an invaluable support.

> They contacted a first cousin of my mother who herself was half Jewish to begin with and who was married to someone who was not Jewish. Not only that, but he was a very prominent person in Social Democratic circles and had a lot of contacts in the Underground. He agreed to help us get out of Amsterdam and find us addresses and false papers.
>
> You see, there are a number of things needed. First of all, it wasn't that easy to just leave Amsterdam because what it meant was taking the train. Nobody had cars of their own anymore. They were all taken by the German army, you know. Family on bicycles couldn't ride in the middle of winter for forty miles or so. But in order to ride a train, you couldn't wear a Star and, of course, in order to take your Stars off, you couldn't have identification papers that are stamped 'J.' So it was taking big risks. And then of course you have to have an address, people who were courageous enough to take people in hiding even though they didn't have too many material resources. [Going into hiding] meant that you didn't have food stamps. You'd have to buy food.

By 1943, the number of hiding spots in the Dutch countryside were shrinking. Members of the Dutch army and Allied personnel looking for refuge were turning up increasingly in the Dutch countryside. But this would be the last window of opportunity for the Steins to go into hiding and they took it. For the next year they ended up finally on a little farm in the west of Holland which had one cow, one pig, six chickens and half and acre of corn. Their 'rescuer' was a fundamentalist Christian known to the Underground through his ties with the Dutch Reformed Church.

> They were so segregated [as a fundamentalist sect] that they didn't even have a minister. They just had Bible readings [laughs]. And they could never have afforded to hide us but the . . . the Underground in that area was very solid. Strangely enough there were . . . there were two . . . two components to that Underground. The one was very devoutly fundamentalist Christian Reformed – the man who represented that group was our contact and he was an exceedingly courageous person. The other component was a group of Communists. And . . . and they worked together. That was the interesting part. They . . . their common enemy was the Nazis and they worked together. [Pause].
>
> But . . . this farmer and quite frankly, although I must say about the man, certainly his life was at risk and he sheltered us and . . . and he never betrayed us, [pause] quite bluntly he needed us too . . . he needed our money.

The farmer had ten children from a previous marriage and though he had promised not to tell that he was hiding Jews, all of the children knew about it. The man had been widowed and remarried with the second marriage being fairly unstable. The house the couple lived in was owned by the wife as part of what she inherited at the death of her first husband. It was impossible to feel completely safe in the situation.

> This couple fought night and day, [like] cats and dogs. My father ... our life depended on [them] ... My father had to be the arbiter for sixteen months between them, that couple, to make sure that this thing would hang together.

But this failsafe did not always work and, at one point, the wife flew off in a fury to her sisters leaving the Steins in fear for their lives, since one word from her might unwittingly betray them to an enemy source. Nothing happened then and the wife returned but Louise's father redoubled his efforts to make the partnership work while at the same time placing more restrictions upon his family. Since neighbours might drop in at any time, the father decided that it was a danger to have books lying around – no reading and no domestic tasks during the daylight hours. Conditions were tense.

> No books! So you know what position that put me in, right? For months and months and months, seeing nobody, and sitting. I had actually been sitting for sixteen months in this room without books, no writing materials, absolutely total sensory ... virtually total sensory deprivation. Not ... never outside, except if it was very dark. We cooked late at night in the dark ... occasionally take some fresh air.
>
> It was a pot-bellied stove to heat the place. It was a little ... see the ... these houses they had a large sort of common room and then there was a smaller sort of Sunday room a few steps up that nobody would ever use other than for funerals or weddings. So that's where we were. And of course, in winter, you can't throw the coal on the stove because it would make a sound. If you had to cough you would put your head in a blanket or else they would hear you. They would sit there til an hour – two hours, having coffee and talking, because that's what's done in that ... that community right? Also you would look strange ...
>
> [Q: Everybody watching everything?]
>
> Oh yah. They would ... Sure. This is farm country. Neighbours know each other intimately. And so they would scratch on the door and then we couldn't make a sound.

In the Fall of 1944 things got worse. Raids were becoming successful in this rural area. Where she was hiding with a family of friends who had taken in twenty or so Jews, Louise's sister had almost been captured. There was fighting not far away and civilians were being billeted to their area.

> So in comes a family, a tailor and his wife and six year old daughter ... billeted in our house! So the whole first day we were sitting there [pause] in utter panic. What ... what should we do? Conclusion eventually was, there is just no alternative. In ... in this house you can't ... we have to take a chance. We have to tell them, you know. Who's to know if they're traitors or ... or talkers or whatever. Well, as luck would have it, they totally accepted it. But we had to take a chance on the six-year-old girl, you know. She plays with other children and you never know what she says. Well, she may even have said ... babbled something about people in her house. But probably nobody even paid much attention to it or maybe she was just not interested in talking about it. Nothing happened anyway. This was from October til April of that winter. But, you know, it could just as well have been a total disaster.

By April 1945 with artillery attacks and Allied bombing in their area, the family decided to move to a trench outside of the house. During a lull in the fighting, her father made a decision to move them to the other side of the nearby river, since he knew something about where the front might be.

We walked through an area, through a forest where there was an institute for mentally ill people there originally. At one point a lot of people went in hiding there, an awful lot of Jews went in there – pretended to be mentally ill, and then they were rounded up and lugged away. Every mentally ill person, Jewish or not... lugged them all out of there. The SS were holed up in there, and the bullets were flying, [pause] whistling around our ears as we were walking, and we could very easily have been killed right then and there. Anyway, we... we weren't killed, and we got behind the lines.

The first Canadian soldier I saw, I'll never forget... as we walked through that forest and at the end of the forest there was a main road with a lot of army vehicles and then eventually we got a ride with some officers who got a jeep to go further. But the first... as we went round the bend, there was one army personnel standing there. Whether he was a soldier or an officer, I don't know, but [deep breath] in my memory [laughing], he is the tallest guy I have ever seen in my life.

Liberation meant being left on their own with the war still raging. They got back to Amsterdam and found haven with an uncle whose daughter had been captured while working with the Underground. She was still in the concentration camps and her father was still doing what he could to assist her cause.

You see he was... he was... because his wife wasn't Jewish, even though they were religious Jews, he managed, you know. Somehow or other, he... he managed to continue living in his house. [Pause]. I really couldn't even tell you how that was possible but... but he was. Course, he was in a terrible state because he didn't know about the fate of his only daughter at that point. Eventually she showed up, and incidentally, that whole experience must have been too much for him. He died of a heart attack at quite a young age after the war. But that was where we went because he was the only close relative who still lived in a regular house that we could move into. And we did that for some months.

All but two of their uncles, aunts and cousins were killed in the camps. Of the 130,000 Jews in Holland by 1940, Louise estimated that only around ten to fifteen percent had survived (see also Oliner and Oliner 1988). Rescue had been fortuitous and was accomplished by Catholics, Protestants and especially the Dutch Reformed Churches, who were outspoken against the Nazis from the start of the War onwards. Accounts of rescue in Holland, including for instance that of Anne Frank, who went into hiding, or Cory ten Boom, who with her family provided hiding spaces for the Dutch resistance, both of whom ended up in concentration camps, show that rescue and being rescued in Holland rested more on the ability to organize successfully than to rely on preached moral standards or any one person's particular heroism, although both were present in each case mentioned.

Looking at rescue in the Holocaust in a general sense, neither age, gender, class, religion, ethnicity, nor place of birth completely predicted when or where individual acts of heroism and heroic rescue would occur. There were facilitating conditions for it. Where resistance networks were strong, rescue was more likely and had a better chance of success. Resistance sprang up where there was clear repression – with a more diffuse focus, the act of organizing would not appear merited. It also emerged where Jews had been incorporated into some part of larger community and where some lines of affiliation continued to function despite the degree of Nazi control.

RESCUE AS A SOCIAL EMERGENT

In attempting to avoid the reification of rescuers' individual traits we may have ignored the larger currents shaping rescue as a social phenomenon. Scholars associated with this insightful reflection on rescue include those who conceptualize rescue in the Holocaust as choosing to act in a certain way (Grob 1997; Zucotti 1987, 1993), in response to situational factors. The seeming unpredictability of rescue in the Holocaust is clearer nowhere more than in the comparison of nations. Denmark, which saved almost all its Jews, was occupied by Germany for almost the entire period 1939–45. The Nazis had expected it to be territory friendly to the Reich. In 1943 when Germany decided to round up all 8,000 of Denmark's Jews, the entire country became an underground movement (Flender 1964) which ferried to Sweden Jews scheduled to be deported to the concentration camps.[10] If we look at the French and Italian cases of rescue in the Holocaust, certain interesting anomalies come to light. France, home of the lofty principles of the Enlightenment, had under the Nazis become collaborationist. The Pétain government and Vichy France became the foil against which the strong humanistic principles of the people of Le Chambon, a rural Huguenot community in the French Alps, were played out. Official France sold out most of the refugees who came expecting safe haven in the arms of wisdom; rescue and resistance (Latour 1970) grew out of community forces that could not be effaced by the shifting tides of politics. Seventy percent of Jews who had been citizens there for centuries were saved (see also Zucotti 1993), yet in no sense was rescue official policy in France. By contrast, as Zucotti points out, the Italians who saved 85 percent of their Jews were soldiers, officers, foreign ministry officials, clergy and farmers, with Italy an Axis power! In short, Italy appears to have been one of the places in Western Europe where helping and rescuing were normative, with Italians themselves becoming a Nazi conquest in 1943. As Zucotti points out, rescuers in Italy came from all levels of society, from Partisans as well as the establishment. Partisans helped find refuge for Jews all through the war years, but were especially helpful during the months of Nazi Occupation in 1943–44.

Rescuers in Zucotti's Italy were acting out of a context where anti-Semitism was not strong or predominant. Italy's Jews may have represented a third of the population two thousand years ago at the height of the Diaspora under the Romans, but in the 20th century had accounted for less than one percent of a population. Assimilation was increasing but also values honouring universalism were present. The humanistic tradition of the Renaissance was strongly reflected in Italy's art and architecture, monuments and collective tastes. The people were unselfconscious and unassuming in their cosmopolitanism. The class system of the 1930s and 1940s included a strong peasantry along with upwardly mobile elements. By contrast, Poland which had been an area of refuge for Jews for more than a thousand years still had to make its (violent) emergence into modernity. As it slowly industrialized it continued to be a churn of ethnic rivalry with rising class ambitions feeding principles of homogeneity leftover from its village past. Universalist values emphasized there, at times by organized religion, were defeated by structural tendencies toward anti-Semitism that echoed in new class rivalry. In Germany of the 1920's and 30's, homogeneity was also an implicit part of national identity. Nazi Germany was mobilized on a folk solidarity ethos that the state took over at the expense of the family (Fitzpatrick and Gellately, 1996). Both of these societies reflected similar structural leanings and political ideologies; both had strong anti-Semitic political movements throughout the century and both had high victimization rates in the Holocaust. Jews though large in number in Poland could never claim they enjoyed more than hostile marginality there in the last hundred or so years. Germany accepted Jews into their industrializing community only under conditions of assimilation rathern than pluralism. Rescue in Germany and Poland was then clearly configured in a different set of understandings than in Italy, with unresolved and unchallenged ethnic hatred left to cast a shadow upon their growth.[11]

DISCUSSION

While the expectation of help and a belief in its certainty is fundamental to the human experience, as Jean Amery tells us in *At the Mind's Limits* (1986), for many in the Holocaust it was a hope that was beyond reach. Community and social life in the times failed to provide basic rights to all its members and especially the Jews, the *tiermenschen* of Nazi racist policies. So great was the longing and the need of the victims for simple human compassion, that in the aftermath of the Holocaust a voice within us answers back, treasuring the act of rescue, identifying with the misery of the suffering and we search through the debris of the past for any sign of that kind of nobility which stood up simply and with modest faith to a behemoth. Amazingly, given the violence of the oppressor, we find heroes as well as those who, not claiming such a vaunted status, performed some small part in a chain of activities organized as part of the resistance effort around them. In my interpretation, rescue in 1933–45 could be construed as both a personal act nourished by the highest of cultural ideals and the confluence of collective tendencies towards a nobility not necessarily part of history before this.

Looking at rescue as a personal act, there are many different kinds of motive structures attributed to the rescuer, including what could be considered far less than heroic. The practical cost of keeping large numbers of people or continuing streams of small numbers of people alive during a period of ration and starvation demanded there be some system of assistance in place – Jewish resistance organizations supplied the Huguenots of Le Chambon (Hallie 1979) with some funds. Yet it is clear that it was not a high profit industry, nor, given the number of official murders of those who were caught or suspected of harbouring 'foreigners', would it stand as a popular pastime. Looking at rescue as a collective emergent, there are converging patterns in the rescue of Jews as we look across nations, but there are as many contradictions and ambiguities as there are constancies.

Rescue in the Holocaust seems perhaps to fit a picture of reluctant bravery, of greatness cast upon the ordinary actor. Rescuers interviewed retrospectively tell us that they were cast upon a dilemma that in their own eyes they could only resolve by taking the stand they did, no matter what the sacrifice. To remain who they were, they had to change their response to authority. It was made easier where extraordinary insight and strength of leadership could be relied on to revitalize flagging spirits and provide a dependable source for the resistance.

CONCLUSION

While there may be no one specific set of correlates that adequately predicts the emergence of heroic rescue in communities or individuals, it did occur during the Holocaust. Rescue is a continually expanding pattern and within complex organic social systems is associated with diversity and inclusiveness. In our present times much of what we do as rescue is normative to our society, during the Holocaust very little of the rescue that occurred was of this vintage. Rescue in the Holocaust came out of a social structural base not quite ready for full-scale normative rescue. What we find is that it exemplifies if not distills the archetype of heroic rescue. As such it was both a personal act and part of a social process. Heroic acts of rescue were called up in such a way situationally that rescuers saw them as a natural outgrowth of already formed convictions. Because of the tight connection between the role and the person, the individuality of the rescuer and the specifics of the actual rescue, we make a false assumption that only by describing the personality type of the rescuer can we say much at all about rescue as a phenomenon. We must instead see that rescue occurs within a community context and involves interpersonal and social network kinds of formations in which personal biographies are played out. Behavioural typologies, as interesting as they are, will not lead to a valid and complete picture of rescue in the Holocaust.

It is important that we grasp this issue correctly, for acts of high purpose and nobility when they occur orient us even in the darkest times. It is suggested that a study of individual rescuers would profit by analysing what happened in terms germane to the sociological analysis of the personal act, taking it as involving turning points, challenged identity (Gallant 1998), conversions or alternations (Travisano 1981) and sustaining structures within the resistance community. In that way we could conceptualize it as involving roles mobilized by identity and guided by already existing understandings about how to accomplish risky goals. Conceptualizing rescue less as a characteristic *in* individuals and more as a choice – a choice within a time that demands emotion management, staging, culturally specified ethics and motives which permit definitions of the act of rescue to be credible and supportable, we can begin to admit social structural elements into the analysis of rescue, taking it as a social and situational rather than a behavioural process.

BIBLIOGRAPHY

Adler, H.G. 1969, *The Jews in Germany; from the Enlightenment to National Socialism*. London: University of Notre Dame Press.
Amery, Jean. 1986. *At the Mind's Limits: Contemplations by a Survivor on Auschwitz and Its Realities*. New York: Schocken Books.
Arendt, Hannah. 1958. *The Human Condition*. Chicago: University of Chicago Press.
Arendt, Hannah. 1963. *Eichman in Jerusalem: A Report on the Banality of Evil*. New York: Viking.
Arendt, Hannah. 1966. *The Origins of Totalitarianism*. New York: Harcourt, Brace and World.
Arendt, Hannah. 1968. *Men in Dark Times*. New York: Harcourt, Brace and World.
Bauman, Zygmunt. 1989. *Modernity and the Holocaust*. Cambridge: Polity Press.
Bauman, Zygmunt. 1991. *Modernity and Ambivalence*. Ithaca, NY: Cornell University Press.
Bellah, Robert N. 1973. *Emile Durkheim on Morality and Society*. Chicago: University of Chicago Press.
Blumer, Herbert G. 1969. *Symbolic Interactionism; Perspective and Method*. Berkeley: University of California Press.
Buber, Martin. 1964. *Philosophical Interrogations*. Edited by Sidney and Beatrice Rome. New York: Holt, Rinehart, Winston.
Buber, Martin. 1988 [1965]. *The Knowledge of Man; Selected Essays*. Atlantic Heights NJ: Humanities Press.
Camus, Albert, 1956. *The Rebel*. New York: Vintage.
Deak, Istvan. 1992. 'Changing Sides and Changing Lives.' *New York Review of Books* 3 9(18): 22–26.
Durkheim, Emile. 1961 [1925]. *Moral Education*. New York: Free Press.
Durkheim, Emile. 1964 [1895]. *The Division of Labor in Society*. New York: Free Press.
Durkheim, Emile. 1966 [1897]. *Suicide*. New York: Free Press.
Durkheim, Emile. 1914. 'Le dualisme de la nature humaine et ses conditions sociales.' *Scientia* 15: 206–221.
Fitzpatrick, Sheila and Robert Gellately (eds). 1996. 'Introduction', pp.1–21 in *Accusatory Practices; Denunciation in Modern European History, 1789–1989*. Chicago: University of Chicago Press.
Flender, H. 1964. *Rescue in Denmark*. New York: Manor Books.
Fogelman, Edith and V.L. Wiener. 1985. 'The Few, the Brave, the Noble.' *Psychology Today* 19 (8): 60–65.
Fogelman, Edith. 1995. *Conscience and Courage*. New York: Doubleday.

Frank, Otto and Mirjam Pressler (eds.). 1995. *Anne Frank; the Diary of a Young Girl*. New York: Doubleday

Friedman, Philip. 1978. *Their Brothers' Keepers*. New York: Holocaust Library.

Gallant, Mary J. 1997. 'Prolonged Trauma in the Holocaust: Effects Fifty years Afterwards.' 27th Annual Scholar's Conference on the Holocaust. Tampa Florida. March.

Gallant, Mary J. 1998. The Meditation of My Heart: Remembering the Holocaust. Work in progress.

Grob, Leonard. 1997. 'Rescue during the Holocaust – and Today.' *Judaism* 46(1): 98–107.

Gutman, Israel. 1990. *Encyclopedia of the Holocaust*. New York: Macmillan.

Hallie, Philip P. 1979. *Lest Innocent Blood Be Shed; The Story of the Village of Le Chambon and How Goodness Happened to be There*. New York: Harper Colophon Books.

Helwig-Larsen, Per, Hendryk Hoffmeyer, Jorgan Kielar, Eigil Hess Thaysen, Paul Thygesen, and Munke Hertel Wulff. 1952. 'Famine Disease in German Concentration Camps: Complications and Sequelae.' *Acta Psychiatrica et Neurologica Scandinavica*. Supplementum 83. Ejnar Munksgaard: Copenhagen.

Keneally, T. 1982. *Schindler's List*. New York: Simon and Schuster.

Latour, Anny. 1970. *The Jewish Resistance in France (1940–1944)*. Tr. Ilene R. Ilton. New York: Walden Press.

Levin, Nora. 1990. *The Holocaust Years: The Nazi Destruction of European Jewry 1933–1945*. Malabar Florida: Robert E. Krieger Publishing Company.

Lifton, Robert J. 1986. *The Nazi Doctors; Medical Killing and the Psychology of Genocide*. New York: Basic Books.

Lindeman, Albert. 1998. *Esau's Tears; Modern Anti-Semitism and the Rise of the Jews*. New York: Cambridge University Press.

Mead, George Herbert. 1938. *The Philosophy of the Act*. Chicago: University of Chicago Press.

Oliner, Samuel P. 1986. *The Roots of Heroism: Rescue Behavior in Nazi-Occupied Europe*.

Oliner, Samuel P. and Pearl M. Oliner. 1988. *The Altruistic Personality; Rescuers of Jews in Nazi Europe*. New York: Macmillan.

Ozick, Cynthia. 1992. 'Of Christian Heroism.' *Partisan Review* 59(1): 44–51.

Porter, Jack Nussan. 1982. *Genocide and Human Rights; A Global Anthology*. Lanham NY: University Press of America.

Richardson, Henry G. 1960. *English Jewry under Angevin Kings*. London: Methuen.

Rubenstein, Richard L. and John K. Roth. 1987. *Approaches to Auschwitz; the Holocaust and its Legacy*. Atlanta: John Knox Press.

Rubenstein, William D. 1997. *The Myth of Rescue*. New York: Routledge.

Stone, Gregory P. 1977. 'Personal Acts.' *Symbolic Interaction* 1:2–19.

Strauss, Anselm 1978. *Negotiations: Varieties, Contexts, Processes, and Social Order*. San Francisco: Jossey-Bass.

Tec, Nechama. 1986. *When Light Pierced the Darkness; Christian Rescue of Jews in Nazi-Occupied Poland*. New York: Oxford University Press.

Travisano, R. 1981. 'Alternation and Conversion as Qualitatively Different Transformations.' Pp.237–248 in Gregory P. Stone and Harvey A. Farberman, *Social Psychology through Symbolic Interaction*. New York: Wiley.

Zucotti, Susan. 1993. *The Holocaust, the French, and the Jews*. New York: Basic Books.

Zucotti, Susan. 1987. *The Italians and the Holocaust; Persecution, Rescue, and Survival*. Lincoln Nebraska: University of Nebraska Press.

NOTES

1 The archetype of rescue exists in many sources but none more accessible and capable of influence over time than the Jewish Torah and the Christian Bible. In it the Passover story celebrates the deliverance of the Jews from captivity, but it is also a depiction of human transcendence as well as Divine rescue of an enslaved people who embraced monotheism and the Mount Sinai covenant of Moses. As rescue, the values it underscores expand within the history of Judaism and, among others, its Christian extensions, bringing us many of the values we recognize as Western civilization today.

Camus (1956) points out that in the past rescue when it was practised as an activity marginal to community life may have been associated with his ideal type 'Rebel'. Today, in the last quarter of the 20th century, rescue is a normative part of life.

2   It is from this vantage point in history with rescue taken as normative practice that we, perhaps unfairly, evaluate the past. We turn away in despair from what we see in that past representing humanity and its civilizations. We displace our revulsion for the city of man using the caveat of a 'few good men' and rescuers stand out well in this light. Heroic rescue assuages our woundedness in looking back at what seems a string of betrayals and inconsistencies as humans from different social groups confronted each other. Heroic rescue becomes the saving image in such a past, all that we might care to salvage there. We gladly accept the rescuer image painted in brilliant colors but not the murky roots in which it stands. To paint a valid picture of humanity as we gaze into the past, we must instead take a wider and more realistic view of rescue, putting it in the context of history and social structure that falls within the reach of the ordinary person.

3   Durkheim in his *Division of Labor in Society* distinguishes between mechanical and organic solidarity which develop as social change leads to a more complex division of labor in society. Cultural change accompanies structural shifts and leads on to individual level growth expressed in what Durkheim refers to as public conscience:

   'Since every advance that society makes results in a higher conception, a more delicate sense of the dignity of man, individualism cannot be developed without making apparent to us as contrary to human dignity, as unjust, social relations that at one time did not seem unjust at all... a given advance in moral education in the direction of greater rationality cannot occur without also bringing to light new moral tendencies, without inducing a greater thirst for justice, without stirring the public conscience by latent aspirations' (Durkheim 1961:12).

   As Robert Bellah (1973: vii–lv) points out, Durkheim is suggesting that as society goes forward, the individual is attached to the whole in terms of a qualitatively different bond, with attachment to groups no longer being blind, uncritical, nor severely exclusionary, as in the earlier mechanical form of social order.

4   Leonard Grob (1997) argues that rescue during the Holocaust was a form of witness. It should not be seen as purely a behavioural issue locked into the exploration of personality typologies. We need instead to seriously examine rescue as a social and historical configuration as we try to describe it during the Holocaust. In addition, because of its symbolic significance, rescue should be seen as an ongoing activity. In the watershed of the Holocaust, it is important for the generations to confront not just the past but the future and to do it using the revitalizing mandate of rescue, configuring this task using the Jewish concept *tikkun olam*. The concept of rescue during the conflagration and as it continues to orient us today helps us articulate creation and renewal (see also Buber, 1964) in the kind of futures we construct.

5   The Warsaw community by 1943 had become a place where many groups came together to form unlikely liaisons that helped Jews and others resist the Nazis in various ways (Paulsson 1998, personal correspondence).

6   Indeed, some writers question whether rescue would be the correct term to use for the altruism of individuals confronting the Nazi genocidal machine since rescue implies saving. Rubenstein (1997) felt that only military intervention could possibly accomplish rescue, that is the saving of the endangered peoples. He also noted the myths connected with what was militarily possible. Istvan Deak (1998) looked at the rescuers in terms of changing sides and changing lives. Others (see also Ozick 1992) note that rescue was more a statistical anomaly than a trendmaking function of the times.

7   Gregory P. Stone (1977) in his article 'Personal Acts' attempted to analyse ordinary life in ordinary times in terms of its capacity to evoke turning points and to being profound meaning to our existence. In part the ability to make ordinary life into a nesting of personal acts has something to do with the individual's ability to seize the moment which may in turn be associated with being able to project a perspective beyond the normative order and bear the consequences. His expansion of the concept allowed him to look at a wide variety of human actors from thieves to lovers, as making personal act-taking a way of dealing with fragmented realities and interrupted flows in expectations as society became complex and the individual rather than the community became responsible for interpreting

the nature of the social worlds spawned by that growing complexity. The villain, the fool, and the hero are all capable of taking identity altering courses of conduct, involving risk, intuition, self-other assessment, values, and the ability to go beyond compliance in handling life's exigencies.

8   This reference harkens back to the distinction in Durkheim's work already mentioned. Mechanical solidarity was the kind of social integration Durkheim saw as supporting community life of the past, one based on commonness of kind and conformity to tradition. By 1939, Europe as a configuration of states was entering a transition period, not quite the old way nor yet completely representing societies which were fully evolved organic solidarities.

9   This is her counterweight for the more familiar term 'banality of evil', which she coined in her work *Eichman in Jerusalem: A Report on the Banality of Evil*. She contributes to a picture of modernity and the times in which she lived in other works as well (e.g. Arendt 1958, 1966, 1968). All are critiques filled with inspiring erudition that is full of doubt and grief concerning modern social forms.

10 Helweig-Larsen et al. (1952) reporting their medically precise study of famine disease and its effects on Danish police imprisoned in Nazi camps implicitly point to the conjunction of national resistance and rescue of Jews. It might also be noted that the horrors described so carefully by the physician researchers applied to prisoners in the 'milder' kinds of camps.

11 The kind of community which Durkheim identifies with the mechanical solidarity of the past predisposed members toward the maintenance of social boundaries, with exclusion of the Other and those not exactly sharing commonality of kind. Religion was an institution central to the old world order and purveyed exclusionism even at the cost of ignoring its central tenets. Works like Richardson's on English Jewry (1960) and Adler's (1969) on German Jewry are among the many (see also Herzer 1992; Zucotti 1987; 1993) which clearly show how this played out in various national contexts. Anti-Semitism (see also Gutman 1990) had many expressions over time and, like any other ill wind may have contributed to rather than debilitated the Jewish way of life in the medieval community. Lindeman (1998) suggests caution in interpreting the Jewish interface with Christianity as a disaster. While Christians did exhibit a predisposition to violent hatred of Jews, historically Jews lived comfortably within Christian societies. If we examine social continuities only from the point of view of the collective behaviour momentarily generated, much is lost. Sociologists accept the contradictions in socio-historical emergence without needing to point out that variation and contradiction are part of social life. They also would point to the patterning of collective behaviour as being influenced by institutionalized forms of discrimination that foster hatred across time and place, putting the onus for positive change on the humanistic reform of institutional structures (Mead 1938). A sweeping new kind of order along the lines Durkheim (1964; 1914) suggested as emerging as the division of labour becomes more complex, would seem to be an important component of the rescue of the future from the abyss of the past.

MOTIVATION IN HOLOCAUST RESCUE:
JAN ZWARTENDIJK IN LITHUANIA, 1940

Jonathan Goldstein

WHAT PROMPTED a Dutch businessman to ignore serious risks in order to assist Jews stranded in wartime Lithuania? In the summer of 1940, Jan Zwartendijk rescued thousands in Kovno. What was his role in the Kovno rescue episode? What was the role of other individuals such as the Japanese Consul-General Sugihara Senpo? What was the attitude of the Soviet government? And how did the State of Israel come to recognize Zwartendijk's courage fifty-seven years after the event?

By late 1939, as agreed under the terms of the Hitler-Stalin pact, the German forces had completed the occupation of western Poland and paused, turning their attention westward. Also in late 1939, the Soviet Union occupied eastern Poland. By May 1940 approximately 6,000 Jews had fled into neutral Lithuania. These refugees had already suffered persecution by the Nazis in the German-occupied Klaipeda (Memel) region of Lithuania or in Poland. M.W. Beckelman, the on-site representative of the American Jewish Joint Distribution Committee, reported that in Nazi-occupied regions,

> the killing of hundreds monthly continue[s] unabated. Forceful expulsions during the arctic spells of December and January of children, aged and ill from Jewish institutions requisitioned by German authorities have resulted in additional hundreds of deaths... The general intent seems to be to expel all Jews from those provinces which have been officially annexed to the Reich and to make life for them in the so-called Gouvernement [of German-occupied but unannexed Poland] so unbearable that they will leave it by flight, suicide or death.[1]

Some had then sought refuge in Soviet-occupied eastern Poland, where some Jewish groups – Bund members, Zionists, rabbis, yeshiva students – faced specific persecution as 'political undesirables'. In the words of the Polish Zionist leader Zorach Warhaftig (later Israeli Minister of Religious Affairs), they felt that 'though rescued from the death penalty, we [had] been sentenced to life imprisonment'. Beckelman's and Warhaftig's observations on Jewish suffering under the Soviets have been corroborated by eye-witnesses Mary Berg and Chaim A. Kaplan, while Masha Greenbaum, Lucy Dawido-wicz, Martin Gilbert, Yisrael Gutman, Shmuel Krakowski and Leni Yahil have documented the brutalization of Jews in areas formally annexed into the Third Reich or under its control, such as the Generalgouvernement of Nazi-occupied Poland.[2]

On 15 June 1940 the Soviet Union occupied of all neutral Lithuania. Five weeks later the U.S.S.R. accepted Lithuania's 'request' to be annexed, a procedure that was completed by August 5th. The Jews who had fled to neutral Lithuania to escape Nazi or Soviet cruelty felt especially vulnerable and desperate during the annexation process. By July virtually all the consulates in Kovno were closed and panic reigned among the Jewish refugees. At this point Jan Zwartendijk took on the role of rescuer.

Zwartendijk had arrived in Kovno in May 1939 as the representative in Lithuania of Philips, the Dutch electronics manufacturer.[3] The Dutch Ambassador to the Baltic states, L.P.J. de Decker, based in Riga, continued to represent the Dutch Government in Exile after Germany overran the Netherlands in May 1940. DeDecker suspected the Dutch consul in Kovno, Dr Tillmanns, a Lithuanian citizen but ethnic German, of pro-Nazi sympathies. In June 1940, only days before the Soviets occupied Lithuania, he dismissed Tillmanns and invited Zwartendijk to become consul in Kovno. When he accepted, Zwartendijk expected only to be involved in minor chores such as extending a Dutch resident's passport.

His appointment quickly provided the opportunity for a rescue operation. In July 1940 Pessla Lewin, a Dutch citizen by birth who had married a Polish Jew and was then living as a refugee in Lithuania with her husband Isaac and son Nathan, wrote to deDecker requesting an immigration permit for the Dutch West Indies. She was informed that no immigration visas were required but that she would need a landing permit from the local governor. Such permits were rarely issued but the ambassador tried to help by noting in her Polish passport 'for the admission of aliens to Surinam, Curacao, and other Dutch possessions in the Americas, an entry visa is not required'.

This annotation, dated 11 July 1940, came to be known among the refugees as a 'Curacao visa'. It gave the impression of being as good as a visa but omitted to mention that to enter Curacao a landing permit was required. On 22 July Isaac Lewin approached Zwartendijk in Kovno. Lewin recalls that Zwartendijk, after seeing what Ambassador de Decker had done, 'copied [the "Curacao visa"] into my Lithuanian safe-conduct pass'.[4] This 'visa' also covered the Lewins' three-year-old son Nathan. Armed with this documentation, Pessla and Isaac Lewin together with her mother and brother, who were still Dutch citizens, went to the Japanese consulate in Kovno, where they were issued 7–15-day transit visas to travel through Japan en route to Curacao. They also went to the Soviet authorities, where they were issued permission to travel by train to Vladivostok, where they would leave for Japan.

The Japanese consul, Sugihara Chiune (also known as Sugihara Senpo, 1900–1986), was until recently far better known than Zwartendijk; he has been featured in the movies *Escape to the Rising Sun* and *Visas That Saved Lives*, in the play *Virtue: Senpo Sugihara*, and in an imaginary dialogue with Boston University Judaic Studies Professor Hillel Levine.[5] Sugihara told Warhaftig in 1969 that he 'had been well aware of the fictitious character of the visas, but as long as his action had not been in any way illegal, he had been prepared to aid the refugees'.[6] Sugihara issued a relatively small number of transit visas based on genuine destination visas for entry into the United States, Palestine, Canada and elsewhere. I was the more than 2,000 fictitious 'Curacao visas' issued by Zwartendijk that enabled him to issue a corresponding number of Japanese transit visas. Zwartendijk's action also enabled the Soviet authorities to issue corresponding numbers of travel permits at a time when Soviet citizens required official permission to travel within their own country and an exit visa to leave its borders.

How did the Lewins' single-family trip turn into a mass exodus of beleaguered Jews? Unaware of the Lewins' experience, Nathan Gutwirth, a Dutch citizen who was then a student at the yeshiva of Telz (Telsiai), Lithuania, asked Zwartendijk if several of his fellow-students, non-Dutch citizens, could accompany him to Curacao. Zwartendijk said he was willing to provide Gutwirth's friends with the same annotation he had given the Lewins. According to Gutwirth, this help was provided with de Decker's concurrence. Gutwirth passed on the news to Warhaftig, and Zwartendijk told Warhaftig he was willing to do the same for anyone who asked. There is no evidence as to whether Zwartendijk sought or received authorization to issue 'Curacao visas' *en masse*.

Word of the escape route spread quickly through the Jewish refugee communities in Kovno and Vilna, although it did not reach some of the more isolated Lithuanian Jewish communities.[7] Within hours, dozens of petitioners lined up at Zwartendijk's office, which is today part of the Red Cross hospital on the main downtown thoroughfare of Kovno. Zwartendijk wrote approximately 1,300 visas by hand between 24 and 27 July and another 1,050 with the help of a rubber stamp between July 29 and 3 August, when the Soviets commandeered his office, obliging Zwartendijk and his family to return to the Netherlands. The highest-known visa number is 2,345, issued to Eliasz Kupinski and his family.

None of the Jews to whom Zwartendik issued bogus visas attempted to enter Curacao. Zwartendijk had made it clear to the recipients of that his 'visas' would not allow them entry – they knew the 'visas' were a way of helping them get to Japan, where they could try their luck at getting legitimate visas for other countries. Armed with the annotations in their passports, which could masquerade as end visas, about half of the 2,200 refugees who reached Japan were successful in moving on to the United States, Palestine, Canada, and other final destinations. The Japanese interned the remaining thousand or so in Shanghai for the duration of the war, among them 250 faculty and students from the yeshiva of Mir, Poland.[7]

Warhaftig records an interview with Dr Kasteel, the Dutch Governor of Curacao and Surinam from 1942, when many years later Kasteel was Ambassador to the State of Israel and Warhaftig was Minister of Religious Affairs:

> After describing to him the type of visas we had received in 1940 for Curacao, I asked him how he would have reacted had a ship actually arrived in Curacao with hundreds of Jewish refugees aboard holding such 'visas.' Would he have accorded them asylum? Nothing of the sort, he answered promptly. He would have forced the ship back into mid-ocean, as had the American and Cuban authorities in the case of the *St. Louis*.[8]

On 22 June 1941, less than a year after the Kovno exodus, the Nazis attacked the Soviet Union and overran Lithuania. The Jews of Lithuania were almost entirely annihilated. Zwartendijk had thus saved more than 2,000 Jews from almost certain destruction.[9]

Zwartendijk and his family returned to the Nazi-occupied Netherlands in September 1940. In 1941/2 he was interrogated by the Gestapo about an unrelated matter, as his son Jan recalls:

> Two Gestapo officers came to see him at home. He feared the worst – that they had found out about the Kaunas affair. But it turned out that the Germans had killed an old friend of his from Prague 'trying to escape' in Romania ['auf der Flucht erschossen' – a common German euphemism for tortured to death during interrogation]. This man had Zwarten-dijk's name and address in his pocket. There was no connection with Kaunas [Kovno] and there were no further consequences of this visit. It was nerve-wracking because drawing attention for any reason meant scrutiny of Gestapo files. Miraculously, his Kaunas activities must have escaped their intelligence. But Zwartendijk did not feel safe until the Allied liberators arrived in southern Holland in September 1944.[10]

Zwartendijk was aware of the risks to himself, his wife, and their three small children. The declaration to which he put his signature 2,345 times was a deliberate deception which was undoubtedly an abuse of his consular authority. The U.S.S.R. and the Netherlands had no diplomatic relations, and he could not hope for protection from the Soviet authorities. Nor could he have any way of knowing that the Soviets would permit Jewish refugees to leave Lithuania.

Zwartendijk was also at risk from the Nazis once the Germans had decided upon the 'Final Solution to the Jewish Question' in January 1942 and High Commissioner Artur von Seyss-Inquart set about systematically exterminating the Dutch Jews. The Gestapo might well have found a file mentioning Zwartendijk's name as the signatory of over 2,000 sham declarations that had enabled many Polish and Lithuanian Jews to escape. It was probably German bureaucratic inefficiency that saved him.

ZWARTENDIJK'S MOTIVATION

What motivated a Dutch businessman to partake in a dangerous scheme to rescue Jews when his own country was already overrun by the Nazis? The President of the Philips Company, Dr Frederik Philips, had taken the initiative in sheltering some 500 Jewish employees from the Nazis and was later forced into hiding, but neither Dr Philips nor his company were aware of Zwartendijk's activities until 1997.[11]

Since Zwartendijk had to destroy all his consular files before leaving Kovno, there are few documents to cast light on events. One clue emerges in a letter written by Zwartendijk from Kovno to Philips headquarters in Eindhoven on 5 July 1940. Zwartendijk speaks obliquely of trying to help folk who were '*in de puree*', colloquial Dutch for 'in the soup'. Even this reference, however, casts little light on motives behind Zwartendijk's altruism.[12]

One possible motivation might be religious faith, such as that which prompted the citizens of Le Chambon sur Lignon in France to shelter many thousands of Jews throughout the war.[13] According to his son Jan this was not the case:

> My father was not religious in the sense of participating in religious activities or going to church. His parents had been strong Protestants, inclined toward the socially-liberal side. He himself never felt comfortable with organized religion and never went to church. I think he could be described as a 'humanist seeker' in his beliefs. In his younger years he was greatly interested in Eastern religions, judging from the books he owned, as well as in the Sufis, the Rosicrucians, and various other groups with mystical overtones. But he was never a member of such a group that I know of. He just picked his own path through their literature.
>
> I believe what guided him in Kaunas was a set of strong personal convictions about what for him was right and what wasn't. He always stuck to his own code without hesitation or compromise, even if that occasionally got him into trouble. But he did not have the slightest inclination to lecture anybody about his values, nor even to discuss them. He just did what he felt he ought to do, period. No discussion or commentary called for, before or after.[14]

Zwartendijk's younger son Robert corroborates his brother's version of events, observing that his father 'did what he felt he had to do as a human being, nothing more and nothing less'.[15]

Perhaps the most telling evidence of Zwartendijk's selflessness is that between 1945 and his death in 1976 he never spoke about what he had done or made any attempt to publicize or glorify his role. Until the year of his death he did not know how many of those he helped had actually succeeding in escaping from Lithuania. Most of those he rescued did not know his name and referred to him as 'Mr. Philips Radio' or 'the angel of Curacao'; some thought 'Philips Radio' was actually his name.

In 1976, through the efforts of Shanghai survivor Ernest G. Heppner and others, Zwartendijk was finally located. Samuel Orlansky, of Bene Berak, Israel, wrote to Zwartendijk on 19 May 1996 of 'what a great feeling it must be if one is privileged to save the life of even one person. And what great merit more was it to save a whole community from the clutches of death.' Pinhas Hirschprung, Av Beth Din of the Montreal Rabbinical Court, wrote to Zwartendijk in June 1976 that 'not only have you saved us, but you literally saved the generations coming from us.'[16] Some months before his death Zwartendijk was made aware of the scale of his rescue operation by historian David Kranzler. On 20 October 1997, through the efforts of Heppner, Kranzler, Israeli diplomat Moshe Yegar, the present author, and others, Zwartendijk was recognized as 'Righteous Among the Nations' by Yad Vashem, the State of Israel's official Holocaust Martyrs and Heroes Remembrance Authority.[17]

THE MOTIVATION OF OTHERS

Over and beyond the question of what motivated a single individual to act heroically, the Kovno rescue episode evokes broader questions of motivation which may never be adequately answered. What were the motivations of the Polish and Lithuanian Jews who did not seek to leave Lithuania and who were subsequently persecuted or slaughtered? What motivated the governments involved in the Kovno rescue scheme?

With respect to the Jews themselves, a perennial question in Holocaust studies is seeking to explain the behaviour not of the Lewins and Warhaftigs who sought to escape but of those who did not make vigorous efforts to leave. Were they too firmly rooted by a feeling of home and security which they did not wish to jeopardize? Did they underestimate the diabolical, ultimately genocidal, nature of European anti-Semitism, in spite of impassioned warnings from Vladimir (Zev) Jabotinsky and other Zionist leaders? With respect to Zwartendijk's specific exit scheme, were some terrified by the idea of having to cross Siberia to get to Japan? Were some convinced they would end up as slave labourers in Siberia? Were some simply unaware that an avenue of escape was available? Mrs. Betty Goodfriend, currently of Atlanta, Georgia, lived in a *shtetl* approximately thirty kilometres from Kovno during the Zwartendijk episode. In conversation with the present author in October 1999 she commented: 'We never heard of Sugihara. We never heard of Zwartendijk.'[18]

The Dutch Government-in-Exile had existed for only a matter of weeks when its Ambassador to the Baltic States asked Zwartendijk to replace the pro-Nazi consul in Kovno – a conscious, anti-Fascist choice. Without consulting his superiors, the Ambassador acquiesced in the issue of phony visas for the Lewin family and for Gutwirth's friends, the precedent for Zwartendijk's voluminous visa-writing. Other Dutch diplomats who later issued 'Curacao visas' to Jewish refugees were A.M. de Jong in Stockholm and N.A.G. de Voogt in Kobe. The issue of these 'visas' was a heroic and commendable act reflecting individual decisions. There was no government policy or structured commitment to issue phony documents to Jewish refugees. Later, the Dutch Government-in-Exile became an active resistance organization, smuggling weapons and personnel into the Netherlands from England, but that was not the case in this initial, nebulous period of of Jewish persecution. Indeed, the Dutch government knew nothing about the Kovno rescue scheme until about 1963, when it first came to official attention and Zwartendijk was asked for an explanation.

What motivated Sugihara? Unlike Zwartendijk, he was a professionally trained diplomat and intelligence officer and his issue of transit visas to Jews should be seen in that context. In an unpublished report, Sugihara explained that he was assigned to open a new Japanese consulate in Kovno in 1939 because 'General Oshima [the Japanese ambassador in Berlin] wanted to know whether the German army would really attack the Soviet Union.' The Japanese General Staff wanted to withdraw its army on the Soviet-Manchurian border and move it to the South Pacific. Sugihara was therefore asked to establish the foreseeable date of the German attack on Russia. 'It was obvious why the General Staff had insisted that the Foreign Office open a consulate in Kaunas. As a consul in Kaunas, where there was no Japanese colony, I understood that my main task was to inform the General Staff and the Foreign Ministry about the concentration of German troops near the border.'[19]

From the outset, Sugihara's intelligence-gathering activities in Lithuania involved agents from the Polish underground and the London-based Polish Government-in-exile. These agents, like many Poles, had crossed the Lithuanian frontier when Poland was overrun in the fall of 1939. Large numbers of Polish troops were interned by the Lithuanian government in camps in Kolotowo, Birsztany and Polaga. Sugihara helped to secure the release of key Polish officers and operatives from internment and get them out of Lithuania, in some cases by issuing them with Japanese identity documents and loaning them his official vehicle. One of Sugihara's closest informants was Polish Lieutenant Leszek Daszkiewicz, whose memoir reveals the close connecton between Sugihara's intelligence operations and his rescue of Polish Jews:

> Apart from supplying the Japanese consul with information from the territory of the USSR, I was to receive a reply from him as to the decision concerning the issue of Japanese transit visas to enable Polish refugees to travel via Russia and Japan to America or to one of the islands off the South American coast ... There had been a positive reply from the Japanese government and he was only waiting instructions from the Foreign Ministry [concerning refugees who had final destination visas] ... The honorary consul of that state in Kaunas agreed to issue residence permits [inaccurate – *J.G.*] against payment, even though he knew that none of the refugees would go there [he did not know that – *J.G.*]. Once in Japan, with the help of the still-operating Polish Embassy there, they would go elsewhere. When the time came and the Japanese Consulate started issuing visas, it was the Jews who came in great numbers, while there were very few Poles. Only a dozen or so applied and I arranged for them to be treated as priority in all matters ... Sugihara told me that it was quite difficult for him to write the customary formula in Japanese in all passports and that caused delays. I suggested making a rubber stamp. He agreed and gave me a master copy. I then gave this to [Polish Army intelligence officer] Captain Jakubianiec who ordered a stamp to be made from it. However, we had two copies made and one sent to Vilnius [Vilna] where Japanese transit visas were issued later following the departure of the consul from Kaunas, but backdated.[20]

Polish documents make clear that aside from humanitarian motives, Sugihara's involvement with Polish-Jewish refugees was part of a coordinated operation to get Jewish and non-Jewish Poles out of Lithuania. It was a by-product of his intelligence-gathering operations with the Polish Government-in-Exile. That cooperation was fully endorsed by the Japanese Foreign Office and military. After the Soviets closed Sugihara's consulate in Kovno, he went on to equally sensitive postings in Berlin and Koenigs-berg and then became Japanese Consul General in Prague.[21] The motivation for Sugihara's activities was thus fundamentally different from that of Zwartendijk, who acted independently and not in conjunction with an intelligence-gathering operation.

An even more intriguing question concerns the motives of the Soviet Union. Who authorized 2,200 Polish Jews to travel thousands of miles across Siberia in order to leave the 'paradise' of the U.S.S.R.? These unusual activities almost certainly could not have been authorized by local party functionaries in Kovno. Who were the higher authorities and why might they have gone along with the scheme?

According to Victor Israelyan, who was Soviet Ambassador to the United Nations and is a historian of the U.S.S.R. in the World War II period, it was Vladimir Dekanozov who would have been responsible in 1940 for approving exit visas for Polish Jews and allowing them to travel across the U.S.S.R. to Vladivostok. Dekanozov was Beria's man from their days in Georgia. When they were called to Moscow, Dekanozov became Foreign Minister Vyacheslav Molotov's long-time deputy (1939–November 1940 and 1941–48) with a short stint as the U.S.S.R.'s ambassador to Germany (November 1940–1941). Beria became head of the NKVD (later named the KGB). Dekanozov became deputy to Beria in March 1953. Both were executed in December 1953.

The broader context in which Dekanozov had to decide about the visas was the Hitler-Stalin Non-Aggression Pact, 'the pact between two scorpions in a bottle'. The agreement stipulated that the Baltic republics were to be within the sphere of influence of the U.S.S.R., not that they were to be annexed by the U.S.S.R. The U.S.S.R. attacked Finland in November 1939 and annexed the Baltic republics in the summer of 1940 when Hitler was preoccupied with overrunning France on his way to invading England. Stalin thought he could get away without a German reaction – as he did – but did not want to push his luck. According to Israelyan, it would have been inconceivable for Dekanozov to allow 2,200 Polish Jews in Lithuania escape across Siberia without Molotov's approval, and Molotov would not have approved it without Stalin's approval.[22]

Why would Stalin have approved? Humanitarian sentiments can be ruled out. What was the deal? With whom? Possible Soviet motives include: (a) a convenient way to get rid of the burden of approximately 2000 desperate and impoverished Polish-Jewish refugees in freshly annexed Lithuania; (b) a good opportunity to try to induce some of the refugees, through intimidation or blackmail, to spy for the Soviets in the U.S., Canada, Palestine, Japan, China, or elsewhere (no one realistically expected the refugees to wind up in Curacao)[23]; or (c) an easy way to raise more than half a million dollars for Intourist, the Soviet state travel agency. Each refugee was charged between U.S.$170 and $240. The money was collected and the tickets bought with the assistance of American Jewish relatives, the American Jewish Joint Distribution Committee and the Vaad Hatzalah.[24] Perhaps all three factors played a part. According to Israelyan, there are probably no Soviet Foreign Office officials left alive who were involved in the authorization. Dekanozov's name has been purged from all official histories and Foreign Office documents. He 'never existed'. Only surviving KGB agents or recently-opened KGB files could tell us more.[25] While such research is beyond the scope of this paper, answers to these questions could clarify one episode in Soviet, Jewish, Dutch, Lithuanian and Japanese history, and contribute to an understanding of motivation in one of the most intense periods of personal and political crisis in 20th-century history.

N O T E S
The State of Georgia Commission on the Holocaust, the Holocaust Educational Foundation, and the Sino-Judaic Institute most generously underwrote the basic research for this article, which was completed while the author was Visiting Scholar at the Oxford Centre for Hebrew and Jewish Studies. The author wishes to acknowledge the research assistance of the late Leila Avrin of the Hebrew University of Jerusalem, Oded Borowski of Emory University, John E. Ferling of the State University of West Georgia, Ambassador (Emeritus) Victor Israelyan of State College, Pennsylvania, Marvin Tokayer of Great Neck, New York, and Jan Zwartendyk of Tucson, Arizona, He also appreciates the bibliographical aid of Charles E. Beard, Nancy Farmer, and Myron House of West Georgia's Irvine Sullivan Ingram Library.

1 'Mr. Beckelman', 'The Refugee Problem in Lithuania', February 1940, 16-page typescript in Joint Archives, New York City, File number JDC: 1937–1950, 730, p.2.

2 Thousands of the Jewish refugees fleeing Nazi or Soviet persecution found temporary haven in Vilna (Vilnius), which was incorporated into independent Lithuania on 10 October 1939. Lithuania ceased to be a safety zone for these refugees when it was occupied by the U.S.S.R. on 15 June 1940. Beckelman noted that of the 9,824 Jewish refugees registered with the American Jewish Joint Distribution Committee in Vilna as of 31 January 1940, '3153 came from territory now occupied by the Russians [and] 6671 from German-occupied Poland.'

For additional detail on the hardships of the Jews under the Soviet occupation, see Zorach Warhaftig, *Refugee and Survivor: Rescue Efforts during the Holocaust* (Jerusalem: Yad Vashem, 1988), pp.91–101, 115–19, and Masha Greenbaum, *The Jews of Lithuania* (Jerusalem and Hewlett, N.Y.: Gefen, 1995), pp.288–301. The situation of the Jews in German-occupied Poland and in the German-occupied Klaipeda (Memel) region of Lithuania was infinitely worse. Murder, brutal forced labour, expulsions, and ghettoization were commonplace. For additional descriptions of the persecution of Jews in the Generalgouvernement and in areas formally annexed into the Third Reich, see Mary Berg, *Warsaw Ghetto* (New York: L. B. Fischer, 1945), pp.12–37; Chaim A. Kaplan, *Scroll of Agony* (Bloomington and Indianapolis: Indiana University Press, 1999), pp.19–236; Lucy S. Dawidowicz, *The War against the Jews, 1933–1945* (New York: Bantam, 1986), pp.112ff.; Martin Gilbert, *The Holocaust: the Jewish Tragedy* (London: Collins, 1986), pp.84–98; Yisrael Gutman and Shmuel Krakowski, *Unequal Victims: Poles and Jews during World War Two* (New York: Holocaust Library, 1986), pp.29 ff.; and Leni Yahil, *The Holocaust: The Fate of European Jewry, 1932–1945* (New York: Oxford University Press, 1990), pp.128ff.

3 Documents about Philips' presence in Lithuania in 1939–40 have been preserved in Lithuania's Central State Archives in Vilna. These are mainly Finance Ministry records bearing original tax stamps and include photographs of Zwartendijk and his wife. I am grateful to Archives Director Riorardas Cipas and Deputy Director Grazine Sluckaite for making these papers available to me during my June 1998 research trip. The Kaunas Regional Archives (Juozas Rimkus, Director), contain some Finance Ministry and other commercial documents from 1940–41 and telephone books for the years 1939–40. For additional background on Orthodox Jewish organizations and their contracts with Zwartendijk, see Efraim Zuroff, *The Response of Orthodox Jewry in the United States to the Holocaust* (New York: Yeshiva University Press; Hoboken, N.J.: Ktav, 2000), pp.83–94, 96.

4 The episode is described in Isaac Lewin's *Remembering Days of Old: Historical Essays* (New York: Research Institute of Religious Jewry, 1994), pp.171–76 and in Nathan Lewin's 'Memories of my Father', *Washington Jewish Week*, 7 September 1995, p.53.

5 Warhaftig, *Refugee*, pp.112–31. Other accounts include Hillel Levine, *In Search of Sugihara* (New York: Free Press, 1996); Christopher Lehmann-Haupt, 'Tackling a Mysterious Mass Rescuei', *The New York Times*, 23 December 1996, C16; Ernest G. Heppner, 'A Rescuer's Image is Gilded', *Jewish Post and Opinion* (Indianapolis), January 1997; Ernest G. Heppner, 'Sine Qua Non', *Hadassah Magazine*, November 1997, p.41; and Mel Gussow, 'Sugihara's List: A Play about 6,000 Saved Jews', *The New York Times*, 21 January 1998, B3.

A widely published but unfootnoted account about Sugihara's activities appears in Marvin Tokayer and Mary Swartz, *The Fugu Plan: The Untold Story of the Japanese and the Jews during World War II* (New York and London: Paddington Press, 1979, reprinted New York and Tokyo: Weatherhill, 1996), also published under the title *Desperate Voyagers* (New York: Dell, 1980) and translated into Chinese by Gong Fangzhen, Zhang Letian, and Lu Haisheng as *Hetun yu Jihua: Dierce Shijie Dazhan Qijian Ribenren yu Youtairen de Mimi Jiaowang Shi* (Shanghai: Shanghai Sanlian Shudian, 1992).

6 Warhaftig, *Refugee*, p.110.

7 Until 1941, when the Japanese closed the gates of Shanghai, this city was a place where a foreigner could legally walk ashore without any documentation whatsoever. For eyewitness testimony, see Ernest G. Heppner, *Shanghai Refuge: A Memoir of the World War II Jewish Ghetto* (Lincoln: University of Nebraska Press, 1993), p.40 and *passim*, translated into German by Roberto de Hollanda as *Fluchtort Shanghai: Erinnerungen 1938–1948* (Bonn: Weidle Verlag, 1998).

8 In fact, Jewish refugees were admitted to Curacao and not turned back to sea. After the German invasion of the Netherlands in May 1940, several Jews with Austrian and German passports were

interned on the Dutch West Indian island of Bonaire. Even more significantly, in late 1941 a League of Nations refugee official in London prevailed on the Dutch Government-in-Exile to cable the Governor of Curacao to admit to Curacao approximately 82 Jewish refugees aboard the Spanish ship *Cabo de Hornos*. The *Cabo de Hornos* incident recalls the arrival of the first contingent of Jewish in New Amsterdam in 1654, when In 23 Jewish refugees were admitted to the colony on orders from Amsterdam over the protest of Governor Peter Stuyvesant. See Warhaftig, *Refugee*, pp.104–05; Beckelman, Asuncion, Paraguay, to Joint, New York, 13 December 1941, 23 December 1941, Joint Archives; 'High Seas', *Time Magazine*, 1 December 1941, p.30; Pamela Rotner Sakamoto, 'The Policy of the Japanese Ministry of Foreign Affairs towards Jewish Refugees', Ph. D. diss., Fletcher School of Law and Diplomacy, Tufts University, 1996, pp.297–300; David and Tamar de Sola Pool, *An Old Faith in a New World* (New York: Columbia University Press, 1955), pp.4–31; Arthur Herzberg, *The Jews in America* (New York: Simon and Schuster, 1989), pp.19–26.

9 Letters from Nathan Gutwirth, Antwerp, to Marvin Tokayer, Tokyo, 24 September and 22 October 1974, both courtesy of Marvin Tokayer; to Mordecai Paldiel, Jerusalem, 28 May 1996 and to Jan Zwartendyk, State College, Pennsylvania, 16 July 1996, both courtesy of Jan Zwartendyk [Zwarten-dijk's eldest son]; David Kranzler, *Japanese, Nazis and Jews: The Jewish Refugee Community of Shanghai, 1938–1945* (Hoboken, N.J.: Ktav, 1988), pp.311–312.

10 Jan Zwartendyk, 'Jan Zwartendijk: His Activities as Dutch Consul in Lithuania, 1940', unpublished ms, 1 October 1996, p.7, courtesy Jan Zwartendyk.

11 On 4 November 1997 the Israeli charitable organization Boys Town Jerusalem sponsored a dinner in Amsterdam to jointly honour Zwartendijk and Dr Philips. At this event, Zwartendijk's children received his posthumous 'Righteous Among the Nations' medal from Yad Vashem. The same honour had been bestowed on Dr Philips earlier that year. Letter from Mordecai Paldiel, Jerusalem, to Jan Zwartendyk, State College, PA., 7 October 1997, copy to author.

12 Letter from J. Zwartendijk, Kaunas, to Philips head office, Eindhoven, The Netherlands, 5 July 1940, courtesy Jan Zwartendyk.

13 See interviews with citizens of Le Chambon sur Lignon, France, recorded by Pierre Sauvage in his documentary film *Weapons of the Spirit*, produced by Friends of Le Chambon.

14 e-mail from Jan Zwartendyk, Tucson, Arizona, to the author 29 December 1998, courtesy Jan Zwartendyk.

15 Robert Zwartendijk quoted in 'The man who saved Judaism', *Jerusalem Post International Edition* no. 1860 (29 June 1996), p.1.

16 Orlansky and Hirszprung letters reproduced in Boys Town Jerusalem testimonial volume to Jan Zwartendijk, New York, 9 September 1996.

17 On the efforts of Heppner, Kranzler, and others, see letters from J. Zwartendyk and Ernest G. Heppner in *The Jewish Post and Opinion*, 30 April 1976, p.2; Ed Stattman, 'Japanese granted Dutchman denied laurels for saving Jews', *The Jewish Post and Opinion*, 21 June 1995, p. NAT4; Ed Stattman, 'Dutchman to be honored for 1940 rescues', *The Jewish Post and Opinion*, 8 May 1996, p. NAT2; Steve Lipman, 'The Decent Thing', *The Jewish Week* (New York), 10 May 1996, p.1; letter from Paldiel to Jan Zwartendyk, 7 October 1997; and Phyllis Braun, 'Yad Vashem gives Righteous Gentile his due', *Arizona Jewish Post* (Tucson), 1 May 1998, pp.1, 8.

18 Betty Goodfriend, conversation with the author, October 1999. On Jewish fears of deportation to Siberia, see Warhaftig, *Refugee*, pp.121–23 and Menachem Begin, *White Nights* (New York: Harper & Row, 1977).

19 Sugihara Chiune, 'Report on the activity in Kovno and on cooperation with the Polish forces' (unpublished, in Russian), pp.1–2, cited in Ewa Palasz-Rutkowska and Andrzej T. Romer, 'Polish-Japanese Cooperation during World War II, *Japan Forum* 7/2 (London, Autumn 1995): 287–88; letters from Gutwirth to Tokayer, 24 September 1974 and 17 January 1975, both courtesy of Marvin Tokayer.

20 Sugihara, 'Report', in Palasz-Rutkowska, p.289; Leszek Daszewicz, 'Placowka Wywiadowcza "G": Sprawodania I Documenta' [Polish: Intelligence Agency 'G.' Reports and Documents], England, 1948, quoted in Palasz-Rutkowska, pp.292–93. According to Warhaftig (pp.167–68), 'sometimes small groups of refugees were helped by the Polish Embassy in Tokyo'.

21 Sugihara Yukiko, *Rokusennin-Inochi-No Biza* [Life Visas for 6,000 People] (Tokyo: Asahi-sonorama, 1990), p.73; quoted in Palasz-Rutkowska, pp.293–94.

22 Victor Israelyan was, as of 1996, a Fulbright Scholar at Pennsylvania State University. Jan Zwartendyk, notes on a conversation with Victor Israelyan, 4 June 1996, courtesy of Jan Zwartendyk.

23 Warhaftig provides some evidence for the theory that the exodus of Polish Jews could have given the NKVD some cover for moving some of its agents out of Eastern Europe. He writes that some of the applicants for Soviet transit permits were called in for screening by an official of the NKVD. 'Two students from the Grodno yeshivah informed me [about] their screening, which had taken an hour or two... The NKVD suggested to [one of the students] that he might act as their agent, whatever his destination. The issue of an exit permit was made dependent on his acceptance of the offer, but he claimed to have declined' (*Refugee*, pp.128–29).

24 'The Refugees earned foreign currency from the sale of jewelry and other items. We also took loans from Jews with foreign currency savings' (Warhaftig, *Refugee*, p.130); see also Kranzler, *Japanese, Nazis, and Jews*, pp.312, 338.

25 Zwartendyk, notes on conversation with Israelyan, 4 June 1996.

JEWISH REFUGEE CHILDREN IN SWITZERLAND 1939–1950[1]

Sara Kadosh

WITZERLAND'S TREATMENT of Jewish refugee children during World War II presents a paradox. On the one hand, Switzerland closed its borders to Jewish refugees, including children, and expelled thousands of refugees who had already entered the country. On the other hand, children who were allowed to remain in Switzerland received humane, even generous treatment. Hundreds of Swiss families opened their homes to them; others donated toys, clothing or sums of money for their welfare.

The story of Israeli journalist Shayke Ben Porat provides an example of this paradox. Shayke crossed the border from France to Switzerland with two other boys on 1 January 1943, when he was fifteen years old.[2] Shayke was allowed to remain in the country; he was taken to a temporary reception camp, then sent to a children's home in Geneva supported by wealthy Jewish donors. He attended the most exclusive secondary school in Geneva at the donors' expense. One of the other boys who crossed the border with him, however, was forced to cross the border back to France because his sixteenth birthday had taken place three months earlier. This boy was promptly arrested by a passing German (or French) patrol and never heard from again.

Between 1939 and 1945, approximately five thousand Jewish children aged six to sixteen found refuge in Switzerland.[3] The majority came from Holland, Belgium and France during 1942–44; others arrived from Italy after the Germans occupied that country in September 1943. Several hundred entered Switzerland from Germany and Austria before the outbreak of the war.

The children were cared for officially by two Swiss non-sectarian organizations: the Schweizer Hilfswerk fur Emigranten Kinder (SHEK),[4] and the Schweizerisches Rotes Kreuz (Swiss Red Cross), Kinderhilfe (SRK, KH).[5] These organizations collected the children from border posts and reception camps, and placed them in Jewish or non-Jewish foster families or children's homes.

This paper will examine Switzerland's treatment of Jewish refugee children during World War II. It will describe how the children succeeded in entering Switzerland, how they were cared for after their arrival, and what happened to them after the war. The paper will also discuss the roles played by Jewish and non-Jewish organizations and by the Swiss Jewish community in the care of the children, and will examine the question of why the Jewish community did not assume exclusive responsibility for the children's welfare.

From the rise of Hitler to the end of World War II, Switzerland's immigration policies attempted to limit the entry of Jewish refugees into the country. Although Switzerland had a tradition of asylum dating from the 16th century, during the years following World

War I the Swiss had developed an exaggerated fear of being overrun by foreigners. In 1919, they had established the Department of Alien Police, later headed by Heinrich Rothmund, to regulate the admission of foreigners into the country.[6]

Rothmund sought to prevent the entry into Switzerland of foreigners who, in his opinion, could not be assimilated into the Swiss way of life. These included Jews, especially East European Jews, communists, gypsies and other 'undesirables'. To implement his policies, he increased the control of the Federal government over the twenty-five Swiss cantons, which traditionally had the right to grant residence permits to foreigners. Unemployment in Switzerland during the 1930s strengthened the argument that foreigners would take jobs away from Swiss citizens.[7]

When the first wave of German Jewish refugees arrived in Switzerland in 1933, Rothmund announced that Switzerland would be only a transit country for Jews until they could emigrate elsewhere. Jewish refugees could not work or own property, they had to live in hotels or board with families and they had to report to the police every three months. When the government hinted that needy Jews would be expelled, the Swiss Jewish community agreed to support the Jewish refugees and to facilitate their speedy emigration.[8]

After the Anschluss in March 1938, thousands of Jews crossed the border illegally from Austria to Switzerland. To prevent their expulsion, the Jewish community assumed financial responsibility for them.[9] The community set up reception camps for the refugees and supported them with the help of the American Jewish Joint Distribution Committee (JDC).

With the outbreak of war in September 1939, Switzerland closed its borders. Rothmund instructed the border police not to admit anyone without a visa, with the exception of deserters, prisoners of war and political refugees. Jews were not to be considered political refugees and therefore could not qualify for asylum in Switzerland. In June 1940, Rothmund softened these regulations and agreed to admit pregnant women, invalids, elderly people, unaccompanied children up to age sixteen and families with children up to age sixteen.[10] However, in the spring and summer of 1942, when the deportations began in Belgium, Holland and France, and thousands of refugees tried to enter Switzerland, the government became alarmed. In August 1942 Rothmund again closed the border, canceling all exceptions, despite evidence in his possession of the mass murders in the East and the probable fate of those who were being deported. Rothmund was urged to close the border by the army, which feared an influx of spies or other undesirable elements and which did not want to spare valuable manpower to guard unwanted refugees. The army also feared an invasion from Germany. Rothmund rejected appeals from the Jewish community leadership to modify his policy.[11]

Many sectors of the Swiss public, the press and even many members of Parliament were appalled at the closure of the borders and the reports of cruel repulsing of refugees by border guards. Heart-rending accounts appeared in the newspapers and there were even demonstrations by Swiss border populations against the sending back of refugees. As a result of this public pressure, Rothmund instructed the border guards to be lenient, but so many refugees entered the country that at the end of September 1942 he reinstated the original rules, allowing only children up to age sixteen, the elderly, pregnant women, etc. to be admitted.[12] During the succeeding months, over a thousand children under the age of sixteen (some with false papers lowering their age) were smuggled into Switzerland by French underground organizations.[13] In December 1942 Rothmund again tightened the regulations. Families would be admitted only if they had a child under the age of six. The underground organizations then tried to create artificial family groups which would include small children.[14]

In September 1943, when refugees began arriving from Italy, Rothmund attempted to close the Italian border, and again was forced to back down by public opinion. Girls up to the age of eighteen were now admitted. Finally, in July 1944, Rothmund gave instructions to admit anyone whose life was in danger (in other words to admit all Jews).[15] Switzerland's refugee policy toward Jews thus followed the fortunes of war. When it was clear that the Nazis would be defeated, Switzerland implemented a more liberal refugee policy.

The regulations concerning refugees were not followed consistently either by the border guards or by the government officials themselves. Sometimes border guards or officials were lenient, at other times stricter than the regulations called for. On one occasion, Rothmund decided to deport a group of young people from Belgium ranging in age from fourteen to twenty-one, in order to discourage groups from entering the country with the help of professional smugglers. Appeals by the Swiss Jewish community on behalf of the youngsters had no effect. On the way back to the border, however, the truck carrying the refugees overturned, the injured refugees were taken to a nearby hospital, doctors who learned of their plight alerted the press and the local authorities, and the young people were allowed to stay.[16]

Sometimes groups were admitted to Switzerland if negotiations were carried out in advance on their behalf. Such was the case with the Youth Aliyah group from Villa Emma, which crossed the Italian border to Switzerland in October 1943. The group consisted mainly of German and Austrian youngsters who had escaped to Yugoslavia, then fled to Italy, and were now in danger of arrest following the German occupation of that country. After extensive negotiations by Zionist and Jewish community leaders in Switzerland, and the intervention of non-Jews such as the consul of Yugoslavia, the entire group, including the older children and the adult leaders, was allowed to enter Switzerland.[17] Similarly, during 1943–44, church organizations in Switzerland submitted lists of individuals in need of asylum – including Jews – to the Swiss government, which passed the names on to border officials. Hundreds of persons on these lists were allowed to cross the border.[18] On the other hand, there were cases of children under the age of sixteen, with close relatives and financial resources in Switzerland, who were nevertheless denied entry to the country.[19]

Statistics demonstrate the discriminatory nature of Switzerland's refugee policies. In the summer of 1942, Federal Councillor von Steiger declared that the country could not support any more refugees than the 9,000 (mostly Jews) who had already entered – the lifeboat was full, he asserted.[20] Yet by the end of the war there were 115,000 refugees in Switzerland, of whom only 22,000 were Jews.[21] In 1944, 13,000 non-Jewish children from border areas of France were allowed to enter Switzerland on very short notice, to escape the fighting near their homes.[22] Yet Jewish children who were in danger of deportation to extermination camps were often turned away from the Swiss border.

The success of refugee children in crossing the border to Switzerland depended not only on Swiss refugee policy but also on the assistance of Jewish and non-Jewish organizations and individuals on both sides of the border. On the French side, Jewish organizations such as the Eclaireurs Israelites, a Jewish scout movement, the Mouvement de la Jeunesse, a consortium of Zionist youth movements, and primarily OSE (Oeuvre de Secours aux Enfants), a Jewish welfare organization, organized convoys of children led by Jewish and non-Jewish volunteers and guided by professional smugglers or members of the French Resistance.[23] Others who smuggled children to Switzerland included the

Protestant youth organization CIMADE, l'Amitie Chretienne and Swiss Red Cross personnel.[24] However, the Swiss Red Cross leadership opposed illegal activities; Swiss Red Cross workers who smuggled children across the border were summarily dismissed.

The children sent to Switzerland were those who were in the greatest danger in France. They included children who could not be hidden in the homes of non-Jewish farmers or in churches or convents because they clung to their Jewish religious practices, had obviously foreign mannerisms, had no knowledge of French, or were suspected of being Jewish by their neighbours. Over one thousand children were smuggled into Switzerland by OSE alone from November 1943 to April 1944.[25] Funds to finance the smuggling effort came largely from JDC representatives in France and in Switzerland.[26]

The unexpected arrival in Switzerland of thousands of Jewish refugees – adults and children – during the summer and fall of 1942 posed a serious problem for the Swiss Jewish community. The Jewish community was small, numbering only 18,000 persons in a population of four and a half million – one half of one percent of the population of Switzerland. (By the end of the war, the number of Jewish refugees in the country – approximately 22,000 – exceeded the entire Jewish population.) Furthermore, the undercurrent of antisemitism that permeated much of Swiss society led to a certain insecurity, a lack of self-confidence on the part of Swiss Jewry.[27] Although the Swiss Jewish community organization, the Schweizerischer Israelitischer Gemeindebund (SIG) viewed its primary task as the struggle against antisemitism, the community's leadership also believed in quiet, behind the scenes diplomacy, in not being too obvious or offensive. Even when thousands of refugees were being turned away from the borders, the community leadership refused to attack the government publicly. In early 1943, critics of this quiet diplomacy forced the resignation of Saly Mayer, the head of the SIG, and elected a new leadership. However, the new leadership did not prove to be any more effective *vis-à-vis* the government than the old one.[28]

When large numbers of Jewish refugee children began arriving in Switzerland in 1942 – some with parents, others in children's convoys – the Verband Schweizerischer Judischer Fluchtlingshilfe (VSJF), the Jewish community welfare organization, was already burdened with the care of the over eight thousand Jewish refugees already in the country and the complete financial support of nearly three thousand of them.[29] Perhaps because of this, there was not much objection when the government assigned responsibility for newly-arrived refugee children to two experienced and well-established child care organizations, SHEK and SRK, KH.

The Schweizer Hilfswerk fur Emigranten Kinder (SHEK), a women's organization headed by Dr. Nettie Sutro-Katzenstein (1890–1967), was founded in Zurich in 1933 to provide medical care to the children of impoverished German and Russian refugees living in Paris; within a few years it had branches in eleven Swiss cities. From 1934–39, SHEK brought nearly five thousand children from France to Switzerland for three-month vacations. The children lived with Swiss foster families, received good food, clothes and medical care and returned to France with their health much improved. Although some forty percent of the children were Jewish, and efforts were made to place them in Jewish families or children's homes, the project was conducted on a strictly non-sectarian basis. The success of SHEK in handling the paperwork, the travel arrangements and the children's placements, earned the organization the confidence of Swiss government officials.[30]

In November 1938, in response to a plea from the Jewish orphanage in Frankfurt, SHEK applied for permission to bring three hundred Jewish children from Germany for a six-month stay in Switzerland, pending arrangements for their emigration to the United States. One hundred of the children were from the Jewish orphanage in Frankfurt, the rest from German cities and towns near the Swiss border. After brief negotiations, permission was granted, and in January 1939, the first group of one hundred children from Frankfurt arrived. Most were children whose fathers had been imprisoned in German concentration camps and whose mothers had brought them to the orphanage for safety. During the succeeding months, small groups of children continued to arrive until, by the outbreak of World War II, two hundred fifty German-Jewish children had reached Switzerland. (The full quota of three hundred children was never reached, partly because of the difficulty in obtaining residence permits for the children from the various Swiss cantons.)[31]

Children from the Frankfurt orphanage were placed in two Jewish children's homes – one in Heiden near Zurich, the other in Basel. Children from the German towns were placed with Jewish foster families and, when these were not available, with non-Jewish foster families. Younger children attended local schools, the older ones received vocational training on the theory that such training would be valuable when they would eventually emigrate overseas. Boys learned carpentry, metalwork, auto repair, baking. Girls were sent to a household arts training course.[32] However, only about thirty of the children were able to emigrate from Switzerland.[33] The rest waited helplessly while their desperate and impoverished parents sought ways of leaving Germany. Most of the parents were eventually deported and murdered. The children, who became orphans during the course of the war, remained in Switzerland for six long years.

The fifty older children from the Frankfurt orphanage were sent to Basel, to the care of the Basler Hilfswerk fur Emigranten Kinder, and its remarkable president, Georgine Gerhard. A childless spinster who was secretary of the local girls' school, Georgine Gerhard devoted herself completely to the care of Jewish refugee children until the end of the war. To accommodate the group from Frankfurt, most of whom were Orthodox, she hired a young educator named Eric Hausmann, who was affiliated with Agudat Israel, and secured the necessary permits for him to open a school. After a few months in the town of Buus, the group was transferred to the Hotel Waldeck in the town of Langenbruck.[34]

Georgine Gerhard provided for all the group's needs, including kosher food, even though this increased her expenses significantly. When the older boys were apprenticed to master workmen, she supported their efforts to find workmen who would allow for Jewish Sabbath observance. In 1942, she opened a dormitory for them in Basel so that they could continue their apprenticeships and avoid being transferred to work camps by the government.[35] The Hotel Waldeck then became a reception camp for newly-arrived refugee children.

Georgine Gerhard's devotion to the Frankfurt group earned her their lasting gratitude. After the war, The University of Basel awarded her an honorary doctorate. The children, who maintained contact with her for many years, dedicated a library in her memory in the ORT girls' school in Pardes Chana, Israel.[36]

The Hotel Waldeck in Langenbruck also benefited from an outpouring of generosity from the local population. Farmers donated fruits and vegetables, housewives collected clothes and linens, doctors and dentists provided their services free of charge or at reduced rates, businessmen gave furniture and equipment. This was symptomatic of the positive attitude to refugees in the German-speaking areas of Switzerland. When the Swiss Centrale,[37] an umbrella organization set up in 1936 to aid refugees, conducted a large public collection in 1942, the Swiss population donated over a million and a half francs for refugee aid, but the largest proportion of this sum came from the

German-speaking cantons. Other cantons were less hospitable, and some refused to accept refugees or to contribute to their support.[38]

After the outbreak of the war, SHEK stopped its vacation programmes from France and restricted its activities to the care of some 350 refugee children in Switzerland, including children of impoverished German and Austrian refugees and a few 'vacation' children from Paris who had remained in the country.[39] During 1940–41, the vacation programme was continued by the Schweizerische Arbeitsgemeinschaft fur krieggeschadigte Kinder(SAK), and from January 1942 by the newly-created Schweizerisches Rotes Kreuz, Kinderhilfe (SRK, KH). However, Jewish children were excluded from the programme at the request of the Swiss Federal Police, who feared that the Vichy government might not allow the children to return to France.[40] Criticism of this discrimination in the Swiss press, by Swiss liberals, by SHEK and by the Swiss Jewish community, led Rothmund to allow a small percentage of Jewish children to participate; but the vacation trips were stopped completely by the Germans following the occupation of Vichy in November 1942. After the liberation of France in 1944, the vacation trips were resumed, with the participation of Jewish children, not only from France and Belgium, but also from Displaced Persons Camps in Germany and even from Jewish orphanages in postwar Poland.[41]

In 1940, the Swiss government decided that refugees already in the country (termed 'emigrants' because they were supposed to be planning to emigrate) should be separated from the general population and isolated in work camps. There, they would provide cheap labour for the army, and gain work experience that would help them obtain visas for other countries.[42] On 1 August 1942, in the midst of the mass flight from France, the Swiss government further announced that all newly-arrived refugees entering Switzerland would henceforth be forcibly interned in work camps.[43] On arrival in Switzerland, they would be sent first to a quarantine camp, then to a reception camp and finally to a work camp.

Most of the work camps were in rural areas. The men built roads and fortifications for the army and did agricultural work, as part of the government's programme to increase Switzerland's food supply during the war. The women, who were placed in empty hotels or chateaux, did laundry and sewing for the men's camps. Men and women ages 20–60 were expected to work; young people ages 17–19, were placed in separate camps where they received some vocational training. Refugees who could not work for health reasons and women with small children under the age of six were placed in hotels or boarded with private families. The reception and work camps were staffed by Swiss military personnel who instituted strict military discipline. Many of the these staff members were unsuited for work with a civilian population, some were excessively harsh and even antisemitic.[44]

Prior to the establishment of the camps, the Jewish community had been completely responsible for the upkeep of Jewish refugees. Now, the Swiss government assumed the cost of housing and feeding the refugees who arrived after August 1942. The Jewish community provided the new refugees with clothing, linens, toiletries, pocket money and ritual objects, and organized Jewish cultural and religious activities in the camps.[45]

The establishment of the work camps led directly to the most problematic aspect of the treatment of Jewish refugees in Switzerland – the separation of children from parents. Within a few months after the establishment of the camp system, there were already nearly a thousand children – with or without parents – in the reception camps. Yet the reception camps had absolutely no facilities for children. The refugees slept in large rooms or barracks on straw, there was no privacy, there were no beds, no play areas, no schools, there was no milk, no proper diet for children. SHEK tried to help by sending food, clothes, children's beds, and medicines to the camps but even Swiss officials agreed that a more permanent solution was needed. Children could not follow their parents to the work camps, where husbands and wives were separated, and where no provision had been made for children.[46] Accordingly, on 1 December 1942, the Swiss government requested that SHEK take charge of all refugee children between the ages of six and sixteen, and place them in foster families or children's homes. Financial support for the undertaking would be provided by the SRK, KH. To facilitate the rapid placement of the children, the government waived the requirement for residence permits from the various cantons.[47]

SHEK immediately appealed for Jewish and non-Jewish families to offer free foster care to the Jewish refugee children. However, while applications were received from nine hundred non-Jewish families, only three hundred Jewish families responded.[48] To increase the number of Jewish foster families, the SIG appealed to the Jewish community, women's and Zionist groups visited Jewish homes, additional subsidies were offered, and articles in the Jewish press called for more Jewish families to come forward. One editorial stated, 'It is a question of honor, we do not have the right to fail . . . we will be judged according to our attitude toward these children, orphans in the true sense of the word.'[49] By the end of 1943, the number of Jewish foster families had increased. But there were still more than seven hundred Jewish children in non-Jewish families and more children continued to arrive.[50]

The non-Jews who offered their homes to Jewish children came from all sectors of the population. Some were wealthy, but many were simple people with large families of their own. Although they did not receive payment for the children, they did expect the children to help with housework and, in rural areas, to participate in farm chores. Younger children attended local schools.

Representatives of the local SHEK branches visited the children periodically. If a child could not adapt to his or her foster family, he was transferred to another family.[51] Children who could not be placed or who could not adjust to a foster family, were sent to the Jewish children's homes in Heiden and Langenbruck or to a children's home in Ascona, near the Italian border, run by Lilly Volkart. The most difficult cases were sent to Lilly Volkart, a gifted woman who often succeeded in transforming disturbed and traumatized children into happier, more normal individuals.[52]

The policy of SHEK was to place the children as much as possible in homes of similar background and, especially, to take the religious wishes of the children into account. Nettie Sutro, the director of SHEK, stated that it was important to respect a child's religious feelings – they were the child's only link to the past and provided the child with emotional stability. Therefore, children from religious backgrounds were placed whenever possible with Jewish families or in Jewish children's homes. Children without strong religious preferences were sent to non-Jewish families.[53]

To increase the placement opportunities for Jewish children, SHEK made use of two existing Orthodox institutions, the Institut Ascher in Bex and the Etz Chaim yeshiva in Montreux, both affiliated with Agudat Israel. Children were also placed in the secular Ecole de l'Humanité in Geneva.[54]

During 1943, additional homes for Jewish children were opened with the financial support of SHEK. Les Murailles, a home for fifty children, was opened in Geneva in early 1943, with the help of wealthy Jewish donors. Several months later, an additional home, La Forêt, was opened by the French child-care organization OSE, which had transferred its headquarters to Geneva in 1943. This home offered vocational training courses provided by ORT (Organization for Rehabilitation and Training), which had also relocated to Switzerland.

To accommodate Orthodox children, SHEK opened a home in Ulisbach, where only vegetarian meals were served. Additional homes for Orthodox children were established by the SRK, KH, which took over responsibility from SHEK for children's homes and for newly arrived refugee children at the end of 1943. During 1944, the SRK, KH opened three homes for Orthodox children in cooperation with Agudat Israel at Schwendibach, Grub and Tavannes.[55]

A number of children's homes were also established by the Zionist organizations. In early 1943, the Swiss Zionist Federation opened a Youth Aliyah home in Versoix, near Geneva, for fifty children who were planning to emigrate to Palestine. Later that year, a second Youth Aliyah home was set up in Bex for the group that had arrived from Villa Emma. These homes were supported by the VSJF as well as by SHEK.[56]

Additional Youth Aliyah homes were established in 1944–45 with the support of the SRK, to accommodate young concentration camp survivors who had arrived from Bergen-Belsen, Theresienstadt and Buchenwald. Nearly 1700 Hungarian Jews arrived from Bergen-Belsen in 1944 as a result of negotiations between Saly Mayer and Nazi officials, and over 1200 Jews were freed from Theresienstadt in February 1945 as a result of negotiations by former Swiss Federal councillor Musy. More than three hundred children arrived in these two groups. Then, in June 1945, over 350 young survivors from Buchenwald were brought to Switzerland by the Swiss Red Cross. Since many of the survivors were Orthodox, several of the Youth Aliyah homes – including those at Krattigen and Engelberg – provided for strict observance of Jewish religious law. ORT also set up a number of training courses for Jewish youth in children's homes and in urban centres.[57]

In addition to the Jewish children's homes, SHEK operated a number of non-sectarian children's homes to meet special needs. There was a home for children with tuberculosis, a home for the mentally ill, and a home for bedwetters. One third of the refugee children were bedwetters, and this was a major problem for the children's homes and foster families. In 1943, SHEK allowed the Zwinglibund, a Christian organization, to set up a children's home, after the organization promised not to do any missionizing. In 1944, SHEK, together with the Italian Jewish welfare organization DELASEM, established a school in Tessin for refugees from Italy.[58]

All these homes were improvised in a very short time. SHEK would rent an empty house, the local population would donate furniture and equipment, and the home would be ready in two or three weeks. The director of the home was always a Swiss citizen, but the staff was chosen from among the refugees in the internment camps.[59] The homes received a major part of their funding from SHEK, and, especially during 1944, from the SRK. SHEK, in turn, received half of its funding from JDC and from the South African Jewish War Appeal. The rest of the SHEK budget was covered by funds raised by its chapters by means of bazaars, theatre parties, and other fund raising activities, and by grants from the Central Swiss agency for aid to refugees. By 1945, there were thirty children's homes in Switzerland, more than half of them created specifically for Jewish refugee children.[60]

The treatment of the Jewish refugee children in the foster families and children's homes differed considerably from place to place. Some families treated the children with great warmth and love as if they were their own children. Others viewed the children as cheap household help, forcing them to work long hours at difficult household tasks and punishing them severely for minor 'infractions.'[61]

Discipline in the children's homes was generally quite strict, in accordance with the prevailing ideas of child rearing in Switzerland. Most of the children's homes, with the exception of Lily Volkart's and some of the Youth Aliyah homes, were directed by Swiss citizens who placed great emphasis on cleanliness, order, and obedience. Children who did not conform received harsh punishments such as not getting food or not being able to receive mail – both cruel punishments for children with Holocaust experiences. Bedwetters had to wear a sign indicating their offence. There was little understanding for the psychological and emotional difficulties of the children. Although the refugees who worked in the homes tried to help the children and to ameliorate the most drastic of the regulations, they were not in charge and could not always help. Often there was a lack of understanding of the children's need for simple warmth and kindness.[62]

Before placing children in families or homes, representatives of SHEK interviewed the children and, if the children had parents in Switzerland, obtained the parents' consent for their child's placement. There was a certain cruelty involved in asking parents who had only recently escaped with their most precious possessions – their children – to now give up these children to strangers. But the women of SHEK explained patiently that in a normal home, any home, the children would at least sleep in a bed, have good food and be able to attend school. The parents would be able to visit them, and the children would be removed from the unhealthy and unpleasant atmosphere in the camps. The parents had little choice but to agree.

However, the good intentions of the SHEK women were mixed with a strong dose of paternalism. Parents had little or no control over where their children were placed. Although they were theoretically able to visit the children, SHEK deliberately placed the children far from the parents to minimize such visits, on the grounds that frequent visits would interfere with the child's adjustment to his or her foster family. Parents received permission to spend a few days with their children only once every three months. In some cases, mothers could also see their children during school vacations. Although parents and children could communicate by correspondence, this too, was strictly limited.[63]

The separation of parents from children was widely criticized in the Swiss press, and even by some officials of the Swiss Red Cross. It was pointed out that no other country that received refugees during this period, such as Sweden or Portugal, separated parents and children. Articles in the press claimed that, with a bit of good will, the Swiss authorities could have arranged for facilities for children even in the work camps. There was some criticism of Nettie Sutro for having acquiesced too easily to the separation of families.[64]

In Jewish circles, the negative reaction to the separation of families was compounded by anxiety regarding the children placed with Christian families. To ensure that these children would not be alienated from Judaism, the VSJF established a Department for Religious Instruction for refugee children. The head of this Department, Georges Bloch, was also the treasurer of SHEK. Classes for six hundred refugee children were opened in Jewish community centres, while traveling teachers gave individual instruction once every two weeks to approximately fifteen hundred Jewish children in rural areas. Some children were brought to Jewish families for Jewish holidays.[65]

With the establishment of the Department for Religious Instruction in September 1943, the official Jewish leadership believed that they had fulfilled their responsibility to the Jewish refugee children. Although acknowledging that Jewish children ought to be in a Jewish milieu, in the absence of Jewish foster families, the leaders believed that Jewish instruction once or twice a month was sufficient to maintain the children's identity.

Zionist and Orthodox (Agudat Israel) circles disagreed, however, insisting that a way must be found to bring Jewish children into Jewish surroundings. Nathan Schwalb, the Hehalutz representative, had argued, as early as 1941 – even before the great wave of refugees arrived – that Jewish youngsters should not be placed in a non-Jewish environment.[66]

The controversy deepened in 1944, when accusations of missionizing activity, some directed at the SRK, appeared in the Jewish press. Many of the foster parents were religious Christians who took the children regularly to church, enrolled them in Sunday School and had them meet with the parish priest. Some children were pressured by the priests and the families to adopt Christianity and, in a few cases, children were baptized. Nettie Sutro claimed that these were only isolated cases and that the children were eventually returned to the Jewish community.[67] However, some observers believed that the SRK, which was in charge of placing refugee children who arrived in 1944, was less scrupulous than SHEK in screening the prospective foster parents and in taking into account the children's religious preferences.[68] Furthermore, children who had arrived from Germany in 1939, had already been in Christian families for five years – and the longer the children remained, the more likely they were to be alienated from Judaism.

During 1945 and 1946, Zionist and Agudat Israel leaders continued to call for the transfer of Jewish children, especially those who were orphans, to a Jewish milieu. The Zionists argued that it was necessary to prepare the children for emigration to Palestine; the Aguda, that it was necessary to educate the children toward an Orthodox way of life.[69] When Chief Rabbi Herzog of Palestine visited Switzerland in the summer of 1946, he seconded the call for the removal of Jewish children from non-Jewish foster families and children's homes.[70]

The Zionist argument accorded well with the government's desire to encourage the emigration of all refugees as soon as possible. Thus, beginning in 1944, orphan children and those who expressed interest in emigrating to Palestine, were transferred from foster families and children's homes to Youth Aliyah homes. There they received vocational training and instruction in the Hebrew language.[71]

However, the transfer of all Jewish refugee children to a Jewish environment was a task that the Swiss Jewish community found impossible to accomplish. The SIG admitted in 1945 that it could not find enough Jewish families willing to take children, and, at the end of 1946, nearly two hundred Jewish children still remained in Christian environments.[72] Zionist leaders from Palestine who visited Switzerland in 1946 were forced to acknowledge that a solution to the problem was simply not available.[73]

Swiss Jewish community leaders agreed that it was important to transfer Jewish children to a Jewish milieu, especially in view of the decimation of millions of children during the Holocaust. The Jewish organizations wanted to ensure that not a single additional child be lost to the Jewish community. At the same time, however, some leaders cautioned that the repeated calls for the transfer of the children would offend the Swiss activists who had cared so devotedly for the children during the war years. Such calls implied gross ingratitude to the hundreds of Swiss families who had taken the children into their homes without any financial remuneration, and could even arouse antisemitism.[74]

The public controversy did, in fact, arouse considerable resentment among the foster parents and the women of SHEK. Dr. Nettie Sutro announced that the attacks on SHEK and the demands for the transfer of children had damaged her work irreparably. She closed the SHEK offices at the end of 1947 and transferred responsibility for Jewish refugee children (including those still in non-Jewish homes) to the VSJF.[75] She even refused to participate in a plan put forward by the Zionist movement and the Swiss Jewish community, to bring five hundred young Holocaust survivors from Poland for a temporary stay in Switzerland, where they could prepare for emigration to Palestine. She declared that she could not work for a nationalist organization after having headed a non-sectarian one. Since the Swiss Jewish community lacked the resources and skills to carry out such a plan without her assistance, the entire project had to be abandoned.[76]

However, the public controversy over the placement of Jewish children, which had begun in 1944, apparently had an effect on the treatment of young concentration camp survivors who reached Switzerland during 1944–45. Unaccompanied children from Bergen-Belsen and Theresienstadt were sent directly to Jewish children's homes – many to Youth Aliyah homes – rather than to foster families.[77] Members of the Buchenwald group spent about two months in an SRK children's home. Then, in response to pressure from the Jewish community, they were transferred to three Youth Aliyah homes according to their religious preferences: the Hehalutz (secular Zionist) home at Bex, the Mizrachi home at Krattigen or the Agudat Israel home in Engelberg. Financial support for the homes was provided by the SRK, while the educational programmes were conducted by the respective organizations.[78] Under the influence of the Zionist representatives, many of the Buchenwald survivors emigrated to Palestine, but some chose to complete ORT training courses in Switzerland and to join relatives in France, the United States or other overseas destinations.[79]

The Swiss Jewish community's difficulty in providing a Jewish milieu for the thousands of refugee children who reached Switzerland during the war years, reflected the community's internal weakness. According to Nettie Sutro, the Jewish community could not provide sufficient places for the children because the community was small – there were only three thousand Jewish households. Some of the people were poor, and some already had refugees – friends or relatives – living with them.[80] When SHEK sought to place Orthodox children with Orthodox families, they generally had to offer the families a financial subsidy.

Other observers were less charitable. Nathan Schwalb stated that some Swiss Jews were ready to pay for the support of Jewish children, but not to take them into their own homes.[81] Instead, they donated books and clothing, organized cultural and religious activities and contributed toward individual sponsorships.[82] Others criticized the VSJF which proved unable to keep pace with the demand for Jewish placements for refugee children.[83] Otto Heim, head of the VSJF, admitted in 1945, 'When Jewish children must be brought to Christian families, the Jews are at fault.'[84]

It is possible that the Jewish community could have established more Jewish children's homes as an alternative to placement in families. Saly Mayer, the JDC representative in Switzerland, supported such a solution, urged the Jewish community to establish such homes, and offered to contribute JDC funds if necessary. We have seen that Agudat Israel, the Zionist movement and OSE all took the initiative in establishing such homes. However, the official Swiss Jewish community (SIG), while requesting that Jewish directors be appointed and offering to contribute financially, preferred to rely on SHEK for the creation of children's homes.[85]

In fact, some of the acculturated Swiss Jewish community leaders, were uncomfortable with the idea that Jews should be openly separatist. When the SIG appealed for Jewish families in 1943, Sylvain Guggenheim, then head of the VSJF, objected to the use of the slogan 'Jewish children in Jewish families'.[86] Guggenheim, Georges Bloch and others minimized the danger to Jewish children of remaining in a non-Jewish environment, provided there was some supervision by the Jewish community. In 1946, the VSJF concluded an agreement with SHEK to the effect that Jewish children would be removed from Christian families only if there was evidence that the Jewish children were being alienated from their religion.[87] In this respect the leaders of SHEK and the Swiss Jewish community shared a common philosophy.

With the end of the war, the treatment of Jewish refugee children in Switzerland entered its third stage – the return of the children to their families or to the Jewish community. Anxious to ensure that all refugees leave the country as soon as possible, the Swiss government set up a commission which included representatives of the Jewish organizations – OSE, JDC, the Jewish Agency, HICEM[88] – and representatives of SHEK, to examine each child's file and to search for individual solutions for the children outside Switzerland. Pressure from the government led SHEK to arrange for the rapid departure of as many children as possible, even though SHEK preferred to give older children vocational training before their emigration. One psychologist even claimed that it was preferable not to uproot young children who had finally adjusted to their foster homes.[89]

The commission's activities were greatly facilitated by the Central Card Index of OSE and by the questionnaires of SHEK. After OSE relocated to Geneva in 1943, it registered every refugee child arriving in Switzerland from France (where many of the children had been in OSE children's homes). OSE staff members interviewed the children in the reception camps and recorded any shred of information that might lead to establishing the child's identity at a later date. Representatives of SHEK also interviewed the children before determining their placement in foster families or children's homes. In addition, SHEK conducted a survey in 1945 of over seven hundred refugee children. Data provided by the two organizations helped establish the children's identity and locate the children's relatives after the war.[90]

During 1945–47, the majority of the Jewish refugee children in Switzerland were reunited with family members in France or Belgium. Some children joined relatives in the United States or other overseas locations, and about five hundred orphans emigrated to Palestine. By the end of 1947, when SHEK closed its doors, several hundred refugee children remained in Switzerland and they now became the responsibility of the VSJF.[91]

In 1947, the Swiss government passed a new law granting permanent asylum to certain categories of refugees. Children up to age sixteen, without relatives, or with mental or physical problems, qualified under the law to remain in Switzerland. Elderly refugees, those with special talents or with spouses who were Swiss citizens, also qualified. As a result of this law, some Jewish refugee children still in Switzerland were adopted by their foster families. Some of the older children, now adults, married Swiss citizens. According to Nettie Sutro, about forty-five refugee children received permanent asylum in Switzerland. According to Saly Mayer, however, in 1950 there were still a small number of Jewish refugee children in non-Jewish families under the supervision of the VSJF. It would seem, therefore, that as a result of the Swiss government's anxiety to ensure the departure of Jewish refugees, nearly all the Jewish refugee children in Switzerland were reunited with their families, sent to Palestine or placed in Jewish community institutions.[92]

Switzerland provides an example of cooperation between Jewish and non-Jewish individuals and organizations in the care of Jewish refugee children. Among the Jewish organizations that helped care for the children were the VSJF, OSE, ORT, Hehalutz, and Agudat Israel. The non-Jewish organizations included, in addition to SHEK and SRK, KH, the Quakers, the Unitarian Service, and Protestant and Catholic Refugee Committees.[93]

However, the most decisive role in the care of the children was played by the women of SHEK. Members of the local SHEK chapters raised funds to support the children and handled all the problems of the children in foster families or children's homes in their respective areas. They dealt with local government and school officials, obtained clothing from the SRK, handled medical emergencies, investigated new families, and visited the children, mostly on a volunteer basis with a minimum of paid staff.[94] SHEK was also the only Swiss organization that arranged for the collective entry of a group of refugees to Switzerland prior to World War II. Nettie Sutro and her co-workers met the children at the border when they arrived from Germany in 1939. As Saly Mayer noted, 'These women had the courage ... to tell the Swiss Government they wanted to have children in Switzerland ... these women had the courage to ask for Jewish children ... How nice to be privileged to report that it's been women who had the courage to do this.'[95]

Switzerland's attitude toward Jewish refugee children was a complex one. It reflected the struggle between conservative elements who wanted to limit the entry of Jewish refugees into the country and liberal groups who welcomed the refugees and were willing to shelter them. It reflected the long-standing Swiss tradition of placing poor and disadvantaged children in foster families for temporary care, in contrast to the refusal of certain cantons to even harbour Jewish refugee children. The Swiss government itself served both as the agent that attempted to exclude Jewish refugee children from Switzerland and the authority that supported the efforts of non-sectarian, Jewish and Christian organizations to care for them.

The treatment of Jewish refugee children in Switzerland also reflected the Swiss Jewish community's internal divisions and its insecurity *vis-à-vis* Swiss government and society. The community's acculturated and assimilated leaders, satisfied that the children's lives had been saved and that their basic needs were being met, were reluctant to challenge either the government or the non-sectarian organizations over issues such as the placement of children in non-Jewish families or the provision of more intensive Jewish education for them. The raising of such issues would have clashed with the image of complete integration into Swiss society which the Swiss Jewish leadership strove to maintain. Although pressure from Zionist and Orthodox groups induced the Swiss Jewish leadership to take a somewhat more active role in the care of survivors and refugee children, the major responsibility for the children remained – until the end of 1947 – with the non-sectarian, government-supported organizations. Thus, the Swiss Jewish community, which might have been the natural address for the care of Jewish refugee children, played only a secondary role in carrying out this historic mission.

NOTES

1 Research for this paper was conducted under the auspices of the International Institute for Holocaust Research, Yad Vashem.

2 Yeshayahu (Shayke) Ben Porat, *Et LeHazkir* (Typewritten Memories), (Tel-Aviv:Zmora Bitan, 1994), pp.74–99.

3 Precise statistics on the number of children who entered Switzerland during the war years are difficult to determine. According to Guido Koller, 'Entscheidungen über Leben und Tod: Die Behördliche Praxis in der schweizerischen Flüchtlingspolitik während des Zweiten Weltkrieges',

Zeitschrift des Schweizerischen Bundesarchivs: Studien und Quellen (Bern: Paul Haupt, 1996), p.88, ten thousand refugee children entered Switzerland, of whom more than ninety percent were Jewish. Approximately six thousand were ages six to sixteen, four thousand below the age of six. According to Nettie Sutro, *Jugend Auf Der Flucht* (Zurich: Chronos Verlag, 1952), p.232, approximately five thousand refugee children were ages six to sixteen.

4 Also known as the Comité suisse d'aide aux enfants d'émigrés.

5 Also known as the Croix-Rouge suisse, secours aux enfants.

6 For a review of Switzerland's refugee policies, see Carl Ludwig, *La politique pratiquée par la Suisse à l'égard des réfugiés au cours des années 1933 à 1955*: Rapport adressé au Conseil fédéral á l'intention des conseils législatifs par le professeur Carl Ludwig, Bale, p.12ff.; Andre Lasserre, *Frontières et camps: Le refuge en Suisse de 1933 à 1945* (Lausanne: Editions Payot, 1995), p.13ff.; Jacques Picard, *Die Schweiz und die Juden 1933–45* (Zurich: Chronos Verlag, 1994), p.58ff.

7 See Lasserre, pp.15–40; Ludwig, p.48.

8 Ludwig, pp.39, 48ff.

9 Lasserre, p.57; Ludwig, p.71.

10 Ludwig, p.169.

11 Ludwig, pp.190ff, 254; Emmanuel Haymann, *Le Camp du Bout du Monde: 1942, des enfants juifs de France à la frontière suisse* (Lausanne: Pierre-Marcel Favre, 1984), pp.229–230.

12 Ludwig, pp.187–88, 195ff., 209.

13 Sutro, pp.91ff.

14 Ludwig, p.218; Sutro, p.97.

15 Ludwig, pp.247–249, 254–255, 279.

16 See Ludwig, p.235; Haymann, 126–27; Letter to Frau Dr. Kurz, 16.7.44, Yad Vashem Archives (henceforth YV), Saly Mayer Archives (henceforth SM), file 24 (JM 117.21). According to this letter, the group was arrested after contacting the Youth Aliyah home in Versoix. A staff member of the home who tried to help them was himself imprisoned.

17 Heini Bornstein, *Ha-ee Schweiz* (Switzerland – An Island) [Hebrew], (Tel Aviv: Moreshet, 1996), pp.143–45; see also Yael Orvieto, *Parashat 'Yaldei Villa Emma': Sippur Hatzalata shel Kevutzat Yeladim Bi-Tekufat Hashoah*, M.A. thesis, Hebrew University, 1996, pp.98–100.

18 Ludwig, pp.212–213.

19 Haymann, pp.143–146; Alfred A. Hasler, *The Lifeboat Is Full: Switzerland and the Refugees 1933–45* (New York: Funk and Wagnalls, 1969), p.173.

20 Hasler, p.175; Haymann, p.74.

21 Ludwig, p.303; Haymann, pp.239–240; Lasserre, p.219.

22 Lasserre, p.205.

23 See Picard, pp.435ff; Also Lucien Lazare, *Rescue as Resistance: How Jewish Organizations Fought the Holocaust in France* (New York: Columbia University Press, 1996), pp.183–202.

24 Sabine Zeitoun, *Ces Enfants Qu'il Fallait Sauver* (Paris: Albin Michel, 1989), pp.268–69; Anne-Marie Im Hof-Piguet, *Fluchtweg durch die Hintertur: Eine Rotkreuz-Helferin im besetzten Frankreich 1942–44* (Frauenfeld: Verlag Im Waldgut, 1987), pp.61ff; Picard, p.439.

25 Picard, p.438. See also Renée Poznanski, 'De l'action philanthropique à la resistance humanitaire', and Laurence Rosengart, 'Les Maisons de l'OSE: parcours d'une enfance fragmentée' in Martine Lemalet (ed.), *Au secours des enfants du siècle: Regards croisés sur l'OSE* (Nil editions, 1993), pp.73–75 and 103–105.

26 Yehuda Bauer, *American Jewry and the Holocaust: The American Jewish Joint Distribution Committee 1939–45* (Detroit: Wayne State University Press, 1981), pp.244–254; Lazare, p.257ff.; Picard, pp.436–437; Poznanski, p.75; See also Judith Hemmendinger-Feist, 'L'Union O.S.E. A Geneve – 1944–1945' in *Notre Mémoire*, OSE (December 1993) pp.74–78.

27 Picard, pp.51–70.

28 Lasserre, pp. 181–82; Bornstein, pp.85–86; Picard, pp.155–156, 231–239, 279–288.

29 See *Dix Années d'activité de l'Aide aux réfugiés en Suisse 1933–1943* (Zurich: Union Suisse d'Aide aux Réfugiés Juifs), p.43.

30 See Eveline Zeder, *Ein Zuhause für Judische Fluchtlingskinder: Lilly Volkart und ihr Kinderheim in Ascona 1934–1947* (Zurich: Chronos Verlag, 1998), pp.37–69 and Sutro, p. 23ff.

31 Sutro, pp.67–74; Lasserre, pp.65–66.

32 See Gernot Romer, *In der Fremde leben meine Kinder… Lebensschicksale kindlicher judischer Auswanderer aus Schwaben unter der Naziherrschaft* (Augsburg: Wissner Verlag, 1996), pp.63–71; also Alfred A. Hasler with Ruth K. Westheimer, *Die Geschichte der Karola Siegel* (Bern: Benteli Verlag, 1976); Interview with Ilse Gutman, 8 December 1998.

33 Sutro, p.75.

34 See Erich A. Hausmann, *Hineni: Erinnerungen eines judischen Padagogen, Ein Bericht aus bewegter Zeit* (Basel: Verlag Morascha, 1996), p.34ff.

35 Sutro, pp.126–28; Hausmann, pp.67–71. The government work camps for teenagers made no provision for Sabbath observance.

36 Hausmann, p.66.

37 Schweizerischen Zentralstelle fur Fluchtlingshilfe.

38 Tätigkeitsbericht, Basler Hilfe fur Emigranten Kinder, Mai 1942 – Mai 1943, YV, M20/60; Picard, p.379; Lasserre, pp.184–185.

39 Sutro, pp.63,80; Lasserre, pp.103, 143. SHEK even set up a school in Zurich for the children of refugees. See also Achten Jahresbericht 1942, Bernische Hilfswerk für Emigranten Kinder, YV, M20/60.

40 The SRK, KH conducted children's homes and other child welfare activities in France. See Lasserre, pp.144–145; Picard, p.431; See also Antonia Schmidlin, 'Dunant oder Helvetia: Welches Geschlecht hat die humanitare Schweiz?: Schweizerische Kinderhilfe in den 1930er und 1940er Jahren' in *Frauen und Staat, Berichte des Schweizerischen Historikertages in Bern, October 1996, Itinera* (Fasc. 20.1998), pp.137–147; Odette Micheli, *Aperçu sur l'activité de la Croix-Rouge Suisse secours aux enfants en France 1942–1947* (Geneva: Croix Rouge Suisse, 1949), p.12; Zeitoun, pp.262–263, SM-Lisbon telephone conversation 29 March 1942 in YV, SM/7 and 15 Feb. 1943, SM/8 (JM 117.14). See also *Israelitische Wochenblatt*, 3 April 1942 ('Judische Kinder bei den Kindertransporten'), 24 April 1942 ('Zur Frage der Kinderhilfsaktion'), 1 May 1942, ('Judische Kinder in die Schweiz').

41 Odeli, p.61; Lasserre, p.324.

42 Lasserre, pp.133–136; Ludwig, pp.165–166.

43 Ludwig, p.261.

44 Lasserre, p.238ff.; Ludwig, pp.237–238, 260–269ff; Haymann, pp.115–121.

45 Katzki (Lisbon) to AJDC (N.Y), 17 September 1943, YV, SM/1; SM – Lisbon conversation, 31 April 1943, YV, SM/6 (JM117.13).

46 Lasserre, p.238; Sutro, p.101; Ludwig, p.260.

47 Sutro, p.97; Lasserre, p.321; Ludwig, p.213.

48 Lasserre, p.329; SM-Lisbon telephone conversation, 16 November 1943, YV, SM/8 (JM 117.14), *Israelitische Wochenblatt*, 18.12.42 ('Neunhundert Judische kinder suchen ein judisches zuhause') and ('Die Unterbringung der Kinder').

49 *Israelitische Wochenblatt* 30 December 1942, ('L'honneur juif'), 4 December 1942 ('Judische Familien für Fluchtlingskinder gesucht'), 8 January 1943 ('Helft dem judischen Flüchtlingskind'), 29 January 1943 ('An die judischen Familien').

50 SM-Lisbon telephone conversation 22 November 1943, YV, SM/4 (JM 117.14).

51 Sutro, pp.110–112; Interview with Ilse Gutman.

52 Zeder, pp.53–54, 73ff. Lilly Volkert, a Swiss citizen, had operated a children's home in Ascona for Jewish and non-Jewish children since the mid-1920s.

53 Sutro, pp.99, 115ff. See also Tätigkeitsbericht 1 Juli 1942–30 Juni 1943, St. Galler Hilfe für Emigrantenkinder, YV, M20/60. Non-Jewish children were also placed according to their religious preferences.

54 See Sutro, pp.145–146; Interview with Shulamit Katan, 8 December 1998.

55 See Bornstein, 211–212. Also see *Hamagid: Blatt der Schweizerischen Aguda-Jugend* (Zurich, December 1944), pp.3–4.

56 See Sutro, pp.100, 115, 250ff; Haymann, pp.179–185; Isaac Pougatch. *A l'Ecoute de Son Peuple; un éducateur raconte* (Paris: Albin Michel, 1980), pp.235–262; Bornstein, pp.144–45; Ben-Porat, pp.84–98.

57 See Lasserre, pp.207–208; Ludwig, pp.286–287; Sutro, p.174, Bauer, pp.408–34; SM-Lisbon conversation 25 June 1945, YV, SM/10 (JM 117.15).

58 Sutro, pp.102, 144–148, 203.

59 See Zentralkommission für Fluechtlingskinder des Schweizerischen Roten Kreuz, Kinderhilfe, und des Schweizer Hilfswerk für Emigrantenkinder, 'Richtlinien betr. Heimleitung und Heimpersonal in der Schweiz,' Histadrut Archives (henceforth HA), Nathan Schwalb Collection, III 37A-1-118.

60 SM-Lisbon telephone conversation, 10 April 1945, YV, SM/10 (JM 117.15).

61 Interviews with Annette Flau, 28 October 1998, and Ilse Gutman.

62 Zeder, pp.90ff.; Interview with Shulamit Katan.

63 Sutro, pp.98–99. 130–138.

64 Picard, p.446–448; Lasserre, p.327; Regina Kagi-Fuchsmann, *Das gute Herz genugt nicht: Mein Leben und mein Arbeit* (Zurich: Ex Libris Verlag, 1968), p.185. See also *Israelitische Wochenblatt* 20 November 1942 ('Zur Frage der Fluchtlingskinder'), 23 November 1942 ('Fluchtlinge in der Schweiz'), 27 November 1942 ('Trennung der Mutter von den Kindern?') See also Protokoll der ausserordentlichen Delegierten versammlung des Schweizerischen Israelitischen Gemeindebundes, 23 January 1944, Bern, nebst Bericht über die Tätigkeit des Verbandes Schweizerischer Judischer Fluchtlingshilfen in Jahre 1943, p.20, in YV, M20/54.

65 See YV, 03/5376; Sutro, p.120; Picard, pp.316, 446; Lasserre, pp 328–329; Zeder, pp.64, 119–120.

66 See conversation with Nathan Schwalb 4 June 1941, YV, SM/24 (JM 1721).

67 Picard, p.446; Lasserre, p.328; YV, 03/9554; Sutro, pp.116–20.
    Some SHEK officials, such as Madame Hohermuth, head of the Geneva Section, minimized the risk of baptism. Even Nettie Sutro contended that religious training was necessary only for children from religious families. See *Israelitische Wochenblatt*, 19 September 1943 ('Fluchtlingskinder und Jomtau-wim').

68 Note by Saly Mayer, 30 June 1944, YV, SM/11a (JM 117.15); Lasserre, p.323.

69 SM-Lisbon conversations 18 April 1945, 9 May 1945, 14 May 1945, YV, SM/10 (JM 117.15); Sternbuch to Heim, 4 October 1945, YV SM/21 (JM 117.20); also Jeschiwah der Waadat Alijat Hanoar mit Dobkin und Silberberg, 6 March 1946, Central Zionist Archives (CZA), L58/877.

70 *Israelitische Wochenblatt*, 31 May 1946.

71 Picard, p.447. See for example R. Kohn to SRK,KH, 14 June 1944, HA III, 37A-1-117B and Liste der für Weggis vorgesehenen Chaverim, HA III-37A-1-118. (There was a Youth Aliyah home in Weggis.) Also Elkan to Landauer, 20 September 1946, CZA, L58/848. Also SM-Lisbon conversation 14 May 1945, YV, SM/10 (JM117.15).

72 There were approximately six hundred Jewish refugee children still in Switzerland. See Elkan to Landauer, 20 September 1946 and Elkan to Youth Aliyah, Jerusalem, 28 November 1946, CZA, L58/848. See also 'Informationsbrief an die Mitglieder unserer Gemeinden', Schweiz. Israel. Gemeindebund, (no.3, November 1945), CZA L58/819.

73 Beyth to Elkan, 10 December 1946, CZA L58/848. See also Notiz über die Jeschiwah der Waadat Alijath Hanoar, 18 June 1946, and Yeshivat Vaadat Alijat Hanoar, 6 March 1946, CZA L58/877. Some SHEK officials and some of the foster parents also objected to removing children from their foster families.

74 SM-Lisbon conversation 14 May 1945, YV, SM/10 (JM 117.15); Heim to Sternbuch, 5 October 1945, YV, SM/21 (JM 117.20); see also Jahresbericht und Rechnungs-Ablage des Schweizerischen Israelitischen Gemeindebundes für das Jahr 1945, YV, SM/3 (JM117.13); also 'Informationsbrief', November 1945, CZA, L58/819.

75 See Elkan to Landauer, 20 September 1946, CZA, L58/848.

76 See Notiz über Besprechungen in Zurich am 4.und 5. September wegen Unterbringung von 500 Kindern und Jugend-Aliyah-Komite und Drive, 5 September 1946, CZA, L58/455. Also Beyth to Landauer, 13 August 1946, CZA, L58/848.

77 This was partly because of the reluctance of foster parents to deal with the difficult behaviour problems of Holocaust survivors. See Sutro, pp.139–41, 183, 208; Picard, pp.317, 447–48; Schwalb to Bleuler, 22 January 1945, HA III-37A-1–118. See also Charlotte Weber, *Gegen den Strom der Finsternis: Als Betreurin in Schweizer Fluchtlingsheimen 1942–1945* (Zurich, Chronos Verlag, 1994), pp.183ff.

78 See 'Informationsbrief', November 1945, p.12, CZA, L58/819; Jahresbericht, SIG, 1945 (see note 74); see also correspondence in HA III 37A–1–118.

79 See Weber, pp.251ff; also Lewinsky to Beyth, 6 September 1945, CZA L58/811. Akiba Lewinsky, who arrived in Switzerland in June 1945 to head the Continental office of Youth Aliyah, was angered by the efforts of various organizations – ORT, OSE, Aguda – to deflect the Buchenwald survivors from the aim of Aliyah.

80 Sutro, pp.114ff.

81 Interviews with Nathan Schwalb (Dror), December 1994 and February 1995.

82 See *Israelitische Wochenblatt*, 30 September 1943 ('Zur Versorgung der Emigrantenkinder'); also 'Die Yiddishe Plitim In Der Schweiz', March 1944, unsigned report in YV, P7/41.

83 The VSJF itself admitted its failure to find places for the children. See Tätigkeitsbericht und Rechnungs – Ablage des Schweizerischen Israelitischen Gemeindebundes für das Jahr 1944, pp.11–12 in YV, SM/3 (JM 117.13). Also Elkan to Youth Aliyah, 28 November 1946, CZA L58/848.

84 Heim to Sternbuch, 5 October 1945, in YV, SM/21 (JM 11720).

85 Tätigkeitsbericht und Rechnungs-Ablage des Schweizerischen Israelitische Gemeindebundes für das Jahr 1943, p.11, in YV, SM/3 (JM117.13). See also SM-Lisbon conversation 18 May 1943, YV, SM/8 and SM-Lisbon conversations 19 March 1944, 16 April 1944 and 17 May 1944, YV, SM/9 (JM117.14).

86 Lasserre, p.329.

87 Picard, p.449, Zeder, pp.64, 119–120. Lilly Volkart objected to requests by Orthodox Jewish groups to transfer some of the children in Ascona to Orthodox Jewish homes.

88 HIAS–ICA–EMIGDIRECT.

89 See Picard, pp.451–454. See also B. Hohermuth, *Aide Aux Emigrés*, '*Zukunftspläne Der Fluchtlinge in der schweiz* (Genf, July 1945), pp.102, 107–121. Also Lasserre, p.447.

90 See 'Central Card Index', 20 December 1944, in YV, SM/26 (JM 117.21). See also Hohermuth, *loc. cit.*; Feist, *op.cit.*

91 According to Saly Mayer four hundred children remained in Switzerland at the end of 1947; according to SHEK statistics, seven hundred. See Address by Saly Mayer to JDC Country Directors Conference, 16 April 1948, p.66, YV, SM/6 (JM 117.14); Sutro, p.234.

92 Sutro, pp.174–179; Ludwig, pp.326–330; Interview with Ilse Gutman; also Jahresbericht und Rechnungs-Ablage des Schweizerischen Israelitischen Gemeindebundes für das Jahr 1950, p.11, YV, SM/6 (JM117.14).

93 Tätigkeitsbericht der Sektion Genf des Schweiz. Hilfswerkes für Emigranten Kinder, 1 September 1942–31 August 1943, YV, M20/60.

94 Interview with Ilse Gutman.

95 Mayer to JDC Conference, 1948 (see note 91).

AN ETHICS OF RESCUE FOR THE FUTURE:
ARISTOTELIAN AND LEVINASIAN PERSPECTIVES

Steven Kepnes

G IVEN THE brutality and coldness with which the Nazis murdered the Jews of Europe and the complicity and apathy of most bystanders, post-Holocaust social science and philosophy has seen renewed attention to ethics and moral psychology. Social scientists such as Stanley Milgram, Robert Lifton and Ervin Staub[1] have focused on the kinds of social and psychological processes which were necessary to produce the Holocaust. Philosophers have taken a slightly different approach and viewed the Holocaust as a kind of moral barometer which revealed the flaws in Enlightenment rationality and ethics. This has led to a re-evaluation of modern Kantian ethics and a search for an ethical theory which could serve as a guide to prevent future genocides. For further resources to this end social scientists and philosophers have jointly turned to investigations of the statistically insignificant yet morally critical presence of non-Jewish rescuers of Jews during the Holocaust. Ethicists and social scientists have been attracted to rescuers not only because they offer some hope for signs of moral life during the Holocaust but also because they believe that the rescuers may be able to provide models for an ethics of rescue which they could employ in the prevention of genocide today and in the future.

The most significant piece of social scientific scholarship to this end has been *The Altruistic Personality* published by Samuel and Pearl Oliner in 1988.[2] This study focuses on the obvious question: when most of Europe did nothing to save Jews, why did the rescuers take the risks to save them? After interviewing 700 rescuers, bystanders, and survivors the answer that the Oliners came up with was that rescue activity was the outgrowth of a combination of psychological and sociological factors that had created 'altruistic personality' types. The Oliners' most significant finding was that rescue activity was not the result of spontaneous acts of kindness by isolated individuals but, rather, rescue was produced by long-standing patterns of behaviour that could be traced back to parental modelling, child-rearing practices and social systems of support. In short, the Oliners found that rescue behaviour was learned behaviour. And in the conclusion of their study, the Oliners suggested that we today could learn from the rescuers how to foster altruistic activity and prevent future genocides.

In the aftermath of the Oliners' path-breaking work, philosophers and social scientists have begun the necessary process of development and critique of their study and its conclusions. This paper follows on the heels of a number of philosophical interpretations of the Oliners' work. After briefly reviewing the Oliners' conclusions I turn to the appreciative philosophical interpretation of Victor Seidler. Seidler used the Oliners' study to critique modern Kantian ethics and argue for an ethics of care based on human feelings and relations.[3] I argue that neither the Oliners nor Seidler go far enough in articulating the import of ethical thought and communal ethical traditions and turn to Aristotle and to Emmanuel Levinas to provide these dimensions. I suggest that Aristotle's notion of the virtuous character supplies a philosophical correlate to the Oliners' notion of the altruistic personality which highlights rational and communal elements which the Oliners miss. Levinas, on the other hand, provides a necessary corrective to Aristotle because he most clearly articulates the responsibilities of the virtuous character to 'the other'. For if altruism and an ethics of rescue begins, as the Oliners and Aristotle suggest, with one's own family and community, it must end with obligations to others who lie beyond the home community.

THE RESCUER AS THE ALTRUISTIC PERSONALITY

Samuel and Pearl Oliner argue that rescue was the outgrowth of an altruistic personality which was developed through a combination of 'personal and external social' factors.[4] Parental modelling, social conditioning, personal characteristics and values led to the development of the 'altruistic personality' who would voluntarily take 'life-threatening risks'[5] to rescue Jews from the Holocaust without expecting any external rewards. What distinguished the altruistic personalities of the rescuers of Jews during the Holocaust for the Oliners was their 'capacity for extensive relationships – their stronger sense of attachment to others and their feeling of responsibility for the welfare of others, including those outside their immediate familial or communal circles.'[6] Of all the factors they enumerate, the key to altruistic behaviour for the Oliners seems to be the psychological concept of 'attachment' – trusting, secure, and affectionate relationships between persons beginning with the parent-child bond and moving outward to others.[7] In the concluding chapter of their book the Oliners give us a recipe for relationships of attachment and for the consequent altruistic personality.

> It begins in close family relationships in which parents model caring behavior and communicate caring values. Parental discipline tends toward leniency.... It includes heavy doses of reasoning – explanations of why behaviors are inappropriate.... [P]arents set high standards they expect their children to meet.... [And they] model such behaviors.... Out of such benevolent experiences children learn to trust those around them. Securely rooted in their familial relationships, they risk forming intimate relationships outside it. Persuaded that attachment rather than status is the source of basic life gratifications, as they mature they choose friends on the basis of affection rather than social class, religion, or ethnicity.[8]

Thus out of supportive emotional attachment with parents and habituation to human caring by parental modelling and discipline the young are able to move outward and engage in altruistic behaviour

EMPATHIC ALTRUISM AND THE LIMITS OF MODERNITY

Victor Seidler, an ethicist from The University of London, finds important advances over modern enlightenment and particularly Kantian ethics in the Oliners' theory of altruism. Seidler argues that the central problem with Enlightenment moral theory is a 'dualistic vision'[9] which pits human rationality, freedom, and morality against human nature. Following Protestant notions of human nature as plagued by original sin, modern ethical and political theorists viewed the human self as filled with selfish and passionate desires and emotions which must be controlled and 'moralized' by reason and external social controls. Seidler outlines the negative affects of this position for ethical theory.

What is crucial is the way that 'reason' is set against 'nature' in such a complete and radical manner . . . It tends to identify the moment of freedom with the moment of choice. It tends to see emotions and feelings as essentially 'selfish' and 'irrational' and so tends to present moral education as a denial of our emotional lives . . . These assumptions . . . set 'egoism' against 'Altruism' and takes [sic] the central task of moral theory to provide 'reasons' for why people would act altruistically toward others.[10]

What Seidler sees as praiseworthy in the rescuers and in the Oliners' theory of altruism is the presentation of altruism as a natural expression of the human personality which is based upon and not opposed to human feeling and emotion. Instead of Kantian reasons, rules, principles and duties as the primary vehicles of ethics, the Oliners provide an affective basis for ethics based on human attachments and mutuality in human relationships. Seidler credits not only the Oliners but Freud, Existentialism and Feminism for underscoring the importance of human feelings and the personal and interpersonal dimensions of existence for the moral life. This provides an antidote to the stress on objectivity, universality, and abstract human rights in modern ethical theory and can lead to the development of ethics of 'care and concern'.[11] What Seidler sees in the rescuers, motivation to help Jewish victims is not universal principles but a deep sensitivity to the pain of another human being and a willingness to help them. Because altruism is based on natural human emotions and feelings of the human self it should be seen as consequent with and not opposed to the 'natural' self. Seidler refers to the work of Mordechai Paldiel, who has argued that 'altruism in its variant forms is an innate human predisposition'.[12] This helps to explain why so many rescuers saw what they did as the unexceptional, unheroic, 'normal' thing for them to do.[13] Seidler suggests that the modern view which suggests that altruism must oppose the natural egoistic self is partially to blame for why we have come to view the rescuers as exceptionally 'righteous' and 'saintly'.[14] Seidler argues that modern ethics suffers from low expectations of the human capacity for good. Since we see the self as naturally selfish we cannot really expect altruism. Where modern ethics are satisfied when persons merely do not infringe on each other's rights, an ethics of care expects that individuals do more than get out of each other's way. An ethics of care requires that persons actively assist one another in times of need and continually pursue the common good. For Seidler, the Oliners' theory of altruism suggests that an ethics of care is a psycho-social norm that we can safely assume as our natural human inheritance.

ALTRUISM AND ARISTOTELIAN CHARACTER ETHICS

In his book *The Moral Limits of Modernity*, Seidler mentions that contemporary ethics must move beyond the Western frameworks provided by Aristotle and Kant.[15] Although he argues extensively why we must move beyond Kant's universalism and reliance on rational principle and duty he does not provide corresponding argumentation for why it is that an Aristotelian framework is equally unworkable. This seems strange because there is much in the Oliners' position which recalls Aristotelian character ethics. Indeed, the Oliners could be seen as providing modern social scientific justification for Aristotle's *Nicomachean Ethics*, and the *Ethics*, correspondingly, can provide philosophical discipline and more refined ethical thinking to the Oliners' theory. Most rescuers appear to us as good people, as 'great-souled people'[16] in Aristotle's terms, people of 'virtuous character' who responded to Jewish victims with a combination of generosity, wit, and courage. They assisted Jews not solely because they were following ethical principles and duties but because of the type persons whom they were. Aristotelian ethics seems so appropriate to the Oliners's position because ethical activity for Aristotle is an outgrowth of a way of life including emotional, social, and philosophical dimensions.

Let us further explore the similarities between the two theories.

In his *Nicomachean Ethics* Aristotle argues that ethical actions are the result of the pursuit of the goal of human happiness.[17] Aristotle does not carry Christian presuppositions about the sinful nature of human beings to his ethical thinking and he shares with the Oliners the assumption that doing good is naturally pleasing and gratifying. Altruism, which we might define in Aristotelian terms as courageous actions for others 'in a terrifying situation,'[18] does not require struggle against some natural egoism. At the same time moral excellence is not something merely given by human nature. It is potential which must be drawn out by habituation and an 'appropriate upbringing.'[19] Furthermore, it must be actualized in ethical activities[20] through the deliberative use of reason and voluntary decisions.[21] Ethical activity, for Aristotle, is aided by friendship[22] with people who share common moral virtues and is supported by moral communities.[23] The Oliners certainly stress the importance of parental habituation and modelling and they also identify social and communal structures as support to altruistic activity. Aristotelian notions of character are helpful in explaining why it is that most rescuers saw what they did as routine and normal behaviour for them. Indeed, rescue activity was 'normal' for these people because it resulted from long standing motivations, sensibilities, and habits.

Aristotelian ethics thus exhibits many features that are common to the Oliners and could be applauded by Seidler. Aristotle does not, of course, articulate the psychological dimension of altruistic activity with any of the depth that the Oliners explore but there are additional advantages to Aristotelian ethics which psychological and social scientific orientations cannot provide. Aristotelian ethics helps to thematize the nature and quality of the feelings associated with altruistic activity and it also allows us to articulate the role of ethics in parental habituation, the import of moral traditions, and the significance of individual human judgement and human decisions in altruistic activity.

The Oliners report on the feelings of 'comfort and gratification' which rescuers received 'from the knowledge that they were able to help some Jews.'[24] Aristotle would help us to understand that this gratification came not only from the feeling of attachment to Jews but from what he would call, 'moral achievement,' a very special but enduring pleasure in knowing that you did the right thing. Aristotle would agree that 'feeling' and gratification is involved in the moral life as the Oliners and Seidler suggest. But the positive feeling and reward of ethical activity is not adequately covered by the psychological notion of 'attachment'. Rescue activity was motivated not only by empathy but by an understanding of the human good and by an acute sense of justice.

For Aristotle it is the approximation of objective moral virtues like generosity, courage, friendship, honesty, truthfulness that gives people gratifying pleasure of happiness and motivates them toward altruistic acts. Furthermore Aristotle helps us to see that rescue activity requires not only certain psychological predispositions but certain moral predispositions and rational thinking as well. Aristotle called this 'practical reason' and he argues that practical reason is gained through moral and intellectual education and habituation. This moral training does not lie behind us as a natural inheritance but is learned through active practice and pursuit of moral norms. Most of the rescuers speak equally forcefully of their parents as warm caregivers as they do of them as ethical teachers and models for moral activity.

For example the German rescuer Maria Countess von Maltzan relates that her father 'built orphanages and an old age home'. She tells of one memorable experience. 'I remember when I was seven, telling my father that the cottage of my nurse had burned down. He asked me how much money I had. I told him 217 marks. He said, "I suggest you go get it. Berta has taken care of you for a long time; now you must take care of her." I gave her 200 marks.'[25]

Aristotelian ethical theory requires us to attend not only to the affective quality of broader contexts of community, society and politics but to the specifically moral quality of these collectivities. The importance of ethical values, moral leadership and the moral quality of community is most clear in larger scale rescue operations such as we see in the town of Le Chambon.[26] Here, the leader of the rescue operation, Pastor André Trocme, began with simple biblical teachings such as 'love thy neighbour as thyself,' the non-violent tenets of Christian pacifism, and the Protestant Huguenot sensitivity to the needs of minorities and refugees. And through his charismatic preaching and his own example of altruistic self-sacrifice, Trocme supplied ongoing moral thinking and leadership to a community of five thousand. Philip Hallie's study of the Le Chambon rescue shows, however, that Trocme's leadership was not enough; the rescue required additional leaders and communal support. Thus Trocme had his Pastor Edouard Theis, the headmaster of the Protestant school, Roger Darcissac, and the simple but strong moral character of Trocme's wife Magda. These people were at the centre of an extended Protestant Huguenot community, which was additionally supported by the Protestant resistance and rescue organization Cimade.

One can of course point out that the rescue operation in Le Chambon was the expression of the strength of the 'intimate contacts' in the community. But it is very clear that it was not just intimacy that motivated the rescue but the specifically Protestant Huguenot moral values that stood behind the rescue mission. The rescue of 5,000 Jews by 5,000 Chambonnais villagers must be seen as an expression of the particular moral traditions and peculiar Huguenot culture that was present in Le Chambon.

This is a point which is suggested by Aristotle's references to the importance of traditions, common beliefs, and the moral habituation that these traditions and common communal beliefs provide.[27] Other Aristotelians, like the medieval religious thinkers Maimonides and St. Thomas Aquinas, stressed the importance of specific moral traditions (here Judaism and Christianity) for the formation of a moral community and for the ethical character of individuals. The argument in contemporary moral theory for the importance of moral traditions has been restated most forcefully by the ethical theorist Alasdair MacIntyre.[28]

What Le Chambon shows is that not only does rescue require the contexts of loving parents of ethical virtue and a supportive moral community but that the community itself benefits from the additional moral context that moral traditions provide. Traditions with their texts, rituals and ethical ideals provide the community and its leaders with support and guidance which is critical to altruistic activity. The Oliners argue that parents provide models to children for ethical activity. But where do the parents get their models from? Certainly religious narratives such as biblical stories of Abraham, Moses and Jesus provide compelling ethical models. And rituals which retell and reenact these stories provide important sources of moral habituation and socialization as well. What the example of Le Chambon suggests is that altruism emerges most naturally and dramatically from communities which support, encourage, and demand altruistic activity from its members and these community themselves require additional support from traditions of altruistic thinking and acting.

Yet as strong as the moral community and moral tradition which supports it is altruistic activity comes down to the judgements and decisions of the individual. This is the final moral meaning of the Oliners' notion of the altruistic personality and Aristotle's notion of the virtuous character. Aristotle tells us that decisions even more than pleasures and actions distinguish the virtuous person.[29] In fact, he argues that it is through ethical decisions that humans differentiate themselves from animals and fulfill their potential as intelligent and moral beings. Traditions, parents, communities, motivations, and habits, can bring a person to the moral crisis with the best of moral equipment but it still comes down to the individual's decision to put that equipment to use and do what is morally necessary. When so many Europeans were either complicit or silent, the rescuers of Jews from the Holocaust decided to act. These decisions required a combination of intelligence, freedom, and judgement which forms a level of excellence above psychological empathy and ethical socialization.

In conclusion, I would argue that what Aristotle adds to the mainly psycho-social approach of the Oliners is the specifically rational and ethical dimension. Aristotle's theory fills in some important empty spaces in the Oliners's notion of the altruistic personality which yields a more complex ethics of rescue which is, I would argue, appropriate to complexity of rescue as an expression of both a moral character and a way of life.

THE LIMITS OF A CHARACTER ETHICS

The character approach suggests that altruistic activity can be expected as natural behaviour for humans who receive adequate emotional gratification and habituation and possess the virtues of character and thought which Aristotle outlines. However, given this recipe we certainly could have expected more cases of rescue out of a population of hundreds of millions of Europeans. After all, the rescue families did not have a monopoly on affectionate parent-child relationships in Europe in the 1930s and 40s. Indeed, we even know that German Nazi ideology applauded the virtues of strong familial ties and the wholesome virtues of honesty, brotherhood, and even altruistic activity for the greater good of German society. Good human relationships and moral parental modelling was simply not enough to get people to involve themselves in the risky venture of rescuing Jews from the Nazi Holocaust.

Aristotelian philosophy can provide some resources to address this problem because the ethics suggests that habituation and parental modeling is only half of the equation of the ethical life. Habituation and parenting helps the individual to form habits and motivations for the ethical life but the individual must use their own reason to make ethical judgements that are appropriate to the present situation. Although past habituation helps the current situation many ethical problems are not adequately covered by past models. At this point Aristotle allows that the moral life requires a certain amount of independence and creativity on the part of the individual.

But one might rightly question whether or not the modicum of independence and moral creativity which Aristotle allows is enough to equip the individual to take the radical step which rescue requires. In the case of the Holocaust the choice to rescue required exceptional risk and sacrifice to self, family, and community. The Aristotelian rule is to choose the middle path between extremes. Aristotle advises the person to choose the middle between profligacy and stinginess, self-deprecation and vanity, recklessness and cowardice. Given the obvious risks, rescuing Jews was sheer recklessness but it also was the right thing to do!

The weakest link in Aristotle's character ethics however, lies in the population which is served by the virtuous person. Aristotle suggests that the proper recipients of altruistic acts are 'fellow-voyagers'[30] in quest for the moral virtues. The proper purview of

Aristotelian ethics thus is one's family, friends, community members and countrymen. What this suggests is what actually happened in Europe and throughout the world during the Holocaust. People directed their attention to the preservation of their own selves, their families, their communities, and their nations. They attended to their own, to those 'like them' and they ignored the Jews who were not like them, who were 'others.' This reveals the true moral challenge of the Holocaust. For it was not only legally legitimate to ignore the plight of Jews who had been deprived of all legal rights, but according to significant traditions in Western ethics, it was morally legitimate to ignore them!

Unfortunately, it is not only Aristotelian character ethics that recommends ignoring those others who lie outside your group. The social science of human relations suggests that humans from infancy onward tend to divide the world into family and stranger, us versus them, ingroup and outgroup, same and other.[31] Thus the 'natural' recipients of our altruistic activities our those in our own group. The social psychologist Ervin Staub has argued that not only is the in group/out group distinction basic to human psychology and social organization but in times of crisis the distinction becomes even more acute and more strongly defended.[32] Thus altruistic activities on behalf of outsiders is even less likely to occur in life-threatening situations.

The social psychologist Krzysztof Konarzewski has argued that the experience of empathy, which is so highly valued by the Oliners as the core of altruistic activity, has inherent qualities which work against acts on behalf of outsiders.[33] Empathy is built out of intimate contact with those with whom one has close contact. Empathy works when one sees the other as a self like oneself. 'The other becomes a vicarious self. Rescuing of the other is rescuing the self-in-the-other.'[34] Konarzewski argues that empathy grows out of conformity to existing familial and communal norms. It, quite naturally, is easiest between like people and becomes more and more difficult as the other person appears more foreign in her appearance, language, and culture. This is another way of saying that warm and intimate family relations and the capacity for empathy are simply not enough to generate rescue activity on behalf of strangers. Konarzewski suggests that altruism for the sake of the stranger requires psychological, existential and philosophical capacities of independence and protest which are actually opposed to the capacity for empathy.[35] Konarzewski argues that rescuers had astute abilities to see through political propaganda and the prevailing ideologies of fascism, Nazism, and anti-Semitism. Rescue activity often required the rescuer to distance herself from oppressive authority structures. Nechama Tec, another important social scientific researcher on rescuers, underscores the importance of independence on the part of rescuers. Contra to the Oliners, her research leads her to the conclusion that rescuers often did not blend into their communities.[36]

It is tempting at this point to turn to a Kantian ethics of universal principles and duties abstracted from the web of human relations upon which a character ethics is built. Kantian ethics defends the independence of the lone rescuer on the basis of the concepts of autonomy and freedom and the duty which the autonomous and free individual owes to the universal ethical principle. But returning to Kant would require us to cut the human bonds back to family and culture and toward the personhood of the Jew which the Oliners, Seidler and we, employing Aristotle, have argued for. Rather than return to the modern abstract and universal ethics of Kant, I suggest that we move forward to create an ethics of rescue which further develops a character ethics of altruism. This requires that we not abandon the hard won insights which the Oliners and Aristotle have brought us but that we further develop and augment them.

THE HUMAN FACE OF THE OTHER

In his face, is the primordial expression, is the first word: you shall not commit murder.[37]

An ethics of care and character underscores the importance consistency in affection and ethical modeling. Social psychologists and Aristotelians converge in the belief that good character requires continuity, connection, and habituation. They further agree that this is provided by home and community and supported by tradition. Like breeds like, and thus goodness leads to goodness. But the weakness of this approach is that it can lead to the tyranny of the same. The good take care of the good alone and the good turn out to be like you. Taken to extremes this ethic leads to an abandonment of all who are not 'like you.' And the apotheosis of this type of thinking is a kind of totalitarianism which seeks the eradication of those not 'like you'. Thus an ethics of care and character requires a way to break through its own tyranny of the same to a positive appreciation for 'the other'. It is precisely the articulation of the importance of the other which has been the centrepoint of the philosophy of Emmanuel Levinas. In his now classic book *Totality and Infinity*, Levinas criticizes Western philosophy for establishing totalities, systems and unities which close thought off from the infinity which otherness represents. Wounded and educating by his own experiences during the Holocaust, Levinas insists that philosophy which is worthy of its claims to the true and the good make ethics its priority. Thus philosophy should begin not with the search for epistemological certainty, the Cartesian cogito, but with the other and the ethical obligations which she makes upon me. Levinas gives us the other not as an abstract concept or principle but as 'the face of the other,'[38] the real living, suffering person whose living complexity by definition can never be captured in a concept, a principle, a totality. This other supplies us with a different route to freedom and goodness than that supplied by Kant's autonomous self. Levinas tells us that we only find freedom and goodness by responding to the ethical demand of the being of the suffering other. 'The being that expresses itself imposes itself, but does so precisely by appealing to me with its destitution and nudity – its hunger – without my being able to be deaf to that appeal. Thus in expression the being that imposes itself does not limit but promotes my freedom, by arousing my goodness.'[39] Levinas suggests that altruism is only altruism when it is a response to the need of the *alter*, the other. When we respond to our own needs and those of our family and communal members we are doing a good but this does not rise to the level of altruism. Thus a Levinasian corrective to Aristotle would require the person of moral character to attend to the needs of the other.

If we return the rescuers of Jews during the Holocaust all of them seemed to have the Levinasian appreciation for the humanity of the Jewish other and a sense for the absolute priority which responding to their need represented. Certainly they did not have Levinas's philosophical terminology to express this priority, they often used much simpler language. Tina Strobos, a rescuer from the Netherlands, put it this way.

> I go out and talk to schoolchildren today and I tell them that people like to join groups which think like they do, and dress the same, just to feel like you belong. And then they become cruel to those who don't belong, who limp, or are different, and we have to be careful not to hurt others who don't belong to our little group.[40]

Magda Trocme the wife of Andre Trome from Le Chambon put it this way: 'I never close my door, never refuse to help... When people come to my door I feel responsible.'[41]

What social science and Aristotle suggests to us is that we can only achieve the sensitivity to the other by habituating ourselves and our children to care for these others.

This is not an easy task and the difficulties are illustrated well by Johtje Vos, a Dutch rescuer who, made the Jews her ethical priority even above her own children.

> When my mother came to visit me and saw we were hiding Jews, she was upset and said, 'You shouldn't do it, even though I agree with what you are doing, because your first responsibility is to your children.' I told her, 'that is exactly why I'm doing it. I thought we were doing the right thing, giving our children the right model to follow.'[42]

Here we see how the ethical priority of the other in need required Vos to place the material needs of the other above her own children. But, paradoxically, she did this for the sake of her own children, for the sake of their moral development, to provide the 'right model' for them to follow. And although this was certainly painful for her children, in the end they came to understand and even appreciate what their mother had done.

> For a time, one of my children felt resentment for what we did. She said we risked her life as well, and that all the Jews in the house came first, before her.... But today my daughter understands perfectly well why we had to do what we did. It all turned out so well.[43]

It is undoubtedly an ethical challenge of the highest order to habituate ourselves and our children to take responsibility for the other who is not only different from us but has also been rendered physically unattractive by his suffering and persecution. Where modern ethics suggested that the best way to accomplish this was to get the autonomous modern individual who himself had been stripped of his ties to community, ethnicity, and tradition to see the humanity of the other underneath his communal, ethnic, and traditional ties, a 'postmodern'[44] ethics of character and care preserves the cultural ties of both the giver and receiver of aid. An ethic of character and care preserves these ties for the giver of aid because, as the Oliners and Aristotelian ethics show, they represent crucial resources for empathy and ethical thinking.[45] On the other hand, Levinas's notion of the 'face' is meant to convey that the other is not an abstract isolated individual but a real human being who comes from a particular family, community, and cultural group.[46] But by preserving the ties to community and ethnicity we run the risk of enforcing divisions and ethnocentricity. We therefore need ethical ideals models and even rituals to correct for this danger. Ervin Staub suggests that altruistic activity between members of different groups is aided by what he calls 'cross-cutting' relations.[47] These are initiated when people from different groups take part in common activities which require them to cooperate and work together. Staub gives the example of his own involvement in building a common playground with people from different communities in his town. Obviously it is harder to get people who have long histories of animosity together for common enterprises but we do see that different group often cooperate with one another despite their differences when matters of common economic gain are at stake. Thus business can be an area for former enemies to meet.

Philosophical and social scientific perspectives on rescue activity suggest that it requires a complex combination of psychological, sociological, and philosophical resources to create a climate for altruistic activity. Aristotle suggests that the master science for ethics is political science. In saying this he recognized that ethical activity is ultimately an expression of a just social order. Thus altruism and the prevention of genocide requires building up a just order which begins with child raising practices and goes through schooling to communal and political structures at the national and international levels.

Ultimately, what we want to produce is people of character who are sensitive to the needs of both their neighbours and those that are designated as 'others'. If we look at the rescuers for models what we see is a peculiar combination of characteristics: empathy and independence, conformity and protest, deep loyalty to family and community and equally deep respect for the other and the stranger. Konarzewski argued that these virtues conflict with one another. Perhaps this is why we have so few cases of rescue of Jews. Yet if these virtues are logically and psychologically contradictory, as an outgrowth of a moral life they do not conflict. Indeed, it does make sense that the highest moral achievement involves our obligations to those who are not 'like us', who stand beyond our ability to empathize with them, who do not immediately draw our affection and who cannot readily reciprocate the good we do for them. But Levinas's suggestion that we focus on the face of the other is meant to tell us that, in the end, the other is not radically other. The face of the other reveals to us the fundamental humanity of the other who is, despite all outward appearances, 'like us' in her humanness. And in responding to the face of the other we not only answer to the call of the other but to the call of the flourishing of our own humanity, goodness, and moral pleasure.

N O T E S

1 Stanley Milgram, *Obediance to Authority* (NY: Harper and Row, 1974). Robert Lifton *The Nazi Doctors* (NY: Basic Books, 1986). Ervin Staub, *The Roots of Evil: The Origins of Genocide* (Cambridge: Cambridge University Press, 1989).

2 Samuel and Pearl Oliner, *The Altruistic Personality* (NY: Free Press, 1988).

3 Victor Seidler, 'Rescue, Righteousness, and Morality', *Embracing the Other*, eds. P. Oliner, S. Oliner, L. Baron et.al. (NY: New York University Press, 1992), pp.48–69.

4 *Altruistic Personality*, p.10.

5 *ibid.*, p.6.

6 *ibid.*, p.249.

7 *ibid.*, p.171–73.

8 *ibid.*, p.250.

9 Seidler, 'Rescue, Righteousness', p.49.

10 *ibid.*, p.50.

11 *ibid.*, p.53.

12 Mordechai Paldiel, 'The Altruism of the Righteous Gentiles', *Holocaust and Genocide Studies* 3:2: 187–96 as quoted in Seidler, op.cit., p.54.

13 Gay Block and Malka Drucker, *Rescuers: Portraits of Moral Courage in the Holocaust* (NY: Holmes and Meier, 1992).

14 Seidler, *ibid.*, p.55.

15 Seidler, *The Moral Limits of Modernity* (London: Macmillan, 1990), p.17.

16 Aristotle, *Nicomachean Ethics*, tr. T. Irwin (Indianapolis: Hackett, 1985), 1123b3.

17 *ibid.*, 1099b9.

18 *ibid.*, 1103b15.

19 *ibid.*, 1103a15.

20 *ibid.*, 1103b15.

21 *ibid.*, 1111b5.

22 *ibid.*, Book 8.

23 *ibid.*, 1159b25.

24 *Altruistic Personality*, p.223.

25 quoted in Block and Drucker, *Rescuers* p.153.

26 Philip Hallie, *Lest Innocent Blood Be Shed* (NY: Harper and Row, 1979).

27 Aristotle, 1095a:25 and 1095b:1–10.

28 Alasdair MacIntyre, *After Virtue* (Notre Dame: Notre Dame University Press, 1981), p.240.

29 Aristotle, 1111b5.

30 *ibid.*, 1159b28.

31 Ervin Staub, *The Roots of Evil*, pp.58–62.

32 *ibid.*, pp.35–51.
33 Krzysztof Konarzewski, 'Empathy and Protest: Two Roots of Heroic Altruism,' *Embracing the Other*, pp.22–30.
34 *ibid.*, p.23.
35 *ibid.*, p.25.
36 Nechama Tec, *When Light Pierced the Darkness: Christian Rescue of Jews* (Oxford: Oxford University Press, 1986).
37 Emmanuel Levinas, *Totality and Infinity* tr A. Lingis (Pittsburgh: Duquesne University Press, 1969), p.199.
38 *ibid.*, p.197.
39 *ibid.*, p.200.
40 As quoted in Block and Drucker, *Rescuers*, p.89.
41 Hallie, *Lest Innocent Blood*, p.153.
42 As quoted in Block and Drucker, *Rescuers*, pp.81–82.
43 *ibid.*
44 Steven Kepnes, Peter Ochs, and Robert Gibbs *Reasoning After Revelation: Dialogues in Postmodern Jewish Philosophy* (Boulder: Westview, 1998).
45 For a carefully argued 'post-enlightenment' defense of the ethical power of particular cultures see Samuel Fleischacker, *The Ethics of Culture* (Ithaca and London: Cornell University Press, 1994).
46 Lawrence Blum has argued that rescue activity during the Holocaust, in its highest form, was not about saving individual Jews but about 'preservation of the Jewish people as a people', and 'culture'. Blum astutely sees that genocide is always about the eradication of a specific group of people and therefore its prevention must involve 'affirming the culture' as well as individuals who are endangered. Blum, 'Altruism and the Moral Value of Rescue', *Embracing the Other*, p.42.
47 Staub, *The Roots of Evil*, p.274.

VERY RELIGIOUS AND IRRELIGIOUS RESCUERS:
AN EXPLORATION OF CULTURAL STYLES

Pearl M. Oliner, Jeanne Wielgus and Mary B. Gruber

O F THE many examples of altruism, the rescue of Jews by non-Jews during the horrendous period of the Holocaust remains among the most compelling. Altruism on behalf of 'insider' groups, groups who share a strong collective identity and a sense of common fate, is not uncommon. What makes rescuer activity particularly important was the fact that it was not only undertaken at grave personal risk, but on behalf of an 'outsider' group, sharply distinguished through long centuries of Christian and European national history as 'them'.

Social scientists generally agree that ingroup altruism (altruism on behalf of any group to which people feel they belong and from which they exclude others) is far more common than outgroup altruism (altruism on behalf of any group to which people feel. they do not belong). Studies of altruistic behaviours often tend to treat altruism as a generalised attribute without distinguishing between ingroup and outgroup altruism. Understanding conditions that promote outgroup altruism is critically important in societies which are increasingly heterogeneous and interdependent. Non-Jewish rescuers of Jews during the Holocaust provide a prime example of outgroup altruism and thus afford a good opportunity for understanding how such activity might occur.

Many studies of rescuers have concentrated on personality characteristics and to a lesser degree on situational variables. The former focus on internal characteristics of individuals, is specific to individuals, and is both inherited and learned; the latter on external matters such as opportunity, political mobilization, availability of resources, and normative considerations.[1] A study by the Oliners that used a comparative sample of nonrescuers, was also in this tradition.[2] Such studies have identified several personal and situational characteristics, as well as socialization practices conducive to rescue with important scholarly and practical implications.

An implicit assumption underlying the above approaches is that personal attributes leading to outgroup altruism and rescue specifically are universally similar. Universality implies that qualities that applied to men would also apply to women, those which applied to Catholics would also apply to Protestants, and those that applied to the very religious also to the irreligious. But is that indeed the case? Phrased differently, did cultural context make a difference?

This paper compares very religious and irreligious rescuers, not as a matter of personality, but as a matter of culture. Understanding culture can lead us to better understand why and how different groups interpreted their sense of responsibility to Jews particularly and to outgroups generally. Interventions that are rooted in the context of a group's culture are likely to be more successful than those that ignore it.

Questions guiding this exploration include: (1) How are very religious and irreligious cultures similar to or different from each other? (2) How did rescuers and nonrescuers within each group compare with each other? (3) What implications might be inferred with respect to group culture and outgroup altruism?

The subjects of our study are respondents included in the Altruistic Personality Project data base, all of them having lived in Nazi Europe during World War II.[3] The very religious included 150 respondents, 111 rescuers and 39 nonrescuers. The irreligious included 58 respondents, 42 rescuers and 16 nonrescuers. Respondents were interviewed in their native tongues; the interview schedule consisted of approximately 450 items; 75 percent of which were forced choices, the remainder open-ended. In addition, each respondent was asked to describe his or her wartime activities in detail. Groups were compared on each measure using analysis of covariance, while holding age and gender constant. Statistically significant findings were further examined with Duncan pairwise, post-hoc comparisons. Descriptions and conclusions given below are based on statistically significant findings at the .05 level or smaller. As a general practice, we use the term 'significant' to refer to statistically significant findings only.

Our study has several limitations that need to be noted before beginning our discussion. Our conclusions are based on small and non-randomly chosen samples. Hence, we do not know to what extent our findings can be found among very religious and irreligious rescuers generally. The research design is ex-post-facto, thus blurring the cause-effect relationship. Since many events have occurred during the forty years or more intervening between World War II and the dates of the interviews, it may well be that the cultural contexts in which respondents answered have been modified. Additionally, interviews depend on self-reports and self-reporters may try to please the interviewer or to conform to presumed expectations; responses may also change depending on mood, fatigue or some external event. The Altruistic Personality Project's interview schedule attempted to address these concerns by including several questions regarding a single variable relative to different times in the respondent's life. Despite such merited cautions, the findings are impressive in that they suggest strong patterns, and in many cases patterns that are consistent with findings in other studies of the religious and the irreligious.

Given the central place given to *culture* and *religion* in this study, we begin with these concepts and how we measured them.

Anthropologists are credited with giving the concept culture its most generally accepted meaning in the social sciences and the study of culture remains the heart of anthropological inquiry. As anthropologists define it, culture means the totality of a group's material (e.g. tools, shelters, art) and nonmaterial (e.g. values, thoughts, emotions) world. They were particularly interested in describing the relationship between culture and personality, and had considerable success in their early years when they confined their studies to small, relatively homogeneous and non-western groups.[4] When they tried to apply similar principles to more complex and western cultures, particularly minority cultures, they confronted a great deal of controversy. Rather than illuminating the groups they studied, they were accused of approaching other groups through their own biased western cultural values, thus confirming stereotypes and legitimating racism and neo-colonialism. Stung by such critiques, they largely abandoned the search for the relationship between personality and culture – at least temporarily – contenting themselves at present with what has come to be called 'thick descriptions' of culture.

More recently, however, making systematic cultural comparisons has begun to be perceived as possible, in large part due to the work of sociologist Geert Hofstede.[5] His work and that of other social scientists, among them Shalom Schwartz,[6] Alan Fiske[7] and Harry Triandis,[8] have many implications for group behaviours, including the relationship of culture to ingroup and outgroup altruism.

People constituting a culture, says Hofstede, share 'a collective programming of the mind;' that is 'patterned ways of thinking, feeling, and acting'.[9] These patterns *incline* participants toward a 'broad tendency to prefer certain states of affairs over others', but they do not determine how they will act. Nor do they determine personality although they influence it. Personalities are unique, says Hofstede, the particular constellation of individual inclinations, influenced by the culture in which the person has been socialized and lives. Triandis calls them a 'tool kit;' a filter through which participants interpret situations.[10] Perhaps so as to avoid any implication that 'collective' means all share it, Fiske proposes that culture is a 'more or less shared systems of models and meaning'.[11] Based on the above, *we define culture as the more or less widely shared beliefs, values and feelings found among a group or category of people who have a sense of common identity which makes them distinct from others.* In this sense, the very religious and the irreligious constitute distinct cultures.

Unlike personality characteristics, which are specific and unique to individuals, learned and inherited, cultural orientations are learned and specific to groups. While they tend to be stable, often showing remarkable generational continuity, they can change but rarely do so radically or within a very short period. They can provide both cognitive and emotional meanings to events, motivating people toward action. Cultural 'understandings', Strauss and Quinn point out can also be 'relatively thematic, in the sense that certain understandings may be repeatedly applied in a wide variety of contexts'.[12] Such understandings, however, need not be necessarily either conscious or consistent. Rather, they are learned reactions, acquired through multiple repetitions over time – in language, stories, song, visuals, dance – and through a variety of societal institutions – family, schools, friends, religious and political groups. In times of chaos, such as that of war, cultural scripts assume particular power to restore order and unify groups. The cultures of both the very religious and the irreligious during the war were thus very influential in helping participants interpret events.

There are hundreds if not thousands of cultures throughout the world, associated with groups who share a common occupation; national, ethnic or political identification; social class, gender, or religion. Each country has many cultures (sometimes called subcultures) within its geographical boundaries, and some cultures (e.g. ethnic and religious) transcend national boundaries. A religious denomination is sometimes a subcultural group within a nation, and often is a nationally transcendent cultural group. Christians fall into both categories, as do Catholics and Protestants. Political groups may also have the same characteristics: socialists and communists are prime examples. As a subcultural group within particular national boundaries, each is likely to be influenced by the dominant national and political culture so that its particular manifestation will be not quite the same as a similar denomination in another country. This, of course, makes it difficult to determine the exact boundaries of a culture; that is where one culture ends and another begins. The boundaries of cultures are thus permeable and inexact but nonetheless real.

To measure cultural orientations, we developed five broad conceptual categories. Categories one and two, respectively called *mastery* and *sharing*, are intended to assess the degree to which the culture supported self-enhancement and/or self-transcendence. Categories three and four, respectively called *primary interpersonal relationships* and *secondary relationships*, are intended to assess the types of primary and secondary institutional relationships that the culture supported. Category five, *outgroup relationships*, is intended to assess the types of relationships with outsider groups which the culture supported. Each is briefly elaborated below:

Mastery: values that support self-enhancement, including achievement, control, assertiveness and material success. It bears some similarity to Schwartz's conception of 'mastery'[13] and to the concept 'agency' as developed by Bakan[14] and Wiggins.[15] The mastery category is derived from ten measures including internal/external locus of control; self esteem; standing up for beliefs; personal potency; leader, follower or independent with respect to friends, economic competence, obedience and propriety.

Sharing: values that reflect the readiness to distribute resources for others' welfare and are associated with self-transcendence and altruism. The term is borrowed from John Tropman's work but used somewhat differently.[16] The sharing category is derived from eleven measures, including empathy, prosocial attitudes, feelings of similarity to the poor, social responsibility and personal integrity.

Interpersonal Primary Relationships: the quality of familial and other personal relationships. This category is derived from eleven measures, including relationships with families of origin and parental discipline, living among and being involved with relatives and close friends.

Secondary Relationships: the degree to which respondents are integrated into the local community, a religious denominational community and a political and national community. This category is derived from nine measures including a general sense of belonging, friendliness of neighbours, feelings of similarity to other members of the same religious denomination, political party membership, patriotism and resistance group membership.

Outgroup Relationships: values and attitudes toward outgroup members, where outgroups include others having a different religious, ethnic, social or political status, and particularly focused on Jews. This category is derived from seventeen measures including feelings of similarity to a variety of outgroups (Jews, Turks, Gypsies) and also include parental values about Jews, time aware of Nazi intentions toward Jews, Jewish friends and empathy for Jews.

What do we mean by *religious* and *irreligious* and how were they measured? No less complex than *culture*, the meaning of *religion* has also changed over time. Social scientists tend to define it in two ways: its function and its substance.

Functional definitions focus on what religion *does* for a group. Religion, most social scientists agree, is a source of identity, social support and integration, providing a group of people with answers to many questions, ranging from the profound – such the meaning of life and the purpose of suffering and death – to prosaic matters – such as proper dress and diet. Religion thus allays anxiety and provides a feeling of comfort and security to its adherents, assuring them that the society in which they live is generally as it should be.

Substantive definitions, on the other hand, focus on a religion's content. Despite their highly varied nature, within and particularly between religions, the content of all religions does share some major substantive elements in common. Notions about who is 'religious' have largely emerged from these commonalties.

At least four elements are commonly associated with a religion's content: (1) a reference to god, gods or some transcendental being, (2) a set of beliefs about the sacred, (3) rituals and practices, and (4) a moral code, that is views about right and wrong.[17] On a popular level, the term 'religious' often refers to individuals who accept core denominational beliefs and practice rituals, but a higher standard is generally invoked to merit the label 'very religious'. In that case, some might insist, people need to manifest all four elements in their lives: a strong relationship to something transcendent, accepting beliefs, practising rituals, and also manifesting behaviour consistent with the denomination's moral code. Others might propose that 'very religious' should be reserved only for those who do these things with exceptional commitment, while still others might suggest that even one of these elements might suffice, provided that it was done intensely. Linguistic conventions which describe these different forms of religiosity include words such as spiritual, having faith, observant (orthoprax), and orthodox.

In light of the above, it is not surprising that measuring religiosity in a scientific way has proved a formidable task. Efforts were already evident at the beginning of the century but the most systematic measures did not emerge until the sixties.[18] Probably the best known and most frequently used scale, the Intrinsic/Extrinsic Scale, measures concepts developed by Gordon Allport.[19] Each of the above instruments proved very useful for the researchers who developed them. But because they were often very lengthy, associated with particular sectarian views, or too narrowly focused on the interests of the developers, other researchers sought a simpler way. The most commonly used measure today is church attendance: those who attend more often are ranked as more religious.

The measure we used was equally simple but less conventional: we asked respondents to categorise themselves as very, somewhat, not very, or not at all religious. Among the major problems of self-identification is the fact that it is subjective, depending on the respondent's own definition of religiosity and thus likely to vary greatly from person to person. On the other hand, it may reflect a more genuine internal religious feeling and commitment, something more akin to the 'intrinsic' religiosity that Allport describes.

Using the above measures, and the statistical procedures described above, we arrived at some conclusions regarding more or less widely shared beliefs, values and feelings found among the very religious and the irreligious which distinguished them significantly from each other. We then compared very religious rescuers with equally religious nonrescures, and irreligious rescuers with equally irreligious nonrescuers, to assess significant differences within these groups.

Very Religious

Christian culture allegedly minimizes materialistic concerns while enhancing self-transcendence on behalf of others. There appears to be more than a measure of truth to this assertion among the very religious and this is reflected to some degree in mastery values and to a larger degree in sharing values. Mastery for the very religious, as compared with the moderately religious, was significantly more associated with assertiveness than with achievement or material success. Economic competence ranked significantly lower among them as compared with the moderately religious, a distinction that also marked very religious rescuers as compared with moderately religious rescuers. This more muted concern with occupational success, which they reported as acquired from their parents, suggests a life perspective in which material success was neither the only nor the essential barometer of worldly achievement.

Beliefs, rather than economic considerations, more often motivated the very religious to act, even when such action meant taking up unpopular causes. Asked if they had ever done anything before the war to stand up for their beliefs, the very religious, as compared with the middle groups, were significantly more likely to say they had. It was a quality they shared with the irreligious but for very different reasons, as we shall see. Asserting oneself can be a means for expressing distinctiveness, a matter of choosing one's own goals rather than those of the community. In their case, however, assertions were often on behalf of the religious community. More than a third claimed to have made a public stand for their religious beliefs, approximately a third identified personal matters, and somewhat less than a third assorted political stands.

Religious cultures are sometimes described as promoting the 'feminine', evidence of which is the disproportionate percentage of women involved in religious activities. 'Feminine' attributes, as compared with masculine ones, are allegedly more tender-hearted, socially directed, and more conducive to altruism generally. Based on their synthesis of several studies, social psychologists Schroeder, Penner, Dovidio and Piliavin conclude that most religious denominations not only teach prosocial values and norms, but that religion is very influential in encouraging more general prosocial action.[20] Our data support such allegations; the very religious, as compared with the irreligious, were significantly more inclined toward sharing with others. Significantly more empathic, more socially responsible, and more concerned with their own personal integrity than the irreligious, they evidenced significantly greater inclinations toward prosocial actions and self-transcendent behaviours. In this, they appear to support what sociologist Lester Kurtz claims to be a central Christian belief nearly universally accepted among Christian believers: namely love of God and love of neighbour.[21]

Very religious culture demonstrated yet other strengths, particularly when compared with the irreligious. In general, the very religious identified strongly with a several key social institutions and felt very comfortable and well integrated into their societies. They were significantly more attached to their families of origin – siblings and parents – generally perceiving them as warm and caring and from whom they learned the value of religion. The schools they attended were more likely to be filled with students like themselves; in significantly largely numbers they attended religious denominational schools with other co-religionists. The political institutions with which they were affiliated also tended to be associated with their religious denominations. And they were significantly more identified with their national communities; even when very young, the very religious in significantly higher percentages than the irreligious claimed very patriotic feelings.

Strong institutional commitments coupled with sharing impulses suggest a communal and collectivist orientation. In collectivist societies, individuals see themselves as inter-dependent and accept personal goals as congruent with communal goals. At its best, individuals within such cultures are indeed more inclined toward altruism, more ready to put the interests of the group ahead of their own even when it involves considerable self-sacrifice. The problem is that their altruism tends to be of a restricted sort; that is directed toward other ingroup members only. At its worst, it becomes exclusionary, hostile and punitive toward outgroups. 'In collectivist cultures', observes Hofstede 'religion takes the form of group worship. Personal salvation is often linked to what happens to relatives, and membership in religious institutions is essential for social life. In fact, it is unthinkable that one would not share the same religion with that of the collective. Thus, it seems "natural" to exterminate those who are apostates, rebels, blasphemers, and so forth.'[22] History unfortunately is replete with such instances; in the case of the very religious in our sample, the worst is not evident. The very religious, as compared with the irreligious, were indeed significantly less egalitarian in their views, but not as exclusionary as the somewhat religious. And while the political parties they belonged to were no advocates of minorities or Jews, they tended toward tolerance rather than exclusion.

Why then did some very religious Christians become rescuers while others did not? In the context of a generally sharing culture, rescuers were significantly more sharing-oriented than nonrescuers, particularly in relation to parental emphasis on caring values.

And in the context of a generally insulated culture – largely unaware of or inattentive to events outside their own collectivities – they were significantly more engaged in the broader social community, were more aware of Jews, and more accepting of outsiders generally. This did not mean less of a sense of belonging in their own communities – in some cases it was in fact a community outreach effort – but rather they had a means for stretching beyond the boundaries of their own collective groups.

The Irreligious

Like the very religious, the irreligious were equally an assertive culture. But whereas religion was a prominent theme among the assertive statements of the very religious, political themes were dominant among a substantial percentage of the irreligious.

More than 80 percent of the assertive stands the irreligious claimed focused on political themes – most of them anti-Nazi, sometimes pacifist and sometimes describing behaviours taken on behalf of Jews. Although as politically affiliated as the very religious, their political parties were significantly different. Economically left and advocates for minorities and Jews, the parties they belonged to were dominantly Socialist and labour, but also included some Communists. Even when respondents themselves did not belong to a political party, they were often socialized in leftist families where one or both parents were politically affiliated.

Unlike the very religious, whose orientation was communal and collectivist, the irreligious tended more toward individualism or self-differentiation. Whereas in collectivist societies individuals see themselves as interdependent and perceive personal goals as congruent with communal goals, in individualist societies individuals see themselves as independent and frequently perceive personal goals as different from communal goals. Individualistic themes are not overwhelming among the irreligious, but they appear frequently. Thus for example, irreligious nonrescuers rarely and significantly less often than either very or moderately religious nonrescuers claim to have learned obedience in their parental households. And irreligious rescuers, as compared with very religious and mildly religious rescuers, ranked themselves significantly higher on self-esteem.

But the most striking differences appeared in the relationships with their families of origin. The irreligious, as compared with the very religious, the moderately and the mildly religious, were significantly less close to their families generally, and to their mothers and fathers. A similar pattern was true for irreligious rescuers, as compared with very religious and moderately religious rescuers, and for irreligious nonrescuers, as compared with all other groups. At its surface, such lack of intimacy with parents and families might suggest abuse, but that is not the case. As compared with those more religious, they were no more or less disciplined and were no more or less subject to authoritarian discipline. As compared with the mildly and moderately religious, they were significantly less subject to physical punishment and as compared with the very religious, their parents were significantly more likely to reason with them. Rather than more abusive than other groups, parents of the irreligious appeared to be more reasonable. Yet in the perceptions of the irreligious, parents but particularly fathers were either too controlling or not quite up to expected standards. What this seems to suggest is that their push for independence began early. Yet despite such breaking away tendencies, their parents and particularly their fathers' politics strongly influenced them.

If independence suggests alleged masculine values, so do their attitudes toward sharing values. There is no single sharing value on which they score significantly higher than any other group, and several on which they score significantly lower. They contrast particularly sharply with the very religious, where they score significantly lower on empathy, social responsibility and perceived personal integrity. A similar pattern is characteristic of irreligious nonrescuers as compared with more religious nonrescuers.

Centred as they are on competition with others to achieve success, individualistic cultures are allegedly less likely to engage in either ingroup or outgroup altruism. They may be more willing to tolerate and even cooperate with outgroup members for reasons of personal gain, says Triandis, but they are not necessarily less discriminatory.[23] And yet studies suggest they are less bigoted and prejudiced generally, more able to live with ambiguity and tolerant of others, more open to experience, less rigid, and more flexible.[24]

Our data support the greater inclusiveness of the irreligious, one mark of which was their lower level of patriotism. As compared with all other levels of religiosity – the very, moderately and mildly religious – the irreligious were significantly less likely to embrace patriotic values. As several of them explained, in the context of the times patriotism meant nationalism, an elevation of the value of their own group above others; a value they could not accept. More importantly, as compared with the very religious they were significantly more egalitarian, socialized with Jews at school, at work and in their political groups, and were significantly more inclined to have Jewish friends. Political sensitivity and party positions, as well as personal friendships, alerted them to Hitler's evil intentions significantly earlier than the very or the moderately religious.

Given the strongly inclusive orientations of irreligious culture, what influenced some to become rescuers while others did not? Irreligious rescuers, as compared with irreligious nonrescuers, were significantly more likely to be self-confident, value personal integrity, and did have closer relationships with their families and their fathers particularly. Unlike irreligious nonrescuers, they grew up with more positive images of Jews, primarily transmitted by their parents, had more empathy for them and claimed learning about their fate earlier.

The challenge for the irreligious was thus largely different than that for the very religious. The latter had far less difficulty with intimate relationships and had to learn to stretch beyond them. Irreligious culture had already largely learned the value of all humankind, at least in the abstract; what they appeared to need was the ability to temper their individualistic impulses and strengthen their capacity to make strong local and personal commitments. Irreligious rescuers appeared to be significantly more equipped in this direction.

In their 1988 study of rescuers, Sam and Pearl Oliner proposed two types of personalities with different implications for ingroup and outgroup altruism. Constricted personalities, they said, 'experience the external world as largely peripheral except insofar as it may be instrumentally useful. More centred on themselves and their own needs, they pay scant attention to others. At best, they reserve their sense of obligation to a small circle from which others are excluded'. Constricted personalities, they implied, were thus unlikely to engage in any form of altruism – ingroup or outgroup. Extensive personalities, they proposed, had a stronger 'feeling of responsibility for the welfare of others, including those outside their immediate familial or communal circles'.[25] Extensive personalities, they implied, were thus more likely to engage in both ingroup and outgroup altruism.

The same concepts, with some modifications, can also be applied to cultures. Constricted cultures also experience the external world as largely peripheral except insofar it may be instrumentally useful. Rather than centring on individual needs, they centre on the needs of the group, thus rendering them quite capable of ingroup altruism but less likely to engage in outgroup altruism. This is the potential danger of a strong collectivity, such as very religious groups often are. Overcoming it requires conscious effort toward more inclusivity in attitudes and behaviour.

Extensive cultures do have a sense of responsibility for the welfare of others, including those outside their immediate familial or communal circles. This suggests their potential for outgroup altruism. Their potential weakness lies in their weaker readiness to become strongly attached and committed to those around them. Without such rooting, much of the inclusiveness orientation assumes a strong abstract quality, divorced from action in real life.

NOTES

1 David A. Schroeder, Louis A. Penner, John F. Dovidio, and Jane A. Piliavin, *The Psychology of Helping and Altruism: Problems and Puzzles* (New York: McGraw Hill, 1995).

2 Samuel P. Oliner and Pearl M. Oliner, *The Altruistic Personality: Rescuers of Jews in Nazi Europe* (New York: Free Press, 1988).

3 For a more detailed description of how the data were collected, see Oliner and Oliner, *ibid.*

4 Two well known examples include Margaret Mead, *From the South Seas* (New York: Morrow, 1939) and Ruth Benedict, *The Chrysanthemum and the Sword* (Boston: Houghton Mifflin, 1946).

5 Geert Hofstede, *Culture's Consequences: International Differences in Work-Related Values* (Beverly Hills, CA: Sage, 1980); *Cultures and Organizations: Softward of the Mind* (London: McGraw Hill, 1991).

6 Shalom H. Schwartz, 'Beyond individualism-collectivism: New cultural dimensions of values', in U. Kim, H.C. Triandis, C. Kagitsibasi, S.C. Choi and G. Yoon (eds.), *Individualism and Collectivism: Theory, Method and Application* (Newbury Park CA: Sage, 1994), 85–119.

7 Alan Page Fiske, *Structures of Social Life: The Four Elementary Forms of Human Relations* (New York: Free Press, 1991).

8 Harry C. Triandis, *Individualism and Collectivism* (Boulder: Westview Press, 1995).

9 Hofstede, *Culture's Consequences*.

10 Triandis, *Individualism*.

11 Alan Page Fiske and Philip E. Tetlock, 'Taboo trade-offs: Reactions to transactions that transgress the spheres of justice', *Political Psychology*, 18/2 (June 1997), 255–297, 261.

12 Claudia Strauss and Naomi Quinn, *A Cognitive Theory of Cultural Meaning* (New York: Cambridge University Press, 1998).

13 Schwartz, 'Beyond individualism'.

14 David Bakan, *The Duality of Human Existence: An Essay on Psychology and Religion* (Chicago: Rand McNally, 1966).

15 Jerry S. Wiggins, 'Agency and communion as conceptual coordinates for the understanding and measurement of interpersonal behavior', in *Thinking Clearly About Psychology: Essays in Honor of Paul E. Meehl* (Minneapolis: University of Minnesota Press, 1991), 89–113.

16 John E. Tropman, *The Catholic Ethic in American Society: An Exploration of Values* (San Francisco: Jossey-Bass Publishers, 1995).

17 More than 100 years ago, Emile Durkheim excluded the reference to god. Religion, he said, is 'a unified system of beliefs and practices relative to sacred things, that is to say, things set apart and forbidden – beliefs and practices which unite into one single moral community called a Church, all those who adhere to them' (*The Elementary Forms of the Religious Life*, 1912, in 1961 New York edition, p.16). Sociologist Lester Kurtz' more recent definition also excludes reference to a god. Religion, he says, 'consists of the beliefs, practices (rituals), the sacred, and the community or social organization of people who are drawn together by a religious tradition' (*Gods in the Global Village: The World's Religions in Sociological Perspective* (Thousand Oaks, CA: Pine Forge Press, 1995), 9).

18 They include among others three scales developed by psychologists Louis L. Thurstone and Ernest Chave (1966) (the Scale of Attitude Toward God, Scale of Attitude Toward the Bible, Attitude Toward the Church), Milton Yinger's (1969) Scale of Nondoctrinal Religion, and five scales developed by Joseph Faulkner and Gordon DeJong (1966) based on the work of sociologist Charles Glock (1962).

19 The concepts intrinsic and extrinsic were developed by Gordon Allport (*The Nature of Prejudice*
    [Reading, Mass.: Addison-Wesley, 1954; *Personality and Social Encounter; Selected Essays* [Boston:
    Beacon Press, 1960, pp.257–267), and subsequently formed into the Intrinsic/Extrinsic Scale by J. R.
    Feagin ('Prejudice and Religious types: A focused study of southern Fundamentalists [*Journal for the
    Scientific Study of Religion*, 4, 1964, 3–13]). For an excellent summary of efforts to measure religiosity
    see David M. Wulff, *Psychology of Religion: Classic and Contemporary Views* (New York: John Wiley
    & Sons, 1991). Wulff's comprehensive work, which synthesizes theoretical and historical aspects of
    the psychology of religion, is a major contribution to the field.
20 Schroeder et al., *The Psychology of Helping and Altruism*.
21 Lester Kurtz, *Gods in the Global Village: The World's Religions in Sociological Perspective* (Thousand
    Oaks, CA: Pine Forge Press, 1995).
22 Hofstede, *Cultures and Organizations*, 138.
23 Triandis, *Individualism and Collectivism*.
24 M. Ross, *Religious Beliefs of Youth* (New York: Association Press, 1950); M. Rokeach, 'Religious
    Values and Social Compassion', *Review of Religious Research* 11 (1969), 24–29; R.L. Gorsuch and
    D. Aleshire, 'Christian Faith and Ethnic Prejudice: A Review and Interpretation of Research', *Journal
    for the Scientific Study of Religion* 13 (1974), 281–307.
25 Oliner and Oliner, *Altruistic Personality*, 251, 249.

HEROIC ALTRUISM:
HEROIC AND MORAL BEHAVIOUR IN A VARIETY OF SETTINGS

Samuel P. Oliner

L ET ME begin with a true story. Stories, we are informed by Sarbin,[1] Vitz,[2] and Tulving,[3] have an important moral impact because they not only explain an event and arouse emotions about moral and immoral acts, but also inform the reader about what reality is. The narrative story serves as a general metaphor for understanding human conduct. Tulving distinguishes between semantic memory and episodic memory. He maintains that people remember episodes and stories better than abstract ideas or semantic memory.

THE KRAKOW STORY

In 1943, as the Nazis were liquidating the Krakow ghetto, approximately a thousand Jews were being led to the railroad station (Umschlagplatz) to be transported to their death in Treblinka. An anxious Jewish woman carrying a six-month-old infant in her arms realized that a tragic end was in store for her and her baby. She noticed a blonde woman, a Catholic Pole, standing on the sidewalk along with other onlookers. She sneaked away from the marching column for a split second and begged the woman to save her child.

The blonde woman took the child to her third-floor apartment. She was neither married nor had she been pregnant, and her neighbours soon became suspicious. In fact, one neighbour informed the Polish police, who were now in the service of the Nazis. The police arrived, arrested her and the baby, and brought them to the police station where she was interrogated by a Polish police captain. Twelve other policemen were sitting in the same room where the captain's desk was. The Polish captain said to her, pointing a finger at the child, 'This is not your child, is it? This is a Jewish child, isn't it?' The blonde woman, as if by divine inspiration, burst into tears, pounded the desk, stared at the captain, and in a rage said, 'You should be ashamed of yourselves, do you call yourselves Poles? Do you call yourselves gentlemen? There is one man sitting right here in this office who is the father of this child, but he stooped so low that instead of admitting his paternity, he would rather see this child labelled as Jewish, and have it exterminated.' Why did she act to save an innocent life?

As a result of this woman's actions, the child was saved and became a scientist as an adult, and the woman/rescuer survived. We had the privilege of interviewing both of them during our data collection period.

This paper, which is part of a larger study, has a twofold purpose: (1) to report results of our long-term study of rescuers of Jews during the Holocaust; and (2) to discuss our current expanded research on heroic and conventional altruism. The first part of my paper will focus on the research on heroism in Nazi-occupied Europe, specifically summarizing the findings that have come from the 14-year study on heroic rescuers published in 1988 by Pearl Oliner and myself.[4]

PART I STUDY OF GENTILE RESCUERS – PSYCHOLOGICAL, SOCIAL AND CULTURAL FACTORS

Between 1980 and 1988, we interviewed rescuers and bystanders in several countries that had been Nazi-occupied during World War II. Rescuers were interviewed in their own homes and languages and compared with a sample of non-rescuers, who were interviewed at the same time, as well as a smaller group of rescued survivors who we felt had some insight into the character and motivation of rescuers.

Our study was guided by the following three questions: (1) Was rescue primarily a matter of opportunity, i.e. external circumstances and situational factors (such as hiding places, food, etc.) and if so, what were they? (2) Was rescue primarily a matter of individual character, i.e. personal attributes, and if so, what were those traits, and how were they acquired? (3) Was rescue a matter of moral values?

Our study involved interviewing over 700 respondents in Poland, France, Germany, Holland, Norway, Italy, Canada and the United States.[5] The comparison between rescuers, bystanders and rescued survivors showed that both rescuers and bystanders in various countries had an equal opportunity to rescue, and were equally aware of the tragedy and plight of Jews. While rescuers knew of the tragedy and took action, bystanders, who had similar knowledge, refrained from helping during that crisis period. We may also say with a degree of confidence that opportunity may have facilitated rescue somewhat, but did not by any means determine it.

Of the many reasons expressed by our respondents, an overwhelming majority of rescuers (87%) cited at least one ethical or humanitarian reason or value for their actions. Ethics cited included justice and fairness – that the persecution of the innocent could not be justified. But the ethic that mattered most was the ethic of care and compassion.

Most of the rescuers' helping was rooted in a need to assume personal responsibility to relieve suffering and pain. Some rescuers felt a particular affection toward Jews they knew; most rescuers felt an obligation toward others in general. Pity, compassion, concern, and affection made up 76% of the reasons rescuers gave for extending help to strangers. More than 90% said they helped at least one stranger, as well as a friend. Typical expressions of rescuers were:

> 'When you see a need, you have to help.'

> 'Our religion says we are our brother's keepers.'

> 'We had to give help to these people in order to save them. Not because they were Jews but because they were persecuted human beings who needed help.'

> 'I sensed I had in front of me human beings who were hunted down like wild animals. This aroused a feeling of brotherhood with the desire to help.'

> 'I was indignant and aroused against this terrible miscarriage of justice. I couldn't stand by and see innocent people destroyed.'

> 'I was always filled with love for everyone, for every creature, for things. I infuse life into every object. For me, everything is alive.'

Caring was not a spectator sport. It compelled action. Rescuers assumed responsibility – not because others had required them to, but because a failure to act would destroy innocent people.

'I couldn't stand by and observe the daily misery that was occuring.'

'I knew they were taking them and that they wouldn't come back. I didn't think I could live knowing that I could have done something.'

Acquisition of Caring Values.[6]   Many of these values of caring and social responsibility were acquired directly from parents. Although parents played a very important role for both rescuers and non-rescuers, significantly more rescuers perceived their parents as benevolent figures who modelled values conducive to forming close, caring attachments to other people.

The values that rescuers learned from their parents and other significant people in their lives also differed significantly from those learned by non-rescuers. One aspect of such values was related to ethics and ethical behaviour. Significantly more rescuers made the point that they owed an obligation to *all people*. We have termed such an orientation involving caring for all human beings and all living things '*extensivity*'.[7] The extensive-personality predisposition comprises attachment to family in an emotionally healthy way as well as inclusion of diverse others as deserving of care.

'They taught me to respect all human beings.'

'I have learned logical reasoning and also to be tolerant, not to discriminate against people because of their beliefs or social class.'

'I have learned from my parents' generosity to be open to people. I have learned to be good to one's neighbour, to be responsible, concerned and considerate. To work and care. But also to help, to the point of leaving one's work to help one's neighbour.

'My parents taught me discipline, tolerance, and serving other people when they needed something. It was a general feeling. When someone was ill or in need, my parents would always help. We were taught to help in whatever way we could. Consideration and tolerance were very important in our family. My mother and father both trust those feelings. My father could not judge people who lived or felt differently than he, that point was made to us.'

Significantly more rescuers than non-rescuers emphasized learning the value of helping diverse others from their parents. More rescuers felt a sense of responsibility toward others, feeling an obligation to help even when nothing could be gained for themselves from such behaviour. In contrast, many non-rescuers felt themselves exempt from such obligations. Non-rescuers, for the most part, were unaffected by such suffering, were more detached and were less receptive to other people's helplessness and pain. Rescuers' attitudes and feelings may well have resulted from the rescuers' general appraisal of others' similarity to themselves. More frequently they perceived themselves as being like other people around the world, sharing fundamental similarities with all humanity, regardless of others' social and economic status, ethnicity, race or religion. A significant number of rescuers had friends from diverse groups.

The role of discipline was also important in inculcating ethical behaviour. As children, rescuers were more likely to have been disciplined by the use of reasoning and explanation of the consequences of their misbehaviour, rather than having been punished verbally or physically as was common among non-rescuers.

Predisposition to Action.   While some of the above characteristics in our sample of rescuers help explain why they helped Jews, the picture is a bit more complex. Not all rescuers necessarily possessed all the above-mentioned values and attitudes. Rescuers' motivations for their actions differed with respect to the ways they characteristically interpreted moral obligation.

In our research, we were able to identify three categories of rescuer motivation based on theoretical concepts outlined by Janusz Reykowski.[8] Those people who entered into rescue activity in response to a highly valued norm, the expectations of a social group, their moral community,[9] or the leadership of a highly regarded authority were termed *Normocentric*. Rescuers who responded to an external event that aroused or heightened their sense of empathy were considered *Empathic*. Rescuers who behaved according to their own over-arching principles, mainly autonomously derived, and who were moved to action by external events which they interpreted as violating human principles, were deemed *Autonomous/ Principled*.

Normocentric Motivation. For some rescuers, witnessing arrest or persecution of Jews triggered a response based on the norms of the social group that they strongly identified with and to which they normally looked for moral guidance. Normo-centric rescuers' motivations arose not from their connection with the victim, but rather from feelings of obligation to the group or community whose implicit and explicit rules the rescuers felt obligated to obey. For instance, an Italian priest stated:

> A monthly meeting of the clergy used to be held in the seminary. After one of these meetings, Bishop Nicolini took Brunacci aside and showed him a letter from the Secretary of State at the Vatican. This letter called upon all bishops to address themselves to the help of Jews, whose safety was becoming increasingly endangered. Thus, Bishop Nicolini said to Brunacci that the instructions from the secretary of state from the Vatican were to be held in the strictest of confidence.

A Dutch rescuer who rescued two Jewish girls said:

> We read from the Bible the story of Elisha. When the Syrians were coming to take Elisha, his servant was very afraid and said to Elisha, 'My Lord, how are we going to survive? They are going to get you.' But Elisha said no, and the Lord opened the boy's eyes, and he saw all the Syrians were dead. My wife said, 'The Lord sickened his enemies with blindness then and he will do so again.' I didn't believe her, but that's what happened. Those girls – the daughters of the local Nazi boss who escorted Mrs. Roth to our house – were also 'stricken with blindness'. They saw nothing strange in what was happening and never understood what was going on. I know the Lord protected us.

Thus for the normocentric rescuer, inaction was considered a violation of the community's moral norms of behaviour. For these rescuers, feelings of obligation or duty were frequently coupled with anticipation of guilt or shame if they failed to act. In such cases, the norms of the larger community, its habits and culture encouraged tolerance and helping. In the case of Italian rescuers, including military officials, religious leaders and diplomats, such social norms legitimated and encouraged them to sabotage, thwart, slow down and resist the deportation of Italian Jews. Approximately 52% of our respondents said they were motivated by obligations that fell into the normocentric category.

Empathic motivation. Empathic motivation involves concern with the fate of another in distress, and feelings of compassion, sympathy and pity are its characteristic expressions. Reactions may be emotional or cognitive, and frequently contain elements of both. The following account demonstrates instances when empathy was the major motivator of rescuer behaviour.

> 'It was unbearable to watch a human being in such a state. When they knocked at our door, we helped them and fed them. Not only them, but others soon came – Jews from Bologna.'

'In 1942, I was on my way home from town and was almost near home when M. came out of the bushes. I looked at him, in striped camp clothing, his head bare, shod in clogs. He might have been about thirty or thirty-two years old. And he begged me, his hands joined like for a prayer – that he had escaped from Majdanek and could I help him? He joined his hands in this way, knelt down in front of me, and said: "You are like the Virgin Mary." It still makes me cry. "If I get through and reach Warsaw, I will never forget you."'

'Well, how could one not have helped such a man? So I took him home, and I fed him because he was hungry. I heated the water so that he could have a bath. Maybe I should not mention this, but I brushed him, rinsed him, gave him a towel to dry himself. Then I dressed him in my husband's underwear, a shirt and a tie. I had to do it for him because I wasn't sure if he could do it himself. He was shivering, poor soul, and I was shivering too, with emotion. I am very sensitive and emotional' (a Polish rescuer).

Empathic reactions are sometimes overpowering feelings that lead people to react spontaneously. Some rescuers could not stand by and see other people in pain, nor withstand the agony and grief it caused them. As can be seen, in many such cases there was a direct face-to-face encounter with a distressed person, which further heightened the impulse to act. Thirty-eight percent of rescuers responded that they were moved empathetically to their first helping act.

Autonomously Derived Principles. Rescuers with autonomously derived principles interpreted the persecution of Jews as a violation of their own moral precepts. Unlike normocentric motivation, which was prescribed by a certain group behaviour, autonomously derived principled motivation involved acting on one's own, without requiring permission or outside validation for actions. The main goal of such rescuer behaviour was to reaffirm and apply the individuals' personal principles. Even when their actions might prove futile, individuals tended to believe that their principles were kept alive so long as there were people who reaffirmed them by their deeds. An Italian rescuer, responding to the statement that what rescuers did was extraordinary, i.e., that rescuing a great number of people was a truly remarkable act, answered:

No, no. It was all something very simple. Nothing grandiose was done. It was done simply without considering risk, without thinking about whether it would be an occasion for recognition or to be maligned, it was, in effect, done out of innocence. I didn't think I was doing anything other than what should be done, or that I was in any special danger because of what I was doing. Justice had to be done. Persecution of the innocents was unacceptable.

Autonomously motivated rescuers felt directly challenged in fundamental ways by the actions they were observing – they felt that letting such acts occur was tantamount to condoning such behaviour. Only a small minority of rescuers – approximately 11% – fell into this category.

It is important to remember that these three theoretical orientations are ideal types and are seldom found in ideal form in any individual case. For instance, elements of empathy were sometimes associated with normocentric considerations, and principled behaviour was not necessarily devoid of normocentric or empathic motivating influences. Concern with self-enhancement or fulfilment of personal needs also appeared in several cases. For example, one rescuer, upon learning that the women living with her were Jewish, said that she was reluctant to ask them to leave since her relationship with them was the only affectionate ones she had.

Moral and Political Climate Conductive to Rescue. Scholars such as Yahil,[10] Zuccotti,[11] A. Ramati,[12] Carpi,[13] Chary,[14] Flender,[15] Friedman[16] and L. Baron,[17] among others, have addressed the climate in which the rescue of Jews was more likely because social, cultural, and political conditions were more conductive to it and anti-Semitism was less rampant. Thus, partly because of such a climate, in October 1943 almost the entire Danish Jewish population (approximately 95%) was rescued by being shipped to Sweden. In Italy, the fact that 85% of the Jewish population was rescued is attributed to the general lack of anti-Semitism and the absence of a sharply drawn distinction between Jewish-Italians and other Italians.

A variety of explanations for Jewish rescue have been put forward. It is our contention that some of those explanations for rescue support each other. Thus, Fleischner[18] concludes that one of the major factors for rescue was compassion for the Jewish victims as do Kurek,[19] Huneke[20] and Tec.[21] Other researchers found that Christian charity, or other similar religious factors, helps to explain rescue. Among them are Huneke, Fleischner and the Oliners in their latest analysis of their data. Several writers (Sauvage, Fleischner, Kurek, Huneke, Tec, Oliner and Oliner; Hallie,[22] Baron,[23] Sauvage,[24] Zeitoun,[25] London,[26] Fogelman[27]) found that morality was an important motivator in the rescue of Jews.

While none of the primary or secondary studies of rescue have arrived at a single reason for rescue, nearly all concur that such motivation is most often associated with a particular type of socialization experience and moral climate in which ethical behaviour was modelled by a significant other such as a parent. Such experiences may help account for the frequently reiterated statements made by rescuers that helping Jews was simply the 'obvious thing to do'.

PART II   CURRENT RESEARCH ON HEROISM AND CONVENTIONAL
ALTRUISM

Recently we have gathered data on five additional groups: Jewish Rescuers of Jews and non-Jews; military heroes, who have won Congressional Medals of Honor or the Victoria Cross for their valour and bravery; Carnegie Heroes, who won the Carnegie Medal for risking their lives to save individuals (other than members of their families) from certain death; moral exemplars, who by their life and actions have made a difference in society; and Hospice volunteers, members of an organization founded by Dr. Cicely Saunders[28] in England, who concern themselves with helping the terminally ill die in peace, an ideal which has spread over the Western world. The purpose for the inclusion of Hospice volunteers is to broaden our understanding of altruistic behaviour which we have defined as behaviour that (1) is directed toward helping another, (2) involves high risk or sacrifice for the actor, (3) is accompanied by no external reward, and (4) is voluntary.

Jewish rescuers. We begin with Jewish rescuers of Jews and non-Jews. The study is based upon in-depth interviews of two rescuers, Wilhelm Bachner and Jack Werber, who risked their lives to save Jews and non-Jews in Nazi-occupied Poland as well as Ukraine, and on review of the literature. Bachner's deeds consisted of wresting individuals from extermination sites, smuggling out Jews from several ghettos, giving them false names and false identity cards, food ration cards, and employment at the Nazi engineering firm for which he worked. The owner of the firm did not know that his right hand man, an engineer, was Jewish.[29] In 1944 Jack Werber,[30] with the assistance of other members of the underground, managed to save 700 young Jewish children who were scheduled for extermination in Buchenwald. When examining statements by Bachner and Werber and hearing from the individuals that they rescued, it becomes clear that both individuals as well as others exhibited extraordinary courage, empathy and social responsibility and that the notion that murdering the innocent was unacceptable to them. When Bachner was asked why he rescued people, he said that he felt confident that God wanted him to help. He said, 'I sometimes felt that God had nothing else to do but look out for Willie Bachner.' In another part of the interview, he said, 'My grandmother said if you are kind to people you will get rewarded back in many ways.'

Military heroes. As of recent date, over 3,027 persons have received the Congressional Medal of Honor for extraordinary valour and courage in the heat of battle; 574 of these medals were received posthumously. The Congressional Medal of Honor was established in 1863 by Congress, and the British Victoria Cross was established by Queen Victoria during the Crimean War. When we examined these two groups for motivational characteristics, we concluded along with Percival[31] that the motivating factors among military heroes are: (1) strong sense of social responsibility for the others; (2) a certain amount of stubbornness; (3) courage; (4) empathy; (5) honour; and (6) a sense of moral code having been inculcated in the individual who acted heroically.

Gal and Gabriel,[32] in their study of heroism in the Israeli army, concluded heroes are not any distinguished species or extraordinary men of courage; neither are they born heroes. Based upon this, it is difficult to predict who might act heroically during crisis conditions in battle. Their study nevertheless suggested that some consistent themes exist and are crucially important to the understanding of behaviour under fire. These include the feeling that their friends would have done the same thing if the situation were called for and the attachment which men feel toward one another and for their leaders in battle. Gal and Gabriel emphasize the point that acts committed by men in battle may reflect a kind of cohesion with their comrades. In the case of the Israeli army, a large percentage of heroes come from the officer corps. This may be because these have been very soundly taught and trained that they are responsible for one another as well as for their entire unit. Gal and Gabriel conclude that the situational effect may have important bearing on understanding military heroism.

Carnegie heroes. Carnegie heroes have performed acts of rescue in a variety of emergency contexts, including, but not limited to, saving people from drowning, burning, assault, animal attack, electrocution and suffocation.

Christian Fetterolf was awarded the Carnegie medal for civilian heroism. He rescued a woman who was being attacked in a New York subway. Later, when he was in the hospital recuperating, he was interviewed by a *New York Times* correspondent who asked him why he risked his life to save a total stranger. Fetterolf replied: 'What I did makes me a human being. I helped someone who needed help. It wasn't heroic. Until now, I didn't know that everybody wouldn't act the same way.'[33]

In order to provide answers to one of our research questions '*What factors prompt ordinary individuals to risk their lives on behalf of others in emergency situations*', one-on-one, structured interviews were conducted with 210 individuals who have received a medal for heroic behaviour from Carnegie.

The Carnegie Fund was established because on 21 January 1904 a massive explosion occurred in one of Andrew Carnegie's mines. It claimed 186 lives. Soon thereafter, Carnegie set aside $5 million under the care of a commission for civilian heroism. The fund offers financial support for those heroic individuals who are injured, and for the families of individuals who die during, or as a result of, their attempts to rescue victims in need. To be awarded the Carnegie medal, one must first be nominated, then investigated by the Carnegie commission in order to establish 'conclusive evidence to support the threat to the victim's life, the risk undertaken by the rescuer, the rescuer's degree of responsibility, and the act's occurrence'.[34] Criteria for being awarded the Carnegie medal include: (1) the act was voluntary; (2) the rescuer risked his or her life; and (3) the act of heroism occurred in the United States, Canada, or the waters thereof.

Needless to say, there are thousands of people who try to aid others, and 71,000–76,000 have been scrutinized by full-time Carnegie staff before a formal review by the commission itself. Only about 8,300 have received this medal. Approximately 20 percent of awards are made posthumously, reflected by a verse from the New Testament on each medal: 'Greater love has no man than this, that a man lay down his life for a friend' (John 15:3). Any individual who voluntarily risks his or her life to an extraordinary degree and beyond the call of duty trying to save the life of another is eligible for recognition by the Carnegie Hero Fund Commission. The act must be brought to the attention of the commission within two years of the date of its occurrence. Persons not eligible for awards are those whose duties, in following their regular vocation, require them to perform such acts, unless the rescues are clearly beyond the line of duty. Rescuers of members of their immediate family, except in the case of outstanding heroism where the rescuer loses his or her life or is injured are also not eligible for consideration. Nor are members of the armed forces or children (who are considered by the Commission to be too young to comprehend the risk involved). There must be factual evidence of the threat to life of the victim, and evidence that the rescuer has undertaken great responsibility in the act of rescuing. Heroes can be nominated by anyone, and frequently they have been nominated by police departments, fire departments, members of the family, the press, and bystanders.

We found that the most prevalent motivational factor for our sample of Carnegie Heroes was a sense of *social responsibility*. A Carnegie Hero who attempted to rescue a woman from drowning expressed his motivation in terms of an overarching feeling of responsibility for her welfare. He said,

> I just felt like it was my duty as a person … It was just a matter of being a human. You've got to help somebody if they need help, if they are in trouble … It's just part of somebody being in trouble. You've got to help somebody in trouble.

Other motivational factors were feelings of *empathy* for the victim, a sense of *efficacy* in the emergency situation, and the possession of *caring norms* by the rescuer. One rescuer who exhibited an empathetic response to a stabbing victim stated:

> But she just had that fear on her face, you know, of helplessness, and you know, the fear in her eyes that something terrible was going to happen. It was just etched in my mind. And I knew that if I didn't do something that something terribly worse would happen. So I just tried all I could.

Another rescuer who rescued a woman from a burning vehicle explained, 'I kept thinking that the car could blow up at any second because, you know, she was on fire also. I don't know, I was raised to help people and that's the first thing that came to mind.'

On the other hand, *reciprocity*, *self-esteem*, and a sense of *autonomy/justice* were each found to be significant factors for less than ten percent of the rescuers we interviewed. They are evidenced by the following examples:

> I just kept thinking what if it was me? What if I got smashed? And if nobody helped me I would just sit there and burn. I just hope and pray that if that ever happened to me, somebody would do the same thing for me.

There are watchers and there are doers. I have always been a participant. I have never been a spectator....I think that there is an imperative that you go after and help someone that needs that kind of help.

What motivated me is that I saw the guy shooting at the White House and I thought 'He shouldn't be doing that.' ...I would think that I was probably concerned about him hurting people. But really it wasn't a matter of him hurting people. It was a matter that he was doing something wrong and I was going to stop him.

In sum, we found that the most prevalent motivational factor for our sample of Carnegie Heroes was a sense of *social responsibility*. Other motivational factors also included feelings of *empathy* for the victim, a sense of *efficacy* in the emergency situation, and the possession of *caring norms* by the rescuer. On the other hand, *reciprocity*, *self-esteem* and *autonomy/justice* were each found to be significant factors for less than ten percent of the rescuers we interviewed. However, through the use of scales[35] we found that although *self-esteem* was not a prevalent motivational factor, the majority of our respondents did rank as having a high degree of self-esteem. Additionally, the scales revealed that all of our respondents had either a high or moderate sense of *social responsibility* and *locus of control*. We also observed that younger respondents and males were more likely to score as high *sensation seekers*, and that respondents who ranked high on the Altruistic Personality Scale were more likely to have reported prior helping behaviour. Lastly, we also noted that the majority of our sample held either a high or moderate *sense of commonality with diverse others*, and that this was related to their self-reported level of *religiosity/spirituality*.

Moral exemplars. In their seminal book, Colby and Damon[36] developed five criteria, which they used to determine those people who are moral exemplars. These are: (1) Sustained commitment to moral ideals or principles that include a generalized respect for humanity; or sustained evidence of moral virtue; (2) the position to act in accordance with one's moral ideals or principles, implying also a consistency between one's actions and intentions and between the means and ends of one's actions; (3) willingness to risk one's self interest for the sake of one's moral values; (4) a tendency to be inspiring to others and thereby to move them to moral action; (5) a sense of realistic humility about one's own importance relative to the world at large, implying a relative lack of concern for one's own ego.[37]

Philosophers, theologians and others have had a long controversy about the nature of human behaviour. Some say that humankind is brutish and inhumane toward each other; others that underneath the surface most people have internalized traditions and ethics of caring for others. Colby and Damon maintain that ordinary people may act selfishly on occasion but most frequently will act for the benefit of other human beings. Their research consisted of interviewing in depth 23 individuals who had a substantial positive effect on people and who have tried to champion justice and aid in various forms. One example was Suzie Valadez, also known as the 'Queen of the Dump', who was deeply concerned about poor people living around dumps and pollutants. She made a forceful effort to 'show the children that there is a better life than they are living now'. In addition, she tried to do something about crime, drugs and alcoholism in the same area. Suffice it to say that moral exemplars help in numerous different ways. Some of the characteristics we see in moral exemplars are: (1) their disregard for risk and their show of courage; (2) their certainty of response about matters of principle; (3) their unremitting faith in positivity in the face of the most dismal circumstances; (4) the capacity to take direction as well as social support from the followers they inspire; and (5) the dynamic interplay between continuity and change in their personal histories. These characteristics of moral exemplars lead them to interpret that it is possible to have an individual personality and also be committed to a moral cause. Colby and Damon maintain that moral exemplars are both highly individual persons as well as highly committed ones. They do not see any conflict between those two attributes, and moral exemplars do not have to necessarily deny their own comfort while they are helping to bring about a better world.

Hospice volunteers. Using a sample of 93 Hospice volunteers and 73 non-volunteers whom we interviewed, our study attempted to find the characteristics and motivations of individuals who devoted time and energy on a regular basis to care for the terminally ill and their families as Hospice volunteers. The Hospice volunteer seems to demonstrate a stronger sense of connection to others and a strong, intensive religious sense.

Volunteerism can be defined as a non-spontaneous helping behaviour for which one receives no material compensation. It can be parochial, within one's own social group, or non-parochial. Non-parochial volunteerism is a form of conventional altruism in that it is directed at others beyond the parochial group and is accompanied by no external reward. It has been established in the literature that volunteers generally score high on measures of empathy, social responsibility and moral development. Piliavin and others[38] state that individuals who have seen their parents volunteer are more likely to volunteer. It wasn't matter of advising their offspring to volunteer, rather they modelled volunteerism.

In our Hospice sample (73% females, with 88% of the sample being 40 years old or older), 85% of the sample described themselves as 'very religious', and 97% had prior volunteer experience. Seventy-five percent reported their mothers had volunteered and 49% said their fathers had done so. A comparison of Hospice volunteers and non-volunteers revealed a most significant difference with regard to self-esteem or internal/external locus of control. Hospice volunteers, and those who volunteered frequently over their lifetimes, scored significantly higher in the measures of empathy and social responsibility than did non-volunteers. They also scored significantly higher on the measures of intrinsic religiosity, that is, religiosity that is implicit in its nature, as opposed to extrinsic orientation, which is utilitarian, explicit and self-justifying in nature. In response to the question, 'what is the most important thing you learned from your mother?', the most frequent response among Hospice volunteers was religion, followed by kindness, compassion and empathy.

The responses to the question regarding motivations for volunteering were placed within four categories: (a) self-enhancement, (b) empathic, (c) normative, and (d) principled. No Hospice volunteer gave any single motive for volunteering and many gave several. Forty-eight percent of Hospice volunteers gave responses that could be categorized as self-enhancing, including responses describing a need to comfort; to learn more about death; desire to feel needed and useful; the need to develop a sense of connection to the community; and a desire for job-related experience. 'I was probably trying to fill a personal need.' 'I was looking for something meaningful to do.' 'I sought it out to become involved in something where I was needed.' One of the most frequent motivations for becoming a Hospice volunteer was the death of a parent, spouse or close friend. Thirty-seven percent of the Hospice volunteers included this as a motivation. One woman, whose husband had died of cancer, said the following: 'I felt I could do something for someone that I wished I could have had [available to us] when my husband died. I wanted to offer what I would have liked to have had.'

It is apparent that there is wide variation in the motivations of volunteers. Other studies seem to conclude that volunteers are more empathic, self-efficacious, emotionally stable and have a high internal standard of morality and a more sensitive attitude toward others than non-volunteers.

The Hospice volunteers demonstrated a lower incidence of physical discipline in childhood than the non-volunteers. Hoffman[39] has said that the development of the caring, altruistic individual requires setting boundaries between right and wrong, moral and immoral, and deviant and normative behaviour. Hospice volunteers were more likely to have been disciplined by reasoning. This finding reflects Oliner and Oliner's 1988 study of rescuers in Nazi-occupied Europe, which found that rescuers are more likely to have been disciplined by reasoning than the non-rescuers. In addition, it should be added that in considering motivation for volunteerism in general, there appears to be a kind of cultural theme that Americans have an obligation, even a divine obligation, to contribute to the betterment of their community.[40] Adams[41] examined 159 articles published in 19 popular magazines between 1980 and 1989. He focused on motivation for volunteering and charitable giving. Among his findings were that Americans make charitable gifts because they want to help other people, especially people with whom they share communities. The truest form of charity in volunteering is found in local, one on one relationships as has been the case throughout U.S. history. Other motivations for volunteering include altruism and natural generosity, an obligation to do good, to benefit other people and the community, and strong ties with other people.

In some ways, this may reflect Albert Schweitzer's statement. He said, 'One thing I know: the only ones among you who will be truly happy are those who have sought and found how to serve.'

SUMMARY AND IMPLICATIONS

What conclusions can we derive from these six groups? It is clear that there is no single motivating factor that triggers people into action – to help. Rather, there are a variety of factors; these can be characterized as learned caring norms; emulation of parents or other moral role models; having acquired a sense of social responsibility; feeling attachment to diverse other groups and including them in their sense of responsibility; and feeling empathy. *Gentile rescuers* risked their lives, and some lost their lives when they were discovered hiding Jews. This was specifically true in Poland. *Jewish rescuers*, who themselves were hunted victims, were able, through ingenious methods, planning, courage and a sense of responsibility and compassion, to help Jews and non-Jewish victims whom the Nazis hunted. *Military heroes* found themselves in situations, which required them to act courageously to save lives. A moral code frequently is inculcated in most militaries around the world. This code consists of virtue, valour, courage, patriotism and social responsibility. The *Carnegie Heroes* exhibited courage, internalized caring norms, compassion, social responsibility and a sense of feeling that they could not just be a bystander and see others perish. To do so would in some way affect them for the rest of their lives.

Moral exemplars are individuals, who because of their existence and their actions have made society a better place. Had Mahatma Gandhi, Nelson Mandela, the Dalai Lama, Martin Luther King, Bishop Desmond Tutu and scores of lesser luminaries not taken a moral stand, the world would have suffered more, and injustice would have been greater. There appear to be several common motivating factors such as an intrinsic religious factor, a sense of empathy, an internalized norm of caring, and a sense of moral courage and personal potency. In the sample of *Hospice volunteers*, we were able to trace the factors of compassion, the need for affiliation, reciprocal helping, self-enhancement, and an internalized norm of care. In the larger study, which is pending, we will be reporting a more detailed examination of these groups and the motivating factors.

What can we learn from studying these six groups that might benefit us in the present and the future? First, acts of heroic or conventional altruism are not the exclusive province of larger-than-life figures. Rather, they are usually the *deeds of ordinary people*, whose moral courage arises out of the routine of their daily lives; their characteristic ways of feeling; their perceptions of what authority should be obeyed; the rules and models of conduct they learned from parents, friends, schools, religion, political leaders, co-workers and peer groups; and what kind of moral code is to be followed. It is primarily through the virtues of connectedness, commitment and the quality of interactions with parents, friends and neighbours in the community that moral courage is born and nurtured. The importance of parents cannot be over emphasized. But, the task cannot be left to parents alone.

If we are to empower people to actively intervene in the presence of divisive and destructive social forces, then social institutions must also assume that obligation. Schools, clubs, religious institutions, the workplace, and the community in general, should share in the inculcation of moral values, especially an extensive, inclusive orientation. Schools should rework their curricula to implement prosocial education as a basic and urgently needed competency. They should instil in their students not only the need and the ability to act on behalf of others, but also the consequences of indifference towards diverse others. Heroic and conventional helpers need to be included in history books and remembered as moral heroes and role models who made a differ-ence, thus helping to correct the distorted image of humanity brought about by the great wars and genocides.

Institutions will need to appeal to the intellect, emotions and moral group norms, emphasizing the obligation due not only to the members of the immediate community, but to those outside it as well. Such institutions will have to recognize that bonds among people are not only created intellectually, through theoretical articulations, but through the experience of caring.[42] Hence, they will need to become caring institutions, which not only talk about caring as an obligation, but also model it, giving, receiving, and expecting caring behaviour from all participants, including the young.

Such an approach represents a challenge to Western thinking, which has traditionally venerated the autonomous individual guided above all by rationality. But, neither autonomous thought nor rationality can guarantee moral virtue. The same, of course, may be said of emotional reactions and empathy or group norms. The road to virtue is not single but multiple; we need to traverse all its paths. Helpers rely on their social norms for moral direction and respond to victims because to do so confirms and supports the values of the social group with which they identify themselves most closely.

Should our social institutions and communities fail to acknowledge this reality, they may also fail to empower ordinary people with the spirit of altruism. Our need to respond to both local and global concerns in the spirit of altruism is an urgent one. The concept of the 'global village' implies not only the sharing of a single environment and ecology, but of a single moral community.[43] More than a century ago Emile Durkheim observed that rather than an 'agreeable ornament of social life', altruism is essential for the survival of any society. What Durkheim failed to emphasize however, and what the research on rescuers demonstrates, is that benefit accrues not only to society as a whole, but also to the participants in it. Reaching out to others can be enormously gratifying, persuading the actors to believe in their own potency, their skills, and above all, their humanity.[44] To understand goodness, caring and compassion, we need to broaden our perspectives and look at examples of helping in other contexts and cultures, both synchronically and diachronically. Rabbi Schulweis said, 'Goodness is rare but sacred in history; it must not be neglected.' To research and understand and reach goodness would be a valuable legacy to leave to our children.

N O T E S :
I wish to gratefully acknowledge the assistance of the following graduate students who have been helping me with this research at the Altruistic Personality and Prosocial Behavior Institute: Kia Ora Zeleny, Anna LoMascolo, Jonathan Mermis-Cava and Alison Gross. In addition, I especially want to acknowledge Kathleen M. Lee for her participation with me on the research on Hospice volunteers.

1 T.R. Sarbin, 'The Narrative as a Root Metaphor for Psychology' in T.R. Sarbin (ed.), *Narrative Psychology: The Storied Nature of Human Conduct* (New York: Praeger, 1986), pp.3–21.

2 P.C. Vitz, *A Critical Review of Kohlberg's Model of Moral Development*, Unpublished report for the Department of Education, Washington, D.C. (1985).

3 E. Tulving, *Elements of Episodic Memory* (New York: Oxford University Press, 1983).

4 Samuel P. Oliner and Pearl M. Oliner, *The Altruistic Personality: Rescuers of Jews in Nazi Germany* (New York: The Free Press, 1988).

5 For detailed discussion of our methodology in this research, see *ibid.*, pp.261–272.

6 By values, I mean an enduring organization of beliefs concerning preferable modes of conduct and/or states of existence along with continued values of importance. Another meaning is a collective conception of what is considered good, desirable and proper, or bad, undesirable and improper, in a culture. Michael Schulman and Eva Mekler, *Bringing Up a Moral Child: A New Approach for Teaching Your Child to be Kind, Just and Responsible* (Reading, MA: Addison-Wesley, 1985) define moral values as consisting of empathy, kindness and responsibility.

7 For a detailed discussion on extensivity, see Oliner and Oliner, *The Altruistic Personality*, pp.249–260. Also, for an excellent discussion on caring and compassion, see Robert Wuthnow, *Acts of Compassion: Caring for Others and Helping Ourselves* (Princeton, New Jersey: Princeton University Press, 1991).

8 For further discussion of empathic, normocentric and principled motivations, see Oliner and Oliner, *The Altruistic Personality*, p.188; J. Reykowski, 'Dimensions of Development in Moral Values: Two Approaches to the Development of Morality' in N. Eisenberg, J. Reykowski and E. Staub (eds.), *Social and Moral Values: Individual and Societal Perspectives* (Hillsdale, NJ: Erlbaum Associates, 1989).

9 For further discussion on moral community, both religious and secular, see Martin A. Johnson and Phil Mullins, 'Moral Communities: Religious and Secular', *Journal of Community Psychology* 18 (April 1990): 153–166.

10 L. Yahil, *The Rescue of Danish Jewry: Test of a Democracy*, tr. M. Gradel (Philadelphia: Jewish Publication Society, 1969).

11 S. Zuccotti, *The Italians and the Holocaust: Persecution, Rescue, and Survival* (New York: Basic Books, 1987).

12 A. Ramati, *The Assisi Underground: The Priests Who Rescued Jews* (New York: Stein & Day, 1978).

13 D. Carpi, 'The Rescue of Jews in the Italian Zone of Occupied Croatia' in Y. Gutman and E. Zuroff (eds.), *Rescue Attempts During the Holocaust: Proceedings of the Second Yad Vashem International Historical Conference*, 8–11 April 1974 (Jerusalem: Yad Vashem,), pp.465–525.

14 F.B. Chary, *The Bulgarian Jews and the Final Solution, 1940–1944* (Pittsburgh: University of Pittsburgh Press, 1972).

15 H. Flender, *Rescue in Denmark* (New York: Manor Books, 1964).

16 P. Friedman, *Their Brothers' Keepers* (New York: Holocaust Library, 1978).

17 Lawrence Baron, 'The Historical Context of Rescue', in Oliner and Oliner (eds.), *The Altruistic Personality*, pp.13–48.

18 E. Fleischner, *Remembering for the Future: Jews and Christians during and after the Holocaust*, Theme 1, International Scholars Conference, Oxford, 10–13 July 1988 (Oxford: Pergamon Press, 1988), pp.233–247.

19 Ewa Kurek-Lesik, 'The Role of Polish Nuns in the Rescue of Jews, 1939–1945', in Pearl M. Oliner, Samuel P. Oliner, Lawrence Baron, Lawrence A. Blum, Dennis L. Krebs and M. Zuzanna Smolenska (eds.), *Embracing the Other: Philosophical, Psychological, and Historical Perspectives on Altruism* (New York: New York University Press, 1992), pp.328–334.

20 Douglas K. Huneke, *The Moses of Rovno: The Stirring Story of Fritz Graebe, a German Christian Who Risked His Life to Lead Hundreds of Jews to Safety during the Holocaust* (New York: Dodd, Mead, 1986).

21 N. Tec, *When Light Pierced the Darkness: Christian Rescue of Jews in Nazi-Occupied Poland* (New York: Oxford University Press, 1986).

22 Philip Hallie, *Lest Innocent Blood Be Shed* (New York: Harper & Row, 1979).

23 Lawrence Baron, 'The Dutchness of Dutch Rescuers: The National Dimension of Altruism' in Oliner et al. (eds.), *Embracing the Other*, pp.306–327.

24 P. Sauvage, 'Ten Things I would Like to Know About Righteous Conduct in Le Chambon and Elsewhere During the Holocaust', *Humboldt Journal of Social Relations* 13 (1985–1986): 252–259.

25 S. Zeitoun, 'The Role of Christian Community in Saving Jewish Children in France during the Second World War' in *Remembering for the Future: The Impact of the Holocaust and Genocide on Jews and Christians, Supplementary Volume* (Oxford: Pergamon Press, 1988), pp.505–525.

26 P. London, 'The Rescuers: Motivational Hypotheses about Christians who Saved Jews from The Nazis', in J. Macaulay and L. Berkowitz (eds.), *Altruism and Helping Behaviour* (New York: Academic Press, 1970).

27 Eva Fogelman, 'The Rescuers: A Socio-psychological Study of Altruistic Behaviour during the Nazi Era', Ph.D. dissertation, University of New York (1987).

28 See C. Saunders and D. Saunders (eds.), *Hospice: The Living Idea* (Oxford: Oxford University Press, 1981).

29 For greater detail, see Samuel P. Oliner and Kathleen Lee, *Who Shall Live: The Wilhelm Bachner Story* (Chicago: Academy Chicago Publishers, 1996).

30 Jack Werber, *Saving Children: Diary of a Buchenwald Survivor and Rescuer* (London: Transaction Publishers, 1996).

31 John Percival, *For Valour, The Victoria Cross: Courage in Action* (London: Thames, Methuen, 1985).

32 Reuven Gal and Richard A. Gabriel, *Fighting Armies* (Westport, CT: Greenwood Press, 1983).

33 Robert D. McFadden, 'Subway Hero Downplays Bravery', *New York Times*, May 18 1993, p.15.

34 World Wide Web, 26 November 1997, *http://trfn.clpgh.org/carnegiehero*

35 The Self-Esteem Scale we used was developed by M. Rosenberg, *Society and the Adolescent Self-Image* (Princeton, NJ: Princeton University Press, 1965), see Oliner and Oliner, *The Altruistic Personality*, p.378. The Social Responsibility Scale was developed by L. Berkowitz and K. Luterman, 'The Traditionally Socially Responsible Personality', *Public Opinion Quarterly* 32 (1968): 169–185, see Oliner and Oliner, *The Altruistic Personality*, p.376. The Internal/External Locus of Control Scale was developed by J.B. Rotter, 'Generalized Expectancies for Internal Versus External Control of Reinforcement', *Psychological Monographs* 80 (1966): 1; we used an adaptation developed by G. Gurin, P. Gurin and B.M. Morrison, 'Personal and Ideological Aspects of Internal and External Control', *Social Psychology* 41(1978): 275–296, see Oliner and Oliner, *The Altruistic Personality*, p.378. The Sensation Seeking scale was developed by M. Zuckerman, 'Sensation Seeking', in H. London and J.E. Exner, Jr. (eds.), *Dimensions of Personality* (New York: Wiley, 1978), and validated by W.F. Straub, 'Sensation Seeking Among High and Low-Risk Male Athletes', *Journal of Sport Psychology* 4 (1982): 246–253. The Altruistic Personality scale was developed by J. Philippe Rushton, Roland D. Chrisjohn and G. Cynthia Fekken, 'The Altruistic Personality and the Self-Report Altruism Scale', *Personality and Individual Differences* 2 (1981): 293–302.

36 Anne Colby and William Damon, *Some Do Care: Contemporary Lives of Moral Commitment* (New York: The Free Press, 1992).

37 *ibid.*, p.29.

38 Jane Allyn Piliavin and Peter L. Callero, *Giving Blood: The Development of an Altruistic Identity* (Baltimore, MD: The Johns Hopkins University Press, 1991).

39 M.L. Hoffman, 'Affective and Cognitive Processes in Moral Internalization: An information processing approach' in E.T. Higgings, D. Ruble and W. Hartup (eds.), *Social Cognition and Social*

Development: A Socio-cultural Perspective (New York: Cambridge University Press, 1983), pp.236–274.

40   David S. Adams, 'Issues and Ideas in the Culture of American Volunteerism', presented at the American Sociological Association, 1990.

41   David S. Adams, 'Why Should Americans Volunteer? A Content Analysis of Popular Magazines', presented at the Annual Meeting of the North Central Sociological Association, 1991.

42   For detailed elaboration about the eight social processes (bonding, empathizing, learning/caring norms, practising care and assuming personal responsibility, diversifying, networking, resolving conflicts, making global connections, see Pearl Oliner and Samuel P. Oliner, *Toward A Caring Society: Ideas Into Action* (Westport, CT: Praeger Publishing, 1995).

43   See M.A. Johnson and P. Mullins, 'Moral Community: Religious and Secular', *Journal of Community Psychology* 18 (April 1990): 153–166. Their research considers the extent to which community groups (social service clubs, professional organizations, churches, etc.) constitute 'moral communities' (relatively coherent social networks which create and support meaningful human relationships by fostering common attitudes, values and practices). It investigates the relationship between belonging to such a group and feelings of 'mass society' (alienation, moral fragmentation, disengagement and segmentation). The data indicate that for many individuals community groups constitute moral communities, that such groups differ in the intensity and frequency of moral community feelings, and that the religious congregation is more likely to inspire feelings of moral community than is any other community group. Feelings of moral community were significantly correlated with reduced feelings of 'mass society' and increased feelings of self-esteem and of meaning and purpose in life. Feelings of 'mass society' were associated with lower self-esteem and a reduced sense of meaning and purpose in life.

44   E. Midlarsky has done research on the connections between helping others and mental and physical wellbeing. There is a strong correlation between helping others and mental health. Her article 'Helping in Late Life' was published in Oliner et al., *Embracing the Other: Philosophical, Psychological, and Historical Perspectives on Altruism*, pp.253–275. Also, see her book, *Altruism and the Elderly*, (Thousand Oaks: Sage Publications, 1994). The following studies show the positive benefits for helpers/volunteers: Samuel P. Oliner and Kathleen A. Lee, 'Conventional Altruism: Hospice Volunteers' (unpublished, 1991). Also see T. Root, *Atomism versus Social Solidarity: A Comparison of Volunteer Workers in Charities and Politics, and non-Volunteers, with reference to Tolerance of Ambiguity*, Master's Thesis in Philosophy, University of East London (unpublished, 1993); and N. Allen and P. Rushton, 'Personality Characteristics of Community Mental Health Volunteers: A review', *Journal of Voluntary Action Research* 12/1 (Jan–March 1983): pp.36–49.

THE FACE OF THE OTHER:
REFLECTIONS ON THE MOTIVATIONS OF GENTILE RESCUERS OF JEWS

Mordecai Paldiel

THE DEEDS and behaviour of those we term Righteous Among the Nations, that is of non-Jewish Holocaust rescuers of Jews honoured by Yad Vashem, have undergone a certain scrutiny in recent years from both sociological and psychological perspectives. Three of the most important studies in this field are those of Nechama Tec, Samuel and Pearl Oliner, and Eva Fogelman.[1] While each of these suggests different explanations for the uniqueness of the actions of the Righteous, they concur in locating the formative nexus of the behaviour of the Righteous in the childhood years. In this paper, I submit that the exceptional response of the rescuers to the plight of the Jews is perhaps predicated on the presence of a deeper and more primal predisposition, perhaps rooted in our genes, which causes some of us to respond instinctively and instantaneously when placed before a situation that is so upsetting to our senses as to constitute a traumatic experience. This is especially the case when the potential rescuer is witness to a situation in which the principle of the right to life is called into question, as it was for Jews on the European continent during the Nazi reign of terror. Hence, altruistic responses under ordinary circumstances should not be compared with similar responses in times of chaotic upheavals brought about by massive onslaughts on the ethical values governing civilized life. Here, one is led to seek explanations of human responses that lie hidden in the subconscious strata of our minds, and which may provide answers to the two extremes of behaviour witnessed during the Holocaust – that of the perpetrators and that of the rescuers; in this paper, the rescuers.

When seeking explanations for the behaviour of non-Jewish rescuers of Jews, the following factors should be taken into consideration, in view of the extraordinary circumstances in which the rescue operation took place.

To begin with, in most cases it is not the rescuers who seek out people who need to be rescued, but quite the contrary: rescuers are suddenly confronted with a direct appeal for aid, and they comply. To repeat – in the majority of cases, rescuers are first approached and sought out; they are chosen by the victims. It is this encounter that triggers the response. This is especially so in Eastern Europe, where the Jew fleeing for his life approached the rescuer – a person he may have known, or a total stranger – and pleaded to be helped. In one such example, in Poland, 21-year-old Felicia Zaltsenberg fled from Hrubieszow, together with her sister and two brothers, on the eve of a German killing raid in August 1943. Not knowing where to turn, she suddenly thought of Wlodzimierz (Wladek, for short) Kozaczuk, a prewar acquaintance with whom she once shared bike rides and who lived in a village some five kilometres away. 'We thought of him as the only person we could turn to,' Felicia stated in her deposition. She and her siblings walked in pitch darkness until they arrived at Kozaczuk's village. Wladek was not home.

His father immediately turned off all lights, telling the frightened arrivals to remain calm until Wladek's return, when it would be decided what to do with them.[2] In Warsaw, Jerzy Lando, after secretly fleeing the Warsaw ghetto in autumn 1942 and wandering the streets on the Aryan side of the city, decided to approach Boguslaw Howil, who owned a large leather goods retail store, and with whom Jerzy's father had once done business. As Jerzy hesitatingly opened the store door and approached Boguslaw, the man looked at Jerzy 'as if he saw a ghost'. In Western Europe, too, in the majority of cases, the rescuer was approached, either by the rescued person or by a clandestine organization which solicited help. This initial setting places the rescue operation in a totally different perspective by contrast to rescue and aid operations initiated by the rescuer; here, persons seek out those they wish to assist. During the Holocaust, in the majority of cases, it was the victimized Jew who took the first step and sought out his or her possible rescuer.

This dramatic meeting is invariably a face-to-face encounter, often involving a direct exchange of gazes between the hapless victim and the possible rescuer. The importance of this proximity and eye contact cannot be overestimated as a triggering event, especially in Eastern Europe, when the Jew fleeing for his life tremblingly approaches his hoped-for rescuer. The desperate situation of the victim, glaringly manifested in the look of his eyes and expression of his face, as exemplified in the Howil story, cannot be mistaken by the individual in whose hands the victim, at this eleventh hour, has placed his fate. The victim has fled either from a sudden raid on his home by the one of the Nazi security agencies, from a ghetto in the throes of violent dissolution, from a cattle train on its way to a death camp, or from a mass execution raid in front of open pits. In Sorginau, East Prussia, on a freezing night in January 1945, the German farmers Albert and Loni Harder are awakened by a knock on their door. Before them stood several women, recently escaped from an execution raid by the Germans on the shores of the Baltic Sea. The three women had lain in the subzero waters of the Baltic Sea, passing for dead, until the Nazi guards had left; they had stumbled upon the first house in this village, and stood facing the Harders in rags. In Western Europe, the eye-to-contact between rescuer and rescued could take place in less frightening but still near-traumatic situations. In Ghent, Belgium, the Podgaetzki couple approached their family doctor in late 1942 to seek advice on where to place their two daughters, aged six and two, to avoid their deportation. As Dr. Jean van de Velde stared into the troubled faces of Zeilie and Ghitlen Podgaetzki, he had to make an immediate decision. Picking up the phone, he called his wife to consult with her. After a brief phone conversation, he told the couple that he and his wife had decided to shelter the two daughters in their home, and add them to their own two children. This was an on-the-spot decision, occasioned by a face-to-face encounter, at a time of large-scale deportations of Belgian Jews.

The appeal of the victim is not just to help him get through a difficult situation; it is to help him stay alive, as his life is in danger through the arbitrary and senseless decisions of others, who unfortunately hold the reins of power. What is at stake here is life itself, the life of the victimized Jew and all his co-religionists. In the situations described above, the potential rescuers know clearly what is in store for the victim. In Poland, the widespread killing of Jews, and the presence of the death camps, makes it clear to all Poles that the Jewish population is being decimated. In Belgium, Jews are violently picked up in their homes and deported to an unknown destination. Similarly when 15-year-old Felix Zandman appeared in front of the forest cottage of Jan and Anna Puchalski, outside Grodno (today in Belarus), it was the second time he had sought refuge from a Nazi killing raid. On this occasion, he had lost his parents to the Nazis. Felix had luckily escaped and was now seeking refuge in the home of former caretakers of his family's summer cottage homes. In this highly charged atmosphere, the potential rescuer may consciously or subconsciously ask himself: 'Without regard to my personal feelings and prejudices on this person's ethnicity (assuming that these are not always positive) – does this living person standing in front of me have the basic and minimum right to continue to live – a privilege heretofore enjoyed by all living creatures, and now, for the first time, contested by a malevolent human agency?'

Before answering his question, the potential rescuer is conscious that the confrontation with the hapless victim is taking place in highly unusual circumstances. Chaos threatens to overtake ordinary life as arbitrary decisions are made on who is to live or die. The rescuer may reflect that whatever the justification of certain measures against the Jews, there is no reason and excuse to warrant the murderous violence against them, regardless of age or sex. This simply does not make sense; persons living under Nazi tutelage cannot fit what they witness with their ordinary sense of life. Conditions prevailing under Nazi rule, especially the Nazi appropriation of the arbitrary right to decide which of the conquered populations is to live, be enslaved or die, is so irrational that it cannot be integrated within the categories one has acquired for making sense of the world. Life has becomes a cheap commodity as the accumulated values carefully cultivated over two millennia are trampled upon and discarded. This results in a situation of traumatic emergency for both rescuer and rescued. In France, John H. Weidner, who spirited many Jews across the border into Switzerland, related a sight he witnessed at a railway station in Lyon. A Jewish woman was holding a baby in her arms, and the baby started to cry. The SS man took the baby, threw it to the ground, and crushed its head with his boot. 'I can never forget the sight and the sound of that baby,' Weidner related.[3] Similarly Marion Pritchard-van Binsbergen, related the incident in Amsterdam which prompted her to change course and become involved in the rescue of Jews:

> One morning on my way to school I passed a small Jewish children's home. I saw the Nazis loading children, from babies to about eight years old, onto trucks. They were all crying, and when they didn't move fast enough, a Nazi would pick them up by an arm or leg, or even hair, and throw them onto the trucks. I was so shocked by this treatment that I found myself in tears. Then I saw two women coming down the street try to stop them, and the Germans threw them into the trucks, too. I stood frozen on my bicycle. Before this I had known of the threats but I hadn't actually seen the Germans in action. When I saw that, I knew that my rescue work was more important then anything else I might be doing.[4]

Similarly, in Poland, Jan Karski, on the eve of a mission to London on behalf of the Polish underground, was shocked by what he witnessed in the Warsaw ghetto. In his words, it was clear to him, that for the Jews, 'this was the end of the world.' The two Jewish leaders he met secretly told him bluntly

> You other Poles are fortunate. Your are suffering too. Many of you will die, but at least your nation goes on living. After the war Poland will be resurrected. Your cities will be rebuilt and your wounds will slowly heal... We [Jews] will be dead... The Jewish people will be murdered... Our entire people will be destroyed. A few may be saved, perhaps, but three million Polish Jews are doomed.

As Karski sat riveted in his chair, he felt 'a painful, oppressive kind of reality that no nightmare ever had... I sank into my armchair. My whole body felt chilled and sore. I was shivering and I felt the pulses in my temples pounding.' A few days later, inside the Warsaw ghetto, secretly witnessing the violent roundup of Jews, 'everything there seemed polluted by death, the stench of rotting corpses, filth and decay.' This confrontation with a world turned upside down, which left him in a state of stupor and shock, had a shattering effect on Jan Karski, and resulted in his mission being transformed into a rescue mission for the doomed Jews of Europe.[5]

The potential rescuer tells himself that he has not chosen this responsibility. He may reflect: 'I have not decided that I want to go out and rescue the other. The other person has either thrust himself upon me, or quite unintentionally I happened to be confronted with a plea by the victimized person. That person's life is now paradoxically in my hands. I can either respond favourably or turn him away to face an almost certain death. I am called to play God.' This terrible and frightening dilemma prevailed in many such encounters between rescuers and rescued, particularly in East European countries under German dominance. An extreme example of this is how in May 1942 the six-year-old Janena Svirska was pushed out by her mother from a column of Jews being led to be murdered, on the outskirts of Rovno in the Wolyn section of Ukraine. The mother told the numbed girl: 'Janutzka, run over to Katia,' a woman who was standing not far from the marching column. This person, Yekatarina Shidlovskaya, realized that Janena's mother had thrust her daughter into her arms, for a very basic and elementary reason – to save the child's life. In Poland, 19-year-old Haim Bzezinski fled with a friend from a liquidation raid in Semiaticze on a cold December night in 1941, to seek out his acquaintance Roch Kosieradzki. When Roch opened the front door, he felt terribly frightened, and did not know how to react. His family had been friends with Haim's family, but they were frightened of the consequences for themselves if Jews were found in their home. In answer to Haim's plea to allow him to hide for just a little while, Roch left to consult with his wife and children, and returned stating: 'I am risking my family's life, but I must help you.' Haim and his friend were led to a potato storage room, where they remained hidden for a long time. The two had thrust themselves on Kosieradzki, who in a dramatic face-to-face encounter, knowing the issue was life itself, responded affirmatively.

In these examples, the rescuer was perfectly aware of the powerlessness of rescued person. He saw the other's vulnerability and his helplessness – similar to that of an infant child. To survive, the person facing him desperately needed his help. In all of the stories recounted above, the rescued person had come to the end of the line. At the moment of the face-to-face contact, his life is practically speaking in the hands of the potential rescuer. In Berlin – to give another example – Kurt and Ursula Reich had despaired of finding a hiding place. 'After finally running out of any possible additional hiding places by the end of August 1943,[6] we had no choice but to give up to the Nazis.' However, they wanted to try to save their little daughter Monica, born the previous December. Through trustworthy people, they contacted Otto and Hedwig Schroedter, who agreed to keep the child and promise to return it to its parents, should they survive the war. As Ursula bid a tearful farewell to her baby, Mrs. Schroedter suddenly remarked that there were was an additional couch in their home, and invited Ursula Reich to move in. To Ursula's inquiry whether her husband could join her, the Schroedters consented. For 19 months, the three Reichs were sheltered in the home of the Schroedters, whose son Herbert was fighting in the German army. The helpless situation of the Reichs, who were on the point of turning themselves over to the Nazis, triggered the Schroedters' offer of refuge.

The rescuer also senses his unique situation – if he doesn't act, it is highly unlikely that anyone else will, for the victim has come to him when all other routes of escape were closed. The victim is now at the last stretch, and needs to be helped in order to survive. The rescuer may think to himself: 'I cannot hand over the task to someone else. There are no alternatives to my acting. The person's life is in my hands, and mine only.' When

20-year-old Moshe Olshevitz, together with his brother, sister and parents appeared at the home of Aleksander Wyrzykowski, after fleeing a German liquidation raid on the Lomza ghetto in November 1942, they had been wandering for days in cold and freezing weather. Moshe's family had decided on a last gambit – to seek temporary help with an old acquaintance. Aleksander readily agreed to the request for a piece of bread, and for a night's stay in his home. In the morning, as the Olshevitz family made ready to quit and continue their aimless wandering, Aleksander and his wife Antonina suddenly stopped them with the words: 'Don't go, children. Whatever we eat you will also eat. Whatever will happen to you will also happen to us. We cannot allow ourselves for you to fall in the hands of the Germans.' In the words of Moshe: 'We fell at their feet, and with tear-drenched words thanked them for their sacrifice.' The Wyrzykowskis, who had two children, cared for the Olshevitzes for two and a half years, who remained hidden in an underground shaft. Made uniquely and irreplaceably responsible, since the Olshevitzes had nowhere else to turn for help, the Wyrzykowskis responded by extending a one-night stay indefinitely – in fact, until the area's liberation, two and half years later.

Whether he was consciously aware of it or not, when he assumed the mantle of a rescuer, he was as though a divine messenger, in the sense of willy-nilly having to decide on the fate of the defenceless person facing him. At this crucial moment, the victim's life was in his hands, and he was called to play God. In deciding to save, he acted in accordance with God the creator – in making possible an extension of life; verily, a new life to the victim. To arrive at such a crucial decision, there was, however, little time to reflect. The decision to intervene had to be taken within the shortest possible time. Facing the distraught women, in their bedraggled clothes, the Harders knew they had to act on the spot – allow them in or not. Similar, when Michal Majercik in Zilina, Slovakia, heard the footsteps of the Gestapo leading down the stairway a young Jewish girl in order to deport her to the camps, his response was instantaneous. Wanting to save the girl, he waited until he heard a Gestapo agent order the 12-year-old Janka Fisch to walk alone down the several floors, so as to be met by another Gestapo man on the ground floor. As Janka passed Michal's apartment, the door suddenly swung open and two hands grabbed her and yanked her inside the Majerciks' home, where Michal and his wife Anna hid her under the crib of their infant child in time for the expected visit of the Gestapo, who rummaged through their home to try to find the missing girl. Here, too, to save the life of this young girl, a decision had to be taken literally within a few brief minutes, perhaps only seconds.

In such highly charged situations, there were several responses open to the possible rescuer. It could be: 'I am sorry, I cannot help, because I am afraid for myself or my family. So please leave right away.' Or: 'Leave after a brief rest' or 'after a night's sleep and some food.' A person captive to his stereotyped opinions could exclaim that he will not help because of his hatred of Jews, or because what is happening to the Jews does not concern him. Finally, the response could take the form of an invitation to take shelter in the rescuer's home for the time being, until an alternative plan for the fleeing victim could be visualized. Shoshana and Shelomo Gon were sheltered for a while by a Ukrainian farmer in the Dubno region. One day, overcome with fear, the farmer told them: 'Here's a piece of bread. Leave! The danger is great.' The Gons continued to a nearby village and, seeking work, tried to pass as Polish refugees. One man told them: 'You're Jews! I already have some people like these.' He gave them a piece of bread, and said: 'Go on; I have no additional place for people like you.' They then accosted a Czech couple, who told them: 'We know you're Jews. It is dangerous to take you in. Go hide in the cemetery; at nightfall we will come to fetch you.' So, indeed, it was. In Shoshana's words, 'These poor people, whom we never met before, took us into their home, and allowed us to stay in their attic for months.'[7] In the Tarnopol region (today in Ukraine), nine-year-old Tova Zehavi-Willner and her mother found temporary refuge in the home of a Polish farmer whom they knew from before. Fearing betrayal by his neighbours, the farmer asked them to leave. They found temporary shelter with another farmer, and were again made to leave. After a while, they learned that a relative was hiding with another farmer. When they approached this man, he adamantly denied he was hiding a Jew, but suggested that perhaps the two women had in mind someone else, with a similar name. Totally exhausted, they reached the other house. There, too, they were told that no Jewish person was hiding with them, but before having them leave, the farmer asked his wife to warm up some milk and food for the two women. As they ate the precious food, the farmer secretly slid off to an underground bunker, where the women's uncle and four others were hiding. He wanted them to verify that the woman upstairs was the sister of one of the hidden men. The hidden people asked the farmer, Michaylo Bomok, to converse loudly with the two women so they could judge whether one of them was indeed his sister. Bomok's suspicions were allayed when this man ventured out of the hiding place to embrace his sister. The two women remained hidden at the Bomok home until liberation. In these stories, we sense the varieties of responses by potential rescuers to the pleas of help – responses conditioned by prejudices, fears and uncertainties.

In taking action to help, the rescuer was confident of his ability to undertake a rescue operation and tip the balance in favour of the fleeing victim. This is to be contrasted with the passive non-rescuer and his feeling of powerlessness to effect a change, as well as his aloofness from the constraints of others around him. The rescuer may initially have thought of a rescue operation limited in time; that would last only for a short period until some other plan was figured out. The rescue may have started in small steps, and then have been extended as the rescuer gained confidence in himself, learned to master his fears, and cement his commitment to the others whose lives depended on him. Jonas Paulavicius, in Panemune, Lithuania, was first approached with a request to shelter a Jewish child from the nearby Kovno ghetto. As the child was constantly weeping, Jonas suggested that its parents join the child. Jonas's son, Kestutis, then asked his father to save a Jewish youth from the ghetto who was very good at the violin. Thinking of the benefit to his son (free violin lessons), Jonas consented. He was then approached with a request to add several more people; his response was for his interlocutors to find professional persons (doctors, engineers), who were worth saving since they would be capable after the war of restoring a viable Jewish community life. As the number of sheltered Jews kept increasing, Jonas built several underground hiding places outside his home, located on the banks of a river, carefully discarding into the river at night the excess soil dug out from the ground. It then struck him that he could add several more Jews to his hiding place. To find the additional persons, he placed himself at road intersections to accost fleeing Jews. One such lucky person was Miriam Krakinowsky, who in July 1944 fled from a forced labour column and was taken by Jonas (at first against her will) to join the others hiding in and near his home. All told, twelve Jews escaped death at the hands of the Germans thanks to an unassuming carpenter, who at first only thought of saving one Jewish child. One small, hesitating step eventually led to giant steps, as the rescuer gained in self-confidence and his ability to save more people. In Buczacz, Poland, Manko Szwiersczak, at first sheltered Jews for short intervals in a cemetery house, where he worked as a janitor, during Nazi killing raids on the ghetto. As the ghetto entered its death throes, he agreed to shelter five persons for an indefinite period inside a tomb which had been emptied of its coffin and enlarged, with Manko secretly providing them with food and comfort for a long period. Here too, a small step at the beginning led to more daring undertakings, as the rescuer felt reassured in his ability to withstand the difficulties and fears associated with the rescue operation.

At the same time, in deciding to shelter one or several Jews in his home, the rescuer was fully conscious of the enormous dangers, not only from the Germans, who made public their threats to deal harshly with anyone trying to prevent the elimination of the Jewish population, but also from elements within their own people – collaborators, antisemites and betrayers of various sorts and colours. Jonas Paulavicius was murdered by a Lithuanian antisemite soon after the war. In Poland, Jan and Stefania Sosnowy were brutalized by a unit of the Polish underground after they learned that he was sheltering a Jew on his farm. Refusing to disclose the whereabouts of the hidden Jew, the couple were taken out of their home to be shot. The hidden Jew, Eli Ashenberg, notes in his testimony that had either one of his rescuers 'decided to confess and give up the Jew (me) to be killed – that would have been the end of it. Unlike the Germans, Poles generally would not kill their fellow Pole who gave up the Jew he was hiding.' After about 15 minutes, Jan and Stefania were released from their ordeal. The death threat was not carried out; perhaps because the raiding party believed the Sosnowys' denials. 'I said to Stefania that after this I would have to leave. Stefania said that after all they went through to save me, she could not consent to my leaving.' The threat emanating from these quarters was open-ended; that is, without a specified time limit, as the rescuer could not tell how long the war will last, nor know, whatever his own hopes, who would be the winner.

An additional factor to take into consideration is that the Holocaust rescuer of Jews cannot be associated with the hero-type who is lauded by society. Above and beyond the fact that the rescuer's action was done in secret – once the action was uncovered, it could no longer continue – his action was not one which had the approval of his surrounding society. This was especially the case in East Europe, with its long history of anti-Jewish pogroms, where the prevailing view was that the elimination of the Jewish presence in their midst was not to be regretted. In addition, most heroic actions, lauded by society, have a foreseen finality. Not so for the Holocaust rescuer; he knows when his rescue operation began, but he cannot be sure how long his commitment to help will last and whether he will survive this dangerous test. Wlodzimierz (Wladek) Kozaczuk did not tell his grown-up children, who lived separately from their parents, of the presence of Jews in his home. Wladek's father, who had penchant for hard liquor, promised not to touch a drop during the 11 months the four Jews hid in the attic of his barn, so as not to reveal the secret inadvertently and bring tragedy upon his family as well as the hidden Jews. Stanislaw Nowosielski, in Poland, came upon two Jews who had jumped a train taking them to the Treblinka death camp and hid them on his farm. With the exception of his wife, none of his family knew of this rescue conspiracy, which lasted for 15 months. In behaviour that did not accord with prevailing social norms – and might even run counter to those norms – secrecy was of prime importance.

All these factors lead us to differentiate between the motivations of the Holocaust rescuer and those affecting the altruistic personality, whose actions take place under normal circumstances. What we commonly term an altruistic personality has a history, which evolved over time, and expresses itself in a certain pattern of behaviour. When a person decides to embark on an altruistic course of action, this is done after much reflection and careful consideration of a type of action which the agent considers most meaningful to his life. Our rescuer does not fit this pattern, as he did not choose this course of action. He does not seek but is sought out, or has been confronted by a situation, unanticipated by him, placed before a moral dilemma and challenged to become a rescuer, and he has little time to reflect and decide.

Bearing all this in mind, how is one to explain the Holocaust rescuer's sudden decision to become a saver of lives; a decision which may even come as a surprise to the author of the rescue? Let us recapitulate one of the basic elements in the dramatic encounter between potential rescuer and victim: the issue at stake is life itself – the animating breath of a living person, in this case a Jew; a life which the rescuer shares with the victimized Jew as a living being. This life is now being threatened with extinction; not brought about through age or sickness, but by the arbitrary decision of a human agency as to who is to live and die – a privilege that to a believing person belongs only to a transcendent and divine figure, to God himself. In this very peculiar face-to-face encounter, where life is at stake, the behavioural patterns of both rescuer and rescued recede to what I would term a primal level of their existence, which is linked to life itself and its preservation – a life which both parties share. Life is, after all, the foundation and ground of all one's human possibilities, including the possibility to experience and make sense of life. Without life, nothing else is possible. Hence, the talmudic motto of 'whoever saves a life saves an entire world.' As such, most people inherently feel that life is sacred, and should not be easily taken away. However, now life itself is being called into question, and this undermines the very possibility of making sense of human existence. The affirmative response by the rescuer is, consequently, an affirmation of life as the foundation of everything, including of making sense of life. Thus, in risking his life for the other, the rescuer reverts to a primal feeling of a common bond which links all human beings. The rescuer experiences an identity with the other; in this case, a hunted Jew. In risking his life for the other, he shares with the other the sense of life as something that is at risk, that cannot be taken for granted, and should be spared. Understood thus, in saving the life of a Jew, the rescuer is saving his own life, in the sense of reaffirming the primacy of life over all other ideological considerations, including the merits and demerits of the victimized person, as in the following story. In a farming village, near Wengrow, Poland, Sevek and Lonia Fishman asked Jan Wikiel whether he could lodge them just for one night. A month earlier, Sevek, a tailor by trade, had cut a suit for Wikiel. It was now Spring 1943, and the killing of Jews in Poland by the Germans had entered its final stages. To Sevek's plea, Jan responded with an offer of payment in return for Sevek's cutting a suit for Jan's son. Sevek said he did not want money but a place to hide for himself and his wife. That evening, Jan learned that on that day the Germans had discovered hidden Jews in a neighbour's home. The house was torched, and all perished. This traumatic experience transformed Jan Wikiel's decision. He no longer asked them to leave on the following morning, but insisted they stay for as long as it might take. Sevek and Lonia Fishman remained hidden in a shaft in Wikiel's home for 18 months. During so long a period, a 'very strong' relationship developed between them. In the words of the Fishmans:

> They comforted us, washed us, and fed us. We became a family. Our love for each other grew, for if we were discovered all of us would die. No one ever found out. We stayed buried all day and the only time we came out for fresh air or to bathe was late at night. The Wikiels would take turns watching so it would be safe.

What started as a one-night stay in the light of the frightening realization of the senseless and criminal destruction of lives, a tentative business arrangement, was transformed into an open-ended rescue operation, lasting until the area's liberation.

This sense of responding out of the depth of one's primal existence is reinforced by the sense of individuality and loneliness which the rescuer found himself after committing himself to the rescue act. This is predicated from the distinction which we draw between the ethics of one's immediate society and the ethics of rescue. Most people, indeed, see themselves as ethical, but it is an ethics dictated by society, of 'following the rules'. Most of the moral decisions we make in our daily lives are not strictly individual but group-programmed norms and rules of behaviour; an ethics which is relative to society – the determiner of our behaviour. However, societies can be decent, or like the Nazi society, they can be murderous. Social ethics cannot, therefore, guard us against the moral collapse of society. By contrast, the rescuer's behaviour is not externally and socially imposed, and not coloured by social approbation. Its content is not determined by prevailing social mores. There is no expectation of social reward for this type of action (as contrasted with participating in underground activity against the enemy). Ethics, as a set of social standards, therefore has no inherent content. On the other end of the spectrum – the deeds of the Holocaust rescuers, who acted independently (or even against) society's standards, are rooted in an ethical content which appears to be inherent and, consequently, the rescuer's action is the closest a person can come to a pure and pristine form of individuality.

In the rescue operation, this special relation between rescuer and rescued, between one individual to another, is absolute. It is as though the totally Other intermingled and was absorbed by the totally I – perhaps consciously unbeknown to the rescuer, since it took place on a subconscious level. Moreover, this unique relationship and bond between the I and the Other, especially against the terrifying background of Nazi terror, individualized the rescuer in a special way – as though a new, and second, person had emerged in the rescue act, even if only for a limited period – a new I, which, as further explained, had already been potentially present in the rescuer's mind. This new I – the one who saves and sustains life, now predominates over the other I – the one with a whole baggage of personal fears, angers, feelings, tendencies, idiosyncrasies, prejudices and stereotyped opinions – which is presently in abeyance.

This may explain the inability of the rescuers to express in everyday terms and motivations what they did. Explanations such as 'anybody would have done what I did,' seem to point to a course of action done without premeditation, almost instinctively. It may be that the trauma of the senselessness of the situation pushed them to a primal and precognitive level in their response to it.

The significance of a personal ethics, rooted in one's relation to others, occupies an important place in the philosophical thinking of Emmanuel Levinas. According to him, the ethical responsibility toward others should be the starting point and primary focus for philosophy; in that 'ethics precedes ontology' (the study of Being). That the search for one's true Self is possible only with its recognition of the Other, a recognition that carries responsibility toward the other person. That other person, in Levinas's thought, is irreducibly different from one's own selfhood, and yet is part of you, in the sense that a true evaluation of one's individuality is only possible by integrating within oneself the presence of the other person, without necessarily trying to control and dominate him. In this context, 'ethics begins with the face of the other,' which includes a recognition and respect of the other's selfhood or, in Levinas's words, the other's Alterity. This recognition of one's relation and obligation to the other is what allows a person to attain a full individuality – of being at one with one's Being. According to Levinas, the face-to-face encounter is the beginning of a personal and authentic ethics which exists beyond every form of a socially conditioned ethics. So viewed, the face of the Other has a special metaphysical and moral significance. The tangible presence and proximity of the Other's face evokes, on a pre-cognitive level, the realization of the Other's and one's own mortality, coupled with a recognition of every person's self individuality, and the preclusion of turning the other person into a tool for the fulfillment of one's egotistical needs. It also evokes the realization of the primordial importance of life itself.

An additional element in Levinas's thought is the importance of speech as a catalyst in the pre-cognitive realization of the importance of the Other's existence and Selfness. Hearing the voice of the other person facing you, and responding to him, is the ground of an authentic relationship based on a common responsibility of one to another, with both sides respecting the Otherness and separate individualities of each other. In the words of Levinas, responsibility is the essence of speech.

In addition, paradoxically, on a very deep level, the other person's face is a reflection of an Otherness (or 'alterity' in Levinas's language) that is within me, coupled with a realization of one's own mortality. As phrased in philosophical language by one interpreter of Levinas' thought, the Other 'is my standing-outside-myself-calling-myself-into-question.'[8] The face of the other, coupled with an authentic relationship with the other, the stranger, integrates his presence inside yourself, and makes him an 'insider', a part of my own worth and self-estimation – or my Being. This, without my being able to fully apprehend that other person. This constitutes the ongoing rupture of phenomenology, a rupture that I experience as the face continually 'tears itself away' from my representation, for I cannot fully grasp it. At the same time, insofar as the Other is within me; that is, an element of my consciousness, this inability to fully comprehend the other person is also part of me. It expresses itself as a limitation of my ability to completely synthesize, grasp, and objectify the other person. As long as I engage in the face-to-face encounter, it prevents my objectification of the other from ever reaching the status of a stereotype. Stereotyping makes the other an outsider, and easily an object for my domination and exploitation of the other person.[9]

A true ethics, according to Levinas, begins with intentionality, which is a turning towards and responding to the Other, since I am only true to myself as long as I carry the other's presence in myself. This encounter with the Other makes possible a true self-dialogue with one's conscience – the soul's dialogue with itself. That takes place when I question myself in light of the Other, who is somehow also present in me, in my consciousness, yet is not of it. My grasp of myself necessarily includes a grasp of the Other who is in me, although as an other than me.

This apprehension of the Other necessitates a commitment, of caring for the other person's needs, when such a necessity arises. This obligation is non-symmetric, in the sense that my help to him is not conditioned by a similar reciprocal obligation by the assisted person. According to Levinas, this concern for the Other is, from a religious perspective, the most authentic form of obeying God's will. God as a transcendent Being is unapproachable, except through the encounter with the Other; with another human being; an encounter which imposes an obligation upon one of the parties. This, according to Levinas, is the essence of a true religious life – the concern for the other's well-being occasioned by the face-to-face encounter.[10]

For a good illustration of how a fleeting face-to-face encounter with victimized Jews, against the setting of unspeakable brutality, transformed an innocent bystander into a grand rescuer of Jews, I have chosen a story which took place, not in Eastern Europe – where conditions for both Jews and the local populations were extraordinarily cruel – but in Belgium, Western Europe, where the German occupation was, relative to Eastern Europe, less harsh.

In late 1942, Alice Van Damme was riding a tramway in Antwerp when, as it approached the central train station, it was suddenly stopped by the Germans, and all occupants were ordered to evacuate the tramway, and line up against a wall for an inspection of their credentials. Curious to know the reason for this, Alice slipped toward the station entrance, and saw lorries lined up. She witnessed an indescribable tumult, as Germans forces separated weeping parents from their children, then forced the parents on the lorries. A crowd watched helplessly and in shock the horror unfolding in front of their eyes. In the confusion, Alice heard one Jewish person shout out a plea to help a certain Dr. Constant, including his address. Returning home, in the nearby town of Belsele, visibly shaken, she decided to look up this stranger Dr. Constant on the following day. The man gave Alice the address of two persons needing immediate assistance. Rushing to the first place, it was too late; the Gestapo having already picked up the residents. Continuing to the second address, Alice met Mrs. Sobolsky, whose husband had already been deported, and who remained with her mother-in-law and her two children, Marcel (four years old) and Johnny (18 months). That same day, Alice brought Mrs. Sobolsky with her two children to her parents' home. Content that her children were safe and secure, Mrs. Sobolsky voluntarily returned to her Antwerp home. 'From this moment,' Alice said, 'I went each week to Antwerp, with provisions for the two women, who did not dare leave their homes.' Two weeks later, Mrs. Sobolski asked Alice to try help another family in distress. From that day, Alice began caring for the Horowitz family, in their self-imposed isolation, with food parcels. Then Mrs. Simonne Horowitz was hidden with Alice's sister, Laura, in nearby Lokeren. A week later, Alice took on an additional assignment – sheltering two children, Henri and Sylvain Grunstein, who were placed with Alice's brother Gaston, who as a married man lived separately. Two weeks later, two more Jewish women were added to Alice's beneficiary list – Mrs. Karfiole and her mother-in-law. The two were sheltered with Alice's mother, who was already caring for the two Sobolsky children (whose mother and the latter's mother's-in-law were eventually deported).

Alice married on 26 February 1943. Hardly a week later, she was summoned by the Antwerp prosecutor's office to submit to an intensive interrogation on her help to Jews. Returning home, she learned that little Johnny Sobolsky had taken ill and needed to be hospitalized. With the consent of her husband, Alice declared Johnny to be her out-of-wedlock son, thus allowing him to be properly registered and admitted in a hospital for surgery. That same year, Alice's parents were betrayed and arrested. A year later, came the turn of Alice's sister Maria to be arrested, together with the two sheltered children, Marcel and Johnny Sobolsky. After a fortnight, Maria was freed; the Germans placed the children in a children home, and their deportation was temporarily halted. Alice's mother Leontine and her sister-in-law Adrienne (Gaston's wife) were incarcerated in an Antwerp jail. Leontine remained there until Belgium's liberation, in September 1944, whereas Adrienne was deported to Ravensbruck camp, which she luckily survived. Of the sheltered Jewish persons, those who survived the Nazi ordeal, thanks to Alice's and her family's intervention included Henri Grunstein, who remained imprisoned on Belgian soil and was later reunited with his brother and parents, and the Sobolsky brothers, who left to be adopted by an aunt in the USA.

Thus the sudden and accidental confrontation with hapless Jewish victims of Nazi brutality transformed an innocent onlooker, first herself, then her relatives, into an extended family of rescuers of lives, with some of the rescuers suffering incarceration in Nazi jails and concentration camp. It was all caused by the shrill cry of help by one of victims; a plea to look up a certain Dr. Constant, during a tumultuous face-to-face encounter with a world of ethical values turned upside down, as mothers were being torn from their children, before their deportation to the camps. Such dramatic encounters did not necessarily provoke all rescue situations – though they did occur in many, perhaps most.

As a final observation, I should like to point out the importance of the stories of these Holocaust rescuers, recognized by Yad Vashem as 'Righteous Among the Nations', as a therapeutic antidote to the unhealed wounds of the Holocaust. These knights of the spirit represent an affirmation of life *contra* death; their stories a tool to make us hope rather than despair. Primo Levi stated it best in his praise of the Italian bricklayer in Auschwitz, with whom he had a fateful encounter and who thereafter gave him additional food and a means of communicating with his mother, who was hidden in Italy. Levi's life was saved through the intervention of this stranger, whom he met accidentally when he was assigned to help out a group of Italian workers who had been contracted to erect a building. After the war, Levi pondered on the meaning of his miraculous rescue at the hands of Lorenzo, initiated by a face-to-face encounter, and drew the following conclusions:

> However little sense there may be in trying to specify why I, rather than thousands of others, managed to survive the test, I believe that it was really due to Lorenzo that I am alive today; and not so much for his material aid, as for his having constantly reminded me by his presence, by his natural and plain manner of being good, that there still existed a just world outside our own; something and someone still pure and whole; not corrupt, not savage, extraneous to hatred and terror; something difficult to define, a remote possibility of good, but for which it was worth surviving ... Thanks to Lorenzo, I managed not to forget that I myself was a man.[11]

In line with Primo Levi's thoughtful words, one ventures the hopeful thought that thanks to the thousands of Lorenzos admitted by Yad Vashem in the Righteous Hall of Fame, whose intervention on behalf of the victimized Jews of the Holocaust was the result, in most cases, of a face-to-face encounter – their example reinforces our hope that man may, indeed, fulfill his true inner essence through an ethics based on a concern and responsibility for fellow man.[12]

NOTES

1 Nechama Tec, *When Light Pierced the Darkness* (New York: Oxford University Press, 1984); Samuel Oliner and Pearl Oliner, *The Altruistic Personality* (New York: Free Press, 1988); Eva Fogelman, *Conscience and Courage* (New York: Doubleday, 1994).

2 Unless otherwise indicated, all rescue stories and their authors appearing in this paper are listed in alphabetical order in note 12.

3 Gay Block and Malka Drucker, *Rescuers: Portraits of Moral Courage in the Holocaust* (New York: Holmes & Meier, 1992), p.55.

4 *ibid.*, page 34.

5 Jan Karski, *Story of a Secret State* (Boston: Houghton Mifflin, 1944); ch.29.

6 This was several months after Nazi Propaganda Minister, Josef Goebbels, had triumphantly declared that Berlin was *Judenrein* – cleaned of Jews.

7 The rescuers were Jozef and Luba Kasper. For many generations, a sizeable ethnic Czech community inhabited the Rovno area. After the war, they were repatriated to Czechoslovakia.

8 James Mensch, 'Rescue and the Fate to Face', unpublished paper, St. Francis Xavier University, Antigonish, Nova Scotia, Canada, p.12.

9 *ibid.*, p.12. Also, by same author, 'Death and the Other: A Shared Premise' (unpublished). I am particularly indebted to Prof. Mensch for his insightful interpretation of Levinas's thought.

10 For more by Levinas, see Emmanuel Levinas, *Total and Infinity* (Pittsburgh: Duquesne University Press, 1969); also: *Alterity and Transcendence* (London: Athlone; New York: Columbia University Press, 1999) and Ze'ev Levy, 'The Concept of "the Other" in Levinas' Ethics', *Daat* 30 (1993): 21–40 [Hebrew]; Elisabeth Goldwyn and Yoram Verta, 'Toward the Other: Emmanuel Levinas', *Shadmot* 10 (1999) [Hebrew]. In interpreting Levinas' philosophy, Mensch advances the interesting observation that it is God that the Holocaust rescuer confronts in the face to face meeting. The God that cannot be represented, the God that transcends the natural world, appears in the form of the Jew who knocks on the door. God's being, as totally other-worldly, can only appear as a lack of worldly content (such as poverty and persecution). Such worldly privation is God's manifestation – in the guise of the abandoned, the unfortunate, and the wretched. It is the God who appears as an appeal, and a call to respond. This God was present during the Holocaust; 'he appeared each time the Jew knocked on the door.' However, only a precious few, the rescuers, recognized this. Mensch, 'Rescue and the Face to Face, page 10. Compare with Pastor John Cazalis' christological perception of his help to Jews in France – the Jew in the form of the Crucified. 'In everyone of them, whoever he was, it was the Christ who came toward us, in the form of the rejected one, the condemned and crucified. In loving them, it is His love that we received. When they invaded our homes and lives . . ., it was His mercy and joy that came into play . . . On each occasion as well, we knew afterwards that He had blessed us' – Georges Casalis, in Emile C. Fabre (ed.), *Les Clandestins de Dieu* (Paris: Fayard, 1968); pp.203–204.
11 Primo Levi, *If this is a Man* (London: Orion, 1959); pp.127–8.
12 Rescue stories appearing in this paper are based on the following files at Yad Vashem, Dept. for the Righteous: Bomok, Michaylo, 8987; Harder, Albert and Loni, 225; Howil, Boguslaw, 5780; Kasper, Jozef and Luba, 6712; Kozaczuk, Wlodzimierz, 4034; Kosieradzki, Roch, 7269; Majercik, Michal and Anna, 2086; Nowosielski, Stanislaw, 4995; Paulavicius, Jonas, 2472; Puchalski, Jan and Anna, 3466; Schroedter, Otto and Hedwig, 5870; Shidlovskaya, Yekaterina, 8296; Sosnowy, Jan & Stefania, 5950; Szwierszczak, Manko, 5950; Van Damme, Alice, 7048; Van de Velde, Jean, 1447; Wikiel, Jan, 2034.

VARIAN FRY IN MARSEILLE

Pierre Sauvage

Viewed within the context of its times, Fry's mission seems not 'merely' an attempt to save some threatened writers, artists, and political figures. It appears in hindsight like a doomed final quest to reverse the very direction in which the world – and not merely the Nazis – was heading.

Pierre Sauvage, *Varian Fry in Marseille*

I. THE MISSION

In February 1941, in Marseille,[1] France, an American wrote to his wife back in New York:

> Among the people who have come into my office, or with whom I am in constant correspondence, are not only some of the greatest living authors, painters, sculptors of Europe...but also former cabinet ministers and even prime ministers of half a dozen countries. What a strange place Europe is when men like this are reduced to waiting patiently in the anteroom of a young American of no importance whatever.[2]

Varian Fry, the young American, was 32 when he arrived in Marseille early in the morning of 14 August 1940 – only two months after France's traumatizing defeat by the Nazis, and a full year and a half before Americans finally allowed themselves to get dragged into the war.

In that summer of 1940, high-level Nazis were talking among themselves about the need for a final solution to the Jewish question, but there is no evidence that anybody was seriously thinking of mass murder. Throughout the coming year, the German policy would remain one of emigration and resettlement.

What was possible when Fry arrived in Europe would, however, no longer be possible by the time Fry left Europe at the end of October 1941. By then, it would not only be the doors of the U.S. and other Western countries that were largely closed to refugees; the doors of departure from Europe would be shut too, and the Final Solution would be under way.

These are the circumstances in which a New York intellectual led what we know to have been the most determined and successful private American rescue operation during World War II. At a time of tragic American apathy about the refugee crisis in Europe, Varian Fry was assisted locally in his struggle by other singular and similarly non-Jewish Americans: the late Miriam Davenport Ebel, the late Mary Jayne Gold, Charles Fawcett, Leon Ball, the late righteous consul Hiram Bingham IV.

Banding together with Jewish and non-Jewish refugees from the Third Reich, as well as early French opponents to Vichy, this tiny group, with erratic assistance from colleagues in New York, may have helped to save as many as 2,000[3] people: Marc Chagall, Max Ernst, Jacques Lipchitz, Heinrich Mann, Franz Werfel, Alma Mahler Werfel, André Breton, Victor Serge, André Masson, Lion Feuchtwanger, Wanda Landowska, Konrad Heiden, Marcel Duchamp, Hannah Arendt, Max Ophuls, Walter Mehring, Jean Malaquais, Valeriu Marcu, Remedios Varo, Otto Meyerhof.... The list – Fry's list – goes on and on.

'There is a fire sale on brains going on here, and we aren't taking full advantage of it,'[4] an American official in Lisbon told Fry in August 1940, long before the Holocaust became established as a metaphor. Even if many of the names on Fry's list have faded into relative obscurity, the list as a whole represents much of the intelligentsia of Europe at that time; the population shifts Fry helped produce would have major ramifications for American and European culture.

Though Fry was not specifically concerned with saving Jews – and indeed the German and Austrian anti-Nazi émigrés in France then seemed the most vulnerable of all, whether Jewish or not – Fry became in 1998 the only American thus far honoured as a Righteous Among the Nations by Israel's Yad Vashem, the Jerusalem memorial to the Holocaust.[5]

Many basic facts about the man and his mission are still unfamiliar even to scholars, while some of what is 'known' is in fact erroneous or misleading. Furthermore, there have been no attempts as yet to place the rescue effort in its historical context. Filling some of these gaps and drawing on extensive research and over one hundred interviews conducted for the author's upcoming feature documentary, *And Crown Thy Good: Varian Fry in Marseille*,[6] this account of the mission will lead naturally enough to some fundamental questions about what we are to make of it, what still remains unknown, and whether the story is more than a mere footnote, however culturally significant, in the history of the Holocaust.

2. THE CALLING

As a student at Harvard, Fry had early on expressed his love for the arts by founding with classmate Lincoln Kirstein a lively avant-garde intellectual magazine, *The Hound & Horn*. In the '30s, he went on to work for small politically-minded publications, hanging out in liberal anti-isolationist circles and making friends within the anti-Nazi exile community.

A trip to Germany at that time made a strong impression on him, according to Mary Jayne Gold, who participated in her own distinctive way in the Fry mission. The American heiress would never forget the tense, quiet voice with which her friend had told her in Marseille about the anti-Jewish rioting he had observed in Berlin in 1935.

Fry singled out one episode. In a café on the *Kurfürstendamm*, in the heart of the city, two Nazi youths had approached a man who was quietly having a beer and who looked as if he might be Jewish. As the man had put out his hand to lift the mug, he had suddenly found that hand nailed to the table by a dagger joyfully and triumphantly wielded by one of the thugs. Though Fry, curiously, never wrote up this particular incident, Mary Jayne Gold thought that the image of the hand pinned to the table had been a factor in Fry's volunteering to go to France.[7]

When he first gazed down into Marseille from the top of the railroad station's majestic staircase, Fry had taken a month's leave of absence from his work, which then consisted of writing and editing substantial political brochures for the Foreign Policy Association, a job he had thoroughly enjoyed. He was an intellectual through-and-through, yet mere analysis no longer satisfied him. Few intellectuals were to wander further from the ivory towers.

He and a few other Americans had noticed the especially ominous Article 19 in the French armistice agreement with Germany. In that clause, adamantly demanded by the Germans,[8] France had ostensibly agreed to 'surrender on demand' any citizens of Greater Germany asked for by the German authorities.

Except for its potential victims, few in France, in those stressful times, had attached much significance to Article 19. Leading French historians of that period recall that the clause had, in fact, been aimed at '*les fauteurs de trouble*' – those few 'troublemakers' or agitators whom the Germans could accuse of having been warmongers against Germany.[9] Indeed, it appears that very few refugees were, in fact, turned over to the Germans by Vichy as a result of Article 19.[10] (Subsequent French complicity in the deportation of Jews from France was not related to the terms of the armistice.)

In New York, however, the apparent threat galvanized those concerned with the plight of the anti-Nazi refugees in France, leading to the creation of an 'Emergency Rescue Committee,' an entirely private, shoestring effort launched at a fund-raising luncheon at New York's Hotel Commodore on 25 June 1940.

In Ingrid Warburg's apartment overlooking the Museum of Modern Art, lists were frantically put together of people who were deemed to be obviously in danger or who might be in danger soon enough.[11] There were many artists and writers on these lists, but also many names belonging to a small, left-socialist splinter group, *Neu Beginnen* (New Beginning).

As is often forgotten, the operation at the outset had been to a large extent political. The Jewish Labor Committee had quickly and remarkably succeeded in obtaining from the Department of State several hundred emergency visitors' visas for prominent political refugees trapped in France. *Neu Beginnen's* Karl Frank (who went under the name Paul Hagen) had been concerned that the help then being worked out for these German and Austrian refugees in France was being refused to his somewhat left-wing (albeit anti-Communist) friends.[12]

Early on, the assistance of Mrs. Eleanor Roosevelt was sought, and at that time she gave it. Because of this early help and encouragement to Fry and the E. R. C. – perhaps also because of the general admiration for Mrs. Roosevelt – she has sometimes been misleadingly portrayed as virtually spearheading the rescue effort, and Fry sometimes and erroneously characterized virtually as her emissary. But despite her involvement in the summer and fall of 1940, Mrs. Roosevelt soon returned to the 'thunderous' silence, as Blanche Wiesen Cook has characterized it, that she had displayed about Nazi persecution in the '30s.[13]

On June 27, Fry brought Mrs. Roosevelt up to date:

> What is urgently needed now is a new Scarlet Pimpernel who will go to France and risk his life, perhaps many times over, in an attempt to find the intended victims of Hitler's chopping block, and either provide them with means to keep alive in hiding or, if [this] is possible, to get them out of France before the French authorities reach them. I have volunteered to go myself and shall do so if no more suitable person can be found.[14]

Did Varian Fry actually risk his life in Marseille, as Hollywood is bound to insist in the dreadful movies we will not be spared? Probably not. Neither Vichy nor the Germans were inclined at that time to interfere to that extent with the rights of even the most meddlesome American citizen; an American passport gave most Americans abroad a reasonably justified sense of invulnerability.

Did Varian Fry *know* that his life was probably not at risk? No, he probably didn't. Indeed, he had been warned by a French friend in New York that he could easily be made to disappear from some dark street,[15] and such disappearances were not rare in any event in Marseille's crime-infested neighbourhoods bordering on murky waters.

3. THE MAN

France's bustling port and second city was then the real *Casablanca*. Many of the Jewish and anti-Nazi refugees who found their way there soon felt, as refugee Hertha Pauli put it, 'like rats on a sinking ship.'[16] She recalled: 'The seas kept rising all around us; whenever a lifeboat showed on the horizon, everyone wanted to be the first to get in — and then the lifeboat would fade away in the mist.'[17]

'These refugees,' Fry wrote to his wife, 'are being crushed in one of the most gigantic vises in history. Unable to leave France, unable to work, and so earn money, they have been condemned to death — or, at best, to confinement in detention camps, a fate little better than death.'[18]

His month's leave over, Fry gave little genuine thought to going home, despite his wife's increasingly pointed pleas and the growing antagonism from almost all sides. He was not afraid to do whatever the situation required; to break the law under these circumstances appeared to him an obvious moral imperative. The pressures suited him, he lied with aplomb, and he knew that the task on which he had embarked was an important one — a matter of life and death. He sensed that fate would never deal him such a role again. Moreover, when Fry put his heart into a task, as somebody close to him later recalled, he was 'amazingly efficient as well as just plain brilliant.'[19]

Yet Varian Fry had neither the manner, nor the temperament that we associate — perhaps under the influence of entertaining but misleading fiction — with secret agents. He certainly didn't appear to have any directly relevant experience. A natty dresser, he had a passion for Latin and Greek and bird watching. He could be stuffy and pedantic, but he loved naughty limericks and had an antic, screwball sense of humour. The image we may retain is one of tweeds and bow-ties, but Fry would sometimes receive his staff in his boxer shorts.[20]

The late literary critic Alfred Kazin was a colleague of Fry's at *The New Republic* magazine in 1943 and 1944. What struck him most about Fry in retrospect was the contrast between Fry's appearance and Fry's reality, a contrast that may have served Fry well in Marseille:

> He was not only elegant, he was foppish. He had an extraordinary upper class distinction. You couldn't miss it. Nobody was ever more surprised [than I] to learn what Varian had done in Marseille. It was not the first time, and certainly not the last time in my life — but it was the most decisive time in my life — that I discovered how little one person's external appearance is a clue to what he really is as such. No one, but no one, who knew Varian Fry as I did — even the very name itself, *Varian Fry* — would ever have suspected him of being able to do what he did.[21]

As with many rescuers, if one scratches a little under the surface, one finds formative influences that were early, deep, and stretch back in time. There always seem to be role models.

When his father died in 1958, Fry recalled in a memorial tribute that his grandfather had worked finding foster homes in the Midwest for homeless New York City children.[22] Though Fry himself, he once wrote, didn't believe in God,[23] his father had grown up 'in an atmosphere of practising Christianity and Christian charity.' His father's greatest pleasure, Fry said, 'had always been in helping others.'[24]

In a frequently astute and moving biography published in the U.S. in 1999 under the inept title 'A Quiet American: The Secret War of Varian Fry' – Fry was neither quiet nor secretive – Andy Marino speculated that aspects of Fry's sexual life and history may have been a major factor in creating in him the sense of being an outsider, leading perhaps to a special sympathy for the plight of other outsiders. Deviancy came naturally to Fry, Marino suggests, and certainly Fry's activities in Marseille, given the political climate, can be characterized as 'deviant'.[25]

Whatever Fry's sexual nature may have been – and it is hard to decide to what extent speculation about such matters is relevant – the stress that Marino puts on Fry *not* being an 'organization man' seems appropriate. Fry himself thought that his 'non-conformist character structure,' which had created problems for him as a youth at Hotchkiss and Harvard, 'produced, later, the... more useful activity [in Marseille].'[26] 'I've always been a non-conformist, I guess,' he wrote to an acquaintance, 'though not, exactly, a revolutionary either.'[27]

He was certainly not the sort of man an established organization, given a range of candidates, would have picked for such a mission. As it happens, Fry's American cohorts in Marseille were also non-conformists. Mary Jayne Gold had escaped the world in which she had been destined to live. Charles Fawcett viewed himself as the 'black sheep' of his distinguished family. Miriam Davenport Ebel felt that they could all be characterized, to some extent, as 'misfits.'

Organizations – including universities – have a vested interest in downplaying this fact: rescue during the Holocaust was not, for the most part, the work of organizations – and successful rescue even less so. As Magda Trocmé, widow of pastor André Trocmé of the Huguenot haven of Le Chambon-sur-Lignon, put it in the author's 1989 feature documentary *Weapons of the Spirit*: 'If we'd had an organization, we would have failed.'[28]

4. THE ORGANIZATION

In Marseille, Fry quickly understood that he needed an organization – which grew into two: the official, cover organization, dispensing humanitarian relief work, and the one working illegally behind the scenes, providing rescue.

His operation, begun in his hotel room and his bathroom at the swank Hôtel Splendide, soon moved to tight quarters at 60, rue Grignan, then finally in January to larger facilities at 18, boulevard Garibaldi. 'Everybody felt a lot better, including the refugees,' staffer Marcel Verzeano recalled about the new office. 'On rue Grignan, they were interviewed in small dark places. But when they came to Boulevard Garibaldi, where there was a lot more light, a lot more space, they felt a lot better. *We* felt a lot better working there.'[29]

A big American flag dominated the scene at the official *Centre américain de secours* – which could legitimately be translated as American Relief Center, although Fry preferred to refer to it bluntly as the American Rescue Center.[30] Locally, Fry's group was often referred to simply as the *Comité Fry* – the Fry Committee.

The word rapidly spread. Some of the long lines outside the American Consulate became long lines outside the American Rescue Center. It was later estimated that some some 20,000 refugees in all made contact with the A.R.C.[31]

The situation was briefly promising. Some U.S. 'emergency visas' came. Transit visas through Spain and Portugal didn't pose a problem. Even the ostensible need for French exit visas could be safely ignored. In those early days, Fry and Leon Ball accompanied Franz Werfel and Alma Mahler Werfel, Heinrich and Nelly Mann, and Thomas Mann's son Golo Mann, to the Spanish frontier; the group was successfully smuggled across, with Fry himself escorting the luggage across the border.

'They were letting us operate without interfering too much,' staffer Verzeano recalled about those early months.[32] (Verzeano, a Rumanian Jewish doctor known then simply as 'Maurice,' played an active role in organizing illegal emigration.) Fry assumed that the lax situation with regard to exit visas was due to simple French confusion at that time.[33] But was it not then unofficial French policy to try to get rid of refugees?

Tension soon mounted. The Spanish border was closed, the 'danger' visas stopped coming in, and even if you were able to get a visa for a final destination, whether genuine (i.e., the U.S. or Mexico) or more or less bogus (Siam, the Belgian Congo, Panama, China . . .), there remained a long wait to get the Portuguese transit visa, and an additional wait to get the Spanish transit visa. The greatest frustration arose when the validity of one document ended while you were waiting for one of the other necessary documents – requiring you to start all over again. Of course, under the best of circumstances refugees were faced with the expense of the trip, and the difficulty of booking passage.

With the onset of an unusually harsh winter and increasingly severe food shortages, Fry's operation mushroomed and changed. Relief work became more and more necessary: one refugee said that what was terrible about the small sums they were given was that you could neither live nor die on them. Emigration became more difficult and more illegal, while legal and illegal activities were increasingly compartmentalized.

There was a flourishing black market in all manner of goods and services – or rather, there was a good black market and a bad one. As refugee Barbara Sauvage later recalled, you could buy a pack of cigarettes, for instance, for which you were charged a fortune – that was the good black market; on the bad black market there would be straw in those cigarettes.[34]

Marseille, to put it mildly, had a very active underworld, and among the gangsters were those who would get paid for their services and deliver (notably Charles Vincileoni, who will later be decorated for his work with the Resistance[35]), and those who merely absconded. (Of Marseille's colourful *milieu*, Mary Jayne Gold quipped to Miriam Davenport that 'It's a bit like high society – everybody knows everybody.')

Thought not always reliable, underworld contacts were useful to the A.R.C. when hiding places had to be found, money changed at black-market rates, documents forged, officials bribed, people smuggled. *Maisons de passe* (where rooms were rented by the hour) were particularly useful places to lay low, as were Marseille's many brothels, which were also hospitable for secretive meetings.

5. THE STAFF

The A.R.C. staff, which had expanded from three to six in September, was overworked at 15 in December. 'Interviewers' saw fifty potential 'clients' a day.[36]

Among the main Frenchmen on the staff were the left socialist Protestant Daniel Bénédite, the key aide at the end, and the liberal Catholic Jean Gemähling, who would go on to become an early and important figure in the French Resistance. Jews from Paris included Lucie Heymann, Paul and Vala Schmierer, Jacques Weisslitz and Charles Wolff (the latter two, after devoting themselves to the A.R.C. till the very end, did not survive those years).

Foreign refugees also contributed in important ways to the survival of others, before mostly escaping themselves when it became possible or necessary: Albert Hirschman, the key aide at the beginning – forever nicknamed 'Beamish' by Fry, who described him privately as 'the best of them all'[37] – Franz von Hildebrand, Lena Fiszman, Anna Gruss,

Heinz-Ernst Oppenheimer, Bedrich Heine, Karel Sternberg, Marcel Verzeano, Justus Rosenberg, Norbert Friedlander, and many others.

Finally, there were those who without formally being part of the Marseille staff were no less essential to the operation. Hans and Lisa Fittko created and ran an astonishingly effective escape route through the Pyrenees.[38] Political cartoonist Bil Spira, then known as Bill Freier, became the main forger for the operation. ('You're Fry, but I'm Frier,' he used to tell his friend, punning on the German word for 'free'.) Caught with his paraphernalia and deported to Auschwitz, Spira survived.[39]

Other Americans recently arrived in Marseille were among the first to join in Fry's mission. While each was very different from the other, what is most striking now is what they had in common. Fry's account, in this regard, is not entirely reliable for a reason that can be easily stated, although it eluded biographer Andy Marino: by modern standards, Fry would be deemed to have been a sexist. In a deplorable lapse, Marino's biography echoes Fry's account in its condescending treatment of Miriam Davenport and especially of Mary Jayne Gold.

The late Miriam Davenport Ebel was a scholarly, witty art lover, with strong political beliefs, deeply held humanitarian inclinations, and remarkable savvy. In a brief memoir entitled 'An Unsentimental Education,' Davenport later recalled her initial visit to the American Consulate in Marseille and her encounter in the early summer with a Consulate official:

> Was anyone, I asked, doing anything for anti-Nazi refugees trapped in France? No. Were there any American organizations in Marseilles looking after their needs? No, none. Oddly, the Consulate's walls were decorated with portraits of Washington, Lincoln, and Herbert Hoover. Franklin Roosevelt's picture was nowhere to be seen. On the way out, I noticed a long queue of refugees, most of them speaking German. I also observed the Consulate's doorman being offensively rude to them. A strong odor of xenophobia and anti-Semitism permeated the premises.[40]

After meeting with Fry shortly after his arrival, Davenport received a note from him urgently asking whether she could type.[41] She couldn't, but she was delighted to join his staff, even briefly being anointed Secretary General of the organization (Fry liked the waspy, ultra-American ring of her last name).

'The book of Ruth was read to me as a fairy tale, when I was a child – when I was a real little girl, four or five years old,' Davenport, a convert to Catholicism, later explained. 'And one of the lines in that is more or less, "Your people are my people." And I felt very strongly that these people were indeed my people. And that I had to do something about it.'[42]

In Marseille, Davenport had met and become friends with the late Mary Jayne Gold, an heiress from the Midwest whose charitable instincts and political inclinations Davenport found entirely compatible with her own. Gold had been enjoying a high-living expatriate's life in Paris when France collapsed. 'You felt it was the end of the world,' she recalled, 'that everything you believed in and everything that had been built up by humanity or decency for centuries was finished. And yet, there was another part of me that said, "We're going to beat 'em." '[43]

Gold had been planning to go home from Marseille, and her reasons for staying on at that time had as much to do with her budding affair with a young French gangster – she rescued him too, and he ultimately became a war hero[44] – as it did with the rescue effort.[45] Fry was initially sceptical of the rich dilettante, but soon drew on her willingness to help financially and to participate in other ways. Most notably, she was asked to go to the repressive French internment camp of Le Vernet and seek permission from the commandant for four highly vulnerable political inmates to come to Marseille, ostensibly just to claim visas awaiting them; to everybody's amazement, she was successful.

It was Miriam Davenport who enlisted Gold to subsidize expanding the relief and rescue effort to encompass more than just the luminaries and politics on Fry's initial lists, creating what Davenport called at the time 'the Gold list,' which Davenport administered and Gold funded. (Years later, Gold asked longtime International Rescue Committee official Karel Sternberg, once himself a refugee in Marseille, who were some of the so-called 'unimportant people' her money had gone to help. He smiled, said nothing, and pointed to himself.)[46]

Gold was not the air-headed blonde evoked in 'A Quiet American.' After all, she understood what few Americans seemed to understand at that time – and perhaps fewer still in her waspy, prosperous social class: civilization as they knew it was at stake with the rise of Nazism. 'She has already given us thousands,' Fry wrote of Gold to his wife in September 1941, 'and she is more interested in our work than any one else I know.'

Moreover, Mary Jayne Gold's flavourful memoir, *Crossroads Marseilles 1940*, edited by Jacqueline Kennedy Onassis for publication by Doubleday in 1980 and published in France in 2001,[47] remains an especially clear-eyed if colourful and idiosyncratic account of Gold's experiences in 1940–41 – a year that she later considered to have been the only one in her life that really mattered. 'I was not there to witness the worst,' she wrote, 'only the beginning, and even then I was sometimes embarrassed into a sort of racialism – like being ashamed of belonging to the human race.'[48]

Throughout his life, Charles Fernley Fawcett – wrestler, Foreign Legionnaire, movie star, socialite, trumpet player, songwriter, composer, artist, expatriate – remained a moral adventurer of sorts, travelling the globe and helping resistance movements in Afghanistan and elsewhere. Independently of his work for Fry, Fawcett also accepted in Marseille to engage in a series of six bigamous and bogus marriages, helping some women to get out of internment camps and allowing all the 'wives' to get out of Europe. (At one point, two Mrs. Fawcetts turned up at the same time in Lisbon.)[49]

Fawcett did all sorts of odd jobs for Fry, but will best be remembered as the doorman receptionist at the A.R.C., decked out in an official-looking if indefinable Ambulance Corps uniform, attempting to keep order while steering people to interviewers. His gracious manner was appreciated even though his Southern drawl made his English especially hard to understand for the refugees – and he was even more indecipherable in poor Southern-accented French: 'They-ah now, you-all. Step back. Take it easy. Evrabody gets his turn. They-ah now. You'll be next.'[50]

'I guess we were from the Promised Land,' is how Fawcett later remembered his status as an American in Marseille. 'We were taught at school, you know, the strong protect the weak. And this is the way it's supposed to be – we are our brother's keeper, let's face it. And America was the strong nation in those days.'[51]

Fawcett's friend Leon Ball, an expatriate lard salesman in France, was an important member of the underground team, adept at border crossings. Little is known about him, because he disappeared after an incident that was embarrassing to him; to this day, none of his Marseille friends have the slightest idea what became of him.[52]

Mary Jayne Gold liked being 'where the action was,'[53] and the same can certainly be said of the other Americans. More surprisingly, Davenport, Gold and Fawcett all happened to have family trees stretching back seemingly all the way to the Pilgrims. If American rescue in Marseille had a sense of *noblesse oblige*, the pedigree was authentic. (It should also be noted, however, that many members of the U.S. foreign service at that time, a body not particularly sympathetic to refugees or to Jews, also had competitively long lineages.)

The stress being placed here on Fry's American friends is not meant to suggest that their roles in Marseille were more important than those of Fry's European colleagues. This was not the case, as Charles Fawcett is quick to tell you. It is just that the greatest significance of the story of the Fry mission may lie in what there is to learn about the *American* response to the crisis – what it was, and what it could have been.

In that respect, it is significant that Fry had one ally at the U.S. Consulate in Marseille – and only one: Vice Consul Hiram Bingham IV; inscribing his book for Bingham in 1945, Fry would call him his 'comrade-in-arms.' It is unlikely that there were many other members of the American foreign service at that time who saw the situation as 'Harry' Bingham put it in a letter to his wife, shortly after the start of World War II: 'We can only pray that the natural goodness of men will fight off the plague before it spreads too far.'[54]

6. THE DO-GOODERS

Tracy Strong, Jr. of the Y.M.C.A. and the European Student Relief Fund did important work in the French internment camps (and also provided support to relief work in the Christian oasis of Le Chambon-sur-Lignon.)[55] He later remembered the atmosphere in Marseille:

> There was complete confusion. Nothing seemed to work. Trains were packed and didn't run on time. Very crowded streets – the whole town was just crowded and noisy and dirty. A lot of beggars or semi-beggars, people trying to make a living one way or another. Every office had refugees – whether it was the Quakers or the Y.M.C.A. office or the Consulate office – the waiting rooms were just packed with people waiting to see somebody and get some help of one kind or another, maybe get a visa, maybe find out how to get through Spain to Portugal, or get a boat to North Africa. The French would have been glad to ship all of [the refugees] anywhere. The Consulate was pretty neutral – you didn't feel they were really pushing themselves.[56]

The growing familiarity of the Fry story has obscured the fact that there were, of course, other American relief organizations and committees active in Vichy France, though their priorities were often different. The American Red Cross was best known in Marseille for its distribution of milk and other needed supplies. (When Miriam Davenport read in a local newspaper about the arrival in Marseille of Varian Fry, she surmised to Mary Jayne Gold that he was 'just another milkman.'[57])

Of course, Jewish organizations such as the local *Comité d'Assistance aux Réfugiés* (supported by the Joint Distribution Committee) and HICEM, were also on the scene. Among the major American organizations represented in Vichy France were the American Friends Service Committee (Dr. Howard and Gertrude Kershner, Rev. A. Burns Chalmers), the Unitarian Service Committee (Dr. Charles R. Joy, Rev. Waitstill Sharp, later Noel Field), and the Y.M.C.A. (Donald A. Lowrie, Tracy Strong, Jr.).

While some of these 'do-gooders' worked closely with Fry, they mostly restricted their activities to relief work rather than rescue, and drew the line at doing anything illegal.[58] One whose agenda was similar to Fry's was Dr. Frank Bohn, who claimed to represent the American Federation of Labor but who had actually been sent primarily by the Jewish Labor Committee, in order to help rescue people on their lists.[59] He blusteringly welcomed Varian Fry to Marseille, but was ineffectual and soon left after a Department of State telegram laid down the law:

While Department is sympathetic with the plight of refugees and has authorized consular officers to give immediate and sympathetic consideration to their applications for visas this government cannot repeat not countenance the activities as reported of Dr. Bohn and Mr. Fry and other persons in their efforts in evading the laws of countries with which the United States maintain friendly relations.[60]

In a memo to the American Embassy in Vichy in May 1941, Marseille Consul General Hugh S. Fullerton reported on the 'under-cover activities of members of certain relief organizations operating in France,' indicating that the State Department would not be likely to approve of such activities by such people. 'Other considerations aside,' he added, 'they are not fitted for such work.' Referring specifically to Fry's involvement in getting British airmen out of France, Fullerton expressed the belief that if Fry stayed on much longer, 'he would find himself in jail.'[61]

But it was Fry's desire to publicize the squalid conditions in French internment camps that finally led to a falling out with most of the other American relief organizations active in Marseille – who did not want to jeopardize their good relations with Vichy, despite the regime's quick and forceful antisemitic measures during that first year. It was those good relations, after all, that made much of their work possible, including the slight ameliorating of conditions in the French camps.

The A.R.C. found itself expelled from the Nîmes Committee (chaired by the well-connected Donald Lowrie), which regrouped the major humanitarian organizations then working in Vichy France. Rev. Howard L. Brooks of the Unitarians wrote in 1942 that Fry was 'ostracized by other relief workers who secretly admired his work.'[62]

7. THE REFUGEES

Two months after his arrival, Fry provided the following report to his wife:

My work reached a crescendo of activity right after I got back from Lisbon, but it has now slackened off a little, so that I am at least able to breathe. I still begin at 8 in the morning and work until 11 at night, and sometimes until one. I still see dozens of people every day, and am witness to displays of every possible quality of character, from heroic to despicable. I still have poor, driven refugees lurking for me in my hotel in the morning when I go out and in the evening when I come in. I still have from six to 12 phone calls an hour, and get 25 letters a day. Sometimes the refugees walk right into my bedroom without knocking or announcing themselves.

But the pressure is slackening – not because the situation is improving but because more and more of our charges are being reinterned – and I am at long last getting an occasional chance to breathe. It is horrible to be glad that anybody has been arrested; but I had reached a point in nervous exhaustion a few weeks ago where I actually was glad to have a few of the most insistent and most pestiferous 'clients' carried shrieking off.[63]

Despite his moments of weariness, Fry felt some real affinity to the complicated refugees of the European intelligentsia. But it would probably be naïve to think that the intellectual émigrés in France – a remarkable crowd of people that would have been remarkable even without the vicissitudes of history – wholeheartedly embraced Varian Fry as one of their own. 'We were slightly contemptuous of American innocents,' Albert Hirschman admitted, 'people who did not really understand Europeans. But I think that on the whole it was a good thing that [Varian] played this "innocent abroad" so thoroughly.'[64]

Lisa Fittko described with amazement Fry's extraordinary *faux-pas* when he assumed that perhaps her husband and she, committed political types, were hesitating about the mission that he was asking them to undertake out of a desire to pry some money out of him. 'How much?' she remembers him saying.

The Fittkos didn't speak much English, but they understood that question. It brought Hans Fittko to a boil. 'He said, "Do you think we're crazy to risk our lives at the border for *money*?" He said something like, "Do you know what anti-fascists are? Do you know what we're about?" '[65]

Fry himself would later make lists of the numerous mistakes he felt he had made in Marseille.

Compounding the challenge to Fry was his realization that his job was 'like a doctor's during an earthquake':[66] one must never forget to reassure. 'See you in New York,' Fry would say to refugees about to attempt an escape over the Fittko route.[67]

Nor was escape experienced by the refugees in heroic terms, *à la* Paul Henreid in *Casablanca*, leaving only to continue the fight. (In real life, Henreid's Victor Laszlo would probably have found his way to a park bench on Broadway and 72nd Street.) What was on Albert Hirschman's mind when he fled in late 1940, as he later recalled, was that his goal since 1933 had been to *win out* over the forces he had been fighting for seven years. 'And the only success I had was the fact of escaping – not one time but three or four times. I had the feeling that I had expended a great deal of energy but in the end without success. I did not feel like a hero at all. A hero has to win.'[68] Deciding not to go off to New York from Lisbon, writer Joseph Kessel put it this way to Fry: 'I have seen too much of refugees already to want to become one of them.'[69]

Their fears, their need to adjust to an almost incomprehensibly different and challenging situation, did not bring out the best in many of the refugees. In her brilliant memoir, *Escape Through the Pyrenees*, Lisa Fittko underscored how difficult some of the refugees found it to be inconspicuous. The greater the intellect, it sometimes seemed, the greater the difficulty adjusting.[70] While some refugees found it difficult to admit to themselves their vulnerable status, others besieged Fry. Daniel Bénédite warned against giving in to a system whereby refugees were given what they asked for, whether money or attention, because they resorted to hysteria or blackmail or repeatedly came back.[71]

Conductor Diego Masson candidly recalled that his father, artist André Masson, a well-known anti-fascist married to a Jew, would get very drunk in the evening when he couldn't work, and would speak out loudly and provocatively at French cafés. 'He never could keep his mouth shut even when he wasn't drunk. I'm quite sure that without Varian Fry, my father would have been arrested, and my mother and my brother and me would have been put in concentration camps, as Jews. With a father like mine, we would not have survived.'[72]

The most famous tragedy of that time involved the prominent German Social Democratic leaders Rudolf Breitscheid and Rudolf Hilferding, who by all accounts haughtily refused to do anything illegal – they weren't going to stoop to Hitler's level. Convinced that the French government would protect them, they were turned over to German authorities and did not survive.

Charles Fawcett, a man disinclined to say anything derogatory about anybody, least of all a refugee, conceded that:

> There were maybe a few that we didn't fall in love with – a few. They wouldn't listen to you. They thought, 'We were so famous, nobody will do anything to us.' Some of them said that! 'The French wouldn't dare to do anything to us – there's world opinion.' World opinion – can you imagine that? Let me tell you, world opinion wasn't standing behind them much in those days.[73]

Writing later in diary form, in a subsequently scrapped draft of his memoirs of that time, Fry recalled the new wave of panic that set in among the refugees with the news of the arrest of Breitscheid and Hilferding. 'The office has been the scene of indescribable hysteria all day; one man actually got down on his knees and with tears streaming down his face begged me to save his life.'[74] The supplicant, prominent anti-Nazi lawyer Alfred Apfel, later died of a heart attack in the A.R.C. office, with Fry holding him.[75]

'Almost everybody wants to be put into hiding,' Fry recounted. 'Even artists and writers who have never had any political activity in their lives are terrified. The difficulty is to know who is in imminent danger and who is not. We can't hide everybody.'[76]

8. THE LANDSCAPE

Fry worked hard but took breaks. He found the time to write a considerable number of extraordinary letters about his life in Marseille, and his own evolution during that time. Some of these letters are surprising. In one of his more depressed moods – Fry's second wife, Annette Riley Fry, concluded that he was manic-depressive[77] – Fry went so far as to suggest that maybe 'the best thing is an early German victory'; he claimed he meant the statement 'quite seriously.'[78]

But he passionately loved virtually all things French – certainly the wine – and even the increasingly difficult times that year didn't make a dent in his enthusiasm. He loved going on bicycle trips through Provence with his friend Stéphane Hessel, who remembered how methodically he would explore churches and Roman ruins.[79]

In October, Mary Jayne Gold, Miriam Davenport, Theo Bénédite (Daniel Bénédite's English wife) and Jean Gemähling stumbled on a large villa on the outskirts of Marseille. It soon came to house Fry, Gold and other A.R.C. staffers, as well as such luminaries as writers André Breton and Victor Serge and their families. Baptized 'Château Espère-Visa' (Chateau Hoping-for-Visa) by Serge, villa Air-Bel became a famous haunt for the refugee Surrealist artists who congregated around Breton. Fry, who enjoyed horticulture, took a particular delight in the garden. Not the least of the house's amenities was that it didn't have a phone.

Fry's life had become a study in contrasts. He wrote:

> I am waiting for Harry Bingham to come with his car. We are going to drive out to Gordes to spend the weekend with the Chagalls. Now that spring is here, Provence is beautiful beyond belief. The almond trees are in bloom, a delicate pink against the soft gray-green and sage-green and dark cypress-green of the Provençal landscape. In this, of all places, it is hard to believe that men, given the beautiful world to live in, can sully and destroy it by war. And yet they do. The same spring which is bringing almond blossoms to Provence is bringing fear and terror to millions of human beings who live not so far away, and to some who live right here. For who knows what spring will bring, but who does not know that it will bring new horrors, perhaps even worse than those of last spring? I hear the sound of tires on the gravel. Harry has come.[80]

9. THE NEW YORKERS

As good as Fry's relations mostly were with the staff and the refugees, it is difficult to overstate how bad his relations were from the beginning with American officials in Marseille – and how quickly and precipitously they declined with the Emergency Rescue Committee that had sent him to France in the first place.

His frustration with his New York colleagues was boundless. To his wife, he railed against 'those boobs in New York'.[81] 'Viewed from here,' he wrote later, 'they seem like a bunch of blithering, slobbering idiots.'[82] For all their sporadic goodwill, as far as Fry was concerned they just didn't get it.

Eileen Fry tried to calm Fry down: 'You really are making a great mistake in being so full of complaints in your letter to E.R.C. They are as good as they can be, which everyone knows is pretty poor.'[83] She had praise, however, for Ingrid Warburg and fund-raiser Harold Oram. 'They are absolutely on your side, absolutely honest, hard-working, and devoted to the same ends as you are...And do remember that in the long run their particular outfit is all you can really count on, at this end at any rate.'[84]

But Fry soon found himself proclaiming that the American Rescue Center was an organization that answered to no one except its 'clients': 'This office is not your office: it is an independent committee consisting of various American citizens residing in France,' he wrote to the E.R.C. 'Please never, even by implication, suggest that I am your representative.'[85] Fry preferred to play up his connections with New York's Museum of Modern Art, the New School for Social Research, the New World Resettlement Fund and other organizations.[86]

Compounding the breach, the Emergency Rescue Committee put pressure on Fry to deliver the big names. 'Casals is probably worth one hundred thousand,' Oram wrote. 'Picasso – fifty thousand. Your trio [Heinrich Mann, Franz Werfel, Lion Feuchtwanger] brought in thirty five thousand. Since their arrival we have had nothing good to offer to the public and they are pretty shopworn by this time.'[87]

And if some really big names elude Fry – Pablo Picasso, Henri Matisse, Pablo Casals, André Gide, André Malraux are among those who have no wish to go to the United States – he does deliver. 'YOUR LETTER MARCH TWENTYFOURTH BRETONS MASSONS EN ROUTE MARTINIQUE,' Fry cabled to the Museum of Modern Art. 'ERNST CHAGALLS LEAVING INCESSANTLY ARPS SOON AS GET EXIT VISAS KANDINSKY NOT TILL AUGUST STOP WILL TRY TO HELP LEONOR FINI.'[88] (Fry never was able to provide Arp, Kandinsky and Fini to his American backers.)

Emergency Rescue Committee Chairman Dr. Frank Kingdon became particularly frustrated with Fry. When Eileen Fry tried to help get her husband's passport renewed, she was able to talk to Mrs. Roosevelt twice on the phone, and with her help thought she was even making headway with the unsympathetic Assistant Secretary of State Breckinridge Long. But Kingdon 'would not back up my request,' Mrs. Fry reported to her husband, 'and refused to see me.'[89]

The breach that developed with the E.R.C. would never heal. Only a few weeks after Fry's return to the U.S., Kingdon, after a trip to Washington, would tell Fry 'that he had been reluctantly forced to conclude that the State Department would grant no visas to applicants presented by the Emergency Rescue Committee as long as [Fry] was connected with it.' Fry, 'European Director' of the E.R.C., was compelled to resign, and would thereafter find himself advising his refugee friends, in their own interest, *not* to mention his name.[90]

There had been a clumsy attempt to replace Fry in early 1941, but after Fry went home, nobody would be sent to succeed him. Despite dwindling support from New York, the remaining French A. R. C colleagues would do their best to continue the work, but the financially ailing Emergency Rescue Committee would soon be taken over by another organization, which in turn would become the current and very active International Rescue Committee.[91]

Indeed, when Fry was astutely recommended to the budding Office of Strategic Services ('Mr. Fry is probably the only qualified American expert on the means of moving people around the continent of Europe despite regulations and occupations'[92]), the possibility of Fry being hired for government intelligence work was not increased by

E.R.C. Treasurer David Seiferheld, who worked very closely with Kingdon. According to an O.S.S. report, Seiferheld had the following to say about his onetime colleague:

> Varian Fry is an intelligent but highly unstable man. He is uncontrollable even with a supervisor on the spot. He has an infinite capacity for intrigue but not very successful intrigue. He managed to irritate American officials to an extraordinary extent.... Despite these handicaps he did a fairly good job, that is he managed to get a considerable number of people out and he managed to hold on to his job and retain his cover intact longer than [the E.R.C] expected, but in doing so he made a good deal of trouble.[93]

But despite the displeasure of the E.R.C. and even when he had to go on without the safety net of an American passport, Fry dug his heels in. 'This job is like death – irreversible,'[94] he wrote to his wife, as the marriage crumbled visibly in the correspondence exchanged between them ('Much love, if you're interested,' Eileen Fry signed one of her letters'[95]).

'We have started something here we can't stop.' Fry went on. 'We have allowed hundreds of people to become dependent on us. We can't now say we're bored and are going home.'[96] On another occasion, he cabled: 'Could no more abandon my people here than could my own children. Leaving now would be criminally irresponsible.'[97] At that time, Fry had no children.

10. THE OFFICIALS

Vichy took its time getting rid of him. Fry would never forget Marseille police chief Maurice Rodellec du Porzic's reproach when the latter told Fry that he was being expelled: 'd'avoir trop protégé les juifs et les antinazis' – that he had provided too much protection to the Jews and the anti-Nazis.[98] That word 'trop' – too much – suggests that exasperation as well as political retaliation may have motivated the expulsion.[99]

Though Vichy probably knew exactly what the Fry Committee had been doing all along, including the illegal activities engaged in, police officials seemed above all to be obsessively troubled by the presence of Trotskyites or former Trotskyites in Fry's entourage. After Fry's arrest, A.R.C. staffer Lucie Heymann was able to meet with the highest Vichy official for the area. She reported that the official 'speculated about Mr. Fry's being either insane, a saint, or an anti-Nazi "Bolshevik" agent.' The feisty Heymann responded 'that [Fry] was probably a saint, probably insane, but definitely not a "Bolshevik" agent of anti-Nazism.'[100]

Astonishingly, Fry was not even precisely expelled; he was *refoulé* – which was a milder form of expulsion that did not preclude his asking for a visa to come back.[101]

What is certain is that by the end of his year in Marseille, everybody – except his A.R.C. colleagues and the refugees! – had wanted him to go home: the State Department, its patience entirely dissipated; the Emergency Rescue Committee; Vichy – and maybe above all the U.S. officials at the American consulate in Marseille.

Even Eleanor Roosevelt's support ebbed. When Fry and Mary Jayne Gold are among those briefly detained by French authorities in December 1940, Mrs. Roosevelt awkwardly writes on his behalf to Undersecretary of State Sumner Welles: 'I'm sure that though he was helping refugees, [Fry] did nothing actually reprehensible.'[102] At a crucial juncture later on, Mrs. Roosevelt reported back to Mrs. Fry that 'there is nothing I can do for your husband.' 'I think he will have to come home,' Mrs. Roosevelt advises, 'because he has done things which the government does not feel it can stand behind.'[103]

Despite what should have been natural affinities of social class, prep school education, wasp and possibly antisemitic backgrounds, Fry immediately rubbed the local American officials the wrong way and it only got worse. Fry's writings are full of disparaging remarks about those officials, and it is unlikely that in France he kept his feelings to himself. American representatives in Marseille and Vichy early on pegged him as a trouble-maker, and some of them soon came to loathe him.

According to Marseille police chief Rodellec du Porzic, with whom U.S. Consul General Fullerton developed good relations, it was as early as December 1940 that Fullerton had asked the police official 'de me débarrasser de [Fry]' – to get rid of [Fry].[104] A few weeks later, a Vichy document indicates that the U.S. Embassy was conveying to the French that it had 'decidedly unfavorable information as to [Fry's] morality and his activities.'[105] For the rest of his stay in France, the American campaign against Varian Fry would never subside.

When after Fry's return to the U.S., the Department of State ordered that a French receptionist at the Consulate be fired as politically suspect, the Consul General wrote to the American Embassy in Vichy to convey his conviction that the dismissal of the employee had been Fry's handiwork. Fullerton did not acknowledge that his furious memo, which he seems to have typed himself, may have had something to do with the fact that the pretty receptionist in question was his mistress.[106] He ended his 'Strictly Confidential' note to First Secretary H. Freeman Matthews as follows:

> In conclusion, dear friend, I think my previous intention to carry with me to Washington a considerable dossier of 'Fryana' should not be shaken[,] as if the snake is attacking minor employees on the Marseille staff he is doubtless saying things far from nice about me, Doug, Woodie and even your august self.[107] I sometimes wonder if it was, after all, wise of me to restrain the Intendant of Police at Marseille from execution of his original intention to put Varian behind the bars [sic.].[108]

One can speculate as to who, of the Vichy police chief or the American consul general, had really wanted Varian Fry behind bars the most. After the war, settled in a job running the American Hospital in Paris, Fullerton would claim to Charles Fawcett that when it came to the Consulate's frosty relations with the A.R.C., he had merely been 'following orders.'[109] If so, those orders appear to have been followed with enthusiasm.

Further research is required to determine whether it was, in fact, American officials in Washington or in Marseille who did the most to undermine Fry's mission.[110] At the time, Fry attributed his 'final defeat' in large part to 'the craven heart of a consul general.'[111]

It is, in any event, an ironic touch that the little square outside the current location of the U.S. Consulate in Marseille was in 2000 renamed in Varian Fry's honour. Consul General Fullerton's successors now receive their mail at *1, place Varian-Fry*.[112]

I I . THE ENEMIES

It is also not clear whether opposition to opening the doors of America to refugees wasn't at times even more insidious and effective in Marseille and other American consulates than it was in Washington. In this regard, though the name William L. Peck has not yet entered the history books, perhaps a place should be found for him or at least for his memo of March 6, 1941, on immigration policy at the Marseille consulate. (Consul Peck had then taken over the Visa Section from Hiram Bingham IV, who was shunted by the State Department to less sensitive posts and soon gave up on a life in the foreign service.)[113]

In his memo, Peck sought to establish his goodwill by stressing at the outset that he did not 'subscribe to the school of thought which advocates refusing visas to all persons whose faces we do not like, on some flimsy pretext or by invoking the technicalities of immigration law to extreme limits.'

Although Peck deplored 'as much as anyone the influx into the United States of certain refugee elements' and protested the notion apparently held in some other American consulates that the Marseille office was 'more lenient' than any other in granting visas, he was 'convinced ... that the Department does desire that visas be issued, when quota numbers are available, to persons legally qualified for admission to the United States.'

Peck also wished to stress his soft spot for old people:

> These are the real sufferers and the ones who are dying off. The young ones may be suffering, but the history of their race shows that suffering does not kill many of them. Furthermore, the old people will not reproduce and can do our country no harm, provided there is adequate evidence of [financial] support.[114]

The memo is not just buried in Consul General Fullerton's files. On April 11, 1941, shortly before going off to Lisbon for the rest of the month – leaving Peck in charge at the consulate[115] – Fullerton sent the memo on to the Secretary of State and to others:

> As of possible interest to the Visa Office I am attaching a memorandum prepared by Consul William L. Peck, in charge of our Immigration Section in Marseille over a considerable period, reflecting in a general way the attitude which we have assumed toward immigration at this particular time. I may add that copies of this memorandum have been sent to the consular officers at Lyon and Nice for their information.[116]

It was during that same month that Fry received from New York a copy of an article in the New York Post outlining the obstructionist policies being carried out by the American consulate in Marseille. He sent it on to Peck, with the following comment: 'I thought you'd be amused.' Peck scribbled a few words next to Fry's: 'I am not amused.'[117]

In June 1941, Fry made a note to himself about what may have been a conversation with Consul General Fullerton (the word 'General' is written but crossed out, as if not to identify the speaker too precisely): 'The [Consul] was giving me advice. "Why do you have so many Jews on your staff?" he asked. I told him I didn't have as many as the police accused me of having. Less than half the staff was Jewish. "Well," the Consul said, "I think you make a mistake to have so many. The Department withdrew all the Jews on the Embassy and Consular staffs in France shortly after Pétain came to power. I think there's only one left, a clerk at the Embassy.'[118]

In August 1941, just before Fry's expulsion, Fullerton passed on some documents to the American Embassy in Vichy, with the following cover note: 'I am enclosing some "fryana" which somebody up there may care to read and which were left with me the other day.'[119] The documents consisted largely of A.R.C. reports, many of them meticulously prepared by Daniel Bénédite, detailing conditions in the French internment camps.

The biggest enemies of Fry's mission to France were not French officials; they may not have been really all that unhappy with what he was doing. Nor were they German officials, who only cared at that point to get their hands on certain definable opponents of the Reich, and perhaps not all that many of them. The biggest enemies of the rescue effort were Americans.

12. THE STAKES

What gives the Fry mission its greatest significance is not just that it highlights the conflicting American refugee and 'Jewish' policy at that time, but also that it was during that very time, in 1941, that the Nazis decided on what has to be characterized as a major change in policy, a change glaringly obvious to most scholars and yet dimly perceived by Americans.

Even major historians stumble into anachronistic lapses with regard to this Nazi change in attitudes. In her Pulitzer Prize-winning book, 'No Ordinary Time: Franklin and Eleanor Roosevelt: The Home Front in World War II,' Doris Kearns Goodwin writes of the summer of 1940: 'It was the summer of high hopes. As long as America and other countries were willing to open their doors to the Jews, the Nazis, at this juncture, were still willing to let them go.'[120]

But the Nazis were not merely 'willing' to let the Jews go at that time – they were eager.

For all of Hitler's dire 'prophecies' and whatever his murderous fantasies and geno-cidal longings, it took time, war, and specific circumstances for the Nazis to begin to imagine – let alone begin to implement – something on the grand scale of the Final Solution as we have come to know it.

Until then, German policy had long been one of 'solving the Jewish question by means of emigration or evacuation,' as historian Michael R. Marrus has summarized it.[121] The old plan of resettling Jews in Madagascar and letting them fester or die off there – should that be what happens – had not been entirely shelved; it was gradually abandoned only when it became clear that continued British sea power made access to the island impossible.[122] Other territorial solutions were also seriously considered.

The objective always was to get the Jews out of the Third Reich and out of Europe – one way or the other. The *hope* undoubtedly was for world domination and the total elimination of the Jews, but hope and fantasies are just that – policies are what people *do*, and policies, ultimately, are what count. 'Nazi policy changed course,' historian Saul Friedländer has stated clearly, 'when it replaced emigration/expulsion with extermina-tion.'

It was in October 1941 that Jewish emigration from Germany and German-held lands was banned, and mass deportations of German Jews to the East began. For historian Yehuda Bauer, 'The decision-making process in Germany probably culminated in the late summer or early fall of 1941 in the consensus that all Soviet Jews should be murdered, and then immediately afterwards into a consensus that all European Jews should be murdered.'[123]

Historian Philippe Burrin has made the case, endorsed in 1994 by Friedländer, that there was a specific decision made by Hitler in mid-September 1941.[124] Burrin argued that even the escalating and violent slaughter of Jews in conquered Russian territories after the German invasion of the Soviet Union on June 22, 1941, did not necessarily constitute a reversal of the overall plan to resettle Europe's Jews after the war.[125]

Historians Christopher R. Browning and Richard Breitman continue to believe that the decision was made earlier in the summer,[126] and Breitman has outlined evidence that seeks to tighten 'the intrinsic connection between the mass shootings of Jews in the Soviet territories and the assembly-line gassings of European Jews in the extermination camps,'[127] which began at Chelmno in December 1941. (Breitman has also detailed how British interception of German radio communications allowed British authorities to know immediately the extent of the massacres – and how British officials chose to keep this information to themselves, not even disclosing it for the Nuremberg trials.[128])

But the precise date of the decision is surely less important than its essential meaning, which Friedländer has put this way: 'Since there was nowhere for them to be sent, the Jews would vanish by the only remaining route: death.'[129]

One year earlier, in October 1940, some 6,500 German Jews had been loaded onto trains and deported to the *West*, bringing them into Vichy France, to the consternation of the French authorities, who first protested to the Germans, then begged the United States to help out by taking in a fair share of these refugees. 'Put bluntly,' Michael Marrus and Robert O. Paxton wrote in *Vichy France and the Jews*, 'the Germans wanted to dump Jews in the Unoccupied Zone; Vichy wanted to keep them out.'[130]

Undersecretary of State Sumner Welles prepared a response to the French Ambassador's plea for help, and submitted it to Roosevelt for the President's approval. The response basically told the collaborationist French regime, with which we had good relations, to get lost, that the U.S. couldn't do anything more than it was doing.

And Welles explained to the President, who approved the response, that if the U.S. gave in to the French on this they would never hear the end of it. The Germans would, in effect, be in a position to keep shoving the poor refugees down American throats.[131]

> Information reaching us is conclusive that if we or the other American Republics yield to these blackmailing totalitarian tactics, the Germans will inaugurate something approaching a 'reign of terror' against the Jewish people, not only those remaining in Germany but those as well in countries under occupation or which may be occupied in the future. Thus hundreds of thousands of unhappy people will be dispossessed of their homes and their goods to be used as pawns in a German maneuver calculated to embroil opinion in the democratic countries overseas.[132]

The greatest fear in high-level American circles was not that Jews wouldn't be able to escape Hitler's Europe; it was that the U.S. might find itself pressured to take in large numbers of these refugees. Moreover, such an influx, it was assumed, would inevitably exacerbate the already startlingly high – and growing – levels of antisemitism in the U.S.

The extent and depth of antisemitic and pro-Nazi sentiment in the United States in the late '30s and early '40s has not yet been fully chronicled and is certainly unfamiliar to most Americans today. The war effort and the flag-waving patriotic hoopla in the American media of the time have obscured the powerful, dark forces that had permeated American life.

In the late '30s, Nazi military attaché in Washington Ulrich von Gienanth encouraged one American fascist leader – there were many aspiring Hitlers around – with the opinion that there was ten times more anti-Jewish feeling in the U.S. then than there had been in Germany before Hitler's rise to power.[133]

According to a Roper poll conducted in July 1939 and not released at the time, 53% of Americans believed that Jews were different – and should be restricted. Ten percent of the public openly declared to the pollster that they favoured expelling Jews from the U.S. Historian David S. Wyman analyzed surveys from the late '30s and early '40s and noted that approximately a third of the American public was in favour of, or at least sympathetic to, 'a general anti-Semitic campaign' (roughly another third was ready to actively oppose such an undertaking, while the rest, presumably, were 'indifferent').[134] In April 1939, the very mainstream *Fortune* magazine reported widespread American opposition to taking in German Jewish refugees – 83 percent of respondents were then opposed to letting in more European refugees – and asked whether Hitler and his American supporters would not be safe in the 'joyful conclusion... that Americans don't like Jews much better than do the Nazis?'[135]

Indeed, all the public opinion polls would chart a continuing *rise* in American anti-Jewish feelings throughout the war years, and regardless of the news from Europe and the increasingly obvious plight of the Jews there.[136] As for the reaction of American Jews to the growing Jewish crisis in Europe, Eleanor Roosevelt – whose passion for civil rights blazed through those years even when her concern for the oppressed European Jews did not – puzzled over it in the fall of 1941. According to a friend, the daughter of American Jewish Congress President Rabbi Stephen Wise, the First Lady confided the following to her during an overnight stay at the White House:

> One of the things that troubles me is that when people are in trouble, whether it's the dust bowl or the miners – whoever it is, and I see the need for help, the first people who come forward and try to offer help are the Jews. Now in these terrible days, when they need help, why don't they come? Or when they come, why do they speak in a lower fashion?[137]

Whatever the reasons, until late 1941 'The door is bolted on the Allies' side, not on the Germans' side,' Christopher Browning stresses. 'The Germans were smuggling more Jews out than all the rescue groups. Certainly, when you're talking about the refugees in the Vichy zone, if the Allies had been willing to take these people, there's no reason why the vast bulk of them couldn't have been rescued. But the Allies were trying to resist what they considered Hitler's totally hostile attempt to flood them with refugees.'[138]

Yehuda Bauer has underscored that while the Nazis had long 'thought that the West might be willing to buy [the Jews],'[139] the Allies, for their part, 'were convinced that one could not negotiate with the Nazis or bribe them.'[140] 'The Allies,' Bauer asserts, 'never understood the Nazis, not even when they defeated them.'[141]

If Adolf Hitler and his pathological hatred were necessary for the Final Solution to occur, as most historians agree, he nevertheless could not have imposed such extreme measures against the will of his people. Who is to say that he could have imposed them against the will of the rest of the world?

Elie Wiesel was once asked what was the most important thing the world had learned from the Holocaust. His answer: that you can get away with it. If that is so, then must we not ask how we let them get away it with it?

To be sure, there may be little evidence that Hitler and the Nazis could be swayed by world opinion, since world opinion seldom opposed them very strongly.[142] Yet Konrad Heiden, the writer and Hitler biographer high on the Nazi 'most wanted' list – who happily was also on Fry's list – had in 1938 summarized the risks of such indifference: 'The lesson is pure and simple. Whenever the world rises against the Jewish persecution in Germany, those persecutions slacken. Whenever the attention of the world wanders, they are resumed.'[143]

In assessments of the Allied response to the Holocaust, the issue often gets reduced to whether mass rescue was possible once mass murder had begun. But rescuing the potential victim of a murderer once the crime is being committed is one thing; it is quite another to have contributed to the climate that nurtured the potential murderer and indeed allowed him to become one.

Referring to Germany, Philippe Burrin has suggested that 'widespread moral indifference' was perhaps 'the most effective facilitator of the Final Solution.'[144] Did the moral indifference outside of Germany not ease the way as well?

Despite the specific obsessions and circumstances that may have led Hitler to his fateful decision, is it not legitimate to ask whether the Nazis weren't influenced in their thinking by the realization that the U.S. and the Western World didn't want these Jews either and certainly wouldn't negotiate on their behalf – that in fact the Western world probably wouldn't care all that much about what happened to the European Jews?

Trained to resist speculation, historians will be uncomfortable with such highly speculative questions. But is it not, in fact, speculative to dismiss out of hand the

possibility that different attitudes outside of Germany – even just in the United States –
could have changed the course of history?

What if America, from 1933 to 1941, had been a nation of Varian Frys, Miriam
Davenports, Mary Jayne Golds, Charles Fawcetts, and Harry Binghams? And was the
American consular corps with which they tangled in Marseille not in the front ranks of
the moral indifference chronicled in historian David Wyman's landmark study *The
Abandonment of the Jews: America and the Holocaust*.[145]

Varian Fry, of course, could not know in 1941 what was happening behind the scenes
and how the world was changing, although he may have retained in the back of his mind
what fellow Harvard graduate and Nazi propagandist Ernst 'Putzi' Hanfstaengl had told
him in Berlin in 1935: 'that the "radicals" among the Nazi Party leaders intended to
"solve" the "Jewish problem" by the physical extermination of the Jews.'[146] (Fry had
only 'half believed him'.)[147]

When Wyman, then a young graduate student, embarked in the '60s on the first
scholarly study of the American response to the Holocaust, he sought Fry's help. Fry
wrote to Wyman that 'The subject of your doctoral dissertation interests me very much
indeed,'[148] and invited Wyman over to his house in Connecticut. The two men pored
over the contents of some cartons Fry had brought down from his attic.[149]

With Wyman's pioneering research, it seemed that Fry's time had finally come, but he
died before *Paper Walls: America and the Refugee Crisis, 1938–1941* was published. We
will never know to what extent Fry would have approved Wyman's challenging closing
words:

> One may level the finger of accusation at Franklin Roosevelt for having done so little and at
> Congress for having done nothing. But the accuser will find himself simultaneously pointing
> at the society which gave American refugee policy its fundamental shape. Like the Pre-
> sident, the majority of Americans condemned Nazi persecution. But most opposed widening
> the gates for Europe's oppressed. Viewed within the context of its times, United States
> refugee policy from 1938 to the end of 1941 was essentially what the American people
> wanted.[150]

Viewed within the context of its times, Fry's mission seems not 'merely' an attempt to
save some threatened writers, artists, and political figures. It appears in hindsight like a
doomed final quest to reverse the very direction in which the world – and not merely the
Nazis – was heading.

13. THE QUESTIONS

But the obvious question arises: can one justify the fact that Varian Fry's initial
motivation was – and primary thrust remained – to assist and save select figures of the
artistic and political worlds? If it is true that the mission wound up encompassing quite a
few anonymous refugees, does the charge of elitism nevertheless carry some weight? For
that matter, is a mediocre artist any less entitled to life than a great one?

Indeed, if there are some whom the Fry group simply was not able to get out of
France, despite its efforts, there were many others whose candidacy for help was
rejected, while they were given meal tickets and sent over to the Quakers: they were
just not deemed to be within the purview of Fry's operation.

Among those who unsuccessfully sought Fry's help were the 'authors' of the author of
these lines, the young journalist Léo Sauvage, a Jewish intellectual without American
connections who had found refuge in Marseille with his wife, a Polish Jew who
ultimately lost much of her family to the death camps. Fry's colleague Jean Gemähling

remembered encountering Léo Sauvage at the American Rescue Center. A list of A.R.C. 'clients' reveals that the Sauvages had gone so far as to include their real names long successfully buried behind French identities: Sauvage-Smotriez, Leo; Sauvage-Suchowolska, Barbara.[151]

Not able to leave France, Sauvage threw himself into Marseille's lively intellectual life at that time, founding a theatrical troupe that staged French medieval farces. Later, he and his pregnant wife found shelter in a singular haven of refuge in the mountains of south-central France, Le Chambon-sur-Lignon. There the determined policy was to turn no one away.[152]

Was the selectiveness of Fry's effort immoral or at least distasteful? Are we wrong to be mesmerized by the fact that Fry and his friends contributed to the survival of so many 'stars' of twentieth-century culture?

Karel Sternberg, a Czech refugee who worked at the American Rescue Center, provided, with some exasperation, what may be the most important answer:

> In any operation you do what you can. You don't measure an assignment by what you cannot do. You measure it by what you *can* do. That you cannot help 50,000 people doesn't mean that you cannot help 2,000 people. Let me repeat, you judge the importance and the meaning of an assignment by what you can do, not by what you cannot do. Because it's always limited, what you can do.[153]

It is also true that a number of the prominent figures in whom Fry and the Emergency Rescue Committee took a special interest were particularly vulnerable *because* of their celebrity status – a major advantage to get an American visa, no doubt, but one still needed to get out of France without an exit visa.

But finally, it may be no less important to remember that if Fry was committed to 'democratic solidarity,'[154] he was also somebody who deeply, passionately cherished the arts and culture. Is it not legitimate to begin by saving those whom one loves?

14. THE TEMPERAMENT

After the war, Fry analysed for his friend Albert Hirschman the components of his own motivation in Marseille:

> You say you wonder what the predominant constituent of my temper was during those times – whether enthusiasm, hope, resignation, or outright cynicism. There was a fair measure of cynicism in it, certainly. I entirely agree with you that it is necessary to have a sense of irony if one is to handle human miseries professionally. But there was a good deal of idealism – less and less as time went on – a certain amount of naiveté, but above all, a common orneriness, which I inherit from my Scotch ancestors. It was a tough struggle, and it took all of my tough Scotch character to stick it out.[155]

Fry would have appreciated that it was the French who have the best, the pithiest – and untranslatable – term for him. He was an *emmerdeur* – somebody who drives you nuts.

This was indeed a time when it was important not to be accommodating, and a man surfaced in the right place, at that time, who was incapable of disregarding his judgment in order to be accommodating. To use the familiar understatement, he didn't suffer fools gladly – but he was as sensitive to moral obtuseness as well as intellectual flaccidity. Even when the stakes were low, Fry would refuse to give in, would not compromise in the slightest, would engage in a barrage of relentless letters.

In Marseille in 1940 and 1941, the stakes had been priceless.

15. THE EXILE

When Fry's train left for Spain from Cerbère, a dozen members of his team were lined up by the tracks to bid goodbye to their leader, a moment captured in the last of the many photographs Fry took during his European adventure.[156] He cried on the train.[157] 'I was very sad at having to leave you and all my friends,' Fry later wrote to the night watchman at the office in Marseille, 'more sad, perhaps, than you were to have me go. For I lost all my friends in going, whereas you lost only one.'[158]

In Spain, on his way to exile in America, Fry reflected on his experience for his wife, conveying that he was no longer the same man that he had been when he'd boarded the Dixie Clipper in New York just a year before:

> The roots of a plant in a pot too small will eventually burst the pot. Transplant it to a larger pot and it will soon fill it. But if you transplant it to a pot altogether too large, it will 'go to root,' as gardeners say, and may even die from the shock. I was transplanted, 13 months ago, to a pot which I more than once had occasion to fear was too large; but I didn't die; in the end I think I very nearly filled it – not entirely, but nearly. At least I didn't die from the shock or the sense of my inadequacy.[159]

In Marseille, after Fry's departure, faithful Daniel Bénédite, Lucie Heymann, Anna Gruss, Paul Schmierer and their colleagues – with invaluable help from lawyer and future Marseille mayor Gaston Defferre[160] – kept the American Rescue Center alive, with no more Americans involved locally, and little or no support from the U.S. According to Daniel Bénédite, there was surprising goodwill from new U.S. Consul General Benton. When the latter introduced Bénédite to a young U.S. Embassy attaché named Cassidy, the Embassy official felt comfortable enough to warmly shake Bénédite's hand with two hands and say, 'I was deeply shocked by the [State] Department's hostility towards your boss, Varian Fry.'[161]

Vichy finally shuttered the operation in June 1942, and formally closed it down with the German occupation of the southern zone that November. Bénédite, Jean Gemähling, Justus Rosenberg (a young German Jew who had served as an office boy), will be among those who enter the Resistance – where patriots, alas, were not encouraged to concern themselves with the fate of refugees or Jews. Schmierer wrote to friends in New York: 'It's curious how very much easier it seems to be to organize emigration toward death than emigration toward life.'[162]

Fry wrote a note to himself: 'Since, silence. I have tried again and again since to reach my friends in France, to have even one direct word from any one of them. I have tried again and again, but I have always failed. Whether I whisper or whether I shout there is not even an echo to reply; only silence, silence so complete that I can hear my blood ringing in my ears.'

In New York, Fry tried doggedly and unsuccessfully to sensitize American public opinion to the refugee crisis in Europe and then to the 'massacre of the Jews' – a cover story in *The New Republic* in December 1942. The article began as follows:

> There are some things so horrible that decent men and women find them impossible to believe, so monstrous that the civilized world recoils incredulous before them. The recent reports of the systematic extermination of the Jews in Nazi Europe are of this order. Letters, reports, cables all fit together and add up to the most appalling picture of mass murder in all human history.[163]

Curiously, Fry, Miriam Davenport and Mary Jayne Gold all went into psychoanalysis during the war years, and Fry considered it one of the great adventures of his life – even greater than Marseille, he wrote to a friend.[164]

Fry's superb and voluminous correspondence and other writings – which cry out for anthologizing – make it especially sad that when he decided to write and publish *Surrender on Demand*, his memoirs of his Marseille adventure, he himself had to surrender to the merciless and censoring scalpel of his Random House editor.[165] Though the editor may have been right that American public opinion was not inclined to hear the complaints Fry wanted to voice on American refugee policy and his 'shame' at being an American citizen in light of that policy, Fry's original manuscript, which has been roughly reconstituted from the successive and jumbled drafts he left in his papers,[166] was more textured than the slim book that was published at the end of 1945.

Despite some good reviews, *Surrender on Demand* didn't sell and quickly went out of print. Fry wrote to a top Hollywood agent, asking 'whether there wasn't anything there which could be adopted for the movies,'[167] but nothing came of that either.

The edition published in 1997, thanks to the pioneering efforts of the United States Holocaust Memorial Museum,[168] wisely included as an afterword the heart-breaking and blunt foreword he had intended for the book. Not mentioned, however, was that in Fry's papers this text, including the following words, had been preserved in a folder marked, in his hand, 'Suppressed Material':

> If I have any regret at all about the work we did, it is that it was so slight. In all we saved some two thousand human beings. We ought to have saved many times that number. But we did what we could. And when we failed, it was all too often because of the incomprehension of the government of the United States. It was not until 1944 that the President created the War Refugee Board, to do in a big way, and with official backing, what we had tried to do in our little way, against constant official opposition. But then it was too late.[169]

16. THE MEMORIES

Among those who had been left behind in France was the young German Jew Justus Rosenberg, who had been befriended by Miriam Davenport and Mary Jayne Gold, and brought in to the American Rescue Center to help out. Rosenberg survived in the *maquis*, and found his way to America after the war, becoming a professor. He had lost touch with his Marseille friends, and in those pre-Internet days it wasn't easy to find people. But in 1952, Rosenberg sent a letter to Miriam Davenport.

> If you recall Marseille, France, 1940/41, 'Le Centre Américain de Secours' with its assortment of sometimes odd, but also original and lovable characters, Mary Jayne Gold and the escapade of the 'Legionnaire' [a reference to Gold's gangster lover], 'then perhaps you might also remember me, a bewildered young chap who went by the nickname of "Gussie" and who acted more or less as a "valet à tout faire." Despite the confusion, those were very formative days and I have kept of them a very lasting impression; among them you always occupied a very central position, since it was partly thanks to you that I survived in those trying days.[170]

A week later, Miriam Davenport sent her response, which included her own reflections on that period, untainted by the growing attention being given to the story today or by any desire for self-promotion. After all, nothing, in 1952, could have been more obscure and of less interest to Americans or anybody else than the Fry mission. Rosenberg found the letter in his papers after Miriam Davenport Ebel's death in 1999 and her burial on a beautiful day in a beautiful cemetery in the corn fields of Riverside, Iowa.

My dear Dr. Rosenberg!

How very formal and improbable it seems to be addressing 'Gussie' as a Herr Associate Professor in Dayton, Ohio!...It was when I came to 'Gussie' that I saw through your reincarnation and simply shrieked with joy!

I remember a great deal about you – you were a symbol of sorts, to me, in those days. Everyone was moving Heaven and earth to save famous men, anti-fascist intellectuals, etc. And there were you, a nice, intelligent youngster with no family, no money, no influence, no hope, no fascinating past. I remember one evening [writer] Hans Sahl tried to tell you how much worse off and in danger he was than you. And I recall telling Sahl (to his horror!) that he was a helluva lot better off, since many Americans would do everything possible for him, but that you were just another kid, a Jew, 'nice boy, but there's nothing we can do...'[171]

This last quote is what Varian Fry had said to Miriam Davenport when she had tried to press Rosenberg's case.[172]

It's strange how that brief period in Marseille looms so large in retrospect. We are 'a people apart' somehow. It was a curious nightmare – it seemed awful at the time, but it must have been happy too. We all had a purpose, a highly moral task to perform. And we and our friends had to survive *no matter how*. We were unencumbered by baggage and freed of all pretense of middle-class respectability. All joy was intense because of imminent danger. Will our wits and vision ever be so sharp again? I wonder.[173]

17. THE END

In Marseille, in 1940, Fry had sent his mother one of those hideously colourized postcards of that time, apologizing for it, and explaining that he had bought it from a war veteran with two medals in his lapel who had limped from table to table in a restaurant where Fry was eating with friends. 'The indifference with which human beings treat the heroes of yesterday always appalls me,' Fry wrote, presumably with no inkling that he himself was to experience that indifference for the rest of his life.

What is true for most rescuers became part of the saga of Varian Fry as well: the rescued did not, for the most part, maintain contact. Few lasting friendships had been established in Marseille with the 'clients'; the affinities were circumstantial and did not survive transplantation to the New World. Only the ties with the key aides remained strong.

Fry separated from Eileen shortly after his return to the States, and after her death in 1948 he married Annette Riley in 1950. They would have three children of whom two survive. His politics, always staunchly anti-Communist, became quite conservative. Ultimately leaving behind the world of editing and political writing for which he was suited, resisting till the end the lure of academia, which should have been second nature to him, Fry instead, with varying success, sought to earn a living in unexpected pursuits for such a man, such as television advertising and the promotion of Coca-Cola.

His friend Stanton Catlin thought that in entering the dog-eat-dog world of business in New York, Fry was determined to show his mastery at something new and original, and also felt the need to assert in that manner a conventional manliness.[174] For his Marseille cohort Albert Hirschman, so successful in America, Fry's postwar years were marked mainly by his desire 'not to play second fiddle to himself'.[175] Daniel Bénédite came to see in him a 'fallen idol'.[176]

Fry seems seldom to have brought up his exploits in France in 1940–41, but this great Francophile decided in the 1960s that he wanted and deserved to receive French honours. The matter had dragged on until it had finally been brought to the attention of André Malraux, then Minister of Culture. Malraux remembered visiting the offices of the A.R.C. in 1941, refusing to leave France, but entrusting Fry with the reels of his dangerous film on the Spanish Civil War, as the film itself was then at risk. It was only a few months before his death that Fry and his family attended a ceremony where he received the *croix de Chevalier* of the French Legion of Honour.

Fry had been divorced from Annette Fry and had just become the Latin teacher at a preppy Connecticut high school when he died on 12 September 1967, at the age of 59, of a cerebral haemorrhage. Shortly before, his old comrade Mary Jayne Gold had sent Varian some cheerful greetings on a postcard. Her last words: 'Well, we shared our finest hours, my friend.'

'In some ways I owe him my life,' the sculptor Jacques Lipchitz, who had remained devoted to Fry, wrote to Annette Fry in his condolence letter. 'I did not want to go away from France. It was his severe and clairvoyant letters which helped me finally to do so. And of what help he was once I decided to go to America! I mourn with you this marvelous man, lost a little in our difficult world, and I will cherish his memory to the end of my life.'

Flying in from Italy for the memorial service, Lipchitz raised his eyes towards the sky and directly addressed his friend, seeking to express what Fry had represented for 'all of us'. At key moments in history, he said, individuals emerge with precisely the qualities required by the situation. In everyday life, Lipchitz added, Fry 'was like a race horse hitched to a wagonload of stones.'

Fry himself had for some reason in 1943 attended a church service and torn out and kept in his papers his whole life a quotation from the programme. The words were from Ralph Waldo Emerson, and in abridged form they could serve as emblematic for Varian Fry in Marseille: 'There are men . . . to whom a crisis . . . comes graceful and beloved as a bride.'[177]

'Heroes of flesh and blood are complex creatures,' Mary Jayne Gold closed her account of her year in Marseille in 1940–41, 'born sometimes to shine brilliantly only for their short and finest hour. Varian Fry went to Marseille to his appointed task and fulfilled his mission, not less glorious because it was brief. Let the record speak.'[178]

NOTES
Abbreviations used are as follows:

CF   Chambon Foundation
COL   Columbia University, Rare Book and Manuscript Library
Crown   Interview videotaped for *And Crown Thy Good: Varian Fry in Marseille*, upcoming feature
          documentary by Pierre Sauvage (Chambon Foundation)

The author apologizes for the incomplete source information.

1   The spelling 'Marseille' will be used throughout, although references to 'Marseilles' in cited texts will
    not be modified.
2   Varian Fry to Eileen Fry, 3 February 1941 (COL).
3   Varian Fry's approximation in 1944 (Varian Fry, *Surrender on Demand*, original draft foreword,
    COL/CF reconstruction). This round number is not likely to be a very precise one, and such
    estimates are further complicated by the overlap between Fry's rescue operation and others.
4   Varian Fry, *Surrender on Demand*, original draft, p.42 (The original papers constituting Fry's
    successive drafts of his manuscript are at Columbia University. The reconstituted manuscript,
    assembled by Pierre Sauvage, exists in photocopy at the Chambon Foundation. Subsequent refer-
    ences will be to the COL/CF reconstruction.). The official is American Minister to Portugal Herbert
    C. Pell, whom Fry at that time found 'very sympathetic about the plight of the refugees.' However,
    documents cited by David S. Wyman suggest otherwise (*Paper Walls: America and the Refugee Crisis,
    1938–1941* [Amherst, 1968], pp.143–145.

5 The Ohio-born Mildred Theis was previously honoured by Yad Vashem as one of the Righteous Among the Nations with her husband Edouard Theis, assistant pastor of Le Chambon-sur-Lignon during the war. She had, however, taken on French citizenship by that time.

6 There is information on the documentary at the Chambon Foundation's Varian Fry Project website at www.chambon.org/fry.htm. Pierre Sauvage can be reached at sauvage@chambon.org or at Chambon Foundation, 8033 Sunset Boulevard #784, Los Angeles, CA 90046–2471.

7 Interview with Mary Jayne Gold (*Crown*). Also, Mary Jayne Gold, *Crossroads Marseilles 1940* (New York: Doubleday, 1980), p.xvi.

8 Interview with Henri Amouroux (*Crown*). Also, Henri Amouroux, *Pour en finir avec Vichy: 1. Les oublis de la mémoire 1940* (Paris: Robert Laffont, 1997), p.269. Anita Kassof points out that the German demand, on its face, was not unprecedented. 'Singularly disturbing about the extraditions ordered under Article 19, however,' she underscores, 'was Vichy's apparent willingness to surrender refugees whom the *Nazis* defined as guilty of crimes.' (Anita Kassof, *Intent and Interpretation: The German Refugees and Article 19 of the Franco – German Armistice, 1940–41*, (M.A. thesis, 1992).

9 Interviews with Henri Amouroux and Jean-Pierre Azéma (*Crown*). See also Amouroux, *Pour en finir avec Vichy: 1.* Amouroux points out that the clause was patterned after a similar clause imposed on Germany by the Allies in the Versailles Treaty after World War I. Azéma underscores that the expectation was that a peace agreement would soon follow, and that France's traditional attachment to the concept of political asylum would then be upheld. It should be noted, however, that Socialist leader André Philip, then visiting the Huguenot village of Le Chambon-sur-Lignon in France, insisted on the iniquity of the clause. (Interview with pastor Edouard Theis in Pierre Sauvage's 1989 feature documentary *Weapons of the Spirit*.)

10 The exact number of refugees handed over to the Germans as a result of Article 19 has yet to be established. Anita Kassof indicates that 'Vichy might ultimately have surrendered as few as thirty German nationals to the Reich under its terms in the period between June 1940 and November 1942.' (Anita Kassof, *Intent and Interpretation*, p.100)

11 Interview with Ingrid Warburg Spinelli (*Crown*).

12 Interview with Jack Jacobs (*Crown*).

13 Blanche Wiesen Cook, *Eleanor Roosevelt, Volume 2, 1933–1938*, (New York: Viking, 1999), p.312, in a chapter entitled 'A Silence Beyond Repair.' If the Fry story is in large measure a story about Americans, the perplexing relationship that the crusading First Lady had with the Emergency Rescue Committee – and indeed with the later massacre of the Jews – is a piece of the puzzle that deserves far greater research and analysis than the shallow and mostly evasive treatment it has received to date. What is one to make of her astounding question to a Zionist in January 1943, at a time when everybody had a sense of what was happening to the Jews of Europe: 'Why can't Jews be members of a religious body but natives of the lands in which they live?' (Letter to Dr. Joseph Dunner, reprinted in his *The Republic of Israel: Its History and Its Promise* [New York: Whittlesey House, 1950]). In 1952, providing a preface to the publication of *Anne Frank: The Diary of a Young Girl* (New York: Doubleday, 1952), all Mrs. Roosevelt saw in the work was 'one of the wisest and most moving commentaries on war.' She also felt no need to make any reference to Anne Frank being Jewish.

14 Varian Fry to Eleanor Roosevelt, 27 June 1940 (COL).

15 Fry, *Surrender*, original draft (COL/CF reconstruction). Also, interview with François and Fanny Charles-Roux (*Crown*).

16 Hertha Pauli, *Break of Time* (New York: Hawthorn, 1972, p.195).

17 *ibid.*

18 Varian Fry to Eileen Fry, 7 September 1940 (COL).

19 Communication to Pierre Sauvage.

20 Interview with Miriam Davenport Ebel (*Crown*). It should also be noted that Fry is not a Quaker, though he has frequently been identified as such.

21 Interview with Alfred Kazin (*Crown*).

22 For information on Charles Fry and the Children's Aid Society, see Annette R. Fry, *The Orphan Trains* (New York: New Discovery Books, 1994)

23 Varian Fry to Jean Gemähling, 9 January 1945 (COL).

24 Varian Fry, *Tribute to the Memory of My Father*, 11 April 1958 (CF photocopy).

25 Andy Marino, *A Quiet American: The Secret War of Varian Fry* (New York: St. Martin's Press, 1999).

26 Varian Fry to Dean A. C. Hanford, 7 September 1945 (COL).

27 Varian Fry to Lansing Warren, 2 May 1945 (COL).

28 *Weapons of the Spirit*, feature documentary by Pierre Sauvage (Chambon Foundation, 1989).

29 Interview with Marcel Verzeano (*Crown*).

30 E.g., American Rescue Center memo, 14 January 1941 (COL).

31 Daniel Bénédite, *La filière marseillaise: Un chemin vers la liberté sous l'occupation* (Paris: Clancier Guénaud, 1984), p.273.

32 Interview with Marcel Verzeano (*Crown*).

33 Daniel Bénédite, Administrative Report, 3 September 1941 (CF).

34 Barbara Sauvage communication to Pierre Sauvage, date unrecorded.

35 Fry disguised him as 'Jacques' in *Surrender on Demand*.

36 Daniel Bénédite, Administrative Report, 3 September 1941 (CF).

37 Varian Fry to Eileen Fry, 9 February 1941 (COL). Hirschman's false name at the time was actually Abel Hermant. Hirschman writes about his work with Fry in *A Propensity To Self-Subversion* (Cambridge, Mass.: Harvard, 1995).

38 Lisa Fittko, *Escape Through the Pyrenees* (Evanston, Ill.: Northwestern U. Press, 1991). Interview with Lisa Fittko (*Crown*).

39 Interview with Bil Spira (*Crown*).

40 Miriam Davenport Ebel, *An Unsentimental Education*. Ebel's brief account of her wartime experiences in Europe is posted at the Chambon Foundation's Varian Fry Project website at www.chambon.org/ebel.htm).

41 Varian Fry to Miriam Davenport, 27 August 1940 (COL).

42 Interview with Miriam Davenport Ebel (*Crown*).

43 Interview with Mary Jayne Gold (*Crown*).

44 Varian Fry had disliked Mary Jayne Gold's boyfriend, Raymond Couraud, nicknamed 'Killer,' who had been a source of problems for Fry. Andy Marino is wrong, however, to cast doubt on whether Couraud really was a deserter from the Foreign Legion and to write that he 'fancied himself in London with de Gaulle.' Couraud's unusual but real military career has been documented by Colonel Roger Flamand in *L'"Inconnu' du French Squadron* (privately published, 1983). Also, Gold, *Crossroads Marseilles 1940*.

45 Gold, *Crossroads Marseilles 1940*.

46 Interview with Mary Jayne Gold (*Crown*).

47 Mary Jayne Gold, *Crossroads Marseilles 1940*. Excerpts are available on the Internet at www.chambon.org/gold.htm. The book, for which rights are available from Pierre Sauvage, is being published in 2001 in France by Éditions Phébus.

48 Gold, *Crossroads Marseilles 1940*.

49 Interview with Charles Fawcett (*Crown*).

50 Gold, *Crossroads Marseilles 1940*, p164.

51 Interview with Charles Fawcett (*Crown*).

52 Interview with Charles Fawcett (*Crown*). Also Fry, *Surrender on Demand*. Although Fawcett and others remember Ball's first name to have been Leon, Fry refers to him as Dick.

53 Interview with Mary Jayne Gold (*Crown*).

54 Hiram Bingham IV to Rose Bingham, 12 September 1939 (Bingham Family Collection).

55 CF (Tracy Strong, Jr. Collection).

56 Interview with Tracy Strong, Jr. (*Crown*).

57 Interview with Miriam Davenport Ebel (*Crown*).

58 How little we know about American relief work in Europe during that time – its strengths, its weaknesses, its dilemmas. Why has there never been an academic conference on this subject? Why is it that to this day, with the exception of the interview cited here, Tracy Strong, Jr. – a vigorous, well-travelled gentleman with a good memory – has never been interviewed by anyone about his significant experiences in France, Switzerland and Germany from 1940 to 1949? Of course, as always,

such action of the few underscores the indifference of the many. Americans, to be sure, still find it easier to ignore all that was done – all that could be done. How else is one to explain how long it has taken the Fry mission to surface?

59 Interview with Jack Jacobs (*Crown*).

60 Department of State telegram to U.S. Consulate, Marseille, 18 September 1940 (CF photocopy).

61 Marseille American Consul General Hugh S. Fullerton, 26 May 1941 (CF photocopy).

62 Howard L. Brooks, *Prisoners of Hope: Report on a Mission* (New York: L. B. Fischer, 1942).

63 Varian Fry to Eileen Fry (COL).

64 Interview with Albert O. Hirschman (*Crown*).

65 Interview with Lisa Fittko (*Crown*).

66 Varian Fry to his mother, 3 November 1940 (COL).

67 Interview with Mary Jayne Gold (*Crown*).

68 Interview with Albert Hirschman (*Crown*).

69 Varian Fry (unsigned), memo, Lisbon, 9 August 1940 (CF photocopy).

70 Fittko, *Escape Through the Pyrenees*, pp.152–3.

71 Daniel Bénédite to Varian Fry (COL).

72 Interviews with Diego Masson and Luis Masson (*Crown*).

73 Interview with Charles Fawcett (*Crown*).

74 Fry, *Surrender on Demand*, original draft, diary, 12 February 1941 (COL/CF reconstruction).

75 Fry, *Surrender*, p.177; Marino, *A Quiet American*, p.264.

76 Fry, *Surrender on Demand*, original draft, diary, 10 February 1941 (COL/CF reconstruction).

77 Annette Riley Fry communication to Pierre Sauvage.

78 Varian Fry to Eileen Fry (COL).

79 Interview with Stéphane Hessel (*Crown*).

80 Fry, *Surrender on Demand*, original draft, diary, 8 March 1941 (COL/CF reconstruction). Adapted by Varian Fry from Varian Fry to his mother, 8 March 1941 (COL).

81 Varian Fry to Eileen Fry, 27 October 1940 (COL).

82 Varian Fry to Eileen Fry, 5 January 1941 (COL).

83 Eileen Fry to Varian Fry, 21 January 1941 (COL).

84 Eileen Fry to Varian Fry, 28 January 1941 (COL).

85 Varian Fry, memo to EMERSCUE [Emergency Rescue Committee], New York, 21 January 1941 (COL).

86 Varian Fry, memo (unsigned), 14 January 1941 (COL).

87 Harold Oram to Varian Fry, 22 January 1941 (COL).

88 Varian Fry cable to Museum of Modern Art, 21 April 1941 (COL).

89 Eileen Fry to Varian Fry, 21 February 1941 (COL).

90 Varian Fry, *Surrender on Demand*, original draft, p.700 (COL/CF reconstruction).

91 Interview with Reynold Levy (*Crown*).

92 CF photocopy.

93 Robert J. Ullman to George K. Bowden, Memo, 16 September 1942, about his talk with David Seiferheld, Treasurer and Active Executive [sic] of the Emergency Rescue Committee (CF photocopy). Fry did, however, do some consulting for government intelligence services. Varian Fry to Herbert H. Lehman, 23 December 1942 (COL).

94 Varian Fry to Eileen Fry (COL).

95 Eileen Fry to Varian Fry, 18 February 1941 (COL).

96 Varian Fry to Elieen Fry (COL).

97 Varian Fry cable, 1 October 1940 (COL).

98 Varian Fry, *Surrender on Demand*.

99 According to Donna Ryan and Serge Klarsfeld, Rodellec du Porzic would vigorously implement Vichy anti-Jewish policies throughout the war years. Interviews with Donna Ryan and Serge Klarsfeld (*Crown*). See also Donna Ryan, *The Holocaust & the Jews of Marseille* (Chicago: U. of Illinois Press, 1996), p.5.

100 Lucie Heymann report, 2 September 1941 (COL).

101 Varian Fry to Albert Hirschman, 31 November 1941 (COL).

102 Eleanor Roosevelt to Summer Welles, 9 December 1940 (CF photocopy).

103 Eleanor Roosevelt to Eileen Fry, 13 May 1941 (COL).

104 Confidential document, *Archives départementales des Bouches-du-Rhône* (CF photocopy).

105 Memo, 3 January 1941 (CF photocopy). It may not be coincidental that there were, apparently, attempts to entrap Fry. 'They are even trying to "frame" me on a morals charge, Fry writes to his wife 'sending both girls and boys. I must sound as though I had gone stark nuts, but it is the plain truth. Needless to say, I don't touch the people sent any more than I touch the "important documents" which people tell me someone told them I could get to the British authorities for them. Yet it is a strain receiving so many provocateurs. I would like to know who it is who sends them.)' 31 May 1941 (COL). Attacks on Fry's 'morality' were apparently circulated, since they even reached his wife. 'Your stories about being attemptedly [sic] framed on morals charges were interesting,' Eileen Fry responds, 'as the stories had already reached me in garbled form, more disturbing than your explanation, which I was glad to get.' 8 July 1941 (COL).

106 Communication from daughter of fired receptionist to Pierre Sauvage.

107 'Doug' was Douglas MacArthur II. 'Woodie' was Woodruff Wallner.

108 Hugh S. Fullerton to H. Freeman Matthews, 15 October 1941 (CF photocopy).

109 Interview with Charles Fawcett (*Crown*).

110 Putting forward a different view of Consul General Fullerton as cowardly but 'relatively amenable,' Andy Marino quotes the Unitarian Service Committee's Howard L. Brooks, who served in France in 1941: 'Fullerton understood Fry's job and was sympathetic to it.' Nothing in the record bears out this assertion.

111 Varian Fry to Eileen Fry, 7 September 1941 (COL).

112 American Marseille Consul General in 2000 Samuel V. Brock was instrumental in obtaining the honours for Varian Fry. Interview with Samuel V. Brock (*Crown*).

113 Born to wealth and social status, Bingham died unrecognized and relatively impoverished.

114 William L Peck, Memorandum on immigration policy at the Marseille consulate, 6 March 1941 (CF photocopy).

115 Hugh S. Fullerton to Fry, letter, 14 April 1941 (CF photocopy).

116 Hugh S. Fullerton to the Secretary of State, 11 April 1941 (CF photocopy).

117 Varian Fry to William L. Peck, date to be determined (CF photocopy).

118 Varian Fry, Handwritten note, Marseille, June 1941 (COL).

119 Hugh S. Fullerton to H. Freeman Matthews, 14 August 1941 (CF photocopy).

120 Doris Kearns Goodwin, *No Ordinary Time: Franklin and Eleanor Roosevelt: The Home Front in World War II* (New York: Simon & Schuster, 1994).

121 Michael R. Marrus, *The Unwanted* (New York: Oxford University Press, 1985), p.232.

122 A bizarre footnote to Fry's stay in Marseille is the allegation put forward independently in the early 1960s by writers Victor Alexandrov and Marcel Wallenstein, and later repeated by Charles Wighton, that Adolf Eichmann met with Varian Fry in Marseille in 1940 thinking that Fry represented the American government (!) and wishing to negotiate the possibility of letting ship-loads of Jews go to Madagascar, in return for $5,000 for each Jew and in the context of the attempt to reach a negotiated peace with Great Britain. Fry later denied that such an encounter or such discussions ever happened, even with Nazi officials other than Eichmann, and there is not a shred of credible evidence that they did. However, the notion of such a discussion taking place between German and American representatives in the summer or early fall of 1940 is not inherently absurd from a strictly political point-of-view, according to historian Yehuda Bauer, and given the good connections that Alexandrov and Wallenstein seem to have had with intelligence services – and the fact that they get some relatively obscure details right, though their accounts are riddled with absurdities – it would certainly be interesting to know how and why this completely forgotten story ever surfaced in the first place. See Victor Alexandrov, *Six Millions de Morts: La Vie d'Adolf Eichmann* (Paris, 1960); Marcel Wallenstein, 'How "the Blackest Nazi" Tried To Bride the U.S. With Jewish Lives,' Kansas City Star, 14 August 1960; Charles Wighton, *Eichmann: His Career and His Crimes* (London, 1961).

123   Interview with Yehuda Bauer (*Crown*).
124   Philippe Burrin, *Hitler and the Jews: The Genesis of the Holocaust* (London: Edward Arnold, 1994). Introduction by Saul Friedländer.
125   Burrin, *Hitler and the Jews*.
126   Interviews with Christopher R. Browning and Richard Breitman (*Crown*).
127   Richard Breitman, *Official Secrets: What the Nazis Planned, What the British and Americans Knew* (New York: Hill & Wang, 1998), p.227.
128   Breitman, *Official Secrets*.
129   Burrin, *Hitler and the Jews*, p.19.
130   Michael R. Marrus and Robert O. Paxton, *Vichy France and the Jews*. (New York: Basic Books, 1981). Also interview with Robert O. Paxton (*Crown*).
131   Amb. Gaston Henry-Haye to Secretary of State Cordell Hull, 25 November 1940 (CF photocopy). Sumner Welles memo to Franklin D. Roosevelt, 21 December 1940 (CF photocopy). Cordell Hull to Gaston Henry-Haye, 27 December 1940 (CF photocopy).
132   Sumner Welles memo to Franklin D. Roosevelt, 21 December 1940 (CF photocopy).
133   Charles Higham, *American Swastika* (New York: Doubleday, 1985), p.82. Some ground-breaking reporting was done by Higham in both *American Swastika* and *Trading With the Enemy* (New York: Delacorte, 1983).
134   David S. Wyman, *Paper Walls: America and the Refugee Crisis, 1938–1941* (Amherst, Mass: University of Massachusetts Press, 1968), p.22.
135   Fortune, April 1939.
136   By D-Day, according to one hopefully inaccurate poll, Americans viewed Jews as a larger threat to the U.S. than the Nazis or the Japanese.
137   Monty Noam Penkower, *The Holocaust and Israel Reborn: From Catastrophe to Sovereignty* (Urbana, Ill. and Chicago: University of Illinois Press, 1994). Penkower cites an interview he conducted with Judge Justine Polier on 17 May 1976.
138   Interview with Christopher R. Browning (*Crown*).
139   Yehuda Bauer, *Jews for Sale?: Nazi-Jewish Negotiations, 1933–1945* (New Haven: Yale University Press, 1994), p.32.
140   *ibid.*, p.61.
141   *ibid.*
142   Nazi invulnerability to public opinion has been overstated. The still little known Rosenstrasse Street public protests in Berlin in 1943, which defied the Gestapo and succeeded in reversing a planned deportation of Jews, suggests that direct challenges to the Final Solution were not necessarily doomed to failure. The story was discovered, researched and recounted by Nathan Stoltzfus, *Resistance of the Heart: Intermarriage and the Rosenstrasse Protest in Nazi Germany* (New York: Norton, 1996). The book will be the foundation of a Chambon Foundation documentary, as well as a dramatic motion picture to be produced by Pierre Sauvage.
143   Konrad Heiden, *The New Inquisition* (New York: Starling/Alliance, 1938), p.174.
144   Burrin, *Hitler and the Jews*, p.151.
145   David S. Wyman, *The Abandonment of the Jews: America and the Holocaust* (New York: Pantheon, 1984).
146   Varian Fry, 'The Massacre of the Jews' (*The New Republic*, 21 December 1942).
147   *ibid.*
148   Varian Fry to David S. Wyman, 29 April 1965 (CF).
149   Interview with David S. Wyman (*Crown*).
150   Wyman, *Paper Walls*. Wyman was tougher on President Roosevelt's record with regard to the Holocaust in the subsequent *The Abandonment of the Jews: America and the Holocaust*.
151   *Deutsche Bibliotek*, Frankfurt, Germany.
152   *Weapons of the Spirit*, a feature documentary by Pierre Sauvage (Chambon Foundation, 1989).
153   Interview with Karel Sternberg (*Crown*).
154   Fry, *Surrender on Demand*, p.ix.
155   Varian Fry to Albert Hirschman, 3 November 1941 (COL).

156 Varian Fry's original negatives from 1940–41 are in the archives of the Chambon Foundation, along with the Miriam Davenport Ebel collection, the Mary Jayne Gold collection, the Justus Rosenberg collection, the Tracy Strong, Jr. collection, and other photographs and documents relating to that time.

157 Varian Fry, *Surrender on Demand*, original draft, p.719 (COL/CF reconstruction)

158 Varian Fry to Adolfo Diaz, 22 January 1942 (COL).

159 Varian Fry to Eileen Fry, 4 September 1942 (COL).

160 Interview with Edmonde Charles-Roux (*Crown*).

161 Bénédite, *La filière marseillaise*, p.333.

162 Paul Schmierer to 'Charlie' and 'Kathleen,' 30 August 1942, cited by Varian Fry, *Surrender on Demand*, original manuscript, p.846 (COL/CF reconstruction).

163 Varian Fry, 'The Massacre of the Jews' (*The New Republic*, 21 December 1942). Why has there never been an anthology of contemporaneous writings about the Holocaust? Could it be, yet again, that there is a reluctance to face everything that a few caring people suspected, knew. said, shouted?

164 Varian Fry, COL.

165 Varian Fry to Robert N. Linscott (COL).

166 COL (original papers) and CF (reconstituted original draft in photocopy, assembled by Pierre Sauvage).

167 Varian Fry to Paul Kohner, 11 July 1945 (COL).

168 The U.S. Holocaust Memorial Museum's first temporary exhibit when the museum opened its doors in 1993, 'Assignment: Rescue – The Story of Varian Fry and the Emergency Rescue Committee' (initiated and supervised by Susan W. Morgenstein) was largely responsible for initiating the growing interest in the rescue mission in the 1990s. Donald Carroll, Cynthia Jaffee McCabe, Henry and Elizabeth Urrows, and Andrew St. George wrote the first important articles on the Varian Fry mission.

169 *Surrender on Demand*, original draft, foreword (COL/CF reconstruction).

170 Justus Rosenberg to Miriam Davenport Burke, 23 June 1952 (CF)

171 Miriam Davenport Burke to Justus Rosenberg, 30 June 1952 (CF)

172 Interview with Justus Rosenberg (*Crown*).

173 Miriam Davenport Burke to Justus Rosenberg, 30 June 1952 (CF)

174 Interview with Stanton Catlin (*Crown*).

175 Interview with Albert Hirschman (*Crown*).

176 Interview with Hélène Bénédite (*Crown*).

177 The full quotation is as follows: 'There are men who rise refreshed on hearing a threat; men to whom a crisis which intimidates and paralyzes the majority, – demanding not the faculties of prudence and thrift, but comprehension, immovableness, the readiness of sacrifices, – comes graceful and beloved as a bride.'

178 Gold, *Crossroads Marseilles 1940*.

THE CATHOLIC CHURCH

Scarcely any topic in Holocaust studies is more controversial than the role of the Roman Catholic Church during the years 1933–1945. Not only do the papers in this section reflect that fact, they also show that the Church's pre-Holocaust anti-Jewish attitudes helped to make Jews vulnerable when the Nazi onslaught came. The Church's post-Holocaust recognition of its own history continues to bring about significant, if wrenching changes, which is another fact confirmed by the recent scholarship found here.

CATHOLICISM'S EMERGING POST-SHOAH TRADITION:
THE CASE OF THE JESUITS

James Bernauer, S.J.

THE CATHOLIC Church entered into an end-of-the-millennium season of repentance and articulated several strong statements of sorrow regarding its conduct during the Nazi period. There was the 1995 statement of the German bishops which commemorated the fiftieth anniversary of the liberation of the Auschwitz camp: Christians 'did not offer due resistance to racial anti-Semitism. Many times there was failure and guilt among Catholics. Not a few of them got involved in the ideology of National Socialism and remained unmoved in the face of the crimes committed against Jewish-owned property and the life of the Jews. Others paved the way for crimes or even became criminals themselves.' The German bishops spoke clearly: 'The practical sincerity of our will of renewal is also linked to the confession of this guilt and the willingness to painfully learn from this history of guilt of our country and of our church as well. We request the Jewish people to hear this word of conversion and will of renewal.'[1] September 1997 brought the powerful confession of the French bishops, who blamed narrow ecclesiastical interests for blinding Church leaders to the call of conscience for a denunciation of the crimes against the Jewish people. The Bishops recognized that such silence was a sin and declared: 'We confess this sin. We beg God's pardon, and we call upon the Jewish people to hear our words of repentance.'[2] More recently, there was the Vatican statement 'We Remember: A Reflection on the "Shoah"' which proclaimed an 'act of repentance (teshuva)': 'At the end of this millennium the Catholic Church desires to express her deep sorrow for the failures of her sons and daughters in every age. . . . We pray that our sorrow for the tragedy which the Jewish people have suffered in our century will lead to a new relationship to the Jewish people.'[3]

The purpose of this paper is to show how this repentance in the face of the Shoah might enter into the very fabric of contemporary Catholicism and transform its vision of ethics and moral formation. I will develop this theme by focusing on one influential group within the Catholic Church, the Jesuits and their relationship with the Jews.

The Jesuits, or the Society of Jesus as it is officially known, is Catholicism's largest religious order and has a long, difficult and important history with the Jews. At the end of 1998, in Krakow, Poland, an international assembly of Jesuits was called together to discuss that history and the future shape of Jewish-Jesuit relations. In his address to the participants, the Superior General of the Order, Peter-Hans Kolvenbach, took note of the meeting's location: 'The fact that you hold your meeting in Krakow, not far from the shameful death camp of Oswiecim, should indelibly fix in your mind the stark reality of what hatred of Jews has accomplished and what we must seek in every way to prevent in the future.' The meeting reminded the Jesuits of the central place which the call to the

Holy Land occupied in the spiritual desires of Ignatius, the founder of the Jesuits, and his first companions. Ignatius fashioned the Spiritual Exercises as a textual pilgrimage to the life and locales of Jesus of Nazareth; with its name, the Society instituted itself as a simple following of Jesus and planted its members in his faith's landscape. We know the depth of Ignatius's personal attachment to his physical Saviour and the appeal exercised for him by an actual sharing in the Jewish lineage ('secundum carnem') of Jesus and Mary.[4] This spiritual desire to labour in the Holy Land provided one question animating the meeting: Had the Jesuits ever reckoned with the deprivation they suffered in the Society's initial failure to establish a ministry in the Holy Land? Did they need to hear the call to Jerusalem once again not just as a place of general pilgrimage but as the sign of a long forgotten dimension in Jesuit identity itself, indeed as the site where the original Ignatian inspiration and consolation might be recovered?[5]

The Jesuits 1995 Thirty-Fourth General Congregation had given them a remarkably rich document in its Decree Five: 'Our Mission and Interreligious Dialogue'. While it recognizes that the dialogue with the Jewish people holds a 'unique place' for Jesuits because it 'enables us to become more fully aware of our identity as Christians', the Decree does not address the dialogue's potential for a fuller experience of their own identity as Jesuits.[6] But there is a striking silence in that document. Strangely, the decree said nothing of the Shoah as the burning event which cried for the Second Vatican Council's declaration 'Nostra Aetate' and which inaugurated the intense dialogue of Christians and Jews during these last thirty years. The Krakow meeting was intended to make up for that deficiency. As a Jesuit and a participant in that meeting, I would like to emphasize how a general repentance for the Shoah needs to be transformed into a concrete grasp of specific attitudes and actions that created the conditions for the Holocaust. My paper has two distinct parts. First, it will give a general historical perspective on the Jesuit-Jewish relationship. The second part will explore one particular dimension of responsibility Christians have for the moral culture that gave birth to National Socialism.

1. *Jesuits and Jews* In order to listen to the past we must learn it, for we are frequently ignorant of the interactions between Jesuits and Jews through the centuries. Its opening moment was both a stance of courage and a leap into cowardice. Ignatius's devotion to the personal figure of Jesus saved him, and initially the Society, from a most common prejudice: the view that Jewish converts to Christianity and their descendants, the so called 'New Christians' of Spain, were more Jewish than Christian for they were of impure blood. Such tainted character justified their exclusion from Church posts and religious orders. Ignatius courageously resisted ecclesiastical and political pressures and refused to exclude Jewish converts or their descendants from the Society's ranks, and thus some of the most distinguished early Jesuits were Jewish.[7] Unfortunately, the Society was to abandon its founder's courage and in 1593, under pressure from its own members, banned the admission of all with 'Hebrew or Saracen stock'; not even the General of the Order could dispense from this impediment of origin. The Fifth General Congregation explained: 'For even though the Society, for the sake of the common good, wishes to become all things to all men in order to gain for Christ all those it can, still it is not necessary that it recruit its workers from any and all human races.'[8]

To my knowledge, no systematic effort has been made to trace the effect on Jesuits of this transformation in the attitude toward Jewish heritage from one of honour to that of curse. We do have occasional glimpses which I would like to indicate here. When the Jesuit historian Francis Sacchini wrote in 1622 that the second general of the Society,

James Laynez, had Jewish ancestry, the 'Spanish Jesuits rose *en masse* to denounce it.' The Provincial Congregation of Toledo called the fact a 'slur', a 'foul blot', a vile imputation', and requested the General to punish Sacchini.[9] An echo of the Spanish sentiment is audible in the pride that the German Ludwig Koch took three hundred years later in the identity of the Society as free of Jews.[10] For one major Jewish thinker, anti-semitism was indeed the special charisma of the Society: 'It was the Jesuits who had always best represented, both in the written and spoken word, the antisemitic school of the Catholic clergy.'[11] Only in 1946 did the Twenty-Ninth General Congregation abrogate the exclusion but without any explanation of why it was done. The Congregation substituted advice to the Provincials regarding the 'cautions to be exercised before admitting a candidate, about whom there is some doubt as to the character of his hereditary background'.[12] The principle of excluding Jews from the Society helps to account for the posture of the single Jesuit institution which evokes the strongest Jewish repulsion: the journal *La Civiltà Cattolica*, which has long been accused of the most vulgar anti-Judaism in many of its articles. One historian makes a common criticism in the literature:

> So powerful were the habits of theological antisemitism that even during the period of mass murder of Jews, after 1940, the Jesuits of *Civiltà* kept up their anti-Jewish crusade. In 1941 and 1942, the journal attacked the Jews for mythic crimes, 'perversity,' 'malice,' 'injustice,' impiety, infidelity, sacrilege'; for, in the eyes of this crucially important Catholic periodical, Jews were deicides whose pariahship could not be eradicated, and whose crimes were repeated in every generation down to the present.[13]

It is not surprising then that Jesuits have been branded as 'precursors of racialism' in fascist Italy.[14]

There is another institution that needs to be considered in any treatment of Jewish-Jesuit relations, the Papacy. Although Pope Pius XII has become the centre of controversy in discussions on the Holocaust, what is really at issue for Jesuits is the special and ongoing relationship they have had with the papacy since their restoration as an Order in the 19th century. The Vatican's assault upon the modern age's liberalism and democracy, and the Society's service to that polemic as well as to an ultramontane Papacy is a very heavy burden for them. They were appreciated: for example, Pope Pius X took consolation in the fact that, faced with evil times, God had delivered to him Jesuits, the 'most select line of soldiers, skilled in battle, instructed for fighting, and ready at the command and nod of the leader even to muster against the enemy where he is most concentrated and to pour out [your] lives'.[15] This was the age of the Papal rejection of modernism and of Vatican authorship of the Syllabus of Errors. Sadly, the enemy of the Church was often identified with emancipated Jewry or Jewish influences. Now that Jews had rights in modern society, it was claimed that special precautions were necessary in order to preserve Christian stability. Jews became a convenient target for the denunciation of a culture which was leaving the Catholic Church behind and attacking them provided a handy vehicle for protecting Catholic identity.[16] Jesuits and Jews are heirs to a history of polemics which made both groups dangerously vulnerable to political assault. The German Kulturkampf put them on opposite sides: after constant Jesuit denunciations of Jewish liberalism and power, Jews reacted with satisfaction, even glee, when, in the summer of 1872, Bismarck enacted a law which closed Jesuit institutions and entrusted to the government wide power over the Jesuits and the right to expel them from Germany as a whole.[17]

A good indication of how pervasive the anti-Jewish animus continued to be is to be found in the recently issued text of the unpublished encyclical on racism ('Humani Generis Unitas') which was commissioned by Pope Pius XI, who entrusted its composition to three Jesuits: John La Farge, Gustav Gundlach and Gustave Desbuquois. The fact that Pius XI died before it was released has probably spared Jesuits from much criticism inasmuch as the document manifests the sorry state of our own attitudes toward the Jews at that time. Israelites had been 'blinded by a vision of material domination and gain' and were doomed to 'perpetually wander over the face of the earth'. 'Israel has incurred the wrath of God, because it has rejected the Gospel.' The Church is not 'blind to the spiritual danger to which contact with Jews can expose souls' and she knows of the need to 'safeguard her children against spiritual contagion'. An especially chilling remark in the document praises the superiority of the Church's historical ways of dealing with the Jews in comparison with the anti-Semitism of the day: while the Church's teaching and practical attitude toward the Jews 'demonstrate the need for energetic measures to preserve both the faith and morals of her members and society against the corrupting influence of error, these same doctrines likewise show the utter unfitness and inefficacy of anti-Semitism as a means of achieving that end. They show anti-Semitism not only as pitifully inadequate, but also as defeating its own purpose, and producing in the end only greater obstacles to cope with.'[18] It is hard to imagine this as part of an effective Papal challenge to Nazi Germany's treatment of the Jews.

And then there is the issue of Pope Pius XII's conduct during World War II. As a result of the central importance his activities have in Holocaust discussions, perhaps historians should be encouraged to investigate Jesuit attitudes during that period, especially because Pacelli relied so often on Jesuits during his reign. The Vatican's recent 'We Remember: A Reflection on the "Shoah"' endorses the Pope's behaviour, and recalls the praise of various Jewish leaders for Pacelli after the war, but does not enter into any analysis of the criticisms which have been made of him.[19] Perhaps Catholic leaders think they have done as much as can be expected by releasing the eleven volumes of material from the Vatican archives which were judged relevant for discussion of Pacelli and the Church. The judges were four Jesuits, each from a different country: Pierre Blet, Robert Graham, Angelo Martini and Burkhart Schneider.[20] The documents paint a vivid picture of the Pope's anguish, his immense work of charity, and the complexity of the political forces with which he had to deal. Historians will long debate his response to those forces.

But perhaps there is need of a broader audience for these documents than that of professional historians. My own review of them has confronted me with the overwhelming diplomatic cast of mind that shaped Vatican approaches to the European struggle and has made me very aware that the charge of inadequate protest by the Papacy against Nazi Germany was certainly not invented by the young playwright Rolf Hochhuth. We know that many leaders, especially from Poland, cried for a more forceful Vatican denunciation of German war crimes and for a clearer identification of the Church of Christ with Germany's victims.[21] If the Papal public silence regarding the Holocaust is justified as a way of preventing even worse crimes, it certainly does contrast with Pacelli's outspokenness to the Allied governments about protecting the City of Rome from bombardment.[22] And then there is the shadow of the regular rejection of Jewish aspirations for a homeland in Palestine: 'Palestine is a Holy Land not only for the Jews, but to a far greater extent for all Christians, and especially for Catholics. To give it to the Jews would be to offend all Christians and infringe upon their rights.'[23]

The wartime American Jesuit Assistant and former Rector of the Gregorian University as well as occasional consultant to Pacelli, Vincent McCormick, suggests in his diary that there is much to explore in the Jesuit ethos in Rome during the war years. He for one felt that the Papacy was in danger of losing its moral authority if it failed to speak out more clearly about the Nazis and that, as a consequence, moral leadership would pass to the Protestant countries. Have we Jesuits ever come to grips with the appeal which Fascism had for some of our members and the animosity they felt for the victorious western democracies? At the beginning of 1943, McCormick wrote about a few Jesuits whom he judged sympathetic to a fascist victory: 'Such blindness is very hard for me to understand. How explain that men with all our intellectual training fail to grasp the real issues, men with our spiritual training are so inordinately nationalistic, while the ordinary intelligent man of the world and the simple folk too see things so much more clearly.'[24]

Perhaps the most regrettable element in the rancorous relationship between Jesuits and Jews is the loss of that special sense of solidarity in suffering which should have emerged from the history they shared. They were both the most frequent victims for those who sought a total, diabolical explanation for how history operated. They formed, as Lacouture has said, a 'tragic couple', both demonized in infamous documents: the *Monita Secreta* for the Jesuits, the *Protocols of Zion* for the Jews.[25] Their diabolical character was charted on the axes of space and time. Spatially, they operated outside of any specific territory and aspired for domination over the world; they lurked behind thrones at the same time that we were quite willing to overthrow those very kings and nations. Jews and Jesuits were preeminently people of the city and, thus, were allied to wealth, loose morality, and a cunning, deracinated intelligence which was contemptuous of the traditions of the rural past. Temporally, they were at home in periods of decadence and collapse and, thus, they were perceived as devotees of modernity: the same spectacles which detected the Jesuits as fathering the French revolution saw the Jews as the creators of the Russian one.[26]

This history echoed in Germany in the years leading to and during the period of the Third Reich.[27] Jesuits and Jews were linked often in the propaganda of the Nazis and other right-wing groups. Identified as international in commitment and urban in attitude, both groups were regarded as disloyal to the German State and as subversive of Aryan culture and morality. Their danger was a shared one as Cardinal Faulhaber warned in a letter of March 1933 to the Bavarian episcopate: 'we confront new situations from day to day, and the present Jew-baiting can turn just as quickly into Jesuit-baiting.' And while no group's losses can compare with that of the Jews, the enmity against the Jesuits did not stop at mere baiting: some 83 of them were executed by the Nazis, another 43 died in concentration camps and 26 more died in captivity or of its results.[28] Apart from them, there was also Jesuit resistance to Nazism and assistance to its victims across Europe, a history that has yet to find a comprehensive study.[29] Of all that might be done to honour our Jewish and Jesuit martyrs, and a sign of our willingness to transform penitential statements into deeds, I believe nothing is more important than a deeper understanding of the forces that erupted into Nazism. That comprehension should emphasize how we who are Catholics might have inadvertently contributed to the appeal which National Socialism had in a culture that was regarded by many as Christian. Raising this issue returns us to some of the intense debates that took place after the war but which were eclipsed by resistance to Allied de-Nazification efforts as well as by the emergence of the Cold War.[30]

2. TOWARD A POST-HOLOCAUST MORAL FORMATION

When Pope John-Paul II visited Germany in June of 1996, he gave a talk in Paderborn in which he praised several people who, 'faced with the totalitarian dictatorships courageously and fearlessly witnessed to the truth of the Gospel'.[31] Among the seven he named was Helmut James von Moltke, who was executed by the Nazis for his resistance activities and for his vision of a post-war German democracy. On 23 August 1940, von Moltke wrote to his wife: 'N(ational) S(ocialism) has once more taught us reverence for what is below us, i.e., material things, blood, ancestry, our bodies.'[32] Initially I was shocked by the statement but I have come to grasp the difficult truth which he is asserting, namely, how Nazism successfully exploited a strong religious alienation from the body and, thus, Christianity's estrangement from its own incarnational tradition. At the end of the war Karl Jaspers differentiated German guilt according to various levels: political, criminal, moral and metaphysical.[33] I would like to argue that there is a fifth level of ethical-spiritual responsibility which explores how our most foundational religious images, concepts and practices for intimate and public lives may contain those seeds of hate and violence which could come to flourish almost automatically in certain cultural crises. But that is to race ahead.

How was it possible for National Socialism to be so successful in capturing the minds and hearts of so many Christians either as committed believers or as tolerant bystanders? The Nazi period forces all of us to ask this question, to confront our dangerous ethical selves: How adequately or inadequately do we fashion ourselves, or are fashioned, intellectually, ethically, spiritually to appreciate or refuse certain types of moral appeal. These practices of the self define how an individual comes to feel that a matter warrants moral concern and what steps one is obligated to take in response to that moral signal. Certainly it is the case that National Socialism appropriated a ready-made set of virtues – honesty, diligence, cleanliness, dependability, obedience to authority, mistrust of excess.[34] Still, if we are to understand why these virtues came to be so characteristic and why people were so prepared to tolerate evil, we must interrogate the dynamics of the spiritual formation that German culture had passed down.

To speak of spiritual life at this time might seem to miss the mark when one remembers the brutal reality of Nazi deeds. What has to be faced, though, is that the beginning of the Hitler regime coincided with a passionate desire among many Germans for a spiritual renewal, indeed for a politics of spirit which National Socialism attempted to define. At this distance it is difficult to appreciate how promising a year 1933 was expected to become. In fact, Paul Tillich at the time accused perhaps the most prominent of his theological colleagues (Emanuel Hirsch) of associating the year so closely with 33, the traditional date of Jesus's death and resurrection, that the year of Hitler's coming to power was given the 'meaning of an event in the history of salvation'.[35] What has to be acknowledged is that there was an intense atmosphere of spiritual transformation that year. Philosophers and theologians felt as though a special invitation had been extended to their talents.[36]

There is not time to look in detail at how this spiritual moment was perceived. For now, let me just say that many philosophers and theologians regarded it as a moment of crisis, and I would claim that that crisis's most important element was how one was to relate to one's self, how one might affirm oneself as worthwhile. But to speak of spirit in the context of a culture which still possessed deep roots in Christianity was also to discuss flesh; cravings for spirit inevitably connect to a discourse of sin, sensuality and sexuality. If spirit expressed vitality and creative force, flesh possessed many satanic features, assaulting reason and proclaiming human weakness. This dualistic reading of the spirit-flesh struggle as soul versus body or sexuality is certainly inadequate to Paul's theology and yet, as we know, it has often characterized Christian discussion of sexual matters both in the past and present.[37] Here we may have, though, perhaps one of the sources of Christianity's own greatest weakness in its encounter with Nazism, for much pathology has flourished in modern religious culture's charting of sexuality. It is the charting with which I am concerned, not the sexual morality that may be put forward as a response to it. Certainly many of the Church's statements since Vatican II have delineated a much more positive appreciation of the sexual realm than had been the case. And I do want to emphasize this: I am not accusing a code of morality but rather the ethical-spiritual foundations of the very self who finds suitable a type of morality or its overthrow.

Having selected sexuality as a privileged route to moral status, the Churches did not create a very sophisticated palette of insight into it. The broodings of moral theology were too frequently isolated from the traditions of Christian spiritual theology.[38] I will not repeat here the series of Christian statements from this period which denounced the social permissiveness of co-education, and its supposed lack of concern for the lust in children and adolescents; nor those which denounced the immodesty intrinsic to public swimming pools; nor those many warnings about the dangers of nudity and male friendships. This determination to exorcise eroticism all too often encouraged a fierce self-hatred. And Jesuit pedagogy in the sexual area contributed to this mood. While Christian moral formation was inadequate, in my judgment, to the sexual domain, the Church's anxiety about it did not come from nowhere and did reflect an awareness that for a century there had been a new sexual challenge in German culture.[39] I cannot examine that challenge here save to note that the Church tended to see in a certain relaxation of sexual moral codes a decline of faith and, thus, a historical intimacy between Christian existence and the spirit-flesh struggle was reconfirmed and strengthened, now with modern sexuality as its unchallenged centre. Pius XI released his 1930 encyclical 'Casti Connubii' with its sharp denunciation of the 'idolatry of the flesh', and five years later he held out an interpretation of celibacy for priests: 'since "God is a Spirit", it is only fitting that he who dedicates and consecrates himself to God's service should in some way "divest himself of the body".'[40] The pivotal role that Christian moral formation conferred upon disciplining sexuality as a result of this had two major consequences.

First, it exposed Christians to a Nazism that could be thought of as either ethically allied with Christianity or as a liberation from religion's inadequacy to the richness of human life. National Socialism found the religious preoccupation with sexuality in moral formation to be helpful in a variety of ways: it sustained the emphasis on those secondary virtues that made people so compliant; it habituated people to an atmosphere of omnipresent sinfulness that seemed to grow with every step beyond childhood; it educated people into a moral pessimism about themselves and what they might be able to achieve; and this issued in what the Jesuit Alfred Delp, who was later to be executed by the Nazis, described as a paralysis of the inner self.[41] While it has been frequently acknowledged that an absence of German self-confidence was a precondition for Hitler's successful career, the focus of responsibility has normally been given to economic factors; the moral-spiritual dimensions should not be ignored.[42] It was this religious subversion of self-confidence which lies behind the primacy given to obedience as a virtue, and an extraordinary insensitivity to the demands of conscience. Many religious and moral practices established a profound alienation from one's self and one's desires. And this self-alienation was also a mode of alienation from the public space: the model for dealing with moral difficulty was set by sexuality: avoidance of danger and cultivation of a tranquil interiority. Often this trained people into a permanent submissiveness or stimulated an intense yearning to get beyond the sexual guilt of Christianity, a state which Nazism held out as one of its promises.

Nazism in effect put forward the bold project of overcoming the dualisms fostered by religion: body versus soul, flesh versus spirit.[43] National Socialism spoke to – and not just flattered – the German tradition of and pride in inwardness, the 'Innerlichkeit' which advocated a strenuous self-cultivation.[44] But the Nazi revolution bound together this celebration of inwardness, of the German spirit, with a profound affirmation of one's historical moment, of one's own German body, social and personal. It was to be praised for its health, its beauty, its utility and, most of all, as the temple for the transmission of biological life. The extent of its sexual ethics could be put forward as what is most distinctive of Aryan ideology.[45]

Its ethics was a strategy of sabotage against alternative relations to sexuality. It made a foe of the sexual libertinism of the Weimar Republic and of the Soviet Union. The sexual laxity which had been identified in the past with that ancient enemy, the French, now was tied to Communism's relaxation of legal restraints.[46] After it had replaced the Weimar Republic, the Third Reich mounted a widespread campaign of sexual purification: denunciations of pornography, homosexuality and any eroticism not governed by the desire for procreation, for those would eclipse the central status which sexuality had on the 'battlefield of life'.[47] This crusade against eroticism was terribly attractive for German Christians – and, I might add, made Hitler appear as a force for moral renewal to Christians in the United States as well.[48] Catholic anxiety about Communism included its perceived sexual license and hostility to family values. Thus, on the eve of the Second World War and the Holocaust, Germany was blanketed with a campaign for decency. But National Socialism was far more cunning than most expected.

The campaign for decency was by no means an acceptance of Christian codes. National Socialism constructed a post-Christian erotic. While Church leaders were regularly denouncing the dangers of immodesty, Nazi culture was celebrating the beauty of the nude body and the benefits of exhibiting it – from galleries of art to the joyful gatherings of youth. The Nazis were very successful in portraying Church views as hopelessly prudish, the Church's sexual teaching as unrelentingly hostile to the joys of sexual life and in encouraging young people to look elsewhere for a wise understanding of their erotic desires.[49] One might have hoped that the long pondering about sexual activities would confer upon Christians a particular sophistication in grasping some of the subtle tones in Nazism's sexual propaganda. I have found few signs of such proficiency.[50] It is as if the long stress on the natural law had made them deaf to the changing sounds of historically contingent evil. Indeed, there seems a special blindness, a general failure to recognize how demonic the unrelenting stress on eroticism's demonic force could also be.

The inadequacy of this moral formation had a second face. In that endless searching after the reasons for why the Jews were so victimized by the Nazis, for why so many collaborated in their murder, and especially for why so many stood aside and failed to do what could have been done, I propose that this issue of sexuality gives an essential answer. Before the Jews were murdered, before they were turned away from as not being one's concern, the Jew had already been defined as spiritless, on the one hand, and sexually possessed, erotically charged on the other hand. In contrast to that special German inwardness I mentioned earlier, the Jew was portrayed not only as empty of spirit but as an enemy of it. German philosophers worried about what was called a 'Verjudung' of 'deutschen Geistesleben', a 'Jewification' of German spiritual life.[51] The Jewish intellectual was both a materialist and a pharisaic rationalist in comparison with

German depth thinking. Deprived of spirit, the Jew was defined in Nazi propaganda as essentially carnal, as excessively sexual, indeed as boundlessly erotic, whose conduct was not under the control of the moral conscience.[52] Lust robbed the Jews of reason and, thus, reduced them to an animal level, a status which would soon come to be reflected in Nazi torture.

Some roots of the Nazi portrayal are in Christianity.[53] I am not able here to trace these roots but I do wish to note the inadequacy of a frequently appearing model in which Christian anti-Judaism and modern anti-Semitism are placed on a chronological calendar where the former is superseded by the latter. In fact they coexisted in the Nazi period and blended in ways that have yet to be adequately mapped. Nevertheless, with that said, the extreme victimization of the Jews by the Nazis comes from the position into which they were placed on the erotic field of modern sexuality.[54] That field need not be isolated, however, from religious discourses and practices. This sexual depiction was not static but functioned dynamically within an ethical field defined as a life and death struggle ('ein Kampf auf Leben und Tod') taking place between the healthy life force of Aryan blood and the disease-laden Semitic death substance.[55] This final element in modern sexual culture may certainly be described as racist but it also relates to the Christian sexual discourse in at least one specific way. This life and death struggle paradigm shows the legacy of that spirit-flesh struggle in which all sexual sin was grave or mortal, that is, condemning the sinner's soul to the death of eternal damnation.

It was in their customary portrayal of Jews as an erotic flood that the Nazis spoke to Christian anxieties about the sexual climate of their culture. Jews were sexually dangerous, their printing companies even blamed for producing far too suggestive pictures of the saints which were displayed in German homes.[56] If we look for the reasons why so few people were troubled about standing on the sidelines, why so many failed to get involved with the victimized Jew, practically or even emotionally, I would claim that this was certainly a major source of that moral indifference. For the Germans who were proud of the spiritual inwardness that was the legacy of their culture and who were humiliated by the sexual war that was waged in their bodies, the carnal Jew represented a contamination, the destruction of the spiritual sense and the eruption of the uncontrollable erotic body. It was to meet one's end as a moral and religious being. In the light of the predominant Christian style of moral formation, one could have predicted that, even while protests were mounted on behalf of the crippled and the insane, the Jews would be abandoned. At best.

Goebbels, Hitler's propaganda minister, claimed that the Third Reich had changed people inwardly, that it had given people the opportunity to escape the bourgeois epoch and embrace a new ethic of 'heroism, masculinity, readiness for sacrifice, discipline'.[57] He was only half right. Certainly, the Nazi movement was successful in absorbing common secondary virtues which, at times, were even defended by Christians as particularly appropriate to the religious sensibility.[58] But these virtues were appealing to people and were developed by them because they were eminently suitable for a struggle with one's flesh, that other self which had to subdued. This campaign's instrumentalization and depersonalization of sexuality was a principal source of that doubling process which some have argued is the key to appreciating how average citizens could function with a good conscience while contributing to mass murder.[59] The split self accounts for how, in the midst of administering the death camps, SS soldiers could be praised for their decency, their loyalty, their truthfulness. Despite the destruction of millions, Himmler could assure his men that 'our inward being, our soul, our character has not suffered injury from it.'[60] This is why the Nazis made a sharp distinction between authorized and illegitimate killings.[61] Strange as it may seem, Hitler's biographer, Joachim Fest, seems justified when he asserts that National Socialism exercised its greatest appeal among those who had a craving for morality.

On the other hand, I do want to stress that Goebbels *is* half-right. One of Nazism's genuine novelties is that it fashioned from a traditional morality of secondary virtues and of sexual asceticism an ethic which evoked from the German people an extraordinary willingness to discipline themselves and, in millions of cases, sacrifice themselves physically. While frequently exploiting the religion's divided self, Nazism created a post-Christian ethic by establishing the opportunity for an intense choice of one's self, in the here and now, an eroticism of one's self in time. There is a major shift in western experience here. Within cultures shaped by Christianity, one's sense of worth was through self-denial and surrender to the vocation one was given by providence. Who one was to *become* in that state free from time and flesh regulated one's commerce with oneself and others. Nazi eroticism was tied to the affirmation of who one *is* biologically, to the embrace of one's body and, through that, one's people. The model of virginity yields to that of breeding. I would claim that their relationship is not one of strict opposition as, for example, Levinas maintains when he contrasts a materialistic bondage to a biological past to a religious spiritual freedom from that bodily burden.[62] On the level of ethical formation, the struggle of spirit with flesh was no less a bondage and, indeed, was prelude to Nazism's own enslavement.

CONCLUSION

Just as a study of our age's culture could not be performed without a treatment of psychoanalysis, I would argue that 20th-century history becomes unintelligible when abstracted from the erotic field. Needless to say, I do not hold that it is reducible to that domain. We have looked at an ethical practice in which National Socialism forged a regime of erotic danger and sexual pleasure and a manner of relating to sexual life which was less indebted to biology than it was to an inherited sphere of spirituality, the struggle of spirit with flesh. Within that field, Nazism presented itself as achieving erotic maturity by overcoming dualisms: a Christian alienation of the soul from the body and a Jewish alienation of the carnal from the spiritual. An ethics that really learns from Auschwitz must take into account this history by establishing a spiritual-moral formation for Christians which does justice to their faith's affirmation of the worth of the human body and which integrates the teaching about sexuality with the Church's discourse on human dignity. Major steps have already been taken in this direction by many Church statements and practices. To give one concrete example of a positive practice, I would point to the search in Jesuit colleges over the last twenty years for a more adequate mode of integrating the pursuit of intellectual excellence and the quest for ethical maturity. It could be argued that recent emphasis on faith and justice as the organizing principle of a Jesuit style of education addresses the double failure of religious and academic cultures. It shifts moral formation from a model in which sex in the drama of flesh versus spirit is privileged as the central seismographic sign of healthy ethical life to the task of integrating the human needs of the historical moment with a personal self-appropriation stressing one's capabilities for meeting those needs and one's personal dignity as sexually embodied. It also unmasks the supposed political-moral neutrality of an academic culture which does not seem to possess the ethical insights and solidarities by which to be critical of its knowledge formations. And perhaps the most important step toward the development of those resources has already been taken by those Jesuit schools which stress as an integral component of their education an engagement and solidarity with communities which are traditionally victimized by our society's most powerful institutions.

The 1995 Thirty-Fourth General Congregation of the Jesuits stated very simply one of the great truths of Jesuit spirituality and tradition: 'Profound experience is what changes us.'[63] The Shoah is that profound experience which is transforming the relationship between Jews and Christians. This paper has stressed the past and certainly it is a past from which Jesuits have much to learn and for which they have much to repent. Still a renewed call to Jerusalem and deeper relationship with Jews is a deeply hopeful one. Jesuits will be led into new understandings of what they might come to share and one of those possibilities comes immediately to mind. In 1925 Rabbi Leo Baeck wrote: 'Whoso has conquered everything corporeal has conquered the God of the Jews.'[64] Is it possible that Christianity's separation from Judaism anticipated the later appeal for Christians of a Platonist dualism? Will its dialogue with the Jewish people give them a richer consent to their own incarnation, to a more profound integration of spirit and body?

NOTES

1 'Letter of Germany's Bishops Commemorating the Liberation of Auschwitz' (23 January 1995). English translation in *Origins* 24/35 (16 February 1995): 585–586.

2 'Declaration of Repentance' (30 September 1997). English translation in *Origins* 27/18 (16 October 16 1997): 301–305.

3 'We Remember: A Reflection on the "Shoah"' (16 March 1998). English translation in *Origins* 27/40 (26 March 1998): 669, 671–675.

4 For the plans of Ignatius and his first companions to work in Jerusalem, see *The Autobiography of St. Ignatius Loyola*, trans. Joseph O'Callaghan (New York: Harper Torchbooks, 1974), pp.24, 46, 47, 75, 80–81. For Ignatius's desire to share in the physical lineage of Jesus, see the citation from Ribadeneyra in James Reites, S.J., 'St. Ignatius of Loyola and the Jews' *Studies in the Spirituality of the Jesuits* 13/4 (September 1981): 17.

5 This notion was initially suggested to me in a reading of *The First Jesuits* (Cambridge: Harvard University Press, 1993) by John O'Malley, S.J., who emphasizes that the Jesuits' image as Counter-Reformation opponents of Protestants was closely connected to the decision to go to Rome: 'When, in 1534, they took a vow to spend some time in ministry in a distant place, they set their eyes on Jerusalem, not Wittenberg. Jerusalem dominated their imagination until the impracticability of passage forced upon them the alternative of going to Rome to find guidance from the wider vision of pastoral need that the pope presumably entertained. With that alternative came the likelihood, almost the inevitability, of enlisting in the battle against Protestantism' (p.16).

6 General Congregation 34: 'Our Mission and Interreligious Dialogue', *Documents of the Thirty-Fourth General Congregation of the Society of Jesus* (St. Louis: Institute of Jesuit Sources, 1995), p.149.

7 See Reites, 'St. Ignatius of Loyola and the Jews'. However, Ignatius too was a man of him times and when it came to the matter of Jews who were not and did not wish to become Christians, he could support the oppressive policy of ghettoization imposed by Pope Paul IV in his 1555 'Cum nimis absurdum'.

8 Decree 52. English translation in *For Matters of Greater Moment: The First Thirty Jesuit General Congregations*, eds. J. Padberg, S.J., M. O'Keefe, S.J. and J. McCarthy, S.J. (St. Louis: Institute of Jesuit Sources, 1994), p.204.

9 James Broderick, *The Progress of the Jesuits, 1556–1579* (London: Longmans, Green & Co., 1946), pp.310–311.

10 See his entry 'Juden' in his *Jesuiten-Lexikon: Die Gesellschaft Jesu einst und jetzt* (Paderborn: Verlag Bonifacius-Druckerei, 1934), pp.939–942.

11 Hannah Arendt, *The Origins of Totalitarianism* (New York: Harcourt, Brace & Company, new edition 1976), p.102.

12 Decree 8. English translation in *For Matters of Greater Moment*, p.625.

13 Robert Michael, '*Theologia Gloriae* and *Civiltà Cattolica's* Attitude Toward the Jews', *Encounter* 50/2 (Spring 1989): 158; see Arendt, *The Origins of Totalitarianism*, pp.116 and 120; Ronald Modras, *The Catholic Church and Antisemitism: Poland, 1933–1939* (Chur, Switzerland: Harwood, 1994), pp. 334–340; Richard Webster, *The Cross and the Fasces: Christian Democracy and Fascism in Italy* (Stanford: Stanford University Press, 1960), pp.122–127; and the discussion 'La Civiltà cattolica, Jews, and anti-Semitism' in *The Hidden Encyclical of Pius XI*, eds. Georges Passelecq and Bernard Suchecky (New York: Harcourt, Brace & Company, 1997), pp.123–136.

14 E. Rossi, *Il magganello e l'aspersorio* (Florence, 1958), cited by Meir Michaelis, 'Christians and Jews in Fascist Italy', in *Judaism and Christianity under the Impact of National Socialism, 1919–1945*, eds. Otto Dov Kulka and Paul R. Mendes-Flohr (Jerusalem:Historical Society of Israel and the Zalman Shazar Center for Jewish History, 1987), p.274.

15 Address to the General Congregation Delegates (16 October 1906). Cited in David Schultenover, S.J., *A View from Rome: On the Eve of the Modernist Crisis* (New York: Fordham University Press, 1993), p.166.

16 See Olaf Blaschke, 'Wider die "Herrschaft des modern-jüdischen Geistes": Der Katholizismus zwischen tradionellem Antijudaismus und modernem Antisemitismus', in *Deutscher Katholizismus im Umbruch zur Moderne*, ed. Wilfried Loth (Stuttgart: Verlag W. Kohlhammer, 1991), pp.236–265.

17 See Uriel Tal, 'The "Kulturkampf" and the Jews of Germany', *BINAH: Studies in Jewish History* I (New York: Praeger, 1989), pp.173–193.

18 *The Hidden Encyclical of Pius XI*, pp.249, 251, 252, 253. See the thoughtful review by Michael Marrus, 'The Vatican on Racism and Antisemitism, 1938–39: A New Look at a Might-Have-Been', *Holocaust and Genocide Studies* 7/3 (Winter 1997): 378–395. For a general consideration of 'Jesuit anti-Judaism' see Reiner Brüggermann and Gerd Spellerberg, 'Die Gesellschaft Jesu und die Juden: Eine Betrachtung über die Folgen des jesuitischen Antijudaismus', *Werkhefte Katholischer Laien* 15 (March 1961): pp.82–89.

19 Robert Leiber, S.J., Pacelli's secretary, provides an important perspective on the Pope in 'Pius XII', *Stimmen der Zeit* 163 (1958–1959): 81–100, and 'Pius XII und die Juden in Rom 1943–1944' *Stimmen der Zeit* 167 (1960–1961), pp.428–436.

20 *Acts et documents du Saint Siège relatifs à la seconde guerre mondiale* (hereafter*ADSS*), volumes 1–11 (Città del Vaticano: Secrétairerie d'État de la Sainteté, 1965–1981).

21 For example, see the introduction to *ADSS* 3, part I, pp.38–55, and document #287: Cardinal Hlond, Primate of Poland, to Cardinal Maglione on 2 August 1941; from part II, document #444: Letter from Apostolic Administrator for German Catholics Breitinger to Pope Pius XII on 23 November 1942; #477: Letter of Bishop Radonski to Cardinal Maglione on 15 February 1943; in *ADSS* 5, see document #449: Polish Ambassador Papée's letter to Cardinal Maglione on 27 August 1942; in *ADSS* 6, document #403: Letter of Polish Ambassador Papée to Montini on 13 December 1940; in *ADSS* 7, document #82: Letter of Polish President Racykiewicz to Pius XII on 2 January 1943. For an example of a strong defence of Pacelli, see Robert Graham, *Pius XII's Defense of Jews and Others 1944–45* (Milwaukee: Catholic League, 1987).

22 See *ADSS* 5, document #104: Notes of Montini of 27 September 1941; the introduction to *ADSS* 7; *ADSS* 11, document 202: Letter of Cardinal Maglione to Apostolic Delegate Cicognani of 31 May 1944, and document #205: Statement of Pius XII to Curia on 2 June 1944.

23 See *ADSS* 11, document #333: Note of the Secretariat of State of 23 August 1944.

24 Entry of 27 January 1943 of McCormick's diary, which is preserved in the New York Province Archives. Large excerpts with commentary in James Hennesey, S.J., 'American Jesuit in Wartime Rome: The Diary of Vincent A. McCormick, S.J., 1942–1945', *Mid-America* 56 (1974): 32–55.

25 Jean Lacouture, *Jesuits: A Multibiography* (Washington, D.C.: Counterpoint, 1995), p.176. For general discussions of the demonization theme and hatred toward one or both groups and the relationship to each other, see Manfred Barthel, *The Jesuits: History and Legend of the Society of Jesus* (New York: William Morrow, 1984); Alexander Brou, *Les Jésuites de la légende*, 2 vols (Paris: V. Retaux, 1906, 1907); Geoffrey Cubitt, *The Jesuit Myth: Conspiracy Theory and Politics in Nineteenth-Century France* (Oxford: Clarendon Press, 1993); Bernhard Duhr, *Jesuiten-Fabeln: Ein Beitrag zur*

Kulturgeschichte (Freiburg im Breisgau: Herder'sche Verlagshandlung, 1892); Léon Poliakov, *La causalité diabolique: essai sur l'origine des persécutions* (Paris: Calmann-Lévy, 1980).

26   As examples of this literature, see René Fülöp-Miller, *The Power and Secret of the Jesuits* (New York: Viking, 1930); E. Paris, *Histoire secrète des jésuites* (Paris: Fischbacher, 1970).

27   As examples of this large literature, see Burghard Assmus, *Jesuitenspiegel: Interessante Beiträge zur Naturgeschichte der Jesuiten* (Berlin: A. Bock Verlag, 1938); Alfred Bass, *An alle Deutschvölkischen! Die Deutschvölkischen im jesuitisch-jüdischen Fangnetz* (Leipzig: Leipziger Verlag, 1920); Ludwig Engel, *Der Jesuitismus eine Staatsgefahr* (Munich: Ludendorffs Verlag, 1935); O. Gröbler, *Jude, Jesuit und Freimaurer im Blitzlicht* (Leignitz: Hahnauer 45, 1932[?]); Erich Ludendorff, *Das Geheimnis der Jesuitenmacht und ihre Ende* (Munich: Ludendorffs Volkswarte Verlag, 1929); Alfred Miller, *Der Jesuitismus als Volksgefahr: Eine Betrachtung zu den Münchener Novembereignissen* (Munich: Deutscher Volksverlag, 1923); NSDAP, *Das zweite Novemberverbrechen: der jüdisch-jesuitische Novemberverrat in München 1923* (Nazi pamphlet, 1923); Alfred Rosenberg, *Schriften aus der jahren 1917–21* (Munich: Hoheneichern-Verlag, 1943); G. Schultze-Pfaelzer, *Das Jesuiten-Buch: Weltgeschichte eines falschen Priestertums* (Berlin: Brunner-Verlag, 1936).

28   31 March 1933 in *Akten Faulhaber*, ed. Volk, I, p.684. Cited in Theodore Hamerow, 'The Conservative Resistance to Hitler and the Fall of the Weimar Republic, 1932–34', in *Between Reform, Reaction, and Resistance: Studies in the history of German Conservatism from 1789 to 1945*, eds. Larry Eugene Jones and James Retallack (Providence: Berg, 1993) p.461. The numbers of Jesuits killed is taken from Vincent Lapomarda, *The Jesuits and the Third Reich* (Lewiston: Edwin Mellen Press, 1989).

29   For a window into Nazi perception of Jesuit activity, see the special 1937 Gestapo report on the Jesuits in *Berichte des SD und der Gestapo über Kirchen und Kirchenvolk in Deutscland 1934–1944*, ed. Heinz Boberach (Mainz: Matthias-Grünewald-Verlag, 1971), pp.242–274. As an example of German resistance, see Augustin Rösch, *Kampf gegen den Nationalsozialismus* (Frankfurt am Main: Verlag Josef Knecht, 1985).

30   See the very helpful thesis by Vera Bücker, *Die Schulddiskussion im deutschen Katholismus nach 1945* (Bochum: Studienverlag Dr. N. Brockmeyer, 1989). Also M. Phayer, 'The Postwar German Catholic Debate Over Holocaust Guilt', *Kirchliche Zeitgeschichte* 8/2 (1995): 426–439, and his 'The German Catholic Church After the Holocaust', *Holocaust and Genocide Studies* 10/2 (Fall 1996): 151–167. Although my focus in section two of this paper will be on Germany, I do not mean to isolate that culture from other western societies, let alone turn it into a pariah. It is clear that anti-Judaism and anti-Semitism are not the exclusive problems of German civilization; equally important to acknowledge is the shared responsibility of other nations for the Shoah. The Vatican's statement on the Holocaust pointed out, for example, that, when the Nazis sought to expel the Jews, it was unfortunate that the 'governments of some western countries of Christian tradition, including some in North and South America, were more than hesitant to open the borders to the persecuted Jews'. Nevertheless, it was in Germany that the victimization of the Jews took on a new death mask and that novelty demands our attention. German Catholicism's experience under National Socialism has the capability of leading us into a more profound understanding of the cultural sources of the evil we call the Shoah.

31   Pope John-Paul II, 'Linking Evangelization and Ecumenism' (22 June 1996), in *Origins: CNS Documentary Service* 26/9 (1 August 1996): 139.

32   Helmut James von Moltke, *Letters to Freya: 1939–1945*, ed. and trans. Beate Ruhm von Oppen (New York: Knopf, 1990), p.110.

33   Karl Jaspers, *The Question of German Guilt* (New York: Dial Press, 1947).

34   See Carl Amery, *Capitulation* (New York: Herder and Herder, 1967), pp.29–34.

35   P. Tillich, 'Open Letter to Emanuel Hirsch' [1 October 1934] in *The Thought of Paul Tillich*, eds. J.L. Adams, W. Pauck and R. Shinn (New York: Harper and Row, 1985), p.364.

36   For a recent discussion of how this spiritual domain coincided with a steady denuciation of 'materialism' see Theodore Hamerow, *On the Road to the Wolf's Lair: German Resistance to Hitler* (Cambridge, MA: Harvard University Press 1997), pp.50–64.

37   For discussion of this theme, see Peter Brown, *The Body and Society: Men, Women, and Sexual Renunciation in Early Christianity* (New York: Columbia University Press, 1988), especially pp.47–49, 86, 296–297, 348–349, 376–77. On the inadequacy of the dualistic view as characterizing all of

Christian tradition, see James Keenan, 'Current Theology Note: Christian Perspectives on the Human Body', *Theological Studies* 55 (1994), pp.330–346.

38 See John Mahoney, *The Making of Moral Theology: A Study of the Roman Catholic Tradition* (Oxford: Clarendon Press, 1987), pp.28–29, 45. Also see Michael Langer, *Katholische Sexualpädagogik im 20. Jahrhundert: Zur Geschichte eines religionspädagogischen Problems* (Munich: Kösel, 1986), p.127.

39 See Langer, Katholische Sexualpädagogik im 20. Jahrhundert: Zur *Geschichte eines religionspädago-gischen Problems*; Michael Phayer, *Sexual Liberation and Religion in Nineteenth Century Europe* (Totowa, N.J.: Rowman and Littlefield, 1977); Walter Braun, *Geschlechtliche Erziehung im katho-lischen Religionsunterricht* (Trier: Spee-Verlag, 1970); Michel Foucault, *A History of Sexuality I: An Introduction* (New York: Pantheon, 1978); Isabel Hull, *Sexuality, State, and Civil Society in Germany, 1700–1815* (Ithaca: Cornell University Press, 1996), and Roy Pascal, *From Naturalism to Expression-ism: German Literature and Society 1880–1918* (New York: Basic Books, 1973) especially pp.198–228.

40 'Ad Catholici Sacerdotii', para. 42.

41 Alfred Delp, *The Prison Meditations of Father Delp* (New York: Macmillan, 1963), pp.118, 146–147.

42 Waldemar Gurian, 'The Sources of Hitler's Power', *The Review of Politics* 4/4 (October 1942): 391.

43 See on this the new study by George Mosse, *The Image of Man: The Creation of Modern Masculinity* (New York: Oxford University Press, 1996).

44 On this topic, see W.H. Bruford, *The German Tradition of Self-Cultivation: 'Bildung' from Humboldt to Thomas Mann* (Cambridge: Cambridge University Press, 1975).

45 See Ferdinand Hoffmann, *Sittliche Entartung und Geburtenschwund* (Munich: J.F. Lehmanns Verlag, 1938), p.51, and W. Hermannsen and R, Blome, *Warum hat man uns das nicht früher gesagt?: Ein Bekenntnis deutscher Jugend zu geschlechtlicher Sauberkeit* (Munich: J.F. Lehmanns Verlag, 1940). These are respectively the fourth and fourteenth volumes in the important series directed at German youth and edited by Heinz Müller as *Politische Biologie: Schriften für naturgestzliche Politik und Wissenschaft (1936–1940).* For a general text on Nazi sexual ethics, see Friedrich Siebert, *Volkstum und Geschlechtlichkeit* (Munich-Berlin: J.F. Lehmanns Verlag, 1938).

46 See Laura Engelstein, *The Keys to Happiness: Sex and the Search for Modernity in Fin-de-Siècle Russia* (Ithaca: Cornell University Press, 1992).

47 Hans Peter Bleuel, *Sex and Society in Nazi Germany* (Philadelphia: J.B. Lippincott, 1973), p.57. The broadest discussion of themes in Nazi sexuality is to be found in the two volumes by Klaus Theweleit, *Male Fantasies* (Minneapolis: University of Minnesota Press, 1989).

48 See Frederick Ira Murphy, 'The American Christian Press and Pre-War Hitler's Germany, 1933–1939', PhD. dissertation, University of Florida, 1970.

49 Wilhelm Arp, *Das Bildungsideal der Ehre* (Munich: Deutscher Volksverlag, 1939); Langer, *Katholische Sexualpädagogik im 20. Jahrhundert*, 115. For examples of Nazi denunciations, see *The Persecution of the Catholic Church in the Third Reich. Facts and Documents Translated from the German* (London: Burns Oates, 1940), pp.440, 464, 472–475. The anonymous editor of this collection was Walter Mariaux, a German Jesuit residing in Rome.

50 It could be argued that an exception would be the resistance shown by German Catholic women, motivated by ideals of virginity, to Nazi efforts to reduce women to the level of mere breeders of children. I cannot develop this issue here but see Michael Phayer's *Protestant and Catholic Women in Nazi Germany* (Detroit: Wayne State University Press, 1990).

51 As an example see Martin Heideggers's letter of 2 October 1929 to Victor Schwoerer, included in Leaman, *Heidegger im Kontext*, pp.111–112. It is also an expression which Hitler used frequently; see for example *Mein Kampf* (Boston: Houghton Mifflin, 1971), p.247. Also see the fine discussion by Steven Ascheim, '"The Jew Within": The Myth of "Judaization" in Germany', in *The Jewish Response to German Culture: From the Enlightenment to the Second World War*, eds. Jehuda Reinharz and Walter Schatzberg (Hanover: University Press of New England, 1985), pp.212–241.

52 For a Jewish defence against these charges, see Chajim Bloch, *Blut und Eros im jüdischen Schrifttum und Leben: Von Eisenmenger über Rohling zu Bischoff* (Wien: Sensen-Verlag, 1935). On the charges, see Sander Gilman, *The Jew's Body* (New York: Routledge, 1991), p.258.

53 See for example Heiko Oberman, *The Roots of Anti-Semitism in the Age of the Renaissance and Reformation* (Philadelphia: Fortress Press, 1984). Gustav Gundlach's 1930 article on 'Anti-Semitism'

for the *Lexikon für Theologie und Kirche* is shocking for its depictions of the Jew; see *The Hidden Encyclical of Pius XI*, pp.47–50.

54 My treatment of modern sexuality follows the categories developed in Michel Foucault's *The History of Sexuality 1: An Introduction* (New York: Pantheon, 1978). I analyse this history in my *Michel Foucault's Force of Flight: Toward an Ethics for Thought* (Atlantic Highlands: Humanities Press, 1990), pp.121–184. Following him, I want to identify the elements of that modern field. First, there is the *body*: the Nazis opposed their view of a trained, classically beautiful body to the Jewish body, weakened by deviant genitalia and unrestrained sexual appetite. Secondly, regarding *children*, there was the juxtaposition of an idealized German innocence with the Jewish invention of a childhood sexuality that was believed to reflect both an actual sexual precocity and Talmudic allowance for intergenerational sex. *Der Stürmer*, Streicher's newspaper utilized medieval tales of Jewish ritual slaughter of Christian children in accounts which stressed acts of torture and the sexual satisfaction they implied. In addition, he emphasized cases of child molestation which involved Jews. Thirdly, in contrast to the image of the German *mother*, who delighted in offspring and their care, and who felt threatened by the sexual advances of Jewish men, especially medical doctors, there was the Jewish *woman*, who was inclined to neurosis, attracted to prostitution, and craving emancipation from the home. The Nuremberg laws prohibited sexual relations between Aryan and Jew in part to prevent contamination by syphilis which was identified with Jews. Fourthly, Jews harboured all sorts of sexual *perversions*, especially homosexuality. These perversions stand behind the Jewish invention of psychoanalysis and sexology. For the Nazis, the Jewish menace was a constructed sexual experience, hidden but omnipresent, camouflaging in other innocuous symptoms the secret causality perverting Aryan life. There are extensive examinations of these themes but reasons of space permit mention of but a few: George Mosse, *Nationalism and Sexuality: Respectability and Abnormal Sexuality in Modern Europe* (New York: Howard Fertig, 1985) and the extraordinary series of works by Sander Gilman, especially *Sexuality: An Illustrated History* (New York: John Wiley & Sons, 1989); *Jewish Self-Hatred: Anti-Semitism and the Hidden Language of the Jews* (Baltimore: The Johns Hopkins University Press, 1986); *The Jew's Body: Freud, Race and Gender* (Princeton: Princeton University Press, 1993). Also see Klemens Felden, 'Die Übernahme des antisemitischen Stereotyps als soziale Norm durch die bürgerliche Gesellschaft Deutschlands (1875–1900)', a 1963 doctoral dissertation at Ruprecht-Karl-University in Heidelberg.

55 Werner Dittrich, *Erziehung zum Judengegner: Hinweise zur Behandlung der Judenfrage im rassenpolit- ischen Unterricht* (Munich: Deutscher Volksverlag, 1937); Barbara Hyams and Nancy Harrowitz, 'A Critical Introduction to the History of Weininger Reception', *Jews and Gender: Responses to Otto Weininger*, p.4; and Jay Geller, 'Blood Sin: Syphilis and the Construction of Jewish Identity', *Faultline* 1 (1992): 21–48.

56 Langer, *Katholische Sexualpädagogik im 20 Jahrhundert*, p.20.

57 Speech given to NSDAP party members on 16 June 1933, cited in James Wilkinson, *The Intellectual Resistance in Europe* (Cambridge, MA: Harvard University Press, 1981), p.112.

58 Jakob Nötges, Nationalsozialismus und Katholizismus (Cologne: Gilde Verlag, 1931), especially pp.170–196.

59 See Robert Jay Lifton, *The Nazi Doctors: Medical Killing and the Psychology of Genocide* (New York: Basic Books, 1986), pp.418–429.

60 Himmler's speech of 4 October 1943 in *Trial of the Major War Criminals Before the International Military Tribunal*, Vol.29 (Nuremberg, 1948), p.145.

61 See Raul Hilberg, *The Destruction of the European Jews*, Vol.3 (New York: Holmes and Meier, 1985), pp.1012–1029.

62 See Emmanuel Levinas, 'Reflections on the Philosophy of Hitlerism' (originally published in 1934), *Critical Inquiry* 17/1 (Autumn 1990): 62–71.

63 Decree Nine: 'Poverty,' #287.

64 'Judaism in the Church', *Jewish Perspectives on Christianity*, ed. Fritz Rothschild (New York: Cross-road, 1990), p.98.

TWO POPES AND THE HOLOCAUST

Frank J. Coppa

I N JUNE 1939, when Nazi Germany's expansionist demands and blatant racism rendered the outbreak of a new cataclysm inevitable, the French Ambassador to the Holy See, François Charles-Roux, lamented the cautious and neutral position of the new Pope, Eugenio Pacelli, who assumed the name Pius XII. The Ambassador appreciated the Pope's determination to preserve the peace, but resented his refusal to pass judgment or assign responsibility, treating aggrieved and aggressor alike. Charles-Roux considered this an unfortunate departure from the course of his predecessor, Achille Ratti, who pontificated as Pius XI (1922–39). 'Without doubt all expected a change, because each has his own temperament and his own methods,' the Frenchman explained, adding, 'to many, however, the differences seemed excessive.'[1]

Others, however, saw little difference between the two popes, criticizing Pius XI for concluding concordats with Fascist Italy (1929) and Nazi Germany (1933), and Pius XII for adhering to them, despite the increasingly atrocious behaviour of these 'totalitarian' regimes.[2] The two were supposedly in basic agreement, the major difference between them being that Pacelli had a more diplomatic approach than his predecessor.[3] Politically conservative if not authoritarian, they were seen to collaborate for decades, with the second serving Pius XI as Nuncio to Germany (1922–1930), and then as the Secretary of State from 1930 to 1939, at which time he succeeded his 'mentor'. Indeed, in 1935 Pius XI honoured his 'closest collaborator' by naming him *Camerlengo* of the Church.[4] Some claimed Ratti groomed Pacelli to be his successor.[5] The controversy continues.[6]

The fact that Pacelli assumed the name of Pius led others to conclude that the new Pope would follow the path of his predecessor, including his confrontation of the anti-Semitism of Nazi Germany, which by 1938 had spread to Fascist Italy. Did the two follow the essentially anti-Judaic policy of the Church – or were there substantial differences in their response to anti-Semitism? How, and to what extent, did the responses of Pius XI and Pius XII to Nazi and Fascist anti-Semitism differ? This paper focuses on these questions.

Problems arise in the pursuit of an objective analysis of the reactions of Pius XI and Pius XII towards anti-Semitism. For one thing, there is a tendency to confuse and to equate the traditional anti-Judaism found in the Church with the racial anti-Semitism of Nazism, and later of Fascism. Members of the World Jewish Congress, among others, perceived the breeding ground of anti-Semitism in some of the dogmas and doctrines of Christianity.[7] Furthermore, the 'silence' during the war has coloured both pontificates, and this is compounded by the fact that the Vatican Archives remain closed for both. In addition, the political agenda of some has led them to blur the distinction between the two. Finally, Pius XII left behind neither an intimate diary nor personal notes that would allow one to penetrate his private thoughts.[8] Still, these obstacles are not insurmountable. One can explore the published record of these popes; the recently uncovered and published Encyclical on racism and anti-Semitism commissioned by Pius XI, and shelved by Pius XII; and the part played by both in concluding the ignored agreement of August 1938, between the Vatican and the Fascist regime on the issue of racism and anti-Semitism.

Although the Vatican Archives remain closed for the period following the Pontificate of Benedict XV (1914–1922), the Holy See has published some of the documents relating to the Second World War. Pius XI's 'encyclical', never officially issued, is not included in these volumes,[9] nor has it been found in the Vatican Archives.[10] Furthermore, the correspondence between father Ledochowski, S.J. and Gustav Gundlach, S.J., who along with La Farge was one of the chief authors of the projected encyclical, remains closed.[11] However, the other encyclicals and discourses of Pius XI (1922–1939) have been published. While the secret agreement between the Vatican and Mussolini's Italy on the racial issue has been long ignored, the context of its approval finally has been explored.[12] Its text has been published by Father Angelo Martini, one of the few allowed to examine the Vatican Archives, for the post 1922 period.[13] The acts of the Holy See appear in the *Acta Apostolicae Sedis*.[14] The newspaper *L'Osservatore Romano*, the daily authoritative voice of the Holy See, is available as well as the Jesuit journal *La Civiltà Cattolica*, which enjoyed a close though autonomous relationship with the Holy See. Finally, the private publication of Pius XI's anti-racist 'hidden encyclical' sheds additional light on responses of these popes to racism and the persecution of the Jews.[15]

Achille Ratti, the Archbishop of Milan who became Pope in 1922, following the Roman adage that 'governments pass away, documents stay', preferred concordats negotiated by the Vatican, to concessions attained by political parties. Both in personal and political matters Ratti proved quick to respond to provocation without necessarily weighing all the consequences, at once volatile and confrontational.[16] Not surprisingly, Pius XI was responsible for the encyclicals launched against the totalitarian regimes, *Non abbiamo bisogno* of 1931 against the abuses of Fascist Italy, *Mit brennender Sorge* of 1937 against those of Nazi Germany, and *Divini redemptoris*, likewise of 1937, against the evils of atheistic communism.[17] In 1938, eight months before his death, and fifteen months before the outbreak of World War II, Pope Pius XI, who suffered from diabetes and heart trouble, commissioned a fourth encyclical to denounce racism and the persecution of the Jews, providing an explicit condemnation of anti-Semitism.[18]

Pius XI proved critical of racism, which he found contrary to the faith. In September 1922, the Pope emphasized that 'Christian charity extends to all men whatsoever without distinction of race....[19] In 1924 he explained that when politics infringed upon the realm of religion, the pope has the right and duty to issue directives to the faithful.[20] In 1926, Pius XI condemned Charles Maurras's allegedly Catholic, but racist and reactionary *Action Française*, which shared many fascist sentiments.[21] Subsequently, in 1928 Pius XI condemned anti-Semitism, when the Holy Office with his approval, suppressed the Friends of Israel.[22] The decree of suppression contains a clear condemnation of anti-Semitism.[23] In the later 1920's, the *Civiltà Cattolica*, which had often depicted the Jews as guilty of deicide, and harangued against their hard-heartedness, moderated its anti-Judaic polemic.[24]

Pius XI negotiated with the Fascists, whom he distrusted, to protect the faith in Italy. In February 1929, following three years of talks, he concluded an agreement with Mussolini's regime.[25] The Pope proclaimed that God had been restored to Italy, and Italy returned to God.[26] However, the Vatican rejected the bellicose tone in Fascist education, complaining that the state should not train its youth to be warriors.[27] In December 1929, the Pope presented the contrasting Catholic position in his encyclical 'On the Christian Education of Youth'.[28] The Pope was disturbed by increasing Fascist infringement on Catholic Action groups, convinced that the totalitarian state was 'unchristian'.[29] Shunting aside conciliation, Pius proclaimed, 'We will not yield to that devil Mussolini! We'll show the world what he is.'[30] This led to his encyclical *Non abbiamo bisogno* of June 1931, denouncing Fascist attempts to dominate all citizen organizations and youth groups. Pius XI would not abandon the young to the totalitarian pretensions of this regime.[31] Eventually a compromise between Rome and the Vatican was effected by Pacelli, even as the Pope declared Catholicism and Fascism incompatible.[32] Cardinal Pacelli also urged Catholic organizations in Germany to reach some accord with the Nazis, on the eve of their accession to power.[33]

During his pontificate Pius XI proved even less receptive to the Nazi programme. Appreciating the influence of the Catholic Church, Hitler sent Hermann Göring to Rome in May 1931, but Pius did not receive him. Since this pope had serious reservations about the Nazi movement, ecclesiastical circles did not applaud the news of Hitler's appointment on 30 January 1933. The Vatican cautiously avoided any public statement.[34] Nonetheless, the *Civiltà Cattolica*, loyal to the Pope, warned the faithful of Nazi abuses.[35] Later, in mid-March 1933, when the Nazis commenced their consolidation of power, the Jesuit journal simply noted that the Führer had assumed police powers following his electoral victory.[36]

In the Spring of 1933, Berlin rather than Rome, assumed the initiative in proposing an agreement between Church and State as the Fuehrer sought to bind the Church to the Reich.[37] Pius XI remained sceptical, even though the pact had the support of his secretary of state, Pacelli. The pope reconsidered his stance following Nazi harassment of the organizational church, which *Civiltà Cattolica* denounced as 'totalitarianism in action'.[38] Pius XI, determined to preserve Catholic youth organizations in Germany, which by 1933 had a million and a half members, and to assure the faithful religious and educational freedom, sanctioned negotiations for a concordat.[39] Its approval in September 1933, did not imply that the Vatican sympathized with Hitler's regime.[40] Father Enrico Rosa, S.J., director of the principal review of the Jesuits, in its columns, emphatically denied that the accord legitimized or approved of the Nazi government.[41]

To the Pope's consternation, the Berlin government almost immediately violated the letter and the spirit of the accord, provoking Pius to complain.[42] The odious Nazi sterilization law was published just days after its conclusion, while the Catholic clergy, charitable organizations, schools, and publications were all attacked.[43] Meanwhile, Nazi racial policy offended the Pope, and the *Civiltà Cattolica* condemned the Nazi mythology of race in a series of articles, while the periodical of the Pontifical Society for the preservation of the faith noted that even those having a mediocre knowledge of Catholic doctrine recognized that anti-Semitism was forbidden.[44] Father Rosa, in an article entitled 'The Jewish Question and National Socialist Anti-Semitism', blasted the Nazi doctrine, which sprang from incredulity and immorality. Another article claimed the Church had long protected the Jews, and prohibited their persecution.[45] As early as 1935, the Holy Office had compiled a syllabus of propositions on racism, national socialism, and statism to be condemned, but its publication was blocked by its secretary, Cardinal Marchetti Selvaggiani, who like Cardinal Pacelli, feared an open conflict with Nazism.[46]

Nonetheless, Pius XI refuted the Nazi assertion that the Jewish question was an internal racial issue, rather than a religious one.[47] In October 1934, when the Pope received the German ambassador, Diego von Bergen, he complained of developments in the Reich. Pius XI was particularly distressed by the Nazi onslaught on Catholic youth organizations, deploring that German propaganda sought to draw them from Christ to heathenism.[48] On this and other issues, the Pope proved unwilling to compromise.[49] Nor did he accept the Nazi contention that the concordat obligated the Catholic Church to obey the laws of the land, as the *Osservatore Romano* protested that Catholics could not be bound by laws at variance with divine right and Christian conscience.[50] As the Church of Pius XI resisted aspects of Nazification, Bergen warned Berlin that without some moderating influence, the prospect increased that 'the Pope will take disastrous decisions.'[51] His analysis proved accurate. Pius XI, who had harboured serious reservations about concluding the concordat with Nazi Germany,[52] considered renouncing it, but was restrained by his Secretary of State, Pacelli, who feared this would aggravate the position of millions of German Catholics. Nonetheless, Father Rosa complained that by developing an immoral racist ideology, Nazism was in fundamental conflict with Church doctrines.[53] In 1936–37, there were frequent attacks by Italian Catholics on Nazi ideology, racism, and anti-Christian policies.[54]

The triumph of Nazism in the Reich, with its anticlerical and anti-Semitic policies, led Pius XI to oppose *Anschluss* between Germany and Austria, which the Holy See had earlier favoured.[55] Rome reversed course once it witnessed the policies pursued by Hitler's Germany. As early as June 1933, *Civiltà Cattolica* warned that the Vienna government had to protect itself from the subversion of the Austrian Nazis, supported by their brethren in the Reich. *Civiltà Cattolica* praised those in the truncated Habsburg State who wished to preserve an Austria, which has as its symbol the Cross of God, and no other. Pius XI now championed an independent Austria, with which Rome concluded a concordat in June 1933.[56]

Pius XI was scandalized by the abortive Nazi coup of 1934 in Austria. His outrage was reflected in a series of articles in the Vatican journal which condemned the murder of Dollfuss, denouncing the Nazis for transferring to Vienna the savage methods they employed in Munich and Berlin. The daily of the Holy See suggested that National Socialism might more appropriately be dubbed national terrorism, branding the assassination an act of defiance against the civilized world. On the other hand, the voice of the Vatican praised Mussolini for dispatching troops to the frontier, and preserving Austrian independence in the face of Nazi aggression.[57] In 1934, the Jesuit-run *Civiltà Cattolica* reported that the anti-Semitism of the Nazis stemmed neither from religious convictions nor Christian conscience, and sought to undermine both religion and society.[58] Pius XI believed the dignity of the Holy See required him to denounce these outrages, confident that the Church would survive the persecution.[59] By 1937–1938 this pope was praised for defending human rights against both Fascism and Nazism.[60] He resented the Nazi laws which violated Church teachings, complaining to the German ambassador that he was 'deeply grieved and gravely displeased'. Diego Von Bergen believed that Pacelli was upset by the Pope's outburst, but did not dare contradict his chief.[61] Continued attacks on Church doctrines led Pius XI to ignore the restraining influence of his Secretary of State; in March 1937, he launched the encyclical *Mit brennender Sorge*.[62]

On Passion Sunday, 14 March 1937, this encyclical which negated the principle of the division of humanity on a racial basis, was read from Catholic pulpits in Germany. 'With deep anxiety and increasing dismay', Pius wrote, he had witnessed the 'progressive oppression of the faithful'.[63] Denouncing the racism of the regime, the Pope catalogued the articles of faith trampled upon by the Nazis. Without mincing words, he insisted that 'the believer had an inalienable right to profess his faith and follow its dictates,' making it clear that God's commandments were not dependent on race. He concluded by urging the clergy to unmask and refute Nazism's errors, whatever their form or disguise.[64] Other denunciations of racism followed, as a series of articles in *Civiltà Cattolica* warned Catholics to remove all traces of anti-Semitism from their hearts, calling upon them to avoid affronting Jews. Another article called for co-existence between Catholics and Jews, observing that the Church condemned every form of anti-Semitism, opposing all civil legislation against the Jews.[65]

The papal encyclical against the neo-pagan racism of the Nazi regime incensed the Hitler government. 'The national and racial formulas of the Reich do not square altogether with the dogmas of the Catholic Church,' the Nazi periodical *Wille und Macht* explained in May 1937, criticizing the pope for addressing those in 'prison cells and concentration camps ... '. Racial issues, it continued, had to be decided by the folk and their state, without Vatican interference![66] Pius XI did not concur, presiding over a special meeting of the Congregation for Extraordinary Ecclesiastical Affairs in June 1937, to discuss the dilemma.[67] By this time, he deplored anti-Christian developments in Germany no less than those in the Soviet Union.[68] Indeed, Nazism seems to have displaced Communism as Pius XI's major concern.[69] Small wonder that relations between the Vatican and the Reich deteriorated during the course of 1938, as Pius condemned the nationalism championed by the Hitler regime as a veritable curse.[70] In April 1938, the Sacred Congregation of Seminaries, under Pius XI, declared eight propositions contained in Nazism's racial doctrine, 'absurd'.[71] In the eyes of the Catholic press, the action represented an encyclical against racism![72] In July, Pius XI made this explicit, charging Nazi policy opposed the spirit of the creed and violated the teachings of the faith.[73] *Der Angriff*, the newspaper of the German Labour Front, in turn, stigmatized the Vatican of Pius XI as the 'Legal Defender of Racial Pollution'.[74] Thus, the last years of Pius XI's reign witnessed increased tension between the Holy See and Nazi Germany.[75]

Meanwhile, the Vatican and the Catholic world viewed the Nazi takeover of Austria in 1938 as disastrous. Not surprisingly, Pius XI repudiated the praise of Cardinal Innitzer and the Austrian bishops, who rejoiced at the forced union of Germany and Austria, constraining them to make a retraction.[76] The *Osservatore Romano* protested the statement of the Austrian hierarchy did not reflect the Vatican's position, while Gustav Gundlach on Vatican Radio, denounced their pro-Nazi pastoral letter as inspired by a false political Catholicism. An angry Pius XI summoned Cardinal Innitzer to Rome, criticizing his unfortunate conduct.[77] These public and private papal denunciations worried his Secretary of State, Pacelli, who feared the grave consequences of a break with the Nazi regime.[78] Nonetheless, Pius XI would not be silenced. During the May 1938 visit of the Fuehrer to Rome, Pius left for Castel Gandolfo, closing the Vatican Museum which Hitler had hoped to visit. From his summer residence, Pius XI lamented it was 'both out of place and untimely to hoist in Rome the emblem of a cross that is not the cross of Christ,' distressed by the glorification in Rome of the 'cross that was the enemy of Christianity'.[79] Subsequently, Hitler revealed his disappointment at not visiting the Basilica of St. Peter during his trip to Rome.[80]

To make matters worse, in mid-July 1938 the 'Fascist Manifesto on Race' was issued, which included ten 'scientific' propositions on the racial issue, preparing the way for Fascist Italy's racial laws. The scandalized Pope responded during an audience to a group of nuns, describing the Fascist propositions as nothing less than apostasy. It was no longer the case of one or more erroneous ideas, he fumed, but the entire spirit of the measure was contrary to the faith of Christ.[81] Small wonder that the Fascist regime prohibited the Catholic press from publishing the talk. The pope returned to this theme when he addressed an group from the Propaganda Fide, praising their universal mission when there was so much talk of racism and separatist nationalism. If there were something worse than the racist formulas being bandied about, he added, it was the spirit of separatism which inspired it. He denounced both the inspiration and its consequences as non religious, non-Christian, and not even human![82] If the Fascists wanted to be Catholics, Pius warned, they had to obey the Church and its head. Pacelli, in turn, sought to moderate the position of the Pope.[83]

Although anxious to avoid a rupture with the Fascist regime, Pius XI proved unwilling to compromise on principle.[84] Anti-Semitism was unchristian, and a slap in the face of the Church, which had acquiesced in the Fascist seizure of power to prevent totalitarianism rather than promote it.[85] Once it became the official doctrine of the Fascist regime, this triggered an energetic response from Pius.[86] His opposition stemmed from the fact that Christianity and its laws were attacked by the racialists.[87] The old and ailing Pope resolved to take additional steps to denounce Fascist racist policies, making no secret of his compassion for the victims of persecution while condemning 'hatred' of the people once chosen by God.[88] Pius selected the physicist Dr. Tullio Levi-Civita for membership in the Pontifical Accademy of Science, the most prestigious scientific body under papal patronage, thus revealing his contempt for Mussolini's Italian Academy, which had rejected Levi-Civita on racial grounds. In fact, he appointed this Jewish scientist chairman of the commission entrusted with awarding the papal prize, the 'premio Pio XI'. In 1938 Pius also admitted the Italian Jewish mathematician Vito Volterra into the Pontifical Academy of Science. 'God is the Master of the sciences,' the pope remarked as he appointed Volterra, adding 'All human beings are admitted equally, without distinction of race, to participate, to share, to study and to explore truth and science.'[89]

Pius XI also kept a close watch on developments across the Atlantic, where the anti-Semitic radio priest Reverend Charles Coughlin found a wide audience in the United States, where millions were mesmerized by his broadcasts. As early as 1930, the Apostolic Delegate, Archbishop Pietro Fumasoni-Biondi, attempted to curb the unruly cleric, but found him protected by his superior, Bishop Michael Gallagher of Detroit. In 1935, Fumasoni-Biondi's successor as Apostolic Delegate, Amleto Cicognani, proved no more successful in moderating the tone and message of the radio priest. The Vatican likewise failed to have the American bishops issue some statement distancing the hierarchy from him. When the American bishops refused to do so, papal authority was invoked. In September 1936, the *Osservatore Romano* denied Coughlin's claim that he had the approval of the Holy See. Furthermore, it was widely believed that the refusal to make Detroit into an archdiocese and the selection of Edward Mooney as Gallagher's successor as Bishop of Detroit, reflected Pius XI's dissatisfaction with Gallagher's refusal to 'silence' Coughlin.[90] Meanwhile, Cardinal Munderlain of Chicago answered Coughlin's anti-Semitic campaign by asserting that Coughlin was 'not authorised to speak for the Catholic Church, nor does he represent the doctrine or sentiment of the Church.'[91] In fact, the Pope revealed that he favoured the position of Father John La Farge, who denounced racism as a myth the Church could not tolerate.[92] In June 1938, as Mussolini embraced anti-Semitism, Pius privately commissioned the American Jesuit to draft an encyclical demonstrating the incompatibility of Catholicism and racism.[93]

Pius XI determined to issue this encyclical without involving his Secretary of State. Pacelli was not included in the Pope's discussion with La Farge when he commissioned the 'encyclical,' even though he had been with the pope moments before.[94] Gustav Gundlach, who along with Gustave Desbuquois collaborated with La Farge in producing the encyclical *Humani Generis Unitas* (The Unity of the Human Race), was convinced that Pacelli, who succeeded as Pius XII, was not informed of their project. Indeed, the new Pope later confessed as much.[95] It is true that Pius XI demanded the strictest secrecy on the matter he deemed of the utmost importance.[96] Still, his deliberate exclusion of his secretary of state from the project is telling, and has hitherto been ignored. Perhaps the Pope feared Pacelli would oppose the encyclical, and attempt to dissuade him from issuing it. This was a reasonable assumption, for his Secretary of State had more than once mitigated the pope's energetic responses, preventing a diplomatic rupture with Nazi Germany. One might also surmise that Pius XI did not want to implicate his likely successor in an enterprise that might not succeed. Or perhaps he recognized that the issuance of the encyclical, making a breach with Nazi Germany inevitable, would have virtually torpedoed the conciliatory Pacelli's prospects for the papacy? If so, this would challenge the prevailing contention that Ratti wanted Pacelli to succeed him. Aside from the testimony of Pacelli's supporters, who claim that Pius XI wanted Pacelli as his successor, one could conclude the opposite. Unquestionably, Pius XI knew that few Secretaries of State assumed the Tiara, and generally the *Camerlengo* was not considered for the position – and yet he had promoted Pacelli to both these posts. Furthermore, it was well known that there were contending factions in the Vatican on how to respond to the provocations of the fascist dictators: with Pius XI championing the confrontational approach, and Pacelli the undisputed leader of those seeking compromise. Pius XI, unlike Pacelli, believed it was necessary to contest the anti-Semitism of the dictatorial regimes, despite the consequences. Are we to believe that the strong-willed Pius XI, at the eleventh hour abandoned his campaign for the conciliatory course of his Secretary of State? The facts suggest otherwise: including his secretly commissioning an anti-racist encyclical, certain to antagonize Fascist Italy and Nazi Germany, the pope's obvious rejection of the pacification pact of 16 August 1938 with the Fascist regime, and finally his projected address condemning Fascist violations of the Lateran Accords. In light of his determination to continue his confrontational policies, one can question the assumption that Pius XI favoured the election of Pacelli, knowing he would pursue a contrary course. Rather, it seems that the physical frailty of the pope, at the close of his pontificate, meant an end to the control that Ratti had earlier exercised in running the Vatican and the affairs of the Church.

At the end of September, 1938, during a time of power brokering and preparation for the new pontificate, the Jesuit authors of *Humani Generis Unitas* presented it to the General of their Order for transmission to the Pope. When they received no response from Pius, they suspected something was amiss, and their draft had not been delivered to him. Their fears proved well founded, for Vladimir Ledochowski, the anti-Bolshevik, Polish head of the Order, sympathized with Pacelli and the conciliarists rather than Pius's confrontational approach towards the fascists. Small wonder, then, that he did not deposit their work in the pope's hands but in those of Enrico Rosa, assigning him the task of moderating its tone in the hope of avoiding a break with Fascist Italy and Nazi Germany. Ratti's later response suggests he had not even been informed that the draft of his encyclical had arrived. It cannot be shown that Ledochowski objected to the traditional anti-Judaic sentiments in the document, as has been recently suggested, for the Jesuits and especially *Civiltà Cattolica* had long been critical of the Jews as a religious group in Catholic Italy.[97] It was the clear condemnation of racism and anti-Semitism that worried the General, and the conciliarists.

The draft of the La Farge encyclical condemned anti-Semitism as reprehensible, arguing that Catholics could not and should not 'remain silent in the presence of racism.'[98] It echoed the position Pius XI had taken throughout his pontificate. This encyclical commissioned by Pius XI, who outlined its main themes, complained that the struggle for racial purity 'ends by being uniquely the struggle against the Jews.'[99] Indeed, the authors warned that anti-Semitism, served as pretext for attacking the Saviour Himself, and thus represented a campaign against Christianity as well as Judaism.[100] Focussing on the evil of racism, it pointed to the clear responsibility that the Church and papacy had in condemning this evil, noting 'that they should point out to mankind the true course to be followed.'[101] 'The Redemption,' the encyclical continued, 'established a universal Kingdom, in which there would be no distinction of Jew or Gentile, Greek or barbarian.'[102] Sentiments and words that were likely to enrage Hitler, as well as Mussolini, who aped his anti-Semitism, and distressed Pacelli. Small wonder that the conciliarists were reluctant to provide the pope with the original version, which offered the contentious pontiff additional ammunition to launch against the fascist regimes.

Gundlach, one of the authors of the 'encyclical,' perceived Ledochowski's action as a blatant attempt to sabotage their work. This was confirmed by the Jesuit, Heinrich Bacht, who was commissioned to translate the document into Latin.[103] Furthermore, this was not the first time that currents in the Vatican sought to restrain, if not silence, Pius XI on the racial issue. In July and August 1938, Pius XI, appalled by the racism of the Mussolini's Italy, which emulated the Nazi regime's anti-Semitism, envisioned a radical revision of Vatican policy towards both Italy and Germany. Unfortunately, few in the Vatican seconded this papal initiative and continued to pursue a conciliatory course towards these dictatorships.[104] These currents hoped for the selection of a more conciliatory successor to Pius XI, and were responsible for the little known agreement concluded with the Fascist government in mid-August 1938, on the racial issue. According to Father Angelo Martini, who was granted access to these Vatican documents, the 'pact' of 16 August 1938 entailed three points: the problem of racism and the Jewish issue, the general question of Catholic Action in Italy, and finally problems between church and state that were particular to Bergamo.[105]

In return for Fascist consideration of papal sensibilties regarding Catholic Action and the Bergamo situation, the Vatican had to promise to leave the Jewish and racial issue entirely to the Regime, which would deal with them 'scientifically and politically'. Consequently, this 'pact' envisioned total governmental freedom in racial legislation and Jewish matters, assuring itself of the non-interference of Catholic forces. As written, only the pope or Holy See was to discuss such issues – but only privately with Mussolini. If accepted, the Church would have had to abandon the safeguarding of human rights and compromise its doctrines in order to safeguard Catholic Action groups.[106] Apparently this 'pact' represents a sort of declaration of interest, written from the Regime's perspective – with some ecclesiastical input, perhaps from father Tacchi-Venturi, who served as an intermediary between Mussolini and the Holy See, and the nuncio Monsignor Borgoncini Duca, under the guidance of Pacelli, Secretary of State.[107]

It seems inconceivable that this pope would have sanctioned an agreement which violated his convictions and his conception of the faith. Even if Pius XI knew of the 'pact' he clearly did not adhere to it in the days which followed. Thus, in his talks of 21 August 1938 and 6 September of that same year, he denounced the Fascist race manifesto as a 'gross error' which violated Catholic doctrine.[108] In his August visit to the students of Propaganda Fide, he branded 'exaggerated nationalism' and racism a curse.[109] In a speech to visitors from Belgium's Catholic Radio, Pius XI again condemned anti-Semitism as a movement Christians had to shirk. Raising his voice with emotion, Pius proclaimed the incompatibility of anti-Semitism with the gospels, concluding 'Spiritually we are Semites.'[110] These words left an indelible impression on Jews and Christians alike.[111] Despite the efforts of the Secretary of State and the Nuncio to heal the breach between the Duce and the Pontiff, a serious wound had been opened as Pius continued the process of disengaging himself from the Fascist regime.[112]

The decisive position that Pius assumed on the racial issue worried others in the Vatican, who feared it would disrupt relations with both the Hitler and Mussolini regimes. Thus, his remark that Catholics were spiritually Semites, was edited by those who printed them in the *Osservatore Romano*, under the direction of the Secretariat of State, excluding his condemnation of anti-Semitism. The other Catholic papers all followed suit. Fearing that his words would be censured, Pius ordered Monsignor Picard's *La Libre Belgique* to publish his remarks in their entirety – and it did. In this fashion the French press, then the Italian, and finally the world press, learned of the pope's position![113] When on 10 November 1938 Mussolini published a decree prohibiting marriage between Italian 'Aryans' with persons of another race, Pius complained both to Mussolini and the King. Indeed, the pope wanted to have the *Osservatore Romano* publish his note of protest, but was dissuaded from doing so by Pacelli.[114] Nonetheless, Pius would not be silenced and determined to use all means to persuade the Mussolini government to change course, including additional diplomatic protests on November 22 and December 4, 1938. Pius publically repeated that this violated the Concordat, in his Christmas eve message. In that talk he also denounced the Swastika as a cross in conflict with that of Christ – even though he was warned that these words were provocative, for the Swastika was the official emblem of the German State.[115] On November 13, Cardinal Schuster condemned racism in a talk in the Duomo of Milan – revealing that he, like the Pope, did not feel bound by the August Accord! The very opposite occurred, as anti-Fascism increased in the closing months of Pius XI's pontificate, which witnessed the old pope contest the racial claims of the regime. Just a month and a half before his death, Pius XI launched a fierce attack against the Nazi regime.[116]

For his condemnation of racism and courageous defence of the Jews, the old Pontiff was not only accused of being a Jew-lover, but of being partly Jewish. In fact, *Das Schwarze Korps* in a poem published before his death, branded him 'The Chief Rabbi of all Christians'. It read:

> 'Go bury the delusive hope
> About His Holiness the Pope
> For all he knows concerning Race
> Would get a schoolboy in disgrace.
> Old, muddled-headed, doddering, ill,
> His knowledge is precisely nil.
> And, gone in years, he can but keep
> His motley flock of piebald sheep;
> Since he regards both Blacks and Whites
> As children all with equal rights,
> As Christians all (whate'er their hues),
> They're "spiritually" naught but Jews.
> The Vatican (e'en blockheads know)
> With verdigris is covered so,
> And wants, no doubt, the faithful band
> Of Christians who around it stand –
> As far as 'ghostly welfare' goes –

To lead 'em by the (hooked) nose.
A pretty picture all men know –
The firm of 'Juda-Rome and Co.'
An 'Old Man' e'er can tell the tale
And, sure his pity will not fail.
The banner is at last unfurled:
'Chief Rabbi of the Christian world.'[117]

Pius XI's campaign against the racist policies of the dictators was frustrated not only by fascist propaganda but by his poor health and advanced age, and sabotaged by the intrigants in the Vatican who were planning for his successor. Various factors point to the increasing isolation of the old Pontiff – which at times amounted to a virtual boycott of his declarations and propositions. Vatican critics charged that the ailing pope was misinformed about Fascist anti-Semitism, placing obstacles in the pope's campaign to combat it.[118] The discussion that Monsignor Borgoncini Duca had with Ciano on 26 August 1938, clearly reveals the lack of consensus in the Vatican concerning the pope and his initiatives. When Ciano warned the papal nuncio that a rupture between church and state was inevitable if the pope continued to denounce racism, the nuncio responded, contrary to the pope's position, that he found nothing wrong with Fascist racism, revealing he was personally very 'anti-Semitic'.[119] 'We know that on the racial issue the clergy is divided into two camps,' Farinacci told the editors of *Das Schwarze Korps* in mid-September 1938, claiming 'the pope was in no position to do anything about it.'[120]

The old pontiff recognized that many in the Vatican, urged compromise with the Fascist regime. Nonetheless, the pope continued to resist this conciliatory course, championed above all by the Secretariat of State.[121] Nor did the division in the Vatican escape the three Jesuits who had written and delivered the anti-racist encyclical, but had not heard a word from the Pope. Most likely, Pius did not know that his antiracist encyclical had been transmitted, until alerted by a letter from La Farge. Only when the Pope demanded that it be delivered at once, did the 'encyclical' belatedly materialize. Reportedly, the pope received it towards the end of January, but it is not known if he read it before his death on 9 February 1939.[122] After his death, it was found on his desk, attached to a note demanding its immediate transmittal.

In March 1939, when Pacelli succeeded as Pius XII, the encyclical condemning racism and anti-Semitism was returned to its authors, revealing that the new Pope did not intend to issue it. The former pope's critique of Fascist violations of the Lateran Accords, was likewise scuttled! Pacelli apparently now read *Humani Generis Unitas*, and incorporated sections of it in his first encyclical *Summi Pontificatus* of 20 October 1939, which rejected the claims of absolute state authority, but abandoned the explicit condemnation of anti-Semitism in his predecessor's planned encyclical.[123] There was considerable disappointment among some, but delight among others. Many believed that Pacelli, having assumed the name of Pius, would follow his predecessor's policies. Perhaps this is why Rome and Berlin had initial reservations about his election.[124] Not surprisingly, Pius XII chose to pursue a different path, reversing Pius XI's unyielding position, and perhaps this is why Catholic opposition to Jews became stronger following the death of Pius XI and the accession of Pacelli.[125]

Following Pius XII's assumption of the papal tiara, both conservative Catholics and critics of the papacy sought to blur the distinction between him and his predecessor by denying that the late pope had found fault with racial anti-Semitism describing those opinions as 'exaggerated' or even basically false. Their propaganda continues to colour the historiography of the two popes. Thus, Father Francescini Gemelli, the anti-Jewish

Rector of the Catholic University of Milan, claimed that the late pope was not democratic, nor anti-totalitarian, nor was he sympathetic towards the Jews.[126] If the first assertion was true, the latter two were not. Still others claimed that the new pope's approach did not reflect a change in the church's attitude from the time of Pius XI, but merely a change in tactics.[127] Many contemporaries disagreed. Rolf Hochhuth, critical of Pius XII, considered it tragic that the resolute Pius XI should have died on the eve of World War II.[128] Jacques Maritain confided to Aryeh Kubovy, of the World Jewish Congress, that Pius XI would have gladly issued a statement on the Church's position towards the Jews, but questioned whether Pius XII would do so.[129] Unquestionably, there was also a striking difference in tone, which led von Plessen of the German embassy to assert that 'a careful diplomat is undoubtedly better than an impulsive, irascible old man.'[130] In fact, the Nazis pursued Pius XI into the grave, continuing their campaign of calumny against him.[131]

Once Pius XII replaced Pius XI, the German Ambassador noted a relaxation of tension between the Vatican and the Reich, and his visit of 5 March 1939 with the pope might be considered the first in a series of steps leading to a détente.[132] The German Ambassador informed his government that Pius XII was prepared to make concessions and favoured a public truce.[133] The very next day, Pius called together the German Cardinals, revealing the primacy of the German problem, which he would deal with himself.[134] Interestingly enough, he contradicted those who claimed there were no real differences between the former pope and himself. Pius XII contrasted his approach and that of his predecessor, explaining that Pius XI had sought to terminate relations with the Reich, but he had restrained him.

> Yes, Pius XI was so indignant about what was happening in Germany that he once said to me, 'How can the Holy See continue to keep a Nuncio there? It conflicts with our honor!' The Holy Father feared that the world would not understand how we could continue diplomatic relations with a regime which treated the Church in such a manner. So I replied to him. 'Your Holiness, what good would that do us? If we withdraw the Nuncio how can we maintain contact with the German bishops?' The Holy Father understood and became quieter.[135]

In an audience granted a number of German pilgrims in April 1939, the new pope avoided the condemnations of his predecessor while offering his sympathy for Germany. 'We have always loved Germany, where we were able to spend many years of Our life, and we love Germany even more today,' he told them.[136] Once the Nazis provoked World War II by their invasion of Poland, the pope refused to condemn their aggression against the Catholic Poles.[137] He revealed his position to the German Pilgrims in September 1939, telling them 'For a priest, it is now more than ever before imperative to be wholly above all political and national passion; to console, to comfort, to help, to call to prayer and to penance, and himself to pray and do penance.'[138] Indeed, when the German foreign minister visited the Pope in March 1940, and complained of the strong words that Pius XI had used against the Germans, Pius XII responded that he had treated the German pilgrims kindly – and von Ribbentrop responded that this had pleased Berlin. In fact, the German Foreign Minister comparing Pacelli to Ratti retorted, 'This is a real Pope.'[139] Von Ribbentrop concluded that 'the Pope has always had his heart in Germany,' claiming that he sought a lasting understanding with Hitler. Himmler, likewise, revealed his appreciation of Pius XII's tact and prudence.[140]

Not all shared the German Foreign Minister's or Police Chief's assessment, distressed that Pius XII's obsessive preoccupation with neutrality, as well as his ideological opposition to communism, combined to steer him away from any explicit condemnation of Nazi abuses. Charles-Roux appreciated the telegrams of sympathy the pope directed to the leaders of the Low Countries, who were the latest victims of Nazi aggression in 1940, but added that sympathy was one thing, but the condemnation of crime another.[141] Furthermore, Catholic circles in Paris were convinced that even these expressions of sympathy were virtually 'wrenched' from a reluctant pope.[142] In fact, Pius chose not to send the stronger message of his own secretary of state, which deplored the violations of international law and natural rights.[143]

Although the Vatican received reports of the Nazi execution of Jews, the feeble-minded, and inmates of insane asylums, no public protest was launched by the Holy See. When Ambassador Taylor complained of the anti-Semitism of Father Coughlin, Cardinal Miglione, in his reply, did not refer to the actions of the present pope, but to his predecessor's efforts on behalf of the Jews, who he cited as the only authoritative voice in Europe raised in their favour.[144] While Pius XII clung to the preservation of diplomatic relations with Germany, some Cardinals urged the pope to follow the example of his predecessor and publicly denounce the Nazi abuses. Silence, they claimed, caused confusion and consternation among the faithful. Cardinal Tisserant contrasted the policy of the present pope unfavourably with that of the more outspoken and confrontational Pius XI.

Some in the diplomatic community and the church continued to urge Pius XII to follow in the footsteps of Pius XI and denounce the persecution, citing the danger his continued 'silence' posed to papal moral leadership. Even Sister Pasqualina, the pope's housekeeper, cook, and closest thing to a companion and confidant, urged the pope to take a stronger stance against Nazi inhumanities. 'The Holy See must aid the Jewish people to the best of our ability,' he supposedly responded, 'But everything we do must be done with caution. Otherwise the Church and the Jews themselves will suffer great retaliation.'[145] This attitude was reflected in the response of Vatican officials who argued that the Holy See could not condemn Nazi atrocities without criticizing Soviet ones; that the charges would have to be investigated, and the difficulties in assembling impartial and accurate evidence would be enormous; that the pope had already condemned major offences against morality in wartime, to which was added the voices of the hierarchy, who spoke on his behalf; and finally, a condemnation of Nazi abuses would further undermine the position of Catholics in these areas.[146] Thus, Pius XII preserved his diplomatic approach, even when the Nazis rounded up the Jews of Rome in October 1943 'under his very windows'. During that unfortunate incident, the Germans themselves commented on the differences between the approach of Pius XI and Pius XII.[147]

Pius XII privately had doubts about his conciliatory approach, fearing his caution would be perceived as anti-Semitism.[148] These doubts were also expressed to the Italian Ambassador Alfieri in May 1940, according to the notes taken by Monsignor Montini, who later became Pope Paul VI. Montini records that Pius said:

> The Pope at times cannot remain silent. Governments only consider political and military issues, intentionally disregarding moral and legal issues in which, on the other hand, the Pope is primarily interested and cannot ignore. His Holiness said, regarding this point, that he had had occasion of late to read St. Catherine's letters, who, writing to the Pope, admonishes him that God would subject him to the most stringent judgment if he did not react to evil or did not do what he thought was his duty. How could the Pope, in the present circumstances, be guilty of such a serious omission as that of remaining a disinterested spectator of such heinous acts, while all the world was waiting for his word?[149]

Later, in March 1944, Pius XII confided to the Archbishop of Cologne that it was 'painfully difficult to decide whether reticence and cautious silence are called for, or frank speech and strong action.'[150] The record reveals that while the temperamental Pius XI resorted to frank speech and strong action, the diplomatic Pius XII relied on reticence and cautious silence.

NOTES

1 *Records and Documents of the Holy See relating to the Second World War, The Holy See and the War in Europe, March 1939–August 1940.* ed. Pierre Blet et al., trans. Gerard Noel (Washington, D.C.: Corpus Books, 1968), I, 169.

2 The controversy engendered by these agreements is explored in Frank J. Coppa (ed.), *Controversial Concordats: The Vatican's Relations with Napoleon, Mussolini, and Hitler* (Washington, D.C.: Catholic University Press, 1999).

3 *Avro Manhattan, The Vatican in World Politics* (New York: GAER Associates, 1949), p.126.

4 As such, he supervised the administration of the Vatican's revenues and was charged with the task of directing preparation for the conclave upon the death of the reigning Pope. Oscar Halecki, *Eugenio Pacelli: Pope of Peace*, (New York: Ferrar, Strauss and Young, Inc., 1951), p.75.

5 *Actes et documents du Saint Siège relatifs à la Seconde Guerre Mondiale*, II volumes, eds. Pierre Blet, Robert A. Graham, Angelo Martini and Burkhart Scheneider (Vatican City: Libreria Editrice Vaticana, 1965–1981). To date only the first of these has been translated into English as *Records and Documents of the Holy See relating to the Second World War, The Holy See and the War in Europe, March 1939–August 1940; Actes et documents du Saint Siège relatifs à la Second Guerre Mondiale, La Sainte Siège e la Guerre en Europe, Mars 1939–Aout 1940*, I, 5; C. Confalonieri, *Pio XI visto da vicino* (Turin: SAIE, 1957), pp.177–179.

6 For the most recent criticism of Pius XII see John Cornwell, *Hitler's Pope: The Secret History of Pius XII* (New York: Viking Press, 1999).

7 Aryeh L. Kubovy, 'The Silence of Pope Pius XII and the Beginnings of the Jewish Document', *Yad Vashem Studies*, ed. Nathan Eck and Aryeh Leon Kubovy (Jerusalem: Yad Vashem, 1967) VI, 18.

8 *Records and Documents of the Holy See relating to the Second World War* I, 85.

9 Burkhart Schneider, S.J. 'Una enciclica mancata', *L'Osservatore Romano*, 5 April 1974.

10 *Actes et documents du Saint Siège relatifs à la Seconde Guerre Mondiale, Lettres de Pie XII au Eveques Allemands, 1939–1944*, II, 407.

11 Georges Passelecq and Bernard Suchecky, *L'encyclique cachée de Pie XI. Une occasion manquée de l'Eglise face a l'antisemitisme*. Préface 'Pie XI, les Juifs et l'antisémitisme' de Émile Poulat (Paris: Editions La Découverte, 1995), pp.53, 67.

12 Giovanni Miccoli, 'Santa Sede e Chiesa Italiana di Fronte alle Leggi Antiebraiche del 1938', *Studi Storici* anno 29, n.4 (October–December 1988): 821–902 and Mariangiola Reineri, *Cattolici e fascismo a Torino, 1925–1943, Biblioteca di Storia Contemporanea* (Milan: Feltrinelli, 1978).

13 Angelo Martini, S.J., 'L' Ultima battaglia di Pio XI' in *Studi sulla Questione Romana e la Concilazione* (Rome: 5 Lune 1963), p.187.

14 *The Papal Encyclicals, 1958–1981*, .5 volumes. ed. Claudia Carlen (Raleigh: The Pierian Press, 1981); *Discorsi di Pio XI*, 3 volumes, ed. Domenico Bertetto (Turin: Società Editrice Internazionale, 1959).

15 After Pius XI's death, copies of this encyclical entitled *Humani Generis Unitas* in French, German, and English were returned to La Farge. In 1973, the *Catholic Mind* determined to publish this 'hidden encyclical' and put it into galleys. It was not published in 1973, and the original was not found in his papers which had been transferred to Georgetown University. However, the galleys were stored at the offices of *America*. Professor Robert A. Hecht of Kingsborough Community College of C.C.N.Y., working independently of Passelecq and Suchecky, uncovered these galleys during the course of his research on a biography of La Farge. I am indebted to him for transmitting a copy to me.

16 Jose M. Sanchez, 'The Popes and Nazi Germany: The View from Madrid', *Journal of Church and State* 38 (Spring 1996): 367.

17 *Non abbiamo bisogno*, 29 June 1931; *Mit brennender Sorge*, 14 March 1937; *Divini Redemptoris*, 19 March 1937, all in *Principles for Peace: Selections from Papal Documents from Leo XIII to Pius XII*, ed. Harry C. Koenig (Washington, D.C.: National Catholic Welfare Conference, 1943), pp.446–448; 498–510; 510–535.

18 Castelli, *National Catholic Reporter*, 15 December 1972, p.1.

19 *Cum Tertio*, 17 September 1922, *Principles for Peace*, p.329.

20 Richard A. Webster, *The Cross and the Fasces*, (Stanford: Stanford University Press, 1960), p.96.

21 Consistorial Allocution of 20 December 1926, *Discorsi di Pio XI*, I, 647.

22 *Decretum De Conosciatione Vulgo, 'Amici Israel' Abolenda*, 25 March 1928, *Acta Apostolicae Sedis*, XX, 103–104.

23 Passelecq and Suchecky, p.144.

24 Miccoli, *Studi Storici* anno 29, n.4 (October–December 1988), 829–833; Daniel Carpi, 'The Catholic Church and Italian Jewry under the Fascists', *Yad Washem Studies*, ed. Shaul Esh (New York: KATV Publishing House, 1975) IV, p.46.

25 The text can be found in Nino Trapodi's *I Patti lateranese e il fascismo* (Bologna: Cappelli, 1960), pp.267–279; an English version is found in Coppa, *Controversial Concordats*, pp.193–205.

26 *L'Osservatore Romano*, 12 February 1929; *Il Monitore Ecclesiastico*, March 1929.

27 'Ecco una', 14 May 1929, *Principles for Peace*, p.388.

28 *Acta Apostolicae Sedis*, XXI, 730–753.

29 George Seldes, *Sawdust Caesar: The Untold History of Mussolini and Fascism*, (New York: Harper and Brothers, 1935), p.260.

30 Paul L. Murphy with Rene Arlington, *La popessa*, (New York: Warner Books, 1983), p.103.

31 *The Papal Encyclicals in their Historical Context*, ed. Anne Fremantle (New York: G.P. Putnam's Sons, 1956), p.249.

32 Arturo Carlo Jemolo, *Church and State in Italy, 1850–1950*, trans. David Moore (Philadelphia: Dufour Editions, 1961), p.257; Seldes, p.256.

33 Carpi, *Yad Washem Studies*, IV, 51.

34 *Anglo-Vatican Relations 1914–1939: Confidential Reports of the British Minister to the Holy See*, ed. Thomas E. Hachey (Boston: G.K. Hall, 1972), p.250.

35 M. Barbera, 'La pedagogia e l'ateismo militante nella Russia sovietica', *Civiltà Cattolica, anno* 84 (1933), I, 99.

36 'Cronaca Contemporanea', 10–13 March 1933, *Civiltà Cattolica, anno* 84 (1933), II, 205–206.

37 John Jay Hughes, 'The Pope's Pact with Hitler: Betrayal or Self-Defense?' *Journal of Church and State*, 17 (Winter, 1975): 64; Klaus Scholder, *The Churches and the Third Reich. II: The Year of Disillusionment: 1934 Barmen and Rome* (Philadelphia: Fortress Press, 1988), p.1.

38 *Anglo-Vatican Relations 1914–1939*, p.250; 'Concordat of the Holy See and Germany', *Catholic World*, August, 1933, vol.137; 'Cronaca Contemporanea', 23 June–6 July 1933, *Civiltà Cattolica, anno* 84 (1933), III, 203–205.

39 *Anglo-Vatican Relations 1914–1939*, p.250.

40 'Concordato fra la Santa Sede ed il Reich Germanico', 20 July 1933, *Acta Apostolicae Sedis*, XXV, 389–408.

41 E. Rosa, 'Il Concordato della Santa Sede con la Germania', *Civiltà Cattolica, anno* 84 (1933), IV, 89; *L'Osservatore Romano*, 27 July 1933.

42 *Anglo-Vatican Relations 1914–1939*, pp.253–254; Camille M. Cianfarra, *The War and the Vatican* (London: Oates and Washbourne, 1945), p.96.

43 Nathaniel Micklem, *National Socialism and the Roman Catholic Church* (London: Oxford University Press, 1939), p.95; A.J. Ryder, *Twentieth Century Germany: From Bismarck to Brandt* (New York: Columbia University Press, 1973), p.377.

44 Luciani Martini, 'Chiesa Cattolica ed Ebrei', *Il Ponte* XXXIV (1978), 1458–1459; Igino Giordani, 'Ebrei, protestanti e cattolici', *Fides*, n. 4, April 1933.

45 Miccoli, *Studi Storici* anno 29.n.4 (October–December 1988), p.839–840.

46 *ibid.*, p.859.

47 *Documents on German Foreign Policy*, Series C, vol., pp.793–794.

48 Micklem, p.104.
49 Scholder, II, 115, 118.
50 Micklem, p.70.
51 Guenter Lewy, *The Catholic Church and Nazi Germany* (New York: McGraw-Hill, 1965), p.126.
52 *Mit brennender Sorge*, 14 March 1937, *Principles for Peace*, p.498; Desmond O' Grady, 'Pius XI – complex and imperious', *National Catholic Reporter*, 15 December 1972, p.15.
53 E. Rosa, 'Ricorsi di Barbarie nella civiltà contemporanea', *Civiltà Cattolica, anno* 87 (1936), III, 356.
54 Miccoli, *Studi Storici* anno 29.n.4 (October–December 1988), p.842.
55 *Principles for Peace*, pp.304–306.
56 'Cronaca Contemporanea', 922 June 1933, *Civiltà Cattolica, anno* 84 (1933), II, 609; 'Cronaca Contemporanea', 25 May–8 June 1933, *Civiltà Cattolica, anno* 84 (1933), II, 609; speech of 29 July 1934 in *Discorsi di Pio XI*, III, 183–185.
57 *Anglo-Vatican Relations 1914–1939*, pp.274–279; Charles-Roux, p.98.
58 Guenter Lewy, 'Pius XII, the Jews, and the German Catholic Church', *Commentary* 37 (February 1964), p.30.
59 'Ai giovani Cattolici di Germania', 8 August 1934, *Discorsi di Pio XI*, III, 188; Passelecq and Suchecky, p.93.
60 Owen Chadwick, *Britain and the Vatican during the Second World War* (Cambridge: Cambridge University Press, 1986), pp.16, 19.
61 *Documents on Germany Foreign Policy*, Series C, IV, n.482; Rhodes, p.199.
62 The original version will be found in *Acta Apostolicae Sedis*, XXIX, 145–167, followed by an Italian version, 168ff.
63 'Lettera enciclica sulla situazione della Chiesa Cattolica nel Reich Germanico', *Acta Apostolicae Sedis*, 1937, XXIX, 168.
64 *ibid.*, XXIX, 182, 185–186.
65 Miccoli, *Studi Storici* anno 29.n.4 (October–December 1988), p.857.
66 *The Persecution of the Catholic Church in the Third Reich: Facts and Documents* (London: Burns, Oates, 1940), p.242.
67 *The New York Times*, 21 June 1937.
68 *Allocution Quod Iterum*, 13 December 1937, Discorsi di Pio XI, III, 671; 'Al Sacro Collegio e alla Prelatura Romana', ibid., III, 679.
69 *Anglo-Vatican Relations 1914–1939*, pp.370, 379.
70 *Principles for Peace*, p.545.
71 'Cronaca Contemporanea', *Civiltà Cattolica*, 9–22 June 1938.
72 Passelecq and Suchecky, p.157.
73 *Discorsi di Pio XI*, III, 770.
74 *The Persecution of the Catholic Church in the Third Reich*, p.418.
75 Miccoli, *Studi Storici* anno 29, n.4 (October–December 1988), p.821.
76 *Anglo-Vatican Relations 1914–1939*, p.387; *Tablet* (of London) 26 March 1938.
77 Charles-Roux, pp.122–123; Micklem, pp.206–207; 96, 99; *Anglo-Vatican Relations 1914–1939*, p.392.
78 William M. Harrigan, 'Pius XII's Efforts to Effect a Detente in German-Vatican Relations, 1939', *The Catholic Historical Review* 49 (July 1963): 177.
79 Cianfarra, p.122; *Anglo-Vatican Relations 1914–1939*, pp.389–394.
80 *Records and Documents of the Holy See relating to the Second World War*, I, 122.
81 *Discorsi di Pio XI*, III, 770.
82 *ibid.*, III, 375.
83 Gianni Padoan, 'Pio XII', *Historia, anno* XIII (November 1969), n. 144, p.25.
84 Martini, 'L'Ultima battaglia di Pio XI', p.203.
85 Meir Michaelis, 'Fascism, Totalitarianism and the Holocaust: Reflections on Current Interpretations of National Socialist Anti-Semitism', *European History Quarterly* 19/1 (1989): 93.
86 Michael R. Marrus, 'The Vatican on Racism and Antisemitism, 1938–39: A New Look at a Might-Have Been', *Holocaust and Genocide Studies* 11/3 (Winter 1997): 382–383.
87 Carpi, *Yad Washem Studies* IV, 54.

88 Meir Michaelis, Mussolini and the Jews: German-Italian Relations and the Jewish Question in Italy, 1922–1945 (Oxford: Clarendon Press, 1978), p.244.
89 Edward D. Kleinlerer, 'Scholars at the Vatican', *The Commonweal* 37 (4 December 1942), 187–188.
90 Earl Boyea, 'The Reverend Charles Coughlin and the Church: The Gallagher Years, 1930–1937', *The Catholic Historical Review* 81/2 (April 1995): 211–13, 216, 218, 222–225.
91 Norman Cohn, *Warrant for Genocide: The Myth of the Jewish world-conspiracy and the Protocols of the Elders of Zion* (New York: Harper and Row, 1967), p.235.
92 John La Farge, *Interracial Justice: A Study of the Catholic Doctrine of Race Relations* (New York: America Press, 1937), pp.59–61.
93 Robert A. Hecht, *An Unordinary Man: A Life of Father John La Farge, S.J.* (Lanham, MD.: The Scarecrow Press, Inc., 1996), pp.114–115.
94 John La Farge, *The Manner is Ordinary* (New York: Harcourt Brace and Company, 1954), p.272; Hecht, p.114.
95 Passelecq and Suchecky, pp.124–126.
96 Hecht, p.115.
97 Lewy, *Commentary* 37 (February 1964), p 30.
98 Galleys of La Farge's copy of the encyclical *Humani Generis Unitas*, p.31, paragraph 123.
99 *ibid.*, p.33, paragraph 131; Passelecq and Suchecky, pp.283–284.
100 Galleys of La Farge's copy of *Humani Generis Unitas*, p.36b, paragraph 147; Passelecq and Suchecky, pp.292–293.
101 Galleys of La Farge's copy of *Humani Generis Unitas*, p.38b, paragraph 154; Passelecq and Suchecky, p.296.
102 Galleys of La Farge's copy of *Humani Generis Unitas*, p.34, paragraph 135; Passelecq and Suchecky, p.286.
103 'Jesuit Says Pius XI asked for draft', *National Catholic Reporter*, 22 December 1972, p.4; Frederick Brown, 'The Hidden Encyclical', *The New Republic*, 15 April 1996, p.30
104 Miccoli, *Studi Storici* anno 29, n.4 (October–December 1988), p.881.
105 Martini, 'L'Ultima battaglia di Pio XI', pp.186–187.
106 Reineri, p.192.
107 Miccoli, *Studi Storici* anno 29, n.4 (October–December 1988), p.878.
108 *Discorsi di Pio XI*, III, 786, 796.
109 'Agli Alunni di 'Propaganda Fide', 21 August 1938, ibid., 784–86.
110 Miccoli, *Studi Storici* anno 29, n.4 (October–December 1988), p.879; Passelecq and Suchecky, p.180.
111 Kubovy, *Yad Washem Studies*, VI, 21.
112 Webster, pp.113–115.
113 Miccoli, *Studi Storici* anno 29, n.4 (October–December 1988), pp.879–880.
114 Martini, 'L'Ultima battaglia di Pio XI', p.219.
115 *L'Osservatore Romano*, 14–15 November 1938; Miccoli, *Studi Storici* anno 29, n.4 (October–December 1988), p.881; Martini, 'L'Ultima battaglia di Pio XI', pp.229–230.
116 Murphy with Arlington, p.162.
117 *The Persecution of the Catholic Church in the Third Reich*, pp.426–427.
118 Miccoli, *Studi Storici* anno 29, n.4 (October–December 1988), p.878.
119 Webster, p.114.
120 Martini, 'L'Ultima battaglia di Pio XI', p.189.
121 Miccoli, *Studi Storici* anno 29, n.4 (October–December 1988), pp.880–881.
122 'Jesuit Says Pius XI asked for draft', *National Catholic Reporter*, 22 December 1972, p.3.
123 *Acta Apostolicae Sedis*, 31 (1939), 413–53; Gordon Zahn, 'The Unpublished Encyclical: An Opportunity Missed', *National Catholic Reporter*, 15 December 1972, p.9.
124 *Records and Documents of the Holy See Relating to the Second World War*, I, 4; Halecki, p.138.
125 Carpi, *Yad Washem Studies*, IV, 54–55; Murphy and Arlington, p.163.
126 Carpi, *Yad Washem Studies*, IV, 55.
127 'Les grands themes des lettres', *Lettres de Pie XII aux Eveques Allemands, 1939–1944, Actes et documents du Saint Siège relatifs à la Second Guerre Mondiale*, II, 21.

128 Patricia Marx Ellsberg, 'An Interview with Rolf Hochhuth', *The Papacy and Totalitarianism Between the Two World Wars*, ed. Charles Delzell. (New York: John Wiley, 1974), p.33.

129 Kubovy, *Yad Washem Studies*, VI, 24.

130 W.A. Purdy, *The Church on the Move: The Character and Policies of Pius XII and John XIII* (New York: John Day Co., 1966), p.27.

131 *The Persecution of the Catholic Church in the Third Reich*, p.427.

132 *Documents on German Foreign Policy*, Series D, IV, nn. 473, 475; *Lettres de Pie XII aux Eveques Allemands, 1939–1944, Actes et documents du Saint Siège relatifs à la Second Guerre Mondiale*, II, 20.

133 Harrigan, *The Catholic Historical Review*, 49 (July 1963): 184.

134 *Actes et documents du Saint Siège relatifs à la Second Guerre Mondiale*, II, 23–24.

135 Anthony Rhodes, *The Vatican in the Age of Dictators, 1922–1945* (New York: Holt, Rhinehart, and Winston, 1973), p.229.

136 George O. Kent, 'Pope Pius XII and Germany: Some Aspects of German–Vatican Relations, 1933–1943', *American Historical Review* 70 (October 1964): 65.

137 *Records and Documents of the Holy See Relating to the Second World War*, I, 281.

138 *ibid.*, I, 293.

139 *Actes et documents du Saint Siège relatifs à la Second Guerre Mondiale, La Saint Siège e la Guerre en Europe, Mars 1939–Aout 1940*, I, 387.

140 *Records and Documents of the Holy See Relating to the Second World War*, I, 166, 359.

141 *ibid.*, I, 421.

142 *ibid.*, I, 431.

143 *ibid.*, I, 415.

144 *ibid.*, I, 381.

145 Murphy with Arlington, p.197.

146 Kent, *American Historical Review* 70 (October 1964): 71–72.

147 John F. Morley, *Vatican Diplomacy and the Jews During the Holocaust, 1939–1943* (New York: KTAV Publishing House, Inc., 1980), pp.180–181; Raul Hilberg, *The Destruction of the European Jews* (Chicago: Quadrangle Books, 1961), p.430; Lewy, *Commentary*, February 1964, p.32.

148 Murphy with Arlington, p.197.

149 *Records and Documents of the Holy See Relating to the Second World War*, I, 423.

150 Stehle, p.213.

MEA CULPA AND THE MAGISTERIUM:
'WIR ERINNERN' AND THE PROBLEMS
OF CONFESSION[1]

Mark R. Lindsay

O N 16 MARCH 1998, the Vatican's Commission for Religious Relations with the Jews issued the document *Wir erinnern: Eine Reflexion über die Shoah*.[2] This was the latest in a long line of papal statements concerning Jewish–Christian relations that extends as far back as the Patristic period in the first few centuries of the Common Era. It was eagerly expected by many to be the most significant prospect for Catholic-Jewish reconciliation since the promulgation of *Nostra Aetate* in 1965.

The first paragraph of the document, as well as the papal letter that accompanied it, emphasized that the imminent dawning of the new millennium rendered the task of repentance and reconciliation both urgent and necessary. Indeed, it was even implied that the process of shaping a future free of genocidal activity obliged the Church to undertake a serious self-examination, so as to expose and seek forgiveness for the evils – particularly of antisemitism – by which she has been corrupted throughout the course of the centuries.

In intent, therefore, the document was both laudable and timely. In content, however, it missed the mark. But why did it fall short of its promise? The necessity of explaining the reasons for the document's shortcomings is urgent given that as prominent a figure as David Novak has come to its defence from the *Jewish* side[3]. It is this explanatory task, followed by a prolegomena to further research, that forms the basis of this paper.

I

The prologue to *Wir erinnern* argues that the tragedy of the Holocaust is one before which the nations of the world cannot remain indifferent. It was 'the worst suffering of all', a persecution which lies 'beyond the capacity of words to convey'.[4] According to the authors, the Church in particular is caught up in the overwhelming tragedy of this event. She is bound in indissoluble solidarity with the victims of the death camps by virtue of both her kinship bond with the Jewish people and her necessary 'remembrance of the injustices of the past.'[5]

It is regrettable that the Church's culpability for fostering the antisemitic prelude to the Holocaust was acknowledged with no greater force than the mere remembrance of past injustices. One could legitimately ask what this overly generalized statement really means *in concreto*. What 'past injustices' are in fact being remembered? And to what extent is 'remembrance' the same as genuine confession? These are just two of the questions which could and should be asked of the opening stanzas of *Wir erinnern*. Nevertheless this opening statement – which attempts in the one breath to capture both the spirit of confession and the spirit of reconciliation – at least points in the right direction. It does, however, *only* point because it is precisely here that the document betrays its fundamental flaw. The minimization of guilt which emerges in the prologue as a vague hint, under this non-specific guise of *Gedächtnis*, becomes in fact the moral base on which the rest of the document proceeds. Correctly, the authors affirm that the occurrence of the Holocaust in Europe has problematized the entire ethical heritage of Christendom, especially in relation to the Church's attitude towards the Jews.[6] Unfortunately, however, the moral foundation of the document, according to which institutional culpability is diluted to become simply 'remembrance', demands that this logic is not carried through to its conclusion in the way in which the document narrates the history of Jewish–Christian interaction. Indeed, evident throughout the statement is a series of historical inaccuracies that not only bowdlerizes the record of ecclesiastical antisemitism but thereby also compromises the integrity of the document's reconciliatory agenda.

So why is this the moral grounding upon which *Wir erinnern* is built? In spite of the Church's self-recognition as a divinely created institution, does the unwillingness of the authors to explicitly accept at the outset the Church's deep culpability for specific and entrenched antisemitism simply demonstrate a very *human* attempt to avoid censure? Theologically, there is more to it than that. Underpinning – and undermining – the whole attempt at guilt confession within this statement is the Catholic doctrine of the *magisterium*. With this as the theological and existential premise upon which the document is predicated, it is impossible for the authors to present anything but the most historically cursory gloss of the Church's role in propagating antisemitism. As a result, institutional guilt confession is relegated to irrelevancy, thus sabotaging the intent of the document as a whole.

Therefore, it is essential to any understanding of *Wir erinnern*'s historiography that the doctrine of the *magisterium* is itself understood. Hans Küng contends that the concept itself is modern, scripturally unfounded and highly confused in its meaning.[7] Nevertheless, in spite of these ambiguities there is a definition of the term. According to Catholic ecclesiology, largely as it was fashioned out of the debates at Vatican I, the *magisterium* came to have 'the meaning sometimes of teaching, sometimes of the teaching function and competence to teach, and finally sometimes ... of the body of prelates who possess public teaching authority: the teaching office.'[8] This diversity of meanings notwithstanding, the term therefore clearly implies an authoritative function of the institutional Church insofar as her public pronouncements to the world and to her own members are concerned.

But from whence this authority? Fundamentally, the Church's role as a locus of authoritative teaching is predicated upon the belief that she is a receptive subject of divine revelation. She is the vessel in which God's self-revelation is enshrined and the medium through which this revelation is proclaimed to the world. Insofar as she is this receptive subject she is also the *ecclesia docens*, to which the 'notes' of the Church – her unity, catholicity, apostolicity, perpetuity and infallibility – are validly ascribed.[9]

Consequently, the question arises whether the Church in her teaching role can ever be in error. Does the *magisterium*, in other words, necessarily imply ecclesiological infallibility? The answer to this is not clear. The decision of the First Vatican Council in 1870 argues that there are specific limits to infallibility. The text of the dogma makes clear that the infallibility and immutability (*irreformabiles*) of papal pronouncements apply only in cases of explicitly *ex cathedra* statements, or where there are disputes over faith and moral norms. As a result, the tendency within Catholicism throughout much of this century has been to assume that the doctrine of the *magisterium* was circumscribed by a 'minimalist' interpretation according to which no one had any real cause to be concerned about a violation of individual conscience – that the imposition of a binding and infallible pronouncement would be rare and something to be expected only in the event of ecclesiastical emergency.[10]

On the other hand, the great but controversial work of Hans Küng in his *Unfehlbar?* has been to show that, these limits notwithstanding, magisterial infallibility impacts on a far greater range of issues and a far larger number of people than has been assumed. 'Even when the Church's claim to infallibility is not explicit, it is always subliminally present.'[11] There is a 'maximalist' interpretation of Vatican I's definition of the *magisterium* that is quite at odds with a large part of professional theology and even some statements of the Second Vatican Council.[12] As Küng himself says, 'the Pope, the Curia and many bishops continue to behave in a largely pre-conciliar fashion . . . [T]he levers of spiritual power are now, as before, in the hands of personalities more interested in the maintenance of the *status quo* than in a serious renewal.'[13] Pesch summarizes Küng's findings as follows: 'if there is such a thing as an infallibility of the church's *magisterium*, then by the nature of the case the limits are wider than people have so far persuaded themselves that they are, and papal *ex cathedra* decisions with what in fact are very narrow limits are then only a special case which does not embrace the whole set of problems.'[14] The result is thus that the *magisterium* as a dogma of the Church impacts upon many more issues and people – both Catholics and non-Catholics alike – than the 'minimalists' would wish to believe, and that therefore the scope of the (teaching) Church's infallibility extends beyond the boundaries as they have traditionally been understood. If Küng is correct, the Church's claim to infallibility suddenly takes on a more worrying aspect and, as *Wir erinnern* shows, enables the Church to justify dogmatically the covering of a multitude of sins by recourse to her magisterial inerrancy.

What does this mean in relation to *Wir erinnern* specifically? The document is clearly intended as a confessional statement, acknowledging antisemitic guilt. But in view of the extension in scope of the *magisterium* which has been persuasively argued by Küng the crucial question now becomes, guilt on whose part? As has been seen, the theological basis of the *magisterium*, that is, the subjective receptivity of the Church to divine revelation, clearly implies that any apology for previous doctrinal mistakes (whether they take the form of systematic theological issues or the 'past injustices' of antisemitism), which is an inevitable implication of a confession of guilt, would by necessity have to be based upon the reception of a higher criterion of truth than revelation itself. The Church would thus be subjecting herself to criteria external to her own essence – a situation which Novak regards as existentially impossible.[15] Thus, if *Wir erinnern* is confessional in intent, it cannot be the teaching Church which is the subject of the censure. The scope of magisterial infallibility will not allow the *ecclesia docens* to be so thoroughly implicated in the moral guilt which surrounds the Holocaust, nor will the revelational premise of the *magisterium* accept an alternative base upon which guilt-confession could be built. The subject of censure can only be, therefore, the more amorphous reality of the Church's individual members. This is the logical result of Küng's interpretation of the *magisterium*, and it is in fact the very thing which we see in *Wir erinnern*.

II

The historical gloss of early Christian–Jewish relations presented by the Commission for Religious Relations with the Jews devolves the blame for the initial expressions of theological anti-Judaism onto individual Christians and their misguided – and, significantly, *unofficial* – hermeneutic of Israel. The Christian mobs who ransacked pagan temples and 'sometimes' also the synagogues (note the defensive implication that the Jews were not the primary target but rather the pagans of the day) were influenced in their behaviour by 'certain interpretations of the New Testament' regarding the Jewish people...'.[16] The Commission then resorts to no less an authority than Pope John Paul II to argue that these 'erroneous and unjust interpretations' by which anti-semitic violence was justified were neither taught nor sanctioned 'on the part of the Church as such...', despite being in common currency.[17] Indeed, such interpretations have been definitively rejected by Vatican II.[18] And of course, this rejection implies that these erroneous interpretations were never part of official Catholic dogma otherwise, by virtue of the infallibility and immutability by which they would thereby be characterized, they could not be rescinded. On the basis of magisterial infallibility, therefore, corporate responsibility has been eschewed. Long-dead individuals carry the blame, while the authoritative teaching institution – the infallible *ecclesia docens* herself – escapes censure. Personal agency is most certainly raised to new levels of significance by this historiographical method, but it comes at the cost of failing utterly to acknowledge the central place accorded within official doctrine to ecclesiastical antisemitism.

One needs only to glimpse at Patristic and early papal pronouncements against Judaism to realize the extent to which *Wir erinnern* refashions the historical record to suit its own ecclesiological paradigm. Early in the third century, for example, Origen proclaimed that 'the blood of Jesus falls not only upon the Jews of that time, but on all generations of Jews up to the end of the world.' John Chrysostom, meanwhile, preached a series of eight sermons in Antioch between 386 and 388 C.E. explicitly against the Jews, arguing that they 'are possessed by the devils'. Even circumcision was redefined by Patristic theology to be no longer a sign of covenantal belonging but rather a new 'mark of Cain' by which the Jews' perdition was visibly demonstrated to the world.[19] All these pronouncements came from the Fathers of the Church – greater theological authority is vested only in the creeds and in Scripture itself. In other words, these were by no means peripheral figures who uttered these statements but, on the contrary, were giants within the history of official doctrinal evolution. And *Wir erinnern* has deliberately omitted them from its record.

It is also significant to note that, despite *Wir erinnern*'s attempts to shift the blame for the destruction of synagogues onto lawless – *fallible* – mobs, Pinchas Lapide contends that the first recorded burnings of synagogues were at the express behest of archbishops, acting with the full authority of the Roman Church. In 388 C.E., Ambrose of Milan defended the destruction of a synagogue in Mesopotamia declaring that 'it was I who gave orders to put fire to that [building].' And again in 415 C.E., Archbishop Cyril ordered the sacking of the synagogue in Alexandria.[20]

It is unmistakably clear that the authors of *Wir erinnern* have written an expurgated version of early Catholic doctrine and actions in respect of Jewish–Christian relations. That as pivotal a leader as Pope Innocent III, whose rule marks the zenith of papal power, saw fit in 1199 to promulgate the *Licet perfidia Judaeorum*[21] bears acute testimony to the persistence and authoritative nature of theological antisemitism within the very walls of the Curia. But again of this, *Wir erinnern* makes no mention. And yet significantly, Hans Küng has argued that according to the definition as proposed by the Second Vatican Council, the infallible teachings of Christ are not simply limited to *ex cathedra* pronouncements of a pope but also include 'those which all bishops, although separated in space, have clearly taught always and everywhere in accord with the pope'.[22] In the light of the 'corrective' to *Wir erinnern*'s history which has been presented above, it could thus legitimately be argued that antisemitism is one of those teachings that has been taught by bishops everywhere and at all times, in accordance with Rome. Therefore, magisterial infallibility is, by this argument, severely implicated in the propagation of antisemitic hatred.

That is to say, in its gloss of Jewish–Christian interaction, *Wir erinnern* has refashioned the story to expunge all traces of institutional ecclesiastical responsibility for antisemitism. In some cases, historical complexities have been ironed out to give the appearance of racial harmony when in fact there was none. In others, where it is impossible to deny the injurious presence of antisemitism, blame has been laid at the feet of everyone but the Church and her official doctrines, when the record unambiguously shows that Christian teachings were employed – and often by prominent Christian leaders – to reinforce antisemitic vitriol. In coming to consider the document's discussion of the Holocaust itself, then, the ground already covered leaves little room for anything but the gravest scepticism that in respect of this most horrendous example of antisemitism, the statement will be genuinely prepared to acknowledge moral culpability 'on the part of the Church as such'.

III

Insofar as the Holocaust itself is concerned, there are two major points of controversy arising from *Wir erinnern*. On the one hand stands the much-debated and still unresolved question of the similarities or otherwise between Nazi and Christian antisemitism. *Wir erinnern* not surprisingly insists that the two were qualitatively different. '[W]e cannot ignore the difference which exists between antisemitism (*sic*) based on theories contrary to the constant teaching of the Church on the unity of the human race and on the equal dignity of all races and peoples, and the long-standing sentiments of mistrust and hostility that we call anti-Judaism, of which unfortunately, Christians have also been guilty.'[23] There is, of course, a fundamental question concerning the accuracy with which one can claim for the Church a constancy of racial equality in her teaching. Quite apart from this, however, there is also an unwillingness once again, not only to acknowledge corporate guilt – the guilty ones are Christians, not the Church – but also to accept that the error was antisemitism. On the contrary, it is the lesser charge of anti-Judaism which is proposed and confessed. There is a self-absolution on the part of the Church at this point which, in later parts of the document, serves to marginalize and minimize every Church association with the *Shoah*. The Holocaust was not, according to *Wir erinnern*, based on anti-Judaism but on antisemitism – and the authors have already shown to their satisfaction that, not only was the Church as such not guilty but that, even when individual Christians were implicated in anti-Jewish hostility, their antipathy was fundamentally religious not racial in content. Logically, therefore, there can be no legitimate censuring of either the Church or her members for participation in the foundational element of the Holocaust.

Worrying though this may be it is not, however, the major problem of the document in respect of its overview of the Holocaust. More problematic by far is the extent to which the authors claim unflinching and open protests by the Church against Nazi antisemitism.

Wir erinnern applauds Cardinals Bertram, Faulhaber and Popes Pius XI and XII for their public repudiations of Nazi racism in, for example, Faulhaber's Advent sermons of

1933 and the 1937 encyclical *Mit brennende Sorge*.[24] But in none of these cases does one find the unequivocal repudiation of antisemitism one would wish, or indeed which the document implies was present. On the contrary, while Faulhaber's Advent sermons defended the canonicity of the Old Testament and the Jews who lived prior to Jesus, he explicitly distinguished them from the Jews of modern Germany. Moreover, in spite of the implication of *Wir erinnern* that these sermons were a deliberate political protest, Faulhaber emphatically denied that he was taking any stance whatsoever on the 'Jewish question'.[25] In a letter to Cardinal Pacelli on 10 April 1933, he argued that the Church did not need to defend the Jews 'because the Jews can help themselves…'[26] Bertram, the other cardinal singled out for praise, can also only be congratulated for his stance if at the same time it is remembered that it was he who, on hearing of Hitler's death, ordered a solemn requiem mass to be said for the Führer so that 'the Almighty's son might be admitted to paradise.'[27] According to Catholic Church law, 'a requiem mass may be celebrated only for a believing member of the Church and only on an important occasion, and if it is in the public interest of the Church…'[28] It is thus surely difficult to reconcile this public call for a requiem mass on the one hand with a thoroughgoing opposition to Hitler's genocidal policies on the other.

On the issue of race, Bertram, Faulhaber and Archbishop Gröber all publicly defended its sanctity. In 1935, Bertram reminded his clergy that the Church had always recognized blood and race to be divine gifts consecrated through Christianity.[29] Gröber, meanwhile, published a book which was sanctioned by the episcopate, in which he argued that 'race and Christianity are not contradictions, but orders of a different kind that supplement one another.'[30]

As for the 1937 encyclical, the language of resistance was undoubtedly powerful and, by being written in German rather than the usual Latin, was clearly intended to provoke a direct confrontation with the German government. But, the objects of condemnation were the deification of the Nazi state, the blood-and-soil theory of racial belonging, and the Nazis' treatment of the Church. The words 'Jew' and 'antisemitism' are noticeably absent. The encyclical was only directed against the Reich's violation of the 1933 Concordat between Germany and the Vatican. There was no explicit denunciation of antisemitism, and there never was any such condemnation in any official Church statement before or during the war, even when the genocidal policy had been put into effect.

This is not to deny or demean the reality of Catholic opposition to various Nazi policies. The widespread protests against the T-4 euthanasia programme, in which the Catholic hierarchy took a leading part, illustrates how powerful and effective public resistance could be. But if anything, this merely implicates the Church even more for, having seen that such protests could work, there was still no concerted effort to repeat the attempt on behalf of the Jews.

Consequently, the most troubling aspect of *Wir erinnern*'s historiography, which some commentators may even feel compelled to label hypocritical, is that insofar as a condemnation of antisemitic racism is ingredient to the document's intention, the authors do not allow themselves to censure the Church 'as such'. Quite aside from the fact that the public declarations of leading Catholic officials against Nazi antisemitism that are championed by the Commission do not in fact have the condemnatory force which is implied, it is surely somewhat self-serving to argue that when it comes to ethical bravery the Church as an authoritative teaching institution is the acting subject, but when it comes to erroneous and discriminatory beliefs and practices it is only individual members who are at fault.

Allied to this is the concern that, while the document acknowledges with deep regret and sorrow the reality of ethical passivity amongst Church members, there is no similar acknowledgment of a more active guilt. There is a grave confession that during the period of the *Shoah* the 'spiritual resistance and concrete action of... Christians was not that which might have been expected from Christ's followers.' Many Christians did not 'give every possible assistance to those being persecuted ... '.[31] While this is a necessary and salutary admission, its force is blunted by the absence of any recognition that Church teaching itself may have been a cause of this quietude and even, if Goldhagen is correct, of active participation of the persecution. In confessional language, there is a commendable sorrow for the sins of omission, but a troubling inability to acknowledge the sins of commission. Once more, we are referred back to the problem of the *magisterium*, and the dichotomy thereby posited between the erring and censurable individual and the infallible, authoritative community of which she or he is a part.

None of these criticisms are intended to underestimate the significance of *Wir erinnern* as a timely progression from *Nostra Aetate*. Displayed in this reflection is a genuine horror of antisemitism and in particular of the Holocaust, as well as a sincere recognition that the fraternal bond between Jews and Christians necessitates an act of repentance – *teshuva* – on the part of the Church for the anti-Judaic sins of prejudice committed by some within her ranks.

Nevertheless, the theological and historical stocktaking is not as comprehensive as it should have been. It is clear that the Vatican's Commission for Religious Relations with the Jews has refashioned history according to the ecclesiastical abstraction of institutional inerrancy. Individuals – the 'sons and daughters of the Church', to use the authors' phraseology – are left to shoulder corporate blame in a way that, although consistent with the motif of magisterial infallibility, makes little sense of the historical realities. To borrow from Emil Fackenheim, the strength of *Wir erinnern* is that it recognizes how essential the task of *Tikkun Olam* is in the wake of the Holocaust. Its weakness is that it does not acknowledge the necessity of *Tikkun* for the Church. There is no real mending of the Church that has taken place because, by virtue of the continuing influence of the doctrine of the *magisterium*, there has as yet been no acceptance of any real rupture in the 'Church as such'.

So where to from here? If the reconciliatory intent of *Wir erinnern* is compromised because of a dogma that, according to Pesch, is inconceivable even to 'countless Catholic[s]'[32], what does that signify for the future of Jewish–Christian reconciliation? The answer possibly lies in a critical rethinking of two foundational elements; the doctrine of the *magisterium* itself, and the revelational premise upon which it is grounded. Can the boundaries of these two issues be redrawn so as to enable the Church to confess institutional guilt without thereby surrendering the integrity of her own internal criteria of assessment? That is what the final part of this paper will explore.

I V

Insofar as the *magisterium* itself is concerned, there is a fundamental problem to be overcome at the outset that is at once public and official. At the public level, the majority of Catholics no longer believe the question of papal or ecclesiastical infallibility to be relevant (if it is a legitimate claim at all!). As an issue it has been sidestepped because of the unwillingness of the laity to submit to the 'maximalist ideologists' who hold office in Rome and who insist on the right to determine the consciousness of the Church's members. Their use of power is, so the argument runs, illegitimate and thus the best way to counter this absolutist use of the *magisterium* is simply to ignore its validity. As for the official side of the debate, it is even simpler – there is none. Disputation over the legitimacy of magisterial infallibility is 'still not allowed by Rome'.[33] So on the one hand, there is an ever growing number of Catholic Christians who refuse to deal with the relevance of the dogma because, for them, it has ceased – or at least, its absolutist usage has ceased – to have any relevance in the modern world. And on the other hand, the official voice of the Church refuses to deal with the issue because to allow debate is to implicitly allow for the possibility that the dogma, or the manner of its employment, is wrong.

There is, of course, also the further question of just how far one can accept the claim to inerrancy when clearly – as Küng and many others have shown – the teaching office of the Catholic Church has made glaring errors in the past. Küng notes as classic examples of past errors the excommunication of Photius, the condemnation of Galileo and the proclamation of the encyclical *Humanae Generis*. Indeed, Küng goes so far as to say that the mistakes made by the Church's *magisterium* have been in every century 'numerous and grave'. And yet, for fear of the consequences an admission of error may have on the claim to infallibility, the Church has nonetheless 'found it difficult frankly and honestly to admit' these mistakes.[34] Surely in addition to the index of magisterial errors must now be added the sin of antisemitism – and yet equally surely, *Wir erinnern* substantiates Küng's belief in the Church's inability to admit institutional error.

But in spite of, or perhaps even because of, these seemingly insurmountable difficulties, the work of Küng and Houtepen[35] among others has put the matter squarely back on the table. It is, in the words of the new edition of Küng's book, an *unresolved* enquiry. And indeed it should be. Irrespective of the internal consistency of the *magisterium* as dogma, the Holocaust begs the question as to whether this aspect of Catholic ecclesiology needs reworking. In the wake of the Holocaust – which, according to Littell, Pawlikowski, Rubenstein and Wiesel was as much a theological as an historical event – doctrinal assumptions are up for grabs. The Curia's stifling of the debate is no longer tenable. Küng has shown that the issue is open to question. And *Wir erinnern* has demonstrated (negatively) that, in contrast to the mass of Catholic Christians who have marginalized the issue because of its seeming irrelevance, the *magisterium* is highly relevant to contemporary questions of reconciliation and global *Tikkun*. And thus we arrive at the crucial question: how can the *magisterium* be reformulated so as to retain its integrity and yet also enable historically accurate confession that, as such, allows the Church herself to be the subject of the censure (and, then, healing)?

Any critical revision of the *magisterium* must come to grips with its foundational premise, the role of divine revelation in constructing the Church's infallible decrees. So what, then, is the nature of this revelation upon which immutable and unerring statements can be based? It is important to note at this juncture that Catholic and Protestant definitions differ significantly from one another. Within the Protestant tradition, the revelation of God has been grouped under the broad headings of presence/ encounter (e.g. Emil Brunner's 'truth as encounter'); experience (e.g. Rudolf Bultmann's adoption of Heidegger's *Dasein* motif, and Paul Tillich's 'courage to be'[36]); and history (e.g. Wolfhart Pannenberg's public-universal 'act of God' theme[37]). Perhaps, however, the most comprehensive and influential definition in recent theological history is that which has come down to us from Karl Barth who, in a very brief condensation of his overall doctrine, explains revelation to be 'the self-unveiling ... of the God who by nature cannot be unveiled to men (*sic*) ... He makes himself present, known and significant to them as God.'[38] And of course for Barth, the most exact locus of this revelation event – the 'primary form' and 'whence of God's Word'[39] – is the incarnation of Jesus.

But what of the Catholic view of revelation? Alistair McGrath has suggested that the most properly Catholic conception of revelation comes under the rubric of 'doctrine', where doctrine denotes 'the accumulated insights of the church over the years...' and which thus can be reduced primarily to propositional logic.[40] But there is much more to it than that. Closely allied to the Protestant idea of revelation as history is the old Thomistic concept of 'natural theology', fixed as dogma by the First Vatican Council in 1870 and according to which valid revelation is mediated through such things as the created world and history. Barth remarks that according to this way in which Roman Catholicism 'ascertains its way of knowledge... it can recognize itself and God's revelation in [a] constantly available relationship between God and man...'.[41] Revelation is not, therefore, (only) transcendentally above humanity but is also present in creaturely form and is thus available in at least one of its forms to humanity without the need for special divine intervention. There have been long and vitriolic debates within professional theology about the extent to which this 'constantly available relationship' sanctions a legitimate perception of revelation in history. These arguments do not need to be reconsidered here. However it can be said that, regardless of the accuracy or otherwise of the Catholic view of revelation, it is surely not inconsistent to suggest that, according to this paradigm, certain revelational truths can be seen within the historical domain. And so why not the Holocaust? Is it in fact possible that the *Shoah* exists within theological discourse, not only because of the credibility crisis it poses to Christianity[42], but much more so because it does indeed reveal certain – perhaps negative? – religious truths about both the Church and her God? The Holocaust would thus become a crucial ingredient to any post-modern, post-Auschwitz natural theology. As Dietrich Ritschl puts it, it is no longer possible to do theology after Auschwitz 'to the exclusion of this fundamental wound'.[43]

There is, of course, a difficulty in this proposition, in that the Second Vatican Council explicitly ruled out any new revelation after 'the glorious manifestation' of Jesus.[44] It is however possible to counter the first part of this problem by asking what is meant by 'new'? Does the Holocaust, if it *is* revelational, supply original material or does it substantiate what is already evident from Scripture? Subsequent questions to be asked here would bear on such issues as the character of God, *theopaschitism*, the nature of covenant theology and the relationship between the two faith communities of Israel and Church. These are issues which are indeed revelational in their content and character and which are equally certainly problematized insofar as their orthodox definitions are concerned, by the Holocaust. But does this problematization contradict the witness of Scripture or rather the interpretation with which Scripture has been loaded? If it is the latter, then the Holocaust can thus be regarded as issuing supportive revelational validity to what the Church's teaching office should have been proclaiming but which traditionally has not. More will be said on this later, when we consider the notion of 'rediscovery'.

The second part of the difficulty with the proposition of the Holocaust as revelational is the prohibition of further divine truths being added to the 'deposit of faith'. But this criticism falls on somewhat unsympathetic ears to those – especially Protestants – who believe that the Catholic Church is clearly willing to make dogmatic additions when she so desires, exemplified perhaps in Marian theology and especially in the dogmatizing of the immaculate conception.[45] In other words, if Marianism is an allowable addition to necessary faith, why not the Holocaust?

We are faced, then, with the prospect of transforming the Holocaust from 'mere' history into something that has revelational import in the construction of theological discourse (although without, of course, surrendering the historical actuality of the *Shoah-*event). How can this be done? Dietrich Ritschl has offered a novel way in which this transformation might occur, with explicit reference to a redefinition of revelation. Revelation 'in the traditional sense', he says, 'should be avoided in theology ... [because] it is a construct produced from a complicated combination of concepts which have become autonomous and which can only be used responsibly and without risk of serious misunderstandings in connection with detailed explanations.'[46] Instead, Ritschl prefers the employment of the concept of 'rediscovery' as a way of explaining revelation. It is only rarely that the words of Scripture – that is, the written word of revelation – make a direct impact upon the believer that then translates into action. More commonly, he argues, there is a 'rediscovery' or verification of scriptural truth through a 'process of inductive knowledge by which a present problem area or task is connected with elements latent in the memory of the church.'[47] For example, war, dispute and reconciliation can be the rediscovery – in either a positive or negative sense – of the prodigal son story. Likewise, hatred, envy and greed can lead, negatively, to a rediscovery of a central message of the Hebrew Scriptures, simply because of their contrasting natures. Such rediscoveries, embedded as they are within the concreteness of practical life, Ritschl terms the 'occasions of revelation'.[48] It seems evident that the Holocaust could easily, by this paradigm, be seen as an occasion of revelation, because it verifies in a negative sense many of the (revelational) truths within the Scriptures, such as covenant theology and philadelphic praxis.

Again, the main point at issue is not whether in fact one must agree with the at least partial legitimizing of natural theology that is thus suggested. What is more important is to stress that this proposed transformation is not self-evidently excluded from a Catholic understanding of revelation but may in fact fit easily into it. If it does so fit, then it becomes logically consistent to utilize the 'revelationalized' Holocaust as a norm by which magisterial statements can be critiqued.

And so we return to *Wir erinnern*. We began our discussion by suggesting that the basic moral-epistemological flaw in the document was the unwillingness of the Commission for Religious Relations with the Jews – speaking on behalf of the Catholic Church, or at least the Curia – to acknowledge institutional guilt for involvement, both passive and active, in the Holocaust and its antisemitic prelude. This unwillingness was predicated upon a reluctance to violate the principle of magisterial inerrancy by confessing that in its history of public pronouncements on the Jews, the Church has largely been wrong. It was further seen that this doctrine of the *magisterium*, upon which the whole document is therefore built, is itself predicated upon the belief in the Church being the accurate receptor and transmitter of divine revelation – not only is the revelational message which she receives by definition infallible, but she must also be an infallible proclaimer of that message to the world. With all this as the theological underpinnings of *Wir erinnern*, it has become clear why the authors cannot logically seek forgiveness on the Church's behalf, but can only devolve blame for antisemitic actions and attitudes onto individual Church members. The document therefore reads as a theologically and ecclesiologically consistent argument, but one which makes a nonsense of the historical record of Church teaching about the Jews, both before and during the Nazi era. The question is thus, how can the Church make accurate confession without surrendering her internal criteria of being and assessment?

One way around this impasse has been to suggest that the definitions of the *magisterium*, and the revelation-concept upon which it is built, be redrawn so as to include the Holocaust itself in the language of theology and revelation. It has been shown that this can be done by referring to Thomas' paradigm of natural theology which seems clearly to allow for historical events to be media of revelational truth. If the Holocaust is transformed into one such medium, it is thereby enabled to offer a critique of magisterial teaching – in this case concerning the Jews and the Church's relationship to them – but crucially, as a revelational event itself, can do so without the internal dynamics of the *magisterium* being upset. Institutional confession could therefore be made, on the basis of revelation, without disturbing the validity of the teaching office. Indeed, it could easily be argued that, were the teaching office to critique itself and subsequently make a genuine confession of guilt, the whole notion of the *magisterium* would regain much of the credibility that, even amongst Catholics, has been lost.

In essence, therefore, the perception of the Holocaust as a vehicle of revelational truth – albeit truth of a very uncomfortable nature – would rupture the Church's self-understanding. But in fact the Church has already been decisively ruptured by the Holocaust – she simply needs to acknowledge it. *Tikkun* can only come when the need for healing has been recognized. By being prepared to use the Holocaust as the means of radical self-critique, the Church would be ideally placed to exhibit true integrity – to herself and her mistakes, to the victims of her mistakes and, most importantly, to her own intrinsic task of *Tikkun Olam*.

NOTES

1 The author would like to acknowledge the generous financial assistance provided by the Tabitha Trust and the Uniting Church of Australia (Western Australian Synod), to enable the author to attend the Remembering for the Future 2000 conference.

2 Commission for Religious Relations with the Jews, *Wir erinnern: Eine Reflexion über die Shoah*.

3 D. Novak. 'Jews and Catholics: Beyond Apologetics', *First Things*, No.89 (January 1999), pp.20–25.

4 *Wir erinnern*, p.2.

5 *Ibid*, p.2.

6 See also F.H. Littell, *The Crucifixion of the Jews: The Failure of Christians to Understand the Jewish Experience*, (Mercer University Press), 1986, p.2.

7 H. Küng, *Unfehlbar? Eine Anfrage* (Zurich: Benziger Verlag, 1970). ET *Infallible? An Enquiry*, trans. E. Mossbacher (London: Collins, 1971), pp.182–183.

8 Y. Congar, *L'Eglise de Saint Augustin à l'époque moderne*, Paris, 1970, p.446, in *ibid*., p.182.

9 L. Berkhof, *The History of Christian Doctrines* (Grand Rapids: Baker Book House, 1975, repr. 1996), p.235. At this point it should be said that the *ecclesia audiens* – the hearing or believing Church – is only secondarily and derivatively the Church.

10 O.H. Pesch, 'The Infallibility of the Papal Magisterium', K-J Kuschel & H. Häring (eds), *Hans Küng: New Directions for Faith and Thought* (New York: Continuum, 1993), pp.21–23.

11 Küng, *Infallible?*, p.23.

12 Pesch, 'The Infallibility of the Papal Magisterium', p.26.

13 Küng, *Infallible?*, p.10. Also p.16.

14 Pesch, 'The Infallibility of the Papal Magisterium', p.23.

15 Novak, 'Jews and Catholics', p.22.

16 *Wir erinnern*, p.2.

17 *Ansprache beim Sympsion über die Wurzeln des Anti-Judaismus*, 31 October 1997, 1: *L'Osservatore Romano*, 1 November 1997, p.6 in *ibid*, p.2–3.

18 *Nostre aetate*, 4.

19 R.R. Ruether, *Faith and Fratricide: The Theological Roots of Antisemitism* (New York: Seabury Press), 1974, pp.123, 128–129, 147; P. Lapide, *The Last Three Popes and the Jews* (London: Souvenir Press,

1967), p.25. See also Cyprian, *The Three Books of Testimonies Against the Jews*; Isidore of Seville, *Contra Judaeos*; Augustine, *Tractatus Adversos Judaeos*.

20 Lapide, *The Last Three Popes*, p.47.

21 This decree expressly prohibited the severe persecution of Jews (*non sunt a fidelibus graviter opprimendi*), but thus implicitly allowed *normal* persecution. The curse of Cain, under which the Jews were to live was, for Innocent, sufficient cause to declare that they 'are under no circumstances to be protected by Christian princes, but on the contrary [are] to be condemned to serfdom.' *ibid.*, pp.48–49.

22 See Vatican II, Consitution on the Church, no.25.2. *The Documents of Vatican II*, ed. W.M. Abbott, S.J. (London: Geoffrey Chapman, 1966), p.48.

23 *Wir erinnern*, pp.3–4.

24 *ibid.*, p.3.

25 *AB Munich*, 15 Novermber 1933, suppl., cited in D.J. Goldhagen, *Hitler's Willing Executioners: Ordinary Germans and the Holocaust* (London: Little, Brown & Co., 1996), p.109.

26 *Kirchliche Akten über die Reichskonkordatsverhandlung, 1933* (Mainz, 1969), p.11, in E.C. Helmreich, *The German Churches Under Hitler* (Detroit: Wayne State University Press, 1974), p.276.

27 Goldhagen, *Hitler's Willing Executioners*, p.454.

28 K. Scholder, 'Ein Requiem für Hitler: Kardinal Bertram und der deutsche Episkopat im Dritten Reich', *Frankfurter Allgemeine Zeitung*, 25 October 1980, in *ibid.*, p.597, n.86.

29 G. Lewy, *The Catholic Church and Nazi Germany* (London: Weidenfeld & Nicolson), 1964, p.162.

30 'Rasse', in C. Gröber (ed.), *Handbuch der religiösen Gegenwartsfragen* (Freiburg, 1937), pp.536–537, in *ibid.*, p.163.

31 *Wir erinnern*, pp.4–5.

32 Pesch, 'The Infallibility of the Papal Magisterium', p.21. Küng puts it in the following way: 'To non-Christians and Christians outside the Catholic Church the attribution of "infallibility" to the Church's teaching office has always been unacceptable. Recently, however, it has to an astonishing extent become at least dubious *within the Catholic Church itself* [italics mine]. Küng, *Infallible?*, p.27.

33 Pesch, 'The Infallibility of the Papal Magisterium', p.16.

34 Küng, *Infallible?*, pp.27–28.

35 A. Houtepen, *Onfeilbaarheid en Hermeneutik. De betekenis van het infallibilitas-concept op Vaticanum* I, Bruges, 1973.

36 P. Tillich, *The Courage to Be* (London: Nisbet & Co., 1952).

37 W. Pannenberg (ed.), *Revelation as History* (New York: Macmillan, 1968).

38 K. Barth, *Church Dogmatics*, 1/1 (Edinburgh: T&T Clark, 1936), p.315.

39 *ibid.*, p.290.

40 A. McGrath, *Christian Theology: An Introduction* (Oxford: Blackwell, 1994), p.154.

41 Barth, *CD* I/1, pp.40–41.

42 See for example, Littell, *The Crucifixion of the Jews*; R. Rubenstein, 'Some Perspectives on Religious Faith after Auschwitz', in F.H. Littell & H.G. Locke (eds), *The German Church Struggle and the Holocaust* (Detroit: Wayne State University Press, 1974), p.262; J.S. Conway, 'Christianity and Resistance: The Role of the Churches in the German Resistance Movement', unpublished, 1995, p.2.

43 D. Ritschl, *The Logic of Theology* (London: SCM Press, 1986), p.128.

44 *The Documents of Vatican II*, p.113.

45 H. Cunliffe-Jones (ed.), *A History of Christian Doctrine* (Philadelphia: Fortress Press, 1980), p.513.

46 Ritschl, *The Logic of Theology*, p.103.

47 *ibid.*, p.76.

48 *ibid.*

A SURVEY OF JEWISH REACTION TO THE VATICAN STATEMENT ON THE HOLOCAUST

Kevin Madigan

I N MARCH 1998, the Vatican released a long-awaited statement on the Catholic Church and the Holocaust. In a preface to the document, entitled *We Remember: A Reflection on the Shoah*, Pope John Paul II expressed his hope that it would 'help to heal the wounds of past misunderstandings and injustices'.[1] Eighteen months after the publication of the document, it seems now possible to conclude that, however sincere the Vatican's intentions, the pope's hopes will almost certainly not be realized. Indeed, far from healing, the document has succeeded largely in re-opening, if not actually deepening, old wounds. Not only did it divide the Catholic intellectual and journalistic communities.[2] More importantly, I think, it bewildered and frustrated many Jewish readers and bitterly disappointed others. It also called forth a literary response from Jewish intellectuals and organizations that, while especially vigorous in the immediate wake of the document's publication, had force and feeling to last more than a year. Since the energy driving these responses appears to have subsided,[3] it seems possible now to undertake a comprehensive survey of Jewish reaction to *We Remember* and to attempt to account for its intensity and duration.

THE FRENCH BISHOPS' STATEMENT

One way of interpreting the Vatican document and of isolating what was distinctive and disappointing to so many about it is by comparing it to prior ecclesiastical statements on the Holocaust and the Church. Probably none of the many documents issued by the various national episcopal conferences of the Church allows us to appreciate by contrast the reaction to the Vatican document than the one issued in October of 1997 by France's Roman Catholic clergy.[4] The impact of this strongly-worded and, it certainly seemed to both Catholic and Jewish auditors, strongly-felt apology was magnified both by the place and time at which it was given, as well as by the identity of those present at the declaration.

The place was the grounds of Drancy, memorialized in a plaque there that calls it 'the antechamber of death'. In 1942 it began serving as the transit camp from which many of the 76,000 Jews who would ultimately be deported from France boarded cattle cars destined for Auschwitz. Among the 1000 Jews and Christians present at Drancy for the French Declaration of Repentance was Jean-Marie Lustiger. Lustiger is now a Catholic; he is, in fact, the Cardinal-Archbishop of Paris. Sixty years ago, however, he was a young Jewish boy menaced by the pro-Nazi government of France, which separated him from his mother. She, once detained, would pass through Drancy on her way to the gas chambers in Auschwitz.

The timing of the apology was also carefully-planned in several ways. Aside from coinciding with the celebration of the Jewish New Year, its delivery came 57 years after

the passage of Marshall Petain's so-called 'Jewish Laws', which not only banned Jews
from the major professions and discriminated against Jews in a variety of other ways –
indeed, in some ways more harshly than the Nuremberg Laws had against the Jews of
Germany – but also facilitated census-taking by Vichy officials, which in turn made it
easy for police to track down French Jews for detention and deportation.[5] Second, the
apology virtually coincided with the trial of Maurice Papon, a former police supervisor
from Bordeaux charged with signing the orders that led to the deportation of some 1700
Jews, including hundreds of children.[6]

Thus, at the very moment the French government was trying the highest-ranking
Vichy official ever accused of complicity in crimes against humanity, the French bishops
were, in effect, delivering a verdict on self-imposed charges that ecclesiastical docility
(their word) in the face of catastrophe had caused the church not just to be complicit in
these crimes but, in so doing, to have violated divine laws and to have failed in its
divinely-ordained mission.

To these serious charges, the French bishops plead, with sober and quite unambiguous clarity, guilty. In fact, the French episcopal document is – especially for those
accustomed to the genteel circumlocution of many Roman episcopal documents – almost
shockingly direct, self-critical and precise in responding to the question, exactly *who* in
the church was guilty of moral dereliction? Throughout, the guilty parties are identified
as 'priests', 'leaders', 'church officials', 'the hierarchy', and 'the bishops of France'.[7]

If the French bishops were blunt about the identity of the guilty ecclesiastical parties,
they were no less direct on the issue of *how* their predecessors had failed. In their view,
the French bishops generally failed – they say *sinned* (36) – above all by their *silence* (a
word used many times in the document), especially in the immediate wake of the
publication of the anti-Jewish laws. 'Silence', the bishops confess, 'was the rule' and
words 'in favour of the victims the exception' (35). If the bishops' preoccupation with
institutional continuity in a time of insecurity was legitimate in itself, their 'docility',
'conformity', and 'loyalism' caused them to ignore the biblical imperative to respect
every human creature in the image of God (32). 'Ecclesiastical interests, understood in an
overly restrictive sense', the bishops say, 'took priority over the demands of conscience'
(33). The moral and political consequences of this silence were profound. Their predecessors' silence, the bishops declare, made them 'acquiescent' in 'flagrant violations of
human rights' and left an open field for the spiral of death (33). Their predecessors failed
to recognize that they had 'considerable power and influence' (32) when the anti-Jewish
laws were promulgated. Although there were 'countless acts of courage later on', they
should, they admit, have offered help immediately, when protest and protection were
possible and necessary (32). Among other things, the impact of a public statement from
them would have been amplified not only by their moral position in French society but
'the silence of other institutions' (32). Indeed, the impact of a public statement, the
bishops conclude, might have forestalled an irreparable catastrophe.

It is important to observe here by way of brief anticipation that this is precisely the
kind of self-inculpatory statement the Vatican document did not make. Some Jewish
commentators, including Robert Wistrich and Roger Cohen, observed that this move is
even more remarkable when it is remembered that several French bishops, including
Archbishop Jean-Geraud Saliège of Toulouse (who declared in August 1942, 'the Jews
are our brothers . . . and no Christian can forget this fact'), Cardinal Gerlier of Lyon and
Bishop Pierre-Marie Théas of Montauban, spoke out strongly against the Vichy regime
in the wake of the roundup of Jews by the French police in July 1942.[8] Their stand,
Cohen observed, stimulated French resistance activity and contributed to the survival of

three-quarters of France's Jewish population, many of whom were sheltered by French Catholics. In general, Wistrich has observed, the record of the French episcopate is, while far from unimpeachable, favourably compared to that of the German bishops.

News of the declaration led television newscasts and made the front page of many French newspapers. If Jean-Marie Le Pen, leader of France's rightist National Front Party, was heard to comment (not unpredictably) that the statement was 'absolutely scandalous', and if Bishop Jean-Charles Thomas of Versailles, who was present at the ceremony, complained that 'Old sensibilities [were] going to be severely ruffled',[9] Jewish reaction to this document was, in a word, overwhelmingly positive. Cohen, for example, called the French episcopal declaration 'an expression of remorse more complete, more uncompromising and anguished than anything previously pronounced by the church.'[10] 'Your words of repentance constitute a major turning point', said Henri Hajdenberg, president of the Representative Council of Jewish Institutions, who was present at the declaration. 'Your request for forgiveness is so intense, so powerful, so poignant, that it can't but be heard by the surviving victims and their children.'[11] However, other Jewish observers present at Drancy, like Serge Klarsfeld, president of the Sons and Daughters of Deported French Jews, perceptively observed that so candid and heartfelt a statement of repentance would 'put pressure on the Vatican' to make 'its public declaration on the Holocaust' and to make it good.[12] Six months later, the Vatican did indeed publish its own declaration of repentance, though to far less enthusiastic reviews.

We Remember

The document begins, uncontroversially enough, by describing the Nazi genocide as 'an unspeakable tragedy' (48) one which the church is urged never to forget. The church is especially urged to remember it 'by reason of her very close bonds of spiritual kinship with the Jewish people' (48) and also because of 'her remembrance of the injustices of the past' (48). The document also acknowledges right at the start that the Shoah took place in 'countries of long-standing Christian civilization' (49) and so immediately raises the question of the relation between the Holocaust and Christian attitudes to Jews over the centuries. The tormented relations of Jews and Christians through the ages the document ascribes to 'erroneous and unjust interpretations of the New Testament in the Christian world' (49). It then hastens to distinguish these interpretations from those held by 'the Church as such' (49) and observes that these interpretations 'have been totally and definitively rejected by the Second Vatican Council' (49).

The document also distinguishes, with a sharpness Jewish commentators almost unanimously found objectionable, between the anti-Judaism of which many Christians have historically been guilty and modern anti-Semitism. The latter, it argues, is a 19th-century development more sociological and political than religious in origin. Indeed, it owes its genesis in part to 'a false and exacerbated nationalism' (50) and to theories which 'denied the unity of the human race' (50), theories used in Nazi Germany for a distinction between the so-called Nordic-Aryan races and other, supposedly inferior ones. Nazi antisemitism, refusing to acknowledge as it did any transcendent reality as the source of life and the criterion of moral good, was 'the work of a thoroughly modern neo-pagan regime. *Its anti-semitism had its roots outside of Christianity*' (50; emphasis mine), the document proclaimed. Indeed, in pursuing its aims, it did not hesitate to oppose the church and persecute her members also.

Nonetheless, the document does ask if the Nazi persecution wasn't 'made easier by the anti-Jewish prejudices imbedded in some Christian minds and hearts' (52), rendering Christians 'less sensitive, or even indifferent' (52) to persecutions launched by the Nazis.

'Did Christians give every possible assistance to those being persecuted, and in particular to the persecuted Jews?' (52) To the bewilderment of some, the document states that 'many people' were 'altogether unaware of the "final solution"' (52) – a statement whose inclusion in the document can now be questioned on historical as well as diplomatic grounds. Still, it goes on, if 'many' individuals gave every possible assistance even to the point of placing their own lives in danger, the behaviour of the rest 'was not that which might have been expected from Christ's followers' (53). Passing from the individual to the collective level, the document is particularly critical of 'the governments of some Western countries of Christian tradition' (52) who hesitated to open their borders to persecuted Jews, though the 'leaders of those nations were aware of the hardships and dangers to which Jews living in the Greater Reich were exposed' (52). The church therefore deeply regrets 'the errors and failures of those sons and daughters of the church' (53). This, the document says, is to be understood as an act of *teshuvah* (54).

At the same time, the document insists that those individuals and institutions who heroically resisted Nazism must not be forgotten. In one sentence that actually has not elicited much comment, the document observed of the German church's response to Nazism, that 'it replied by condemning racism' (50) – surely one of the cruder and even erroneous statements the document makes. And it singles out Cardinals Bertram of Breslau and Cardinal Faulhaber of Munich as well as other regional episcopal conferences for criticism of Nazi anti-semitic propaganda and celebrates Bernard Lichtenberg's public prayer for Jews in the wake of *Kristallnacht*. Similarly, it acknowledges Pius XI's encyclical *Mit brennender Sorge*,[13] read in German churches in 1937 and quotes his famous assertion, delivered to Belgian pilgrims in September 1938, 'Spiritually we are all Semites' (50–51).

Much more controversially, it also celebrated Pius XII not only for warning, in his very first encyclical (*Summi Pontificatus*),[14] against theories which 'denied the unity of the human race and the deification of the State' but for 'all that he had done' either personally or through representatives to save hundreds of thousands of Jewish lives.' (53). Then, in a footnote, roughly ten times longer than the next longest footnote, *We Remember* documents the praise by Jewish leaders given to 'the wisdom of Pius XII's diplomacy', quoting, among others, Golda Meir (55–56, note 16).[15]

POSITIVE JEWISH REACTION

A number of Jewish commentators, even those who were critical of certain elements of the document, nonetheless praised it as a whole and for its good intentions. Wistrich spoke for many in observing that 'whatever one's final judgment' on the document, 'one cannot but commend both its tone and its basic aims.'[16] Similarly, Michael Berenbaum of the Survivors of the Shoah Visual History Foundation remarked: 'Jews didn't get everything they wanted, but what they got was so significant,'[17] and Yehuda Bauer, head of the Holocaust Research Institute at Yad Vashem and professor of Holocaust studies at Hebrew University concluded: 'The document has to be evaluated positively.'[18] Contradicting the sentiments of many Jewish commentators, who called the Vatican document a step backward,[19] Dr. Jonathan Sacks, the Chief Rabbi of Britain, celebrated *We Remember* as 'a step forward.'[20] These sentiments were echoed in substance by France's Grand Rabbi Joseph Sitruk, who observed that his disappointment was blunted by his excellent rapport with the bishops of France and their courageous statement[21] – precisely what had caused feelings in others that expectations had been so hopefully raised, only to be disappointed.

More specifically, some Jewish groups, like the American Jewish Committee and the Tanenbaum Center for Interreligious Understanding hailed the Vatican document, one hopes not too optimistically, for rendering impossible the obscenity of Holocaust denial among Catholics in the next century. Rabbi A. James Rudin, who is interreligious affairs director of the American Jewish Committee and a member of the International Jewish Committee on Interreligious Consultations, remarked that, '50, 75, 100 years from now, there can never be any doubt that the Holocaust took place, because here is a definitive statement from the Catholic Church by a pope from Poland.'[22] Finally, David Gordis, President of Hebrew College, argued that 'the statement must not be read in isolation but in the context of an extraordinary and epochal change in the Catholic Church's teaching and behaviour... if read in the context of history, the document 'represents both a true act of Xn repentance and an act of *teshuvah*', sentiments echoed by Rabbi David Rosen, director of the Anti-Defamation League in Israel, who read the document as a step in a continuing process of ecclesiastical self-criticism and repentance.[23]

CRITICAL JEWISH REACTION

Despite these expressions of generalized approval, Jewish reaction to this document was largely negative. Lord Janner, of Britain's Holocaust Educational Trust, confessed that he was 'deeply disappointed' and denounced *We Remember* as an 'unworthy document.'[24] Ignatz Bubis, Chairman of Germany's Central Council of Jews, likewise condemned the document as 'completely unsatisfactory.'[25] Many Jewish commentators expressed frustration that the document as a whole was so nebulous, so equivocal, so partial and so euphemistically formulated that it amounted to a lower-order sort of denial. Robert Rifkind, President of the American Jewish Committee, commented: 'It only begins to address many issues and questions concerning the role of the Catholic Church in the evolution of antisemitism throughout the ages and its culmination in the Holocaust.'[26] Phil Baum, Executive Director of the American Jewish Congress likewise observed: 'Without derogating from the Church's efforts at atonement, some of the most troubling questions of responsibility and complicity in those horrendous events still have not been addressed.[27] And Israel's Chief Rabbi, Israel Lau, said, 'We expected a more specific apology,' one that was less equivocal about 'the silence of the Christian world and those who headed it during the Holocaust.'[28]

As these comments suggest, the problem here really is the diplomatic and legalistic character of the document. Indeed, one of the main reasons this document touched such a nerve is undoubtedly that many Jews sensed, as Holocaust survivor Pierre Sauvage tells us he did, in its feebleness and vagueness an expression of diplomatic hesitation, equivocation and timidity all too painfully redolent of papal attitudes toward Nazi policy during the war.[29] As Efraim Zuroff, director of the Israel office of the Simon Wiesenthal Center, has bluntly put it, 'the statement still lacks the guts that would make it satisfactory.'[30] Some commentators felt particularly and painfully surprised by these features of the document, ironically in part because of the perceived excellence of John Paul II's record on Jewish–Christian relations. Abraham H. Foxman, national director of the Anti-Defamation League and a Holocaust survivor, for example, observed, 'We expected more from this pontiff, who has been so courageous in reconciling the church with the Jewish people.'[31] Other commentators noted that expectations had been heightened by the French Catholic Bishops' document. Elan Steinberg, executive director of the World Jewish Congress argued, that *We Remember* compared unfavourably both with it and with the apology issued by the German Bishops' Conference.[32]

In terms of specific criticisms, virtually all Jewish commentators faulted the document for failing to acknowledge the deep connection between ecclesiastically-sponsored anti-Judaism and the anti-semitism that achieved such disastrous expression in the Shoah.

Foxman, for example, observed that 'Two thousand years of teaching contempt of Jews by the church was part of the underpinning of the Holocaust ... The people who killed Jews during the day then went to church on Sunday ... They were not aberrations. They were part and parcel of what Western civilization was.'[33] Bauer noted that, despite the examples of Catholic heroism, 'it is still true that the vast majority of individual priests and Catholic faithful were completely indifferent, or downright hostile to Jews' and that this indifference is traceable to the 2000-year tradition of contempt for the Jews.[34] Zuroff added that doctrinal antisemitism 'enabled Catholics' not simply to be passive or indifferent but to *participate* in the Holocaust, not only in Germany, but 'more especially in places like Lithuania and Croatia,' where the Nazis almost effortlessly found enthusiastic collaboration.[35] In short, Nazi ideology, policy and genocide all presupposed a cultural framework that had been fashioned, as Wistrich has summarized the matter, 'by centuries of medieval Christian theology, ecclesiastical policy and popular religious myth.'[36]

However, it was over *We Remember's* flawed representation of the ever-heroic and compassionate behaviour of the hierarchy that Jewish commentators generally expressed their profoundest frustration. While most Jewish commentators focused on the picture of Pius XII, a few, though very few, found unconvincing and even offensive the portrayal of the German bishops the document lionized for their heroism. If the document was surely right to honour the memory of Bernard Lichtenberg, they thought, for speaking out from his pulpit against anti-Jewish atrocity – that eventually sealed his fate, and he perished in a train en route to Dachau – it again attempted, so to speak, to fudge the facts by mentioning Cardinals Faulhaber of Munich and Bertram of Breslau in speaking of these two in the same breath as the martyred Provost of Berlin Cathedral. Robert Wistrich talks at some length about the ambiguous legacy of both of these princes of the church, and then, widening his scope to the German episcopate in general, observes that the elevation of these two is anomalously accompanied in the document by 'utter silence about the German church's acquiescence and, at times, complicity in the Shoah.'[37] Unlike their counterparts in France, Belgium, Italy and Holland, Wistrich observes, leaders of the German Catholic Church, 'rather than attempting to guide their flock, tamely chose to follow it.'[38] They accepted the Nuremberg race laws and offered virtually no protest in the wake of *Kristallnacht*. Worse still, the German Catholic Church collaborated with the Nazis in helping to establish who in the Third Reich was of Jewish descent.[39] At best, Wistrich concludes, the German bishops were disastrously naive; at worst, they were complicit in genocide. Either way, they should not have been candidates for glorification in *We Remember*.

Still, the criticism of the Vatican document for its portrayal of the German bishops was rare and then mild compared to the ubiquitously critical response evoked by its image of Pope Pius XII. Virtually no Jewish commentator, even those who responded favourably to *We Remember* as a whole, applauded the document for its representation of Pius, and very, very few spoke favourably of his activities on behalf of menaced Jews during the War. In fact, the responses to these aspects of the document were, for all intents and purposes, uniformly negative. The only complexities and distinctions came in the degree of criticism, ranging from the view that, in this respect, the document was soft, defensive or partial to the view that it was mendacious and insulting to readers, to historical memory and to the victims.

Typical of this latter view was the opinion of Meir Lau, who commented of the pope that, 'His silence cost millions of human lives.'[40] Zuroff described *We Remember* as 'a total cop-out' on the role of Pope Pius XII and also adds he 'could have saved millions.'[41]

B'nai Brith International President Tommy Baer remarked that the document, 'sadly attempts to varnish the controversial wartime conduct of Pope Pius XII.'[42] If the American Jewish Congress does not go that far, it certainly was not alone in finding the portrait of Pius as a tireless and heroic labourer on behalf of menaced Jews wildly exaggerated and even false. So far from being tireless, it observed, he was virtually passive. As Phil Baum put it, 'The historical record does not allow us to disregard the harsh fact of the refusal of important church leaders to take even those minimal steps of compassion and rescue that were clearly within their power to provide.'[43] As for the claim that Pius XII saved hundreds of thousands of Jewish lives, many called for at least some documentary evidence to support that claim.[44] Robert Wistrich was certainly not alone in observing that, while we may never know exactly how many Jewish lives he was responsible for saving, 'the number is almost certainly far smaller than that implied by the Vatican.'[45]

If few Jewish commentators portrayed Pius either as criminally complicit with the Nazis or altogether passive in the face of atrocity, and fewer still as courageously heroic and active, many faulted him for extreme and naive caution and timidity. While acknowledging that Pius's Christmas message of 1942 does, in general terms, deplore the condemnation to death of hundreds of thousands solely because of their nation or race, Wistrich, for one, has noticed that this was the protest that lasted 'for the duration of a breath and mentioned neither Jews, nor Nazis nor any Nazi ally.'[46] Given the obvious ambiguity of this record, Wistrich observes, it is odd that not only the Vatican but many Catholics have felt the need to defend him at all costs. After all, he notices (though not quite accurately), 'no one is blaming the wartime Pope or the Catholic Church for the destruction of European Jewry, or even suggesting that Pius XII could have done much to stop the slaughter. Nor can one reasonably object to his quiet diplomacy where it did actually save the lives of Jews and other victims of the Nazis.' But what *is* undeniable, he argues, is the 'paucity of moral courage displayed by the Vatican when it came to the fate of the Jews.'[47] Many Jewish commentators have deplored Pius' prudence and discretion. It was not a time, they agreed, for diplomats but for prophets.[48]

One commentator, Susannah Heschel, in an article published in *Dissent*,[49] has argued that the Vatican Statement failed to come to grips with 'the most damning piece of evidence' regarding the Vatican: namely how it, or at least some of its priests, behaved at the *end* of the war. 'Pius XII might have been intimidated before the spring of 1945, but why did he remain silent after Hitler's defeat?' The 'most incriminating insight' into the Vatican's real attitudes is its effort to secure safe passage out of Europe for former SS officers being hunted by the Allies. 'No less a figure than Franz Stangl,' former commandant at Treblinka, wanted for the murder of 600,000 people, was, Heschel points out, 'spirited to South America by an underground railroad of Catholic priests, under the guidance of the Vatican's own bishop, Alois Hudal.' The 'intriguing question is what might have motivated the Vatican to assist those murderers... Could it be that the Vatican felt closer ties to the Nazis than the Jews? Which lives did the Church really want to save?'[50]

Other commentators deplored the document's decision to point out that Nazi hostility was expressed toward Christianity as well as Judaism. Some saw it as a Catholic attempt to appropriate the Holocaust, a literary analogue to installing crosses outside of Auschwitz. Again, some perceived in this a subtle form of denial, for it cannot be forgotten that, if thousands of Catholics died in the Holocaust, the Shoah was overwhelmingly a Jewish, not a Christian, catastrophe.

Finally virtually all Jewish commentators called on the Vatican to open its archives to historians.[51] Baer declared, 'We therefore call again on the Vatican to tear down [its] archival wall and let the light of truth in for the world to see,' adding that while not presuming to suggest what the archives may disclose, 'suspicions can only continue to grow about what they may contain.' 'Only when the Vatican archives are opened to historians,' Heschel has said, 'and the record set straight in all honesty, can a genuine Catholic reflection on the Shoah take place.'[52]

DEFENSIVE JEWISH REACTION TO JEWISH CRITICISM

One of the most challenging reactions, both intellectually and morally, comes from the pen of the University of Toronto scholar David Novak. Delivered first as the Swig Judaica lecture at the University of San Francisco and then published in revised form in the periodical *First Things*, this essay is one of the longest and most complicated of all the responses to the Vatican document.[53] 'My own view,' Novak says, 'is that the Jewish response is largely mistaken, and that it reflects a misunderstanding not only of Catholic theology but Jewish theology as well. The Jewish leaders' reactions were not just uncharitable, they were also unjust' (21).

The error of the Jewish response Novak assigns to an imperfect understanding of what the Vatican statement meant when it refused to apologize for the actions or passivity of 'the Church as such.' When Catholics use the term 'the church', he argues, they mean one of two things. First, a human association, a collection of fallible human beings. Second, her *magisterium*, her teaching authority, the expression of God's will (as Catholics see it) in scripture and in developing church doctrine. Putting aside the important question of whether Novak is historically or theologically correct in identifying the church as such with the *magisterium*,[54] understanding the term 'church' at either of these levels allows one, he argues, to 'see why an apology is inappropriate.'

If we understand church in the first sense, as a collection of fallible human beings, Novak remarks, we are still driven to ask, 'Now just *who* would apologize to *whom?*' (21) It is not clear. A Catholic who actually participated in Nazi atrocity could not apologize to someone capable of accepting his apology. Those who were murdered are obviously now in no position 'to absolve anyone' (21). For their part, present-day Jews, who were only potential victims of Nazi atrocity, cannot exonerate a participant in atrocity for what he or she did to someone else. In addition, if an apology was made by people who did not commit any such crimes, and who do not even sympathize with the murderers, then what would they be apologizing for? 'The Jewish tradition on this point is quite clear,' Novak says. 'We do not believe in inherited guilt...Each person is responsible only for his or her own sins. Consequently, 'an apology makes no sense.' It could, Novak says, only be 'empty rhetoric' (21).

If we understand 'the church' as more or less coterminous with its teaching authority or *magisterium*, then it becomes obvious why the church, according to Novak, 'cannot possibly apologize based on her own theological assumptions' (22). For, Novak says, that would presuppose a criterion of truth and right 'higher than the revelation upon which the Church bases its authority' (22). Just as a Jew committed to the Torah as the Word of God 'cannot in good faith criticize anything taught within the Jewish tradition from a standpoint external to that tradition, so the Vatican could not have judged itself by 'someone else's standards' or 'the way an uncommitted outsider might criticize her' (23). One can only look into the tradition itself for sources of a careful and responsible reappraisal and criticism of past teaching and past activity.

Once 'one sees how moral logic within religious traditions like Judaism and Christianity operates, then it is possible to understand why it is not an apology that is called for' (23). It is not an apology that is called for, argues Novak, but instead an act of repentance, or *teshuvah*. To expect an apology rather than *teshuvah* is to 'call for something quite cheap when there is the possibility of something much more precious. Only Jews who are theologically sensitive can appreciate what the Church is trying to do in this statement' (23–4).

This, Novak concludes, is a document which has resonance with Jewish theology and Law. Moreover, because it was a statement that recognized the chosenness and vocation of the Jewish people *qiddush ha-shem*, the sanctification of the Holy Name,' (24) Jews must see this document as making a positive contribution to the relationship between Jews and Christians. 'Its integrity and wisdom should not be missed,' Novak concludes, 'because of the moral and political antagonism stemming from those having less integrity and less wisdom' (25).

CONCLUSION

Despite the reaction of Novak, it remains true that the overwhelming majority of Jewish commentators expressed disappointment, ranging from mild to severe, with the document. Their disappointment had several sources. First, both the perceived excellence of John Paul II's record on Jewish–Catholic relations and the candour and contrition expressed by the various national episcopal documents raised expectations that the Vatican would issue a document which fully came to terms with its conduct during the War. Few Jewish commentators thought it did. Many of them found themselves in agreement with Catholic journalist Peter Steinfels, who remarked that the document read as if crafted by a cadre of lawyers 'whose job it was to protect Catholicism from the theological equivalent of civil suits.'[55] Indeed, it seems to many to be, in the most literal sense of the term, a *jurisprudential* document which constantly forced its genuine expressions of remorse to compete with its less honorable impulse to self-exoneration.

So far as the theological flaws of the document are concerned, many Jewish commentators found the main problem with *We Remember* was its reiterated distinction between 'the church as such' and its sinful members. Cardinal Cassidy, in a reflection given two months after the publication of the document, and addressed to the vigorous and voluminous criticism that had already been published, insisted that the church as such did *not* refer to the hierarchy, and that the sinful sons and daughters of the church could include popes, cardinals, bishops, priests and laity. But it is understandable that almost all Jewish (and many Catholic) readers felt, not only because of the intrinsically hierarchical and filial character of the sons and daughter language used here, but also because the heroes celebrated by name in *We Remember* are, without exception, popes, bishops and priests, that this theological distinction was an attempt to absolve the institutional church of blame, as was the distinction between historic, ecclesiastically-sponsored anti-Judaism and modern, secular anti-semitism.

Finally, the deepest frustrations of many Jewish commentators with the document come on historical grounds. Of course, all recognized that *We Remember* is not a historical analysis of the Shoah. Nonetheless, it did make historical statements, many of them shockingly selective and partial. In their eyes, nothing so undermined the credibility of the document as the selectivity and gross crudity of many of those statements, especially those connected with the behaviour of the German episcopate and, especially, of Pope Pius XII. The historical statements made should either have been accurate and nuanced, many felt, or not included at all. The ones that were made again made it appear as if the church was primarily interested, not in a courageous confrontation with its past, but in prudent self-protection. Even more seriously, they seemed to involve the church in a subtle, lower-order form of denial. Worst of all, many perceived in the diplomatic waffling of the document a parallel to papal attitudes towards the Jews and to Nazi policy in the hour of extreme Jewish agony.

For these reasons, especially, I have to agree with most Jewish commentators that a precious opportunity has been missed. 'After centuries of prejudice and hostility, culminating in the murder of European Jewry,' Robert Wistrich has observed, 'the prospect has tantalizingly appeared of a day when anti-Semitism will no longer hold a place in Christian hearts.' But, he adds: 'the arrival of that day depends not only on repentance and a generalized will to change but, ultimately, on an honest reckoning with the past.'[56] That honest reckoning will eventually come, I hope, not only because of widespread Jewish desire for it, and the influence of the radiant example of the French bishops but also, one hopes, because of the eternal obligatory force of an ancient Jewish text binding on us Catholics too. I am thinking of Exodus 20:16: 'Thou shalt not bear false witness.' To which I might add in concluding, nor partial witness either.

NOTES

1 See *Catholics Remember the Holocaust*, ed. Secretariat for Ecumenical and Interreligious Affairs, National Conference of Catholic Bishops (Washington, D.C.: 1998), pp.47–55. Page numbers for quotations from this document will be cited in parentheses in the text. Except in references, I will abbreviate the document hereafter as *WR*.

2 For critical Catholic reaction, see John T. Pawlikowski, 'The Vatican and the Holocaust: Putting *We Remember* in Context', *Dimensions* 12/2 (1998): 11–16; Garry Wills, 'The Vatican's Dismaying Statement', *Outrider*, 25 March 1998; Michael Phayer, 'Pope Pius XII, the Holocaust and the Cold War', *Holocaust and Genocide Studies* 12/2 (Fall 1998): 223–56. Roughly one year before the publication of *We Remember*, James Carroll published a critical assessment of the Pope's wartime passivity; entitled 'The Silence', it appeared in *The New Yorker*, 7 April 1997. For a moderately critical reaction, see John F. Morley, '*We Remember*: Reaction and Analysis', *Dimensions* 12/2 (1998): 3–10. For defensive Catholic reaction to Catholic criticism, see Kenneth L. Woodward, 'In Defense of Pius XII', *Newsweek*, 30 March 1998; and Joseph Sobran, 'The "Silence" of Pius XII', *Conservative Current*, 19 March 1998.

3 Though one of the most thorough, careful and scholarly responses was published shortly after the writing of this paper was completed. See Randolph L. Braham, 'Remembering and Forgetting: The Vatican, the German Catholic Hierarchy, and the Holocaust', *Holocaust and Genocide Studies* 13/2 (Fall 1999): 222–51.

4 'Declaration of Repentance', in *Catholics Remember the Holocaust*, pp.31–37. Page numbers for quotations from this document will be cited in parentheses in the text. For the French original, see, 'Les évêques de France et le statut des juifs sous le régime de Vichy', *La Documentation Catholique* 2168 (October 19, 1997). Statements by the Hungarian, German, Polish, Dutch, Swiss and Italian bishops are also included in the volume *Catholics Remember the Holocaust*.

5 See Michael R. Marrus and Robert O. Paxton, *Vichy France and the Jews* (New York: Basic Books, 1981).

6 Papon was later elevated to Budget Minister under Valery Giscard d'Estaing. This, naturally, did much to embarrass the Republic's pretenses to being a wholly distinct entity from Vichy, a distinction that had been exploited by both church and state to avoid an honest confrontation with the past. Papon also made international headlines on 20 October 1999 for having fled France rather than serve his 10 year prison sentence. He would soon be discovered hiding in Switzerland.

7 See 'Declaration of Repentance', *passim*.

8 R. Wistrich, 'The Pope, the Church and the Jews', *Commentary* 107/4 (April 1999); R. Cohen, 'French Catholic Church Apologizes for Silence on Holocaust', *New York Times*, 1 October 1997.

9 'French Catholic Church Apologizes', *New York Times*, 1 October 1997.

10 *ibid.*
11 Marilyn August, 'French Bishops Make Unprecedented Apology for World War II Silence', *Associated Press*, 1 October 1997.
12 'French Catholic Church Apologizes', *New York Times*, 1 October 1997.
13 Dated 14 March 1937. See *Acta Apostolicae Sedis* 29 (1937): 145–67.
14 Dated 20 October 1939. See *Acta Apostolicae Sedis* 31 (1939): 413–53.
15 The Vatican was also presumably relying on the testimony of the former Israeli consul Pinchas E. Lapide, who estimated that the Church under Pius was instrumental in saving the lives of 860,000 Jews, or at least in preserving that many from Nazi detainment in the camps. See *Three Popes and the Jews* (New York: Hawthorn Books), p.214.
16 'The Pope, the Church and the Jews', p.24.
17 Thomas O'Dwyer, 'Vatican's Struggle to Save the Church's Soul', *Jerusalem Post*, 23 March 1998.
18 *ibid.*
19 To give just one example: Rabbi Leon Klenicki, director of the Department of Interfaith Affairs of the Anti-Defamation League, commented, 'The document falls short of the mark; it's taking a step backward.' *BBC News*, 16 March 1998.
20 'Vatican Apology to Jews "Rings Hollow",' *The Times*, 17 March 1998.
21 'Leading Rabbi Defends Vatican on Holocaust', *The Irish Times*, 18 March 1998.
22 'World Jewish Group Chastises Vatican's Shoah Stance', *Jewish Telegraphic Agency*, 4 September 1998. This is a point Rudin made in an interview on *The News Hour with Jim Lehrer*, 8 April 1998.
23 Richard Owen, 'Vatican Apology to Jews "Rings Hollow",' *The Times*, 17 March 1998.
24 *BBC News*, 16 March 1998.
25 'Leading Rabbi Defends Vatican on Holocaust', *The Irish Times*, 18 March 1998.
26 W. Drozdiak, 'Vatican Gives Formal Apology for Inaction during Holocaust', *Washington Post*, 17 March 1998.
27 American Jewish Congress Press Release, 16 March 1998.
28 Anton La Guardia, 'Jews Cool on Apology', *The Age*, 18 March 1998.
29 'An Equivocal Apology Hurts More than It Heals', *Los Angeles Times*, 20 March 1998.
30 'Vatican's Struggle', *Jerusalem Post*, 23 March 1998.
31 Diego Ribadeneira, 'Vatican Falls Short of Jewish Hopes', *Boston Globe*, 17 March 1998.
32 *BBC News*, 16 March 1998. This was a point made from the Catholic point of view by Notre Dame theologian Richard McBrien in an interview on *The News Hour with Jim Lehrer*, 8 April 1998: 'the bar has been raised in recent years . . . This document does not' acknowledge 'the guilt of the Church as such.'
33 'Vatican Falls Short', *Boston Globe, 17 March 1998*.
34 'Vatican's Struggle', *Jerusalem Post*, 23 March 1998.
35 *ibid.*
36 The Pope, the Church and the Jews', p.24.
37 'The Pope, the Church and the Jews', p.25. Wistrich observes that Cardinal Bertram of Breslau, ranking prelate in German Catholicism throughout the period of the Third Reich, condemned Nazism in print in 1931, but after Hitler rose to power his objections became 'increasingly timid and inaudible.' Never did Cardinal Bertram speak out (as Lichtenberg had) from the pulpit, and he celebrated a solemn requiem mass for Hitler shortly after his suicide.
38 *ibid.*
39 The supply of genealogical records was crucial to the Nazi genocide and continued through the war years, a fact that has led some historians to place certain ecclesiastical officials in the category of 'perpetrator.'
40 'Vatican Gives Formal Apology', *Washington Post*, 17 March 1998.
41 'Vatican's Struggle', *Jerusalem Post*, 23 March 1998.
42 Rabbi Marvin Hier, head of the Simon Wiesenthal Center in Los Angeles, also remarked: 'To take 10 years to study the critical question of the Vatican's role in the Holocaust and not to criticize Pius XII is in my view incredible.' See 'Vatican Apology "Too Little, Too Late", Jews Say', in *The Salt Lake Tribune*, 17 March 1998.

43 'Vatican Falls Short', *Boston Globe*, 17 March 1998.
44 See, e.g., Rudin, 'Reflections', p.521.
45 'The Pope, the Church and the Jews', p.26.
46 *ibid.*, p.27.
47 *ibid.*
48 Still, the process of beatification, the penultimate step to sanctification or canonization, has been going on for several years, under the leadership of the Vatican's Father Gumpel. A recent report, however, suggested that the Church had decided to slow down the process toward sainthood. See 'Vatican Slows Beatification for Pius XII-Group', *Reuters*, 27 October 1999. The timing of this decision coincided with widespread publicity given to the British journalist John Cornwell's controversial new book, *Hitler's Pope: The Secret History of Pius XII* (New York: Viking, 1999).
49 See Heschel, 'The Vatican and the Holocaust', *Dissent* (Summer, 1998): 13–14.
50 On this story, see Gitta Sereny: *Into that Darkness* (New York: Vintage, 1983); Phayer, 'Pope Pius XII', pp.233–56; and Mark Aarons and John Loftus, *Unholy Trinity* (New York: St. Martin's 1991). In the 15 November 1999 number of *US News and World Report*, an article was published that suggests a soon-to-be-released Argentine government report has confirmed the involvement of the Vatican in seeking Latin American visas for fleeing Nazis, many made by the Vatican Secretariat of State. Some were also made for Vichy collaborators, and much intercession occurred on behalf of the Ustasha criminals. The Argentine report has not, however, yet been published.
51 As did some prominent Catholics, including John Cardinal O'Connor, Archbishop of New York. See *The Jewish Week*, 9 October 1998. The Vatican responded by declaring itself the judge of the timing and scope of archive accessibility. See Eric J. Greenberg, 'Vatican to U.S.: No Archives', in *The Jewish Week*, 11 December 1998. Morley, who has worked with the eleven volumes of diplomatic documents related to the War published by the Vatican between 1965 and 1981 [*Actes et Documents du Saint-Siège relatifs à la Second Guerre mondiale*, edited by Pierre Blet, Vatican City: Libreria Editrice Vaticana, 1965–1981)] has observed: 'I fear sometimes that this contribution of the Vatican to historical research has not been clearly appreciated. Moreover, I suspect that the very existence of these primary sources is not as well known as it should be.' See Morley, '*We Remember*', p.6. At the time of the writing of this paper, the Vatican had appointed a team of three Catholic scholars, which included Morley, and three Jewish scholars, which included Michael Marrus, to discuss the issue of full access to Vatican archives relating to the War and the Holocaust.
52 'The Vatican and the Holocaust', p.14.
53 'Jews and Catholics: Beyond Apologies', *First Things* 89 (January 1999): 20–25. Page numbers for quotations from this article will be cited in the text.
54 Novak's understanding of *magisterium* could be critiqued on at least two points. First, the church *is* not a *magisterium*; it *has* a *magisterium*. Secondly, the question of just which part of the *magisterium*, if any, is considered to be infallible will be answered differently depending on *which* Catholic happens to be responding. It needs to be observed, too, that the term *infallible* itself has a complicated history (on which, see Brian Tierney, *The Origins of Papal Infallibility* [Leiden: Brill, 1972]). The pope was declared to be infallible only at the very late date of 1870, at the First Vatican Council, and Catholics have differed *in bona fide* about what part of papal teaching, if any, should be considered infallible. See Hans Kung, *Unfehlbar? Eine Anfrage*. English Title: *Infallible? An Inquiry*. Translated by Edward Quinn. (Garden City, N.Y.: Doubleday, 1971).
55 'Beliefs', *New York Times*, 3 April 1999.
56 'The Pope, the Church, and the Jews', p.28.

ADDRESSING THE DEMONIC IN SACRED TEXTS:
THE NEXT STEP IN CATHOLIC-JEWISH RELATIONS AFTER THE HOLOCAUST

Ronald Modras

GESTURES OF friendship among Catholics and Jews have become commonplace enough in the last several years as to receive scant attention from the secular press. Such was the fate of two press releases sent out the same day, 15 July 1999, one from the American Jewish Committee in New York, the other from the National Conference of Catholic Bishops in Washington, D.C. One related the contribution of a hundred thousand dollars by the American Jewish Committee to the Kosovo Relief Fund of Catholic Relief Services.

The other press release likewise involved inter-faith finances. In mid-June three synagogues in Sacramento, California, were severely damaged by firebomb attacks. The accused perpetrators, a pair of brothers, have been described as the products of fundamentalist Christian upbringing. Searches of their homes turned up anti-Semitic propaganda denouncing Jews as 'subhuman'. The Roman Catholic bishop of Sacramento, William K. Wiegand, responded to the arson not only with words of condemnation but with a check for twenty thousand dollars, ten thousand for a 'Unity Fund' to rebuild the burned synagogues and ten thousand toward the establishment of a Centre of Tolerance being planned to fight violence and hatred in the Sacramento area. The National Conference of Catholic Bishops joined the Catholic diocese of Sacramento by contributing another twenty-five thousand dollars toward the synagogue rebuilding efforts. Conference President Bishop Joseph Fiorenza underscored Bishop Wiegand's condemnation of the arson as 'cowardly and blasphemous' and stated, 'When synagogues are burned, all Christians are Jews.'

Again, the media did not give the bishops' donation particular notice. If anti-Semitic violence erupts anywhere, we have come to expect words and gestures of Catholic solidarity with the Jewish victims. It goes without saying, however, that words and gestures are one thing, forty-five thousand dollars something else altogether. So too is humanitarian aid to Jews in need something altogether different from Catholics helping to rebuild a synagogue, a place of non-Catholic, non-Christian worship. There is no question but that the bishops' donation verged on the historic.

Both these news stories exemplify the sea change that has taken place in Catholic-Jewish relations. More than speeches and gestures, they demonstrate what one prominent expert on the matter, Rabbi David Rosen, has called 'one of the greatest revolutions in human history'. A revolution, I would add, that is still going on. Revolutions require a before and after. I intend in the following essay to sketch some of the outlines of that before and after and to point out one highly sensitive area where I believe that Jews and Catholics can work together, where Jews in particular can be of help to Catholics and other Christians, namely, in addressing the demonic in our sacred texts.

SYNAGOGUE OF SATAN?

For those with a sense of history, the bishops' donation toward rebuilding burned-down synagogues was a particularly apt though ironic symbol of the revolution I am describing. It serves as a mirror image in reverse of an incident in 388 when, in the Mesopotamian town of Callinicus, a Christian mob, led by the bishop, burned down the local synagogue. At the time such attacks were against the law but not uncommon. The Emperor Theodosius ordered the bishop to rebuild the synagogue. But Saint Ambrose, the eloquent and redoubtable Archbishop of Milan, intervened.

Ambrose wrote a letter to the Emperor, exhorting him to revoke his order. He described the synagogue as 'a home of unbelief, a house of impiety, a receptacle of folly, which God Himself has condemned'. He appealed to the fact that during the reign of the Emperor Julian the Apostate, Jews had burned down churches without being compelled to make recompense. Should the synagogue be 'avenged' and not the church? Ambrose' appeal went unheeded by the Emperor. But some time later, he had occasion to preach at a Mass with Theodosius in attendance. Once again Ambrose brought up the imperial order to rebuild the synagogue. He threatened Theodosius to his face not to continue with the worship service until the order was withdrawn. Ambrose prevailed and the Emperor promised to rescind his order.[1]

It bears noting here that, despite the Emperor's capitulation, the law against burning synagogues remained part of the Theodosian Code, compiled in 438, which would govern the empire in both East and West. It set down statutes that determined Christian Jewish relations for centuries to come. Judaism was decreed to be 'not a prohibited sect'; Jews who conducted themselves peacefully were not to be molested; their Sabbath and feast days are not to be disturbed; synagogues were not to be attacked, burned, or violated. At the same time, the Code prohibited Jews from throwing stones at Jewish converts to Christianity, from interfering with the sacraments, and from mocking or burning the cross during the feast of Purim.[2] Hostility between Christians and Jews was apparently mutual and occasionally overt.

Also noteworthy is the fact that, though he accuses the synagogue of impiety, and folly, nowhere in his letter or sermon does Ambrose refer to it as demonic. The same cannot be said for his contemporary, Saint John Chrysostom (*c*.345–407). Before becoming the Patriarch of Constantinople, Chrysostom served as a priest in Antioch, where he found so-called Judaizing Christians, i.e. Christians attracted to Jewish rituals and worship, attending the synagogue services, observing Jewish festivals and fast days. Even more worrisome, Christians were also going to rabbis for cures from disease. The rabbis were already achieving a reputation as physicians – one that would reach its pinnacle in the 12th century with Moses Maimonides.

The rabbis of Antioch were known for being able to heal ailments with amulets and charms and by expelling demons. Chrysostom reacted with a series of eight sermons or discourses generally recognized to be the shrillest example of rhetorical violence to be found in that whole genre of Christian literature known as *Contra Judaeos* (Against the Jews).[3] He described the synagogue as a 'brothel', a 'theatre', a 'den of robbers and a lodging for wild beasts' (I, 3,1). The cures which the Jews were effecting were not genuine, Chrysostom insisted. He apparently could not deny or dismiss the rabbis' success in achieving cures, so he attacked their source of origin with a conventional ploy. They were the work of the demons, and it would be better to die of a disease than to be cured by the 'Jews' witchcraft' (VII, 8,5). To those who countered his argument and claimed that Jews too worship God and God heard their prayers, Chrysostom answers with an appeal to the eighth chapter of John's gospel, where John has Jesus say of the Pharisees, 'you know neither me nor my Father' (John 8:19).[4]

That Chrysostom based his argument on the eighth chapter of John's gospel is not surprising. Here we read that Jesus' adversaries are not truly children of Abraham because they do not do what Abraham did. Neither is God their Father, because they do not accept Jesus. On the contrary, 'You are of your father the devil, and your will is to do your father's desires' (John 8:44). It is noteworthy that Chrysostom does not quote this particular text. Neither does he quote the texts from Revelation, referring to the 'synagogue of Satan' (Rev. 2:9; 3:9). That fact deserves some brief consideration.

Chrysostom's sermons against the Jews are lengthy; his knowledge of both the Hebrew and Christian scriptures impressive. If he wanted to paint Jews as essentially demonic, why did he not cite the two most likely passages in the New Testament that would allow him to do so? One can only conjecture. Was it because in two places the gospels have Jesus say to the apostle Peter, 'Get behind me, Satan' (Mt. 16:23; Mk. 8:33)? Chrysostom associated the demonic not with Jews per se but with the rabbis' healings and does not develop or dwell on the charge, because, as I will argue below, it was a stock charge against any wondrous deeds accomplished by one's adversaries. Calling the synagogue demonic was simply one vilification among many and not the central image by which the church would come to see Jews.

With good reason, Joshua Trachtenberg, in his influential study *The Devil and the Jews*, focused on the popular medieval conception of the Jew as associated with the demonic.[5] This, however, was not the over-riding conception of the Jew in the first thousand years of Christianity; nor was it the predominant view of the church and civil leaders. If that were so, the church and civil leaders would never have tolerated the existence and building of synagogues. Jews would have been treated like pagans, who were not tolerated, since the pagan gods were identified with demons. Jews would have been executed like those accused of witchcraft, precisely for being in league with the devil.

The principal conception by which the institutional church interpreted Jews and by which Christian relationships with Jews were governed was much more ambiguous than a simple association with the demonic. For Saint Augustine of Hippo (354–430), another contemporary of Ambrose and Chrysostom, Jews were to be interpreted as under the sign of Cain. Cain, in the Genesis story, (Gen. 4:1–16), was guilty of murder and punished by exile, compelled to wander the earth homeless. But he was not to be killed. 'If anyone slays Cain, vengeance shall be taken on him sevenfold. And the Lord put a mark on Cain, lest any who came upon him should kill him' (Gen. 4:15). Augustine viewed Jews as bearing peculiar guilt for the death of Jesus. He read the text in Matthew's gospel as historical: 'And all the people answered, "His blood be upon us and upon our children"' (Mt. 27:25). On the strength of that text, Augustine regarded Jews of all generations as compelled to wander the earth exiled from their homeland. They were a 'witness people', destined by their lot to testify to the validity of Christian claims. Cursed by their own words, they could be expelled, but they were not to be killed.

Augustine's view of Jews as under the sign of Cain came to be shared by most church fathers and leaders, above all by the influential Pope Gregory the Great (*c*.540–604). Gregory insisted that the legal rights of Jews, as stipulated in the Theodosian Code, be respected. He forbade bishops to interfere in internal Jewish affairs. Jews were to be allowed to celebrate their feasts freely. On several occasions when synagogues were confiscated or damaged by Christians, Gregory insisted that they be returned or restored. In one case, when a synagogue in Palermo had already been consecrated as a church, Gregory ordered the bishop to pay for it, implicitly disavowing the example of Saint Ambrose in this matter.[6] He could not have done so if it was, without qualification, the synagogue of Satan.

IDOLATROUS CHRISTIANS?

Christianity can raise no high-sounding claims to a tradition of tolerance. Jews, pagans, and heretics were all viewed as mired in error. But in the era of Constantinian Christianity, Jews alone were tolerated as erroneous but licit. Even for someone like Saint Pope Gregory, every effort was to be made to convert Jews from their 'superstition'. But at the same time they were protected by civil and church law – allowed to live and worship within Christian society, to celebrate their feasts, to build and maintain synagogues. In short, Christian tradition regarding Jews, while overwhelmingly negative, was also ambiguous. Can the same thing be said about Jewish tradition with respect to Christians?

If there is a Jewish counterpart to the voluminous writings of the church fathers, it is the Talmud. Comprising sometimes as many as twenty folio volumes, the Babylonian Talmud embodies the thought and labours of some eight centuries of Jewish teachers. Traditional or orthodox Judaism views revelation (Torah) as coming down from God on Mount Sinai not only in written form (the Penteteuch), but orally as well. Passed down from one generation to another, the oral Torah was committed to writing (*ca.*200 C.E.) in the Mishna, both an interpretation and augmentation of the written Torah. In relating the discussion of the sages on what constituted divine will and holiness for Israel, the Mishna reported divergences of opinion as well as majority decisions. Subsequent rabbinical discussions and commentary on the Mishna (Gemara) were compiled together with the Mishna to form first the Jerusalem Talmud (*ca.*400 C.E.) and later, the larger, more influential Babylonian Talmud (*ca.*600 C.E.).

The single most authoritative document in Judaism, the Talmud can be compared to an immense hall filled with hundreds of voices, as one commandment after another is analysed, debated and applied to changing circumstances. In it one finds conflicting interpretations placed side by side, rejected opinions alongside the accepted. To an outsider the Talmud could hardly appear as anything else but chaos. Its chaotic form is precisely what rendered it open to Christian misunderstanding and antagonism in the past and continues to do so today.[7]

Several times in the middle ages, the Talmud was literally put on trial by Catholic inquisitors at the behest of monarchs. The most famous was the disputation at Paris in 1240, when Rabbi Yehiel ben Yosef was called upon to defend the Talmud against charges made by one Nicholas Donin, a Christian convert from Judaism. The matter was serious. Judaism was tolerated so long as Jews did not blaspheme Christianity or do anything to hinder its practice. Donin charged that the Talmud contained blasphemy against the Christian faith: that it made slurs against Jesus and Mary, equated Christians with pagan idolaters, and cursed them during their daily prayer.

The Talmud, in the words of a pioneer Christian scholar, 'has preserved only a very vague and confused recollection of Jesus. His name was doubtless held in abhorrence as that of a dangerous heretic and deceiver; but extremely little was known of him, and that little is mentioned more by way of casual remark than as being of importance on its own account.'[8] There are very few references to 'Jesus of Nazareth' (Jeshu ha-Notzri) in the Talmud. But there are also references to a 'Jesus ben Stada' who is also called 'Jesus ben Pandera' and the son of 'Miriam the hair-dresser'. When Donin confronted Rabbi Yehiel with these Talmudic references, Rabbi Yehiel argued that Jesus was a common name in

1st-century Israel and that these Talmudic passages did not refer to the Jesus of Christianity. The wily rabbi foiled Donin and the Paris inquisitors, we are told, by pointing out that 'not every Louis is King of France.'

Confronted as Rabbi Yehiel was with very real danger to his people and the Talmud, his claim of more than one Jesus in the Talmud may be understandable, but it was at least questionable.[9] According to these various references, Jesus was illegitimate, led a checkered career as a sorcerer, and was eventually put to death by Jewish authorities. Probably the most offensive Talmudic passage refers to a necromantic vision of Jesus as being punished in hell in boiling excrement (Gittin 56b). Another Talmudic passage refers to Jesus as a deceiver and magician who was executed by stoning on the charge of seducing Israel to idolatry (Sanhedrin 43a).[10] The unhistorical nature of both these passages indicates that by the third century anything like an independent Jewish memory of Jesus had died out. Both references were obvious attempts to counter Christian missionary efforts among Jews. In any case, even if all the references are to Jesus of Nazareth, they are so few as to be deemed a negligible theme in the Talmud.

As for attacks against Christians, the Talmud undoubtedly contains references hostile to gentiles, pagan idolaters ('worshippers of stars and constellations') and Jewish heretics (the so-called *minim*). The Talmud forbids certain forms of business and social intercourse with idolaters. Jewish tradition also calls for the daily recitation of the Eighteen Benedictions (*Shemone Esreh*), in which there is included a curse against the Jewish heretics. Rabbi Yehiel countered Donin's charges by pointing out correctly that many Talmudic laws in relation to idolaters were not being applied to Christians, the prohibition of trading with them, for example. Yehiel maintained that the Talmudic sayings about gentiles and idolaters referred to the nations of the ancient world and must be read in that context.

Again, Rabbi Yehiel's sharp distinction between Christians and idolaters, while understandable, was, in the thirteenth century at least, ahead of its time. The *minim* or Jewish heretics, mentioned in the curse of the *Shemone Esreh*, certainly included Jews who had become Christian. It corresponds to the anathema or excommunication which the church imposed on Christian heretics and apostates. Certainly it was no more harsh than the 'bull' of Pope Boniface VIII (*Unam Sanctam*), which declared that Jews, pagans, schismatics and all who die outside the Catholic church, are damned forever, that there was no salvation outside the church. That papal teaching has undergone considerable historical revision, as did rabbinical teaching about Christians, although the rabbinical revision preceded Catholic rethinking by several centuries.

As the late Israeli historian and rabbinic scholar, Joseph Katz, has demonstrated, the Talmudic tradition on Gentiles is complex.[11] The Babylonian Talmud quotes from the earlier (late 2nd century?) rabbinic work, the *Tosefta*, that the sons of Noah were given seven commandments, among them prohibitions against idolatry, blasphemy, sexual immorality, bloodshed, and robbery. Gentiles who observed them are regarded as righteous among the nations and having a place in the world to come.[12] In virtue of Talmudic teaching on the Noahide laws, medieval Jews distinguished among the Gentiles, and therefore Christians, taking them as they found them. When Gentiles, including Christians, treated life, including Jewish life, as cheap, the rabbis regarded them as idolaters, to be identified *tout court* with the wicked as enemies of Israel and enemies of God. Immorality was indicative of idolatry.

But what of Christians who respected the moral values contained in the Noahide laws? Were they thereby numbered among the righteous? Not if one took the thinking of Moses Maimonides as normative. Maimonides (1135–1204) taught that 'the righteous of all people have a part in the world to come.'[13] But he was ambivalent in his overall assessment of Christianity. He valued Christianity for its acceptance of the Hebrew Bible. He saw both Christianity and Islam as providentially inspired to carry knowledge of the Hebrew Scriptures to the world and thus prepare the world for the Messiah. But Maimonides distinguished between Muslim and Christian monotheism. In his opinion the Christian doctrines of a trinitarian God and a divine incarnation as well as Christian use of icons and statues vitiated Christian claims to being monotheistic.[14] Maimonides refused to acquit Christians of idolatry, and in this opinion he was not alone. If some adjustments had been made by Rabbi Yehiel's time in the 13th century, they were made for reasons of economic expediency. Some laws regarding relationships with idolaters still pertained to Christians, such as the prohibition against drinking gentile wine for fear it had been used for idolatrous worship. According to the common rabbinic opinion of the time, Jewish merchants who engaged in commerce with Christians during the 13th century were doing so with idolaters.

First in the 14th century, in southern France, were Christians acquitted of the sin of idolatry, by one Rabbi Menahem Meiri of Provence. Relationships between Jews and Christians in Provence were positive, marked by mutual respect and intellectual interchange. Jewish law had for some time come to identify gentile idolatry with immorality. Rabbi Meiri turned the equation around. Meiri regarded Christian morality as indicative of freedom from idolatry. Unlike Maimonides, Meiri did not look at Christian theology but only at behaviour. He created a new legal category that distinguished peoples with a moral code from the ancient pagan idolaters. In taking upon themselves the moral code found in the Hebrew Scriptures, Christians and Muslims distinguished themselves from the pagan idolaters of the past. They could be numbered among the 'righteous among the nations' who abide by the seven Noahide laws and have a place in the 'world to come'.

Rabbi Meiri's expansive and humane view of Christianity remained largely unknown for centuries. It took time to become commonly accepted rabbinic teaching.[15] Nevertheless, it is noteworthy that Jewish reassessment of Christianity began six hundred years ago, whereas the Christian reassessment of Judaism, by contrast, is of much more recent vintage. In both cases, however, for the greater part of two thousand years, Jews and Christians saw each other as outsiders, as quintessentially other, and it is this broad category of the 'other', the 'alien', those who are not of God, that I describe with the term 'demonic'.

One need not make a case for a moral equivalence between the Christian 'teaching of contempt' (Jules Isaac) and the Talmudic view of Gentiles to point out that both Christian and Jewish traditions looked upon the other as precisely that – 'the other,' excluded from the community to which one owed loyalty and concern. Contempt, more often than not, was mutual. Certainly, Christians, as the dominant force in the culture, had the greater opportunity and therefore the greater responsibility for making a change in that relationship. It is not coincidental that the same century that saw the virtual destruction of European Jewry in the heart of what was once Catholic Christendom is also the century that first saw Christians attempt to make that change.

THE REVOLUTION IN CATHOLIC JEWISH RELATIONS

What Rabbi Rosen has called 'one of the greatest revolutions in human history' goes back to 1965 and the Second Vatican Council's decree, *Nostra Aetate*. In that decree the highest teaching authority in the Catholic Church denounced anti-Semitism and spoke of a spiritual 'bond' between Christians and Jews. It repudiated the long popular tradition that rendered all Jews peculiarly guilty of the death of Jesus. *Nostra Aetate* also taught that 'Jews should not be presented as rejected or accursed by God, as if this followed from the Holy Scriptures.'[16] The decree made no mention of the Holocaust nor of Jewish attachment to the land of Israel.

On the tenth anniversary of *Nostra Aetate*, in 1975, the Vatican's Commission for Religious Relations with Jews published a document entitled 'Guidelines and Suggestions for Implementing the Conciliar Declaration *Nostra Aetate*'.[17] The Vatican Guidelines made up for the prior omissions by placing the Council document in the context of the Holocaust, acknowledging that for two thousand years Catholic Jewish relations were 'too often marked by mutual ignorance and frequent confrontation.' The Guidelines also described Jewish [rabbinic] tradition as living, not ended with the destruction of the Second temple, and 'rich in religious values'. Christians were encouraged to acquire a better understanding of that tradition through dialogue, striving 'to learn by what essential traits the Jews define themselves in the light of their own religious experience.' Though not explicitly, certainly by implication, that self-definition would include the millennial Jewish attachment and relationship to the land of Israel.

Vatican II's *Nostra Aetate* acknowledged indirectly that certain texts in the New Testament had been interpreted to mean that Jews were rejected or accursed by God, 'as if this followed from the Holy Scriptures.' The 1975 Vatican Guidelines were more explicit in admitting some of the problem passages. Without mentioning the gospel of Matthew as primarily responsible, they recognized that the word Pharisee has taken on a largely pejorative meaning. The Guidelines also pointed to the problematic use of the term 'the Jews' in John's gospel, which 'sometimes, according to the context, means "the leaders of the Jews" or "the adversaries of Jesus," terms which express better the thought of the Evangelist and avoid appearing to arraign the Jewish people as such.' Not surprisingly, the Guidelines were definitive in stating, 'Obviously, one cannot alter the text of the Bible.' They left it to preachers and educators to put problematic passages into context.

In 1985 the Vatican marked the 20th anniversary of *Nostra Aetate* with a document entitled 'Notes on the Correct Way to Present Jews and Judaism in Preaching and Teaching in the Roman Catholic Church.' The Notes too built on the foundation of Vatican II. They emphasized that Jesus' relations with Pharisees were not always or wholly polemical, that 'an exclusively negative picture of the Pharisees is likely to be inaccurate and unjust.' Reaping the benefits of modern biblical scholarship, the Notes acknowledged that 'the Gospels are the outcome of long and complicated editorial work' and that 'certain controversies reflect Christian–Jewish relations long after the time of Jesus.' Here for the first time the Holy See formally recognized that many of the polemical statements attributed to Jesus in his relationship with his co-religionists (*c*.30 C.E.) in actuality are drawn from the conflicts between the New Testament church and synagogue sixty to seventy years later, at the end of the first century, after the destruction of the Second Temple (70 C.E.).

It bears noting here that the Jewish reception for every one of these Vatican documents was negative. When it first appeared, no less an ecumenical spirit than Rabbi Abraham Heschel criticized *Nostra Aetate*, the watershed Vatican II document that started the revolution; Rabbi Heschel called it too little, too late. Viewed from a distance, however, we see that these Vatican documents acquired a cumulative momentum. They often sparked statements by national conferences of Catholic bishops that went beyond the Vatican documents. A case in point is the United States Bishops' 1988 document, *God's Mercy Endures Forever: Guidelines on the Presentation of Jews and Judaism in Catholic*

Preaching.[18] Here we read that 'Jesus was perhaps closer to the Pharisees in his religious vision than to any other group of his time.' We are reminded that the Synoptic gospels mention only the Roman and temple authorities in conjunction with Jesus' crucifixion, not the Pharisees. The U.S. bishops' document on preaching also looked at John's gospel and its formulaic references to 'the Jews.' It stated, 'The bitterness toward synagogue Judaism seen in John's gospel (e.g. Jn 9:22; 16:2) most likely reflects the bitterness felt by John's own community after its "parting of the ways" with the Jewish community.'

Even so cursory a review of Catholic teaching suffices to justify the claim that a 'revolution' is taking place in Catholic Jewish relations. And it is this astounding turn-about that one must keep in mind when reading the most recent 1998 Vatican document, 'We Remember: A Reflection on the Shoah'.[19] By any measure it is the most important document pertinent to Catholic Jewish relations since Vatican II. 'We Remember' represents the first serious attempt by the Holy See to come to grips with the fact that some Catholics were actively complicit in the attempt by Nazi Germany to perpetrate the genocide of European Jewry, and many more passively acquiesced. And like all preceding Vatican documents of its kind, it was met by trenchant, sometimes even acrid criticism, both by Jewish and Catholic commentators.

This is not the place for a detailed summary let alone critique of 'We Remember'.[20] Suffice it to say, on the plus side of the ledger, that the Holy See allied itself with the Jewish community against an onslaught of Holocaust denial and revisionism. To the Catholic faithful and the world at large, the Holy See has said, 'It happened.' The Vatican put its moral authority solidly behind the importance of holocaust remembrance and education, so that, in the words of Pope John Paul II in a letter accompanying the document, 'the unspeakable iniquity of the Shoah will never again be possible.' The Pope's letter frames 'We Remember' with a call to 'repentance of past errors and infidelities.' The document itself uses the Hebrew word *teshuva*, which means not only repentance but conversion and change of heart. None of which, of course, makes any sense, unless there is an at least implied acknowledgement of guilt for sins, whether of omission or commission. The question, however, is – whose repentance, whose guilt, and whose sins.

'We Remember' has been faulted by critics for its quasi-Platonic distinction between the 'church as such' and the 'sons and daughters' of the church. The former is a pure, mystical, disembodied entity, identified with the saving Christ, and therefore above history and blame; the latter are the church's weak, sinful members. 'We Remember' expresses regret for the 'errors and failures' committed by its sons and daughters at the time of the Shoah but admits of no blame in the church itself. Contrary to the suspicions of some Jewish commentators, the distinction was not specially invented for this document. It goes back at least a century to a time when theologians began focusing on the church as the 'Mystical Body of Christ.'[21]

A distinction between 'the "church"' and the '"children of the church"' has been out of fashion with most contemporary theologians, ever since the Second Vatican Council highlighted the church as the 'people of God.' But it is a distinction on which Pope John Paul II insists. It does not exculpate churchmen in high places; popes, bishops, even saints like John Chrysostom are considered 'children of the church.' But it does seem to acquit the 'institutional church' and Christian tradition of guilt. Even if, for the sake of argument, one accepts the distinction, the Vatican document suffers from a severe limitation, as theologian Father John Pawlikowski has incisively pointed out: '*We Remember* could have, and should have, made it clearer that the "sons and daughters" of the Church who espoused anti-Semitism did so because of what they had learned from teachers, theologians (including the Church Fathers), and preachers sanctioned by the institutional Church.'[22]

Critics have also faulted 'We Remember' for its distinction between anti-Semitism and anti-Judaism. The Vatican document defines anti-Judaism as 'mistrust and hostility' toward Jews and their religion and accepts that there were 'sentiments of anti-Judaism in some Christian quarters.' This anti-Judaism led to 'a generalized discrimination' which led in turn to 'suspicion and mistrust' and 'ended at times in expulsions or attempts at forced conversions.' But anti-Judaism, the document insists, is quite different from anti-Semitism, which it defines as a form of racism that denies the unity and equality of all races. In the words of 'We Remember': 'The Shoah was the work of a thoroughly modern neo-pagan regime. Its anti-Semitism had its roots outside of Christianity and, in pursuing its aims, it did not hesitate to oppose the Church and persecute her members also.'

There is clear and compelling merit to the Vatican's case for making a distinction between traditional Christian anti-Judaism and modern, racist anti-Semitism. Jewish historian Yosef Yerushalmi pointed out two decades ago that if the logic of Christian anti-Judaism led directly to genocide, it would have been attempted in the middle ages, when church leaders in much of Europe actually had the political power to carry it out. They did not and, at their worst, did not even contemplate such a possibility. Only in our own secularized 20th century did it happen, after the breakdown of the Christian world-order, when Europe's political leadership lost anything like a God-centred vision and the moral restraints that vision imposed.[23] When society is stripped of respect for a transcendent God, unchecked secular authority becomes absolute and, in the words of Rabbi Irving Greenberg, leads 'directly to the assumption of omnipotent power over life and death on the part of the state'.[24]

'We Remember' can claim the support of important Jewish and Christian scholars in its insistence on an essential difference between Christian anti-Judaism and racist anti-Semitism, above all, the genocidal racist anti-Semitism of the Nazis. The document's emphasis on the distinction, however, coupled with its silence on any links between them, leaves the impression that there was no relationship, no inherent connection between the two. And here serious historical scholarship takes issue with the Vatican document. It is unlikely that Jews could have been singled out so easily and rendered scapegoats by the Nazis without the long tradition of Christian anti-Judaism that preceded and accompanied the more modern racial anti-Semitism.

Despite the distinction and essential difference between Christian anti-Judaism and Nazi racist anti-Semitism, there is not a total disconnect. Scholars who have studied the matter have come up with a variety of metaphors, trying to describe the relationship. They speak of Christian anti-Judaism as one of the 'roots' of Nazi anti-Semitism or one of the 'approaches to Auschwitz' (Richard L. Rubenstein and John K. Roth); it served as an 'indispensable seedbed' for the Nazi genocide (John Pawlikowski) or it 'helped prepare the ground' (Donald Dietrich). Yosef Yerushalmi described the relationship in terms of causality. He has no doubt that Christian anti-Judaism helped create a cultural mentality in which the genocide of the Jews, once conceived, could be carried out with little or no opposition. 'But even if we grant that Christian teaching was a necessary cause leading to the Holocaust, it was surely not a sufficient one.'[25]

Rather than that of causality, my own preferred metaphor has been one taken from the field of contract law. Christian anti-Judaism was a pre-requisite or condition, one of a complex of conditions, that contributed to a climate that made the Holocaust possible. It was not the principal or most important condition, as some would claim without empirical demonstration of any kind. But it was a necessary condition, a *conditio sine qua non*.[26] The matter is sensitive, of course, to the point of being neuralgic. And the careful search for appropriate metaphors is indicative not only of the sensitivity of the question for Christians but also of its complexity. For the issue is not one of holding individual Christians (like Pope Pius XII) accountable for their actions or inactions, but the institutional church and its long anti-Judaic tradition.

That there was an historical link between Christian anti-Judaism and the anti-Semitism behind the Holocaust is, in the opinion of Catholic historian Donald Dietrich, with which I agree, now almost universally recognized.[27] The Vatican scholars and authors behind 'We Remember', however, could not bring themselves to that admission. One can only speculate why they could not and why that Vatican document treated Christian anti-Judaism in so summary a fashion, in only a paragraph. Was it to avoid making moral judgments about saints like Ambrose or John Chrysostom? My own suspicion is that any more thorough an investigation would require looking more carefully at the origins of Christian anti-Judaism. Those origins do not originate *ex nihilo* in the second century in one or another church father or theologian. And once again one encounters metaphors like 'roots,' as one confronts those origins in the pages of the New Testament itself.

ANTI-SEMITISM IN THE NEW TESTAMENT?
Vatican II, as pointed out above, explicitly taught that 'Jews should not be presented as rejected or accursed by God, as if this followed from the Holy Scriptures.' Pope John Paul II has spoken of 'erroneous and unjust interpretations of the New Testament' as having engendered 'feelings of hostility' toward Jews. Has Christian anti-Judaism been based on only misinterpretations of the New Testament texts? A number of scholars have not been so benign in their assessment of those texts. Nor as careful in making nuanced and fine distinctions between anti-Judaism and anti-Semitism.

Fifty years ago Protestant theologian James Parkes, a pioneer in the field, drew a direct line between the pages of the New Testament and the death camps of Auschwitz.[28] Richard Lowry drew a similar line from John 8:44 ('You are of your father the devil') through medieval woodcuts illustrating that charge, up to a 1936 children's book published in Nazi Germany announcing on the first page that 'Der Vater der Juden is der Teufel.' Rosemary Radford Ruether created considerable controversy when she called anti-Semitism the 'left hand' of Christology and claimed that the theological roots of anti-Semitism constitute an inherent element of traditional Christian belief. Assessing the New Testament in general and John's gospel in particular, John K. Roth, in collaboration with Richard L. Rubenstein, claimed: 'There is no defamation of comparable severity of one religion by another. The ascription of a satanic nature to Jews had the effect of legitimating even the most obscene violence against them.'[29]

The late Samuel Sandmel, Jewish historian and theologian, found such accusations against the New Testament to be exaggerations. Sandmel distinguished sharply between the anti-Jewish texts in the New Testament and the racist anti-Semitism of the Nazis. But given such criticism by Christian scholars, can one blame Jewish scholar, Lillian C. Freundmann, for assenting to the charge that the author of John's gospel is the 'father of anti-Semitism'? No wonder, she writes, that pious Christians have considered it acceptable to attack Jews, what with 'virulent' passages like John 8:44 regarded as 'inspiration.'[30] A New Testament text 'virulent,' poisonous? Can reading an inspired text be dangerous to your health? Or to somebody else's health? Here is a most nettlesome point not yet addressed by any Vatican document, problematic or what I call demonizing passages in what we Christians regard as our inspired and normative sacred texts.

As any glance at the literature will indicate, scholars, both Christian and Jewish, have been deliberating over the anti-Jewish texts in the New Testament for the better part of fifty years. Perhaps because the debate is still going on, one can excuse the Vatican authors of 'We Remember' for not even acknowledging the problem. Even without final conclusions, however, there is growing scholarly consensus on several key points and these deserve to be given wider notice by Christian leaders and educators within the broader church community.

The New Testament contains only a very few references to Jews and Judaism that can be construed as positive, e.g. Paul boasting that he was a Pharisee; his analogy of the Gentiles being grafted on to the 'cultivated olive tree' that is Israel; the Jesus of John's gospel proclaiming that 'salvation comes from the Jews.' The overwhelming majority of references to Jews and Judaism in the New Testament are harshly negative. One Jewish author counted a hundred and two references which he describes as 'degrading, malevolent and libelous' and conducive of 'ineradicable hatred towards the Jewish people.'[31] Without granting or gainsaying the accuracy of that count, one must acknowledge that two gospels in particular, Matthew and John, have been the repository from which Christians have drawn most of the weaponry and justification for their anti-Semitic assaults.[32]

Thanks to Matthew's gospel, especially chapter 25, the word Pharisee has become synonymous with hypocrite. The scribes and Pharisees, the forerunners of rabbinical Judaism, are also labelled as 'blind guides' who are 'full of iniquity', a 'brood of vipers' who will scourge and persecute Jesus' disciples. It is also in Matthew's gospel, in its account of Jesus' passion and death, that a Jewish mob shouts 'let him be crucified' (Mt. 27:23) and 'his blood be on us and on our children' (Mt. 27:25). John's gospel describes Jesus' opponents not as scribes, Pharisees, high priests or elders, but simply as *Judaioi*, usually translated as 'the Jews.' And it is in John where 'the Jews' are described as being 'of your father the devil' (Jn. 8:44).

Both the 1985 Vatican 'Notes' and the 1988 U.S. bishops' 'Guidelines' recognize the fact that the gospels not only contain historical memories of Jesus but also reflect the situation of the early Christian church in conflict with the synagogue, especially after the destruction of the Second Temple (70 C.E.). Critical New Testament scholarship recognizes that the so-called self-curse by a Jewish crowd at Jesus' trial (Mat. 27:25) is thoroughly unhistorical. Rather it represents the interpretation by Matthew's gospel (written around the year 90 C.E.) as to how and why God could have allowed the calamities that occurred some twenty years earlier – the Jewish uprising, the siege of Jerusalem, and the destruction of the temple.

If Jerusalem lay in ruins, it was because of the complicity of the temple leadership in the crucifixion of Jesus and the subsequent Jewish rejection of Christian claims for Jesus. Traditional Jewish theology explained affliction as punishment for sin, and Matthew's gospel was happy to name the sin.[33] Quite outside the meaning of the text, however, subsequent generations of Christians used the Matthean self-curse passage to justify their imposing further hardships on the Jewish people. Here the Second Vatican Council and Pope John Paul II are correct to insist that the text is being misinterpreted. For this the gospel writer bears no responsibility. If any are to be held accountable, it is those Christian preachers and educators who know better and allow the text to be misinterpreted by standing by and saying nothing.

Not so easily exonerated is what Matthew's gospel says about scribes and Pharisees nor what John's gospel says simply about 'the Jews.' Here we are dealing not with subsequent misinterpretation or historical impact (*Wirkungsgeschichte*) but with disparagement pure and simple embedded in the gospel texts themselves, what Catholic New Testament scholar Luke Timothy Johnson aptly calls the rhetoric of anti-Jewish slander.[34] Johnson has no misgivings about describing the anti-Jewish language in Matthew and John as 'scurrilous' and 'a source of shame (finally) to Christians'. He disagrees, however, with those critics who would go on to characterize the authors of the offending passages as anti-Semites. Such labels, and here I agree heartily with Johnson, are anachronistic. They assume that Christianity and Judaism were well-defined and distinct entities in the first century when the New Testament's polemics against the synagogue were written, that Judaism was one thing and Christianity something else altogether. On the contrary, Judaism in the 1st century was utterly divided. The Pharisaic movement that would become normative Judaism was but one sect among others. They along with Sadducees, Zealots, Essenes, Samaritans, and the Hellenized Jews of the diaspora – all claimed to represent the true way to be Jewish. The Jews and their Gentile converts who professed Jesus to be the Messiah regarded themselves as 'the Israel of God' (Gal. 6:16). They were just one more voice, one more rival claimant in a fierce debate over the question who is a real Jew.

Scholars have recognized for some time now that the anti-Jewish invective of the New Testament bears all the earmarks of being part of a particularly rancorous (sometimes even vicious) family feud.[35] Luke Johnson's particular and quite helpful contribution to the scholarly discourse on the issue has been to point out that such invective was both throughly Jewish and quite conventional. He points out that 1st-century diaspora Jews and Christians both perceived themselves and were perceived by their Hellenist contemporaries as constituting distinct schools of philosophy. Philosophy in the Hellenistic period was a way of life, a prescription for health and salvation, less a matter of metaphysics than of morals. Both Judaism and Christianity fit that category.

The various schools acknowledged the general character and goals of philosophy, but they disagreed fiercely on how to best realize that character and reach those goals. If the term sophist (like Pharisee) has acquired a pejorative meaning, it is thanks to the polemics of the Platonists. But the Sophists could give back in equal good measure to the Platonists, describing them as inwardly corrupt, worthy of scorn, making a show of virtue without practising it. Plutarch, a most urbane and sympathetic philosopher, could become quite ugly when he defended his own Platonic tradition by writing lengthy treatises against the Stoics and Epicureans, calling them 'buffoons, charlatans, assassins, prostitutes, and nincompoops'.[36] In the context of 1st-century Hellenism, certain standard categories of vice were automatically attributed to any opponent. They were lovers of money and lovers of glory, corrupt (like the Epicureans) if they lived up to their doctrine, and, if they did not, they were hypocrites.

The polemical charges we find in the New Testament against Pharisees and Jews were routinely attributed to any opponent. Their function was not so much to describe or rebut that opponent as to edify and differentiate one's own school, in the case of Matthew to make clear to Matthew's Christian readers that the scribes and Pharisees were rival teachers in a rival school. In short, they were conventions of 1st-century Hellenistic rhetoric. But being Hellenistic did not make them any less Jewish. Similar polemics are well attested in the Jewish literature of the first century as well. Josephus relates some of the slanders made against Jews by hostile Gentiles (*Against Apion*): Jews were atheists and misanthropes; Moses was a charlatan, circumcision was silly, the sabbath ridiculous. In rebuttal, Josephus resorted to the same kind of slander. He calls hostile Gentiles 'rivilous and utterly senseless specimens of humanity'. He says to the Gentiles of Alexandria antagonistic to Jews, 'We refuse to call you . . . collectively men because you worship and breed with so much care animals that are hostile to humanity.' And of his adversary Apion, Josephus says he has 'the mind of an ass and the impudence of a dog.' Similarly Philo of Alexandria calls the Gentiles of his city 'more brutal and savage than wild beasts'. He writes, 'Alexandrians are adepts at flattery and imposture and hypocrisy,' and the Egyptians 'are a seed bed of evil in whose souls both the venom and the temper of the native crocodiles and wasps are reproduced . . .' Josephus and Philo were both responding to serious Gentile attacks against Jews, but their language shows them able to give as well as they got.[37]

Jews could be no less abusive when talking about one another, when they disagreed. Josephus blamed the Zealots and Sicarii for the war against Rome and ultimately the destruction of the Temple. He calls them 'imposters and brigands'; more wicked than Sodom, they are 'slaves, the dregs of society, and the bastard scum of the nation.' Josephus' views on the destruction of the Temple are of particular interest, when compared to those of the gospel writers. He says that the Zealots profaned the Temple so that it was no longer the dwelling place of God. God had turned from the sanctuary deciding to 'condemn the city and purge the sanctuary by fire.' The destruction of the city was God's punishment for the guilt of the Zealots.

The Palestinian Jewish material, though more fragmentary, complements Josephus in revealing first century Jews to be, in Luke Johnson's words, 'a fanatically divided and fratricidal population.'[38] Besides disputes between Jews and Samaritans, there are disputes between Pharisees and Saducees, between the Pharisees of the school of Shammai and those of the school of Hillel. It puts John 8:44 into a different light when one knows that a follower of Hillel could call a follower of Shammai a 'first-born of Satan' (*bekor satan*).[39]

Not the Pharisees, however, but the Essenes at Qumran best reveal how malicious 1st-century Jews could be toward other Jews, those whom they called 'the ungodly of the covenant' (1QM 1:2). The rule of thumb at Qumran seemed to be that one could not say enough bad things about outsiders. They were marked by 'wickedness and lies, haughtiness and pride, falseness and deceit, cruelty and abundant evil' (see 1QS 4:9–14). It should be emphasized here that all this invective is directed not only at Gentiles but at all other Jews who do not adhere to the Essenes' ideas of purity. Again, one hears John 8:22 differently when one knows that the Jews at Qumran regarded all other Jews as 'sons of darkness' (1QS 1:10; 1QM 1:7) and 'sons of the pit' (see 1QS 9:16), ruled by an angel of darkness (1QS 3:19–21), to know that one of the rituals at Qumran involved shouting curses at such 'men of the lot of Satan' (see 1QS 2:4–10).

If the anti-Jewish language of the New Testament has become jarring to our ears, it is because other 1st-century voices are silent. Josephus, Philo, and the Qumranite scrolls did not become canonized as inspired and normative. Indeed, measured by contemporary standards of Hellenistic and Jewish rhetoric, Luke Johnson finds the New Testament's slander against fellow Jews 'remarkably mild.' He finds the harsher polemic reserved for Gentiles: Thus the Jesus of Matthew's gospel urges his disciples not to pray with many words and empty phrases like the Gentiles (Mt. 6:7). Paul describes Gentiles as 'full of envy, murder, strife, deceit . . . foolish, faithless, heartless, ruthless' (Rom. 1:29–31); they are 'strangers to the covenants of promise, having no hope and without God in the world' (Eph. 2:12). In 1 Peter we read that Gentiles are given to 'living in licentiousness, passions, drunkenness, revels, carousing and lawless idolatry' (1 Pet. 4:3).

Harsher yet are what authors in the New Testament say about other members of the Christian movement whom they regard as deviant. The 1st-century Christian movement was just as fragmented as Judaism and just as fractious. Paul describes his antagonists at Corinth as 'deceitful workers, disguising themselves as apostles of Christ,' these 'false apostles were in fact ministers of Satan' (2 Cor. 11:13–14). The author of Second Timothy describes his fellow Christian antagonists as corrupt in mind, with a counterfeit faith, ensnared and held captive by the devil to do his will (2 Tim. 2:26; 3:8). For the author of Second John, deviant Christians who deny Jesus had a body of flesh and blood are deceivers and the anti-Christ (2 Jn. 1:7).

Jews, in other words, are not the only people demonized within the pages of the New Testament. Nor are 1st-century Jewish–Christians the only Jews who do the demonizing. 'The world into which the New Testament was born was one of rhetorical hardball, and the earliest Christians learned to play it expertly.'[40] But does that fact eliminate altogether the responsibility of Christian leaders, preachers and educators of addressing or dealing with those demonic texts any further? I think not. Luke Johnson's literary and historical analysis goes a long way toward taking the bite out of the New Testament's anti-Jewish polemics by relativizing them. Grasping their conventional nature not only makes them more intelligible but deprives them of their capacity for mischief. But it takes a bigger pulpit than those offered by academic journals and college classrooms to halt the damage that can be done by Christians quoting the Bible out of context. It will take an army of preachers and the biggest pulpit of all, the chair of Peter, to address the problem of what I call here the demonic in sacred texts.

ADDRESSING THE DEMONIC IN SACRED TEXTS
So what are Catholic leaders and educators – above all those at the church's highest level – to do about the anti-Jewish passages in the New Testament? Painful as it may be, the first and most important step, I would suggest, is to admit their existence. It does no good simply to claim that Christian anti-Judaism began as a misinterpretation of the Christian Scripture. Just as anti-Semitism has its roots in Christian anti-Judaism, so too does Christian anti-Judaism have its roots in the hateful images and references to Jews in the New Testament, a literary witness to the rancorous falling-out between two Jewish sects, Phariseism and the Jesus movement. One of them would become normative, rabbinical Judaism and the other would become a Gentile Christian church, both claiming to possess the authentic interpretation of the Hebrew Scriptures on how to live a godly life.

Once church leaders admit there are anti-Jewish passages in the New Testament, the next question is – what do they do with them. No one seriously suggests censorship as an option. Marcion in the second century was declared a heretic for eliminating biblical passages that offended him. The Merchant of Venice will not be cut out from the Shakespearean canon, nor will the Prophet Mohammed be transferred from Dante's Inferno to the Paradiso. Like all classic texts, the Bible will stay intact.

Another possible solution is to ignore the offending passages by excluding them from use in church worship. It is telling that the official Roman Catholic lectionary has done just that. Used by a variety of Protestant churches as well as all Roman Catholics, the lectionary omits altogether the saliently anti-Jewish John 8:44 and the 'synagogue of Satan' passages from Revelation. Roman Catholics never hear them either at Sunday or daily Mass. But is ignoring the offending passages and the history they generated the best way to deal with that history? In any case, there are other anti-Jewish passages which will never be omitted from the Christian liturgy, most notably in the passion narratives which are read every Holy Week. At those liturgies, the congregation hears about Pilate washing his hands as the Jewish crowd calls out, 'crucify him'. Because the readings are unusually long in Holy Week, Catholic priests are notorious at simply ignoring the problematic passages, preaching only briefly or perhaps excusing themselves from preaching altogether. But not commenting on those passages can lead a congregation to infer Jews to be Christ-killers even without sermons calling them that explicitly. And silence can be construed to mean consent.

Even though they are omitted from the lectionary, the issue is bigger than John 8:44 or the 'synagogue of Satan' references in Revelation, bigger even than the more or less 108 instances of anti-Judaism in the New Testament. When I use the term demonic in this essay, I do so in the broadest sense to refer to passages capable of dividing people into us and them, with God on our side and not on theirs. Research by the social scientists in the United States has shown that Christians who most loudly claim the Bible as the sole basis and center of their faith and thinking are often found to be among the most bigoted and intolerant people in the country. They are adept at quoting the Scripture to justify their hatreds. That is not an accident.

There are texts in the Bible, in both Testaments, that lend themselves to justifying discrimination and intolerance. Phyllis Trible limits her study to only the Hebrew Bible in her feminist reading of passages that have been used to support the suppression of women, passages she aptly calls 'texts of terror.'[41] The New Testament offers a similar mine of passages used to demean women. Bible Christians quote from both testaments in their certitude that 'God hates fags.' They cite Scripture to justify white supremacy and to vilify Catholics. They can quote passages to support a claim that anything that is not explicitly Christian is implicitly in service to the devil (1 John. 5:19).

There is a long history of religious intolerance among Christians of every stripe – Catholic, Protestant, and Orthodox. Certainly a case can be made that xenophobia and intolerance are rooted in our common condition of human sinfulness. But it can also be argued that Christianity's history of anti-Semitism, anti-feminism, crusades, inquisitions, heresy- and witch-hunts arises out of a strain of intolerance embedded in our normative texts. In other words, the issue is larger than anti-Judaism or anti-Semitism. And it is in the context of this wider problem, I would argue, that Christian anti-Judaism and anti-Semitism can most successfully be addressed. Rather than ignoring or excusing the demonic in our sacred texts, Christians need to acknowledge them as such, do them the courtesy of taking them seriously, and deal with the issues they raise. In doing this, Christians can take some valuable lessons from the rabbis.

Judaism has a long tradition of addressing sacred texts critically, even the Torah, and of questioning sacred heroes, like the patriarch Joseph in Egypt. How could Joseph have lived for so many years in luxury and power in Pharaoh's court when his father mourned him as dead? Couldn't he have at least sent a letter, a messenger? What kind of son was he? More germane to our considerations here, the rabbis had to look long and hard at what the Torah has to say about the descendants of Amalek (Exodus 17: 14–16; Deut. 25, 17–19). When Israel was in the desert, on its way to the Promised land, the Amalekites were the tribe that attacked them without warning from the rear, where the most vulnerable were. The Torah says that remembrance of Amalek is to be blotted out, they and all their descendants. King Saul was instructed by the prophet Samuel to slay every man, woman, and child among them (1 Sam. 15:3).

Committed as it is to the canonical text, Rabbinic tradition had to deal with the fact that, if given a literal reading here, the Torah seems to justify genocide. Is God in this instance acting independent of morality? How can these verses be reconciled with

Jeremiah's prophetic injunction that 'every one shall die for his own sin' (Jer. 31:30)? From Talmudic to more recent times, rabbis questioned the text and came up with a variety of interpretations to resolve their moral dilemma. Some have suggested that Amalek is symbolic of metaphysical evil or the evil instinct; others decided that, since the time of Assyrian King Sennacherib (7th century BCE), the nations have all been mixed and Amalek no longer exists. Despite a variety of individual differences among them, the rabbis agreed that the text should not be divorced from the broader context of the Torah and rabbinic tradition, that this text like all others should be interpreted and understood as being in accord with Judaism's moral assumptions rooted in the Torah.[42]

The difficulty, however, is wider than just Amalek and includes all the Canaanites. Israel did not try to appropriate any one else's religion or status as God's chosen people, but it did seek to justify its appropriation of the lands of Canaan, and it did so using the same rhetorical methods the early church used. The anti-Judaic texts of the New Testament have a counterpart in the Torah's demonizing of Amalek and slander of the Canaanites. In the words of biblical scholar John D. Levenson, 'the parallels are not perfect, but neither are they unreal. Like the Jews in some New Testament and much patristic literature, the Canaanites in the Hebrew Bible are, without exception, wicked in the worst of ways.'[43] As the New Testament church vilified Jews in its attempt to justify its claims to supplanting Judaism, Israel earlier vilified the Canaanites. Fortunately for Jewish tradition, the Canaanites have been assimilated, and the rabbis have said that Amalek no longer exists. The question for Christians is, do the *Judaioi* (Judeans) of John's gospel still exist?

Like the rabbis with respect to Torah and their own tradition, Catholic scholars need to question and criticize the texts of the biblical canon and admit the moral dilemmas they sometimes pose. We need to put the anti-Jewish texts of the New Testament into context and then broaden that context. For we have learned too well in this century that not only can the devil quote Scripture, but so too can Nazis and Neo-Nazis, racists, homophobes and misogynists. Certainly, despite its contemporary critics, the New Testament is about more, much more, than anti-Judaism and sexism, more than the suppression of religious and sexual diversity. Christianity's sacred texts witness to the power of God to transform human life from self-centredness into loving service.

Precisely because those sacred texts have transformed lives, ecumenically oriented Christians must not abandon them to those Christians who would exploit them for purposes of hate. At the same time, my co-religionists in the Catholic church and I need to make amends for those Catholics in the past who did just that, who quoted the Bible to justify their hating Jews and demeaning women. If the Holy See can ally itself with the Jewish community against those who would deny the Holocaust, it can also ally itself with modern scholarship against those Bible Christians who would misuse the Bible to excuse their hatred of others, whomever those 'others' might be.

Enlisting the aid of rabbis as well as biblical scholars in addressing the demonic in sacred texts may be a novel idea for cardinals at the Vatican; some might even consider it outrageous. But more remarkable things have happened in the course of the revolution that is occurring in Catholic-Jewish relations. I merely suggest it for consideration as a salutary next step.

N O T E S

1 Philip Schaff and Henry Wace (eds.), *Nicene and Post-Nicene Fathers*, volume 10, *Ambrose: Select Works and Letters* (Peabody: MA: Henrickson, 1994), 440–450.

2   Edward H. Flannery, *The Anguish of the Jews: Twenty-three Centuries of Antisemitism*, revised edition (New York: Paulist Press, 1985), 56–57.

3   Saint John Chrysostom, *Discourses against Judaizing Christians*, transl. Paul W. Harkins (Washingon, D.C.: Catholic University of America Press, 1977).

4   Chrysostom, *Discourses*, 11.

5   Joshua Trachtenberg, *The Devil and the Jews: The Medieval Conception of the Jew and its Relation to Modern Antisemitism* (Cleveland/New York: Meridian; Philadelphia: Jewish Publication Society, 1961).

6   Flannery, *Anguish of the Jews*, 73.

7   Among the more accessible English introductions to the Talmud are Hermann J. Strack, *Introduction to the Talmud and Midrash* (Philadelphia: Jewish Publication Society, 1945); Moses Mielziner, *Introduction to the Talmud* (New York: Block, 1968); and the many works of Jacob Neusner, especially his *Invitation to the Talmud* (New York: Harper and Row, 1984).

8   R. Travers Herford, *Christianity in Talmud and Midrash* (Clifton, NJ: Reference Book Publishers, 1966), 83.

9   Herford has no doubts about the matter, expressing his indebtedness to the work of Heinrich Laible, *Jesus Christus im Talmud* (Berlin, 1891).

10 Even if once accepts the argument of more than one Jesus in the Talmud, the Ben Stada and Ben Pandera references in the Talmud influenced the development of Jewish folktales in the post-Talmudic, medieval Toledot Yeshu, best described as a polemical counter-gospel. The main scholarly work on the topic is Samuel Krauss, *Das Leben Jesu nach jüdischen Quellen* (1902). See also Morris Goldstein, *Jesus in the Jewish Tradition* (New York: 1950).

11 Jacob Katz, *Exclusiveness and Tolerance Studies in Jewish–Gentile Relations in Medieval and Modern Times* (Oxford: Oxford University Press, 1961).

12 For an extensive treatment of the Noahide laws and their implications for Jewish–Christian dialogue, see David Novak, *The Image of the non-Jew in Judaism: An Historical and Constructive Study of the Noahide Laws* (New York/ Toronto: Edwin Mellen Press, 1983) and *Jewish–Christian Dialogue: A Jewish Justification* (New York/ Oxford: Oxford University Press, 1989).

13 Katz, *Exclusiveness and Tolerance*, 174.

14 For a full treatment of Maimonides' view of Christianity, see David Novak, *Jewish–Christian Dialogue: A Jewish Justification*. (New York/Oxford, Oxford University, 1989), 57–72.

15 Katz, *Exclusiveness and Tolerance*, 164.

16 Walter M. Abbot, S.J. (General Editor). *The Documents of Vatican II* (New York: America Press, 1966), 660–668.

17 'Guidelines and Suggestions for Implementing the Conciliar Declaration Nostra Aetate', Secretariat for Catholic-Jewish Relations, National Conference of Catholic Bishops of the United States, 1967. Useful sources for this and other documentation on Jewish Christian relations can be found in Helga Croner (ed.), *Stepping Stones to Further Jewish–Christian relations*, (London/New York: Stimulus Books, 1977) and Helga Croner (ed.), *More Stepping Stones to Jewish–Christian Relations: An Unabridged Collection of Christian Documents, 1975–1983* (New York: Paulist Press, 1985).

18 Bishops' Commitee on the Liturgy, National Conference of Catholic Bishops (Washington, D.C.: United States Catholic Conference, 1988).

19 The full text of 'We Remember', together with a Vatican statement clarifying the intent of the document and relevant statements from European and U.S. bishops, is available in 'Catholics Remember the Holocaust,' publication no.5–290 (Washington, DC: U.S. Catholic Conference, 1999).

20 Among the more valuable critiques attempting to balance and contextualize the Vatican document are John Pawlikowski, 'The Vatican and the Holocaust: Putting We Remember in Context', *Dimensions*, 12: 2 (11–16); Eugene Fisher, Catholics and Jews Confront the Holocaust and Each Other,' *America*, 11 September 1999; Judith H. Banki, 'Catholics and Jews: Vatican Holocaust Statement will help,' *Commonweal*, 28 April 1998, 10–11.

21 The classic expression of this theology is to be found in Charles Journet, *L'Eglise du Verbe Incarné*. 2 vols. (Bruges: Desclee, 1941). Vol.1 translated by A.H.C. Downes as *The Church of the Word Incarnate* (London/ New York: Sheed and Ward, 1955).

22 Pawlikowski, *The Vatican and the Holocaust*, 15.

23 Eva Fleischner (ed.), *Auschwitz: Beginning of a New Era?* (New York: KTAV, 1977), 103–4.

24 *ibid.*, 29.

25 *ibid.*, 103.

26 Ronald Modras, 'Christian Antisemitism and Auschwitz: some Reflections on Responsibility,' *New Theology Review* 10:3 (Aug., 1997) 58–72.

27 Donald J. Dietrich, *God and Humanity in Auschwitz: Jewish–Christian Relations and Sanctioned Murder*. (New Brunswick, NJ/London: Transaction, 1995) 5.

28 James Parkes, *Judaism and Christianity*, (Chicago: University of Chicago, 1948), 167. The literature on the topic is too massive to list here. Some of the notable sources I have used here are: Gregory Baum, *Is the New Testament Anti-Semitic? A Re-examination of the New Testament.* rev. ed. (Glen Rock, NJ: Paulist Press, 1965); Rosemary Radford Ruether, *Faith and Fratricide: The Theological Roots of Anti-Semitism* (New York: Seabury, 1979); in response to Ruether, Alan T. Davies (ed.), *Antisemitism and the Foundations of Christianity* (New York: Paulist Press, 1979); Samuel Sandmel, *Anti-Semitism in the New Testament?* (Philadelphia: Fortress Press, 1978); Stephen Motyer, *Your Father the Devil: A New Approach to John and 'the Jews'* (Carlisle, UK: Paternoster Press, 1997).

29 Richard L. Rubenstein and John K. Roth, *Approaches to Auschwitz: The Holocaust and Its Legacy*. (Atlanta: John Knox Press, 1987), 43.

30 Cited in Motyer, *Your Father the Devil*, 1–2.

31 Cited in Sandmel, *Anti-Semitism in the New Testament*, 156.

32 John Pawlikowski argues, however, that the book of Acts is the most anti-Jewish book in the New Testament and poses more difficulties than the fourth gospel. *Catholic Biblical Quarterly* 49 (1987), 138.

33 Raymond Brown, 'The Narratives of Jesus' Passion and Anti-Judaism,' *America* (April 1, 1995), 12. See also Stephen J. Patterson, *The God of Jesus: The Historical Jesus and the Search for Meaning*, (Harrisburg, PA: Trinity Press International), 207.

34 Luke Timothy Johnson, 'The New Testament's Anti-Jewish Slander and the Conventions of Ancient Polemic,' *Journal of Biblical Literature* 108 (1989): 419–423.

35 See Franklin Littell, *The Crucifixion of the Jews* (New York: Harper & Row, 1975).

36 Johnson, 'The New Testament's Anti-Jewish Slander,' 431.

37 *ibid.*, 435.

38 *ibid.*, 437.

39 *ibid.*, 439, n.62. For a sense of how vigorous debates within the Pharisaic party could be, see Harvey Falk, *Jesus the Pharisee: A New Look at the Jewishness of Jesus*, (New York: Paulist Press, 1985).

40 Luke Timothy Johnson, 'Religious Rights and Christian Texts,' in J. Witte, Jr. and J.D. van der Vyver, *Religious Human Rights in Global Perspective*, 2 vols. (The Hague: Martinus Nijhoff, 1996), 1:76.

41 Phyllis Trible, *Texts of Terror: Literary-feminist Readings of Biblical Narratives*, (Philadelphia: Fortress, 1984).

42 For a recent review of the rabbinic tradition on this matter, see Avi Sagi, 'The Punishment of Amalek in Jewish Tradition: Coping with the Moral Problem,' *Harvard Theological Review*, 87:3 (1994), 323–46.

43 Jon D. Levenson, 'Is There a Counterpart in the Hebrew Bible to New Testament Antisemitism,' *Journal of Ecumenical Studies*, 22:2 (1985), 242–260, here 250.

THE VATICAN STATEMENT ON THE *SHOAH* AND PIUS XII

Richard L. Rubenstein

O N 16 March 1998 the Vatican Commission for Religious Relations with the Jews issued the Holy See's long awaited statement on the *Shoah, We Remember: A Reflection on the Shoah* with a prefatory letter by Pope John Paul II.[1] The document contains five sections. The first is entitled 'The tragedy of the Shoah and the duty of remembrance'. Citing Pope John Paul II's Apostolic Letter of 10 November 1994, *Tertio Milennio Adveniente*, the Commission declares that

> the Church should become more fully conscious of the sinfulness of her children recalling... when they departed from the spirit of Christ and of his Gospel and... indulged in ways of thinking and acting which were truly forms of counter-witness and scandal.

In this statement, the Commission appears to make the highly debatable claim that insofar as the Church's 'children' were perpetrators they conducted themselves in a thoroughly un-Christian manner. The reflection then continues:

> Before this horrible genocide, which the leaders of nations and Jewish communities themselves found hard to believe at the very moment when it was mercilessly put into effect, no one can remain indifferent, least of all the Church, by reason of her very close bonds of spiritual kinship with the Jewish people and her remembrance of the injustices of the past.

The above sentences contain an implicit note of self-exculpation, suggesting that the Holy See could not have been expected to denounce or otherwise take action against the slaughter in view of the fact that leaders of powerful nations as well as of the Jewish communities found it 'hard to believe' what was happening. Apart from the fact that those Jewish leaders who found it 'hard to believe' were speedily and tragically disabused of their illusions, when representatives of the United States and Great Britain urged the Pope to speak out, their requests were politely turned aside.

The first section concludes with 'a call to all Christians to join... in meditating on the catastrophe that befell the Jewish people, and on the moral imperative to ensure that never again will selfishness and hatred grow to the point of sowing such suffering.'

In view of the durability of the Christian teaching depicting Jewish suffering and degradation as ultimately divinely inflicted chastisements for the alleged role of the Jews in crucifying Christ as well as for their continuing 'disbelief', a statement of this sort can be considered helpful in fostering improved inter-religious relations.

The second section is entitled 'What we must remember' and deals with the issue of historical memory. Taking note of the sufferings inflicted on the Jewish people over the centuries 'for the sole reason that they were Jews', the Commission declares that 'the very magnitude of the crime' demands much 'scholarly study'. Although well intentioned, this statement rests on a weak historical foundation. Jews were not persecuted in Christendom simply because they were Jews but because they were faithful to beliefs and values deemed inimical to the maintenance of the Christian symbolic universe. In reality, the leaders of the Church did not act out of malice when they instituted or approved of anti-Jewish measures. On the contrary, the fundamental purpose of such measures was to prevent the Jews from being in a position to lead the faithful astray. Such measures were regarded as defensive in character. That, incidentally, was one of the most important reasons for the Church's vehement opposition to the emancipation of the Jews following the French Revolution. Emancipation bestowed upon the Jews an altogether unprecedented opportunity to enter professions such as journalism, teaching and politics within European Christendom and with it the freedom to influence the faithful.

The Commission then takes note of the question of the relation between the Nazi persecution and traditional Christian attitudes towards the Jews in view of the fact that the *Shoah* took place in Christian Europe. The Commission offers its answer in the third section, 'Relations between Jews and Christians' which contains a very brief encapsulation of the history of Jewish–Christian relations. The Commission observes that the relations between Jews and Christians over two millennia have been 'quite negative', starting with the earliest persecutions of the Church by 'Jewish leaders and people who, in their devotion to the Law, on occasion violently opposed the preachers of the Gospel and the first Christians.' When Christianity became the established religion of the Roman Empire, the situation was reversed and the 'Christian mobs' that attacked pagan temples 'sometimes did the same to synagogues'. According to the Commission, these attacks were 'influenced by certain interpretations of the New Testament regarding the Jewish people as a whole'. Pope John Paul II and the Second Vatican Council are cited as rejecting 'erroneous and unjust interpretations of the New Testament regarding the Jewish people and their culpability'. Nothing is said about the fact that it took the *Shoah* to rethink the 'erroneous and unjust interpretations' or that they were regarded as authoritative for almost two millennia before Vatican II and Pope John Paul II.

The Commission statement also acknowledges that the anti-Jewish disabilities included expulsions, 'attempts at forced conversion', the absence of a 'fully guaranteed juridical status', and a tendency to take the Jews as scapegoats in times of stress so that they sometimes became the victims of 'violence, looting and even massacres'. According to the document, the situation began to change at the end of the 18th and the beginning of the 19th century when Jews generally 'achieved equal status and some even rose to positions of influence in society'. However, the new situation led to 'a false and exacerbated nationalism' in which 'Jews were accused of exercising an influence disproportionate to their numbers'. Nevertheless, the Commission maintains that the new anti-Judaism was 'more sociological and political than religious'. We shall return to this issue. For the moment, let us simply note that the crux of the implicit argument is that while Christian anti-Jewish hostility is to be deplored, the *Shoah* was the result of a very different and infinitely more malignant 'pagan', racist anti-Semitism. The Commission further notes that the appeal of extremist nationalism was intensified in Germany by defeat in World War I and 'the demanding conditions imposed by the victors', thereby placing some blame on the Allies for what took place in Germany at the end of the war. Regrettably, the document ignores both Imperial Germany's territorial ambitions in Belgium and Northern France during World War I and the far harsher peace terms Germany imposed on Russia in the Treaty of Brest Litovsk.[2]

The Commission cites pastoral letters 'condemning racism' by Adolf Cardinal Bertram of Breslau, Michael Cardinal Faulhaber of Munich, and the Bishops of Bavaria, the

Province of Cologne and the Province of Freiburg in February and March 1931, as well as Faulhaber's 1933 Advent sermons and Provost Bernhard Lichtenberg's martyrdom in order to document the German Church's opposition to extremist nationalism. This section concludes by citing Pope Pius XI's Encyclical Letter *Mit Brennender Sorge* of 14 March 1937, his statement to a group of Belgium pilgrims that 'Anti-Semitism is unacceptable. Spiritually, we are all Semites' (6 September 1938), as well as Pope Pius XII's warning in his very first encyclical *Summi Pontificatus* (20 October 1939) against theories which deny 'the unity of the human race' and against the deification of the state. However, the condemnation of racism is not necessarily inconsistent with approval of National Socialism's imposition of legal disabilities against Jews that effectively removed them from business, commerce and the professions and deprived them of their political rights. Moreover, although the statement points to the opposition of the German hierarchy until 1933, it says nothing about the Holy See's role in rendering Catholic opposition to National Socialism impotent through the signing of the *Reichskonkordat* of 1933.

In the fourth section, 'Nazi anti-Semitism and the *Shoah*', the Commission stresses the enormous difference between Nazi anti-Semitism and Christian anti-Judaism 'of which, unfortunately, Christians also have been guilty'. Unlike Christianity, National Socialism denied the unity of the human race and 'the equal dignity of all races and peoples' and refused to acknowledge 'any transcendent reality as the source of life and the criterion of moral good'. It was, according to the Commission, animated by a 'hatred directed at God himself' and a 'desire to see the Church destroyed or at least subjugated to the interests of the Nazi state'.

Having established the difference between Nazi anti-Semitism and Christian anti-Judaism, the Commission asserts that:

> The *Shoah* was the work of a thoroughly modern neo-pagan empire. Its anti-Semitism had its roots outside of Christianity and, in pursuing its aims, did not hesitate to oppose the Church and persecute its members also.

The members of the Commission apparently understood that more was needed than the bald and controversial assertion that Nazi anti-Semitism 'had its roots outside of Christianity'. Hence, they pose the question of whether the Nazi 'persecution of the Jews' was facilitated by 'the anti-Jewish prejudices imbedded in some Christian minds and hearts'. Having posed the question, the Commission argues that the complexity of the issue precludes an overall response.

The question is then asked whether Christians gave 'every possible assistance' and the response is that '. . . many did, but others did not'. Among those who did was Pope Pius XII whom the document singles out and credits with saving 'hundreds of thousands of Jewish lives'. The accolade is expanded in the document's longest footnote in which Jewish expressions of gratitude are cited, including a 1958 tribute by Golda Meir. The defence of Pius XII is arguably the most controversial part of the entire document. Having praised Pius XII, the document cites Pope John Paul II's acknowledgement that 'the spiritual resistance and concrete action of other Christians was not that which might have been expected from Christ's followers'.

As noted above, the document's fundamental claim is that the behaviour of the perpetrators and even the bystanders was somehow inconsistent with Christian morality. Both *Nostra Aetate* and Pope John Paul II's strong condemnation of racism and anti-Semitism are cited to validate this claim. Taking the side of the angels, the Commission then offers a utopian condemnation of 'persecution against a people or human group anywhere, at any time'. Among the examples cited are the Armenian massacre, Stalin's assault against the Ukrainians in the 1930s, the genocide of the Gypsies, the 'tragedies' resulting from racist ideas in 'America, Africa, and the Balkans' and 'the millions of victims of totalitarian ideology in the Soviet Union, in China, Cambodia and elsewhere'. The Commission's final reference is to 'the drama of the Middle East' and the comment that even today 'many human beings are still their brothers' victims'.

This section is almost as problematic as the defence of Pius XII. It implies that the Shoah was but one among a number of horrible examples of mass slaughter in the 20th century, thereby evading the question that is central to the document, namely, whether Christianity itself rather than errant Christians made a significant contribution to the extermination of Europe's Jews. It also adds a gratuitous note by lumping together human rights abuses that led to some loss of life and much suffering with the Holocaust, which had as its objective the unremitting slaughter of every single Jew in the world wherever domiciled. Some observers have also commented that the reference to the 'drama of the Middle East' in a consideration of the Shoah and modern programmes of mass murder is inappropriate if not offensive. There is no denying that the Arab-Israel conflict resulted in much suffering but whether it deserves mention in the context of genocide is another matter. One is moved to ask what were the political motives that compelled the insertion of this reference in the document.

Having found a hook with which some Church leaders could imply a measure of fault in contemporary Jews, the fifth and final section of the document expresses the hope that the Church's 'sorrow for the tragedy which the Jewish people has suffered in our century will lead to a new relationship with the Jewish people'. The concluding sentence expresses the resolve that 'the spoiled seeds of anti-Judaism and anti-Semitism must never again be allowed to take root in any human heart'.

Clearly, this problematic document is the outcome of multiple interests and compromises, although there is little evidence that the document's critics understood this. Writing in the *Canadian Jewish News*, for example, Rabbi Leon Klenicki, Director of Interfaith Affairs of the Anti-Defamation League of B'nai B'rith, expressed 'profound disappointment'. He noted that 'so much progress' had been made in Catholic-Jewish relations since Vatican II that 'expectations of a dramatic conclusion to the recent progress were raised'.[3] The rabbi commented that after the French Bishop's Declaration of Repentance (30 September 1997) and the declaration of the German Bishops Conference (24 January 1995) acknowledged regret and responsibility, the Vatican document is 'disappointing'.[4] Apparently, the rabbi failed to understand that it is easier to achieve consensus among bishops of national churches like France and Germany than for a Vatican commission that must take account of many more constituencies within the Church. The European Conference of Rabbis meeting in Prague on 25 March 1998 offered a more balanced opinion. Rabbi Moshe Rose, director of the conference, acknowledged that the Commission could not have condemned Pius XII by name. At the end of their meeting the rabbis issued a statement that read in part:

> While we must express our disappointment that the Vatican did not accept responsibility for the centuries of persecution of the Jewish people, we recognize the significance of this declaration as a first step in the right direction.[5]

The rabbis were justified in their caution. This document is the work of many hands. Every word had to be weighed. By virtue of the extraordinary range of communities, memories and commitments that find their spiritual home in the Roman Catholic Church, it was impossible for the document to be the kind of clear-cut decisive statement that many Jews and Christians had hoped for. Moreover, it would have been impossible for a Vatican commission to condemn Pius XII. In the eyes of the Church, he was the Vicar of Christ on earth in his time. Throughout his life he was the faithful servant of the Church at a time when it was confronted by some of its most dangerous opponents in its entire history. Many Catholics today believe he merits canonization however controversial his policies may seem to his critics. Some undoubtedly seek his canonization partly *because* of his critics. Father Andrew Greeley, an important Catholic sociologist, novelist and commentator has recently observed:

> It would appear that some people in the Vatican are determined that Pius should be beatified; that they are willing to shove beatification down the throats of protesting Jews is, I think, another terrible mistake.[6]

The question of the canonization of Pius XII is an internal Catholic issue. Jews and, indeed, many Catholics are more likely to rejoice at the canonization of John XXIII than that of Pius XII, but the sensibilities of outsiders are ultimately irrelevant to the canonization process. Nevertheless, if we are to understand the role of the leaders of the Christian Church during the Holocaust it will be necessary to examine the claim implicit in the *Shoah* Statement that the behaviour of the perpetrators and even the bystanders was somehow inconsistent with Christian morality. But, what if the reverse were true? What if those who remained silent knowing that the slaughter was taking place believed that their silence and even the deeds of the perpetrators were actions that, however regrettable, were committed in defence of Christendom if not the Christian religion itself? Let us recall that when the Inquisition handed heretics over to the secular arm for excruciatingly painful capital punishment, its actions were seen by the Church as a necessary defence of Christianity.

The American ethicist Peter Haas has sought to understand how an entire society, not just Nazi party members, willingly participated for over a decade in a state-sponsored programme of mass torture that culminated in genocide without serious opposition from political, legal, medical or religious leaders. According to Haas, the Nazis offered the Germans a new definition of good and evil that facilitated their participation in and acceptance of the *Shoah*. He argues that the Holocaust was not an example of 'the banality of evil' (Hannah Arendt) but of the human ability to redefine good and evil and act accordingly. They were motivated by an ethic that legitimated their behaviour. Crucial to his theory is his definition of an ethic as any *formal* system that permits human beings to characterize some actions as good and others as evil, *irrespective of the system's contents*. 'The power of an ethic', he writes, 'ultimately resides in the fact that it provides a system for judging every action in a coherent, non self-contradictory and intuitively correct way'.[7]

Normally, when confronted with real persons or actions, most people tend to modify the absolute character of the binary opposition of good and evil. Nevertheless, when pushed to an extreme, as often happens in times of acute political or social stress, good and evil come to be mutually exclusive and the world is divided into the children of light and the children of darkness or the elect of the Lord and Satan's spawn.

Something analogous to that division was operative in Germany between 1933 and 1945 when the overwhelming majority of its citizens became convinced that their country was in a life and death struggle with powerful internal and external enemies, the most dangerous being the Jews. In this they were joined by millions of other Europeans for whom the twin struggles against Bolshevism and Judaism were ultimately one. As is well known, the Nazis did not invent the idea of the Jews as the enemies of European

Christian civilization. Nor, according to Haas, were the Nazis alone in believing that the elimination of Europe's Jews was a justifiable benefit. Haas argues that there was a formal congruity between the Nazi ethic and the ethical system of their wartime opponents. Most European and American political and religious leaders shared the Nazi ethic to some extent. There was general agreement concerning the need to fight Bolshevism, the alien character of Judaism, and the principle that the internal policies of a sovereign state were its own affair. Moreover, the Nazi ethic presupposed the 'fully accepted moral category of the just war' which held that killing an enemy in defence of one's community was not morally wrong. Because of the age-old tradition of Christian anti-Judaism, Jews could easily be portrayed as mortal enemies. By so depicting the Jews, the ethical problem of even murdering Jewish children could easily be resolved: If permitted to survive the children would grow up to be enemies of Christian civilization.

Undoubtedly, many people will be uncomfortable with Haas's portrayal of mass murderers as sincerely committed to an ethical system and working for what they believed to be the defence of their community. If, however, we consider the example of participants in a holy war who identify their opponents with radical evil and ruthlessly set out to destroy them, we will have an analogy with the situation Haas seeks to explain. Within their own community, active participants in a holy war are likely to be viewed as selfless defenders of their community's traditions and values.[8]

Perhaps the most serious shortcoming of the *Shoah* statement is its understandable failure to consider the unpleasant question of whether the majority of the leaders of the Christian Church during World War II, and most especially Pius XII, regarded the elimination of Europe's Jews as a benefit for European Christendom. When the Vatican document characterizes the Shoah as 'the work of a thoroughly modern neo-pagan regime' whose anti-Semitism 'had its roots outside of Christianity', that question is clearly ignored. In this essay, I propose the hypothesis, and given the gaps in the archival evidence it cannot be more than an hypothesis, that, contrary to the *Shoah* statement's defence of Pius XII, the Pontiff did indeed regard the elimination of Europe's Jews as a benefit and acted accordingly. I have developed this thesis in previous essays but my understanding of the issue has been deepened by a rereading of Klaus Scholder's *The Churches and the Third Reich* and a reading of John Cornwell's *Hitler's Pope*.[9] I am especially indebted to their contributions to our understanding of the importance of canon law and the politics of concordat diplomacy for an understanding of Pius XII's role in the Holocaust. I would remind my readers that the purpose of an hypothesis is to offer the most plausible interpretation of the known facts. An hypothesis can be falsified by the discovery of new facts. However, it seems highly unlikely that the Vatican would keep hidden any documents that would validate its claims about Pius XII's wartime role.

Because of Cornwell's harsh condemnation of the Pope, his work has been attacked by conservative critics. Nevertheless, it is highly significant that Owen Chadwick, Regius Professor of Modern History at Cambridge from 1968 to 1983 and a church historian of the highest repute, has written in *The Tablet*, the United Kingdom's leading Roman Catholic weekly:

> ... this book is not another conventional tirade about silence during the Holocaust. It is a serious study of a very complex character tossed about in the most tragic series of crises ever to afflict Europe.[10]

Chadwick's evaluation is especially significant in view of the fact that his own book *Britain and the Vatican during World War II* presents a relatively sympathetic view of the Pope.[11]

The accusation that Pius XII did not do enough to save the Jews first attracted international attention in 1963 as a result of a sensational play, *Der Stellvertreter* (in English, *The Deputy*) by Rolf Hochhuth, a German Protestant.[12] Hochhuth's portrayed the Pope as a heartless cynic who never issued a statement explicitly condemning the mass extermination of the Jews or urged Catholic non-cooperation in the Final Solution concerning which he was very well informed. Hochhuth depicts Pius XII as more concerned with the falling price of the Vatican's equity holdings in Hungarian Railroads as the Red army advances than with the fate of the Jews.

Hochhuth's play sparked a controversy about Pius XII that continues to this day. Hochhuth's condemnatory portrait of the Pope entered deeply into the popular imagination. The play also had the effect of eliciting the early publication by the Holy See of its wartime documents, an exception to the rule that Vatican archives remain secret for 75 years.[13] The play was followed by a number of scholarly and not so scholarly works on the role of both the Catholic and Protestant Church during the Holocaust.[14] Until the recent publication of John Cornwell's book, *Hitler's Pope: The Secret History of Pius XII*, most of the debate on the wartime role of Pius XII centered on the period between 1933 and 1945. Unlike almost all other explorations of the subject of Pius XII and Nazi Germany, Cornwell stresses the importance of the Pope's family background and the 19th-century history of the Church for an understanding of his career.

The relevant part of Pius XII's family history begins with the arrival of his grandfather Marcantonio Pacelli in Rome in 1819 to study canon law. Marcantonio quickly rose in the Vatican bureaucracy, becoming a trusted official in the service of Giovanni Maria Mastai-Ferreti, Pope Pius IX, popularly known as Pio Nono. When Pio Nono became Pope in 1846, he was the sovereign of a band of territory across the middle of Italy that included Rome, Bologna, Parma, Ancona and Modena. However, the revolutionary upheavals throughout Europe in 1848 led to popular demands for constitutional government in Rome. Pio Nono acceded to the demands. One of his liberalizing measures was to order the gates to Rome's ghetto torn down. Popular opinion soon turned against him after he denounced Italian nationalism. When Pellegrino Rossi, his prime minister, was assassinated in November 1848, Pio Nono fled to the Kingdom of Naples accompanied by Marcantonio Pacelli.

Protected by French forces, the Pope returned to Rome on 12 April 1850, where he encountered a cold, if not hostile, reception. Partly as a result of his experiences, Pio Nono came to view the political and social changes introduced into Europe by the French Revolution and the Enlightenment as the work of the devil.[15] His views were shared by Marcantonio Pacelli. Whatever willingness Pio Nono might have had to compromise with the forces of liberalism and nationalism evaporated in exile. Upon his return, for example, he forced the Jews of Rome back into the ghetto. Like other members of the hierarchy, Pio Nono firmly believed that Jews might be tolerated as *resident aliens* in Christian lands under strictly regulated conditions that prevented them from leading the faithful astray. Nevertheless, they had absolutely no right to a political voice in a Christian state. This principle had been rejected in the political emancipation of the Jews during the French Revolution. Having experienced at first hand what he regarded as the Revolution's bitter legacy, Pio Nono was firmly and consistently committed to undoing the revolution's political legacy, one of whose most objectionable features was Jewish emancipation. Pio Nono's enforced return of the Jews of Rome to the ghetto epitomized a fundamental attitude shared by all his successors until Pope John XXIII. In this regard, it is interesting to note that when the Commission states that by the beginning of the 19th century Jews had achieved an 'equal standing with other citizens in most States', it omits any reference to the harsh civic disabilities imposed upon Jews in the only 19th-century political entity in which the Vatican was free to define Jewish rights, namely, the Papal states.[16]

Simply stated, throughout the 19th century and until the middle of the 20th, those at the helm in the Vatican regarded the political emancipation of the Jews as a tragic mistake that they were determined to terminate if they could. This objective was repeatedly affirmed in the pages of *Civiltà Cattolica*, a Jesuit political journal founded in 1850 by Carlo Curci, a priest from Naples, with the active encouragement of Pio Nono. The journal speedily became and for decades remained the unofficial organ of the Holy See. If one wishes to understand the attitude of the Vatican towards Jews and Judaism in the second half of the 19th and the first half of the 20th centuries, there is no better source than *Civiltà Cattolica*, save perhaps *L'Osservatore Romano*, one of whose founders in 1861 was Marcantonio Pacelli.

The hostility of the Holy See to the modern world was enormously intensified by the founding of the Kingdom of Italy in 1861 and its seizure of Rome as its capital on 20 September 1870. Pio Nono refused to accept Italian sovereignty and withdrew into the Vatican where he proclaimed himself a prisoner in the Vatican. He and his successors maintained that position until Fascist Italy recognized the Pope's sovereignty over Vatican City in the Lateran Treaty of 1929. Having lost temporal authority, Pio Nono was determined to assert an ever greater claim to unconditional spiritual authority culminating in the promulgation of the dogma of papal infallibility in 1870. The dogma asserts that when the pope acts as supreme teacher of the Church, he cannot err in matters of faith and morals. Even before its promulgation, Pio Nono had published the Syllabus of Errors (8 December 1864) listing 80 of the 'principal errors of our times'. The concluding eightieth article effectively summarized the entire text. It characterized as error the view that 'the Roman Pontiff can and should reconcile himself to and agree with progress, liberalism, and modern civilization'. In effect, the Syllabus of Errors was a call to undo the political and social consequences of the French Revolution. Had the political programme implicit in the Syllabus ever achieved its intended objective, the emancipation of the Jews would have been completely nullified.

Eugenio Pacelli was born in Rome on 2 March 1876 to Filippo and Virginia Graziosi Pacelli. Like his father Marcantonio, Fillipo was a lay canon lawyer. As Vatican lawyers, both Marcantonio and Filippo were poorly paid. Nevertheless, both declined the opportunity to become well-paid bureaucrats of the new Italian state after the establishment of Rome as its capital, preferring the respectable penury of papal employment.[17] The Pacelli family was intensely loyal to the papacy and the Church which they saw 'as threatened on all sides by the destructive forces of the modern world'. Nevertheless, true to their vocation, they saw the universal application of canon law as the key to the Church's survival and future prosperity.[18]

Eugenio Pacelli surprised no one when he decided on the priesthood at the age of 18. Upon ordination in 1896 he began his studies in canon law at St. Apollinaris Institute where he came under the influence of a Jesuit authority on canon law, Franz Xavier Wernz, S.J. According to Cornwell, Pacelli credits Rome's Jesuits as being his special mentors both as a seminarian and throughout his life. Cornwell stresses the importance of *Civiltà Cattolica* on Pacelli during the future Pope's formative years. As the most important journal in the circles that most deeply influenced his development, in reality, the only circles to which he had access, the pages of *Civiltà Cattolica* offer clues concerning many of Pacelli's most enduring attitudes.

Civiltà Cattolica's extreme hostility towards Jews and Judaism until the 1950s has often been documented.[19] Nevertheless, a brief review is in order. Between February 1881 and December 1882, *Civiltà Cattolica* published a series of articles by Giuseppe Oreglia di San Stefano S.J., claiming that, especially in Eastern Europe, the ritual murder of Christian children under conditions of extreme cruelty was a Jewish religious obligation. The author claimed that the children's blood was used in the Passover meal. The Jews were also accused of stealing and desecrating consecrated Hosts, the Communion bread that becomes the 'body and blood' of Christ in the Mass. Implicit in these libels, which had persisted since the twelfth century, was the belief that the Jews used magic in order ultimately to destroy Christianity. These beliefs were pervasive in parts of Eastern Europe and even the Holocaust could not eradicate them.[20]

In addition to ritual murder, *Civiltà Cattolica* published a series of articles in 1890 entitled *Della questione ebraica in Europa* (Concerning the Jewish Question in Europe) that were widely disseminated in pamphlet form. With no basis in reality, the author alleged that the Jews started the French Revolution to gain civic equality, place themselves in key positions in most state economies in order to control them, and institute a 'virulent campaign against Christianity'. Identified as a 'race that nauseates', the author called for their segregation from the rest of the population and the abolition of their civic equality.

Civiltà Cattolica was deeply involved in the celebrated case of Captain Alfred Dreyfus, the only Jewish member of the French General Staff, who was falsely accused of espionage for Germany in 1894 and sentenced for life to hard labour on Devil's Island. When the real culprit, Major C.F. Walsin-Esterhasy, was discovered and confessed before fleeing the country, the Army refused to admit error. Commenting on the Army's refusal, on 5 February 1898 *Civiltà Cattolica* expressed the opinion that 'The Jew was created by God to serve as a spy wherever treason is in preparation'. The journal commented:

> The Jews allege an error of justice. The true error was that of the *Constituante* which accorded them French nationality. That law has to be revoked.... Not only in France, but in Germany, Austria, and Italy as well, the Jews are to be excluded from the nation. Then the old harmony will be re-established and the peoples will again find their lost happiness.

Although Dreyfus was pardoned by the President of the Republic in 1899 and restored to rank in 1904, the affair was a foretaste of what lay ahead for Europe's Jews in the 20th century.

Civiltà Cattolica saw only one solution to the Jewish problem in Europe, conversion to Christianity. A newspaper correspondent at the first Dreyfus in 1894, Theodor Herzl had another solution. Herzl was deeply sensitive to the rising antagonism against the Jews throughout modern Europe. Convinced that Jews had no future in Europe, Herzl became the founder of the modern Zionist movement whose ultimate objective was the emigration of Europe's Jews to Palestine. The revolutionary new movement did not escape the notice of *Civiltà Cattolica*. In May 1897 the journal published one of the earliest expressions of Catholic opposition to Zionism. It remains one of the most succinct statements of the conservative Catholic position on the subject:

> 1827 years have passed since the prediction of Jesus of Nazareth was fulfilled, namely that Jerusalem would be destroyed ... that the Jews would be led away to be slaves among all the nations, and that they would remain in the dispersion till the end of the world ... According to Sacred Scriptures, the Jewish people must always live dispersed and wandering among the other nations, so that they may render witness not only by the Scriptures ... but by their

very existence. As for a rebuilt Jerusalem, which would become the center of a reconstituted
state of Israel, we must add that this is contrary to the prediction of Christ Himself.[21]

In another article on Zionism published in 1899, the journal referred to the Jews as 'a
race of murderers', echoing John 8:41–45.[22]

The tradition that the sufferings and wanderings of the Jews are divinely inflicted
punishments for their rejection of Jesus Christ as Messiah and their alleged participation
in his crucifixion was central to Christian doctrine until Vatican II. Moreover, there is no
reason to doubt that the Pope who proclaimed as infallible the dogma of the Assumption,
namely, that Mary's body did not corrupt and die but was incorruptibly *assumed* into
heaven where she sits enthroned as Queen, could have had any doubt that the sufferings
of the Jews, no matter how severe, were divinely inflicted providential chastisements.
There is nothing in the *Civiltà Cattolica* article to which the young Pacelli could have
taken exception. Moreover, it was undoubtedly the interpretive matrix used by Pius XII
to understand what was happening to the Jews during World War II and reflected the
attitude of Vatican leadership during most of the 20th century.

Moreover, *Civiltà Cattolica's* hostility towards Jews and Judaism did not abate with the
advent of the Third Reich. In 1936 the journal spelled out the difference between
National Socialism's racial anti-Semitism and Christian anti-Semitism. The journal
complained that the Jews 'have become the masters of the world' whose supreme ideal
'is to turn the world into an incorporated joint stock company'.[23] Like the Pope himself,
Civiltà Cattolica was silent about the fate of the Jews during World War II although it is
hard to believe that the editors lacked relatively accurate information on the subject. The
slaughter was mentioned in 1946 in an article that questioned the objectivity of the
Nuremberg trials and sought to exonerate Germany for the crimes. The editors commented: 'conceding even that, on diplomatic grounds, Germany had been the one to set
the gunpowder on fire, historically, they had been compelled to do so'.[24]

In estimating the degree to which the views of *Civiltà Cattolica* coincided with those of
Pacelli, it must be remembered that *Civiltà Cattolica* was not a marginal rag but one of
the most respected and authoritative organs of the Church. Moreover, had its views been
in any way objectionable to the Holy See, the editors would have quickly altered them.
Freedom of the press was not highly valued by the Vatican in the period in which the
dogma of papal infallibility was formulated. John Cornwell is not wide of the mark when
he asserts that a ground swell of vicious antipathy towards Jews was promoted in the only
circles to which Pacelli had access.

Pacelli's career was on a fast track from the start. Can anyone seriously believe that
Pacelli would have risen so high or so rapidly if he had not fully shared the opinions and
values of his superiors? In 1901 Monsignor Pietro Gaspari, the Vatican equivalent of
Foreign Minister, took the highly unusual step of calling on the young priest at the home
of his family and inviting Pacelli to join him in the Secretariat of State. The partnership
was to last thirty years until Pacelli himself succeeded Gaspari as Cardinal Secretary of
State in 1930. In 1904 Pacelli completed his doctoral dissertation and was then appointed
secretary to Gaspari in the latter's capacity as President of the Papal Commission on
Codification. His thesis subject, the nature of concordats, was prophetic for his
later career and for an understanding of his relations with the Third Reich in its initial
phase.

The Commission on Codification laboured from 1904 to 1917 to bring forth the
monumental *Corpus iuris canonici*, the Code of Canon Law, whose principal architects
were Gaspari and Pacelli. The code was a comprehensive law-book that exhaustively
regulated conditions within the Church in the spirit of Pio Nono's very conservative

First Vatican Council. It is undoubtedly one of the most important documents in the history of the modern Church. Codification was a rationalizing and modernizing strategy that enhanced centralized bureaucratic control of the entire Church by the Holy See. According to Cornwell, Pope Pius X created the code as a modernizing device to foster conformity, discipline, and centralization, thereby enhancing papal power and religious uniformity to an unprecedented degree.

As noted above, throughout the 19th century Church authorities saw their institution as threatened by the political and cultural forces of modern life. In response they regarded as indispensable a strengthened, authoritarian Church based upon the belief that Christ Himself had established and, through the inspiration of the Holy Spirit, continued to guide His Church. The doctrine of Papal Infallibility was a corollary of the Church's self-understanding, but the doctrine could be rendered impotent were the bishops to treat it with reservation or ignore it altogether. In consequence, it became necessary for Rome to control the appointment of bishops. Ironically, the secularization of the nation state in the 19th century and the diminution of the state's interest in interfering with the governance of the Church left the Church free to stipulate the way bishops were appointed. Pius X grasped the significance of the new situation and sought a total separation of sovereignties with the Pope as the head of the Church and relations with the world mediated through the papal diplomatic service and bishops. Pius X had little use for the Catholic political parties in France, Italy, or Germany, because he could not control them. Their understanding of the interests of French or German Catholics was often different from that of the Vatican. On one occasion, Pius X remarked, 'I do not like the *Zentrumspartei* (the German Catholic Centre Party) because it is a Catholic party.'[25] Within the pyramid of papal power, the Pope saw no role for lay-clerical pluralism. As we shall see, papal distaste for Catholic political parties was to have momentous consequences in 1933 when Pius X's successor, Pius XI, and Cardinal Secretary of State Pacelli agreed to Hitler's demand that the German Catholic Centre Party dissolve itself as the price for agreeing to the kind of concordat that the Vatican wanted.

Canon 329.2 of the *Corpus iuris canonici*, the Code of Canon Law, endows the Pope with the sole right to appoint bishops. Among others, John Cornwell looks with disfavour on this development as fostering an unduly authoritarian Church. There is, however, another side to the story. There are situations in which local appointment of bishops may endanger the integrity of the Church. For example, on January 6, 2000 just hours before Pope John Paul II consecrated twelve new bishops in St. Peter's Basilica, Beijing's state-sanctioned Catholic Church consecrated five new bishops without the consent of Rome. There can be little doubt that the new Chinese bishops' fundamental loyalty will belong to the Communist regime rather than to Rome.[26] Similarly, without an agreement with Hitler guaranteeing the right of the Holy See to name Germany's bishops, Hitler rather than the Pope would ultimately have determined the appointment of bishops in Nazi Germany. However, the Holy See's right to name bishops could not be implemented in many jurisdictions without the renegotiation of some major concordats. That would not prove to be an easy task. The first concordat negotiated by Pacelli was with Serbia in 1914 and involved the *de facto* abrogation of Austria-Hungary's ancient protectorate rights over Catholic enclaves in Serbia. Moreover, the Austrian government and the Papal Nuncio to Vienna were kept in the dark for over a year while Pacelli conducted negotiations with the Serbs. The accord was signed in the Vatican on 24 June 1914, four days before the assassination of Archduke Franz Ferdinand in Sarajevo that triggered the start of World War I. *The negotiations and the signing of the accord revealed that Pacelli was willing to compromise the long-term interests of one of the most important Catholic states in Europe for the sake of the expansion of papal power.* The Austrians were understandably furious over what they regarded as a double betrayal, the secret Vatican negotiations and the weakening of Austrian influence in the Balkans. The concordat with Serbia marked the ominous beginning of Pacelli's pattern of utter aloofness from the far-reaching political consequences of his diplomatic efforts on behalf of the Pope and the institution of the papacy.

Pius X died in August 1914 and was succeeded by Benedict XV, Giocomo della Chiesa, on 3 September 1914 just as World War I was commencing. One of the new Pope's first acts was to appoint Gaspari Papal Secretary of State. At Gaspari's insistence Pacelli remained in Rome until the completion of the *Codex iuris canonici* in 1917. Shortly thereafter Pacelli was consecrated an archbishop and appointed Papal Nuncio to Bavaria.

In his official capacity, Pacelli met many of the principal leaders of Imperial Germany in its last two years, including Kaiser Wilhelm II, King Ludwig III of Bavaria, Matthias Erzberger, a leading figure in the Catholic Centre Party, and German Chancellor Theobold von Bethmann-Hollweg. However, the event that made the most profound impression on him took place at the very end of the war. On 7 November 1918, the royal house of Bavaria was overthrown and Kurt Eisner, a socialist Jewish writer from Berlin, found himself at the head of the provisional revolutionary government of Bavaria. In addition to Eisner, a number of other Jewish intellectuals, *literati*, and revolutionaries took highly visible leadership roles in the three successive revolutionary regimes in Munich. They included Gustav Landauer, Eugen Leviné, Ernst Toller, and Towia Axelrod.[27] Eisner was assassinated by Count Anton von Arco Valley, a right-wing extremist of partly Jewish descent. After his death, a Bavarian Soviet Republic was established without the Communists. A second Soviet Republic led by Eugen Leviné, a Russian-born, Jewish-educated Communist, was established in April. On Palm Sunday 1919 posters signed by Leviné appeared all over Munich proclaiming:

> Finally today Bavaria has also elected the dictatorship of the proletariat. The sun of world revolution has risen: Long live the world revolution![28]

To frighten the bourgeoisie into submission, the Munich Soviet's action committee announced an indefinite general strike. The police were disbanded and replaced by a Red Guards. When the Whites declared a blockade, the Reds ordered the confiscation of all hoards of food, wherever found. When the milk supply was reduced to a tenth the normal amount, Leviné declared:

> What does it matter if for a few weeks less milk reaches Munich? Most of it goes to the children of the bourgeoisie. We are not interested in keeping them alive. No harm if they die-they'd only grow into enemies of the proletariat.[29]

The revolution ended in a right-wing bloodbath, but not before the Reds entered Pacelli's compound, pointed a gun at his breast, demanded his limousine, and threatened to kill him. In later life Pacelli often alluded to this incident. In the eyes of the victorious right, the Bavarian Republic and the two subsequent Soviet Republics constituted a 'pogrom against the German people staged by Jews'.[30] A violent wave of anti-Semitism ensued in Munich, then becoming the birthplace and spiritual capital of the National Socialist movement.

Pacelli was acutely conscious of the Jewish character of much of the rebellion's leadership. In a letter to Gaspari, Pacelli described a meeting in April 1919 between his assistant, Monsignor Scioppa, and Max Levien, one of the ruling triumvirate of the Munich Soviet, at Levien's headquarter as 'absolute hell':

> ...a gang of young women of dubious appearance, Jews like all the rest of them, hanging around in all the offices with lecherous demeanor and suggestive smiles. The boss of this female rabble was Levien's mistress, a young Russian woman, a Jew and a divorcée. And it was to her that the nunciature was obliged to pay homage in order to proceed.[31]

> This Levien is a young man of about thirty or thirty-five, also Russian and a Jew. Pale, dirty, with drugged eyes, hoarse voice, vulgar, repulsive, with a face that is both intelligent and sly...he listened to what Monsignor Schioppa told him, whining repeatedly that he was in a hurry and had more important things to do.

Finally, Pacelli wrote to Gaspari that a right-wing, White Brigade was battling the Red Brigade for control of the city. In this letter Pacelli wrote that Munich is 'suffering under a harsh Jewish–Russian revolutionary tyranny'.[32]

Like Cornwell, Carlo Falconi and many others, I believe Pacelli's Munich experience was enormously influential in framing the context of his policies towards the Jews during World War II.[33] Cornwell comments that Pacelli's 'constant harping' on the Jewishness of the Red leadership is consistent with the German belief that the Jews were the instigators of the Bolshevik Revolution and that their principal aim was to destroy Christian civilization. Cornwell also notes that Pacelli's repeated references to the Jewishness of the Reds, describing them as physically and morally repulsive, 'gives an impression of anti-Semitic contempt'.[34] Cornwell is correct in noting Pacelli's resort to anti-Semitic stereotypes, but that was hardly surprising under the circumstances. As Papal Nuncio to Bavaria, with a firm commitment to order and hierarchy, he had known many of the most important leaders of Imperial Germany. Suddenly, they were deposed and an unkempt, rag-tag group of revolutionaries, some highly idealistic, others less so, all wholly ignorant of the fundamental social and political realities of Germany even in defeat, seized power in the quixotic belief that they could change the world. In addition, the world they sought to build had no place for religion. Nor did the presence of so many Jews in the Red leadership help matters for Pacelli. Rightly or wrongly, these were people of little or no standing in Imperial Germany. Suddenly, they were in command.

Nor was Bavaria the only predominantly Catholic European nation that was threatened by a Bolshevik takeover. A Hungarian soviet republic came to power on 21 March 1919 under the leadership of Béla Kun, a doctrinaire Bolshevik and the son of a Jewish village clerk. Kun succeeded to power after the demise of Hungary's first post-war regime led by the liberal provisional president Count Mihaly Karolyi. With Serb, Czech and Romanian troops installed in defeated Hungary, Kun claimed that Bolshevik Russia would come to Hungary's aid if a communist government was installed. No help came, but Kun, a rigid communist ideologue, applied 'brutal and extreme' measures against both the nation's rural and urban populations.[35]

In July 1919 Kun led an unsuccessful military campaign against the Romanians. The Hungarians were defeated 1 August 1919 and Kun fled to Vienna. Unfortunately, 18 of 29 leading members of the short-lived communist regime were Jewish. In the eyes of the Hungarian public, communism was equated with Judaism. On 16 November 1919, Admiral Miklos Horthy entered Budapest at the head of a counter-revolutionary army and installed a government whose aim was to purify Hungary from communism. In the ensuing White Terror, supported by Horthy, most victims were Jews. In addition, a large number of 'patriotic' organizations were formed, with the dual aim of nullifying the Treaty of Trianon and 'purifying' Christian Hungary of the allegedly harmful influence of Jews and Judaism.

The Munich revolution proved to be a disaster for the Jews of Europe, the great majority of whom had no sympathy for Bolshevism. And, its effect on Pacelli was to prove enduring. *For Pacelli, the Communist revolution was not something that happened in distant Russia.* He had experienced it directly. He also saw the right-wing nationalist forces that suppressed the revolutions in Bavaria and Hungary as the defenders of Christian civilization against the assault of rootless, godless communists, many of whom were Jews. That lesson was never to leave him. If he had any doubts concerning the destabilizing consequences of Jewish emancipation and their entrance into European intellectual and political life before Munich 1919, he had none thereafter. His experience certainly added credibility in his eyes, if indeed he needed further credibility, to *Civiltà Cattolica*'s views on the place of Jews in Europe.

Nevertheless, Pacelli's most important business in Germany was not to witness a revolution but to bring about a fundamental change in the relations between the Vatican and the German Catholic Church. Before the war German Catholics had been Europe's most generous community in their support of the Holy See. In spite of military defeat, they remained the one of the most important Catholic populations in Europe. Pacelli's ultimate goal was to negotiate a concordat with the Reich satisfactory to the Holy See that would be binding on all Germany. Although there had been a Prussian legation to the Vatican since 1882, there had never been a Reich legation and hence no Reich Concordat. Pacelli realized that, unlike Imperial Germany, the new constitution of the Weimar Republic, with its separation of Church and state, left the Church free of political interference in the appointment of bishops. Pacelli also realized that any attempt to strengthen the Vatican's control over the German Church would meet with strong opposition from Protestant conservatives, the Social Democrats, and even some German Catholics zealous of the German Church's hereditary prerogatives.

Pacelli's strategy was to negotiate concordats one state at a time, thereby playing off each state against the Reich. With few friends after defeat in the first World War, Germany was interested in cultivating Rome's good will and on 27 September 1919, Diego von Bergen became the first ambassador of the Reich to the Holy See. At the same time, the Reich government informed Pacelli that it was amenable to a Reich Concordat and a restructuring of church-state relations. The Nuncio preferred to negotiate first with Catholic Bavaria and then use the Bavarian concordat as leverage to compel the predominantly Protestant Prussian and Reich governments to sign favourable concordats. Pacelli also suggested that Bavaria maintain its legation at the Vatican with the Reich legation representing the rest of Germany. That arrangement made it possible for the Vatican to send two Nuncios to Germany, one for Berlin, the other for Munich. If the arrangement was unacceptable, Pacelli warned, the Holy See would prefer no Reich legation. The Reich government gave in. Then in May 1920 Gaspari appointed Pacelli Papal Nuncio to the Reich as well as Bavaria thereby enabling Pacelli to play Bavaria, Prussia, and the Reich against each other.[36]

On 30 June 1920, Pacelli became the first diplomat to present his credentials to the Reich government. He thereby became the doyen and senior member of the diplomatic corps in Berlin, a position he held until December 1929. Thus, Pacelli saw the rise of National Socialism in two pivotal German cities, Munich and Berlin, and was undoubtedly one of the best-informed Vatican officials on Germany of his time.

Pacelli commuted from Munich to Berlin as often as necessary but did not take up residence in Berlin until 1925. Initially, he devoted most of his time to securing a concordat with Bavaria. He demanded that the Bavarian state guarantee the application of canon law to the faithful and that it be bound by all of the bishops' proposals regarding teachers of religion. Although the state paid for Catholic education, Pacelli insisted that the state must fire teachers the bishops found objectionable. The Bavarians found Pacelli's demands excessive but agreed to sign when Pacelli threatened to break off negotiations. However, the concordat required the approval of the Reich government in order to come into effect. The approval was forthcoming when Pacelli threatened to appoint a French bishop in the Saar, an historically German district temporarily occupied by the French. In his dealings with both the Bavarians and Reich authorities, Pacelli demonstrated that he was not averse to playing hardball effectively concerning issues he considered of vital interest to the Church.

Pope Benedict XV died on 22 January 1922. The new Pope, Achille Ratti, took office as Pius XI on 6 February 1922, retaining Gaspari and Pacelli in their respective posts. Pacelli and Ratti shared a deep hatred for Bolshevism. Pacelli had already been approached in 1921 by the Reich Chancellor, Joseph Wirth, concerning a concordat. When Wirth inquired concerning the Vatican's terms, Pacelli stipulated that the Vatican must have the same control over Catholic schools and teachers in Prussia as he was proposing for Bavaria. Once again, Pacelli resorted to threats. Without a concordat on the Vatican's terms, Pacelli declared a German bishop would not be appointed in French-occupied Trier. The threat moved the Reich government to express a willingness to discuss the school issue.

Bavaria signed the concordat on 24 March 1924. His harsh bargaining tactics had paid off, but Rome's victory did not play well in predominantly Protestant Prussia, the largest and most important state in Germany. His task completed in Munich, Pacelli moved on to Berlin on 18 August 1925. Convinced that the time was not opportune for a concordat with the Reich as a whole, he next sought a concordat with Prussia. However, Pacelli found negotiating a concordat with the Protestant Prussians far more difficult. Otto Braun, the Prussian Prime Minister, informed him that the Prussian government would not agree to any concordat provision that dealt with Catholic schools. Moreover, the government refused to agree to the Holy See having the sole right to appoint bishops. Instead, it stipulated that the Vatican could choose three candidates and the canons would make the final choice. In addition, the Prussian government insisted on the right, when necessary, to veto the canons' choice. Although this was hardly the concordat Pacelli sought, the two sides signed the agreement on 14 June 1929. That was not to be the end of the matter. In August Pacelli wrote to Braun declaring that he had signed under pressure and that he had not renounced his 'fundamental principles'.[37]

Approaching 80, Gaspari retired late in 1929 and died soon thereafter. Shortly thereafter Pacelli returned to Rome where on 7 February 1930 Pope Pius XI named him to succeed Gaspari as Cardinal Secretary of State. One of Gaspari's final achievements was the signing of the Lateran Treaty with Fascist Italy, a treaty drafted and negotiated by Francesco Pacelli, Eugenio's brother. Under the terms of the accord, the Papacy finally recognized the Kingdom of Italy with Rome as its capital. In return, Italy recognized the Pope's full sovereignty over the 109-acre Vatican City. The state also agreed to permit Catholic religious instruction in primary and secondary schools while ceding to the bishops the right to appoint or dismiss teachers of religion in the schools. The treaty acknowledged the unhindered right of the Church to impose the Code of Canon Law within Italy and Catholicism became the sole officially recognized religion. Article 43 of the treaty included the commitment of the Holy See 'to renew for all clergy, and all those in religious orders in Italy, the prohibition against registering in and being active in any political party.'[38] The article resulted in the disbanding of the Catholic Popular Party, thus effectively bringing to an end an important centre of opposition to Mussolini and Italian Fascism. In the election following the treaty, the Vatican encouraged priests to support the Fascists and the Pope characterized Mussolini as 'a man sent from Heaven'.[39]

The Lateran Treaty was a forerunner of the Reich Concordat of 1933. As noted, both Pacelli and the Pope had a strong aversion to Catholic parties and political Catholicism. In addition, the Vatican unconditionally favoured Fascism over Bolshevism. The vicious persecution of the Church in the Soviet Union had no counterpart in a Fascist Italy that was willing to come to terms with the Holy See. Moreover, Adolf Hitler grasped the significance of the treaty for Germany and commented upon it at length in a speech delivered at a party meeting in Munich on 21 February 1929. The next day the Nazi newspaper *Völkischer Beobachter* reported on Hitler's speech in an article with the headline 'A Speech by Hitler on the Roman Question'.[40] In discussing the significance of the treaty, most commentators stressed the establishment of Vatican City as a sovereign entity. By contrast, Hitler emphasized the fact that Mussolini had, with the consent of the Vatican, eliminated Catholic political opposition and had demonstrated that Fascism was closer to Christianity than the 'Jewish liberalism' of the German Catholic Centre Party. He went on to chastise the Catholic Centre Party as mistaken in its pro-democratic attitudes.

According to Scholder, Hitler's views on the relevance of the Lateran Treaty for a future National Socialist Germany were accurately presented in December 1930 in a publication from the Party office entitled *National Socialism and the Catholic Church* written by Johannes Stark, a Nobel Laureate in Physics and a convinced Nazi. Scholder argues for the authenticity of the document as an authoritative reflection of Hitler's own views from the fact that, as a Nobel Laureate, Stark had neither political ambition nor expertise in the subject of concordats. Stark commented that the Holy See had never approved of the 'Black–Red' coalition of the Social Democratic Party and the Catholic Centre Party that had governed Germany through most of the 1920s. He promised that things would be different in a National Socialist state:

> As soon as Marxism, the declared enemy of the Church, is forced out of power and the Catholic Church declares its connection with the German Volk...the leaders of the Catholic Church can conclude treaties with the new power in Germany which is friendly to the Church and can do without the political support of the Center Party. Then, as in the concordat with the Fascist state in Italy, in a treaty with the National Socialist state of Germany the Vatican can declare that it will prohibit all clergy and members of religious orders in Germany from joining any political party or being involved in it. That will mean the end of the Center Party.[41]

As we shall see, the thinking of Hitler and Pacelli largely coincided on the conditions necessary for a *Reichkonkordat*.

The period between 1930 and 1933 was a time of turbulence for the world and especially for Germany. By July 1930 the Nazi Party had become the second largest in Germany and the question of its participation in government had become urgent. In August 1931 Heinrich Brüning, Germany's chancellor and a leader in the Catholic Centre Party, visited Rome to called on Pope Pius XI and Mussolini. As a result of Brüning's deflationary policies and a growing international bank crisis, the German economy was facing disaster. 4.5 million were unemployed and industrial production had declined drastically. Brüning hoped for the assistance of the Pope and Mussolini in alleviating the burden of the war reparations the victorious allies had imposed upon Germany.[42] Before the papal audience, Brüning spent forty-five minutes with Cardinal Secretary of State Pacelli who demanded that German military chaplains report to their local bishops rather than to the military bishop as had been customary. Brüning warned Pacelli that were he, a Roman Catholic Chancellor, even to raise the issue, he would enrage the conservative Protestants and meet with strong Socialist opposition at a time of extreme national economic distress. Brüning told the prelate that he was determined to avoid doing anything that would impose even the slightest additional stress on the domestic political situation in Germany. Indifferent to the German political situation, Pacelli was so fixated on achieving a Concordat that he gave Brüning's words no heed. He then told Brüning that he 'ought to form a government of the Right simply for the sake of a Reich concordat, and in doing so make it a condition that a concordat be concluded immediately'. According to Brüning, Pacelli indicated his willingness to see Hitler in the cabinet. The Chancellor replied to Pacelli 'that he mistook the political situation in Germany and, above all, the true character of the Nazis'.[43]

After the papal audience at which German bishops were in attendance, Brüning returned to Pacelli and told him that upon reflection he had decided to drop all negotiations concerning the military chaplains and the Reich concordat. He also told Pacelli with more than a little bitterness that he believed 'the Vatican would fare better at the hands of Hitler and Hugenberg than with the Catholic Brüning.'[44] Ironically, this opinion was shared by Pacelli.

Cornwell cites a chilling reflection on Pacelli from the manuscript version of Brüning's memoirs that was not included in the published version:

> All successes [Pacelli believed] could only be attained by papal diplomacy. The system of concordats led him to despise democracy and the parliamentary system.... Rigid governments, rigid centralization, and rigid treaties were supposed to introduce an era of stable order, an era of peace and quiet.[45]

In spite of Brüning's opposition, the Pope and Pacelli continued to urge the leadership of the Catholic Centre Party to explore the possibility of cooperating with the National Socialists. In December 1931 the Pope told the Bavarian ambassador that cooperation between the Church and the National Socialists could prevent 'a still greater evil'.[46] According to both Scholder and Cornwell, this view reflected Pacelli's opinion but not that of the German bishops.

Brüning resigned under pressure on 30 May 1932 and was succeeded by Franz von Papen, a conservative Catholic who favoured a deal with Hitler. One of Papen's first acts was to lift the ban on Hitler's brownshirts, the S.A. He also dissolved the Reichstag, necessitating new elections in which the Nazis became the largest political party in Germany with the ability to create chaos in the streets with the newly enabled brownshirts. In spite of the seeming inevitability of the National Socialist seizure of power, the German hierarchy repeated its denunciation of National Socialism in the published edition of the minutes of the bishops annual conference at Fulda.

The bishops notwithstanding, Papen continued to seek an alliance with Hitler. He had an important ally in Monsignor Ludwig Kaas, the Chairman of the Catholic Centre Party since 1928, an expert in canon law and a representative in the Reichstag. According to Cornwell, by 1931 Kaas had for all practical purposes become Pacelli's personal assistant and companion. In spite of his responsibilities as party leader, Kaas represented the interests of the papacy rather than the party. Moreover, after the signing of the Reich Concordat, Kaas left Germany permanently for Rome where he served Pacelli as translator and in other capacities.

Both Scholder and Cornwell stress the importance of an influential essay written by Kaas in the summer of 1932 on the political significance of the Lateran Treaty in which

Kaas argued that German Catholics could learn some lessons from what took place in Italy.[47] Kaas maintained that there was a genuine affinity between Fascism and the Church. Both are based upon an hierarchical ordering of power concentrated at the top. This, he claimed, is the reason why Mussolini could have no objection to the Church's insistence on the state's recognition of Canon Law in the religious sphere:

> Nobody would have better understood the claim to comprehensive law, such as that demanded by the Church, than the dictator who in his own sphere had established a radical, unchallenged and unchalleable, hierarchical Fascist edifice.

Kaas saw the Lateran Treaty as an ideal agreement between the modern totalitarian state and the modern Church in which the central issue was acceptance by the state of the Code of Canon Law for its Catholic citizens. Cornwell comments:

> Nowhere had the ideology of papal supremacy... been so clearly compared with the fascist *Führer-prinzip* – leadership principle – or the necessity for withdrawal from social democracy more frankly urged.[48]

Given the closeness of the relationship between Pacelli and Kaas, both canon lawyers, and the strict provisions of the code itself, Cornwell argues that Kaas' article could not have been written without the prior consultation and approval of Pacelli. As events were to prove, Pacelli was about to act in accordance with Kaas' insights. In reality, they were his own.

Adolf Hitler became chancellor of Germany on 30 January 1933. In February, Hitler publicly declared that Germany's churches were an integral part of German life. Privately he vowed that he would eradicate Christianity.[49] In spite of Hitler's assurances, most leaders of the German Catholic Church were undeceived about National Socialism and the Catholic Center Party constituted an important part of the German democratic opposition to National Socialism in the nineteen-twenties and early thirties.

In the elections held on 5 March 1933, Hitler failed to get the absolute majority he sought. Although determined to render political Catholicism impotent, Hitler was reluctant to use the methods the Nazis had used against the Communists and Social Democrats. He believed that Germany had lost the first World War because of divisions within the German *Volk*. He did not want one third of the *Volk* to be resentful of him or in opposition in view of the dangerous adventures he had planned for Germany. For Hitler, the ideal solution was a treaty similar to the Lateran Treaty in which Catholics themselves abandoned independent political action. At least on paper, Hitler was willing to grant Catholics a degree of religious freedom and to agree to the Holy See's terms on the imposition of Canon Law on the German Church. His price was the complete withdrawal of Catholics from social and political action.

With Hitler in power, Pacelli knew that he finally had the one German politician in office who was both willing and able to sign a concordat on terms agreeable to the Vatican. Nevertheless, the German bishops continued to oppose a deal. On 7 March Hitler told his cabinet that the Center Party could only be defeated if the Vatican were persuaded to abandon it. For his part, Parcelli sent out signals that he was ready for a deal.

After the unsuccessful Munich Beer Hall Putsch of 1923, Hitler was determined to come to power by legal means, but Hitler wanted absolute power. The Enabling Act, passed by the Reichstag on 24 March 1933, was Hitler's method of attaining absolute power 'legally'. In retrospect, it is possible to theorize that Hitler sought political legitimacy because he understood that without it he could not have brought ordinary Germans willingly and with a good conscience to commit the heinous crimes they perpetrated. The Enabling Act gave Hitler the power to enact laws and conduct foreign policy without the consent of the Reichstag. Put differently, Hitler successfully demanded that the German parliament effectively put itself out of business.

Brüning urged the Catholic Centre Party not to cooperate with Hitler, characterizing the Enabling Act as 'the most monstrous resolution ever demanded of parliament'. The collective leadership of the party also opposed passage. However, Ludwig Kaas, in his capacity as Party Chairman, demanded that the party support the act. Because Kaas was in close contact with both Hitler and Pacelli, the party leadership finally decided that he was in the best position to judge the situation and endorsed the Enabling Act. In reality, a deal was in the making, as Kaas was later to admit, in which the Center Party would vote for the Enabling Act, effectively committing political suicide, in exchange for the government's agreement to negotiate a Reich Concordat. Before the negotiations could proceed, the German bishops had little choice but to change their policies towards Catholic members of the Nazi party. On 28 March the bishops revoked the ban on membership by Catholics in the Nazi party. Two days earlier, the Protestant churches had formally accepted the Hitler regime.

The first major test of the churches' attitude towards the Jews under National Socialism came when the government called for a boycott of all Jewish business establishments on 1 April. A few Catholics protested individually but there was no official Church protest. This was followed on 7 April by the dismissal of all civil servants 'who are not of Aryan descent' and a series of similar laws that by 25 April excluded the Jews from the professions. There was no church response. On the contrary, there was almost universal approval.[50] Referring to the boycott, Cardinal Faulhaber wrote to Pacelli, '... the Jews can help themselves'.[51] The prelate did, however, express concern that baptized Jews would be subject to the same disabilities.

Concordat negotiations began in the same month and continued until Papen and Pacelli signed the document in the Vatican on 20 July 1933 with Kaas sitting on Pacelli's right. The finalized Concordat stipulated that only purely 'religious, cultural and charitable' Catholic organizations were entitled to the protection of the Reich. All others were to be abandoned or merged with Nazi organizations. Moreover, Hitler interpreted Article 31, the depolitization clause, to mean that 'the Holy See will ensure a ban on all clergy and members of religious congregations from political activity.'[52]

Pacelli had no illusions concerning Hitler's price and no objections to Hitler's interpretation. As a prelude to the signing, the German bishops announced the end of their opposition to the National Socialist regime on June 3 and signalled their acceptance of the depolitization clause. When many Center Party politicians threatened to defect to the Nazis, Brüning reluctantly agreed to the party's dissolution. Kaas then left Germany for Rome never to return. The Holy See thus became the first major international institution to sign a treaty with National Socialist Germany, an action widely interpreted as the Church's endorsement of National Socialism.

Hitler had achieved an extraordinary, multi-dimensional victory. With the voluntary dissolution of the Catholic Center Party, he had secured the end of official Catholic opposition to his regime. He had also demonstrated to the international community that the Holy See, one of the world's most influential institutions, had seen fit to conclude a treaty with his regime on terms favourable to him. On 22 July 1933, Hitler wrote to the Nazi party claiming that the treaty amounted to an endorsement by the Roman Catholic Church of the National Socialist state and a rejection of the claim that National Socialism is hostile to religion. He also told his cabinet that as a result of the treaty 'a sphere of confidence has been created that will be especially significant in the urgent struggle against international Jewry.'[53]

When Pacelli learned of Hitler's claims he wrote a two part article in *L'Osservatore Romano* on 26 and 27 July denying that the treaty in any way constituted moral approval of National Socialism. Instead, he stressed that 'the Code of Canon Law is the foundation and essential legal presupposition of the concordat.' The concordat, he claimed, involved the Reich's official recognition of the Church's legislation as well 'the adoption of many provisions of this legislation and the protection of all Church legislation.' Pacelli was not dissembling. On the contrary, his entire career had been so focused on securing a concordat that assured the Holy See centralized control over the appointment of bishops and state recognition of the authority of the Code of Canon Law over Catholics that he failed to take serious account of Brüning's warnings or the admonitions of Germany's bishops concerning Hitler's regime. In my opinion, both he and Kaas also made the mistake of believing that signing a treaty with Hitler was like signing one with Mussolini. In spite of his thirteen-year sojourn in Germany Pacelli failed to see the fundamental difference between Mussolini's regime and Hitler's. Mussolini's Fascism was totalitarian and brutal but never as brutal as Hitler's National Socialism or, until Mussolini became Hitler's puppet in 1943, as profoundly anti-religious and anti-Semitic.

There is, however, no evidence that Pius XII was either pro-Nazi or favoured a Nazi victory in World War II. There is much evidence to the contrary. For example, in November 1939 the Pope expressed a willingness to act as a go-between on behalf of the anti-Hitler German resistance that would approach Neville Chamberlain and seek assurances of an honourable peace following a successful anti-Hitler plot. In so doing, he took an extraordinary risk both for his person and the Church as an institution.[54] However, Pius XII did favour a negotiated peace that would have left Germany intact as a bulwark against Soviet communism. Under no circumstances did he want a total victory for National Socialist Germany. *Pius XII's willingness to come to terms with Hitler was largely a consequence of the centrality of the concordat issue throughout Pacelli's career as Nuncio and Papal Secretary of State. For Pacelli securing a concordat acceptable to Rome overrode all other considerations. Hitler wanted the kind of Reich Concordat that he easily extracted from Pacelli.* For very different reasons, Pacelli wanted the same kind of document as badly as did Hitler and was prepared to pay a very high price for it.

In this essay, I have dealt primarily with the religious and historical motivations that drove Pius XII to become the first major international figure to sign a treaty with the Nazi regime. In so doing I have, as noted, followed the lead of Klaus Scholder and John Cornwell. Their contributions call our attention to important issues that the *Shoah* statement ignored in its defence of Pius XII and in its dichotomous distinction between the pagan, racial anti-Semitism of National Socialism and the religiously based traditional anti-Judaism of the Christian Church. The *Shoah* statement also ignores the degree to which the pre-Vatican II Church looked with favour on political movements that sought to curtail the civic and political rights Jews had gained in Europe since the French Revolution. If one wishes to understand the Vatican's conception of the proper place of the Jews in Europe before World War II, one need only consider the conditions under which Jews were compelled to live in the only political entity where the Church had full freedom to regulate their status, the Papal States. And, it was the demise of the Papal States that the Pacelli family found so distasteful that Pius XII's grandfather and father refused to enter into the employ of its successor, the Kingdom of Italy.

There was a very good reason why both Pius XI and Pius XII found little motive to object to those Nazi measures designed to bar Jews from the professions and dismiss those in government employ. This was precisely the kind of ghettoization that the Church had everywhere employed when it had the power so to do. Before the war there was only one issue on which the Church vehemently opposed National Socialism. It refused to capitulate on the transforming power of the sacrament of baptism. For the Church, once baptized a Jew became a Christian; for the Nazis baptism changed nothing. The Church was prepared to permit baptized Jews full entrance into Christian society although its opposition to the deportation of baptized Jews was often less than whole-hearted.

Implicit in the *Shoah* statement is the assumption that Pius XII would have saved Europe's Jews if he could have. I believe that assumption is unexamined. Before making it we would do well to consider the influence of the following events and documents in shaping the Pope's policies vis à vis Jews and Judaism: Pio Nono's vehement rejection of the political legacy of the French Revolution; his *Syllabus of Errors*; his decision to become a 'prisoner in the Vatican'; the promulgation of the doctrine of Papal Infallibility; the very conservative first Vatican Ecumenical Council; the intense commitment of the Pacelli family to Pio Nono and its defensive psychology with regard to the papacy; the influence of the Jesuits on Pacelli, Pacelli's work on the *Corpus iuris canonici*, his efforts to achieve its implementation through a series of concordats, and his response to the Bolshevik threat. Pacelli had few illusions about Hitler and National Socialism, but he was prepared to make a pact with the devil because he was convinced that the long-term interests of the Church were at stake.

There is also the question of whether Pius XII was an anti-Semite. Implicit in the Shoah statement is the view expressed by many of the Pope's defenders that the Pope was not motivated by anti-Jewish hostility but was limited in what he could do to help them. By contrast, John Cornwell holds that Pacelli displayed a 'secret antipathy toward the Jews' and that his was 'an antagonistic policy toward the Jews, based on the conviction that there was a link between Judaism and the Bolshevik plot to destroy Christendom'.[55] Furthermore, Cornwell argues that Pacelli's concordat policy guaranteed Hitler's rise to absolute power and effectively thwarted any potential Catholic protest on behalf of the Jews. According to Cornwell, Pacelli believed that 'the Jews had brought misfortune on their own heads'. Hence, he was determined to refrain from any public appeal on behalf of the Jews. He was, however, willing to permit the alleviation of Jewish sufferings on 'the level of basic charity'. Cornwell concludes that the Pope's

> failure to utter a candid word about the Final Solution in progress proclaimed to the world that the Vicar of Christ was not moved to pity and anger. From this point of view he was the ideal Pope for Hitler's unspeakable plan. He was Hitler's pawn. He was Hitler's Pope.[56]

Cornwell is especially offended by the Pope's post-war attempt to claim 'retrospective moral superiority for having spoken candidly' about the Holocaust when, in reality, he offered neither apology nor explanation for his failure to speak. The Pope's attempt after the war to portray himself as 'an outspoken defender of the Jewish people', Cornwell argues, revealed him to be 'not only the ideal Pope for the Nazis Final Solution, but a hypocrite'.[57]

I am inclined to concur in Cornwell's judgement concerning Pope Pius XII's wartime policies vis à vis the Jews although I do not see him as a hypocrite. On the contrary, I believe he was convinced that he was defending the Church against its enemies. I would add that in no way were the Pope's hostile attitudes toward the Jews and Judaism uniquely his. We have documentary evidence that important groups in the wartime American and British governments were apprehensive lest a successful effort at rescue might result in the emigration of millions of unwanted Jews to their respective countries and territories under their control.[58] The Pope's attitudes were partly culturally determined, partly a response to the history of Europe since the French Revolution, and partly the result of his own experiences. There was little, if anything, in his culture that would have fostered a sympathetic view of the Jewish situation in the 1930s and 1940s.

Nowhere in the *Shoah* statement is there any acknowledgement of the fact that until Vatican II, the Holy See regarded the political emancipation of the Jew as a tragic mistake that the leaders of the Church in Europe were determined to bring to an end. The statement does observe that non-Christians 'did not always enjoy a fully guaranteed juridical status' before the end of the 18th century. However, a 'fully guaranteed juridical status' is not the same as equality before the law. Such a status is not inconsistent with explicit legal disabilities such as the *Statut des juifs* of 3 October 1940 and other anti-Jewish measures of Vichy France or even the Nazi laws barring Jews from the civil service, the professions and even depriving them of full Reich citizenship as long as the basis of discrimination was religious rather than racial. Although the *Statut des juifs* excluded French Jews from professions that influence public opinion, barred them from the ranks of the officer corps, and limited their entrance into the liberal professions, the highest circles in the Vatican offered no objections after receiving inquiries concerning the regulations. On 7 August 1941, Marshall Henri Phillipe Pétain directed Léon Bérard, Vichy's ambassador to the Vatican, to inquire concerning the papal view of Vichy's measures. Bérard responded in a lengthy report that stated there is every reason 'to limit their activity in society' and that it is legitimate to deny them access to public office... to admit them only in a fixed proportion to the universities (*numerus clausus*) and the liberal professions.'[59] When Monsignor Valerio Vallat, the Papal Nuncio to Vichy and an opponent of the *Statut*, inquired of Luigi Cardinal Maglione concerning the source of Bérard's opinion, he learned that Monsignor, later Cardinal, Domenico Tardini and Monsignor Giovanni Battista Montini had given it to him. Both prelates were very close to Pius XII. Tardini served as Deputy for Foreign Affairs in the Secretariat of State. Montini succeeded Pius XII as Pope Paul VI.

Such views can be characterized as reactionary but those who at the time regarded Roman Catholicism as the one true religion did not see it that way. From their perspective there was nothing intolerant in barring the political participation of non-Christians in a Christian state, especially when Christianity was perceived as under moral threat from both Bolshevism and Judaism. I have long believed that the Bolshevik Revolution and the Red uprisings in Bavaria and Hungary at the end of World War I convinced Pacelli and his colleagues that Jewish emancipation had unleashed upon Europe a power potentially capable of bringing about the moral and spiritual destruction of Christendom. Emancipation had allowed Jews to become intellectuals, teachers, writers, politicians, financiers and revolutionaries. As such, the Church regarded them as *internal enemies within Christendom with the unprecedented ability* to lead the faithful astray. When confined to the ghetto, they had no such power.

Not only did the Vatican see the hand of the Jews in the Bolshevik Revolution, they also saw it in the hated movement of secular Italian nationalism that deprived the Holy See of its temporal realms and made Pio Nono a 'prisoner of the Vatican'. As the new Kingdom of Italy, with Count Camillo Benso di Cavour as its first Prime Minister and a Calvinist in religion, extended its jurisdiction throughout the peninsula, the emancipation granted to its Jewish subjects in 1848 was extended to the new territories. The Jews were beneficiaries of the unification of Italy and the Holy See the most important loser. That was not a situation upon which the papacy could look with favour and it was in this atmosphere that the young Pacelli was nurtured in a family intensely loyal to the papacy.

At no time in its entire history did the Church perceive itself as under a greater threat than when Europe's most populous empire fell into the hands of the Bolsheviks whose virulently anti-religious revolutionary movement actively sought the destruction of Christianity. Even the conquering Muslims had constituted less of a threat. In the lands the Muslims conquered, they sought to subordinate Christianity not destroy it. Not so, the Bolsheviks. Pacelli believed that the Church and National Socialism shared two common enemies, Bolshevism and Judaism Ultimately, both saw Bolshevism a bastardized form of Judaism. As noted, there was nothing in the anti-Semitic policies of the Nazis concerning the Jews *before* World War II to which the Church would or could object as long as baptized Jews were excluded from the Nazi-mandated disabilities. In effect, the Nazis were implementing a long cherished Vatican goal, the disenfranchisement of non-believing Jews in Christian Europe and their ultimate return to the ghetto.

Violence and extermination was another matter. Or was it? The Inquisition or the Congregation of the Holy Office never executed condemned heretics, those regarded by the Church as its internal enemies. Instead it handed the condemned over to the secular arm that alone was authorized to impose the death penalty. Moreover, the Inquisition was alive and well in the Papal States until 1870. After Pio Nono's restoration, the responsibilities of the Holy Office included oversight of the Jews who were forbidden to provide Christians with food and lodging, own land, spend the night outside the ghetto, or have 'friendly relations with Christians'.[60] That was the state whose passing the Pacelli family mourned and whose restoration they sought.

Finally, neither the Commission responsible for the *Shoah* statement nor Cornwell ask the fundamental question about Pius XII, a question concerning which, as stated above, it is possible to offer a plausible hypothesis, one that cannot be said to be falsified by what we now know of the man, although hypothesis it must remain: *Did Pope Pius XII regard the elimination of Europe's Jews as a demographic presence a benefit for European Christendom?* The overwhelming body of evidence suggests an affirmative answer. Unlike the Inquisition, he was not required to turn the internal enemy over to the secular arm. All that was required of him was to do nothing and say as little as possible. The secular arm did the rest.

In fairness to the Church, it must also be stated that the Shoah statement is also evidence of the vast difference between the way the Roman Catholic Church has dealt with the issue of religious pluralism before and after Vatican II and most especially its relations with Judaism. Although the statement's positive evaluation of Pius XII's wartime role remains divisive, the new spirit that animates the Church's attitude towards Judaism is well expressed in the statements concluding expression of hope for the future:

> We pray that our sorrow for the tragedy which the Jewish people suffered in our century will lead to a new relationship with the Jewish people. We wish to turn awareness of past sins into a firm resolve to build a new future in which there will be no more anti-Judaism among Christians or anti-Christian sentiment among Jews, but rather a shared mutual respect, as befits those who adore the one Creator and Lord and have a common father in faith, Abraham.[61]

NOTES

1 Commission on Religious Relations with the Jews, *We Remember: A Reflection on the Shoah* (Vatican City: Liberia Editrice Vaticana, 1998). The text is available on the World Wide Web at http:www.cin.org/docs/shoah.html.

2 On the treaty of Brest-Litovsk, see John W. Wheeler-Bennett, *Brest-Litovsk: The Forgotten Peace March 1918* (New York: W.W. Norton, 1971; 1st edition, 1938). On Germany's war aims in World War I, see Fritz Fischer, *World Power or Decline: The Controversy over Germany's Aims in the First World War*, trans. Lancelot L. Farrar, *et. al.* (New York: W.W. Norton, 1974), originally published as *Weltmacht oder Niedergang* (Frankfurt am Main: Europäische Verlagsanstalt, 1965).

3 Leon Klenicki, 'Document Disappoints Profoundly', *Canadian Jewish News*, 26 March 1998.

4 John-Thor Dahlburg, 'French Bishops Beg Forgiveness: Church Says It Should Have Done More', *Toronto Star*, 1 October 1997; 'German Catholic Bishops: Church Shares in Guilt for the Annihilation of European Jewry', *This Week in Germany* (New York: German Information Center, 27 January 1995).

5 'European Rabbis Express a Differing View', *Canadian Jewish News*, 26 March 1988.

6 Andrew Greeley, 'Pope Pius XII failed in not denouncing the Holocaust', *The Times Union* (Albany, NY: 13 November 1999).

7 Peter J. Haas, *Morality After Auschwitz: The Radical Challenge of the Nazi Ethic* (Philadelphia: Fortress Press, 1988), p.4.

8 This writer made the same point more than two decades ago. See Richard L. Rubenstein, *The Cunning of History* (New York: Harper and Row, 1975).

9 Klaus Scholder, *The Churches and the Third Reich*, trans. John Bowden (London: SCM Press, 1987), 2 volumes, and John Cornwell, *Hitler's Pope: The Secret History of Pius XII* (New York: Viking Press, 1999).

10 *The Tablet*, 25 September 1999.

11 Owen Chadwick, *Britain and the Vatican during the Second World War* (Cambridge: Cambridge University Press, 1986).

12 Rolf Hochhuth, *Der Stellvetreter* (Reinbek bei Hamburg: Rowohlt Verlag GmbH, 1963); English translation, *The Deputy* (New York: Grove Press, 1964).

13 *Actes et Documents du Saint Siège relatifs à la Seconde Guerre Mondiale*, ed. Robert Blet, Robert A. Graham, Angelo Martini and Burkhard Schneider, 11 vols, in 12 (Vatican City: 1965–81). There is, however, continuing controversy concerning the integrity and comprehensiveness of some elements of the collection. A summary of *Actes et Documents* by Pierre Blet, S.J., the last surviving editor of the collection, has recently been published in English. Blet's volume stresses the extraordinary complexity of the situation confronting the leader of a universal church with millions of communicants on both sides engaged in a bitter and devastating war against each other. Pierre Blet, S.J., *Pie XII et la Seconde Guerre Mondiale* (Paris: Academique Perrin, 1997); English translation, *Pius XII and the Second World War: According to the Archives of the Vatican*, trans. Lawrence J. Johnson (New York: Paulist Press, 1999).

14 Among the many volumes that have appeared are Saul Friedländer, *Pius XII and the Third Reich: A Documentation*, trans. Charles Fullman (New York: Alfred A. Knopf, 1966); John F. Morley, *Vatican Diplomacy and the Jews During the Holocaust: 1939–1943* (New York: KTAV, 1980); John Conway, *The Nazi Persecution of the Churches* (New York: Basic Books, 1968); Victoria Barnett, *For the Soul of a People: Protestant Protest Against Hitler* (New York: Oxford University Press, 1992); Doris L. Bergen, *Twisted Cross: The German Christian Movement in the Third Reich* (Chapel Hill: University of North Carolina Press, 1996) and Ernst Christian Helmreich, *The German Churches under Hitler: Background, Struggle and Epilogue* (Detroit: Wayne State University Press, 1979).

15 A useful account of Pio Nono' attitude towards liberalism can be found in David Kertzer, *The Kidnapping of Edgardo Mortara* (New York: Alfred A. Knopf, 1997), p.78.

16 In Rome under Pio Nono, not only were the Jews confined to the ghetto and severely constrained economically, but their rabbis were forced to submit to humiliating indignities. At Carnival the rabbis were compelled to make an appearance grotesquely dressed with the crowd at liberty to pelt them with rotten food and other objects. See the chapter 'Jews in the Land of the Popes' in David I. Kertzer, *The Kidnapping of Edgardo Mortara* pp.13–22.

17 According to John Cornwell, Eugenio was raised in an 'ambiance of penurious respectability and an enduring sense of injured papal merit'. *Hitler's Pope*, p.14.
18 Cornwell, *Hitler's Pope*, p.14.
19 See article 'Civiltá Cattolica, La' in *Encyclopaedia Judaica*, (Jerusalem: Keter, 1972), vol. 5, pp.559–600.
20 In July 1946 after the Germans had killed more than 3,000,000 Polish Jews, Poles killed 70 Holocaust survivors in Kielce on the basis of a false rumor that Jews had kidnapped a Christian boy and killed him in a 'ritual murder'. Bishop Stefan Wyszynski of Lublin, later Cardinal and Primate of the Polish Church, refused to stem the ongoing violence by condemning the Kielce massacres adding that he was not altogether convinced that Jews did not commit ritual murder.
21 *Civiltá Cattolica*, 1 May 1897, cited by Sergio I. Minerbi, *The Vatican and Zionism: Conflict in the Holy Land 1895–1925* (New York: Oxford University Press, 1990), p.96.
22 *Civiltá Cattolica*, September 1899, p.749. cited *Encyclopaedia Judaica, loc. cit.*
23 *Civiltá Cattolica*, vol.87 (1936), nos. 37–39, cited *Encyclopaedia Judaica, loc. cit.*
24 *Civiltá Cattolica*, vol.97 (1946), issue 2297,
25 Carlo Falconi. *Popes in the Twentieth Century, from Pius X to John XXIII*, trans. Mildred Grindrod (Boston: Little, Brown, 1968), p.76.
26 Mark Landler, 'Beijing – Backed Church, Defying Vatican, Installs 5 New Bishops', *New York Times*, 7 January 2000.
27 On the red revolution in Munich see Allan Mitchell, *Revolution in Bavaria, 1918–1919* (Princeton: Princeton Univeristy Press, 1965); Ruth Fischer, *Stalin and German Communism* (Cambridge: Harvard University Press, 1948); Charles B. Maurer, *Call to Revolution: The Mystical Anarchism of Gustav Landauer* (Detroit: Wayne State University Press, 1971); Rosa Leviné-Meyer, *Leviné the Spartacist* (London: Gordon and Cremonesi, 1978); Richard Grunberger, *Red Rising in Bavaria* (New York: St. Martin's Press, 1973).
28 Grunberger, *Red Rising*, p.116.
29 Grunberger, *Red Rising*, pp.124–25.
30 Karl Dietrich Bracher, *The German Dictatorship* (New York: Praeger, 1973), p.82.
31 Letter of Pacelli to Gaspari, 18 April 1919, cited by Cornwell, *Hitler's Pope*, pp.74–75.
32 Pacelli to Gaspari, cited by Cornwell, *Hitler's Pope*, p.78.
33 See Carlo Falconi, *The Silence of Pius XII*, trans. Bernard Wall (Boston: Little, Brown, 1965), p.86.
34 Pacelli to Gaspari, cited by Cornwell, *Hitler's Pope*, p.78.
35 For an account of the Communists' rule in Hungary, see Rudolf L. Tökés, *Béla Kun and the Hungarian Soviet Republic: The Origins and Role of the Communist Party in Hungary in the Revolutions of 1918–1919* (New York: Praeger, 1967).
36 See Scholder, *The Churches and the Third Reich*, vol.1, p.61.
37 Scholder, *op. cit.*, vol.1, pp.66–73.
38 Scholder, *op. cit.*, vol.1, p.163.
39 Cornwell, *Hitler's Pope*, p.114.
40 *Völkischer Beobachter*, no. 45, 22 February 1929, Bavarian edition. Cited by Scholder, *op. cit.*, pp.164–65.
41 J. Stark, *Nationalsozialismus und katholische Kirche* (Munich: 1931), pp.31, 20. Cited in Scholder, *op. cit.*, pp.165–66.
42 Scholder, *op. cit.*, p.152.
43 Heinrich Brüning, *Memoiren, 1918–1934* (Stuttgart: Deutsche Verlags-Anstalt, 1970), p.358.
44 Historians are at odds concerning the reliability of Brüning's account of his meeting with Pacelli. Cornwell accepts the judgement of historian Klaus Scholder that Brüning accurately indicated Pacelli's intentions. Scholer's opinion is not shared by Ludwig Volk, a respected Jesuit historian who expresses incomprehension that the Pacelli could have been as politically inept as Brüning depicts him. I am more inclined to accept Scholder's magisterial judgement as being consistent with Pacelli's behaviour not only with Brüning but also with Wirth and others. See Cornwell, *op. cit.*, p.394, n.24; see also Scholder, *op. cit.*, vol.1, p.612, n.25.
45 William L. Patch, Jr., *Heinrich Brüning and the Dissolution of the Weimar Republic* (Cambridge: Cambridge University Press, 1998), pp.295–296, cited by Cornwell, *Hitler's Pope*, p.124.

46 Scholder, *op. cit.*, p.154.
47 Ludwig Kaas, 'Der Konkordatstyp des fascistischen Italien', *Zeitschrift für ausländisches öffentliches Recht und Völkerrecht, III, I, 1933*, 488–522.
48 Cornwell, *Hitler's Pope*, p.129.
49 Martyn Housden, *Resistance and Conformity in the Third Reich* (London: Routledge, 1997), p.46, cited by Cornwell, *Hitler's Pope*, pp.105–6.
50 In addition to Scholder, *The Churches*, see Victoria Barnett, *For the Soul of a People: Protestant Protest Against Hitler* (New York: Oxford University Press, 1992) and Doris L. Bergen, *Twisted Cross: The German Christian Movement in the Third Reich* (Chapel Hill: University of North Carolina Press, 1996).
51 Ernst Christian Helmreich, *The German Churches under Hitler: Background, Struggle and Epilogue* (Detroit: Wayne State University Press, 1979), pp.276–77; cited in Cornwell, *Hitler's Pope.*, p.140.
52 Cornwell, *Hitler's Pope.*, p.151.
53 Scholder, *The German Churches*, vol 1, p.404.
54 See Owen Chadwick, *op. cit.*, pp.86ff.
55 Cornwell, *Hitler's Pope*, pp.295–96.
56 Cornwell, *Hitler's Pope*, pp.296–97.
57 Cornwell, *Hitler's Pope*, p.297.
58 Historian David Wyman cites a British Foreign Office memorandum written after William Temple, Archbishop of Canterbury rose in the House of Lords on March 23, 1943 to plead for immediate efforts aimed at the rescue of Europe's Jews. The memorandum reads in part: 'There is the possibility that the Germans or their satellites *may change over from the policy of extermination to one of extrusion*, and aim as they did before the war at embarrassing other countries by flooding them with alien immigrants.' See David Wyman, *The Abandonment of the Jews: America and the Holocaust 1941–1945* (New York: Pantheon Books, 1984), p.105.
59 See Michael R. Marrus and Robert O. Paxton, *Vichy France and the Jews* (New York: Basic Books, 1981), pp.200–201.
60 'Editto della Santa Inquisizione contro gl'Israeliti degli Stati Pontifici' in Achille Gennarelli, *Il governo pontifico e lo stato romano, documenti preceduti da una esposizione storica* (Rome: 1861), part I, pp.304–5, cited by David Kertzer, *The Kidnapping of Edgardo Mortara* (New York: Alfred A. Knopf, 1997), p.190.
61 *Origins: CNS Documentary Service*, March 26, 1998, p.674.

THE ATTITUDE OF THE RUSSIAN ORTHODOX CHURCH AND THE UKRAINIAN GREEK CATHOLIC CHURCH TO THE HOLOCAUST DURING WORLD WAR II

Mikhail Shkarovski

L ITTLE ATTENTION has been paid by historians to the subject of this paper, despite the fact that the Russian Orthodox Church was at the centre of events in World War II and was forced to react very directly in one way or another to the Holocaust. It should be emphasized that at that time the Russian Orthodox Church was not a united body and had broken up into several jurisdictions. Even before the beginning of the war between Germany and the USSR, many Russian emigré priests in different countries of Europe had expressed their opinion on the persecution of Jews. They belonged to two jurisdictions: that of Metropolitan Evlogy in Paris and that of the Synod of Bishops of the Russian Orthodox Church Abroad in Belgrade.

Several Russian parishes situated on German territory were under the jurisdiction of the Western European Exarchate of Metropolitan Evlogy, who had submitted to the jurisdiction of the Ecumenical Patriarch in Constantinople. Soon after the National Socialists came to power these communities began to suffer various persecutions and legal limitations. The pretext for these persecutions was the myth that the Evlogian parishes in Germany were an important link in a large-scale conspiracy against the Third Reich, directed and financed by international Jewish Masonic organizations and French Intelligence with the help of Russian emigrés. The Gestapo accused Metropolitan Evlogy of having belonged to the Masonic Order as early as 1913.[1]

The Nazis were right to suspect the Evlogian parishes of not sympathizing with their regime, its anti-liberal ideology and its aggressive aspirations in the sphere of foreign policy. Metropolitan Evlogy's parishioners had a negative attitude towards the Nazis' racial theory and in particular towards cultivating a hatred of the Jews. There were several Jews among the lecturers of the famous St. Sergius Theological Institute in Paris which was under Metropolitan Evlogy's patronage. The Nazis knew this only too well and soon after the occupation of Paris they arrested Professors Zander and Zenkovsky. It is true that we cannot speak of any kind of widespread opposition from the Evlogian communities in Germany itself. Their clergy maintained a strictly apolitical attitude and concentrated their efforts on religious life. The only exception was the question of their attitude to the Jews.[2]

The head of the Evlogian parishes in Germany, Archimandrite Ioann (Shakhovskoy), never concealed his extremely negative attitude to the antisemitism in Nazi ideology and policy. The same can be said of his parishioners. Two years after the Nazis had come to power, Archimandrite Ioann gave his pastoral response to Nazism by publishing in Berlin in 1934 a brochure called 'Judaism and the Church', in which he wrote of the incompatibility of nationalistic religion and racism with the Christian faith.

Unfortunately, in his post-war memoirs, Archimandrite Ioann, who by that time was already Archbishop of San Francisco, wrote modestly and little about his attitude towards the persecution of Jews:

> How many people in the towns and villages gave selfless help to the less fortunate.... Even now I can still see one deaf, middle-aged Jewish woman with a hearing aid wandering from house to house. Christians gave her shelter. It was one of the awful apocalyptic visions of those years, people wearing the yellow star of David, doomed to slaughter.
>
> I recall how I secretly consecrated as a nun one Jewish–Christian woman, my spiritual daughter, the servant of God Elizabeth. She had been summoned by the Gestapo and we had no doubts about the meaning of that summons. Giving her my blessing for martyrdom, I gave her a new name, Michaela, in honour of the Archangel Michael, the leader of the Jewish people. Of course, at that time, along with everybody else, I had to show documents to prove my Aryan origins and speak of my convictions and of the faith of the Church. One day the investigator interrogating me, who knew that I received anyone into the Church without regard to their race, asked me, 'What if Litvinov wanted to be baptised (In Germany at that time Litvinov[3] was the personification of so-called Judaeo-Bolshevism) would you baptise him too?'. 'Of course,' I replied, 'if Litvinov repented and wanted to live the life in Christ, then the Church would accept him along with all others.'[4]

In July 1938, the Gestapo began to raise the question of deporting Archimandrite Ioann from the country. In a letter of 27 July to the Reich's Ministry of Church Affairs it was stressed that,

> Ioann, especially lately, has been causing unrest among the Russian emigrés with his sermons and pronouncements which are extremely friendly to the Jews. He has been consciously trying to upset the efforts of anti-Bolshevik groups among the emigrés. He has been sharply criticised for many years by nationalist-minded Russian emigrés because of his friendly disposition towards Jews.

The Gestapo viewed Fr. Ioann as 'a striking example of the ecclesiastical trend led by Metropolitan Evlogy, influenced by the Masonic Order and hostile to Germany'.[5]

The Ministry of Church Affairs had its own plans to unite the Russian Orthodox community in Germany and incorporate, if possible by peaceful means, the Evlogian parishes into the Diocese of Germany and Berlin of the Russian Orthodox Church Abroad. It therefore proposed to the Gestapo to 'observe the development of the Shakovskoy affair' without resorting to deportation. In July 1939 the Gestapo's second attempt to have Archimandrite Ioann and other Evlogian priests deported, also met with failure. The deportation was prevented by a compromise agreement concluded on 3 November 1939 according to which the Evlogian parishes were to be incorporated into the Diocese of Germany and Berlin, but Metropolitan Evlogy's jurisdiction over them was still recognized. But Archimandrite Ioann continued to be subject to repression. In 1941 the publication of his missionary journal *For the Church* was forbidden and in 1943 the Gestapo searched his apartment and the place where his books were stored. Archimandrite Ioann's papers and letters were confiscated and, after a long interrogation, he was forced to sign a document saying that he would not leave Berlin.[6]

The Evlogian clergy in Nazi-occupied France were especially active in showing their attitude towards the Holocaust. People close to Metropolitan Evlogy described his mood during the days that Paris was occupied in the following way: at present the Metropolitan is gloomy, sad and anxious. When we speak of what is happening all around, he makes a wry face and begins to fret, 'Oppressors... oppressors... and what they're doing to the Jews doesn't bear thinking about.' In one of his letters of 26 October 1944, the Metropolitan wrote, 'whilst being a convinced nationalist i.e. a faithful and loyal son of my own people, I do of course entirely repudiate that brutal kind of nationalism which the Germans are now showing towards the Jews, just as being Orthodox, any kind of religious fanaticism is alien to me. Above all, I revere freedom in Christ.'[7] Almost all the representatives of the Evlogian clergy shared the Metropolitan's position. For example, the heroic work of Mother Maria (Skobtsova, Kuzmina-Karavaeva) is well known. Her name has been immortalized by the tree planted in the Grove of the Righteous at the Museum of the Victims and Heroes of the Shoah, Yad Vashem in Israel.

Mother Maria led the work of the Paris-based charitable, cultural and missionary organization 'Orthodox Action' which helped Jews during almost all the time that France was occupied. For registration purposes the term 'Jew' was defined for the first time in a decree of 27 September 1940 which laid down that anyone belonging to the Jewish faith was considered to be a Jew. As a result there was a great demand for baptism certificates which could help to avoid humiliation and repression. The priest at the 'Orthodox Action' church, Fr. Dmitrii Klepinin, began to receive urgent requests to grant such certificates to non-Christian Jews. With Mother Maria's full approval, he decided to give out certificates of membership of his parish. Soon, Fr. Dmitrii's card index contained details of 80 new 'parishioners'. According to the 17 April 1948 issue of the New York Jewish newspaper *Forward*, Fr. Dmitrii gave out hundreds of false baptism certificates. Furthermore, Fr. Dmitrii resisted any interference or control over his actions. When the diocesan administration requested lists of the newly baptized, he categorically refused.[8]

From March 1942, French Jews had to wear the distinguishing mark of the yellow star of David. Mother Maria, who from the very start had considered persecution of Jews a burden to be borne by all, said on this issue,

> There isn't a Jewish question. There is a Christian question. Do you really not understand that the battle is being waged with Christianity? If we were real Christians, we would all wear the yellow star. Now has the time come for us to confess our faith.[9]

On the night of 15–16 July 1942, mass arrests of Jews took place in Paris. The majority of them were herded onto a winter cycle-track. Due to her monastic habit, Mother Maria managed to get access and spent three days there. She comforted the children, encouraged the adults and distributed food. With the help of refuse collectors, she was twice able to help children escape. After 15 July the Jews desperately needed reliable hiding places and opportunities to escape. Orthodox Action's house at Lourmel became such a hiding place. One of the workers there, Mochulskii, wrote,

> Lourmel is full to overflowing. People are living in the outhouses, in the barn. They are sleeping on the floor in the living-room . . . Both Jews and non-Jews. Mother Maria says, 'We have a severe housing crisis. It's surprising the Germans haven't clamped down on us yet.'[10]

The Orthodox Action house became a link in a whole network of hiding places and escape routes which formed throughout France. I.A. Krivoshein wrote in his memoirs,

> It wasn't just a matter of giving material aid anymore. We had to obtain false documents for the Jews, help them escape to the unoccupied zone in the south, and hide in the remote parts of the country. Finally, we needed to take care of children whose parents had been caught on the street or during raids.[11]

In the end the Gestapo got to know of these activities. From 8–10 February 1943 the house was searched and arrests took place. Fr Dmitrii Klepinin, Mother Maria and the laymen Yury Skobtsov, F. Pianov, A. Viskovsky and Yu. Kazachkin were arrested. They proposed to release Fr. Dmitrii on condition he would not help Jews in future; he showed them his cross with the crucifixion depicted on it and said, 'But do you not know this Jew?' The others arrested displayed the same strength of spirit. When accused of helping Jews, F. Pianov replied, 'We gave help to all in need, both Jews and non-Jews – it is the duty of every Christian to help in such a way.' When Mother Maria's mother, Sophia Borisovna Pilenko, was being interrogated the Gestapo officer shouted, 'You've brought up your daughter very badly. She helps only Jews.' To which she replied, 'My daughter is a true Christian and for her there is neither Greek, nor Jew but only the unfortunate person. If you were in trouble, she would help you too.' Mother Maria smiled and said, 'I very likely would,' for which she was almost slapped in the face.[12]

A few days after the arrests, the famous theologian Fr. Sergei Bulgakov held a 'moleben' (a service of intercessory prayer) for the release of the captives. Shortly afterwards the occupying authorities ordered that Orthodox Action should be closed down and the prisoners were sent to concentration camps. Fr. Dmitrii Klepinin died in Buchenwald on 8 February 1944 and Mother Maria died in the gas chambers of Ravensbruck on 31 March 1945, the eve of Easter. She left behind her many writings.[13]

This example of how the Evlogian clergy helped Jews is far from being the only one. In Paris, not far from Lourmel, false baptism certificates were issued by Archimandrite Afanasy (Nechayev), the senior priest at the Church of the Three Holy Hierarchs on rue Petel. And on 20 September 1941 the senior priest of the Church of the Holy Trinity in Clichy, Fr. Konstantin Zambrzhitsky, who was himself in prison at the time, baptized a Jew, I. Fondaminsky, in the camp at Compiegne. Plans were made to help Fondaminsky escape through the 'free' zone of France to the USA but Fondaminsky resolutely refused such plans. He wanted to share the fate of his brothers and relatives and died in Auschwitz on 19 November 1942.[14]

At the same time, the Evlogian clergy's attitude to Judaism was quite distinctive. Many of them, including Mother Maria, believed that with the unprecedented horrors of the World War, the inevitable conversion of the Jews to Christianity was beginning. The famous Orthodox theologian Sergei Bulgakov developed this idea most fully in his articles, 'The Persecution of Israel' and 'Racism and Christianity', which were written in occupied Paris in winter 1941–42. He saw the Jewish people, chosen by God for the incarnation of the Saviour, as 'the axis of world history'. The Jews continue to be God's chosen people even though they did not accept Christ. The Jewish question would only finally be resolved with the conversion of the whole Jewish people to Christ as announced by the Apostle Paul, and therefore antisemitism is anti-Christianity and unacceptable.

> On the one hand, by fighting with Christianity, Israel is a laboratory for all kinds of spiritual poisons that contaminate the world, especially Christendom. On the other hand, they are a nation of prophets in whom the spirit of prophecy is never extinguished and the religious element never weakens. However, in their state of blindness, it is Christianity without Christ and even against Christ, although it is Him alone for Whom they are searching and waiting. The conclusions that can be drawn about the persecutors of Israel are clear: they are persecuting Christ Himself in Israel, just as the Jews themselves, in as much as they are fighting Christ, are fighting their own election.[15]

Fr. Sergei was extremely harsh in his condemnation and denunciation of Nazi ideology, maintaining that 'Hitlerism' as a religious phenomenon was much more negative than even the militant atheism of Bolshevism. He emphasized the central place occupied by enmity towards Judaism in the 'spiritual armoury' of German racism:

> All racism is nothing other than antisemitism. It is a sublimated envy of the Jewish people and competition with them, not positive but negative competition. Such is the secret of

racism, its source. Hitler and the zealots of antisemitism are religious, or to be more precise, antireligious maniacs. In its spirit, as well as in its practical outworkings antisemitism is not only a temptation for, but is also in direct opposition to the Christian spirit.'

Fr. Sergei Bulgakov also wrote about the antichristian crimes of the Jews themselves:

> The Jewish people are still worshipping the golden calf and have fallen away from faith, even in the God of Israel. For Israel, all these new troubles are not only perhaps the final trials before their conversion to Christ and spiritual resurrection, but perhaps also the inevitable punishment for that awful crime and terrible sin that they have committed against the body and soul of the Russian people in Bolshevism.

The theologian's final conclusion is full of faith in the fulfilment of the Apostle Paul's prophecy, 'In historic Christianity a new force will appear which will become its spiritual focus just as it was in its early days – Judaeo-Christianity.'[16]

The position of the Russian Orthodox Church Abroad was rather different from that of the Evlogians. Its leadership was extremely anti-Soviet and frequently spoke out against the 'Jewish-Bolshevik' government in Russia. For example, in a message to Orthodox Russian people adopted by a meeting of the Bishops of the Russian Orthodox Church Abroad on 25 October 1943 in connection with the election of Metropolitan Sergi (Starogorodsky) as Patriarch of Moscow, it was said, 'His long-standing close connection with the bloody tyrant Stalin's Communist government which has several Jews in it who fanatically hate Christianity and are mercilessly exterminating the Russian people, casts a particularly gloomy shadow over the figure of the new Patriarch whom our conscience will not allow us to call our true father and spiritual leader[17]. In the 1942 Easter message of Metropolitan Anastasios, the Chairman of the Synod of Bishops of the Russian Orthodox Church Abroad, a different point was made, 'In vain Christ's enemies the Jews, who continued to persecute Him even after his death, sealed His body in the tomb and deliberately guarded Him hoping to keep Him in the grave.'[18]

In such statements there was undoubtedly a certain anti-Judaism which had both political and religious motives. However, the thinking of the Russian ecclesiastical emigration was completely free of the racism so characteristic of Nazism. The leadership of the Russian Orthodox Church Abroad never gave its approval to the Holocaust. Among the Church's parishioners in Germany there were people of Jewish origin who took part in the Resistance movement. For example, Liana Berkowitz belonged to the Berlin 'Rittmeister Group' of the Resistance organization 'Rote Kapelle'. She began to take part in underground activities such as distributing leaflets from the age of 16. On 30 March 1943 she was arrested and on 5 August 1943 she was executed in the Plotzensee prison in Berlin.[19]

The aim of the Russian Orthodox Church Abroad as a whole and the vast majority of its hierarchs was the revival of Great Russia and the reconstruction of a strong, united Russian Church, and therefore it was irreconcilably opposed and deeply hostile to Nazi Germany with its goal of enslaving the peoples of Russia, although at first the Russian Orthodox Church Abroad had some illusions about the policy of the Third Reich. Only one of the hierarchs of the Russian Orthodox Church Abroad is known to have been clearly pro-German, the Metropolitan of Western Europe, Seraphim Lukyanov. But even he, in his 'Plan for the organization of the higher ecclesiastical authorities of the Orthodox Church in Russia' of 9th September 1941 which he sent to the German administrative authorities, wrote, 'In order to reconstruct Russia, immediately after the overthrow of Soviet power and the formation of a national Russian government, we need to organize a single higher ecclesiastical authority for the Orthodox Church.'[20] The

Metropolitan did not suspect at that time that Hitler's government had no intention of allowing a Russian government to be formed. Later on, as Metropolitan Seraphim gradually discovered the truth, he began to take a more sober view and repented of his former position (he returned to the Moscow Patriarchate in 1945). By 1943 the Metropolitan had already handed over the practical running of his Metropolitan District to his closest assistant – the pro-English Archpriest Timofeyev whose daughter was in a concentration camp. In June 1943, Timofeyev baptized six young Jews so saving them from extermination. Metropolitan Seraphim (Lade) of Germany wrote to Metropolitan Anastasios on 18th July 1943, saying that Metropolitan Seraphim (Lukyanov) was anti-semitic in words but not in action, whilst Timofeyev baptized Jews and even gave them certificates to prove their Arian origins.[21]

Special attention should be paid to the activities of the hierarchs of the Diocese of Berlin and Germany of the Russian Orthodox Church Abroad – until 1938 Archibishop Tikhon (Lyashchenko) and from 1938 to 1945 Metropolitan Seraphim (Lade). The former's secretary and lawyer until 1937 was N.N. Masalsky who was deported from Germany for his partly Jewish origins. Archbishop Tikhon did everything he could to keep Masalsky with him. K.Kromiadi writes that in order to help the Jews,

> Archbishop Tikhon of Berlin and Germany baptized and gave baptism certificates to Jews who asked him. Unfortunately this did not help them and the Gestapo demanded that the Synod remove Tikhon from Germany. As a result, Archbishop Tikhon was transferred to Sremski Karlovci and his closest assistants suffered repression.

This statement is not quite correct. There was a whole host of reasons for the Archbishop's dismissal and it has not been possible to find information in the archives about repressions against his closest assistants.

Metropolitan Seraphim, who replaced Metropolitan Tikhon, had a positive attitude towards the Evlogian clergy and often saved them from the Gestapo. His first conceleb-ration of a divine service with Evlogian clergy and in particular with Archimandrite Ioann Shakovskoy was due to take place on 28 July 1938. The evening before, both Metropolitan Seraphim and the Gestapo received an anonymous letter demanding that they should 'defend our Church from the intrusion of Judaeo-Masonic forces who are trying to camouflage themselves by concelebrating with our clergy.' But the service nevertheless took place and it was one of the reasons that Archimandrite Ioann was not deported.[22]

Still more characteristic is the case of the Evlogian Bishop of Brussels and Belgium, Alexander (Nemolovsky). In 1938–40 he repeatedly condemned Nazi activity in his sermons and addresses to his flock. For example, in a sermon on 31 July 1938 he said, 'We are going through terrible trials. In Germany the cruel barbarian Hitler is wiping out the Christian faith and spreading paganism. We implore God to save this country from this terrible man as the situation is even worse than in Soviet Russia.' In other speeches the Archbishop also condemned Hitler's racial theory. After the occupation of Belgium, the Archbishop was arrested by the Gestapo on 4 November 1940. They attached a board saying 'Enemy No.2' to his chest and sent him to prison in Aachen and then on to Berlin. Metropolitan Seraphim was able to rescue Archbishop Alexander from imprisonment, going bail for him and sending him to the Russian church in Tegel, where he remained until the end of the war.[23]

At the same time, Metropolitan Seraphim sometimes used antisemitic rhetoric in his official correspondence with the institutions of the Third Reich, although he did not approve of Nazi policy and did not share their goals. In particular, in October 1940 he wrote to the Ministry of Church Affairs about his opponent, the Ukrainian Professor I. Ogienko who later became the Archbishop of Kholm of the Autocephalous Orthodox Church of the General-Government:

> I cannot trust such a person who not long ago swore faithfulness to the Polish government, or who only four years ago informed the public that he was a friend to the Jews, took their interests into consideration, promised to found a Department for the study of Jewry at the University of Kamenetz-Podolsk and that 25% of students accepted at the university would be Jewish, convinced a Jewish rabbi that the university would be of great material and spiritual benefit to the Jewish people. I cannot trust such a person even if at present he enjoys the good graces of the highest authorities.[24]

After the Nazi occupation of Poland in September 1939, part of Poland's territory was incorporated into the Third Reich. The Orthodox parishes there were placed under the jurisdiction of the German Diocese of the Russian Orthodox Church Abroad. Archival documents show that the priests of some of these parishes, for example, Fr. Michael Boretsky from Lodz, baptized Jews and saved them. Until September 1940, Metropolitan Seraphim was head of the Orthodox Church on the territory of the General-Government which was formed out of the other part of Poland, but then he was forced to leave this post due to the hostility of the Governor-General Frank and the Ukrainian nationalists. The Nazis tried in all kinds of ways to arouse national dissension and sometimes handed over closed synagogues to the Ukrainians for use as Orthodox churches. One example of this took place in Krakow in December 1941.[25] Unfortunately, such a policy bore poisonous fruit at times.

But assistance to the Orthodox from the authorities of the General-Government was just an exceptional episode. Archival documents show that the Nazi government considered that the Russian Orthodox Church itself had been 'infiltrated by Jewish dogmatists' and therefore they planned to create a new pseudo-religion for the occupied Eastern territories. A directive of the Reichssicherheitshauptamt of 31 October 1941 said that:

> ...under no circumstances should the masses receive teaching about god that is rooted in Judaism and borrows its understanding of religion from Jewish ideas. In sermons, teaching about god must be free from all Jewish influence and so preachers must be found who will be given appropriate education and guidance before they are released to teach the Russian masses. Therefore it is absolutely necessary to prohibit priests from bringing any hint of doctrinal teaching into their preaching and at the same time we must take care to create as soon as possible a new kind of preacher who will be able to teach a religion free of Jewish influence after appropriate, albeit brief, training. It is clear that the confinement of 'god's chosen people' to ghettos and the eradication of this people who are the main culprits of Europe's political crimes, are compulsory measures which will further the cause of liberating the eastern regions of Europe. It is also clear that under no circumstances should the clergy be allowed to interfere with these measures, particularly in the regions infected by Jews, where on the basis of Orthodox teaching, they are preaching that the healing of the world begins with the Jews. It is clear from the above that the solution of the church question in the occupied Eastern regions is a task of extreme importance for the political liberation of those regions. It is a question which, if skilfully handled, could be wonderfully resolved in favour of a religion free from Jewish influence although, as a prerequisite, churches in the eastern regions infected by Jewish dogma would have to be closed.[26]

The undisguised racism of the directive leaves no doubt as to the fate of Orthodoxy if Hitler's Germany had been victorious. Orthodoxy would have been wiped out and a 'new religion' free of many basic Christian dogmas implanted. We can agree with the authors of 'The History of Christianity' that after exterminating the Jews, removing all leadership, both Christian and non-Christian, and enslaving believers, Himmler's dream was to actually create here a territory of Aryan supremacy[27]. On a practical level, German church policy in the East from 1941 until 1945 was shaped by this attitude.

The Moscow Patriarchate took a very clear anti-Nazi stand and condemned the persecution of Jews (although the attitude of the Soviet authorities did not allow it to express its views publicly nor to publicly distance itself from growing Soviet anti-semitism. It should be pointed out that there had traditionally been a group of priests of Jewish background in the Russian Orthodox Church. At the same time, as Archpriest Sergei Hackel rightly pointed out in his paper at the Second International Conference 'Theology after Auschwitz and the Gulag' (St. Petersburg, 1998), many opportunities to collect information about Orthodox clergy and laypeople's efforts to save Jews during the war years have been lost:

> for example, Joseph Stalin, the head of the godless persecutors of the Church and himself Orthodox by background, appointed a representative of the Russian Orthodox Church, Metropolitan Nikolai Yarushevich to the state commission for the investigation of crimes committed by the Nazis on the occupied territories of the Soviet Union. Metropolitan Nikolai was allowed to be appalled by Fascist brutalities, but almost exclusively by those of an anti-Orthodox character. This was a requirement of Soviet policy at the time. He was not supposed to speak of the mass extermination of Jews taking place on the same territory at the same time. Even this witness was deprived of the opportunity of drawing public attention to righteous people among the Gentiles.[28]

This is why now, 55 years after the end of the war, it is difficult to establish the names of many Russians, Belorussians, Ukrainians – believers under the jurisdiction of the Moscow Patriarchate – who saved Jews from extermination. A painstaking search has to be made for shreds of information in archival documents, memories of eyewitnesses, in periodicals. The author of this paper heard about one such situation from the St. Petersburg Professor I. Levin.[29] During the years of the occupation he was living in the town of Pechory in the Pskov region. The son of the Deacon at the local Orthodox Church was shot by a Nazi soldier because he looked like a Jew. After this, the priest spoke out sharply in his sermon against the actions of the occupying forces. Levin himself, as well as several other Jews in Pechory, survived due to the action of Orthodox clergy.

We can read about another noteworthy event in an article devoted to the death of Archbishop Philotheus (Narko). During the war he was head of the Mogilev and then the Minsk Diocese, and then in 1942–43 Panteleimon, the Metropolitan of Minsk entrusted the running of the entire Metropoly of Belorussia to him. In the article it is underlined that, 'His particular service was that he baptized thousands of Jewish children, thus rescuing them from death in Hitler's gas chambers.'[30]

There was a similar situation to that of the Moscow Patriarchate in the 'Renovationist' Church (Obnovlencheskaya Tserkov or Living Church) which was led by Metropolitan Alexander Vvedensky, a Jew by origin. In the Renovationist Church the proportion of priests with Jewish origins was higher and the Nazis persecuted it particularly actively in the occupied territories. For example, a Renovationist clergyman from Zhitomir in the Ukraine who began to serve as priest after the German occupation, was arrested. The Kuban and Northern Caucasus was the only region where the activity of the Renova-tionist Church was in some form allowed by the occupying forces.[31]

The Russian Orthodox Church's attitude to the Holocaust was more evident in the Ukraine where the majority of Soviet Jews lived. During the occupation there were two Ukrainian Orthodox Churches – an autocephalous church and an autonomous church which was subordinate to the Moscow Patriarchate. The latter condemned outright the extermination of Jews. Many of its priests tried to save them in different ways. The most famous example is that of Alexey Glagolev in Kiev. In a speech given in 1991 to a predominantly Jewish audience in New York[32], Alexis II, Patriarch of Moscow and All Russia spoke of him together with Fr. Dmitrii Klepinin and Mother Maria (Skobtsova) as examples of those who had made heroic efforts to save Jews. Fr. Alexey, Senior Priest at the Church of St. Nicholas in Podol', and his wife Tatiana managed to save dozens of people from death over a period of several years. Fortunately, they both survived.

But several priests and laymen in the Ukraine were killed by the Nazis for trying to save Jews. For example, on 6 March 1942 the Security Police and the SD made a report on the execution of Sinitsa, the Mayor of Kremenchug in the Poltava region, for baptizing Jews together with the local priest, giving them Christian names and so saving them from extermination. In the report there was no information about how the priest was punished. A. Arkhangelsky, a senior priest from the Crimea, reported to the Metropolitan of Leningrad, Alexey (Simansky) on 13 July 1944 that during the occupation the senior priest of the cemetery church in Simferopol, Fr. Nikolai Shvets, read an anti-Nazi appeal made by the Patriarchal Locum Tenens Metropolitan Sergi to his parishioners, and then Deacon A. Bondarenko helped him to distribute it. 'Their patriotic deed was supported by the elder Vikenti, a former 'Renovationist' Bishop. They were all shot by the German Gestapo. Fr. N. Shvets was also accused of baptizing Jews.[33]

However, some Ukrainian nationalists voluntarily took part in exterminating Jews. Most of them belonged to the Greek Catholic Church but some belonged to the Autocephalous Ukrainian Orthodox Church. In a horrific report made by the SS operational command No.5 in autumn 1941 we read about the actions of the latter. The report speaks of the extermination of 229 Jews in the town of Khmelnika, and of how the inhabitants of the town received the news of the murders with such enthusiasm that a thanksgiving service was held.[34] Whilst the leadership of the Autocephalous Ukrainian Orthodox Church did not approve the anti-Jewish actions, it also did not condemn them.

In Galicia in the Western Ukraine the majority of the Ukrainians belonged to the Greek Catholic Church. Its head Andrei Sheptitsky, Metropolitan of Lvov, personally saved the lives of Jews in Lvov and he resolutely condemned the Holocaust in his conversations and letters. Lvov was occupied by German troops on 30 June 1941. And on the morning of 1 July thousands of Jews living in the town were herded into the courtyard of the prison by Ukrainians wearing German uniforms and almost all of them were shot. The next day, the Ukrainian auxiliary police, subordinate to the SS operational group, also took part in anti-Jewish pogroms. Some of the victims, among them Rabbi David Kahane and the son of a murdered Rabbi, I. Levin, took refuge in the Metropolitan's residence where they managed to survive these persecutions[35]. The Metropolitan also encouraged Greek Catholic monks who gave shelter to Jews in their monasteries.

In February 1942, Sheptitsky wrote a letter Himmler in which he protested that 'the Ukrainian auxiliary police are being forced to shoot Jews'. In a reply by the Reichsfuhrer of the SS the Metropolitan was told not to interfere with business 'that has nothing to do with him'. On 29 August 1942, Metropolitan Andrei called upon the highest moral authority in his church, Pope Pius XII: 'Today the whole country unanimously considers the German regime to be possibly a greater evil than the Bolshevik regime and to be almost diabolic... The number of murdered Jews in our small country already exceeds

200,000. 130,000 men, women and children were murdered in Kiev in the space of a few days.' The Metropolitan described the Nazi regime as a 'system of lies, deception, injustice, robbery, a caricature of all ideas of civilization and order . . . a system of national chauvinism taken to absurd extremes, of hatred towards all that is good and beautiful.'[36] The Pope did not reply to this dramatic letter.

Sheptitsky continued to protest against the extermination of Jews. In this respect his interview with the French journalist of Ukrainian origin, Vsevolod Frederic, in September 1943 is significant. The latter worked for the German Ministry of Foreign Affairs and a detailed record of the interview was passed to various Nazi offices. One of Sheptitsky's main reproaches of the Germans was their 'inhumane attitude to the Jews'. He said that in Lvov alone 100,000 Jews had been killed, and in the Ukraine as a whole, one million. One young man had told him at confession that 'he personally had killed 75 people in one night in Lvov.' According to the record of the interview, Frederic asked, 'But aren't the Jewish people a dangerous threat to Christianity?' The Metropolitan agreed but held to his opinion that the extermination of the Jews was impermissible.[37] It should also be remembered that the Metropolitan published a passionate pastoral appeal 'Thou shalt not kill'. However, the majority of his parishioners were extremely antisemitic and the Metropolitan's example did not have the necessary effect on them.

During the war years, part of the Southwest Ukraine was occupied by Romanian troops. This territory came under the jurisdiction of the Romanian Orthodox Church which had a cautious and unfriendly attitude towards the Jews during the war but did not approve of their extermination. Evidence of this can be found in a report made by the head of operational staff of Rosenberg's department, Dr. Zeiss, about his trip to Bucharest in June 1944:

> The national Orthodox Church has a helpful attitude. They are more hostile towards the Jews than the Roman Church but on the other hand they don't go as far as agreeing with our point of view. Two years ago they forbade the baptism of Jews which obviously does not exclude individual cases of Jews being baptised in return for a bribe. People living in the villages are extremely antisemitic. The inhabitants of Bucharest are indifferent.[38]

On the whole the Romanian Church did not have a great influence on the Ukrainian population which rightly saw it as a weapon of Romanianization.

Thus though the situation differed in the various branches of the Orthodox Church in the USSR, it can be said that on the whole between 1941–45 the Russian Orthodox Church condemned the extermination of Jews, although its practical action in this respect was clearly insufficient. Further research on this subject is undoubtedly necessary as there are still many gaps in our knowledge. Above all, we need to establish the names of Orthodox faithful in the occupied territories who risked their lives to save Jews. Most of them are still unknown.

N O T E S

1 Preservation Centre of Historical-Documentary Collections (TsKhIDK), f.1470, op.1, d.10, 1.234.
2 A.K. Nikitin, *Natsistskiy rezhim I russkaya pravoslavnaya obshchina v Germanii (1933–1945 gg)* (Moscow: published by the author, 1998), p.96.
3 M. Litvinov, People's Commissar of the Foreign Affairs in the 1930s, was an ethnic Jew.
4 Archbishop Ioann (Shakhovskoy), *Izbrannoye* (Petrozavodsk: Svyatoy ostrov, 1992), p.375.
5 TsKhIDK, f.1470, op.1, d.17, 1.236.
6 A.K. Nikitin, *op. cit.*, pp.218, 251–253; Archbishop Ioann (Shakhovskoy), *op. cit.*, p.378; 'Materialy k biografii arkhiepiskopa Ioanna (Shakhovskogo)', *Tserkovno-isotoricheskiy vestnik* 1 (Moscow, 1998), p.83.

7 Metropolitan Evlogy (Georgievski) *Put' moej zhizni. Vospominanija mitropolitan Evlogija, izlozhennye po ego rasskazam T. Manukhinoj* (Paris: YMCA Press, 1947), pp.663, 670.

8 Protohierarch Sergy Gakkel, *Mat' Maria (1891–1945)*, (Paris: YMCA Press, 1980), pp.160–162.

9 *ibid.*, pp.162–164.

10 *ibid.*, pp.164–167.

11 I.A. Krivoshein, 'Tak nam velelo serdtse', in *Protiv obshchego vraga. Sovetskie lyudi vo frantsuzskom dvizhenii Soprotivlenia* (Moscow: Politizdat, 1972), pp.270–271; I.A. Krivoshein, 'Mat' Maria (Skobtsova) (K 25-letiu so dnya konchiny)', *Zhurnal Moskovskoy Patriarkhii* (Moscow, 1970), p.39.

12 Protohierarch Sergy Gakkel, op.cit., pp.169–171; *Mat' Maria, Stikhotvorenia, poemy, misterii. Vospominania ob areste v lagere Ravensbrück* (Paris: La Presse Française et Etrangère Oreste Zeluck, 1947), pp.151–152.

13 *Mat' Maria*, p.164–165; See *Mat' Maria (Skobtsova). Vospominania, stat'i, ocherki*, 2 vols. (Paris: YMCA Press, 1992).

14 Protohierarch Sergy Gakkel, *op.cit.*, pp.157–158, 174.

15 Protohierarch Sergy Bulgakov, *Khristianstvo I evrejskij vopros* (Paris: YMCA Press, 1991), pp.6, 82–83.

16 *ibid.*, pp.137–140.

17 *Russkoye* delo, 23 dd.7 November 1943, Belgrade.

18 *Pravoslavnaya Rus'* 10 (1942), p.2

19 Käte Gaede, 'Russische orthodoxe Kirche', in *Deutschland in der ersten Hälfte des 20. Jahrhunderts* (Köln: Edition Orthodoxie, 1985), pp.246–247.

20 Bundesarchiv Berlin (BA), R501/22183.B1, 16–20.

21 TsKhIDK, f.1570, op.2, d.17, 1.96, 101–102.

22 *ibid.*, f.1470, op.1, d.17, 1,238, 242; K. Kromiadi, *Za zemlyu i volyu . . .* (San Francisco, 1980), pp.23–24.

23 Käte Gaede. *op.cit.*, pp.244–245; A.K. Nikitin, *op.cit.*, p.226, 367; A. Kazem-Bek, 'Znamenatel'ny yubiley. K poluvekovomu sluzheniu arkiepiskopa Bryussel'skogo i Bel'giyskogo Alexandra v arkhiyereyskom sane', *Zhurnal Moskovskoy Patriarkhii* 11 (1959), pp.13–16.

24 TsKhIDK, f.1470, op.2, d.14, 1.261.

25 TsKhIDK, f.560, op.3, d.456, 1.247; F. Heyer, G. Weise, 'Kirchengeschichte der Ukraine. Acht Jahrzehnte vom ersten Weltkrieg bis zu den Konflikten der Gegenwart', manuscript (Göttingen, 1997), pp.216–217.

26 Russian Centre of Preservation and Study of the Documents on the Contemporary History (RTsKhIDNI), f.17, op.125, d.92, 1.23–25.

27 Jean-Marie Mayeur, *Die Geschichte des Christentums*, Bd.12: *Erster und Zweiter Weltkrieg – Demokratien und totalitäre Systeme (1914–1958)* (Freiburg-Basel-Wien: Herder, 1992), p.976.

28 Sergi Gakkel, 'Zapadnoye bogoslovie posle Oswencima i Russkaya Pravoslavnaya Tserkov', *Stranitsy* 3/3 (Moscow, 1998), p.403.

29 Oral narrative, St. Petersburg, 25 January 1998.

30 'So svyatymi upokoy . . . Konchina arkhiepiskopa Filofeya', *Vestnik Germanskoy Yeparkhii Russkoy Pravoslavnoy Tserkvi za granitsey* 5 (Munich, 1986), pp.9–11.

31 State Archive of the Russian Federation (GAFR), f.6991, op.1, d.6, 1.25; V.I. Alekseev, F.G. Stavru, 'Russkaya Pravoslavnaya Tserkov' na okkupirovannoy nemtsani territorii' *Russkoye Vozrozhdenie* 18 (New York-Moscow-Paris, 1982), pp.117–119.

32 Preservation Centre of Historical-Documentary Collections (TsKhIDK), f.1470, op.1, d.10, 1.234.

33 *Religioznye organizatsii v SSSR v gody Velikoy Otechestvennoy voiny (1943–1945 gg.)*. Publication by M.I. Odintsova, Otechestvennye arkhivy, Moscow, 1995, N 3, p.55; V.I. Alekseev, F.G. Stavru, *Russkoye Vozrozhdenie*, 17 (1982), p.106. A.K. Nikitin, *Natsistskiy rezhim i russkaya pravoslavnaya obshchina v Germanii (1935–1945 gg.)* (Moscow: the author's edition, 1998), p.96.

34 See R. Headtand, *Messages of Murder: A Study of the Reports of the Einsatztruppen of the Security Police and the Security Service, 1941–1943* (London and Toronto, 1992), p.114.

35 Hansjakob Stehle, 'Der Lemberger Metropolit Sheptytskyj und die national-sozialistische Politik in der Ukraine', *Vierteljahreshefte für Zeitgeschichte* 34/3 (München, 1986), p.411.

36 *ibid.*, pp.415, 418–419; S. Redlich, *Sheptitskyi and the Jews*; P.R. Magusi, *Morality and Reality* (Edmonton 1989). 145–164; Taras Hunczak, *Ukrainian–Jewish Relations during the Soviet and Nazi Occupations*; Y. Boshyk, *The Ukraine during World War II* (Edmonton, 1986), pp.49–51.

37 Bundesarchiv Berlin (BA) R6/179, B1.105.

38 BA 62 Dil/82 Film 3307, Anfn. Nr.4907437.

TO SERVE GOD OR HITLER:
NAZI PRIESTS, A PRELIMINARY DISCUSSION

Kevin Spicer, C.S.C.

I N 1934, Wilhelm Stockums (1877–1956), Auxiliary Bishop of Cologne, stated that 'every incumbent of the priestly office is by virtue of sacramental consecration another Christ in his supernatural life and vocation', and, therefore, 'he should be another Christ in the moral order also by his personal life of virtue'.[1] In the history of the German Catholic church in Nazi Germany, however, there existed a small number of priests whose actions in both professing allegiance to and joining the Nazi party became a blatant anomaly to Stockums's understanding of their consecrated office. These renegade or Nazi priests, who publically professed their allegiance to the National Socialist movement, differed from the many priests who had initially shared in the wave of national enthusiasm for Hitler when he first came to power as Reich Chancellor. Thus by the end of 1933, when most of those priests who had first welcomed the new government withdrew their support because of their disillusionment with the state's encroachment into areas formerly reserved to the church (i.e., youth groups, parish associations), these Nazi priests became, conversely, more militant in their association with the party and stayed that way until the very end.[2]

This essay seeks to open up a discussion on the life of these priests by examining their motivations for joining the Nazi party. This investigation includes a study of their activities on behalf of the Nazi party and how these actions affected their relationship with their church superiors and parishioners. What will be shown is that these men were exceptions to the norm, who often placed their own careers and welfare above ministry and service to the people whom they were called to serve. To carry out this examination, this essay will first discuss how widespread Nazi membership among the German Catholic clergy was and then review the literature that has previously dealt with priests who joined the Hitler party. Thirdly, it will examine what encouragement a priest received to join the party and the difficulties he had to surmount to become a member. Finally, this essay, through brief case studies centering on the diocese of Berlin, will discuss the motivations, actions, and fate of these priests who openly supported the NSDAP.

I.   It is difficult to determine just how many individuals were among the ranks of these Hitler or Nazi priests, as they were often referred to by their fellow clergymen and parishioners. Primarily, this has been attributed to an earlier lack of access to diocesan church archives and personnel data. The actions of these individuals, as one can imagine, are not a high point in church history that many church archivists wish to explore. A 1942 unsigned article in *The Tablet* investigated the relationship between German priests and the Nazi party and speculated that there were 'less than a hundred who openly expressed their sympathy with the party', and only half of these were members of the Nazi party.[3] In 1973, Frederic Spotts stated that according to his research there were approximately 150 Roman Catholic priests who had actually become members of the Nazi party. He based this number on American military documents that indicated that 'an average of five priests in each diocese, as well as some seminarians and members of orders, belonged to the party'.[4] This number is relatively small when compared to the 21,461 diocesan priests along with several more thousand religious order priests who served the Catholics of Germany.[5] According to the continuing research of this author, however, Spotts was correct in his speculation.[6]

II.   No author has devoted a single study to discussing the history behind and impetus for the activity of these Nazi priests in the NSDAP. Instead, most discussions of these clergymen are found in works that offer general or regional histories of the Catholic church in Nazi Germany. These survey studies include early endeavours by John Conway, Guenter Lewy, and Alois Natterer and later studies by Donald Dietrich, Gerhard Hetzer, Georg May, and Klaus Scholder that briefly discuss some of the more infamous priests as they pertain directly to their narrative or argument.[7] More recently, as church archives have opened their doors to researchers, regional studies have appeared investigating the lives of individual Nazi priests in either chapters or articles. These short biographical studies include efforts by Raimund Baumgärtner, Roman Bleistein, S.J., and Werner Tröster.[8]

The most significant study of Nazi clergymen was a recently published comparative study of Catholic and Protestant pastors in the diocese of Speyer. Thomas Fandel, the author, seems to have had unrestricted access to diocesan archive and clergy files for his investigation. Fandel said that among the 346 personnel files that he analysed, he found twenty-six priests who supported the NSDAP outright. He was able to reconstruct the histories of sixteen of these men. In his analysis, Fandel argued that there was not one specific reason why these men supported or joined the NSDAP. According to Fandel, their support was less determined by an attraction to Nazi ideology, and more determined by an individual's troubled past with diocesan officials. Thus, through contact with the party, these priests attempted to gain its support against church superiors and to ensure future employment.[9] A letter of 21 November 1935 from Hans Kerrl (1887–1941), the Reich Minister for Church Affairs, to Josef Goebbels (1897–1945), Minister for Propaganda, supported Fandel's findings. Kerrl warned of priests who wished 'to use the party as a screen' after difficulties with church superiors concerning non-political issues.[10]

Other authors of many of the publications discussed above have attributed a wide range of reasons for priests' adamant support of and enrollment in the Nazi party. *The Tablet* article found that many of the Nazi priests had previous disciplinary problems with their bishops, but it also added that the majority were 'young, ambitious teachers of religion' who welcomed the prospect of advancement. Few of them, it argued, were 'to be found among priests occupied in pastoral work'. Instead, they kept themselves 'aloof from the clergy's monthly conferences and thereby cut themselves off from the influence of a more loyal clergy'.[11] In an overly apologetic tone, Georg May insisted that priests supported the NSDAP based solely on its political aims: to rectify Versailles and to rid Germany of 'ungodliness and corruption'.[12] Offering a more realistic assessment, Tröster showed that the party's response to Germany's political situation in the Weimar Republic, coupled with its blame and hatred of the Jews, attracted Dr. Lorenz Pieper (1875–1951) of the Paderborn archdiocese, as early as 1922 to the NSDAP.[13]

III.   Regardless of a particular priest's reasons for supporting National Socialism, both the church and the state made it difficult for Catholic clergy to add their name to the NSDAP membership card index in Munich and to agitate publicly for the party. On the part of the state, Hitler himself, in the infancy of the Nazi movement, encouraged priests who were 'old-fighters' to delay their membership in the party or desist from explicit agitation in order to avoid conflicts with their own church superiors. This decision most likely had more to do with Hitler's decision to keep the party and religion totally separate, than with an actual concern for arousing the ire of a diocesan bishop and his chancery.[14] Even if this was Hitler's reasoning, the priests attributed his request to a desire to prevent conflict with diocesan officials. For example, in the Fall of 1923, Hitler encouraged Dr. Pieper, who had seven months earlier resigned from his assignment as assistant priest at St. Peter's Church in Hüsten to travel to Munich and agitate for the Nazi movement, to return to Paderborn to avoid any further difficulties with his bishop. Hitler allegedly stated that he could not have a 'suspended' priest working for his party.[15] In the case of Fr. Josef Roth (1897–1941) of the archdiocese of Munich and Freising, sometime before 1933 Hitler had allegedly encouraged Roth not to join the party, evidently to avoid problems with church superiors, despite the young priest's zealous enthusiasm for the movement.[16]

Until 1931, each diocese had to contend individually with the few priests, such as Dr. Pieper and Dr. Philipp Häuser (1876–1960) of the Augsburg diocese, who agitated for National Socialism and other right-wing organizations. Finally, at different times in or near March 1931, the bishops individually released common pastoral guidelines for Catholics who wanted to associate themselves with National Socialism. In point two, for example, they 'strongly forbade priests to work with the National Socialist movement in any manner'.[17] This decree stayed in effect until 28 March 1933 when the joint German episcopacy, through their Fulda Bishops' Conference, issued a statement that repealed the prohibition against membership in or activity for the NSDAP.[18] However, this reprieve for Catholic priests to join the Hitler movement was short-lived. On 20 July 1933, after an amazingly brief period of negotiations, the German government and the Holy See signed a concordat to protect the interests of the Roman Catholic church in the Reich. Upon Hitler's express bidding, article thirty-two excluded priests and members of religious congregations from 'membership in political parties and activity for such parties'.[19] After that, the German bishops, who chose to reprimand their priests for publicly speaking out on behalf of National Socialism, regularly turned to this article for support. According to Church Affairs Minister Kerrl, whose assistant Josef Roth was experiencing difficulties in extending his bishop's permission to continue his work for the government, this reference was a 'completely inappropriate' misuse of article thirty-two.[20] Kerrl was not the only government official who held this opinion. A May 1940 memo from an official in the Reich Chancellory concerned itself solely with the history of the question of membership of clergy in the NSDAP. According to this memo, in December 1933, Hitler requested an interpretation of article thirty-two that would not preclude membership in the NSDAP. This interpretation, at least on the part of the state, seems to have been adopted. The memo added that in 1938, a government official determined that the NSDAP was 'not a party in the sense of article thirty-two' and, therefore, did not affect Catholic priests' membership in the Nazi party.[21] Yet, even if Catholic priests managed to join the party and stay active members, a doubt concerning their authenticity still lingered in the minds of many fellow party members. For example, in 1939, as Roth lectured on the theme of 'The Catholic Church and the Jewish Question' at a symposium for the Reich Institute for History of the New Germany, an

attendee who had also lectured on the same subject and who was 'surprised that Roth
received so much applause', abruptly confronted Roth afterwards and reminded him of
what an SD official had once told him that one needed to proceed with 'the utmost
caution' in reference to anyone who had been 'a Jesuit'.[22]

For those who did join and supported the party openly, this often meant a great deal
of difficulty with their church superiors. Often this had less to do with the nature of a
priest's specific activity and more to do with the priest's direct disobedience against the
wishes of his diocesan superiors. Kerrl realized that anyone who worked 'full-time or in
visible ways for National Socialism' had to expect 'unpleasant reprimands and punishments'. At times, Kerrl added, the conflicts that ensued from this activity between the
priest and his church superiors were 'indeed sometimes a burden for the party'. This
disruption also often caused removal of the priest from his parish – the very place
'among the Catholic population' where he could promote the aims of the movement.[23]
More often than not, a priest who had encountered problems with his bishop and
chancery on account of his pro-Nazi stance received no support from the NSDAP. A
memo of 13 June 1936 from Kerrl to Rudolf Hess (1894–1987), Deputy to the Führer,
revealed this dilemma. In his letter, Kerrl requested that Hess reply to two previous
requests for a remedy to assist Nazi priests who had been reprimanded by their superiors
on account of their political attitudes or activities. According to Kerrl, the party had a
'certain moral obligation to help such priests who have actually become a victim of their
National Socialist convictions'.[24] On 22 August 1936, Kerrl finally received a reply from
Martin Bormann, then Chief of Staff to Hess, who ultimately offered him no guidance
when he advised Kerrl to deal with the matter himself or in 'special cases' to turn to the
Gestapo for further investigation.[25]

IV.   The actual situation of Nazi priests can best be understood when studied in the
context of a particular diocese, such as that of Berlin. In 1933, in the newly established
Berlin diocese, there were 260 active diocesan clergy (including priests from other
dioceses who worked full-time in Berlin parish ministry) involved in parish work, sixty
five additional priests serving as teachers or chaplains or in full retirement, and over one
hundred members of men's religious communities involved in a variety of apostolic
works.[26] Unfortunately, bombing raids towards the end of the war destroyed the majority
of diocesan records and personnel files concerning these men. Therefore, the activities of
the Nazi priests active in Berlin have to be reconstructed from extant files in state
archives, newspaper articles, and the remaining files of the Berlin Diocesan archive. In
reviewing archival evidence, it has been determined that four priests openly pronounced
their support for the NSDAP: Wilhelm Knobloch (1890–1957); Walter Leonards (1887–
1965); Anton Scholz (1891–1980); and Johannes Strehl (1887–1951). The last three were
confirmed Nazi party members. An additional six priests were also active in the NSDAP:
Robert Chrysostomus Conrath, OP (1880–1956); Paul Arthur Drossert (Tournai, Belgium 1883–1969); Karl Johannes König (Paderborn 1876–1939); Simon Pirchegger
(Graz, Austria 1889–1949); Josef Roth and Anselm Vriens, OCSO (*b*. 1880). These latter
priests were either members of a religious community or from outside dioceses. And
although they resided in Berlin, they held no official ministerial position through the
diocesan chancery. Besides these individuals, there were also at least four ex-priests:
Albert Hartl (Munich-Freising 1904–1982); Friedrich Murawski (Paderborn 1889–1945);
August Wilhelm Patin (Munich/Freising 1879–1946) and Sebastian Schröcker
(Munich/Freising *b*. 1906), who deserted their priesthood for the Nazi party and who
lived and worked in Berlin for the Nazi state.[27]

It is quite possible and probable that there were additional priests in the Berlin diocese who openly supported National Socialism. Evidence of this fact may be found in a July 1934 SD situation report for Potsdam. In this report, an SD official stated that there was a 'small section of Catholic pastors' who were 'oriented in a good German sense' and who supported 'the National Socialist movement with all their energy'. The SD informant also pointed out that because these pastors did not wish to suffer any 'setbacks from superiors' they did not make known their support of the NSDAP.[28] In June 1936, another example surfaced in the correspondence of the SD that detailed the activities of Dr. Simon Pirchegger, a diocesan priest from Graz-Seckau, Austria. In 1936, after experiencing difficulties with his Austrian church superiors over his pro-Nazi activity, Pirchegger immigrated to Berlin and moved shortly thereafter to Bonn to assume teaching duties at the University there.[29] Upon arriving in Berlin, the SD reported that Pirchegger had 'assembled around himself a group of twenty-five Catholic priests' who were 'loyal to the National Socialist state'. However, only Dr. Pieper's name was mentioned as a member of this group. In March 1936, the SD asked these priests to promote a 'yes' vote from among the Catholic population to confirm Hitler's policies (i.e. reoccupation of the Rhineland). According to the letter, the Nazi priests at the last minute 'withdrew their appeal in order not to jeopardize the authority of the German bishops' who in many dioceses had issued individual statements promoting the referendum.[30] Although no additional evidence of this group's existence has surfaced, their hesitation to aid the state by acting jointly as a group in the face of possible reprimand by their bishops revealed how segregated they were – from the party whose support they could not always count on and from their own bishops who in the end supported the referendum. As the SD official exclaimed in his letter, their 'attitude indicates how ideologically weak' this group was.[31] These men were outsiders, but outsiders who were afraid to break with the Catholic church.

V. In 1933, the most prominent Nazi priest in the Potsdam vicariate was Johannes Strehl who, as both an opportunist and aspirant to higher positions, promoted himself as the first National Socialist Catholic priest appointed as pastor.[32] The portrait of Strehl that developed was that of an individual who cared much less for his pastoral duties to his parishioners than his desire to advance under the National Socialist government. Ordained in 1914, Strehl served in a variety of parishes as parochial vicar during and after the war years. In 1931, Bishop Christian Schreiber (1872–1933) offered Strehl his first position of leadership by appointing him the administrator of St. Ann's church in Lichterfelde-Berlin. While serving in this relatively small community of Catholics (1,500 parishioners), Strehl received word that Fr. Karl Warnecke (1873–1949), pastor of St. Peter and Paul (6,000 parishioners) in Potsdam, had decided to retire.[33] Realizing the importance of the position and the opportunity to advance, Strehl began to manoeuvre in order to obtain the new position.

Utilizing his connections through his membership in the Catholic Association for National Politics,[34] a conservative, right-wing, pro-Nazi group of Catholic professionals who promoted rapproachement between German Roman Catholicism and National Socialism, he became a favoured candidate of Dr. Ernst Fromm, the District Governor (*Regierungspräsident*) of Potsdam for the position. According to a law of 21 March 1931, the state held patronage rights over certain delegated parishes including Potsdam. On 28 April 1933, Fromm wrote to Wilhelm Kube (1887–1943), NSDAP District Commander (*Gauleiter*) and Provincial Governor (*Oberpräsident*) of the Province Brandenburg and Berlin, to recommend Strehl for the pastorship of St. Peter and Paul. Fromm described him as a 'pastor who will hold firm to the guidelines of the government and who will strive for the coordination of church and state'.[35] Kube, who himself had been involved in party, state, and religious questions in regard to the Protestant church, eagerly took up Strehl's cause to obtain for him the vacant pastorship in his district.[36]

In the meantime, on 1 May 1933, in order to ensure the state's support for his candidacy as pastor of St. Peter and Paul and to solidify his own support for National Socialism, Johannes Strehl joined the Nazi party and was assigned number 2,658,955. Strehl, confident he would receive the position in Potsdam, preempted this appointment and had his profession listed as 'Catholic pastor' on his enrolment card.[37] In waiting until May to join the party, Strehl honoured the prohibition against membership in the Nazi party, especially for clergy, that was repealed in March 1933. His membership, however, seemed a bit too opportune in relation to his candidacy for the Potsdam position. A June 1933 letter to Hitler from Georg Lossau, President of the Catholic Association for National Politics, supported this interpretation. In the letter praising Strehl, Lossau described him as one who 'has openly declared his allegiance to the NSDAP since the days of the repeal of the bishops' prohibition'.[38] Lossau, however, did not offer any insight or information about Strehl's pre-1933 stance toward the Nazi party. Strehl, therefore, like so many Germans, most likely viewed the rise of the Nazi movement into power as an opportunity for advancement and thus joined to further his own goals. This is not to say, however, that Strehl did not support the aims and ideology of the movement, since his future activities clearly helped the party.

On 5 May 1933, confident that Strehl would support the aims of the Nazi party, Kube wrote to Bishop Schreiber to present Strehl as his candidate for the position. In the letter, Kube mentioned nothing of Strehl's political orientation.[39] Several weeks later, on 30 May 1933, the Berlin chancery office appointed Strehl as pastor of the Potsdam parish.[40] There are no records to show whether or not the diocese had any knowledge of Strehl's support of the NSDAP. A recommendation for his appointment from Kube, however, known for his involvement in Protestant church affairs, should have sparked some interest in this question. According to comments in a letter (written after the appointment) from Paul Steinmann (1871–1937), Vicar General in the Berlin Diocese, to Adolf Cardinal Bertram (1859–1945), Archbishop of Breslau, Strehl told him that he wanted to 'stand by the church with advice and action' on church and state relations in his new position.[41] Steinmann, who himself was sympathetic to the new state in its early years and who was in fact running the diocese in the absence of Bishop Schreiber whose health continued to fail, perhaps took this comment as a positive sign, especially during the lapse of time between the repeal of prohibitions against the NSDAP and the conclusion of the concordat.[42] High hopes existed in the minds of many churchmen for good working relations with the state.

Soon after Strehl assumed his pastorship in Potsdam, rumours began to circulate in church circles that the government was planning to name Strehl as state commissioner for the Catholic church. On 23 June, Steinmann wrote to Cardinal Bertram and stated that he had received 'confidential information' concerning Strehl's possible appointment and suggested that the bishops preempt any move by the state by designating a representative of their own choosing to the Reich government.[43] On 25 June 1933, Bertram informed the Metropolitan bishops of the German church provinces of this information and suggested the appointment of Steinmann to this position.[44] The bishops, however, did not immediately act on Bertram's suggestion, nor did the government pursue creating such a position.[45] Bertram's suggestion, however, reflected the bishops' disapproval of someone not of their choosing.

Unfortunately, the extant documents do not offer much insight into Strehl's activities as pastor of St. Peter and Paul. However, several documents reveal how relentless he could be in supporting the concerns of the state and of the Nazi party. For example, in January 1934, Strehl refused to read from the pulpit during Sunday Mass the mandated pastoral letter concerning marriage that contained a new paragraph against sterilization. Instead, Strehl informed the Potsdam Gestapo of the impending reading of the pastoral letter and denounced Steinmann, Dr. Georg Köhler (1892–1958), Monsignor Bernard Lichtenberg (1875–1943) and Monsignor Georg Banasch (1888–1960), all diocesan chancery officials, for their part in preparing and disseminating the document to be read.[46] The Potsdam Gestapo forwarded Strehl's letter and copy of the pastoral letter to their Berlin Headquarters, which in turn sent the information with a cover letter to Hans Lammers (1879–1962) in the Reich Chancellery. In the cover letter, a Gestapo official noted that Strehl 'always speaks in exemplary ways in favour of harmonic cooperation of the Catholic church with National Socialism'.[47] In August 1935, in a separate incidence, Strehl even brought charges against his own parishioners who allegedly defamed his character. Evidently, Strehl took a liking to alcohol and was known to enjoy drinking in the local taverns. Allegedly, Cornelius M. and Otto E. accused Strehl of drinking so much that he collapsed outside a tavern. According to his 'slanderers', Strehl was so inebriated the night before that he was unable to preside at Sunday Mass the following day. On a different occasion, they again alleged that Strehl had drunk so much alcohol that he had to be helped home by two SA men. These rumours had enough credence in the city for an artist to create a caricature of Strehl drinking beer at the local tavern with a caption reading: 'That is the drunken Catholic pastor of Potsdam', which was published in a city newsletter. A subsequent trial convicted Strehl's accusers and sent both of them to jail, albeit for two months and one month respectively. The *Potsdamer Beobachter* that reported the story, condemned Strehl's accusers and at the same time upheld the character of Strehl. According to the author of the article, Strehl had been attacked solely because he was 'a National Socialist, and that does not suit the Centre Party Catholics in Potsdam'.[48]

On 31 March 1936, Strehl at forty-eight years of age suddenly resigned from his Potsdam pastorship. It is unclear from the documentary evidence whether the new Bishop of Berlin, Konrad Preysing (1880–1950), noted for his anti-Nazi stance, forced Strehl to resign as he did with other Nazi priests or whether he resigned for health reasons (i.e., alcoholism). Unlike some of his Nazi priest colleagues, on 15 May 1937 Strehl was appointed chaplain of a nursing home run by the Grey Sisters in Berlin-Spandau, a position he held until the end of the war. Again, it was unclear whether this was a state appointment or an assignment delegated by the diocese. In either case, Strehl no longer had influence over a large congregation.[49]

The process that ensued to replace Strehl and find an acceptable candidate for both the state and church offers insight into how a local bishop could still control the appointment of candidates for a parish pastorship (though with approval from the state) and how there existed a lack of communication between government bureaus. On 15 April 1936, Dr. Johannes Allendorf (1894–1978), decorated veteran of World War I, recipient of a doctor of philosophy from the University of Freiburg (21 August 1926), former secretary to the bishop and at the time pastor of St. Joseph in Tegel-Berlin (1,600 parishioners), sent his application directly to Kube. In his application, Allendorf enclosed a brief curriculum vitae, listed three Nazi party members as referees, and concluded his letter with '*Heil* Hitler!'.[50] The use of the Hitler greeting does not immediately signify an individual's allegiance to Nazism, but could have been used to attract Kube's sympathy for his candidacy for the Potsdam position. The testimonies of the witnesses, however, present Allendorf in a different light.

In the extant correspondence concerning Allendorf's application, two out of the three listed referees wrote a recommendation for the priest. The earliest reply came from Mr. F., a teacher, who related how in 1931 Allendorf helped to establish a relationship between the Theatre of Youth (*Theater der Jugend*), an organisation sympathetic to National Socialism, and the Berlin diocesan chancery, despite resistance from within the diocese. Furthermore, he declared that Allendorf was a 'genuine and honest supporter of the new Germany' who after Hitler's assumption as Chancellor flew the Swastika from his parish buildings and declared himself 'faithful to the government', again despite resistance from a number of his parishioners.[51] Dr. Z., a school administrator, was much more reserved in his response. According to Dr. Z., Allendorf was a Catholic priest who sincerely made 'an effort to bring his religious views in harmony with the *völkische* events of our time'. Allendorf, he continued, was of the opinion that the *Führer* saw 'in both Christian denominations important factors for the preservation of the German ethnicity'. Dr. Z. also found that Allendorf worked for unity between church and state, including an extraordinary show of respect for the Protestants in his community.[52]

Though these responses reveal that Allendorf supported the early endeavours of the new state to unify the nation and strengthen Germany, they do not present a definite portrait of an individual who overtly supported National Socialism. From his voluntary military service and experience in the war, it is understandable how Allendorf could be so nationalistic in his support of the state. However, in the eyes of others, to continue to manifest this support of the state while this same state persecuted many Catholic priests and religious (i.e., in currency and morality trials) and encroached on the activities of the church (i.e., youth groups, charity associations), led to the conclusion that Allendorf was sympathetic to the new government.

Despite his application and enthusiasm, Allendorf was not the first candidate for the government. For example, in May 1936, the SD in their promotion of candidates did not even consider Allendorf, but instead suggested Anton Scholz, pastor of Holy Family church (290 parishioners) in Strasburg/Uckermark, who, according to a SD report, was already active as an informant on church matters to the SD Section East. It was the SD's hope that Scholz would continue providing 'extraordinarily valuable material' that up to this point 'was supplied by Strehl'.[53] For some unexplained reason the SD did not immediately pursue Scholz's candidacy.

Instead, on 2 June 1936, Kube forwarded to Fromm a copy of Preysing's nomination of three priests for the Potsdam pastorship. It contained the names of Johannes Wittenbrink (1888–1962). Alfons Maria Wachsmann (1896–1944), who was later executed by the Nazis for an offence against the prohibition on listening to foreign radio transmissions, and Johannes Allendorf.[54] Clearly, from the contents of this letter, Allendorf had been in consultation with Preysing concerning filling the vacant pastorship. A few days letter, on 6 June, Kube suggested a fourth name for the candidacy, Paul Arthur Drossert, a priest from Tournai, Belgium, who had been released from his diocesan duties since 1927 and was living privately in Potsdam. In 1932, Drossert had lost his residency in the St. Joseph House with the Sisters of Charity of St. Karl Borromaeus on order of the Berlin chancery because of his pro-National Socialist talks and, more specifically, for signing an appeal for Hitler that appeared in *Der Angriff* and the *Völkischer Beobachter*.[55] Kube admitted that it appeared 'hardly possible to achieve the candidacy of Fr. Drossert'. With this realization, he focused on choosing from among the three candidates presented by Preysing. Interestingly enough, in his correspondence with Fromm, Kube showed evidence that he wanted not only a man loyal to the party and state, but also one who would be qualified to fulfill his pastoral duties in the parish.[56] By the middle of July, Kube had determined that Wittenbrink was 'politically unreliable' and Wachsmann was 'politically questionable', even though he was a known member of the NSV.[57]

In August 1936, Scholz's name returned to the discussion at least in the understanding of the SD. Then the SD informed the Kurmark district leadership of the Nazi party that Scholz should be appointed, if only temporarily, as pastor of the Potsdam parish. Immediately, an official from the district leadership wrote Fromm of their concerns about Scholz who, because of his political views, had already been 'repeatedly transferred'. Instead, they wanted to appoint a pastor like Strehl who in addition to his faith and his church would also 'fight with full conviction and fervor for the movement and Adolf Hitler'.[58] In the same month, Scholz himself sent in an application for the position.[59] This was shortly followed by a letter from the Local Nazi party in Zossen, where Scholz had once served as pastor, to Fromm, advocating the candidacy of Scholz for pastor of St. Peter and Paul.[60] In the midst of these suggestions, Kube was forced to resign from his position as *Oberpräsident* over party-political matters, and was succeeded in August by Emil Stürtz (1892–1945). Despite this change of power, on 29 August Fromm decided in favour of Dr. Allendorf for the position and informed Stürtz of his choice.[61] At the same time, Fromm wrote to the NSDAP in Zossen to inform them that it was too late to add Scholz to the list of candidates.[62] On 1 September 1936, Stürtz accepted this recommendation and informed Bishop Preysing of his choice.[63]

There are no extant records that offer insight into Allendorf's pastorship of St. Peter and Paul. Nor are there any state documents that record any problems between Allendorf and the state. Clearly, from the material presented, Allendorf was a strongly patriotic German who supported the new government. The portrait that Nazi party members painted of him was also positive. Unfortunately, the extant documents do not offer any insight into understanding his response to Nazi ideology. His inclusion on the list of candidates by Preysing, a noted anti-Nazi, however, prompts a second opinion of Allendorf. This opinion cannot be solidified until further documents become available to make a full judgement of Allendorf's activities during the Third Reich. This same conclusion has to be reached about Wilhelm Knobloch (1890–1957), pastor of St. Anthony church in Nowawes in the vicariate of Potsdam, who on 6 February 1939 was forced into retirement by Bishop Preysing on account of his activity for the Nazi party.[64] Little else is known about Knobloch's activities in the Third Reich.

VI. Although Strehl joined the NSDAP apparently for opportunistic reasons the documentary evidence does not allow for a definite conclusion in this regard. In the cases of the next two priests, Karl König and Josef Roth, who came from dioceses external to Berlin, their writings help reveal what aligned them with National Socialism: an adamant antisemitism and belief that Nazism would solve the perceived ills that plagued Germany toward the end of the Weimar Republic.

Following his early retirement in 1926 from his pastoral duties in the diocese of Paderborn, König first moved to Cologne and then to Berlin.[65] König was frustrated with the state of German society and culture and had convinced himself that Germany was spiralling downward into destruction. He attributed this decay to the 1918 revolution, the institution of a liberal democratic government, political Catholicism, Bolshevism, and the Jews. In National Socialism, König saw the saving force that would rescue Germany from ruin and restore her to greatness.[66] König believed that Hitler and his party would rid the nation of those liberal elements that attacked the core of German society. To this end, König made the pledge to direct all his energy to help the state combat those forces he perceived were against it. Therefore, he joined the NSDAP[67] and provided the Reich Chancellery and other government agencies with regular reports under the title 'Chronicle of the Centre' that detailed the events in the German Catholic church that he considered political and harmful to the Nazi state.[68] These reports were also used by the SD to gather information against the church.[69]

Although a contemporary described König as an 'unsavoury figure' who openly expressed his glee over the government's persecution of elements in the Catholic church who acted against the state[70], König continually argued that no one, including the state, was persecuting the Catholic church. Instead, he pointed out that never in history was the church more 'involved in the welfare of the human soul than today in Germany'. He argued that the state attacked only those people and groups that were harmful to Germany. König stated proudly that the *Führer* had smashed everything that was 'evil in Germany, the terrible literature, the terrible theater, the terrible art, the terrible parties, and the terrible government and laws'.[71]

In his analysis of the situation, König continually lumped together the Jews, Free Masons, and the Jesuits as groups that concentrated their 'attack against our *Führer* and against his *Volk*'.[72] According to his rambling, the Jews influenced and infiltrated the former Catholic Centre party, which he still saw as a force working to harm Germany. He argued that German Catholics could be brought in line with the Nazi state only if 'the Lord God, the *Führer* and his comrades as well as the German Volk can unconditionally rely on' the German Catholic bishops, if church newspapers and the Centre press were banned, if the Jesuits were expelled from the schools, and if Catholics would agree to leave a church whenever a Centre-influenced priest spoke against the state or party. Furthermore, he believed that Germany knew how to solve its Jewish question: through force, terror and intimidation. He then listed a series of headlines from newspapers throughout the world detailing attacks and terror against Jews in Germany.[73]

König also introduced similar patterns of thought into his sermons and talks. In an October 1935 talk to a Nazi party gathering in Rottach-Egern, he spoke against the 'baneful connection of the Centre with the SPD, Jews, and the other powers of disbelief and subversion'.[74] Again, on 8 March 1936 in Bad Neuheim, König attacked Jews and Bolsheviks in the context of a sermon in which he compared the transfiguration of Christ to the revitalization of Germany under Hitler.[75]

Both the Paderborn and Berlin dioceses made attempts to control König's actions with little success. On 12 November 1935, he received a letter from the Paderborn chancery that demanded he stop making speaking appearances at political rallies. On 16 November, König sharply replied to the rebuke and assured the chancery that his words were always 'purely of a pastoral nature'. He also described himself as a 'priest-private man' who did not speak from an official ministerial position. In December, the chancery wrote an even sharper letter back to König, again demanding he refrain from speaking at political rallies. The diocesan official also rejected his creation of the term 'priest-private man' as detrimental to the priesthood. König refused to follow the requests of his diocesan superiors who gave up their inquiry in the new year.[76] In June 1938, the Berlin chancery tried to encourage the city government to withdraw its offer to König to teach Catholic religious instruction at two schools in Berlin-Schöneberg. According to the chancery, König did not possess the required approval of the local ordinary or his diocesan bishop in Paderborn to teach religion.[77] The chancery also informed Church Affairs Minister Kerrl of the situation.[78] At the same time, the Paderborn chancery office informed König that he did not hold the required permission to teach religious education.[79] König, of course, ignored the concerns of his superiors and, with the city government's permission, accepted the new teaching posts.

Living away from his local ordinary, König was impossible to control. König simply refused to obey the wishes of his superiors, and entangled them in an endless correspondence that never fully resolved a difficult situation. As a result, König devoted his entire life to serving the goals of the Nazi movement and providing it with information to further limit the activity of the Catholic church. His reward was praise from Nazi officials. The more he was praised, the greater his hatred and intensity toward those elements in Catholicism and in German society grew. In many ways, through these actions, König formed his own notion of church that incorporated the ideology of National Socialism and attributed salvation to Hitler and the Nazi party. Finally, on 18 February 1939 death suddenly stopped König's fanatical efforts to aid the goals of National Socialism.[80]

Josef Roth was even more fanatical than König in his dedication to National Socialism, in his detestation of the Versailles Treaty and the Weimar Republic, and in his anti-semitism.[81] Roth had served voluntarily in the First World War, and as with many soldiers, the defeat and its aftermath left a lasting impression upon him. Roth saw a great weakness in German society and attributed all of his country's ills to the permeating influence of Jews in every aspect of German life. As early as 1923, as a parochial vicar, Roth published a vile antisemitic tract entitled 'Catholicism and the Jewish Question'. In it he argued that people had to leave their 'catacomb antisemitism' and embrace a radical antisemitism that would lead to the removal of Jews from any influence in public life, including their 'enjoyment of the rights of citizens, . . . exclusion from all state offices, . . . refusal of licenses for any trade and industry, . . . and prohibition of any literary and propaganda activity'. According to Roth, it was permissible for a Catholic to adopt racial antisemitism because the Jews transmitted immorality – that which the Catholic must resist – through their blood. Therefore, for Roth the Christian command to love one's neighbour did not apply in the case of Jews because from the beginning every Jew was 'already a latent danger for the Christian religion and morality' and, therefore, 'the Jewish race on account of its naturally demoralizing influence inherent from nature must be eliminated from the public life of our religion and our *Volk*'.[82] Cardinal Faulhaber reprimanded Roth for publishing such a tract without the church's approval. Roth learned his lesson from this and afterwards only published under pseudonyms. In response to the Cardinal, Roth did as he would always do, respond with a letter pledging fidelity, denying all wrongdoing, and promising to obey the church in the future.[83]

In 1934, Roth, who had already been agitating for the party before the takeover of power, joined the SA and more publicly aligned himself with the NSDAP.[84] In the same year, he began teaching religion at the National Socialist Leadership School in Feldafing.[85] Soon thereafter, in August 1935, he was invited by Kerrl to join the newly established Ministry of Church Affairs. To accept this position, he asked Cardinal Faulhaber to grant him time off from his regular diocesan duties of teaching. At first, Faulhaber denied the request, but through encouragement of his chancery who believed Roth's assignment could prove useful for the diocese, Faulhaber relented and granted permission for Roth to move to Berlin and assume the new position.[86] In 1936, Roth, upon receiving a more permanent position as head of the Catholic division, requested an extension through the Berlin chancery for permission to continue his work in the Ministry of Church Affairs.[87] This time Faulhaber was not as agreeable and denied Roth's request after the chaplain admitted that he did not regularly preside at daily

Mass.[88] Faulhaber had also been privy to information from another Nazi priest Alban Schachleiter, who advised the Cardinal through a chancery official not to give approval to Roth's new position on account of his disloyalty to Rome, his careerism and his advocacy of a German National Church.[89] Faulhaber also suspected that Roth had been publishing and working against the church, but did not have evidence to support his suspicions.[90]

In the Ministry of Church Affairs, Roth worked against what he considered to be political Catholicism and the encroachment of the Catholic church into areas of the state. He viewed the Reich Concordat as an outdated agreement, concluded by a state in its infancy and in his own words strove 'to sabotage, to undermine, and to work for the annulment of the Concordat through my entire professional activity'.[91] Not only had the Concordat been overtaken by the development of the new National Socialist state, but in 1935, under the pseudonym of Walter Berg, Roth published an article that argued that the church herself had grown ancient and ineffective and was currently being replaced by the National Socialist revolution.[92]

For Roth, Christianity was not only ancient and lacked significance, but it was also permeated by Judaism, which left it weak. As early as 1923, Roth had presented an image of Christ as a 'heroic strongman' calling upon people not to mourn but to be strong in spirit.[93] In his essay on Roth, Raimund Baumgärtner also saw that Roth called for more manly virtues and ideals to be reclaimed by Christianity, which he believed had become effeminate with its stress on charity and good work. In contrast, Roth argued that masculine Christian virtues 'rebel against institutions and endeavours that do not fight suffering with all their might, but only offer good words and support to those who suffer'.[94]

By 1940, Roth had come to the conclusion that Christianity could not be saved from the influence of Judaism, which continually weakened and distorted it. In a 1940 lecture for the Institute for the History of New Germany that was also published in the same year, Roth again addressed the issue of 'The Catholic Church and the Jewish Question'. According to Roth, the church was permeated by Jewish influences to her core. This included hundreds of years of overtures of the Jesuits to allow Jews in its ranks. Despite a history of anti-Jewish church law, the church now had lost the battle against Judaism and preached tolerance of Jews. He concluded, 'the Catholic church will never come to a clear and determined struggle against Judaism and will never become an ally in the national ideological struggle because it would have to give up its own mission and its own spiritual substance'.[95]

In 1940, Roth not only turned his back against the church on account of its alleged Jewishness, but according to diary fragments left by Roth, he was also struggling with his own celibacy. Somehow, despite his own involvement in his agency's measures enacted against the Catholic church and his own approval as an official in the Church Affairs Ministry of the arrest of individual Catholic priests, Roth never withdrew from the Catholic priesthood. In 1939–41, his own vow of celibacy was questioned when he entered into a relationship with a recently divorced woman, Käthe S. From Roth's diary entries and recorded testimony of his fellow employee, Dr. Sebastian Schröcker, Roth endured a pang of conscience whether to marry this woman. Käthe seemed to make his decision even harder, for though she professed her love for Roth, she constantly returned to live for short periods with her former husband. Roth's diary fragments revealed that he was torn and confused by the situation.[96] Before he had the chance to make up his own mind as to what to do (or to create more problems for his own church) on 20 August 1941, Roth suddenly died in a canoe accident in Tattenberg am Inn in Tirol.[97]

CONCLUSION

This essay has shown that the priests under discussion supported National Socialism for a variety of reasons: nationalism, antisemitism, anti-liberalism, anti-Bolshevism, and opportunism. Though these individuals had different reasons for joining and supporting the Nazi party, they did have one point in common: alienation from their faith tradition. For varied reasons, including the ones mentioned above, they no longer saw their church and faith tradition as the sole means of salvation. Whether consciously or not, they also imposed this messianic role on Adolf Hitler and the Nazi party, believing that their *Führer* could offer them and their country the means to a better society, happiness and life. In turn, they allowed Nazism to become the all-important guiding factor in their lives. Despite this factor, all of them were unable to break away from their religious tradition. Catholicism had a grip on them. These Nazi priests, however, distorted their own perception of Catholicism to accommodate their love, faith and trust in National Socialism.

NOTES

1 Wilhelm Stockums, *The Priesthood*, trans. Joseph W. Grundner (London: Herder, 1942), p.20.

2 Ulrich Wagener, 'Unterdrückungs-und Verfolgungsmaßnahmen gegen Priester des Erzbistums Paderborn in der Zeit des Nationalsozialismus', *Theologie und Glaube* 75 (1985), p.56.

3 *The Tablet*, 'Catholic Priests and the Nazi Party', reprinted in *Catholic Mind* 40 (8 January 1942), p.17.

4 Frederic Spotts, *The Churches and Politics in Germany* (Middletown, CT: Wesleyan University Press, 1973), p.109.

5 The Catholic statistical yearbook for Germany listed that in 1933 there were 16,887 priests in parish ministry with an additional 4,574 priests (not including religious) who served as chaplains and teachers or were in retirement. Hermann A. Krose, S.J., *Kirchliches Handbuch für das katholische Deutschland*, 19 (Cologne: J.P. Bachem, 1936), n.p., statistical foldout.

6 Utilizing both church and state archives I have collected information on approximately fifty priests who were either members of the NSDAP or outspoken in their support of the National Socialist movement.

7 See John S. Conway, *The Nazi Persecution of the Churches 1933–45* (New York: Basic Books, 1968), pp.133, 169, 406–407; Guenter Lewy, *The Catholic Church and Nazi Germany* (New York: McGraw-Hill, 1964), pp.6–7, 10, 101, 155, 272; Alois Natterer, *Der Bayerische Klerus in der Zeit dreier Revolutionen 1918–1945. 25 Jahre Klerusverband 1920–1945*, (Munich: Katholische Kirche Bayerns, 1946), pp.283–295; Donald J. Dietrich, *Catholic Citizens in the Third Reich. Psycho-Social Principles and Moral Reasoning* (New Brunswick, NJ: Transaction Books, 1988), p.55; Gerhard Hertzer, *Kirchenkampf in Augsburg 1933–1945. Konflikte zwischen Staat, Einheitspartei und christlichen Kirchen, dargestellt am Beispiel einer deutschen Stadt* (Augsburg: Hieronymous Mühlberger, 1982), pp.35–36; Georg May, *Kirchenkampf oder Katholikenverfolgung? Ein Beitrag zu dem gegenseitigen Verhältnis von Nationalsozialismus und christlichen Bekenntnissen* (Stein am Rhein: Christiana, 1991), pp.308–309; and Klaus Scholder, *The Churches and the Third Reich*, trans. John Bowden (Philadelphia, PA: Fortress, 1988), Volume I: p.135; Volume II: p.228.

8 Raimund Baumgärtner, 'Vom Kaplan zum Ministerialrat Joseph Roth – eine nationalsozialistische Karriere', in *Politik – Bildung – Religion. Hans Maier zum 65. Geburtstag*, eds. Theo Stammen et. al. (Paderborn: Ferdinand Schöningh, 1996), pp.221–234; Bleistein, 'Abt Alban Schachleiter OSB', *Historisches Jahrbuch* 115 (1995), pp.170–187, and ' "Überläufer im Sold der Kirchenfeinde" *Jahrbuch* 115 (1995), pp.170–187, Josef Roth und Albert Hartl: Priesterkarrieren im Dritten Reich', *Beiträge zur altbayerischen Kirchengeschichte* 42 (1996), pp.71–109; and Werner Tröster, ' "…die besondere Eigenart des Herrn Dr. Pieper!" Dr. Lorenz Pieper, Priester der Erzdiözese Paderborn, Mitglied der NSDAP Nr. 9740', in *Das Erzbistum Paderborn in der Zeit des Nationalsozialismus*, ed. Ulrich Wagener (Paderborn: Bonifatius, 1993), pp.45–91.

9 Thomas Fandel, *Konfession und Nationalsozialismus. Evangelische und katholische Pfarrer in der Pfalz 1930–1939*, VKZ B76 (Paderborn: Ferdinand Schöningh, 1997), pp.467–468.

10 Kerrl to Goebbels, 21 November 1935, BArch Berlin R5101 22314, n.f.

11 *The Tablet*, 'German Priest and the Nazi Party', pp.18–19.

12 May, p.309.

13 Tröster, pp.51–52, 73.

14 See Scholder, I: pp.88–98.

15 Tröster, p.54.

16 Ludwig Brandl, 'Josef Roth', in *Biographisch-Bibliographisches Kirchenlexikon*, Volume 8, Friedrich Wilhelm Bautz, ed. (Herzberg: Traugott Bautz, 1994), p.743.

17 Schreiber to Berlin Clergy, 21 March 1931, in Gotthard Klein, ed., *Berolinen. Canonizationis Servi Dei Bernardi Lichtenberg. Sacerdotis Saecularis in Odium Fidei, Uti Fertur, Interfecti (1875–1943)*, Volume II: Documenta (Rome: Congregatio de Causis Sanctorum, Prot. N. 1202, 1992), p.40.

18 *Amtsblatt des bischöflichen Ordinariats Berlin*, 1 April 1933, p.23.

19 Alfons Kupper, *Staatliche Akten über die Reichskonkordats Verhandlungen 1933*, VKZ A2 (Mainz: Matthias Grünewald, 1969), p.273.

20 Kerrl to Goebbels, 21 November 1935, BArch Berlin R5101 22314, n.f. On Roth's concerns see Roth to Heß, 13 December 1935, BArch Berlin R5101 22268, f.84.

21 Note, May 1940, BArch Berlin R43 II/155, ff.72–73.

22 Baumgärtner, p.234.

23 Kerrl to Goebbels, 21 November 1935, BArch Berlin R5101 22314, n.f.

24 Kerrl to Heß, 13 June 1936, BArch Berlin R5101 22268, f.128.

25 Bormann to Kerrl, 22 August 1936, BArch Berlin R5101 22268, f.135.

26 *Schematismus des Bistums Berlin für das Jahr 1933*, pp.69–77; 96–108.

27 On the exploits of these individuals see David Alvarez and Robert A. Graham, S.J., *Nothing Sacred. Nazi Espionage Against the Vatican, 1939–1945* (London: Frank Cass, 1997); Heinz Boberach, 'Organe der nationalsozialistischen Kirchenpolitik. Kompetenzverteilung und Karrieren in Reich und Ländern', *Staat und Parteien. Festschrift für Rudolf Morsey zum 65. Geburtstag*, Karl Dietrich Bracher, et. al. eds. (Berlin: Duncker & Humblot, 1992), pp.305–331, especially 324–325; and Robert A. Graham, S.J., 'Documenti di Guerra da Mosca: Spionaggio Nazista Antivaticano', *La Civiltà Cattolica* 4 (1993), 542–550; Wilhelm Patin, *Beiträge zur Geschichte der Deutsch-Vatikanischen Beziehungen in den letzten Jahrzehnten* (Berlin: Nordland, 1942).

28 Lagebericht July 1934, GStAPK I/Rep. P Lageberichte Provinz Brandenburg 2, 5 Potsdam, f.144.

29 On 1 May 1932, Pirchegger joined the NSDAP (Number 901,259). See Pirchegger Karte, BArch Berlin, NS-Akt, personenbezogene Unterlagen aus der NS-Zeit (PBU). On Pirchegger see Harold Anton Hofmüller, *Steirische Priester befürworten den Nationalsozialismus und den Anschluss an das Deutsche Reich Adolf Hitlers* (Diplomarbeit, Universität Graz, 1997), pp.93–101.

30 On the 1936 referendum and the German bishops see Lewy, pp.201–205 and also the correspondence in Bernhard Stasiewski, ed., *Akten deutscher Bischöfe über die Lage der Kirche 1933–1945*, III, VKZ A25 (Mainz: Matthias-Grünewald, 1979), pp.299–303, 310.

31 SD Berlin to SD-Section East Berlin, 28 June 1936, SAPMO-BArch Dahlwitz, Z/B1 1691, f.757.

32 Strehl to Hitler, 6 June 1933, BArch Berlin R43 II/174, f.31.

33 See Johannes Allendorff, 'Katholisches Leben in Potsdam im Wandel der Jahrhunderte', *Archiv für schlesische Kirchengeschichte* 19 (1961), 260–292.

34 On this organization see Lewy, p.6.

35 Fromm to Kube, 28 April 1933, BLHA Pr. Br. Rep. 2a Regierung Potsdam II Pdm. 525, n.f.

36 On Kube's religious activity in regard to the German Protestant denominations and the German Christians see Scholder, I: pp.197–209, 287–290.

37 Strehl Karte, NS-Akt, BArch Berlin, PBU.

38 Lossau to Hitler, 6 June 1933, BArch Berlin R 43 II/174, f.34.

39 Kerrl to Schreiber, 5 May 1933, BLHA Pr. Br. Rep. 2a Regierung Potsdam II Pdm. 525, n.f.

40 Strehl to Hitler, 6 June 1933, BArch Berlin, R43 II/174, f.31.

41 Steinmann to Bertram, 23 June 1933, in *Akten Deutscher Bischöfe über die Lage der Kirche 1933–1945*, I: 1933–1934, VKZ A5, Bernhard Stasiewski, ed. (Mainz: Matthias-Grünewald, 1968), p.255.

42 See his comments in the *Kreuz Zeitung*, 5 October 1933, BArch Berlin R5101 21675, f.194.

43 Steinmann to Bertram, 23 June 1933, in Stasiewski, I, p.255.

44 Bertram to Faulhaber, Gröber, Hauck, Klein and Schulte, 25 June 1933, Stasiewski, I, pp.253–254.

45 See Martin Höllen, *Heinrich Wienken, der 'unpolitische' Kirchenpolitiker. Eine Biographie aus drei Epochen des deutschen Katholizismus*, VKZ B33 (Mainz: Matthias-Grünewald, 1981), pp.54–69.

46 Strehl to Gestapo Potsdam, 15 January 1934, BArch Berlin BA R43 II/174, f.193.

47 Gestapo Berlin to Lammers, 3 February 1934, BArch Berlin R43 II/174, f.192.

48 *Potsdamer Beobachter*, 24 August 1935 in BArch Berlin R5101 22384, n.f.

49 See *Schematismus des Bistums Berlin*, 1937: p.129; 1938: pp.41, 120. After the war, Strehl went into full retirement and lived in Königshausen über Schwabmünchen in Bavaria until his death on 18 May 1951. See *Schematismus des Bistums Berlin*, 1947: p.158; *Zum Gedächtnis der verstorbenen Priester im Bistum Berlin* (Berlin: Bischöfliches Ordinariat, 1986), p.19.

50 Allendorf to Kube, 15 April 1936, BLHA Pr. Br. Rep. 2a II Pdm. 525, n.f.

51 F. to Fromm, 24 April 1936, BLHA Pr. Br. Rep. 2a II Pdm. 525, n.f.

52 Dr. Z. to Fromm, 5 May 1936, BLHA Pr. Br. Rep. 2a II Pdm. 525, n.f.

53 Sd Report to C., 9 May 1936, SAPMO-BArch Dahlwitz Z/B1 1691, f.813.

54 Kube to Fromm, 2 June 1936, BLHA Pr. Br. Rep. 2a Pdm. 525, n.f.

55 From the 'Chronik des St. Josephshauses, II' 1932, pp.58–59. Diözesanarchiv Berlin (DAB) VI/1 Paul Drossert.

56 Kube to Fromm, 6 June 1936, BLHA Pr. Br. Rep. 2a II Pdm. 525, n.f.

57 Gauleiter Pommerania to Fromm, 15 July 1936; Gauleitung Groß-Berlin Personalamt to Fromm, 20 July 1936, BLHA Pr. Br. Rep. 2a II Pdm. 525, n.f.

58 Kreisleiter Gauleitung Kurmark to Fromm, 21 August 1936, BLHA Pf. Br. Rep. 2a Pdm. 525, n.f.

59 Fromm to Stürtz, 29 August 1936, BLHA Pr. Br. Rep. 2a II Pdm. 525, n.f.

60 Ortsgruppe NSDAP Zossen to Fromm, 28 August 1936, BLHA Pr. Br. Rep. 2a II Pdm. 525, n.f.

61 Fromm to Stürtz, 29 August 1936, BLHA Pr. Br. Rep. 2a II Pdm. 525, n.f.

62 Fromm to Ortsgruppe NSDAP Zossen, n.d., BLHA Pr. Br. Rep. 2a II Pdm. 525, n.f.

63 Stürtz to Preysing, 1 September 1936, BLHA Pr. Br. Rep. 2a II Pdm. 525, n.f.

64 *Schematismus des Bistums Berlin* 1939, p.123.

65 The documentary evidence does not offer any insight into why König, in 1926, left his pastoral duties in the diocese and retired from active ministry shortly thereafter. König Lebenslauf, Erzbistumsarchiv Paderborn (EAP), Sammlung zu Karl König.

66 Undated obituary for König, EAP, Sammlung zu Karl König. Also see König to Lammers, 15 March 1935, BArch Berlin R43 II/1636, ff.11–12.

67 König's NSDAP membership card is lost. Contemporary articles from Nazi publications regularly describe him as a member of the party. See *Schwarze Korps*, 2 March 1939.

68 König Easter Letter, Easter 1934, BHStAM 107255, n.f.

69 SD to Ziegler, 19 June 1936, SAPMO-BArch Dahlwitz, Z/B1 1691, f.709.

70 Adolph, p.163.

71 König to Lammers, 4 July 1935, BArch Berlin R43 II 1636a, ff.122–123.

72 König to Lammers, 25 July 1935, BArch Berlin, R43 II/1636a, f.41.

73 König to Lammers, 9 August 1935, BArch Berlin, R43 II/1636a, ff.2–4.

74 *Tegernseer Zeitung*, 18 October 1935 in EAP, Sammlung zu Karl König, n.f.

75 Sermon, 8 March 1936, EAP, Sammlung zu Karl König, n.f.

76 See the following letters: Gierse to König, 12 November 1935; König to Gierse, 16 November 1935; Gierse to König, 17 December 1935; König to Gierse, 13 January 1936; consecutively printed. See BHStAM 107257, n.f.

77 Lichtenberg to Stadtpräsidenten Abt. für höheres Schulwesen Berlin, 18 June 1938, BArch Berlin, R5101 22341, f.166.

78 Lichtenberg to Kerrl, 18 June 1938, BArch Berlin R5101 22341, f.165.

79 Prange to König, 16 July 1938, BArch Berlin R5101 22341, f.170.

80 Böring to Klein, 22 February 1939, EAP, Sammlung zu Karl König, n.f.

81 Roth was a rabid antisemite who during his career in the Ministry for Church Affairs would regularly refer to a colleague in the Protestant Division of the ministry whom he believed had Jewish blood as

'*Jude*' (Jew) any time he encountered him in the corridors of the ministry building. Recollection of Dr. Sebastian Schröcker, BArch Koblenz, Roth Nachlaß, n.f.

82   Josef Roth, *Katholizismus und Judenfrage* (Munich: Franz Eher, 1923), pp.2, 5, 10.

83   Bleistein, 'Überläufer', pp.74–75.

84   Roth joined the SA on 1 April 1934, Number 287, 274. Roth, SA-Akt, BArch Berlin PBU, n.f.

85   Brandl, p.742.

86   See the series of correspondence between Faulhaber, Munich chancery and Roth in Erzbistum Archiv München und Freisung (EAM) Akte Faulhaber 7269, n.f.

87   Steinmann to Neuhäusler, 23 April 1936, EAM Akte Faulhaber 7269, n.f.

88   Roth to Faulhaber, 17 May 1936; Faulhaber to Roth, 28 May 1936, EAM, Akte Faulhaber 7269, n.f.

89   Report of Neuhäusler, 28 August 1935, EAM Akte Faulhaber 5539, n.f.

90   See Faulhaber to Roth, 7 May 1936, EAM, Akte Faulhaber 7269, n.f.

91   Persönliche Erinnerungen. BArch Koblenz, Roth Nachlaß 898.

92   See Walter Berg, 'Die Kirche ist alt geworden', *Deutsche Glaube* 3 (1935), 125–1927.

93   Sermon of Roth, during the Memorial Mass for the German Day in Nuremberg on 4 September 1923, *Bayern und Reich* 1 (1923), BArch Koblenz, Roth Nachlaß 898, n.f.

94   Baumgärtner, p.227.

95   Josef Roth, 'Die katholische Kirche und die Judenfrage', *Forschungen zur Judenfrage IV* (Hamburg: Hanseatische Verlaganstalt, 1940), p.175.

96   BArch Koblenz Roth Nachlaß 898, n.f.

97   Roth Obituary, EAM Akte Faulhaber 7269.

DIFFERING WAYS OF READING, DIFFERING VIEWS OF THE LAW:
THE CATHOLIC CHURCH AND ITS TREATMENT OF THE JEWISH QUESTION DURING VICHY

Richard H. Weisberg

I. INTRODUCTION: HOW FRENCH LAWYERS DURING VICHY AVOIDED THEIR OWN BEST INSTINCTS AND TRADITIONS

THE REACTION of the Roman Catholic Church to the Holocaust is a vast and contentious subject. With a natural focus on the Pontiff, Pope Pius XII, many historians have tried to parse the often baroque political and diplomatic record of the years 1933–1944; playwrights and theologians have added their words to this attempt at veracity. And now the Vatican itself has convened a distinguished commission to peruse documents hitherto closed to scholars.

Furthermore, the Church in almost every country in Hitler's Europe has been separately studied, although perhaps with less passion and less available evidence than apply to inquiries that centre on the Vatican itself. Among Europe's predominantly Catholic populations, the Church in France, Italy, and Poland has been scrutinized. This paper will add to the empirical base of knowledge about France, as my archival research from 1982–94 uncovered interesting and as-yet largely unpublished documentation about the French Church; I have also benefited from – and am in surprising relevant agreement with – the recent study of Vesna Drapac on the local French parishes,[1] to which I shall turn in some detail below.

This paper, at its heart however, will develop – theologically – arguments I have already made about the surprising and disheartening behaviour of French *lawyers* during Vichy. I link this behaviour to an ensconced, peculiarly French and Catholic *manner of reading*. This 'hermeneutic', I will argue, not only affected the Church's response to the Vichy regime but also influenced lawyers and many other Catholics to behave with less vigor than French traditions otherwise demanded against the unprecedented statist racism of the Vichy laws against Jews.

Some of my findings about the French Church, and about Vichy's relationship to the Vatican, were published in my 1996 study, *Vichy Law and the Holocaust in France*.[2] That work, which has been translated and published in Paris under the title, *Vichy, la Justice et les Juifs*,[3] employed archival findings to expose the workings of the French legal system during the War. My central thesis based on the empirical work was that the system pervasively, and without substantial deviation from its pre-war institutional and formal patterns, participated in the persecution of Jews on French soil. Across the spectrum of the legal profession, from the Justice Minister to Vichy legal functionaries (including judges, law professors and others) to private practitioners of law, France accommodated and in fact took the lead from the Germans on questions of racial and religious status.

But in order to do this, French lawyers first needed to leap a hurdle not present in other countries victimized by Hitler. They had to reckon with their ingrained belief in *egalitarianism*, a staple of the French legal system since 1789 and one that endured throughout the 20th century, up to and including Dreyfus (which did not involve any statist racial legislation) and even the Vichy years, during which government lawyers consistently invoked the 'rights of man' while contemporaneously ejecting the Jew from the circle of traditional protection. My findings firmly indicate that the *private* reaction to Vichy racial laws of most lawyers (even those in the Vichy bureaucracy) was one of aversion to such a fundamental and distasteful change in French legal tradition. Even among antisemites at the bar, for example, there was regret that Jews were being singled out, especially those many hundreds of respected colleagues who were not foreign-born. Many felt that discriminatory legislation was simply 'not French'; if the Nazis insisted on singling out the Jews, perhaps nothing could be done, but surely the French themselves would not initiate and then instantiate such a gross deviation from the basic egalitarian principle of French law.

So how did so many thousands of lawyers manage to deform their own best legal instincts? In my book, I first show that traditional explanations do not work to explain this shift. There were very few rabid antisemites at the bench and bar, for example; although some saw the laws as giving them or their clients a chance to benefit economically at the expense of the Jews, lawyers were thriving anyway in wartime France: opportunism does not explain the system's four-year commitment to these laws, even after Stalingrad and even after D-day; the Germans put very little pressure on the French – in either zone – and came to see that the Vichy approach, although very different from their own on the Jewish question, would save them in manpower, treasure, and political provocation. Finally, the treatment of Jews by the Vichy legal establishment could not be fully explained by the tradition of 'positivism' – the existence alone of specific laws addressing the Jews. Countries with analogous positivistic legal traditions such as Italy had similar laws and (to a large extent) did not apply them until the Nazis took over in 1943. In Belgium, protest by prominent figures at the bench and bar *immediately followed* from the posting of Nazi antisemitic ordinances in that country. The participation of so many thousands of French legal actors already ensconced in a libertarian legal tradition might have led to the same results under Vichy. Instead, the French rejected their best interpretive instincts and decided (almost universally) to 'go with' the new statutory scheme.

My thesis was and remains that a form of *flexible* deformation of ensconced textual understandings gradually permitted lawyers (and others) to overcome their native hostility to Vichy's racial scheme. This flexibility derived in large part from a tradition of Catholic reading strategies that influenced even lay and largely anti-clerical professionals. As inbred as the story itself of egalitarianism, this strategy of manipulating foundational texts and concepts allowed lawyers during Vichy to work with the notion of equality and *at the same time* develop an intricate four-year-long pattern of discrimination against Jews.

Far from merely theoretical, this flexibility in Catholic reading strategies emerged explicitly from the Vatican in the Summer of 1941 and in the French church itself at other points.

The question was how the Vatican at its highest levels would respond to the racial laws promulgated against the Jews by the Vichy regime. The answer, at its heart, was 'There's a problem, but the Church's way of reading its own doctrine eliminates the problem immediately as a matter of interpretive strategy. So go ahead and persecute the Jews.' This letter, which has been selectively cited by earlier scholars such as Saul Friedlander, will shortly be quoted here in a crucial, hermeneutic paragraph that is usually omitted but which virtually concludes the letter in its full, archivally preserved version.

The theory – and the wartime practice – of Roman Catholic hermeneutics thus influenced behaviour among lawyers and others in France who might instead have let their egalitarian instincts overcome and overwhelm a bizarre-seeming set of Vichy laws. Instead, *French lawyers managed to interpret the still extant constitutional principles of their training flexibly, i.e., in a manner permitting relatively open-ended understandings of once-ensconced concepts such as 'equality'.*

As I shall further argue here, with the perhaps surprising assistance of Drapac's recent book and its conception of a 'flexible', 'coded' discourse among Catholics during the War, hermeneutic creativity of this type originates in a form of French Catholic reading of central texts, and it dates to at least the manner in which early Christians such as St. Paul managed to 'read' the Old Testament to produce striking and disharmonious understandings of the Bible and to promote the new religion.

Why not Italy, too? French Cartesianism

Of course, not all Catholic countries persecuted Jews in this singular manner. Italy has already been mentioned. Harsh antisemitic laws existed there on the books, but they went largely unenforced. Italy, in this sense, *does replicate Catholic flexibility,* but they chose to ignore or manipulate texts on the level *of the statutes themselves.* The French could have done that, too. They had their own government, and they considered themselves as autonomous agents in developing their own laws. But here another overwhelming aspect of French cultural tradition balefully joined with the hermeneutic flexibility they showed toward their own constitutional ideals.

This converse of the flexible hermeneutic brought the skills and eloquence of *Cartesian logic* to the task of interpreting the actual racial and religious legislation. Exactly to the contrary of their flexible readings of foundational texts, French lawyers insisted on narrow, almost myopic readings of their statutes that lost in potential power of protesting argument anything they may have gained by technical acuity and rhetorical coherence.

Liberated to deconstruct its own traditions, as I showed in my book, lawyers proceeded across the entire spectrum of their practice to produce narrow, positivistic readings of Vichy's antisemitic laws. The flipside of the Catholic-influenced flexible hermeneutic, this inflexible literalness left the Jewish population largely bereft of any 'mercy' from French law. *The peculiar but not unique combination during Vichy of interpretive flexibility as to foundational concepts – e.g. equality – but narrow formalism as to lower-level texts – e.g., statutes – will also be examined further here as to its potential theological significance for the understanding of temporal law in Christian countries.*

The Jew-as-Talmudist

As Pierre Birnbaum has shown, French xenophobia worked with French anti-semitism to bring pain to Jews on French soil throughout history.[4] But the emphasis of Vichy legal theory was upon the 'legalistic' traits of the Jewish outsider. On this view, the Jew deserved a particularized legal status because of his 'Talmudism', defined as an overly literal allegiance to a code of law and practice. Puzzling to Catholics even in our post-Holocaust world,[5] the Jew's perceived commitment to text, law and practice was especially galling to Vichy legal theorists, who were in the business of rationalizing not only anti-semitic laws but also the quick (non-Talmudic) change in their own legal traditions that would permit such a breach of French egalitarian beliefs.

In a book-length doctrinal treatment of Vichy's new antisemitic laws, lawyers Henri Baudry and Joannes Ambre[6] identify 'Talmudism' as a kind of literalistic allegiance to a daily system of laws foreign to the French notion of a more 'spiritualized' law;[7] their approach is replicated by legal scholar André Broc, who contemporaneously condones the laws against Jews as correctly symbolizing the *essential religious differences* between Christian and Jew:

> Judaism has no real mystical aspect, which might somehow correspond directly to religious needs. . . . On the contrary, Judaism consists since the Exile essentially of a system, supported by the Talmud, designed to maintain the patriotic goal of the social cohesiveness of the Jews, dispersed in the midst of the Gentiles. This system, although intellectualized, has so marked the Jewish people that it seems objectively today to be their moral law, at least as regards the essential rules, the details having been nitpicked to death by them. One might ask if this system, by its corporeal restaints, particularly as regards sexual matters, has not itself contributed to the enforcement of racial categories . . .[8]

Not surprisingly, these non-theologians often seem to misquote or to distort the Talmud itself,[9] but the Jew's ineffable 'otherness' is always proved this way. And why not a loose 'interpretation' of the Talmud? After all, anti-Talmudism virtually requires a flexibility in the reading of texts. Inaccurate or distorted understandings of fundamental texts – far from being anathema to Vichy law – becomes a badge of honour! For the Jews, every act is dictated by the letter of the law, whereas French law has risen to an elevated level of spiritualistic generalization.

This rationalizing of antisemitic legislation brought with it an analogous legitimizing of Vichy's non-literal approach to the still extant constitutional ideal of egalitarianism; to avoid any tint of Talmudic literalism or even devotion to a long-accepted understanding of foundational beliefs, Vichy law simply reinterprets a 150-year-old idea of egalitarianism *without completely revoking it*. Somewhat like the early Christian hermeneutical imperative of preserving the Old Testament while utterly distorting its accepted meanings, legal analysts under Vichy preserve egalitarianism[10] but find a way to *read the Jews out*. Baudry and Ambre provide a helpful formulation – 'it seems that what is desired, as Christian Renaudin has put it, is to define the limits of the French community before legislating for it.'[11]

The double-barrelled emblematics of the Talmud then both reveals the need for a special law to regulate a group that has defined itself as legally special and legitimates persecution of that group through loose, amorphous, and often incoherent readings of history, religion, and sacred texts. French law seems to play a special role – given French culture and religion – in the special definition of Jew-as-Talmudist, a role that logically pushes French law beyond even the Nazi precedents: 'quite naturally, the extent of the French laws is greater than that of the German ordinances.'[12]

For these Vichy legal theoreticians, the Jew *cannot be redeemed from his Talmudism*. It is a universal element that has often distanced the Jew from his (temporary) European domicile. It shifts the blame, as it has throughout history, from the persecutors to the persecuted. For is not the Jew finally responsible, through his stiffnecked non-assimilation, for his own suffering?[13] So Baudry and Ambre remind their legal readers that precedents going back a millenium or more also justify Vichy's approach.

While the relationship between the Jewish population and various monarchs had its ups and downs, the ecclesiastical authorities rarely softened in their hatred.[14] At the time of the Crusades, the first anti-semitic measures were promulgated in France. These statutes saw nuances of strictness from the 12th century until the Revolution, with property occasionally stripped away, or the entire Jewish population expelled in some cases, whereas occasional monarchs treated them more benignly. What was universal is highlighted by these legal analysts in a one-sentence paragraph:

> Let us again note that civil disputes between Jews were adjudicated by Rabbinic courts, relying on a special law.[15]

The authors take their brief survey from the Revolution through the recent hostilities, emphasizing the golden period for Jews under the law, while noting that the Dreyfus affair 'split France in two, renewing hatreds, planting in the whole country the murderous seeds of anger and doubt.'[16] Church legislation against the Jews through the centuries has not, or so say these lawyers, quieted the problem now faced by the new state of Marshal Pétain's Vichy.

The Vichy-era book-length works cited thus far deal, of course, with the minutiae of an ever-expanding *positivistic* base of Vichy antisemtic legislation, a groundswell of legalism that would eventually number almost 200 home-grown laws, decrees and regulations about every component of Jewish life (and death) on French soil from 1940 to 1944. So we have the remarkable combination of an anti-Talmudist Catholic spiritual rationalization of the laws and a detailed reading of how the laws actually are to be implemented by everyday lawyers and judges.

Vichy's scrupulous attention to every ambiguity in the statutes ironically would recreate a dessicated form of Talmudic literalism. France's case-by-case cartesian thoroughness merited a German response of antipathy to what the Nazis thought was the undue literalism of Vichy's inquiry into the question 'Who is a Jew?'. Thus the French became, for the 'spiritual' Nazi jurisprudence that was heavily influenced by Carl Schmitt and focussed less on positive texts than on the person himself of the Fuhrer, 'plus juif que les Juifs'. Vichy was to the 'elevated' Nazi lawyers what the Talmudists were to a more 'spiritual' French approach to law. But the irony was lost on the French, who proceeded over four years to produce and elaborate a logically admirable but morally and constitutionally dessicated antisemitic structure of law.

II. ANTI-TALMUDISM IN PRACTICE UNDER VICHY

Lawyers Adapt to a Bizarre Innovation

Ways of reading affect *ways of action* – or non-action. Vilifying as 'Talmudic' an allegiance to long-established ethical practices, Vichy legal theory opened the door to a reversal of its own 150-year-long ethical traditions. Lawyers proved vulnerable to the double-edged theories of the treatise-writers. Only one of them managed to protest forcefully the (anti-Talmudic) reversal of decades of egalitarian tradition in France.

Prof. Jacques Maury of the Toulouse Law School, in the authoritative *Journal officiel* for the late-1940 period just after Vichy promulgated its first anti-Jewish laws, concludes that no French lawyer will be willing to enforce such strange legislation.[17] Maury's lengthy statement – elaborated over several articles – in one of the profession's most prominent publications surely stood as a challenge to the already tangible legislative policies dividing citizen from citizen (and citizen from 'non-citizen') on the basis of race.

Maury's courageous protest must have seemed quite natural to him at the beginning. Unfortunately, no one joined with Maury. It is hard to sustain the discursive high ground in a non-Talmudic environment. As reported at length in my book, the progression in Prof. Maury's discourse itself over the next few years indicates that internal professional pressures led even a right-minded analyst such as himself to adapt to an apologetic way of speaking about religious definition.

Tragically – and surprisingly during a period in which there were no precedents but in which French law had already firmly re-established itself as an autonomous, going concern – no other mainstream lawyer joined Maury's protest on this high level of egalitarian generalization. Not that Maury was in any way punished for his words, either by the French or by the German authorities. Worse than this, his articles failed to inspire any public response. What Maury felt would be a natural, common reaction from his colleagues would prove to be far more complicated and nuanced.

Failing in an opportunity to protest together, legal actors turned to the statutes on a detailed basis. Although the key point remains the professional community's equivocation in the face of grotesquely untraditional French legislation, there were remaining interpretive options. All of the data tends to support the conclusion that legal actors could have rendered the religious statutes a virtual nullity: French lawyers had all the options at their command, and the laws' language could have opened protective doors. Instead, the statutes were read in a niggardly and literalistic manner, each stingy interpretation leading to yet another, until more Jews were persecuted than the literal language of either German or Vichy law required. Everything, always, was under the control of French lawyers, judges, and bureaucrats; their choices involved a flexible[18] sense of their options. They managed to get around their own training and professional ethics.

The Work of Vesna Drapac

It is all too easy to 'generalize' about the response of so many people. While conclusions about French lawyers flow – I hope with some plausibility – from my twelve-year inquiry and its ensuing empirical data, broad assertions about *religious* motivations are more treacherous. I have been aided by an unlikely source, however, both in articulating and perhaps justifying the *methodology* of culturally based influences that informs both my earlier study and this present paper.

Vasna Drapac's recent *War and Religion*[19] studies the discourse and the actions of what have been called 'Petain's little parishoners,' local churchmen and ordinary Catholics during the Vichy period. The first part of her book criticizes those who have made negative generalizations about this population. She urges, with the help of her data, an understanding of the practical and cultural conditions that make the local Catholic response to Vichy a more nuanced question than earlier analysts have supposed.

> This [earlier] understanding of French religious history and Catholic resistance is full of holes and distorts many aspects of religious life. It generalizes about Catholic Petainsim from the (sometimes extreme) examples of prominent clerics or notables. It fails to take account of the multiple ways in which faith was translated into action . . . It conveniently dispenses with the need to account for the many instances of resistance activities among Catholics from all walks of life and integrate them into a more general appreciation of religious practice and motivation at the time.[20]

Drapac correctly, or so it seems to me, urges a reversal in what she sees as the traditional historian's prior view of 'Catholic' activity. Instead of reasoning *backwards* – from assertions of the Catholic population's *political* activity to a judgment about Catholic belief, she insists on fathoming the religious and cultural impulses that influenced individual Catholics (whether the millions of believers or simply those many who thought of themselves as motivated still by Catholic ways of believing and reasoning) and only then making judgments about the highly nuanced varieties of *political* response to Vichy. For example, instead of dividing the Catholic population grossly into collaborators or resistance fighters, this methodology permits recognition of a very wide spectrum of words, acts, and private behaviour ranging from joining the *milice* to blowing up German trains – but with the vast majority of Catholics somewhere in between.

However, in setting forth a defence of 'conditions on the ground,' Drapac herself – as is almost inevitable in work of this type – engages in an inductively earned set of judgments about (almost all) of France's Catholic population during the war. Her generalizations are not casual; they are well thought through, and they are of great interest to historians of Vichy.

Remarkably, Drapac's main conclusions are *discursive* in nature. She asks the same question I am asking here: compared to other discourse and belief systems, would Catholics appreciate (more or less than other groups) certain common elements within the challenges of wartime France that *bore within them long-developing and deeply-ensconced* influences upon their response to Vichy and the Nazis? Furthermore, her primary example of such deeply held and influential patterns of behaviour and belief *relate to the way Catholics used words*, that is to the way they spoke, prayed, read texts, and understood hermeneutically the world around them.

Here are Drapac's main conclusions:

> A distinctly Catholic approach to social and civic action was not confined to the Vichy period and was certainly not a product of it.... The Church's... interests are themselves values, a moral framework, a defense of human dignity, rights, and liberties.... The language that is peculiar to the Church must be understood if its pronouncements are to be appreciated fully. It constitutes a sort of code, and one must have the key to the code. Much in that language was not new but developed new significance in changed circumstances. Some was deliberately unspecific – often the occupation was referred to as 'the current situation' (*les circonstances actuelles*) or the ordeal (*l'épreuve*) – though Catholics listening to or reading the messages knew what was meant.[21]

Drapac proceeds in this defence of Catholic discourse, which she insists was deliberately ambiguous. She does so with perhaps less than sufficient understanding that the historians whom she is answering both fathomed this coded equivocation and still thought themselves able to criticize it. But she does so with great accuracy. Her contribution, perhaps seasoned with the more sceptical response that I have provided in the tenth chapter of my book, is to shift the focus of analysis of wrongdoing from *political leaders* to the millions upon millions of individuals who wound up participating in evil while at the same time thinking themselves either as resisting it or at least as continuing the belief and speech patterns of a noteworthy religious institution:

> Meanings were 'hidden' or 'ambiguous' only to those unfamiliar with the language's devices. Under authoritarian regimes (in this case an occupation regime) language becomes complicated.... Religious language contained the message the Church considered most crucial to the times. The message was that obedience to the gospels would set Europe free. Language as code, as prayers and sermons, and as images and gestures, was a potent force that, it could be argued, itself constituted spiritual resistance to nazification, if not a form of spiritual resistance.[22]

The key recognition here, helpfully tending to reverse mainstream analyses of Vichy, is that France during the war – and perhaps Europe more broadly – must be fathomed *less as an authoritarian, submissive, simplistic response to dictatorial evil at the top echelons of leadership* than as *a collective, highly nuanced, deliberately complex reaction* to evil, a response *whose very hermeneutic complexity permitted evil to exist and expand.*

Is it only because Drapac focuses her study on Paris that she refers to 'an occupation regime'? The best evidence for her correct generalizations about Catholic discourse lies, perhaps, in the unoccupied zone where, as I have endeavoured to demonstrate, a coded, complex and nuanced set of justifications emerged (and were accepted) for a *franco-French* – indeed an overwhlemingly 'Catholic' – promulgation and elaboration of statist anti-semitism. We cannot forget that so powerful a figure as Vichy's second justice minister, Joseph Barthelemy, was a devout Catholic, who may well have considered himself 'spiritually resisting' as he promulgated over 100 of Vichy's increasingly detailed antisemitic laws and regulations.[23] Where does such a complex discourse find a begin- ning of responsibility for events as they happened? Was everyone, as I heard consistently when I started interviewing Vichy lawyers and bureaucrats in 1982, *was everyone in the resistance, spiritual or otherwise?*

Drapac's answer makes sense, but only if one assumes that 'nazification' in France consisted of terrible invaders and necessarily docile French Catholics. The reality of France – in both zones (for the Nazis simply did not need to do much, even in Paris, once they say how aggressive Vichy legislation was and once they saw how passive the millions were in the face of antisemitism) – was that at any time *a less coded, less ambiguous* response would have served to undermine Nazi evil, or at least to call on Berlin to invest far more heavily in manpower and treasure than they had to do once French Catholics remembered and saw before them a theology of 'coded' responses to evil, responses that always primarily furthered 'obedience to the gospel'.

Drapac proves perhaps more than she wishes. A discourse of ambiguity and equivoca- tion from the top is received as licence for ambiguity and equivocation in the masses. In between, meanwhile, we have temporal leaders – such as Vichy's lawyers – brought up as French Catholics and hence trained to understand that words are powerful but that they *can be flexibly used and understood.* Nothing, neither a constitutional ideal nor a long pattern of egalitarian belief, nor a sense of professional ethics, needs to operate as a *considered force in opposition to radical change* of the type represented by Vichy antisemitic law.

> It was not fragmentation [Drapac continues] but cohesion, continuity, and the ways in which a basic belief system was sustained that stood out.... I attempt to show.... choices and options in terms of a common cultural experience, tradition, and norms of behavior that were flexible and inclusive enough to take account of social diversity, and differences in class, gender, and geography.... Survival did not necessarily indicate loss of integrity.[24]

Opportunities Missed: Catholic Discourse prevails over Simple, Jugular Protest
So we return to Jacques Maury. Unpunished, indeed increasingly prominent as the war years progress, Maury – just three months before D-Day – is asked to opine about the Jewishness of three young issue of a mixed marriage in Toulouse. He has come far from his stance of jugular protest to the first fruits of Vichy legislation. Too much has happened in those almost four years since the regime launched its programme. In March 1944, there is no longer any doubt of the religious laws' 'Frenchness,' no longer any talk of the unacceptability of distinguishing one person from another on the basis of immutable characteristics. The discourse has softened; lawtalk, like parish talk, has accomodated. The issues have sorted themselves out on a far lower level of general- ization.

Jugular protest, although rare, did attend the promulgation of the 1940 Vichy anti- semitic statutes. Foundational attacks on Vichy legislation were published and abided, and they would continue (in very small doses) throughout the four years of the regime. The 1941–42 political trials, against Third Republic leaders at Riom, inspired some prominent lawyers publicly to pick up on Maury's 1940 theme of the non-French nature of the regime's laws, although the Riom courtroom resistance unfortunately did not specifically address the religious laws *per se*. But Maury's own rhetorical shift, over the years, to a neutral tone accepting the racial premise as a given (where he once saw it as grotesque and aberrational) is typical of French professional discourse during the period.[25] It is not so much that some protested, continued to protest and then gave up or were somehow silenced; rather the anti-Jewish, anti-egalitarian laws became a viable reality because the discourse of direct protest *never caught on*. Instead, moving in the gradual way that professional rhetoric will, French lawyers and courts found racism tolerable. Their traditions as flexible Catholic readers – as those used to undermining textual literalism, accepted stories, and even ethical absolutes – learned to accommodate those few colleagues whose nausea in the face of what they were seeing placed them increasingly at the margins of polite legal discourse.

III. THE FLEXIBLE HERMENEUTIC AS PREACHED: LÉON BÉRARD, THE VATICAN, AND THE FRENCH CARDINALS

Catholic 'flexibility' at the highest levels

Interestingly for one who is surveying, and everywhere sensitive to, French Catholic discourse, Drapac in her recent study does not even mention perhaps the most famous example of Catholic rhetoric associated with Vichy anti-semitism: the 1941 statement of Vatican emissary Leon Berard to Marshal Pétain himself. As Saul Friedlander describes the incident:

> On July 31 [1941], Rabbi Jacob Kaplan, assistant to Chief Rabbi Isaiah Schwartz, addressed to Vallat[26] a letter in which he tried to demonstrate that the measures taken against the Jews were contrary to the injunctions of Christianity. Were not Jesus and his apostles Jews, asked the Rabbi? Rabbi Kaplan's letter appears to have caused some embarrassment in the inner councils of the Vichy government[27]... Consequently, on August 7, Marshal Pétain asked Léon Bérard, his ambassador to the Holy See, to enquire about the attitude of the Vatican in this matter.[28]

Friedlander proceeds to quote different sections of the lengthy Bérard response than the one I am about to cite here. (He points out that Nobecourt had already published parts of the letter in the early post-war period.) My reader will need to have refreshed the memory of a full-fledged *hermeneutic* of flexible acceptance that is quite explicit in the letter. For, coupled not only with Church declarations in France but also with much more recent Vatican assertions (even apologetic) about the Jews, the letter amply indicates how a culture accustomed to accommodation as a hermeneutic principle could have proceeded with all the vigour that was Vichy's to subjugate an entire people.

Why August, 1941? It culminates a busy legalistic period for Vichy. Its major dominant pieces of religious legislation, the 2 June statute relating to definitions, professions and census, and the 22 July statute relating to property aryanization, have recently been promulgated. Joseph Barthélemy, a signatory to both, now suffers the self-described dual ordeal of learning at the opera of Pétain's declaration of the Riom defendants' guilt and being forced to sign the 'special section' jurisdictions into law.[29]

Vichy legal actors have become suffusively engaged in the rhetorics of religious exclusion. Whatever protests might have been lodged on the level of constitutional law no longer emanate from Vichy pens, which have been quieted as the community increasingly accepts the hermeneutics of Jewish absence. Reams of words, on the other hand, have attended the 'delicate' new statutory materials, lower level talk that lawyers love, because it engages their narrowest creative impulses and because it keeps them in business.

Curiously, it is Marshal Pétain himself who finds the time to seek the moral high ground. Given his Riom-related behaviour that summer, given the paucity of individuals he permits to gain exemptions from the harsh strictures of the religious laws, given the advice and consent of a man like Barthélemy to the programme, what besides an inkling of Catholic conscience would motivate him to heed a mere Rabbi's challenge and then to charge his ambassador to the Vatican with the task of determining Papal attitudes about Vichy legislation? Early that August, Pétain initiated such an inquiry. In a letter that has been cited sparsely, but that is of sufficient importance to our study to cite at some length, Vatican Ambassador Léon Bérard replies to Pétain:

> 2 September, 1941. M. le Maréchal: By your letter of 7 August, 1941, you honored me by requesting information touching questions and problems that might be raised, from the Roman Catholic perspective, by the measures your government has taken regarding the Jews. I have had the honor of sending you a preliminary response where I observed that nothing has ever been said to me at the Vatican that would imply, on the part of the Holy See, a critique or disapproval of those legislative and regulatory acts. Now I can affirm that at no time has the pontifical authority been either concerned or preoccupied with that part of French policies and that no complaint or request coming to it from France has so far given it such an opportunity. [Bérard now notes that it has been difficult to get a copy of the Italian laws, but that he is ready to articulate the 'complex' stance of the Church on] the contradictions or divergences that might be found between the teachings of the Church on this question and the fascist legislation, on the one hand, and the French legislation on the other. . . .

> A. The Church and Racism. There is a fundamental and basic opposition between Church doctrine and 'racist' theories. The Church, by universal definition, professes the unity of all human beings. The same Redeemer died for all men; the Gospel is announced to 'every creature.' . . . All these precepts are incompatible with a concept that could derive from the conformity of the skull and the nature of the blood and the aptitudes and the vocation of peoples, their religion itself, to establish finally a hierarchy of the races, at the top of which is found a pure and royal race called 'aryan.' . . . The Church thus has condemned racism as it has condemned communism.

> From its teachings about racist ideas one should be far from deducing, however, that it necessarily condemns any specific measure taken by any particular state against what it calls the Jewish race. Its thinking on this involves distinctions and nuances that must now be noted. The subject must be treated clearly.

> B. The Church, the Jewish Problem, and Anti-Semitism.
> It would be vain to extract from Canon Law, theology, pontifical acts, a group of precepts that resembles legislation on Judaism or the Judaic religion. . . .

> The first principle that appears, and the surest, is that in the eyes of the Church, a Jew who has been authentically baptized ceases to be a Jew and becomes part of 'Christ's flock.' But one should not conclude from this that the Church regards religion alone as the thing marking Israel off in the midst of the nations. It does not believe that Jews constitute simply a 'spiritual family,' as do in our case, for example, Catholics and 'reformed' Christians. It recognizes that among the distinctive traits of the Jewish community there appear not so much *racial* as *ethnic* particularities. It discerned this long ago and has always taken this into account. [Bérard then recounts various periods in which such measures as the *numerus clausus* or special signs on apparel were adopted by Catholic authorities such as, respectively, St. Thomas of Aquinas and the Lateran Council.] . . .

It would be possible now, with the help of these precedents, to determine whether the French laws on Jews contradict or not, and in what ways they contradict, Catholic tenets. [There follow two pages on Mussolini's racial laws, to which the Church objected on two discrete grounds not relevant to the Vichy example.]

D. What Disjunctions Can One Find Between Catholic Doctrine and the French Law of 2 June, 1941 on the Jews?
[Bérard reviews the law's exclusionary sections.] In principle, there is nothing in these measures that the Holy See would criticize. It believes that in promulgating such measures a State uses its legitimate power and that a spiritual force should not interfere with the internal politics of States. And, then too, the Church has never professed that the same rights must be given to or recognized in all citizens. It has never ceased teaching dignity and respect for the individual. But it surely does not understand matters in the fashion, strictly speaking, of the spiritual followers of Rousseau and Condorcet.... Yet the law of 2 June 1941 begins with the legislator's giving a juridical definition of the Jew as expressly linked to the notion of 'race'.... It remains the case that a Jew, if duly converted and baptized, will still be considered a Jew, if he is the issue of at least three grandparents of the Jewish race, that is having belonged to the Judaic religion.
There, one must admit, is a contradiction between French law and Church doctrine.

E. Practical Result of This Contradiction.
Conclusion. I just pointed out the sole point at which the law of 2 June 1941 contradicts a principle held by the Roman Church. But it does not follow from this doctrinal divergence that the French state is threatened with ... even a censure or disapproval that the Holy See might express in one form or another about the Jewish laws.... As an authorized person at the Vatican told me, they mean no quarrel with the Jewish laws.[30]

Bérard's letter apparently gave considerable solace to Pétain.[31] Although flagging the contradiction on the question of 'race', the letter not only denies its significance to the Vatican but, more importantly to our thesis, plays into the dominant understanding of the French statutes anyway: that they were religious more than racial and that they responded to special qualities in the Jew (Bérard calls them 'ethnic') that eject him from the circle of constitutional equality.

Indeed, the only dissonance between Vatican thinking – as summarized by Bérard – and Vichy jurisprudence is in the distinct distaste the Church explicitly brings to the generation of 1789, embodied in Rousseau and Condorcet. Vichy never formally broke with that republican generation, even as it was excluding Talmudists from the circle of its benign protection. For the French wartime legal thinker, there was ample room for both Rousseau and anti-semitism, for the great foundational ideals of egalitarianism, and for an exclusionary interpretive principle that read Jews out of any such majestic vision. Pétain's resistance to a merger of Church and State always permitted Vichy to innovate its basic programme without departing from the discourse of human rights and due process. It is enough for Church and State to agree on a *Christian* sense of human dignity, and there is simply no disagreement from the Holy See with what Vichy has wrought.

Saul Friedlander, omitting from Part E of the letter its *crucial hermeneutic* point, recommends 'great caution' in assuming that it reflects Vatican thinking at the highest level but says that 'it must nevertheless be admitted that the last paragraphs of the Bérard report [to the cited point above] provide a significant insight into the attitude of the Holy See concerning the discriminatory legislation.'[32] As the letter proceeds into *theology*, it becomes even more significant; here are the lines left out from Friedlander's cited version of Bérard's letter:

E.... One could find in our legislation as a whole, as in that of many other states, and for example in our still very much extant Napoleonic codes, many statutes that would not be approved of by the Vatican. Also, [the Vichy] rule denying to everyone who might be baptized the status of Catholic is perhaps, from a theological point of view, not the most serious breach.[33] *The Church has never ceased to practice an essential distinction, full of wisdom and reason: the distinction between* thesis *and* hypothesis, *the thesis, in which the principal is invariably affirmed and maintained, and the hypothesis, where practical considerations are comprehended [ou s'organisent les arrangements de la pratique'].*[34]

The Church thus both asserts an opposition to 'racism' and – on the 'realistic' plank it calls 'hypothesis' – accepts it! Vichy, meanwhile and reciprocally, vaunts its constitutional retention of virtually every individual right proclaimed by the generation of the 1790's and also manages to exclude the Jew. The hermeneutic is ingrained, like the Maurrassian 'antisémitisme de peau'[35] and requires no clear articulation on such high levels of authority. Church and State, preserving their historical functions, can reach a détente.

Cardinal Gerlier of Lyon was one of the first clerics (as Maury, Duverger, Baudry and Ambre and André Broc were among the first academic writers) to bring closer to the world of real people the vague hermeneutics of the hierarchical leadership. Just as Maury, in October of 1940, was able to attack the exclusionary texts in advance of the imposition of an entrenched way of reading them, so Gerlier had the power to suggest ways of reading Church rhetoric and doctrine that might have helped his parishioners and others to recognize the debased quality of the new environment.

On 6 October 1941, this 'brilliant lawyer'[36] and cleric sat down and conversed with Xavier Vallat about the religious laws. The conversation – as narrated by the CGQJ chief – reveals both Gerlier's Pétainist leanings and the complex interpretive vision of religious persecution that I claim was more central to the suffering than even the positive statutes of which he spoke:

> His Eminence: I believe that M. Léon Bérard makes many allusions ... No one knows better than I the enormous harm the Jews have done to France. It's the damned Union générale the Jews wanted that ruined my family.
>
> No one supports more zealously than I the policies of Marshal Pétain. I have compromised myself for him, and I have been bitterly reproached for certain strong words I used about the French people's duty to him. But on this terrain of justice and charity, I cannot follow you ... Your law is not unjust, I know you did not write it, the Germans supposedly imposed it [*les Allemands l'auraient imposée*] and even harsher [sic.], but it is in its application that justice and charity are lacking. I said this just the other day to the Maréchal in front of Admiral Darlan, and although the latter did not completely agree with me, the Maréchal said: 'That's right. That question needs to be looked at.'
>
> ... By the way, Pastor Boegner came to see me, also troubled like me, by numerous visits from poor types who see no other choice but suicide.
>
> Me [Vallat]: To my knowledge, there have not yet been any suicides of Jews in the free zone, and if there were, there are certainly fewer than in Germany at the time of the new laws. And, although Your Eminence knows that I feel deference and even zeal about the advice You are giving me, I am absolutely indifferent to the opinion of Pastor Boegner, who has written to us that 'all Christians, we have been spiritual Semites.'
>
> His Eminence smiled.[37]

Part of the legal hermeneutic in Vichy depended on what we have just seen: the acceptance by Catholic authorities, with a few noble exceptions and with some reservations, of the 'hypothesis' of legalized Jewish persecution. Surely this consoled many working Frenchmen, as it did their Marshal, both spiritually and pragmatically. Other Catholic prelates continued to add rhetorical fuel to the legalistic fires.[38] There was good and bad, private and public, and we are just beginning to amass the necessary data from which a historical (as opposed to a philosophical, moral, or even theological) conclusion might be based. But one thing seems clear until the present moment: there is no forthright condemnation by the Catholic Church of Vichy anti-semitism.

French Catholics as Directly Affected by Vichy Anti-semitism
There were many acts of Christian charity towards individual Jews.[39] Some Jewish writers have begun to note the complexities of the situation during Vichy, including the varying positions taken on the question of proselytizing Jewish children who were brought under the protection of devout Catholics.[40]

The relation of Christianity to Vichy law does, however, pose profound questions relevant to this study. Clerics tried in many cases to assist mixed-heritage individuals by providing baptismal records to carry the evidentiary burden on the issue of Jewishness raised by the law of 2 June 1941. Vichy law's diminution of the value of these clerical records finally surprised even the Germans and moved the Nazis to recommend less legalistic nitpicking about such evidence.[41]

There were yet more direct confrontations between the clerics and Vichy legal actors. The Church hoped that the new régime would look more favourably on longstanding sources of ecclesiastical resentment. For example, they wanted repeal of some early 20th century laws that had affected the rights of congregations to obtain the status of individual associations;[42] this and other changes would have assisted the Church to regain property rights. More expansively, they sought a rescission of the law of 9 December, 1905 (which was a key date of departure in the 2 June 1941 racial statute requiring 'suspected Jews' to prove they belonged to a religion recognized as an established one prior to that date); they sought restoration of church-state relations harking to the medieval age of Charles VII and Louis XII. and on this, they received strong lay support from several of the members of Vichy's constitutional reform committee, notably Joseph Barthélemy's colleague as law professor, Achille Mestre, who believed in a Catholic state.[43] But Justice Minister Barthélemy, himself a practising Catholic, apparently decided not to grant substantial legislative concessions to the Church.[44]

Frustrated institutionally by what they saw as an insufficient Vichy attack on laicity, the Christian sects saw the anti-semitic laws themselves affect more than a few practising clerics and faithful parishioners as well. These appeared to come under the definition of Jew, despite their Christian faith or even priestly professional callings. Thus the head of the Missionary Priests of Notre Dame of Zion in Aubenas had to plead for three colleagues in his religious order in the Ardèche. His case went all the way to Xavier Vallat, head of the CGQJ, who was willing to protect two of Hungarian origin but not the third, a father Jean de Menasce, about whom:

> it is not possible for us not to consider him Jewish according to the law, for it is race, contrary to what you seem to think, which is the decisive factor under French law in determining the legal Jew. Yet the only sanction that might affect Father Menasce would be against teaching in a public facility. It does not seem that he would be actually affected by this prohibition.[45]

As pointed out by André Broc, one of the legal rationalizers cited extensively in this paper, Christians (and even priests) might have reason to fear racial categorizations implicating ancestral heritage.[46] Father Menasce's case indicates this, and there were hundreds of files of Catholics and other Christians who were imperilled by the peculiar racial approach of the Vichy statutes, an approach that became increasingly 'rigorous' as courts, lawyers and academicians brought their cartesian logic to bear on the interstices of the statutory language itself. The immediate threat to devout or at least believing Christians did not, however, produce a sense of solidarity with persecuted Jews.

Catholic congregants felt the tincture of alleged 'racial' Jewishness. In a representative situation, the vicar general of the diocese of Marseille, Audibert, writes in early 1943 to a parishioner in distress, the converted writer Albert Lopez:

> My dear friend: You have shared with me your intense and legitimate hope, having made all the declarations needed on the subject of your Jewish racial origin,[47] to be recognized by all and incontestably as a good Frenchman and a good Catholic. No one who knows you can raise the slightest doubt about this double claim.... For my part, I want to reassure you and give you my witness in order to satisfy justice and friendship. [Audibert recounts Lopez' conversion at the age of 19, his marriage to a Catholic and the baptism of their many children.] In your literary works, among your poems, biographies, critical articles, and novels, you have expressed your Provençal spirit, your feel for the Mistral as we might say. You have always been as regional as you have been French, in the manner that Marshal Pétain likes so much.... Good Frenchman, good Provençal, you have also been a good Catholic at the cost of much sacrifice – this I know. You have suffered, and this is understandable, from the incomprehension, and sometimes the hostility, of some of your race. Yet you have always kept mastery of yourself, in patience and in empathy.[48]

What Drapac might call the 'code' of hierarchical French Catholic discourse about Vichy anti-semitism is everywhere present in this letter. As we shall see below, the penultimate cited sentence in particular re-invokes the kind of implicit anti-semitism that we first find in such gospel-writers as St. John, who never missed an opportunity to turn the knife in the image of the Jewish population at the time of Jesus. It is noteworthy, but perhaps understandable in a letter designed to help Lopez, that the villains of the piece are Lopez' former co-religionists, and not the bizarre laws the Marshal had set in place.

Audibert's letter, in fact, situates the French Church comfortably within Pétain's 'new' France. Reciprocally, and well aware that much was expected of his régime from its devout Catholic constituents, Pétain (with the help of his Catholic justice minister, Barthélemy, played a double game. He declared, in remarks touching on the proposed new constitution, that Vichy would not go all the way to a Catholic state, but that it did seek greater détente with Christianity than had other recent French governments and especially with the Church to which he belonged and whose Pope he would soon look to for support:

> The State declares loudly its respect for individual humanity, the first triumph of Christian civilization. It remains completely separated from the churches. But it retains the right to take, in accord with them if the need arises, such actions and such measures that seem to it to conform to the profound and permanent interests of the Nation.[49]

For our limited purposes here, it seems correct to state that Vichy air breathed a growing closeness in church–state relations, although little actually changed on the level of legislation. In what we are calling the spiritual hermeneutics of exclusion, however, the Marshal's view of the churches as an integral part of 'the Nation' served to bring all Vichy policies – including the persecution of the Jews – under the umbrella of 'Christian civilization.' Vichy both distinguished its programme in this way from the gross barbarities of the Germans and encouraged the internalization by all legal actors of the Jew as religious 'other'.

If much was only implicit in the Marshal's view of the churches, we have just seen his reliance on his own Church to legitimize Vichy's religious laws. Perhaps the 1941 appeal to Vatican authority was disingenuous, not only because Pétain was far from a devout Catholic,[50] but also because in some ways institutional Catholicism's response to the Jewish question in France was already situated, knowable, and quiescent.[51]

But what about the 'mass' of Catholics in France? The myth of 'universal resistance' perhaps forever debunked[52], what can we say of some potential lasting validity and meaning about their response – on the ground – to Vichy anti-semitism? We turn to the ultimate implications of the Vichy hermeneutic.

IV. THE THEOLOGICAL ROOT OF VICHY PREJUDICE

The Logical Absence of Catholic Protest

Henry Rousso – in polite dialogue with Serge Klarsfeld – has recently opined that the population of Catholics, undoubtedly influenced by their leaders, largely failed to act on behalf of Jews, particularly at the beginning stages, when history now teaches us it might have most counted. There were no Jacques Maury's among devout Catholics, none – that is – who spoke up in direct language, anticipating a similar response from their audiences.

There are, of course, many explanations for this failure. But I believe (unlike Drapac, for example) that the absence of 'plain talk' protesting the anti-semitic policies of Vichy *did* constitute a clear failure of Catholic moral integrity. On the other hand, as I shall now try to show, the overwhelming acceptance of laws that contradicted their basic (egalitarian) traditions by so many millions of French Catholics *does follow* logically from an ensconced pattern of anti-textualist prejudice that finds its origins in the Gospels themselves.

Catholic reading strategies assisted Vichy not only morally and pragmatically in affirming its anti-semitic programme but even more integrally in providing a way to effectuate the programme politically. By isolating the Jew as *Talmudic* other, Vichy played into an almost universal sense within the Catholic polity that the worst moral trait is sticking to a text. A new regime and a new Europe called for rapid charge, not ethical textualism!

Few other defeated, satellite or allied countries in Hitler's Europe had to face the formidable task of taking a home-grown set of egalitarian political beliefs and – without expunging the institutions at all (except, temporarily, parliament) – distorting them to fit a new scheme. Benefitting from Catholic models of reading, France flexibly accommodated to the programmatic ostracism of the Jew.

Long before Vichy, after all, a certain capacity to work flexibly with foundational texts and to make them 'fit' some new vision had become commonplace in Christian Europe. In its signally most memorable and indeed seismically original form, this ability to work creatively with basic texts had rendered possible the complete distortion of the 'Old Testament' in order to validate a new spiritual condition. As Friedrich Nietzsche brilliantly articulates what (for him) was the debased hermeneutic revolution brought to the West by Christianity:

> However much the Jewish scholars protested, everywhere in the Old Testament there were supposed to be references to Christ and only to Christ and particularly to His cross.

Whenever any piece of wood, a switch, a ladder, a twig, a tree, a willow, or a staff is mentioned, this was supposed to indicate a prophecy of the wood of the cross; even the erection of the one-horned beast and the brazen serpent, even Moses spreading his arms in prayer, even the spits on which the Passover lamb was roasted – all are allusions to the cross and as it were preludes to it. Has anyone who asserted this ever *believed* it? Consider that the Church did not even shrink from enriching the text of the Septuagint (e.g., in Psalm 96, verse 10) so as afterwards to employ the smuggled-in passage in the sense of Christian prophecy. For they were conducting a *war* and paid more heed to their opponents than to the need to stay honest.[53]

My contribution here, having reflected on my empirical findings as to lawyers, is to suggest that Vichy anti-semitism, and its acceptance among the masses of the people, was a *hermeneutic*, as much as it was a xenophobic, racist or even traditionally anti-Jewish, problem. The ability to shift one's ground – fairly quickly and without a sense of profound, seismic change – as to foundational ideas and texts originated, as I see it, in the early Christian ability to distort the sacred text upon which Christians chose to base their vision: the Jewish Bible. Their contribution instantiated a *way of reading* that wove distortion into the very moral fabric of the emerging religion's followers. This hermeneutic, at its origins and as it continued – with the best example being Catholic France – into the 20th century – involved a *rejection of close reading itself*, a discomfort with textual fidelity masked in many of Christianity's founding texts as a rejection of *Jewish law*.

The Pauline paradox: rejecting textualism while retaining the text
Common to an otherwise highly variegated set of early Christian writers is a deep skepticism about *the law*. To the extent these writers perceived 'legalism' in the Jewish traditions and also in the practices of some Jews who lived at the same time as Jesus, they often associated the law with an allegiance to *textualism*, that is to a kind of literalism that they felt sometimes overrode the spiritual or more essential elements of the Jewish religion. As A.N. Wilson, a very comprehensive and sympathetic observer of Paul, puts it:

> It occurred to Paul, however, who saw that, with the world in its current condition of pain, aching sorrow, confusion, bloodiness, dirtiness, and moral anarchy, any God who took reponsibility for it would have to be the First Cause of more Evil than Good. Either the Law or the Commandments of such a human figment would be completely null – because he could not be a good God who presided over such a chaos as our present universe – or the human race itself was a write-off, impossible to save or to justify, since its failure to be good or wise was demonstrated on an hourly basis throughout the world.... Paul's readers, particularly the cleverest of them such as Marcion or Augustine, have tried to draw a 'logical conclusion' from all this. Marcion... who lived from c.85–160, believed that what *Romans* really taught us was that there were two Gods: a God of Justice, the Old Testament God, who was really incapable of mercy or love, and the Good God to whom we all respond in the love of our hearts. This Good God, who was made manifest in Jesus, destroyed the old God with his bloodcurdling Commandments....[54]

Though Wilson allows that this reading of Paul may be inaccurate, he also concludes that it is inevitable. Earlier, he describes Paul's task as: 'the attempt to translate Hebrew ideas into a Gentile setting. [This involved] using words either with new senses or with great boldness.'[55]

On this reading, Paul's rejection of the Jewish law and of its textual base carried with it a programme of *retention* of Hebrew ideas and even a retention of the *full material text* of the Hebrew Bible.

It is this paradox that I believe lies at the origins of the French Catholic hermeneutic exemplified tragically during Vichy. It may help to explain later developments – like Vichy – in which a Catholic culture based on Pauline 'love' but nonetheless acting governmentally within the world, far exceeds in cruelty anything imagined by the original Jewish textualists against whom Paul rebelled.

I am very mindful, in speaking of Paul in particular, of the caution expressed by post-Holocaust Christianity's true prophet and inspiring leader, Franklin Littell. This pioneer allowed that Christianity has much to answer for after the Holocaust ('the French Catholic community,' he reminds us as just one national example, 'has a long record of Anti-semitism'[56]), and he did not hesitate to date virulent Christian theological anti-semitism to as early as certain first century epistles;[57] he is more equivocal in pondering 'the question whether the New Testament is necessarily antisemitic, an issue which is increasingly exercising the skills of exegetes.'[58] But Littell dissociates Paul from later Christians like Marcion (cited as we have seen by Wilson in connection to Paul) by denying as to Paul any 'supercessionalist' impulses. 'That he taught the rejection of the Jewish people cannot truthfully be asserted.'[59]

Still, even for Littell (on the hermeneutic issue I foreground here), Paul needed to use 'considerable skill' in order 'to graft believing gentiles into an essentially Jewish history of salvation.'[60] What seems at first to be an admirable, nay brilliant career of textual manipulation, must – in view of the thousands who followed Paul's *hermeneutic* example during the Holocaust – be reconsidered. To do this, I believe we must pass briefly through the more transparent window of the Gospel according to St. John.

The example of John: using the Hebrew text while attacking the textualists at every turn
As Nietzsche observed, retaining a sacred text while fundamentally altering its meanings took some work, at least at the beginning of Christianity. By the time we get to John, the methodology is easier (even for an 'outsider' like myself) to find, although still as paradoxical as it seems to some when handled by Paul's anti-platonic, chaotic but in every way remarkable soul.

Any set of verses from the Gospel according to St. John will reveal the bifurcated hermeneutic aim of *re-interpreting the Hebrew Bible to make it fit Christian beliefs* while also *attacking wherever possible as legalists and textualists the non-accepting Jewish community*. The first prong instantiates the Jesus-story – against all the textual odds – as having been 'predicted' by the older text; but the second prong *justifies sloppiness in the readings of those older texts by attacking, precisely, the 'Jewish' reading strategy of textual legalism*. John, so to speak, has his cake and eats it, too. In case – as for most knowledgeable readers of the Hebrew texts – the alleged allusions to Jesus-as-Messiah simply will not do – he attacks the very idea of sticking closely (label it, say, legalism) to a text altogether.

While John, perhaps in particular, has been the critical object of much commendable post-Holocaust Christian commentary – from all of which I have benefitted and will continue to learn[61] – I am not sure on the readings as yet called to my attention that this twinned hermeneutic has been noticed as an essential contribution to anti-semitism, just as important to it as the increasingly discredited, more direct, anti-Jewish verses in the New Testament.

In John 7, for example, Jews respond to the idea that Jesus might be the Messiah with some textualist scepticism. They nitpick (in verses 40–44), for example, about whether the Messiah was supposed to descend from David and come from Bethlehem. John tells the story as though opposition to Jesus derives from some awful tendency to remain loyal to ensconced textual understandings. Today's commentators continue to refer to this Jewish quibble : 'there is a division among the people over superficial matters,' says one.

Now the textual basis for Jesus-as-Messiah is usually given as a compendium of allegedly prophetic verses in such Hebrew texts as Isaiah, chs 52–53 or Psalms (e.g., 69:9); both of these are evoked in John. Yet any reader of these two texts must grapple with the long tradition of understanding – still adhered to by Jewish exegetes – that denies any plausible prophesy of someone like Jesus, however admirable, as the Messiah. Thus, in a superb Jewish commentary on Isaiah 53:3 ('he was despised...') and the surrounding verses, the traditional understanding is espoused that Isaiah is conjuring no single individual at some future time; what is going on, instead, is that 'the Babylonians, or their representatives, having known the servant, i.e. exiled Israel idealized, in his humiliation and martyrdom, and now seeing his exaltation and new dignity, describe their impressions and feelings.'[62]

John is annoyed that some Jews just cannot see these sacred texts his way. But to take them with his understanding required more flexibility than they (or, I imagine, most reading communities up until then) were willing to show. These were, after all, *sacred texts received not without creative variation but nonetheless within certain hermeneutic bounds* that were being stretched to fantastical limits.

John needs, in the face of such opposition, to go further. Not only must the textual understandings be distorted; *distortion as a hermeneutic principle must be ensconced and ratified*. 'By no means,' Paul wrote, has God abandoned Israel (*Romans*, 21:1), but apparently all the time-honoured rules of understanding Him have been changed in the twinkling of an eye. For most Jews, methods of reading are indistinguishable from ways of living life morally, so is there a distinction?

This is not to say that Jewish tradition abjures creative and, indeed, 'flexible' readings, often embodied in the oral as opposed to the written tradition. To compare the imaginative embellishments of Jewish and Christian interpretation is the task of a lifetime. But it may well be quite fair to say that the work done by early Christian exegetes on the Tanakh, or Hebrew Bible, broke all the rules revered then – and now – by traditional exegetes. As Samuel Hoenig, a recent respected thinker on the Talmud, recently puts it:

> A viable system of law must not sacrifice either its spirit or its letter. Hasty compromises, unfounded alterations, and whimsical abandonment of legal traditions lead only to chaos. In order for a legal system to endure and flourish, it is necessary for the law to be flexible, elastic, and fluid, as well as definitive, clear, and steadfast.[63]

Perhaps impatient with the traditional Jewish mix, John goes on to pepper his account of the Jews with a kind of gratuitous distaste, mostly centred around the Law and people's textual allegiance to it. A reader coming fresh to the Gospels wonders about John's strategy:

> 5.1. After this there was a feast of the Jews. and Jesus went up to Jerusalem. 2. Now there is in Jerusalem by the Sheep Gate a pool... which has five porticoes. 3. In these lay a multitude of invalids, blind, lame, paralyzed. [Jesus sees a man who had been lying there sick for 38 years.]... 8. Jesus said to him, 'Rise, take up your pallet, and walk.' 9. And at once the man was healed, and he took up his pallet and walked.

This is a beautiful story. But what follows is not:

> Now that day was the sabbath. 10. So the Jews said to the man who was cured, 'It is the sabbath, it is not lawful to carry your pallet.' 11. But he answered them, 'The man who

healed me said to me 'Take up your pallet and walk'... 15. The man went away and told the Jews that it was Jesus who had healed them. 16. And this was why the Jews persecuted Jesus, because he did this on the sabbath.

This gratuitous slur, which is at best a weird wrinkle in a wonderful tale and at worst an incredible misintrepetation designed only to hate, articulates and forever ensconces the anti-Jewish anti-textual principle:

39. You search the scriptures, because you think that in them you have eternal life; and it is they that bear witness to me.[64]

In other words, Jews, you need to be more flexible in the way you interpret your own texts so that you will see me in them.

40. Yet you refuse to come to me that you may have life.

From now on, even if you cannot accept the new view of the old text, it has become outmoded even to *look* to the text. Everything, from now on, has become personalized. The new situation mandates a distorted look at the old texts. More than this, it mandates departure from text always and altogether.

What chance did ethical behaviour have, from then on, on this earth that Paul himself knew was so imperfect?

V. CONCLUSION

I have endeavoured to trace a pattern of *strategies of reading* from Paul and John to the Vichy Catholic community (and the Vatican wartime response to Vichy racial laws). This 'Vichy hermeneutic', more – I believe – than other attempts to fathom the breakdown of France from 1940–44, helps to understand the quick reversal of an earlier-understood story by the French legal profession and by millions of other French men and women who grew up under the Third Republic. The notion of 'equality', which had stood in France for 150 years, was never repudiated by Vichy, and indeed was invoked at the highest levels of government. Attached as they were to this tradition, people nonetheless found the reading strategy that *at the very same time* excluded the 'Talmudic Jew' from the circle of egalitarian protection. This strategy, adopted by most Catholic voices in France, was confirmed at a theological level by the Vatican, when it was asked explicitly to comment on Vichy's antisemitic legislation and was able to condone it despite its own precepts. The strategy of deforming still extant, foundational (and even sacred) texts originates – as Nietzsche most directly observed – in early Christian exegetical strategies of distorting and condemning text and law while still retaining the actual texts whose traditional reception was being condemned.

NOTES

1 Vesna Drapac, *War and Religion: Catholics in the Churches of Occupied Paris* (Washington, D.C.: Catholic University of America Press, 1998). I am indebted to Michael Marrus for calling my attention to this work.

2 London: Gordon & Breach; New York: New York University Press.

3 Editions des archives, 1998.

4 Birnbaum, *Anti-Semitism in France* (Oxford: Blackwell, 1992), chapter 4 and *passim*.

5 The recent statement from the Vatican apologizing in part for the Holocaust, reiterates the view that the Jew's very allegiance to his own practices largely explains and even justifies the Christian's perennial need to ostracize and persecute the Jewish people. In 'We Remember: A Reflection of the Shoah' (12 March 1998) the Vatican observes, for example: 'In a large part of the "Christian" world,

until the end of the 18th century, those who were not Christian did not always enjoy a fully guaranteed juridical status. Despite that fact, Jews throughout Christendom held on to their religious traditions and communal customs. They were therefore looked upon with a certain suspicion and mistrust.' This implicitly anti-Talmudic syllogism seems to beg the question why the Jews did not in the first place enjoy full equality by blaming prejudice among Christians on the Jews' simple desire to stick with their own tradition at all costs.

6 Baudry and Ambre, *La Condition publique et privee du Juif en France (le statut des Juifs): Traite theorique et pratique* (Lyon: Desvigne et cie., 1942), p.15.

7 *See*, e.g., *ibid.*, pp.15–17, 35, citing Xavier Vallat, first head of the Vichy-created commission on the Jews, the Commissariat général aux questions juives (CGQJ): 'Le Juif est un type confessionel: tel qu'il est, c'est la loi et le Talmud qui l'ont fait plus fort que le sang ou les variations climatiques...' For a complete discussion of the Vichy legal theorists in this respect, see Weisberg, *Vichy Law*, chapters 2 and 10.

8 André Broc, *La Qualité de juif; une notion juridique nouvelle* (Paris: Presses universitaires de France, 1943), p.14.

9 These references in seemingly 'neutral' and 'scientific' legal treatises had their spiritual origins in antisemitic writings and speeches from the 1930s in France. For example, lawyers Baudry and Ambre cite the organic anti-semitism of Charles Maurras – an 'antisémitisme de peau' in their *La Condition publique et privée du Juif en France*, p.13. And they, as well as Broc, evoked the kind of broad-brush smearing used by Darquier de Pellepoix, eventually to become the second head of CGQJ; in 1937, he included the following series of 'quotations' in his publication, *L'Antijuif*:

'It's a commandment for every Jew to try to wipe out everything that concerns the Christian church and those that serve it.' (Talmud)...

'To bolster their trusts, their guilds, the Jews have decided to ruin trade. Small businessmen are inept, they constitute a social anachronism and it would be good if they disappeared.' (Léon Blum)

'Non-Jews have been created to serve Jews, night and day.' (Talmud)

'Only Jews are people; other nations are a species of animal.' (Talmud)

Cited in Jean Laloum, *La France antisemite de Darquier de Pellepoix* (Paris: Syros, 1979), p.18.

10 The most intriguing example of this method, as described in a full chapter of my earlier study, is Joseph Barthélemy who – as Vichy's second and most important and respected justice minister – tried consistently to invoke the ideals of 1789 while at the same time he elaborated a complex scheme of antisemitic law and practice. *See* Weisberg, *Vichy Law and the Holocaust in France*, chapter 4 and *passim*.

11 *ibid.*, p.25.

12 *ibid.*

13 *See especially*, *La Condition publique et privée du Juif en France*, pp.13–15.

14 *ibid.*, p.20. See also Birnbaum, *Anti-Semitism in France*, p.19.

15 *La Condition publique et privée du Juif en France*, p.21.

16 *ibid.*, p.22.

17 *Journal officel*, 18 October 1940; Doc. # 169.

18 In case one might conclude that the legal community simply craved antisemitic outcomes, and hence interpreted both French constitutional tradition and the new statutes accordingly, reference must be made to the sections of my work that report *some* pro-Jewish legal outcomes, e.g. landlord/tenant law and the laws relating to illegitimate children.

19 Op. cit.

20 *ibid.*, p.15.

21 *ibid.*, 21, 23.

22 *ibid.*, p.24.

23 See Barthélemy, *Ministre de la Justice* (edited by his grandson, Jean Barthélemy), (Paris: Pygmalion, 1989), where he speaks of his Catholicism and of 'working from within' to make a bad situation better.

24 Drapac, pp.29–30.

25 For much more on this, see my *Vichy Law*, chapters 2 and 10.

26 We shall return to Vallat later, as he converses about the 'Jewish question' with Cardinal Gerlier.

27 My book is full of examples of debate and even inner turmoil among Vichy *government officials* and lawyers as they nonetheless both strove to and indeed accomplished a full-fledged, franco-French system of elaborate anti-semitism. And this combination of moral doubt coupled with consistent evildoing is exactly what I am trying to fathom in the French Catholic, professional and bureaucratic spirit.

28 Friedlander, *Pius XII and the Third Reich* (New York.: Knopf, 1966), p.92.

29 Barthélemy, *Ministre de la Justice*, op. cit; Weisberg, *Vichy Law and the Holocaust in France*, ch.9.

30 CDJC CIX–102, all emphases in the original.

31 See, e.g., Marrus and Paxton, *Vichy France and the Jews*, p.202.

32 Friedlander, p.99.

33 Perhaps Bérard, by the Summer of 1941, had in mind arrests and encampments – in inhuman conditions eventually leading to the death of 3000 Jews *on French soil* – all under color of Vichy law, beginning with the antisemitic statutes of 3–4 October, 1940.

34 Bérard letter in full, Centre de documentation juive contemporaine (CDJC) # CIX–102, p.10 of letter emphasis added.

35 See note 9.

36 Marrus and Paxton, *Vichy France and the Jews*, p.200.

37 CDJC CIX–106.

38 For other statements by Church officials, see e.g. Marrus and Paxton, *Vichy France and the Jews*, pp.271–79; Drapac, *War and Religion*, op. cit.

39 Philip Hallie's account of the leadership of Pastor André Trocmé in saving Jewish lives in the Protestant town of Le Chambon is well known. See *Lest Innocent Blood Be Shed: The Story of the Village of Le Chambon and How Goodness Happened There* (New York: Harper, 1979). Another Protestant pastor, Marc Boegner, denounced the Jewish laws, as did anti-Pétainist Catholic prelates such as Jules-Gérard Saliège of Lyon. See, e.g., on the latter righteous Christians, Marrus and Paxton, *Vichy France and the Jews*, pp.203–05. The Catholic reaction to Boegner was mixed; see below, the extended transcript of the conversation between CGQJ's Vallat and Cardinal Gerlier; see also Henry Rousso's perceptions, below.

40 See, most recently, Maurice Rajsfus, *N'Oublie pas le petit Jésus* (Paris: Manya, 1994).

41 See my *Vichy Law and the Holocaust in France*, ch.6.

42 The laws in question were those of 1 July and 16 August, 1901. See Dayras file, National Archives (AN) BB30 #1708.

43 Mestre called explicitly for repeal of the law of 1905, which he felt 'created an obstacle to the concordat,' see AN 72 AJ #412, doss. #5.

44 *ibid.* Barthélemy two-page memorandum of late Summer or early Fall, 1941. A legal advocate for the Church's cause, who seems to have travelled to Vichy to plead with Dayras for its interests, was Auguste Rivet of Lyon, Dean of the Catholic Faculty of Law in that city (*ibid.*).

45 Vallat letter of 13 August 1941. CDJC CXIV #46.

46 *La Qualite de Juif*, pp.16–18.

47 The word 'origine' is in the typed text, crossed out and the word 'race' handwritten in the margin.

48 Letter written by Audibert and approved by Monsignor Delay on behalf of the archdiocese of Marseille, January 8, 1943. CDJC CXV #93.

49 Pétain's written observations about the Vichy constitutional program. AN 72 AJ #412, doss. #2.

50 An excellent, and representative, account of Pétain's view of Catholicism is rendered in Lépagnot, *Histoire de Vichy* (Geneva: Editions Idegraf, 1978), I, pp.35–41. 'The Marshal was not noted for his religious piety,' *ibid.*, p.40; but he had learned much during his years as French ambassador to Franco about 'how a dictator leaning on the Church, the army (that one victorious), and on all conservative forces, could impose himself on a torn people, broken by war.' *ibid.*, p.37.

51 The bulk of Vichy's legislative scheme against the Jews was in place by the Summer of 1941, and already dozens of judicial and administrative decisions were published, people had been arrested on the streets, Drancy prison camp and many others were going (French-administered) concerns, etc. The German occupiers noted periodically the reactions of powerful institutions and of individual Frenchmen; they were not concerned about anti anti-semitic responses. The Church had been quiet;

perhaps its encoded language – along with the 'spiritual resistance' it often helped to inspire – were lost on people as they acted in the world and on the governments they might have tried more forcefully to divert from their terrible racist tasks.

52 From 100% in the resistance, the figure given to me time and again when I started my empirical interview work in 1982, the figure more realistically has been reduced to somewhere between 10% and 5% (the latter reported to me by a real French war hero on 6 June, 1994 when we dined together in New York during his D-day reunion trip with American and French liberators of the continent).

53 Nietzsche, *Dawn of Day*, aphorism 92, my translation. See on Nietzsche's author-centred philological programme, Hendrik Birus, 'Nietzsche's Concept of Interpretation,' *Texte-Revue de critique et de Théorie littéraire*, vol.3 (1984), p.87. Nietzsche's prose often contrasts New to Old Testament values and hermeneutic strategies. See, e.g., *Beyond Good and Evil*, aphorism 52.

54 A.N. Wilson, *Paul: the Mind of the Apostle* (London: Pimlico, 1998), p.196.

55 *ibid.*, p.28.

56 Littell, *The Crucifixion of the Jews*, (New York: Harper & Row, 1975), p.84–5.

57 *ibid.*, pp.26–7.

58 *ibid.*, p.24.

59 *Ibid.*, p.29. Note that sympathetic analysts of Paul such as Sidney G. Hall III have nonetheless spoken of 'Paul's insistence on the Jewish acceptance of his gospel,' *Christian anti-semitism and Paul's Theology* (Minneapolis: Fortress Press, 1993), p.61.

60 Littell, p.29.

61 See, for example, Henry F. Knight, 'Facing the Holy Whole: Reading *John* 8 with Chastened Eyes' (unpublished paper distributed at the Holocaust Scholars Conference, March 2000, Philadelphia); George Smiga, *Pain and Polemic: Anti-Judaism in the Gospels* (N.Y.: Paulist Press, 1992); Robert Kysar, 'Anti-Semitism and the Gospel of John,' in Evans and Hagner, eds., *Anti-Semitism and Early Christianity* (Minneapolis: Fortress Press, 1993).

62 I. W. Slotki, ed., *Isaiah* (London: the Soncino Press, 1949, p.261) – the Soncino version being a respected commentary on the Tanakh – no Jewish reader, even after the long centuries of Christian interpretation (and surely not at the origins) would even *imagine* that this text has anything to do with a figure like Jesus. See e.g., Rabbi A.J. Rosenberg, 'So-called Christological Inferences', in 'Preface', The Book of *Isaiah* vol.2 (New York: The Judaica Press, 1995), pp.xiv–xv. Most Jews have not even thought about the idea. John, however, indicates that some *had to* in the days of the historical Jesus. He does not seem very sympathetic with their quite traditional and utterly mandated scepticism in the face of such uses of sacred texts.

63 Samuel N. Hoenig, *The Essence of Talmudic Law and Thought* (N.J. and London: Aronson, 1967), p.13.

64 See also, for example, John ch.9, where the Pharisees (at 13–16) say of Jesus, after he cures a blind man, 'This is no man of God, he does not keep the Sabbath.'

THE PROTESTANT CHURCHES

If the pluralism of Protestant Christianity diffused its responsibility in comparison with the more hierarchical and centralized authority of the Catholic tradition, Protestant denominations have their share of Holocaust-related burdens, too, for that catastrophe involved a moral collapse that will haunt Christianity forevermore. How did Protestants cope with the rise of Nazism and the Holocaust that followed? How are they responding to their Holocaust-related histories as the 21st century unfolds? Such questions govern this set of essays.

HOW ARE THE PROTESTANT CHURCHES
RESPONDING 50+ YEARS AFTER?

Alice L. Eckardt

Plenary Address, Oxford, 18 July 2000

I N THE years since the Shoah most churches of the West have been responding to that event one way or another, fortunately in an increasingly thorough-going manner. As we now read the earlier documents[1] we find much to dismay us, but we also observe a slow but difficult awakening, as if God were enticing the churches onto untried paths. The last few decades show significant development in recognizing the more foundational issues to be dealt with, and much more readiness to engage in groundbreaking, even revolutionary, thinking such as the acknowledgment that Israel remains God's people. (We will find a mixture of consequences drawn from that acknowledgment.)

While earlier documents spoke about antisemitism a great deal, they did not face up to it as the heritage of the church's teachings and actions over centuries.[2] By contrast statements of the '80s and '90s acknowledge, repent of, and repudiate the church's 'teaching of contempt' with all its terrible consequences.[3]

Paul van Buren has suggested that 'the pattern of revelation which shaped the Scripture and the church's beginning has once again reasserted itself' in the Holocaust and the establishment of the State of Israel (events I have referred to as the nadir and zenith of Jewish history.). The criteria generally accepted for qualifying as a revelational event involve an initiating historical happening followed by a 'profound reorientation.' In both the events of this mid-century the profound reorientation is evidenced in many of the church council and synod statements. Both of these events put human responsibility at centre stage. Van Buren acknowledges that such a claim as he makes must be handled carefully, but he also points out that Emil Fackenheim dares to use the language of a new revelation when speaking of 'a commanding Voice from Auschwitz'.[4] To be sure, the church statements themselves do not claim to be responses to revelation, and confirmation of that suggestion may await the full response of the Christian community as the statements are tested in the life of the churches and their people. (However, I wonder if full response of that sort is necessary; may not the statements stand on their own merit even without full church support?) Certainly the new acknowledgments together with the rejection of the church's 'teaching of contempt' and its assertions that the Jewish people were cast off by God would appear to be the kind of response revelation would elicit.

What happens when the churches begin to pay attention to the consequences of that rejection/contempt theology? (Remember that many churches are only beginning to ask this question, such as the Uniting Church in Australia.[5]) The Reformed Church of the Netherlands led the way in really new thinking in a lengthy study document of 1970. Ten years later two German Synods carried this forward: The Rhineland Synod of the Evangelical Church not only recognized the 'historical necessity of attaining a new relationship of the church to the Jewish people' but did so on the basis of *acknowledging them as the permanently elected people of God* who have continuing significance for salvation history, and into whose covenant the church has been taken. It not only admitted 'responsibility and guilt' for the Holocaust, but in an astounding about-face insisted that the church 'may *not* express its witness toward the Jewish people as it does its mission to the peoples of the world.' Also in 1980 the Baden Provincial Synod spoke of obeying 'the command of history ..., in conformity with biblical teaching', to gain a new relationship towards the Jewish people, and to realize the 'inseparable link between the New and Old Testament.' Israel has not been rejected by God or by the church's election.[6] (I will have more to say on this in the section on 'Church Mission'.)

The State of Israel

Further, the 1980 Rhineland Synod addressed the State of Israel issue by confessing that 'the continuing existence of the Jewish people, its return to the Land of Promise, and also the creation of the State of Israel, are signs of the faithfulness of God toward His people.' The Synod let this affirmation of the State's significance stand without mentioning the Palestinians, whereas the Baden Synod did not mention the State at all. But even earlier, in 1975, the Evangelical Church in the Federal Republic of Germany insisted that with regard to 'justified claims on both sides' Palestinian Arabs should not have 'to bear the consequences of the conflict' alone nor 'should only Israel be held responsible for the situation.' No other statement before or since has made such an observation.[7]

The 1970 Netherlands document focused a good bit of attention on the issue of the State of Israel. It saw land as part of the election of the Jewish people by God, and rejoiced in the 'reunion of people and land' in the post-World War II years, 'a sign ... that it is God's will to be on earth together with man' as well as a sign of 'God's lasting election' of this people. (The Dutch church did not disallow the possibility of the Jews' later loss of the land.) While speaking from a theological perspective the Netherlands Church insisted that 'faith has consequences in the political realm.' Again in 1981 Dutch Protestants warned against criticisms of the State of Israel that either negated the right of its existence or forgot the tie between the Jewish people and the land. They also observed that the history of Christian antisemitism and the annihilation of six million Jews in the mid-twentieth century combined with 'excessive expectations' of the Jewish state give Jews a reason for suspicion of Christian intent.[8]

In 1982 the Texas Conference of Churches, in a move similar to that of the Netherlands Reformed Church, insisted that 'the Spirit of God moves among us' in the nitty-gritty events of worldly and political events. And even earlier, in 1977, the Union of Evangelical Churches in Switzerland said that it is the 'duty of the Christian Churches and all Christians ... to stand by Israel in her growing isolation.'[9] In 1993 the International Council of Christians and Jews (ICCJ) theology committee produced a statement recognizing 'an intrinsic relationship between the Jewish People and the Land of Israel, which is linked to God's covenant with them, a reality which is often not well understood by Christians.' The statement went on to refer to some of the biblical commandments regarding the use of land which the ICCJ saw as 'paradigms' that others might apply toward land and people elsewhere (e.g., the sabbatical year which is based on divine ownership of land, release of slaves, and cancellation of debts, as well as recognizing the rights and dignity of 'others' living in one's land).[10]

Generally, European churches have been more supportive of Israel than those of North America or the World Council of Churches. Most documents of the American churches as well as of the World Council have tended to focus on the purely political dimension of the Jewish return to the Land and the consequences for the Palestinian Arabs, sometimes in an unbalanced way. For example, the World Council of Churches' 1983 'Statement on the Middle East' was definitely more one-sided on the Palestinian Arab and Lebanese side and negative toward Israel, referring to the 'repressive action of the occupying power in East Jerusalem and other occupied territories' without any mention of the Arabs' refusal to accept a negotiated peace settlement in the aftermath of the 1967 Six Day War or their continuing hostile actions against Israel. And in 1994 a resolution passed by the General Convention of the Episcopal Church in the U.S. insisted that Israeli settlements in Gaza, West Bank, and East Jerusalem were illegal and obstacles to peace.[11]

The United Church of Christ statement of 1987 deliberately omitted any reference to the State or Land of Israel knowing what a hot issue that would be to handle at the national meeting. Nevertheless the issue came up in the three public hearings on the 1987 document after its passage. And when the Theological Panel issued its 'Message to the Churches' in 1990 it dealt with that subject fairly extensively (in sections 1 and 5) though without being able to represent any consensus in the church on it. The 'Message' did state appreciation for the 'compelling moral argument for the creation of modern Israel . . . for a victimized people.' But it also recognized the 'entailing . . . dispossession of Palestinians from their homes and the denial of human rights.' It reported that successive General Synods of the Church have asserted both peoples' right to self-determination as well as 'security and justice'.[12]

The British Working Group of the WCC's Consultation on the Church and the Jewish People issued its 'Guidelines/Recommendations on Jewish–Christian Relations' in 1977. It contained three positive statements about the State including the following: 'the most remarkable of all such [Jewish] resurgence is the emergence of the State of Israel which . . . has made it possible for Judaism to regain its wholeness.'[13]

Speaking more theologically, the Presbyterian Church in its study document of 1987 recognized the central place of 'the covenant promise of land' in Jewish life over the centuries, and it affirmed 'the continuity of God's promise of land.' But it hedged that statement with the caveat that possession is dependent on the people's adhering to God's expectations. It then went on to insist that it is 'inadequate' to see the promise of land 'solely in terms of a specific geographical entity on the eastern shore of the Mediterranean'; instead they held that ' "land" ' is a biblical metaphor for 'sustainable life, prosperity, peace and security' and that since the 'State of Israel is a geopolitical entity' it is *'not to be validated theologically'*.[14] Hence this church implicitly denies any revelational status to the Jewish state.

Other churches have tried to balance their acknowledgment of the meaning of the land and nationhood to the Jewish people, its right to secure borders, and acceptance of the State's legitimacy with recognition of the Palestinian people's right to and need for nationhood. The Disciples of Christ statement does not mention Palestinian statehood but speaks of the Bible's insistence that God's gift of land to Israel is made 'in trust' that Israel will live there responsibly with regard both to the land itself and to the poor and the stranger, connecting this to relations between Israel and 'the Palestinian people.' (The Disciples point out that while this is a theological statement it should be taken in the context of the U.N. General Assembly's 'moral concern for justice and peace'.)[15]

Church mission

With regard to mission and conversion (which I touched on briefly earlier) most churches have not followed the Rhineland Synod in rejecting 'mission' to the Jewish people (as it continued to do in two documents of 1996 and 1997);[16] in fact, this remains probably the biggest hurdle. The mission of the church to *all* peoples, including Jews, and in some cases especially to Jews, is seen as so central to the church's being called into existence that it is not easily rethought even in light of the new and fairly widely accepted recognition that God's covenant with the Jewish people has *not* been rescinded (a view that is the absolute opposite of the centuries' long Christian position). Thus we find various churches affirming the Jewish peoples' continuing covenant with God while insisting that the Church has been called to bear witness to Jesus Christ among *all* people. As the Episcopal Church did in 1988 when it said 'The Church must bear witness by word and deed among all people to Jesus Christ,' though it insisted that 'coercive proselytism' should not be used. In 1991 The Presiding Bishop's Committee on Jewish-Christian Relations expressed concern about the 'Decade of Evangelism', and went on to express gratitude for Anglicanism's tradition ('in its more enlightened moments') of respect for 'God's truth as it exists outside of the Church.' In that same year the world-wide Anglican communion at Canterbury, England acknowledged two opposite views within the church on this subject, and while not opting for one, it rejected 'aggressive' proselytizing. At the same time it issued a resolution on 'Inter-Faith Dialogue: Jewish/Christian/Muslim' in which many of the admissions made by the Episcopal Church in the U.S. regarding mistreatment and misrepresentation of Jews were echoed. (The Canterbury document also recognized that Islam claims to supersede both Christianity and Judaism.)

The Presbyterian Church study (which initially came out of the Southern Presbyterian Church in 1982, was reworked and then issued by the united church in 1987) has positive statements regarding God's 'irrevocable' election of both peoples; sees the reign of God being attested by both the Jewish people's continuing existence and the church's proclamation of the gospel; and affirms the church as engrafted into Israel's covenant. Yet when it comes to the conflict between the Scripture's commission 'to witness to the whole world about the good news of Christ's atoning work for both Jew and Gentile' and its representation of Jews as 'already in a [permanent] covenant relationship with God', Presbyterians choose to adhere to what they see as their commission to bear witness. In a somewhat similar manner United Methodists affirm: 'We are clearly called to witness to the Gospel of Jesus Christ in every age and place. At the same time we believe that God ... continues today, to work through Judaism and the Jewish people.' It then adds two modifiers: (1) we realize that 'evangelization of persons of other faiths, and of Jews in particular' often involves sensitive and difficult issues, and (2) we 'can never presume to know the full extent of God's activity outside the Christian Church.'[17] In each of these instances we find that even forthright affirmations of the enduring covenant of God with Israel and recognition of the evils that followed from the Church's long denial of that have not usually led to a clear-cut rejection of the view that Jews need to accept Christ.

Dr. Robert Willis argued in 1975 that, if after the death camps Christians 'still cling to the pretension that their story undergirds a responsibility for the conversion of Jews, then it is questionable whether we can learn anything from the events of history.'[18]

That kind of thinking led the United Church of Christ in 1987 – one of the most explicit statements – to forthrightly affirm that 'Judaism has not been superseded by Christianity; that Christianity is not to be understood as the successor religion to Judaism; God's covenant with the Jewish people has not been abrogated.' Further rejection of the previous supersessionist pretension is asserted in three very recent documents. In 1995 the Society for Christian–Jewish Cooperation in Hamburg, Germany issued a 'Renunciation of "Mission to the Jews"' in which it warned that 'only if the churches clearly refuse to missionize Jews is their fight against anti-Judaism within the church and against every form of antisemitism in society really plausible.' It claimed that all efforts (in Germany) to get a 'governing church body or synod' to adopt a firm stance against missionizing Jews had failed. In 1998 the Evangelical Church A.B. & H.B. of Austria most explicitly insisted that 'missionary activity among Jews is theologically unjustifiable and must be rejected as a church program' precisely because God's covenant with Israel stands 'to the end of time.'[19] The 1997 United Church of Canada's position is initially a bit more confusing as it affirms that it is called to 'bear faithful witness to *all* people... to God's reconciling mission in Jesus Christ' but the sentence continues by saying '[thus opening] the door in a new way to those previously *outside' Israel's irrevocable covenant* with God. To avoid any misunderstanding on this point the document adds Appendix C to its full study which states that the United Church 'does *not* support' efforts to evangelize Jews since it recognizes that 'conversion from Judaism to Christianity is not needful for salvation.'[20]

The Lutherans' struggle with this central issue can be followed by examining documents from 1964 through 1982 and on into the 1990s. At Løgumkloster, Denmark in 1964 the Lutheran World Federation took a traditional *replacement* position, although its 1969 final draft of one section was a bit more ambiguous and perhaps leaned toward the new theology of *recognition*. The 1973 document (Neuendettelsau) affirmed a low-key theology of *recognition* while the 1975 Oslo statement reverted to *replacement* theology, and the 1982 Bossey report mixed the two views. In North America Lutheran statements of the 1970s espoused traditional *replacement* theological views on the relationship of Christianity to Judaism and its people but in a restrained manner (except for the Missouri Synod branch). In the mid-1990s North American Lutheran churches focused on repudiating Luther's diatribes against Jews, on proclaiming antisemitism to be 'an affront to the Gospel', and on sponsoring interfaith dialogues. The Evangelical Lutheran 'Guidelines' of 1998 acknowledged strong Jewish reactions to conversion efforts, and recognized that the Jewish people are 'a diverse, living community of faith' with whom an encounter is 'profoundly enriching' for Christians. *Recognition* seems to be implied though Lutherans have not yet made such outright statements as the previous three I have mentioned.[21]

By contrast, we find the Synod of the Evangelical Church of the Rhineland again in 1996 and 1997 insisting on its 1980 view on this point. In 1996 its 'Ecumenism and World Mission' Committee instructed its representatives to bring the Rhineland position on the relationship between the church and Israel, Christians and Jews into the discussion with several Assembly and Council groups so as to emphasize: that 'Christian mission could never replace God's covenant-history with Israel'; that regarding salvation history there is 'only one distinction' between people – that between 'the people of God and the [people of] the Gentile world'; that there are no 'chosen people' besides Israel; that the church 'cannot do missionary work on its own, but always within a partnership of testimony with Israel.' It pointed out that church mission 'repeatedly followed national claims and prepared for or followed colonialist practice'. The Rhinelanders further observed that 'Christian mission can learn from Israel how as a minority to live in exile, without any ambition for power, and still to become a blessing for many....'[22]

The one exception to all of the above positions is found in the Southern Baptist Convention's 1996 outright avowal to continue to pray for salvation of the Jewish people and to direct its 'energies and resources toward proclamation of the gospel' to them. On June 16, shortly after the Southern Baptists issued their resolution, three church communities in New York – the Roman Catholic archbishopric, the bishops of the Evangelical Lutheran Church, and the Episcopal Church – objected to this singling out of Jews for evangelization. Their joint statement (after citing one source for each church) opted for dialogue instead. They saw 'no conflict between a dialogue based on mutual respect for the sacredness of the other and the Christian mission to preach the Gospel.' And then added: 'An aggressive direct effort to convert the Jewish people would break the bond of trust built up for over thirty years and recreate enmity between our "elder brothers and sisters" and ourselves...'.[23]

A much more effective and affirming statement had been made by the Alliance of Baptists in the previous year (March 1995). Recognizing that the Holocaust was the 'culmination of centuries of Christian teaching and church-sanctioned action directed against the Jews' the Alliance accepted Baptist responsibility for transmitting 'a theology which has taken the anti-Jewish polemic of the Christian Scriptures out of its first century context and has made it normative for Christian–Jewish relations; a theology which has usurped for the Church the biblical promises and prerogatives given by God to the Jews; a theology which [views] Jews as modern versions of their first century co-religionists;...a theology which has valued conversion over dialogue, invective over understanding, and prejudice over knowledge [and] does not acknowledge the vibrancy, vitality, and efficacy of the Jewish faith.' They offered this confession 'with humility and with hope for reconciliation between Christians and Jews.' At the same time they went on to affirm that Christian Scriptures teach that God has not rejected the 'community of Israel, God's covenant people' and therefore they renounced 'interpretations of Scripture which foster religious stereotyping and prejudice against the Jewish people and their faith'.[24]

Liturgical reform

If any long-term change is to be accomplished, major reformulations of liturgy, hymns, and services of the church will be essential since so many continue 'the traditional Christian view of Jews and Judaism', as the WCC British Working Group observed in 1977. The Disciples of Christ warn about the 'language of invective, condemnation, and rejection' used against Jews in the New Testament and in most church traditions, especially the 'deicide' accusation (killing of God) which it insists is a 'theological and historical error.' The Disciples go on to point out that history 'has witnessed the same crucifying actions by Christians toward Jews.' United Methodists insist the church has an 'obligation to ensure that the preparation, selection, and use of liturgical and educational resources' do not 'perpetuate misleading interpretations and misunderstanding of Judaism.' The Episcopal Bishop's Committee on Christian–Jewish Relations expresses concern about lectionary readings with antisemitic overtones, and both Evangelical Lutherans and the British Columbia Conference of the United Church of Canada advise that care must be used and explanation given when New Testament texts reflect the early conflicts between synagogue and the early church or when Jesus' death is dealt with.[25]

But such advice and warnings are only prescriptive. By contrast, the United Church of Canada document of 1997 devotes eleven pages of substantive instruction to 'anti-Judaic moments' in the four Gospels and Paul's letters, and another six pages to guidelines for the use of Scripture in general. In addition, the document provides for a six session study, or alternatively one of three sessions. The study affirms that the story of Christ 'recapitulates the Hebraic stories...newly revealing the content that God always saw in them. "Fulfilment" then is revealed again and made available more widely to gentiles.' The document further elaborates on how the time of separation of the two communities led to writings that made no attempt 'to be fair to opponents' and that later these passages seemed 'to validate Christians in their animosity toward Jews.'[26]

I suggest that in addition to these types of efforts the churches periodically combine with the Scripture selections a reading of one of the more helpful and forward-thinking of the church statements (including from denominations not their own) perhaps calling them 'Letters to the Churches.' Thus the church will demonstrate that it is a living organism that is continuing to grow in understanding, just as it does with many of the recently-adopted confessions of faith.

None of these efforts address the problem of the language of many hymns, and yet congregations sing them week after week without being aware of how their fundamental thinking is being affected. Many of the most loved hymns create the biggest problems. While many churches have changed wordings to take account of the need for language inclusive of women, none have done so (to my knowledge) related to the rethinking of Christian theology regarding Judaism. Yet that need not be an unsurmountable problem.

German Protestant churches led the way liturgically in observing the new relationship between Christians and Jews each year.[27] In 1988 the Episcopal Church 'Guidelines' recommended that this be done annually in its churches, either at the time of Yom HaShoah/Day of Remembrance of the Holocaust or in the fall on the Feast of St. James of Jerusalem.

American Lutherans have discussed the appropriate wording of prayers in civic settings, and have recognized the value of Christian attendance at Bat and Bar Mitzvahs, Seders, and Yom HaShoah observances.

With regard to the training of clergy, Episcopalians and Evangelical Lutherans have urged their theological schools to promote greater understanding and appreciation of the common heritage of Jews and Christians. The Episcopal General Seminary and Protestantism's Union Theological Seminary have established dialogue relationships with the seminaries of both Conservative and Reform Judaism, the Russian Orthodox Church, and the Roman Catholic Church (in Yonkers). This, combined with considerable attention to Judaism and Jewish–Christian relations in a number of GTS's courses, has had a very formative effect on the ministry of their students. A number of them, from 1965 to the present, with whom I have been in touch speak very positively when they tell of the impact this has had on their ministry – the way they preach and teach Scripture as well as relationships they have developed with neighbouring Jewish congregations, rabbis or individuals (as well as with Muslims, Buddhists, etc. in some cases). Three of the four Disciples of Christ schools also take the issue seriously.[28] But the foregoing appear to be exceptional (though, to be sure, most seminaries have at least one faculty member attuned to the new thinking). By contrast, Beverly Asbury's 1992 survey of some 15 major theological schools (Protestant and Roman Catholic) in the United States found that few of those in training for the ministry know anything about contemporary Judaism, the church statements we've been discussing, or the scholarship that undercuts triumphalism and supersessionism. Indeed, just a few years ago most candidates for the position of Protestant chaplain at Vanderbilt University seemed 'never to have questioned' such assumptions. Moreover, seminary curricula generally remain preeminently traditional with regard to the Christian–Jewish issue.[29]

Dr. 'Coos' Schoneveld of The Netherlands has argued forcefully for reading the New Testament with newly-opened eyes. He advises that it is time we see Jewish survival over so many dire centuries in the light of a new understanding that in the Resurrection God affirmed the Torah which Jesus upheld, the people of Israel of which Jesus was one, and Jewish existence as such. Schoneveld sees Jesus as having been vindicated *as a Jew* (not as a Christian) who underwent martyrdom, as so many Jews have done, for the justification of God's name (*kiddush ha-Shem*).[30]

I have just a few more remarks about two additional documents: A brief statement issued jointly by Hungarian Roman Catholic Bishops and the Ecumenical Council of Churches in Hungary in 1994 called the Holocaust 'an unpardonable sin' and 'the greatest shame of our 20th century'. It stated that 'all those who... failed to raise their voices against the mass humiliation, deportation, and murder of their Jewish neighbours' are responsible along with the perpetrators, and it asks for forgiveness. It upholds those who 'rescued lives at the cost of their own, or endangering it, and... protested with universal and general effect against the diabolical plots.' It further stresses the need to develop 'true humaneness' so that such crimes 'will never happen again'. However none of the theological issues is touched on.[31]

In 1998 the Lutheran Church of Bavaria issued a Declaration which stresses that a 'fresh start' in relations between Christians and Jews 'has to begin with an understanding of the complicity of Christians in the persecution and destruction of children, women and men of Jewish origin (the *Shoah*/Holocaust). The *Shoah* represents a deep challenge to Christian teaching and practice' extending over centuries. 'The Lutheran Church of Bavaria has a share in this guilt – as Lutheran and as German.' It goes on to insist that 'anti-Judaism [is] in opposition to the deepest essence of the Christian faith'; therefore the church's responsibility is 'to fix [its] understanding of itself in such a way that [the self-understanding] of the Jewish people is not thereby set aside.' It follows that 'Christians have... to think through anew how they are to understand their witness that Jesus Christ is the savior of all [persons] in respect to the Jews.'[32]

One other Protestant project is presently being carried on among the many Reformation churches of Europe (the Leuenberg Church Fellowship) and is not yet finalized. Since the churches see themselves as 'the community of those who believe in Jesus Christ' and hence the 'people of God', they recognize that the question of how close they are to, or differ from, the people of Israel who also see themselves as the 'people of God' calls for further clarification.[33]

Conclusion

All of these developments are very important. The big question is: What impact are they having? Have the churches acted as if a new revelation has been given to them? The Berlin-Brandenburg Synod admitted in 1984 that despite its endeavours, 'there has, as usual, been little progress beyond the initial stages. The burden of centuries of ecclesiastical and political antisemitism is still upon us.'[34] While this is still largely true, some of the signs I've noted may give us more hope. However even these accomplishments are almost entirely within the main-line churches of the West. Among the biblical/fundamentalist churches we find two camps: those who hold that conversion of Jews is a prerequisite for the Second Coming of Christ; and those who, while hoping for Jews' ultimate acceptance of Jesus, leave the matter up to God and insist that their 'mission' is to stand fast *with* Jews. All in all, Charles Obrecht has observed that the 'troubling story of the Jewish-Christian encounter is perhaps the most vexing and enduring problem in western history.'[35]

Ultimate changes depend on the permanent effect of the new thinking on the life and faith of the whole church. Consequently major work still lies before us and the momentum toward change must not be stopped. We still need to rediscover God's will for the world in a radically new way. As the Disciples church puts it, 'History under God [requires] a continuing reclaiming of the truth and power of God in every generation.'

An openness to new understandings that may seem radical at first is part of the 'unending task of interpretation' as God works to accomplish redemption.[36]

NOTES

1 In the immediate aftermath of World War II churches for the most part remained imbued with centuries-old theological convictions even while they acknowledged the horrors of the recent years of Nazism and what they entailed for Jews. The Protestant Evangelical Church of Germany in October 1945 spoke of the guilt it shared with the nation for the 'unending suffering' imposed on 'many peoples and countries', yet it never mentioned the particular suffering imposed on the Jews of Europe (Franklin Hamlin Littell, *The German Phoenix* [Garden City: Doubleday & Co., 1960], Appendix C, p.89). And when the World Council of Churches' executive, prior to its first Assembly in Amsterdam in 1948, requested some input, the Protestant Federation of France responded. Its paper saw the sufferings of the Jewish people as God's judgment (though *not* His 'vengeance') for their unfaithfulness in rejecting Jesus, and considered this suffering to be an 'appeal to conversion' and for Jews to 'turn from their unfaithfulness in refusing to recognize [Jesus] as the Messiah foretold by the prophets.' The French statement candidly stated that the aim of general conversion 'cannot be anything less than the spiritual destruction of Israel' (*The Theology of the Churches and the Jewish People* [Geneva: WCC Publications, 1988], p.128). The World Council's own final document insisted that the churches must proclaim to the Jewish people that 'The Messiah for Whom you wait has come' (*ibid.*, pp.6–7).
   For documents from 1965 to 1975 see *Stepping Stones to Further Jewish–Christian Relations*, Helga Croner compiler (London: Stimulus Books, 1977); for documents 1975 to 1983 plus a 1947 interfaith document, see *More Stepping Stones to Jewish–Christian Relations*, Helga Croner compiler (New York: Stimulus Books/Paulist Press, 1985). Also see *Stepping-Stones to Further Jewish–Lutheran Relations*, Harold H. Ditmanson, ed. (Minneapolis: Augsburg Fortress, 1990), and *The Theology of the Churches and the Jewish People: Statements by the World Council of Churches and its member churches*, Allan Brockway, Paul van Buren, Rolf Rendtorff, Simon Schoon, commentators (Geneva: WCC Publications, 1988). Sources for additional documents that are not included in these volumes will be noted as mentioned. A new volume in the *Stepping Stones* series is presently in preparation; it will include many of the earlier statements from the first two volumes plus the many that have been issued since then.
2 See the World Council of Churches 1948 statement.
3 See Lutheran World Federation, 1984; Presbyterian Church (USA), 1988; Anglican Church at Lambeth, 1988; World Council of Churches and the Consultation on the Church and the Jewish People, 1988 and 1992; Disciples of Christ, 1988/1993; Evangelical Lutheran Church in America, 1994; Alliance of Baptists, 1995; Evangelical Lutheran Church of Canada, 1995; United Methodist Church, 1996; United Church of Canada 1997/2000; Austrian Evangelical Church, 1998.
4 Van Buren, *Discerning the Way* (San Francisco: Harper & Row, 1980), pp.176–79; Fackenheim, *God's Presence in History* (New York University Press, 1970).
5 Statement of the Uniting Church in Australia, July 1997 specifically asks 'What are the implications for us, as a church, when we enter into a new relationship with Jewish people?'
6 *More Stepping Stones to the Jewish–Christian Relations*, p.161; *Stepping Stones to Further Jewish–Christian Relations*, p.145. Some may object that the Rhineland Synod statement is not a clearcut renunciation of mission hopes and efforts, though that is not my reading, nor my understanding of the Synod's intentions on the basis of conversations with some of the participants.
7 *ibid.*; for the Evangelical Church statement see *Christian Jewish Relations* 17, 3 (1984): 33–34.
8 Synod of the Reformed Church, Holland, 1970 (*Stepping Stones...*, pp.103, 92; Declaration of the Council of Churches in The Netherlands, 1981, *More Stepping Stones...*, p.214.
9 For both the Texas Conference of Churches and the Union of Evangelical Churches in Switzerland statements see *More Stepping Stones...*, pp.186, 203.
10 'Jews and Christians In Search of a Common Religious Basis for Contributing Towards a Better World', *Current Dialogue*, 28 (June 1995): 13.

11 The Sixth Assembly of the World Council of Churches, 1983, *The Theology of the Churches*, 43–46; and the Episcopal News Service, Sept. 7, 1994. The Episcopalian Presiding Bishop's Committee on Jewish–Christian Relations acknowledged the criticism of Israel in its 1991 report.

12 'A Message to the Churches', Jewish–Christian Theological Panel, May 1990, *New Conversations* 12, 3 (Summer 1990): 5–8.

13 *More Stepping Stones...*, p.161.

14 'A Theological Understanding of the Relationship Between Christians and Jews' [1987] in *The Theology of the Churches...*, pp.116–17. This study has never been adopted as a church statement, largely due to opposition from Middle Eastern congregations. In it the Israeli–Palestinian issue was not discussed, but in 1997 the church's General Assembly adopted an informative, thorough-going, and unbiased study entitled 'Resolution on the Middle East.'

15 The Disciples of Christ 'Statement on the Relations Between Jews and Christians' of 1988/93 is to be found in *The Church and the Jewish People: A Study Guide for the Christian Church (Disciples of Christ)*, Clark Williamson, ed. (St. Louis: Christian Board of Publications, 1994), Appendix, pp.87–93. For other mentions of the State of Israel issue see also: Episcopal General Convention, 'Guide for Christian–Jewish Relations', 1988; United Methodist Church, 'Building New Bridges in Hope', 1996; United Church of Canada, 'Bearing Faithful Witness', 1997/2000; The Evangelical Church A.B. & H.B. in Austria, 'A Time to Turn', 1998; Evangelical Lutheran 'Guidelines', 1998.

 It is most surprising to find the United Church of Canada affirming the right of the State of Israel on the basis of U.N. resolution 181 (1947) which, while it envisioned Israel's 'right to exist in safety and well-being', also included the creation of a Special International Regime for the City of Jerusalem.

16 See later discussion on these recent Rhineland Church actions.

17 'Building New Bridges in Hope', 1996.

18 Willis, 'Auschwitz and the Nurturing of Conscience', *Religion in Life* 44/4 (1975): 438.

19 For the Austrian church document 'A Time to Turn' see *SIDIC*, 17/1 (1999): 28.

20 'Bearing Faithful Witness: United Church–Jewish Relations Today' (Etobiocoke, ON: The Committee on Inter-Church and Inter-Faith Relations, 1997) and its Revised Proposed Statement, 2000.

21 The terms *replacement* and *recognition* were suggested by Dr. Harold Ditmanson in his 'Introduction' to *Stepping-Stones to Further Jewish–Lutheran Relationships* (Minneapolis: Augsburg, 1990], p.13).

22 'Israel and Christian Mission', 1996. The 1997 study document of the same church spelled out more of the details of the history of the relationship between the two peoples, its own questions about why the churches had kept silent during the Nazi era, and its conclusion that they had done so because they 'had marked Judaism as hostile, at least as strange and opposing to the Christian belief.' Moreover, the author commented on his observing the 'sometimes conscious, sometimes unconscious hostility, or at least, differentiation [toward Judaism and its people] found within the ecumenical movement' at the World Council of Churches meeting in Canberra in 1991.

23 Both of these documents can be found on the Internet under <jcrelations.net>.

24 See statement at <jcrelations.net>.

25 The Presiding Bishop's Committee on Christian–Jewish Relations, *The Blue Book*, 1991, p.534. 'Guidelines for Lutheran–Jewish Relations', Evangelical Lutheran Church in America (1998) avers that those who had a hand in Jesus' death are 'representative of humanity as such.' The British Columbia Conference of the United Church of Canada urges that congregations be reminded that it was Gentile Roman authorities who killed Jesus (1996).

26 'Bearing Faithful Witness', pp.9–32.

27 Previously 'Israel Sunday' was mission oriented.

28 John Townsend points out that Harvard Divinity School requires superior knowledge of some other world religion than the students' own, and has numbers of professors from these religions teaching the courses.

29 Beverly Asbury, 'The Revolution in Jewish–Christian Relations: Is It To Be Found in Christian Theological Seminaries? A Preliminary Study', *Theological Education* 28/2 (1992).

30 J. Schoneveld, 'The Jewish "No" to Jesus and the Christian "Yes" to Jews', *Quarterly Review: A Scholarly Journal for Reflection on Ministry*, 4/4 (1984): 60.

31 Joint Statement on the Occasion of the Fiftieth Anniversary of the Holocaust, Hungarian [RC] Bishops and Ecumenical Council of Churches in Hungary, November 1994.

32 'Christians and Jews', *Journal of Ecumenical Studies* 36/3–4 (1999): 481, 482, 484.

33 'Church and Israel' of the Leuenberg Church Fellowship has a 43 page draft document (dated 1999) which is being circulated among participating churches (including the Church of Scotland, Czech Brethren, Ev. Kirche A.B. in Austria, Evangelical Reformed Church in Poland, Lutheran and Reformed Churches of France, Church of Denmark, Evangelical Augsburg Church in Poland, Ev. Kirch im Rheinland, Nordelbische Ev.-Luth. Kirche, Vereinigde Protestantse Kerk in Belgium, Iglesia Evangélica Luterana Unida, Argentina, and others). This is a very thorough-going study and statement which will merit considerable attention.

34 *SIDIC* 17/3 (1984): 32.

35 Charles Obrecht, *Explorations* (Institute of Christian and Jewish Studies, Baltimore): 11, 1 (1997): 5.

36 Disciples of Christ (Christian Church) statement, 1988/93, op cit.

THE IMPACT OF THE HOLOCAUST ON THE CHURCH OF ENGLAND

Marcus Braybrooke

W HEN I said to a friend that that I was writing a paper on the impact of the Holocaust on the Church of England[1], her answer was 'Has there been any?' Alan Ecclestone also in his *The Night Sky of the Lord* – a book we shall consider – says 'it is difficult to find evidence of a realistic approach to the Jewish problem or to show how it has affected the learning processes of the churches in Britain.'[2] I think this is somewhat unfair because there has been a real attempt to purge the church's teaching and liturgy of its traditional anti-Judaism and some effort to learn about Judaism as a living religion. There has been little reflection, however, on the more properly theological question of how God's character and purpose for the world is to be understood in the shadow of the Shoah.

I begin with the 1988 Lambeth Conference document 'Jews, Christians and Muslims: The Way of Dialogue', as it may serve as a bench mark of the church's teaching about Judaism. Then, having considered the contribution of some church leaders, I will look at the writings of a few seminal thinkers, who represent three stages of rethinking Christian attitudes to Judaism. James Parkes helped Christians recognize their responsibility for the age-long evil of anti-Semitism. Peter Schneider encouraged members of the church to appreciate the spiritual riches of Judaism as a living religion and to recognize the significance of Israel in Christian-Jewish relations. Ulrich Simon and Alan Ecclestone tried to address the theological questions that are presented by Auschwitz.

'JEWS, CHRISTIANS AND MUSLIMS'

Although 'Jews, Christians and Muslims' is a document of the Anglican church, approved by the 1988 Lambeth Conference of bishops of the Anglican Communion, much of the preparatory work was done by the Bishop of Oxford, Richard Harries, and a small team of advisers, most of whom were British. It can, I think, therefore, be taken as indicative of the 'best' teaching of the Church of England, although many members of that church have little awareness of the dramatic changes that have taken place in Christian–Jewish relations in Britain in last half century.

The document was originally intended only to deal with relations with Jews. Many Anglican bishops, however, were from parts of the world where Islam is dominant and they were afraid that the emphasis on Judaism would cause offence to their Muslim neighbours. The original draft was, therefore, considerably revised and extended to include relations with Muslims, although I will concentrate on the references to Judaism.

The final document begins with a sensitive description of dialogue. It is 'the work of patient love and an expression of the ministry of reconciliation . . . The essential condition of any true dialogue is a willingness to listen to the partner; to try to see with their eyes and feel with their heart. For understanding is more than intellectual apprehension. It involves the imagination and results in a sensitivity to the fears and hopes of others. Understanding another means allowing them to define themselves in their terms rather than ours, and certainly not in terms of our inherited stereotypes.'[3]

The document is in three parts. The first, 'The Way of Understanding', affirms that Judaism is a living religion with the Mishnah and the Talmud as its definitive works. This implicitly rejects the popular equation of Judaism with the religion of the Old Testament. Judaism, which is not only a religion but also a people and a civilization, is seen in a positive light. The 'Profound changes and potential for good' in modern Biblical study, which is increasingly a joint Jewish-Christian enterprise, are acknowledged. The division between the early church and the Jewish people is recognized to have been 'contingent on specific historical developments.'[4] This suggests that the real 'parting of the ways' happened after the fall of Jerusalem in 70 CE and that the Gospels reflect the polemic of that period. It also implies that Jesus did not consciously intend to found a new religion.

The second section, 'The Way of Affirmation', recognizing the special bond between Judaism and Christianity, suggests that this relationship would be strengthened if both traditions gave a central place to their hope for God's kingdom. It affirms that God's covenant with the Jewish people is still effective. Recognizing that Christian anti-Jewish propaganda contributed greatly to Jewish sufferings, the document confesses that this provided the soil in which 'the evil weed of Nazism was able to take root and spread its poison'.[5]

The third part, 'The Way of Sharing', reflects the different views in the church about whether or not missionary attempts to convert Jews to Christianity are appropriate:

> At one pole there are those Christians whose prayer is that Jews, without giving up their Jewishness, will find their fulfilment in Jesus the Messiah... Other Christians believe that in fulfilling the law and prophets, Jesus validated the Jewish relationship with God, while opening up this way for Gentiles through his own person. For others, the Holocaust has changed their perception, so that until Christian lives bear a truer witness, they feel a divine obligation to affirm the Jews in their worship and sense of the God and Father of Jesus.[6]

The document, which was watered down by various revisions, calls for more teaching about Christian-Jewish relations, for care in preaching, the purging of anti-Jewish material from the liturgy and suggested possible common action. Instead of a whole section on Israel, all that is said is that 'the importance of the land of Israel to the majority of Jews throughout the world needs to be understood'.[7]

'Jews, Christians and Muslims', which was, at least in part, a response to the horror of the Holocaust, deplores the anti-Judaism which has stained much of the traditional teaching of the church and has caused so much Jewish suffering. It reflects a significant change in its renewed emphasis on the Jewishness of Jesus, its recognition that the Gospels reflect the polemic of the early church and that the picture of the Pharisees is unfair and in exonerating the Jews from blame for the crucifixion. There has also been a new appreciation of the spiritual contribution of Judaism through the centuries. There is, however, little reflection on the deeper theological issues raised by the Holocaust – such as for example whether belief in a loving God is still credible.

CHURCH LEADERS

From its beginnings, the Archbishops of Canterbury have played an important role in the Council of Christians and Jews (CCJ). As Archbishop of York, William Temple hosted a lunch at which he and the Chief Rabbi and other leaders discussed the possibility of forming a council. Temple was reluctant just to focus on anti-Semitism, which he saw as symptomatic of an even deeper evil. He hoped that members of the two religions could express 'the principles which they had in common and which lay at the basis of a just civilisation'.[8]

Temple mapped out the path that CCJ was to follow. It has set itself against all forms of discrimination and has tried to promote the fundamental ethical teachings which are common to Judaism and Christianity. It has also engaged in extensive educational work to encourage members of both religions to have a proper understanding of the teaching and practice of the other religion. This, because it had to clear away traditional prejudices, has led to rethinking in the churches. CCJ has not, however, usually been a body for theological reflection and dialogue, partly because the Orthodox Jewish leadership had no wish for such dialogue.

Temple was vocal in expressing outrage at the Nazi atrocities. He urged that refugees from Nazi-controlled areas should be welcomed to Britain and he suggested the possible prosecution after the war of those responsible for the atrocities. He was well aware that what he said might make little difference but that even so 'it ought to be said for the sake of the principles of justice itself.'[9] His concern was recognized by many members of the Jewish community who shared in the mourning which attended his death.

Temple's successor, Geoffrey Fisher was a strong supporter of CCJ, especially during the difficulties created by Catholic withdrawal from the Council.[10] Fisher also took a great interest in the Israel/Palestine situation and was a strong advocate of international control of Jerusalem.

Michael Ramsey also supported CCJ. In 1964 he was persuaded to issue a statement, regularly reissued, which made clear that the Jews were not to be blamed for the crucifixion:

> It is always wrong when people try to lay the blame upon the Jews for the crucifixion of Jesus Christ. In the event the Roman Governor was no less responsible for what happened.
> The important fact, however, is that the crucifixion was the clash between the Love of God and the sinfulness and selfishness of the whole human race. Those who crucified Christ are in the true mind of the Christian Church representatives of the whole human race, and it is for no one to point a finger of resentment at those who brought Jesus to his death, but rather to see the crucifixion as the divine judgement upon all humanity for choosing the ways of sin rather than the Love of God.
> We must all see ourselves judged by the crucifixion of Christ.[11]

Donald Coggan, a fine Hebrew and Biblical scholar, who on retiring from Canterbury became an active chairman of CCJ and president of the International Council of Christians and Jews (ICCJ), continued this support. In 1980, whilst he was archbishop, the first official Anglican-Jewish Consultation, chaired by the Archbishop of York, Stuart Blanch, and the Chief Rabbi took place at Amport House, Andover on the theme 'Law and Religion in Contemporary Society'.

Robert Runcie became so involved in Christian–Jewish relations that he talked of his 'Jewish period'.[12] In 1988, he addressed the CCJ Annual Meeting, preached at the West London Synagogue, spoke at the *Kristallnacht* memorial meeting and a little later lectured to the World Union for Progressive Judaism's biennial international conference. He also conferred a Lambeth degree on the Chief Rabbi, Lord Jakobovits. During Runcie's time in office the Lambeth Conference agreed to 'Jews, Christians and Muslims', and the Joint Presidents of CCJ, who distanced themselves from the missionary activities of 'Jews for Jesus', started their pattern of an annual meeting. Liturgical revision also removed the Good Friday Reproaches.

Archbishop Runcie's willingness to raise theological issues was particularly valuable. Speaking to CCJ, he explored the significance of the creation narratives in the Jewish-Christian understanding of the world. At the *Kristallnacht* meeting, he unambiguously acknowledged Christian responsibility for Jewish suffering.

> Without centuries of Christian Anti-Semitism, Hitler's passionate hatred would never have been so fervently echoed... The travesty of *Kristallnacht* and all that followed is that so much was perpetrated in Christ's name. To glorify the Third Reich, the Christian faith was betrayed... And even today there are many Christians who fail to see it as self-evident. And why this blindness? Because for centuries Christians have held Jews collectively responsible for the death of Jesus. On Good Friday Jews have, in times past, cowered behind locked doors for fear of a Christian mob seeking 'revenge' for deicide. Without the poisoning of Christian minds through the centuries, the holocaust is unthinkable.[13]

George Carey has continued this concern. Soon after taking office, he declined an invitation to become Patron of The Church's Ministry Among Jewish People (CMJ) – a society which has traditionally adopted a missionary approach to the Jews – as inconsistent with his role as a Joint President of the Council of Christians and Jews. He made clear that the 'Decade of Evangelism' was primarily addressed to lapsed Christians and not targeted at Jews or members of other faith communities. He himself took part in the third Anglican-Jewish Consultation, which was held at St George's House, Windsor in 1992.[14]

PARKES AND SCHNEIDER

A leading pioneer of a new Christian approach to Jews and Judaism was James Parkes, who was an Anglican clergyman although he never held a parochial appointment.

In one sense, it could be said that during the last fifty years, the church has been absorbing the major conclusions that James Parkes reached in his pioneering study *The Conflict of Church and Synagogue*, first published in 1934.[15] It is significant, as Robert Everett observes, that Parkes began his research even before the Nazis came to power.[16] In 1928 Parkes went to work for the International Student Service in Geneva, where he quickly became aware of the rising tide of anti-Semitism[17] and began serious study of this phenomenon. He was, he wrote later, 'completely unprepared for the discovery that it was the Christian Church and the Christian Church alone, which turned a normal xenophobia and normal good and bad community relations between two human societies into the unique evil of Anti-Semitism, the most evil, and as I gradually came to realise, the most crippling sin of historic Christianity.'[18]

This was the major conclusion of his detailed study, *The Conflict of Church and Synagogue*. The main cause of Anti-Semitism, he argued, was the teaching of the Christian church. The hostility to the Jews that existed in the Graeco-Roman world had in his opinion 'reasonable historical causes.'[19] He also rejected an economic explanation for medieval hatred of the Jews. Nowhere was the term 'Jew' coupled with any term of economic significance. 'The new factor', he insisted, 'was religious.'[20] The first believers in Jesus, who were Jewish, found in Him something new to their experience which they had lacked in Judaism. They insisted that Gentile believers in Jesus did not need to observe the Jewish ceremonial and ritual law. But, when Gentiles took over the leadership of the Christian church, 'the entirety of the religious conceptions of Judaism as proclaimed in the Old Testament was rejected as superseded by the Church.'[21] 'Out of this artificial separation of history into two parts, on the simple principle that what was good belonged to one group and what was bad to the other, grew the caricature of the

Jew with which patristic literature is filled.'[22] The theological conceptions of the first three centuries were the foundations upon which an awful superstructure was reared, which showed itself in ecclesiastical and secular legislation as well as in religious fanaticism, which was expressed in forced baptisms, burning of synagogues and acts of violence against Jews. The major responsibility for anti-Semitism rested, in Parkes's view, 'upon the theological picture created in patristic literature of the Jew as being perpetually betraying God and ultimately abandoned by Him.'[23] In the 9th century, new legislation was introduced which further discriminated against the Jews and fresh supposed crimes were added, such as ritual murder and the poisoning of wells.

Parkes summarized his study in a memorable final sentence:

> The Christian public as a whole, the great and overwhelming majority of the hundreds of millions of nominal Christians in the world, still believe that 'the Jews' killed Jesus, that they are a people rejected by their God, that all the beauty of the Bible belongs to the Christian Church and not to those by whom it was written; and if on this ground, so carefully prepared, modern anti-Semites have reared a structure of racial and economic propaganda, the final responsibility still rests with those who prepared the soil, created the deformation of the people, and so made these ineptitudes credible.[24]

Parkes never wavered from his view that what distinguished Anti-Semitism from other forms of ethnic hatred and prejudice was the theological fiction perpetuated by the church. He was also clear that there was a direct line from the teaching of the church to the death camps of Hitler. He put this clearly in an item on Anti-Semitism written for *A Concise World History*.

> That which changed the normal pattern of Jewish-Gentile relations was the action of the Christian Church. The statement is tragic, but the evidence is inescapable. What is still more tragic is that there is no break in the line which leads from the beginning of the denigration of Judaism in the formative period of Christian history, from the exclusion of Jews from civic equality in the period of the Church's first triumph in the fourth century, through the horrors of the Middle Ages, to the Death Camps of Hitler in our own day.[25]

Parkes was a prolific writer. He struggled to remove Christian misconceptions about Judaism. He rejected the view, which was widespread at the time, that post-exilic or so-called 'late' Judaism was moribund. That period 'saw the development of synagogue worship . . . evolved the idea of Holy Scripture and included history as a sphere of revelation . . . It found that religion was not an affair of priest and cult, but of the moral living of ordinary men.'[26] He wrote his *History of the Jewish People*[27] to show that throughout the history of Christendom Judaism had continued to be a fertile spiritual religion. 'I had to explain', he said later, 'that Judaism was *not* an incomplete form of Christianity, that it was *not* unchanged "Old Testament" religion . . . and that it had to be treated as an equal in any discussion between Jews and Christians.'[28]

Parkes also felt the need to correct Christian misapprehensions about the New Testament. He argued that it was a mistake to think of Jesus as the Jewish Messiah;[29] he criticized the way in which Christians normally spoke and wrote about the Pharisees;[30] he suggested that the Gospels were discoloured by anti-Jewish polemic and he rejected the charge of 'deicide' which falsely blamed the Jews for the death of Jesus. 'It was only when the Church was trying to ingratiate itself with the Roman authorities – which was just at the period when the traditions were crystallising into our present Gospels – that Pilate tended to be exonerated and the Jews to be blamed.'[31] Parkes also suggested that a careful study of what Paul wrote did not support the usual Christian derision of the Law nor the view that the church had replaced Israel in God's purposes.

He argued that Paul never attacked the religion of his ancestors nor the importance of the Law. Paul's objection was to the attempt to impose the Law on Gentile believers in Jesus. In Romans 9.11, Paul, in Parkes's view, argued for one salvation history in which both Jews and Gentiles would be saved.[32]

Parkes held that both Judaism and Christianity had a continuing place in God's purposes. He developed what has come to be known as the 'Two Covenant theory', arguing that both religions stemmed from the same divine origin and revelation and neither possesses the whole truth. The covenant at Sinai was essentially about God's will in community life, the covenant at Calvary about the individual's relation to God. Because the Jewish people were still in a covenant relationship with God, Parkes opposed missionary attempts to convert the Jews.[33]

After the Second World War, Parkes wrote a great deal about the situation in Israel/ Palestine, which he first visited in 1946. He explained the historical background to the situation and the great importance of Israel to most Jewish people. At that time there was much Christian sympathy for the new state, although the mood changed after the Six Day War, when Israel's occupation of the West Bank and Gaza became prolonged.

From his time as a student at Oxford, Parkes's thinking was much influenced by Modernism. The horrors of the First World War had made him an internationalist and keen supporter of the League of Nations. He stressed God's concern for the whole of life and saw an intimate link between politics and religion, saying that the Kingdom of God was central to Jesus' preaching. He was critical of the theology of the churches as being Christological rather than theological. The dangers of this, he suggested, were threefold: (1) it created a doctrine of Divine activity in which Christ occupies an exclusive position; (2) it created a situation in which the Church preached that Christ is the solution to every problem in human life, in spite of the evidence to the contrary; (3) it introduced the concept of 'salvation in Christ' whose exclusive nature consigns the majority of humanity to Hell.[34]

Parkes held that a more theocentric theology would allow the church to recognize other revelations besides that in Christ. Parkes himself held that Sinai, Calvary and the Renaissance were all revelations of God and he made occasional reference to other world religions.

In emphasizing God's concern for the whole of life, Parkes recognized God's responsibility for the world being as it is – even with all its suffering – and he affirmed that God would eventually achieve his purposes and lead his whole creation to perfection.[35] In this Parkes reflected the optimism of Modernism and one might have expected him to have modified these views in the shadow of the Holocaust, although it is unfair to suggest that because Parkes anticipated so many issues in the field of Christian–Jewish relations he should also be expected to have anticipated this subject, which has only become a matter of discussion in the last twenty-five years. Parkes's lasting work was to recognize Christian responsibility for Anti-Semitism and then to help Christians come to a better appreciation of Judaism and to purge the falsehoods of their own teaching.

In many ways Peter Schneider, who spent some years in Israel and then became secretary to the Archbishops' Consultants on Interfaith Relations carried on the work of Parkes, to whom he expressed his indebtedness in his book on Judaism, *Sweeter than Honey*.

Schneider was Jewish by birth but adopted by a Christian family. He was brought up as a Christian and was ordained. A number of Christians who are Jewish by birth have made a significant contribution to rethinking Christian attitudes to Judaism. They have, however, often been made to feel uncomfortable in dialogue circles because of Jewish fear of Christian missionary activity and because, as Bishop Hugh Montefiore, a convert from Judaism says 'For a Jew to become a Christian is to go over to the enemy.'[36]

Sweeter than Honey, written as part of the 'Christian Presence' series of books which were edited by Canon Max Warren, was a good statement of the most 'progressive' thinking of the mid-sixties on this subject. Schneider reiterated Parkes's indictment of Christianity's responsibility for anti-Semitism and then argued for a more sympathetic picture of the Pharisees and of Jesus' attitude to the Law. Not surprisingly his treatment of Paul does not anticipate the writings of Krister Stendahl and Lloyd Gaston, but he insisted that in Paul's view, God's rejection of the Jews was only temporary.

His book is significant for arguing that Christians should 'not only correct the past but go on to an inner appreciation of Judaism'.[37] He contributed to this in *Sweeter Than Honey* by a fine section on Jewish views of Jesus. Jewish animosity against Jesus, he claimed, derived from the 'wholly fictitious and unworthy representation of Jesus' in the medieval *Toldot Yeshu*,[38] and not from the Talmud, which hardly mentions him.[39] Although Jesus' teaching is considered by the Talmud 'sufficiently heretical to be the cause of his death, the fact that he continued some of the Pharisaic teaching tradition is not forgotten. What is, however, of far greater significance than these meagre details, is the consistent agreement of all the evidence that Jesus remained a Jew. It was as such that he was valued and as such that his place "in the world to come" was not denied.'[40]

It was the 19th-century Jewish historian Heinrich Graetz who reclaimed Jesus as a great Jewish seer, saying that 'Jesus made no attack upon Judaism.'[41] Schneider, in his survey, contrasted the sympathetic studies of the teaching of Jesus by the liberal Jewish scholar Claude Montefiore with the writings of Asher Ginsberg, usually known as Ahad Ha-Am, who emphasized the immense gulf between Judaism and Christianity. Schneider also summarized Joseph Klausner's *Jesus of Nazareth*, which was published in Jerusalem in 1922 and the novel *The Nazarene* by Scholem Asch.[42]

Besides this summary of some Jewish views of Jesus, Schneider devoted nearly a quarter of the book, as well as a valuable appendix, to a sympathetic section on 'The Message of Judaism'. The concept of the *Shechina* is discussed in some detail and its similarity to 'the Christian doctrine of the indwelling Spirit in the life of the saints' is noted.[43] Attention is also given to the *Shema* and to the meaning of *Torah*.

The book ended with a chapter on 'Christians and Jews', which included some discussion of the significance of the state of Israel to Christian-Jewish relations, a subject to which Schneider returned in a number of talks and articles.[44]

Peter Schneider also made a lasting contribution to improving Christian-Jewish relations by his active participation in both the Jerusalem and London Rainbow dialogue groups and in the World Council of Churches' Consultation on the Church and the Jewish people. His influence on the Bristol Report, which was one of the first Protestant documents to acknowledge that God had not revoked his covenant with the Jewish people, was especially significant.[45]

The recognition that God's covenant with the Jewish people is still valid and that they remain a people of God – a view that Schneider was one of the first Anglicans to advocate – has gradually gained ground and has required the Church to rethink its attitude to mission.

Yet, for all its sympathy with contemporary Judaism and the Jewish people, Schneider's book only devotes about a page to the Holocaust, which is mentioned in the chapter on 'Christianity and Anti-Semitism'.[46] It is easy now – with the rapid growth of Holocaust studies – to forget that for twenty years or more there was great reluctance to discuss the subject. For example, in 1961, CCJ refused to support an exhibition about the concentration camps because it was felt likely that the exhibition would only perpetuate hatred and bitterness. The Council also turned down a suggestion that the Ten Points of Seelisberg be reprinted with a brief commentary feeling that the subject was so difficult that it should only be discussed at a university faculty of divinity.[47] All this makes the more remarkable the ground-breaking book by Ulrich Simon, *A Theology of Auschwitz*, first published in 1967.[48]

SIMON AND ECCLESTONE

Simon, who was Jewish by birth, was clear that the Holocaust raised profound theological questions, which he addressed as a Christian theologian. 'The problem of Auschwitz is theological in the fullest sense because it posits the ambiguity of human historical existence in a world created and sustained by God. Its meaning or lack of it cries out for transcendental reference. But transcendental terms, such as Providence, for example, must be examined afresh in the light of the great catastrophe.'[49]

> The theologian must ask the great 'Why', rather than be content to know how and why certain crimes were perpetrated. He extends the 'why' to the root of the historical drama and to the actors in it. He will compare and contrast his findings with the declared Christian doctrines. How does Auschwitz stand in the light of the Fatherhood of God, the Person of Christ, and the Coming of the Holy Ghost... These norms are not an excuse to blur the facts.[50]

Auschwitz, for Simon, was the comprehensive and realistic symbol of the greatest possible evil which still threatens humankind.

Simon discussed some traditional theories about the cause of suffering, such as whether it is the result of sin and the view that evil is a deficiency or an absence of being. In one sense, he said, Auschwitz's only purpose was to cause death and was essentially meaningless in terms of life. Divine power, he argued, is opposed by another power hostile to God and man – although the tradition has resisted an absolute dualism saying that God neither makes nor condones evil, though he permits its manifestation in the interest of freedom.

Recognizing some people's distrust of all metaphysics and theories, Simon warned of the dangers of moral relativism and the view that 'everything is permitted'. He argued that to reject all attempted explanation of our ills is intolerable:

> A belief in the rule of chance, coupled with that in the survival of the fittest and made respectable by our awareness of the almost endless varieties of customs among the people of the world, created the mentality which understands, condones and pardons all... this so-called liberal substitute for traditional theodicy is one of the causes of Auschwitz... The lasting significance of Auschwitz for humanity lies in its disclosure of the human condition as something incomprehensible and insoluble in merely human terms.[51]

The attempt to hold on to meaning, Simon insisted, was in no sense a denial of the grim reality of the Holocaust, which represented the unimaginable and total degradation of humanity. 'If we protest against an anthropology of despair, based upon the sight of heaps of skeletons and smoking furnaces, and press for a vindication of mankind, a restatement of meaning and destiny, it is based upon a belief reacting to the facts.'[52]

Simon touched on Hitler's fanning of Jew-hatred and on the tragic way in which Christians had forgotten their Jewish spiritual roots. Most of the perpetrators were 'as banal as the rest of the world's little men' but open to the charismatic or 'religious ecstasy', which for Hitler was hatred of the Jews. Hitler fused the historical Christian antagonism to the Jews with Nietzsche's contempt for 'the morality of the weak' together with economic jealousy.[53]

> By fusing all existent resentments and traditions connected with Anti-Semitism, Hitler introduced a spiritual factor. By his racial criterion not only the Jews but also the Christian religion is thoroughly condemned. For the first time, but too late, it dawned upon responsible Christian circles that Israel is not only the cradle of Christianity, but that Jesus and the apostles, Jews, had bequeathed to the Christian tradition precepts irreconcilable with the new ecstatic faith of Nordic Superman. It may now seem unbelievable, but it is nevertheless true, that Christian churches, and especially theologians, were enticed to such an extent that they saw too late that Law, Prophecy, Wisdom, Gospel were rejected in common with the Jews.[54]

Simon's main aim was to place aspects of the Holocaust in relation to key events in the story of Jesus, as theological interpretation should avoid too many abstractions. The concrete reality, as given by history, had to be compared and contrasted with the concrete reality of divine self-disclosure.

In chapter four the Arrest of Jesus is considered. Jesus and other martyrs 'know that by handing over their body their only remaining freedom lies in the obedience which turns the arrest into a voluntary dedication in sacrifice. Thus they achieve a theological interpretation by their intention and imitation of Christ'[55] This, however, was not true of the majority of the victims of the Holocaust. They had no freedom to escape arrest. Equally the prophetic indictment of the sinful people of Israel 'does not apply to any modern community'. The victims' fate is 'not the arrest of Christ re-enacted',[56] but closer to Rachel's mourning for her children and the suffering of the Servant of God.

> These helpless people resemble the Servant of God, weak, poor and less attractive than any man. This tentative identification enables us to reconcile God's providence with the sufferings of Israel. The salvation of Israel cannot look to success in armed conflict, but must be found beyond the great endurance in spiritual victory. Hence the arrest of the many fulfils, as did the self-oblation of Christ, the Servant prophecies: 'despised, rejected, struck with grief, smitten of God, afflicted, taken.'[57]

Theology had to accuse both the criminal authors of the arrest as well as the society which allowed it and also theology's own muffled voice. Such criticism was essential to avoid a mystique of necessary suffering. The search for meaning is not to be found in propositional theology, but in lamentation and prayer.

Chapter Five focused on the Trial of Jesus, although the deportees faced no trial and unlike Jesus they did not confront their enemies face to face. They were on trial against the enemy within. Their sufferings were like the beating of Christ, showing 'up the degree of evil in the whole human race'. God used their agony for the 'humanisation of mankind. The *via dolorosa* of the railway is the *via dolorosa* of God.'[58]

Chapter Six compares the arrival of Jesus at Calvary and of the victims at Auschwitz. Simon saw the cross as the symbol of horror and asked are their limits to forgiveness? Could Jesus' words 'Father, forgive them, for they know not what they do' be applied to the perpetrators? Simon's answer is 'no'.

> I do not myself believe that there can be forgiveness for Auschwitz, and I do not think the words of Christ apply here. Not only the monstrosity, but also the impersonal 'nothingness' of the evil renders this remission immoral and impossible. There is a sin against Man and the Spirit which Christ declared to be unforgivable, and Auschwitz is this sin against Man and the Spirit. It is the supreme act of blasphemy, and the men and the tools who caused it neither desire nor can receive forgiveness of their sin.[59]

The perpetrators are 'their own executioners, and the vindication of the righteous and of the righteous cause occurs on a higher plane than the exposure of their nothingness'. They enter into nothingness. 'In the darkness the shades blend with the blackness until complete indifference engulfs them. "May they never arise again!" '[60]

Just as we cannot know Jesus' inner thoughts as he was crucified, so we cannot know what the victims thought as they died. Without a belief in God, Simon insisted, no meaning can be found in the wanton destruction. 'Nothing can be made of this mass of dying if man is the measure of all things, except the message of an anthropology of despair: the only thing that matters is to be outside, not inside, the cage.'[61] Some must have felt that despair, others died with a burning hatred.

> Others knew, however inarticulately in the many languages assembled there, that they were witnesses to God, that they died for God, his law, the prophetic message, the wisdom from of old. They drowned their resentment in holding on to a transcendental cause. They could commit themselves to Truth with a 'It is finished' which espied the dawn, the beginning of a better age...Even Auschwitz held and holds the secret of redemption. The final credo bursts here all denominational ties and distortions. Man appears before God.[62]

For Simon, the victims' deaths have to be understood in terms of sacrifice. 'God incorporates the terror into the pattern of meaningful sacrifice.'

> This meaning, however, is perceptible only to faith. It is grounded in the belief that God has himself entered human history in the sacrifice of Jesus...We can appropriate this pattern partly for the victims of Auschwitz, not in the sense that they are now gods or that their work aspired to perfection...The claim is that all these, at the point of life-giving, enter into the supreme sacrifice by way of a sharing analogy.[63]

> We come to the dying Christ as we do to the dead of Auschwitz with a restrained *De Profundis* in our hearts: but we know we come to a place of transformation whose heart is an altar with an atoning sacrifice.[64]

In Chapter Eight, Simon turned to the Resurrection. 'The dead at Auschwitz', he wrote, 'died also for the sins of others... Their voices plead the cause of the unity of the whole human race. Not one life given there can cease to speak to the world as an accusation and as a warning.'[65] He also found hope in the creation of the State of Israel and the new relations between Jews and Christians. Further, literature about the Holocaust had renewed awareness that human life is sacred and that all discrimination is to be rejected. Yet he warned of the dangers of fine words and of moral relativism. 'The resurrection from Auschwitz' is still more a demand than a given fact. 'The test of its reality is, as after the resurrection of Christ, the love of the brethren as shown by the deep interchange of mercy... Grace and Love are the *sine qua non* of human existence.'[66] 'Resurrection does not obliterate the marks of tragedy but translates them from the level of passing incident to that of eternal worth. Auschwitz is overcome not by tragic resignation but by victory over impersonal and meaningless torment in personal love.'[67] Simon strongly affirmed that the victims are raised to glory:

> We claim that God reigns throughout the catastrophe...We venture to attribute the glory of the ascended Christ to the gassed millions. We deny that the dead are still dead.[68]

> Only He Who Is, God, creates and sustains such an order of things as fulfils the aspirations of the believer's hopes. The God of Auschwitz is not made in the image of our despair, but rather meets our despair by his total Otherness and Reality. He is not the ground of our rotten and rotting being, but the Ground of what we are not and must yet become. The transcendental 'Nevertheless' is, therefore, always known in our repudiation of sin and unreality, which is the first step to faith. To say 'No' to Auschwitz is already to say 'Yes' to our ascent in faith, hope and love.[69]

Simon returned to this subject in his book *Atonement. From Holocaust to Paradise*, published in 1987.[70] It begins with a moving *cri de coeur*.

> I did not die at Auschwitz, but I have shared the burden of the Holocaust. My father was murdered there in 1943. My brother had already been killed earlier in Stalin's terror. But these disasters are not confined to one family. On the contrary, an uncountable throng of innocent victims pleads for remembrance. It is as if all the graves and pits of concentration camps and Gulags open and a universal cry is heard.[71]

Simon warned of the dangers of evading the theological demands of Auschwitz.

> The possibility of spiritual defeat stares us in the face even after the defeat of the enemy and the punishment of some of the criminals... Silence and ignorance must gladden the damned in their hell... Many Jews... cannot believe, they cannot hope and they can hardly love. The bereaved, too, mourn without ceasing and without consolation. Even those less directly involved are tempted to capitulate to the very nihilism which Hitler and his gangs stood for.[72]

Simon argued strongly against the denial of human guilt and against those Christians who set no limit to the possibility of God's mercy.

> The biblical and Christian tradition has never been at a loss to set historical faces to the Satanic usurper of the creator... Cain, Belshazzar, Judas, Nero... According to this Christian faith, this brutish parody of power cannot be eligible for reconciliation, for it is a sham, a nothing, despite its temporary terror. It is condemned and subject to retribution.[73]
>
> Christians seem to be too good-natured to come to terms with the devil, although, as we shall see, the New Testament concentrates on the meaning of the struggle on every level of experience. But the work of Christ as seen by most Christian theologians seems to spell Atonement and reconciliation even behind the worst excesses. Universal restoration and the love of God bring even Judas, i.e. traitors and desperate men, into the fold. Thus, surprisingly, even Karl Barth flirts with Origen's *apokatastasis*... In our century of unprecedented evil such sham solutions repel.[74]

Even more strongly Simon goes on to say, 'Christians can become involved in deadly sin when they wish to extend the Atonement of Christ to the perpetrators of unrepented evil.... All our moral instincts are outraged if the pardon of devils and devilry is envisaged as a Christian virtue.'[75]

Simon did not deny the possibility of genuine repentance and forgiveness. Jesus responded to the thief who repented with a dramatic promise of pardon but 'no acquittal or promise is extended to the guilty who remain unrepentant. The Passion appeals to the freedom of repentance.'[76]

Simon rejected 'subjective' views of the atonement, which hold that Christ's death works an inner change in the person who comes to faith at the foot of the cross, which both convicts people of their sin and assures them of God's forgiveness. 'Objective' views of the atonement affirm that Christ's death made an actual difference to the status of humanity in God's sight. To those who repent and have faith in Christ, God offers pardon. The grim reality of the Holocaust, for Simon, shattered any confidence in human perfectibility. Hope is grounded solely on the action of God, not on human change.

Although Simon does not refer to Anthony Phillips, his book *Atonement: From Holocaust to Paradise* appeared two years after Philips wrote an article in the *Times*, which was headed 'Why the Jews must forgive.' Canon Dr Anthony Philips was at that time Chaplain of St John's College, Oxford and Consultant to the Archbishops on Jewish affairs. In 1985, fifty years after the end of the Second World War, President Reagan planned a visit to Germany which was to include a visit to the cemetry at Bitburg where both members of the SS and some of their Jewish victims had been buried. Rabbi Albert Friedlander had written an article protesting that this would blur the distinction between victim and victimizer. Philips acknowledged this, but suggested that there could be no lasting peace until the Jews were able to forgive their persecutors.

> A theology unwilling to come to terms with the oppressors, however heinous their crimes, imprisons itself its own past, jeopardising the very future it would ensure. Without forgiveness there can be no healing within the community, no wholeness...Failure to forgive is not a neutral act: it adds to the sum total of evil in the world and dehumanises the victims in a way the oppressors could never on their own achieve.[77]

Several Jewish writers made clear that in Jewish thinking no one could forgive on behalf of the victims, who were dead. They insisted that forgiveness, both human and divine, requires evidence of repentance. It was not obvious that the perpetrators had repented.

This is the crucial difference between Phillips and Simon. Phillips spoke for those Christians who believe the initiative for reconciliation may have to lie with the one who has been injured. Phillips quoted from an Editorial in *Common Ground*, which said that 'Bitter, unfair, unreasonable though it may seem to be, the healed relationship can only come through the activity of the sufferer. This is a point of anguish – something which can scarcely be said though it is necessary to say it.'[78] Such an approach reflects the Christian belief that 'Christ died for us whilst we were yet sinners' (Romans 5.8), as well as the teaching of Jesus in the parables of the Lost Sheep and the Prodigal Son. It is as a person knows that they are still loved by one whom they have hurt that they become aware of the enormity of their actions. Further if such is the quality of God's love, revealed in Jesus Christ, it follows that God goes on loving the sinner for all eternity in the hope that he or she will turn to the mercy of God. This approach also sees the efficacy of the cross primarily in changing people's self-understanding rather than as a sacrificial offering – a 'subjective' rather than an 'objective' view of the atonement.

Simon, as we have seen, insisted that the perpetrators of the Holocaust are beyond the hope of forgiveness. He complained that many contemporary theologians ignored the power of evil and failed to recognize that wicked men show no remorse for their deeds and do not respond to love. The only ground for hope, according to Simon, is not in the possibility of human improvement, but in the saving action of God.

For Simon that action is focused in the atoning death of Christ on the cross. He recognized God's presence in the history of the Jewish people and was very aware of Christian responsibility for Jewish suffering, but he writes self-consciously as a Christian theologian, who 'if he can show the pattern of Christ's sacrifice, which summarizes all agonies, as the reality behind Auschwitz fulfils his obligation to the Here and Now.'[79] The horrors of Auschwitz are a challenge to Christian belief in God. If God's ways are to be justified and faith in the goodness of God is to be upheld, then the Christian will reflect on these atrocities in relation to the death and resurrection of Jesus. Yet, as Rabbi Dr Albert Friedlander has written, 'When it (Christianity) presses Judaism into its own construct, denying Judaism integrity and identity, and when it utilises and misuses Auschwitz in a celebration of Christian triumphalism and supersessionism, we take issue with Christianity.'[80]

I do not think Simon is guilty of triumphalism, and it is unreasonable to expect a Christian theologian to try to interpret these terrible events other than in the categories of Christian thought. Christians and Jews still have to struggle to understand their different approaches to redemptive suffering, to forgiveness and to the nature of evil. Today, however, the differences are often as much within each religion as between them. Traditionally, Christian theology with its teaching on original sin has taken a more pessimistic view of human nature than Judaism. Contemporary Christian thought now seems the more optimistic. I do not myself share Simon's 'objective' theory of the atonement and unlike Simon, I hope that no one, not even the greatest sinner, is ultimately beyond the reach of God's love. But this hope is not in humanity's powers to change the world for the better, but in the Love of God revealed in Jesus Christ. As I have argued in *Dialogue With a Difference*, I do not think that traditional ways of speaking of God as omnipotent, impassible and omniscient are still viable. Instead, I find it more helpful to speak of God as suffering Love and to think that the freedom of the world is greater than we have usually perceived. God entrusts to humanity the future of our world. But Simon is right to warn us to take seriously the reality of human evil.[81]

Like Simon, Alan Ecclestone in his *The Night Sky of the Lord* is trenchant in his criticism of the facile theology that blinded the church to the viciousness of the Nazis:

> Auschwitz is perhaps for the churches in Europe their last chance to learn to pray responsibility for mankind. Its very occurrence reveals the extent of the poverty and blindness of their spiritual life hitherto. The gas ovens that burned up human bodies could be, under God, redemptive did they also burn up the fantasies and false dreams of the world we have known.[82]

Ecclestone wrote as much as a parish priest as a theologian. His book is a personal reflection and he was made particularly aware of Jewish suffering when a Jewish refugee lodged with his family. Ecclestone admitted that he did not have first hand experience of much of what he wrote, having been shielded from the terrible evils of the world. Even so, 'the suffering and horrors that others have known and still face are part of the world in which I live...We cannot sleep off the anguish of mankind.'[83] Further, the Jewish question, he wrote, should be of personal concern to Christians, partly because Christians have been too ignorant of Judaism and because of the monstrous character of the Holocaust which threatened the annulment of all things human. Ecclestone was also very aware of the threat of nuclear destruction that hung over the world as he wrote.

Much of the book deals with the dangers of Anti-Semitism and the need for a new appreciation of Judaism and of the Jewishness of Jesus. Its distinctive feature is its emphasis on prayer as the essential means by which people can see through the false values of the world. Quoting Rabbi Hugo Gryn's words that, 'Auschwitz is about Man and his idols', Ecclestone wrote:

> It is about abominable things set up in the place of God. This brilliant powerful, clever, sophisticated world of ours stands so nearly in the grasp of inconceivable Evil and time is so short that no other talk can compare in urgency with this. In a quite special sense the ancient Biblical choice of life against death is ours today. We make the choice only by learning to pray, by turning to God.[84]

He pleaded for a pattern of prayer that faced the grim reality of the world instead of a Christianity that was often a spiritual affair with little to do with the real world. 'Religion has actually insulated Christians from any possible sense of pain arising from what has happened.'[85] Ecclestone suggested that Christians could learn from Jews how to pray in a post-Auschwitz world – not by imitating Jewish prayers, but by looking at human life in the presence of God. A changed style of praying required a new vision of the involvement of Christianity with the history of humankind and a new readiness to use poetry, drama, dance and music. Ecclestone wanted prayer for the coming of God's kingdom to be more central in the Christian liturgy. The Churches were largely silent at the time of the Holocaust because their life of prayer did not concentrate on the real world. Christians needed to learn from Jews and mission to Jews hindered this. Christians and Jews 'both have a necessary witness to make to the Kingdom of God in the world. One day what we now regard as the separate vocations of the Synagogue and the Church will cease.'[86] Jesus himself preached about the coming of the Kingdom, although after his resurrection the Church's preaching centred instead on the person and work of Jesus.[87]

Despite these hints, Ecclestone skirted round this question and avoided discussions of Christology, such as those raised by *The Myth of God Incarnate*.[88] His point was that, cut adrift from its Jewish foundation, the Church turned away from hopes of God's kingdom on earth. Instead, 'men's attention was turned towards a Heavenly Kingdom, towards a theology of Heaven, hell and purgatory, to notions of immortality and a life after death. The Church, like an Ark of God, preserved the souls of those appointed to life till the times of their trials should cease.'[89] When Christianity became the official religion of the Roman Empire, the gap between the Christian faith and a prophetic hope for the Kingdom became even greater. By idealizing the Kingdom, the Church largely abandoned the life of the world to human ambition. Admitting that Christians on the whole had not yet recognized their share of responsibility for the sufferings of the Jewish people, Ecclestone concluded his chapter on the Kingdom of God by saying that

> What Christians must set about doing because of the Holocaust is an immediate matter. We cannot afford to grow careless to what it revealed of ourselves. We cannot neglect the reminder that the earth is the Lord's and that our real business is to prepare for His coming. Only so far as the Kingdom of God is made central to all Christian thinking and praying may we hope to be faithful servants.[90]

After a sensitive chapter on 'Israel and the Nations' and on the changes in Jewish-Christian relations, Ecclestone returned in the final chapter to his urgent concern that the Church should grapple with the realities of life. The Holocaust, he wrote, happened 'because men and women failed utterly to understand the situation in which they lived'.[91] Ecclestone took Buber's metaphor of 'the eclipse of God' to characterize the present situation. God was eclipsed by the fearful folly of professed disciples who wasted time and energy in sectarian battles, thereby abandoning great areas of human life to other agents. The moral and spiritual impoverishment allowed crude substitute religions such as Nazism to fill the vacuum. By rejecting its Hebrew heritage a fatal flaw developed in the culture which Christianity had nourished. When that civilisation broke away from its Christian roots, it rejected the Bible's fundamental teaching about human relations. The sanctity of life was abandoned and human life used for social experiment and the cruel fantasies of dictators.'[92] The need, as Bonhoeffer saw, was for Christians to regain a sense of 'worldiness' and by sharing in the world's suffering to teach that the whole of life has to be redeemed by God.

CONCLUSION

For Ecclestone, the Jewish question was 'supremely *the* religious question'.[93] The Kingdom of God, the question of prayer, the differences that historically divided Jews and Christians and the concept of man that has been influential in both cultures were, he claimed, of supreme importance for the future of mankind. 'Are we convinced', he asked, 'that radical change in Christian thinking, behaviour, teaching, church-life and mission will be needed if Christianity is to do more than repeat the sad spectacle of the churches of Europe looking helplessly, tongue-tied, on the triumph of Evil spelled out in the murder of the Jews?'[94]

Simon and all the writers whom we have considered likewise saw the central importance of Auschwitz and Jewish-Christian relations. Simon insisted that 'the failure of theology has been and remains at the root of our enslavement' and the Christian thinking needed to grapple with the realities of the world, including its evil, and make the Kingdom central to its concerns, which it could only do as it recovered its Jewish roots.[95]

Writing after the tragic events of 1999 in Kosovo, aware of the genocidal acts and ethnic cleansing in other parts of the world and the poverty and starvation of millions of human beings in the world today and conscious of the priorities of the churches and the indifference of the majority of the population in Western Europe, it is not easy to be optimistic. Slowly dialogue between Christians and Jews and members of all the great faiths is growing and there is a greater commitment to bringing a spiritual and moral dimension to the critical issues facing humanity. Yet only a minority of any faith are involved in this, just as a real concern to purge anti-Semitism and to build a new relationship between Jews and Christians is only a minority interest in the Church. Even after the Holocaust, Church life centres around personal and family occasions and is on the margin of economic and political life. Only as the evil symbolized by Auschwitz is confronted and theology regains the Hebrew concern to discover God's will in every day life will prayer and work for the coming of God's kingdom become central to the life of the Church.

NOTES

1   In this paper, the word 'church' usually refers to the Church of England.
2   Alan Ecclestone, *The Night Sky of the Lord* (London: Darton, Longman and Todd, 1980), p.10.
3   'Jews, Christians and Muslims' in *The Truth Shall Make You Free. The Lambeth Conference 1988*, Anglican Consultative Council. Appendix p.299.
4   *ibid.*, p.300.
5   *ibid.*, p.303.
6   *ibid.*, p.305.
7   *ibid.*, p.300.
8   Quoted in my *Children of One God: A History of the Council of Christians and Jews* (London: Vallentine Mitchell, 1991), p.11.
9   *ibid.*, p.23.
10   *ibid.*, pp.33–41.
11   Issued from Lambeth Palace on 18 March 1964.
12   Graham James, 'Tilling the Ground of Dialogue: Reviewing a Fertile Period', in *Christian-Jewish Dialogue: a Reader*, ed. Helen Fry (Exeter: University of Exeter Press, 1996), pp.277–283.
13   *Children of One God, op.cit.*, p.131.
14   The second consultation was held at Shallowford House near Stafford in April 1987.
15   James Parkes, *The Conflict of Church and Synagogue* (London: The Socino Press, 1934).
16   Robert A Everett, *Christianity Without Anti-Semitism* (Oxford: Pergamon Press, 1993), p.191.
17   For the sake of consistency I keep the spelling anti-Semitism, although Parkes disliked the hyphen.
18   John Hadham (Parkes's *nome de plume*) *Voyages of Discovery* (London: Victor Gollancz, 1969), p.123.
19   *ibid.*, p.371.
20   *ibid.*, p.373.
21   *ibid.*, p.373.
22   *ibid.*, p.374.
23   *ibid.*, p.375.
24   *ibid.*, p.376.
25   James Parkes, *Anti-Semitism: A Concise World History* (London: Vallentine Mitchell 1963), p.60.

26 'Christendom and the Synagogue', *Frontier*, Vol 2, No 4 (Winter 1959): 272.
27 James Parkes, *A History of the Jewish People* (London: Weidenfeld and Nicolson, 1962).
28 *Voyage of Discoveries, op.cit.*, p.220.
29 See Everett, p.264.
30 'Christendom and the Synagogue' and *Jesus, Paul and the Jews* (London: SCM, 1936).
31 An unpublished review of Paul Winter's *On the Trial of Jesus*, Everett, *Christianity*, p.210.
32 *ibid.*, pp.213–18.
33 See his University sermon at Oxford in 1939 in *Voyages of Discovery*, pp.154–55.
34 James Parkes, *Prelude to Dialogue: Jewish-Christian Relationship*, (London: Vallentine Mitchell 1969), p.208.
35 See his *Good God, passim*.
36 Hugh Montefiore, *On Being A Jewish Christian* (London: Hodder and Stoughton, 1998), p.15; see also pp.99–100.
37 Peter Schneider, *Sweeter Than Honey* (London: SCM Press, 1966), p.113.
38 *ibid.*, p.91.
39 *ibid.*, pp.85–6.
40 *ibid.*, p.87.
41 Heinrich Graetz, *The History of the Jews*, ed. and tr. Bella Loewy, 5 vols (London: David Nutt, 1891), vol 2, p.155.
42 Joseph Klausner, *Jesus of Nazareth*, ed. and tr. H Danby (London: Allen and Unwin, 1925); Scholem Asch, *The Nazarene*, ed. and tr. Maurice Samuel (London: Routledge, 1939).
43 Schneider, *op.cit.*, p.119.
44 For example, his *The Christian Debate on Israel*, published by The Centre for the Study of Judaism and Jewish Christian Relations, Selly Oak, Birmingham (no date) or *Jerusalem Perspectives*, which he edited with Geoffrey Wigoder, published by the London Rainbow Group, 1976.
45 See my *Time to Meet* (London: SCM Press, 1990), pp.24–25.
46 Schneider, *op.cit.*, pp.37–8.
47 See my *Children of One God*, pp.52–3.
48 Ulrich Simon, *A Theology of Auschwitz* (London: SPCK, 1978; first published London: Victor Gollancz, 1967).
49 *ibid.*, p.38.
50 *ibid.*, p.11.
51 *ibid.*, p.27.
52 *ibid.*, p.30.
53 *ibid.*, p.31.
54 *ibid.*, pp.36–37.
55 *ibid.*, p.42.
56 *ibid.*, p.43.
57 *ibid.*, p.44.
58 *ibid.*, p.55.
59 *ibid.*, p.71.
60 *ibid.*, p.75.
61 *ibid.*, p.82.
62 *ibid.*, p.83.
63 *ibid.*, p.84.
64 *ibid.*, p.89.
65 *ibid.*, p.91.
66 *ibid.*, p.101.
67 *ibid.*,
68 *ibid.*, p.105.
69 *ibid.*, p.107.
70 Ulrich Simon, *Atonement: From Holocaust to Paradise* (Cambridge: James Clarke & Co., 1987).
71 *ibid.*, p.1.

72   *ibid.*, pp.2–3.
73   *ibid.*, p.19.
74   *ibid.*, p.41.
75   *ibid.*, p.49.
76   *ibid.*, p.92.
77   Anthony Phillips, *The Times*, 8 June 1985. Albert Friedlander's article appeared on 4 May 1985. I give a fuller account of the discussion in *Time to Meet*, pp.106–113.
78   Anthony Philips, 'Forgiveness Reconsidered', *Christian–Jewish Relations*, Vol 19, No 1, p.17, quoting from *Common Ground* (CCJ, London), 22/3 (1968): 4.
79   See note 17.
80   Albert Friedlander, *Against the Fall of Night*, 1984 Waley Cohen Lecture, CCJ, p.5.
81   See Braybrooke, 'The Power of Suffering Love' in *Dialogue With a Difference*, eds. Tony Bayfield and Marcus Braybrooke (London: SCM Press, 1992). I am much influenced by Jewish thinkers such as Arthur A Cohen and Hans Jonas.
82   Alan Ecclestone, *The Night Sky of the Lord* (London: Darton, Longman and Todd, 1980), p.134.
83   *ibid.*, p.1.
84   *ibid.*, p.133.
85   *ibid.*, p.138.
86   *ibid.*, p.153.
87   *ibid.*, pp.159 ff.
88   See *The Myth of God Incarnate*, ed. John Hick (London: SCM Press, 1977). See also *Time to Meet*, ch. 5.
89   *The Night Sky of the Lord*, p.165.
90   *ibid.*, p.167.
91   *ibid.*, p.209.
92   *ibid.*, p.221.
93   *ibid.*, p.210.
94   *ibid.*, p.210.
95   *ibid.*, p.138.

THE UNITED CHURCH OF CANADA AND
THE STATE OF ISRAEL:
THE IMPACT OF THE HOLOCAUST

Haim Genizi

URING THE Holocaust, the United Church of Canada, the largest Protestant
denomination in that country, did not speak in one voice: there were harsh
antisemitic and pro-Nazi expressions on the one hand, and protests against anti-
Jewish persecution and support for the admission of Jewish refugees into Canada on the
other. While individuals stood out as exceptions, the institutional United Church (UC)
was part of the general silence in Canada. Statements by official UC members and courts
were rare and vague. United Church members who sympathized with the suffering of the
Jews during the Holocaust and felt guilty for their own silence supported the establishment of the State of Israel. They realized that the only guard against a repeat of mass
destruction was a strong Israeli nation with secure borders. A strong opposition rose in
the United Church against this uncritical support of Israel. Led by Ernest M. Howse, a
former Moderator, and A.C. Forrest, editor of the *United Church Observer*, this group
maintained that an attempt to meet one refugee problem has created another similar
injustice. The result of the establishment of the State of Israel was the creation of
injustice to Arab refugees. The arguments of this group prevailed, and from 1956 the
United Church adopted a constant pro-Arab policy. The aim of this article is to show
how the shadow of the Holocaust hovered over the debate regarding the attitude of the
United Church towards the State of Israel.

The United Church of Canada, formed on 10 June 1925, was the first organization of
its kind. Political, economic and evangelical considerations led to the union of the
Presbyterian, the Methodist and the Congregational Churches of Canada. A strong
liberal point of view and an emphasis on social gospel were characteristic of the UC,
which became the largest Protestant denomination in Canada. But unlike other denominations, the UC did not have a united voice: its members and clergy ranged from the left,
with its belief in social justice, to the right, whose position was fundamentalist and highly
traditional.[1]

The attitude of the United Church to the Zionist idea and to the establishment of the
State of Israel was partly based on Christian theology. The destruction of the Second
Temple in 70 AD and the subsequent Jewish exile was interpreted in the New Testament as a divine punishment for the crucifixion of Jesus and the refusal to accept his
redemption. Christians believed that they had inherited the legacy of Jewish people,
becoming the New Israel. The Jews lost not only their identity as Israel, but also their
divine right to Palestine, which the Christians gained, calling it the Holy Land. Even
after centuries of Muslim occupation of Palestine, Christians never gave up their claim to
the country. This theological perception did not leave room for the new phenomenon of
a Jewish claim to a sovereign state in Palestine, and for the right of the Jewish people to

play a role in the world history as a nation. The appearance of the dynamic Zionist movement, with its claim for an independent state in Palestine, confronted the churches with a theological challenge.

The nationalistic character of the Zionist movement also seemed to contradict the universalism preached by the Prophets and by Jesus. The resurgence of Jewish nationalism was viewed as a repetition of the same fatal error that had led to the Jewish rejection of Jesus. 'His own people, the Jews, want to set up again a narrow Jewish political nationalism, against which He protested at the cost of His life', wrote A.E. Prince, a historian at the University of Toronto, in the *United Church Observer* (*UCO*), the official journal of the UC.[2]

Liberal members of the United Church who believed in internationalism – a popular ideology after World War Two – rejected the 'narrow' nationalism of the Zionists. They regarded Zionism as divisive, and they opposed the Jewish State because it was created at the expense of the Palestinians. 'They desire to swamp or expel the existing inhabitants', maintained an article in the *UCO* in 1945.[3] Prince argued that the Zionist movement was a 'putting back of the clock many centuries to the earlier more primitive concept of a religious nationalism, based on the narrow "racism" of a "Chosen People"'. Zionism caused 'ill-will', and was a 'tragic obstacle to closer cooperation' between the three religions. 'If the Jews would only relinquish their political ambitions to establish a separate state in Palestine, then the New Year of 1946 would indeed be an *Annus Mirabilis*', for the Jews, the Arabs, for England and for the whole world. Prince called upon the Jews to give up their two millennia of prayer and dreams on behalf of the peace of the world.[4]

With the growing tension between Eastern and Western powers after the war an editorial in the *UCO* of December 1947 asked Zionists to give up their demand for an independent state in order to save humanity from the danger of a world war.[5] A.J. Wilson, editor-in-chief of the *Observer*, expressed his opposition to the Jewish State a month before its establishment: 'At a time when small nations are being absorbed into large national units, it seems contrary to historic processes that a new sovereign state should be set up for the Jews in Palestine.' The editor complimented the Jews for doing 'a phenomenal job in Palestine, building up the waste places, and making the desert blossom as the rose'. But why did they need a state?

> If they would be satisfied to live and work, and to enjoy the prosperity they have wrested from the soil, without fanatically insisting on the status of a sovereign state, all would be well. For the sake of the peace of the world, the Jews should renounce their claims for an immediate sovereign state. Such a renunciation would do more than any other single act, to restore confidence in an essential goodness of human nature.[6]

Liberal church circles enthusiastically supported the process of decolonization and the national liberation movements in Asia and Africa, including that of the Palestinians. Yet the Jews were asked 'for the sake of the peace of the world' to renounce their demand for a sovereign state, because it was 'contrary to historic processes'. This kind of inconsistency was the result of traditional theological prejudices.

Yet during the Nazi era, there were certain UC ministers who did support the idea of a Jewish State in the light of the persecution of the Jews, the refugee problem, and growing antisemitism in Canada. Those members of the United Church who sympathized with the victims of the Nazi terror in the 1930s and called for the admission of a certain number of Jewish refugees to Canada, were the ones who supported the Zionist desire to open the gates of Palestine to large-scale migration of European Jews.[7]

There were exceptions, such as Claris E. Silcox (1888–1961). A renowned clergyman and journalist, Silcox was one of the most outspoken supporters of the cause of Jewish refugees during the Nazi era. After World War II, however, he became a strong anti-Zionist. He insisted that the Zionist claim to Palestine had no foundation historically, legally or practically. The Zionists, by their 'most extreme positions' were 'creating a new focal centre of antisemitism in the Middle East, and alienating a vast body of sympathy with Jewry built up during the Hitlerian persecution on the part of non-Jews'. Silcox remained vehemently opposed to the State of Israel,[8] believing its establishment would increase antisemitism and destroy the friendship of Christians who had sympathized with Jews during the Holocaust. He added sarcastically: 'Let it not be said tomorrow that the Jews seem to have a positive genius for making enemies'![9]

When reports of the mass murder and cruelty of the Nazis became known after the war, sympathy among members of the UC for a haven for the persecuted Jews in their own homeland increased. 'The horror of our people expressed itself in the support of the establishment of Israel. The only guard against a repeat of such mass destruction was a strong Israeli nation with secure borders,' recalled A.B.B. Moore, a former Secretary of the United Church General Council.[10] Moore's recollection probably reflected the private feelings of some of his colleagues, and should not necessarily be regarded as an expression of the views of the UC; no official resolution was adopted and the articles and editorials on the subject in the *United Church Observer* were rare, and not sympathetic.

With the establishment of the State of Israel in May 1948, an authoritative statement from the United Church General Council was expected. However, the year-old Committee on the Church and International Affairs (CCIA), which was responsible for the formulation of foreign affairs policy, was unable to produce an adequate policy recommendation. A neutral position was therefore adopted, selecting the official statements of Jewish, Arab and British leaders without any commentary.[11]

The noncommittal approach soon changed. The CCIA's report of 1954 pointed out that the foundation of the State of Israel was supported by Christians who sympathized with Jewish suffering during the Holocaust. Thus 'an attempt to meet one refugee problem has created another of similar injustice'. The result of Israel's establishment was the creation of one million refugees. The report criticized Israel's use of force, its retaliatory massacres, its expansionism, and its refusal to comply with UN resolutions, including repatriation of Arab refugees and the internationalization of Jerusalem. The existence of Israel was considered to be 'an unalterable fact of history, and a new, real political entity'. Therefore, the report called upon the Arabs to accept the existence of Israel 'and learn to live with her as a neighbour'. Israel should participate in the compensation of those Palestinians that could not return to their homes. As for Jerusalem, since its internationalization was impossible, the United Church would be satisfied with UN supervision and protection of the holy sites. The report of 1954, which was approved by the General Council, was generally an effort at a balanced position.[12]

The transformation of the United Church from a relatively even-handed to a pro-Arab point of view of the Israeli–Palestinian conflict took place in 1956, partly due to Ernest Marshall Howse. During the Nazi era Howse had worked for the entrance of Jewish refugees to Canada and strongly condemned antisemitism. In the mid 1950s, however, he switched his support from the Jews to the Arabs. He became the champion of Palestinians in Canada. A former Moderator and an influential member of the CCIA, he was in a position to shape the course of the United Church Middle East policy, and between 1956 and 1960, Howse played a major role in the formulation of the United Church official policy, changing the balance in favour of the Arab cause. The report on the Middle East, which appeared in the UC *Record of Proceedings of the 17th General Council, 1956*, stated that since the Israeli side was much more publicized, the United Church would put more emphasis on the Arab cause. Indeed, the pro-Arab point of view dominated the report and reveals that Howse was its author. The Western countries were blamed for sacrificing the interests of Arab refugees 'for partisan advantage in domestic policies'. In spite of Western compassion for the survivors of the Holocaust, no country was ready to provide a haven for them. To soothe their conscience, the Western countries sent the Jewish refugees to Palestine, causing the Arab refugee problem. 'The Western world therefore has an inescapable share of responsibility for the Arab refugees, the Semites, who have become the ultimate victims of antisemitism.' Israel was accused of expansionism and being responsible for the war of 1948.[13]

Thus the United Church adopted a position that delegitimized Israel's right to exist, on the grounds that the establishment of the State was based on moral injustice to the Palestinians. Furthermore, its establishment had no historical, religious or national justification but was solely the outcome of Christians' guilt because of their silence during the Holocaust. These arguments appeared time and again in discussions relating to the Middle East crisis.

Another person that had an important role in the formulation of the pro-Arab policy of the United Church was A.C. Forrest (1916–1978), who used his position as the editor of the influential *United Church Observer* to propagate his pro-Arab and anti-Israel ideas. Particularly after the Six Day War of 1967, Forrest became the champion of the Palestinian cause and a critic of the Israeli approach to the refugee issue. From the fall of 1967 onwards, the *Observer* was preoccupied with the Middle East problem. Almost every issue carried articles and editorials on the subject. The October 1967 issue was entirely devoted to the Palestinian refugee cause, the first time a special issue had been devoted to a foreign country.[14] The *Observer*'s coverage of the Arab–Israeli conflict was almost without exception unsympathetic to Israel and to the Zionist movement. Forrest became obsessed with the Arab refugee problem.[15] Reuben Slonim, a journalist and a friend of Forrest, admitted that the *Observer* lost its sense of proportion on the Arab–Israeli conflict: 'If a reader since 1967 were to obtain his information on the Middle East from the *Observer* as his only source, the picture would be distorted beyond recognition.'[16] Forrest soon became the centre of a heated quarrel between the Canadian Jewish community: the Jewish community was agitated by the *Observer*'s constant criticisms of Israel and Zionism, regarding them as antisemitic, and were particularly disturbed by the fact that neither the United Church courts nor any UC leader confronted Forrest and his accusations.

Forrest maintained that 'Jews and Zionists should not be confused'. He blamed Canadian Jewry for branding as antisemitic anyone who criticized Israel's policies.[17] The contention that anti-Zionism was not antisemitism, and that no one was entitled to criticize Israel's policy without being accused of antisemitism, was supported by the majority of members of the United Church. Ernest M. Howse wrote in his support:

> It is ironical that Forrest might have criticized any other country on earth, including his own, without arousing the torrent of abuse with which he was deluged as soon as he tried to tell the facts as he had seen them in Palestine.
> ...He could have criticized Great Britain, and not been slandered as anti-British. He could have criticized the United States, and not been suspected of nurturing an uncontrollable hatred of Yankees. But one thing he could not do. He could not criticize Israel. After that the deluge.[18]

Angus J. MacQueen, a former Moderator and chair of the Editorial Advisory Board of the *Observer*, insisted that anti-Zionism was not a cover for antisemitism. He sympathized with Forrest, who could not understand why the Jews reacted more heatedly than the Scots or the English when their country was criticized.[19] The issue was so important that the General Council of the UC found it necessary to justify the *Observer*'s criticism of Israel after the Six Day War. At the 23rd General Council in 1968, a resolution was adopted that read: 'We deplore suggestions that those who criticize Israel's policies are necessarily antisemitic. . . . The policies of Arab and Israeli governments are always open to the judgment of public opinion.'[20]

There were occasions when people, including Forrest, referred to the Jews or to Israel as 'arrogant Zionists'. Canadian Zionists resented this, as Rabbi Gunther Plaut, a leader of the Toronto Jewry, clearly expressed in an editorial in the *Canadian Jewish News*, the organ of the Canadian Jewish Congress:

> . . . All too frequently anti-Zionism (as distinguished from ordinary criticism of Israel's policies) has become the cover for antisemitism, and the *Observer*'s tendency to depict Zionism as a historical evil has strengthened the heritage of latent and overt antisemitism in many readers. Surely, given the bitter facts of history, any material, which evokes such sentiments, ought to be firmly out of bounds in a Christian publication.[21]

Not only Jews but some Christians, among them devoted United Church ministers, saw in anti-Zionism 'a convenient vehicle to develop an antisemitic theme', as Roland de Corneille, an Anglican priest, stated.[22] Edward H. Flannery, a prominent Catholic historian and leader in the reconciliation of Christians and Jews, argued that Christian uneasiness to the restoration of Jews to Palestine and Jerusalem, was the basis for a Christian anti-Zionism and the cover for various 'reasons' supplied for disfavouring the State of Israel. He maintained that the similar reaction of Christendom to the Holocaust and to the emergence of the State of Israel was symptomatic of 'determinative unconscious forces, specifically, of an unrecognized antipathy [to] the Jewish people'. The Holocaust and the State of Israel were at opposite poles in the existence of Jews. 'One is its nadir; the other, its zenith; Israel prostrate and Israel triumphant.' Yet even though the incentives are opposite, the response to them is identical: apathy, and even hostility.[23]

Gregory Baum, a Catholic theologian, reacted to Howse's and Forrest's arguments in a sermon at the Eglinton United Church, Toronto in 1972, when he said that he expected a Christian writer or editor 'to wrestle with his own ideological past' of centuries of Christian antisemitism before approaching the political situation in Israel. If Forrest insisted that he was 'only' anti-Zionist and not anti-Jewish, 'he will eventually reveal the ideological origin of his attitude'. Baum maintained that because of the ideological past of Christian anti-Jewish teaching it was impossible to consider Israel as being the same as any other society. Christian preaching was not hostile and prejudiced against Muslims or British, but against Jews. 'If, therefore, the Christian wants to express his own critical views of Israeli policies, he can do so with honor only if he reveals that he is also wrestling with his own ideological past.'[24] David Demson, professor of theology at Emmanuel College, a UC institution in Toronto, challenged Forrest's position on the grounds that as a clergymen and as the editor of a church magazine he should take into consideration the history of Christendom, which was not anti-British or anti-American, but which was anti-Jewish. Since after Auschwitz it was politically incorrect to be an antisemite, many preferred to use the cover of anti-Zionism. Demson warned Christian writers to be 'careful, then, to avoid any continuance of an anti-Jewish attitude'.[25]

Alan T. Davies, a United Church minister and professor of religion at Victoria College, the University of Toronto, belonged, along with Demson, to a minority of young intellectuals in the UC who supported Israel and who criticized the pro-Arab stance of the official UC courts. In a thoughtful essay in the *Christian Century* in 1970, titled 'Anti-Zionism, Anti-Semitism and the Christian Mind', Davies investigated the relationship between the two 'isms'. He dismissed the argument, frequently used by Forrest, that since there were anti-Zionist Jews, opposition to Zionism could not be antisemitic. 'Anti-Zionism sooner or later reveals a distressing tendency to shade into antisemitism', maintained Davies. The fact that there were some Jews critical to Zionism gave no legitimization for Christians to oppose Zionism. Davies analysed the feelings of the Jews regarding the Jewish State, particularly after the Holocaust. 'Israel stands in juxtaposition to Auschwitz as, to imply a Christian analogy, the Resurrection stands in juxtaposition to the Crucifixion.' Jews considered the Zionist idea as the affirmation of Jewish existence, interwoven with strong attachment to Jewish history and Palestine. 'Given this reality, it is exceedingly difficult on the emotional level for the victims of the Holocaust to distinguish anti-Zionism from the antisemitism, however clear the distinction may seem to Gentiles'. He emphasized the difficulty for Christians to comprehend Jewish sensitivity after Auschwitz. Like Demson, Davies also maintained that since after the Holocaust it was inappropriate to appear as an antisemite, anti-Zionism was chosen as a substitute: 'Antisemitic convictions can be transposed without any difficulty into the new language of anti-Zionism.'[26]

Franklin H. Littell, the American Holocaust scholar at Temple University, enthusiastically reacted to Davies' analogy of crucifixion and resurrection to the Holocaust and the establishment of Israel. 'That is as succinct a statement of recent Jewish history as I have seen, and I was most excited when I ran into it because I had been using the symbol of crucifixion and resurrection rather hesitantly myself, when I saw that it hit you the same way, I took courage', wrote Littell to Davies.[27] Not everybody agreed with this analogy. Several United Church ministers stated that the establishment of the State of Israel presented a challenge 'in the area of ethics concerning the right use of power. Is the restored State of Israel to represent a new triumphalism of power among the nations? Or is it not rather to be a servant among the peoples exercising a prophetic and rabbinical function?', asked a member of a United Church theological group.[28]

It seems that United Church leaders refused to accept the argument that Israel deserved special consideration because of the Holocaust. W. Clarke MacDonald, chair of the Committee on the Church and International Affairs and a future Moderator, was 'deeply moved' by the tragedy that had happened to the Jews and 'what we need to do is simply acknowledge that fact, express profound contrition for it and move on.'[29]

In November 1971, Forrest took another step which alienated the Jewish community in Canada. Reacting to criticism that the churches did not do anything during the Holocaust, Forrest editorialized:

> We hear this slander repeatedly, especially from Christian Zionists who emphasize that the Church did so badly by the Jewish people in times of the past it must now throw all its support behind Israel.... Just for the record it should be remembered that in order to stop Hitler, a good many hundreds of thousands of Western soldiers, sailors and airmen died.[30]

The editorial caused a storm of angry protests. Professor H. Weinberg blamed Forrest for repeating 'blatantly antisemitic canard that the Allies fought the war in defense of Jewish interests. This is not only a perversion of the truth, but a grave insult to the Jewish people'.[31] Dolores Nicholls, the wife of a United Church minister, declared that 'the one thing the church did not oppose was the destruction of Jews'. She maintained that the war was to save Britain 'and our own skins'.[32] To be sure, the editorial did not specify that the Allies entered the war in order to save Jews. However, 'the implication was clear: ... All the dead of the war could be laid at the Jewish doorstep', wrote Gunther Plaut, adding: 'The West owned nothing to us.'[33] Even Reuben Slonim, who defended Forrest, admitted that although the editorial was not antisemitic, 'it did, however, display a lack of sensitivity to a tragic era'.[34]

Criticism was not confined to Jews or to known supporters of Israel. Even leading United Church members disagreed with the editor. In a private letter, Angus J. Mac-Queen, former Moderator and Chair of the Editorial Advisory Committee of the *Observer*, expressed in March 1972 his truthful opinion of Forrest's handling of the magazine:

> Al Forrest and I have disagreed on a number of things, one being his November editorial. There are times when I question his judgment, his objectivity, his sensitivity to the feelings of the Jewish community, and his naivete in not realizing that certain articles and emotive words are bound to create a storm among the Jewish people, and forment anti-Jewish prejudice among our own people.[35]

While MacQueen confided his disagreement with Forrest privately, Donald R. Keating, a United Church minister and a community worker in Toronto, did it publicly. In 'An Open Letter' to the heads of the major Protestant denominations Keating protested against the refusal of the church to silence or dismiss Forrest. Why 'nobody is doing anything about him? ... Is he not lighting the candles that stoke the fires that turned to smoke and ashes the bodies of six million Jews in the Holocaust? ... I can no longer stay even on the outside of the same house. I'm resigning today'.[36] Keating's resignation made headlines and church leaders were embarrassed. It contributed to the polarization between the Jewish and the United Church communities, because Keating criticized not only Forrest and his magazine, but also the silence of the church leaders to censure Forrest. However, the impression of the resignation did not last long, because Keating had no influence within the church.[37]

As a gesture of reconciliation, the St. Andrew's College, a United Church institution in Saskatoon, offered an honorary doctorate in philosophy to Emil Fackenheim of the University of Toronto, an internationally renowned Jewish philosopher who had dealt intensively with the meaning of the Holocaust in both Jewish and Christian theology. In honouring Fackenheim, St. Andrew's appreciated his theological and philosophical contribution to Holocaust scholarship. The statement of St. Andrew's College read, among others: 'We Christians live with the mark of Cain on us as we contemplate our guilt through indifference, acquiescence and theological irresponsibility in that anti-Semitism, which manifested itself so incredibly in the murder of six millions. And we confess how quickly we have forgotten Auschwitz.'[38]

Fackenheim consulted Gunther Plaut on whether to accept the degree. 'I strongly urged him to go to Saskatoon, accept and make the kind of strong statement of which he was eminently capable,' recalled Plaut.[39] On Plaut's advice, Fackenheim received the honorary degree and utilized the public relations opportunity, delivering a strong attack on the United Church and the *Observer*. He discussed the deeply seated anti-Jewishness of Christian theology, and pointed out that the church still continued it in practice, under the guise of anti-Zionism. The *Observer* has shown an ever-increasing anti-Jewish bias, and the United Church officials, while seeking refuge behind the editor's freedom of speech have either themselves kept silent, or else used their own freedom of speech only to defend the policies of the editor, or even to attack, often vociferously, those who opposed these policies.[40]

There were mixed reactions, both to the United Church award of honorary doctorate to Fackenheim and to his address. Alan T. Davies was enthusiastic. But not everyone in the United Church was as happy as Davies. W.W. Sedwick maintained that Fackenheim himself was the reason for the growing antisemitism in the United Church. Earl S. Leuteschlager, of Emmanuel College, the University of Toronto, had a similar complaint. When Fackenheim 'threw at us... all the old Jewish accusations against the Christians, I then and there stopped giving support to the Jews. They don't welcome supporters evidently'.[41]

The offer of an honorary doctorate to Fackenheim did not improve relations between the Canadian Jewish community and the United Church. The growing criticism of Forrest's anti-Israeli and anti-Jewish publications, not only from Jewish circles, but from his own church leaders as well, pushed the editor to grave mistakes. The more he was criticized the more adamant he was. His eagerness to publish anti-Zionist material drove him to cross the line between anti-Zionism and antisemitism. The publication of John Nicholls Booth's article in the *Observer* 'How Zionists Manipulate Your News', was a case in point.[42] According to Angus J. MacQueen, Forrest made 'a serious mistake, but it was obviously a reaction by an editor who has got his back up and is determined not to be intimidated or pushed around'.[43] Booth, a pastor of a Unitarian-Universalist congregation in Gainesville, Florida, was known for his antisemitic sermons and articles. They were printed in the right-wing *American Mercury* and in the antisemitic and anti-Black *Cross and the Flag*.[44] 'How Zionists Manipulate Your News' opened with accusation that during her few years of existence, Israel

> has left a trail of global tensions, the longest and blackest record of international censures against any nation. Unable to challenge the truth about their territorial greed, maltreatment of refugees and defiance of UN resolutions, they have tried instead to silence their critics, ... and discredit those who manage to be heard with the red herring cry of anti-semitism.

The article elaborated on the Zionists' efforts to suppress anti-Israel reports through character assassination against distinguished people. The author focused his attack on the Anti Defamation League of B'nai Brith, saying that it 'exercised surveillance of Israel critics' and that its files contained 'dossiers on thousands of North Americans. ... Israeli intelligence, through B'nai Brith ... penetrates every part of our nation.'[45]

The Booth article raised 'temperatures in both communities to fever pitch', recalled Reuben Slonim.[46] The Jews unanimously accused Forrest of antisemitism. For them, the Booth article clearly demonstrated that anti-Zionism and antisemitism belonged to the same family of ideas.[47] Gregory Baum, the Catholic theologian, criticized Forrest for printing a 'plainly antisemitic' article. He denounced the *Observer* for failing to fulfil the vital task of eliminating the centuries-old Christian bias against Jews, particularly in the face of the Holocaust.[48] Leading members of the United Church, such as F.B. Brisbin, of the UC Division of Communication, George Morrison, the Secretary of the General Council, Angus J. MacQueen and A.B.B. Moore, former Moderators, privately criticized Forrest. MacQueen regarded the Booth article 'a serious mistake', and Moore thought that Forrest 'had gone too far in publishing an antisemitic article in the *Observer*.'[49] B. Robert Bater, minister of Eglinton United Church, Toronto, a theologian and a distinguished member of the UC, regretfully pointed out that 'we seem to be at such distance from one another both in thinking and feeling'. Bater was particularly disturbed that Forrest was not able 'to see that after Auschwitz confessed Christians can only take sides against Jews when it is clear that there is human tragedy which will be intensified if they don't act... and even then with terrible agony and heart-searching that everything could align a Christian against Jews again'. He regretted that he did not find such an awareness in Forrest. Bater wondered whether Forrest had not increasingly developed strong anti-Jewish not anti-Zionist or anti-Israel bent.[50]

We can see the connection that theologians, including United Church leaders, made between the Holocaust and the right attitude to the State of Israel. This connection was particularly clear after the Yom Kippur War of October 1973.

In contrast to official hesitations and 'balanced' positions of United and Anglican Church leaders during and after the war,[51] a group of fourteen Catholic and United Church theologians and academians, published on 19 October 1973 in the *Globe and Mail* (Toronto) a 'Statement of Christian Concern About the Middle East'. It rejected the anti-Zionist myth that Zionist imperialism was a Nazi-type racism, which dispossessed the poor Arab population. 'Zionism is not a dirty word', it said. Modern Zionism was born as an answer to Christian antisemitism. Israel 'is a resurrection symbol following the near extinction of the Jewish people' in the Holocaust. Therefore, 'Christians must affirm Israel as the visible and tangible manifestation of both Jewish survival and Jewish security.' Israel could be criticized just like any other nation, but it would be wrong to object to it because of its Jewish foundation. The Statement recognized the plight of Arab refugees, but it rejected the moral force of the churches as an objective body to mediate between the two sides. The signatories of the document concluded that since the Arabs were threatening to drive the Jews into the sea, 'Christians must... stand with Israel... without equivocation'.[52] Emil Fackenheim complimented Alan Davies, who was the author of the 'Statement', saying that it was 'by far the best and most profound that I have ever seen on this subject from any Christian source.... It has been heart-warming and encouraging to countless people beside myself.'[53]

Five days after the publication of the 'Statement', a pro-Arab response appeared in the *Globe and Mail*, produced by L.M. Kenny and signed by thirteen other professors of the Department of Islamic and Near Eastern Studies at the University of Toronto. The 'Statement' of Davies was termed 'a surprising apology for Zionism'. It was 'rife with prejudice, often subtle, but nonetheless virulent anti-Semitic prejudice against the Arabs (for they too are Semites)'. Kenny complained that since the Balfour Declaration Arab rights had constantly been denied. 'Should Christendom not feel some guilt for this denial?' Kenny's letter objected to the accusation that the Arabs were perpetuating a second Auschwitz, since they were not guilty of the first one. 'It is mere obfuscation to claim that Christian opinion is seeking solace in the guilt with regard to the Jews'.[54]

The war of letters in the pages of the *Globe and Mail* led W. Clarke MacDonald, secretary of the UC Committee on the Church and International Affairs to join in, aiming to clarify the official policy of the United Church. The church emphasized its deep sensitivity to the tragedy of Jews and Arabs alike, praying for 'peace and justice'. He blamed the pro-Israel letter, which 'has served to polarize local feeling.... We feel that their statement is not adequate'. MacDonald declared that 'there would be no peace without justice for the Palestinians'. The United Church resolved that 'while guaranteeing the security of Israel, [it] aims to secure justice and self-determination for the Palestinian Arabs'.[55]

Gradually, the United Church abandoned any effort for a balanced position on the Israel–Palestinian conflict. It criticized Israel's retaliatory policy. MacDonald expressed the UC's 'unequivocal opposition to the spirit of revenge on the part of Israel'.[56] Jewish leaders angrily reacted to the moral preaching of church officials. Gunther Plaut stated that because of world silence during the Holocaust, 'Jews will not listen to any kind of Christian moralizing'. Christians had lost their credibility. They could not instruct Jews on how to be moral or how to act in a glorious fashion.[57] Responding to Rabbi Plaut's remark, MacDonald said: 'that must not dissuade us from doing so'.[58]

Indeed, the argument that because of the Holocaust the United Church must stand with Israel 'without equivocation' was rejected, as the various resolutions of the General Council attested. In August 1977 the General Council of the United Church adopted a resolution that the Palestinian people be represented in the Geneva Peace Conference by the Palestinian Liberation Organization (PLO).[59] The insistence of inviting the Palestinians as partners of the Geneva Peace Conference had already appeared in the General Council of 1974. However, the recognition of the PLO as the representative of the Palestinian people was a new development in the United Church Middle East policy. 'The UC is, I understand, the first Western Church to recognize the PLO,' boasted Forrest. Due to Forrest, the United Church was the forerunner of the pro-Arab approach.[60]

After Forrest's death in December 1978, a definite effort was made by both sides, the United Church and the Canadian Jewish community, to improve mutual relations. The *United Church Observer* went through a metamorphosis. Under the editorship of Hugh McCullum (1979–1992) the Middle East almost totally disappeared from the pages of the magazine.

These efforts notwithstanding, the pro-Arab policy of former decades prevailed. With the Israeli invasion of Lebanon in 1982, and with the beginning of the *Intifada*, the Palestinian civilian uprising against the Israeli occupation, in December 1987, Christian attitudes to Israel underwent a meaningful change. Even Gregory Baum, who had supported Israel and had criticized Howse, Forrest and their followers for their attacks on Israel's policy, changed his mind. Since many Jews in Israel and in North America also began to criticize the Israeli government for its suppression of the civilian uprising, 'Christians are now free to speak out', declared Baum.[61]

In 1984 the General Council adopted a resolution of the World Council of Churches, that included the withdrawal of Israel from the occupied territories, the right of all states, including Israel and the Arab states, to live in peace and to have secure boundaries, and the 'implementation of the Palestinians to self-determination, including the right of establishing a sovereign Palestinian state'.[62] Thus, the process of gradual recognition of Palestinian claims was completed. The process had grown from supporting the cause of miserable refugees, through recognition of their right to self-determination, to recognition of their right to a homeland, and now to endorsing their right to a sovereign state.

The critical attitude to Israel of the 1990s was apparent at the Toronto Regional Conference of the United Church, one of the largest UC Conferences. At its Annual Meeting on May 30 1993, the Conference adopted a resolution critical of Israel's 'gross violations of basic human rights' in the West Bank and Gaza. If Israel disregarded the Geneva convention in regard to human rights, the Canadian Government should turn to the UN to send 'protecting power' to defend the Palestinian people in the occupied territories. The Conference stated that there was wide international consensus that Israel's practices constituted a 'major block to peace'. The motion was adopted in spite of warnings from several delegates that it might upset ongoing Christian-Jewish dialogue.[63] This resolution was 'disappointing but not surprising' to the members of the Canada-Israel Committee (CIC). It was 'consistent with the one-sided, unbalanced and excessively judgmental statements made in recent years by the United Church', read a

CIC inter-office memo. It saw in the motion either a naive and superficial attitude, or an effort to discredit Israel's very legitimacy.[64] The Canadian Jewish Congress officially protested to the President of the Toronto Conference, saying that the 'grossly un-balanced resolution contains a shameful denunciation of Israel'. The Congress, was 'shocked and saddened' by the anti-Israel resolution. It warned that such 'unbalanced and hostile attacks' by the United Church would encourage Arab terrorism and might undermine the continuation of inter-faith dialogue.[65] Even fifteen years after Forrest's death, the United Church maintained the unbalanced approach to the Arab-Israeli conflict that it had begun in the mid-1950s.

While still critical to Israel, the United Church progressed in its attitude to Jews and Judaism. In 1997 the General Council considered a study entitled *Bearing Faithful Witness: United Church-Jewish Relations Today*. The Council approved it as a study document to be send to the churches for comments. It aimed to mend fences with Jews. The document proposed 'guidelines for the relationship with Jews and Judaism and for the related interpretation of Scripture within the United Church'. After examin-ing various anti-Jewish passages of the Scriptures, the study concluded that they were 'argumentative and often present a skewed picture of Judaism'. Therefore, it recom-mended to the UC congregations 'to adjust the picture of Judaism that they present with information from the Hebrew Scriptures' and from other contemporary sources. 'It clears away potential use for disrespect.' In the guidelines for the use of Scripture the document indicated that *'We must be ready to revise our understanding of the Palestinian context . . . in which Jesus lived'*.[66]

The study recommended that the church stop trying to convert Jews to Christianity, stop interpreting the Scriptures in a way that would lead to anti-Jewish feelings, and that it departs from the belief that Christianity had replaced Judaism. 'Christianity does not supersede Judaism', declared Bill Phipps, Moderator of the United Church. Phipps, a member of the committee that drafted the document, pointed out that the study did not compromise the Christian faith, but rather it abandoned the effort to criticize other faiths and to cast aspersions on other traditions. He said that the most important aspect of the document was making congregations aware of the fact that anti-Jewish teachings could be found in most worship services. The Canadian Jewish community hailed the report as a major breakthrough in relations between the two communities. 'I think it deserves the highest accolades,' observed Rabbi Reuven Bulka, chair of the Religious and Interreli-gious Affairs Committee of the Canadian Jewish Congress.[67] According to Alan Davies, who had a role in drafting the document, the chances are good and the efforts of the church leaders were sincere and convincing.[68] This new trend of mutual understanding is promising.

Although this article focuses on the impact of the Holocaust on the attitude of the United Church to Israel, this subject was marginal to the main concerns of the church in the 1990s. In that decade the United Church faced serious internal problems. The internal divisions between evangelists (conservatives) and social activists (liberals) were deeper than ever before. The church had to determine what its attitude would be to Native Canadians, whether the Bible should be 'the' fundamental authority for church life, and what approach to take with gays, lesbians, and the same-sex covenant. These controversial debates led to a sharp decline in church membership, church school enrolment and church income. The circulation of the *Observer* drastically declined.[69]

In 1990, John Webster Grant, the historian of the United Church, stated that 'after 65 years of union the United Church seems less *united* than ever before. Our current disagreements have brought to light such a diversity of convictions and such an intensity of emotion that pain, alienation and a measure of schism have been the only possible results'.[70] Thus, the United Church's attitude to the Middle East, particularly in the 1990s, was not high in the church's agenda and should be considered in that light.

To conclude, the subject of the Holocaust was discussed in United Church circles time and again in regard to the church's attitude to the State of Israel. The pro-Israel group maintained that because of Christian silence during the Holocaust, criticism of Israel's policy should be made with caution and respect. The pro-Arab group, on the other hand, argued that Jews had neither historical nor moral right to Palestine, because it was founded on Christian guilt. Therefore, the establishment of the State of Israel was an act of injustice to the Palestinians. What was the role of this debate on the actual policy taken by the United Church towards the Middle East? Which group was more influential on the formulation of official resolutions? To be sure, there was no single cause to the adoption of a resolution on the Israel–Palestinian conflict. Although most of the resolutions of the General Council were pro-Arab, the Council always insisted upon Israel's right to exist. The Israeli clause was added not only for the impression of a balanced statement, but probably due to the Holocaust. N. Bruce McLeod, a former Moderator of the United Church maintained that 'vigorous criticism of Israel is not antisemitism as long as the criticism is grounded in recognition of the country's right to exist within secure borders'.[71] While during the 1960s and 1970s Auschwitz was mentioned many times in the polemic literature of the UC, later, during the 1980s and 1990s, it almost entirely disappeared. Thus, the Holocaust was in the minds and hearts of many United Church members, but this sympathy to the Jews did not find actual expressions towards the State of Israel in the official resolutions adopted by the UC courts, particularly in the last two decades.

NOTES

1 John Webster Grant, *The Canadian Experience of Church Union* (Richmond, VA: John Knox Press, 1967), pp.5–101; J.W. Grant, 'What's Past Is Prologue', in *Voices and Visions: Sixty Five Years of the United Church of Canada*, ed. by Peter G. White, *et. al.* (The United Church Publication House, 1990), pp.125–129.

2 A.E. Prince, 'The Global War: Is Political Zionism a Denial of the Best Judaic Tradition?', *United Church Observer (UCO)*, 15 December 1945: 4.

3 *Ibid.*, pp.4, 25, 28.

4 Prince, 'The Global War', *UCO*, 1 January 1946: 28.

5 Editorial, 'The World Scene', *UCO*, 15 December 1947:8.

6 Editorial, 'Palestine', *UCO*, 1 April 1948: 4.

7 Lorna Francis, 'A Challenge to Christians', *UCO*, 15 March 1944: 11; See also, 'Palestine and Post-War Jewish Problems', *Fellowship* (Monthly Bulletin of the Canadian Conference of Christians and Jews, Toronto), November–December 1944: 5.

8 Claris E. Silcox, 'Address on Palestine and the Balfour Declaration', pp.7–11 (The archives of the United Church at Victoria University, the University of Toronto. Hereinafter cited as, UCA. The files of Claris Silcox, 86, 208, b.6, f.68); See also, Silcox, 'Crisis in the Middle East', *United Church Observer*, 15 February 1956: 5, 24–26.

9 Silcox, 'The Impasse in the Holy Land', *The University of Toronto Quarterly* 16 (January 1947): 132.

10 A.B.B. Moore to the author, 10 May 1995.

11 Henry Langford and J.R. Mutchmor to the Members of the Committee on Church and International Affairs, 1 June 1948 (UCA, the files of the Committee on the Church and International Affairs, 88,088C, box 1, folder 1. Hereinafter cited as CCIA); United Church of Canada (UCC), *Record of Proceedings of the 13th General Council, September, 1948*, pp.138–140.

12 UCC, *Record of Proceedings of the 16th General Council, September 1954*, pp.141–143, 148–149.

13 UCC, *Record of Proceedings of the 17th General Council, September 1956*, pp.141–143. See also, 'The situation in the Middle East Today', CCIA, Minutes, 5 January, 7 April, 17 May 1956 (UCA, CCIA, 88,088C, b.1, f.1).

14 *UCO*, 1 October 1967.

15 Arnold Ages, 'The *United Church Observer* and the State of Israel' (1969), p.2. (13-page MS., Ontario Jewish Archives, Toronto, MG8/S, b. 53, f.161. The archives hereinafter cited as OJA.)

16 Reuben Slonim, *Family Quarrel: The United Church and the Jews* (Toronto: Clarke, Irwin & Co., 1977), pp.52–53.

17 Editorial, 'Egypt-Israel: Two Sides of it', *UCO*, 15 December 1955:6. Forrest, 'What Happened When I Criticized Israel', *UCO*, 1 April 1968: 27–28.

18 E.M. Howse, 'Torrent of Abuse', The *Toronto Star*, 12 January 1972.

19 Angus J. MacQueen to the author, 2 May 1995.

20 UCC, *Record of the Proceedings of the 23rd General Council, 1968*, p.444.

21 Quoted in W. Gunther Plaut, *Unfinished Business: An Autobiography* (Toronto: Lester Orphen Dennys, 1981), p.290.

22 Interview with Roland de Corneille, 20 July 1995. See also, A Roy Eckardt, *Your People, My People: The Meeting of Jews and Christians* (New York: Quadrangle, 1974), pp.102–103.

23 Edward H. Flannery, 'Anti-Zionism and the Christian Psyche', *Journal of Ecumenical Studies*, 6:2 Spring 1969: 174, 178–179, 181.

24 Gregory Baum, 'Salvation is From the Jews: A Story of Prejudice', *The Christian Century*, 89, 19 July 1972: 775–777.

25 David Demson, 'A Reply to Dr. Ernest M. Howse', The *Toronto Star*, 30 January 1972; Interview with Demson, 30 March 1995.

26 Alan T. Davies, 'Anti-Zionism, Anti-Semitism and the Christian Mind', The *Christian Century*, 89, 19 August 1970: 987–989.

27 Franklin H. Littell to Alan Davies, 12 January 1972 (Alan Davies's private collection. I thank Prof. Davies for his kindness in showing me this collection.)

28 United Church of Canada, *Yearbook, 1977*, p.140.

29 Clarke MacDonald to Reuben Slonim, n.d. (UCA, CCIA, 82,250C, b.7, f.9).

30 Editorial, 'For the War Record', *UCO*, November 1971: 10–11.

31 Editorial, 'Was This Anti-Semitic?', *UCO*, March 1972: 11–12.

32 Dolores Nicolls to the editor of the *London Free Press* (Ontario), 8 November 1971; see also the *Canadian Jewish Press*, 18 November 1971.

33 Plaut, *Unfinished Business*, p.288.

34 Slonim, *Family Quarrel*, p.8.

35 A.J. MacQueen to Donald Keating, 22 March 1972 (UCA, the files of A.C. Forrest, 86, 104C, b.20, f.2).

36 Donald Keating, 'An Open Letter' to A.B.B. Moore, Moderator of the United Church, E.W. Scott, Primate of the Anglican Church of Canada, H.C. Hyman, and members of Halton Presbytery, Hamilton Conference, The UCC, 25 November 1971 (UCA, Forrest, 86, 104C, b.19, f.14).

37 Plaut, *Unfinished Business*, p.288.

38 Joy De Marsh, 'Details of the Message Honouring Emil Fackenheim in Saskatoon', *Globe and Mail*, 6 May 1972.

39 Plaut, *Unfinished Business*, p.289.

40 Cited in Slonim, *Family Quarrel*, pp.33–34.

41 Alan T. Davies to the Faculty and Governing Boards, St. Andrew's College, Saskatoon, 12 May 1972 (Davies' private collection.); W.W. Sedwick to the editor of the *Globe and Mail*, 9 May 1972: Earl S. Leuteschlager to Forrest, 4 May 1972 (UCA, Forrest, 86,104C, b.20, f.3).

42 John Nicolls Booth, 'How Zionists Manipulate Your News', *UCO*, March 1972: 24–26.

43 MacQueen to Keating, 22 March 1972.

44 Booth to Forrest, 17 March 1972 (UCA, Forrest, 86,104C, b.23, f.4).

45 Booth, 'How Zionists Manipulate Your News', *UCO*, March 1972: 24–26.

46 Slonim, *Family Quarrel*, p.9.

47 Plaut, *Unfinished Business*, p.290.
48 'Father Gregory Baum Criticized Forrest for the Booth Article', n.d. (UCA, Forrest, 86,104C, b. 20, f.8); Editorial, '*Observer* Controversy: It's United Church's Dilemma', *Canadian Jewish News*, 21 April 1972.
49 F.G. Brisbin to Forrest, Re: '*Observer* article about Zionism', 9 March 1972 (UCA, Forrest, 86,104C, b.23, f.4); MacQueen to Keating, 22 March 1972 (UCA, Forrest, 86,104C. b.20, f.2); A.B.B. Moore to the author, 19 May 1995; George Morrison to the author, 24 June 1995.
50 B. Robert Bater to Forrest, 11 April 1972 (UCA, Forrest, 86,104C, b.20, f.3). See the criticism of Kenneth Bagnell, a former managing editor of the *Observer*, Keneth Bagnell to Alan Davies, 7 January, 23 October 1972 (Davies' private collection).
51 See the statement of E.W. Scott, Primate of the Anglican Church in Canada, and of N. Bruce McLeod, UC Moderator, on 9 October 1973. 'Anglican News Service', For Immediate Release, Toronto, 9 October 1973 (OJA, MG8/S, b.54, f.41).
52 Signatories to the document included Edward A. Synon, President of Pontifical Institute of Medieval Studies, Gregory Baum, St. Michael College, University of Toronto, John M. Kelly, President of St. Michael College, Alan T. Davies, Victoria College, University of Toronto, William O. Fennell, Principal, Emmanuel College, University of Toronto, David Demson, Emmanuel College, and Robert B. Bater, minister, Englinton United Church, Toronto. 'Statement of Christian Concern About the Middle East', The *Globe and Mail*, 19 October 1973.
53 Emil Fackenheim to Alan Davies, 23 October 1973 (Davies' private collection).
54 'Fourteen University of Toronto Professors See Anti-Arab Bias in Pro-Israel Argument', The *Globe and Mail*, 24 October 1973.
55 W. Clarke MacDonald, 'Statement of United Church Official on Mideast', The *Globe and Mail*, 30 October 1973.
56 MacDonald to N. Bruce McLeod and George Morrison, 21 May 1974 (UCA, CCIA, 82,250C, b.7, f.9).
57 Plaut, *Unfinished Business*, pp.291–292. 'Plaut Urges United Church to Phase Out Middle East Role: Jews Will Not Listen to Christian Moralizing', *Canadian Jewish News*, 27 October 1972.
58 MacDonald to McLeod and Morrison, 21 May 1974.
59 UCC, *Record of Proceedings of the 27th General Council, August 1977*, p.617.
60 Editorial, 'Lets Welcome the PLO', *UCO*, August 1975: 9; 'News', *ibid.*, October 1977: 20.
61 Gregory Baum, 'The Churches, Israel and the Palestinians', *Catholic New Times*, 8 January 1989: 8–9.
62 UCC, *Record of Proceedings of the 30th General Council, August 1984*, p.452.
63 Michael McAteer, 'United Church Conference Seeks Aid for Palestinians', The *Toronto Star*, 31 May 1993.
64 Confidential Memo from Research and Communication Departments to CIC Ad Hoc Media Committee, 31 May 1993, re: United Church Motion on Human Rights in the Territories (Canadian Jewish Congress, The National Archives, Montreal (CJCNA), DA5, b. 31, f. 73).
65 Irving Abella to James Ritchie, 4 June 1993 (CJCNA, DA5, b. 31, f. 7b).
66 *Bearing Faithful Witness: United Church-Jewish Relations Today*; for discussion, prepared by The National Task Group on United Church-Jewish Relations (February, 1997), pp.24, 26. Emphasis in the original.
67 Joan Breckenridge, 'United Church Reaches Out to Jews', The *Globe and Mail*, 23 May 1998.
68 Interview with Alan Davies, 30 July 1999.
69 UCC, *Yearbook 1991*, p.37; *Record of Proceedings of the 34th General Council, August 1992*, p.351.
70 John Webster Grant, *Voices and Visions: 65 Years of the United Church of Canada* (The United Church Publishing House: 1990), pp.146–147.
71 N. Bruce McLeod to the author, 29 May 1995.

JAMES PARKES AND THE HOLOCAUST[1]

Tony Kushner

I N JUNE 1977 Franklin Littell wrote to James Parkes: 'You'll be interested to know that we have just gotten approval for the first PhD program in Holocaust Studies in the USA.' Parkes was intrigued by this development and wrote back that he would be particularly interested 'if there were any way in which I could keep in touch with what your researchers define as "the psychological situation which made the holocaust possible". That seems to me the key from a practical point of view.' Subsequently Parkes was invited to be an advisor to Littell's newly formed National Institute on the Holocaust in Philadelphia which aimed to encourage the 'study and discussion of the Holocaust and the lessons to be learned from it at all levels and in all sectors of public life'.[2]

From the perspective of the early 21st century, the novelty of creating such an institute and the apparent innocence of Parkes's interest is surprising. Unbeknown to either man – Parkes was one of the leading authorities on the history of antisemitism, and Littell was one of his protégés in the field of Christian–Jewish relations – interest in the Holocaust was about to escalate, especially in the USA.[3] Almost as an absent-minded aside, Parkes mentioned to Littell that 'I see that I was already writing on the subject in 1944.' Parkes repeated an anecdote that had appeared in his autobiography, *Voyage of Discoveries*, nearly a decade earlier about the refusal of the British Foreign Office in the latter stages of the war to accept the figures he gave about the number of Jews murdered by the Nazis in a publication that required official approval.[4]

Parkes, in this correspondence with Littell as well as in *Voyage of Discoveries*, was circumscribing his own scholarly and practical involvement in responding to the Holocaust. In turn, the partial suppression of the event in the shaping of his own life reflected an ambivalence towards confronting the destruction process that Parkes never fully resolved. This paper will outline Parkes's writings on the Holocaust from the days of mass murder through to his death in 1981 and seek to explain his silences on the subject. It will, in particular, highlight Parkes's concerns about the potential abuses to which the study and representation of the Holocaust could lead. Parkes's analysis of the nature of the European Jewish catastrophe, I will argue, has a wider resonance well beyond the study of the man himself, and has contemporary relevance. It has potential importance for a wide range of academic disciplines as well as for the popular portrayal and teaching of a subject that now, in contrast to the world Parkes experienced, generates an intense if not an obsessive interest.

James Parkes, if remembered at all today, is seen as a pioneer in the study and betterment of Christian – Jewish relations. His work outlining the history of antisemitism and in particular the Christian roots of modern hatred of Jews is occasionally acknowledged, although the originality of his contribution is often lost sight of as those that followed his lead have been given credit for work that he pioneered in the most difficult of academic circumstances.[5] What has been almost totally forgotten, however, is his life of activism which brought him into direct contact with the crisis of European Jewry resulting from the politicization of antisemitism during the 1920s and 1930s, and his continued involvement in rescue work during the war itself. There is no mention of Parkes, for example, in the newly open Imperial War Museum Holocaust Gallery in London. Parkes and other British campaigners on behalf of European Jewry such as the maverick orthodox Jewish communal leader Solomon Schonfeld are absent in a permanent exhibition which cost over £5 million to mount.[6]

Parkes, as we will see, would not necessarily have welcomed excessive attention to Christians who *helped* Jews during the Nazi era. To him, facing the Holocaust honestly meant confronting the silences, antipathies and sheer hatred of the church which enabled the Holocaust to happen without meaningful opposition. Remembering activists such as Parkes today is partly about honouring their humanity but equally if not more so in illustrating the failure of their contemporaries to act. Parkes, like many other British travellers in the inter-war period, stumbled across the ferocity of continental antisemitism. Unlike many of his contemporaries, however, Parkes was unwilling to blame Jews for their own misfortune.

His work for the Student Christian Movement and then the International Student Service brought Parkes into direct contact with the virulent extreme nationalism and racism of campus life in central and eastern Europe. He was clear after some initial research into the causes of this widespread hatred that its roots were to be found in the nature of Christianity, a deeply disturbing conclusion for an individual who was an ordained minister in the Church of England. In this respect, Parkes was, as Colin Richmond suggests, by so blatantly going against the grain 'a great English eccentric'. His eccentricity went further, however: he 'was also an activist: he was one for whom thinking was not enough'. Through his publications outlining the injustices faced by European Jewry which appeared even before the Nazis came to power, Parkes attempted to undermine the antisemitic discourse that permeated the western world in the inter-war period. But reasoned argument, whether in print or in court, as with the so-called 'Protocols' trials in Switzerland during 1935, were not his only contributions to fighting the prejudices of the time. Throughout the 1930s Parkes was active in helping refugees, particularly students and academics, escape from Nazi persecution.[7]

His defence work combatting domestic antisemitism continued in the war and Parkes was also instrumental in setting up the Council of Christians and Jews. Galvanized initially in response to the first news about the 'Final Solution' which reached the British public in the summer of 1942, by the end of that year its campaigning on the issue had all but evaporated. Publicity on the issue was left to Eleanor Rathbone and her newly established National Committee for Rescue from Nazi Terror[8] and to the publisher Victor Gollancz through his impassioned and brilliant pamphet, *Let My People Go*, written feverishly on Christmas Day 1942.[9] Gollancz and his fellow Jewish publicist, Arthur Koestler, had been deeply moved by meeting Jan Karski, a non-Jewish Pole who had been smuggled into the Warsaw ghetto and into what later emerged was a satellite camp of Belzec.[10]

Belzec, we now know, was the first purpose-built death camp, which along with Sobibor and Treblinka was designed through 'Operation Reinhard' to murder the Jews of Poland.[11] Gollancz, Rathbone and Koestler of course did not have the clarity of hindsight, but they were convinced that the Nazis were intent on killing all of Europe's Jews and that the death camp was an integral part of this process and the climax to the murderous intent of the regime. Parkes had no contact with Karski and for most of the war lived quietly in the Cambridgeshire village of Barley. But the relative peace and harmony around him and the lack of direct contact to someone such as Karski did not prevent his deep identification with the fate of European Jewry. Parkes knew Eleanor Rathbone through his earlier refugee work and was a founder Executive Member of the National Committee for Rescue from Nazi Terror.[12] Like Gollancz and Rathbone, he employed his typewriter to campaign for the British people to demand that their government help the Jews of Europe. Reflecting the marginality of this small group of activisits, his essay 'The Massacre of the Jews: Future Vengeance or Present Help?', dated January 1943, was never published. Parkes himself never referred back to it, yet as with all his writings on the Jews, it showed remarkable perception and empathy.[13]

Although influenced by Gollancz and Rathbone's writings, Parkes revealed his own particular knowledge and understanding of the Holocaust at the point at which the extermination process was at its most intense. Parkes outlined the development of Nazi policy during the war from brutal ghettoization through to slave labour, mass shootings and finally the deportation of Jews from eastern and western Europe and the use of poison gas: 'Hitler was not only threatening but actually carrying out the policy of destroying the whole Jewish population within his power.' By grasping the full nature of the Nazi intent, though underestimating the size of the Jewish population, Parkes stumbled on a figure that predicted the scale of Jewish losses under the Nazi onslaught: 'Six million human beings, from infants in arms to old men and women, were to be deliberately killed in cold blood.'[14]

It is a reflection of the speed of the destruction of Polish Jewry rather than Parkes's unwillingness to face reality that he, and other activists, probably underestimated by half the number of Jews murdered by the start of 1943. Indeed, the *proportion* of Jews killed in his narrative was reasonably accurate, indicating that he was well aware of the overall impact this whirlwind of destruction was causing on the Jewish world. Parkes suggested that

> By the ghastly passions of this madman, and the brutality of those who had been specially trained to become his executioners, it is believed that one third of the whole Jewish population of Europe – two millions of men, women and children – have already perished.[15]

Parkes was driven to write following the Allied Declaration on behalf of European Jewry on 17 December 1942 and the failure of the British government to promise any meaningful action to help other than a promise of post-war retribution. Debate in the House of Commons following the Declaration was deliberately stifled. Rathbone, hinting at a philosemitism which was alien to Parkes, had a carefully prepared speech calling for rescue and juxtaposing the British war effort and experience with that of the Jews: 'I suggested the other day, when the ringing of Church bells at Christmas was under discussion, that if the Church bells were considered . . . joy bells, it would be a mockery to ring them when the nation which gave us the Bible was in [the] course of extermination.'[16] Rathbone was not allowed to deliver this speech.

Parkes was similarly appalled by the response of his government: 'Vengeance after the war will not save a single Jewish life.' Dismissing the case that could have been made by any recent British Home Secretary in relation to the entry of refugees, Parkes confronted those that would appease racism:

> It is said that if we offered unlimited asylum in our own country or the territories we control, it might lead to a dangerous increase of antisemitism. It is even said – as though the

idea should terrify instead of rejoicing us – that Hitler might take us at our word, and send us all the Jews still alive in Europe, several million of them.

Like Rathbone, he wanted to make the fate of the Jews part of British war effort:

> There is only one answer for men who still believe there is any nobility in the cause for which we are fighting: we will receive them. And if there really be three million of them we will thank God that we have been able to save so many from Hitler's clutches. And if there be a Jewish Problem to solve, we will solve it as civilised men and not as murderers.[17]

There are two aspects to this last part of Parkes's article that merit further attention. First, Parkes and other campaigners were not mistaken in identifying the fears of senior British politicians and civil servants that the Nazis planned to 'flood' the western Allies with Jews. It is certainly the case that when the Nazis did suggest huge transfers of Jewish people, as with the Hungarian Jews in 1944, the offers were not genuine. But it is equally clear that the British government took such offers seriously and were mightily relieved when they came to nothing. For Herbert Morrison, writing at a time when the open deportation and murder of Hungarian Jews at Auschwitz was at its height, it was 'essential that we should do nothing at all which involves the risk that the further reception of refugees here might be the ultimate outcome'. Parkes, with his usual restraint, simply referred to Morrison in *Voyage of Discoveries* as 'a very obdurate Home Secretary' in matters relating to the rescue of Jews.[18]

The second point relates to Parkes's somewhat disturbing reference to the possible creation of a 'Jewish Problem' in Britain should a mass influx of Jews occur. Parkes, it must be stressed, saw antisemitism as a problem for non-Jews and especially for Christians to solve. He was, however, a man of his age in tending to see minority problems in the nation state as coming out of the mass numbers involved rather than from the nature of nationalism itself. He was thus tempted, as were so many of his liberal contemporaries, to see territorial solutions to the needs of oppressed minorities, often involving the potential transfer of populations in their millions. It is partly for this reason that to Parkes Zionism appeared as a sensible *practical* solution to the so-called 'Jewish problem'.[19] Whilst Parkes sincerely believed ultimately that Jews were not responsible for antisemitism, in his earlier writings particularly on the modern period there was an assumption that some of the antisemitism of pre-1939 eastern European countries, especially Poland, was due to the size and concentration of the Jewish population.[20] Thus in his campaigning during the war, whilst he had enough faith in the British population that some three million refugee Jews could be allowed entry without necessitating a violent response, he still assumed that it might lead to a 'Jewish problem'.

At its most extreme, the tendency to see solutions to minority difference in the movement of populations led to the Nazis' attempt to re-order the 'racial' map of Europe. The recent scholarship of a younger school of German historians has revealed the enormity of what the Nazis intended and how far it was carried out, providing a more general layer of racialism in which to place the attempted extermination of European Jewry.[21] In liberal circles, of course, such genocidal policies were anathema but it has not stopped well-meaning western politicians, statesmen and others from advocating ethno-religious separation of countries and regions with disastrous human rights consequences. In the case of Parkes, for example, his humanitarian support of Zionism and support for the new Jewish state limited (although it certainly did not destroy) his understanding of the tragedy of the Palestine refugees displaced during and after 1948.[22] Conversely, however, it also enabled him to look dispassionately at the demographics of Jewish life and to assimilate with incredible speed the full implications of mass murder and its effect on the global geo-politics of the future Jewish world.

In 1944 the Royal Institute of International Affairs (Chatham House) approached Parkes to write a survey of the Jewish world since 1939. The Zionist underpinning of Parkes's essay was not to the taste of this semi-official organization and Sir John Hope Simpson wrote a response to it which ignored the basic premise of Parkes's argument – that most of European Jewry had been destroyed – and instead tried to demolish the 'myth' of Jewish national identity.[23] For similar reasons, and also to undermine the case for rescue of the Jews left on the continent, the Foreign Office rejected Parkes's overall figures of the Jews murdered by the Nazis. Nevertheless, Parkes was aware that by 1944 in eastern Europe, with the exception of the Jews in the Soviet Union, 'it is the survivors who are to be numbered only by hundreds of thousands, the casualties by the millions.' Again, Parkes slightly overestimated the number of survivors – in the case of Poland he believed that some half a million would still be alive in the country itself, perhaps ten times the actual figure. To Parkes, however, thinking in global demographic terms, the number was still pitifully low: Polish Jewry he wrote 'has been exterminated as a living force'. It is hard to reconcile this bleak but ultimately accurate analysis with the view that the article had, in essence, nothing 'to say about the Holocaust'.[24]

Dan Stone has recently commented on the absence of Holocaust references in the immediate post-1945 writings of James Parkes: 'Most striking ... perhaps because he was such a tireless campaigner on behalf of the Jews, was the fact that James Parkes evinced an initial difficulty in facing up to the reality of the Holocaust.' On one level, Stone is right. Parkes did not write at length about the destruction process until he produced a succinct and, given the scarcity of secondary literature available (it was researched and written before the early works of Gerald Reitlinger and Leon Poliakov appeared), remarkably well-informed essay, 'The German Treatment of the Jews', which was published by Chatham House in 1954, utilizing material from the International Military Tribunal at Nuremberg and a variety of Jewish sources.[25] Parkes outlined clearly and accurately the process of extermination and its development from the pre-war period, providing 'in cold terms of statistics' how the figure of six million could be broken down by adding together the losses of the pre-war Jewish communities of the continent. Beyond such numbers, however, Parkes reflected as only one who had known and understood the Jewish world before 1939, that 'To estimate in terms either of human suffering, or of destruction of spiritual, historical, cultural and economic values, the full consequences of Nazi anti-semitism during these war years will for ever remain impossible.'[26]

In the second edition of his history of antisemitism, published in 1963, Parkes provided perhaps his only reference to the liberation of the Nazi concentration camps: 'In 1945, with all the horrors of the Death Camps still present to our minds and imaginations, men felt that while the present generation lived there could be no danger of a recrudescence of the violent antisemitism of the Nazis'.[27] But does Parkes's failure to write immediately of this horror show, as Stone argues, that he 'was less insight-ful ... than he had been in the years immediately preceding the Holocaust'?[28]

At the time of the Eichmann trial in Jerusalem, Parkes pondered on 'the mentality of persecutor and persecuted' and especially on the frightening normality of the murderers, spectators and victims. They were, he argued, connecting his much-loved garden and countryside in Dorset to the killing fields of the continent, 'nothing other than men, women and children, families and neighbours, such as I would meet if I walked down my village street'. Anticipating the classic work of Christopher Browning by over a quarter of a century, Parkes commented that 'Ordinary men did and watched these things and then went home to supper, played with their children, listened to music, while the victim went to death'.[29]

Yet Parkes was wary of examining the specific and bloody terror of the Holocaust for its own sake in a message which is perhaps even more relevant than when he wrote in 1961. 'If I need lavish the superlatives of horror on the story I indulge in escapism by separating myself artificially from those who did such things, or watched them unmoved.'[30] Parkes, as ever, was a practical man. He saw the ease, especially within Britain, of blaming the Holocaust on easy targets – most obviously the Germans – and thus both avoiding the responsibility of others and the potential relevance to contemporary concerns when confronting the involvement of ordinary people in new forms of prejudice.

Moreover, rather than lacking insight, Parkes's immediate response to the impact of the Holocaust was frighteningly realistic. Refusing to dwell on the horror at this stage, as early as 1946/1947 in the Charles William Eliot Lectures he assessed where the dynamics of the Jewish world now rested with two-thirds of European Jewry massacred. The 'heart of the Jewish people', eastern Europe, 'that immense reservoir is, to all intents and purposes, empty'. There were now three potential Jewish centres: the Soviet Union, Palestine and the USA. The first Parkes rejected, realizing that Jewish identity had been undermined by Soviet assimilation and antisemitism. The future was to be between Palestine, the USA and to a far lesser extent, other parts of the 'free world' diaspora.[31] Parkes's stress on post-war Palestine as a Jewish home was not, as Stone suggests, a form of diversion from facing the reality of the destruction process: or Zionism as redemption and the 'return' to the Promised Land as something he would draw religious comfort from. Quite to the contrary, it reflected Parkes's *political* confrontation with a hostile world in which the survivors found themselves and his analysis, as a liberal nationalist, of where they were most likely to find a place in which he hoped they could live freely and develop Judaism and Jewishness beyond the previous restraints of hostile neighbours. It was, in fact, true to Parkes's life as a whole, the very opposite of escapism. That Parkes in 1945 did not ponder the nature of modernism, or man's destructive potential as revealed by the camp exposures – images that he did *not* need to tell him of the scale of the European Jewish disaster – is to misunderstand the nature of an activist, albeit one who when the time required it, could offer a profound analysis of the human condition.[32]

In the Charles William Eliot Lectures, Parkes was to articulate for the first time after the war how his analysis of antisemitism had been affected by what would now be called the Holocaust. Revealing the clarity of his position as well as the courage of his convictions he refused to alter his pre-war position:

> In our own day and within our own civilisation, more than six million deliberate murders are the consequence of teaching about Jews for which the Christian Church is ultimately responsible, and of an attitude to Judaism which is not only maintained by all the Christian Churches, but has its ultimate resting place in the teaching of the New Testament itself.[33]

This unambiguous statements is one of the most heavily quoted amongst the extraordinarily large and varied writings of James Parkes. It both opens and closes Lionel Steiman's generally well-informed and balanced *Paths to Genocide* (1998), perhaps one of the most successful one volume accounts of the history of antisemitism since those attempted by Parkes himself.[34]

To be fair to those who quote Parkes in such a way, he made similar statements about the roots of the Holocaust until his death. In his *Antisemitism* (1963) Parkes argued:

> That which changed the normal pattern of Jewish-Gentile relations was the action of the Christian Church. The statement is tragic but the evidence is inescapable. What is still more

tragic is that there is no break in the line which leads from the beginning of the denigration of Judaism in the formative period of Christian history, from the exclusion of Jews from civic equality in the period of the Church's first triumph in the fourth century, through the horrors of the Middle Ages, to the Death Camps of Hitler in our own day.[35]

In his very last publication, *Christianity, Jewish History and Antisemitism* (1976), Parkes confirmed that it was his conviction that for antisemitism, including the Holocaust, 'the Christian church retains an inescapable theological responsibility'.[36]

Yet for all the explicitness of such statements, Parkes has been used selectively for those who want scholarly underpinning for their 'staight path' route through the history of antisemitism. It is no surprise, for example, to find the quotation above from *Antisemitism* appearing as supportive evidence in Daniel Goldhagen's *Hitler's Willing Executioners* (1996). It is significant, however, that Goldhagen misses out the line immediately following Parkes's bold outline: 'Other causes indeed came in during the passage through the centuries: the motives and climate of the Nazi period owed nothing to Christian teaching.'[37] Similarly, in the Charles William Eliot Lectures, as the Parkes scholar Robert Everett has pointed out, Parkes highlights how 'In general, it must be said of modern antisemitism that its strength lies in the political and economic rather than the religious field.'[38]

Indeed, as we have seen in his response to the Eichmann trial, Parkes was well aware, thirty years before the appearance of Zygmunt Bauman's work, of how modernity and 'civilization' in an increasingly secular age had enabled the Holocaust to be implemented with such ease. Reviewing Raul Hilberg's *The Destruction of the European Jews* in 1961, he agreed with the author that 'killing's not as difficult as it used to be'. Parkes as a left-leaning liberal modernist within the Church never gave up his faith in human betterment, but he was too honest a man not to confront the challenge of the Holocaust. As he wrote in response to Hilberg, which Parkes saw as 'an essential work of reference and . . . an impossible one to read':

> the whole idea of an inevitable betterment based on the nature of the universe itself has to be ruled out of the picture . . . Here is a long factual record of what men could organise and do, could watch and plan, and could find allies in the whole operation among the 'civilised' [but notice the quotation marks] countries of Europe. Only if these factors are taken into account dare men hope for a better future for humanity.[39]

To understand Parkes on the Holocaust we have to see him working at two levels – the historical and the political-theological. With regards to the former, Parkes's post-war writings (which whilst not overly plentiful, are far more substantial than he at the end of his life seemed willing to acknowledge) if looked at carefully provide a balanced and, given the paucity of contemporary scholarship in the area, reasonably well-informed account of modern antisemitism allowing for continuity *and* change.[40] In terms of the latter, we return to Parkes as the committed scholar and activist. Parkes believed that 'the Nazi destruction of the Jews is an event which must not only be factually known but must be spiritually felt by anyone who seeks to understand the world we live in'.[41] For Christians this meant acknowledging their past role in the harm done to the Jewish people, including the Holocaust.

What Parkes wanted was a fundamental appraisal of the nature of Christianity, a root and branch purging of its teachings about the Jews in the past and its ongoing conversionist approach to present day Jews. Writing 'After the Eichmann Verdict', but with even greater relevance to the contemporary obsession with apology, he was not against penitence *per se* for past guilt, but stressed it 'would be an empty gesture if it were not accompanied by a determination to understand wherein and how and why we so sinned that six million of our fellow-men died horribly and uncomforted – over a million of them children'.[42]

Parkes knew that he was asking a lot:

> There will be some who will say that all this is too difficult and in any case would launch the Church on to a slippery slope from which it might be impossible to recover. It is much better to remain where we are. They are entitled to do so; but they must accept the reverse also of the picture. They must accept the ultimate responsibility for the massacres in Hitler's death-camps which are the result of the attitude they are unwilling to change. And they must accept that they are the allies – however reluctantly – of the Fascism which is still alive and still making use of antisemitism.[43]

To him, however, Christians could not take refuge in the Holocaust purely as a German crime, although it was 'a specifically German responsibility to examine truthfully and humbly what in German traditions, attitudes and outlooks made so appalling a regime possible'.[44] Nor could they simply blame modern secular society where 'the official becomes more powerful and the infliction of suffering becomes an impersonal response to an order'. All this was avoidance, and the desire to find a scapegoat: 'The question to ask is: What really is our responsibility?'.[45]

In 1963, Rolf Hochhuth's play *Der Stellvertreter* (in English, 'The Deputy'), was performed in Germany. Dealing with the role of Pope Pius XII in relation to Nazi persecution during the war, it provoked much concern in the world of Christian–Jewish dialogue in Britain in the months before its performance in London. Parkes again was anxious that the actions of the war-time Pope did not become the focus of the debate: 'We shall only be adopting the well-known evasion of seeking a scapegoat if we turn the discussion on to whether he has been unfair to Pius XII.'[46] As ever, and in marked contrast to the 1998 Vatican's statement 'We Remember: A Reflection on the *Shoah*',[47] Parkes did not want Christians to avoid their personal responsibility. The challenge in relation to *Der Stellvertreter*,

> The real issue, for each Christian individually, is: *Has he been unfair to me?* . . . In the end the Churches cannot evade [the] question 'Did you survive Nazism with your lives and property intact? If so, why?'[48]

Parkes acknowledged that 'Inevitably the main burden of an examination of conscience falls on German Christians, Catholics or Protestants, then on European Christians in countries which the Nazis overran.'[49] But even here Parkes saw an easy way out for Christians. First, he was more than aware that 'individual Christians risked and forfeited their lives in rescuing [Hitler's Jewish] victims', but he firmly believed that 'Jews can forget antisemitism only when Christians and humanists remember it. The most cowardly thing we do is to remind them that many Christians and others risked their lives to save Jews.'[50] Second, he did not want Christians in Britain to see this only as a question of continental church responsibility: 'We in England have no right to tell them what they should have done . . . we, as well as they, are heirs of the impotence of the Churches in the face of the open evils of Nazism'.[51] Indeed, he wrote to his close collaborator, William Simpson, who had also faced the indifference and antipathy of British society towards the fate of the Jews during the war, 'we can do nothing from the safe distance of our security and "victory". We can only admit humbly that it is unlikely that we would have done any better.'[52]

Before drawing this paper towards a conclusion, it is worth pondering how far we still are from Parkes's vision of Christians taking meaningful responsibility for the Holocaust.

This is not the place to discuss the progress and limitations of recent Vatican statements and actions, nor to examine how far the churches in west, central and eastern Europe have come to terms with their role in the Jewish catastrophe. I will limit attention to Britain itself and in particular, the Church of England, in which Parkes was a clergyman for all his professional career.

The Lambeth Document on the Jews (1988) owes much to Parkes's intellectual legacy, even if it is not explicitly acknowledged.[53] His influence is especially clear in the acknowledgment of the hurt caused to the Jews by past attempts at Christian conversion and more generally in acknowledging Christian guilt in creating an antisemitic tradition. But what has been missing from the Church of England and indeed churches in Britain as a whole is a recognition of their own failings during the Nazi era. Instead, attention has focussed on the help given to Jewish refugees and the proclamations made by prominent church figures denouncing Nazi antisemitism in the 1930s and the extermination process during the Second World War. The dominant tone was set by Richard Gutteridge in 1987:

> What was by and large the good record of the Churches in England during the Hitler period was encouraged by the favorable circumstances in England compared with other countries, the benefit of a tradition of liberal toleration, a lack on the whole of official discrimination, a welcome absence of persecution, and the minimum of overt antisemitism among the population as a whole.[54]

Since Gutteridge wrote, although there have been some dissenting voices, the positive assessment is still dominant. More detailed research, however, reveals the ambivalent response of Christians, collectively and individually, to *Jewish* refugees as well as the limitations of Christian protest against Nazi antisemitism.[55] Yet what is significant is how the danger outlined by Parkes – that the Holocaust is someone else's problem – has been realized. As Tom Lawson has suggested, many church historians explicitly point towards the allegedly positive response of Christians in liberal countries such as Britain as the counter-example to the failings of their co-religionists on the continent. In the process they help to restore confidence and integrity in the response of Christianity to the Nazi onslaught as a whole.[56]

It is because of Parkes's recognition of the failings of Christianity before, during and after the Nazi era that makes him so uncomfortable a figure to confront today. His legacy flourishes at the centre named in his honour at the University of Southampton but he is all but forgotten in the Christian world today. The Church of England has failed to mark his significance in spite of opportunities to do so. Indeed, Parkes would have been distressed that the vast proportion of the funding of the Centre for the Study of Jewish/non-Jewish relations at the University of Southampton has come from Jewish and secular sources – Christians have been notable by their almost total absence. In 1960, a few years before the agreement to transfer his unique library to Southampton, Parkes declared 'that it was one of the shames of Christendom that the Jews were forced to bear the burden of combating anti-Semitism'.[57] As we have seen, Colin Richmond has described Parkes as an eccentric – a description which the former sees as a positive attribute. Others have used this term to dismiss Parkes, to suggest he is unworthy of serious consideration – a quirky man with quirky views.[58] To do so, and to continue to do so would be another form of denial of past and current responsibility.

To summarise: Parkes has much to offer those who want to confront the nature of the Holocaust. One can sympathize with Colin Richmond's exasperation that 'I wish James

Parkes had not been so bloody polite'[59] – on many levels he was restrained by a surface Englishness that disguised the radicalism of what he was demanding of society, of his own religion and of the individual. Yet that radicalism and challenge is still there. Nicholas de Lange is partially right in arguing that the reason that Parkes is rarely cited is 'really a kind of tribute. His work has not been rendered obsolete or cast aside, it has simply been institutionalised to the point that it is taken for granted'[60].

Nevertheless, I would argue that the greater challenge of Parkes for Christians – to avoid pious platitudes with regard to the Holocaust (such as, in the light of the intensification of post-1945 genocide, the increasingly fatuous slogan, 'Never Again') and to look to personal and collective responsibility both then *and* for the horrors of racism and discrimination in the contemporary world – has yet to be seriously confronted. Parkes demanded penitence for past sins in the form of a revision of Christian thinking and teaching about the Jews. He wanted Christians and others to face up to the reality and integrity of the Jewish presence in the post-Holocaust world and he wanted people to see the evil of any form of prejudice. Underlying all his concerns in dealing with the Holocaust was that the response should be, as he wrote to Franklin Littell, as we have seen at the start of this paper, 'from a practical point of view'. For Parkes, remembering was for now, not for the future: for the victims themselves and not, as a form of moral masturbation, to make those responsible or who looked on without taking action, feel better about themselves.[61]

Parkes in his last published work wrote that he had not at any point dealt theologically with the Holocaust.[62] I hope in this overview I have shown that he was being unduly and frustratingly modest, although his comparatively sparse but incisive writing on the subject has a message in itself to us today: with regard to writing and speaking about the Holocaust, as well as memorialising it, less is often more. In his classic *The Foundations of Judaism and Christianity* (1960), Parkes argued that 'Bad history cannot be the foundation for good theology.'[63] It is a maxim that many in the world of theology, perhaps especially so in Holocaust studies, would do well to remember and to keep in mind the example of Parkes himself, who was both a good historian and a deeply challenging theologian.

NOTES

1 I would like to thank Colin Richmond for his interest in James Parkes and our informal discussions about the man. Colin Richmond is planning a much needed biography of Parkes, as is Haim Chertok. Their works will be complementary rather than rivals.

2 Littell to Parkes, 7 June 1977; Parkes to Littell, 24 June 1977 and Littell to Parkes, 2 August 1977; circular on National Institute on the Holocaust, 5 November 1977 in University of Southampton archive (SUA), MS 60/31/30.

3 See, for example, Edward Linenthal, *Preserving Memory: The Struggle to Create America's Holocaust Museum* (New York: Viking, 1977); Tony Kushner, *The Holocaust and the Liberal Imagination: A Social and Cultural History* (Oxford: Blackwell, 1994), chapter 7; Peter Novick, *The Holocaust and Collective Memory* (London: Bloomsbury, 2000), chapters 10 and 11.

4 Parkes to Littell, 2 August 1977 in SUA MS 60/31/30; James Parkes, *Voyage of Discoveries* (London: Gollancz, 1969), p.180.

5 This is partly explained by his own personality. Parkes was willing to risk a permanent outsider status in the Christian world for his views on Jewish issues but he never promoted himself as personality above his life work. He was, as Colin Richmond suggests, 'too well mannered', almost too 'English', in spite of his Guernsey background, to engage in self-publicity, an approach that I might add others in areas he pioneered could take note of. *Voyage of Discoveries* is 'so unassuming it reveals virtually nothing'. See Colin Richmond, 'Parkes, Prejudice and the Middle Ages', in Sian Jones, Tony

Kushner and Sarah Pearce (eds), *Cultures of Ambivalence and Contempt: Studies in Jewish-Non-Jewish Relations* (London: Vallentine, Mitchell, 1998), pp.212, 241.

6 The absence of reference to such figures was the basis for a feature on the new exhibition by Sancha Berg on *Today*, BBC Radio 4, 29 May 2000.

7 See *Voyage of Discoveries*, chapters 4–6; SUA MS 60/17/3 and 4, concerning his work with Jewish and other students 1926–1935.

8 For the limitations of the Council of Christians and Jews, see Kushner, *The Holocaust and the Liberal Imagination*, p.191; Eleanor Rathbone, *Rescue the Perishing* (London: National Committee for Rescue from Nazi Terror, 1943).

9 Victor Gollancz, *Let My People Go* (London: Gollancz, 1942); Ruth Dudley Edwards, *Victor Gollancz: A Biography* (London: Gollancz, 1987), p.375. See Karski's testimony in Brewster Chamberlin and Marcia Feldman (eds), *The Liberation of the Nazi Concentration Camps: Eyewitnesses of the Liberators* (Washington, DC: United States Memorial Council, 1987), p.179.

10 David Cesarani, *Arthur Koestler: The Homeless Mind* (London: William Heinemann, 1998), pp.189, 202–3; E.T. Wood and S.M. Jankowski, *Karski: How one man tried to stop the Holocaust* (New York, J. Wiley, 1994).

11 Yitzhak Arad, *Belzec, Sobibor, Treblinka: The Operation Reinhard Death Camps* (Bloomington, IN: Indiana University Press, 1987).

12 See SUA MS 60/15/57.

13 SUA, MS 60/9/5/1. The essay is dated January 1943.

14 *ibid.*

15 *ibid.*

16 Eleanor Rathbone, 'Speech Notes on the Jewish Question', December 1942, Rathbone papers, XIV/3/85, University of Liverpool archive.

17 MS SUA, 60/9/5/1.

18 See Yehuda Bauer, *Jews for Sale: Nazi-Jewish Negotiations, 1933–1945* (New Haven: Yale University Press, 1994), chapter 10, esp. p.188 for the Morrison quote; Louise London, *Whitehall and the Jews 1933–1948: British Immigration Policy and the Holocaust* (Cambridge: Cambridge University Press, 2000), chapter 8; Parkes, *Voyage of Discoveries*, p.175.

19 For an astute analysis with a brief reference to Parkes, see Mark Levene, 'The Limits of Tolerance: Nation-State Building and What It Means for Minority Groups', *Patterns of Prejudice* vol. 34 no. 2 (2000), pp.19–40, esp. p.19 note 1.

20 See, for example, James Parkes, *The Jew and his Neighbour: a study of the causes of anti-Semitism* (London: Student Christian Movement Press, 1930).

21 See, for example, Gotz Aly, *The Final Solution: Nazi population policy and the murder of European Jews* (London: Arnold, 1999).

22 For Parkes and the Palestinian refugees, see SUA 60/9/10/15; 60/17/49 and 50.

23 James Parkes, 'The Jewish world since 1939', *International Affairs* vol. 21 no. 1 (January 1945), pp. 87–99 and Simpson response, pp.100–105. See also SUA MS 60/11/1.

24 Parkes, 'The Jewish World Since 1939', p.90; Dan Stone, 'The Domestication of Violence: Forging a Collective Memory of the Holocaust in Britain, 1945–6', *Patterns of Prejudice* 33/2 (April 1999), p.21.

25 James Parkes, 'The German Treatment of the Jews' in Arnold and Veronica Toynbee (eds), *Survey of International Affairs 1939–1946*, vol. 4 *Hitler's Europe* (London: Oxford University Press, 1954), pp.153–64.

26 *ibid*, pp.163–4.

27 James Parkes, *Antisemitism* (London: Vallentine, Mitchell, 1963), p.158.

28 Stone, 'The Domestication of Violence', p.21.

29 James Parkes, 'The Mentality of Persecutor and Persecuted', *The Scotsman*, 24 May 1961; Christopher Browning, *Ordinary Men: Reserve Battalion 101 and the Final Solution in Poland* (New York: HarperPerennial, 1993).

30 Parkes, 'The Mentality of Persecutor and Persecuted'.

31 James Parkes, *Judaism and Christianity* (Chicago: University of Chicago Press, 1948), chapter 7. This book was based on the Charles William Eliot Lectures at the Jewish Institute of Religion, New York, given by Parkes in 1946 and 1947.

32 Stone, 'The Domestication of Violence', pp.26–7.

33 Parkes, *Judaism and Christianity*, p.167.

34 Lionel Steiman, *Paths to Genocide: Antisemitism in Western History* (London: Macmillan, 1998), pp.1, 242; Stone, 'The Domestication of Violence', p.22.

35 Parkes, *Antisemitism*, p.60.

36 James Parkes, *Christianity, Jewish History and Antisemitism* (Southampton: The Parkes Library, 1976), p.7.

37 Daniel Jonah Goldhagen, *Hitler's Willing Executioners: Ordinary Germans and the Holocaust* (London: Little, Brown and Company, 1996), p.52; Parkes, *Antisemitism*, p.60.

38 Parkes, *Judaism and Christianity*, p.137; Robert Everett, *Christianity Without Antisemitism: James Parkes and the Jewish–Christian Encounter* (Oxford: Pergamon Press, 1993), pp.240–41.

39 Parkes review of Hilberg, November 1961, in SUA MS 60/10/2; Zymunt Bauman, *Modernity and the Holocaust* (Oxford: Polity Press, 1989); Richmond, 'Parkes, Prejudice and the Middle Ages', pp.219–20, 223–7 for Parkes, Modernism and the Holocaust. See also Everett, *Christianity Without Antisemitism*, passim for a sensitive reading of Parkes in this respect.

40 Curiously in his last publication, he wrote of the Holocaust 'My own treatment of it comes only in my volume entitled *Antisemitism*' which ignores his perceptive articles and reviews on the subject. See Parkes, *Christianity, Jewish History and Antisemitism*, p.5.

41 Review of Hilberg in SUA, MS 60/10/2.

42 James Parkes, 'After the Eichmann Verdict', *Observer*, 7 December 1961.

43 Parkes, *Judaism and Christianity*, p.176.

44 Parkes, 'After the Eichmann Verdict'.

45 *ibid.*

46 James Parkes, 'The Vicar', May 1963, unpublished typescript in SUA MS 60/15/32.

47 The Vatican Document was published on 16 March 1998 under the Presidency of Cardinal Edward Cassidy.

48 *ibid.*

49 *ibid.*

50 Parkes, *Antisemitism*, p.60; idem, 'After the Eichmann Verdict'.

51 Parkes, 'The Vicar', in SUA MS 60/15/32.

52 Parkes to Simpson, 25 May 1963, in SUA MS 60/15/32.

53 *The Truth Shall Make You Free: The Lambeth Conference, 1988* (London: Church House Publishing, 1988).

54 Richard Gutteridge, 'The Churches and the Jews in England, 1933–1945', in Otto Dov Kulka and Paul Mendes Flohr (eds), *Judaism and Christianity Under the Impact of National Socialism* (Jerusalem: Historical Society of Israel, 1987), p.353. For a summary of the existing historiography on British Christianity and the Jews under Nazi control, see Chana Kotzin, 'Christian Responses in Britain to Jewish Refugees from Europe, 1933–1939' (unpublished PhD thesis, University of Southampton, 2000), Introduction.

55 See Kotzin, 'Christian Responses'; Kushner, *The Holocaust and the Liberal Imagination*.

56 Tom Lawson is a doctoral student at the University of Southampton assessing the impact of Anglicanism on the development of Holocaust historiography.

57 Parkes quoted in *AJR Information* vol XV no. 4, April 1960.

58 Richmond, 'Parkes, Prejudice and the Middle Ages', p.241. Nicholas de Lange, 'James Parkes: A Century Lecture', in Jones et al, *Cultures of Ambivalence and Contempt*, pp.45–6 comments on the absence of reference to Parkes but is more benign in his interpretation.

59 Richmond, 'Parkes, Prejudice and the Middle Ages', p.214.

60 de Lange, 'James Parkes's', p.46.

61 Parkes to Littell, 24 June 1977, SUA MS 60/31/30.

62 Parkes, *Christianity, Jewish History and Antisemitism*, p.5.

63 James Parkes, *The Foundations of Judaism and Christianity* (London: Vallentine Mitchell, 1960), p.x.

ON THE JEWS AND THE LUTHERANS:
THE ELCA CONFRONTS HISTORY

Rochelle L. Millen

E VER SINCE the Confessing Church in Germany issued the Barmen Declaration in 1934, Lutherans, both European and American, have struggled with issues surrounding the role of the church during the rise of Nazism and World War II. Most recently, here in the United States, this struggle led in 1994 to the official condemnation by the Evangelical Lutheran Church in America[1] of Luther's 1543 anti-Semitic pamphlet. Continuing along the path of repentance and reconciliation, the ELCA in April 1998 issued the draft of a document on Lutheran–Jewish relations, requesting comment from academics and clergy associated with the church. A final version was adopted on 16 November 1998.

This paper will give the background of the dispute surrounding the condemnation of Luther's 'On the Jews and Their Lies' and analyse the text of the 1994 statement, comparing it to earlier statements of the Lutheran Church, especially the 1984 declaration of the Lutheran World Federation. It will also critically examine the 'Guidelines for Lutheran-Jewish Relations,' commenting on various sections of the text. For purposes of comparison, and as a means of highlighting the complexity of Jewish–Christian relations, the Missouri Synod and its attitudes towards Jews and Judaism will also be discussed. Thus this study will give the context for current developments in Jewish–Christian relations in American Lutheranism, as well as focus upon details of the most recent recommendations.

The Barmen Declaration of the German Evangelical Church in 1934 was decisive in how the German Lutheran establishment was to deal with National Socialism. Organized primarily by Karl Barth, the meeting at Barmen was neither banned nor policed by the Nazis. This was a sensible choice, as little was said at the meeting that could have been considered subversive. The situation of Jews in Germany did not merit a mention and there was no criticism of Nazi racial ideology. Political loyalty to the state, regarded as divinely sanctioned, was expressed, and whatever criticism was articulated was hidden in ecclesiastical and theological language, with the accompanying proviso that no attack upon the new state was intended. National Socialism was not condemned, but rather the false ideology of the new state, which arrogated to itself the power to supersede Christian teachings and ethics. 'We reject the false teaching that the State has the right or power to exceed its own particular function, and become the sole and total authority in human life,' the Barmen Declaration proclaimed.[2]

While the Barmen Declaration is significant in expressing the opposition of the Confessing Church to the rise of Nazism and the anti-Judaism of the 'German Christians', its focus on doctrine resulted in a lack of empathy toward and action on behalf of those who were being increasingly marginalized in German society. The 'German Christians' had met earlier in Berlin and enthusiastically endorsed the Aryan clause calling for the segregation of all Christians of 'alien' blood. Reinhold Krause, one of their leaders, declared that 'Those of Jewish blood do not belong to the German *Volkskirche* either in pulpit or in pew.'[3] But Barth's theology tended to be other-worldly and esoteric, emphasizing a transcendental christology and tabling – perhaps even ignoring – concerns of this world, such as legal measures against the Jews of Germany. While not embracing the Aryan clause as did the official Church, the Confessing Church moved in 1934 from tepid opposition[4] to the clause to the issue of confessional integrity. The way to express resistance to the official Church and its *volkisch* orientation was to emphasize pure doctrine based on Scripture. The path of practical action was eschewed in favour of theological reformulations. In 1967, toward the end of his life, Barth expressed in a letter to a friend his feelings of guilt for not having included the issue of the Jewish question in the Barmen Declaration.[5]

At subsequent meetings of the Confessional Synod, both several months prior to and following the passing of the Nuremberg Laws on 15 September 1935, Barth's anti-activist dictum that 'the Church has in no way whatever to serve mankind, nor the German People. It has alone to serve the Word of God,'[6] seemed to serve as a fundamental guideline. At the first post-Nuremberg Laws meeting, Dietrich Bonhoeffer, Eberhard Bethge, Heinrich Vogel and Martin Niemöller were unable to get Vogel's substantive statement expressing concern for German Jews passed. Niemöller commented on that occasion, '...our mouths will only be really opened when we have to undergo suffering ourselves.'[7]

In his essay on the German Protestant churches during the Hitler years, Richard Gutteridge laments the paucity of opposition to the increasingly impassioned anti-Semitism with its increasing restrictions on all aspects of life for Jews. Words or actions of direct resistance were rare.[8] Gutteridge's reading of the material on the German Protestant churches finds no rejection of antisemitism as such, no rebuttal of Luther's anti-Jewish writings, no appeal to the Hebrew Prophets or to Paul's Epistle to the Romans, chapters 9–11. The latter, after all, had been consistently used in the Catholic Church in medieval times to protect the Jews – to whatever extent it was possible to restrain the uneducated by espousing doctrine. As Gutteridge notes, the rather succinct Declaration of Guilt at Stuttgart in October 1945 made no direct reference to the failure of the churches that represented Protestants to support the cause of the Jews; nor was there an apology for – or even an acknowledgement of – the failure to oppose the unrelenting racial antisemitic measures.

The attitudes of the Protestant churches and of the German population in general toward the increasing marginalization of the Jews and then violence against them remained ambiguous. Various documents show frequent criticisms against the new government voiced by representatives of the Church. An example is a letter found in the files of the Main Office of the Gestapo in Berlin. It was sent to Hitler and his ministers in December 1938, subsequent to the organized outbursts of Kristallnacht. Authored by a Protestant clergyman from Berlin, it is signed with his full name and address:[9]

> The events that occurred amongst our people on and after November 9th of this year force me to take a clear stand. Far be it from me to disregard the sins that many members of the Jewish people have committed against our Fatherland, especially during the last decades; also, far be it from me to deny the right of orderly and moderate proceedings against the Jewish race. But not only will I by no means justify the numerous excesses against Jewry

that took place on and after Nov. 9 of this year (it is unnecessary to go into details), but I reject them, deeply ashamed, as they are a blot on the good name of the Germans.

First of all, I, as a Protestant Christian, have no doubt that the commitment and toleration of such reprisals will evoke the wrath of God against our people and Fatherland, if there is a God in heaven. Just as Israel is cursed and on trial because they were the first who rejected Christ, so surely the same curse will fall upon each and every nation that, by similar deeds, denies Christ in the same way.

I have spoken out of the ardent concern of a Christian who prays to his God every day for his people and his rulers (*Obrigkeit*). May God hearken to my voice, hopefully not the only one of this kind. With due respect to the authorities (*Obrigkeit*).

Erich Klapproth
Pastor[10]

When the Nuremberg Laws were passed in 1935, some objections had been voiced by representatives of both Catholicism and Protestantism in Germany. The voices of opposition to the Nazi racial proclamations often took the form of noting the 'neo-paganism' of the regime, or of expressing support for or empathy toward the 'Old Testament People of Israel'.[11] These expressions clearly convey the ambivalence of their authors. No overt objection is made to the present persecution of actual Jews; rather, ideological arrows against Alfred Rosenberg's racial theories are sent forth. Surely it was correct to see the Nuremberg Laws as resulting from pagan sources in German history. But at the same time, the Nuremberg Laws adhered to the firm principle of medieval Church policy against the Jews based on Romans 9–11: Jews may be humiliated and degraded, but not done away with. After all, their presence was needed for the Second Coming.[12]

In addition, the phrase 'Old Testament People of Israel' represents the refusal, in both German philosophy and theology, to acknowledge the identity of its Jewish community – indeed the identity of Jews in general – as something other than an anachronistic group whose history allegedly had ended with the destruction of the Second Temple by the Romans in the year 70 CE. The phrase surely follows in the footsteps of Kant, Hegel and others whose views on Judaism neither took account of the development of rabbinic Judaism nor acknowledged that Old Testament Israelites had long ago ceased to exist, and certainly were absent in the Germany of their time.[13]

Indeed, 'orderly and moderate' actions against the German Jewish population were deemed acceptable since Jews, after all, had rejected Christ and still carried the burden of Matthew's words in 27:25: 'His blood be on us and on our children.'[14] While Klapproth's letter is commendable as representing a Protestant clergyman who would not keep silent, what seems to have bothered him were the 'excesses', the violence, the messiness, the lack of orderliness, the unsystematic qualities that define a pogrom. The systematic and more 'moderate' measures against Jews of 1933 and 1935 had been both appropriate and deserved. It must also be noted that the racial designation of Jews is unquestioned, and that Jewish culpability, both theological ('Israel is cursed') and social ('the sins that many members of the Jewish people have committed against our Father-land') is presumed. Given the ambiguity of such protests against the violence of Kristallnacht, and the weak dissent of a religious leader, it is little wonder that other leaders – and laypeople – were and continued to be bystanders as the situation for Jews became increasingly difficult.

While the above letter and analysis serves as an indicator of the attitudes prevalent among the religious leadership in Germany during the war years, the question of the attitudes of the population in general must also be commented upon. As implied above, the ordinary person, possessing the same ambiguous feelings as his/her religious leader, although in a less sophisticated manner, followed a similar path.

Although the relationship between the Churches and the Third Reich during the war years has often been characterized as one of armistice (*Burgfrieden*),[15] the historical evidence once again presents a paradox. Despite the presumed armistice or truce, there were frequent criticisms against the regime voiced by both Church leaders and laity. Yet the increasing ostracism and eventual deportation of Jewish friends and neighbours garnered little attention. A kind of apathy prevailed, in which little note was taken of the fate of real people, German people, who also happened to be Jewish.

It is well-known that the Churches were successful in halting the euthanasia programme and the order to remove all crucifixes from schools. The moves to accomplish these goals must be contrasted with the passivity and acquiescence of the population when deportations of the Jewish population were carried out in full view. In almost all cases, the Christian German population knew that Jews were being rounded up and taken away. Documents to support this contrast are brought by Otto Kulka in his essay, 'Popular Christian Attitudes in the Third Reich'. Kulka quotes from a report dated December, 1941 from the district of Augsburg:

> As a result of the removal of crucifixes from the schools in Litzendorf, in the district of Bamberg, on the 9th of November, new demonstrations broke out in which 150 people participated. When the demonstrators dispersed there were some cries of denunciation . . . , 'The cross must be returned to the school . . . We thought that only Communists do such things.'[16]

The removal of crosses from schoolrooms was seen as anti-Christian and worthy of public protest; the legal structure that had increasingly isolated and harmed German Jews since 1933 was not.

This dichotomy is further supported by the continuation of the same report from December 1941: 'In the course of the evacuation of the Jews, a special train with 1001 Jews and 9 children left Nuremberg for Riga. Three Jewish women committed suicide, apparently in fear of the impending evacuation.'[17] Another source, which Kulka describes as 'a parallel report from Nuremberg,' comments: 'The matter was not concealed from the population, which noted the fact and acquiesced in it.'[18]

Thus it cannot be claimed that Germans who were Christian did not know what was happening to Germans who were Jews. The greatest efforts of the Churches were not to halt the increasing isolation and humiliation of German Jews, but to try to protect Jews who had converted to Christianity from the impact and implications of the Aryan clause. Jews who had not converted could be classified as subhuman on racial grounds, but Jews who had been baptized ought to be immune to racial nuances. Perhaps the repeated calls over the years for the solution of 'the Jewish problem' and the 'total disappearance' of Jews from German life had created an unconscious concurrence with acts leading to those goals, unless they manifested 'excesses'[19] Orderly deportations brought almost no active opposition.[20] As Kulka states so eloquently: 'The many outspoken responses concerning the fate of only the relatively few converted Jews among the millions of persecuted Jews highlights the power of religious antagonism to overshadow the universalist Christian principles of the sanctity of life and responsibility for your fellowman.'[21] Indeed, it is against this background of general indifference fuelled by theological principles, however unarticulated, that the protests of a small number of clergy stand out. It may be assumed, based on the results of the protests against the euthanasia program and the removal of crucifixes from schools, that a proliferation of objections from Church leaders might have influenced the populace and led to a diminishing, however temporary, of the implacable movement forward in accomplishing the 'Final Solution.'

The reaction – or lack thereof – of the Churches during the war years in the Third Reich is a problem to which the Churches themselves must attend; indeed, this paper is a study of just such an effort on the part of the ELCA. Before turning to the events of the last fifteen years within the ELCA, it is important to balance the above brief discussion of the role of the Protestant churches in Germany during the war years with a glimpse into what was happening with Lutherans in Denmark and among Protestants in the United States. The latter is of course a much more diverse group than the former; in Germany, most Protestants were Lutheran. Such was also the case in Denmark, in which the responses of Lutherans to Nazi persecution of Jews took a turn markedly different from that in Germany.

An examination of the Protestant press in the United States during this time reveals a Christian perspective similar to that evident in Germany. That is, the passage of the Aryan clause in 1933 caused much consternation and comment, but it was restricted almost entirely to concern for baptized, confessional Christians who, as originally Jewish, were especially targeted, in Christian eyes, by the racial distinctions. Great distress was expressed by Protestants in general, and especially by Lutherans and members of the Reformed churches, in regard to the exclusion of non-Aryan Christians from the churches.[22] Concern for Jews as Jews, however, was a secondary matter, as was criticism of the use – or misuse – of the concept of race.

Nonetheless, it can be stated that the several hundred items about the persecution of the Jews in Europe between 1933 and 1945 published in the Protestant press were accurate accounts of the events.[23] From the very beginning – the pogroms of April 1933 and the establishment of the Aryan clause – readers of *The Friend* (Quaker), *The Lutheran* (United Lutheran Church), *The Presbyterian* (Presbyterian, U.S.A.), *The Watchman-Examiner* (Baptist), and *Advance – Christendom* (Congregationalist), among others, had access to the facts of what was occurring. As Robert W. Ross writes, 'Virtually no detail discovered in 1945 had not been already reported in the American-Protestant press by 1943, with the one exception of the total number of death camps....'[24]

It is interesting to note that in 1937, *The Churchman* (Episcopal), began a series of articles on fascism, focusing particularly on antisemitic groups in the United States which had become both vociferous and active. The first piece identified Germany as the source of much of the antisemitic propaganda being spread in America. *The Churchman* was a strident voice opposing that propaganda. On 15 September 1938, it criticized Father Charles Coughlin[25], 'who had reissued the Protocols of Zion while admitting that he could not vouch for their authenticity.' *The Churchman* continued to analyse, critique and discuss both antisemitism and fascism during those years. Other Protestant papers, such as *The Lutheran Companion* (Augustan Swedish Lutheran), published statements opposing antisemitism, both in Europe and the United States. Samuel McCrea Cavert, in *The Lutheran Companion*, reminded Christians of their indebtedness to 'the spiritual heritage of the Hebrews'.[26] Although Cavert's article – and the others – are laudable, they too, as in the case of German Lutheran statements, point to ambiguities. The use of the word 'Hebrews' rather than 'Jews' is one indication of ambivalence, paralleling the appellation of 'the Old Testament People of Israel' in Pastor Klapproth's letter. A fundamental attitude of non-acceptance and non-acknowledgment of the Jewish people is conveyed. A second indication, although less overt in the examples cited here and expressed also by the term 'Hebrews'[27] is the unarticulated but pervasive notion of supersessionism. Designating the Jewish people by the term 'Hebrews' – or, sometimes, 'Israelites' – conveys the notion that Judaism effectively ended in the first century, having been superseded by its derivative but 'true' religion, Christianity. The appellation 'Jews' or 'Jewish' acknowledges the continuity and validity of Jewish tradition after the destruction of the Second Temple, through the on-going rabbinic tradition.[28]

The general comments above in regard to the Protestant press in the United States during the war years, and the issue of what was known and what was not, provide a framework through which to view a group to the right of those that in 1988 came together to form the ELCA. Founded in 1839 by German immigrants to Missouri, the Lutheran Church-Missouri Synod reports a membership of 2.6 million across the United States, as of 1993, with the largest concentration in the Midwest.[29] While it belongs to the International Lutheran Council, it is not a member of the Lutheran World Federation, the National Council of Churches, or the World Council of Churches, thus setting itself apart from the umbrella organizations both of Lutheranism specifically and Protestantism generally. The Missouri Synod affirms Luther's view that 'the Bible is the Word of God and that it does not mislead or deceive us;' at the same time it believes that 'the reliability of the Bible is not possible apart from faith in Jesus Christ.'[30] While all branches of Lutheranism declare allegiance to grace, faith, and Scripture, the Missouri Synod sees the centrality of Scripture compromised by the legitimization of historical criticism in the study of the Bible. This includes the view that the Bible may be in error in matters of science and history. While the ELCA accepts a diversity of approaches based on evolving modern biblical scholarship, the Missouri Synod does not, seeing such a perspective as a blurring of the proper distinctions between Law and Gospel.[31] Incorporating modern biblical scholarship into one's views of the Bible also leads to views on the ordination of women and the nature of church fellowship which the Missouri Synod sees as inimical to its understanding of Lutheran confession.

The strict stand of the Missouri Synod in regard to biblical interpretation led, in the early 1970s, to a walkout of most of the faculty members and students from Concordia Seminary in St. Louis and the eventual departure of close to 100,000 members, who later formed the Association of Evangelical Lutheran Churches. The tensions in the Missouri Synod between liberal and conservatives were evident as early as 1959, when a Missouri Synod convention passed a resolution 'binding all pastors, teachers, and professors to a doctrinal statement, written by Franz Pieper and first adopted by the Synod in 1932, that was scholastic and even fundamentalist in its approach to the Bible.'[32] The conflict that emerged, although ostensibly over methodologies of biblical interpretation, was in essence about power and authority. At the end, 'Old Lutheran conservatism tinged with American fundamentalism triumphed in the Missouri Synod; the moderates were forced out of all positions of influence or authority.'[33]

The differences between the ELCA and the Missouri Synod find expression as well in regard to Christian ecumenicism and Lutheran-Jewish relations. The Missouri Synod fears merging, or having fellowship, with those with whom they disagree on doctrinal issues, although it affirms the unity of Christian believers: 'Despite all of the external divisions in contemporary Christendom, we . . . believe that there is . . . only one church in heaven and on earth.'[34] But this is a theoretical claim only, as practical unity, according to the Synod,[35] is dependent upon the ability to 'confess the truth and expose error', 'truth' and 'error' as defined by the Synod. This leads to an isolationism bordering on sectarianism. A member of the ELCA, as an example, cannot receive communion in a Missouri Synod church. If there is a problem in relating to other Christians, even to other Lutherans, Jews are 'off the radar screen'.[36] The Committee on Church Relations and Theology of the Synod is a powerful group, seeing itself as gatekeepers of the Old Lutheran traditions rather than reaching out toward consensus. This group writes the publications and statements which are concerned with other Christian groups as well as Jews.

At the Missouri Synod convention in 1977, for example, the church's leadership encouraged its member congregations 'to prepare themselves for effective witness to the Jewish people.'[37] The church issued 3000 instruction manuals, which it claimed, after complaints by the American Jewish Congress, could not be recalled. The executive secretary of the Synod's Board for Evangelism later reported that the board was 'considering writing letters to those people [who had ordered the manuals], with explanations about the offensiveness of the material.' He promised that in subsequent editions of the manual 'we will remove offensive material that presents unfavourable stereotypes of Jewish persons . . . . we have come to see that this material is offensive.'[38] At the time of *The Christian Century* article quoted, i.e. 3 May 1978, no such corrected manual, or letter of apology to Jewish organizations, had been received.

A 'Statement of Jewish–Lutheran Concerns', however, had been issued and adopted in January 1978 by the Commission on Witnessing to Jewish People of the Board of Evangelism of the Synod. This statement assured Jews that 'we are not singling out the Jewish people as a special target for our evangelistic endeavors,' and 'we are not mounting a campaign to convert Jewish people with techniques of evangelism which involve manipulation, pressure, and disrespect of the individual. Unfortunately, most of our people are not aware of past injustices.'[39] The proclamation affirms its desire to be sensitive to 'the danger that witnessing to Jewish people can result in misunderstanding and potential nurturing of anti-Semitic attitudes',[40] but it proceeds in articulating a theology of supersessionism which persists in making Jews legitimate objects of Christian efforts at conversion. It declares 'we love the Jewish people',[41] but its 'love' is defined by domination, not the acknowledgment of autonomous identity. Another resolution in regard to the evangelism of the Jews was adopted by the Synod in 1983, in commemoration of the 500th anniversary of the birth of Luther. Additional declarations were affirmed in 1986 and 1989.[42]

The three resolutions of the 1980s offer minor changes from the affirmations in the 1978 statement. Most interesting to me was a phone conversation on 20 August 1999 with Dr. Jerald C. Joersz, Director of the Synod's Commission on Theology and Church Relations. Dr. Joersz asserted that documents of Luther are 'purported' to be anti-semitic because Luther repudiated his earlier stands in regard to the Jews on his deathbed. Unless Dr. Joersz is referring to some general confession of sin which is customary at the bedside of the dying, there is absolutely no reference to any such statement on Luther's part. No biography of Luther of which I am aware makes reference to any such repudiation of earlier statements. Rather, in discussing Luther and the Jews, the noted historian Roland Bainton is often quoted. Referring to the 1543 pamphlet *Concerning the Jews and Their Lies*, Bainton, a great admirer of Luther, writes, 'One might wish that he had died before ever he wrote it.'[43] Bainton is thus unaware of any repudiation or remorse expressed by Luther.

Subsequent to this exchange, I wrote Dr. Joersz and he e-mailed me a response, which follows:

> Thank you for your August 24 letter, in which you inquired concerning Luther's comments on the Jews before he died.

What I had in mind were Luther's comments made in connection with his last sermon in Eisleben on February 15, 1546, three days before he died. He added some comments under the heading 'Eine Vermahnung wider die Juden.' Although he has some stern things to say about those Jews who blasphemed Christ, he also makes statements like this (St. Louis Edition, Vol.XII):

Nun wollen wir christlich mit ihnen handeln, und bieten ihnen den christlichen Glauben an, dasz sie den Messiam wollen annehmen, der doch ihr Vetter ist und von ihrem Fleisch und Blut geboren, und rechter Abrahams Same, dessen sie sich ruhmen ... (1265)

Noch wollen wir die christliche Liebe an ihnen uben, und für sie bitten, dasz sie sich bekehren, den Herrn annehmen, den sie vor uns billig ehren sollten. (1265)

Wollen sich die Juden zu uns bekehren, und von ihrer Lasterung und was sie uns sonst gethan haben, aufhoren, so wollen wir es ihnen gerne vergeben ... (1266)

It is in light of such statements that our church in 1983 concluded Resolution 3-09 'To Clarify Position on Anti-Semitism' with the encouragement that 'we personally and individually adopt Luther's final attitude towards Jewish people ...'

I hope that this response is helpful to you in some way.

Kindest regards.

Dr. Jerald C. Joersz[44]

The German translates as:

Now we want to treat them in Christian fashion and offer them in the Christian faith, so that they will accept the Messiah, who is after all their cousin and born of their flesh and blood and of Abraham's seed, of which they too boast ...

Further we want to practice Christian love with them and pray for them so that they convert, accept the Lord, whom they should honor before us as is right and proper.

If the Jews were to convert and cease their blasphemy and other misdeeds, we would gladly forgive them.

Dr. Joersz describes the words of Luther's sermon three days before his death with the mild adjective 'stern'.

One must also take note of the letter written to Katherine upon Luther's arrival in Eisleben two weeks earlier.

Dear Kate,

I was faint on the road close by Eisleben. It was my fault, but had you been there you'd have said the Jews were to blame, or their god. We had to pass through a village close by Eisleben where many Jews were dwelling – perhaps it was they blowing at me so hard. Right this minute here in Eisleben there are more than fifty Jewish residences. And it is a fact that when I passed that settlement such a cold blast came into the back of the coach and through my beret that I thought it would turn my brain to ice. That probably aggravated my vertigo. But now I am, praise God, in good shape, except the pretty women are such a trial to me that I have no problems with libidinousness whatsoever.

The persistence of the Missouri Synod in understanding proselytizing to be its mission to the Jews and denying both the content and the virulence of Luther's last three tracts[45] is evident in the above correspondence. One is compelled to conclude that contemporary adherents of the doctrines of the Synod might claim, as did Luther is his letter to Kate, that 'the Jews were to blame' for their own fate. Even the 1989 Missouri Synod Resolution[46] sees its work of proselytizing as holy work. The resolution, entitled 'To Strengthen Witness to Jewish People' states (in part), '... God has blessed this work with the result that Jewish people have come to faith in Jesus Christ as their Savior...'[47] Thus the Missouri Synod offers no apologies either for Luther's aim of converting Jews or his vitriolic words about

Judaism and Jewish people; rather, it sees itself as carrying out his policies in the proper fashion.

A final note about the Missouri Synod: In 1945, Concordia Publishing put out a volume entitled *Marching Side by Side: Stories from Lutheran Chaplains on the Far-flung Battlefronts*. A compilation of the experiences and recollections of Lutheran chaplains during World War II, it is noteworthy for the complete absence of any reference whatsoever to the murder of European Jewry. The word 'Jewish' appears but once in the text: ' "Chaplain," said one Jewish medic, "there's a fine lad in my ward who carries his church identification on his dog tag. It says something about notifying a Lutheran chaplain..." '[48]

The silence of this volume and the ambiguities of the responses evident among Lutherans in Germany and in the Protestant press in the United States stand in stark contrast to the directness of both word and action within the Lutheran Church in Denmark. The story is well-known: how nearly all the Jews in Denmark were ferried to safety in Sweden; how the Torah scrolls, prayer books, synagogues and Jewish homes were meticulously maintained; how the small number of Jews deported to Theresienstadt were constantly inquired about by the King, who would ask how his Danish citizens were faring under German care. Danish Lutheran policy was activist and humanitarian. On October 3, 1943, the Danish Lutheran bishops sent a letter to the German occupation officials in Denmark. In addition, it was read from every Lutheran pulpit in the country. The letter stated:

> We will never forget that the Lord Jesus Christ was born in Bethlehem of the Virgin Mary, according to God's promise to the Chosen People of Israel. Persecution of the Jews conflicts with the humanitarian conception of the love of neighbors and the message which Christ's church set out to preach. Christ taught us that every man has a value in the eyes of God.
>
> Persecution conflicts with the judicial conscience existing in the Danish people, inherited through centuries of Danish culture. All Danish citizens, according to the fundamental law, have the same right and responsibility under the law of religious freedom...
>
> Notwithstanding our separate religious beliefs we will fight to preserve for our Jewish brothers and sisters the same freedom we value more than life... It is evident that in this case we are obeying God rather than man.[49]

Some Lutherans – both German and American – saw the role of bystander in the murder of the Jews as a way of obeying God: a fulfilment of God's decree against a stubborn, rejected, people, an announcement of the Second Coming, the destruction of the Temple in 70 CE in modern guise. Or, in more gentle terms, the essential holiness of all human life did not beckon as an ultimate reason to defy and speak out against systematic human brutality directed towards one group. Danish Lutherans, in contrast, cut through theological justifications to the fundamental Christian message as they understood it: the sanctity of every human life. It is not the purpose here to attempt to ascertain why Lutheranism manifested such different attitudes, but rather to note the wide variation within this one branch of Protestantism.

It is within this broad context that the condemnation of Luther's 1543 document by the ELCA in 1993 must be understood. The decision was the result of a long, gradual process, and the resolution of repudiation was not unanimously adopted[50]; yet it does express the majority view of the close to 5.2 million members of the Evangelical Lutheran Church in America at the close of the twentieth century. The passage of the resolution has led to numerous sermons in churches, discussions in Lutheran divinity schools and universities, publications, and moves forward in Lutheran-Jewish dialogue.

As greater understanding and respect continue to develop, one can only be grateful for the steps taken.

That the repudiation of *Concerning the Jews and Their Lies* comes 450 years after its publication is the result of many factors. The enormity of the Holocaust – the pervasiveness of anti-Judaism among nearly all European peoples (as well as some non-European nations which severely limited entry of Jews into their borders) – led to a slow recognition among Christians world-wide that Christian doctrine and ideology had contributed to the success of the Nazi machine: indeed, after the war, Europe was, for all intents and purposes, *Judenrein*. What might be called the first stage of this post-Shoah process culminated in Vatican II, meeting from 1962–65. The impetus of Vatican II forced churches everywhere to deal with the meaning and consequences – both practical and theoretical – of Christian texts, biblical and extra-biblical.

One might ask, in regard to Lutherans, why were people for the most part unaware of Luther's anti-Jewish statements and the violence they recommend? A first and common sense response is that one tends to focus upon positive contributions; it is only recently, to make an analogy, that historians have begun to uncover and make public Thomas Jefferson's liaison with a female slave on his plantation. Second, Luther's writings are voluminous, and until the official translation into English in 1971,[51] were only partially available in English to the student of theology or the interested layperson. Third, study of Luther tended to concentrate on his life until 1529, with little attention given to his last 17 years.[52] One might say that the decision of the editors of the 1971 English translation, Jaroslav Pelikan and Helmut T. Lehmann, to include the anti-Jewish works, especially the 1543 essay, was an act of historical, moral consciousness, a kind of 'owning up' to that which Luther had indeed stated and affirmed and suggested as commendable Christian (Lutheran) behaviour. It is estimated that when John Stendhal proposed an official repudiation of the 1543 document in 1993 to the nearly 1000 delegates present at the ELCA Churchwide Assembly in Kansas City, 85% knew vaguely of some anti-Jewish writing of Luther's, but 95% had neither read nor heard Luther's actual words.[53]

Under discussion at the Assembly was whether or not to approve the Lutheran World Federation statement on Lutheran-Jewish relations issued in Stockholm in 1983. The meeting of representatives of the world Jewish community[54] and world Lutheran community had convened on the occasion of the 500th anniversary of the birth of Luther to discuss the theme 'Luther, Lutheranism, and the Jews'. After three days of conversations, the 12 Jewish and 15 Lutheran participants, put forth three statements, Jewish, Lutheran, and joint. Following is the Lutheran Statement which in 1993 in Kansas City was judged inadequate and which was not passed by the ELCA Churchwide Assembly.

Lutheran Statement

We Lutherans take our name and much of our understanding of Christianity from Martin Luther. But we cannot accept or condone the violent verbal attacks that the Reformer made against the Jews.

Lutherans and Jews interpret the Hebrew Bible differently. But we believe that a christological reading of the Scriptures does not lead to anti-Judaism, let alone anti-Semitism.

We hold that an honest, historical treatment of Luther's attacks on the Jews takes away from modern anti-Semites the assumption that they may legitimately call on the authority of Luther's name to bless their anti-Semitism.

We insist that Lutheranism does not support racial anti-Semitism, nationalistic, anti-Semitism and political anti-Semitism. Even the deplorable religious anti-Semitism of the 16th century, to which Luther's attacks made important contribution, is a horrible anachronism when translated to the conditions of the modern world. We recognize with deep regret, however, that Luther has been used to justify such antisemitism in the period of national socialism and that his writings lent themselves to such abuse. Although there remain conflicting assumptions built into the beliefs of Judaism and Christianity, they need not, and should not, lead to the animosity and the violence of Luther's treatment of the Jews. Martin Luther opened up our eyes to a deeper understanding of the Old Testament and showed us the depth of our common inheritance and the roots of our faith.

Yet a frank examination also forces Lutherans and other Christians to confront the anti-Jewish attitudes of their past and present. Many of the anti-Jewish utterances of Luther have to be explained in the light of his polemic against what he regarded as misinterpretations of the Scriptures. He attacked these interpretations, since for him everything now depended on a right understanding of the world of God.

The sins of Luther's anti-Jewish remarks, the violence of his attacks on the Jews, must be acknowledged with deep distress. And all occasions for similar sin in the present or the future must be removed from our churches.

Hostility toward the Jews began long before Luther and has been a continuing evil after him: The history of the centuries following the Reformation saw in Europe the gradual acceptance of religious pluralism. The church was not always the first to accept this development; yet there have also been examples of leadership by the church in the movement to accept Jews as full fellow citizens and members of society.

Beginning in the last half of the 19th century antisemitism increased in Central Europe and at the same time Jewish people were being integrated in society. This brought to the churches, particularly in Germany, an unwanted challenge. Paradoxically the churches honored the people Israel of the Bible but rejected the descendants of those people, myths were perpetuated about the Jews and deprecatory references appeared in Lutheran liturgical and educational material. Luther's doctrine of the Two Kingdoms was used to justify passivity in the face of totalitarian claims. These and other less theological factors contributed to the failures which have been regretted and repeatedly confessed since 1945.

To their credit it is to be said that there were individuals and groups among Lutherans who in defiance of totalitarian power defended their Jewish neighbors, both in Germany and elsewhere.

Lutherans of today refuse to be bound by all of Luther's utterances on the Jews. We hope we have learned from the tragedies of the recent past. We are responsible for seeing that we do not now nor in the future leave any doubt about our position on racial and religious prejudice and that we afford to all the human dignity, freedom and friendship that are the right of all the Father's children.[55]

The issue of repudiating Luther's anti-Jewish writings was brought to the attention of the full Assembly initially by a group from New England led by John Stendhal. In the ensuing discussion, some delegates suggested approving the 1983 Lutheran World Federation Statement rather than formulating a new one. Others recommended sending the resolution to committee for further discussion; it then would have come up before the Assembly at its next meeting in two years' time. The New England based group, however, prevailed in getting the Assembly to act immediately, without further consultation or procrastination; for them, it was an urgent matter. The urgency was most forcefully conveyed by the reading aloud, to the entire Assembly, of sections of the 1543 essay. The coarseness of Luther's language and violence of his suggestions were shocking to the many who had but the faintest notion of the existence and/or content of this writing. When the resolution authored by the New England group and others was then read, the proposal that it be adopted by the Assembly was passed by a vote of 905 in favour, 38 opposed, and three abstentions.[56] The text of the declaration officially adopted by the Church Council of the ELCA on 18 April 1994, reads:

In the long history of Christianity there exists no more tragic development than the treatment accorded the Jewish people on the part of Christian believers. Very few Christian communities of faith were able to escape the contagion of anti-Judaism and its modern successor, anti-Semitism. Lutherans belonging to the Lutheran World Federation and the Evangelical Lutheran Church in America feel a special burden in this regard because of certain elements in the legacy of the reformer Martin Luther and the catastrophes, including the Holocaust of the twentieth century, suffered by Jews in places where the Lutheran churches were strongly represented.

The Lutheran communion of faith is linked by name and heritage to the memory of Martin Luther, teacher and reformer. Honoring his name in our own, we recall his bold stand for truth, his earthy and sublime words of wisdom, and above all his witness to God's saving Word. Luther proclaimed a gospel for people as we really are, bidding us to trust a grace sufficient to reach our deepest shames and address the most tragic truths.

In the spirit of that truth-telling, we who bear his name and heritage must with pain acknowledge also Luther's anti-Judaic diatribes and the violent recommendations of his later writings against the Jews. As did many of Luther's own companions in the sixteenth century, we reject this violent invective, and yet more do we express our deep and abiding sorrow over its tragic effects on subsequent generations. In concert with the Lutheran World Federation we particularly deplore the appropriation of Luther's words by modern anti-Semites for the teaching of hatred toward Judaism or toward the Jewish people in our day.

Grieving the complicity of our own tradition within this history of hatred, moreover, we express our urgent desire to live out our faith in Jesus Christ with love and respect for the Jewish people. We recognize in anti-Semitism a contradiction and an affront to the Gospel, a violation of our hope and calling, and we pledge this church to oppose the deadly working of such bigotry, both within our own circles and in the society around us.

Finally, we pray for the continued blessing of the Blessed One upon the increasing cooperation and understanding between Lutheran Christians and the Jewish community.[57]

What was judged inadequate in the 1983 Lutheran World Federation statement that was seen as rectified in the ELCA proposal a decade later? The 1983 proclamation, while expressing 'deep regret' and 'deep distress', nonetheless contained more explanation than apology. It focused upon the historical context of Luther's 1543 essay, affirming that 'Lutherans and Jews interpret the Bible differently,' and 'Many of the anti-Jewish utterances of Luther have to be explained in the light of his polemic against what he regarded as misinterpretations of the Scriptures. He attacked these interpretations. . . .' Those who lobbied for a specific ELCA proclamation over and above that of the LWF felt the earlier statement did not go far enough; it was equivocal, perhaps even grudging. It was important to affirm that Lutherans were not only doing history (it is important, of course, to place Luther within historical context), but also, in assuming responsibility, participating in a process of repentance. The 1993 document accomplishes this aim. While averring its agreement with the LWF statement, the words of the ELCA declaration go further, referring to 'our deepest shame,' asserting the 'complicity of our own tradition,' and expressing the 'urgent desire to live out our faith . . . with love and respect for the Jewish people'. The language is more direct, the recounting of historical context much less an explanation, the apology complete. As officially adopted by the ELCA in 1994, the 1993 declaration represents an authentic move forward in Jewish–Lutheran relations and a meaningful development in post-Holocaust Christian theology.

The capstone of this movement both of responsibility and reconciliation is the 'Guidelines for Lutheran-Jewish Relations' drafted by the Consultative Panel on Lutheran-Jewish Relations of the Department of Ecumenical Affairs of the ELCA and officially adopted by the ELCA Church Council on 16 November 1998. These Guidelines concretize the 'urgent desire' expressed in the 1994 repudiation of Luther's anti-Judaism, 'to live out our faith in Jesus Christ with love and respect for the Jewish people.' Containing introductory remarks and a list of 15 suggestions for interfaith interaction, the Guidelines conclude by stating that they 'have been issued so that those who desire to engage in interfaith dialogue might benefit from the experience of those who have gone before. They are intended to provide practical assistance as well as the encouragement needed for a rewarding journey.'[58] The list of suggestions is sensitively explicated and astutely formulated, including brief discussion of the Passover Seder, Messianic Jews, emphasis in Judaism on communal survival, and use of New Testament texts by Lutheran pastors. To indicate the tone of the Guidelines, the introductory remarks follow:

> As Lutherans, we seek to renew and enhance our relationship with the Jewish people, a relationship long distorted by misunderstanding and prejudice. In its 1994 *Declaration to the Jewish Community*, the Evangelical Lutheran Church in America publicly repudiated the anti-Jewish views of Martin Luther, expressed repentance for Christian complicity in hatred and violence against the Jews through the centuries, and committed itself to building a relationship with the Jewish people based on love and respect. For Lutherans to read, understand, and acknowledge this Declaration...can be a first step in renewing our relationship with the Jewish community. Reconciliation always begins with an understanding of the offense and a willingness to repent and amend one's ways. Only then can further steps be taken to forge a new relationship.
>
> We as Christians share deep and common roots with Jews, not least books of Scripture revered by both communities. There is much to be gained in exploring those common roots, as well as the reasons for the 'parting of the ways' during the first generations of the followers of Jesus. New Testament texts reflect at many points the hostility between the two communities, but also point to ways in which a new spirit of mutual respect and understanding can be achieved.
>
> We as Christians also need to learn of the rich and varied history of Judaism since New Testament times, and of the Jewish people as a diverse, living community of faith today. Such an encounter with living nd faithful Judaism can be profoundly enriching for Christian self-understanding. It is to nurture this blessing that we offer these guidelines or honest and faithful conversation and cooperation between Lutherans and Jews.

The journey of Lutherans from the Barmen Declaration of 1934 to the ELCA Guidelines of 1998 traverses not only 54 years of the 20th century, but also centuries of misunderstanding. In the Guidelines, Judaism is affirmed as a living, vital faith, not an historical vestige. Lutherans are advised to learn about Jewish history and practice so as to '...enrich[ing]..Christian self-understanding.'[59] Understanding of the Christian tradition is seen as enhanced by understanding the complexities of the historical experiences of Jews and historical development of Judaism. The Guidelines are neither patronizing nor condescending, but put forth with genuine sincerity and caring. Lutheran educators and clergy are cautioned against misuse of certain texts of the Greek Bible or New Testament, and urged to develop curricular materials which avoid the old anti-Jewish stereotypes.[60]

In confronting its own history since the rise of Hitler – and over the past half-century – Lutherans have moved toward altering the collective memories of their shared traditions. The past cannot be denied; as in all instances of authentic repentance, it must be faced directly, with full acknowledgment and responsibility. These components of repentance then become part of the new collective memories of the tradition, one which deals with rather than denies its past. The reworded memories as expressed in the 1994 and 1998 ELCA documents express contrition, the recognition of Jewish identity – both personhood and peoplehood – and a clarion call to action.

In so articulating its confrontation with its own history, the words of the ELCA 'manifest great courage. For they involve changing the direction in which the historical memories of a shared tradition have moved for centuries developing, as it were, a new self-identity. . .'.[61]

Contemporary Lutherans of the ELCA 'Remember the days of old' (Deuteronomy 32:70). May their remembrance – and the efforts of Jews and Christians together – inspire us to ever greater responsibility toward one another.

NOTES

1 The ELCA was officially formed in January, 1988. An amalgamation of the American Lutheran Church, the American Evangelical Lutheran Church, and the Lutheran Church of America, the merger plans were approved by each of these groups in 1986.

2 Quoted in Richard Gutteridge, 'German Protestantism and the Jews', in Kulka and Mendes-Flohr (eds.), *'Judaism and Christianity under the Impact of National Socialism, 1919–1945* (Jerusalem: Historical Society of Israel, 1987), p.234.

3 Quoted in Gutteridge, p.233.

4 Almost none of the pamphlets commenting upon the Aryan clause in 1933 were free of racial overtones and anti-Jewish slurs. Even Martin Niemöller referred to the Jews as a guest people within the German nation and said: 'We as a nation have been made to suffer considerably under the influence of the Jewish people. It is a matter of real self-denial to champion their cause.' Quoted in Gutteridge, p.232.

5 R. Zvi Werblowsky, 'New Territories, New Maps, New Realities,' in Kulka and Mendes- Flohr (eds.), p.532. See as well the reference in Gutteridge, p.235. According to Gutteridge, Barth claimed that had he advocated including references to measures against the Jews in the Barmen Declaration, 'it would not have been acceptable to the confessing way of thinking at that time.'

6 Gutteridge, p.234.

7 Gutteridge, p.237.

8 Gutteridge records the actions of the Pastor of Gemarke Church in Barmen immediately after Kristallnacht on p.248.

9 The following letter is quoted in Otto Dov Kulka, 'Popular Christian Attitudes in the Third Reich', Kulka and Mendes-Flohr, eds. p.257.

10 Kulka's source is cited on p.257, n.10, which states: *Geheimes Staatsarchiv der Stiftung Pressischer Kulturbesitz*, Rep.90, No.71.

11 Kulka, 'Popular Christian Attitudes in the Third Reich', p.255.

12 See Kenneth R. Stow, 'Hatred of the Jews or Love of the Church: Papal Policy Toward the Jews in the Middle Ages', in Shmuel Almog, ed., *Antisemitism Through the Ages* (New York: Pergamon Press, 1988), pp.71–90.

13 See, for instance, Immanuel Kant, *Religion Within the Limits of Reason Alone* (New York: Harper Torchbooks, 1960) and Emil Fackenheim, *Encounters Between Judaism and Modern Philosophy* (New York: Basic Books, 1973), esp. chs 2 and 3.

14 See Judith H. Banki, 'The Image of Jews in Christian Teaching', in Naomi W. Cohen (ed.), *Essential Papers on Jewish–Christian Relations in the United States: Imagery and Reality* (New York: New York University Press, 1990), 43–59, esp. p.55. Also, Amy Newman, 'The Death of Judaism in German Protestant Thought from Luther to Hegel', *Journal of the American Academy of Religion* 61/3 (Fall 1993): 455–84.

15 This is the term used by Kulka, 'Popular Christian Attitudes in the Third Reich', p.257.

16 Quoted in Kulka, p.259; see his n.14 also on that page.

17 *Loc cit.*

18 Quoted in Kulka, p.259; see his n.16 on that page.

19 See Klapproth's letter earlier in the text.

20 A wonderful fictionalized account of the conflicts in a German town resulting from acts against its Jewish population is Ursula Hegi's *Stones from the River* (New York: Simon and Schuster, 1994).

21 Kulka, 'Popular Christian Attitudes in the Third Reich', p.266.

22 Robert W. Ross, *So It Was True: The American Protestant Press and the Nazi Persecution of the Jews* (Minneapolis: University of Minnesota Press, 1980), pp.17–19.

23 *ibid.*, p.271.

24 *ibid.*, p.170.

25 *ibid.*, p.95.

26 *ibid.*, p.97.

27 All of our children were born in a Catholic hospital in Hamilton, Ontario in the 1960s. When asked my religion at the pre-admission meeting, I said 'Jewish'; the person on the other side of the desk wrote 'Hebrew' in the space on the form. It was the first time I had seen that designation. Immediately perceiving the theological implications of the term, I asked that it be written as I had stated it, i.e. 'Jewish'.

28 An excellent analysis of the issues surrounding the notion of supersessionism is to be found in Clark M. Williamson, *A Guest in the House of Israel: Post-Holocaust Church Theology* (Louisville, Kentucky: Westminster/John Knox Press, 1993).

29 Samuel H. Nafzger, 'An Introduction to The Lutheran Church-Missouri Synod' (St. Louis, Missouri: Concordia Publishing, 1994), p.4.

30 Nafzger, p.12.

31 'The Law tells what God demands of sinners if they are to be saved. The Gospel reveals what God has already done for our salvation.... It is in the proper distinction between Law and Gospel that the purity of the Gospel is preserved and the three *solas* of "grace alone", "faith alone", and "Scripture alone" are united' (Nafzger, pp.12–13).

32 Donald J. Huber, 'John H. Tietjen', in George H. Shriver (ed.), *Dictionary of Heresy Trials in American Christianity* (Greenwood Press, 1997), p.423. Huber's entry gives an excellent and detailed discussion of the liberal/conservative controversy in the Missouri Synod.

33 *ibid.*, p.428. Huber concludes his article with the statement: 'Whether it was a victory for Christian truth was a question that continued to trouble thoughtful observers, who wondered if politicized church conventions and packed committees are any better equipped than fallible seminary faculties to determine the will of God for the life of the church,' pp.428–29.

34 Nafzger, op.cit., p.15.

35 *Loc. cit.*

36 Conversation with Dr. Donald J. Huber, Professor, Trinity Lutheran Seminary, Columbus, Ohio, 30 August 1999.

37 Quoted in 'Missouri Synod Evangelism Singling Out the Jews', *The Christian Century*, 3 May 1978, p.460.

38 *Loc. cit.*

39 Harold H. Ditmanson (ed.), *Stepping-Stones to Further Jewish–Lutheran Relationships: Key Lutheran Statements* (Minneapolis: Augsburg Fortress, 1990), p.80. The last sentence quoted echoes of apologetics. It seems bizarre to imply that the 'injustices' referred to were secrets of a sort, when most of the evangelizing of Protestant denominations was done by ordinary folk. In addition, part of the task of the Commission on Witnessing to the Jewish People might be seen as correcting previous abuses, thus making church members aware of them in the first place.

40 *Loc. cit.*

41 Ditmanson, *op.cit.*, p.81.

42 I was finally able to obtain the full text of these later three statements from Reverend Bruce Lieske, Executive Director of an organization called Lutherans in Jewish Evangelism. Reverend Lieske told me in a phone conversation on 25 October 1999, that he is especially proud of the language at the conclusion of the 1978 statement, which reads, ' . . . we do love the Jewish people . . . and will continue to love them even when they choose not to accept our witness' (quoted in Ditmanson, p.81). According to Lieske, these words manifest 'the true *agape* (love) of the Saviour'. Perhaps what is appealing here to him and others is the insistence that Missouri Synod Lutherans remain committed

to converting Jews, but without resorting to the violence recommended by Luther. The objective is the same, but the means are infused with true Christian 'love.'

43 Quoted in H.G. Haile, *Luther: An Experiment in Biography* (Princeton, New Jersey: Princeton University Press, 1980), p.292.

44 Personal e-mail correspondence, 26 August 1999.

45 *Against the Sabbatarians: Letter to a Good Friend* (1538), *Against the Antinomians* (1539), and *On the Jews and Their Lies* (1543). Titles are taken as translated in Volume 47 of *Luther's Works*, Franklin Sherman and Helmut T. Lehmann (eds.), (Philadelphia: Fortress Press, 1971).

46 Resolution 1–12, passed in Wichita.

47 Bruce J. Lieske, 'Witnessing to Jewish People', (Orlando, FL.: Lutherans in Jewish Evangelism and LCMS World Mission, 1995), Appendix A, p.53.

48 Frederick C. Proehl (ed.), *Marching Side by Side: Stories from Lutheran Chaplains on the Far-flung Battlefronts* (St. Louis: Concordia Publishing, 1945), p.122.

49 Quoted in Harold Flender, *Rescue in Denmark* (New York: Holocaust Library, 1963), p.69.

50 The vote was 'Yes–905; No–38; Abstain–3'. Minutes of Plenary Session Eleven, Response of the Memorials Committee, p.465.

51 Jaroslav Pelikan and Helmut T. Lehmann, General Editors, *Luther's Works* (in 55 volumes), (Philadelphia, Concordia Publishing and Fortress Press, 1971).

52 Conversation with Dr. Franklin Sherman, 25 August 1999.

53 Conversation with Dr. Sherman, 25 August 1999, and earlier conversation with Dr. Paul Nelson.

54 The International Jewish Committee on Interreligious Consultation (IJCIC) is composed of World Jewish Congress, the Synagogue Council of America, the American Jewish Committee, the B'nai B'rith Anti-Defamation League, and the Jewish Council in Israel for Interreligious Consultations.

55 Quoted in Ditmanson, *op.cit.*, pp.102–103.

56 Minutes of 1993 Churchwide Assembly, Assembly Action (CA93.7.46), p.465.

57 In pamphlet, 'Guidelines for Lutheran-Jewish Relations' published by the Department for Ecumenical Affairs, ELCA, Chicago (1999)

58 'Guidelines for Lutheran-Jewish Relations', Affairs, p.3.

59 Guidelines, p.1.

60 Guidelines, #13, p.3.

61 Rochelle L. Millen, 'Remembrance, Responsibility, Reconciliation: Reflections on Memory and History', Trinity Lutheran Review, February, 2000.

ONCE MORE:
MARTIN LUTHER AND THE JEWS

Andreas Pangritz

ARTIN LUTHER's attitude towards the Jews has often been examined as an example of the role of theology in the history of antisemitism in general and in the preparation of the Holocaust in particular.[1] The authors of the article on Luther in the *Encyclopaedia Judaica* rightly state that.

> Inconsistency and violence characterized Luther's utterances in all fields, but perhaps in none with more disastrous consequences than in his statements on the Jews...Throughout the subsequent centuries Luther's ferocious castigation of the Jews provided fuel for anti-Semites and the vicious force of that legacy was still evident in Nazi propaganda.[2]

Lutheran theologians, however, are still inclined to qualify or even excuse Luther's attitude towards the Jews, employing a whole set of apologetic strategies. One version of these strategies has consisted in stressing the obvious inconsistencies in Luther's theological development, particularly the obvious contrast between the early reformer and the later embittered political advisor. This explanation results in an attempt to play down the disaster and excuse Luther's unpleasant aberrations in psychological terms. Another version is the historical comparison of Luther's position with the 'normal' antisemitism of the time. Was not Luther simply a child of his time, sharing in the literary 'brutalism' (*Grobianismus*) of the time? Others point to the fact that the polemic between Jews and Christians was mutual, passing over in silence the extremely unequal balance of power within the social reality of the time.[3] Another version of playing down the problem are references to the economic context of Luther's attitude in respect to his polemics against usury. Here the question should be asked, 'why were the Fuggers cursed, whereas the Jews were expelled?'[4]

The most disturbing problem, however, is posed by another strategy, which is the separation of Luther's decisive theological discovery – 'justification by faith alone' (*solus Christus, sola gratia, sola fide*) – from his statements on the Jews, which are played down as tied to the time. The obvious purpose of this strategy is to maintain the reputation of Luther the Reformer, without any reservations, on the grounds that the theological essence of the Reformation movement has nothing to do with its antisemitic form. We can read, for instance, that 'It is not the Reformer Luther, but the church politician Luther, who in an historically given situation proved to be anti-Jewish. The Reformer and the gospel proclaimed by him are pro-Jewish.' Moreover: 'The Reformer Luther is a different person from the church politician Luther. It is scientifically untenable to construct a harmony between the Reformer Luther and the enemy of the Jews in relation to church policy.'[5] Well, if this is scientific, I prefer to risk scientific untenability, simply presupposing that Luther and Luther are the same person. The question of whether there is an inner connection between Luther's theological approach and his antisemitism must be permissible. Oberman, for instance, points out that the theme of 'the Jews' is 'not a dark, special page' in Luther's work, but a 'central theme of his theology'.[6]

The purpose of the paper is a critical assessment of these apologetic strategies, based on a *relecture* of Luther's 1523 treatise in comparison with his later, explicitly antisemitic writings. A close reading of Luther's statements will prove that as early as 1523 he was interested in the Jews simply as objects of conversion. It may turn out that there is much more continuity than apologists of the Reformer would admit between Luther's allegedly pro-Jewish attitude in 1523 and the explicitly antisemitic writings of his later years.

A clarification with respect to terminology is necessary in advance: It is unusual – at least among Protestant theologians – to speak of Luther's 'antisemitism'. Certainly, the use of this term in the context of the 16th century is an anchronism, as the term has its historical roots in 19th-century racism. It has therefore become popular among Christian theologians, and sometimes is regarded as the only 'scientific' attitude, to speak of 'anti-Judaism' rather than 'antisemitism', as far as theological motives are concerned. Qualifications in the use of the term 'antisemitism' are obviously necessary and useful. On the other hand, it seems not unreasonable to suspect that the neat and tidy distinction between racist antisemitism and theological anti-Judaism may sometimes serve as a tranquillizer in order to play down the role of theology in the history of antisemitism. The difference may be important with respect to the psyche of the perpetrators, while for the victims the question of motives does not make much difference. At least in his later years Luther would not hesitate to find theological reasons in order to proclaim eliminationist actions against the Jews. And these were not shallow words, but propaganda with immediate political effects. Therefore – in spite of necessary distinctions – it seems to be appropriate to speak of 'antisemitism' with respect to Luther's position as well.[7]

In what follows I will first give an account of how Luther's attitude towards the Jews developed over time. In the second section I will inquire into the strongest aspect of Luther's theological view of the Jews as it is expressed in his early treatise 'That Jesus Christ Was Born a Jew' (1523). In a third section I shall compare Luther's early essay with his later, explicitly antisemitic writings, particularly with the treatise 'On the Jews and Their Lies' (1543). In our century particularly, Luther's later writings against the Jews would provide fuel for Nazi propaganda: They were used by the German Christians, the Nazi party within the Protestant church, as ammunition for the persecution of the Jews.[8] And even among more conservative Lutherans the Reformer's antisemitic attitude was applauded.[9] No wonder then that Julius Streicher, the editor of the *Völkischer Beobachter*, would be able to quote from Luther's writings in support of his own attitude during the trial of the major war criminals at the International Military Court in Nuremberg in 1946 with the words, 'Dr. Martin Luther would certainly be at my place in the dock today....'[10]

I. THE DEVELOPMENT OF LUTHER'S ATTITUDE TOWARDS THE JEWS

Many attempts have been made to defend Luther against the reproach of dealing with the Jews in an antisemitic way. Most popular among these strategies – as mentioned above – is the reference to Luther's allegedly pro-Jewish early treatise 'That Jesus Christ was Born a Jew' (1523), whereas the later violent attacks are played down as the regrettable aberrations of an embittered old man.

Let us look first at the way Luther's attitude towards the Jews developed during his lifetime. It is true that 'during the first period of his activity' as a university teacher in Wittenberg, 'Luther often condemned the persecution of the Jews and recommended a more tolerant policy toward them...'.[11] For example, in the 1513 controversy between the humanist Johannes Reuchlin and the converted Jew Pfefferkorn, Luther takes sides with Reuchlin against the Dominican monks of Cologne and strongly disapproves of the confiscation of the Talmud and rabbinic literature. His reason, however, is at least ambiguous: Luther does not see any chance of 'improving', that is, converting the Jews; God alone is able to bring about the inner conversion of the Jews and end their blasphemies. For the time being, Jewish blasphemies and invectives against Christ must be regarded as the fulfilment of the predictions of the prophets against this people. Human beings should not anticipate the actions of God. Obviously, Luther's early practical tolerance with respect to Jewish writings already includes an anti-Jewish theological position, or, more precisely: it is exactly his anti-Jewish theology which paradoxically enables him to take sides in favour of the Jews.

Around 1520 Luther's attitude towards the Jews seems to have changed. His reflection on the Jews in the context of the commentary on the Magnificat, written in 1521 during his stay at the Wartburg, for instance, sounds rather friendly. Of the final words of Mary in Luke 1.55 – 'As he has spoken to our fathers, Abraham and his seed, in eternity' – Luther remarks:

> That is why we should not be so unfriendly to the Jews, because among them there are still future Christians and day by day there are more of them. In addition it is they alone and not we Gentiles, who have the promise that there should be Christians in Abraham's seed for ever...Who would become a Christian, observing Christians treating people in such an un-Christian way? Not this way, beloved Christians! Tell them the truth gently, and if they do not want to listen, let them go their way![12]

Luther's most tolerant remark on Jewish–Christian relations I know can be found in his treatise 'On Married Life'. Here he even accepts intermarriage between Jews and Christians, as between Christians and Pagans, Turks and Heretics. He hopes, however, that a Christian wife by her good Christian behaviour would convert her Jewish husband to Christianity.[13]

It is also in the early 1520s that Luther wrote his treatise 'That Jesus Christ was Born a Jew'. Luther's relatively gentle attitude in this period even caused some positive expectations among the Jews with respect to the Reformation: 'Luther's disruptive impact in Roman Catholicism...was welcomed by Jews as a break in the monolithic power of the Church. Others hoped that the turmoil arising in the Christian world through the spread of Lutheranism would lead to toleration of all forms of worship. There were even some...who regarded Luther as a Crypto-Jew....'[14] This was certainly a misunderstanding.

As time went by, Luther's attitude towards the Jews changed again. It seems that especially after the troubles of the Peasants Revolt of 1525 his position hardened more and more. For example, in 1537, after the electoral prince of Saxony, Frederic the Magnanimous, had issued a ruthless edict of expulsion against the Jews, Joseph (Josel) b. Gershom of Rosheim in Alsace, the spokesman of German Jewry at the time, dared to ask Luther for a letter of recommendation to the prince in order to receive permission to pass through Saxony. Luther, gentle in style but uncompromising in content, rejected Josel's suggestion: In his heart he was still convinced that the Jews should be treated gently, but only in order to convert them to their Messiah, not in order to confirm them in their error. His 'good friend' Josel might find other persons to help him.[15]

This rejection marks the beginning of Luther's explicitly antisemitic propaganda as shown in his writings against the Jews of the late 1530s and 1540s. More examples are available from Luther's table talk of the time: In one talk he expresses his conviction that Jews could not really be converted: he does not believe in the possibility of their inner conversion, whereas external conversion alone will lead to simulation.[16] This argument, derived from the suspicions of the Spanish Inquisition of the Marranos, clearly represents a prelude to modern racist antisemitism. In another table talk Luther even expresses his desire to kill a 'blasphemious Jew'.[17]

On 14 February 1546, on the occasion of a visit to Eisleben, Luther publicly read his 'Admonition against the Jews', an appendix to his last sermon on Matthew 11.25–30. It seems that a sudden feeling of weakness forced him to break off the sermon, but he found enough strength to read the 'Admonition', which in view of his death three days later may be regarded as his theological testament. It ends with the words: 'As soon as the Jews will convert themselves to us and end their blasphemies and their other deeds, we will forgive them. Otherwise we will not bear nor tolerate them any longer.'[18]

2. 'THAT JESUS CHRIST WAS BORN A JEW' (1523)

As mentioned above, Luther's treatise 'That Jesus Christ was Born a Jew' (1523)[19] is often referred to as a document displaying his friendly attitude towards the Jews in his younger years. The problem with this characterization of the treatise is that there is only poor evidence in the text. Readers of the treatise who consider only the introduction and the conclusion, where Luther speaks up for a humane treatment of the Jews, and take these phrases out of their context, tend to misjudge his attitude to the extent that they praise the alleged tolerance of the Reformer. They ignore the threat already immanent in 1523 to reverse this tolerance, since Luther warns that if the mild treatment does not work, it will not be worthwhile employing it any longer. In addition, it seems that these interpreters have hardly any knowledge of the treatise as a whole, the corpus of which consists of an extended anti-Jewish theological polemic in the tradition of the ancient and medieval '*adversus Iudaeos*' literature.[20]

The treatise contains two main parts, one concerned with the evidence of the Christian doctrine that 'Christ was a Jew, born of a virgin', the other with the rejection of the messianic expectations of the Jews. In his introduction Luther indicates that the reason that prompted him to write the treatise was 'a new lie...being circulated' about him: 'I am supposed to have preached and written that Mary, the mother of God, was not a virgin either before or after the birth of Christ, but that she conceived Christ through Joseph, and had more children after that.'[21] The purpose of the treatise therefore is apologetic. It is primarily addressed not to the Jews but to Christians, who might be confused by the rumours spread by theologians of the Roman Church on Luther's allegedly heretic teachings. Luther adds that his arguments might have an additional effect: 'that I might perhaps also win some Jews to the Christian faith.'[22]

At this point Luther claims that 'our fools, the popes, bishops, sophists, and monks – the crude asses' heads – have hitherto so treated the Jews that anyone who wished to be a good Christian would almost have had to become a Jew.' He even adds that 'if I had been a Jew and had seen such dolts and blockheads govern and teach the Christian faith, I would sooner have become a hog than a Christian.'[23] Again, it is clear that the primary direction of this polemic is against the Roman church.

The theological connection between the two main parts of the treatise is also interesting. The parts are like the two sides of a coin, one working as the theological evidence of the other: If Jesus really was born a Jew, more precisely: borne by a Jewish virgin, he obviously was the true Messiah and the messianic expectations of the Jews are erroneous and politically dangerous. And conversely: as the messianic expectations of the Jews have been disproved by history, there is no remaining reason why the Jews should not accept Jesus as their true Messiah.

In the first main part Luther provides his reasons from Scripture for the doctrine that Jesus was borne by a virgin. It is important to note that the series of arguments already resembles those employed in his later overtly antisemitic writings. Luther's four points for the virginity of Mary are:

(1) 'Christ is promised for the first time soon after Adam's fall, when God said to the serpent, "I will put enmity between you and the woman, and between your seed and her seed; he shall crush your head, and you shall bruise his heel" [Gen 3:15].'[24] According to Luther, this promise refers to Christ. He is the seed of Eve, who will crush the head of the serpent:

> This seed of the woman . . . because he is to crush the devil's power, that is, sin and death, must not be an ordinary man, since all men have been brought under the devil through sin and death. So he must certainly be without sin . . . How, then, can this be? . . . The solution must ultimately be that this seed is a true natural son of the woman; derived from the woman, however, not in the normal way but through a special act of God . . . This is thus the first passage in which the mother of this child is described as a virgin.

Christ in fact could not be 'a distinctive man, without sin . . . had he been begotten like other men because the flesh is consumed and corrupted by evil lust, so that the natural act of procreation cannot occur without sin.'[25]

(2) Luther's second argument is God's promise to Abraham, Genesis 22.18: 'In your seed shall all the Gentiles be blessed.' – Here again, according to Luther, the mother of Christ 'is proven to be a pure virgin'. For 'human nature', as such, 'has nothing but cursed seed and bears nothing but unblessed fruit . . . Therefore, apart from Christ, all who are born of man must be under the devil, cursed in sin and death.' Christ was to be 'the blessed seed which should bless all others'; therefore 'he could not be begotten by man, since such children . . . cannot be conceived without sin . . .'.[26]

The word 'by which God promises his blessing upon all Gentiles' requires that 'this blessed fruit' – the seed of Abraham – 'had to be the fruit of a woman's body only, not of a man, even though that very woman's body came from man, indeed, even from Abraham and Adam . . . Now this passage [Gen. 22.18] was the gospel from the time of Abraham down to the time of David, even to the time of Christ.'[27] And Luther remarks that 'Scripture does not quibble or speak about the virginity of Mary after the birth of Christ . . . Scripture stops with this, that she was a virgin before and at the birth of Christ; for up to this point God had need of her virginity in order to give us the promised blessed seed without sin.'[28]

The Christian doctrine of 'original sin', in the sense of biologically hereditary corruption, is thus decisive in Luther's understanding of God's blessings on Abraham. As we will see later, this Christian doctrine of sin forms at the same time the other side of the teaching on righteousness by God's grace alone, as revealed in Christ.

(3) Accordingly, the passage addressed to David, II Samuel 7.12–14, promising that God would establish the kingdom of David's seed for ever, that God would be 'his father' and that he sould be the 'son' of God, 'must' in Luther's view, refer to Christ. Moreover, it would be possible to show that David's seed 'had to be the son of a woman

only in order to be called here God's child'.[29] In other words, the teaching on the 'virginity of Mary' seems to be only the other side of the doctrine that Christ is God's son. But Luther is here very brief and does not yet wish to enter into detail.

(4) The fourth and most important passage is Isaiah 7.14: 'God will give you a sign. Behold, a virgin [*jungfrau*] is with child, and shall bear a son.' – The pregnancy of a young maiden, promised here, refers to the virgin Mary. Here Luther explicitly attacks the Jews, who 'contend that the Hebrew text does not read, "A virgin is with child," but, "Behold, an *almah* is with child." Almah, they say, does not denote a virgin; the word for virgin is *bethulah*, while *almah* is the term for young damsel [*dyrne*]. Presumably, a young damsel might very well have had intercourse and be the mother of a child.'[30] In contrast to this linguistic argument, Luther insists that both Matthew and Luke in their gospels 'apply the passage from Isaiah to Mary, and translate the word *almah* as "virgin". They are more to be believed than the whole world, let alone the Jews. Even though an angel from heaven were to say that *almah* does not mean virgin, we should not believe it. For God the Holy Spirit speaks through St. Matthew and St. Luke; we can be sure that He understands Hebrew speech and expressions perfectly well.'[31]

Luther concedes that the Jews would not be convinced by this evidence, as they 'do not accept the evangelists'. Therefore Luther insists that also the term *almah* 'means a young woman who has never had intercourse; call her by whatever term you please, in her person she is still a virgin'. Luther concedes that the translation, 'Behold, a maiden [*Magd*] is with child' would certainly be most accurate, but again he insists that even in this case 'Isaiah means a damsel who is nubile but still wears her crown . . . Hence the mother of God is properly called the pure maiden, that is, the pure *almah*.'[32]

So far, this seems to Luther 'enough for the present to have sufficiently proved that Mary was a pure maiden, and that Christ was a genuine Jew of Abraham's seed'. We can see here that the title of the treatise – 'That Jesus Christ was born a Jew' – is only the other side of Luther's main purpose: the evidence of the doctrine of Christ being born of a virgin. Luther concludes this part of his treatise summarizing: 'So certainly no one can doubt that it is possible for God to cause a maiden to be with child apart from a man, since he has also created all things from nothing. Therefore, the Jews have no ground for denying this, for they acknowledge God's omnipotence. . . .'[33]

We can ask: Why should the Jews be interested in Luther's representation of the Christian doctrine on the miraculous birth of Christ so far? Once more: Luther's primary concern is not to convince the Jews but 'to answer the futile liars who publicly malign me in these matters'. But at this point of his argument Luther goes on adding that 'we would also like to do a service to the Jews on the chance that we might bring some of them back to their own faith, the one which their fathers held.'[34]

This is the beginning of a second main part, where Luther disputes the messianic expectations of the Jews:

Luther's first argument refers to Genesis 49.10ff, 'where the holy patriarch Jacob says: "The scepter shall not depart from Judah, nor a teacher from those at his feet, until the Shiloh comes; and to him shall be the gathering of the nations"'.[35] Here Luther argues from historical evidence that 'The Jews cannot deny that for nearly fifteen hundred years now, since the fall of Jerusalem, they have had no scepter, that is, neither kingdom nor king. Therefore, the *Shiloh*, or Messiah, must have come before this fifteen hundred year period, and before the destruction of Jerusalem.'[36]

Luther asserts that 'This prophecy can therefore be understood to refer to none other than Jesus Christ our Lord, who is of the tribe of Judah and of the royal lineage of David . . . He has been king these fifteen hundred years, and will remain king on into eternity.'[37] 'It is the kingdom of Christ which is here described in masterly fashion.'[38] And Luther concludes from this passage a prediction of death and resurrection of the Messiah: 'For since he is to come from the tribe of Judah [Gen. 49.10], he must be a true, natural man, mortal like all the children of Judah. On the other hand, because he is to be a special king, distinguished above all who have held the scepter of Judah before him, and he alone is to reign forever, he cannot be a mortal man, but must be an immortal man.' The only solution of these two contradictory statements is that 'he must through death put off this mortal life, and by his resurrection take on immortal life, in order that he may fulfil this prophecy and become a *shiloh* to whom all the world shall be gathered.'[39]

The kingdom has been taken from the Jews and transferred to Jesus in all eternity. 'Because *shiloh* was to come when Judah's scepter was ended, and since that time no other has fulfilled these prophecies, this Jesus must certainly be the real *shiloh* whom Jacob intended.'[40]

At this point we meet the crucial argument. Luther asks the Jews: 'When was there ever such a man of Jewish ancestry to whom so many nations were subject as this Jesus Christ?' And Luther gives the answer himself: 'The Jews will have to admit . . . that the Gentiles have never once yielded themselves so willingly to a Jew for their lord and king, as to this Jesus.'[41] Why is this important? The fact that Jesus was born a Jew is important not so much with respect to the Gentiles but with respect to the Jews. It forms a strong argument in the attempt to convert the Jews. I quote the crucial passage: 'It is amazing that the Jews are not moved to believe in this Jesus, their own flesh and blood, with whom the prophecies of Scripture actually square so powerfully and exactly, when they see that we Gentiles cling to him so hard and fast and in such numbers that many thousands have shed their blood for this sake.'[42] In other words: When great numbers of Gentiles were ready to become followers of a Jew, there is no excuse left for Jews to reject this Jew.

Luther makes the anti-Jewish background of his argument very clear, when he continues:

> They [the Jews] know perfectly well that the Gentiles have always shown greater hostility toward the Jews than toward any other nation, and have been unwilling to tolerate their dominion, laws, or government. How is it then that the Gentiles should now so reverse themselves as to willingly and steadfastly surrender themselves to this Jew, and with heart and soul confess him king of kings and lord of lords, unless it be that here is the true Messiah, to whom God by great miracle has made the Gentiles friendly and submissive in accordance with this and numerous other prophecies?[43]

It is clear that in Luther's view the Gentiles would refuse to follow any other Jew except Jesus. So Jesus was born a Jew, but he was an exception of the Jews.

Luther has yet another argument, taken from Daniel 9.24–27, a vision on the future of Jerusalem and the Messiah, which contains the theory on the seven weeks of history, which – in the sense of year-weeks – always have provoked theological speculations on a messianic timetable. For Luther it is clear from this passage 'that the true Messiah must have come over one thousand and five hundred years ago, just as we hold that our Jesus Christ did'. In addition it seems clear to him that Gabriel in this passage 'can surely be referring only to that destruction of Jerusalem which subsequently took place under the Roman emperor Titus' about forty years after the ascension of Christ.[44]

Luther constructs from Daniel's vision a clearly anti-Jewish theology of history. His conclusion 'that the true Messiah came after the rebuilding of Jerusalem [by Nehemiah] and prior to its destruction [by Titus]' is not simply a matter of historical calculations but also a crucial theological statement in order to 'thus mightily overcome the error of the Jews'.[45] Luther interprets Gabriel's announcements:

> They [who cut him off] shall not be his – that is, those who crucify him and drive him from this world will no more belong to him and be his people, but he will take unto himself another people ... All of this happened just that way. Jerusalem and the temple were destroyed with frightful severity, and to this time have never come into the hands of the Jews or been restored to the former position of power despite the earnest efforts made in that direction. The city today is still the ruin it was before, so that no one can deny that this prophecy and the actual situation before our eyes coincide perfectly.[46]

Clearly Luther here repeats the anti-Jewish theological tradition on the Jews as the people who crucified Christ. In any case the destruction of Jerusalem is interpreted as punishment of the Jews by God himself. And it is clear on the other hand that – on the level of such theological speculations on history – we would have to admit that Luther's perspective has been refuted at least in part by the foundation of the state of Israel in our century. The question however is, if such theological speculations on history are legitimate at all.

What makes this argument so cogent in Luther's view is the fact that this traditional Christian theology of history easily fits with the central theological discovery of the Reformation: righteousness by grace alone without works of the law. When Gabriel announces that 'seventy weeks are determined concerning your people and your holy city, that transgression may be finished, forgiveness sealed, iniquity atoned for, and everlasting righteousness brought in ... ', Luther interprets: 'This is as if he were to say: Your nation of the Jews and the holy city of Jerusalem have yet four hundred and ninety years to go; then they will both come to an end.' And it is clear that Luther understands 'everlasting righteousness' in the sense that 'the righteousness of faith' is 'preached, that righteousness which is eternally valid before God', whereas 'before it there has been nothing but sin and work-righteousness, which is temporal and invalid in the sight of God'.[47] Therefore, when Gabriel announces that 'in the middle of the week the sacrifice and offering shall cease', it is clear in Luther's view that the meaning is that 'the law of Moses will no longer prevail, because Christ, after preaching for three and one-half years, will fulfill all things through his suffering, and thereafter provide for the preaching of a new sacrifice, etc.'.[48] Clearly we can observe at this point how Luther's teaching on righteousness by grace alone works as the other side of his teaching against human work-righteousness as the central symbol of sin.

Luther is so convinced by his own anti-Jewish theology that he concludes:

> Scripture and history agree so perfectly with one another that the Jews have nothing they can say to the contrary. They certainly are painfully conscious of their destruction, which is immeasurably greater than any they have ever endured ... It would be unthinkable that God would leave them so long without prophets unless they were finished and all Scripture fulfilled.[49]

After this nearly completed destruction of the Jews by Scripture and by history in the two main parts of the treatise Luther suddenly reaches a conciliatory conclusion: In a pedagogical tone he admits that the Jews might feel offended 'because we confess our Jesus to be a man, and yet true God'. It goes without saying that Luther is ready to 'deal forcefully with that from Scripture', but – as he allows – 'in due time'. It would be 'too harsh for the beginning. Let them first be suckled with milk, and begin by recognizing this man Jesus as the true Messiah; after that they may drink wine, and learn also that he is true God.'[50] And it is in this context of a soft version of Christian mission to the Jews that Luther finds some friendly formulations which have always been quoted as testimony of Luther's allegedly pro-Jewish attitude: 'I would request and advise that one deal gently with them and instruct them from Scripture; then some of them may come along . . . So long as we thus treat them like dogs, how can we expect to work any good among them? . . . If we really want to help them, we must be guided in our dealings with them not by papal law but by the law of Christian love.' In the context of the treatise as a whole and in knowledge of Luther's further theological development, however, the concluding phrases sound like a threat: 'Here I will let the matter rest for the present, until I see what I have accomplished.'[51] It would be less than 15 years before Luther drew the consequences from his lack of success. Then he would no longer spare the Jews the Christian doctrine on Jesus as God's son.

Provisional stock-taking: 'For Luther conversion is the main subject, along with which the method disappears as irrelevant or at least trivial. We firmly draw attention to this fact, because here . . . a point is reached, where the danger of a reversal becomes threateningly close. Should the new means not work, and leniency fails, as did the harshness and cruelty of former times, then it will not be worth employing it any longer. . . .'[52] 'The conversion of the Jews . . . forms the keystone of the marvellous building that he has erected. The Papacy has failed to accomplish the task, not only because it employed the wrong methods but rather because its foundation is based on fake and heresies.' Luther, having discovered 'true Christianity' again, would regard 'the final victory of the church against the synagogue' as 'the most splendid confirmation' of the truth of the Reformation.[53]

I fully agree with this interpretation by Reinhold Lewin. Luther's antisemitism gains its explosive force from its connection with the anti-Roman Catholic polemics, which was indispensable in the context of the Reformation movement. The desperately expected conversion of the Jews seemed necessary to Luther as documentary evidence of the theological truth and right of the Reformation against Rome. The other side of the coin, which I would add to Lewin's perspective, is the following: The fact that the Jews remained obstinate even after the Reformation must have led Luther into a state of severe uncertainty about the truth of the Reformation itself. That is the reason why his attitude towards the Jews became more and more urgent and violent.

3. 'ON THE JEWS AND THEIR LIES' (1543)

In 1538 Luther published his first explicitly antisemitic treatise, the letter 'Against the Sabbatarians to a good friend'. Since 1532 Count Schlick zu Falkenau had warned Luther of a group of Moravian 'Jews' who allegedly persuaded Christians in Moravia to observe the Sabbath and to be circumcised. This is why Luther calls them 'Sabbatarians'. It is likely that these Moravian 'Jews' were not Jews at all but radical Reformers, that is: anti-trinitarian Christians, who according to Luther's source even believed that the Messiah had not yet appeared and the Mosaic law would prevail for ever and should be adopted by the Gentiles as well. Interestingly, in his conviction that the dispersal of the Jews is the consequence of God's definitive judgement, Luther swears that 'as soon as the Jews return to Jerusalem to re-establish the temple, priesthood, and statehood, the Christians will follow them' and become Jews themselves.[54]

This letter 'Against the Sabbatarians' turned out to be only a forerunner of a whole series of unscrupulous antisemitic pamphlets published in 1543. Most infamous is the first: 'On the Jews and Their Lies' (*Von den Juden und ihren Lügen*), followed by 'On the Shem Ha-Mephoras'' (The Ineffable Name; *Vom Schem Hamphoras und vom Geschlecht*

Christi) and 'On David's Last Words' (*Von den letzten Worten Davids*) – a treatise on Christ being God.

The immediate cause for this series of pamphlets was Luther's receiving a message that a rabbi had written a polemic response to his letter 'Against the Sabbatarians'. Now Luther pleads for a 'sharp mercifulness' and repeats all the accusations and invectives of medieval antisemitic polemics: Jews are in his eyes well-poisoners, kidnappers etc. In addition he makes 'practical suggestions' such as forced labour, confiscation of Jewish books, the burning of synagogues and outright banishment. And these suggestions bore fruit: 'As many of the Protestant rulers of the times relied on Luther's political advice, his attitude resulted in the expulsion of the Jews from Saxony in 1543 and the hostile *Judenordnung* of Landgrave Philip of Hesse in the same year.'[55]

It would be disgusting to deal extensively with Luther's boring explanations, full of repetitions, in the treatise 'On the Jews and Their Lies'. The editors of the *Weimar edition* of the pamphlet were well aware of the continuity between Luther's later explicitly antisemitic writings and his earlier more friendly attitude towards the Jews and of the convergence of his antisemitism with his theological approach. They write in their introduction:

> This treatise ... ends with a serious warning against the Jews. But before that Luther creates a basis for his advice in an attempt to prove that the prophecies of which the Jews still await fulfilment, already have found their fulfilment in Christ and in his kingdom. He repeats a lot of what we already know from his treatise 'Against the Sabbatarians' or even from his first treatise on the Jews, 'That Jesus Christ was Born a Jew'.[56]

In fact, it is only in the introduction of 'On the Jews and their Lies' that Luther addresses the Jews directly: 'Do you hear, Jew, do you know that Jerusalem and your kingdom together with the temple and the priests has been destroyed about 1460 years ago now?' This 'cruel wrath of God' should show them 'clearly enough that they are certainly mistaken and on the wrong way'.[57] Luther refers in this context to Hosea 1.9: '*Lo ami*. You are not my people, and I am not your God.' But then he makes clear: 'It is not our intention to talk to the Jews now, but about the Jews and about their doing that our Germans also should know.'[58]

With respect to the content of Luther's treatise we ask again: Is there an inner connection between Luther's theology and his antisemitism? The answer seems to be unavoidable: there is such a connection. We can already see this connection in the structure of the treatise 'On the Jews and Their Lies', which in some respects resembles the early treatise 'That Jesus Christ was Born a Jew': again we have two main parts, where the second exposes the false messianic expectation of the Jews and particularly its dangerous political components. Again, the first part forms the other side of the coin, but this time the topic is not Christology – 'Jesus Christ was a Jew, born of a virgin' – as in 1523; this time the topic is the doctrine of 'justification by grace alone' and therefore the attack against the so-called 'self-righteousness' of the Jews, who believe that 'good works' may help.

Again Luther employs biblical references in support of his argument. In the second main part some of these references are the same as in the earlier treatise. Most important in our context is the exposition on Daniel 9.24–27, which had played a decisive role in his earlier treatise. Here the connection between theology and antisemitism becomes particularly evident. Now Luther confronts explicitly Jesus Christ, the true Messiah, who according to him had been crucified by the Jews,[59] with the wrong, political messianism of the Jews, and particularly with Bar Kochba, the revolutionary Messiah, who allegedly – like Thomas Müntzer in Luther's day – had 'slaughtered very many Christians, who were not willing to deny Jesus Christ', until he and his prophet Rabbi Akiba were killed by the Romans.[60] This disaster should have humiliated the Jews, had they not been blind in their self-righteousness. They should have recognized that their worldly messianism was erroneous and that Jesus was the spiritual Messiah.[61]

In addition, we can observe a connection between Luther's Christology and antisemitism. This becomes clear particularly in his profession of Jesus as God's son, which constitutes a new feature in his polemics compared with the earlier treatise. Luther's threat at the end of the treatise 'That Jesus Christ was Born a Jew' now becomes reality: Now the fact that the Jews cannot accept Jesus as the only begotten Son of God is condemned as blasphemic. 'Luther's antisemitic utterings, as they can be found particularly in his treatise "On the Jews and Their Lies" are not the regrettable aberrations of a disappointed man who has become old, rather they are the almost compulsive consequences from his central theological discoveries. According to Luther the Jews, as long as they continue to be Jews, are necessarily unbelievers.'[62] 'Luther identifies God himself and Christ directly'[63], and at the same time he almost identifies the Christians who profess Christ with Christ himself. Therefore he states: 'He who blasphemiously denies and curses us at this point, denies and curses Christ, that is: God himself as an idol.'[64] Or, at another place: 'Cursing God's Son, that is the same as cursing God himself, the father, the Creator of heaven and earth.' And: 'Everything happening in honour or dishonour to the Son, certainly happens to God the father himself.' Finally: 'We Christians know that they [the Jews] publicly curse and blaspheme God, when they curse and blaspheme this Jesus.'[65]

Klaus Wengst rightly comments of such phrases: 'It is to be noted that according to this logic the blasphemy of the Jews simply consists in not accepting Jesus, that is in their very existence *as Jews*.' And that is the reason, why Christians are not permitted any longer to be tolerant with respect to the Jews, because otherwise they would 'be cursed with someone else's sin' (*fremder Sünde teilhaftig*). Wengst continues: 'It is exactly from this definition of God exclusively in the perspective of Jesus Christ or rather from this identification of Jesus Christ as God that Luther's wicked advices against the Jews follow.'[66] Wengst refers in this context to the connection drawn by Luther between Christology and the practical advices: tolerance with regard to the Jews would imply dishonouring God's son, whereas honouring the Son means persecution of his enemies, the Jews.[67] In other words, Wengst concludes: 'It has to be noted with absolute clarity that the harshness of [Luther's] advices follows from the theological basis, from the *"Solus Christus"* which is emphasized particularly against the Jews... These consequences result necessarily, when God is defined exclusively from the perspective of Jesus Christ...'[68]

The treatise ends with Luther's infamous practical advices on how the Jews should be persecuted. However, not only are these final passages explicitly antisemitic, so is much of the phraseology in the preceding theological parts of the treatise. As an example of the antisemitic style of the treatise I will quote only one paragraph from the second main part:

> Shame on you here, shame on you there and wherever you are, you damned Jews, for you have ventured to interpret this solemn, magnificent, consoling word of God so shamefully to satisfy your mortal, maggotty, greedy belly, and for that you are not ashamed of displaying your greed so vulgarly. You are unworthy to look at the outside of the Bible, let alone read inside it. You should read only that Bible which is under a sow's tail, and the letters that fall from there you should gobble up and gulp down...[69]

The passage is interesting particularly with respect to the association between Jews and pigs, constructed by Luther. In fact the City Church of Wittenberg was decorated by a so called '*Judensau*', an antisemitic symbol spread in medieval Germany. Luther refers to this symbol again in his pamphlet 'On the Shem Ha-Mephoras'. Here he asks regarding the mystic tradition on the ineffable name of God: 'Where have the Jews got this high wisdom, that they so divide the words of Moses, the holy blameless letters, into three verses and make out of it arithmetical signs or numbers, and also name seventy-two angels and, in short, reconstruct the whole *Shem hameforash*?' At first he refuses to give an answer: 'Let me in peace, ask the Rabbis about it, they will certainly tell you.' Then, however, he announces his own explanation:

> There is here in Wittenberg, on our parish church, a sow carved in stone, young piglets and Jews lie under it and suck teats. Behind the sow stands a Rabbi who lifts the sow's right leg up, and with his left hand pulls the tail over himself, bows and stares with great attentiveness under the tail of the sow into the Talmud, as if he wanted to read and understand something intricate and extraordinary. From this, certainly, they got their *Shem hameforash*. For in the past there have been many Jews in these lands . . . and some learned and esteemed man, who was an enemy of the dirty lies of the Jews, had such a sculpture made . . . .[70]

In his study on *The Judensau* Isaiah Shachar points out that Luther's explanation of the '*Judensau*', although it would become very influential, 'does not shed light on the original meaning of the relief. The inscription *Rabini Schem HaMphoras* (The Rabbi's expounded name of God), at least two hundred years later than the relief, is clearly inspired by Luther's passage.' As for the original meaning of the relief, Shachar points out that:

> this *Judensau* is placed outside the church but is not part of an allegorical cycle of vices. The emphasis on the activity round the animal's tail and hind-quarters . . . leaves little doubt about a derisive intention . . . It was in Wittenberg for the first time . . . that the motif was publicly exhibited not as a symbol of a particular vice but as a defematory representation of the Jews. Here the isolation of the motif from a wider moralizing context and the elaboration of the obscene theme make the Jews sole target . . . The Jews were expelled from Wittenberg in 1304, but were allowed to re-settle there a short time after; evidence exists of a community in 1339 . . . A link between the expulsion and the sculpture should not be totally discounted. The special location of the sculpture and its lack of a symbolic context suggest such a link.[71]

Luther adds to this interpretation the suggestion that the Wittenberg sow was meant to stand for the Talmud or Jewish teaching in general, especially with respect to mystical speculations on the name of God. But the 'culminating point' in Luther's explanation, according to Shachar, is the following:

> In this way one may also easily relate, and turn round, the word *Shemhamphoras* namely 'Peres schama' or, as they do, master it boldly and make it into 'Schamha Peres'; so that it sounds very similar . . . This is how the Devil makes fun of the Jews his prisoners; he lets them say *Shem hameforash*, believe in it and hope for great things. But *he* means 'Sham hapheresh', meaning [in Hebrew]: 'here is dirt'; not the kind that lies in the streets, but that which comes out of the belly . . . .[72]

It must be said in this context that other reformers of the time got sick of Luther's antisemitic pamphlets. Heinrich Bullinger for instance, Zwingli's successor in Zurich, wrote in 1545: 'There is Luther's swinish, filthy Schemhamphorasch, which, had it been written by a herdsman of swines, not of souls, would have only a weak excuse.' Martin Butzer in Straburg and Andreas Osiander in Nuremberg likewise detested Luther's pamphlets.[73] Josel von Rosheim, after reading Luther's antisemitic pamphlets, expressed undisguised hostility to the Reformation, calling Luther 'the unclean' (*Lo-Thahor*, a word play on his name)'.[74] He successfully intervened with the magistrate of Strassburg in order to forbid Luther's pamphlets there.

In conclusion, 'the conversion of the Jews', on which Luther had placed his hopes in 1523, would have been 'the most splendid confirmation' of the truth of the Reformation in his eyes. This 'final victory of the church against the synagogue' (Lewin) had not taken place and Luther had to abandon his hopes. After the Reformation movement had failed with respect to the Jews, aggressive antisemitism in honour of Jesus Christ, which had already lurked in Luther's earlier more tolerant attitude, became – in his view – the only way to save Christians.

NOTES

1 Cf. Reinhold Lewin, *Luthers Stellung zu den Juden. Ein Beitrag zur Geschichte der Juden in Deutschland während des Reformationszeitalters.* Neue Studien zur Geschichte der Theologie und der Kirche, ed. N. Bonwetsch and R. Seeberg (Berlin: Trowitzsch & Sohn, 1911). Cf. also: Heiko A. Oberman, *Wurzeln des Antisemitismus. Christenangst und Judenplage im Zeitalter von Humanismus und Reformation* (Berlin: Severin und Siedler, 1981) and H.A. Oberman, 'Three Sixteenth-Century Attitudes toward Judaism: Reuchlin, Erasmus, and Luther', in Oberman, *The Impact of the Reformation* (Grand Rapids: Wm. B. Eerdmans, 1994), pp.81–121. Cf. also: Walther Bienert, *Martin Luther und die Juden. Ein Quellenbuch mit zeitgenössischen Illustrationen, mit Einführungen und Erläuterungen* (Frankfurt am Main: Evangelisches Verlagswerk, 1982).

2 'Luther, Martin', *Encyclopaedia Judaica* (Jerusalem: Keter, 1982), vol.11, col.586.

3 Walther Bienert, *Martin Luther und die Juden*, p.192.

4 Heiko A. Oberman, *Wurzeln des Antisemitismus*, p.16.

5 W. Bienert, pp.181 and 190.

6 Oberman, *Wurzeln...*, p.125.

7 It has long become usual to speak of 'antisemitism' with respect to the expulsion of the Jews from Spain in 1492, in spite of the obvious anachronism. There is no reason why such anachronism should not be permitted with respect to Luther as well. However, speaking of Luther's 'antisemitism' we should stay aware of the fact that historically (and in Luther's biography as well) we can distinguish different forms and motives of antisemitism.

8 Cf. the statement of the Protestant churches of Saxony, Hesse-Nassau, Mecklenburg, Schleswig-Holstein, Anhalt, Thüringen and Lübeck, 17 December 1941, on occasion of the *Reichspolizeiverordnung* on marking the Jews with the yellow star: '...as already Dr. Martin Luther after bitter experiences raised the demand to take harsh measures against the Jews and to expel them from German countries' (German text cited in Ernst Ludwig Ehrlich, 'Luther und die Juden', in Heinz Kremers (ed.), *Die Juden und Martin Luther – Martin Luther und die Juden* (Neukirchen-Vluyn: Neukirchener Verlag, 1985), p.86).

9 Cf. the statement of the church leaders of Hannover, Braunschweig and Kurhesse, 23 June 1939: 'In the realm of faith there is no harsher opposition than the conflict between the gospel of Jesus Christ and the Jewish religion of legalism and political messianic expectations' (German text cited in Ernst Ludwig Ehrlich, 'Luther und die Juden', op. cit., p.87).

10 Julius Streicher, 29 April 1946: 'Antisemitische Presseerzeugnisse gab es in Deutschland durch Jahrhunderte. So wurde bei mir zum Beispiel ein Buch beschlagnahmt von Dr. Martin Luther. Dr. Martin Luther sässe heute sicher an meiner Stelle auf der Anklagebank, wenn dieses Buch von der Anklagevertretung in Betracht gezogen würde' (*Der Prozess gegen die Hauptkriegsverbrecher vor dem Internationalen Militärgerichtshof Nürnberg*, Nürnberg 1947, vol.12:346, cited in Martin Stöhr, 'Martin Luther und die Juden', in H. Kremers (ed.), *Die Juden und Martin Luther – Martin Luther und die Juden* (Neukirchen-Vluyn: Neukirchener Verlag), 1985, p.89).

11 *Encyclopaedia Judaica*, vol.11, col.584.

12 M. Luther, 'Das Magnificat, verdeutschet und ausgelegt' (1520 and 1521), in *Luthers Werke in Auswahl*, ed. Otto Clemen, vol.2 (Bonn: A. Marcus und E. Weber's Verlag), 1920, p.184.

13 M. Luther, 'Welche Personen verboten sind zu ehelichen. Vom ehelichen Leben' (1522), in: *Luthers Werke in Auswahl*, ed. O. Clemen, vol.2, p.342: 'As I may eat, drink, sleep, go, ride, buy and deal with a pagan, Jew, Turk, Heretic, so I may become married with him as well . . .'.

14 *Encyclopaedia Judaica*, vol.11, col.584f.

15 Cf. M. Luther, 'An den Juden Josel' (Wittenberg, 11 June 1537), in *Weimar edition, Correspondence*, vol.8 (Weimar: Hermann Böhlaus Nachfolger, 1938), pp.89–91.

16 M. Luther, 'De Iudaeo baptisando et altero, qui fuit impostor' (summer 1540), in *Weimar edition, Table Talk*, vol.5 (Weimar: Hermann Böhlaus Nachfolger, 1919), p.83. Cf. also Bienert, p.126f.

17 M. Luther, 'De Iudaeis' (spring 1543), p.257. Cf. also W. Bienert, p.172.

18 M. Luther, 'Ermahnung wider die Juden' (1546), in *Weimar edition, Table Talk*, vol.51 (Graz: Akademische Druck-und Verlagsanstalt [reprint], 1967), 195f.

19 M. Luther, 'Dass Jesus Christus ein geborner Jude sei' (1523), in *Weimar edition*, vol.10/2, p.314–346). – English translation: 'That Jesus Christ Was Born a Jew', in *Luther's Works* [American edition], Saint Louis: Concordia Pub. House, and Philadelphia: Fortress Press), 1955 and later, vol.45, ed. Harold J. Grimm, Theodore Bachmann, et al., p.199–229.

20 Luther's patterns were drawn among others from Nikolas de Lyre's treatise '*Contra perfidiam Iudaeorum*' (printed in Nuremberg 1497) and Paulus de Burgos, '*Dialogus qui vocatur Scrutinium scrutinarum libris duobus contra perfidiam Iudaeorum*' (printed in Mantua 1475). Both books are quoted extensively in Luther's later treatise 'On the Jews and Their Lies'.

21 M. Luther, 'That Jesus Christ was Born a Jew', in: *Luther's Works* [American edition], vol.45, p.199.

22 M. Luther, *op. cit.*, p.200.

23 *ibid.*

24 *ibid.*, p.201.

25 *ibid.*, p.202.

26 *ibid.*, p.203f.

27 *ibid.*, p.204.

28 *ibid.*, p.205f.

29 *ibid.*, p.206.

30 *ibid.*, p.207f.

31 *ibid.*, p.208.

32 *ibid.*, p.209f.

33 *ibid.*, p.213.

34 *ibid.*

35 *ibid.*

36 M. Luther, *op. cit.*, p.214.

37 *ibid.*, p.215.

38 *ibid.*, p.217.

39 *ibid.*

40 *ibid.*, p.220.

41 *ibid.*

42 *ibid.*, p.220f.

43 *ibid.*, p.221.

44 *ibid.*, p.222.

45 *ibid.*, p.223.

46 *ibid.*, p.227f.

47 *ibid.*, p.226.

48 *ibid.*, p.228.

49 *ibid.*

50 M. Luther, *op. cit.*, p.229.

51 *ibid.*

52 Reinhold Lewin, *Luthers Stellung zu den Juden*, p.30f.

53 *ibid.*, p.36.

54 M. Luther, 'Wider die Sabbather. An einen guten Freund', *Weimar edition*, vol.50, p.323. Cf. H.A. Oberman, *Wurzeln* . . . , p.62 and p.82 (note 137); cf. also Oberman, 'Three Sixteenth-Century Attitudes toward Judaism . . . ', in Oberman, *The Impact of the Reformation*, p.116. In his protest against these radical Reformers Luther did not hesitate to use sexual allusions: He would never be so stupid to accept circumcision; rather he would have his Käthe and every woman cut off their left breast.

55 *Encyclopaedia Judaica*, vol 11., col.585.

56 F. Cohrs and O. Brenner, in M. Luther, *Weimar edition*, vol.53 (Weimar: Hermann Böhlaus Nachfolger, 1920), p.413.

57 M. Luther, 'Von den Juden und ihren Lügen', *Weimar edition*, vol.53, p.418.

58 M. Luther, *op. cit.*, p.419.

59 *ibid.*, p.494.

60 *ibid.*, p.496.

61 *ibid.*, p.498.

62 Klaus Wengst, 'Perspektiven für eine nicht-antijüdische Christologie. Beobachtungen und Überlegungen zu neutestamentlichen Texten', in *Evangelische Theologie*, vol.59 (1999), p.240.

63 Wengst, p.241.

64 M. Luther, 'Von den Juden und ihren Lügen', *Weimar edition*, vol.53, p.540: 'Wer uns in diesem Artickel abgöttisch beleuget und lestert, der beleuget und lestert Christum, das ist: Gott selbs, als einen Abgott.'

65 M. Luther, *op. cit.*, p.531.

66 Wengst, *op. cit.*, p.241.

67 M. Luther, 'Von den Juden und ihren Lügen', *Weimar edition*, vol.53, p.536.

68 Wengst, *op. cit.*, p.241f.

69 M. Luther, 'On the Jews and Their Lies', quoted in Isaiah Shachar, *The Judensau. A Medieval Anti-Jewish Motif and its History* (Warburg Institute Surveys, ed. E.H. Gombrich and J.B. Trapp; Worcester and London: The Trinity Press) 1974, p.86, note 232; cf. 'Von den Juden und ihren Lügen', *Weimar edition*, vol.53, p.478.

70 M. Luther, 'On the Shem Ha-Mephoras', quoted in I. Shachar, *op. cit.*, p.86f., note 237; cf. 'Vom Schem Hamphorasch', *Weimar edition*, vol.53, p.601.

71 I. Shachar, *op. cit.*, p.31.

72 M. Luther, 'On the Shem Ha-Mephoras', quoted in I. Shachar, *op. cit.*, p.86f., note 237; cf. 'Vom Schem Hamphorasch', *Weimar edition*, vol.53, p.601.

73 Cf. H.A. Oberman, 'Three Sixteenth-Century Attitudes toward Judaism . . . ', in *The Impact of the Reformation*, p.114: 'We have good reason to assume that Melanchthon was as embarrassed as some of the leading city reformers by the ferocious anti-Judaism of the later Luther.'

74 *Encylopaedia Judaica*, vol.11, col.585. Cf. R. Lewin, p.90f.

A PARTING AT THE CROSS:
THE CONTRASTING NATIONAL CULTURES OF LUTHERANISM IN GERMANY AND DENMARK DURING THE HOLOCAUST

Leon Stein

T HIS BRIEF exercise in comparative history attempts to achieve three goals. First, it seeks to explain how the interplay of national culture and religious ideas and institutions played a crucial role in the differing outcomes of Lutheranism in Germany and Denmark with regard to attitudes and behaviour of those countries toward the Jews before and during the Holocaust. Second, it tries to illustrate how seemingly similar Christian religious beliefs and practices can be interpreted and exercised in radically different ways by distinctive national cultures that can result in opposite impacts. Finally, this essay should serve as a warning for the future as to how Christian ideas and institutions can be shaped for purposes of prejudice, hate, and indifference – or instead put to the service of humanitarian, tolerant, and life-saving ends.

HISTORICAL CONTEXT AND VARIABLES

Any foray into comparative history runs the risk of being weakened by facile generalizations. Therefore, the complexities, context and variables within the topic must first be considered. During the period of the persecution and the murder of the Jews from 1933 to 1945, the majority of the Lutheran Churches in Germany were antisemitic or silent, but so was the Catholic Church in Germany and in some other countries. It would be incorrect to attribute the formation of modern German antisemitism to Lutheranism alone. Luther drew on the legacy of medieval Catholic antisemitism. And it was in Austria particularly that both Catholic Jew-hatred and racist antisemitism flourished in the 19th and early 20th centuries. In addition, the rise of racism in the 19th and 20th centuries resulted in a radical antisemitism that sometimes became anti-Christian as well as anti-Jewish.

During the Holocaust a few individual German Lutherans spoke out and tried to help Jews.[1] In Denmark the overwhelming majority of Lutheran laymen and pastors and the official institutional church opposed the Nazi persecution of the Jews and, when Denmark was occupied by the Nazis, joined the Danish resistance and rallied to help save the Jews of that country. Still, Denmark contained a small Nazi movement in the 1930s and a small number of Nazi sympathizers and collaborators during the Holocaust. Moreover, the Norwegian and Slovakian Lutheran churches also spoke out on behalf of the Jews. The Norwegian Lutheran church attempted to rescue many Jews as well; so did some other churches in Europe, such as the Bulgarian Orthodox Church.[2]

The variables of the situation of the Lutheran Churches in Germany and Denmark can be summarized as follows: In Germany Lutheranism had for the most part fused with xenophobic nationalism, antisemitism and elitist authoritarianism.[3] During the Nazi regime, the Lutheran churches were split in at least three major ways: most Lutheran laymen and leaders went along with the regime or remained passive; some formed a nazified 'German Christian' group that tried to combine antisemitic racism with Lutheranism and some founded a Confessional Church that struggled to protect church autonomy and Lutheran doctrine from destruction by the Nazi state. Moreover, the Nazi government used both inducements and terror to keep the Lutheran churches in line. In Denmark, on the other hand, the Lutheran State Church had developed within a framework of democracy and enlightenment and remained united and steadfast in helping to save the Jews during the German occupation of that country from 1940 to 1945.[4] This contrast tends to confirm the characterization of German nationalism (to 1945) as ethnic, that is, defined collectively by birth, blood, religion and ancestry, while Danish nationalism can be classified as of a civic variety, in which citizenship and national tradition are also tied to equal rights, tolerance, participation in public affairs, traditions of constitutional protections of freedom and the freely given consent of individuals and parliamentary bodies.[5]

Still, the circumstances of the Danish rescue of the Jews also depended on the favourable German attitude toward the Danes (as fellow 'Aryans'), the relatively benign occupation of the German army (up to 1943), the German need for Danish raw materials and agricultural products, the participation of anti-Nazi Germans such as Captain Georg Ferdinand von Duckwitz and Count Helmuth von Moltke in warning the Danes about the danger to the Jews in October 1943 and even the reluctance of the Nazi Plenipotentiary, Dr. Werner Best, to risk failure and chaos in the face of Danish opposition to the Nazi plans to round up the Jews. These favourable conditions included the geographical proximity of Denmark to Sweden and the policy of the Swedes – pressured by the Danish-Jewish physicist Niels Bohr – to accept Danish Jewish refugees by 1943. Also, the Danes had offered no real initial active resistance to the Nazi occupation. Ironically, this benefited the Jews of Denmark in the long run. Finally, despite their admiration for some aspects of German culture, the Danes had engaged in a bitter territorial rivalry with Germany over the duchies of bordering Schleswig-Holstein. Prussia had taken these territories from Denmark by force in 1864. The Danes had never forgotten this attack on their territory and on their sense of national self-respect.

With most of these variables considered, the age-old question as to whether history is made by structures or conditions, or whether history is made by men and women who make decisions and choices, must also be addressed. In Germany most Lutheran leaders and laymen either supported or ignored the persecution and murder of the Jews. In Denmark most chose to oppose this central programme of the Nazis. In the case of the churches particularly, it came down to a matter of interpreting and implementing Christian values as such and as they related to the prevailing national and political culture.

THE NATIONAL CULTURE OF LUTHERANISM IN GERMANY BEFORE AND DURING THE HOLOCAUST

Martin Luther (1483–1546), that towering figure in both Christian and German history, became a key founder and significant influence on modern German antisemitism. He derived his anti-Jewish demonology from a vast storehouse of learned and popular medieval beliefs. His rage against the Jews was caused primarily by the Jewish refusal to interpret the Old Testament in his Christian theological way. For Luther, the fact that the Jews would not accept the divinity of Jesus became proof of their malicious character.

When Luther wrote his violent tracts and sermons against the Jews in the 1540s, most notably 'Against the Jews and Their Lies' (1543), he was directing his fury against the Jews not only as a reprobate religion but also an evil people. Raul Hilberg aptly summarized Luther's ideas about the Jews as 'an enemy, a criminal, and a plague' that must be dealt with by radical national means such as expulsion, enslavement, and even killing.[6] In his last sermon, delivered only a few days before his death in 1546, Luther exclaimed that if given the opportunity, the Jews of Germany would massacre the Christians. Thus Luther ranked the Jews next only to the devil as the enemies of Christendom and of Germany.

His later writings were the first works of modern antisemitism for they presented a detailed set of political, social, and economic proposals. These were directed to the German princes and the wider public and were written in German in a violent popular idiom, characterizing the Jews as an incorrigible and satanic threat to Christendom as a whole and to the German people in particular. His pamphlets were later reprinted under different titles in the later 16th and 17th centuries and revived under the Nazis – especially the 'German Christians'.[7] Luther also contributed to German political and social theory, developing the noted doctrine of the 'Two Kingdoms', in which the individual should be obedient to the divinely ordained state (*Die Obrigkeit*), while the soul alone should be accountable to God. In contrast to the other Protestant Christian groups such as the Calvinists and Zwinglians who were more mildly disposed to the Jews and sought to reform the political order, German Lutheranism reinforced and supplemented the older Catholic medieval legacy of antisemitism in Germany and glorified the state and its ruling elites. In fact, other Protestant reformers such as Zwingli and Bullinger were shocked by Luther's outbursts against the Jews.

Luther also became an ancestor of the tradition of German idealism which fostered great philosophical and religious works but also helped cast the Jews as enemies of morality and spirituality in Germany. Finally, the impact of Luther's antisemitism on Protestant Germany helped to encourage the 'history of an obsession' with any threat of *Verjudung* (Jewification) in German culture.[8]

Thus Luther Germanized and unwittingly modernized the vast legacy of Christian Jew-hatred. In a nation riven with territorial divisions and strife between Protestants and Catholics, hatred against the Jews could give many Germans of both denominations a sense of national self-awareness in the definition of a common enemy. (Germany was the only nation in Europe in 1939 that was both heavily Protestant at 60 percent and heavily Catholic at 40 percent). The Austrian-born Catholic Adolf Hitler was to acknowledge the three 'truly great' Germans of all time who were all Protestants – Frederick the Great, Richard Wagner, and Martin Luther.

From the later 16th century to the early 20th century most of the German Lutheran clergy were hostile to the rationalism of the Enlightenment and the emancipation of the Jews. Most became spokesmen for the ultra-conservative interests of 'throne and altar', particularly in authoritarian Prussia. The Lutheran churches became appendages of the state.[9] During the nationalist upsurge in 19th century Germany many Lutheran clerics and intellectuals turned to antisemitism, particularly after the unification of Germany in 1871. The Jews in Germany were now blamed for the problems of modernity. One leading Lutheran, Adolf Stoecker, the court preacher of the ruling Prussian dynasty in Berlin, blamed the Jews for all the social and economic problems of Germany. He reached out to a wider audience in his attempt to create a 'Social Christian' party and helped make antisemitism respectable within the German Conservative Party and in German society generally. Here was a role model who was both a Christian leader and a notable representative of the German Emperor himself.[10] This important Lutheran leader pioneered the new political and social antisemitism of the 1880s.

The spread of racist antisemitism in the later 19th century was fostered both by Protestant intellectuals in Germany and by Catholic writers in Austria. In Austria, Georg von Schoenerer, the leader of the antisemitic and racist Pan-Germans, sought to convert Austrians to Lutheranism, which he deemed the true national Germanic religion. One striking manifestation that this racism took among intellectuals in Germany of Lutheran background was that of the 'Aryan Christ'. The idea that Jesus was a German and was really anti-Jewish was propounded by influential German nationalists, theologians and polemicists such as Johann Gottlieb Fichte, Paul de Lagarde, the Germanophile English racist Houston Stewart Chamberlain, and Richard Wagner. These beliefs had the effect of blurring the lines that distinguished the old Christian antisemitism from the newer racist variety. They also had the effect of denying the Jewish roots of Christianity and of justifying the complete exclusion of the Jews from German and Christian society and, in the case of Lagarde and others, their extermination. This suggests that 'Anti-Semites did not so much replace Christian anti-Judaism with secular racism as many claim; they adjusted Christianity to create a new racist faith. Racists who publicly scorned Christianity had little success.'[11]

With the bitter defeat of Germany in the First World War and the rise of the democratic Weimar Republic the Lutheran churches in Germany were disestablished and bereft of the old authoritarian constitution. In addition, the German Jews finally received their complete emancipation in the Weimar Republic. Most Lutheran pastors and bishops responded to this new state of affairs by allying with the ultra-conservative German Nationalist Party, by bitterly attacking the new Republic and by blaming the 'soulless materialism' and the 'decadence' of the Republic on the participation of Jews in it. The Evangelical Lutheran press and Lutheran leaders such as Church Superintendent Otto Dibelius proudly proclaimed their antisemitism throughout the 1920s. A creative 'Luther renaissance' led by such progressive theologians as Karl Barth, Dietrich Bonhoeffer and Ernst Troeltsch was paralleled by the rise of antisemitic and racist Lutheran professors, among them Paul Althaus, Emanuel Hirsch and Gerhard Kittel, who advocated that Christianity be purged of its Judaic heritage. Under Hitler these antisemites formed an 'Institute for Research on Jewish Influence on the Life of the German Church'. A large number of academics joined this institute and prepared a revised version of the New Testament in which references to such Jewish terms as 'Israel', 'Zion' and 'Jerusalem' were expunged. This institute also held conferences to which students from Sweden and Denmark were invited. Gerhard Kittel, a leading expert on Judaism and the Old Testament and who played a leading role in this antisemitic institute, 'produced a body of work between 1933 and 1944 filled with hatred and slander toward Jews and warmly supportive of National Socialism and anti-Jewish policies'.[12] Emmanuel Hirsch, the leading German expert of his generation on the Danish religious thinker Kierkegaard, attempted to Germanize Kierkegaard's teachings by portraying him as an anti-modern antisemite. These leading theologians distorted Christianity for prejudicial and opportunistic reasons and tailored their ideas to fit Nazi ideology.

'By 1930 the Nazis had a substantial following among the Protestant clergy.'[13] The historian Hajo Holborn noted that 'Such [extreme nationalist] opinions would not have been so widely held if in modern German Protestantism Lutheranism had not so often been declared to be the national German religion. This assertion could easily degenerate into the conception of a German God.'[14] Symptomatic of this tendency was the rise of the 'German Christian' group who declared Jesus to be Nordic, excluded the Old Testament from the Christian Canon and opposed the ecumenical teachings of Saint Paul. Pastors of this persuasion allowed Nazi Storm Troopers to decorate their churches with swastikas. In the ecclesiastical elections of 1932 this movement, sponsored by the Nazis, captured one third of the seats in the synods.

At first, most of the Lutheran pastors and bishops were attracted by Adolf Hitler's characterization of Nazism as a form of 'positive Christianity' and his promise to respect the interests of the German churches. Most Lutherans also turned a blind eye to the extreme Nazi pronouncements on and violence to the Jews – so permeated was German Lutheran culture by German nationalism, antisemitism, and authoritarianism. For example, in the early, decisive days of the Nazi regime in 1933, the pastor Hermann Umfried spoke up against the beating deaths of two Jews in his small town of Nieder-stetten. The local district party leader forced the pastor to resign. No church institution of any kind came to his support, nor did any official speak out against the persecution of the Jews in Germany as a whole. Anxious for the safety of his family, the pastor committed suicide.[15] Lutherans such as Paul Tillich and Karl Barth, who criticized Nazi ideology and tried to preserve Christianity, left Germany, lost their positions, or withdrew inward. Some were sent to prison and others to camps. Non-conformist Christian sects such as Jehovah's Witnesses and Seventh Day Adventists were subjected to systematic persecution, arrest and internment in concentration camps, where thousands died. No official church voices were raised on their behalf.

The beginnings of Church opposition to Hitler occurred when the Nazis strove to unify the Lutheran churches by insisting on Ludwig Müller, a 'German Christian', as Reich Bishop in 1933 and later in 1935 appointing Hanns Kerrl, a committed Nazi, as 'Minister for Church Affairs'. Although the churches were officially unified they splintered into three major groups. Most Lutheran pastors and bishops remained either passive or loyal to the Nazi regime, 85 percent swearing a personal loyalty oath to Hitler in 1938. As noted earlier the 'German Christians' attempted to restructure Lutheranism by injecting neo-pagan and racist practices into their observances. Finally, a 'Confessional Church' was formed that opposed the government incursions into the identity of the church itself. Most scholars of the 'German Church Struggle' have concluded that these divisions and conflicts were waged within the Lutheran churches themselves, over issues of church governance, autonomy, teaching and dogma – but not against the Nazi regime *per se*. That is to say, the church struggles were theological and interdenominational, but not political and civic, as was the opposition of the Danish Lutheran Church to the Nazi occupiers.[16]

With regard to the persecution of the Jews from 1933 to 1939, most Lutherans approved or were silent or, as was the case of the German Christians, aided and abetted the persecution as they invoked Luther's original exhortations to burn the synagogues and to exclude, impoverish, expel and even kill the Jews. The Confessing Church was particularly concerned with the 'Aryan Paragraph' of the Civil Service Law of 1933 and the influence of the 'German Christians' that excluded Jews converted to Christianity (of which there were thousands) from holding church offices or even church membership. With the exception of a few courageous individuals the Confessing Church as an institution did not speak out against what was happening to the Jews themselves. Most of the Confessing Church supported the initial Nazi measures against the Jews and the concerns of the Confessing Church were officially limited to Jews who had been converted to Christianity. 'Criticism of the Aryan paragraph did not prevent the survival of a traditional anti-Semitism; the Protestant and Catholic objections to euthanasia were not matched by any similar protests against the Jewish policy.'[17]

In contrast, the Danish Lutheran Church made no distinction whatsoever between defending converts and Jews who practised the religion of their forbears. Nor did the Danes make any distinction between those Danish Jews who were citizens and the 2200 Jews who did not hold Danish citizenship. Unlike the democratically minded Danes, the German Church resisters failed to realize that the loss of civil rights could lead not only to persecution, but also to mass murder. Moreover, the resistance of the Confessing Church was often reluctant because of fear, the rationale of self-preservation and the Lutheran tradition of subservience to the state.

The German church opposition understood that the Nazi racist ideology was a blatant attack on the power of Christ and on the sacrament of baptism, but began to realize only too late that the persecution and murder of the Jews struck at the heart not only of Jews but of the existence of Christianity. Even Dietrich Bonhoeffer, the most radical theological exponent of the Lutheran resistance to Hitler, evolved from a position of theological antisemitism in 1933 and non-opposition to the Nazi state to solidarity with the Jews and full political resistance later on.[18] Martin Niemoeller, one of the most courageous leaders of the Confessional Church who was imprisoned in two concentration camps, remarked at his trial in 1938 that the Jews were to him an 'unpleasant and alien' force in Germany. Only by the end of the war did he proclaim Germany's responsibility for the Holocaust and his own guilt in not speaking out on behalf of the Jews. In the words of pastor Heinrich Grueber, who risked his life to save Jews during the Holocaust, 'What were the few who protested in comparison with the millions who cooperated or kept silent, and at best stuck their heads ostrich-like into the sand, or clenched their fists in their pockets?'[19]

The institutional Lutheran Churches did not criticize the Nuremberg Racial Laws of 1935, nor did they take a public stand against the 1938 *Kristallnacht* pogrom and the burning of the synagogues. During the Holocaust itself many of the regional churches issued proclamations blaming the Jews for instigating the war. Bishop Wurm, a leading Lutheran, wrote to Hitler protesting against the mass murders yet affirmed his theological antisemitism and his loyalty to the regime. A confidential memorandum, issued by about ten percent of the militants of the Confessing Church and submitted to Hitler, condemned the Nazi doctrine of blood, race, and hatred of the Jews as opposed to Christian morality and to 'love of one's neighbour'. In 1943 the Twelfth Confessing Synod of the Prussian Evangelical Church took issue with the murder of the Jews but weakened this by saying that Jews were a 'foreign race' who had 'rejected God's Christ'.[20]

A remarkable manifesto drawn up by a group of Lutheran laymen in Munich was drafted in 1943 and contained an extensive condemnation of the murder of the Jews. This was the most detailed and forthright statement that condemned the treatment of the Jews of Germany during the persecutions and the Holocaust. Significantly, it began by attacking the silence of the church and then went on to condemn the German people themselves:

> As Christians we can no longer tolerate the Church in Germany keeping silent about the persecution of the Jews... Consequently we recognize our share of the blame for neglect in this respect... Every non-Aryan, whether he be Jew or Christian has today in Germany 'fallen among murderers...'. The recognition that there is a 'Jewish Problem' cannot absolve us from such a decision. On the contrary, the Church has to make use of this situation, in order to testify that the Jewish Question is primarily an Evangelical concern and not a political issue...
>
> The Church has in particular to oppose that version of 'Christian' antisemitism in the Congregation itself that excuses the passivity of the Church respecting the procedure of the

non-Christian world against the Jews...Over against the State, the Church has to bear witness to the redemptive (*heilgeschichtlich*) significance of Israel, and to withstand to the utmost every attempt to solve the Jewish Question according to a self-manufactured political gospel involving the annihilation of Jewry, and to reveal it as an attempt to resist the God of the First Commandment.... The Church may no longer try to promote her security in the face of the attack directed against Israel. She must on the contrary testify that along with Israel she and her Lord Jesus Christ Himself are being attacked.... The testimony of the Church against the persecution of the Jews in Germany thus becomes an exceptionally important special instance of the witness that she is required to give against all violation of the Ten Commandments by the State Authority (*Obrigkeit*).... The Church has to admonish the state...in its legal protection of the oppressed and in its respect for certain basic rights of its subjects...This witness of the Church must be made publicly either from the pulpit or by means of a special word from those who hold the office of bishop, shepherd, and watchman. Only thus can the Church fulfil her obligation towards all those who have a legislative or executive part in the persecution, and at the same time supply the Jews concerned and the Christian congregation assailed in its faith, with the due instruction of their consciences....[21]

This 'Christian Proclamation', presented to Bishop Meiser in the Easter of 1943, was not composed by churchmen or theologians. Despite its eloquent protests it was non-political and stated that a 'Jewish Problem' actually existed. In strong contrast, the Danish Church and King insisted adamantly that Denmark had never had a Jewish problem. Unlike Danish statements about their own traditions, this document would have found it difficult to appeal to a history of strong German democratic institutions and deep traditions of tolerance for the Jews. There is no evidence that Bishop Meiser ever acted on this anonymous and unsigned recommendation of his churchgoers. At any rate, such strong protests were very rare and were not shared by the majority of church resisters. These courageous and idealistic protests came out of the marginally dissenting groups within German Protestantism. Most Lutherans remained loyal to the Third Reich and many saw the Jewish sufferings as caused by the Jews themselves and not central to Christian concerns. On the 'German Christian' side, many members approved of the persecution and some of the killing of the Jews. One Protestant pastor, Ernst Biberstein, served in the killing squads of the SS Einsatzgruppen. Many 'German Christians' were able to filter back into respectable German society after the Second World War.[22] The Danish Church saw saving of lives as a Christian duty; many 'German Christians' viewed the persecution and sometimes the killing of Jews as their Christian obligation.

After 1945 some Lutheran Churches of Germany attempted to issue statements of repentance and contrition, acknowledging the guilt, responsibility and complicity of the churches in the face of the persecution and the murder of the Jews. Other responses continued to harp on Christian triumphalism and supersession, and the stiff-necked refusal of the Jews to recognize the divinity of Jesus. 'Among Christians, the neo-orthodox [Reformed anti-Nazi] Karl Barth was unorthodox enough to describe the Holocaust as the greatest Jewish catastrophe in history; that it might also be a Christian catastrophe does not seem to have entered his mind.'[23] Thus, the culture of German Lutheranism, despite some hopeful signs, had difficulty in fully coming to terms with the challenge of the Holocaust to Christian theology.[24]

For the sake of perspective, it might be helpful to contrast the behaviour of the German Lutheran churches toward the Jews with that of the Catholic Church. Many Catholics in Germany also welcomed the Nazi regime. In 1933 the Vatican reached an accommodation with Hitler in return for a degree of autonomy. Thus a relatively unified

Catholic church was able to avoid the divisions of the Protestant Churches. In this way the Catholic Church was better able to weather the storm of the Nazi Years. Some of the Catholic bishops in Europe and some individual Catholics spoke out and helped Jews. Yet the Vatican was silent for the most part. On the one hand the Catholic church did not espouse the extremist antisemitic and neo-pagan ideas of the 'German Christians' with their 'Aryan Christ'. On the other hand, however, some of the Confessional Protestant resisters such as Bonhoeffer, Albertz, Grueber and van Sylten went further in their resistance and in their opposition to Nazi antisemitism than the German Catholic leaders, who tended to remain neutral.[25]

In the judgement of Primo Levi, echoed by Pastor Wilhelm Niemoeller and others after the war, 'The true crime, the collective general crime of almost all Germans of that time was that of lacking the courage to speak.'[26] Still, this was facilitated by the fusion of antisemitism, German nationalism and German Lutheranism that had created a culture of intolerance and illiberalism before 1945. In the words of Saul Friedlander, '[German] redemptive antisemitism was born from the fear of racial degeneration and the religious belief of redemption.'[27]

THE CONTRASTING NATIONAL CULTURE OF LUTHERANISM IN DENMARK BEFORE AND DURING THE HOLOCAUST

The Protestant Lutheran Reformation began in Denmark in 1536, when King Christian III called a council of one thousand nobles, merchants and peasants. The Danish Reformation was at first German inspired, looking to German universities and German theologians (the celebrated Prince Hamlet himself was a student at Luther's University of Wittenberg).

But the Danish Reformation developed into a distinctly national and popular movement. Luther's tracts on the Jews made no impact on Denmark. Quite to the contrary; in 1690 the Danish Parliament passed a resolution condemning the very idea of establishing a ghetto for the Jews in Copenhagen as 'an inhuman way of life' and fired the police chief who sought to follow the example of other European countries. In 1814 the Danish parliament passed a bill making all racial and religious discrimination punishable by law. In that year the Jews of Denmark were given full Danish citizenship. When Denmark abolished its absolute monarchy in 1849 and promulgated its first free constitution, the Jews were given full political, social, educational and commercial equality. In Danish public law Jews were defined as Danes who went to a 'Jewish church' on Saturday rather than to a Christian church on Sunday. The Danish constitution was the first Scandinavian document to enshrine the idea of religious liberty. The contrast with Germany should be apparent here. The Danish Jews were granted freedom and equality well before that of the German Jews and were accepted rather than merely tolerated. During the course of the 19th century the Danish Jews became well integrated into most of Danish society, though the established elites tended to be somewhat exclusionary.[28]

There might be an interesting similarity of the Jewish community of Denmark with that of Italy. In Italy the community was also small, relatively assimilated and highly integrated into Italian society. Despite the race laws issued by Mussolini in 1938, most Italians and many Italian priests considered Nazi antisemitism as alien to their culture. They considered Italian Jews as Jewish Italians, and helped save most of the Jews of Italy.[29]

The population of the Jews of Denmark was relatively small. By 1940 there were fewer than 8000 Jews in a population of 4.5 million Danes. Most were concentrated in the capital city of Copenhagen. Even by today's American standards the incidence of Jewish intermarriage in early 20th century Denmark was extraordinarily high, an indication of the rate of assimilation of the Danish Jews. This led to Jewish familiarity with a large network of Danes who would prove very helpful during the Nazi occupation. The rate of intermarriage between Jews and non-Jews in Weimar Germany was also high and this would sometimes prove helpful to Jews, but not on the Danish scale, given the widespread legacy of antisemitism in Germany and the power and popularity of the Nazi dictatorship.

The Germany of 1933 contained 550,000 Jews in a nation of 60 million Germans – barely one percent of the population. German Jews tended to be more 'visible' by dint of their greater numbers, their prominence in the professions and commerce, their concentration in the cities, their associations with German liberalism and social democracy and the strong traditions of antisemitism in German society that reached back into medieval times.

During the first half of the 19th century Denmark experienced a remarkable national revival characterized by a flood of political, social and cultural reforms. Not only was the absolute monarchy abolished in 1848 but throughgoing land reforms and universal male suffrage established a strong democracy. Again, this stood in contrast to Germany, where the revolutions of 1848 failed to achieve both German unification and true German democracy. The German peasants looked back to the past and tended to be antisemitic, while most Danish farmers became educated and democratically inclined.

The Danish State Lutheran Church remained the official church of the nation headed by the King, but much of Danish Lutheranism was transformed into a democratic, popular, enlightened and tolerant culture. The two most prominent Danish Lutheran religious figures who influenced the character and culture of the nation were Nikolai F.S. Grundtvig (1782–1873), who put the stamp of his personality and ideas on his own time, and Soren Kierkegaard (1813–1855) whose impact was made in the 20th century.[30]

Grundtvig was an author, poet, educator, church official and theologian. He became the major figure in the Danish national revival. A Danish nationalist, he nevertheless expressed a strong tolerance for other cultures and religious traditions. His greatest creation was that of the Danish folk high schools for young adults. His motto was 'First a human being, then a Christian: this alone is life's order...People are bound to one another with ties more profound than any of the barriers that human history, including the history of religion, may have constructed.'[31]

In the schools established by Grundtvig, rote learning was replaced by discussion and community singing to instill pride in the nation's past. At first Grundtvig attempted to combine the early Nordic pagan religions with Christianity, but abandoned this effort and concentrated on Christian humanitarianism. The Viking heroes celebrated by Grundtvig were praised for their struggle for freedom, not for their *volkish* racial purity. 'Let freedom be the watchword in the North', he proclaimed. Grundtvig also admired English political culture.

Ironically, this intellectual revolt of nationalism, romanticism, and religious revivalism reached Denmark by way of Germany. Like Luther, Grundtvig believed that faith was more important than reason. But in contrast Grundtvig supported progressive innovations in theology, believed in democracy and a true 'peoples' church' and rejected the Lutheran dichotomy of the 'Two Kingdoms' in which Luther had argued that man is subject to the ruling powers, but spiritually free. Grundtvig believed that the church should be active in the affairs of the world, and that it must uphold the sanctity of life. He believed that there could not be spiritual freedom without political freedom. He played an important role in forging the constitution of 1849 that granted complete equality to the Jews, as did other liberal Danish clerics, such as D.C. Monrad. Grundtvig had a democratic view of the church, saying, 'the State Church is not a Church State.'[32] Here he clearly departed from the practices of German Lutherans and pietists.

Finally, Grundtvig was a great admirer of the Hebrew Bible and particularly of the Jewish prophets. He believed that the most important peoples in history were the Jews, the Greeks, the Anglo-Saxons and the Norsemen. Grundtvig wrote many influential hymns which were based on the Old Testament. Palle Dinesen, the current pastor of Trinity Lutheran Church in Copenhagen remarked:

> The strong spirit of the Old Testament which pervades his [Grundtvig's] hymns contributed to the Danes' feeling a sense of identification with the Jewish people and with Biblical Jewish history. We also have a tradition in Denmark of telling Old Testament stories to our children.[33]

Grundtvig's impact on Danish Lutheran culture and education was enormous and epoch-making. His ideas were revived by young Danish theologians and professors during the time of the German occupation, and with great effect.

In contrast, Grundtvig's German contemporary counterparts were the nationalist figures of Friedrich Ludwig 'Father' Jahn, Johann Gottlieb Fichte and Friedrich Schleiermacher. Jahn founded the influential gymnastic societies and espoused a narrow, pro-Prussian, antisemitic, xenophobic and neo-pagan German nationalism. Fichte, an influential rector at the University of Berlin, boasted in his 'Addresses to the German Nation' in 1807 that Germany had invented the Protestant Reformation and was entitled to the future leadership of Europe because of the profundity and originality of its national character. Like Luther, Fichte perceived the Jews as a deadly enemy of 'Germanness', accusing them of immoral self-interest and materialism that was antithetical to both the German and Christian spirit.

> It was Schleiermacher more than any other at this time who elaborated a philosophy of national education intended to infuse a common spirit into the people by transmitting to the succeeding generations the values and spirit that had become part of the national heritage.[34]

His nationalism and romanticism were much more introspective and politically passive than Grundtvig's. With regard to the Jews, Schleiermacher believed that they were a petrified religion, and that a Jew who sought to embrace German culture should be required to adopt Christianity. He also disparaged much of the Old Testament. As the greatest German theologian of his time his ideas were bound to make their impact on modern German Lutheranism.

Soren Kierkegaard was not as influential as Grundtvig on Danish culture and politics but was arguably the greatest Christian theologian of modern times. As a Lutheran, Kierkegaard stressed faith and Christian integrity, but criticized Luther for his emphasis on grace alone and his subservience to secular authority. Kierkegaard criticized the Lutheran Church of his day as well as modern Christianity for its 'spiritless torpor'.[35] His theology urged the steadfastness of individual and authentic Christian ethical responsibility no matter what the cost, the willingness to suffer for the truth and the insistence on love of neighbour as a commandment equal to love of God. Kierkegaard's models were Abraham and Jesus. These principles of Kierkegaard were consciously revived during the Holocaust by Dietrich Bonhoeffer and Karl Jaspers in Germany and the Danish theologians and anti-Nazi resisters Hal Koch and Kai Munk in Denmark.[36]

Emmanuel Hirsch, a German-Christian theologian of the Nazi period, attempted to portray Kierkegaard as antisemite but this was a gross distortion. Kierkegaard did remark on the differences between Judaism and Christianity, noting that Judaism did not emphasize suffering as a way to salvation and that it put less of an emphasis on the other world In his interesting Jewish perspective on Kierkegaard, the great Jewish rabbi and theologian Abraham Joshua Heschel noted:

> [Kierkegaard] once told Israel Lewin, his secretary, who was a Jew, that he envied him because he did not have to be concerned with Jesus Christ; meaning that he thereby escaped the suffering which is always the Christian's lot because of the collision between Christ (and the Christian likewise) and the world.[37]

It was the radical Christian integrity and courage of Kierkegaard with its emphasis on personal responsibility as well as on human sinfulness – rather than any of his observations on the Jews – that became translated into action in the years of the German occupation of Denmark.

During the 1920s and the 1930s Denmark became one of the most progressive social democracies in the world. Social insurance, medical care and old age insurance were expanded. The Social Democratic party also introduced 'Civil Confirmation' as an option to the traditional religious ceremonies. The Orthodox teachings of the Church of Denmark were weakened by the currents of modernism and secularization. Still, the Church remained a considerable influence in the life of the people In the aftermath of the Great Depression a small, yet vocal antisemitic movement and Nazi party arose. Anti-democratic movements developed a small following among farmers and the youth. At their height, the Danish Nazis had about 22,000 members and received less than two percent of the votes cast. Antisemitic articles in Danish Nazi publications were largely ignored. Though the Danish Church opposed antisemitism it did, following the tradition of pietism, have an organization called 'The Inner Mission' whose goal was to convert the Jews. The German Lutherans under Nazism were forced to abolish their similar organization due to the racist belief that even if a Jew converted to Christianity, he remained a Jew.

Denmark adopted restrictive policies against immigration of Jewish refugees. Yet, during the 1930s the church leadership along with many theologians strongly and openly condemned the Danish Nazis, exposed the Protocols of the Elders of Zion as a vicious lie and vigorously denounced the burning of the synagogues on *Kristallnacht* in 1938. Bishops of the Danish church instructed pastors to pray for the Jews, characterized antisemitism as a 'poisonous pestilence' and affirmed the kinship of Jews and Christians by asserting that 'Our Lord and Saviour Jesus Christ was David's Son after the flesh, and those who love Him cannot hate his people.'[38] Thus, the Danish Church was spiritually arming the Danish people before the German invasion and the Holocaust. It now appeared that the hierarchy of the Danish church was doing everything in its power to discredit Luther's earlier pronouncements on the Jews that were now being applied in Nazi Germany.

The Germans occupied Denmark in 1940. In December 1941 (when the Jews were still unharmed), Danish Lutheran theologians held a conference at the University of Copenhagen to protest publicly that the Danish government would not tolerate any future Nazi discrimination or persecution of the Jews. Throughout the occupation church gazettes denounced Jew hatred, again strengthening the humanitarian resolve of the Danes. In the autumn of 1943 when rumours of the impending persecution of the Jews were circulating, Fuglsang-Damgaard, the Bishop of Copenhagen, contacted German and Danish authorities and Jewish leaders to voice his concern and his support for the Jews.

Church newspapers were so outspoken in their call for a struggle against antisemitism that in 1942 the State Ministry of Religion issued a warning to church newspapers to tone down their remarks.

> It is clear that the anti-Semitic press foamed with rage against the Church. In the *Faedrelandet* of 3 January, 1943, the well-known anti-Semite Frits Heide wrote, in an article on the Church called 'The Jewish Poison in the Danish Spirit'; 'It is quite impossible to understand how it has come about that this poison has penetrated so deeply into the Church; nothing in any of our social institutions is fought for with such fanaticism as this cause of 'the safety and freedom of the Jews.'[39]

Once the Nazis decided to persecute and 'resettle' the Danish Jews, the Lutheran bishops, pastors and laymen participated overwhelmingly to save the Jews. 'The clergy had about ninety percent of its membership participating in the underground.'[40] Paul Borchsenius, nicknamed 'the fighting priest', whose underground activities forced him to escape to Sweden, believed that both the Christians and the Jews took legitimate and authentic roads to salvation. The Danish religious leadership and its rank-and-file refused to be intimidated by the German occupiers when the persecution of the Jews seemed imminent.

A secret meeting of the Protestant higher clergy was convened in the home of the Bishop of Copenhagen, Fuglsang-Damgaard. Many clergy organized to rescue Jews and Jewish religious objects. Churches hid Jews and stored Jewish sacred objects such as Torah scrolls. Protestant ministers opened their homes to entire Jewish families. In one instance a church that hid Jews was besieged and invaded by Danish Nazi collaborators.

> It is interesting to note . . . that for some of the rescuers, many of whom were indeed drawn from the ranks of the clergy or were from rural areas where fundamental Evangelist teachings held sway, theological considerations played not an insignificant and positive role in their position on the Jews and on anti-Semitism.[41]

This resulted from a distinctive blend of religion, nationalism and humanitarianism.

The Rabbi of Copenhagen, Dr. Marcus Melchior, was hidden together with his family by Pastor Gildeby in his Jutland home. The pastor's superior, Bishop Flums, established the headquarters of an organization to ferry Jews to Sweden. A biblical scholar, Dr. Aage Bertelsen, Principal of Aarhus Cathedral College, formed a rescue organization that smuggled 1200 Jews past a flotilla of German warships. His wife was captured and tortured by the Gestapo.[42] Some Danish pastors also provided needed financial aid to the Jews.

Hal Koch, a theologian and professor and noted authority and disciple of both Kierkegaard and Grundtvig, held a series of public lectures in 1940 to revitalize Danish youth. Using the language of biblical morality and citing the Nazi threat to Danish democracy he urged the protection of the Jews as vital to the very survival of Danish democracy and Christianity. His lectures and charismatic personality electrified Danish public opinion, especially students. Koch shared some of Kierkegaard's pessimism about human nature but believed passionately that evil must be fought and resisted, in contrast to the German Lutheran view that political and social evil should be tolerated and endured.

Another great Danish cultural leader who spoke up for the Jews in the strongest terms was the minister and playwright Kai Munk. His novel *Toys*, written in 1936, analysed the nature of a totalitarian regime by portraying the way in which a firm of toy manufacturers builds itself up, rules by terror and finally self-destructs. Using the pulpit to denounce the Germans, he said that if the Germans tried to do to the Danish Jews what they had done to the Jews of Norway (deporting them to camps), the Danes would not only wear the yellow star of David, but would also resist the Nazis *en masse*.[43] This scholar and disciple of Kierkegaard stated:

> When here in this country pogroms have been started against a special group of our fellow countrymen, only because they belong to a special race, then the church has a right to cry out. This is breaking the constitution of Christ's kingdom and is abominable to the Nordic way of thinking. The Church must here be indefatigable.[44]

In 1944 the Gestapo dragged Munk from his home, shot him and threw his body in a ditch. Munk was one of the 3213 Danish resisters who were executed by the Nazis.

The officials and theologians of the Danish church fully identified with Danish democratic traditions and realized that any danger to the Jews of Denmark was a grave threat to them, striking at the heart of the integrity and existence of Danish democracy and national character itself. The Danish Church was a true 'Peoples' Church' not because it espoused ties of a *Voelkisch* national identity and loyalty to an authoritarian state, as was the case with most of the German churches, but because it helped organize the people in conjunction with a civic, democratic resistance and because it had its own mind and served an educational function. In that capacity the Danish church became a force in the leadership of the nation, a key role that the German churches failed, or perhaps never even sought, under Hitler. In the last analysis, Nazism was a pseudo-religion that tried to cooperate with, then co-opt, and then finally substitute itself for traditional Christianity. Most of the German Churches failed to realize this. The Danish church did because it held to the oneness of God, a belief it stated in its 1943 proclamation when it affirmed its kinship with the Jews.

In the Denmark of 1943 a courageous film entitled *Day of Wrath* was produced by the noted movie maker, Carl Dreyer. Its theme was the epidemic of witch-burning religious hysteria that had swept over Europe in the 17th century and had resulted in the deaths of thousands of women. The reference to the Nazi and, indeed, European obsession with characterizing the Jews as demons and latter-day witches was unmistakable. Such leading figures of Danish culture now mobilized to fight Nazi fanaticism and antisemitism.

The Danish intellectuals and clerics also looked upon themselves as guardians of the nation who opposed laws contrary to the Christian faith as interpreted by that Church, especially if those laws were directed against Danish citizens. Civic nationalism played its part here. Unlike the German churches which were fragmented historically and weakened by Nazi totalitarianism, the Danish Church remained unified with a strong sense of mission and morale.

All these efforts of the Danish Lutheran leaders reached their peak in the pastoral letter on behalf of all of Denmark's bishops that was drafted by the Bishop of Copenhagen and read from the pulpits of all the state churches on Sunday 3 October 1943. It proved to be the most comprehensive church protest written during the Second World War in any of the countries occupied by the Nazis and contained three major principles that can be summarized as follows: (1) The Old Testament prepared the way for Jesus the Jew; Jews and Christians are peoples related by a sacred history who simply received the covenant differently; the Jews play a vital role in the salvation of the Christians. (2) The persecution of the Jews is 'irreconcilable' with the humanitarian love of neighbour commanded by Christ. 'Our different religious views notwithstanding, we shall fight for the cause that our Jewish brothers and sisters may preserve the same freedom which we ourselves value more highly than life itself.' (3) The persecution of Danish-Jewish citizens also strikes at the Danish democratic way of life, and is contrary to the Danish constitution that guarantees religious freedom and human rights. Danes are a law-abiding people, but when human rights are violated 'they must obey God rather than man.'[45] This was sent to the Nazi occupation officials and was read from all the pulpits to great popular approval.

A similar pastoral letter was drafted by the Bishop of Zeeland, scoffing at the Nazi 'barbarians' and affirming that there were no distinctions between Jewish and Christian Danes. Such strong official political as well as religious pronouncements were never issued by the churches in Nazi Germany either before or during the Holocaust. The pronouncement of 1943 contained none of the negative comments about the Jews that characterized some of the protests of the other Churches in Europe, such as the Dutch Reformed Church of Holland and the Orthodox Church of Greece. The Norwegian Lutheran Church, however, issued a proclamation very similar to that of the Danish Church.

Despite the relative failure of Hitler's order to round up the Danish Jews for future extermination, the Nazi intentions had the effect of exacerbating Danish opposition to the Germans. Resistance against the Germans increased and notes were sent to known collaborators. Coffins decorated with crosses were drawn on those threatening letters. There could be no doubt about their ultimate meaning.

It should be remembered that the Danish King, Christian X, who had always proclaimed his great solidarity with the Jews, was also the official head of the Danish State Lutheran Church. The King always insisted that there was no Jewish problem in Denmark, not only because Jews were also considered Danes but – in an insight of psychological irony – remarked that the Danish Christians had never felt inferior to the Jews. Both the King and the Bishop of Copenhagen also made it clear to the Germans that the 472 Danish Jews who were captured and sent to the concentration camp at Theresienstadt outside Prague, Czechoslovakia, must not be harmed. It is very likely that the unshakeable resolve of the Danes and their Church had a sobering effect on the German occupying officials in their policies toward Danish Jews.

After the war the Jews were welcomed back by the Danish Church and the Copenhagen synagogue was rededicated with the King and with officials of the church. Soon after, the democracies celebrated the Danish example as a beacon of hope, perhaps unmindful of the fact that most churches and Christians in Nazi-occupied Europe did not go the way of the Danes. It has been established that the mythical tale that King Christian X donned the yellow star in protest was a creation of British wartime propagandists, who sought to strengthen morale and to glorify Western democracies. The King did not have to wear the yellow star; his other actions were sufficiently effective.[46]

Some major post-war statements of Scandinavian Lutheranism were very critical of past Christian attitudes and practices and very positive toward Jewish tradition. The Danish '*Logumkloster* Report' (1964) regarding the relations between the Church and the Jewish people condemned Luther's anti-Jewish utterances, urged the responsibility of Christians to understand the Jewish people and their faith, condemned antisemitism as 'spiritual suicide' and interpreted the continuing existence of the Jews as a reminder of the origins of Christianity and as 'a profound cause of wonder and hope'. The Oslo Report of 1975 stated that 'We cannot confess our guilty involvement in the Holocaust of the 1940s without committing ourselves to action that will prevent the repetition of such a tragedy. We must say, never again.'[47]

CONCLUSIONS

The interplay of national culture and religious ideas and institutions played a crucial role in the radically different outcomes of Lutheranism in Germany and Denmark with regard to attitudes and behaviour toward the Jews. A warning to the present and the future is contained in this parting at the cross: For example, many of the hate groups in present day America such as the 'Aryan nations', the Ku Klux Klan and the National Alliance seek to present themselves as authentic representatives of a true Christianity. Some have attempted to align themselves with the religious right-wing of American politics. The currents of prejudice that combine racism, antisemitism and Christianity still live. The Holocaust revealed that Christianity could easily be perverted and adulterated by extreme nationalism, racism, and neo-paganism – in addition to indifference and to passive acceptance of radical evil that were at odds with the original teachings of Christ.[48] 'The Holocaust repudiated the concept that the teachings of Christ were practised in the daily lives by most of those who professed to be believers.'[49] Both German Christians and anti-Christians, together with their nominally Christian European collaborators and bystanders perpetrated the disaster. The Danes responded with their Christian answer and we must listen, always.

NOTES

1 See J.S. Conway, *The Nazi Persecution of the Churches, 1933–1945* (New York: Basic Books, 1968), Richard Gutteridge, *The German Evangelical Church and the Jews, 1879–1950* (New York: Harper and Row, 1976) and Klaus Scholder, *A Requiem for Hitler and Other New Perspectives on the German Church Struggle*, tr. by John Bowden, (London: SCM Press, 1989). Also, *Dimensions: A Journal of Holocaust Studies: The Churches and the Holocaust: A Reconsideration*, vol.12, no.2, 1998. A useful, wide-ranging series of essays was compiled by Franklin H. Littell and Hubert G. Locke, *The German Church Struggle and the Holocaust* (Detroit: Wayne State University Press, 1974). For an updated analysis of Protestant resistance and eyewitness testimony see Viktoria Barnett, *For the Soul of the People: Protestant Protest Against Hitler*, (New York: Oxford, 1992).

2 For a good comparative survey of the attitude and behaviour of the Churches during the Holocaust see Helen Fein, *Accounting For Genocide: National Responses and Jewish Victimization During the Holocaust* (New York: The Free Press, 1979). The responses of the German and Danish Churches to the 'Jewish Question' are ably summarized by Wolfgang Gerlach, 'The German Protestant Church and the "Jewish Question"' and Jorgen Glenthoj, 'The Danish Church in the Critical Years, 1940–1945', in Franklin H. Littell, Irene Shur, and Claude R. Foster Jr., (eds.), *In Answer...Is the Story True? Why Did the World Community Not Respond? What Are the Lessons?* (West Chester, Pa.: Sylvan Publishers, 1989). For a good summary of the response of the Norwegian Lutheran Church see Samuel Abrahamsen, 'The Role of the Norwegian Lutheran Church During World War II', in *Remembering for the Future: Jews and Christians During and After the Holocaust*, vol.1 (Oxford: Pergamon Press, 1988), pp.3–17.

3 For the fusion of Lutheranism, antisemitism and German Nationalism see Paul Lawrence Rose, *Revolutionary Antisemitism in Germany, From Kant to Wagner*, (Princeton, New Jersey: Princeton University Press, 1990), Uriel Tal, *Christians and Jews in Germany: Religion, Politics, and Ideology in the Second Reich, 1870–1914)*, tr. by Jonathan Jacobs, (New York: Cornell University Press, 1975) and John Weiss, *Ideology of Death: Why The Holocaust Happened in Germany*, (Chicago: Ivan Dee, 1996).

4 On the rescue of the Danish Jews see Harold Flender, *Rescue in Denmark* (Washington D.C.: Holocaust Library, 1963), Leo Goldberger (ed.), *The Rescue of the Danish Jews: Moral Courage Under Stress* (New York: New York University Press, 1987), and Leni Yahil, *The Rescue of Danish Jewry – Test of a Democracy* (Philadelphia: Jewish Publication Society, 1969). Good surveys of Danish history and culture are provided in John Danstrup, *A History of Denmark*, second edition (Copenhagen: Wivels Forlag, 1950) and W. Glyn Jones, *Denmark* (New York: Praeger, 1970).

5 This distinction between civic and ethnic nationalism is analysed convincingly by Liah Greenfield, *Nationalism: Five Roads to Modernity* (Cambridge, Mass.: Harvard University Press, 1992), pp.9–14.

6 On Luther's writings on the Jews and their impact, see Johannes Brosseder, *Luther Stellung zu den Juden im Spiegel seiner Interpretation* (Munich: Hueber, 1972), Harold H. Ditmanson (ed.), *Stepping Stones to Further Jewish – Lutheran Relationships* (Minneapolis: Fortress, 1990), and Richard Marius,

Luther (Philadelphia: J.B. Lippincott Co., 1974). Luther's characterization of the Jews is summarized in Raul Hilberg, *The Destruction of the European Jews* (Chicago: Quadrangle Books, 1967), pp.2–11.

7   See Doris Bergen, *Twisted Cross: The German Christian Movement in the Third Reich* (Chapel Hill: University of North Carolina Press, 1996).

8   See Klaus P. Fischer, *The History of An Obsession: German Judeophobia and the Holocaust* (New York: Continuum, 1998).

9   See Hajo Holborn, *A History of Modern Germany, 1648–1840* (New York: Alfred A. Knopf, 1968), pp.128–146.

10   See Gutteridge and Weiss, *op.cit.*

11   Weiss, *op.cit.*, p.139. On the 'Aryan Christ' see Susannah Heschel, 'When Jesus was an Aryan', in *Betrayal: German Churches and the Holocaust*, eds. Robert P. Eriksen and Susannah Heschel (Minneapolis: Fortress, 1999), pp.68–89.

12   Robert P. Ericksen, *Theologians Under Hitler: Gerhard Kittel, Paul Althaus, and Emmanuel Hirsch* (New Haven: Yale University Press, 1985), pp.30–31.

13   Weiss, *op.cit.*, p.295.

14   Hajo Holborn, *op.cit.*, p.662.

15   The account is reported in Saul Friedlander, *Nazi Germany and the Jews, Vol.1: The Years of Persecution, 1933–1939* (New York: Harper Collins, 1997), p.36.

16   See Conway *op.cit.*

17   Karl Dietrich Bracher, *The German Dictatorship: The Origins, Structure, and Effects of National Socialism* (New York: Praeger, 1970), p.384. Also, Shelly Baranowski, 'The Confessing Church and Antisemitism: Protestant Identity, German Nationhood, and the Exclusion of Jews' in Ericksen and Heschel, *op.cit.*

18   See Gutteridge, *op.cit.*, p.92.

19   *ibid.*, p.181.

20   *ibid.*, p.249.

21   A long extract of this manifesto is in Gutteridge, *ibid.*, pp.350–351.

22   See Bergen, *op.cit.*

23   Emil L. Fackenheim, *To Mend The World: Foundations of Post-Holocaust Jewish Thought* (Bloomington: Indiana University Press, 1994), p.192 and passim.

24   See Micha Brumlik, 'Post-Holocaust Theology: German Theological Responses since 1945', in: Ericksen and Heschel, *op.cit.*, pp.169–188.

25   See Guenther Lewy, *The Catholic Church and Nazi Germany* (London: Weidenfeld and Nicholson, 1964).

26   Primo Levi, *The Drowned and the Saved* (New York: Summit Books, 1988), p.182.

27   Friedlander, *op.cit.*, p.89.

28   See Nathan Bamberger, 'A Cultural History of the Jews of Denmark, 1622–1900', D.H.L. Dissertation, New York: Yeshiva University, University Microfilms, 1974.

29   See Susan Zucotti, *The Italian Jews and the Holocaust* (New York: Basic Books, 1987).

30   On Grundtvig, see Ernest D. Nielsen, 'N.F.S. Grundtvig on Luther' in *Interpretations of Luther: Essays in Honor of Wilhelm Pauck*, ed. Jaroslav Pelikan (Philadelphia: Fortress Press, 1968). On Kierkegaard, see Ernest B. Koenker, 'Soren Kierkegaard on Luther' in the same volume. Also Alastair Hannay and Gordon D. Marino (eds.), *The Cambridge Companion to Kierkegaard* (Cambridge: Cambridge University Press, 1998).

31   Quoted in Jaroslav Pelikan, 'Grudtvig's Influence', in Goldberger, *op.cit.*, p.175.

32   *ibid.*

33   Quoted by Linda Friedman Shah, 'Wartime Denmark: Resistance and Rescue', in *Dimensions: A Journal of Holocaust Studies: The Rescue of the Danish Jews – A Fiftieth Anniversary Commemoration*, vol.7 no.3, (1993): 13.

34   Koppel S. Pinson, *Modern Germany: Its History and Civilization* (New York: Macmillan, 1954), p.35.

35   Quoted in *The Cambridge Companion to Kierkegaard, op. cit.*, p.250.

36   See Roger Poole, 'The Unknown Kierkegaard: Twentieth Century Receptions', in *The Cambridge Companion to Kierkegaard*, pp.48–75.

37 Abraham Joshua Heschel, *A Passion for Truth* (New York: Farrar, Straus, and Giroux, 1973), p.245.

38 Quoted in Fein, *op.cit.*, p.117.

39 Yahil, *op.cit.*, p.234.

40 Goldberger, *op.cit.*, p.6.

41 *ibid.*, p.199.

42 See Philip Friedman, *Their Brothers' Keepers* (New York: Holocaust Library, 1968), pp.153–154. Also Marcus W. Melchior, *A Rabbi Remembers* (New York: Lyle Stuart, 1968).

43 Yahil, *op.cit.*, p.233.

44 Quoted in Flender, *op.cit.*, p.70.

45 Quoted in Johan M. Snoek, *The Grey Book* (New York: Humanities Press, 1970), p.168.

46 See Richard Petrow, *The Bitter Years* (New York: Morrow, 1979), p.227–229.

47 Quoted in Ditmanson, *op.cit.*, p.31.

48 See Theodore H. Gill, 'What America Can Learn From the German Church Struggle,' in Littell, *The German Church Struggle, op.cit.*, pp.278–289.

49 Rita Steinhardt Botwinick, *A History of the Holocaust: From Ideology to Annihilation* (Upper Saddle River, New Jersey: Prentice Hall, 1996), p.217.

STEWART W. HERMAN, PASTOR OF THE AMERICAN CHURCH IN BERLIN 1935–42, AND HITLER'S PERSECUTION OF THE JEWS

Ronald Webster

LTHOUGH THIS paper focuses on the attitude and involvement with the Jewish 'question' of one American Lutheran clergyman, Dr. Stewart Herman, it should not be assumed that on this issue Herman stood apart from the mainstream in his homeland. He has been singled out here because, as a representative of this mainstream, he held a unique position in Hitler's Germany in the crucial years between 1935 and 1941. As the pastor of a non-denominational Berlin Protestant church, a relatively prominent figure in the city's social and diplomatic world, Herman became deeply engaged in the events surrounding the plight of Berlin's Jews. Before considering his experiences, however, it is important make some brief introductory observations about the sentiments on the Jews of leading contemporary American Lutherans.

It is safe to generalize that until Hitler came to power in 1933, American Lutheran leaders seldom departed from the most conventional public and private opinions about the Jews, opinions that were for these times either 'moderately' antisemitic or even philosemitic. As an example of the latter, Dr. Lauritz Larsen, in 1921 the general secretary of the recently founded National Lutheran Council [NLC],[1] displayed a decided antipathy towards his predecessor's enthusiasm for the strident antisemitism of Henry Ford's *Dearborn Independent*. 'Whatever we may think of the position of the Jews in our country and in the world in general at present,' he wrote, 'I do also think that it is necessary for us to be on guard lest we be guilty of racial or religious discrimination, if not persecution.'[2]

Alas, by the 1930s there was a dramatic change and some of the most internationally active American Lutherans leaders were now inclined to respond sympathetically, initially at least, to Nazi treatment of the Jews. For example, in 1933 Reverend Dr. Lars Boe, prominent Norwegian-American member of the NLC and of the Lutheran World Convention [later Federation][3] described to a friend his recent impressions of a trip to Germany.[4] In respect to the Jews, he wrote: 'Justice is being done without regard for person or position . . .', and 'Those who are guilty are sent to concentration camps and their ill-gotten gains are taken for use for the public good.' Moreover, in 1934 Dr. Boe was to allege to the German Lutheran Bishop of Bavaria, Hans Meiser, that before Hitler had systematically launched his campaign against them, the Jews had achieved an all-powerful international position, and that 'We in America are so subject to Jewish propaganda that I thank God for the opportunity given to me to know the truth.'[5] This could only encourage men such as Meiser to condone Hitler's acts, at least passively.

The German Professor Michael Reu of the Lutheran Wartburg Seminary in Dubuque, Iowa, a participant in numerous Lutheran World Convention sessions before 1933 and long-time editor of the U.S.-based, German-language periodical *Kirchliche*

Zeitschrift, took Boe's views significantly further. For if in 1933–34 Boe was merely alleging that the Jews were 'getting out of hand', Reu became downright fanatical. In late 1933, in the pages of his journal, he accused the Jews of cornering German culture. Indeed, employing tones virtually identical to *Mein Kampf*, he wrote that 'In the European struggle which is mainly a struggle between the Jews and the Germanics, the German will only be victorious if, by expelling all Jewishness, he restores the purity of his race and its Indo-Aryan basis....' He capped this diatribe with the sweeping political (and popular German) allegation that the Jews were among the chief protagonists of the hated Versailles Treaty.[6] In the next year, in a language again ominously echoing 'Nazi-speak', Reu wrote approvingly of Hitler's demand for 'the relocation of the non-German elements, especially the Jews'.[7]

Dr. Ralph Long, NLC head from 1930, was no supporter of such extreme antisemitic views and was usually more attuned to the attitudes expressed by his predecessor, Lauritz Larsen. In a lengthy address in September 1933, Long expressed an admixture of cautious, mollifying and modestly critical views of Nazi antisemitic policies. While he did indeed begin by attempting to place a positive emphasis on Hitler's plans for the German churches, including the latter's early attempts to have 'non-aryan' Christians weeded out of the ranks of the church, Long also expressed some dismay at these measures when he said: 'We cannot help but deplore and regret that under the pressure of a great revolution in the German nation a fanatical and unchristian attitude toward the Jew has accompanied the movement even to the extent of being brought into the regulations of the church.' Long also blamed the German churches themselves for not having worked hard to achieve conversions before Nazi regulations were beginning to make this prohibitive.[8]

Soon, however, Long began to retreat from his measured censure of Nazi antisemitic policies. In a 1934 letter, attempting to mollify a colleague who was concerned about Hitler's attacks on 'non-aryan' Christians, Long assured him that while his church did not approve of what was happening, U.S. Lutheran bodies would not take a stand on this issue due to what he claimed was the prevalence of antisemitism in the United States. Moreover, he attempted to reassure his correspondent that the Lutheran churches in Germany were actually involved in a 'valiant fight' against Nazi purges of Christian 'non-aryans', moreover that 'Lutheran pastors of Jewish extraction' still enjoyed full rights. But Long's concluding comment sums up clearly the aloofness of the NLC and the wider American Lutheran movement at this time: 'In view of all these circumstances, I personally think it is the wisest policy to stay by principles and not become involved in episodes.'[9] Nor did Long appear to take up this issue during the next few years.

Long's remarks were no exaggerations, for polls of American public opinion between 1940 and 1944 indicate that the Jews were more unpopular than America's enemies, the Germans and Japanese.[10] Thus it is no wonder that in this era of American neutrality, Lutheran church leaders, who were inclined to be highly sensitive to public sentiments, would be so circumspect in their criticisms of German antisemitism. It also helps to cast some light on the serious ambivalence we shall come to witness in Pastor Herman's attitudes.

HERMAN'S EARLY EXPOSURE TO NAZI ANTISEMITISM

Born in 1909 in Harrisburg, Pennsylvania, at the time of his arrival in Europe in 1934 Stewart Herman had recently graduated from and been ordained by the well-known Gettysburg Lutheran Seminary. After graduation he had obtained scholarships to study at the Universities of Strassburg, Göttingen and Berlin. Preceding this first extended journey to Continental Europe were longer trips to Latin America and the U.K. Therefore, by 1934-Herman was an experienced traveller, who strove to make himself more than conventionally knowledgable about international political and cultural affairs. Moreover, since his student days, he had cultivated his skills as a writer on student newspapers and also more widely read publications. Thus on his way to Europe in the autumn of 1934 he was deliberately writing home very detailed letters that would constitute the main basis for his subsequent publications.[11]

Arriving in Germany in the wake of Hitler's notorious September 1935 racial laws, it was inevitable that Herman would become aware of the plight of German Jews. In the spirited language of college graduates of those times, and perhaps befitting an unprejudiced newcomer, Herman in his early letters largely confined himself to brief comments such as one about a shipboard romance between a Frenchman whom he felt had regrettably gotten himself 'entangled with a German Jewess'.[12] But in this darkening season of escalating Nazi persecutions, and predictably after arriving in Germany, Herman's curiosity became more deeply aroused because he now made a habit of going to the Jewish sector in every German city he visited. For example, during a late October 1935 visit to Berlin's Jewish quarter, he wrote home, somewhat lightheartedly, 'I saw few Jewish noses on the streets and none of the uproarious hilarity that usually characterizes the ghetto because of many children.'[13] But lighthearted though these comments might sound, they do seem to reveal at least the first signs of a deeper curiosity about the German Jews who, following the Nuremberg racial laws, had been relieved of their basic rights of citizenship, including the right to marry and/or cohabit with gentiles. As the subsequent evolution of Herman's sentiments will reveal, it was the poorer ghetto Jews rather than their more privileged counterparts who elicited his greatest sympathy.

After leaving Strassburg to continue graduate studies at Göttingen and Berlin, in early 1936 Herman became the temporary and eventually the full-time pastor at the Berlin American Church,[14] where the plight of the Jews was to confront him with an intensity he had not experienced as a travelling student. In 1936 Herman was also coming to realize that his church had the potential to become a minor focal point in the escalating 'Jewish question': he mentioned at this time the appearance of Jewish supplicants at his church door, some of whom he acknowledged helping, others whom he said he could not.[15]

A dramatic personal experience heightened the young American clergyman's awareness of the extremes of the Hitler cult which, of course, fuelled German antisemitism. In March 1936, Herman was physically assaulted on the streets of Berlin by an unidentified super-patriot for neglecting to respect a national moment of silence during the broadcast of a Hitler speech. Indeed, the assault created a minor international incident, no doubt also establishing for Herman a certain profile otherwise not so easily attainable by the very young pastor of a small American church in Hitler's capital.[16]

But one comes to realize that in the longer evolution of Herman's attitudes towards the Jews in Germany, and alongside his witness to the pernicious influence of extreme German nationalism and antisemitism, he also appears to have brought with him across the Atlantic the negative images of the richer Jews typified by such stereotypes as the Jewish Hollywood film moguls. Thus, in a letter home at the time of the 1936 assault, Herman noted that when he once approached an American movie executive for church support, he was relieved to find that 'When I had thought to find a bunch of "hard boiled Jews" in the film business, I discovered him.'[17] While this particular antipathy was to prove to be very persistent in Herman's thinking, his church was at the same time soliciting patronage from American Jews situated in Berlin. Even well-situated Jews were to be found among the church's benefactors.[18]

In the months that followed Herman was also to show decidely philosemitic qualities. In September 1936 he wrote home about the appearance at his church of a Jewish–American woman married to a German. Now seriously ill, the woman wished to be baptized. This could cause serious personal and professional dilemmas for the pastor, including the opposition of parishioners to the baptism.[19] Unable to enlist the assistance of her German family pastor, a 'German-Christian',[20] and having consulted the U.S. Ambassador, William Dodd, Herman was left alone to weigh the fact that the woman's American citizenship had lapsed against the couple's pleas. Finally he agreed to perform the ceremony, and reported home how deeply affected he was by the tears of gratitude the couple shed.[21]

This touching event conveys something about his character. Firstly, he displayed here genuine compassion in the face of congregational and diplomatic opposition. Secondly, he began to reveal an emerging pattern on this thorny question: while he continued – sometimes gruffly – to disparage Jews who tried to seek baptism solely as a means of avoiding persecution, he also proved willing to take risks in assisting those who genuinely sought conversion. Commenting on a related case, he elaborated on his wider philosophy on Jews who genuinely sought baptism: 'To all intents and purposes, these people are not Jews. They don't look it, they don't live like them or with them, and they often are grounded in Christian training.' While such a philosophy was in itself a revelation of some mildly antisemitic overtones, at least Herman appears to have decided that he would not budge on his determination to support 'non-aryan' Christians who came to him for help. He even speculated, along the lines already recommended by Ralph Long, that perhaps the Christians should now be pursuing a more proactive Jewish conversion strategy,[22] presumably for both religious and humanitarian reasons. Certainly in 1936 Herman could not have known that such a strategy was doomed, as Hitler was later to demonstrate that baptism was not to be a shield against the Final Solution.

By the autumn of 1936, Herman was beginning to question seriously the whole facade of Nazi racial policies. Thus, in contrast to the published sympathies of Dubuque's Michael Reu, Herman commented rhetorically: 'how much truth is there in this doctrine of race deterioration through any kind of social intercourse?'[23] Yet on this he appeared to be still wavering, for in 1937 he was still prepared to concede that race purification was perhaps 'a fine idea', even though he thought what the Nazis were attempting did not appear to fulfil this ambition.[24] Certainly he appeared to be enduring a most difficult time coming to a final judgement.

If in 1937 it was still possible to avoid taking a categorical stand against Jewish persecution, the events of 1938 were to challenge profoundly this 'open mindedness' vis-à-vis Hitler. As early as June 1938 Herman was reporting dramatically on outrages against Berlin Jews which clearly represented a run-up to Kristallnacht. But characteristic of his ambiguous view of the victims, he noted that at this point nastier treatment was visibly being meted out to the Jews in the poorer compared to the upscale districts of the city.[25]

One consequence of the intensified persecution was that unconverted 'non-aryans' were more indiscriminately appealing to him for baptism. Given his views on the subject as outlined above, he often declined such religiously unmotivated entreaties, pointing out to the supplicants 'the error in having waited so long'.[26] Moreover, hinting also at public pressures working against such baptisms while revealing nonetheless a good deal of personal anguish, he wrote home in some desperation: 'I feel very helpless and wonder whether a good diplomatic reputation is worth saving in the face of evident distress.'[27]

Herman's allusion to his 'diplomatic reputation' was not merely offhand, as from the very outset of his stay he had cultivated extensive and valuable contacts with 'official' Berlin and with the U.S. diplomatic community. By September 1939 he was to join the U.S. Embassy staff.[28] Such contacts placed a threefold burden on his work: firstly, a too-public identification with Hitler's victims could endanger his church with the regime; secondly, he needed to be circumspect on the 'Jewish question' due to his contacts to the Berlin officials of his own neutrality-minded government; thirdly, as already mentioned, he had to take into account the hostility of his American parishioners towards a 'non-aryan' presence within the church.

There was another significant constraint, perhaps fuelled by strong American neutralist sentiment: a lingering, widely held illusion that not Hitler but his paladins were behind the Jewish persecutions. For in his report on the mistreatment of Jews in Vienna in March 1938, Herman was still willing to believe that Hitler had played a 'moderating' role. Referring to the riff-raff who had allegedly exploited the Jewish plight in Vienna, he wrote: 'I admire the way the government has put its foot down and thrown many of the scavengers in jail.'[29] Thus, back in Berlin Herman could also attribute the pressures that then prompted the small flood of baptismal requests not to orders on high, but to the chicanery of Hitler's local satraps (admittedly hard to sustain in the epicentre of the Führer's regime!).

Perhaps in the light of such sentiments, Herman clearly continued to find it troublesome to divest himself of his lingering antipathies towards more privileged Jews. For example, in July 1938 he reported on a conversation he had recently had with two 'Jewish rabbis [sic.]' who, he wrote, 'were simply venomous with a hatred that the Nazis come nowhere near duplicating'. Claiming that he had tried to impose some moderation on his interlocutors, he continued that all rational arguments were impossible with these men 'in the face of a flow of statistics and propaganda and sheer prejudice equal to the renowned Stürmer'.[30] However, he did admit that 'Maybe I've been "corrupted" by propaganda', yet he went on: 'I can't stomach so much pure poison as these Jews were spouting.' Thus at this juncture he appeared to sense that his own antipathies – perhaps influenced by Nazi propaganda – had now exceeded the levels of stateside anti-semitism.[31]

A week later, Herman reported on a visit from a German pastor, who came to plead with him to influence Americans not to close their doors to German 'non-aryans'. Despite his sympathy with this collegial entreaty, Herman nonetheless felt it necessary to add that the German pastor had assured him that these victims were not however the 'infamous' international Jews.[32] To underscore the clear demarcation line he had established for himself between 'genuine' victims and their more privileged counterparts, he proceeded in this letter to cite pointedly an American newspaper which had just reported that a 'Jewish rabbi' had been arrested trying to smuggle narcotics into the United States.[33] Nevertheless, he continued to report home on examples of courageous acts by other foreign pastors in Germany and Austria, acts he freely admitted unable to emulate.[34]

Right up to the very day before Kristallnacht hints of the dramatic fate of the Berlin Jews continued to confront Herman and his congregation. He reported the visit to his church of a suicidal 'non-aryan' Christian with his 'aryan' wife. While commiserating with the man's desperate state of mind, Herman added: 'I doubt whether he has anything to fear.'[35] In the light of what had happened to Austrian Jews since the Anschluss in March 1938 and what he had witnessed in Germany since that summer, how could he have been so reassuring? The events of the following day were to trouble greatly anyone who had expressed such unwarranted optimism.

KRISTALLNACHT, NOVEMBER 1938

To use a metaphor from the Christian Bible, for Reverend Herman the Jewish pogrom of 9–10 November 1938 was to resemble, in the immediate term at least, a Pauline experience on the road to Damascus. As the details became known, all his previous reservations about the Jews, and his sometimes fulsome admiration for the Germans, seemed quickly to disappear in the light of the carnage he witnessed.[36] He also seems to have believed that Kristallnacht was an object lesson for his fellow Americans, so in his sermon on the Sunday after this terrible event he berated his parishioners and reduced them to tears in describing its consequences for them. He also sought out positive things for earnest reflection: the 'aryan' holding fast to a Jewish spouse, the sense of shame he witnessed among even ardent German patriots. He also excoriated German public indifference to the sight of the carnage, including its willingness to believe that Herschyl Grynzspan was the sole cause of this rampage. Herman also commented ironically about the subsequent huge fines imposed on the Jews by the Nazis, belittling the regime's attempts to label the Jews as the authors of their own destruction. He also reported that concentration camps were now being set up for the eventual incarceration of all of the 500,000 German Jews, rather than being 'limited', for the time being, to all the adult Jewish males the Nazis could apprehend. In this long report he stated that 'The least excusable act of all was the burning of the synagogues.' This last admission was all the more profound as Herman and other ardent Christians had been traditionally inclined to display at best grudging respect for either the Jewish religion or its physical symbols. He also assured his American family and friends that this scene of destruction was in no way being exaggerated by the American press. A month later he was even more categorical when, referring to Jews who might still endeavour to stay in Germany after Kristallnacht, he made perhaps the most prescient and ominously accurate statement of his whole Berlin stay: 'there is no doubt that the eventual fate of those who remain is . . . death.'[37]

Jews now began to flood into his parish. In his unpublished history of the church,[38] Herman relates how on the Sunday after Kristallnacht 'fully one third of the 200 people present were obviously German', also that 'many of these newcomes were "non-aryan" Christians who were effectively banned or no longer felt welcome in their own parish churches.' Once again the clergyman and his parishioners were painfully reminded of the dilemma created by the programme, for it would 'threaten our ability to serve' the 'non-aryan' and 'our American community'. The only solution Herman felt prepared to recommend to his congregation was to remain strictly neutral, neither refusing nor encouraging German attendance at American services, while at the same time accelerating all efforts to enlist the assistance of German pastors.

However, his instinctive dislike of the privileged Jews, who also were appearing at his doors in greater numbers, appears to have remain unaltered in these dramatic weeks. Variously describing these persons as 'snivelling' with 'fatty, flabby hands which haven't done a day of manual labour,' he even managed to liken their post-pogrom demeanour to a cornered mouse he had been once obliged to kill.[39] These old antipathies were also reinforced when he learned that some of them had attempted to bribe embassy officials for exit visas,[40] indeed commending the latter for not succumbing to such bribes.[41]

At the same time he was also witness to some curious examples of *mea culpa* among his parishioners. In December 1938 he related how Fred Kaltenbach,[42] later to become notorious as an American version of Lord Haw-Haw, came to his church shortly after Kristallnacht. Noting that, although Kaltenbach aspired to be a 150% Nazi, he had broken down in Herman's presence, telling him that in the light of the destruction his sense of shame had led him to absent himself from the church. For the clergyman this particular incident seemed to arouse hopes that, without any international interference, the Hitler regime was about to disillusion even its most ardent supporters.[43] An understandable and commendable hope, but yet another which subsequent events were to utterly destroy.

THE WAR YEARS 1939–42

As the ominous year 1939 began, Herman's references to the Jewish plight continued to grow. In January he reported home on the many recent applications for exit visas, while still unable to resist a dig at the 'soft' Jews who were apparently refusing to accept manual labour as a condition for a visa.[44] In the new year he also turned to other aspects of Nazi antisemitism, for which he reserved some of his richest and most bitter irony. Attending a meeting at the University of Berlin 'solemnly opened' by the notorious Jew-baiter, Julius Streicher, Herman ridiculed the university for launching a series of lectures intended to purge the Old Testament of all Jewish references. Perhaps the lecture was for Herman a mirror of a serious personal religious conflict, for it was at this time that he made perhaps his most damning comment about the illustrious founder of the Lutheran faith when he wrote bitterly that, on reflecting on Luther's antisemitism, even a Julius Streicher resembled 'a "mere babe" in vituperation and indictment.'[45] Herman was also becoming exercised about the Jewish pogroms, and was busy collecting material on them.

Yet his hopes, however faint, of some way out of this vicious circle of Nazi persecutions continued to linger, as he seems to have shared with many others the fading illusion of reaching a settlement with Hitler. Herman placed unfounded hopes on the success of an obscure Rublee Committee that was then convening in Berlin. Apparently an attempt to negotiate secretly with Hitler about solving the 'Jewish problem', public silence reigned over the details. Herman had learned from his numerous Berlin contacts that the meetings were somewhat protracted and he contrived to believe this was a positive sign and that the Committee might reach an amicable settlement.[46] At the end of January, however, this hope proved illusory and Herman reported home on Hitler's two-hour harangue commemorating the sixth anniversary of his seizure of power, in which the Führer predicted a 'Final Solution' for the Jews if they were to cause a new war. Herman added trenchantly that this 'ought to silence those who think he didn't approve of last November'.[47]

As a possible consequence of antisemitic policy since Kristallnacht, Herman seems to have decided in early 1939 to commit his American church to an official stand in respect of 'non-aryan' Christian supplicants and caused the following statement to be included in the church bulletin of 12 January:

> Anyone who has been baptised in any Christian church and still stands by that confession of faith is eligible for membership in the American Church. This involves no severance of church connections at home. We invite your allegiance and your support, both at the service and in our activities.[48]

This public statement confirmed unequivocally that all 'Jewish–Christians' would qualify to become members of Herman's church, and presumably would thus enjoy the protection of that church, of its pastor and also of the U.S. diplomatic apparatus in Berlin. The statement also boldly contravened the practice if not the official policy of the German Protestant churches at this time of finding ways to separate 'non-aryan' Christians from their fellow-believers, even urging them to form separate 'non-aryan' Christian congregations.[49] Unfortunately, as events were to prove, the American church did not manage to serve as a haven for these unfortunates,[50] and there is no evidence that before Herman's internment in December 1941 any significant numbers were able to take advantage of his humanitarian offer. We can only speculate from the scattered references in his letters home whether this stemmed from the often-mentioned opposition of his American parishioners to accepting these unfortunate people among their ranks, or to the pressures of the Nazi regime, or from pressures that may have been exerted on Herman by the U.S. diplomatic representatives in Berlin.

As an example of the congregational hostility, Herman reported in early 1939 on an interview with a professor's widow, Mrs. S., whose late husband had taught in both the United States and Germany: 'She wondered why the Germans in America didn't arise to wipe out Roosevelt, the Jews, and all non-Germans.'[51] Herman vehemently opposed such utterances, but they document the kinds of opinion among his parishioners his official declaration was intended to counter. Moreover, Herman's known animus toward privileged Jews may have prompted this woman to make such wild assertions.

A few weeks later he wrote home about another incident that deeply aroused his ire. A young American singer, Miriam Verne, had recently sung before Hitler. This led to a serious professional crisis for her as she was under contract to the famous Jewish–American orchestra leader, Billy Rose, to sing at the 1939 New York World's Fair. Rose threatened to annul her contract unless Miss Verne promised never to sing again in the Führer's presence. Incensed, Herman wrote to his family: 'Of course this was a stupid thing to say.' He went on to make the outlandish assertion: 'of the two gentlemen I prefer Mr. H[itler]...Rose is typical of the sort of rotten Jewry that we could well dispense with in America.'[52] Painful as such utterances sound today, no doubt in the late 1930s they were not unknown within and without clerical circles.[53] Yet one cannot pass this over in silence, as we know that in 1939 the pastor was in a much better position than his compatriots to comprehend the true nature of Hitler's antisemitic measures.

After war broke out in September the intensification of Nazi persecution was obvious to Herman and the American community in Berlin. Evidence of Hitler's wider plans for the Jews was now abundantly revealing itself. In early 1940 the pastor reported home that columns of Jews were being obliged to remove snow from the Berlin streets.[54] In May he described the desperate plight of Jews attempting to reach the United States via Italy, and mentioned the spread of antisemitic propaganda: 'I have just listened to a German broadcast in French inciting the French to stop dying for Jews, British plutocrats, and American aeroplane manufacturers.'[55]

Returning to his reports on the escalation of anti-Jewish measures within Germany itself he wrote in July 1940: 'The Jews have had the screws turned on them again; they are allowed to shop between the hours of 4–5 p.m. only. In these days when housewives usually have to stand half an hour or 45 minutes for a few vegetables or a bit of fruit, one can well imagine how much the Jews will get to eat.' In this letter Herman also referred to the decision of the U.S. government to curtail Jewish emigration: as a consequence, 'many nonaryans who were due to leave have nearly gone crazy.'[56] Once again, in the light of this atmosphere of human desperation, it is patently clear that the pastor and others based in the German capital could have had no reason to delay seeking immediate help for the Jews, for whose tragic plight Herman blamed the Washington government.

In August 1940 he reported home the rumours circulating about the Nazi policy of euthanasia. He mentioned a possible 750,000 that had been 'put to death'[57] – a good twelve months before the Roman Catholic Bishop Count Galen spoke out publicly about these executions.[58] While in 1940 it was not publicly known that murder was to be systematically imposed upon the Jews, previous references to their terrible fate under Hitler must have led Herman and others to the conclusion that this might well be the Jews' fate too.

Another dramatic topic alluded to at this time was the establishment of the eastern ghettos.[59] Referring to Warsaw, he indicated that after the September 1939 bombings its reconstruction had been desultory, but 'The one piece of construction for which time was found is the wall of brick and mortar seven feet high surrounding approximately 200 streets which constitute the ghetto. Eighteen German police can now close off this section at a moment's notice.' Nevertheless, he continued to add disparaging comments, noting that as the ghetto inhabitants had to present themselves for delousing, some Jews were managing to sell delousing certificates for profit. It was also in this period that Herman reported on the first example of the mass deportation of German Jews, in this instance from southwest Germany to a ghetto at Gurs in Vichy France.[60] Herman's revelations about euthanasia and the ghettos once again document the amount of information then more or less in the 'public domain', which puts paid to the myth that no one knew what was transpiring.

As persecution escalated, Herman had to contend with very difficult situations within his parish. For example, he reported in late 1940 the plans of a Jew to marry a girl from the Embassy:

> Our church has been responsible to a certain extent for a romance with which I am not so pleased. I told you of the two Americans who, in trying to escape from Belgium at the time of the invasion, were subsequently overtaken by the Germans in Boulogne and brought to Berlin. One of them was Jewish. We took him in of course and lent our aid. He proceeded to fall in love with a sweet girl...and they decided to get married. By calling himself a 'Catholic' he got permission from the German authorities to marry and yesterday they asked me to be a witness![61]

Herman explained that he had tried to persuade the couple to wait, but to no avail. This incident also shows that as late as 1940 Jews still clung to the hopeless illusion that conversion would save them from persecution. Somewhat puzzling in this case is the fact that, as an American citizen, this young man was apparently still able to evade one of Hitler's most stringent laws (against racial intermarriage), yet at the same time he had not been allowed to repatriate, though the United States was not then at war with Germany. The tone of regret in Herman's report on this romance is also evidence of the constant conflict he must have felt between his own sense of Christian brotherliness and the priorities of a diligently neutral America.

By 1941 the unfolding drama was constantly impressed upon the American pastor in Berlin. In February Herman reported home on another 'non-aryan' who was planning suicide as his family was either abroad or dead. The clergyman noted that his story 'was the most moving thing I have ever heard'. After receiving money for the church from this desperate man, Herman added pithily: 'And many people in our colony wonder why I don't turn out of [the] Church the few non-aryans who come to service....'[62]

Perhaps Herman was now trying to educate his parishioners, and in the same month gave a sermon in which he took as his theme 'Conversion'. Avoiding specifically naming the Jews, he rather spoke approvingly of conversions of heathens in Africa and Asia, of Protestants to Catholicism and *vice versa*.[63] Obviously he was obliged to be circumspect in the light of congregational sensitivities, the likely presence of Nazi spies among his hearers, and the tense diplomatic situation between Washington and Berlin in 1941. However, between the lines his intent was fairly obvious.

Another example of the Jewish plight in 1941 comes from a letter he received from a young woman who, while never explicitly mentioning her 'non-aryan' status, found herself in dire straits. In her desperation she raised the idea of marrying Herman, still an eligible bachelor.[64] Couched otherwise in a very indirect language, moreover in an tone of apparent forced lightheartedness, her letter included the phrase: 'Would it be very unpleasant for you if I came to church next Sunday once again, for the last time? Please, I want to so very much! Today I sought out Pastor Schultz, but he was not home. He has otherwise, of course, little time.'[65] From this we can easily deduce that her German pastor was avoiding the young woman, and she needed to implore Herman to permit her to enter his church, although she had obviously been converted at some earlier point. In the German original of her letter her youthfulness comes out clearly, both in her suggestion about marriage as well as in the rather obsequious, even child-like tone. The letter also reflects a very young person's attempt to make light of her desperate situation in full knowledge of the sombre consequences of her plight. It is also likely that this letter represented a final desperate plea to avoid deportation to the East, which became increasingly frequent after the summer of 1941.

As the last weeks of American neutrality drew to a close Herman (and everyone else in Berlin) had more evidence of the dramatic escalations of Hitler's persecutions when, in late September, Herman reported 'the appearance of the "yellow badge" on every non-aryan breast'. He added that 'there has been a flood of anguished inquiries from British Jews', for up to this juncture foreign Jews had believed 'their foreign status protected them from the anti-semitic laws'.[66] In fact, by now they only differed from their German counterparts in their exemption from wearing the yellow star.[67] In his capacity as pastor of an interdenominational church, and moreover as an embassy official since September 1939, Herman had been charged with looking after the interests of enemy citizens still in the Reich, so this situation was also tangential to his official position.

This measure also had the effect of noticeably reducing the number of 'non-aryan' Christians in his congregation, which, to his personal regret, was met with approval by those of his parishioners who had always disliked the 'non-aryans' in their midst. With a heavy heart Herman therefore left to these unfortunate people 'the final decision' whether they still wished to attend his church. He added that these people 'invariably showed their understanding of our delicate position', adding sombrely that 'they have withdrawn...to their homes which, also, are consistently being commandeered.'[68] The American church, like its German counterparts, was no longer to be a refuge for Nazi victims; as before, there was clear and gloomy realization of the consequences.

This realization obviously continued to cause serious personal conflicts for the American churchman, for a few days later Herman discovered himself actually becoming progressively angry, even impatient, with the reappearance of 'non-aryan' Christians at his church doors. Rather petulantly he wrote home: 'I can do nothing for them,' adding that 'It is hard to have to listen helplessly to their whining, moaning, hand-wringing despair.' On reflection, however, he admitted that this was 'probably unnecessarily gruff and ungracious'.[69] He likened his inaction to the feeling a surgeon would have if he were obliged for some reason to stand by helplessly at an operation. By October 1941 Herman's options were almost exhausted, and the combined pressures of his diplomatic post, his parishioners' antagonisms against the victims, and his constant exposure to their hopeless situation, had led him to mingle anger with sorrow and deep pity.

The situation of the Berlin Jews now was entering its fatal phase, and in his next letter home Herman mentioned the Jewish roundup of 16 October 1941: that they were taken off 'one cold morning into a disastrous future in which death is the single pleasant prospect.' Herman related that he was personally involved in a last-minute but alas unsuccessful effort to secure the evacuation to England of some 200 orphaned 'non-aryan' children.[70] However, having revealed the terrible fate of the Jews and of his own brave efforts, in the very next sentence of this letter he abruptly concluded somewhat crassly, 'these troubles... need not concern me'.[71]

But the Jews could not be put out of his mind so easily, for in mid-November Herman reported on the heroic efforts of a German clergyman, a Reverend Kurtz, who was 'fighting for the Christian non-aryan' and had even managed to turn a closed school 'into a home for evicted old folk'. In the very same paragraph Herman also reported on an elderly couple who had escaped the recent Berlin roundups and had come to his church for help.[72]

Finally, on 6 December 1941, in his last Berlin letter, and on the eve of his own incarceration as a part of the U.S. diplomatic community, Herman had to field the bitter observation of a 'half-Jew' that the Jews of Berlin considered him an antisemite 'because I brace myself to refuse their impossible pleas for help'. Characteristically, Herman ended this letter too on a rather jarring note by writing angrily: 'Unfortunately, when Jews are in trouble, they think they are the only ones in trouble.'[73] Whether 'trouble' is the appropriate description of what he was witnessing in December 1941 the reader may judge. In the light of his own admission immediately before this final letter, a more ominous description would have seemed to have been in order.

AFTER REPATRIATION, 1942–45

After his repatriation to the United States in May 1942, Herman must have been bitterly disappointed to encounter unsettling opinions on the Jewish tragedy in his congregation, for in the scattered references to this topic he ceased to make categorical references to the Jews. Since only a few of his letters from the period after his repatriation are on file, some of the sermons he gave in the United States have been analysed to indicate the need he apparently continued to feel to exercise public caution on the subject.

Thus, less than a week after arriving in the United States Herman gave a sermon in his father's Harrisburg church in which he mentioned the crimes of the war, without direct reference to the Jews, and spoke laconically of 'the helpless victims of racial hatred who are dying of cold and disease in the sub-cellars of Polish ghettos'.[74] In another sermon, which he gave on at least two occasions (in summer 1942 and in 1943), Herman again began by obliquely mentioning the sad plight of 'Polish' refugees to Israel, of the murder of family members by the Germans etc., but once more he avoided stating that these refugees were Jews.[75]

Indeed, when he did manage to make a rare direct reference to the Jews, this had a somewhat dismissive air about it. Thus, in a July 1943 sermon Herman did refer briefly to the Jews by making somewhat disparaging comments about their early forebears. Referring to the period when Greek culture was in decline and Rome was ripe for a new revelation, Herman said that 'the Jewish religion was given the opportunity to present its God of universal justice and righteousness to the world', but failed and 'degenerated into a quibbling priesthood of ecclesiastical lawyers'.[76] This demonstrates that a persistent and pernicious Jewish–Christian rivalry was apparently still popular in the churches Herman visited after his return home.

Finally, in a June 1945 sermon,[77] Herman reached a certain peak in the process of glossing over the real consequences of World War II for all of Hitler's victims, not only the Jews. Adapting a sermon he had given in Berlin in September 1939, Herman offered in 1945 the vista of a world which had now survived the experience of the Hitler era and in which he believed the gloomiest prophesies of 1939 had not come true. To do this he also managed to manipulate some by summer 1945 well-known facts. For example, he alleged that 'although tens of thousands of people have died under the weight of collapsing cities, only a minor fraction of them – except in Russia – have been citizens of the United Nations.' To make this claim was to ignore the appalling extent of the slaughter: the 20 million Russians, the six million Jewish victims, the several million Poles, Yugoslavs, and the thousands of Greeks who were martyred by Hitler's onslaught. Nor can one comprehend his exclusion of victims in states not then part of the U.N. Here too it is indeed significant that the pastor did not again explicitly name the Jews in his recounting of these grisly statistics.

When on this occasion he finally spoke of the Jewish survivors, he said: 'I can't think of one threat of Hitler's that was finally fulfilled; there are even 150,000 Jews left alive in Germany itself, a small remnant, but a remnant.' He even alleged that the survivors of slave labour, which must surely have included Jews, 'even prefer to stay on German farms until they know a bit more about the uncertain future.' Here it is not the facts themselves that are in dispute but the way they are presented. Either willingly or in response to his congregation's mood, it sounds as if Herman were inviting his audience to don rose-coloured glasses. Finally, in this sermon Herman also touched upon a theme that was to be evoked so profoundly by Elie Wiesel: where was God amidst the carnage? Clearly unwilling to reject divine intervention, in June 1945 the pastor believed he saw the Creator's hand in preserving at least the essence of European culture and its peoples, even if severely diminished in numbers. His faith in God is admirable, but then and since he and many other Christians have failed to face this terrible question which the Jewish survivor of Auschwitz was forced to pose.

POSTSCRIPT AND CONCLUSIONS

Herman's postwar career has not been given close treatment here as it has received important scholarly attention.[78] Briefly, after spending some time in Geneva in the early postwar years, Herman occupied a number of important posts with the U.S. government, the World Council of Churches and with the Lutheran World Federation. Here he laboured tirelessly and effectively, especially to bring the German churches out of the isolation into which Germany's war guilt had plunged them. In these years he won many friends among the German churchmen, and became a major figure in international Lutheran church circles. The published evidence of some of this work does not reveal, however, that his pre-1945 experiences and his attempts to ameliorate the bitter fate of the Jews was a central focus of his productive postwar career. Of his three published (and one unpublished) writings, two of which appeared after 1945, only his book *It's Your Souls We Want* (1943) expresses the outrage he felt at Hitler's crimes against the Jews.

In conclusion, during his German years, Stewart Herman clearly did not manage to divorce himself entirely from certain anti-Jewish sentiments. Ironically, these sentiments were actually fortified by the fact that he found himself in a terrible dilemma: while his Berlin church had had over the years of his stewardship a constant presence of 'non-aryan Christians' in its midst, Herman's diplomatic contacts and formal embassy status (from September 1939), his perceived need to mollify the less than philosemitic sentiments among his American parishioners, and his own uneven sense of empathy for some of the victims, managed to severely limit his sometimes vigorous efforts on behalf of many of his Jewish contacts. Yet his papers certainly testify to deep self-examination on the subject, as the example of his 1939 'heretical' and unequivocal condemnation of Martin Luther's antisemitism indicates. Perhaps, during the months of internment in

Bad Nauheim, it was given to him and to many others to ruminate further on and to resolve this most persistent of western civilization's dilemmas: an antisemitism often unreflected and thus unresolved.[79]

NOTES

1 On the NLC see Frederick K. Wentz, *Lutherans in Concert: The Story of the National Lutheran Council, 1918–1966*. (Minneapolis: Augsburg Publishing House, 1968).

2 NLC [National Lutheran Council Archives, Chicago], 2/1 Box 9, 'Larsen General'. Larsen's predecessor, H.J. Stub, to Larsen, 23.1.1921, Larsen to Stub, 28 January1921.

3 See J. H. Schjorring, P. Kumari and N. Hjelm (eds.), *From Federation to Communion. The History of the Lutheran World Federation* (Minneapolis: Fortress Press, 1997).

4 Lars Boe Papers, St. Olaf College, Northfield, Minn, Box 110, 23 December 1933. Boe sent Dr. Ylvisaker a 14-page report of his recent German trip.

5 Boe Papers, Box 97, Boe to Meiser, 13.12.1934.

6 Reu, 'Wer sind die "deutschen Christen"?' *Kirchliche Zeitschrift* [KZ], October and December 1933, pp.593–4.

7 Reu, 'The Place of the Lutheran Church in the Third Reich', *KZ*, vol.58 (May 1934), p.275. It must also be stressed that Reu made these blatant utterances in a public forum, while Dr. Boe and other Lutheran leaders mostly confined their views to their private correspondence.

8 NLC 2/3/1, Box 2, 'General W – Z 1933', Long addresses a Lutheran 'Long Island Conference' of 27 September 1933.

9 *ibid.*, Box 3, 'General S 1934' 8 5.1934, Long to Rev. Simen, Pittsburgh.

10 See Deborah Lipstadt, *Beyond Belief* (Detroit: Free Press, 1986), p.127.

11 The value of Herman's letters home is heightened by the fact that he could largely avoid the German censors even after September 1939 since right up to the very moment of his internment in December 1941, he was able to use the U.S. diplomatic pouches. Herman's book-length publications are *It's Your Souls We Want* (New York: Harper and Brothers, 1943), *Rebirth of the German Church* (New York: Harper and Brothers, 1946) and *Report from Christian Europe* (New York: Friendship Press, 1953.

12 Stewart Herman Papers [hereinafter 'Herman Papers'], A.R. Wentz Library, Gettysburg Lutheran Seminary, Gettysburg Pennsylvania, Box 17, 23 September 1935.

13 *ibid.*, Box 17, 30 October 1935.

14 An interdenominational church, it had been established in the 1870s with American funds.

15 Herman uses his privately published 'American Church in Berlin' to recount these days. See p.65, where he briefly alludes to Jews who sought help. In a letter he also mentioned being able to help a German Jewess to find lodging in Berlin with a U.S. family, while unable to do so for a woman seeking a visa for a Jewish youth. Herman Papers, Box 17, 3 March 1936.

16 Herman Papers, Box 17, 30 March 1936. The Nazi regime, in the 1936 Olympic year, was then solicitous of its own image, and Hitler instructed his then foreign press attaché and acquaintance of Herman's, Ernst [Putzi] Hanfstangl, to apologise formally to Herman. Louis Lochner, the UPI head in Berlin, reported the incident which prompted the Nazis to try to smooth over the matter, including an unsuccessful attempt to find the perpetrator.

17 *ibid.*, Box 17, 3.March 1936. His contact was Mr. Valler of Paramount films.

18 *ibid.*, Box 17, 10 February 1936.

19 In a recent interview, Dr. Herman came back to this considerable reluctance of his parishioners to embrace Hitler's Jewish victims. Interview S. Herman, Shelter Island, New York, 7. March 1999.

20 Herman Papers, Box 18, 21 June 38. Known for their ideological affiliations with National Socialism. Respecting Jewish baptisms, it was not unknown for individual German Christians ['Deutsche Christen' = D.C s'] to condone them if, as in this case, they could avoid performing the ceremony themselves.

21 *ibid.*, Box 17, 24 September 1936.

22 *ibid.*, Box 17, 24 September 1936.

23 *ibid.*, 24 September 1936

24 *ibid.*, Box 17, 11 November 1937.
25 For example, while showing modest sympathy for the victims, he also expressed how surprised he was to see that many Jews were still in business in Berlin. He even slightly minimized their plight by claiming that their tormenters had 'decently done' antisemitic scribblings on Jewish store windows in the better districts. *ibid.*, Box 18, 21 June 1938.
26 *ibid.*, Box 18, 21 June 1938.
27 *ibid.*, Box 18, 28 June 1938.
28 *ibid.*, Box 18, 11 September 1939; announces his employment at the U.S. Embassy.
29 *ibid.*, Box 17, 28. June 1938.
30 An allusion to Julius Streicher's virulent antisemitic organ.
31 Herman Papers, Box 18, 19 July 1938.
32 *ibid.*, Box 18, 26 July 1938. The pastor is not named.
33 *ibid.*, Box 18, 19 July 1938.
34 For example, Herman relates how 'Old Dr. Bruce of Dresden [church] has been forced to retire because he took it upon himself to break up picketers in front of Jewish stores. The man in Vienna got in very hot water because he baptised too many Jews without discrimination....' *ibid.*, Box 18, 3 November 1938.
35 *ibid.*, Box 18, 8 December 1938.
36 *ibid.*, Box 18, 14 November 1938.
37 *ibid.*, Box 18, 8 December 1938.
38 S. Herman, 'The American Church in Berlin', privately published, 1978, pp.72–3.
39 Herman Papers, Box 18, 25 November 1938 1938.
40 *ibid.*, Box 18, 8 December 1938.
41 *ibid.*, Box 18, 9 November 1938.
42 *ibid.*, Box 18, 20 December 1938. In the last volume of his memoirs *A Native's Return*, 1945–88 (Boston: Little Brown & Co., 1990), pp.39–40, William Shirer writes of Kaltenbach that '(h)e was a fanatical convert to Nazism', who was moreover to die a prisoner of the Russians. While also moving in the same Berlin circles as Herman, Shirer probably was not aware that Kaltenbach had appeared in Herman's church in December 1938, or that at this time he had shown any remorse for Kristallnacht.
43 Reiterated by Dr. Herman to the author in a letter of 25 April 1999.
44 Herman Papers, Box 18, 18 January 1939. Herman reported here that some 70,000 applications for exit visas had piled up in the Berlin embassy, some 50,000 in Stuttgart and no less than 150,000 in Vienna.
45 *ibid.*, Box 18, 18 January 1939.
46 *ibid.*, He noted that neither the German public nor the press corps in Berlin was privy to the meeting's agenda.
47 *ibid.*, Box, 18, 30 January 1939.
48 *ibid.*, Contains the programme for the service of 12 January 1939.
49 See R Gutteridge, *Open Thy Mouth for the Dumb! The German Evangelical Church and the Jews 1879–1950* (Oxford: Blackwell, 1976), and R. Ericksen, *Theologians Under Hitler* (New Haven: Yale University Press, 1985).
50 See below for reference to one such unfortunate and apparently very young 'nonaryan' supplicant.
51 Herman Papers, Box 18, 22 January 1939.
52 *ibid.*, Box 18, 15 March 1939. In Dr. Herman's Papers someone attempted to ink out the last sentence of this letter although it was exceedingly easy to decipher the original text. The word 'rotten' was also underlined in pencil.
53 An example of a published stateside antisemitic diatribe comes again from Professor Michael Reu. As late as the autumn of 1940 Reu allowed himself the following 'reflection' on the pro-British stand of the Roosevelt government: 'World Jewry stood behind the war mongering under whose iron grip our government allowed itself to be made entirely captive', *Kirchliche Zeitschrift*, October 1940, p.636.
54 Herman Papers, Box 18, 14 February 1940.
55 *ibid.*, Box 18, 25 May 1940.

56 *ibid.*, Box 18, 12 July 1940. On 15 August he also reported that, as of 1 September 1940, the Jews 'will have all telephones taken away'.

57 *ibid.*, Box 18, 17 August 1940.

58 *ibid.*, Box 18, 15 August 1940. Count Galen made his famous public protest on 3 August 1941. He too did not allude to the Jews.

59 *ibid.*, Box 18, 16 October 1940.

60 *ibid.*, Box 18, 30 October 1940: Here he wrote with considerable irony of '(t)he latest manoeuvre in the "Voelkerwanderung"; the expulsion of some 7000 Jews from Wurettemberg, Baden and the Pfalz'. Like so many observers, both within and without Germany, he incorrectly speculated that they were en route to Madagascar.

61 *ibid.*, Box 18; written between 22–25 October 1940.

62 *ibid.*, Box 18, 21 February 1941.

63 *ibid.*, Box 8, Sermons 1941; sermon of 16 February 1941 'Conversion is a Word'.

64 In the course of his Berlin years Herman reported on a number of relationships, among them, Nancy Bird, a much-fêted Australian aviatrix. [See Herman Papers, Box 18, Nancy Bird to Herman, 9 January and 18 December 1938]. He also severally reported home having had to fend off marriage proposals from members of his Berlin parish.

65 Herman Papers, Box 18. Letter of 25 June 41, from a Miss Brigitte Meyer.

66 *ibid.*, Box 18, 22 September 1941.

67 *ibid.*, Box 18, 22 October 1941.

68 *ibid.*, Box 18, 6 October 1941.

69 *ibid.*, Box 18, 20 October 1941.

70 *ibid.*, Box 18, 24 October 1941. He wrote 'I have undertaken to sponsor a project for rescuing Christian children but there is little hope, I fear, of success.' On this, see also Herman's *It's Your Souls We Want*, p.234.

71 *ibid.*, Box 18, 24. October 1941. In his *The Holocaust. The Jewish Tragedy* (London: Collins, 1986), p.213, Martin Gilbert mentions the Berlin and other roundups at this time.

72 Herman Papers, Box 18, 17 November 1941. He told his parents nothing about what he did or did not do for these desperate people.

73 *ibid.*, Box 18, 6 December 1941.

74 *ibid.*, Box 8, Sermons, 7 June 1942.

75 *ibid.*, Box 8, Harrisburg Sermons of 16 August, 6 September 1942 and 4 July 1943.

76 *ibid.*, Box 8, 4. July 1943.

77 *ibid.*, Box 8, 19 June 1945

78 An exhaustive documentary treatment of Herman's role in immediate postwar German affairs is provided by Clemens Vollnhals (ed.), *Die Evangelische Kirche nach dem Zusammenbruch. Berichte ausländlischer Beobachter aus dem Jahre 1945* (Gottingen: Vandenhoeck & Ruprecht, 1988).

79 In our March 1999 interview, due to his advanced age (Dr. Herman turned ninety in August 1999), the author did not feel comfortable with raising such extremely unsettling issues with him.

POST-HOLOCAUST THEOLOGY

Disastrously, the Holocaust showed that Christians and Jews could inhabit the same cities and countries and yet be so divided from one another that the attempt to destroy European Jewry nearly succeeded in a culture steeped in Christian tradition. After Auschwitz, however, Jewish-Christian dialogue has intensified and deepened. Where is this dialogue headed? What pitfalls and promises has it contained and discovered?

Post-Holocaust theology unavoidably leads to the issues that the authors in this section lift up for consideration. How have the Holocaust and genocide affected religious faith? How should their devastating histories influence what people think about God, how Scripture should be interpreted, and what it might mean to be a Christian or a Jew in the 21st century? These questions are not completely new. For some time, history has forced versions of them upon us. But the responses to such fundamental questions are still very much in the making. In distinctive ways, the authors who come next use and refashion their own traditions to make constructive contributions to the ongoing development of post-Holocaust theology and Jewish-Christian dialogue.

THEOLOGY, PAST PRESENT AND FUTURE

Edward Kessler

Plenary Address, Oxford, 20 July 2000

A T THE opening of the theology plenary I mentioned that I represented a younger generation of scholars and felt humble in the presence of such a distinguished and eminent panel consisting of John Pawlikowski, Richard Rubenstein and Alice Eckardt. This afternoon, I am delighted to say I have the pleasure of introducing two younger and extremely significant thinkers. Their writings have already begun to make an impact on students and scholars alike and I am certain that their influence will continue to grow in the future.

And this, of course, is the point. We are after all considering Remembering for the Future.

What are the lessons to be drawn from the Holocaust for the future? – this has been the subject of our discussions in theology and ethics. The lessons in terms of human responsibility, in terms of theology – theologies of protest, of resistance, of the victim and the perpetrator, the lessons in terms of the legacy of Christian anti-Judaism and antisemitism and the lessons in terms of theological education and the theological curriculum.

Our seminar was particularly concerned with the lesson of the Holocaust for today and tomorrow not only for Jews, but also for humanity in general.

This conference has shown that while the Holocaust has special unique and profound meaning for Jews it is not only for significant to Jews. Indeed, Jews should not fall into the trap of believing that the Holocaust is a Jewish monopoly. Jews were of course the victims of the Holocaust but we can never let it be forgotten that the Holocaust was a tremendous tragedy for humanity as a whole.

Apart from the fact that five million non-Jews perished in the Holocaust it was a tragedy for humanity because it was a negation of all that has a right to be called human. It is therefore appropriate that there are so many non-Jewish scholars here. Indeed, it gives us grounds for optimism to acknowledge we have participated in a broad-based conference. But let me give you a warning, there are still too many scholars and thinkers (some of whom are controversial) who are not here but who need to be here; whose voices are not heard but whose voices need to be heard.

Apart from the fact that the Holocaust must remain in our memory because it undermined the moral underpinnings of what it meant to be human, we also agreed that it would be a mistake, especially a political mistake, if it were seen solely as a Jewish tragedy. If it is treated as such it will be dismissed over time as an historical event of interest only to Jews and of no consequence to the rest of humanity. This mistaken perception must be answered.

There is also another danger – that by focusing solely on the victim, Jews and Christians will gain a distorted view. For example, a young Jew will construct a negative Jewish identity, which without the positive side of Judaism, will not be a value to be handed down over the generations. A young Christian will come away with an exclusive picture of the Jew as victim without an awareness of the positive aspects of Jewish culture. If the Jew disappears from the horizons from the end of the biblical period and only reappears again in 1933, what are we remembering for the future?

I also noted a concern at the use (for some, abuse) of the Holocaust when Holocaust language is incorporated in the mass media and in popular culture. I hear complaints when we read about or hear mass murder, ethnic cleansing and genocide described in terms of the Holocaust. We should resist the temptation of claiming that the suffering of genocide victims cannot be compared to the suffering of the Holocaust victims because of its special character.

This means that the Holocaust has now become the paradigm and the model for the study of genocide in the 20th century. This means that the Holocaust has become the subject of general study, an inter-disciplinary study. Is this not simply the outcome of what Elie Wiesel asked for the other day – you cannot understand the Holocaust, you will not understand the Holocaust – but you must try to understand it. The general teaching of the Holocaust, whilst inadequate, has resulted in this phenomenon.

Our discussions have also made clear that it is incumbent upon us *all* not to be indifferent to the suffering not only of the victims of the Holocaust but also to contemporary suffering. Indifference, played a key role in the Holocaust and it is the indifference, in our churches and synagogues, as well in society in general which must be combatted. We must speak out whenever there are signs of genocide and suffering. This is our duty and is one of the lessons of the Holocaust and a lesson for the future.

One of my own concerns has been the issue of dialogue after the Holocaust. How does contemporary interfaith dialogue differ from the interfaith disputations of earlier times? How does it differ from the bargaining of the market in which the aim is to find a mutually acceptable compromise? In fact it is neither.

First, the word 'dialogue' and dialogue activity have been both misconstrued and ill-defined. A casual conversation between Jews and Christians that may add up to no more than a loose restatement of entrenched theological positions is sometimes claimed as dialogue. Any communication between persons of two differing religious points of view that does not involve a genuine hearing of the other is all too easily claimed as dialogue. Today, one can communicate with others either by phone, fax or e-mail but dialogue requires more effort, and most of all, a face to face contact. Dialogue is not simply a method of communication.

Second, is the sloppy way in which the word is used as almost an umbrella term to cover a whole host of related word activities that are good in themselves, some of them even providing an essential framework for dialogue, but are not the equivalent to dialogue. For example, some adopt the term Jewish-Christian relations as synonymous with dialogue. You can after all have good or bad relations (as often the case with relatives) but relations in themselves are not the equivalent of dialogue; nor is the comparative study of religions, which is also taken by some as a synonym for dialogue. Of course, dialogue does involve the serious study of the religion of others, but understanding is required before dialogue can take place.

In reality, dialogue involves a respect that takes the other as seriously as one demands to be taken oneself. This is an immensely difficult and costly exercise. We find it all too easy to relate to others in a casual way with a lack of concentration on the reality and good of the Other. However difficult this is, it illustrates the foundational principle of Jewish–Christian dialogue today: Judaism and Christianity must be understood on their own terms.

Dialogue consists of a direct meeting of two people and involves a reciprocal exposing of the full religious consciousness of the one with the 'Other'. Dialogue speaks to the Other with a full respect of what the Other is and has to say. This is never less than personal but can develop in such a way as to be extended to a group and even to communities. However, it begins with the individual and not with the community. This is not an original definition for the biblical prophets were experts in this full personal communication and encounter. Isaiah in a famous passage powerfully commends Israel to enter into a personal relationship with God stating, 'come now let us reason together' (Isaiah 1:18).

Our two speakers will fulfil this task. They will engage in a dialogue – to be honest, I have no idea what they are going to say but I know that you will be stimulated and I for one am looking forward to hearing to what they have to say. According to rabbinic tradition we are commended as follows, *aseh l'cha chaver*. 'Find yourself a partner (friend)'. I think both Katherina von Kellenbach and David Blumenthal will show us what the rabbis may have had in mind and I welcome you both.

FUTURE DIRECTIONS FOR CHRISTIAN THEOLOGY AND ETHICS AFTER THE HOLOCAUST

Katharina von Kellenbach

Plenary Address, Oxford, 20 July 2000

A S THE next generation of Jewish and Christian thinkers is taking on the legacy of the Holocaust, there is good reason to rejoice in the increased dialogue between Jews and Christians and the diversity of methodologies that characterize religious wrestling with the Holocaust. Christian theologians have much to learn from Jewish thinkers such as David Blumenthal, Richard Rubenstein, Emil Fackenheim and Elie Wiesel in their quest to formulate religious responses to the Shoah. There is some hope that the Holocaust will serve to increase Christian consciousness of Judaism as a separate, vital religious tradition and that the study of Christian anti-Judaism may play a greater role in Christian education. Such greater openness on the part of Christian theologians to listen to Jewish voices and to take the experience of the Jewish victims of Christian and racist persecution seriously was long overdue and constitutes a necessary first step. But there is also a certain temptation among Christian theologians to integrate the Jewish struggle with the Holocaust too easily into an essentially Christian framework. Such an embrace of the Jewish victim perspective would erase the peculiar perspective of the Christian tradition *vis à vis* the Holocaust. Christian theologians must be vigilant against any attempt to expropriate the theological perspective of the Jewish victims.

I want to draw attention to three areas of concern peculiar to the Christian struggle with the Holocaust. These three areas of concern are: the dangers of narratives of meaning that codify the complexity of history; Christian responsibility for and towards the perpetrators; and the increasing depoliticization of the Holocaust.

THE CODIFICATION OF MEANING AND THE COMPLEXITY OF HISTORY

One challenge confronting religionists is the temptation to describe the Holocaust as one coherent event whose meaning can be grasped and categorised, analysed and absorbed theologically (i.e. theology after Auschwitz, as if Auschwitz could stand symbolically for the entire experience of the Holocaust). The quest for meaning that is properly the domain of religious language abstracts from historical complexities and turns historical reality into narratives of value and significance. While historians insist on biographical detail and differentiated political analysis, religionists abstract from the thickness of human experience. This movement from historical thickness into spiritual simplicity is always in danger of falsifying the experience. As the Holocaust moves into cultural and religious memory, the temptation to simplify and codify grows. The danger to smooth the totality of this historical disaster into one coherent event or to create one consistent tale that can be absorbed into cultural memory is fraught with difficulties. Religious master narratives that 'explain' the Holocaust along the lines of the primordial struggle between good and evil, of destruction and redemption, of death and resurrection, or of (the state of) Israel reborn would be intrinsically wrong because they gloss over the totality of destruction. Equally problematic are theological explanations that focus exclusively on God's abandonment and silence as the final message of the Holocaust, thereby erasing the experience of pious victims and survivors.

The Holocaust should make us suspicious of any and all explanations and ideologies that conceal the Face of the individual Other. Any master narrative, including religious explanations that exclude, overlook and ignore the face of the littlest among us must be suspect. The study of the Holocaust must not lead into abstraction but into concreteness, the thickness of human suffering and human evil. It will be crucial that the religious approach to the Holocaust remains closely tied to historical research and that the spiritual lessons drawn from the Holocaust do not detach from the hundreds of thousands of experiences that make up this phenomenon called the Holocaust.

CHRISTIAN RESPONSIBILITY FOR AND TOWARDS THE PERPETRATORS

Most perpetrators of the Nazi genocide were Christian before they engaged in mass murder, some remained active Christians during the killings, and many perpetrators rejoined the churches after the war. Christian 'Theology after Auschwitz' has begun to rethink Christian doctrine in solidarity with the Jewish victims, but has not considered the theological and ethical challenges arising from the experiences of the perpetrators. What are the churches' responsibilities towards the perpetrators? This question is especially relevant because Christian communities are faced with similar situations in other parts of the world. What is the appropriate ethical response to ordinary policemen who engage in mass executions, who participate in torture, who commit atrocities against ethnic minorities or political opponents on massive scales in so many different states around the world?

The Christian knee-jerk reaction to perpetrators of political mass violence is to talk about 'forgiveness'. In Germany, immediately after the war, both Protestant and Roman Catholic churches used their moral capital to mobilise nationally and internationally on behalf of forgiveness for the perpetrators. Their campaign for amnesty and mercy was partly motivated by political sympathies and entanglement with the elites of the Nazi State, but partly fuelled by the conviction that 'forgiveness' is the central message of the Gospel. One could cite the Secret Memorandum of the Evangelical Church in 1949 signed by none other than Martin Niemoeller calling on the US Military Government to repeal the verdicts of the Nuremberg Trials or the Pope's appeal on behalf of the prisoners in Landsberg. The Clemency Board of the US Military government received thousands of letters from laity and clergy, who used Christian arguments in their denunciation of Allied punishment for the perpetrators.

These voices endorsed a theology of 'forgive and forget' based on faith in Christ's vicarious sacrifice on behalf of all sinners. Since Christ's blood takes away the sin of the world, the salvific power of his sacrifice must include the Nazi perpetrators who therefore deserved mercy and another chance in life. Oftentimes, anti-Judaism and Christian supersessionism buttressed this theological reasoning. The Christian God of the New Testament was seen as a God of Love and Mercy who transcended the primitive Jewish God of Revenge and Wrath supposedly characteristic of the Old Testament. Christian attitudes of mercy and forgiveness were presented as superior to 'Jewish' calls for justice and judicial prosecution of perpetrators. The Jewish survivors' refusal to forgive was seen as a hateful attitude rooted in revenge rather than a form of necessary justice.

The result of this Christian endorsement of forgiveness was the wholesale cultural, spiritual and legal acquittal of the perpetrators of the Holocaust. Although theological discourses of forgiveness should be kept separate from judicial proceedings, such attitudes influenced the German justice system's treatment of perpetrators as well. According to an official statistic published by the West German ministry of justice in 1986, German prosecutors opened 90,921 investigations against National Socialist perpetrators between 1945 and 1986. However, only a fraction of these initial investigations reached the courts. Of those that were brought to trial only 6,479 defendants were convicted. This low number, disturbing as it is, is further reduced when one excludes defendants who were prosecuted for charges of robbery and assault. Court cases concerning capital crimes, i.e. murder, amounted to only 912 cases involving 1,875 defendants. Of those 1,875 defendants 150 received life sentences, 842 temporary prison terms, and 1,117 were acquitted or let go because of alleged ill health. In other words, the German justice system practised a version of forgiveness and saw little value in punishing perpetrators of National Socialist crimes. Luke's 'Judge not, and you will not be judged; condemn not and you will not be condemned; forgive and you will be forgiven; for the measure you give will be the measure you get back' (Lk 6: 37–42) takes on a distinctly disturbing quality in such a post-genocidal situation, when no institution, least of all the justice system, welcomes scrutiny. The injunction against judgement leads to moral paralysis, and not as the Gospel-writers undoubtedly intended, to spiritual humility. A practice of forgiveness may be a spiritual virtue for victims and victim cultures, but perpetrators and their cultures must be encouraged to engage in judgement and moral discernment in order to liberate them from oppressive ideologies and structures that entangle them. Religious-based counsel against judgement has debilitating effects on moral reasoning in families and institutions. It is ultimately a betrayal of the perpetrators because it feeds into their denial. And instead of facilitating a new beginning, it prevents genuine transformation of perpetrator cultures.

This theology of forgiveness also abdicates responsibility to the legal system. Increasingly secular courts and United Nations War Crimes Tribunals are charged with the responsibility to 'deal with' the perpetrators. Yet, secular law can only hold individual criminals accountable. It is ill equipped to grasp the intricate chains of command in modern genocide and overwhelmed by the sheer numbers involved in political mass violence. How can the Rwanda justice system ever do justice to the 90,000 Hutu perpetrators of the Tutsi genocide currently kept in prison camps? Even in affluent societies, secular criminal law is an inept tool to respond to the difficult questions arising from the modern phenomenon of genocide and other forms of institutionalized, political mass killings.

What are the churches' responsibilities towards the thousands of men and women whose hands have been bloodied in mass violence and who live with the memories of horrific acts of cruelty and barbarity? What is required to facilitate moral and political insight prerequisite for any genuine insight among perpetrators?

First, theologians and ethicists are challenged to think creatively about the peculiar moral predicament of perpetrators of genocide. While secular law looks (and convicts) individual criminals, religious leaders have the tools to address entire communities. How can moral culpability in genocide, the peculiar mixture of individual moral agency and political action be grasped ethically? How do we maintain the dialectic tension between individual moral agency and the reality of political ideologies and the powers of modern nation states? It is equally wrong to convict the lone camp guard as if he was an individual murderer as it would be to exonerate him because he acted on orders. We need a new ethical language to account for moral culpability in an era of mass violence where individuals are swept up in an orgy of destruction. Theologians and ethicists must develop communal rituals of expiation, communal forms of acknowledging guilt that transcend the legal narrowing on individual criminal behaviour.

Second, religious communities must tackle the modern phenomenon of what Howard Ball called, 'unrepentant participation in genocide.' The experience of 20th-century genocide demonstrates that perpetrators of state sanctioned and legitimated mass violence show no consciousness of wrong and do not feel remorse for their actions. Theological insistence on the importance of justice conveys to perpetrators the fact that their acts of destruction are wrong. And the pursuit of justice affirms the dignity and traumatised humanity of the victims. Only firm commitment to punishment creates real possibilities to restore relations between victims and perpetrators (especially important in countries such as Rwanda and Bosnia where victim and perpetrator are forced to live in close proximity). Again the Christian churches are called to develop symbolic acts of atonement and restitution and to engage in the process of elaborating new, restorative acts of restitution.

Third, Christian theology is obliged to break the link between forgiving and forgetting and to place greater value on memory. The remembrance of traumatic events is never easy. One should never underestimate the effort it took and takes survivors to tell their stories. We are forever indebted to them for their commitment to remember despite the nightmares and sleepless nights, the ocean of despair that threatens to swallow them each time they reenter the horror of the Holocaust.

For perpetrators, such truthful memory is virtually unprecedented. As a rule, perpetrators lie, not only to their families and the courts, but also eventually to themselves. Denial and deception become part of their identity. Christian communities must actively engage with perpetrators in a process of recovery in order to help perpetrators to confront the truth. There may only be small openings for truth in the lives of many perpetrators, but such short moments of truth are sacred and worth fighting for. These moments of truthful insight can only be accomplished if Christian theology places greater weight on truth finding as opposed to forgiveness. Only then will this painful process of truth recovery appear worthwhile to the perpetrators.

DEPOLITICIZATION OF THE HOLOCAUST

The Holocaust should not be reduced to 'man's darkest moment' in history, to quote a leaflet circulated during the Survivors Gathering in London, preceding the Remembering for the Future 2000 conference. The Holocaust was neither a cataclysmic eruption of evil nor the inevitable climax of centuries of satanic anti-Semitism. It was the result of a political movement that espoused not only anti-Semitism but racism as an ideological platform for world renewal. It is a mistake, in my view, to divorce the Holocaust from the overall program of National Socialism. The destruction of the Jews did not happen by itself and, I would venture to say, could not have happened in isolation. For Nazis and Neo-Nazis anti-Semitism, racial supremacy, homophobia, sexism and hatred of all, who are physically, socially and politically different, belong intrinsically together. By focusing exclusively on anti-Semitism one not only distorts the historical record, but also undermines the political battle against an ideological and political movement that is far from extinct. For the various Nazi reincarnations, the neo-Nazis, the US Aryan Nation, Ku Klux Klan and white Militias, the hatred of Jews is of central importance. But the hatred of Jews is always connected to profound disgust and hatred of other differences: blacks, foreigners, racial and sexual minorities. Anti-Semitism cannot be separated from racism. Neither can it be separated from the hatred of homosexuals. The people, who would kill Jews, also kill gays and lesbians, people of colour and progressives. To minimise the interconnection of anti-Semitism, racism, homophobia (as well sexism) flies in the face of history and contemporary political reality. The academic debate over the uniqueness of the Holocaust, which ignores these political interconnections, weakens political resistance. It misreads the enemy and potentially strengthens their position by dividing important political coalitions of resistance.

For Christian theologians, the task of uprooting the 'Teaching of Contempt' for Jews in the Christian tradition – an ongoing task, to be sure – is tied to the equally important project of tackling the teachings of contempt for homosexuals, women, the handicapped, and of those who think or believe differently. These teachings of contempt belong together. Theological and political responses to National Socialism must commit to all of its victims and must not ignore particular victim groups. Theologians must tie the critical analysis of anti-Judaism to scrutiny of sexism and homophobia, including that found in Jewish-Christian dialogue and Holocaust studies. Diversity is what the Nazis set out to destroy and we must be ever vigilant about our own tendencies to silence those who don't fit into our own master narrative.

POST-AUSCHWITZ CATHOLIC–JEWISH DIALOGUE:
MIXED SIGNALS AND MISSED OPPORTUNITIES

Alan L. Berger

'There is nothing so whole as a broken heart.'
– Reb Nahman of Bratzlav

T HERE IS, perhaps, no better metaphor for Catholic–Jewish relations both during and after the Holocaust than that of mixed signals. Nechama Tec, the distinguished sociologist who as a young girl survived the *Shoah* by passing as a Polish Christian, describes the nature of these signals. On the one hand, the Church has advocated 'Jewish hatred', yet on the other hand, it required its members 'to reassess their own sins, to love, and to sacrifice for their fellow human beings'.[1] During the Holocaust, and absent any clear message from the Vatican, observes Tec, 'the clergy and lay Catholics could base their reaction on religious anti-Semitism or on Christian teachings of charity and universal love.'[2] Three events of the last fifteen years reveal the ongoing impact of the legacy of mixed signals. Indeed, the two major controversies engendered by the Carmelite convent and the planting of crosses at Auschwitz, and by the promulgation of the papal document 'We Remember: A Reflection on the *Shoah*', continue – and deepen – this legacy.

This paper examines the issues raised by what these controversies reveal concerning underlying theological assumptions which historically have poisoned the possibility of dialogue between the two faith groups. Focusing on 'We Remember', it argues the document itself appears both as an absolute departure from, as well as an espousal of, mixed signals and missed opportunities. Inquiry is made into the possibility of authentic Catholic-Jewish dialogue. The paper concludes by examining the feasibility of applying Emanuel Levinas's insight into the role of the Other as a possible source of helping move the controversy beyond stereotypical thinking and bridging the gap between Catholicism and Judaism.

AUSCHWITZ AND COMPETING MEMORIES

A common assumption among people of good will is that if Auschwitz cannot bring people together, then nothing can. Both Catholics and Jews view Auschwitz as a site of anguish and pain. For Poles it is a site of national martyrdom at which upwards of eighty thousand Polish people perished. Jews view Auschwitz as a vast necropolis in which approximately one million Jewish people were murdered. Yet, ironically, the two faith communities *share no common memory* of Nazism's murderous onslaught. Quite the contrary is the case: as Carol Rittner and John Roth have shown in their book *Memory Offended*, Catholics and Jews have trampled on each other's memory.[3] Moreover, Catholics and Jews commonly do not refer to the same place when speaking of Auschwitz, which itself was divided into three unequal segments. The main camp (*Stammlager*) is called Auschwitz I. This was the site of Polish suffering. Auschwitz-Birkenau (Auschwitz II), located three kilometres away, was a vast expanse dedicated primarily to eradicating Jews from the face of the earth.[4]

Furthermore, on the theological level the stories that Catholics and Jews tell about themselves frequently exclude an understanding of the other. In fact, Christianity's construction of Judaism as the paradigmatic Other has enabled much of the destructive behaviour towards Jews and Judaism. Consequently, as the 20th century drew to a close the Auschwitz controversies engendered behaviour which at times bordered on medieval religious warfare. It is reasonable to expect that additional controversies will erupt unless and until the two communities understand their theological and historical differences. Although resolutions of both the convent and crosses have been achieved through religiously motivated dialogue, these settlements appear more the result of political and diplomatic compromise rather than an attempt to explore the theological issues which have proved so divisive and deadly. This is one reason that Pope John Paul II's promulgation of 'We Remember' was awaited with great expectations.

Morally ugly and divisive arguments concerning Auschwitz arose publicly in the decade of the 1980s. These controversies centred on two primary issues: who 'owned' the death camp, notwithstanding the fact that in 1979 UNESCO officially declared that Auschwitz is a 'world heritage site', and what role, if any, should be played by religion in commemorating the victims and martyrs of the largest of Nazism's vast system of death camps. These issues, while analytically separable, are in reality two sides of the same coin. Both Poles and Jews suffered at Auschwitz. Yet for Polish Catholics the suffering of their compatriots seemed an embodiment of the identification of Poland as the 'Christ of Nations'.[5] Consequently, many Poles view the Jewish claim on Auschwitz as an assault on Catholicism and the cross. For Jews, Auschwitz was the terrible culmination of centuries of Church teachings of contempt and antisemitism. Therefore, what emerges is a volatile combination of religion, nationalism and politics in which neither side can understand, or accept, the perceived insensitivity of the Other.

Focusing on the impact of the *Shoah* on classical theological paradigms, one again sees a clash between Jewish and Catholic perceptions. For example, Jewish thinkers such as Arthur Cohen, Emil Fackenheim, Irving Greenberg, Richard Rubenstein, Elie Wiesel and others have attested that after Auschwitz everything needs to be re-evaluated. These thinkers raise questions about the relationship of God to the death camps and the meaning of classical liturgical statements. In contrast, there has until recently been relatively little Christian self-critiques in light of the *Shoah*. Among the pioneers in this area are Gertrude Luckner. Jacques Maritain and James Parkes, whose work actually preceded the Holocaust; more recent contributions include Harry James Cargas, Eugene Fischer, Father Edward Flannery and John Pawlikowski among Catholic scholars. In the Protestant world, the work of Roy and Alice Eckardt, Franklin Littell and Paul Van Buren comes to mind. But until the advent of Pope John XXIII and the Second Vatican Council, the concept of the 'Church untouched by history' reigned supreme.[6] Yet, if the Carmelite convent case demonstrates anything, it is the belief on the part of the nuns and also on the popular level that theologically the *Shoah* changed nothing; pre-Holocaust forms of prayer and piety remained acceptable. Both the convent and the crosses at Auschwitz revealed the extent to which Christian triumphalism remains firmly entrenched at the popular and, in certain cases, clerical leadership at the parish level.

THE CARMELITE CONVENT

In 1984 a Carmelite convent was established in the Theatergebaude (old theatre building) near the grounds of Auschwitz I. During the Holocaust this building had been used to store both the belongings of those who were gassed and canisters of Zyklon B, the poison used in the gas chambers. The convent plan was approved by the Polish authorities and the Catholic church. However, no communication or dialogue with the Jewish community took place. The nuns announced that it was their religious duty to pray for the souls of those murdered in Auschwitz and to do penance. Moreover, one aim of the convent appears to have been the conversion of the Jews, as in the statement issued by a Catholic organization in Belgium, 'Aid to the Church in Distress', which announces that the convent 'will become a spiritual fortress and a guarantee of the conversion of strayed brothers...'.[7] This statement is, at the very least, ambiguous given the church's long history of mission to the Jews.[8] In 1985 this organization issued an appeal for financial assistance for the Carmelite convent. Jewish, and a few Catholic, protests were raised. While this is not the place to rehearse the long and tortured history of negotiations that eventually led, eleven years later, to the convent's removal, it is instructive to note that discussions between Belgian Jewish leaders, Cardinal Franciszek Macharski, Archbishop of Cracow, the diocese which includes Auschwitz, and the Polish Minister of Religious Affairs had failed to reach an accord.[9]

Political negotiations continued. In 1986 a meeting was held in Geneva between a high-level Roman Catholic delegation and several Jewish leaders. All present, including Cardinal Macharski, recognized the uniqueness of Auschwitz-Birkenau, and agreed that no convent should be built there. In retrospect, however, 1987 was the crucial year of this controversy. On February 22 of that year a document was signed by Jewish and Catholic leaders agreeing that within two years the Catholic side would raise substantial funds to achieve the movement of the convent outside the area of 'Auschwitz-Birkenau camps' and become part of a new centre of 'information, education, meeting and prayer'.[10] This interfaith centre was envisioned as a place devoted to fostering mutual understanding and trust. The declaration went on to state that 'There will, therefore, be no permanent Catholic place of worship on the site of the Auschwitz and Birkenau camps. Everyone will be able to pray there according to the dictates of his own heart, religion, and faith.' In November of the same year a large cross was installed on the convent building. Subsequently it was removed, but another cross was planted in the convent garden. Six more years elapsed before the Pope wrote to the nuns asking them to move. In 1995, eight years after the deadline, the convent was gone but the cross (inaccurately referred to as the papal cross) remained.

At this point it is appropriate to note another event that occurred in the late summer of 1987. Reacting in part to the issue of the Carmelite convent at Auschwitz, but in the main to the Pope's ill-advised welcome of Kurt Waldheim to the Vatican, a summit meeting between the pope and international Jewish leaders was held at Castelgandolfo. This gathering was called because Pope John Paul II's planned meeting in Miami with leaders of American Jewry was on the verge of being cancelled owing to strongly negative Jewish reaction to the above-mentioned events. On September 1 the Holy See declared its intention of producing an official document on the relationship of the Catholic Church to the *Shoah*. Furthermore, this document would soon be published. This message was received in the Jewish community as a clear, positive and strong statement. A few days later, and in response to this declaration, the Pope and the Jewish leaders had a successful meeting in Miami.[11]

Returning to the Carmelite convent issue, it is instructive to focus on Jewish and Catholic responses to this saga. The Jewish response consisted of negotiations with church and government officials, and various protests. The best-known of these protests was led by Rabbi Avraham Weiss, who in July 1989, along with six students, scaled the wall of the convent and studied Torah on the convent porch. The protestors wore prayer shawls [*tallis*] and head coverings [*kipa*]. Rabbi Weiss attested that workers threw buckets of paint at the protestors and evicted them from the convent grounds. Further, there were charges of antisemitic slurs being uttered. Two days later, the protestors returned without incident. Many in both the Catholic and Jewish communities viewed Rabbi Weiss's action in storming the convent as insensitive and inappropriate; an American-style protest launched in a culture that views convents as places of sacrality and holiness.

During this same period Pope John Paul II was sending a variety of signals. On the one hand, he spoke of reconciliation between Catholicism and Judaism. He became the first pope to visit a Jewish synagogue when, in April 1986, he went to Rome's main synagogue and embraced Chief Rabbi Elio Toaff. The pope referred to Judaism as Christianity's elder brother, and underscored the Church's rejection of antisemitism. Yet, curiously he made no reference to the still unresolved Carmelite convent situation. Approximately one year later, however, the Pope beatified Edith Stein, a Jewish philosopher who converted to Catholicism and became Sister Teresa Benedicta of the Cross in the Carmelite order. Yet Edith Stein was murdered as a Jew in Auschwitz. Pope John Paul II also canonized Father Maximillian Kolbe, a Polish Franciscan priest who gave his life to save a married prisoner in Auschwitz. Kolbe, however, was also at least a 'conversionist', i.e., his wish was to convert Jews, who edited a pre-war journal that had published antisemitic articles.

The Pope's actions led to charges that he was attempting to Christianize the Holocaust. Further, in the case of Edith Stein, the Pope's speech of 1 May 1987 explicitly states that Judaism is an incomplete religion whose fate is to find fulfilment only in the cross. In the Pope's words,

> Her life and her cross itinerary are intimately linked to the destiny of the Jewish People. In a prayer she recognizes to Christ the Saviour what she knew: 'It is His Cross that now is placed over the shoulders of the Jewish people.'[12]

Sergio Minerbi contends that by comparing Edith Stein to the biblical Esther who saved her people, the Pope implies that Edith Stein saved her people by her conversion to Christianity.[13] Salvation is possible, as indicated by Edith Stein, and lies in the Cross. That Pope John Paul II has sent mixed theological signals is undeniable. During the month of August 1989, Pope John Paul delivered two homilies at the Vatican in which he claimed that the Old Testament 'shows many instances of Israel's infidelity to God'. Nothwithstanding the continuation of the supersessionism found in the *Adversos Judaeos* tradition, the very use of the term Old Testament is offensive and triumphalistic.

The insensitivity of both sides in the convent issue can be seen in statements made by Cardinal Jozef Glemp, the polish primate, who addressed a religious gathering at Jasna Gora, the shrine of the Black Madonna, Poland's holiest icon, and by Yitzhak Shamir, the then Israeli Prime Minister. Cardinal Glemp stated that 'pronouncements against the [Carmelite] nuns at Auschwitz offend the feelings of all Poles.' The primate's message clearly implied that Jews were interfering with a purely internal, Polish, matter, as if the murder of a million Jews at Auschwitz were insignificant. Prime Minister Yitzhak Shamir responded by saying that Poles 'suck [antisemitism] in with their mother's milk'. This exchange clearly did nothing to foster Catholic–Jewish relations, and Shamir's remarks were clearly undiplomatic, although it is instructive to note what Tec terms the existence of 'diffuse cultural antisemitism' even among the Polish rescuers.[14] After the nuns finally moved and the convent was relocated outside the grounds of Auschwitz, half of the fourteen nuns returned to the mother convent in Posnan. Sister Maria Teresa, the superior, then rented the building to a right-wing nationalist group. The Polish government subsequently invalidated this agreement.

Focusing on the theological lessons of this situation, one can observe the following. Both the nuns and those who opposed the convent viewed each other as doing the work of the Devil. This indicates that, unfortunately, old stereotypes still play an important and disruptive role in Catholic–Jewish relations. Furthermore, apart from intellectuals such as Father Stanislaw Musial, S.J., of Cracow, one of the signers of the 1987 Geneva accords, Cardinals Jean-Marie Lustiger, and Albert Decourtray of France, the Vatican itself showed little interest in engaging in a self-critique concerning the role its traditional teachings played in sewing the seedbed of the Holocaust. To even imply a post-Auschwitz mission to the Jews is a theological obscenity. The Polish Church itself appears deeply divided. On the one hand, many parish priests, especially those in rural areas, remain antisemitic and are hostile to any change in perception of Jews or Judaism. On the other hand, the 'Pastoral on Jewish–Catholic Relations', issued by the Polish Bishops on 30 November 1990, forthrightly addresses both the ties between Christianity and Judaism, as well as the wartime failure of many Polish Catholics to aid the Jewish people. In the words of the bishops' Pastoral, 'If only one Christian could have helped and did not stretch out a helping hand to a Jew during the time of danger or caused his death, we must ask for forgiveness of our Jewish brothers and sisters.'[15] Since then, the Polish bishops have issued additional letters, January 1995 and August 2000. The August letter which was read in all Polish churches on the 27th of the month, asks forgiveness for the church's historic toleration of antisemitism. The statement also contends that 'anti-Semitism, just like anti-Christianism, is a sin'.

On the Jewish side, it is important to develop a more nuanced understanding of both Poland and Polish–Jewish relations. If any sort of meaningful dialogue is to emerge, Jews need to recognize that there were Polish rescuers and helpers during the Holocaust. Although the rescuers comprise less than one percent of the population, the fact that they did rescue is crucial. Moreover, there was a national organization, ZEGOTA, that helped save Jews during the war. Poland is also one of two countries that has the most trees planted in memory of the righteous at *Yad Vashem*. Jews need to incorporate this into their story of the Holocaust. Listening to the voice of the other helps humanize the relationship and allows for the possibility of mature dialogue.

THE CROSS AND THE CROSSES AT AUSCHWITZ

That the transfer of the Carmelite convent was not the same as resolution of Catholic–Jewish tensions was made abundantly clear by the continuing antagonism concerning the role of religious symbolism at Auschwitz. The so-called papal cross, which in fact is not a papal cross, located in the garden of the former convent remains. Additionally, hundreds of crosses have been planted in Auschwitz I. The tale of these so-called baby crosses reveals much about the possibility of meaningful Catholic–Jewish dialogue. Originally, a group of Polish boy scouts put up some crudely made Stars of David and crosses inside

Auschwitz-Birkenau as a memorial to the victims. Although done with good intentions, this act provoked criticism. On the technical level, placement of these religious symbols had not been officially authorized. The Polish bishops' conference played an important role in getting rid of these baby crosses. The Auschwitz Museum, which has authority to maintain the integrity of the camp within its barbed wire fences, removed these symbols in December 1997. Symbolically, however, the matter re-raised all of the unresolved issues and tensions that appeared in connection to the Carmelite convent.

The issue is complex and goes far beyond any simplistic notion of 'good' versus 'bad' people. At stake here are deeply held beliefs, whose adherents are by no means uneducated or unworldly. Quite the contrary is the case; highly educated people who do not view themselves as insensitive can say remarkably naive things. For example, I note the comment of an official of the Auschwitz Museum in a conversation with me dealing with the matter of religious symbols at the death camp. The reason that Elie Wiesel is opposed to crosses at Auschwitz, my informant opined, is because 'he does not believe in God'. Jan Karski, when informed of this, responded, 'I suppose she [the official] thinks that she does believe.'[16]

These tensions erupted with great fury in 1998. Right wing nationalist Poles, led by Kzimierz Switon, planted hundreds of crosses adjacent to Auschwitz I. Switon has established a sort of primitive headquarters among the crosses, living there in a tent, and vows not to leave the site unless church officials provide written guarantees that the cross and crosses will never be removed. Many of the crosses bear a legend reading, 'only under this cross, only under this symbol, Poland is Poland and a Pole is a Pole.'[17] This statement is reminiscent of slogans which appeared in Poland immediately after the *Shoah* which proclaimed Poland is for Poles, i.e., not for Jews. According to many survivor memoirs, this same sentiment was articulated shortly after the war by groups of Poles who warned the few Jews who had survived the Holocaust that they were not welcome in Poland.

It should be noted that there have been two conflicting responses to this situation. On the one hand, intellectuals, including Karski, and certain church leaders such as Father Musial, have roundly criticized this shameful and destructive nationalism. On the other hand, many in the ruling majority in the Polish Parliament support the presence of the crosses as do many in the Polish countryside.[18] As of this writing, the Vatican has had no public reaction to this inflammatory situation. But it is noteworthy that Cardinal Cassidy, speaking as President of the Vatican Commission, has urged transferring the large, so-called 'papal', cross to the re-located carmelite convent. As with the convent issue, so with the cross and the crosses; no consultation, either formal or informal, was undertaken with Jewish communal leaders.

Negotiations over the cross and crosses issue appear to have followed the pattern established by the convent controversy. Political and diplomatic discussions, rather than theological self-critique, are the norm. International in scope, representatives of the Polish Government, the World Jewish Congress, the Vatican, and the then head of the United States Holocaust Memorial Museum engaged in intense negotiation. Again, as with the Carmelite convent, incendiary statements were made on both sides. Rabbi Weiss proclaimed that Jews would 'not negotiate in the shadow of the cross'. On the Polish Catholic side, there is disturbing evidence that Switon may appeal to a far larger segment of the population than merely the lunatic fringe.

On the positive side of the matter, one can point to some important developments. For example, the Auschwitz museum now conducts educational seminars for teachers on how to educate their students about the Holocaust. Increased attention is being paid to the Jewish experience. Furthermore, many of the intellectual and government leaders are embarrassed by the crosses and are seeking to educate the public about the evil of antisemitism and what role Poland's own history played in fostering such hatred. The fact that Pope John Paul II is a Pole who lived during the *Shoah* as a priest near Cracow, and had Jewish friends who perished in Auschwitz, means that he can play an important part in addressing the role and teachings of the church during those terrible years.

WE REMEMBER: A REFLECTION ON THE *SHOAH*

On 12 March 1998, eleven years after being announced, the Vatican's public statement on the Catholic Church and the Holocaust, 'We Remember: A Reflection on the *Shoah*', appeared. In a prefatory letter to the document, addressed to Cardinal Edward Idris Cassidy, Pope John Paul II correctly referred to the *Shoah* as 'an indelible stain on the history of the century that is coming to a close.' Furthermore, he expressed his 'fervent hope' that the document, which was prepared under the direction of Cardinal Cassidy and the Commission for Religious Relations With the Jews, will 'help to heal the wounds of past misunderstandings and injustices.' Finally, 'We Remember' rightly contends that the 'common future of Jews and Christians demands that we remember'. The document cites Pope John Paul II's pronouncement – very Jewish in content – that 'there is no future without memory'.

'We Remember' generated many responses both within the Church and among Jewish leaders. However, the one thing it did *not* achieve was the healing of the wounds of the past and historical injustices. Quite the contrary is the case. The document appears to have hardened old lines of suspicion. Praised by some and condemned by others, 'We Remember' appears to continue the tradition of mixed signals and missed opportunities.[19]

In order to understand why this is so, it is important to recognize several points. At the close of the second millennium the Catholic Church was still conflicted about how to deal with Judaism and the Jewish People. On the one hand, the post-*Shoah* record of the Vatican is extraordinary. One need only recall the new era in Catholic–Jewish relations heralded by Pope John XXIII's convening of the Second Vatican Council, out of which emerged *Nostra Aetate* [October 1965], which set forth the church's relationship with non-Christian religions, especially Judaism. Furthermore, the Guidelines for Implementation [no. 4, October 1974] absolved Jews from the charge of deicide. 'We Remember' continues the quest for better Catholic–Jewish relations. Moreover, the Vatican, guided by Pope John Paul II granted diplomatic recognition to the State of Israel. Further, the pope's recent visit to Yad Vashem was a heartfelt, deeply moving and symbolically important event.

But 'We Remember' itself is comprised of various theological and literary strata. Divided into five sections; the first two of which appear to be genuine calls for penance, the document embraces both the light of repentance and the darkness of dogma. Indeed, Rabbi Irving Greenberg terms it 'a split document emotionally and theologically'.[20] The pope's above cited letter to Cardinal Cassidy demonstrates the pontiff's personal sorrow over the Holocaust. Furthermore, the Church's acknowledgment that the *Shoah* is a 'major fact of the history of this century' is a rebuke to Holocaust deniers and other antisemites. Additionally, the pope's emphasis on the necessity of the church becoming 'more fully conscious of the sinfulness of her children when they departed from the spirit of Christ and his Gospel' [part I] and his raising of the 'question of the relation between the Nazi persecution and the attitudes down the centuries of Christians towards the Jews' [part II] suggests that he is encouraging a Catholic self-critique in light of the *Shoah*.

Coupled with his desire to rid the church of antisemitism, however, the pope simultaneously embraces a reading of history which, at best, is disingenuous. For instance, sections three and four of 'We Remember' are, unfortunately, not marked by a commitment either to historical accuracy or theological candour. The conflict between liberal and conservative elements in the church is clearly seen in the portions of the document dealing with the history of the relations between Jews and Christians, and Nazi Anti-Semitism and the Shoah. To cite but two examples, the document clings to the Pauline distinction between devotion to the *Law*, which, according to Paul, on occasion caused Jews to violently oppose the preachers of the Gospel and the first Christians, and the *Spirit*. Further, as Rabbi James Rudin observes, 'By using the words "violently opposed", the Vatican text transmits the not-so-subtle message of a moral equivalency between historic, often deadly, Christian persecution and denigration of Jews and Judaism and the anti-Christian attitudes and behavior of some Jews.'[21]

Further, in distinguishing between Christian anti-Judaism and the antisemitism of Nazism which is 'secular and neo-pagan', the document implies two highly questionable positions. First, Christianity is exonerated from any blame for the impact of its anti-Jewish doctrines after the 18th century. Secondly, Christianity itself was a victim of Nazism which, 'in pursuing its aims,... did not hesitate to oppose the Church and persecute her members also'. Consequently, Christians and Jews, alike were victims of the Holocaust. Is this not a further step towards Christianizing the *Shoah*?

'We Remember' is also deeply flawed in suggesting that Christian resistance to the Holocaust was active and vigorous. The document contends that the German church responded to Nazism 'by condemning racism;' singling out Cardinals Bertram of Breslau and Faulhaber of Munich. The report also extols Domprobst Bernhard Lichtenberg's public prayers on behalf of the Jews following *Kristallnacht*. Lichtenberg perished en route to Dachau where he had been sent by the Nazis. Pius XI's encyclical 'With Burning Anxiety' read in German churches in 1937 and his 1938 assertion, made to a group of Belgian pilgrims that 'Spiritually we are all Semites' is also cited as proof of Catholic resistance. The actual facts present a vastly different picture of the German Church where silence was the rule and protest the exception. Moreover, the assertion that many individual Christians helped their Jewish brothers and sisters while some did not, is demonstrably false. The fact of the matter is the reverse; most Christians did nothing to aid Jews or to embrace the teachings of love and compassion articulated in normative Christian teachings.

It is, however, the document's portrayal of the role of Pope Pius XII which has most angered critics and enfeebled the Church's own moral position. Pius XII is credited with saving hundreds of thousands of Jewish lives by his own actions and through the activities of his representatives. In the largest footnote in 'We Remember', approximately ten times longer than any other note, the authors assemble praise of Jewish leaders concerning 'the wisdom of Pius XII's diplomacy'. It is true that the pope's appeal to Regent Horathy at the end of the war was an attempt to save Hungarian Jews. Yet it is also correct that Pius XII never openly spoke out against Nazism, never threatened to excommunicate any of the Catholic murderers, and was a staunch admirer of German culture.

The literature on the role of Pius XII is enormous, much of it being polemical in either blaming or praising the pontiff. Three scholarly works deserve careful attention on this issue. Father John Morley's *Vatican Diplomacy and the Jews during the Holocaust:*

1939–1943 (New York: KTAV, 1980) contends that Pius XII's record was not good. John Cornwall's *Hitler's Pope* (New York: Viking, 1999), dismissed by the Vatican as 'rubbish', argues that Pius XII was a germanophile, uninterested in aiding the Jewish people. Michael Phayer's *The Catholic Church and the Holocaust, 1939–1965* (Bloomington: Indiana University Press, 2000), is a sober look at Pius XII's persona and policies. Phayer concludes that political considerations were paramount in any concern that the pontiff displayed toward the rescue of Jews. Any informed judgement about Pius XII, however, cannot be made until the Vatican opens its archives to qualified scholars. Cardinal Bernadin in 1992 was the first to issue a call to open the archives. Seven years later, Cardinal O'Connor echoed this plea. Significantly, a team of scholars has been chosen to examine pertinent Vatican documents. It is not clear that other relevant documents located in various European cites will also be made available. What is undeniable however, according to Robert Wistrich, is 'the paucity of moral courage displayed by the Vatican when it came to the fate of the Jews'.[22]

Two questions arise from this section of 'We Remember'. Why is the Vatican so keen to defend Pius XII? Why list other 20th-century horrors such as the murder of the Armenians, the massacre of the Ukrainians, the murder of the Gypsies and racist ideas in America, Africa, and the Balkans . . . the millions of victims . . . elsewhere? Concerning the first question, James Carroll provides a helpful clue. He writes: 'That John Paul II has reasserted the idea of infallibility, on the one hand, while demonstrating an unprecedented and genuine sympathy for Jews, on the other, is the great paradox of his papacy.'[23] In other words, the mixed signal is systemic; John Paul II wishes both to reach out to the Jewish people and to retain the conservative notion of papal infallibility which prohibits any far reaching self-critique on the part of the Church.

Lumping other tragedies into this section serves merely to dilute each of them. Further, it detracts from the pope's contention that the Holocaust was 'an indelible stain' on the history of the 20th century. More preferable is the assertion of Elie Wiesel who attests that 'every tragedy deserves its own name'. Further, if evil is ubiquitous, then everyone is its victim. The Jews, therefore, cease being Nazism's principal victim. If this is the case, could it not be argued that Polish Catholics emerge as the primary victims? Could this be a late 20th century attempt at historical alchemy whereby Christianity ceases to be complicit in the Holocaust and becomes instead the *Shoah*'s main victim? Finally, 'We Remember' curiously omits any reference to the Vatican's post-War actions and attitudes towards Nazi war criminals. Was there an official response to the horrors of the Holocaust? Were any Nazi leaders excommunicated?

Minerbi views the reign of John Paul II as aiming to Christianize the Holocaust. He writes: 'the holocaust could become a Polish-Catholic martyrdom, the Catholic Church as a whole becoming thus a victim and not merely a witness of the holocaust, and therefore Pius XII would pass into history as the chief-martyr.'[24] Irrespective of the merit, or lack thereof, in Minerbi's position, suspicion could have been allayed and trust built if 'We Remember' had not been insistent on raising the issue of Pius XII in a document that aims at repentance. The complexities of Pius XII deserve a separate study. Instead of shrouding the discussion in legalisms, it would have been far healthier for Catholic Jewish dialogue if Nahman of Bratslav's admonition were heeded. One can only build the basis for genuine hope after knowing, and acknowledging, the worst.

Comparing 'We Remember' to the earlier statements of the German and French bishops (1995, 1997), one sees the difference in tone and in historical and theological veracity. The French bishops declaration was made at Drancy, 'the antechamber of death', and its proclaimers included Cardinal Lustiger, whose Jewish mother died in

Auschwitz. These statements admit the churches many failings during the Holocaust, especially the sin of silence.[25] The even earlier paper by Harry James Cargas, 'My Papal Encyclical' (1989) specifically calls for the admission of errors on the part of Christian teachers including Church Fathers.[26] Cargas also calls for examination of scriptures in order to interpret them in a non hateful or hurtful manner. While not carrying the weight of the Vatican document, these other statements courageously engage in a theological self-critique and thus offer a firmer foundation for trust and dialogue in the manner suggested by Reb Nahman.

POST–AUSCHWITZ CATHOLIC–JEWISH DIALOGUE

Writing in *Telling Tales*, Jacob Neusner contends that the time is ripe for dialogue. This is so because of the Holocaust. 'From Vatican II onward', he writes, 'important Christianities have formulated a theologically valid Christian alternative to a teaching of contempt.' On the Jewish side, argues Neusner 'in response to gestures of reconciliation, Judaism's position of implacable rejection awaits modification, adaptation to facts never before encountered among Christianities.'[27] In face of the mixed signals sent by 'We Remember', Neusner's position appears only partially accurate. Although the teaching of contempt, a phrase penned by Jules Isaac, a French Jew who had lost his family during the *Shoah*, has been doctrinally discredited, the inability of the Church to own its part in contributing to the Holocaust and in failing to speak out against the terror, means that Neusner may be overly sanguine about Catholicism.

Of what does authentic dialogue consist? Neusner suggests three criteria: '(1) each party proposes to take seriously the position of the other, (2) each party concedes the integrity of the other, and (3) each party accepts responsibility for the outcome of the discussion: that is, remains open to the possibility of conceding the legitimacy of the other's viewpoint.'[28] Yet, as our survey has shown, these criteria have not been uniformly met. Further, it is not clear how far beyond 'We Remember' the Church is willing to carry the discussion. Nor is it clear that many Jews who have little or no experience reading Church documents can appreciate the sincerity of Pope John Paul II and Cardinal Cassidy. It is perfectly legitimate to inquire about the future of Catholic Jewish dialogue in light of the three events analysed in this paper.

EMMANUEL LEVINAS AND THE 'OTHER'

It is clear from the three events described that a fundamental stumbling block for Catholic Jewish relations is the inability to grant credence to the viability of the Other. Historically, the burden of this inability has been born by Jews and Judaism since the 4th century of the Common Era. Determined literally to exterminate alterity, Nazism focused its murderous efforts on the Jews, the exemplary Other in European and Christian history. Emmanuel Levinas, the Lithuanian-born Jewish philosopher who himself was a prisoner of war near Hanover, Germany, was greatly concerned with the relationship between ethics and the Other. Identity stems from one's encounter with alterity. He views the Holocaust in terms of a crisis in ethical relations. He asks, *not* 'Where was God?' Rather, the question for Levinas is, Where was man as an ethical being, during – and after the *Shoah*? Although Levinas, like Elie Wiesel, contends that it is immoral to get any 'lesson' from Auschwitz, both thinkers contend that systems are not to be trusted. Theological totalities are never good, attests Levinas, because they are unable to deal with alterity. Rather, Levinas stresses that personal responsibility is crucial.

A Levinasian reading of the end of the century crises in Catholic Jewish relations may provide some insight useful to both parties. For Levinas ethics was prior to metaphysics. In Levinas's view, 'the subject is defined by the other yet also unique and singular.' Consequently, his ethics were grounded in dialogue. Radicalizing Martin Buber's dialogical position of I–Thou, Levinas embraces the view articulated by Alyosha Karamazov in Fyodor Dostoyevsky's *The Brothers Karamazov*: 'We all are responsible for everyone else – but I am more responsible than all of the others.' Personal ethics and social justice are prior to any 'totalizing system'. For Levinas ethics entails the 'obligations and responsibilities that one person has for another person encountered face-to-face and that ultimately each person has for all humanity.'[29] Ethical obligations obliterate the demands of reason. If this principle were operative during the *Shoah*, then far more Christians would have been rescuers.

Contrasting Levinas and the attitudes engendered by the Carmelite convent and the crosses, one can see that for the Jewish philosopher alterity is the source of one's humanity and responsibility, whereas precisely the opposite position emerged in the two crises. In those cases alterity led not to fulfillment of one's identity but to claims of superiority and triumphalism. A Levinasian approach to the Catholic-Jewish dialogue would contend that for genuine dialogue to occur, one must recognize the priority of the Other. In Richard Cohen's trenchant phrase, 'for Levinas the self is its brother's keeper; the other's material requirements are the self's spiritual requirements.'[30] Thus, dialogue in the genuine sense of the word has nothing to do with religious narratives but everything to do with ethics in terms of responsibility for the Other.

Beyond, and prior to, arguments over convents, crosses, and papal documents, Levinas attests that 'in the access to the face there is certainly also an access to God'.[31] God as alterity is a summons to respond. This God is 'otherwise than being', and, in the words of Sandor Goodhart, 'a God who demands of us nothing less than shouldering God's own responsibility for others, for their lives, for their responsibility, even for their deaths.'[32] It remains to be seen if the Catholic Jewish dialogue can embrace alterity as an opportunity for growth rather than an occasion for hate.

NOTES

I am grateful for the observations of the following scholars who read and offered valuable comments on earlier drafts of this essay: Dr. Eugene J. Fisher; Professors Asher Z. Milbauer, Susan E. Nowak, Harold M. Stahmer; and Dr. Sigmund Stahl. However, none of these individuals is responsible for any errors or for my interpretations.

1 Nechama Tec, 'The Vatican, the Catholic Religion, the Jews', in *Holocaust Scholars Write to the Vatican*, ed. Harry James Cargas. (Westport, CN: Greenwood Press, 1998), p.27.

2 *ibid.*

3 Carol Rittner and John K. Roth (eds.), *Memory Offended: The Auschwitz Convent Controversy* (New York: Praeger, 1991). Hereafter *M.O.*

4 Auschwitz was divided into three sections. Auschwitz III, the industrial complex, comprised the various factories where German industries utilized slave labourers.

5 Michael C. Steinlauf cites Adam Mickiewicz, the 19th-century Polish National Poet, who used the phrase in *Bondage to the Dead: Poland and the Memory of Holocaust* (Syracuse: Syracuse University Press, 1997), p.9.

6 Rabbi Irving Greenberg, discussion with Alan L. Berger, 27 November 1998; henceforth cited as Greenberg discussion.

7 The mission statement is cited by S. I. Minerbi, 'Pope John Paul II and the Shoah', *Remembering for the Future: Working Papers and Abstracts*, ed. Yehuda Bauer, Vol. III (Oxford: Pergamon Press, 1989), p.2978.

8 Dr. Eugene Fisher observes that the phrase 'conversion of strayed borthers' has a specific meaning: lapsed Catholics. Letter to the author, 6 June 2000. Hereafter, this source will be cited as Fisher letter.

9 This meeting took place on 17–18 February 1986. *M.O.*, p.21.

10 Fisher letter.

11 A. James Rudin, 'Reflections on the Vatican's *Reflection on the Shoah*. *Cross Currents*. Winter, 1998/99. p.519.

12 Minerbi, *op. cit.*, p.2983.

13 *ibid.*

14 Tec, pp.25–26. Tec notes the complexity of the issue in writing that: 'Most rescuers consciously tried to dissociate themselves from the prevailing anti-Semitic climate, and succeeded in dissociating themselves from anti-Jewish actions and ideologies. However, only a few of them managed to steer clear of the influence of diffuse cultural anti-Semitism.'

15 English translation of this text, by Thomas Byrd, appears in Rittner and Roth, *M.O.*, p.265. For purposes of this paper I omit the larger question of whether it is possible to forgive a crime in someone else's name. The Jewish theological tradition distinguishes two types of sins, one that is committed between 'man and man' and one that is committed by an individual against God. Further, only the person who has been transgressed against has the right to forgive his/her transgressor. On this issue see Alan L. Berger, 'Response' in *The Sunflower*, ed. Simon Wiesenthal (New York: Schocken Books, 1997), pp.118–120.

16 Terest Swiebocka comments to A.L. Berger, Auschwitz Museum, 10 August 1998; Karski response to A.L. Berger, telephone conversation, 31 August 1998.

17 'Poles and Jews Feud About Crosses at Auschwitz', *The New York Times*, 20 December 1998, p.12.

18 John Pawlikowski, 'The Struggle for Memory and Memorialization at Auschwitz', unpublished paper, p.6.

19 See the excellent study by Kevin Madigan, 'A Survey of Jewish Reaction to the Vatican Statement on the Holocaust', paper presented at the American Academy of Religion, November 1999.

20 Greenberg discussion.

21 Rudin, *op. cit.*, p.522.

22 Wistrich is cited by Madigan, *op. cit.*, p.7.

23 James Carroll is cited by David Gordis, 'Pope John Paul II and the Jews' in *John Paul II and Interreligious Dialogue*, eds. Byron L. Sherwin and Harold Kasimo. (Maryknoll, New York: Orbis Books, 1999), p.137.

24 Minerbi, *op. cit.*, p.2974.

25 Madigan. *op. cit.*, p.2.

26 Harry James Cargas, 'My Papal Encyclical', in Harry James Cargas, *Reflections of a Post-Auschwitz Catholic* (Detroit: Wayne State University Press, 1989). For a fascinating study of three Catholic thinkers and their attempt at a post Auschwitz theological self-critique see Samuel Edelman, 'The Rhetoric of "Almost" Redemption and rebirth: Catholics and the Shoah, The Speeches of Pope John Paul II, Harry James Cargas, and the Cassidy Report, "We Remember"', unpublished paper. Association of Jewish Studies Conference, December 1999.

27 Jacob Neusner. *Telling tales: The Urgency and Basis for Judeo-Christian Dialogue*. (Louisville: Westminster/John Knox Press, 1993), pp 9–10.

28 *ibid.*, p.27.

29 Levinas is cited by Richard A. Cohen, 'Emmanuel Levinas', in *Interpreters of Judaism in the late Twentieth Century*, ed. Steven T. Katz (Washington: B'nai B'rith Books, 1993), p.212.

30 *ibid.*, p.217.

31 Emmanuel Levinas, *Ethics and Infinity*, trans. Richard A. Cohen (Pittsburgh: Duquesne University Press, 1985), p.92.

32 Sandor Goodhart, '*Conscience*, Conscience, Consciousness: Emmanuel Levinas, the Holocaust, and the Logic of Witness', above, pp.98–113.

CHRISTIANITY AND THE INSTITUTIONALIZATION OF ANTI-SEMITISM: A CONTEMPORARY THEOLOGICAL PERSPECTIVE

Donald J. Dietrich

E VER SINCE Christianity and Judaism diverged and began to compete with one another, Christianity has developed and sustained its identity in confrontation with Judaism. As a result of this relationship, the theological teachings of the Christian churches have designated the Jewish people as 'different' and, perhaps, even dangerous to religious and secular interests. Very early in the common era, Jews were assigned a defined place in 'salvation history', and their ultimate conversion was viewed by Christians as validating the ongoing divine superiority of Jesus' message. The alleged involvement of 'the Jewish people' in the death of Jesus with all that such an accusation connotes as well as the so-called 'collective guilt' demanded that Jews in subsequent generations were frequently to be consigned to live in segregated communities and in a demeaned state as punishment for those deeds labelled 'diabolical' by Christians.[1] Fortunately, such a view is now considered antediluvian by most Christians, even though the sources of such perceptions remain living in the texts and traditions of the Christian churches.

For centuries before 1945, Christian antisemitism thrived and was reinforced through religious as well as cultural norms, which ultimately politically matured into the self-fulfilling prophecy that is called the Holocaust or the Shoah. Ironically, even the *philosophes* during the Enlightenment found that they could utilize the traditional Christian defamation of the Jewish people as a weapon useful in the attack on Christianity, an example that the Nazis would subsequently emulate. Modern nationalism, ethnocentrism, and racism, therefore, continued to stress the stateless situation of the Jewish people as well as the 'insider-outsider' distinction earlier nurtured and developed by Christianity. Over the last few decades, scholars have been able to make a compelling case that strong historical continuities have existed between Christian as well as more modern political and racial antisemitism, at least with respect to terminology and images.[2]

The Holocaust has compelled a rethinking of theological-ethical, political, and socialization principles and, thus, of the holistic human condition. Scholarly attempts in disparate areas seem to be converging on common questions, reflections, and values as men and women have tried to analyse the Shoah and have laboured to erect defences against a recurrence. Humanists have tried to re-establish more vigorous conceptions of and increased sensitivity to issues of human dignity. Anxious to prevent a recurrence of such a tragedy, scholars have offered preventative prescriptions rooted in the social sciences. Such social science contributions have attempted to be diagnostic and predictive, and have focused on agents with specific values that have seemed to incite genocide. Two questions quickly emerge. If values are known, what predictions can be made? Social scientists have addressed this question. What can be done theologically to construct or reinforce a value structure that can, at least religiously, safeguard us from sanctioned murder? Theologians have been reflecting on this issue.

Any relevant and comprehensive analysis today has to include theological, political, psychological and social dimensions, if a future disaster of this magnitude is to be averted. Since the Holocaust did occur in what could be termed, at least nominally, a Christian culture that also helped support such beneficent values as human dignity, which developed through two thousand years of European history, the response of post-World War II Christian thinkers and institutions was initially to assess the derailment from as well as the perversion of the original message of Jesus, which focused on love and compassion. They have sought to analyse critically the historical Jewish-Christian relations that developed in order to understand the symbiosis that produced such hatred toward the Jewish people.[3]

Such research has helped clarify Christian normative standards, rooted in historical experiences, which now presumably should be institutionalized in reconfigured theological systems. Ultimately, when faced with such dissonance as 'good' Christians exterminating Jews and creating an environment that supported or permitted the Shoah, theologians have increasingly been finding that they can no longer manipulate information, emotions and attitudes to compel theological consistency.[4] Only by revealing the roots of antisemitism and comprehending politically motivated genocidal evil can there even be a possibility of shaping the future so that such sanctioned evil as the Holocaust will not again occur. The Holocaust itself offers us a horrific event that compels our reflection, so that we can seek ways to help avoid further incidents of sanctioned murder.

II. A few observations from social psychology would probably be useful at this point to help ground how values, attitudes and behavioural activities are formed. A person, for example, in a society that is highly aggressive toward a targeted group has a good chance of inculcating hostile values as part of the socializing process. Moral formation is very intricately connected to our social activities. Psychological research also seems to suggest that persons may exhibit altruistic moral characteristics, but that these can be dissolved when individuals identify with a group which may emphasize serving the interests of its members without moral obligations toward others. A diffusion of authority can typify group activity. Members of a group, therefore, often relinquish authority and control to the group and its leaders.

In such a context, Ervin Staub has analysed what he labels a 'continuum of destruction'.[5] On such a continuum, a person might accept boycotts, then legal changes, then physical assaults, then segregation, and finally extermination. Once a person relinquishes the defence of another's dignity, the slippery slope effect can begin. In some cases, persons abandon themselves to the 'group decision', even if only articulated by an individual, and proceed to develop a commitment that can enable them to sacrifice even their own lives.[6] It would seem, then, that some personal values normally accepted by an individual may not suffice to safeguard a society from group biases and aggression unless the more transcendent nature of personal morality can be recognized. Personal and communitarian morality, the century has shown, do not inhibit violence and may actually accelerate a society into disaster. A morality sensitive to systemic evil may have to counterbalance the varieties of institutional oppression that have assaulted human dignity so vigorously in this century. In response to evidence of brutalizing oppression, scholars have increasingly become interested in understanding how morality develops in a cultural context.

Philosophers and theologians have traditionally claimed to ground their arguments in appeals to actual human experiences in the faith traditions of their religions. These appeals, of course, have tried to go beyond the tangible empirical knowledge of individual cases or the statistically documented studies of human behaviour and attitude formation carried out by social scientists. Religious traditions in large measure rely on the experiences that humans have had of the divine. Philosophers and theologians, therefore, may draw on social science databases as well as historical material, but their efforts usually require them to raise and reflect on questions that are ethical in nature and touch the very core of humanity.

On the theological and philosophical level, facts do not always speak for themselves; nor are they always self-interpreting. Faced with the tragedies of this century, philosophers and theologians have unpacked the Holocaust experience so that its most basic features – structural and normative – can be clarified. Along with social scientists, who have focused on the social, economic and political dynamics that shape behaviour, theologians and philosophers have been seeking to comprehend the values that energized the Holocaust in order to shed light on past experiences and have sought to develop theological and socio-ethical normative principles and methodologies, which can help persons in all religious traditions plumb the depths of the mysteries of God and the human condition. The result of this work over the last two decades may help enable us to form and nurture societies that might help provide a theological environment for authentic human development. In essence, social scientists and theologians have been trying to ground their disciplines in the 'historical event'.

III. Historical reality itself can help provide the critical tool to reveal the deficiencies of a theological hermeneutics. Jürgen Habermas, for example, has critiqued any hermeneutics that interprets a text that has been isolated from its historical environment and severed from the cultural issues that initially nurtured the written reflection. Ignoring the generative historical experience would, he has insisted, eliminate any real possibility for critically challenging the ideological agenda that birthed the text. A critical analysis, sensitive to the dominant ideology, seems requisite for any sociopolitical emancipation from political dominance.[7]

Theory alone, whether political or theological, cannot change the world; such an approach would merely reduce political activity to instrumental manipulation. In fact, as can be seen in this century, theory and ideology have historically tended to become authoritarianism in practice. Theory needs the corrective of praxis, i.e., real world experience. The history of the twentieth century has given warning about any promotion of ideology as *the* system of principles that should be organizing society.[8] Habermas's discussion of political and social theory has informed Christian theologians as well.

In light of the need for a coherent and meaningful theology that is responsive to political repression, Johannes Metz, a German theologian, has used Auschwitz as the reality that has epitomized brutalized repression in this century and has pointedly condemned the antisemitism nurtured by Christianity. He has suggested that Auschwitz might seem religiously unfathomable, if we merely hypothesize that the executioners performed their evil deeds while God apparently remained silent. Metz has insisted that Christian antisemitism was part of the problem. Even more disturbing than the outright murder, in the opinion of Metz, was the compliance of subordinates and the silence of the bystanders as the Jewish people were slaughtered. The Final Solution has compelled theologians to examine critically the moral values embedded in the Christian tradition.

Historical actions can be condemned, but they should also help produce new standards of behaviour. After Auschwitz, Metz has asserted, theologians cannot ignore the defects in Christianity, which helped lead to oppression in the Third Reich. According to Metz, theologians now have to affirm that there is at least one authority (those who suffer) that can never again be rejected. The Holocaust, therefore, is not just another historical fact, nor a subject for arcane research with no moral implications. The event itself has to be used by Christians to create an authentic theology that responds to the victims. With his sensitivity toward historical process, Metz sees the concrete world as the horizon for any consideration of God's creative activity.[9]

Alert to the theological pitfall aimed at saving doctrine not people, Metz has insisted that Christians need to be cautious about which terminology they use and must avoid sweeping comparisons, which might urge any type of intellectual assimilation of Judaism. Attempts to establish any 'theological common ground' between Christians and Jews also should be viewed with suspicion. We have to recall, he has insisted, that the 'common ground' present at the inception of Christianity did not serve to prevent disaster.[10]

Historically, Christians have posited their faith as a theological *Weltanschauung* that has or can provide universal answers. In hindsight they should now see that it really avoided the agonizing questions that should have been posed as the acts of cruelty were committed. For example, Christians have historically viewed human suffering from the perspective of the cross, which allowed them to share discipleship with Jesus as they approached the triumphal Second Coming. The unforeseen consequence of this attitude has been that Christians have historically been insensitive and indifferent to the suffering of others, because in their minds it somehow could only be related to Christ's redemptive mission. Suffering had no atoning power unless it could somehow be connected to the cross, and then it was to be endured. Such an approach is illegitimate, since its premise would be to establish all religious identity on the mission of Jesus Christ and thus drastically reduce the integrity of non-Christian religious traditions. Metz has helped force Catholics to realize that the suffering that Christians inflicted on the Jewish people down through the ages was justified by church leaders, who saw it rooted in the Christian faith in the eschaton. From the perspective of Metz, the relationship between the Christian faith and the world was to be seen as a creative and militant eschatology whose purpose was to induce reform. In fact, the gospel's message should have a political and liberating relation to a person's present and practical life in society.[11] Metz has asked that Christians now rethink the meaning of the human condition, freedom, faith and suffering in light of such historical events as the Holocaust, which have epitomized the capacity of humans to oppress other humans.

Conscious of the betrayal of the intended meaning of Christianity, Metz has tried to construct a political theology that would help support a relentless opposition to any extreme interiorization of a religious mission. This earlier spiritual tradition of interiorization carried with it the danger of the uncritical and all-too-frequent reconciliation of Christianity with the reigning dominant political interest. The political theology that he has proposed argues that it is the non-dialectic interiorizing of doctrine that historically has prompted Christianity to enter into uncritical alliances with morally hostile political regimes. In the past, Christianity has tended to focus solely on its spiritual faith, which has encouraged it to ignore its sociopolitical environment as long as its 'eternal values' were not impacted. One lesson to be learned is that Christianity probably should not model the patterns of power constellations that have enjoyed historical triumphs. Even so, Christianity has to operate in the world of politics. But Christianity should also reflect on its spiritual essence so that it can assume a fundamentally critical stance. To achieve this, Christianity should probably assume a marginal position and never be part of the dominant power complex.[12]

A case could be made that the original Christian faith was to be enacted in the praxis of discipleship, but in practice this has not happened with any degree of frequency. As a cognitive or philosophically permeated faith, Christianity became a part of an institutional superstructure that served its own interests. Christianity became an ideology and not a living discipleship. It supported dominant elite groups, not those which confronted victimization.[13]

Metz has urged changes in theology. Christians should avoid doing a theology that would be unaffected by or neutral toward the barbarities of political oppression. If Christians and Jews hope to construct a relationship that has originated in their root experiences, and they hope that they can both react to the horror of Auschwitz, they should avoid relying on a sense of reconciliation based solely on terminological and conceptual manipulation or on a generalized friendliness that does not grapple with the significant issues that can serve to unite them on some level as well as can serve to maintain their separate integrity on others.

To avoid a superficial reform that verbally obfuscates major divisions, Christian theologians, inspired by Habermas and Metz, have been developing concrete and foundational theologies that can help create a healing Christian consciousness. This theology would recognize that legitimate separations may rest on an act of faith and may simultaneously provoke the realization that the Jewish faith experience, for example, is still living and continues to offer important insights to Christians as they struggle to gain a deeper insight into the mystery that is God. Using such a methodological approach, theology could then be proactive and not defensively exclusivistic. Auschwitz would then be remembered as an event that has had moral and theological repercussions and would not be consigned to the history of humanity as just another tragedy.[14] To move forward, theory and praxis have to be related.

From the perspective of political theology, the meaning of praxis as a technical concept has become crucial as scholars have delved into the implications of such systemic evils as the Holocaust. Gustavo Guitiérrez, for example, has said that in a profound sense praxis is dedicated to seeing the becoming of humanity as a process of emancipation through history. Humanity has a task to create a constantly improving society that works to eliminate servitude and oppression. Humans, then, seem to have an obligation to become the artisans or co-artisans of an authentic humanity. John Pawlikowski has referred to humans and God as the co-creators of the world. A focus on praxis would serve to remind us that theory and action exist in a symbiotic relationship. Theory at its best embodies the subject's orientation toward the object. Praxis represents human action with respect to what is currently done or could be done. In its most complete sense, praxis demands committed involvement, because only morally oriented actions can make persons truly human. Praxis can be seen to encourage intersubjectivity because an individual's interactions will or will not produce authentic persons. Critical theory combined with subject-oriented praxis can help create knowledge and values by in effect 'doing the truth', i.e., implementing values and theory.[15] To be really human, then, theory must be enacted in the world and reconfigured in light of human responses. Given this principle, the dialectical relationship between theory and praxis goes to the very core of what it means to be human.

Both Bernard Lonergan and Johannes Metz have insisted that the learned theological tomes, which call for explicating theology within the traditional ecclesial contexts, are too limiting. In fact, theory by itself has in the past created an evil that has impregnated the social order. After the degrading events of this past century, theologians cannot really advance their enterprise by merely including a reflection on the Holocaust as a supplement to an academic text and thus ignore the basic cognitive corpus that has been part of Christian culture. Only authentic religious, moral, and social praxis, in which theory responds to the concrete world, can provide an adequate foundation for doing theology and so help prevent future genocidal policies and sanctioned murder.[16]

This transcendental and subjective focus in contemporary theological treatments discloses that humans work out their salvation in God's presence and so virtually demands a transformative function for theology. Such a theological enterprise could help support persons and help them become attentive, responsible, and loving subjects, who as people of faith, can respond to their historical and social experiences. Their presence and relationship to God should help summon these people of faith to be responsible humans. Such social sins as racism or antisemitism as well as political and economic structural oppression cannot be confronted simply with pious ideals devoid of any driving force for their application. To consider critically social or systemic evils, therefore, would seem to require conversion to a social and political praxis rooted in God-centredness. For Christians, such theocentric anthroprocentrism would respond to the needs that the Holocaust has inserted into our culture.[17]

Praxis as just the implementation of theory into concrete activity has generally been labelled technique. Praxis is not merely 'putting faith into practice' or making Christianity relevant. Rather, praxis is delineated as reflective, dialectical, and intentionally transformative. Christ's own constructively conflictual responses to his culture should help suggest that praxis at its best is a critique of the prevailing society and culture. Within its specific social context, liberating praxis has as its goal the commitment to and solidarity with others. Liberation and political theologies are today being asked to address the personal, social and economic evils in the world while they stimulate a praxis of liberating transformation that can then address the restatement of an authentic theology. Authentic praxis, therefore, should change both society and the person, because truth can only be recovered in the very experience of furthering social liberation. Such theologians as Metz, Lonergan and Karl Rahner have argued for a social dynamism that has not previously characterized Catholic theology.

IV. Changing the way persons think is generally the necessary prelude to changing the way they act. If Christian antisemitism led to contempt, then it is important to revise theology and the values that it sustains. Such a process can also show us how to deal with other phenomena of xenophobia and ethnocentrism. In light of the potential for brutalization, such a journey is mandated because religious symbols and doctrines can and do inform political and ethical reflection. Knowing what values are crucial to sustain the human person and understanding how evil values can be expunged ought to give us clues for institutionalizing the normative moral values that can form the foundation for a society that allows men and women to develop their full potential. Some very recent creative theological initiatives rely at least implicitly on the theory-praxis model that is sensitive to historical events and human dignity.

In the incarnational viewpoint of the theologian John Pawlikowski, Christians have to realize a responsibility for the shaping of human culture and also have to insist that this freedom to be conditioned by the healing and affirming power of God, who remains a direct source of strength and who influences the conduct of human affairs, is necessary as well.[18] Such a theological anthropology can offer healing to the atomistic culture of modernity that has given birth to the self-referent morality responsible for the Holocaust.

The presence of Jesus Christ in human history should exemplify for Christians the union of God and humanity and their respective roles as co-creators of history. To confront properly the cultural dissonance that contributes to the feeling of isolation among individuals as well as their self-referential freedom, the Incarnation in the Christian tradition deemphasizes the exclusionary. To insist that any part of the Jesus-Event is a completely self-sufficient, self-sustaining root-experience that has no need to be complemented by supportive traditions from other faith experiences would help to perpetuate the 'traditional Christian supercessionism'. A fundamental mistake of past Christologies, Pawlikowski feels, has been to consider their unique perspective as exclusive and universal; such hubris has made the tragedy of the Holocaust possible.[19] The Incarnation, however, offers a resolution to the fragmentation and isolation inherent in modern society as well as a remedy for traditional Christian exclusivism, since the intimate relationship between God and humans, at least biblically, can be viewed as a shared thread of the common Judeo-Christian experience. The Incarnation stresses a communal salvation with God, who is engaged with creation, and reflects the Genesis experience where God and creation were in an interactive relationship. The path to such fullness in life viewed from the Christian perspective also resonates with the sense of salvation in and through the feeling of community, which was central to the covenantal faith of Judaism.

The Incarnation can best be understood in contemporary Christian theology, only if the Jewish tradition of community is kept in mind. In union with God through Jesus, Christians can feel that humans are able to achieve freedom and responsibility for the creation of history. Through this freedom they can work toward the elevation of all humanity toward a unity of God and creature. The current studies of the Holocaust and our reflection on the unfortunate results of adhering to the individualistic modern perspective should encourage Christians to look to the Jewish ideal of communal faith that can help overcome the tendency to any false privatization of religious or moral values.[20]

Pawlikowski, for example, has maintained that the sense of the human person as a co-creator with God definitely has its roots in the Jewish covenantal tradition. The volatile nature of history in this past century seems to suggest that the early claim of Christianity that Jesus had completed the salvation of humanity has to be rejected. The reappropriation of the Jewish co-creatorship notion within the Christian tradition and a sensitivity to the proactive meaning of the Incarnation seem critical for Christians who oppose the religious triumphalism that has wreaked such havoc on the Jewish people. The salvation of humankind can now be seen as a task yet to be accomplished. Thus, the Jesus-Event did not complete, but only helped further, the process. The premature claims of Christianity that the messianic kingdom had fully arrived in Jesus or would shortly come through him hindered Christians from accepting any type of ongoing and inclusivistic responsibility directed toward the entire human community. Instead, they formulated the disastrous triumphalistic doctrines that have wreaked such havoc in our history. Sensitive to the religious meaning of the Holocaust, many theologians have been trying to discard simplistic notions of fulfillment and have assiduously been searching for a model based on the Jesus-Event, which can provide a legitimate basis for dialogue as well as for the elimination of any improper notion of self-referential morality. Moral values, many feel, should be rooted in the historical interaction of God and humanity. For Christians, the Incarnation can provide a theological tool that opposes an atomistic view of humanity and that fastens onto a communal approach that can be useful in constructing a morality with transcendent roots, which will highlight the Jewish-Christian concept of co-creation.[21]

Such theologians as Karl Rahner and John Pawlikowski have developed a viable incarnational theology of witness that can help stress the intimate connection between God and humanity in society, since in their opinion the life of Jesus in history is as meaningful as his death and resurrection.[22] Helping to understand this union of God and humanity in Jesus was his own historical life of witness, which can help prepare Christians to realize that a really meaningful Christology has to be rooted in a theological anthropology that can lead humanity to a solidarity with marginalized victims as humans join with God in an unceasing act of co-creation.

V. The notion of co-creation should help deepen the dialogue between Christians and Jews around several issues. Incarnational theology offers a vantage point for Christians, which may be useful, but it does not provide a complete response. In fact, Incarnational theology may provide only a beginning, albeit an important step, that will have to be nuanced as we reflect on the connections between Christians and Jews from the very beginning. At the most fundamental level of theology rooted in the Hebrew Bible and Christian Scriptures, Christians need to emphasize God more than they have and to see Jesus Christ as saviour within the context of God's relationship to all humanity. Christians too frequently centre everything on Jesus to the detriment of the God who sent him, guided him, and sustained him. Jesus subordinated himself to God's will to rule, conserve, and care for humanity. The rule of God and his kingdom should help shape current theological reflection. In essence, God rules over, loves, and cares for Israel, the Church, and all nations.[23]

From this perspective, Jews and Christians can be seen as attached to the same God. For Christians, the corollary to God's love for Israel is clear: what Jesus Christ did as well as what Jesus Christ is in his Church today takes place in some fashion within Israel. Christians can see this in the life of Jesus, a Jew, in the history of the early combined Jewish and Christian communities, and in the deeply Jewish roots of the Christian tradition. The Israel that nourishes the Christian Church and that co-exists with it is not some conceptual abstraction, but the living community of Jews, with whom Christians still live in a permanent relationship. The Sinai Covenant and the Incarnation are crucial for both traditions and are rooted in discrete experiences of the same God. The historically conditioned separation of the two traditions, however, has meant that Christianity has in some way relinquished part of its own heritage and meaning.[24] The goal of Christian theology, therefore, no matter which route it takes, should be to seek its origins in the Jewish tradition and to critique its subsequent development from the perspective of the Christ-Event that occurred in Israel as part of Jewish history, at least before the cleavage opened between the two traditions. The Jewish identity of Jesus somehow has to bear on such Christian doctrines as the Incarnation and redemption. Developing the meaning of Christianity's Jewish roots has not been completed.

The co-creation and theory/praxis models currently being discussed among Catholic theologians really have to advance one more step in order to ensure that Christian theologians remember that the Christ-Event took place in a Jewish community and was nurtured in that culture. When this happens, Christian insights about Jews and Jewish insights about Christians can then begin constructively to help develop more fruitful ideas about religious pluralism and the fact that God's revelation has been communicated in a variety of ways.[25] At that point, theologians can tentatively construct a foundational and comprehensive theological methodology that can help them more aggressively address the issues raised by the Holocaust. A Christianity that developed its identity through antisemitism now has to seek nourishment from its Jewish origins.

NOTES

1 Helen Fein, *Accounting for Genocide: National Responses and Jewish Victimization during the Holocaust* (New York: Free Press, 1979), p.4. For the relations between Jewish communities and the early Christians, see John Gager, *The Origins of Anti-Semitism. The Attitudes Toward Judaism in Pagan and Christian Antiquity* (New York: Oxford University Press, 1983); Alan Segal, *Rebecca's Children: Judaism and Christianity in the Roman World* (Cambridge: Harvard University Press, 1986); Randolph Braham (ed.), *The Origins of the Holocaust: Christian Anti-Semitism* (New York: Columbia University Press, 1986); James H. Charlesworth, *Jesus within Judaism. New Light from Exciting Archaeological Discoveries* (New York: Doubleday, 1988); Franz Mussner, *Tractate on the Jews: The Significance of Judaism for Christian Faith* (Philadelphia: Fortress Press, 1984); Edward H. Flannery, *The Anguish of the Jews: Twenty-Three Centuries of Anti-Semitism* (New York: Paulist Press, 1985), p.33. Flannery has candidly acknowledged that the New Testament reflected an anti-Judaic theology and anti-Jewish pronouncements, prophetic in nature, which made it into a seedbed of antisemitism; see also Herbert Strauss, ed., *Der Antisemitismus der Gegenwart* (Frankfurt: Campus Verlag, 1990); Frank Manuel, *The Broken Staff: Judaism Through Christian Eyes* (Cambridge: Harvard University Press, 1992).

2 Jacob Katz, *Out of the Ghetto: The Social Background of Jewish Emancipation: 1770–1870* (Cambridge: Harvard University Press, 1973), pp.57–79; Uriel Tal, *Christians and Jews in Germany: Religion, Politics, and Ideology in the Second Reich, 1870–1914* (Ithaca: Cornell University Press, 1975); John Pawlikowski, 'Christian Ethics and the Holocaust: A Dialogue with Post-Auschwitz Judaism', *Theological Studies* 49 (1988): 649–70.

3 For a comprehensive analysis of the relationships among religious/racial antisemitism, social science contributions that aid in understanding the Shoah, and current theological reflections on these issues, see Donald J. Dietrich, *God and Humanity in Auschwitz: Jewish-Christian Relations and Sanctioned Murder* (New Brunswick: Transaction Publishers, 1995).

4 Ervin Staub, *Positive Social Behavior and Morality*, vol.1, *Social and Personal Influences*, vol.2, *Socialization and Development* (New York: Academic Press, 1978–79); Emil Fackenheim, *The Jewish Return into History: Reflection in the Age of Auschwitz and a New Jerusalem* (New York: Schocken Books, 1978), p.279; Emil Fackenheim, *God's Presence in History. Jewish Affirmation and Philosophical Reflections* (New York: New York University Press, 1970), pp.84–92; Amos Funkenstein, 'Theological Interpretations of the Holocaust: A Balance', in Francois Furet (ed.), *Unanswered Questions: Nazi Germany and the Genocide of the Jews* (New York: Schocken Books, 1989), p.302; Richard Rubenstein, *The Age of Triage: Fear and Hope in an Overcrowded World* (Boston: Beacon Press, 1983), p.131; Leon Festinger, *A Theory of Cognitive Dissonance* (Stanford: Stanford University Press, 1957), p.3. For two provocative works that have begun to connect the research insights produced by theologians and social scientists, see Darrell J. Fasching, *Narrative Theology after Auschwitz: From Alienation to Ethics* (Minneapolis: Fortress Press, 1992) and Christine Gudorf, *Victimization: Examining Christian Complicity* (Philadelphia: Trinity Press International, 1992). For a study of the socio-political and cultural foundation needed for the Holocaust, see Zygmunt Bauman, *Modernity and the Holocaust* (Ithaca, NY: Cornell University Press, 1989). For an older review of the literature, see Michael Marrus, *The Holocaust in History* (Hanover: University Press of New England, 1987). To keep current with research on the Holocaust, see the journal *Holocaust and Genocide Studies*. See Helen Fein, Introduction to *Genocide Watch*, ed. Helen Fein (New Haven: Yale University Press, 1992) for an analysis of the difficulties in defining genocide.

5 Erwin Staub, *The Roots of Evil: The Origin of Genocide and Other Group Violence* (Cambridge: Cambridge University Press, 1989), pp.17, 24, ch. 4.

6 M.A. Wallach, et al, 'Group Influences on Individual Risk Taking', *Journal of Abnormal and Social Psychology* 65 (1962): 75–86; B. Latane and J.M. Darley, *The Unresponsive Bystander: Why Doesn't He Help?* (New York: Appleton-Century-Crofts, 1970); D.T. Campbell, 'Ethnocentric and Other Altruistic Motives,' in David Levine (ed.), *Nebrasksa Symposium on Motivation* (Lincoln: University of Nebraska Press, 1966).

7 D. Misgeld, 'Critical Theory and Hermeneutics: The Debate between Habermas and Gadamer', in John O'Neill (ed.), *On Critical Theory* (New York: Seabury Press, 1976).

8   Richard J. Bernstein, *The Restructuring of Social and Political Theory* (New York: Harcourt Brace Jovanovich, 1976), p.217; J. Hellesness, 'Education and the Concept of Critique', *Continuum* 1970: 40.

9   Johannes Metz, *The Emergent Church: The Future of Christianity in a Post-Bourgeois World* (New York: Crossroad, 1981), p.18. A great deal of revisionist historical literature can be found in *The Journal of Historical Review*. For an analytical survey of some revisionist issues, see Deborah Lipstadt, 'Deniers, Relativists, and Pseudo-Scholarship,' *Dimensions* 6 (1991): 4–9; Johannes Metz, *Theology of the World* (London: Burns & Oates, 1969), pp.21–22, 128–29.

10   Metz, *The Emergent Church*, 22.

11   Ibid., 23–24; Metz, *Theology of the World*, pp.91, 95.

12   Metz, *The Emergent Church*, 27; Charles Davis, *Theology and Political Society* (Cambridge: Cambridge University Press, 1980); Dermot Lane, *Foundations for a Social Theology: Praxis, Process and Salvation* (New York: Paulist Press, 1984).

13   Johannes Metz, 'Political Theology of the Subject as a Theological Criticism of Middle Class Religion', in Johannes Metz (ed.), *Faith in History and Society: Toward a Practical Fundamental Theology* (New York: Seabury Press, 1980), pp.32–48; Johannes Metz (ed.), *Christianity and the Bourgeoisie* (New York: Seabury Press, 1979).

14   Metz, *The Emergent Church*, pp.28, 30, 32; Max Horkheimer and Theodor Adorno, 'Elements of Anti-Semitism: Limits of the Enlightenment', *Continuum* (1975): 168–208.

15   Gustavo Gutiérrez, *A Theology of Liberation: History, Politics and Salvation* (Maryknoll, NY: Orbis Books, 1973), p.88; Jürgen Habermas, *Theory and Practice* (Boston: Beacon Press, 1973), pp.253–82; Jürgen Habermas, *Knowledge and Human Interests* (Boston: Beacon Press, 1971), pp.301–17; Bernard Lonergan, *Method in Theology*, (New York: Herder and Herder, 1972), pp.265–92; John Pawlikowski, 'Christian Ethics and the Holocaust: A Dialogue with Post-Auschwitz Judaism', *Theological Studies* 49 (1988): 651, 653, 656–657, 661–667.

16   Lonergan, *Method in Theology*, pp.24, 125–45, 332, 355–368; Johannes Metz, and Trutz Rendtorff (eds.), *Die Theologie in der Interdisziplinären Forschung* (Düsseldorf: Bertelsmann Universitäts-Verlag, 1971); Bernard Lonergan, 'The Ongoing Genesis of Methods', *Studies in Religion* 6/4 (1977): 341, 351; Matthew Lamb, *Solidarity with Victims: Toward a Theology of Social Transformation* (New York: Crossroad Press, 1982), p.84.

17   Lamb, *Solidarity with Victims*: pp.120–121. For a study of compassion, see Karl Morrison, '*I Am You': The Hermeneutics of Empathy in Western Literature, Theology, and Art* (Princeton: Princeton University Press, 1988).

18   John Pawlikowski, 'Toward a Theology for Religious Diversity: Perspective from the Christian-Jewish Dialogue', *Journal of Ecumenical Studies* 26 (1989): 145–146.

19   John Pawlikowski, *Jesus and the Theology of Israel* (Wilmington: Michael Galzier, Inc., 1989), p.88; Dietrich, *God and Humanity*, pp.159–198.

20   Pawlikowski, *Jesus and the Theology of Israel*, pp.89–91.

21   Dietrich, *God and Humanity*, pp.115–124, 187–198.

22   Metz, *The Emergent Church*; pp.18–27; David Tracy, 'God of History, God of Psychology', in Hermann Häring and Johannes Metz (eds.), *Reincarnation or Resurrection* (London: SCM Press, 1993), pp.102–111; Elisabeth Schüssler-Fiorenza and David Tracy (eds.), *The Holocaust as Interruption* (Edinburgh: T. & T. Clark, 1984).

23   See Anthony Saldarini, 'Christian Anti-Judaism: The First Century Speaks to the Twenty-First Century', paper presented at the Joseph Cardinal Bernardin Jerusalem Lecture, Chicago, IL, 14 April 1999.

24   John Pawlikowski, 'Vatican II on the Jews: A Dramatic Example of Theological Development', paper presented to the 1999 Convention of the Catholic Theological Society of America, Miami, Florida, 12 June 1999; Carlo Maria Cardinal Martini, 'Christianity and Judaism: A Historical and Theological Overview', in James H. Charlesworth, *Jews and Christians: Exploring the Past, Present and Future* (New York: Crossroad, 1990), p.19.

25   *Conference Proceedings: Examination of Conscience: Polish Church Confronts Anti-Semitism, 1989–99*, ed. Boddan W. Oppenheim (Loyola Marymount University, Los Angeles, 20 January 1999), p.81.

READING THE BIBLE AFTER AUSCHWITZ

Jacques B. Doukhan

C AN WE still read the Bible after Auschwitz?[1] The very fact that the event took place in the heart of the most biblically literate country of the world, a country where the reading of the Bible was promoted for the first time in history in Christian civilization, a country with the largest quota of biblical scholars, and a country with the most developed biblical scholarship, justifies this arrogant question.[2] That the Holocaust was produced in a civilization characterized by an intense reading of the Bible may suggest, indeed, that the reading of the Bible played some role in the origination of the event. And this observation leads to a subsequent question even more troubling than the first: why did the reading of the Bible lead to Auschwitz? It will not be easy to answer this question. Is it because of what the Bible is, or what it says, or is it because of the way it was perceived, (mis)understood and (mis)applied? Whatever answer one is tempted to offer to that question, the fact remains that the reading of the Bible appears to be a significant factor in the production of Auschwitz. And if reading the Bible had an impact on Auschwitz, then Auschwitz should have an impact on the reading of the Bible. Even if the reading of the Bible had no effect on Auschwitz, the 'unique' nature of the event,[3] and the magnitude of the crime, would affect the reading of the Bible. For after Auschwitz, nothing can be the same, including the reading of the Bible. Indeed, for the first time since the Inquisition and Voltaire, the traditional reference to the Bible has once again been shaken. Expressions used to describe the impact of the Holocaust, such as 'new Revelation'[4] or 'new Sinai',[5] implicitly bear witness to the force of the Holocaust in relation to the Bible. This revolution has taken place not only in secular circles, where the Bible was already discarded and barely read, but also among the theologians and religious thinkers, where a new Bible criticism and a new hermeneutic has emerged out of Holocaust awareness.

In the wake of these recent currents of Jewish and Christian post-Holocaust theology,[6] this paper will expose and explore the main features of this 'new awareness' as it has affected or as it should affect the way we read the Scriptures; namely,

(1) the way we receive the Scriptures, our view of the authority of Scripture;
(2) the way we interpret the Scriptures, our principles of hermeneutic;
(3) the way we move within the Scriptures, our post-Holocaust selections of the Bible.

I. AUTHORITY OF SCRIPTURE

After Auschwitz, the Bible has lost its authority.

I. SHARED AUTHORITY

Certainly one of the most significant effects of the Holocaust in the Church has been the reconsideration of 'how the authority of the New Testament is to be understood in relation to that of the Old Testament'.[7] The old Marcionite idea that the New Testament had replaced the Old Testament as Holy Scriptures[8] – and by implication the teaching of supersessionist theologies[9] – has been denounced as perhaps the most important determining factor in the teaching of anti-Semitism which ultimately led to Auschwitz. For it contained the spiritual germs of what later became the physical Holocaust.[10] The process was twofold. It was first a process of ecclesiological and political capitalizing on the idea that the Church replaced Israel. This way of thinking, which predominated in Catholicism, was not expressed only in religious and liturgical terms. It was often accompanied by violent actions. Synagogues were destroyed and 'replaced' by churches, while the Crusades were based on the claim that the Holy Land belonged to the Church. The process was also theological, especially in Protestantism, where it revolved around the theology of Salvation versus Creation, and the teaching that the Christian freedom of grace and love had replaced the Jewish burden of Torah. This emphasis on Salvation (grace, love, spirit) at the expense of Creation (law, justice, flesh) often implied that the abstract principle, the ethereal truth of the Spirit was more important than concrete life and real people – a set of values that has also often been advocated in fascist ideologies (in the camps, Nazis with advanced academic degrees and even doctors of medicine often showed more sensitivity towards music and art and great spiritual ideals than to the physical fate of the inmates). Indeed, Auschwitz, as the ultimate outcome of this Marcionite influence, warns us against the latter as the effect warns us against its cause. As James A. Sanders puts it: 'Christianity has become so systematically Marcionite and anti-Semitic that only a truly radical revival of the concept of canon as applied to the Bible will, I think, counter it.'[11]

Christian theologians who have become aware of the lethal nature of the Marcionite impact have suggested a number of solutions to counter it. One of 'the most radical proposals'[12] was offered by systematic theologian Paul Van Buren,[13] who reacted against the traditional current in Christianity that rejected the Old Testament, and who emphasized instead the authority of the Old Testament, the only Holy Scriptures, over and against that of the New Testament, 'the Apostolic Writings'. His thesis was mainly based on the argument that the Old Testament was the original Bible of the early Christians and as such deserved more attention, more reverence. Christian and Jewish scholars have criticized Van Buren's proposal from various perspectives.[14] But in spite of all the flaws which may be pointed out in Van Buren's proposal, this position is a symptom that shows new moves in Christian circles.[15] And if Sanders is right in his prognostic that 'only a truly radical revival' will counter the Marcionite trend that ultimately produced the Holocaust, the lesson of history should be to go back before the Marcionite disruption-when the early Christians did not yet oppose the two documents,[16] when they called the Old Testament with the technical Jewish term *graphai*[17] (from the Hebrew *ketubim*, Scriptures) then used in Jewish circles,[18] and considered the New Testament writings as a mere addition to 'the rest of the Scriptures' (2 Pet 3:15–16).

After Auschwitz, the Christian reading of the Bible should aim at recovering the reverence the early Christians entertained towards the Old Testament Scriptures. This new discovery would bring Christians next to the Jews in the same appreciation for their common heritage. As the Old Testament will receive the same authority as the New Testament, in theology but also in liturgy and in daily worship, its word will finally be taken seriously by Christians and will ultimately affect their mentalities: the values of Creation and life will be raised to the same status as Salvation and the spiritual truths; the reference to the Torah's justice and ethics will weigh as heavily as the reference to grace and love. Christians will then indeed work and push against the currents that promoted the Holocaust.

2. CHALLENGED AUTHORITY

Yet even if the ideal balance is restored, even if the Christians agree to recognize the authority of the Old Testament and abandon traditional supersessionist intentions, the problem of the authority of Scripture after the Holocaust remains as serious as ever. Apart from the Holocaust, the authority of Scripture had already been shaken. As Williamson notes, 'the collapse of authoritarian ways of doing theology in the modern and post-modern eras in itself poses the question of whether scripture can any longer be regarded as authoritative, and if so how and in what sense'.[19] Now after Auschwitz, the authority of Scripture has been questioned for one more reason: for what the Scriptures may say that does not make sense or is incompatible with what we learned from Auschwitz.[20]

For many Christians and Jews, the Holocaust has become an important factor in their religious reflection and more particularly in their approach to the Scriptures. Yet, because of the different nature of their respective Scriptures, and also because of their different rapport with the Holocaust, Christians and Jews do not address the question of the authority of the Scriptures in the same terms.

For Christians, the question of the authority of Scripture is essentially concerned with the *adversus Judaeos* mode of reading the biblical texts, whether it applies to the issue of the relation between the Old Testament and the New Testament (see above), or to the meaning of a particular text.[21]

For Jews on the other hand, the question is rather of an existential nature. Emil Fackenheim's reflections on that matter are characteristic: 'After the Holocaust, Jews cannot read, as once they did, of a God who sleeps not and slumbers not; ... So enormous are the events of recent Jewish history ... that the Jewish Bible must be ... struggled with, if necessary fought against.'[22] The key words are 'struggled with' and 'fought against'. Fackenheim does not provide any exegetical solution to the problem he encounters in the Scriptures, nor does he reject the authority of the Scriptures. His proposal is a struggle with, a fight against, with no compromise on his part. The text is accepted as it is, 'a naked text', and the Jews come to the text as they are, 'naked'. The approach proposed by Fackenheim is therefore to challenge and to question the biblical text, to struggle with it and even to fight against it. At that stage, Jews and Christians stand together with the same passion to understand, and the same duty to interpret in the raw light of Auschwitz. For both Jews and Christians, the question of the authority of Scripture stumbles then on the meaning of the biblical text and is ultimately a hermeneutic problem.

II. HERMENEUTICS

After Auschwitz, the 'truth' has lost its innocence.

We have learned from that event that the reading of the Bible can be dangerous, and the Bible can be misunderstood; or worse, it can be misused. The exegetical assignments of searching and interpreting the divine 'truth' perceived in the biblical text should therefore proceed under the control of the data taken from without, namely, the value of life and ethics, and the meaning of the text in its actual application; and from within, namely, the testimony of alternate biblical texts, and to the 'other' side of the biblical text itself which may carry an ambiguous meaning.

I. ETHICAL CONTROL

After Auschwitz, any biblical interpretation that would promote or even imply hatred, discrimination, or superiority of one group over another is suspect.[23] The way many churches have used the Bible to maintain African-Americans as slaves or as second-class citizens, to hold women in subjection to men, or to mark the Jew as rejected by God urges for a 'return to Scriptures'[24] to be reread and reinterpreted. And this return to the text should be monitored by the awareness of this potential abuse or distortion. In other words, the hermeneutical assignment should be conducted in close and permanent contact with the acute consciousness of ethics and the value of life.[25]

This hermeneutic principle is in fact implied in the rabbinic doctrine of *pikuah nefesh*, the sacred duty to preserve life that should take precedence over and even annul all other laws. The rabbis[26] established this principle on the basis of the verse 'You shall therefore keep My statutes and My judgments, which if a man does, he shall live by them: I am the Lord' (Leviticus 18:5). The idea is that man shall 'live' by these commandments, by the word of God, and not die as a result of observing them. In the New Testament, Jesus seemed to have referred to the same principle when he stated that 'The Sabbath was made for man, and not man for the Sabbath' (Mark 2:27). When human dignity and life are at stake in our interpretation of the Word of God, such a reading is suspect and should therefore be reevaluated.

This hermeneutic principle does not suggest that the human measure should control and govern the divine word; it simply intimates that the actual fruit of a methodology in its concrete human application has something to say in regard to the quality or the adequacy of that methodology. To be sure, the need for this hermeneutic principle goes beyond the issues directly related to the Holocaust. It may apply to issues such as parental abuse, health risks, sexual or civil misconduct, etc. – indeed all ethical misbehaviour which has been or might be supported by a biblical reference.

2. THE RELATION OF MEANINGS

The return to the biblical text implies first of all the duty to reexamine what it meant then and compare it with what it would mean now,[27] after Auschwitz, that is, in the light of its potential damage. The most obvious and perhaps the most important case concerns the prophetic denunciations of Israel (e.g., Jonah, Amos, Matthew, Revelation, etc.) which have often 'been taken up, literalised, and used to demonize this community'.[28] These denunciations have been carried by Jews but also preserved by Jews who elevated them to the status of Holy Scriptures; this wonder should be seriously taken into consideration as one prepares to reinterpret these denunciations today. That these prophetic words once 'meant' denunciations against Israel does not necessarily mean that they are still relevant against the Jews today. Also, the fact that they were given in specific contexts and by specific spokesmen, the prophets, should prevent us, biblical interpreters who are outside the dispute, from using the same prophetic denunciations even against the Israel of that time. Furthermore, the fact that those who carried the denunciations as well as those who preserved these denunciations are Jews themselves constitutes an ironical warning against those who are prone to present a negative picture of the Jews (in general, including the Jews of that time) on the basis of these denunciations. It would be inappropriate if not ridiculous for an outsider to denounce those who denounce themselves. And today, after

Auschwitz, this argument carries even more weight than the argument of a mere intellectual or homiletic reference to a family dispute.

Does this mean that we are now forbidden to read these texts and to understand them as denunciations of Israel? Certainly not. They have been preserved for that very purpose. But as we read them and theologize about them we should bear in mind that these texts have been used and exploited for anti-Semitic purposes. The memory of Auschwitz being the direct consequence of these biblical manipulations therefore serves as a control to orient and keep our interpretation within a safe path.

A similar case could be presented on the usage of the word 'Jews' in the gospel of John. The same methodology applies here. The return to the Scriptures requires first a research about the meaning of the word 'Jew' in the historical, theological, and geographical context of that time. Second, about what it meant for John, who used it in his writings. Then, whatever conclusion we may reach – whether it was a mere geographical term to distinguish the Judaens from the Galileans,[29] or a *terminus technicus* to designate the Jewish leaders in their opposition to Jesus,[30] or even some sort of *vaticinium ex eventu*, a meaning projected a posteriori from a later situation[31] – it is important to evaluate to what extent this interpretation of 'what it meant' does not convey a reading leading to Auschwitz.

3. THE CANONICAL WORD

The return to the Scriptures should aim also at searching alternate biblical passages, which will help to nuance the suspect passage or to discuss it under the control of 'canonical' hermeneutics or criticism.[32] For instance, passages suggesting the rejection of Israel (Romans 9–10) should be treated in tension with other passages supporting on the contrary 'the affirmation of Israel' (Romans 11). The two hermeneutic axioms as defined by James A. Sanders, namely, the 'prophetic' and the 'constitutive',[33] illuminate his view of the canonical process and are pertinent to our discussion.[34] The 'prophetic axiom' stresses universalism, teaching that God is the God of all, and the 'constitutive axiom' stresses particularism, teaching that God is the personal God of Israel. Each voice testifies to the same grace of God. At times, the prophetic mode is heard and Israel is reminded of God's interest for Egypt and Assyria (Isaiah 19:25); at other times, the constitutive mode is sounded and Israel is called the first among the other nations (Exodus 4:22, Jeremiah 31:9). The same hermeneutic modes can be used when we read exclusivist 'constitutive' passages of the Scriptures, such as 'No one comes to the Father except through Me' (John 14:6) or 'Nor is there salvation in any other, for there is no other name under heaven given among men by which we must be saved' (Acts 4:12), and when we balance them with universal 'prophetic' passages, such as 'Other sheep I have which are not of this fold' (John 10:16) or 'How then shall they call on Him in whom they have not believed? And how shall they believe in Him of whom they have not heard?' (Romans 10:14). This principle may even apply to larger sections of the Scriptures. The retributive theology of the book of Deuteronomy[35] or of the book of Proverbs[36] or, within the book of Job, of the three friends, should be challenged by the questions of Job himself (9:22–24), or Ecclesiastes (8:14; 7:15; 9:11–12, etc.). To be sure, this reading of the Scriptures in canonical context is not easy or comfortable, because it does not provide us with a quick, clear, and well-settled interpretation but rather leaves us with an unresolved tension or a very complex idea. One of the lessons of this tension is that we cannot, we should not, reach a 'final' conclusion on the basis of only one passage. To make a sound judgment one should always be ready to hear and take into consideration also the opposite party (Proverbs 8:14). The 'other' passage annihilates our suspect text or puts it in a new perspective; and as a result, the suspect text will hardly be able to survive as such.

4. THE AMBIGUOUS WORD

The return to the Scriptures implies also to be attentive to the 'other' side of the suspect text itself; for the biblical text is often ambiguous.[37] The text which carries a meaning 'against' the Jews may well hide another meaning which would instead testify on their behalf. A classic example of this 'double entendre' is the text which reports on the curse the Jews called upon themselves in the Praetorium: 'His blood be on us and on our children' (Matthew 27:25). From this text it has often been concluded that the Jews alone are guilty of the death of Jesus, for they all wished vengeance upon themselves. 'There may be no more fateful verse for the history of Jewish-Christian relations in the entire Bible than this one'.[38] This particular text has, indeed, often been used to justify Christian anti-Semitism and persecution down through the centuries; and as such, it is a suspect text. The immediate historical interpretation of the text ('what it meant') should first take into consideration a number of specific data provided by the context:[39] (1) those who are demanding Jesus' death are in fact the Jewish leaders and not the people; (2) these Jewish leaders are not representative of the people; (3) according to the gospel stories, the majority of the Jews were on the side of Jesus; (4) Jesus had forgiven those who demanded his death (Luke 23:34); and 5) the place of the event, the courtyard of the Praetorium, allowed only a limited number of people to attend. To these 'direct' interpretations which may still contain the idea of the Jewish responsibility should be added the perspective of the ambiguity of the statement on the 'blood of Jesus'. Indeed, the New Testament idea of the blood of Christ does not convey the idea of 'curse' or condemnation but is rather associated with the idea of salvation.[40] It is, therefore, possible that the text carries here a double entendre;[41] for the idea of the blood of Jesus upon the Jews may also have a redemptive sense.[42]

The need for ambiguity in regards to the Holocaust can also be illustrated by the ambiguous words of Job 13:15. The double entendre is here rendered through the testimony of the *qere/Ketiv* traditions. If we accept the Masoretic vocalization of the *qere*[43] (*lo'eyael*) we understand that Job has hope 'though He slay me, yet will I trust Him' (NKJV). If on the other hand we follow the consonantal text of the *Ketiv* (*lo'eyael*) like many modern interpreters,[44] we understand that Job does not have hope: 'See, he will kill me; I have no hope' (NRSV).

It is noteworthy that a passage of the Mishnah has assumed the ambiguous meaning of the biblical text and recognized that both renderings were possible: 'The matter is undecided – Do I trust in Him or not trust?' (*Sotah* 5:5). According to André Neher, 'in this verse...Job pronounces two words which signify *simultaneously* hope and hopelessness...*I hope in Him*, he shouts, but also do not hope in Him.'[45] This contradiction is meaningful as it expresses the tension of the one who is crushed and torn between his hopes and doubts, his faith and his revolt, the very tension that would inhabit any religious thinking about the event of the Holocaust.[46] The dilemma of biblical interpretation after Auschwitz has forced us to realize that the immediate, explicit, and plain meaning of the text is not the final stage of its interpretation. The Holocaust point of view has urged us to return to the text and search it until a safe and yet biblical meaning is ensured. This approach may be suspected to bring foreign and therefore unacceptable paradigms into the process of interpretation – unless we find in the biblical document texts that witness to similar concerns and sensitivities as those found in the Holocaust experience and reflection.

III. POST-HOLOCAUST SELECTIONS

After Auschwitz, the biblical texts have lost their muteness.

Post-Holocaust thinkers and Bible interpreters are paying more attention and are referring more often to biblical texts which were until now generally neglected. These new texts suddenly respond to their concerns and sensitivities; they speak to them. These new concentrations include the following:

1. THE *AKEDAH*

The 'binding of Isaac' (Genesis 22:1–19) is perhaps the most important post-Holocaust biblical reference. Although they differ in interpreting the connection between the *Akedah* and the Nazi Holocaust, Jewish and Christian writers agree in viewing the Holocaust as some kind of re-enactment of the *Akedah* and the *Akedah* as a prefiguration of the Holocaust. The connection is somewhat controversial, for the Jews did not offer themselves freely like Isaac and the sacrificer was not obeying God and a loving father like Abraham but an enemy of God who was full of hatred. Also, the Nazi destruction is not a religious act as the Holocaust of the *Akedah*. Yet, the reference to the *Akedah* knows a long history in Jewish tradition. Already in the Middle Ages, against the background of the massacres, the crusades and the stakes, the reference to the *Akedah* had produced a literary genre among the penitential hymns (*selihot*) where the themes of revolt and anguish were associated with the themes of salvation and hope.[47] It is Elie Wiesel who for the first time returned to the *Akedah* and applied it to the Holocaust, a choice he and other thinkers find unfortunate and now regret.[48] At any rate, many philosophers, poets, and theologians, Jews and Christians, have since constructed their post-Holocaust reflection around the reference to the *Akedah*.

Holocaust Themes:
1. The innocence of the victim slaughtered for no reason; cruelty and madness of the event (Genesis 22:1).
2. The poignant father-son relationship in a drama that surpasses them (Genesis 22:7–8).
3. The human silences and the questions suspended in the void; problem of faith towards the unexplained (Genesis 22:7–8).[49]
4. Terror and impotence in the face of the disaster (Genesis 22:7).
5. Sacrificial motif in relation to redemption (Genesis 22:8, 13, 14).

2. JOB

From the sculpture of Job at the door of Yad Vashem to the modern Jewish and Christian commentaries on the book,[50] Job has been identified with the Jewish suffering at Auschwitz. Martin Buber wrote his *Job of the Gas Chambers* (1951). In *Night*, Elie Wiesel at Auschwitz identifies himself with Job. Eliezer Berkovits pondering over the book of Job speaks of the 'two Jobs' at Auschwitz: 'The one who belatedly accepted the advice of Job's wife and turned his back on God, and the other who kept his faith to the end, who affirmed it at the very doors of the gas chambers, who was able to walk to his death defiantly singing his *Ani Mamin – I Believe*.'[51] And Emil Fackenheim stumbles on the death of the children of Job and wonders about the ethics of their replacement: 'How can Job die "full of days" (Job 42:17), when his first seven sons and three daughters are dead, remain dead – and are irreplaceable?'[52]

Holocaust Themes:
1. Suffering of the innocent 'for nothing', '*hinam*' (Job 1:9; 2:3; 9:17; 22:6).
2. Theology of *chutzpah* (audacity, boldness) challenging God (Job 10; 31:35–37).[53]
3. The silence of God (Job 30:20; 19:7; 31:35).[54]
4. Hope and the longing for God's presence (Job 14:7; 19:17).
5. The question of theodicy (Job 1:20–21; 9:17, 24; 42:7–8).[55]

3. ESTHER

The 'strange' book of Esther is a good example of how Auschwitz has affected the reading of the Bible. Before Auschwitz, this book was almost ignored and even to a certain extent discarded for two reasons: (1) the absence of any reference to God; and (2) the nationalistic tone of the book.[56] After Auschwitz, these are, in fact, the reasons why it has become relevant. Reflecting on Buber's 1926 'Man of Today', Emil Fackenheim remembers that the book of Esther was then 'a strange book in the one Book'.[57] In 1938, Schalom Ben Chorin wrote a critique against the book,[58] but forty years later, in 1986, under the impact of the Holocaust, he will write *Als Gott Schwieg*, a positive assessment of the book precisely because of its silence about God. Fackenheim explains that this change is essentially due to the impact of the Holocaust: 'In my view, this is the total and wholly adequate cause for the sharp contrast between a 1938 fideism so close to a Christian as to demand the elimination of Esther from the canon, and *Als Gott Schwieg* in which surviving Jews have much to say – "after God was silent"'.[59]

Holocaust Themes:
1. God's presence in His absence.[60]
2. Cosmic conflict between Good and Evil.[61]
3. God's providence and chance (Esther 4:14; 6:1; 9:24–26).[62]
4. Immanent judgment: persecution returns on the hand of those who initiate it (Esther 3:7–11; 7:10).
5. Survival from the threat of genocide: joy of life (Esther 9:18–22).

4. ISAIAH

Two series of texts from the book of Isaiah have been used in the post-Holocaust reflection. The first series of texts focuses on the motif of the 'suffering servant' (Isaiah 52:13–53:19). These texts are often associated with the passion stories, 'Golgotha' (see below). Yet beyond the common evocation of unjust suffering, most of these writers emphatically note the difference between the two cases. According to Berkovits, the Jewish people who bear witness 'to God's elusive presence in history' are His suffering servant.[63] But he insists that the suffering of the Jewish people is in no way comparable to the suffering endured by Jesus,[64] and he responds to those who argue that Jesus was God, that 'to torture and to kill one innocent child is a crime infinitely more abominable than the killing of any god'.[65] Christian theologian James F. Moore applies the text of the suffering servant to both the Jews as victims of the Holocaust and Jesus on the cross, but recognizes that this connection is inappropriate because 'Jesus is not a victim; he is a rescuer'.[66] For Maybaum, the text of Isaiah 53 applies to the Jews who suffered vicarious death for the sins of mankind. Maybaum contends that the *churban* of Auschwitz replaced the cross and 'is the pagan Golgotha of our time'.[67] Likewise, for Irving Greenberg, 'the Suffering Servant in Isaiah 53 sounds like a passage out of Holocaust literature', and the vicarious function of this suffering is interpreted in the sense that the Holocaust serves as a warning to save the world.[68]

The other series of texts of Isaiah focuses on the motif of the 'hidden face of God'.[69] The *Hester Panim* of Isaiah is interpreted by Berkovits as an attribute of the God of Israel, 'a quality of being assumed by God in his own initiative'.[70] For André Neher, this 'metastasis' is the expression of the silence of God as experienced in the 'silence of Auschwitz'.[71]

Holocaust Themes:
1. Suffering as a key for redemption (Isaiah 53:5–8).
2. Mystery of 'the hidden face' (Isaiah 53:3).[72]
3. Suffering of the righteous (Isaiah 53:4, 7, 9).
4. Universalism (Isaiah 53:3, 6, 11).
5. Christian-Jewish controversy on the relation between the suffering servant, Israel, and the cross.[73]

5. THE CRUCIFIXION

The Passion story has become a common reference in Jewish as well as in Christian post-Holocaust thinking.[74] One of the first, perhaps the first text that associates Jesus' crucifixion with the suffering of the Jews has been written in 1949 by Jules Isaac in the conclusion of his book *Jesus and Israel*.[75] Elie Wiesel's conversation with French writer François Mauriac testifies to the same connection and raises the problem it implies: 'Sir . . . you speak of Christ. Christians love to speak of him. . . . In your religion, that is all you speak of. Well, I want you to know that ten years ago, not very far from here, I knew Jewish children every one of whom suffered a thousand times more, six million times more, than Christ on the cross.'[76] In an often quoted text, however, Elie Wiesel tells the story of the death of a child at Auschwitz in terms that evoke the passion story. Behind the hanging child he perceives the mysterious presence of God: 'God is there!'[77] This text has received abundant commentaries by both Jews and Christians. Moltmann calls it 'a shattering expression of the *theologia crucis*',[78] and Neher qualifies it as 'a strange evocation of the Passion'.[79] Christian theologian Paul M. Van Buren urges us then to take the lessons from Auschwitz as from Golgotha: 'God's omnipotence is such that God can and does enter into the pain and suffering of his children'.[80]

Holocaust Themes:
1. The suffering of the righteous (Matthew 27:4).
2. The silence of God and the question of theodicy (Matthew 27:49; Mark 15:30–32).
3. The 'Why?' (*lama*) on the cross challenging God, expression of revolt and of hope (Matthew 27:46).[81]
4. Theology of redemptive sacrifice (Romans 5:6–10).
5. Israel, Jesus, and the Church.[82]

6. THE GENESIS CREATION STORY

Significantly, it was the events in Germany in the 1930s that brought back theological interest to the doctrine of Creation, 'as it provided a focal point for the struggle within the church and between *the Church and the Nazis*'.[83] For it was precisely in the doctrine of Creation blended with ingredients from the philosophy of Hegel and Nietzsche that Nazi ideology had found its theological justification; indeed, the 'Gott mit uns' was seen at work in the history of nations as it was in the creative forces of Creation. Against these views, Dietrich Bonhoeffer[84] among other Christian theologians responded by insisting that it was in God, in Jesus-Christ that we had to start and not from Creation or nature or history; for in Him only we would find the right criteria against which any human 'Führer' or any claim for authentically creative life should be measured.

After the Holocaust, the reference to Creation took another turn. The question was no more 'Was God at work in Creation, or in this history?' but 'Why did the omnipotent and the benevolent God of Creation allow this history to happen?' To this question, Holocaust thinkers responded in two ways.

For some, the idea of God's omnipotence and benevolence was incompatible with the evil that was experienced at Auschwitz. To solve this problem these thinkers resorted to models like the Lurianic *tsimtsum* (the divine shrinking or contraction) and/or the paradigm of process theology.[85]

Others have preserved the conventional positive reading of the biblical Creation stories and retained the idea of life and goodness of God's Creation.[86] Advocates of this view have only one way out of the Holocaust: call God to account regarding evil and challenge Him 'to reconcile this observation with His claim that the world is "very good" (Genesis 1:31). Believing in God in spite of God, they cajole God to emerge from His silence'.[87]

All these post-Holocaust reevaluations of Creation lead to the same lesson, urging for human responsibility to repair (*tiqqun*)[88] the work of Creation. For process theologians, the *tiqqun* concerns an original 'imperfect' world; for the others the *tiqqun* concerns a 'broken' world which will be brought back to its original flawless state. All of them would concur with Berkovits, who reacts against the death load of the Holocaust and in tune with the biblical Creation story appeals for life: 'The act of creating a life or enhancing its dignity is the counter-testimony to Auschwitz.'[89]

Holocaust Themes:
1. The question of theodicy: God's omnipotence, the goodness of Creation, and evil (Genesis 1:1, 31; 2:17).
2. Nostalgia for life without death, and hope (Gensis 1:29–30; 2:17).
3. Human responsibility in working with God (Genesis 1:26; 2:15).
4. Ethics: man created in God's image, equality of all human beings, and respect for difference (Genesis 1:27, 28).
5. The 'Yes' to Creation: affirmation of the value of life (Genesis 1:29–30; 9:6–7).

7. APOCALYPTIC

It is certainly not without some significance that theology and Bible scholarship after the Second World War has been marked by 'the renaissance of Apocalyptic',[90] with the main contribution of German theologians such as Pannenberg and Moltmann[91] and New Testament scholars Wilckens and Käsemann[92] who found in the Apocalypse a response to their actual concerns and needs for the future in a devastated Germany, and an echo to their still fresh memory of the Holocaust.[93] For the Holocaust had, indeed, an apocalyptic character with its systematic destruction accompanied by an astronomic number of deaths[94] and the pervasive presence of 'radical evil'.[95] It was, essentially, 'a prophetic warning'[96] against the threat of Ellul's technical city.[97] For our city strangely resembles the frightful cold organizations of the technical experts of Auschwitz.[98] Also, after Auschwitz one does not expect redemption any more from the power of this world. This is the lesson taken by Leo Baeck in his commentary on the book of Daniel. Salvation is now to be sought 'upwards' and 'vertically' outside of human time in the 'end of days' (Daniel 2:8; 8:17), from the world to come (*olam haba*).[99]

Holocaust Themes:
1. Reality of radical evil (Revelation 12:9).
2. Hope in the God of above (Daniel 7:13–14; Revelation 14:14–16).
3. Cosmic view of war and destruction (Revelation 8–9, 16; Daniel 11).
4. 'Utopian liberation' towards a radical change of our city (Revelation 21:1; Daniel 2:44–45).
5. Martyrology (Daniel 7:25; 12:1; Revelation 6:10).

To be sure, these texts are not the only biblical passages that have responded or would respond to the Holocaust connection. Many other biblical texts have qualified or would qualify.[100] The reading and rereading of these often neglected texts which have been saved by the Holocaust awareness will not only broaden the biblical horizon, but will also guide and influence the reading of the Bible in general from within the Bible itself and thus make the biblical text more relevant and therefore more vibrant on the troubling path of our post-Holocaust/post-modern age.

SUMMARY, A MIDRASH AND CONCLUSION

To the question raised in the beginning, Can we still read the Bible after Auschwitz?, the answer is definitely 'Yes', provided, however, that this reading works under three conditions. First, the reading should for Christians embrace the whole Bible, the Old as well as the New Testament, with the same degree of reverence and receptivity, and the same readiness to be shaped by the Old Testament as they are by the New Testament.

Second, the biblical texts should be interpreted with 'suspicion' under the control of life and ethics; the meaning of the text (it meant) should be confronted with its potential understanding and exploitation today after Auschwitz (it means); it should be compared with the lesson of other texts dealing with the same theme; and should be nuanced or challenged by the ambiguity of its words.

Third, the reading of the Bible should explore new biblical texts which are inhabited with the spirit of the Holocaust, texts that have become relevant precisely because of the Holocaust.

After Auschwitz, the reading of the Bible is therefore more total, more demanding, and more responsible than it was before Auschwitz or could be outside of this parameter. Yet, reading the Bible after Auschwitz means more than the above, more than a theoretical exercise, more than just questioning the authority of Scripture, or sharpening/finding a new meaning, or even discovering new biblical texts. The lessons of the post-Holocaust reading should be heard and received beyond the circles of the theologians or the Bible exegetes, and reach the public domain through 'liturgy,[101] homiletics and lectionaries,[102] and catechetics and adult education.[103]

Now, does this mean that the mere observance of these rules and principles will guarantee the 'correct' reading of the Bible and will prevent us from another Auschwitz? Were these principles always absent in the pre-Holocaust reading of the Bible? These questions take us to another, more disturbing and certainly more complex and almost ominous question we also raised in our introduction; namely, Why did the reading of the Bible lead to Auschwitz? Why did the reading of the Word of God lead to killing people? There is no easy answer to that question. This essay has not answered this question, at least not explicitly, not completely.

To address this question, I will therefore proceed indirectly, suggestively, by means of a midrash on the Bible story of the crime of Cain,[104] a relevant text indeed in regard to our Holocaust interrogation.

The chronicle of the crime is given in the form of a dialogue between God and Cain, or rather what is supposed to be a dialogue (Genesis 4:6–8). For our text is articulated by the technical mark of the dialogue '*wayyomer*', 'and he said'. The words of God invite and require an answer; they are made of questions 'Why?' (v. 6), 'Will you not?' (v. 7). And indeed the indication of the forthcoming answer is given: '*wayyomer* Cain' ('and Cain said', v. 8). In the normal flow of the dialogue, the *wayyomer* of Cain is designed to respond to the other *wayyomer* of God; Cain's response to God is expected. Yet, nothing of that sort happens. Cain does not answer to God. Instead, he turns to Abel and kills him. The mechanism of the act pertains to a psychoanalytic process. Cain has transferred his vertical relation into a horizontal relation. Instead of fulfilling his duty to answer God, Cain preferred to ignore his 'religious' calling and transposed the vertical requirement onto a horizontal level. Cain was to respond to God, yet instead Cain spoke to Abel. And therefore killed him.

The Bible story of the crime of Cain reveals the psychological mechanism which may have led to the Crusades, the wars of religion, and ultimately to Auschwitz. They turned to the other; they called the other because they failed or simply refused to respond to the call of God. Had Cain, instead of calling his brother, responded to God's call, he would not have killed his brother and 'mankind would have been spared much horror and tragedy.'[105] If indeed, reading the Bible is hearing the Word of God, the next step after that should not be to turn to the other and speak to him even 'about God', but rather to respond to God, for in the words of Elie Wiesel: 'After Auschwitz, I do not believe that we can speak about God; we can only . . . speak to God'.[106]

NOTES

1 Auschwitz (the German name of the Polish Oswięçim) was one of the six 'killing centres' with large-scale gassing facilities operated by the German National Socialist state. More than half of the slaughter of the Jews (about 3.5 million out of the six million) was perpetrated there. Auschwitz has therefore become a symbol of the Nazi programme of Jewish genocide (on these statistics, see Lucy S. Dawidowicz, 'Thinking about the Six Million: Facts, Figures, Perspectives', in *Holocaust: Religious and Philosophical Implications*, ed. John K. Roth and Michael Berenbaum (New York: Paragon House, 1989), pp.51 ff.

2 For the moral implications of this geographical location, see Alan T. Davis, *Antisemitism and the Christian Mind* (New York: Herder and Herder, 1969), p.37.

3 On the uniqueness of the Holocaust, see Michael Berenbaum, 'The Uniqueness and Universality of the Holocaust', *American Journal of Theology and Philosophy* 2/3 (September 1981): 85–96.

4 See James F. Moore, *Christian Theology After the Shoah*, Studies in the Shoah, no. 7, ed. Zev Garber (New York/Lanham, MD: University Press of America, 1993), p.2.

5 Michael Berenbaum, *The Vision of the Void: Theological Reflections on the Works of Elie Wiesel* (Middletown, CT: Wesleyan University Press, 1979), p.78.

6 On the definition and scope of (post)-Holocaust theology, see Stephen R. Haynes, *Prospects for Post-Holocaust Theology* (Atlanta, GA: Scholars Press, 1991), pp.6 ff.

7 Clark M. Williamson, *A Guest in the House of Israel: Post-Holocaust Church Theology* (Louisville, KY: Westminster/John Knox Press, 1993), p.140.

8 See especially Marcion's *Antithesis*, for a summary of Marcion's views, see Justo L. Gonzalez, *A History of Christian Thought*, vol. 1 (Nashville: Abingdon Press, 1970), pp.140–144.

9 For a summary of the history of the supersessionist doctrine see John Pawlikowski, *Jesus and the Theology of Israel* (Wilmington, DE: Michael Glazier, 1989), pp.10–11.

10 On the murderous mechanism of supersessionist thinking, see Darrel J. Fasching (ed.), *The Jewish People in Christian Preaching*, Symposium Series, 10 (New York: Edwin Mellen, 1984), p.x.

11 James A. Sanders, *Canon and Community: A Guide to Canonical Criticism* (Philadelphia, PA: Fortress Press, 1984), p.xv.

12 The expression is used by Gaston Lloyd in 'Jesus the Jew in the Apostolic Writings', *Religion and Intellectual Life* 3 (1986), p.58.

13 See especially his book *A Theology of the Jewish–Christian Reality, Part 1: Discerning the Way* (New York: Seabury Press, 1980).

14 For a critique of Van Buren's thesis, see Clark M. Williamson, *A Guest in the House of Israel*, pp. 148–150.

15 See also Gaston Lloyd; Albert A. van Ruler, *The Christian Church and the Old Testament*, trans. Geoffrey W. Bromiley (Grand Rapids, MI: Wm. B. Eerdmans, 1971).

16 According to New Testament scholar Norman Perrin, 'the very concept of a New Testament as distinct from the Old may well go back to Marcion's repudiation of the Jewish Scriptures' (*The New Testament: An Introduction* [New York: Harcourt Brace Jovanovitch, 1974], p.33); likewise, patristic scholar Cyril C. Richardson notes 'that the first New Testament canon comes from gnostic sources' ('Introduction to Early Christian Literature', in *Early Christian Fathers*, Library of Christian Classics, vol. 1 [Philadelphia, PA: Westminster Press, 1953], pp.24–25).

17 See Luke 24:27; John 5:39; 1 Cor 15:3; 2 Tim 3:15.

18 See *Peah* 8:9; *Sanh.* 4:5; *Avot* 3:7, 8, etc.

19 Clark Williamson, 'The Authority of Scripture After the *Shoah*', in *Faith and Creativity: Essays in Honor of Eugene H. Peters*, eds. George Nordgulen and George W. Shields (St. Louis, MO: CBP Press, 1987), p.125.

20 In that connection, two groups of people are irrelevant for our enquiry, for in both cases the reading of the Scriptures is or has been voluntarily disconnected from the event of the Holocaust. Those who reject the authority of Scripture altogether. This position has been justified either on the simple reference to the Holocaust (see for instance Richard L. Rubenstein's 'atheistic' reaction in his 'death of God' theology [*After Auschwitz: Radical Theology and Contemporary Judaism* (New York: The Bobbs-Merrill Company, 1966), pp.113–129]) and/or upon reasons elaborated essentially from critical paradigms that originated in our 'modern and post-modern' cultural settings (see Glenn D. Earley's proposal of 'perspective relativism' inspired by Gadamer's hermeneutics ['The Radical Hermeneutical Shift in Post-Holocaust Christian Thought', *Journal of Ecumenical Studies* 18 (Winter 1981): 18–21, 31]). And those who defend the traditional views of the authority of Scripture. This position has been held by Jewish theologians who refuse to grant the Holocaust any 'privilege' of an impact on the authority of Scripture. For 'the voices of the prophets speak more loudly than did Hitler' (Michael Wyschogrod, 'Faith and the Holocaust', *Judaism* 20 [Summer 1971], 294; see also Jacob Neusner, 'The Implications of the Holocaust', *The Journal of Religion* 53/3 [July 1973]: 307–308). It is also noteworthy that in the various developments in Protestant theology since 1950 no special reference to the Holocaust, if any, has been noted (see Robert E. Willis, 'Christian Theology after Auschwitz', *Journal of Ecumenical Studies* 12 [Fall 1975]: 500 ff.).

21 See Clark M. Williamson, *A Guest in the House of Israel*; Rosemary R. Ruether, *Faith and Fratricide: The Theological Roots of Anti-Semitism* (Minneapolis: Seabury Press, 1974); Gregory Baum, *Theology After Auschwitz* (London: Council of Christians and Jews, 1976); and James F. Moore.

22 Emil L. Fackenheim, *The Jewish Bible after the Holocaust: A Re-reading* (Bloomington, IN: Indiana University Press, 1990), pp.vii–viii.

23 James F. Moore qualifies this principle as a 'hermeneutic of suspicion' which he explains in the following manner: 'Interpretations that are unable to hold in the light of that challenge must be considered suspect, impossible to retrieve at least in the way presented' (p.139).

24 Stephen R. Haynes, p.279.

25 This approach implies the rejection of the Kierkegaardian idea of 'suspension of ethics', for God never suspends ethics (see Manfred Vogel, 'Kierkegaard's Teleological Suspension of the Ethical, Some Reflections from a Jewish Perspective', in *The Georgetown Symposium on Ethics [In Honor of Henry B. Veatch]* [Lanham, MD: University Press of America, 1984], pp.19–48; see also Milton Steinberg, 'Kierkegaard and Judaism', *Menorah Journal* 37/2 [1949]: 163–180).

26 See *Yoma* 85b; *Sanh.* 74a.

27 On the issue of the relation between what the text 'meant' and what it 'means' today, see Krister Stendahl, 'Biblical Theology, Contemporary', in *The Interpreter's Dictionary of the Bible*, vol. A-D (New York: Abingdon Press, 1962), pp.419–420.

28 Fredrick C. Holmgren, *The Old Testament and the Significance of Jesus: Embracing Change-Maintaining Christian Identity* (Grand Rapids, MI: Wm. B. Eerdmans Publishing Company, 1999), p.10.

29 See, for instance, C.J. Cuming, for whom the word 'Jesus' means Judaen as opposed to Galilean, quoted in Leon Morris, *The Gospel According to John* (Grand Rapids, MI: Wm. B. Eerdmans Pub. Co., 1975), p.131.

30 George G. Beasley-Murray, *John*, Word Biblical Commentary, vol. 36 (Dallas, TX: Word Books, 1987), p.lxxxix.

31 David P. Efroymson, 'Let *Ioudaioi* Be *Ioudaioi*: When Less is Better', *Explorations* 11/2 (1997): 5.

32 In recent years, a call to read the biblical texts as canonical Scripture has been vigorously advocated from a variety of perspectives. Terms like 'canonical criticism', 'canonical hermeneutic', etc., were used. See James A. Sanders, and also Brevard S. Childs, *Old Testament Theology in A Canonical Context* (Philadelphia, PA: Fortress Press, 1985).

33 James A. Sanders, p.xv.

34 See Clark M. Williamson, *A Guest in the House of Israel*, pp.161–166.

35 J.G. Gammie, 'Theology of Retribution in the Book of Deuteronomy', *Catholic Biblical Quarterly* 32 (1970): 1–12.

36 R.N. Gordon, 'Motivation in Proverbs', *Biblical Theology* 25/3 (October 1975): 49–56.

37 On the relevance of ambiguities in post-Holocaust hermeneutic, see James F. Moore, pp.29 ff.

38 Donald A. Hagner, *Matthew*, Word Biblical Commentary, vol. 33A (Dallas, TX: Word Books, 1993), p.827.

39 See Jules Isaac, *Jesus and Israel*, ed. Claire H. Bishop, trans. Sally Gran (New York: Holt, Rinehart, and Winston, 1971), pp.274–284.

40 See Karl H. Schelkle, 'Die "Selbstverfluchung" Israels nach Matthäus 27, 23–25', in *Antijudäismus im Neuen Testament?*, ed. W.P. Eckert, et al. (Munich: Kaiser, 1967), pp.148–156; and W. Sanders, 'Das Blut Jesu und die Juden: Gedanken zu Matt. 27, 25', *Una Sancta* 27 (1972): 168–171.

41 In the same context of Jesus' crucifixion, Jules Isaac draws the attention to another double entendre concerning the name 'Barabbas' which means 'son of the Father' (a son of God) thus creating another confusion in the minds of the people (see *Jesus and Israel*, pp.341–342).

42 See R.H. Smith, 'Matthew 27:25: The Hardest Verse in Matthew's Gospel', *Currents in Theology and Mission* 17 (1990): 421–428; cf. T.B. Cargal, ' "His Blood Be upon Us and upon Our Children": A Matthean Double Entendre?', *New Testament Studies* 37 (1991): 101–112.

43 See E. Edouard Dhorme, Hoist, Andersen, Fohrer, AV, RV, NAB, NIV, NKJV, etc.

44 See John E. Hartley, *The Book of Job*, The New International Commentary on the Old Testament (Grand Rapids, MI: Wm. B. Eerdmans, 1988), p.221; cf. Richard Jacobsen, 'Satanic Semiotics, Jobian Jurisprudence', in *The Book of Job and Ricoeur's Hermeneutics*, Semeia 19, ed. John D. Crossan (Chico: Scholars Press, 1981), pp.67–68. Cf. W.B. Stevenson, *The Poem of Job: A Literary Study, with a New Translation* (London: Pub. for the British Academy by Oxford University Press, 1947); NEB, etc.

45 André Neher, *L'Exil de la parole: Du silence biblique au silence d'Auschwitz* (Paris: Editions du Seuil, 1970), p.215 (translation from the French is ours).

46 The same tension may be recognized in the ambiguity of the word *brk* (bless/curse) in Job 2:9. There also the suffering human condition is made of the contradiction between the faith that accepts and blesses God and the revolt that rejects and curses God. (See André Neher, *L'Exil de la parole*, p.210.)

47 See André Neher, *L'exil de la parole*, p.227; cf. Wilhelm Zuydema, 'Isaac à nouveau sacrifié', *Foi et Vie* 81 (January 1982): 39–40.

48 For a significant discussion on the appropriateness of terms, see Zev Garber and Bruce Zuckerman, 'Why Do We Call the Holocaust, the Holocaust? An Inquiry into the Psychology of Labels', in *Remembering for the Future*, vol. 2 (New York: Pergamon Press, 1988), pp.1879 ff. See also John Roth and Richard Rubenstein, *Approaches to Auschwitz* (Atlanta: John Knox Press, 1987), pp.4–7.

49 See Jacques Doukhan, 'The Center of the Aqedah: A Study of the Literary Structure of Genesis 22:1–19', *Andrews University Seminary Studies* 31 (Spring 1993): 17–28.

50 See especially André Neher, 'Job: the Biblical Man', *Judaism* 13 (1964): 37–47; Richard L. Ruben-stein, 'Job and Auschwitz', *Union Seminary Quarterly Review* 25 (1969–70): 421–437; P. Watté, 'Job à Auschwitz: Deux constats de la pensée juive', *Revue théologique de Louvain* 4 (1973): 173–190; Margarete Susman, *Das Buch Hiob und das Schicksal des jüdischen Volkes*, 2d ed. (Basel: Herder, 1968); R. Dedmon, 'Job as Holocaust Survivor', *St. Luke's Journal of Theology* 26 (1982–83): 165–185.

51 Eliezer Berkovits, *Faith after the Holocaust* (New York: Ktav Publishing House, 1973), p.69.

52 Emil L. Fackenheim, p.93.

53 See likewise Abraham (Genesis 18:17–33); Jacob (Genesis 32:26), Moses (Exodus 3:11–14; 32:11–14); Habakkuk (1:1–3), etc. Beldon C. Lane comments on what he calls 'an audacious faith, almost bordering on insolence,... "*hutzpah k'lapei shamaya*" it is called in the Jewish tradition – a boldness with regard to heaven' ('Hutzpa K'lapei Shamaya: A Christian Response to the Jewish Tradition of Arguing with God', *The Journal of Ecumenical Studies* 23/4 [Fall 1986]: 567, 568).

54 See André Neher, *L'exil de la parole*, p.211.

55 On theodicy in the Old Testament see, among other works, James L. Crenshaw (ed.), *Theodicy in the Old Testament* (Philadelphia: Fortress Press, 1983); see also Byron L. Sherwin, *Toward a Jewish Theology: Methods, Problems, and Possibilities* (Lewiston, NY: The Edwin Mellen Press, 1991), pp.63–77.

56 See Bernard Anderson, 'The Place of the Book of Esther in the Christian Bible', *Journal of Religion* 30 (1950): 32.

57 See Emil L. Fackenheim, p.62.

58 Schalom Ben Chorin, *Kritik des Estherbuches* (Jerusalem: Heatid, 1938).

59 Emil L. Fackenheim, p.115, n. 13.

60 See André Neher, *L'exil de la parole*, p.27; Angel M. Rodriguez, *Esther: A Theological Approach* (Berrien Springs, MI: Andrews University Press, 1995), p.96.

61 See Yehezkel Kaufmann, *History of the Religion of Israel*, vol. 4 (New York: KTAV Publishing House, 1977), p.519.

62 See Abraham D. Cohen, ' "Hu Ha-goral": The Religious Significance of Esther', *Judaism* 23 (Winter 1974): 87–94.

63 Eliezer Berkovits, p.125.

64 Ibid., p.126.

65 Ibid., p.127.

66 James F. Moore, p.90.

67 Quoted in Dan Cohn-Sherbok, *Holocaust Theology* (London: Lamp Press, 1989), p.32.

68 Irving Greenberg, 'Cloud of Smoke, Pillar of Fire', in *Holocaust: Religious and Philosophical Implica-tions*, ed. John K. Roth and Michael Berenbaum (New York: Paragon House, 1989), pp.326–327.

69 See especially André Neher, *L'exil de la parole*, p.148.

70 Eliezer Berkovits, p.101.

71 André Neher, *L'exil de la parole*, pp.148–149.

72 For the theme of 'the hidden face of God', see also Isaiah 54:8; 57:17; 45:14–15; 8:16–17.

73 See Irving Greenberg, p.328; Eliezer Berkovits, pp.125–126.

74 See the significant title of Franklin Littell, *The Crucifixion of the Jews* (Macon, GA: Mercer University Press, 1986); see also Michael Brown, 'On Crucifying the Jews', *Judaism* 27/1 (Fall 1978): 476–488.

75 Jules Isaac, p.400.

76 See Robert McAfee Brown, *Elie Wiesel: Messenger to All Humanity* (Notre Dame, IN: University of Notre Dame Press, 1983), pp.167–168.

77 Elie Wiesel, *Night*, American edn., trans. Stella Rodway (New York: Hill and Wang, 1960), p.71. Cf. Eliezer Berkovits, p.126.

78 Jürgen Moltmann, *The Crucified God: The Cross of Christ as the Foundation and Criticism of Christian Theology* (London: SCM Press, 1974), p.273.

79 André Neher, *L'exil de la parole*, p.236.
80 Paul M. Van Buren, *A Theology of the Jewish-Christian Reality, Part 3: Christ in Context* (San Francisco: Harper and Row, 1988), p.166.
81 James F. Moore, pp.86–87.
82 See John Pawlikowski, especially pp.79 ff.
83 Norman Young, *Creator, Creation and Faith* (Philadelphia: Westminster Press, 1976), p.17.
84 See his radio broadcast entitled 'The Idea of Leader in the New Germany' (quoted in Norman Young, p.200, n. 7); cf. Gerhard von Rad, *The Problem of the Hexateuch and Other Essays*, trans. E.W. Trueman Dicken (New York: McGraw-Hill, 1966), p.142 ff.
85 See Paul M. Van Buren, *A Theology of the Jewish-Christian Reality, Part 2: A Christian Theology of the People of Israel* (New York: Seabury Press, 1983), pp.62 ff.; see also Jon D. Levenson, *Creation and the Persistence of Evil: The Jewish Drama of Divine Omnipotence* (San Francisco: Harper and Row, 1988), p.141; and Clark M. Williamson, *A Guest in the House of Israel*, p.220.
86 See Douglas A. Knight, 'Cosmogony and Order in the Hebrew Tradition', in *Cosmogony and Ethical Order*, ed. Robin W. Lovin and Frank E. Reynolds (Chicago: University of Chicago, 1985), p.142; Paul Ricoeur, *The Symbolism of Evil* (Boston: Beacon, 1969), p.203.
87 Byron L. Sherwin, p.74. This Theology of Protest has essentially been that of Elie Wiesel, see Dan Cohn-Sherbok, *Holocaust Theology*, pp.92–103.
88 See Clark M. Williamson, p.212; Byron L. Sherwin, p.70; André Neher, *L'exil de la parole*, p.159.
89 Irving Greenberg, p.331.
90 See Klaus Koch, *The Rediscovery of Apocalyptic: A Polemical Work on a Neglected Area of Biblical Studies and its Damaging Effects on Theology and Philosophy*, Studies in Biblical Theology, Second Series, no. 22 (London: SCM Press, 1972), p.13.
91 Ibid., pp.101 ff.
92 Ibid., pp.73 ff.
93 As recently as 1988, Jürgen Moltmann has recognized the influence of the Holocaust on his theological thinking: 'For us young Germans who began the study of theology after the war, "Auschwitz" became a turning point in our thinking and acting…"After Auschwitz" became our concrete context for theology' ('Political Theology and the Ethics of Peace', in *Theology, Politics and Peace*, ed. Theodore Runyon [Maryknoll, NY: Orbis, 1989], p.34).
94 See Darrell J. Fasching, *The Ethical Challenge of Auschwitz and Hiroshima: Apocalypse or Utopia?* (Albany, NY: State University of New York Press, 1993), pp.28 ff.
95 On the phrase 'radical evil', see James F. Moore, pp.2, 9.
96 Darrell J. Fasching, *The Ethical Challenge of Auschwitz and Hiroshima*, p.28.
97 See Jacques Ellul, *The Technological Society* (New York: Random House, Vintage Books, 1964).
98 See Jean-François Steiner, *Treblinka*, trans. Helen Weaver (New York: Simon and Schuster, 1967), pp.23, 169.
99 Dan Cohn-Sherbok, *Holocaust Theology*, pp.36–37.
100 For instance, the Exodus story which is told in the Passover Haggadah, the texts of the Day of Atonement (see Richard L. Rubenstein, *After Auschwitz*, pp.93–129) and the texts dealing with the covenant with Israel (Daniel 9:24–27); the Epistle to the Hebrews and Romans 9–11 (see Jacques Ellul, *Ce Dieu injuste…? Théologie chrétienne pour le peuple d'Israël* [Paris: Arléa, 1991]; F. Lovsky, *La déchirure de l'absence: Essai sur les rapports de l'Église du Christ et du peuple d'Israël* [France: Calmann-Lévy, 1971]; Clark M. Williamson, *A Guest in the House of Israel*, pp.107–114).
101 See, for instance, Marcia Sachs Littell and Sharon Weissman Gutman, eds., *Liturgies on the Holocaust: An Interfaith Anthology*, new and rev. ed. (Valley Forge, PA: Trinity Press International, 1996).
102 See, for instance, Fredrick C. Holmgren and Herman E. Schaalman, eds., *Preaching Biblical Texts: Expositions by Jewish and Christian Scholars*, forewords by Elie Wiesel and Joseph Cardinal Bernardin, intro. by David Tracy (Grand Rapids, MI: Wm. B. Eerdmans Publishing Company, 1995).
103 Glenn D. Earley, p.31, on the 'implications for preaching and teaching'; see also the invaluable comments of Clark M. Williamson, *A Guest in the House of Israel*, pp.46–47.
104 Cf. André Neher, *L'exil de la parole*, pp.103–104.

105 Eliezer Berkovits perceives the same mechanism in the Holocaust: 'Had Christianity, instead of being preoccupied with what it believed to have been a deicide, concentrated its educative attention on the human crime of homicide, mankind would have been spared much horror and tragedy' (p.127).

106 Quoted in Hans Küng, *Judaism*, trans. John Bowden (London: SCM Press, 1992), p.605.

OUR FAILURE TO REACT:
METHOD IN CHRISTIAN MORAL THEOLOGY
AFTER THE HOLOCAUST

Mark E. Gammon

I SPENT LAST summer working for an organization called Seeds of Peace; its purpose is to bring Arab and Israeli teenagers together to a summer camp in Maine. While there is a regular camp programme, much like any other summer camp in the United States, there were religious services for Jews and Muslims on Fridays and for Christians on Sundays. Although I was not hired to do so, I found myself serving as the unofficial pastor for the small Christian population of the camp, meaning a few of the Arab campers and a small number of the staff. Part of what I did was to preach at the Sunday services, which I came to call 'exhibition worship' due to the presence of more Jews and Muslims than Christians.

Wanting to give an authentic experience to the interested onlookers, I preached like I would to a given Christian congregation. I preached the lectionary texts for each Sunday, and my sermons featured the theme of the cross prominently. Much of the staff of the camp was Jewish, and my emphasizing the cross was met with some polite hostility by a few of the Jews in attendance. One woman, who is very bright and articulate and holds a masters degree in Jewish education, asked me, 'What's with all the suffering stuff? What do Christians know about suffering?' Of course she had a point. In fact, by the final Sunday of the summer, I was dreading preaching, especially because I knew that Matthew 16: 21–28 was coming up in the lectionary. How could I proclaim Jesus' words ('If any want to become my followers, let them deny themselves and take up their cross and follow me. For those who want to save their life will lose it, and those who lose their life for my sake will find it.') to a room half full of Jews? Then I remembered that in all honesty, the cross does not make a lot of sense to most of the *Christians* I've encountered through the years, and in the end, all I could do was proclaim the message of the cross honestly and faithfully.

My situation – preaching to Jews – was certainly atypical, at least for one who eschews the call to convert the Jews. The incident did, however, bring into sharp relief the discomfort I have felt with most of the self-identified 'post-Holocaust' Christian theology. Few deny the critical role that the greatest historical manifestation of evil should play in the way Christians do theology; however, few agree what effect the Holocaust does or should have. There is a spectrum of responses, from those who proclaim that as something that happened to a different community entirely, the Holocaust should have very little to do with theological method to those who wish to run every bit of Christian doctrine by the Jewish community for its approval. As is to be expected, the polarized extremes are neither useful nor appropriate. As we proceed, then, there are two fundamental points at issue with regard to the way Christian moral theology should proceed after the Holocaust. The first is the role and value of dialogue with Judaism – what can the two traditions offer each other, and to what degree should the experience of either be normative for the other? The second is what the Holocaust has to say about the fundamental aims of Christian 'ethics' – what is it that we hope to accomplish? A review of the literature shows that, for the most part, Christian theologians have failed to find a way to think about the Holocaust that brings an appropriate critical judgment of pre-Holocaust theology without throwing out the most distinctive element of Christian theology, namely the cross.

DIALOGUE

That Christianity should engage in ongoing dialogue with Judaism seems to have been a nearly foregone conclusion in the second half of the 20th century. Indeed, the very gesture of engaging in dialogue is important insofar as an encounter with the 'other' is informative and humanizing. To enter into dialogue is to show respect, to recognize that we have something to learn from the experience of the other, and to take the first steps toward a mutually beneficial friendship.

There is no doubt that Christianity does have something to learn from post-Shoah Jewish theology, especially its struggles with the theodicy question – a question made more complex and difficult by Judaism's self-understanding as the chosen and covenanted people of God. Here, theologians such as John T. Pawlikowski have done a nice job of surveying Jewish theology and critically appropriating what is judged important for Christian theology. Pawlikowski's attempts to engage the thought of David Hartman, Eliezer Berkovits, Emil Fackenheim, Arthur Cohen, and others are sensitive and informative (although, as I shall make clear below, I do not like where Pawlikowski goes from there).

On the other hand, there is a tendency to take 'dialogue' a step too far – the danger being that Christianity's distinctiveness from Judaism is downplayed to the point that the Christian's ability to take a critical stance is severely hampered. James F. Moore, for example, writes, 'All Christian theology is to be done in the context of a community of Jewish–Christian dialogue. Any reading of a Christian text, then, becomes a tentative reading subject to examination by this expanded community of interpretation.'[1] Here, Moore is treading on dangerous ground and making a number of epistemological assumptions about which Christians should be suspicious. Moore's move assumes that something like a unified Judeo-Christian tradition is both possible and desirable – and, of course, we know that if all Christian theology had been subject to Jewish approval, there would be no such thing as Christian theology. In other words, in watering down Christian distinctiveness, we lose something critical to the tradition.

John Milbank, in his essay 'The End of Dialogue', stands at the opposite extreme of Moore's position, and while his rhetoric is inflammatory, his points are valid. According to Milbank, the very concept of interreligious dialogue is fraught with difficulty precisely insofar as it is a covertly imperialistic enterprise. When representatives of different religious traditions sit down in order to dispel theoretical disagreement through 'practical' agreement, the entire project is tainted by a Western, liberal bias. Milbank writes that:

> dialogue obscures the truth-of-difference. One can only regard dialogue partners as equal, independently of one's valuation of what they say, if one is already treating them, and the culture they represent, as valuable mainly in terms of their abstract possession of an autonomous freedom of spiritual outlook and an open commitment to the truth. In other words, if one takes them as liberal, Western subjects, images of oneself.[2]

Milbank decries 'sympathy' as dangerous, for 'too often we sympathize with what we can make to be like ourselves.'[3] The assumption behind most interreligious dialogue is that the religions of the world are but cultural manifestations of one generally humanistic truth; therefore, the goal of dialogue is practical agreement on just what this generic truth entails. In the process, however, each tradition gives away something of its ability to critique others – for a 'religion' is already a cultural critique of that which is different from it. There can be no valuation of one tradition over another for any reason other than cultural familiarity, which, according to Milbank, renders the whole project unintelligible:

> Indeed, if it were accepted that all cultures (religions) have equal access to the (religious) truth, then all critique, including critique of sexist and racist constructs, would become impossible. And since religions are such readings, deeply embedded in habitual practices and attitudes, it is clear that the idea of a universal religion free from cultural attachments, or even of an essential Christianity that could be expressed in non-Western cultural terms, is just nonsensical.[4]

To Milbank, the Christian ecclesial project *is* unique, as it is the only tradition able to recognize peaceful differentiation – the integration of difference through harmony. Because of the Church's Christocentric claims,

> it is apparent that at least as important a site of uniqueness is the ecclesial project itself; no other religious community comprehends itself (in theory) as an international society, independent of political regimes and legal codes, including as equal members (in some sense) men, women, and children, without regard to social class and committed to the realization, within this society, of perfect mutual acceptance and cooperative interaction.[5]

Certainly Judaism, with its burgeoning Zionism and almost complete delimitation to one ethnic group, cannot sign on to such a project.

We cannot simply whitewash the fact that Christianity and contemporary Judaism are the result of a two thousand-year disagreement, though of course the disagreement is not the sum total of the identity of either. Therefore, Milbank warns us to be careful, because our attempts at dialogue can lead to something else:

> For every major religion is *already* the result of a confronting of the fact of religious differences and an attempt to subsume such differences.... Just because of these universalizing aspirations, their conceptual frameworks cannot readily be dissolved through dialogue, whose only possible outcome must be either disguised conversion by the rhetorically strong discourse (Christianity), or else a new hybridization, yielding a new, and of course just as *particular*, elite religion for the votaries of dialogue themselves.[6]

It follows that those who see anti-Semitism as an essential component of Christianity are often neither accurate nor fair with their accusations,[7] but neither can the crucial differences between the two faiths be negotiated away.

As has been well established, the condemnation of 'Jews' as a group in the New Testament must be placed in a specific historical context. This argument has been well stated many times over, so I will only summarize it here. First century Judaism was not a monolithic entity, but rather a diverse, dynamic set of religious practices. Christianity began as one sectarian movement within Judaism. By late in the first century, the Christian mission had found success with the mission to the Gentiles, but relative failure in its mission to the Jews; this state of affairs led to a crisis in communal identity for the early Christian church. While there is no evidence of persecution of Jews by Christians during this early period, there is evidence that Christians were persecuted by Jews (something to which Paul admits). The anti-Jewish rhetoric to be found in the New Testament, especially in the gospels of John and Matthew, must be read in light of the 'sibling rivalry' between the nascent Christian community and its more established rival Jewish sects. To speak of 'anti-Semitism' in the New Testament is to use an anachronism – the disagreements were not about ethnic or racial divisions, but rather about doctrine and practice, especially Christology, which makes no sense removed from its Jewish foundations.[8]

At the heart of Jewish–Christian antipathy is a critical, non-negotiable foundational point – the question of whether Jesus is or is not the Christ. This point itself comes down to how one deals with the cross. While the cross made little sense to first-century Judaism, it should make even less sense to contemporary Judaism, which has a history of unfathomable suffering at the hands of those who have failed to take the moral implications of the cross seriously. There is a tragic irony here, which we must explore more below, but the implications of this situation for dialogue are problematic for two reasons. The first is that for many, the aims of dialogue are untenable insofar as they would threaten Christian distinctiveness. As Richard Hays writes, dialogue is important and useful, but it nonetheless must be approached with the recognition that it is 'tense and risky.'[9] The second, and perhaps the more important for this audience, is that dialogue since and about the Holocaust often fails to recognize the fact that the experience of the Holocaust was very different for Jews and Christians. We often enter into dialogue with the assumption that in learning from one another, we can develop common goals and aims. This assumption ignores the fundamental differences between Judaism and Christianity, both in terms of their respective histories and traditions before the Holocaust and in terms of how each should proceed after it.

The lessons to be learned from being a victim, a victimizer, and the silent bystander are all very different, and it is my assertion that Christians have taken the wrong lesson from the Holocaust. In the case of the Holocaust, the Christian call for dialogue is too often the attempt to integrate the victims' narrative into our own, to heed the call to suffer with the Jews after the fact – and in so doing, to avoid the need for confession and repentance about the Church's multiple failures. The great challenge for *Jewish* theology after the Holocaust is to deal with the question of how a good and just God could let God's chosen people suffer such evil. The great challenge for *Christian* theology after the Holocaust is to deal with the question of how a good and just God could let God's chosen people at worst perpetrate such an evil and at best stand by and watch silently while such evil was perpetrated by those who called themselves Christian. This latter question is precisely the one that Christian theologians have, for the most part, failed to engage, and it is a question the answer to which should have profound implications for the way we think about Christian 'ethics' today.

CHRISTIAN 'ETHICS' AFTER THE HOLOCAUST

The rallying phrase for political ethics after the Holocaust has been 'Never again'. We hear this phrase whenever there are virulent outbreaks of anti-Semitic activity, and sometimes we hear it used as a cry for action in any situation which threatens to escalate to 'genocide' – though its use in the latter is often selective.[10] 'Never again' is of course an appropriate call to action, and no one should argue that it is not something for which Christians should hope, pray, and act. As Stanley Hauerwas has stated, however, it should not be a promise that Christians make.[11] Following on Hauerwas's point, I would argue that it is here that otherwise well-meaning and sensitive theologians have made the mistake noted above – the mistake of confusing Jewish and Christian experiences, or, perhaps more accurately, assuming that they lead to the same conclusions.

John Pawlikowski is a representative case in point. Pawlikowski goes through great pains to engage and understand post-Shoah Jewish theology, though he seems to be somewhat baffled by the failure of many of such theologians to move from the theodicy question to the political question. In Pawlikowski's work, one can feel the struggle to respect and understand the position of someone like David Hartman, who writes: 'Auschwitz, like all Jewish suffering of the past, must be absorbed and understood within the normative framework of Sinai. We will mourn forever because of the memory of Auschwitz. We will build a healthy new society because of the memory of Sinai.'[12] Pawlikowski says that he stands 'in partial sympathy' with these thinkers, but that:

> they have seriously underestimated the degree to which the Holocaust forces us to readjust some of our understanding of our biblical heritage. The Shoah is not merely the most gruesome and troubling example of the classical theological problem of evil. To stop there in probing the Holocaust is, in my judgment, to endanger our humanity. For we will fail to appreciate fully enough the degree of power and consequent responsibility that has come into our hands. And not to attain such realization may allow this power to pass once again into the hands of new Hitlers.[13]

In other words, it seems that Hartman and others do not take 'never again' seriously enough:

> To confine our response to the Shoah to the renewal of covenantal faith as Hartman prescribes would be to endanger human survival. For we would remain unprepared to deal with the magnitude of the power and consequent responsibility that has come into the hands of humanity.[14]

Pawlikowski finds more of value in those who radically rethink theology in light of the Holocaust, theologians like Rubenstein and Cohen, insofar as they have not underestimated the problem; still, he thinks they go too far in rejecting the tradition. He agrees with their rejection of an interventionist God, writing, 'Stopping such destruction is now clearly the burden of the human community. Humanity must learn to save itself from future instances of holocaust, nuclear or otherwise. We no longer have the luxury, in fact it would be the height of human irresponsibility after the Holocaust, to imagine that God will do it in response to simple petitions of prayer.'[15] The key point is that humanity has achieved greater power over its own destiny than ever before, and therefore this 'creative potential' must be 'influenced by a genuine encounter with the living and judging God'.[16] The Holocaust shows us that we must be willing to assume and use our co-creational power, but that we must use it responsibly. We also learn that 'ethics must now stand at the center of any authentic systematic theology.'[17]

Therefore, Pawlikowski speaks positively of such theological projects as the one presented by Darrell Fasching. Fasching argues that one of the things Christianity can learn from dialogue with Judaism is the tradition of dialectic and questioning of God, or *chutzpah*.[18] According to Fasching, the more dominant theological model in Judaism has been that of contending with God, whereas in Christianity, the emphasis has been on unquestioning obedience: 'Where the Christian tradition tended to focus on answers formulated as doctrine, the Talmudic tradition focuses on questions and the vigorous debate over, and with, God's word.'[19] This tendency led to a situation where the authority of God and the authority of the state were identified, such that Christianity fostered an unquestioning obedience to the state 'as an aspect of obedience to Christ.'[20] Fasching mentions the Anabaptist ecclesial position, but relegates it to an anomaly within the dominant strains of the tradition, by which he means Roman Catholic, Lutheran, and Reformed.[21]

Insofar as pre-Holocaust Christianity allowed such complicity with evil, according to Fasching it is 'an obscenity. Full continuity with that tradition is fundamentally immoral.'[22] We must ask what it is in Christianity that needs to be changed in order to prevent such complicity from ever occurring again. Fasching argues that what needs to go is that part of the tradition which calls for submission of the will: 'All faith that asks for total surrender of will is, finally, not only pagan but also demonic, even if it is faith in Jesus or the God of Jesus. For, all such faith is a training ground in fanaticism that blurs the distinction between God and the state and leads to the dehumanization of the *chosen* victims of the state.'[23] He concludes that the 'test of authentic faith is the possibility of dissent against *all* authority in the name of a human dignity that reflects the image of a God without image.'[24] All doctrine must be held up to examination based on a humanistic standard.

There are several problems with Fasching's position, not the least of which being that it is an awful oversimplification of the Christian tradition. More importantly, however, his evidence is insufficient and does not hold up to close scrutiny. While he is right to conclude that we should look to encourage those aspects of the tradition which bring human authority into question, it does not hold true that the strains of the tradition which promote submission of the will and obedience to God lack the resources to do just that. Fasching presumes that the habits cultivated in learning obedience to God automatically transfer to obedience in general, including obedience to corrupt secular authority. Studies of the theological motivations of rescuers, however, contradict Fasching's assumption. In fact, a disproportionate number of rescuers with Christian motivations came from the Calvinist and Anabaptist communities, and within those communities, it was strong identification with a particularistic communitarian ethic of obedience that led rescuers to act.[25]

David Gushee notes that many rescuers are unable to explain the reasons for their actions – their characters had been nurtured in such a way that the question whether or not to act never presented itself.[26] Christian rescuers, in other words, seldom engaged in the kind of casuistry that would allow them to evaluate the option to refuse to help those in need – the option simply never occurred to them. There is some evidence to suggest that the character of rescuers was such that they were as likely to help fleeing Nazis after the war as to help fleeing Jews during the war; their inclination was to help those in need, irrespective of who they were. Fasching ignores the strongly prevalent aspects of Christianity which encourage a critical evaluation of state authority, notably the call to obedience found among the Anabaptists, whom he mentions in passing but fails to engage, and the Calvinists, whose obedience to God inspired the Puritan and Huguenot revolts in England and France respectively and arguably has had considerable influence toward radical political activity since. Robert E. Willis argues that what is required for Christians is an understanding of moral development which reaffirms the connection between story and moral agency in the nurturing of the conscience.[27] Willis's use of the word 'conscience' resembles that used by the Puritans in the 17th century. In short, it is precisely the aspect of the tradition that Fasching would have us reject which history has shown to be most effective in bringing the authority of secular government into question.

All of which I present as a prelude to returning to Pawlikowski and others who would have us assume worldly power and wield it responsibly that we may promise 'never again.' First, it is unclear who it is that Pawlikowski would have assume and wield this power. He suggests that such power has fallen into the hands of 'humanity' as a generality, but he appears to be writing for a Christian audience. That 'humanity' is to wield this power is a troubling notion, for it is precisely because factions of humanity disagree and subsequently seek to assume and use violent power that wars break out. Either we then revert to a Niebuhrian realist mode of politics, as Pawlikowski seems to suggest, or we attempt to 'convert' the world to this titular Christian politics, which amounts to cultural imperialism. These two choices amount to little more than a choice between the two primary foreign policy options faced by the United States in the early part of the twentieth century – realist isolationism versus Wilsonian idealism. In other words, Pawlikowski is an example of how the way we think about Christian ethics has changed very little since the Holocaust. He calls for conditions and guidelines that would ensure the responsible use of violent power. The Holocaust has not been fundamentally transformative; rather, it is an example of what happens when we let power get into the wrong hands. It is a justification for continuing to think about Christian ethics just as it was thought about before, the one crucial difference being that we now perhaps are willing to let Jews in on the conversation about what constitutes the responsible use of violent power.

Pawlikowski speaks approvingly of Stanley Hauerwas's call for humility as a response to the Holocaust, but he really misses Hauerwas' point. As a pacifist, Hauerwas means to say that we must stand humble before the God of history, saying that 'What we require is not a god that underwrites our pretensions, but is capable of calling us from our false notions of power and control.'[28] Hauerwas does *not* mean that we should wield violent power humbly; we are not to be a church of penitent killers, sadly and dutifully instrumentalizing violence for God's good ends.

Most political 'Christian ethics' since World War II has amounted to an attempt to reclaim moral influence over the state. Both the Wilsonian and the realist postures on the part of theologians come with Constantinian assumptions which have become untenable. Christendom has crumbled, and many continue to try to rebuild it as best they can, even if we now call it Judeo-Christendom. If the Holocaust teaches us anything, it is that Christians should leave this tactic behind. This is what Hauerwas means when he calls for humility – the wedding of Christian ethics and state power has proven to be an unworkable alliance, both in terms of its consequences and the original conception of the project. The Christian narrative is precisely that which shows that humans are capable of living in community without the threat of violence holding things together, but Christian political thought has proven unable to trust in that confession.

One classic anti-Semitic line is that 'the Jews killed Christ'. In the suffering of Jews during the Holocaust, Christians should be reminded that Christ stands in solidarity with those who suffer – therefore, in this case, that formula has been reversed. Christians killed Christ by refusing to suffer with those in need. The Church's sin in the Holocaust was not that it let power fall into the wrong hands, for power was in the hands of Christians all along. Rather, the Church's sin was in seeking its own interests, bargaining and turning its back in order to ensure its own survival. Better that the Church be destroyed than it fail to speak out and suffer with those in need.

Lest one think that I am laying the responsibility at the feet of only one group of Christians, I need to make one essential clarifying point. The Church must bear collective responsibility and guilt for its failures during the Holocaust – and, indeed, for the entire history of Christendom. This is the crucial element that seems to be lacking in Hauerwas and others' writings on the subject. There is a tendency on the part of the more so-called 'sectarian' factions of the Church to claim the mantle of 'authentic' Christianity. Instead, Christians must accept guilt, as Willis puts it, 'at the level of shared memory and participation in the ongoing life of a community rather than at the level of interpersonal assessment and judgment of the actions of others.'[29] We bear responsibility for the way in which we have failed to let the Christian story profoundly shape our lives *and* for the way that the Church has failed to embody the way of the cross at the institutional level.

This is perhaps the most uncomfortable task we face as Christians in the aftermath of the Holocaust. The ongoing story of the Church includes its greatest moral failure. As Willis writes, 'the effects of the Christian story through time in creating a potent seedbed for contemporary anti-Semitism, and the actions of those who professed allegiance to it during that crisis, can become, through intentional appropriation, part of my (and our) history as well.'[30] The act of repentance is something that each Christian does in living out the faith on a daily basis. This is our *primary* moral task after the Holocaust:

> The acceptance of one's complicity in Auschwitz provides no basis for assessing the intentions and actions of others. It is an action that each of us must perform for herself or himself, but it is done in the name of, and on behalf of, our participation in the community as a whole. Nevertheless, it is not a merely religious action devoid of moral import. Rather, it is, following Karl Barth's analysis, the *primary* moral deed – repentance, *metanoia* – which must precede and inform all subsequent thinking and doing.[31]

Here is where Christians can benefit most from dialogue with Jewish theologians. The greatest challenge to the ongoing life of the Church is dealing with its history of complicity in evil committed against other humans. In the case of the Holocaust, we must learn how to narrate the un-narratable. Jewish authors have wrestled with the horror of the camps, which represents the greatest *aporia* in history – meaning the events that have so destroyed personal identity that they absolutely resist emplotment in a narrative. To have been the victims of such horrors no doubt represents the greatest narrative challenge, but to integrate the role of the victimizer into the Christian narrative is a challenge nonetheless significant. How this integration will play out remains to be seen, because this is the work in which too few Christians engage; nonetheless, I believe that as we move into an increasingly secularized, post-Christian Western culture, we will find that the moral legacy of the Holocaust will lead us to true penitent humility of a more peaceful kind than Pawlikowski recommends.

It seems that Christianity's greatest moral failure has become its greatest temptation. We somehow have come away from the Holocaust with the notion that its horrors are the result of our not monopolizing enough of the violent power in the world, meaning that the event has not been transformative on any fundamental level. The moral import of the cross is not to call us to the humble exercise of violent power, for when we preach the Gospel of the cross from a position of power, we do it harm – it becomes a tool for oppression rather than a proclamation of divine truth. The type of dialogue that Christians have entered into with Jews has been less about understanding our own moral failures and more about collecting evidence for why power must remain in our hands. As I learned this summer, the cross is a disproportionately large part of the difference between Jews and Christians, and the cross makes even less sense to Jews precisely insofar as Christians have sold it out and forgotten its political meaning. If the Church is to be the embodiment of a different kind of community, one which overcomes racial and ethnic divisions, then its message is a hard one: Christians must stand in solidarity with those who suffer everywhere, even those who suffer at the hands of the so-called 'just' powers of the world. Christians need to be in solidarity with not only Kurds and Kosovars who suffer at the hands of Iraqis and Serbians, but *also* with Iraqis and Serbians who suffer at the hands of Americans. We must speak out against both the continuing anti-Semitism that rears its head in too many places worldwide *and* the continuing oppression of Palestinians by Israel. Our prayers must be precise but indiscriminate. Of course, prayers are not enough. Christians must also engage in political activity, but such activity must be within the bounds of the life Jesus has called us to live. The importance of prayer is not to bid the services of an interventionist God, but to ask that God for the strength to lead the type of life each of us is called to lead. Contemporary 'secular' society offers, as Hauerwas has noted, the first chance in seventeen centuries for Christians and Jews to encounter one another in freedom, without the threat of one group dominating the other. Our temptation is to use the Holocaust as an excuse for not allowing that to happen. Our failure was not that we neglected to kill the right people, but rather that we saw the need to kill at all. What, indeed, have Christians known about suffering? In Latin America and Africa, perhaps quite a lot, but when it comes to those who are prepared to dictate 'ethics' for the rest of the world, the fact of the matter is that we do not know enough.

NOTES

 1 James F. Moore, *Christian Theology after the Shoah* (New York: University Press of America, 1993): 137.
 2 John Milbank, 'The End of Dialogue', *Christian Uniqueness Reconsidered: The Myth of a Pluralistic Theology of Religions*, ed. Gavin D'Costa (Maryknoll, NY: Orbis Books, 1990): 177–178.
 3 *ibid.*, 178.
 4 *ibid.*, 184.
 5 *ibid.*, 179.
 6 *ibid.*, 180.
 7 I have in mind Rosemary Ruether, *Faith and Fratricide: The Theological Roots of Anti-Semitism* (New York: Seabury Press, 1979). Ruether gives a nuanced and sophisticated argument, and there is much truth in what she has to say, especially with regards to the role of emerging nationalism in oppressing Jews (page 220); however, one could argue to what extent Christian theology and the biblical tradition is to blame for nationalism.
 8 These points are summarized in Richard B. Hays, *The Moral Vision of the New Testament: A Contemporary Introduction to New Testament Ethics* (New York: HarperCollins, 1996): 409–410.
 9 *ibid.*, 439.
10 Which is to say, there were few international calls for action before the outbreak of violence in Rwanda, whereas the Holocaust was invoked repeatedly as an example of why NATO needed to intervene in Kosovo.
11 Stanley Hauerwas, *Against the Nations* (New York: Winston Press, 1985): 66.
12 David Hartman, 'New Jewish Religious Voices II: Auschwitz or Sinai?' *Ecumenist* 21, no.1 (November/December 1982): 8; cited in John T. Pawlikowski, 'Christian Ethics and the Holocaust: A Dialogue with Post-Auschwitz Judaism', *Theological Studies* 49 (1988): 654.
13 Pawlikowski, 655.
14 John T. Pawlikowski, 'The Shoah: Continuing Theological Challenge for Christianity', *Contemporary Christian Religious Responses to the Shoah*, ed. by Steven L. Jacobs (New York: University Press of America, 1993): 145.
15 Pawlikowski (1988): 657.
16 *ibid.*, 661.
17 *ibid.*, 667.
18 Darrell J. Fasching, 'Faith and Ethics after the Holocaust: What Christians Can Learn from the Jewish Narrative Tradition of *Hutzpah*', *Journal of Ecumenical Studies*, 27:3 (Summer, 1990): 453–479. See also Fasching, *Narrative Theology after Auschwitz: From Alienation to Ethics* (Minneapolis: Fortress Press, 1992).
19 Fasching (1990): 456.
20 *ibid.*, 463.

21 Fasching (1990): 465.

22 *ibid.*, 469.

23 *ibid.*, 470.

24 *ibid.* Curiously, Luther does not apply in Fasching's argument. While Luther is perhaps the exemplar of the struggle with God, according to Fasching his struggle ends in submission of the will. Of course, one would hardly wish to have Luther as a poster-boy for post-Holocaust theology.

25 David P. Gushee, *The Righteous Gentiles of the Holocaust: A Christian Interpretation* (Minneapolis: Fortress, 1994): 142.

26 *ibid.*, 161. Gushee also suggests that the Calvinist tradition, because it had done much to reclaim the Old Testament as a source for moral theology, better prepared Christians to recognize the humanity of Jews.

27 Robert E. Willis, 'Auschwitz and the Nurturing of Conscience', *Religion in Life* 44 (1975): 434.

28 Stanley Hauerwas, 'Jews and Christians among the Nations', *Cross Currents* 31 (Spring 1981): 34.

29 Willis, 440.

30 *ibid.*, 441.

31 *ibid.*

THE SHOAH AND THE CHRISTIAN DRAMA OF THE REDEMPTION

Massimo Giuliani

OR MY contribution, I would like to answer to the following questions: Can we consider the Shoah as a novelty and a caesura for Christian theology, Christology, and the Christian doctrine of the redemption? If so, what will the implications be? The essay is a development of a methodological premise and three issues: the uniqueness of the Shoah as a crisis for the Christologies of the churches; the Shoah and the rethinking of a Christian theology of the Jewish people; mutual legitimacy and messianic responsibility of Jews and Christians after Auschwitz.

ON METHODOLOGICAL RIGOUR: HERMENEUTIC AWARENESS
In the field of Christian theology it is difficult to avoid the risk of wrong beginnings. Methodological rigour (needed by all theological reflections if they are not to be weakened or even disproved for wrong presuppositions) must be pursued, especially when we are trying to propose a criticism of traditional Christologies in the light of a contemporary historical event. This methodological rigour has the feature of a deep hermeneutic self-understanding, that is, the awareness of the hermeneutic context in which all critical thought fits. Such a hermeneutic context, which no theological reflection can escape, also constitutes the limit of every criticism of traditional Christologies. It serves as an act of humility of reason before religious faith, understood as research and witness to a meaning of the world and history. I would like to sum such hermeneutic awareness (or methodological rigour) with a self-quotation:

> If a theological discourse did not care about the truth (of God), it would simply be mythology. But a theology that would also care about the truth without consideration for history would be destined to become mythological or ideological. The possibility 'to do theology' is always between truth and history. For centuries we were educated to think that the foundation of the theology was the truth, and that only a very certain presupposition guaranteed the theological reflection. And for centuries the risk and weakness of such a reflection were relegated to the dimension of language and linguistic codes. Between the end of the 20th and the beginning of 21st century, the suspicion arose that the certainty of the presupposition was relative in nature (is faith not a risk, a leap, a *pari*?), and that, on the contrary, the only certainty was the code where presupposition was thought of – and passed on – by history. After Heidegger and Gadamer, who can ignore the fact that truth – including theological truth – is dependent on language? And that language is the grammar of history? The truth of faith and the accident of history cannot be separated. On the contrary, the nexus linking a fact to its interpretation or an event to its narration is insoluble and structural. The truth and the authority of theology do not depend on the assumed ahistoricity of its affirmations, but on taking on linguistic historicity as the ultimate and

not-transcendable context in which truth manifests itself. As an interpretative striving of the faith of the churches, theology has nothing to lose from its recognition of historical evidence if one accepts that 'truth is historical' (according to John's verse: *Verbum caro factum est*). Instead, it has everything to lose when it settles on an idea of truth that denies or opposes the historical datum. This means, again: a theology that would deny its own status as interpretation would be pure ideology, and would not share anything with faith.[1]

This premise removes any objection to the legitimacy of rethinking the fundamental credo of Christianity in light of a historical event. Moreover, because the Shoah belongs to the history of the relations between Christians and Jews (and not only to world history), it is the primary need of contemporary Christian self-understanding to interpret – or re-interpret – the truth of that relation in light of such an event.

THE JEWISH UNIQUENESS OF THE SHOAH AS A CRISIS FOR THE CHRISTOLOGIES OF THE CHURCHES

Truth about oneself

My reflection, therefore, starts from Christian self-understanding and not directly from the Shoah as an event of Jewish history. It is Christian self-understanding that, in its urgent need to be faithful through Christ to God, the same God of the Jewish people, feels the duty to 'verify itself'. To verify itself for the churches has a double meaning: firstly to examine their behaviour, attitudes and thoughts (and here the critical function of theological reflection intervenes); and secondly 'to do the truth' (John 3: 21) on themselves (and this could imply the special witness of martyrdom). In order to be loyal to Christ's teachings and to return to God the Christian churches must allow history – and especially the Shoah – to put them in crisis. The Shoah constitutes that unique event in which the history of the Jewish people and the history of Christianity collide and are placed face to face with their own will, in a manner that never happened before. Moreover, in the Shoah the two histories crash and interweave so that, from that point forwards, it will be impossible for the churches and Israel to think about themselves without recalling that event, or at least without taking into account all its implications.

The so-called 'Christian theology after Auschwitz' is an attempt to grasp and develop the implications pivoted around the undeniable fact that the Shoah is the summit of many centuries of anti-Jewish (and anti-Semitic) teachings and attitudes.[2] Indeed, without the theological prejudice and the religious discrimination against the Jews the 'final solution of the Jewish question' performed by the Nazis and their collaborators would not have been possible, at least with the modalities that we know. For the churches and Christian theologies, 'doing the truth' means realizing this fact. It means searching and discovering the deepest causes, even the most remote ones, of this prejudice and discrimination. It means analysing them in relation to the entire corpus of the Christian credo in order to remove them. And it means trying to understand why and how they were able to remain for so long among the communities of the believers in Christ. The task is not only to focus on errors and uproot them (as the ecclesiastical hierarchies and many Christian thinkers and theologians have honestly done in recent years). Above all, the task is to offer a new interpretation of the relationship that links Israel to the churches, a relationship that so far was misunderstood and misinterpreted precisely in terms of prejudice and contempt, or even of 'theological negation' of which the entire history of Christian anti-Judaism is an open, tragic manifestation.

The theological error

Until the day after the Shoah, the churches taught and passed on to their fellows an error, a 'theological error' regarding Jews and Judaism whose results have become the entire history of anti-Judaism, anti-Semitism and, in the end, the Shoah. A process of 'theological revisionism' inside the churches denounced and corrected that error – that God has rejected Israel and nullified the covenant with the Jewish people, that Christianity has superseded Israel in the heritage of the promises and is now the *verus* Israel of whom the ancient Jewish people were a mere prefiguration – by offering a new, positive and appreciative teaching about Jews and Judaism. This revisionism was urgent and necessary. Today, while the former error is corrected through a new understanding of the relation between Israel and the churches, Christian theology has the duty to re-interpret such a history, that is, to interpret the same 'theological error' that was taught by Christianity for centuries. Indeed, such an error – paradoxically but not too much – was the only ecumenical truth shared through the centuries by the Christians in their many diverse and conflicting theological discussions. This ecumenical truth was, of course, negative and perverse not only for Jews, but it was also unifying and founding, as unique and basic as it was and is, for Christianity, the *kerygma* of the faith in Jesus as Christ dead and resurrected.

What does this theological error mean? What is hidden under the seemingly linearity of the superseding logic that generated it? How do we re-open the serious case of the separation between the two religions at the beginning of the first millennium of the Christian era? How can we evaluate the drama of Christian self-legitimacy before the Jewish people? How can we remove the causes of such an error inside the same Christian Holy Writings? Who has the moral and magisterial authority for such a removal? All of these questions burn in contemporary Christian self-understanding and force theology (in all its branches: biblical, liturgical, moral and systematic) finally to face the meaning of that error. That is, to face 'what the error stands for', because an error is always a deviation from a truth just as a sin is always the result of a missed act of obedience or a neglected virtue. In other words the theological error that was taught by churches for centuries does nor stand for itself, but is nothing more than the upside-down of a truth. It is the negative of a positive. It is the absence of a *pleroma* of theological meaning and grace to which the churches are called and from which they were separated as the result of such a sin. A sin against God and against Israel.

Illuminating the most deeply hidden causes and theological motivations of the sin of anti-Judaism is for the Christian churches and theologians a compelling and mandatory task 'to do the truth' of the Gospel by enlightening so that loyalty to Christ and conversion to God can be sincere. Also in its negativity, the error bears witness to the counter-truth still to be discovered and performed, a 'truth to do' as *veritas in fieri*. The error alludes to plenitude that is not yet reached, not yet revealed. Perhaps the theological error about Jews and Judaism is the Christian form of resistance to God and the divine process of redemption. What does amending this error mean, if not making room for a more complete revelation? But in this case returning to God entails first of all a serious revision of our own (wrong) self-understanding, a revision made possible by a sincere opening to Jewish diversity. As it is known for all true conversions, nobody can convert alone, *sua sponte* and without suffering.

Revelation of a veritas in fieri

If the Christian churches had existed since their beginning in the plenitude of the truth they would be without sin. But the fact that they have lived for so long in sin of anti-Judaism constitutes the proof that even for the churches the truth is more a mission than a datum, more a process than a possession, more a re-velation (*aletheia*) and a confirmation (*emunah*) than a doctrinal corpus that is unalterable and impenetrable. The Christian theological error about Jews and Judaism is a kind of 'reversed truth' that is still waiting to be reversed and revealed. For this reason, only when they accept not having all the truth and 'doing the truth' through the returning through Christ to the God of Israel, do the churches participate in the major event of the history of salvation: the revelation of the divine initiative to redeem the world.

Certainly, Christians and Jews have two different visions of how such a revelation happened and such an initiative developed in history. Nonetheless, both historically and theologically Christian revelation depends on Jewish revelation because the event of Christ was possible in the history of Jewish people, and is understandable to this day. This implies that even the Jewish refusal of Jesus as Christ has a theological meaning for the churches, a positive meaning. It attests that revelation and redemption living in a Christian context are not all of revelation nor all of redemption according to God's intention. It is not the reason for God's rejection of God's people but constitutes instead the principle of incompleteness of Christian revelation and redemption and, at the same time, it suggests an idea *in fieri* of the revealed truth. Redemption indeed is only partially accomplished in history and is still being developed. To this *veritas in fieri*, therefore, the churches are called together with Israel and precisely when they face the loyalty of Israel to its own calling. By accepting the principle that truth is not 'at the beginning' but 'at the end', the churches can also accept the idea that their theological error is understandable within the way toward the truth, and as such, can be overcome. Overcoming it is an increase of Christian truth itself. The recognition of this sin against God and Israel is for the churches the first, necessary condition to have access to the plenitude of the revelation. The un-veiling and the re-versing of this error is a prelude to a new chapter of revelation, or perhaps a new hermeneutics of the ancient revelation, and therefore a new self-understanding of Christianity as a religion of the salvation of the world.

Soteriological relativity

What is this new hermeneutics of Christian revelation? To what kind of truth is it bringing the unveiling of the theological error of anti-Judaism, that is not a given truth but one to be achieved, nay, to be added to the gift of the revelation 'in Christ'? Now the sin of anti-Judaism committed in history by the Christian churches is nothing but the missed recognition that not one and just one soteriological way exists in God's intention, but at least two. At least because 'two' means plurality. The churches commit the sin of anti-Judaism every time they deny that Israel is a legitimate way established by God to save the world. But the churches also commit the sin of anti-Judaism when they exclude someone from the possibility of being saved beyond themselves, that is, every time they reduce the ways of divine mercy to their own way. The sin of anti-Judaism is, for the churches, this pretended soteriological *reductio ad unum* – to themselves – while, on the contrary, every time they recognize Judaism as a legitimate way of salvation, they open up to a new hermeneutics of themselves and their mission in the world. Under the sin of anti-Judaism is hidden a need of legitimacy to which ancient Christians gave satisfaction by putting the burden of proof on Israel's shoulders: the proof of divine election. The destruction of the Temple in Jerusalem and the Diaspora were believed to be God's punishment of Jewish people and was for Christian theology proof of the delegitimacy of Israel and the consecration of the Church as *novus et verus* Israel that superseded the ancient (old) one. Once Israel was delegitimated the Church elected itself as the universal heir to the promises and the gifts of God that already belonged to Israel, which was now apostrophized with the negative term 'according to the flesh' in opposition to 'according to the spirit'. Of course, the Christian spirit.

The Shoah was the tragic epilogue of this long delegitimating process. In its tragic manner, the Shoah put Christianity before a very ancient and unresolved problem, that is, it re-opened in the self-understanding of the churches the undeniable need of theological legitimacy, or, in other words, of knowledge of its own root. The sin of anti-Judaism was exactly this 'blinding scream'[3] by the churches toward their own roots, translated in an open mis-recognition of the theological primacy of Israel. As the last and the most radical attempt to delegitimate Israel and the emblem of the price paid by Israel of its own mission in the world, the Shoah is the biggest confutation of the soteriological self-sufficiency of Christianity and the churches. It made clear how deep the crisis of the idea is that God only reveals Himself with plenitude inside the churches. It forces the churches to recognize Israel as suffering servant of God (according to Isaiah's prophecy) and as the privileged witness of the divine freedom of salvation. And finally it forces the believers in Jesus as Christ to recognize the permanent theological meaning of Israel in the 'economy of salvation'. As a corollary, all of this implies the soteriological relativity of Christianity, or – in more positive terms – underlines the value of the soteriological pluralism of the Jewish-Christian tradition. This soteriological pluralism is the true matter at stake in the long, hard conflict between Christianity and Judaism.

For the churches the re-interpretation of the sin of anti-Judaism also has the goal of a honest recognition of the structural conflict existing between the two religions, a conflict in which the history of anti-Judaism and anti-Semitism is only one aspect, one manifestation, the substance of which is precisely divine election for the salvation of the world. (For the Jews, the Torah is the tool given by God for the sanctification of the world; for the Christians, instead, God redeems the world in Christ and the churches have the duty to announce this 'news' to as many individuals as possible.) The reversed truth of the Christian error concerns this conflict. The error is not to be reversed in a generic religious peace, or in a cheap reconciliation, but has to be converted into the recognition that, precisely through the conflict, Israel and the churches struggle together with God for the liberation of the world from evil, that is, from injustice. The condition of this recognition after the Shoah from now on is an acceptance by the churches of their own soteriological relativity, that is, of their subsisting 'before Israel'. Israel is not a super-seded soterological reality that God wanted earlier than the churches and next to the churches. Denying to Israel this soteriological status constitutes the historical nucleus of any theological anti-Judaism. Affirming it, again or *ex novo* constitutes the novelty of the Shoah as a revelation of the structural theological dependence of the churches on the mystery of Israel.

The implications of the soteriological relativism of Christianity
In our reflections we rely on the presupposition (that we cannot take for granted) that a link exists between Israel and the churches, Judaism and Christianity – a unique link theological in nature that goes beyond specific historical circumstances. It is a true overlapping of identities: Christianity was thought of as a particular experience of Judaism, and inside Judaism, the new religion was ostracized (together with other Greek elements) as a necessary step to survive and preserve the Jewish identity. There-fore it is in light of the uniqueness of the relationship between the two religions that we can explain the theological relapse of what happens – has happened and will happen – in Judaism to Christianity. All that is Jewish, we can say, has an impact on Christianity and

the churches.[4] Thus the Shoah as an essentially Jewish tragedy has a double impact on Christianity, both in the traditional way in which Christians think of Jews and Judaism and, more deeply, in the way in which the churches think of themselves as 'the people of God', called in Christ to participate in the same promises made to the Jewish people and in a mission that, close up, is not qualitatively (better, ethically) distinguished from the Jewish mission. If such a particular historical-theological link did not exist between Israel and the churches the Shoah would not have touched the nature and the mission of Christianity so deeply. And this is true without considering also the specific theological responsibilities that Christianity – that is, the churches – has had in the history of the anti-Judaism and anti-Semitism.[5] Instead the Shoah touches and modifies this nature and mission because the self-understanding of the churches passes through the conflict with Israel. This conflict can no longer be thought of in terms of negation of the theological value of Judaism *per se*. From now on it has to be thought of – because of Auschwitz – as a manifestation of soteriological pluralism. Precisely in virtue of this pluralism non-Jews participate 'for grace' in the Jewish 'covenant that was never revoked'.[6] In this context, 'for grace' represents the *unicum*, the specific and the irreducible of the Christian faith, that is, the soteriological value of the Cross. 'For grace' means, in Paul's language, 'in Christ'. If all this is true and if it is true that 'the theological problem of the churches is not the Shoah *per se* but through the Shoah the re-discovery of Israel and the Christian historical dimension',[7] then it will not be difficult to understand the impact that the Shoah had and has on the way Christians believe that Jesus is the Christ and that the Cross is redemption. At this point, we do not have to discuss whether this impact exists, but only how it is articulated within the Christological architectures of the churches.

Christology is the Christian doctrine about Jesus as Messiah and Lord. It is the living heart of every Christian theology because, in this doctrine, the three moments of every theological Judeo-Christian reflection converge: redemption, revelation and creation (in this exact order).[8] Albeit with the variations of the different Christian churches some constant themes exist in every Christology. Two themes, it seems to me, are basic: the first, in Christ the drama of the co-presence of God and evil in the world is – so to speak – resolved. The second, in Christ the role of the Jewish people among the others is revealed. The first theme primarily refers to the moments of redemption and creation. The second theme has a narrow nexus with the moment of revelation. My intention is to show how the Shoah has an impact on each of these basic themes that the diverse churches share.

Evil in the world

The first theme is, once again, theodicy. I do not mean the 'problem of theodicy' in the traditional sense used in the philosophical treatises. My context is essentially theological. And for Christian theology this 'problem' is not a problem at all because Christ is the only theo-dicy. In other words, Christ is the full revelation of the justice of God, and evil in the world (*peccata mundi*) does not constitute a problem any more, at least not for God. Certainly, nobody can deny that evil did not disappear from the world despite the redemption of the Cross. Nor can one deny that this world, created by God – in Christ or in view of Christ – is a world inhabited by evil. But Christology also has a solution for this seeming contradiction, an eschatological solution.

Evil is a historical fact not a divine entity or one with a transcendental nature. It entered into the world through the human freedom to choose, contrary to God's law for the world. Such an evil would be irredeemable if God Himself did not take care of it in order to atone for it. In Jesus as Son and Christ, God ontologically assumes evil and wins against it through a voluntary atoning sacrifice. Jesus' death is this atonement of the Son while the resurrection is the act through which God consecrates Jesus as His messiah, the winner against a death that is emblematic of evil. Thus the sacrifice of Christ has a universal theological value: Jesus is not just a lamb, not the first of lambs, but is the only Lamb of God (*Agnus Dei qui tollit peccata mundi*). There is no room for other lambs. History becomes 'before' and 'after Christ'. The sacrifice of the unique *Agnus Dei* of Easter has been overlapped by and superseded the lambs of *Pesach*, the Jewish Passover. This superseding – or the principle of substitution at work here – is not a marginal element in Christian theology. It is, its explicatory logic, its main pillar, its hermeneutic key. Thus, the death and the resurrection of Jesus as Christ resolve the *aporeia* (contradiction) of a thought that is shocked by the fact that God and evil cohabit the same world, or that God tolerates evil within His world. Now, if even after the sacrifice of Christ evil does not seem defeated, this is because only the eyes of faith are able to see the mystery of redemption and the reign of God implanted on earth. In addition, this truth will be openly revealed only at the end of this world, even if already now the community of the believers mystically participates in this victory and reign. Every contradiction is solved: God is God and evil is only in function of good. The key of this solution of the problem, the ultimate word of this 'perfect theodicy', is the Cross of Christ whose sacrifice was accepted by the God who resurrected him.

The Shoah arose as a very unique evil before this 'perfect theodicy': it is an evil that does not tolerate being used as a means of any good, neither an eternal, spiritual, nor superior good. It is an evil committed against those who do not accept Christianity and its Christology (they have already paid a very high price for the principle of substitution). And finally, it is an evil that has its remote origin precisely in the Christian doctrine of Christ, through the allegation that the Jews are deicides and killers of Jesus. The tragedy of the Shoah awakened in the heart of Christians the doubt and suspicion that this kind of evil is not redeemed at all, nor is it redeemable by the Cross of Jesus. And this for no reason other than that such an evil was committed in the name of the Cross and perpetrated by the baptized. This evil is not theological fiction. The Christological theodicy does not reach it, nor does it solve it within Christian redemption. Doubt and suspicion cause an impact that is more than sufficient to force us to rethink about Christology from its very base: its superseding logic and the soteriological value of the Cross of Christ.

Israel, the churches, and the rest of the world
The second theme is the revelation in Christ (Christ as revealer and what is revealed), who enlightens, explains, and absorbs – that is, supersedes – the role of Israel in the divine economy of salvation. Indeed, both the revelation of Sinai and the subsequent mission of Israel among the nations find their accomplishment in the Christological doctrine. The election of Israel was functional, in this scheme, in the preparation of the coming of the king-messiah, the envoy of God, and the diffusion of this 'good news'. In Christ the intimacy of relation between God and Israel is opened and becomes the intimacy between God and every human being. The prophetic, sacerdotal and royal function of Israel as a people is passed over by the figure of Jesus as Christ and after him (through him) by the Church as *ecclesia*, the community mystically called on to develop the same work of redemption in the world. This 'work' is the faith in Jesus 'constituted Christ by God' (Acts 2: 36). There is no contradiction, therefore, between Israel and Christ since the true mission of Israel was to prepare the advent of the messiah and leave

the spot for him at the right moment. And there is no theological contradiction between Israel and the churches because they are the *verus* Israel, and all nations are called in and by Christ to become the unique Israel of God. Thus, the 'carnal' Israel is transformed into a simple, introductory chapter of ecclesiology and its function as the 'light of the nations' is absorbed by the same mission of Christ and the churches. It is always the principle of substitution at work: in election, in the process of revelation and the uniqueness of the mediation between God and the world. The consciousness of churches' mission rests on this chapter of the Christology.

Once again however this consciousness confronts the Shoah as a tragic revelation of the permanent theological value of Israel that God did not at all want to repudiate nor substitute with the Church/churches. By surviving and returning into history[9] as the people of God Israel reaffirmed its loyalty to the covenant, even in the largest plurality of its interpretation. And these – surviving the Shoah and returning to the land of Israel – are, for the churches, the most evident signs of the weakness of their own self-legitimacy at the expense of Judaism. These signs challenge the idea of the uniqueness and universality of Christian soteriology, that is, of the traditional Christologies. As a realization of the permanent presence of Israel beside the churches, the Shoah stirs in them the question about the limits of their pretension of worldly salvation and poses a theological limit to the redemption of Christ. And this, *per se*, is something really new in Christian theology! We can say that the cause of this question is the Shoah as a Jewish tragedy. As I mentioned above, all that is Jewish touches revelation and subsequently, for Christians, touches Christ and his mystery. Therefore the Shoah should also be considered a Christological problem from a primarily theological point of view. Indeed it has posed in traditional Christologies the doubt of soteriological relativity and the suspicion that the sin of anti-Judaism made the churches blind to a deeper comprehension of God and His presence in the world.

At this point, every Christian theologian who is able to stand before Israel after the Shoah cannot avoid the most crucial questions. How can the churches affirm their identity without expropriating Israel, by spoiling it of its identity? For Christology, what is the meaning of the fact that the suffering of Israel is not reachable by the redemption of the Cross? And how can one face the suspicion that perhaps it was precisely the Cross of Christ that has contributed to the Shoah as 'irredeemable evil?'

THE SHOAH AND THE RETHINKING OF A CHRISTIAN THEOLOGY OF THE JEWISH PEOPLE

At the stage of questions
'What we need,' Paul Van Buren once said, 'is not a theology of the Holocaust, whatsoever, but a Christian theology of the Jewish people.'[10] Even better, we need a Christian theology built in light of the 'tragic revelation' of the Shoah, that is, by assuming the fact that Israel is the first partner of the covenant with God and that its election continues having a theological meaning *per se* and for the churches. The *pars destruens* made by the Shoah on contemporary Christian self-understanding is the unavoidable point of departure. It is not surprising, nor is it unreasonable to be shocked, that so far Christian theologians have been able only to ask questions but not to elaborate a holistic theological vision as the *pars construens*. The recognition of the theological error and the consequent loss of the credibility of the churches have been so devastating that very few have dared to ask questions. Thus, only from here is it possible to depart and try to give an adequate answer to the contemporary Christian crisis of identity.

Reinterpreting the theological error – or, in a more religious language, repenting for the sin of anti-Judaism – is the most urgent priority for the theology of the new century. The sin committed 'in the name of the Cross' against the Jewish people is not one sin among others. It is instead a real threat to the entire system, having already determined the decline of credibility of the churches during the second millennium and made the building of Christian redemption, that is, the Christology, tremble like a giant with clay feet. No doctrine about Jesus can continue to be affirmed by the churches on the basis of the principle of substitution and soteriological exclusivity, pushing the Jewish people into the corner of protology (Israel as preparation and pre-figure of the churches) or eschatology (the final conversion of the Jews to the gospel).

Therefore we have to accept the risk and the scandal of these crucial questions. To what extent does the renouncing of anti-Judaism – with all its implications for Christian life – touch on the truth and legitimacy of Christianity? Does such a renouncing entail a revision and correction of the Tradition, depriving it of its status as a 'pillar of revelation' together with the Scriptures? And with which conceptual and linguistic instruments is such a revision even possible (given that nobody is free from the influences of a tradition)? Should this revision not start precisely from a 'deconstruction' of the New Testament? But is this not a process of self-destruction, operated under a true or alleged sense of guilt? And again: if the sacrifice of Christ is not universal – because it cannot reach all of the evil in the world, or at least it cannot reach the sin committed against the Jews – what is the true meaning of this sacrifice? How can Christians affirm that 'Christ achieves the Scriptures' without stealing what belongs to Israel? The problem of the Christian identity is so interwoven with the Jewish identity that there is no point in any Christian doctrine (not only in Christology) that does not become problematic when the principle of substitution is given up. Indeed, when soteriological pluralism is inserted into Christianity it is not a banal principle of relativity but is a 'standing again next to Israel' – as it did two thousand years ago – facing the conflict of co-habitation: the same Scriptures, the same patriarchs, the same prophets, the same promises and also the same messianic hope. Certainly, the error and shame of the long history of anti-Judaism and anti-Semitism can be removed from the churches. Fear, prejudice and contempt toward Christianity can also be removed from the Jewish people. But nobody can remove the theological conflict that is born from what the two religions have in common and what precisely constitutes the *substantia* of the conflict. Like two different flowers blossoming on one tree, they are – according the expression of the Italian scholar Paolo De Benedetti – 'more than one, less than two'.

In search of a new hermeneutics
Facing these and other difficult questions (often without a satisfactory answer by Christian theologians and official representatives of the churches) we are tempted to formulate a kind of 'negative theology of Israel'. At this stage, the Shoah forces us to admit what Israel is no longer for us, by denying the error we taught for so long. But this does not enable us to formulate a new Christian theology of the Jewish people, one that is positive. Now, if we seriously and without reservation affirm that the Torah is still compelling and engaging for non-Jews, because God's word is always valid and God does not deceive anybody in order to save someone else (that is, God does not disprove the Jewish people to credit Christians), then the non-Jews should honestly recommence to practice the *mitzvot*,[11] all the commandments, beginning from circumcision! But it was the renouncing of circumcision in favour of the faith in Christ that made Christianity different from Judaism![12] On which basis, therefore, can we renounce the principle of

substitution and with what does it have to be substituted? It seems to me that, for now, theology has to be satisfied with and rest upon a simple but unavoidable hermeneutic criterion, perhaps minimal, but not easy to apply. It echoes the famous criterion given by Rabbi Irving Greenberg more than 25 years ago,[13] but it lays out a new awareness that is widespread among Christians. I would formulate it as the following: a Christian affirmation is no longer legitimate if it is the positive of an anti-Judaic negative, in other words if it is the result of a negation or exploitation of one or more characters of Judaism. To give an example: even the soteriological principle of the 'faith in Christ' becomes theologically illegitimate if it is moulded as the positive versus a negative, for example, the observance of the *mitzvot*. Or again: the value of the uniqueness of the sacrifice of Christ versus the meaning of the multiple sacrifice of the victims of the Shoah or, in a remote but not completely surreal hypothesis, versus the possible sacrifices in a future third temple in Jerusalem.

The fact is that, on the one hand, the dialectics of Judaism today, after the 'return of the Jewish people into history', causes a crisis in the eschatological pro-lectics of Christianity, by showing the whole hermeneutic relativity – that is, soteriological relativity – of the latter. On the other hand, the Cross of Christ is, for Christians, an offer of grace made by the God of Israel and signifies the entrance into the covenant. The Cross, like the election of Israel, is unique. And this perhaps suggests that, for Christian theology, the relation Christ-Israel precedes, founds and orients all other relations, including that between Israel and the churches, or between church and church, or even between the churches and the world (and maybe also that between the churches and God). The implications of that (seemingly) simple 'criterion in negative' are complex because they touch the very essence of Christianity: the relation of Christ with Israel and its God. By breaking the prolectics of Christian escatology, the dialectics of Jewish history produces the effect of changing dogma into drama, theodicy into *Choaskampf* and opens the redemption to the risk of failure. Israel is no longer pushed into the corner of the protology and the eschatology of Christian theology and becomes – as it was first in the election – the co-partner in the covenant with God. Of course, it was always so, even in the most anti-Judaic theology, but in a contemptuous manner as a tool of evil in view of good: the Christian redemption. The churches do not yet know how to rethink it in a positive, appreciative manner, reversing the long history of Christian anti-Judaism. But 'if it is not up to the generation after Auschwitz to accomplish the work, it is certainly up to it to begin to work on it'.[14]

Christology and theocentrism

To what consequences will this theological effort expose Christianity? Is it not a mere deconstruction, with no possibility of substituting anything else for a destroyed Christology? A theology seriously facing Auschwitz is a theology that knows the risks of becoming a form of ideology, or, in a more religious language, a form of idolatry. On this point, the pastor Martin Cunz recalled the lesson of Dietrich Bonhoeffer: 'He raised his voice in favour of the Jews [during the Shoah] so that he could sing in Gregorian. Without this act of protest, the Gregorian would have been transformed into a chant that was not different from the Nazi ones.'[15] For Cunz, a post-Auschwitz theology – a theology of listening to the Jewish people – is a theocentric theology that is able to unmask 'Christolatry', the Christian ideology that made idols of God and Christ available for consumption of the churches.[16] For Christian theology after the Shoah theocentrism means rethinking Christology in biblical terms by recognizing Jesus's Jewish blood and bones, returning him to his people, its land and history. It means rethinking Christ in light of his faith in God, in the God of Abraham, Isaac and Jacob, in the God of Moses and David, in the God of the covenant. He did not come to revoke but to accomplish by observing all the commandments (see Matthew 5: 17–18). The Christ of Paul's letters does not supersede God, exactly as the gospel narration does not supersede the Bible understood as Torah and Prophets. The re-discovery of the theocentrism lived by Jesus and the renouncing of an exaggerated Christocentric worship can constitute a good start to rethinking Christian theology and a renewed Christology in listening to God in light of the tragic lesson of the Shoah.[17]

The Cross of Christ does not have a worse enemy than itself if and when it is used ideologically, out of context, as an instrument of oppression and discrimination instead of as an admonition for justice, liberation and love 'until death'. Thus, the Cross reverses against those who brandish it 'in the name of God' and becomes an emblem of failure. This is why the Cross erected in the extermination camp of Auschwitz, far from symbolizing redemption or God's love for the victims of the Jewish people, in the very moment of its extreme abjection became an emblematic claim of theological superiority. It can become, in the words of Martin Cunz, 'a declaration of bankruptcy for the baptized people, a bankruptcy that began with the inquisition and that was confirmed by Nazism, which the baptized were unable to seriously resist'.[18] Again, as Robert E. Willis recalls: 'We cannot proceed as if the passion of Christ would provide a model that is symbolically innocent to interpret the Holocaust. Symbolically, it became part of the same evil that it tried to enlighten.'[19] This affirmation is only a different way of asking the question above. How can we predicate the Christian meaning of the death and the resurrection of Christ, and at the same time affirm that the suffering of Israel is not touched by it? Moreover, is predication precisely the ultimate root of such suffering? This gap, that appears unbridgeable, poses a new challenge to Christian theology and its ability to comprehend and convey the Christian drama of redemption.

RECIPROCAL RECOGNITION AND MESSIANIC RESPONSIBILITY OF JEWS AND CHRISTIANS AFTER AUSCHWITZ

The theological value of Jews and Judaism for the Christian churches
The entire reflection of Christology developed thus far pivots around the tragic discovery by the churches of their own sin of anti-Judaism, a sin against God and against Israel and at the same time a theological error. This error is at the heart of the faith in Jesus, who Christians recognize as the Messiah and the Lord. For the churches, therefore, rethinking their own Christology is a consequence of that dramatic recognition and the first result of what we are used to call – along with the rabbinical theology – *teshuvah*, that is, repentance and return to God, in Greek *metanoia*. The inspiring principle of this rethinking of Christology is an ancient truth but forgotten and obscured by centuries of theological error: the Jewish people – not only the people of the Bible, but the current living people of Israel – are the active partners of God and have a theological value *per se*, as the entire Bible (New Testament included) attests. They also continue to have a theological meaning for the churches, their identities and mission. The attempt, under the sin of anti-Judaism and anti-Semitism, to exterminate the Jewish people from the face of earth has a double meaning for the churches. On one hand, the Shoah was a consequence – its directness or indirectness is up to the historians to debate – of a theological error that was taught for almost two thousand years by these very churches. On the other hand, it was a kind of revelation of the permanent theological value of Israel, whose destiny and suffering cannot be thought of as a function for the identity and

mission of Christianity. From here stems the urgent need for the churches to rethink themselves from their root, from Christology. As I said above, Israel is not a chapter of the ecclesial protology, as preparation and prefiguration of the coming of Christ and the Church. Nor is it a chapter of eschatology, when their conversion to Christ will signify the resurrection from death (according to a too-quick interpretation of Paul's letter to Romans).

After the Shoah, the churches find Israel in front of them again, not as an unconscious witness of Christ, but as an active partner in the covenant between God and humanity. Israel has a theological value *per se*, in virtue of its unique and eternal relationship with God. Moreover, after the Shoah the churches sit in front of Israel as 'a disciple sits in front of the teacher', because they know now that the mystery of the relation between Jesus and Israel is deeper than they thought thus far. And it still must be explored. Because the Scriptures, the patriarchs, the prophets, the promises and also the messiah are a 'gift of Israel' to the world, the churches realize that they are dependent on Israel in a symbolic but none the less real form. Christian anti-Judaism was a clumsy, tragic way through which the churches have tried to legitimate themselves without Israel, nay, against Israel. Today, as a result of their act of repentance and the recognition of their historical sin, the churches are able to see the vital relationship that links them to Israel at the same level to their own identity and *raison d'être*. In order to be faithful to God through Christ, the churches must recognize such a relationship and recognize that they are partners with Israel in the divine project on the world. For Christians a task is directly derived: they have the responsibility to recognize the theological value that Jews and Judaism have *per se* and to keep it with esteem and love, given that it is the 'root that bears' the value of the very Christianity. Even if such an affirmation seems hard and paradoxical from a theological point of view Christianity is a chapter in Jewish history; Judaism is not a chapter in Christian theology or ecclesiology. The *teshuvah* made by the churches after the Shoah implies this task: to recognize Judaism *per se* – for what it says it is – and recognize in Judaism the holy root of Christianity, with which it shares the partnership in the only covenant with God. This covenant was made known to Christians as non-Jews through Jesus, who represents for them the 'door of the covenant'. What else and what more can the attribute 'Christ' for Jesus mean (see Ephesians 2: 14)? By recognizing in a new manner the theological value of Israel, the churches 'do the truth' on themselves and, religiously speaking, give to God that worship of truth and justice that was denied for so long by the sin of anti-Judaism.

The legitimacy of Christianity by the Jewish people
What is the other face of the problem? The history of discrimination and persecution inspired by Christian theology and condensed into the pseudo-scientific language of the Shoah has 'negatively revealed' to the Jewish people of this century its relationship with Christianity, a relationship that is both historical and theological. It cannot be overlooked any more. Precisely its negation by Christians was the basis of the sin of anti-Judaism. For such a negation to be overcome and transformed it is also necessary that the Jewish people do not deny but recognize the relation that links it to Christianity. How? By recognizing Christianity and the churches as partners in the covenant with God, in a partnership that is symbolic but real,[20] to which Israel was called first, but not alone. Israel saw evil face to face in the tragedy of the Shoah and felt with urgency the need of redemption in the world. And inside this tragedy Israel realized how evil is too large to be fought by one alone. During and after the 'final solution', many Jewish thinkers and theologians tried to interpret that event and to put it in the framework of the long Jewish

history. This meant looking for a meaning of the Shoah. Many believed they had seen a theological meaning: a negation of God's existence, or a confirmation of faith in God and Israel's destiny. I believe that a theological meaning also exists in the fact that the Shoah changed the relationship between Israel and the churches, marking an impact on the religious consciousness of contemporary Christians (at least on those who made *teshuvah* from the sin of anti-Judaism). Jews suffered for a long time at the hands of Christians because of the almost desperate need of Christians to be theologically legitimized. Indeed, from whom can this legitimacy come from but the Jewish people, to whom the Scriptures belong, the patriarchs, the prophets, the promises and the very messiah? From another perspective the Shoah increased in Judaism the need for a 'theology of history' in which Christianity and Islam can also find a place[21] beside the traditional doctrine of Noah's laws.

Both Christian messianism and Islamic prophetism have a special link to the God of Israel. The former in particular is a direct offspring of the messianic longing of Israel, although it became another religion from the beginning. Another, but not enough to be something else. If it really had to become something else then it would not have developed and kept alive for centuries a jealousy towards and aversion against its very root. Christian messianism is not too different from all other Jewish messianisms except for its ability to become autonomous and successful. But success is not a theological reason. It is only a historical fact. In this perspective even two thousand years later and after the Shoah a Jewish responsibility exists toward Christianity, a responsibility of legitimacy that can accelerate the end of the 'theological hate' of Christians against Jews and will also perhaps open a new conception of the covenant for Judaism. I think that, just as the churches cannot think of the God's intention of salvation through Christ without Israel and its history, Israel cannot think of redemption in the world as if Christianity and Islam did not exist. And just as the Shoah forced Christians to take responsibility for the future of Judaism and Jews without secondary goals (for example the conversion), the tragedy of European Judaism in the heart of Christian Europe also opened to Jews the possibility of theologically recognizing Christianity – or at least those churches that made *teshuvah* – as a partner in the larger mystery of the redemption of the world. Or, in a more modest language, as a partner in the messianic hope to better the world.

THE HERITAGE OF THE 20TH CENTURY
The acceptance of a soteriological relativity by churches and synagogues, tragically implied by Auschwitz, is a condition such that the historical conflict between Judaism and Christianity ceases to be a history of suffering and becomes a 'dialectic covenant' rooted in a reconciled memory and inspired by the hope of God's victory against evil. As I mentioned above, the end of the long history of anti-Judaism and anti-Semitism does not mean the end of the confrontation of the two religions. Their conflict is an effect of their real and undeniable diversity. But this conflict is *dans l'ordre des choses*. It is a constitutive part of the identity of both. We do not have to demonize the conflict, understood as dialectics of different interpretations. We have to prevent the conflict from degenerating into hate and persecution, into a history of suffering. A quick look into each religious tradition will show that all affirmations are a result of a conflict: theological, religious, linguistic. Often only the *polemos* allowed each religion, Judaism and Christianity, to define itself and survive in history. For Christianity the correction of its structural anti-Judaism will be an inner battle and will request a radical, deep turn. Professor Maureena Fritz said: 'a change of paradigm'[22] is needed at the heart of the

Christian theology, inside Christology (which is not, of course, a doctrine written by Christ, but a human effort to think about redemption, revelation and creation). But history, hand in hand with tradition, is not an extraneous principle in the structure of Judaism and Christianity. Change – the idea of the reform – is typical of Jewish as well as Christian histories. After the Shoah the two histories are destined to approach each other in positive terms and perhaps to share some ideas by mutual contagion, or maybe to reform those old ideas that the historical events broke and shattered.

A strong relation exists between theocentrism and soteriological pluralism. It is not my task to develop it here. The debate about Christology and the soteriological value of the sacrifice of Christ is intense and causes some suffering. But it has always been so in the long history of Christian dogma. Today the spirit is different, especially because Christianity has developed a more acute awareness of evil that it can procure in the name of the Cross when dogmatism prevails. I would like to repeat: theology has nothing to lose by accepting the evidence of history. It has everything to lose when it defends an idea of truth that denies or opposes the historical datum. The Shoah is a historical datum whose theological implications must still be explored and interpreted, but cannot be removed or denied. Evil is a historical fact of which the 20th century has been a tragic manifestation and a painful realization. The theology of the 21st century faces this challenge: to assume the heritage of the past century and to reconcile memories by taking the responsibilities about which we spoke. In the hard *Chaoskampf* of history, God and the human being – Jew or Christian – are still allied. If it is not up to the generations after Auschwitz to accomplish the work, it is up to them to begin it.

N O T E S

1   Massimo Giuliani, 'L'interpretazione di Auschwitz nel pensiero cristiano. Contributi per il revisionismo teologico delle chiese', *Humanitas* 5 (1998):791–792.

2   Regarding Christian theology after Auschwitz, the author of this essay considers the following names essential: Roy A. and Alice L. Eckardt, Rosemary Radford Reuther, Gregory Baum, David Tracy, Franklin Littell, John Pawlikowski, Michael Ryan, Paul Van Buren, Martin Cunz, Dirk Ansorge. For a synthetic presentation of these thinkers, see the essay mentioned in endnote 1 above. For Pawlikowski and Ansorge, see the contributions in the proceedings of the 1997 symposium, *Good and Evil after Auschwitz: Ethical Implications for Today*, (Hoboken, NJ: Ktav, 2000) (Italian edition, Milan, 1998).

3   'Blinding scream'. 'Blinding' refers to the Middle Age sculptures on the façades of gothic cathedrals representing the synagogue as a veiled woman; when instead it was the Church that was blind, unable to see the mystery of Israel. 'Scream' because the voice of the Jews was hidden and unheard.

4   Below I will explain how the reciprocal is also true, that is, what happens in Christianity has an impact on Judaism (although so far it has only been a negative one).

5   A large literature exists on the specific responsibilities of Christian theology for anti-Judaism and anti-Semitism. See, for example: Edward Flannery, *The Anguish of the Jews* (New York: Macmillan, 1965); Alice and Roy A. Eckardt, *Long Night's Journey into Day: A Revised Retrospective on the Holocaust* (Detroit: Wayne State University Press, 1988); Malcolm Hay, *The Roots of Christian Anti-Semitism* (New York: Freedom Liberty, 1981); Julie Isaac, *Teaching of Contempt: Christian Roots of Anti-Semitism* (New York: Holt, Rinehart and Winston, 1964).

6   The expression 'a never-revoked covenant' refers to Paul's letter to Romans 11:29. John Paul II used it for the first time during a speech given to a Jewish community in Mainz, Germany (1980).

7   Giuliani, op. cit., 792.

8   In both Judaism and Christianity the redemptive event (the exit from Egypt, the Calvary and the empty tomb) constitutes the theological *prius* and is the context for revelation (the gift of the Torah on Mount Sinai; the Pentecost in the Upper Room and the *kerygma*). Creation is also located inside this context, as what already existed 'at the beginning' did so precisely in view of the redemption

(creation for love of Israel; creation 'through wisdom', where *wisdom* corresponds to a feminist interpretation of Christ).

9 See Emil Fackenheim, *The Jewish Return into History. Reflections in the Age of Auschwitz and a New Jerusalem* (New York: Schocken Books, 1978).

10 See Paul Van Buren, 'Affirmation of the Jewish People. A Condition of Theological Coherence', *Journal of the American Academy of Religion* 45, 3 (1977).

11 I refer at the least to the commandments included in the Torah.

12 See Acts 15.

13 See Irving Greenberg, 'Cloud of Smoke, Pillar of Fire. Judaism, Christianity and Modernity after the Holocaust', in Eva Fleischner (ed.) *Auschwitz: Beginning of a New Era?* (New York: Ktav, 1977). Greenberg's criterion says: 'No theological affirmation should be made if it cannot be credible in the presence of the children that were burnt alive in the crematoria.' For a presentation of Greenberg's thought, see my book: *Auschwitz nel pensiero ebraico: Frammenti dalle 'teologie dell'Olocausto'* (Brescia: Morecelliana, 1998), pp.103–109.

14 Massimo Giuliani, op. cit., p.973.

15 Martin Cunz, 'Solo chi alza la voce per gli ebrei può cantare in gregoriano', *Qol* (1996): 62–63. The article is part of a contribution given at the Monastery of Camaldoli, Italy (1995).

16 Ibid.

17 On this point see the contribution of Maureena Fritz in the proceedings of the symposium mentioned above, *Good and evil after Auschwitz*. She refers to the debate about inclusive and or exclusive Christologies. The same discussion is traceable in different books by Jacques Dupuis S.J. on religious pluralism and its implications for the Catholic Christology. For one of these books the Jesuit was made object of a disciplinary intervention by the Vatican Congregation for the Doctrine of the Faith.

18 See M. Cunz's article, op. cit.

19 See Robert E. Willis, 'Christian Theology after Auschwitz', *Journal of Ecumenical Studies* 12/4 (1975).

20 Twice I use the word 'symbolic' in speaking about Christian participation in the covenant between God and Israel. More precisely, it stands for 'sacramental' and refers to the richness of the symbolic and theurgic language typical of the sacramental doctrine of the Christian churches.

21 See my interview with Rabbi Irving Greenberg, 'Le religioni dell'alleanza', *Jesus* 5 (1999).

22 See the contribution of Maureena Fritz already mentioned. She expressly speaks about 'new paradigms' in Christian theology in regard to the new attitude toward Jews and Judaism after the second Vatican Council.

CHRISTIAN DISCOURSES OF FORGIVENESS AND THE PERPETRATORS

Katharina von Kellenbach

T HIS PAPER will argue that the Christian emphasis on forgiveness has dubious side effects for perpetrators of genocide and their communities. The Christian focus on forgiveness undermines the painful process of truth finding and examination by encouraging premature closure and an attitude of forgetfulness. My observations on Christian teachings on forgiveness are based on popular culture and discourse rather than on academic theological literature. Specifically, I will revisit Simon Wiesenthal's *The Sunflower* and draw on my personal experiences with perpetrators in German families and the court system. A more detailed historical analysis of theological literature in post-war Germany and the attitude of the churches towards the prosecution of NS perpetrators is planned for my upcoming sabbatical year.

Wiesenthal's autobiographical tale in *The Sunflower* forces the question of forgiveness by recounting his encounter with a dying SS man who requested that a Jew – any Jew – be brought to his bedside from the nearby concentration camp in order to hear his confession. Young Simon Wiesenthal quietly listened to the young Catholic man's account of killing Jews but refused his plea for forgiveness. Instead he walked out of the room in silence and issued the challenge to his readers 'What would you have done in my place?' In two volumes, the first published in 1969, the second in 1997, he solicited responses by an international array of theologians, rabbis, journalists, psychiatrists and activists who wrestle with the issues of repentance, forgiveness and justice.

For several of the Christian respondents, human beings have a moral obligation to forgive each other and the refusal to forgive a repentant sinner creates new guilt. Catholic theologian Ed Flannery expresses this position in the following question succinctly: 'Can one morally and with full deliberation refuse forgiveness to a repentant sinner? It is a cardinal principle of the Judeo-Christian ethic that those who sincerely repent should be granted forgiveness... To refuse pardon after repentance is a form of hate, however disguised.'[1] German Catholic author Luise Rinser equates Wiesenthal's refusal to grant forgiveness with the very guilt of the SS man: 'your guilt was a great as his, because he had acted in ignorance and you were acting with your eyes open. You could not be forgiven, because you had refused to forgive.'[2] This reversal of culpability arises out of a (misunderstood?) reading of Matthew: 'Judge not, that you not be judged. For with the judgment you pronounce you will be judged, and the measure you give will be the measure you get'. (Matt 7: 1 and Lk 6: 37) Therefore Wiesenthal's decision to judge must itself be judged harshly. Rinser chastises him:

> Your dead folk will know whether at that moment you acted with mental clarity and ethical honesty, or whether you were blinded by hate (that too might be understandable). But I

shudder at the thought that you let that *repentant* young man go to his death without a word of forgiveness. I must admit that you found yourself in one of those situations, which are too difficult for a human being, when in judging, though innocent, one is guilty. There was once a Man who said: 'Father, forgive them, for they know not what they do.'[3]

Her thinking is rooted in the Gospels' strong warnings against judgment and exhortations to forgive one's brother 'seventy times seven.' (Matt 18: 22) These repeated admonitions against judgment, a certain fear of retribution ('judge and be judged') and a perception of forgiveness as a morally and spiritually superior attitude run through many of the Christian contributions of *The Sunflower*.

This general Christian bias in favour of forgiveness is heightened by some Protestant theologians, such as Gregory Jones in *Embodying Forgiveness* (1995). He takes the above mentioned statement by Jesus on the cross one step further and argues that Jesus forgives even those who are 'ignorant' and therefore 'without requiring prior repentance.'[4] Jesus, he argues, 'diverge[s] from Israel's understanding and practices ... [because] he both claimed divine authority to forgive sins and offered forgiveness *without necessarily presuming prior repentance*' (emphasis added).[5] This theological combination of claiming authority to forgive sins (thereby sidestepping the victims) and the (especially Protestant) depreciation of repentance has harmful consequences for perpetrators of state-authorized mass violence.

In post-war German churches and families this theological reasoning justified massive forgetfulness. The New Testament imperative to forgive was deployed as a tool to prevent further questioning of particular persons' involvement in NS activities. These 'Christian' arguments usually arose in the context where someone attempted to find and name perpetrators of atrocities. Such historical questioning was understood as a spiteful attack on the wartime generation and as a judgmental attitude rooted in the younger generation's arrogance and ignorance. The (Christian-coded) obligation to forgive effectively undercut attempts at truthful confrontation with 'the past' and it crippled moral discernment.

In the following I want to describe the German legacy of forgetfulness and impunity mingled with discourses of 'forgiveness' in the concrete example of family history. I grew up in the comforting belief that the 'bad guys' had simply vanished. By 1960, the year of my birth, West Germany had comfortably joined the Western political and economic world, and my aspiring, hard-working, middle-class world seemed to have little connection with the horrors of the war. And while we were duly shocked upon the introduction of historical facts and materials about the Third Reich in schools, churches and youth groups, these horrors had nothing in common with my present life and contemporaries. Those who had committed these crimes were obviously brutes, monsters, inhumane beasts, and nobody I knew fitted that description. The personal connection between the past and the present, the perpetrators and my post-war environment remained obscured.

Contrary to Wiesenthal's tale about the repentant SS man, most perpetrators were not particularly bothered by their conscience and returned to civilian and family life on the basis of elaborate deceptions. Their immediate and extended families colluded in their duplicity and actively facilitated their reintegration by a widespread conspiracy of silence.[6] 'There would be no discussion of that shameful past, no analyzing, no reflecting, no mourning, and no regretting. There would be no need for answers because there would be no questions.'[7] 'Forgive and forget' became the policy that paved not only German economic recovery from the war but also its psychological, social and political restoration. Germany's judges, engineers, medical doctors, bureaucrats, teachers, policemen, military personnel and church leaders were all more or less reinstituted after a short *Anstandsperiode* (period of politeness) around a consensus of forgiving and forgetting.

Although theological discourses of forgiveness should be kept separate from judicial proceedings, such attitudes influenced the German justice system's treatment of perpetrators as well. According to an official statistic published by the West German ministry of justice in 1986, German prosecutors opened 90,921 investigations against NS perpetrators between 1945 and 1986. However, only a fraction of these initial investigations reached the courts. Of those that were brought to trial only 6,479 defendants were convicted.[8] This low number, disturbing as it is, is further reduced when one excludes defendants who were prosecuted for charges of robbery and assault.[9] Court cases concerning capital crimes, i.e. murder, amounted to only 912 cases involving 1,875 defendants. Of those 1,875 defendants, 150 received life sentences, 842 temporary prison terms, and 1,117 were acquitted or let go because of alleged ill health.[10] In other words, the German justice system practised a version of forgiveness and saw little value in punishing perpetrators of NS crimes.

Luke's 'Judge not, and you will not be judged; condemn not and you will not be condemned; forgive and you will be forgiven; ... for the measure you give will be the measure you get back' (Lk 6: 37–42) takes on a distinctly disturbing quality in such a post-genocidal situation, where no institution, least of all the justice system, welcomes scrutiny. The injunction against judgment leads to moral paralysis, and not as the Gospel-writers undoubtedly intended, to spiritual humility. A practice of forgiveness may be a spiritual virtue for victims and victim cultures, but perpetrators and their cultures must be encouraged to engage in judgment and moral discernment in order to liberate them from oppressive ideologies and evil structures that entangle and suffocate them.

Such religious-based counsel against judgment has debilitating effects on moral reasoning in families and institutions. Among the many abortive NS trials was one affecting me personally. I learned about this trial involving an uncle of mine as a teenager during a family gathering when somebody handed me a newspaper article. The article reported that my uncle, Alfred Ebner, was accused of killing 20,000 Jews, and that his trial was to be discontinued because of health considerations.[11] Alfred Ebner was sitting across the table from me while I was reading this news release. He was a regular guest at family gatherings and I had often visited his family's house in Stuttgart before my family moved to Munich. I remember my confusion and inability to make sense of this information while he sat peacefully (and apparently healthy) among my family. What was I to make of the fact that my family did not censure him? Would not my family treat him as a murderer if he had killed one person? Would he not be ostracized as a serial killer if he had killed ten? The fact that he sat among us unperturbed implied that the murder of 20,000 never happened. I wondered how does one person kill 20,000 people? Where did he do it? Who were his victims? But my attempts to make sense of this information were brushed off. 'Of course, he didn't do these things, these are all lies. Leave this old man his deserved peace, he has suffered much during the war ... all of this is long past and forgotten ... there is no point in raking up muck from the past.' The newspaper article was taken from me and my questions ran into stony walls of silence. For years, I pestered family members with questions about this subject to no avail. Eventually, I 'forgot' this incident.

Few theologians would explicitly condone such 'cheap grace' or a theology of forgiveness that invites forgetfulness. However, in the absence of concrete pressures that force perpetrators (their families, churches, societies) to confront the evil of their theory and practice, remorse and repentance will not arise spontaneously. As Howard Ball has pointed out in *Prosecuting War Crimes and Genocide: The Twentieth Century Experience*, 'In all these genocides, there was the specter of "unrepentant participation" by the overwhelming majority of ordinary men and women.'[12] Politically motivated violence appears justified and legitimate to the actors. In the aftermath of genocide, remorse is not a given and it cannot be presumed as the starting point of the process of forgiveness and healing. Rather, repentance is the end goal of a process of moral discernment and education in moral judgment.

In my case, the pressure to re-member came years later in dialogue with Jewish survivors and their children as a graduate student in religious studies in the United States. As I saw myself through the eyes of my Jewish dialogue partners, I realized that my ignorance was not innocent. Forgetting did not equal forgiving and my lack of knowledge colluded with the perpetrators' desire to conceal their crimes. In fact, I was guilty by association to the extent to which I accepted the silence surrounding these crimes. It was the carrot of genuine friendship with Jewish peers and the stick of their disapproval or possible rejection that propelled me to acknowledge the 'unknown,' forgotten skeletons in my closet.

In retrospect, my family's claims of Ebner's innocence are as laughable as the German courts' legal manoeuvres to minimize his responsibility. Based on the historical record, Ebner was directly responsible for the implementation of Nazi extermination policies, and he killed both by virtue of his position as well as on personal impulse – yet, he was never convicted and, as far as I know, he never regretted his actions. Here is a summary of the historical record:

Alfred Ebner was indicted before the Regional Court of Stuttgart between 1964 and 1966 and, beginning in 1968, tried in the Regional Court of Frankfurt together with members of the police battalion 306 for 'several hundred cases of malicious and cruel murder'.[13] The biography that emerges from the court documents shows Ebner as an early and passionate member of the National Socialist movement. Born poor in a village in Southern Germany in 1913, he left school after seven years, became an apprentice mechanic and joined the masses of unemployed young men. He enlisted in the party and the SS in 1931 and enrolled in an NS elite educational facility, called *Ordensburg* in 1936. The four-year training course for future leaders (*Nachwuchsführer*) was disrupted by the outbreak of the war. After his brief army service in France, he was trained for a post in the civil administration of the Occupied Territories in the East. He was appointed deputy area commissioner (*stellvertretender Gebietskommissar*) to the city of Pinsk in Byelorussia and arrived there in September of 1941. The area of Pinsk was part of the *Reichskommissariat Ukraine* and as 'deputy area commissioner' Ebner was the responsible official for the Jewish inhabitants of the entire region of Pinsk. He was considered the 'specialist for Jewish affairs'.[14]

He was in control of the lives and deaths of approximately 20,000–30,000 Jews who had survived the first mass killings of August 1941. As part of the Einsatzgruppen killings behind the frontline, 11,000 Jewish men between the ages of 16 and 60 were shot on 7 and 8 August 1941, by the Second SS cavalry regiment.[15] Between the fall of 1941 and December of 1942, Alfred Ebner oversaw the systematic expropriation of Jewish property (gold and various other 'taxes' were imposed), the exploitation of Jewish labor and the methodical starvation of the Jewish population.[16] He organized the ghettoization of Jews in May 1942, which forced more than 18,000 people into a mere 240 wooden houses within twenty-four hours.[17] Finally, he helped implement the mass shootings of all Jewish inhabitants of Pinsk lasting four days between 29 October and 2

November 1942. The order to 'liquidate' the ghetto of Pinsk was signed by Heinrich Himmler, head of the SS himself.[18] A few Jews were allowed to live because of their work skills. They were killed on Christmas Eve, 1942.

The city of Pinsk was originally settled by Jewish families in 1506 and maintained a majority (70–80%) Jewish population for several centuries. Pinsk achieved remarkable religious, cultural and legal autonomy for its Jewish community.[19] Its economic strength as an industrial town, its timber and shipping industry that imported raw materials and exported industrial goods along the waterways of the Pripjet fostered cultural, religious and political diversity. There were longstanding conflicts between famous houses of *Hasidim* and *Mitnaggedim*, a growing *Haskalah* (Jewish enlightenment) movement, various conservative and progressive Jewish political parties, different socialist and a variety of Zionist groups, all of which fostered a diverse and fertile culture. Traditional religious schools (*hadarim*) were reformed and transformed into secular Zionist schools teaching in Hebrew as well as the Polish and Russian languages, but Yiddish remained the dominant language in Pinsk. All of this was destroyed when Pinsk became effectively '*judenrein*' by the end of 1942.

The presentation of these historical facts is accompanied by conflicting emotions. And within the German context, one must be prepared to defend such factual presentation of the historical record against accusations of judgmental attitudes. How else would one explain the following *caveat* by Heinrich Missala in his preface to a collection of enthusiastic war sermons given by Catholic military priests:

> This [collection] intends to be neither defense nor justification, neither exposure nor accusation, this is not about assignment of guilt – no human being can judge guilt, co-guilt (*Mitschuld*) or innocence of the individual participants – and even less is it about condemnation. No 'moral index finger' is raised here (*wird kein moralischer Zeigerfinger erhoben*) and no censure is administered from the greater knowledge of hindsight.[20]

Would the preface to a study of Napoleonic texts begin with an admonition not to judge the participants? Why should the editor of church documents find it necessary to warn against any moral evaluation? Without a doubt, the suspension of judgment is a necessary step in historical research and one would expect these same standards in any historical period, including those lives lived during the Third Reich. One must always strive for an unbiased record of historical events. Yet, there must at some point also be the possibility of moral judgment. If we do not apply the greater knowledge of hindsight to our study of history, why engage in it in the first place?

Christian theology and practice must come to a different, more positive evaluation of judgment. In the Jewish tradition moral judgment is an intrinsic and morally praiseworthy activity. I found a revealing passage in Rachel Adler, *Engendering Judaism*, where she describes judgment as a positive and necessary act:

> Judgment, we know, is a holy act. God judges. The *bet din*, the law court, judges. We judge our society, our community. How is it fulfilling its obligations? How is it progressing towards righteousness and fructifying social vision transmitted to us by the prophets? In our secret depths we judge ourselves. We seek courage to assume responsibility for what we do. We ask ourselves if we are becoming the people we are supposed to become.[21]

Such an understanding of judgment emerging from the Jewish tradition may be an appropriate starting point to counteract Christian discourses of forgiveness in perpetrator communities. Persons born into perpetrator communities not only have the right but the responsibility to judge the actions of our forebears (and, one may want to add, contemporaries). One must do so only after thorough investigation and with empathy. But the moral judgment of choices made by a person like Alfred Ebner is necessary if we want to move into the future. Without moral discernment that pronounces these policies, principles, structures and individual actions as evil, without insistence that perpetrators be held accountable for these crimes, without condemnation of the impunity and atmosphere of denial that shielded them, even those born after the war are caught in guilt by association. Such moral judgment is not an attitude of moral superiority but of moral discernment. It is a precondition of change and transformation.

Let me end with reference to a different cultural context where a similar gap with regard to issues of forgiveness exists between victims and perpetrators. Bishop Tutu's *No Future without Forgiveness*, based on his experiences as Chair of the South African Truth and Reconciliation Commission, champions Christian forgiveness. As the beloved bishop of the Anglican Church, Tutu played a central role in convincing his country to submit to the amnesty requirement of the Truth and Reconciliation Commission. He argued forcefully that forgiveness enhances goodness in the world and that it has the potential to open people's hearts and to move beyond the violence of the past (although he acknowledges the political exigencies that precluded judicial prosecution of perpetrators as happened in the Nuremberg Tribunal). The accounts of graphic violence of oppression characteristic of South Africa's jails and police tactics and of the terror of armed struggle against the apartheid regime are punctuated by stories of

> people who by rights should have been filled with bitterness because of untold and unnecessary suffering they had endured. Instead they were to demonstrate a remarkable generosity of spirit, an almost unprecedented magnanimity in their willingness to forgive those who had tormented them.[22]

It should be noted (although it is self-evident) that such incidents of forgiveness, where hatred gives way to forgiveness, involve victims. Not all the victims who forgave were black. Some of them were white and had suffered because of terrorist attacks by the ANC. Nevertheless, forgiveness was initiated and expressed by victims. The perpetrators, however, the white majority who upheld and benefited from apartheid were mostly absent and curiously uninterested in forgiveness. Tutu laments:

> There were splendid things about the commission and it has notable achievements to its credit, but there were alas, things we might have done differently, and things that might have been done a great deal better . . . For me, one of the greatest weaknesses in the commission was the fact that we failed to attract the bulk of the white community to participate enthusiastically in the process. It might very well be because of faults on our side. It was certainly one on the side of our white compatriots. It paralleled the way in which, on the whole, they have refused to embrace the new dispensation wholeheartedly. They have spent far too much time, in my view, whining, being quick to find fault and gloating shortsightedly at the imagined and real shortcomings of those at the helm nowadays. They are filled with far too much resentment at the fact that they have lost some political power.[23]

For perpetrators of state crimes, the dominant issue is not forgiveness but insight into the error of their ideologies and the evil of their actions. Without moral judgment and the realization that racism, antisemitism, oppression, ethnic cleansing and genocide are wrong, there is no need for forgiveness. Politically motivated perpetrators act convinced of their righteousness, irrespective of the gruesome and brutal nature of their deeds. Contrary to Christian criticism of judgment as hasty, haughty and hypocritical, moral judgment requires sustained empathy, love and support for the perpetrators. Moral judgment does not mean to write off the perpetrator but to treat them as moral agents and to insist on their human freedom to choose good and evil. Moral judgment must become the starting point of healing and transformation for perpetrators, their families, churches and cultures.

NOTES

 1 Simon Wiesenthal, *The Sunflower* (New York: Schocken Books, 1976, orig. 1969), p.113; Simon Wiesenthal, *The Sunflower: On the Possibilities and Limits of Forgiveness* (New York: Schocken Books, revised and expanded Edition 1997), p.136.

 2 Simon Wiesenthal, *The Sunflower* (1969), p.195.

 3 *ibid*, p.198.

 4 Gregory Jones, *Embodying Forgiveness: A Theological Analysis* (Grand Rapids, MI: Erdmans Publishing Company, 1995), p.102.

 5 *ibid.*, p.102.

 6 Dan Bar On, *Legacy of Silence: Encounters with Children of the Third Reich*. Cambridge: Harvard University Press, 1989. Bar On, 'Holocaust Perpetrators and their Children,' in *The Collective Silence: German Identity and the Legacy of Shame*, edited by B. Heimannsberg and C. J. Schmidt, translated by C. Oudejans Harris and G. Wheeler (San Franscisco: Jossey-Bass Publishers, 1993), p.195–208.

 7 Sabine Reichel, *What Did You Do in the War, Daddy?: Growing up German* (New York: Hill and Wang, 1989), p.5.

 8 Götz Aly, *Bilanz der Verfolgung von NS-Straftaten* (Köln: Bundesanzeiger Verlags-Gesellschaft, 1985), p.149, Adalbert Rückerl, *The Investigation of Nazi Crimes 1945–1978*, (Hamden, Connecticut: Archon Books, 1980).

 9 Jörg Friedrich, *Die kalte Amnestie* (Munich: Piper, 1994), p.367.

10 C.F. Rüter D.W. deMildt, *Die westdeutschen Strafverfahren wegen nationalsozialistischer Tötungsverbrechen 1945–1997* (Amsterdam: Holland University Press, 1998).

11 I cannot remember my exact age, but the court decision to discontinue the trial for health considerations was made on December 2, 1971. I must have been 12 or 13 years old when I saw the article.

12 Howard Ball, *Prosecuting War Crimes and Genocide: The Twentieth Century Experience* (Kansas City: University of Kansas Press, 1999), p.222.

13 13 (19) Js 22/62 Landgericht Stuttgart, Indictment, Hessisches Hauptstaatsarchiv Wiesbaden.

14 13 (19) Js 22/62, Indictment, LG Stuttgart, Hess. Hauptstaatsarchiv.

15 2 Ks 1/63 LG Braunschweig, in Karl Bracher, P.M. Brilman, et al., *Justiz und NS-Verbrechen: Sammlung deutscher Strafurteile 1945–1999* (Amsterdam: Holland University Press, 1968 ff.); Vol.XX, 570, Christian Gerlach, *Kalkulierte Morde: Die deutsche Wirtschafts-und Vernichtungspolitik in Weissrussland 1941–1944* (Hamburg: Hamburger Edition, 1999), pp.555–566. See also http:www.pinsk-jew.com/e/4.htm (March 15, 2000).

16 Nahum Boneh (Mular), *The Holocaust and the Revolt: Offprint from the Book 'Pinsk'*, Vol.1 Part 2 (Tel Aviv, 1977), pp.107ff.

17 Rozenblat E.S., Yelenskaya, I, *Pinskie Evrei: 1939–1944* (Brest: Brestskii Gosurarstvennyi Universitet, 1997), pp.119–148.

18 Christian Gerlach, *Kalkulierte Morde*, p.719.

19 W.Z. Rabinowitsch, *Studies in Pinsk Jewry*, Haifa: Association of the Jews of Pinsk in Israel 1983, S.6ff. 'Pinsk' in *Encyclopedia Judaica*, Vol.13 (New York: Macmillan Co., 1971), pp.539–546.

20 Heinrich Missala, *Fur Gott, Führer und Vaterland: Die Verstrickung der katholischen Seelsorge in Hitlers Krieg* (Munich: Kösel, 1999).

21 Rachel Adler, *Engendering Judaism: An Inclusive Theology and Ethics* (Boston: Beacon Press, 1998), p.17.

22 Desmond Tutu, *No Future without Forgiveness* (New York: Doubleday, 1999), p.144.

23 *ibid.*, pp.231–232.

A THEOLOGY OF JEWISH–CHRISTIAN DIALOGUE FOR THE 21ST CENTURY

Edward Kessler

ANY STUDY of Jewish–Christian dialogue will point to the existence of a significant imbalance between the number of writings, which consider a Christian theology of Judaism and those which consider a Jewish theology of Christianity. Much more has been published on the former than the latter. One thinks immediately of Christian authors such as Pawlikowski, Thoma and Kung (from the Catholic perspective), and Van Buren and Eckardt (from the Protestant perspective), all of whom have made significant contributions to a Christian theology of Judaism.

As far as Jewish authors are concerned, the names of Novak, Borowitz and Lapide come to mind but although all have touched on the subject of a Jewish theology of Christianity none have offered a detailed study. Indeed, Claude Montefiore's call for the creation of a Jewish theology of Christianity has remained unanswered for over 75 years.[1] Montefiore (1878–1938), like James Parkes (1896–1981), was a pioneer in Jewish–Christian relations in the UK. Montefiore was the founder of Liberal Judaism in England and offered a radical re-assessment of Christianity. Although his writings on Christianity caused great controversy among his Jewish and Christian contemporaries even Montefiore did not attempt to create a Jewish theology of Christianity but limited himself to a number of important studies on the New Testament as well as a few short lectures on Jewish attitudes towards Christianity.

It is important to understand the reasons for the imbalance, which are twofold. First, the stimulus for dialogue has arisen, inevitably, from the Christian side. From the Christian perspective, the re-awakening to the fact that Christianity arose out of Judaism as well as the realisation that Christian teaching made a significant contribution to the suffering of Jews contributed to a renewed interest in Judaism. For Jews, however, the new Christian interest was met with suspicion – a legacy of the consequences of the 'teaching of contempt'.

As well as highlighting this imbalance, a study of Jewish–Christian dialogue should concern itself with other aspects, which result from the fact that dialogue is an activity to be experienced and lived, rather than talked about, lectured on, analysed and appraised. It is only out of actual and continuous involvement in dialogue that one can reflect on the issues involved for they affect both the quality of religious life as well as the communal relationship. This means that a theology of Jewish–Christian dialogue must also reflect the impact of dialogue on the living communities as well as the more philosophical issues.

KEY ISSUES IN DIALOGUE IN THE LAST FIFTY YEARS

There are two themes in Jewish–Christian dialogue, which in the last 50 years have come to the fore of theological reflection: Christian antisemitism and the Shoah, and the creation of the State of Israel.

The Shoah resulted in a general awareness of the immensity of the burden of guilt which the Church carried not only for its general silence, with some noble except- ions during 1933–45, but also because of the 'teaching of contempt' towards Jews and Judaism which it carried on for so many centuries. As Jules Isaac showed im- mediately after the war, it was this that sowed the seeds of hatred and made it so easy for Hitler to use antisemitism as a political weapon.[2] Although no one would deny that Nazism was opposed to Christianity, it is well-known that Hitler often just- ified his antisemitism with reference to the Church and Christian attitudes towards Judaism.[3]

As a result of the soul searching which took place after 1945, many Christians began the painful process of re-examining the sources of the teaching of contempt and repudiating them. Christian institutions, most notably the Vatican, the World Council of Churches and certain Protestant denominations have, since then, issued declarations against the perpetuation of this teaching.[4]

This meant from a Christian perspective that before dialogue could take place the history of the Church and its attitude towards the Jews had to be publicly acknowledged. This involved a proper appraisal of antisemitisim, anti-Judaism and the significance of the Shoah. Recent Christian institutional statements have consistently condemned antisemitism and documents such as *We Remember* illustrate a willingness to tackle this subject. Most Christian theologians involved in Jewish–Christian dialogue have acknowledged that the slaughter of 6,000,000 Jews in the Shoah would not have been possible were the roots of antisemitism not deep within the Christian tradition. Such views are nearly always mentioned in the forewords and introductions of modern Christian writings on Jews and Judaism, many of which begin with a personal reflection on this reality.

It is, therefore, not surprising that many studies, which have been published on Jewish–Christian relations examined, in particular, Christian antisemitism. This ten- dency was reinforced by the publication of a number of key works including specific institutional statements such as *Nostra Aetate* and individual studies such as Ruether's *Faith and Fratricide*. The agenda of Jewish–Christian dialogue was heavily influenced by such works.

The Shoah not only caused Christianity to reassess its relationship with Judaism but also stirred greater Jewish interest in Christianity. Jonathan Sacks spoke for many when he stated that, 'today we meet and talk together because we must; because we have considered the alternative and seen where it ends and we are shocked to the core by what we have seen'.[5]

The need to tackle such issues as the Shoah in Jewish–Christian dialogue is self-evident but there are dangers if they are not conducted in perspective. Fackenheim's proclamation that the Shoah resulted in a new commandment, the 614th, which stressed that it was incumbent upon Jews to survive as Jews, is a case in point. According to Fackenheim one remained a Jew so as not to provide Hitler a posthumous victory. However, as a result, Jewish identity became Shoah-centred and, at the same time, Jewish–Christian dialogue became Shoah-centred. The danger is that by focusing solely on the Holocaust Jews and Christians will gain a distorted view. For example, a young Jew will construct a negative Jewish identity, which without the positive side of Judaism, will not be a value to be handed down over the generations. A young Christian will come away with an exclusive picture of the Jew as victim without an awareness of the positive aspects of Jewish culture. If the Jew disappears from the horizons from the end of the biblical period and only reappears again in 1933, where is the Jew and what is Jewish–Christian dialogue?

It is a result of this emphasis on the Shoah and antisemitism that Jewish–Christian dialogue often appears to consist of an attempt to educate Christians about Judaism in order to prevent, or at the very least, to reduce Christian antisemitism. Thus, Jews and Christians have become involved in dialogue on account of defensive factors, in other words, to stop the possibility of antisemitism from breaking out in churches in the future. Although Jewish–Christian dialogue has proceeded at many levels, one should realise that whilst reaction to the Shoah is an important driving force, a theology of dialogue cannot be built solely on responses to antisemitism and Christian feelings of guilt. Indeed, no healthy and enduring relationship between people is built on guilt. If recent Christian soul-searching in the aftermath of the destruction of European Jewry leads to a new approach and a revision of traditional anti-Jewish teaching so much the better. However, the future relationship cannot be built on the foundations of guilt. The sense of guilt is transient and does not pass to the next generation; moreover, it is unstable, inherently prone to sudden and drastic reversal.

A second key issue in Jewish–Christian dialogue is the establishment of the State of Israel. There is little doubt that whilst the Church has for many years been grappling with issues related to Christian antisemitism, attitudes towards the Land and State of Israel have, from the theological perspective, proved more difficult to tackle. Theological difficulties have made a Christian re-orientation to Israel problematic. Simply put, it has been easier for Christians to condemn antisemitism as a misunderstanding of Christian teaching than to come to terms with the re-establishment of the Jewish State. As a result, the subject of Israel has probably caused as much disagreement and division within the Church as any other topic in Jewish–Christian dialogue.

The Christian reluctance to accept the implications of the new State in the Jewish–Christian relationship has only served to reinforce its centrality in discussion. In addition, its significance lies in the fact that, first, Israel is the only State in which Jews form the majority and this has important consequences for the Jewish–Christian relationship. For example, Jews have more confidence in their dealings with Christians. Also, all the Christian holy places are now in Israel or in Israeli controlled territory, which means that the entire Christian world takes a close interest in developments. This has led to strong reactions – both of a favourable and unfavourable nature – but the very existence of this spotlight shining so strongly on Israel, and especially on Jerusalem, gives particular importance to any attempt at mutual understanding between Christian and Jew inside Israel. The recent controversies over the Nazareth mosque are a good example of this phenomenon. At the same time there is always the potential hope of a future meeting with the other great monotheistic faith, Islam.

However, there are a number of dangers with basing a theology of Jewish–Christian dialogue primarily on Israel. One is the fact that dialogue becomes linked to certain stages of achievement, which give an impression of a direct line of progress. Valuable as the stages of achievement are, they are often far from the complexities of the reality itself. For example, there is great danger in arguing that what was once an interpretation about the nature of the biblical word and promise is now in the situation of Israel concretised in a contemporary event. The challenge to Jewish–Christian dialogue as a result of an emphasis on fulfilment of biblical prophecy can be seen in the writings of some evangelical Christians as well as fundamentalist Jews.

For example, what happened a hundred years ago to the Jews outside of Israel is considered by some as historically remote compared to biblical events, which are viewed as almost contemporary. The present becomes transformed into biblical language and geography, which leads to the danger of giving metaphysical meaning to geographical places. The fundamentalist Jew in Israel interprets the ownership of the Land of Israel in terms of a divine gift. This creates a great danger of bestowing divine importance to Israel and the vocation of the Jew becomes a dedication to the existence and the restoration of the cosmic state. Thus, the return to the Land is a fulfillment of the divine promise and reflects a return to the original fullness. However, the biblical promises do not define the same borders and by choosing the widest ones the fundamentalist abuses the idea of the promise, which is related to the Land.

The dangers of Israel-based dialogue are also illustrated by those who, in the name of dialogue, move from a position of commitment for the well being of Israel to one of almost Israel can do no wrong. This is not conducive to dialogue for it is not an honest and sober conversation firmly related to present realities.

The 1994 Vatican recognition of the State of Israel marks a significant shift in Christian thinking and is important for this study. Its significance is explained by David Rosen, who was intimately involved in the negotiations with the Vatican:

> This is the end of the beginning. The implications of *Nostra Aetate* and the subsequent documents called out for full relations between the Holy See and the State of Israel. Their absence had suggested that the reconciliation between the church and the Jewish People was not a complete one. Accordingly, for the last three decades, Jewish representatives have called on the Vatican to take this step. The agreement that was signed last week, therefore, has historical and philosophical importance as well as diplomatic significance. Now we can address the meaning of our relationship and get on to many other matters of common interest.[6]

The question is, what are the 'other matters of common interest'?

PARTICULARITIES OF FAITH

To be sure, both the Shoah and the State of Israel will continue to be pillars of Jewish–Christian dialogue, but they will no longer bear the load on their own and be the only items on the agenda. In my view, other factors will increasingly be taken into consideration and these arise from what might best be described as 'particularities of faith'. This term can be defined as those points which Christians and Jews claim to have a universal significance and finality.

For too long dialogue has ignored the existence of 'particularities of faith'. From a Jewish perspective they include, for example, an emphasis on Torah, on God's ongoing covenant with the Jewish people and on divine sanction for the attachment to the Land of Israel.

From the Christian perspective, they include the Christian conviction that in the life, death and resurrection of Jesus God acted decisively for all humanity. Christianity is a religion that combines a claim to be universal in scope with the demand of exclusiveness in belief: Christ is Lord of all and the Saviour of all. The ending of Matthew's Gospel attributes to Jesus the command to 'go and make disciples of all the nations' (Matt. 28:19). The same Christ is also depicted as stating that 'I am the Way, the Truth, and the Life: no one can come to the Father except through me' (Jn. 14:6) and the record of early Christian preaching includes the oft-repeated text that 'there is salvation in no one else, for there is no other name given to men by which we can be saved' (Acts 4:12).

This means that dialogue cannot simply be limited to the areas of common ground, though these will always provide a bridge. The existence of these 'particularities of faith' results in two significant conclusions:

- Both Judaism and Christianity contain features, which although shared in principle divide in practice, as for example, the issue of the identity of the people of Israel.
- From the perspective of both these features are central to their understanding of God's purpose. All such convictions are strictly irreducible.

Although from the outside the particularities of faith might seem narrowly possessive, from within, however, they reflect an experience, which cannot be denied nor ignored. It is totally unhelpful to condemn such features as arrogant for their meaning is of such relevance that to deny them would appear to be an act of denial of one's own faith. Genuine dialogue will not be prevented by the acknowledgement of these particularities of faith and the assumption of each partner in dialogue that the ultimate and deepest insight into God's purpose lies on its side.

Thus any attempt to ignore the existence of the 'particularities of faith' will result in an increased likelihood of the failure of dialogue. It takes a high degree of maturity to let opposites co-exist without pretending that they can be made compatible. At the same time, it takes the same degree of maturity to respect an opinion that conflicts with one's own without attempting to achieve a naïve accommodation.

UNDERSTANDING THE MEANING OF DIALOGUE
Having described the significance of the particularities of faith in Jewish–Christian dialogue we now move on to consider the theological basis for dialogue.

- How does modern interfaith dialogue differ from the interfaith disputations of the Middle Ages?
- How does it differ from the bargaining of the market in which the aim is to find a mutually acceptable compromise?

In fact modern interfaith dialogue is neither disputation nor seeking for compromise.

First, the word 'dialogue' and dialogue activity have been both misconstrued and ill-defined. A casual conversation between Jews and Christians that may add up to no more than a loose restatement of entrenched theological positions is sometimes claimed as dialogue. Any communication between persons of two differing religious points of view that does not involve a genuine hearing of the other is all too easily claimed as dialogue. Today, one can communicate with others either by phone, fax or e-mail but dialogue requires more effort, and most of all, a face to face contact. Dialogue is not simply a method of communication.

Second, the word is sloppily used as almost an umbrella term to cover a whole host of related word activities that are good in themselves, some of them even providing an essential framework for dialogue, but are not the equivalent to dialogue. For example, some adopt the term Jewish–Christian relations as synonymous with dialogue. After all you can have good or bad relations (as often the case with relatives) but relations in themselves are not the equivalent of dialogue; nor is the comparative study of religions, which is also taken by some as a synonym for dialogue. Of course, dialogue does involve the serious study of the religion of others, but the understanding required before dialogue can take place consists of more, for example, than the understanding of the major festivals and life-cycles of Judaism and Christianity.

Third, dialogue is not new, nor is it an institutional development which owes its origin to the establishment of various committees such as the WCC sub-unit of *Dialogue with People of Living Faiths and Ideologies* or the Vatican's *Pontifical Commission for Religious*

Relations with the Jews or the World Jewish Congress' *Committee on Interfaith Relations*. All of these august bodies have helped to channel group dialogue and to stimulate global dialogue but they are not the equivalent of dialogue neither did they originate the dialogue process.

In reality, dialogue consists of a direct meeting of two people and involves a reciprocal exposing of the full religious consciousness of the one with the 'Other'. Dialogue speaks to the Other with a full respect of what the Other is and has to say. This is never less than personal but can develop in such a way as to be extended to a group and even to communities. However, it begins with the individual and not with the community.

This is not an original definition for the biblical prophets were experts in this full personal communication and encounter. Isaiah in a famous passage powerfully commends Israel to enter into a personal relationship with God stating, 'come now let us reason together' (Isaiah 1:18). We should also refer to Leviticus 19:33–34: 'When a stranger lives with you in your land, do not ill-treat him. The stranger who lives with you shall be treated like a native-born. Love him as yourself for you were strangers in the land of Egypt. I am the Lord your God.' These verses provide the theological basis for dialogue – indeed, the command to love the stranger is found on 36 occasions in the Written Torah. Dialogue consists of embracing the dignity of difference and is dependent upon a willingness to understand the difference and to get to know the Other.

Such a quest is never easy because it is not merely about the Other, nor where the Other differs from us. The thoughts and experience of dialogue are well expressed in the writings of Franz Rosenzweig. According to Nahum Glatzer, who produced the definitive biography, Rosenzweig's emphasis is not on 'the subject matter that connects the speaker with the listener but the I confronting the Thou. The word is not only an expression of reality but also a means by which to express it.'[7]

Speech for Rosenzweig consisted of articulating an awareness and comprehension in living contact with another person, which he called *sprachdenken*. Thus the use of words in a live encounter was for him more than just talking, in other words something is not only said but something happens. This means that dialogue is dependent upon the presence of another person. It is not difficult to see how Rosenzweig became one of the main sources out of which Martin Buber developed his 'I and Thou' formula.

Buber in his exposition of the I–Thou relationship maintained that a personal relationship with God is only truly personal when there is not only awe and respect on the human side but when we are not overcome and overwhelmed in our relationship with God. This is illustrated by a famous story found in the Talmud in which Rabbi Eliezer appeals to heaven and the voice of God declares that he is right. However, the *halakhah* (Jewish law) still follows the majority opinion (in opposition to Rabbi Eliezer) because of the principle 'it is not in heaven' (Deut. 30:12). Many years later, the story concludes, Elijah tells Rabbi Nathan that when the incident took place God laughed and declared, 'My children have conquered Me'.[8] The significance of the story for our study lies in its presentation of the personal relationship between God and humankind.

This has implications for human–human dialogue because it means that two people must meet as two valid centres of interest. Thus one should approach the Other with respect and restraint so that the validity of the other centre is in no sense belittled. Further, not only is the essential being of the other respected but the world of faith is also treated as valid and genuine; not an 'it' to be carelessly set aside but a distinctive value of belief. An I–Thou relationship is a meeting not of religions but of religious people. The emphasis is placed on the individual.

Dialogue, therefore involves a respect that takes the other as seriously as one demands to be taken oneself. This is an immensely difficult and costly exercise. We find it all too easy to relate to others in a casual way with a lack of concentration on the reality and good of the Other. However difficult this is, it illustrates the foundational principle of Jewish–Christian dialogue today: *Judaism and Christianity must be understood on their own terms*.

Thus genuine dialogue between Christians and Jews only started when Christians showed a willingness to improve their knowledge of Judaism. The task of achieving a greater understanding was (and is) not easy since an understanding of Judaism as it defines itself is not simply an intellectual pursuit. The difficulty was magnified for the Church when Christianity became the religion of the Roman Empire after the conversion of Constantine (312 CE) and after the edicts of Theodosius the Great (380–92 CE).

Ironically, during the first few centuries of the Church's history Christians viewed dialogue as the norm because they were surrounded by people of religions different from their own. They had to face questions about their own practices and beliefs, questions which were posed by the Jewish environment first of all. Although Christians and Jews developed separate means for survival, they both learned how to reconcile their spiritual experience within a framework of ideas that supported these other faiths. As a result, religious pluralism was the milieu of the first Christians.

However, the history of the relationship between Judaism and Christianity was not one of open pluralism but of hostility and animosity. Mutual ignorance and suspicion bred an increasing isolation, and as a result when Jews and Christians communicated with each other they did so in a state of ignorance and were burdened with past histories and the fears which had been engendered.

A striking example of how the application of the foundational principle of Jewish–Christian dialogue can overcome this burden is seen in the letters of Franz Rosenzweig.[9] For example, when discussing the saying of Jesus in the Gospel of John (6:14) that 'No one can reach the Father except through me' Rosenzweig does not simply reject it as false. He asserts that it is true, particularly when one remembers the millions who have been led to God through Jesus Christ. However he argues that the situation is quite different for a Jew who does not have to reach God because he is already with God. Indeed, he asks, does the alternative of conversion even exist for one who has been chosen?

Rosenzweig raises the foundational principle by asking the fundamental question: can Christians view Judaism as a valid religion in its own terms (and, we might add, *vice versa*)?

Questions also need to be considered from the Jewish perspective. What was the purpose behind the creation of Christianity? Does the fact that Jesus was a Jew have any implications for Jews? Jews are rightly proud of Jewish heroes and heroines but Israel's most famous Jew is generally ignored. Now, in a freer climate as far as Jewish–Christian relations are concerned, is it not time that there was a greater Jewish interest in the Jew Jesus?

For Christians, the question of the validity of Judaism challenges some of the proclamations of Christian triumphalism. The issue which we need to address, is whether Christianity can differentiate itself from Judaism without asserting itself as either opposed to Judaism or simply as the fulfilment of Judaism. We need to ask whether, in the language of Rosemary Ruether, antisemitism stands at the centre of Christianity and represents 'the left hand of christology'?[10]

The challenge of such questions has resulted in a dramatic rethinking as can be seen, for example, in the reconsideration of Paul's argument that God has not forsaken the people of Israel (Romans 11:25–6). The call for Christianity to abandon its historical religious animosity and misleading caricature of Judaism has been overwhelming. These are now admitted as being wrong and their full and public rejection was required before the possibility of dialogue might exist. Positively this might be expressed as the essential necessity to understand the faith of the Other in terms of his or her own self-understanding.

Thus, Christian dialogue with Judaism began only after it shifted from what was, for the most part, an inherent need to condemn Judaism to one of a condemnation of Christian anti-Judaism. This process has not led to a separation from all things Jewish but, in fact, to a closer relationship with 'the elder brother'.

It is possible to trace the gradual emergence of this insight with increasing clarity and emphasis in the primary church documents.[11] So for instance *Nostra Aetate* has a brief paragraph:

> Since the spiritual patrimony common to Christians and Jews is thus so great, this Sacred Synod wants to foster and recommend that mutual understanding and respect which is the fruit above all of biblical and theological studies as well as of fraternal dialogues.

That statement was further developed by the 1975 *Guidelines*, which state:

> Christians must therefore strive to acquire a better knowledge of the basic components of the religious tradition of Judaism: They must strive to learn by what essential traits the Jews define themselves in the light of their own religious experience.

The 1985 *Notes* reinforces this view and calls on preachers and catechists to 'assess it carefully in itself and with due awareness of the faith and religious life of the Jewish people as they are professed and practised still today'. Such concerns continue to be expressed in the most recent institutional statements, such as 'We Remember' (1999) and in comments expressed by Pope John Paul II during his pilgrimage to Israel (2000).

There is a similar progression in the documents of the World Council of Churches. The 1948 Amsterdam statement has a fleeting reference in its first recommendation to the member churches that they 'encourage their people to seek for brotherly contact with and understanding of their Jewish neighbours, and co-operation in agencies combating misunderstanding and prejudice'. The 1967 Bristol Document goes further:

> For a real encounter with the Jews we consider it imperative to have knowledge and genuine understanding of their thinking and their problems both in the secular and in the religious realm. We should always remain aware that we are dealing with actual, living people in all their variety, and not with an abstract concept of our own.

Similar statements have regularly been issued by individual denominations since then: witness the recent statements by the General Conference of the Methodist Church in the United States (1996) and the Uniting Church in Australia (1997). All we have said above can be summarily stated as the occurrence of a demonstrable shift from a Christian monologue about Jews to an instructive (and sometimes difficult) dialogue with Jews. A monologue, which generally fails to exhibit an understanding of the reality of the Other, is therefore replaced by a dialogue. This begins with the respect for the Other as it understands itself.

At the same time, the difficulties in attempting to achieve this goal are immense and should also be appreciated. First, of course, was the need for a massive change in attitude among Christians, but there were also other difficulties, not least of which concerns the self-understanding of Jews. Judaism, as is well known, is not easily defined and wide ranging views of its definition can be found. Thus a Christian understanding of Judaism needs to deal with the varieties and contradictions that exist within Judaism just as a

Jewish approach to Christianity needs to take into account the varieties that combine to make up 'Christianity'. It is noticeable, from even a cursory glance at the forewords and introductions to the increasingly numerous Christian writings about Judaism that there exist an awareness of this issue as well as a desire to respond to it.

The need for changing attitudes and a more accurate understanding of the other faith is not limited to Christianity but is also required among Jews. Many Jews today retain an infantile understanding of Christianity, which is often based on primary school education. In addition, there is an urgent need to confront the mark that the centuries of Christian antisemitism have left on the Jewish psyche. As a result, there has been an abundance of Jewish writings which consider the political, sociological and historical relationship with Christianity but few which can be categorised as theological. Indeed, a number of Jews involved in dialogue with Christians do not wish to engage in any theological discussion. Jonathan Sacks, for example, advocates an ethical dialogue with Christians and argues that the problems are theological. His views, which are articulated most fully in *Tradition in an Untraditional Age* (1990), represent a common view amongst many Jews involved in Jewish–Christian dialogue in the twentieth century. He has clearly been influenced by one of the foremost Orthodox Jewish theologians of the 20th century, Joseph Soloveichik who argued that it was impossible for faith communities to communicate with each other and that theology could not be a subject of dialogue.

The efforts of Sacks and others often appear to be directed towards the education of Christians rather than dialogue. Perhaps partly as a result of a natural desire to retain the involvement of such people, the agenda of Jewish–Christian dialogue has been influenced by them and has remained focused primarily on responses to Christian antisemitism and the Shoah as well as on responses to the significance of the Land and State of Israel.

However, as argued above, issues associated with 'the particularities of faith', will be increasingly considered in dialogue, and as a result, dialogue will return to the mainstream of Judaism and Christianity.

DIALOGUE IN THE MAINSTREAM OF JUDAISM AND CHRISTIANITY
From a Christian perspective the justification for Jewish–Christian dialogue is quite clear: there exists an urgent need to understand Judaism and Christian relations with Jews since Christianity was born of Judaism. Indeed, an understanding of Christianity is, to some extent, dependent upon a proper understanding of Judaism. From a theological perspective this view would be understood as follows: that God's revelation through Christ was for all humanity. Since God's revelation came first to the Jews (and since God does not break His promises), it is essential to explore the meaning of God's mission to Israel. Christians need to enter into dialogue with Jews in order to preserve and understand God's faithfulness with Israel.

In the earlier stages of dialogue in the 20th century, Christian re-acquaintance with Judaism resulted primarily in an increased awareness of the Jewish origins of Christianity. That Jesus was born, lived and died a Jew; that the first Christians were Jews; that the New Testament is, for the most part, a Jewish work. However, more recently, there is a growing realization that for nearly two thousand years – not only the first 100 years – living Judaism has interested Christians and has influenced Christianity in one way or another. Paul described this as 'the mystery of Israel' and it is the significance of this mystery that has continued to challenge and engross Christians.

Thus, the justification for Jewish–Christian dialogue is unambiguous from a Christian perspective. However, the issue from a Jewish perspective is more complicated. At first glance, there is no theological nor other imperative to view the relationship with Christianity as more special than the Jewish relationship with any other faith group. This view is reinforced by the popular assumption that the influence was wholly one-way: Christianity did not influence Judaism; rather, Judaism influenced the development of Christianity.

However, this is an inaccurate assumption because Christianity has influenced Judaism in a number of ways including, most significantly, influencing the development of Rabbinic Judaism. It is well known that after Christianity became the official religion of the Roman Empire the position of the Jewish communities became more and more precarious. However, it is not so well known that the rabbis allowed, consciously or not, Christian ideas and interpretations to enter into Jewish thought and life. This happened because dialogue was part of the mainstream of Jewish life.

This development is particularly important because both Orthodox and Progressive[12] Jews view Rabbinic Judaism as the cornerstone of Judaism today. One example of the Christian influence on Rabbinic Judaism can be seen in exegetical encounters, which took place between Jewish and Christian interpreters. These encounters took place on the basis of a shared textual tradition – the Hebrew Bible even though each faith community interpreted these writings in different ways. The rediscovery of this interaction, from the Jewish perspective, will prove significant to the Jewish contribution to Jewish–Christian dialogue.

A new reading of the rabbinic writings offers an insight into these exegetical encounters. They illustrate not only awareness of Christian teaching but also a rabbinic ability to listen, learn and incorporate those teachings and traditions, which were deemed relevant to Jewish life. Jewish–Christian dialogue is, therefore, not a modern phenomenon. If Jews and Christians examine post-biblical interpretations they will discover a shared emphasis on the importance of certain biblical texts as well as a willingness to be open to, and influenced by, each other's teachings. The exegetical encounters, which took place so long ago, point the way forward.

One example of the exegetical interaction between the classical rabbinic and patristic traditions can be seen in the interpretations of the *Akedah*, the Binding of Isaac (Genesis 22). The story of Abraham's attempted sacrifice of Isaac is one of the most well known stories of the Bible. It has been important for Judaism and Christianity from an early period. For Jews, from at least as early as the third century CE, the passage has been read on Rosh ha-Shana. For Christians, from around the same period, the Sacrifice of Isaac, as it is called, has been mentioned in the Eucharist and read in the period leading up to Easter.

The focus of the biblical story concerns Abraham's relationship with God and how his faith in, and commitment to God is demonstrated by his willingness to sacrifice his long awaited son at God's command. Little attention is given to Isaac.

Both the rabbis and the Church Fathers reflected a great deal on the story. In the rabbinic writings, Isaac is no longer portrayed as a peripheral figure but becomes equal, if not superior, to Abraham. The rabbis portray Isaac as the willing martyr who volunteers to give up his life for his people. Indeed, such is the merit of Isaac's action, (*zecut avot*), that Israel benefits from his actions in the future.

The rabbinic portrayal of Isaac parallels a number of aspects of the Christian understanding of Jesus. Like Jesus, Isaac was willing to give up his life.[13] Like Jesus, Isaac was not forced by human hand to carry the wood for the burnt offering but carried it freely. Like Jesus, Isaac was not forced to offer himself as a sacrifice but willingly gave himself up to his father.[14] Like Jesus, Isaac was described as weeping bitterly when told by Abraham that he was to be sacrificed.[15] Like Jesus, Isaac shed blood.[16] Like Jesus, Isaac is depicted at the gates of Hell (*gehinna*).[17] In a similar way to Paul's assertion concerning baptism the Akedah was described as atoning for all, Jew and non-Jew.[18] Finally and perhaps most remarkably, Isaac is described as having died and having been resurrected.[19]

There is one other example, which provides further evidence that the rabbinic interpretation of the Akedah was influenced by Christian teaching. Among the interpretations there is one comment, which is particularly striking, for the rabbis discuss Isaac carrying the wood for the sacrifice on his shoulders: '"And Abraham placed the wood of the burnt-offering on Isaac his son." Like a man who carries his cross (*tzaluv*) on his shoulder.'[20]

The reference to a cross is clearly influenced by the Christian description that Christ carried his cross to the crucifixion.[21] The rabbi who offered this interpretation, whose name is not mentioned, decided that the comparison between Isaac carrying the wood and a man (Jesus) carrying a cross to his execution was valuable. The editors/redactors of Genesis Rabbah concurred since they did not censor the comparison in the final redaction.[22]

Thus, Jewish interpretations of Isaac at the Akedah cannot be understood properly without reference to the Christian context. Indeed, they are more easily understood when viewed as illustrating an exegetical encounter since the rabbis were not only aware of Christian exegesis but were influenced by it. These exegetical encounters between Jews and Christians in bygone times should inspire Jewish–Christian dialogue in the future. Since the writings of the rabbis and the church fathers provide the cornerstone for Christianity and Judaism today, a study of Jewish and Christian biblical interpretation should become a pillar of Jewish–Christian dialogue in the future. I suggest the growing realization that Rabbinic Jews were concerned with and influenced by Christian interpretations (and *vice versa*) will result in Jews and Christians becoming reacquainted with each other's interpretations of Scripture.

CONCLUSION: THE WAY FORWARD
What is the way forward? I have argued that the future dialogue will not only deal with Christian antisemitism, the Shoah and the State and land of Israel but will:

• Consider the issues associated with the particularities of the Christian and Jewish faiths.
• Bring dialogue into the mainstream of the religions, perhaps by re-examining the shared textual tradition.

Most importantly of all, however, the future of dialogue depends upon *education*; not only an education of the elite but an education for all. How should this be achieved?

It means that Jews should examine the writings of the church and be willing to examine these writings in a new light. There can be no escaping the obligation in the new framework and this includes an examination of Jewish education concerning Christians and Christianity. In Jewish classrooms, little has been done to change negative or infantile perceptions of Christianity. The yeshiva doors need to be opened to the winds of change blowing through. To achieve this Jewish scholars are needed who can offer a theology of Christianity; who are willing to put dialogue back into the mainstream.

I call upon Jewish thinkers to face the world of contemporary Christian ideas and to create a Jewish theology of Christianity. Although it is understandable that some Jews look upon dialogue with an element of mistrust, perhaps viewing it as a veiled attempt at Christian conversion, our Christian partners are beginning to say, 'we have made many changes and offered new thinking, isn't it your turn now, to respond?'

On the Christian side, it means that Christian seminaries should not only offer courses in Judaism as it developed since the Common Era but should consider rabbinic interpretations of Scripture. The results of these studies must find their way not only into the classrooms of seminaries, universities and teacher training colleges. They must also be discussed in the churches as well as the synagogues. Only then shall we truly begin to discover the significance of a shared textual tradition.

New attitudes are of little use if they are confined to an elite and the true test is the extent to which they have affected teaching at all levels. This means we have to tackle the 'nitty' issues and not only teach Christian ordinands about the Jewish understanding of the Sabbath, Passover, life cycle and so on. We have to tackle the subject of the Pharisees, the relationship between Jesus and other Jews, the two covenants; how to deal with polemical texts. We have to tackle the fact that the plain text of the New Testament and the teachings of churches leaves the Jews in a position of inferiority and will induce feelings, if not of genocide, then at least of scorn.

I call upon Christian teachers to implement those statements of their religious institutions which discuss the place of Jewish–Christian dialogue. The serious study of Judaism as a living faith, and its relationship with Christianity are an essential non-marginal part of Christian formation today. Perhaps it is best to conclude with the words of the Vatican's Pontifical Commission for Religious Relations with the Jews:

> Christians must strive to acquire a better knowledge of the basic components of the religious tradition of Judaism; they must strive to learn by what essential traits the Jews define themselves in the light of their own religious experience.[23]

NOTES

1 Claude G. Montefiore *The Old Testament and After* (London: Macmillan, 1923), 560–64.

2 Jules Isaac *The Teaching of Contempt* (New York, 1964).

3 See excellent summary in Richard L. Rubenstein and John K. Roth, *Approaches to Auschwitz* (London: SCM, 1987), 199–228.

4 For a summary of Vatican statements, see Eugene Fisher and Leon Klenicki eds,. *In Our Time* (New York: Paulist, 1990); for a summary of Protestant statements, see *The Theology of the Churches and the Jewish People* (Geneva: WCC, 1988). Also, *Stepping Stones to Further Jewish–Christian Relations*, compiler, Helga Croner (New York/London: Stimulus Books, 1977); *More Stepping Stones to Jewish–Christian Relations*, compiler, Helga Croner (New York: Paulist Press, 1985); *Stepping-Stones to Further Jewish–Lutheran Relationships*, ed. Harold H. Ditmanson (Minneapolis:Augsburg Press, 1990). For the most recent statements see the web-site: *www.jcrelations.com*.

5 Helen Fry *Christian–Jewish Dialogue* (Exeter: Exeter University Press, 1996), xi.

6 Quoted from David. O'Brien *The Hidden Pope* (NY: Daybreak, 1998), 383.

7 Foreword to *The Star of Redemption* (University of Notre Dame Press, 1985), xiv.

8 Babylonian Talmud, Bava Metzia 59b.

9 See in particular Nahum Glatzer *Franz Rosenzweig: his Life and Thought* (New York: Schocken, 1955) Eugen Rosenstock-Huessy ed., *Judaism Despite Christianity* (New York: Schocken, 1975).

10 Rosemary Radford Ruether *Faith and Fratricide* (NY: Seabury, 1979), esp.246–251.

11 The primary church documents can be found at *www.jcrelations.com*. All the following quotations are found at this excellent web-site.

12 I use this term to include all non-Orthodox religious groupings.

13 Lamentations Rabbah Proem 24.
14 Fragmentary Targum 22:10: 'In that hour the angels of heaven went out and said to each other: Let us go and see the only two just men in the world. The one slays, and the other is being slain. The slayer does not hesitate, and the one being slain stretches out his neck.'
15 Midrash Composed under the Holy Spirit, 65.
16 Mekhilta de Rabbi Ishmael, Pisha 7.
17 Song of Songs Rabbah 8:9.
18 Leviticus Rabbah 2:11: 'whosoever, Jew or Gentile, man or woman, slave or maidservant, reads this scriptural text . . . the Lord remembers Isaac's Akedah' and Galatians 3:28: 'There is neither Jew nor Greek; there is neither bond nor free; there is neither male or female; for you are all one in Christ.'
19 Pirkei de Rabbi Eliezer 31.
20 Genesis Rabbah 56:3. Some modern Jewish commentators have suggested that this interpretation merely explained why Abraham did not place the wood on the donkey. Cf. Moses Mirkin *Midrash Rabbah* Vol.2, Heb. (Tel-Aviv Yavneh, 1980) 286, offers two suggestions – firstly, that it enabled Abraham to fulfil God's command in every way and secondly, that condemned men carry their stake to their own execution. However, such explanations fail to explain why such a clear reference to Christianity was retained by the midrash.
21 John 19:17.
22 Cf. Irving Jacobs *The Midrashic Process* (Cambridge: Cambridge University Press, 1995), 17.
23 Vatican 'Guidelines and Suggestions', 1974.

FACING THE WHIRLWIND ANEW:
LOOKING OVER JOB'S SHOULDERS FROM THE SHADOWS OF THE STORM

Henry F. Knight

HROUGH THE ages people of faith have turned to Job (the biblical figure and the story about him) for a voice to confront the suffering around them and the anguish within their souls. At the close of arguably the most violent century of the millennium, Job/*Job* beckons to searching eyes with an all too familiar text. They face Job/*Job* with their questions and their hopes, their fears and their sorrows. However, in the shadows of Auschwitz, Job's story turns on itself as those who live like Job in the aftermath of a world-rending, catastrophic event, question the story's capacity to address their anguish without breaking under the strain.

READING *JOB* AFTER THE SHOAH

In 1970, Richard Rubenstein argued that Job failed in this regard. 'Unfortunately,' he wrote, 'the radically novel experiences of the twentieth century could not have been anticipated by the biblical writers even in their most demonic fantasies. Job does not provide a helpful image for comprehending Auschwitz.'[1] Rubenstein's critique was radical, challenging the very notion of viewing the Shoah through the lens of a story that could recount the death of ten children and never stumble over their loss. In the shadows of Auschwitz any use of Job's story must acknowledge that Job's children were multiplied by a factor of six hundred thousand.

Elie Wiesel, writing shortly thereafter,[2] developed a less radical stance. As a survivor, he recognized that Job's story was a survivor's tale, applicable to survivors and accountable to them as well. In that spirit, he challenged the traditional ending of the story where Job repented on the ash heap. Wiesel raised the possibility that such an ending was a later addition to soften the protest that Job, the survivor, brought before God (and out of step with the Job God upholds in the end).

Their questions demonstrate what thoughtful people of faith[3] discover when they turn, almost instinctively to Job/*Job*: there are significant stumbling blocks. More specifically, these stumbling blocks raise the central questions that people of faith must confront regarding God's ways with the world. We read *Job* over their shoulders. And we hear Job's story from the lips of a narrator, who himself is looking over Job's shoulder as he relates Job's difficult tale. And in our context, we stand in the shadows of other survivors who know Job's story as if it were their own. So we read looking over their shoulders as well. Eliezer Berkovits expressed this feature as a double bind recognizing that non-survivors who read *Job* after the Shoah, especially when they are family members, do so with a double responsibility to the Jobs of the Shoah. They must refrain from judging those who were unable to sustain their faith in the aftermath of the Shoahs; at the same time they dare not give up on their faith if others who endured its destruction did not turn their back on theirs. Nonetheless, the stumbling blocks remain as we peer at this classic text ever aware that our gaze is always at more than one remove.

Recounting a storied text. The text of the story is familiar. It begins with a stylized, prose introduction that scholars have come to refer to in shorthand as the prologue. It then moves after two chapters to a lengthy, poetic middle and concludes with another short prose section identified as the epilogue. The opening gambit begins in legendary fashion, 'There once was a man from Uz named Job', and develops into a parabolic encounter featuring God, a troubling figure called the Adversary (*ha Satan*), and Job.

In the prologue we learn the narrative facts of the story – the givens of the tale. Job is a righteous man with ten children – seven sons, three daughters. He is blameless and upright before God and provides for his family's material welfare, which is great, and their spiritual well being as well, regularly offering sacrifices on their behalf to atone for even the possibility of sin and thus to assure their welfare in their covenantally measured world.

The scene shifts to heaven where God is visited by attendant heavenly beings (*b'nai ha elohim*). One of them called the Adversary (*ha Satan*), approaches God, responding to God's pride in the man named Job, and offers an accusatory challenge. God approaches this member of the heavenly court and asks the Adversary where he has been. He replies that he has been roaming the earth [in what guise we can only speculate, the text doesn't say]. God, with divine pride, asks if he has seen his servant Job, pointing out Job's loyalty and righteous ways. The Adversary suggests other reasons for Job's uprightness: divine favour, declaring to God 'You have fenced him round' (Job 1:10; NRSV), suggesting Job's loyalty is a consequence of that; one should not be surprised. If his good fortune were otherwise, he would not be faithful. With this taunt, the gauntlet is thrown and the challenge engaged. God then declares to the Adversary that the power to test Job is in the Satan's hands, imploring his adversary not to hurt his servant Job.

Immediately, the story relates the ensuing catastrophe. Tragedy befalls Job's children. Each one is victim to an unexpected disaster, with the news of each tragedy related in a compounding style designed to heighten the sense of overwhelming loss. Messengers arrive to communicate one calamity with each tragic announcement interrupted in its recounting by more grievous news. Not one single child survives. Yet Job's faith does. He tears his garments and mourns as his faith directs. Then he declares: 'Naked I came from my mother's womb, and naked shall I return there; the LORD gave and the LORD has taken away; blessed be the name of the LORD' (Job 1:21; NRSV).

Still the Adversary persists, arguing that Job's response was possible because he was not bodily affected by what happened. If Job, in his person, suffered, then he would fall away – or so argues the Adversary. Again God replies, 'Very well, he is in your power, only spare his life' (Job 2:6b; NRSV). Immediately Job's body is attacked; he is afflicted with sores. His body becomes an adversary to itself.

From here the story unfolds in greater, more realistic detail in a series of poetic dialogues. The heavenly figures are replaced by four recognizable ones: three erstwhile counsellors (Eliphaz, Bildad and Zophar) and a fourth, more elusive figure. An un-attributed poetic interlude (perhaps the narrator's off-stage soliloquy) separates the exchange between Job's three counselors and the pedantic Elihu, further compounding the wrestling. Then comes the transformative encounter with the whirlwind from which God responds to Job. Job responds, retracting either his complaint, or some other previous action, and the story draws to an end. God upholds his servant Job, restoring his health and prosperity, and reprimands the three counsellors, directing them to turn to Job for spiritual guidance and support. And the pretentious arbiter, Elihu, is disregarded completely.

Acknowledging the context. Except for the possibility of two obscure references to a legendary figure named Job in Ezekiel (Ez. 14:14,20),[4] there is nothing known about Job that is not provided by the canonical text. The limited narrative detail, the unspecified time period, the highly stylized descriptions of his family (seven unnamed sons, three unnamed daughters) and Job's long life all suggest legendary qualities associated with the pre-patriarchal period in Genesis. In fact, *The Talmud* records a number of options in this regard, among them the possibility that Job never existed and that his story is an elaborate parable.[5]

Although Job is most probably not a Jew but a pre-patriarchal hero, his narrator seems to be a critically aware Israelite rooted in the wisdom tradition. The ironically self-conscious use of material from the Hebrew Scriptures and the restricted use of the divine name in the sections that frame the story suggest a thoroughgoing familiarity with *Torah*. At the same time, the use of pre-patriarchal designations for God in the poetic middle, in contrast to the more particularly covenantal ones whose boundaries he is exploring, suggest a sophisticated texturing of the story he tells, not unlike that achieved in music's use of counterpoint in developing its full harmonic voice.

A number of scholars view the poetic middle (chapters 3: 1–42:6) to be an expression of an earlier folk legend incorporated into a later parabolic frame supplied by the prose chapters at the beginning and end of the story. Even if this is the case, the canonical form exhibits a sophisticated tapestry woven into what is now a single, though complex, narrative. One might even wonder if the Hebraic placement of *Job* between the *Book of Psalms* and the *Book of Proverbs*[6] is intended to be a literary bridge, expressing *in nuce* the re-configuration of faithfulness that occurs as one moves from conventional piety of the psalter to the critical life of faith represented in the wisdom writings. Our attention, however, is focused at the boundary beyond which the wisdom writings may not go without betraying their witness in the process. At that boundary we meet two major stumbling blocks: the concluding act of Job, as Job responds to the voice from the whirlwind, and the wager that serves as the pretext for the story, initiating the action that follows.

Recognizing the pretext. The action in this story is set up by the encounter between God and the heavenly figure the text designates as the Adversary or Accuser (*ha Satan*). After roaming the earth, the Adversary challenges God in the face of God's delight in the man from Uz named Job. The narrative recounts the encounter with God replying, 'Very well, all that he has is in your power; only do not stretch out your hand against him!' (Job 1:12; NRSV). Immediately, tragedy engulfs Job's children; all ten are killed in a mix of natural and political disasters. And to heighten the pain, the news of their deaths is reported in a heart-rending cascade of interrupted messages. Then, the scene between the Adversary and God repeats itself in a subsequent encounter in which the Adversary presses the point that even though Job lost his children and all his possessions, he escaped bodily harm, and so remained untouched. Again, the Adversary questions Job's loyalty. God replies, 'Very well, he is in your power; only spare his life' (Job 2:6; NRSV).

Most scholars, and the weight of tradition, interpret this exchange to imply that God has taken on the challenge of God's adversary as if it were a wager, with God setting the limits of what may unfold next. Some, like Carol Newsom in the *New Interpreters Bible*,[7] view the exchange as a test, not a wager. Nonetheless, the dynamics are viewed in similar ways. The test or wager is between the Adversary and God, as God reacts to the

Adversary's challenge. Habel's translation of this exchange reveals the operative assumption: '*Hinne* can hardly mean "behold" in contexts where seeing is not implied. *NEB* "so be it" seems to catch the idea of the original.'[8] Habel interprets the exchange as a specific challenge that God accepts, granting to the Adversary the power to act against Job, but within specified limits.[9] The plain meaning of the text is dismissed because it does not fit the presumed action – a heavenly usurper's challenge to God's providential care of the man named Job. Other translations that retain the plain meaning of 'behold' or 'see' do so making the same assumption. But Habel's caution raises the possibility that another reading is possible. However, before exploring such an option, it would be wise to consider these stumbling blocks more carefully.

CONTENDING WITH JOB/*JOB*

After providing the narrative facts regarding Job's life, the narrator recounts the dramatic encounter that drives the remainder of Job's story. God, attended by a court or council of heavenly beings, is challenged by one of them known simply as *ha Satan*, the Adversary. Who was/is this figure?

Coming to terms with the adversary (ha Satan).   According to Peggy Day, 'The noun *satan* could mean both "adversary" in general and "legal accuser" in particular, and it was used to refer to various beings both terrestrial and divine when they played either of these adversarial roles.'[10] Day, in her research on this figure, cites nine instances where this figure is employed in the biblical narrative. Five of the settings refer to an earthly figure, as distinct from a celestial one (1 Sam. 29, 2 Sam. 19; 1 Kings 5 & 11; Ps 105) and four refer to a celestial one (Num. 22: 22–35; Zech. 3: 1–7; Job 1–2; I Chron. 21–22: 1). Depending on the context, the adversarial role could refer to a forensic and legal office or a problematic relationship. Day concludes that Job 1–2 clearly has forensic connotations, as in Zech. 3.[11] The adversarial role is expressed in reference to an office of 'accuser' in the divine council. But Day, reviewing the biblical and extra-biblical textual evidence concludes that there was no public office of 'accuser' (like a prosecutor). Rather, any litigant could bring an accusatorial complaint. In other words, any member of the royal court could fill the role of the *satan*.[12] Still, the definite article (*ha*) indicates that the narrator has a specific figure in mind, even if that figure can be applied in more than one instance. Day cautions against too simple an identification of the figure in this regard, suggesting instead a *gestalt* of related meanings, each of which can be applied in specific fashion, depending upon the circumstances.

In this context, then, we must ask, who (or what) is the Adversary in Job's story? The plain meaning of the text remains our guide: even the heavenly beings are hospitable to the voice and presence of the adversary. The adversary is an intimate of the heavenly court.[13] Many readers focus first on the literal qualities of this scene, and then in their discomfort proceed to allegorize or demythologize the polytheistic implications. Some simply discount the notion of a heavenly council as the cultural background of near Eastern court theologies. We may find it more fruitful, indeed more faithful, to face the scene literally enough to recognize its expression of radical hospitality in the realm of heaven. Room is made in God's presence for others, even the opposing, adversarial other identified as *ha Satan*. In other words, God has made a place in God's own domain for otherness, even the adversarial other that rejects the very gift of its own place.[14]

Biblical scholars (Jews and Christians) refer to the pretext generating the story of Job as a wager with Satan or with the Adversary, concentrating their attention on this adversarial figure to differentiate it from later personifications of evil embodied in an evil, supernatural character who bears the name Satan. To do this, some scholars emphasize the title; some the role. However, they concur that the figure serves the creator in this and other scenes in the Hebrew Bible where this term is used. Each explains that the text is not referring to an independent evil power, but to one of God's heavenly servants. In doing so, they still implicate God in the decision to test Job, which is, of course, the stumbling block in the story.

Job's experience of '[e]vil tells him about an Other whom the friends do not see',[15] that is, an adversary embraced by God. In his innocence, Job sees that God has embraced an adversarial other that can rend life asunder. But his counsellors are unable and unwilling to face Job and his complaint. We and the narrator know otherwise – by virtue of the prologue. Without the prologue and its parabolic frame, we might join these representatives of tradition in their interpretations of Job's plight. Instead, we are in position, with the narrator's help, to recognize that Job, as he confronts his companions with their own lack of hospitality toward him, is faced with adversarial others of his own. In fact, as the dialogues with his three counsellors unfold, we discover that even though the Adversary disappears from the text, the adversarial other is present throughout the remainder of the story in one guise or the other.

Each of Job's erstwhile friends and counsellors approaches Job after sitting with him in solidarity and grief for seven days. However, they quickly demonstrate their inability to relate to Job except through the assumptions of their conventional piety in which righteous behaviour is to be rewarded in this life and unrighteous behaviour is to be punished. The expectation of a one-to-one correlation of sin and punishment prevents the three counsellors from seeing Job as an innocent victim.[16] As a result, each of them unwittingly becomes Job's adversary, even as they perceive Job, with his unyielding insistence on his own integrity, to be their adversary.[17]

Through the use of verbal and dramatic irony, even occasional parody,[18] the narrator employs the three 'friends' as representatives of conventional, covenantal Jewish piety: God will make manifest in human history the covenantal reciprocity of blessing for righteous behaviour and judgment or curse for sinful actions. 'If you are pure and upright, surely then he will rouse himself for you and restore you to your rightful place' (Bildad, Job 89:6; NRSV). Anyone who might hold such a conventional view is captured by their comments and presumptions. When a fourth figure, Elihu, is introduced, the adversarial character of that relationship is soon encountered as well. While a number of scholars have posited Elihu as a later addition to the story, Habel contends that he is the longed-for arbiter.[19] But he also becomes Job's adversary, only to be undercut by his pretentious legal posturing and then by claiming that God would never contend with a mere mortal. In short, the narrator, in skilful fashion, discloses the ongoing presence of the adversarial other in Job's life, now in the fully embodied, yet inadequate ways of viewing the sacred held by steadfast representatives of traditional, covenantal piety.

In subtle and even suggestive ways, the readers and hearers of Job's narrative are brought into the story as potential adversaries. Through the dramatic irony of the presentation, we hear Job's pleas for intermediaries to intervene on his behalf with a narrative advantage. In each case, because we know what the narrator knows, the perspectives of these roles are provided to the reader or hearer of the story – who may very well be frustrated by not being able to fulfil them. Eventually, the narrator introduces a figure, Elihu, to attempt the arbitration that Job has requested; and the reader is invited to stand in ironic solidarity with the narrator as we view Elihu hoisted on his own petard.

With the representative use of Job's four counsellors, conventional piety is represented and shown to be at odds with the reality of Job's situation. Because of what we know, the sustained apologetics of Job's theological advisers is exposed as spiritual violence,[20] humiliating and shaming an already distraught victim and blaming him for his own victimization. Indeed, this violence indicts any person or providential scheme that, in defending its view of the world, refuses to relate to Job in his distress. To further intensify the scene, Job is trapped by the same theological scheme as he views himself attacked by God (Job 19:21). As long as the traditional structure of providence is operative God must be viewed as the Agent directly responsible for his suffering. Though Job does not yet see this implication, we do, with the narrator's help.

Job is frustrated and desperate. Clinging to his own integrity, he cries out at least to face God, his hidden adversary – to confront the Holy One directly, and not through the inadequate expressions and representations of his counsellors, nor their pietistic posturing. Eventually Job finds himself in the final adversarial relationship of his story, facing the whirlwind in and through which he encounters the Eternal One he has tried to serve in spite of every obstacle otherwise.

In other words, the entire story is marked by Job's struggle with the adversarial other, and the narrator, by telling the story in the way he has, makes that struggle the one the audience faces as well, looking over Job's story as it unfolds. Furthermore, because of the self-conscious inclusion of the figure of the Adversary (*ha Satan*) in the prologue, we are forced to grapple with the incongruity posed by the unfolding action and the apparent premise of the story. That is, we are forced to ask if it is wrongly, or too narrowly, conceived as we are drawn further into the narrator's web and back to the beginning of the story.

RECONSIDERING THE WAGER

Moshe Greenberg, in his introduction to the 1980 Jewish Publication Society edition of *The Book of Job*, states:

> Satan's wager and God's assent to it dramatize a terrible quandary of faith: a pious man whose life has always been placid can never know whether his faith in God is more than an interested bargain ... unless it is tested by events that defy the postulate of a divine moral order. Only when unreasonable misfortune erupts into a man's life can he come to know the basis of his relation to God, thus allaying doubts (personified here by Satan) that both he and others must harbor toward his faith.[21]

This is, of course, the presumption that most scholars make. The problem is captured, albeit ironically, in a later comment in the same essay. 'To the very end, Job remains ignorant of the true cause of his misfortunes, for he never learns of Satan's wager.' As Greenberg admits, the narrator and the reader know more: 'Job's suffering was the result of a divine bet on Job's disinterested piety.'[22] After Auschwitz, this implication cannot be glossed over without participating in a theological blindness comparable to that of Job's counsellors.

When we read the pretext of Job's story in the traditional way, we encounter God portrayed as the victim of the Adversary, falling for the power play and stooping to engage in the Adversary's game. In addition, God's decision exhibits a quality that turns Job into an instrument for proving the loyalty of one of God's creatures to the Adversary of heaven. Whereas Job demonstrates the steadfastness of his relationship with God, God does not! Job is but a pawn. Levinas has put the matter clearly: '[it] is a moral outrage to

justify anyone's suffering for some transcendent reason.'[23] 'Habel, we will recall, translates the critical exchange between God and the Adversary: So be it! All he possesses is in
your hand. Only do not lay a hand on him.'[24]

He explains that translating the term *hinne* literally as 'behold' is problematic because
it does not carry the meaning of God deciding to accept the challenge offered by the
Adversary in the scene. '[Adonai's] immediate acquiescence to the Satan's proposition is
surprising. The narrator does not leave [Adonai] struggling with his decision to strike
Job.'[25] However, if we read the text otherwise, guided by the plain meaning of the text
that Habel wants the reader to disregard, another option appears. Instead of God reacting
to the challenge of the Adversary, we may read God pointing out to the Adversary a
reality that already exists.

When we honour the plain meaning of the text by rendering it this way, we do not
portray God stooping to a petty challenge nor using Job as an instrument in a contest of
will. Rather we view God acknowledging what already lies within the Adversary's power,
and in this context God pleads with him not to hurt Job. In other words, instead of
reading the exchange as one in which God grants the Adversary power at a moment of
challenge and then sets limits to a subsequent wager, we may read the exchange as
involving God's acknowledgment of the power that the Adversary already has, imploring
the Adversary not to abuse that power. Why else, we might ask, would the creator say,
'do not hurt him'? Surely, it implies a limit that the adversary must be capable of
transgressing. Otherwise, why say it?

If this option is chosen, there is no specific wager between God and the Adversary
driving the action in Job's story. Still, there may be a wager, if that is the best term for it,
that we may view God making with every manifestation of the adversarial other in the
reality we identify as creation. The wager, in this sense, is a ventured risk that embraces
the full range of possibilities that otherness embodies by choosing to relate Godself to
that which is other than God – creation. The wager: creation, not a power game in which
individual creatures are pawns.

Furthermore, the prologue by referring to *b'nai ha elohim* (literally, sons of the
Gods, or heavenly beings), suggests that even in God's own domain, God has embraced the other. That is, God's embrace of life extends even to that aspect of otherness
that denies even its own place. In other words, the literal use of the figure[26] of
the accuser (*ha satan*) invites recognition of creation's essential embrace of its negating
other.

UNMASKING THE VIOLENCE

In every turn of his story, Job has faced an adversary. After facing three myopic
representatives of theological orthodoxy, Job then faced Elihu, a supposed arbiter but
no less an adversarial presence. In each case, Job was not honestly faced as the innocent
victim he was. Instead, he was viewed as a preconceived figure who, in the accounting of
their theology, could not be blameless. In the end, however, Job stood his ground by
assuming an adversarial posture himself as one who would bring a legal complaint before
the One his adversaries supposedly represented – the creator and judge of the universe.
Job faced his counsellors, and through them, their orthodox perspectives, which prevented them from seeing the person who stood before them.

Guided by their traditional piety, Job's counsellors could not account for the experience of Job – neither his blamelessness nor his anguish. As a result, the one-to-one
correlation between sin and punishment, righteousness and divine favour, collapses. Job
confronts this providential structure and becomes, as it were, its adversarial other,

challenging God to a legal suit. Eventually, he calls for an arbiter to intervene between God and him as the anguish builds and the conflict between he and his three counsellors reaches a breaking point. Job, having confronted his counsellors, calls out for help and redress, still looking through the orthodox paradigms that prevented his counsellors from facing him. 'Oh, that I had one to hear me! Let the almighty answer me!' (Job 31:35; NRSV). Elihu steps in to fill this role, declaring orthodox, theistic truths in the process (among them that Job is asking for the impossible, to face God in court). Then in one final, ironic touch, the narrator abruptly announces: God spoke to Job from the whirl-whind.

With every step dogged by an adversary, Job eventually received his wish: first an arbiter to hear his case, and second, the opportunity to bring his complaint before God. As Elihu represented the conventional piety of his time in a belaboured legal voice, he only underscored the inability of that theology to deal with Job's complaints. When he confronted Job with his trump, that God, the transcendent one, would never respond to the complaint of a mere mortal, God trumped the arbiter and responded directly to Job from the whirlwind.

FACING THE WHIRLWIND
Why does God speak from a whirlwind? No figure of a storm has been introduced, except as a source of calamity in the deaths of Job's children. Some scholars point to the imagery of the exodus presence: a pillar of fire and cloud of smoke. While this is plausible, we can identify other possibilities directly from the imagery of the story and the narrator's delight in dramatic irony and double entendre.

A whirlwind is wind (*ruah*) turned in on itself with primal force. And in the Hebrew Scriptures *ruah*/wind is also a way of referring to spirit. What happens when *ruah*/spirit is turned in on itself with elemental fury? If we listen closely to the text, we can hear the rush of this storm brewing in Job's narrative as one of its primary overtones. In this same vein, a whirlwind configures the otherness of nature encountered in extreme moments. A whirlwind, in this sense, could be a natural symbol for the otherness of God expressed from God's own self.

In a story as attentive to its language as this one is, we must ask further, 'Why "the" whirlwind and not "a" whirlwind?' When we turn to the story and how it has been told, we are reminded that the text has wrapped Job in a storm-like *gestalt* of its own. First, Job experienced a whirlwind of destruction, re-enforced by the way in which it was relayed, building traumatically and dramatically as its anguish intensified. Second, Job experienced his own unsettling questions about God's providence in what happened. In the guise of aid and counsel, he faced one adversary after another. As a person whom we can presume to be as conventionally faithful as his so-called advisers were, he would have experienced sharp dislocation between his own theological expectations and the anguish he was enduring. In other words, Job would have experienced the theological assumptions of his life turned against him in the face of three counsellors and one myopic arbiter. Still, he knew he was not to blame. Nonetheless, he felt himself accused by God, albeit mistakenly, because he was trying to make sense of his experience through the same providential paradigm that prevented the others from facing him. Surely, the narrator, in identifying 'the' whirlwind, would have been alluding to this storm of questions, feelings, frustrations, explanations that Job had been facing from the beginning of his story. If so, God would be speaking in ultimate irony, from the midst of all that, confronting Job with yet another series of forceful questions:

> Who is this that darkens counsel by words without knowledge?
> Gird up your loins like a man,
> I will question you, and you shall declare to me.
> Where were you when I laid the foundation of the earth?
> Tell me, if you have understanding...
>
> (Job 38:2–4; NRSV).

In the course of God's response, God confronted Job with the fundamental majesty of creation's primal acts. Indeed, all the aspects of divine sovereignty previously attributed by Job to God in his earlier comments are claimed by God, in Job's presence, but in new, forceful, and more immediate ways. Conventional views of this encounter record God's fury overwhelming Job with divine majesty. Job is confounded by God so powerfully that he withdraws the complaint that he so desperately sought to bring to God. Eliezer Berkovits represents this attitude poignantly: 'Job was, in a sense, silenced by divine omnipotence.'[27] But the text is more ambiguous in this regard.

The ambiguity of the closing scene of Job before the Eternal One of creation is captured by Zachery Braiterman and Carole Newsom as they each summarize the range of possible meanings that can be legitimately supported by Job 42:6, the critical verse in Job's reply to God. Braiterman writes: 'A brief look at a number of possible translations shows that the meaning of this verse proves notoriously unclear:

'al ken 'em 'as me-nihamti 'al 'aphar wa 'epher	Job 42:6
Wherefore I abhor my words; and repent, Seeing I am dust and ashes.	(JPS 1917)
Therefore, I recant and relent	(JPS 1985)
Therefore I retract And repent of dust and ashes.	(Habel)
Therefore I despise and repent Of dust and ashes.	(Good)[28]

And Newsom in her commentary for the *New Interpreters' Bible* adds more:

Therefore I despise myself and repent Upon dust and ashes (i.e., in humiliation)	(NRSV; NIV)
Therefore I retract my words and repent Of dust and ashes (i.e., the symbols of mourning)	(Patrick)
Therefore I reject and forswear dust and ashes	(Janzen)
Therefore I retract my words, and I am comforted Concerning dust and ashes	(Perdue)[29]

In other words, one can read this verse in a number of ways, ranging from Job's resignation regarding God's ways with the world, to an affirmation of Job's protests and a repudiation of a closing, penitential attitude. The key, depends upon how one understands the context provided by the larger narrative. Newsom puts it this way: 'The ambiguities inherent in the divine speeches and Job's reply resist every attempt to reduce them to a single, definitive interpretation.[30] In other words, how one interprets the closing scene depends upon the narrative that frames Job's story as well as its more immediate manifestations in the speeches that precede the last scene. We are left, concludes Braiterman, 'to wonder if Job retracts his complaint before the God who appears to him out of the whirlwind. Has he won or lost his suit?'[31] We are not left without clues for how we might proceed. But they may not appear where we might think to look first.

In this case, a return to *peshat* (the plain meaning of the text)[32] does not provide an answer though it does clarify the problem. *How* one reads the text makes all the difference. If we read with Braiterman, Good and Patrick, that Job retracts the penitential act of dust and ashes, then we are left with a Job who retains his integrity even in the face of the creator. On the other hand, if we read with the NRSV and others that Job retracts his complaint (i.e., his law suit), then we are left with a penitent Job. In the first case, Job is left unreconciled with God and God's ways with the world at the same time he honours other victims with his solidarity on their behalf. In the latter case, we are left with a Job who, in turning to God, abandons those who rely on his voice to express their pain. Job betrays them even as he fails to uphold his own integrity. Either way is unsatisfactory, or so it appears.

Other options remain, however. First, we may read Job as penitent, but not necessarily retracting his complaint. We can, quite plausibly, view Job faced with the fury of a grieving creator who has lost more than Job can imagine. Such an encounter could force Job to recognize the smallness of his complaint in the face of God's, but not its inappropriateness. We may also argue that, in the face of a grieving creator, Job could have discovered that he was so caught up in the pain he had endured he had forgotten the ten children whose loss he had earlier failed to protest. In this case, God's attention to even the most adversarial of creatures (Behemoth, Leviathan) expressed more (com)passion than Job did for any of his ten children. Either possibility points to a shame[33] that could drive Job to sackcloth and ashes, without his having to view his earlier complaints as sinful.

Philippe Nemo argues that Job is not retracting his accusations and rebellion against God but the reactions to his counsellors that participated in their hostility to him. He contends that what Job retracts is something in his discourse 'that too often resembled the senseless remarks made by [them] . . . He repents of having spoken with them in *their* language' [Nemo's italics].[34] In other words, Job repented of participating in their spiritual violence. Levinas, in response to Nemo, points to the re-ordering of his anguish as it is turned outward by the creator's relationship with creation. According to Levinas, Job, from his anguished viewpoint has his eyes turned outward to link his life to others. In doing so, he sees not simply God's greater embrace of life but God's deeper anguish. Job's steadfast integrity enables him to view God's steadfast commitment to all of life, whereby he is able to hear the even greater anguish of divine lament.[35]

Levinas's reading of *Job* suggests an added dimension in this regard. Job's complaint may be read as his *hineni*, albeit adversarial. ('Here is my signature': Job: 31; 35; NRSV.) It answers the divine question posed to every human being via Adam: 'Where are you?' God's forceful 'Where are you when . . . ?' turns Job outward in the full presence of revelation – God's *hineni* – expressing not the disdain of reclaimed sovereignty and power, but the pride and pain of the one who has created all life and must bear its crises and peril, its promise and loss. In this way, the divine *hineni* is expressed in a fury whose context is the lament of creation.

Such an encounter can be restorative, since it puts Job's anguish in a larger, life-affirming light. In other words, as God's anguish dwarfs Job's, it does not humiliate him, but rather reconnects him with life in what Levinas calls 'fraternal solidarity with creation.'[36] Job may experience shame as a result, but not humiliation as he recognizes that the face of God is reflected in the fragile and wounded other for whom God laments. As Levinas notes, Job 'never [puts] the suffering of the other in the foreground.'[37] God's lament provides that 'face' by reminding Job of others of God's creatures that are in some fashion God's children. And in the process, Job's children cry out for recognition, by Job and the reader. We hear that cry from our post-Shoah vantage point with important overtones.

In this spirit, then, we may also read Job retracting his complaint, but not because he was wrong to protest the suffering that occurred, nor misguided in resisting the short-sighted theology that explained it as an expression of divine judgment. Rather, Job could be recognizing that God was not directly responsible for evil, except in providing a creation that embraced the other so extensively that life could deny itself in myriad ways and multiple dimensions. In this case, Job would not be retracting his suit because he had sinned in bringing it. Instead, he would be acknowledging that he had not fully grasped the deeper significance of creation, that from the beginning it has been a risky venture, a wager with the adversarial other every step of the way.

We may never be able to know why the story makes Job's righteousness irrefutable only to move toward Job's penitent response to the voice from the whirlwind. Some commentators argue that what Job has sought throughout his story is the presence of God who has been painfully absent until the encounter with the whirlwind. Some point to the inscrutability of God. Some continue to resist offering any answer, even that of God's inscrutable will, claiming it to be a later addition. In the end, the text does not resolve the matter for us. Instead it leaves us with its ambiguity. But the closing epilogue does make clear what is not an acceptable reading. The three counsellors are admonished for their behaviour and for their apologetics. And to underscore the matter, they are charged to relate to Job as their spiritual guide while Job is embraced for his steadfast refusal to surrender to the ways that their conventional piety has disallowed the integrity of his own experience. In short, any interpretations that support the stances represented by Job's counsellors are unacceptable.

The story ends, as stories do, with all Job's possessions being restored in abundance. Even a new family is given. And Job is blessed with a long and full life. Survivors may recognize that some of this can be appropriate. Many of them have been able to rebuild their lives. Some have even thrived. However, anticipating the protests of the Jobs of more recent times, we must draw the line and reject the easy notion of a replacement family. Job's first ten children remain lost. After Auschwitz, with over a million children lost to that long night, the ten lost children of Job cannot be dismissed as ciphers in a story.

FACING JOB/JOB ANEW

A great deal is at stake in our contending with these matters. If there is merit in unpacking the apparent pretext of the story to reveal a more nuanced view of creation as a divine wager in which otherness is abundantly risked, then we are presented with a different way of viewing God and God's ways with the world. Instead of the deistic turn suggested by many conventional readings, we are in position to consider that God may be active as the hospitable host of life who, from the beginning, has been making time and space for life to unfold in its full panoply of otherness. In other words, if God works in history by way of hospitality, God does not have to be removed from the sphere of human affairs in order for divine action to continue having meaning at the same time as human responsibility grows in importance. But God's ways must be re-configured. They can no longer be viewed through a simple lens of covenantal reward and punishment. Instead, like Job we must turn to the radical hospitality of life we know as creation for guidance.

The turn towards a providence of hospitality is not a veiled attempt to argue that suffering serves a necessary role in an otherwise incomprehensible design of God. Rather, it is a reconfiguration of God's ways with the world that relates to God as an ever-hospitable advocate of life, in its fullness. The Deuteronomic configuration of covenantal theology gives way to a creational *gestalt* in which the direct, causal linkages of reward and punishment are replaced by covenantal responsibilities for life accepted by God's representatives in the face of an inclusive, embrace of creation that welcomes the full range of otherness in life. Importantly, a providence of hospitality does not remove the anguish from Job's witness. Indeed, it intensifies it, adding the divine anguish of the creator to the already overwhelming angst of every Job.

In other words, a providence of hospitality does not provide a grand design in which Job's anguish finally makes sense. Rather it offers a perspective that places Job's individual experience of loss and grief in the perspective of the One who has borne this pain from the very beginning. To hear God cry 'where were you when...?' is not for Job to encounter a divine put-down but for him to hear a divine cry pent up from the beginning of time. Such a cry would rightly overwhelm any mortal. And yet each one, Job and God, remain present to the other – Host to host; Father to father. Job's lament is not dismissed. Instead it provides God with an other who will understand and not be destroyed by the divine cry when it is heard.

As we look over Job's shoulders and ask 'where is Job's God now?' we hear overtones of another scene. In *Night*, Wiesel describes the haunting execution of three camp inmates at Auschwitz, among them a young boy implicated in an act of sabotage. As the three victims hang from the nooses around their necks, the inmates, Wiesel among them, are marched before the victims. The young boy was not yet dead; he was too light. 'For more than half an hour he stayed there, struggling between life and death, dying in slow agony before our eyes.' Someone behind Wiesel asked, as he had asked before, 'Where is God now?' Somewhere within, Wiesel heard his reply, 'Here He is – He is hanging here on this gallows...'[38].

For Job as for Wiesel, their traditional tapestry of God and providential order unravelled before their eyes. Even though Job did not recognize it then, the loss began with his missing children. For those of us who look over both of their shoulders, the tearing apart of traditional piety is still tied to the missing children – a hundred thousand times over. A reconfiguration of Job's God into the steadfastly faithful host of creation does not, however, remove the anguish of this unsettling scene. Instead, it deepens and extends it.[39] Anguish for the missing ten, unnamed children extends in our time to over a million. And with ever-attentive hearts, the anguish deepens to include every missing child living east of Eden.

A providence of hospitality does not call for abandoning Job. Instead it calls for a partnership of hospitality in which we join the host of life in making time and room for Job (old and new). And the spirit of such a partnership pushes Job to extend this hospitality to other victimized and anguished survivors. Its violation directs Job's and our anguish outward as well to other Job's and other children.

However, the adversarial other need not inflict violence, nor oppose all others absolutely. There are various of ways of contending with the other, many of which serve life. The key is to recognize and honour this tension by placing it in the service of life. Sometimes this may lead us to contend with Job as well as with God, but not in an argument that demands that life become subservient to some theological view reversing their proper relationship. Likewise, we must hold our faith tenaciously and let it guide us in wresting meaning and hope from life when experience seems devoid of either. In short, we must find our way to contend with Job and God together,[40] never abandoning either for the sake of the other.[41]

Job's story brings us face to face with the intentionality of creation as a fundamental commitment to the life of the other. But as Job's story shows, not every other can sustain a reciprocal response to life. Some expressions of otherness oppose the very hospitality that welcomes its creative presence. And yet, this is the way of the Creator, and the way creation unfolds. There are adversarial others that serve life by calling forth more creative responses to the world around them. There are others, however, that do not. When we come face to face with the radically adversarial possibilities of otherness, we are driven to the awareness that stalks Job and his world. It is the same awareness that stalks the landscape of the valley of dark shadows, the landscape of evil and death scarred by Nazi hatred. At the same time as we stand before the power of the other to detroy life, we are driven, as people of faith, to confront a radical and fundamental meaning of creation – the choice for creation is a wage from the beginning. That is the turn that saves this 'undeceived lucidity'[42] from unmitigated and life-denying cynicism and nihilism. In the end, it is the difference between the unrepentant Nazi and the penitent, yet steadfast person of faith.

WORKS CONSULTED

Berkovits, Eliezer, *Faith After the Holocaust* (New York: KTAV Publishing House, 1973).
Berkovits, Eliezer, *With God in Hell: Judaism in the Ghettos and Deathcamps* (New York: Sanhedrin Press, 1979).
The Book of Job: A New Translation According to the Traditional Hebrew Text with Introductions by Moshe Greenberg, Jonas Greenfield, Nahum M. Sarna (Philadelphia: The Jewish Publication Society, 5740/1980).
Braiterman, Zachary, *(God) After Auschwitz: Tradition and Change in Post-Holocaust Jewish Thought* (Princeton: Princeton University Press, 1998).
Crenshaw, James L. (ed.), *Theodicy in the Old Testament* (Philadelphia: Fortress Press, 1983).
Day, Peggy L. *An Adversary in Heaven: Satan in the Hebrew Bible* (Atlanta: Scholars Press, 1988).
Glatzer, Nahum N. ed. *The Dimensions of Job: A Study and Selected Readings* (New York: Schocken Books, 1969).
Gutiérrez, Gustavo. *On Job: God-talk and the Suffering of the Innocent* (Maryknoll: Orbis Books, 1987).
Habel, Norman C., *The Book of Job: A Commentary* (Philadelphia: The Westminster Press, 1985).
Humphreys, W. Lee, *the Tragic Vision and the Hebrew Tradition* (Philadelphia: Fortress Press, 1985).
Levinas, Emmanuel, *Entre-Nous: On Thinking of the Other*, trans. Michael B. Smith and Barbara Harshav (New York: Columbia University Press, 1998).
Levinas, Emmanuel. *Nine Talmudic Readings*, trans. Annette Aronowicz (Bloomington & Indianapolis: Indiana University Press, 1990).
Nemo, Philippe, trans. Michael Kigel with a postface by Emmanuel Levinas, *Job and the Excess of Evil* (Pittsburgh: Duquesne University Press, 1998).
Newsom, Carol A., 'The Book of Job: Introduction, Commentary, and Reflections', in *The New Interpreter's Bible* Vol.IV (Nashville: Abingdon Press, 1996), pp.319–637.
Pagels, Elaine, *The Origin of Satan* (New York: Vintage Books, 1995).
Rubenstein, Richard L. *After Auschwitz: History, Theology, and Contemporary Judaism* (Baltimore and London: The Johns Hopkins University Press, 1966, 1992.
Rubenstein, Richard L and Roth, John K. *Approaches to Auschwitz: The Holocaust and Its Legacy* (Atlanta: John Knox Press, 1987.
Scheindlin, Raymond P. *The Book of Job: Translation, Introduction and Notes* (New York: W. W. Norton & Company, 1998.
The Babylonian Talmud: Seder Nezikin, Vol.II, *Baba Bathra*, trans. Rabbi I. Epstein (London: Soncino Press, 1935).
Westermann, Claus. *The Structure of the Book of Job: A Form-Critical Analysis*, trans. Charles A. Muenchow (Philadelphia: Fortress Press, 1981).
Wiesel, Elie. 'Job', in Zev Garber and Richard Libowitz, *Peace, In Deed: Essays in Honor of Harry James Cargas* (Atlanta: Scholars Press. 1998).
Wiesel, Elie. *Messengers of God: Biblical Portraits and Legends* (New York: Random House, 1976).
Wiesel, Elie. *Night*, trans. Stella Rodway (New York: Avon Books, 1958).

NOTES

1 Richard L. Rubenstein, 'Job and Auschwitz', *Union Seminary Quarterly Review*, 25(4), (Summer, 1970): 421. A more recent expression of Rubenstein's views on these matters is found in chapters 8 and 9 of the second edition of his book *After Auschwitz: History., Theology, and Contemporary Judaism* (Baltimore and London: The Johns Hopkins University Press, 1966, 1992) pp.157–200. While the heart of his criticisms remains the same, 'the pagan spirit that dominated in *After Auschwitz* receded into the background.' Nonetheless, 'the dialectical-mystical elements' of his perspective have endured (*After Auschwitz*, second edition, pp.174–5).

2 Elie Wiesel, 'Job', *Messengers of God*.

3 Zachery Braiterman, in a new and compelling work entitled *(God) After Auschwitz*, has characterized three postures with regard to these matters positing a form of faith he terms anti-theodic. By anti-theodicy he refers to theological positions which resist the more traditional theodicies which account for suffering and defend God by way of reference to a design of creation in which suffering has its place: a radical anti-theodicy he associates with Richard Rubenstein; a mixed stance in which anti-theodicy and theodicy are held in active tension, which he associates with Emil Fackenheim; and a conservative theodic stance, which he associates with Eliezer Berkovits. See *(God) After Auschwitz: Tradition and Change in Post-Holocaust Jewish Thought* (Princeton: Princeton University Press, 1998).

4 Habel, Norman C., *The Book of Job: A Commentary* (Philadelphia: The Westminster Press, 1985) p.39.

5 *Baba Bathra 15a–15b – The Babylonian Talmud: Seder Nezikin*, Vol.II, trans. Rabbi Dr. I. Epstein (London: Soncino Press, 1935), p.73.

6 The Christian Old Testament locates *Job* between *Esther* and the *Book of Psalms*.

7 Carol A. Newsom, 'The Book of Job: Introduction, Commentary, and Reflections', in *NIB* (Nashville: Abingdon Press, 1996) pp.344ff.

8 Habel, p.78.

9 Habel, pp.79f.

10 Peggy L. Day, *An Adversary in Heaven: Satan in the Hebrew Bible* (Atlanta: Scholars Press, 1988), p.15.

11 Day, p.33.

12 Day, p.39.

13 Elaine Pagels emphasizes this point in her study of the origins of this figure. '... this greatest and most dangerous enemy did not originate, as one might expect, as an outsider, an alien, or a stranger. Satan is not the distant enemy but the intimate enemy – one's trusted colleague, close associate, brother.' See Elaine Pagels, *The Origins of Satan* (New York: Vintage Books, 1995), p.49.

14 Pagels' insight regarding the intimacy of this contending other reaches not only the realm of creation but the realm of God as well. Note the care that the narrator makes in recording the Adversary's departure from the presence of God. Each occasion follows the acknowledgment of the power held by this adversarial other.

15 Philippe Nemo, *Job and the Excess of Evil*, trans. Michael Kigel with a postface by Emmanuel Levinas (Pittsburgh: Duquesne University Press, 1998), p.149.

16 Eliphaz, Bildad, and Zophar accurately express the content of their faith – they get the words right. But they fail to see the relationship with God that Job embodies, even as he seeks to stand as an adversary before God. The very hospitality that makes the prologue possible demands no less than welcoming the complaint of Job.

17 In contrast, Job's wife makes a single, enigmatic appearance in the story. She too is Job's adversary, overtly contending with him to curse God and die. Ironically, her comments express more solidarity with and understanding of Job than anyone else in his story. But she disappears from the narrative – cause for more wrestling with this text. She too has lost ten children, her home, and all else in her household, even her name – save Job.

18 Psalm 8 is clearly referenced in this manner in Job 7:17–18: 'What are human beings that you make so much of them, that you set your mind on them, visit them every morning, test them every moment.' NRSV. In similar fashion, Job 1:10 is parodied by Job 3:23 and then later by Job 13:27.

19 Habel, pp.438, 459–463.

20 Wiesel emphasizes this feature in a later essay on Job. He writes: 'For they did to Job psychologically, mentally, what Satan had done physically. They tormented him. They tortured him . . . . At best, they allowed themselves to be used as instruments of victimization. Of the worst kind.' See Elie Wiesel, 'Job', in Garber and Libowitz, *Peace, In Deed: Essays in Honor of Harry James Cargas* (Atlanta: Scholars Press, 1998) p.124.

21 Moshe Greenberg, 'Reflections on Job's Theology', in *The Book of Job: A New Translation from the Traditional Hebrew Text*, Introductions by Moshe Greenberg, Jonas Greenfield, Nahum M. Sarna. (Philadelphia: The Jewish Publication Society, 5740/1980) p.xviii.

22 *ibid.*, p.xxi.

23 'Useless Suffering', in *Entre Nous: On Thinking of the Other*, trans. Michael B. Smith and Barbara Harshav (New York: Columbia University Press, 1998), p.98.

24 Habel, p.76.

25 *ibid.*, p.91.

26 Note what is literal here: the figure. We must let the literal qualities of the language speak without forcing them to render a simplistic literalism of the world they represent.

27 Eliezer Berkovits, *With God in Hell: Judaism in the Ghettos and Deathcamps* (New York: Sanhedrin Press, 1979), p.119.

28 Zachery Braiterman, , *(God) After Auschwitz: Tradition and Change in Post-Holocaust Jewish Thought* (Princeton: Princeton University Press) 1998), p.48.

29 Newsom, p.629.

30 *ibid.*

31 Braiterman, p.52.

32 The *peshat* refers to the plain meaning of the text, meaning not simply the original wording of the text but also the givenness of the text.

33 We must be alert to more than one way to view shame. Shame can be a healthy signal to re-adjust how one relates to the significant others in his or her life. Shame can also refer to a debilitating experience of humiliation. Here I mean the former. See my essay, 'From Shame to Responsibility and Christian Identity: The Dynamics of Shame and Confession Regarding the *Shoah*', *Journal of Ecumenical Studies*, 35(1), (Winter 1998): 41–62.

34 Philippe Nemo, *Job and the Excess of Evil*, trans. Michael Kigel with a postface by Emmanuel Levinas (Pittsburgh: Duquesne University Press, 1998) p.156.

35 Emmanuel Levinas, 'Postface: Transcendence and Evil' in Nemo, pp.180f.

36 *ibid.*, p.180.

37 *ibid.*

38 Elie Wiesel, *Night*, trans. Stella Rodway (New York: Avon Books, 1958), p.76.

39 In this regard we must be careful to distinguish the continuing action of hospitality from the initial establishment of a state of freedom that reigns supreme thereafter.

40 The reader may note that this essay is structured in precisely this manner, contending with Job/*Job* and with God as we know God. Indeed, I have also tried to reflect my understanding that this is the narrative structure operating in the biblical text.

41 Levinas has described this double commitment as the hermeneutical strategy of sacred scripture. While one grants authority to sacred writ before one understands it, one may also resist troubling texts (and pieties) insisting that one continue wrestling with and wresting from them a meaning which does not force one to abandon the persons or concerns which forced the wrestling in the beginning. See Emmanuel Levinas, 'The Temptation of Temptation' in *Nine Talmudic Readings*, trans. Annette Aronowicz (Bloominton & Indianapolis: Indiana University Press, 1990), pp.30–50.

42 I am indebted to Richard L. Rubenstein and John K. Roth for this phrase. See their *Approaches to Auschwitz: The Holocaust and Its Legacy* (Atlanta: John Knox Press, 1987), p.364.

OF FIRE AND WATER:
HOLOCAUST TESTIMONY, BIBLICAL TEXTS AND GERMAN 'AFTER AUSCHWITZ' THEOLOGY*

Björn Krondorfer

> Do not fear, for I have redeemed you;
> I have called you by name, you are mine.
> When you pass through the waters, I will be with you;
> and through the rivers, they shall not overwhelm you;
> when you walk through the fire you shall not be burned,
> and the flame shall not consume you.
> For I am the Lord your God,
> the Holy One of Israel, your Saviour.
>
> (Isaiah 43: 1–3)

IN THE context of reflecting on the Holocaust, or Shoah, certain biblical texts lose their innocence. Passages like the prophetic words of Deutero-Isaiah quoted above have the power to evoke images which we – as a post-Holocaust generation – connect with what we know about Nazi Germany's systematic attempt to annihilate European Jews. The Shoah seems to have turned words of solace into a mockery: the fire that shall not burn has burned the innumerable.

Jews and Christians who are conscious of being a post-Holocaust generation may have difficulty affirming the vision of a protective God as spelled out in Isaiah 43. We may wonder: how was it possible to revitalize the covenantal relation between God and Israel after the unthinkable and unprecedented had happened? The temple had been destroyed, the promised land, kingdom and nation lost, and the people made homeless. How could faith in a Saviour God be renewed as the people experienced the Babylonian exile? And yet, into this crisis Deutero-Isaiah spoke those words: flames shall not consume you, fire shall not burn you, rivers shall not overwhelm you, and through waters you shall move unharmed.

In a post-Holocaust world, it seems we have lost the confidence to read, speak or listen to these words in good faith. Can Jewish and Christian believers return to biblical notions of covenant, God, or redemption as if nothing had happened? Or are the prophetic words irrevocably contaminated by images and stories by which we remember the Shoah? It can be argued that the Holocaust demonstrates the ultimate triumph of a secularized, technological world,[1] forcing us to reevaluate traditional religious visions of a good, just, and redemptive cosmic order.

The image of fire and flames – one of the most prevalent cultural images of the mass killings of Jews – has been seared into our collective memory. 'The past,' Anton Kaes remarked in the context of postwar German film making, 'is in danger of becoming a rapidly expanding collection of images, easily retrievable but isolated from time and space.'[2] Biblical references to fire and flames recall pictures and stories of crematories, chimneys and burning pyres. 'So this was to be our new home,' wrote survivor Judith Sternberg Newman about her arrival in Auschwitz-Birkenau. 'A little farther back the sky was blood red. Giant flames were rising high in the air.'[3] To which we can add the words of Elie Wiesel: 'In front of us flames. In the air that smell of burning flesh. . . . We had arrived at Birkenau, reception center of Auschwitz.'[4] Can we approach Hebrew Scriptures unchanged after reading these accounts?

RHETORIC OF RUPTURE AND CONTINUITY

We are no longer innocent of the new terrifying dimension that is imposed on biblical texts by the reality of the ghettos and camps, the *Einsatzgruppen* and death marches. Contrary to the prophetic vision, Jews died in the flames of Auschwitz; and the God of Isaiah 43 was – according to many post-Holocaust Jewish thinkers and Christian theologians – silent, indifferent, passive, absent, in exile, or dead.[5] Whether we add a 614th commandment, question the traditional notion of God's chosen people, or face an abusing God, it becomes apparent that for many the Holocaust has taken on an authoritative voice equal (almost) to biblical texts.[6] More than a particularly gruesome historical event, the Holocaust is interpreted as a rupture.[7] As a negatively sacred event, or 'radical counter-testimony to both Judaism and Christianity',[8] the Shoah has assumed an aura of authority that calls into question the universe which the biblical texts affirm. What we remember collectively and individually as 'the Holocaust' shapes our reading of and responses to biblical notions of God, the covenant, redemption, faith, hope or justice. The image of fire in Deutero-Isaiah has turned into a strange fire indeed.

It would be tempting to continue along the lines of a rhetoric of rupture and continuity, presenting and discussing numerous theological attempts at reading Hebrew Scriptures after the Holocaust. We could distinguish between different 'after Auschwitz' discourses: those that continue to write about central tenets of their respective faith traditions as if little has changed, thus bypassing and downplaying the significance of the Holocaust (which we could call the *evasive* approach); those that adopt a pessimistic view, debunking God's promise to Israel and arguing for modernity's anti-covenantal legacy (the *cynical* approach); or those that imaginatively and compassionately descend into the hell of Auschwitz and ascend with a fragmented but strengthened faith, convinced of the necessity to act responsibly in light of the Shoah, irregardless of one's theological certitude (the *ethical* approach).

Each of these three suggested approaches would have, for example, a different take on Isaiah 43. The evasive pathway would evoke the comforting voice of the prophet by relying on traditional theodicies and theologies of suffering to explain the Shoah, thus employing a rhetoric of continuity. The cynical view would dismiss Isaiah 43 as a particularly naive vision of a peaceful world, perhaps best exemplified in the voice of 'the faceless one', the unnamed prisoner in Elie Wiesel's barrack in Birkenau, who put more faith in Hitler's promises to the Jewish people than in the biblical covenant.[9] His voice would represent the most radical articulation of the Shoah as rupture. And finally, the ethical approach would carefully negotiate the tension between a rhetoric of continuity and rupture, attentive to the fact that the Shoah alters our understanding of Isaiah's certitude in a protecting God, yet convinced that post-Shoah generations must find the courage to say with Isaiah, 'Do not fear.' Rather than lamenting the absence of a caring God in the face of burning children, we should, as Greenberg proposed, 'pull a child out of a pit, clean its face and heal its body.'[10]

Elaborating on these differences, it would be relatively easy to convince the reader of the merit of the ethical approach. After all, once confronted with the testimony of victims and survivors, what matters most is the courage to act ethically – not out of theological certitude but out of practical necessity. Who would seriously object to a theological reasoning that calls on post-Shoah generations to act responsibly and ethically? Who would object to a faith tested by the fires of Holocaust narratives? We would assume that most 'Christian Holocaust theologies' would want to claim that they are the result of having been touched, shamed, or wounded by Holocaust testimonies.[11] To choose what I have called the ethical pathway would almost seem like a strategic necessity for Christian theologians – and especially for Germans theologians – so as to avoid being criticized for trivializing the Shoah.

Surprisingly, among postwar German theologians it has not been self-evident to make a sincere effort of integrating the Shoah into their theological thinking. 'Beginning in the early 1970s,' observes Britta Jüngst, 'an awareness for a "theology after Auschwitz" developed among a few West German theologians, but the mainstream of established theology in Germany has continually disregarded it.'[12] But even among the few, marginalized 'after Auschwitz' theologians many are concerned more about saving the theological enterprise than understanding the history and legacy of the Shoah. 'Regrettably, in Germany we have taken the second step before the first,' writes Moltmann self-critically in a recent essay. 'We have started with Jewish-Christian dialogue... and have left Holocaust conferences to the Americans, where victims speak.'[13]

When the Holocaust is not recognized as a *Zivilisationsbruch*, as radical counter-testimony, theologians do not feel compelled to discontinue with previously held doctrinal beliefs or methodological presumptions, according to a recent study by Norbert Reck, a young German Catholic scholar.[14] But should not Christian theologians in general – and German theologians in particular – start with the assumption that the fire and flames of Auschwitz have the power to burn theological language itself? Or that Holocaust narratives subvert the position from which German theologians make statements about biblical notions of God and faith? How trustworthy are German theological writings that state how they have been challenged by the Holocaust but are, in the end, not willing to abandon conventional theological solutions?

THE VOICE OF CULTURAL CRITICISM

In this article, I propose to bring to bear upon Christian Holocaust theologies the voice of cultural criticism. Such a voice does not accommodate simply to the internal logic of theological reasoning but invites us to step outside in order to raise questions about the cultural location from which a particular theological position is produced. It does not treat theology solely as an independent text but considers also the particular cultural moment in which a theological work originates. This process, which interrupts the accepted structure of theological discourse (and hence may be resisted by theologians themselves), draws our attention to issues that are invisible as long as one moves within established perimeters of the theological system itself.

My interest is in viewing German 'after Auschwitz' theology from the perspective of cultural criticism. In particular, I will assess critically two short pieces on biblical theology. Doing so, I do not intend to make a judgment on the validity and sincerity of German post-Holocaust theology in general, which, over the years, has produced an impressive list of Catholic and Protestant authors, such as Johann Baptist Metz, Jürgen

Moltmann, Dorothea Sölle, Rolf Rendtorff, Martin Stöhr, Clemens Thoma, Peter von der Osten Sacken, Friedrich-Wilhelm Marquardt, and Johanna Kohn (noteworthy also are recent responses of third-generation theologians such as Norbert Reck, Britta Jüngst, Tania Oldenhage, Kirsten Hannah Holtschneider, Gregor Taxacher, Reinhold Boschki, Paul Petzel, Regina Ammicht-Quinn, Jürgen Maneman and others).[15] These theologies are rich in detail, elaborate and differentiated in their argumentation, and combative with each other as they try to come to terms with a difficult legacy. But I also hope to show that my criticism is relevant beyond the scope of my two examples, calling for some rethinking about the ways post-Shoah theology is practised in Germany today.

The problem of German Holocaust theology, as I see it, cannot be found alone in the specifics of internal theological arguments (though one cannot, of course, ignore substantive theological issues). Rather, it is rooted in a fundamental blindness to one's cultural location as postwar and post-Shoah Germans. This blindness is not so much due to a lack of Christian theological sophistication but to the absence of reflecting one's German identity when writing contemporary Christian theology. In other words, the problem does not lie with the answers provided but with the questions that are *not* being asked. A shifting of perspective is required, one that foregrounds the social location of living in a (former) perpetrator culture. It is my hope that the voice of cultural criticism may help to provoke such a shift.

Since I argue here that the historical–cultural positioning of German theologians is not adequately reflected in their work, it is only fair to insert a few words about my own social location and about my motivation for writing this chapter. I was born and grew up in Germany, and I studied Protestant theology for five years in Frankfurt and Göttingen. But I no longer live in Germany, and theology is no longer my primary language with respect to my scholarly endeavours. When I came to the United States in the early 1980s, originally with the intention to stay only a year, I switched to a doctoral programme in (comparative) religious studies. With the completion of my doctoral thesis on hermeneutical issues relating to religion, art and culture, and with the eventual acceptance of a teaching position at an American college, a return to Germany became less feasible and realistic. Perhaps I could be described as a bi-cultural religious studies scholar with a strong interest in Holocaust studies and cultural criticism.

After arriving in the United States, I met Jewish people for the first time consciously in my life (I was 24 at the time), an encounter which triggered a series of intellectual and emotional upheavals. I later learned that such personal crises are not untypical for Germans of my generation who have come in contact with the American Jewish community. In my case, these initial experiences have motivated me to become deeply involved in understanding and facilitating relations between Jews and Germans, particularly with respect to the so-called third generation.[16]

I continue to read theological works on an occasional basis, especially if they concern themselves with aspects of the Shoah. Admittedly, many of these works tend to put me to sleep quickly, although the topics they discuss matter to me. I usually do not take my soporific response too seriously, but the question has crossed my mind whether I am simply the wrong audience for these books (a possibility I am not discounting) or whether these Christian Holocaust theologies are less relevant than they ought to be. What would happen, I wondered, if I tried to understand what it is that tires and bothers me when reading German 'after Auschwitz' theology? The writing of this chapter, then, is also a response to this personally motivated curiosity.

I am aware that it is difficult, though not impossible, for Germans to write a persuasive post-Shoah theology today. There are many battles to be fought: with and against a Christian tradition that has instrumentalized, marginalized and demonized Jews long before racial antisemitism emerged during the 19th century; with and against a German history of genocidal antisemitism and the role of the German churches *vis-à-vis* the *Endlösung*; with and against a postwar society unsure of its attitude towards remembering and forgetting; with and against the specific German church-state relations that directly impact on the academic creativity of theological curricula at universities; with and against an audience of regular German churchgoers who purchase theological books; with and against colleagues who have marginalized 'after Auschwitz' theology; with and against Jewish voices inside and outside of Germany that have taken German theologians to task. Keeping all of these difficulties in mind, it is still important to point out that a fundamental blindness plagues German 'after Auschwitz' theologies, a blindness that is linked to the reluctance of theologians to problematize explicitly their cultural and national identity as Germans.

BIBLICAL THEOLOGY AFTER AUSCHWITZ: TWO EXAMPLES

Two entries on biblical theology in a 1997 collection titled, *Als Gott weinte: Theologie nach Auschwitz* (When God Wept: Theologies After Auschwitz), illustrate different levels of rhetorical employment of 'after Auschwitz' discourses. According to the editors, *Als Gott weinte* is the first German volume in which Catholic and Protestant representatives of diverse disciplines address the legacy of the Holocaust: biblical theology, church history, systematic theology, and pastoral/practical theology. The two contributions under the heading of biblical theology are written by Protestant theologian Ferdinand Hahn, professor emeritus of New Testament, and Catholic theologian Manfred Görg, professor of Old Testament.[17] Whereas Hahn presents five condensed theses on the significance of a theology after Auschwitz for New Testament exegetical work, Görg reflects on his coincidental discovery of the liturgical formula 'God with you' in a prisoner's letter from Auschwitz, a formula which the author traces in the Hebrew Scriptures.

In their 'after Auschwitz' biblical-theological studies, Hahn and Görg address the legacy of antisemitism and the Holocaust in different ways. Whereas Hahn employs a theological rhetoric of continuity (thus following what I have called the *evasive* approach), Görg is more attentive to the disrupting force of the Shoah, adopting the *ethical* approach. As I want to show, however, both studies misjudge the relevance of the Shoah for doing theology in Germany today, mainly due to their choice of using a Christian rhetoric that hides the authors' specific backgrounds. Hahn and Görg, like so many of their colleagues engaged in 'after Auschwitz' discourses, appropriate and handle biblical texts, Jewish traditions, and narratives of victims with the confidence of professional *Christian* theologians without reflecting on their cultural, historical and moral location as post-1945 *German* theologians. They do so, I suspect, not because of individual inadequacy but because they are part of the universalizing language of Christian theology and part of a society that remains uncomfortable about the shadows that are cast upon it by its dictatorial and genocidal past. These two moments – Christianity's universalization and Germany's discomfort about remembering the past – are not incentives to render visible the context and descent of the individual author. However, it is precisely the disappearance of the writing subject in German 'after Auschwitz' theology that leads to a misjudging of hermeneutically relevant questions.

Example 1: Not a Different Theology

Let us turn our attention now to Ferdinand Hahn, the first case study on biblical theology. Hahn's major point is that the importance of the Shoah for Christians today is to remind them that Christianity is bound to Judaism. Hahn calls on Christians not to divorce their reading of the New Testament from its Jewish context, so as to eschew the long tradition of antisemitic interpretations and to be able to renew Jewish-Christian relationships. Auschwitz, he writes, made us realize the terrifying silence of God. Yet, despite God's silence, Christians can hold on to faith. This persistence in faith is possible because it is linked to 'a theology of suffering, which does not lead to passive submission or fatalism, but to responsibility for the humanness of humans'.[18] Contrasting responsibility with fatalism, Hahn seems to adopt what I have called the ethical approach. Rhetorically, all elements are present: for Hahn, neither the evasive nor the cynical pathways are appropriate options for Christians because a 'correctly understood theology of the cross'[19] prevents them from falling into cynicism in the face of God's terrifying silence in Auschwitz. The cross reveals that even in moments of seemingly utter abandonment by God, faith can prevail. Christian can neither evade the cross (and, by extension, Auschwitz), nor do they turn cynical at its sight. Instead, they become responsible humans.

But we do not get the sense of existential urgency and vulnerability from Hahn's study that usually emerges out of a confrontation with Holocaust testimonies, challenging the foundation on which faith has traditionally been built upon. This confrontational encounter, which characterizes the ethical pathway, is missing in Hahn's piece. Instead, the larger context of Hahn's theological construction reveals that he pursues a rhetoric of continuity rather than rupture. Structurally and strategically, Hahn's brief thoughts on Auschwitz are placed in between two continuities: he first shows that New Testament writings and the development of early Christianity cannot be understood outside the context of the Hebrew Scriptures and the Jewish environment (this makes up the largest part of his study), and he concludes by saying that early Christianity has always insisted on being perceived as the continuation of Israel's *Heilsgeschichte*. In between, he inserts his thesis about the persistence of faith in light of God's terrifying silence in Auschwitz. Auschwitz, in other words, should remind Christians of the Jewish embeddedness of early Christianity (the retrospective gaze) and, progressively, of Christianity's attachment to Judaism by a *heilsgeschichtliche* continuum. The specific task of biblical theology after the Holocaust, then, is to point out that Judaism and Christianity share a 'common faith in God', a 'common faith in creation', and 'common eschatological expectations'.[20]

In the spirit of inter-religious dialogue, Hahn's focus on a shared faith in Judaism and Christianity seems praiseworthy and appropriate. Yet, by folding early Christianity into its Jewish context and simultaneously claiming that Christianity continues Israel's *Heilsgeschichte*, Hahn engages in a language of continuity that presents Judaism and Christianity as indistinguishable *vis-à-vis* the Holocaust. God's terrifying silence in Auschwitz seems to affect Jews and Christians equally. The Shoah is not perceived as having severed the ties between Jews and Christians but has been turned into a historical event that challenges both faith communities in equal ways. The Shoah as equal opportunity challenger? No space is left for reflecting on differences between a Christian theology that emerges from the past of a perpetrator culture and Jewish responses that are coming forth from a community severely victimized. It is not surprising, then, that Hahn can conclude that the Holocaust has not fundamentally changed theology. 'Theology after Auschwitz is not a different theology, but a correctly understood biblical theology which takes seriously the challenge of the Shoah.'[21] This sentence, which opens the last paragraph of Hahn's study, is a masterpiece of theological rhetoric: Hahn simultaneously claims to take the Shoah seriously as he affirms that nothing has changed.

Aren't we led to conclude that the Shoah is just one historical misfortune among others rather than an event that shakes the foundations of doing theology in the land of the perpetrators?

Hahn's theological position exemplifies the ease with which the ethical approach can be rhetorically employed while lacking in substance. In the end, Hahn's biblical theology turns out to follow the evasive rather than an ethical pathway. The Shoah, far from being perceived as *Zivilisationsbruch*, is absorbed by conventional theologies of suffering and the cross. The central paradoxical intervention of (a silent) God remains the crucifixion of Jesus, not Auschwitz.

Other questions emerge: how viable is a post-1945 German theology that speaks in the name of both Judaism and Christianity but obscures their different historical, cultural, and moral locations *vis-à-vis* Nazi Germany's genocidal antisemitism? Is the lack of self-reflectivity of one's German identity linked to the author's desire to renew Jewish-*Christian* relations without problematizing Jewish-*German* relations? Is the claim that 'after Auschwitz' theology is 'not different' from other theology a strategy that is primarily protective of Christian theology or of German identity?

Downplaying or obliterating references to one's German identity enables 'after Auschwitz' theologians to move within the universalizing language of Christianity without grounding themselves in their own history. Such deliberate[22] social dislocation frequently results in a blend of old triumphalism, where Christians continue to speak in the name of Judaism, and modern religious hegemony, where Christian Germans appropriate unself-critically Auschwitz as a symbol – as if this place belonged to the tradition of Christian martyrdom.

Example 2: Thanks Be to God

Manfred Görg's short and unconventional contribution to biblical theology is cognizant of the disruptive impact of the Holocaust on post-Shoah generations. But the word 'German' also does not appear as a marker for self-identification. As a result, questions about the specific burden and responsibility of doing biblical theology in Germany today remain absent.

Görg's essay opens with a detailed description of two letters he obtained at a stamp auction. These handwritten letters from Auschwitz, dated 1943, are apparently trade objects among philatelists. In the official philatelist language they belong to a genre called *Lagerpost* or *KZ-und Ghettopost*. The letters in Görg's possession are from a prisoner who pleads with his parents and sisters to send him cigarettes and bread, ending one of his pencilled messages with the phrase, 'God with you, my loved ones.'[23] Görg, who is genuinely touched by the prisoner's plea, takes the concluding phrase 'God with you' (which the person had probably used out of convention rather than spiritual conviction) as an opportunity to elaborate on the apparent absurdity of writing about God's presence from the zone of death. Görg's reflections, which are more suggestive than systematically argued, raise important issues: can the old liturgical phrase 'God with you' reveal something about God's presence or absence in the death camps? Can theologians truly understand the reality to which documents and narratives of victims testify? Are theologians allowed to reflect on God's presence without becoming '*Schreibtischchristen*',[24] that is, Christians who will not dirty their moral conscience by remaining safely behind their desks (like the infamous *Schreibtischtäter*, the masterminds of the Final Solution, who never bloodied their hands directly)? Can any precedence be found in the Hebrew Scriptures when contemplating God in light of such calamities?

Görg turns his attention briefly to passages in Job and Isaiah 43, wondering whether biblical faith in God has credibility in the face of crematoria. Hebrew Scriptures, Görg writes, can testify to the paradoxical nature of God, as both a 'creator of light' and as 'a dark God.'[25] This apparent paradox can be understood existentially but not resolved academically. Perhaps only those who have been in the zone of death can speak with authority and understanding of God's absence or presence in the camps. To his credit, Görg realizes that theological reasoning alone cannot grasp the existential despair experienced in the camps, and he allows his own reasoning to be disrupted repeatedly by questions about the futility of imposing theological meaning on the Shoah. 'After Auschwitz' theology is, as an academic discipline, always in danger of trivializing that which it tries to comprehend. This insight differentiates Görg's biblical theology from the rhetorics of his Protestant colleague Hahn, who, as I have shown, resorted to a language of continuity. But Görg is not free from a desire for continuity either. In the concluding paragraph, he cannot refrain from hinting at some vague cosmic order and justice. 'I am taking again the letter from Auschwitz into my hands,' he writes. 'The letter has survived until today, and with it its wish to the loved ones. Thanks be to God.'[26]

Thanks be to God? After having raised profound doubts about God and questioned the comforting words of Isaiah 43, why does Görg conclude by thanking God? Is he suggesting, like his Protestant colleague, that the mysterious face of God is revealed even in Auschwitz, and hence also present in this prisoner's letter? What is he thanking God for? That the letter survived? That there is yet one more piece of historical evidence for us to contemplate? That the letter has served as a stimulant for our theological imagination? Görg does not tell us, and the reader is left to her own devices, perhaps puzzled like me, perhaps comforted by the enigma of an omnipresent God. Rhetorically speaking, Görg's inconclusive ending is, of course, a clever move: the reader may find comfort in such vagueness, and the author is not committed to a clear position. But the inconclusiveness also reveals a weakness that runs through much of Görg's essay: the author says little about how he as a German theologian relates to the letter he had obtained at a stamp auction. We may wonder: isn't it a bit self-serving to thank God for the preservation of the letter when, in all likelihood, the prisoner who wrote it did not survive?

As readers, we learn in some descriptive detail about the letter's form and appearance but we learn nothing about the person who wrote it. Selected aspects of the prisoner's background, however, must be known to Görg. For example, he mentions in passing that the address, though fading, is still legible. We can also deduce from the type of orthographic errors of the handwritten messages cited by Görg that the prisoner could not have been a native German speaker. But who was this prisoner, and where did he come from? What was his name, religion, nationality? Was he Jewish, or Polish, or Russian? To whom did he send his request? To a ghetto, the Wartheland, or another part of Nazi-occupied Europe? Do such specificities matter?

They do. They would tell us, for example, whether the letter was written by a Jewish inmate from the death camp of Auschwitz-Birkenau (an unlikely scenario), or, say, from a Polish Catholic prisoner of the smaller camp Auschwitz I. The ability to ask for packages from the outside may point to a few privileges the prisoner may have enjoyed within the camp hierarchy. For all we know, the prisoner may have even survived.

Perhaps none of Görg's theological insights would have been affected by such knowledge. And still the specificities matter. Or better, it is the absence of specificity that matters. Is it a simple oversight that the prisoner remains nameless and faceless? Or is the lack of effort of identifying the prisoner a result of a hermeneutic blindness in Görg's biblical theology? After all, alternative approaches are conceivable. For example, Görg could have chosen to gather and present as much information about the prisoner as possible in order to give him back his subjectivity. Or he could have tried to find surviving relatives or other members of the prisoner's family, regardless of how success-ful this search would have been (the address, as we know, is still legible). These or similar efforts would have forced the author to relate to the prisoner, to step into a personal relationship with one particular victim of the Holocaust, rather than treating the letter as an object.

Görg's study on biblical theology does not contemplate acts of relationality, and as readers we are left with the impression that the letter has served the purpose of stimulating theological thought at the neglect of the person who wrote it. Rather than lifting one person from the masses of nameless victims, what matters seems to be the preservation of the letter, now in the hands of a German, thanks be to God. Holocaust testimony as trophy? What if the theologian had tried to give the prisoner a face, or had searched and found surviving relatives? He would have become vulnerable. 'But theolo-gians,' Carol Christ once wrote, 'fear vulnerability.'[27]

STEPPING TO THE WINDOW

The objectifying treatment of this letter exemplifies what plagues much of German 'after Auschwitz' theology: the Holocaust remains an object. I am reminded of Zygmunt Bauman's compelling distinction between the Holocaust as 'a picture on the wall' and as 'window', with which he described his discovery of the significance of the Shoah for the discipline of sociology. To Bauman, the Shoah had always been 'like a picture on the wall: neatly framed', until he began to understand 'beyond reasonable doubt that the Holocaust was a window ... [and] what I saw through this window I did not find at all pleasing.'[28] In Bauman's case, this shift of perspective led him to view the Holocaust not as marginal but central to sociological inquiry, bearing on the 'self-awareness and practice'[29] of social theory, public institutions, and contemporary society. A similar shift, I think, has not yet occurred in the field of theological inquiry. The two examples of this article – Hahn's embedding of 'Auschwitz' in a rhetoric of continuity and Görg's use of the Auschwitz letter as theological stimulant – illustrate the distance at which the Holocaust is kept. The authors have not stepped to the window to discover how perilous the history and memory of the Holocaust can be to themselves and their profession.

Granted, it is difficult to judge objectively the depth of a personal crisis of individual theologians: the conventions of language or other professional and societal restrictions may not always allow people to express what they have actually experienced. Görg, for example, seems genuinely saddened by the plight of the victims. And yet I can't help thinking that the letter on Görg's desk is little more than a picture on the wall, neatly framed: he, like other 'after Auschwitz' theologians, fails to give back subjectivity to the people victimized.

If Ferdinand Hahn is an example of Christian Holocaust theology (mis)appropriating Auschwitz as a place overdetermined by Christian imagery, Manfred Görg's treatment of the Auschwitz letter points to the general problematics of the Christian embrace of victim narratives – as if these narratives belonged to the Christian tradition. The danger of using historical documents or accounts by survivors to illustrate theological points is that one falls easily into the trap of lamenting the absence of faith in God rather than mourning the absence of people's faces. When the writer is German, the situation is even more delicate, because it puts the difference between communities of victims and of perpetrators in even sharper contrast.

German theologians rarely explain why they have made certain textual choices when it comes to citing and inserting Holocaust narratives in their works. It seems that any documents, testimonies, or accounts of victims and survivors may do as long as they serve to stimulate, provoke and inspire theological thought. I am certainly not the first person to point out the hazard of appropriating Jewish stories for a Christian agenda, with the result that Auschwitz has been turned into a Christian Golgotha. We only need to recall one of the better-known controversies between German theologian Jürgen Moltmann and his American colleagues Alice and Roy Eckardt. In his book *The Crucified God*, Moltmann cited Elie Wiesel's account of the hanging of a Jewish boy in Birkenau for a christological and trinitarian discussion of God, concluding with the (in)famous sentence that 'even Auschwitz is taken up into the grief of the Father, the surrender of the Son, and the power of the Spirit.' In response, the Eckardts accused Moltmann of Christian triumphalism.[30] The boy's Jewishness had been rendered invisible, disrespectful to both the victim and Judaism.

I do not need to rehearse the details of this debate here.[31] But we can learn from it that a lack of self-critical reflectivity can (inadvertently) lead German 'after Auschwitz' theologians to misjudge the relevance of the Shoah. The hanging of the Jewish boy remains a picture to be gazed at for theological inspiration. But why has this particular story been chosen? Because of its dramatic quality? Because Wiesel's bestselling book is widely known among readers? Or because of the story's emotional appeal to Christians due to its similarity to imagery of the crucified one? Without reflecting on the hermeneutic relevance of particular choices, appropriation can swiftly turn into cultural subjugation. Randomly chosen Holocaust narratives are in danger of becoming largely ornamental.

I need to return to Görg's biblical theology, lest I be misunderstood. Görg, one could object, did not shy away from the Holocaust and did establish a relationship to the Auschwitz letter in his possession. But beyond this fact, we know little. Is the letter meaningful to him because he can hold it in his hands and touch it? Is it the tactile sensation of touching this document that has stimulated the theological mind? Is the theologian disturbed by it because it intrudes into the tranquillity of his home? Is he proud that he rescued the letter from oblivion? Is his ownership an attempt at domesticating the horrifying reality to which this letter testifies? We do not know. We are left to speculation because there is no biblical-theological reflection on what it means to have obtained the item at a stamp auction. Had the theologian stepped away from his desk and moved to the window, he might have seen what has remained invisible to him before: the prisoner, or perhaps the prisoner's relatives, may have looked back at him, questioning his motivations, attitudes, beliefs. Their questions, we can assume, would have been different from those he has brought to the letter, and, in effect, changed the power relation between the theologian as an active agent and testimony as a passive resource. Görg's question about faith in the camps would have faded in favour of recognizing the face of a single victim or survivor.

Doing theology in the face of victims and survivors is, for precisely the reason of recognition, central to the efforts of Catholic scholar Norbert Reck, who has made the encounter with survivor testimony a key to doing 'after Auschwitz' theology. Working on the (yet to be published) memoir of a Jewish survivor residing in Munich, Reck has simultaneously developed a dogmatic/practical theology in face of witnesses, published in 1998.[32] For a theology after Auschwitz, Reck so eloquently and persuasively argues in his book, one must step to the window and wrestle with theological responses under the confronting gaze of survivors and witnesses. Once theologians relate to and respect the voices of victims, survivors and witnesses as equal others,[33] they may discover that what they hear from the witnesses is incompatible with theological assumptions. Christian theologians, Reck asserts, cannot pick and choose from Holocaust testimony at will so as to smooth over differences. Rather, these differences are an opportunity to reflect on inadequacies of one's own theological position. 'A conversation in the face of the victims', Reck writes, 'would cause, with respect to the central event of Christianity, self-critical examinations.'[34]

When stepping to the window, we do not only see 'others' outside, and thus expose ourselves to their gaze, but we may also get a glimpse of ourselves in the reflection of the glass. In other words, 'after Auschwitz' theologians cannot have a true conversation or encounter with Holocaust testimony without having to speak about themselves. To return again to the example of Görg's biblical theology: Görg does not see the prisoner, and he does not see himself. Görg, the author, does not appear in his writing in a deliberate and conscious manner. We may wonder: what questions might emerge if some kind of self-examination had been in place? As readers, we may want to know, for example, why the theologian had obtained the prisoner's letter. Did he find it coincidentally? Does he specialize in so called *KZ- und Ghettopost*? In the case of the latter, was money exchanged to procure the item? What is its market value? And what does the owner intend to do with it? Keep it? Trade it? Donate it to a museum? Or forward it to family members in case they can be identified?

These questions are far from being irrelevant for doing a post-Shoah biblical theology. Asking them opens new dimensions for theological and ethical inquiry: the engima of the presence of God in the camps would become less prominent than one's own position *vis-à-vis* appropriate forms of remembering and memorializing a nation's genocidal legacy. For instance, purchasing, possessing and trading objects that could be called Holocaust memorabilia is for many people, including survivors, an appalling idea, for it is perceived as an insult to the people who perished. It is a moral question. So we ask again: does it matter whether Görg stumbled accidentally across the letter or whether he purchased it intentionally as a stamp collector? Depending on the answer, issues of morality and relationality would come differently into focus.

Considering the issue of Holocaust memorabilia, it is obvious that Isaiah 43, the text that Görg had chosen to illuminate his theological queries about God's presence in the camps, cannot provide any models and insights. It is the wrong textual choice. We would have to identify different passages from the Hebrew Scriptures as counter-reading to the situation as it is now presented. Our gaze might, perhaps, fall onto Isaiah 44:9: 'All who make idols are nothing and the things they delight in do not profit; their witnesses neither see nor know. And so they will be put to shame.' This passage – though not a perfect parallel (for it assumes, among other things, an intentional malice on Görg's part, which he never exhibits) – points us into a direction we must take: to abandon the objectifying treatment and appropriation of the Holocaust as idol (read 'image'), and to bear witness in such a way that we can 'see and know.'

OUTLOOK: DOING THEOLOGY IN THE FACE OF PERPETRATORS
I hope that is has become apparent why resistance to making one's German identity an explicit part of one's theologizing serves a protective function: the writer removes himself from being socially, morally or biographically implicated in a culture that continually struggles with coming to terms with having perpetrated a genocide. The universalizing tendency of Christian theology is one mechanism that assists in turning a blind eye to one's own particular historical, cultural and moral situatedness. Post-Shoah German

theologians seldom examine themselves over against a background of a perpetrator culture and, instead, prefer to place themselves in the context and conventions of Christian theology. Within these perimeters, they lose sight of the uniqueness and the otherness of the Jewish victims as well as of the uniqueness and sameness of the German perpetrators.

A central story that Christianity tells of itself is that it has struggled against victimization, suffered martyrdom and death, but emerged triumphant nevertheless. This story tempts Christian theologians to imagine themselves on the side of the victims of Auschwitz, even at the expense of replacing the Jewishness of the victims with Christian imagery. The Christian story does not, however, provide models for looking at oneself as a perpetrator or descendant thereof. In a perversely nostalgic and pathetic way, it is more comforting to theologize about the hanging of a Jewish boy in Birkenau than to theologize, for instance, about Rudolf Höss's confessed 'moral' dilemma of having to act against his own emotions when ordering a sergeant to tear two little, screaming children from their mother's arms and put them in the gas chamber. The mother, camp Kommandant Höss writes in his memoirs, 'was weeping in the most heart-breaking fashion. Believe me, I felt like shrinking into the ground out of pity, but I was not allowed to show the slightest emotion.'[35]

How can German 'after Auschwitz' theology respond to this scene in Höss's memoirs? What christological models ought to be employed, what biblical text quoted? How can we respond theologically to Höss's religious sentimentality that peaks occasionally through his memoirs and is, no doubt, traceable to his strict Catholic up-bringing? How dangerous would it be to locate oneself as a German theologian in the cultural tradition of the Auschwitz Kommandant rather than that of the Jewish mother and her children? Would it be possible and permissible to identify, if only for a moment, with Höss's spark of 'moral' conscience, as perverted and nauseating as it may be? How could a balance be struck between recognizing one's religio-cultural roots in a tradition that led to Höss's behaviour, yet keeping a critical and healthy distance to the mentality of perpetrators? The challenges that are buried in these questions may illustrate why German theologians are reluctant to acknowledge the lives and deeds of perpetrators as a ground for theologizing. Testimony and narratives of Jewish victims and survivors can be integrated into a 'Christian' story with less of an intellectual effort than the accounts of perpetrators, whether we find the latter in memoirs, interviews, trial records or archival documents.

I am not suggesting to replace Holocaust testimony of victims and survivors with testimony of perpetrators – for surely, we do not want to learn or teach how to become 'good' perpetrators. A German theological position that cuts out the victim perspective is untenable. But limiting oneself exclusively to the victim perspective raises, as I tried to show, hermeneutical dilemmas about textual choices and about one's cultural perspective, always at risk of misappropriation and false identification. Without positioning oneself as theologian consciously and explicitly in the tradition of perpetrators, German 'after Auschwitz' theology remains disingenuous and incomplete.[36]

A theology that dares to probe the limits of theologizing in the face of perpetrators will bring new insights to the often rehearsed debate over continuity and rupture. Such a theology cannot engage in a language of continuity, if by this is meant that theology after Auschwitz is 'not a different theology', or that post-Shoah Jews and Christians struggle equally with questions of faith and God. But a theology done in the face of perpetrators can also not adopt unqualifiedly the idea of the Shoah as rupture, as *Zivilisationsbruch*, because it must look for continuities in new areas: how, for example, German society has integrated perpetrators;[37] how the churches have helped to facilitate this re-integration on individual and social levels;[38] how selective stories about World War II have been transmitted within German families from generation to generation, while a partial amnesia descended upon stories about one's family's knowledge of and participation in the Shoah;[39] and how standard theological works written before and during the Nazi dictatorship have poisoned generations of postwar German theologians with their subtle or not so subtle antisemitism.[40] Looking through the window also means to examine such continuities. Or, as Zygmunt Bauman put it: 'The more depressing the view, the more I was convinced that if one refused to look through the window, it would be at one's peril.'[41]

As far as biblical theology is concerned, an obvious place to start implementing such a shift of perspective, as I have argued, is choosing biblical passages that speak to the issue of doing theology in the face of perpetrators. We can now, at the end of this chapter, return to Isaiah 43. We would not, however, as in the beginning, evoke the image of fire and flames, and read this image counter to narratives of victims. Rather we would turn our attention to the verses which promise that the rivers shall not overwhelm you and the waters leave you unharmed; and a passage from Höss's memoirs would serve as our counter-reading. 'When you pass through the waters, I will be with you; and through the rivers, they shall not overwhelm you' (Isa. 43.2). As we can see in the brief scene below, the waters of the river Sola – passing in front of Höss's villa and the Auschwitz *Stammlager* (main camp)—provide pleasure and do not harm. But it is the perpetrators who enjoy such protection. We would be challenged not to dismiss the bitter sarcasm of such parallel reading as a cynic's attempt to destroy theological inquiry but a critic's attempt to ground German 'after Auschwitz' theologies in their particular moment in history, and thus to make them relevant again. Höss writes:

> Yes, my family had it good in Auschwitz, every wish that my wife or my children had was fulfilled. The children could live free and easy.... [They] constantly begged me for cigarettes for the prisoners... The children splashed around in the summertime in the small pool in the garden or the Sola River. Their greatest pleasure was when daddy went into the water with them. But he had only a little time to share all the joys of childhood.[42]

NOTES

* An earlier, shorter version of this paper was originally published as 'Of Faith and Faces: Biblical Texts, Holocaust Testimony and German "After Auschwitz" Theology' in a volume entitled *Strange Fire: Reading the Bible after the Holocaust*, edited Tod Linafelt, ©2000, Sheffield Academic Press Ltd., and is reproduced here with kind permission of the publishers.

1 See Zygmunt Bauman, *Modernity and the Holocaust* (Ithaca: Cornell University Press, 1989).
2 Anton Kaes, *From Hitler to Heimat: The Return of History as Film* (Cambridge: Harvard University Press, 1990): 198.
3 Judith Sternberg Newman, *In the Hell of Auschwitz* (New York: Exposition Press, 1963): 16.
4 Elie Wiesel, *Night*, trans. Stella Rodway (New York: Bantam Books, 1982): 26.
5 Rather than listing the many Jewish and Christian scholars who have contributed to religious and theological inquiry regarding the Holocaust, let me point the reader to some selected books. The volumes by John K. Roth and Michael Berenbaum, eds., *Holocaust: Religious and Philosophical Implications* (New York: Paragon House, 1989), and by Elisabeth Schüssler-Fiorenza and David Tracy, eds., *The Holocaust as Interruption* (Edinburgh: Concilium and T. & T. Clark, 1984) contain selected writings of some of the important voices of the early generation. For critical summaries and discussions of Jewish and Christian thought, see Steven Katz, *Post-Holocaust Dialogues: Critical Studies in Modern Jewish Thought* (New York: New York University Press, 1983); Zachary Braiterman, *(God) After Auschwitz: Tradition and Change in Post-Holocaust Jewish Thought* (Princeton: Princeton University Press, 1998); Donald J. Dietrich, *God and Humanity in Auschwitz: Jewish-*

Christian Relations and Sanctioned Murder (New Brunswick: Transaction Publishers, 1995); Eva Fleischner, ed., *Auschwitz: Beginning of a New Era? Reflections on the Holocaust* (New York: KTAV, 1977): Ellen Z. Charry, 'Jewish Holocaust Theology: An Assessment', *Journal of Ecumenical Studies* 18/1 (Winter 1981), 128–139; and Britta Jüngst, *Auf der Seite des Todes das Leben: Auf dem Weg zu einer christlich-feministischen Theologie nach der Shoah* (Gütersloh: Chr. Kaiser, 1996): 136–143. A book less often discussed is Arthur A. Cohen, *The Tremendum: A Theological Interpretation of the Holocaust* (New York: Crossroad, 1981). A controversial post-Shoah Jewish theologian is Marc H. Ellis, *Ending Auschwitz: The Future of Jewish and Christian Life* (Louisville, Kentucky: Westminster/John Knox Press, 1994); for a discussion of Ellis's work, see Richard L. Rubenstein, *After Auschwitz: History, Theology, and Contemporary Judaism*, 2nd ed. (Baltimore: John Hopkins University Press, 1992): 266–280.

6   The 614th commandment refers to Emil L. Fackenheim, 'Jewish Values in the Post-Holocaust Future: A Symposium', *Judaism* 16 (Summer 1967), reprinted in Roth and Berenbaum, eds., *Holocaust*, 291–295. See also Fackenheim, *God's Presence in History: Jewish Affirmations and Philosophical Reflections* (Northvale, New Jersey: Jason Aronson, 1997): ix–xvi. The questioning of traditional Jewish notions of the covenant refers to Richard L. Rubenstein, *After Auschwitz*. The notion of the abusing God refers to David R. Blumenthal, *Facing the Abusing God: A Theology of Protest* (Louisville, Kentucky: Westminster/John Knox Press, 1993). See also Eliezer Berkovits, *Faith After the Holocaust* (New York: KTAV Publishers, 1973), who rejects the idea of giving the Holocaust a singularly authoritative voice.

7   Stephen R. Haynes, 'Christian Holocaust Theology: A Critical Reassessment', *Journal of the American Academy of Religion*, lxii/2 (Summer 1994), who criticizes overly dramatic terminology to describe the effects of the Shoah on Christian faith, such as 'endpoint, interruption, crisis, break, rupture, [or] paradigm shift' (554).

8   Irving Greenberg, 'Cloud of Smoke, Pillar of Fire', in Fleischner, ed., *Auschwitz*, reprinted in Roth and Berenbaum, eds., *Holocaust*, 305–345.

9   Wiesel, *Night*, 76–77.

10   Roth and Berenbaum, eds., *Holocaust*, 331.

11   The quote is from Haynes, 'Christian Holocaust Theology', 553–555. An example of a wounded and shamed Christian post-Shoah theology is the recently published, thoughtful work of Henry F. Knight, *Confessing Christ in a Post-Holocaust World: A Midrashic Experiment* (Westport, Connecticut: Greenwood Press, 2000).

12   Jüngst, *Auf der Seite des Todes*, 158.

13   Jürgen Moltmann, '"Die Grube:" "Wo war Gott?" Jüdische und christliche Theologie nach Auschwitz', in *Als Gott weinte: Theologie nach Auschwitz*, eds. Manfred Görg and Michael Langer (Reenburg: Pustet, 1997): 53.

14   Norbert Reck, *Im Angesicht der Zeugen: Eine Theologie nach Auschwitz* (Mainz: Grünewald, 1998), 14.

15   Important titles of the authors can be found, among others, in the excellent bibliography of Reck, *Im Angesicht*. Reck, and in *ibid.*, 'Lernt zu lesen: es sind heilige Texte. Die Theologie nach Auschwitz und die Zeugen', in Görg and Langer, *Als Gott weinte*; Jüngst, *Auf der Seite des Todes*; Tania Oldenhage, 'Parables for Our Time? Rereading New Testament Scholarship After the Holocaust' (Ph.D. diss., Temple University, 1999); and Kirsten Holtschneider, who is currently completing her Ph.D. thesis in Birmingham, United Kingdom, on a third-generation perspective on German Protestant identity in relation to the memory of the Holocaust.

16   For details about my work with the 'third generation', see Björn Krondorfer, *Remembrance and Reconciliation: Encounters between Young Jews and Germans* (New Haven: Yale University Press, 1995); and *ibid.*, 'Third-Generation Jews and Germans: History, Memory, and Memorialization', in Working Papers of the Volkswagen-Foundation Program in Post-War German History (Washington, D.C.: German Historical Institute and AICGS/John Hopkins University, 1996). See also my afterword to Edward Gastfriend's, *My Father's Testament: Memoir of a Jewish Teenager, 1938–1945*, ed. with afterword by Björn Krondorfer (Philadelphia: Temple University Press, 2000).

17   Ferdinand Hahn, 'Theologie nach Auschwitz und ihre Bedeutung für die neutestamentliche Exegese: Eine Thesenreihe', and Manfred Görg, '"Gott mit euch, meine Lieben:" Die Formel vom Mitsein Gottes in, vor und nach Auschwitz', in Görg and Langer, eds., *Als Gott weinte*.

18 Hahn, 'Theologie nach Auschwitz', 92.
19 *ibid.*
20 *ibid.*, 92–93.
21 *ibid.*, 93.
22 The term 'deliberate' is not meant here to convey intentionality on the part of the individual but to point to a strategic convention of postwar German theology.
23 Görg, 'Gott mit euch', 83.
24 *ibid.*, 85.
25 *ibid.*, 86.
26 *ibid.*, 87.
27 Carol Christ, 'Whatever Happened to Theology?', *Christianity and Crisis* 35 (May 1975): 114.
28 Bauman, *Modernity*, vii–viii.
29 *ibid.*, xii.
30 Jürgen Moltmann, *The Crucified God*, trans. R. A. Wilson and John Bowen (New York: Harper and Row, 1974), 278; A. Roy Eckardt, 'Jürgen Moltmann, the Jewish People, and the Holocaust', *Journal of the American Academy of Religion* 44/4 (December 1976): 675–691; and Alice L. and Roy A. Eckardt, *Long Night's Journey into Day: A Revised Retrospective on the Holocaust* (Detroit: Wayne State University Press, 1982): 109–117.
31 For an apologetic response in behalf of Moltmann, see Haynes, 'Christian Holocaust Theology', 560; and *ibid.*, *Prospects for Post-Holocaust Theology* (Atlanta: Scholars Press, 1991): 114–122. For repetition and some clarification of Wiesel's story in Moltmann, see Moltmann, 'Die Grube: Wo war Gott', 51–52.
32 Reck, *Im Angesicht*.
33 For the victims, Reck uses the German term *Gegenüber*, which may be best translated as 'equal other' ('die Opfer sind als *Gegenüber* zu begreifen und zu respektieren', *Im Angesicht*, 121).
34 *ibid.*, 230.
35 Rudolf Höss, *Death Dealer: The Memoirs of the SS Kommandant at Auschwitz*, ed. Steven Paskuly, trans. Andrew Pollinger (New York: Da Capo Press, 1996): 162.
36 Recently, some tentative reflections on doing theology in the face of perpetrators appear in German 'after Auschwitz' theologies. See Peter von der Osten Sacken 'Christliche Theologie nach Auschwitz', and Moltmann, 'Die Grube: Wo war Gott', both in Görg and Langer, *Als Gott weinte*. Jüngst, *Auf der Seite des Todes*, and Reck, *Im Angesicht*, also bring awareness to this issue. But a theological perspective in light of perpetrator testimony is, to my knowledge, nowhere fully and systematically developed.
37 See Ralph Giordano, *Die zweite Schuld oder von der Last ein Deutscher zu ein* (Hamburg: Rasch und Röhring, 1998).
38 See, for example, Doris L. Bergen, *Twisted Cross: The German Christian Movement in the Third Reich* (Chapel Hill: University of North Carolina, 1996): 206–230.
39 For new research on intergenerational transmission and German family history, see the work of Gabriele Rosenthal, ed., *Der Holocaust im Leben von drei Generationen: Familien von Überlebenden der Shoah und von Nazi Tätern* (Giessen: Psychosozial Verlag, 1997); *ibid.*, ed., *Als der Krieg kam hatte ich mit Hitler nichts mehr zu tun: Zur Gegenwärtigkeit des 'Dritten Reiches' in Biographien* (Opladen: Leske + Budrich, 1990); Dan Bar-On, *Legacy of Silence: Encounters with Children of the Third Reich* (Cambridge: Harvard University Press, 1989); Barbara Heimannsberg and Christoph J. Schmidt, eds., *The Collective Silence: German Identity and the Legacy of Shame*, trans. Cynthia Oudejans Harris and Gordon Wheeler (San Francisco: Jossey-Bass Publishers, 1993); and Björn Krondorfer, 'Biographische Arbeit in jüdisch/deutschen Begegnungsgruppen nach der Shoah', in *Biographische Arbeit in der Erwachsenenbildung: Beispiele aus der Praxis* (Berlin: Bundesministerium für Bildung, Wissenschaft, Forschung und Technologie, 1998).
40 Charlotte Klein, *Anti-Judaism in Christian Theology* (Minneapolis: Augsburg Fortress Publishers, 1978).
41 Bauman, *Modernity*, viii.
42 Höss, *Death Dealer*, 164.

JEWS AND CHRISTIANS AFTER AUSCHWITZ:
REFLECTIONS FROM A POLITICAL–
THEOLOGICAL PERSPECTIVE

Jürgen Manemann

JOHANN BAPTIST Metz, the founder of the new political theology, starts his essay 'Facing the Jews' (1984) with a quotation by Soren Kierkegaard: 'In order to experience and understand what it means to be a Christian, it is always necessary to recognize a definite historical situation.'[1] For the new political theology, theology means speaking of God, speaking of God in our time. Speaking of God in our time always means to give a diagnosis of our time, to find out what is going on in history and society. From this perspective, speaking of God means always to speak about the so-called 'signs of our time' and the sign without which no Christian in our context should speak of God today is Auschwitz.[2]

Political theology is a theology after Auschwitz, brought about by the terrible questions: How could it happen that Christians prayed and celebrated liturgy turning their backs to Auschwitz? And how was it possible that theology after 1945 made this catastrophe appear to be merely the echo of a departing thunderstorm and continued to do theology as usual?[3] Political theology first faced National Socialism from a Hitler-centred perspective but more and more it began to realize that it was not Hitler but Auschwitz that was the centre of this period. Furthermore, political theology came to the conclusion that Auschwitz overshadows everything after 1945. Thus Auschwitz is to be considered not only as a challenge to religion, but a challenge to history and politics as well.

Political theology, conceived as a theology after Auschwitz, needs to develop a theology which is unable to distance itself from the suffering of people in society and history and the harm that has caused. Therefore it argues that the so-called theodicy question must be the foundation of contemporary God-Talk.[4] The neglect of this question in Christian theology has led to a forgetting of the messianic tradition which could be described as a falling behind Judaism. Since the resurrection of Christ, salvation has seemed to be given automatically. Sadly, Christianity virtually silenced those who suffered because their suffering was already regarded as fulfilled in the suffering of Christ. So each time a solitary cry of rebellion against human suffering was uttered, the answer came in the form of an even more terrible suffering: the crucifixion of Christ.[5] Thus Christianity appeared as if it would not expect anything. It had forgotten that the history of salvation is not a history beyond this history or above this history, but this history itself.[6] If the German philosophers Theodor W. Adorno and Max Horkheimer are right, this forgetting is one of the main reasons for anti-Semitism. Their famous philosophical book *Dialectic of the Enlightenment* written in 1944 is in fact a sustained meditation on progress, asking 'why mankind, instead of entering into a truly human condition, is sinking into a new kind of barbarism'. Concerning the origins of anti-Semitism they argue that Christians persuaded themselves with a heavy conscience that Christianity was their own sure possession:

> [they] had to affirm their eternal salvation as against the worldly damnation of all those who did not make a dull sacrifice of reason. This is the religious origin of anti-Semitism. The adherents of the religion of the father are hated by those who support the religion of the son – hated as those who know better. It is the hostility to spirit, grown obdurate in the conviction of salvation. For christian anti-Semites truth is the stumbling-block, truth which resists evil without rationalizing it, and clings to the idea of undeserved salvation against all the rules of life and salvation which are supposed to ensure that blessed state. Anti-Semitism is meant to confirm that the ritual of faith and history is right by executing it on those who deny its justice.[7]

In response to this critique political theology forces theology to face history and society, but in order to know what history is alike we must hear the testimonies of the victims to avoid evading history's disasters.[8] But instead of listening carefully to the voices of the victims the Catholic Church, although emphazising the need to remember in a moral way practises much more confidence in the historical science without realizing the dialectic of the enlightenment. Every scientific method implies violence and 'there are hardly any easier ways to dehumanize the dead after their murder than by unconsciously imitating the Nazis and turning them into objects again – this time objects of historical, sociological, (theological) or other research'.[9] Based upon this insight, a historiographical description of National Socialism has to start with the testimonies of the victims and has to lead to the testimonies of the victims – if it would lack the connection to the testimonies the stories told by the historians must be viewed with caution. This has to be taken into account when one makes use of the research of the historians in theology.[10]

IN ORDER TO DEVELOP A POLITICAL THEOLOGY AFTER AUSCHWITZ WE FIRST HAVE TO FACE THE CATASTROPHE[11]

Auschwitz is the biggest annihilation camp in human history. It is a symbol for National Socialism because it was the centre of it. Auschwitz is not a notion, it is a name of a place not comparable with other places. Auschwitz is unique. Again and again Jewish victims bear witness to the uniqueness and incomprehensibility of this catastrophe knowing that language is unable to describe it. This is why Elie Wiesel says: 'The more – and the more carefully – people listen to us, the more we realize that our words are not "getting through"; what we try to say is not what you think you have heard.'[12]

But to talk of uniqueness raises many historical and philosophical questions. If we deal with these more abstract questions we will avoid evading the catastrophe. By becoming aware of its aporetical character we become sensitive to the rupture caused by this catastrophe. The following remarks will illustrate the complexity of this interruption.

A basic philosophical preliminary of historical research is that every event of history is unique and that therefore in a general way every event is, as far as its uniqueness concerned, incomprehensible.[13] But Auschwitz is both significantly unique and unprecedented. Furthermore it represents a *caesura* in universal history, an event that changed everything or – as Fackenheim calls it – an 'epoch-making event'. In order to distinguish Auschwitz linguistically from other historical events which might also be significantly unique, we could speak with the theologian Roy Eckardt of a 'uniquely unique' event.[14] Auschwitz is not only unique in the framework of Jewish existence. It is unique outside this framework too. Certainly there have been massacres before throughout history, but never before did a national state represented in its elected leader both decide and act on its decision to murder an entire group of people including women, the old, the children and the babies, with every means at its disposal. They killed the people in an industrial way – Auschwitz was a killing-factory.

The Nazis decided that every available Jew had to be murdered. This was unprecedented as well as incomprehensible and irrational. Or: Is it 'a rational decision for Hitler to decide that even if Germany goes down, every Jew has to be murdered?'[15] And could we assume that the answer is that Hitler really believed it? Would this be a face value? The Canadian philosopher Emil Fackenheim said: 'If Hitler was crazy, how come they let him run a whole country? Almost conquer the world? Or were they all crazy? That doesn't answer anything.'[16] Auschwitz is unique because it is incomprehensible. The only things we can understand are the economic and technical precautions taken, for example the technical improvement of capacities. But the meaning of this annihilation, annihilation for the sake of the annihilation, is not comprehensible. Perhaps if we could comprehend it we would go mad – as Elie Wiesel suggests. He says that the impossibility to comprehend might be caused by God's mercy because it saves us from becoming insane. The philosopher Steven T. Katz writes:

> The Holocaust remains always 'beyond comprehension', an event as much revealed as mysterious, much as we must insist that it be open to scholarly investigation and ordinary rules of historical and philosophical enquiry.... By contrast, the Gulag generates rage and dread, anger and sorrow, but no mythification.[17]

However, to speak of the uniqueness of Auschwitz does not mean to say that the victims in Auschwitz suffered more than, for example, the victims of the Gulag. On the contrary, it is merely to emphasize that all suffering is unique.[18] Speaking of uniqueness illustrates that there is a difference we have to acknowledge which makes Auschwitz a precedent. Facing differences is a necessary precondition for facing catastrophes. Negating differences leads to indifference!

Facing the uniqueness of Auschwitz we become aware that National Socialism bears deep theological, philosophical-methodological, political-ideological and moral problems which make this event an abnormal occurrence in history.[19] There are two particularly important theories concerning this catastrophe which are often used in an evasive way. These are the theory of totalitarianism and the theory of fascism. Both are of course, heuristically valuable, but only if we acknowledge their limits. Both are – according to Max Weber – ideal-typical concepts and two-sided notions. On the one hand they are historical and sociological concepts; on the other they are political notions. As such they are not sufficient to meet the case in its uniqueness. The theory of totalitarianism, for example, investigates the structures of dictatorship, but it does not ask why Auschwitz has been possible. As far as the theory of fascism is concerned, we notice that the annihilation of the Jews is a *novum* despite all the anti-Semitic hatred that characterized other fascist movements. Furthermore we have to take into account that both theories were already fully developed before Auschwitz. Looking for similarities they are unable to face the catastrophe in its uniqueness.

One main problem of the historiography of National Socialism is that all historical research is rooted in some kind of longing for continuity and identity. Some historians, for example, view history as a way of building up a national identity. It is obvious that a historiography grounded in the longing for an unbroken, positive identity is incapable of viewing a negative catastrophe because this is a counterpart of such a longing and would contradict and interrupt it. There is no possibility of building up a positive national identity in the face of Auschwitz. This leads to the insight that to face up to Auschwitz means to face meaninglessness: to learning about Auschwitz means to realize a process of unlearning. Another reason for not recognizing Auschwitz is so-called egocentric inevitability, the inability to face the world through the eyes of the other, to view history from the perspective of the victims.[20]

Despite these arguments and facts the uniqueness is often criticized, but the critics are mostly unaware that their compulsion to comprehend is grounded in a scientific approach unable to grasp the blind spot of its epistemology. If this event is indeed unique our methods might not be sufficient to reach the case. Maybe some day we will be able to explain how it happened – but will we ever be able to explain why it happened? Fackenheim gives three reasons for the negation of uniqueness:

> First, it is hard to believe that a unique event of catastrophic import should have happened in one's own lifetime...Second, if nevertheless the event must be confronted by thought, then an appropriate category...seems sufficient to meet the case; the ingrained habit of thought resists the insight that, in case the event is in fact unique, these categories, simply because they are categories, are not sufficient to meet the case but are actually a means of escape from it. Third, there is the well-known philosophical problem of whether 'the unique' – the unique of any kind – can be thought at all.[21]

And Fackenheim closes this passage with the question: 'But what if the Holocaust is unique?'[22]

The dead of Auschwitz should have brought upon us a total transformation; nothing should have been allowed to remain as it was, neither among our people nor in our churches.[23] Yet, what has happened to us Germans and Catholic Christians? Auschwitz was no turning point. After 1945 there has been sorrow, not about the victims, but about our own losses like the loss of the national identity. The restoration of our society and the survival of the church as an institution are celebrated as heroic acts. Since the unification of Germany Auschwitz threatens to become only a detail of history. The critique of Adorno has died away. Already anticipating this development he wrote in 1944:

> The idea that after this war life will continue 'normally' or even that culture might be 'rebuilt' – as if the rebuilding of culture were not really its negation – is idiotic. Millions of Jews have been murdered, and this is to be seen as an interlude and not the catastrophe itself. What more is this culture waiting for?[24]

– and we should add: 'What more is theology waiting for?'

The task of a theology after Auschwitz is to protect remembering and retelling from suspicion of reductionism and homogenization. According to such a point of view theologians have the following main duties.[25]

First, there has to be a radical transition from system concepts to subject concepts, from theology to political theology. The second duty has to do with discernment: a theology after Auschwitz must have the capacity to provide a broad and deep analytical grasp of the present in the light of the past. Thirdly, theology must protect the narratives. In order to protect narratives we theologians have to brush history against the grain (Walter Benjamin). Fourthly, we have to criticize every act of distancing ourselves from the suffering of others: The condition of truth is to allow the suffering to speak. But this does not mean that those who suffer have a monopoly on truth. It has to be understood that for truth to emerge it must be in tune with those who were and who are undergoing misery.[26] According to Cornel West we could formulate the fifth duty as hoping against hope or, as Walter Benjamin puts it, hoping for the sake of the hopeless. Sixth; keeping track of hypocrisy (this is very important for theologians) by accentuating the gap between principles and practice.

Political theology as I envisage it suggests recognizing that our findings are missing 'something'. To resist the processes of forgetting Christianity needs to foster an anamnestic culture (a culture of remembrance) which keeps track of the forgotten – the victims. Johann Baptist Metz points out that the Catholic Church has preserved its memory liturgically but that is has not cultivated it publicly.[27] As an anamnestic culture the church could concern itself with the catastrophe because the kind of anamnestic culture which is indicated here is rooted in biblical remembrance. Biblical remembrance entails an inability to distance itself successfully from the terror and abyss of reality through mythologization or idealization. Metz calls this mentality 'poor in spirit'.[28] Biblical remembrance is *memoria passionis* – memory of suffering. This memory is dangerous. Doing theology in the light of dangerous memory means that mysticism returns to logic, praxis returns to theory, the experience of resistance and suffering returns to the experience of grace and spirit.[29]

Biblical memory is an expression of a conscience which consisted in the ability to take into account the true interests of others. This memory interrupts our 'high-order-interest' in self-determination and self-preservation and our view of the world. An anamnestic reason based on memory of suffering is aware that the need to lend a voice to suffering is the precondition to all truth and justice. This means that there is no understanding without compassion. The first epistemological principle is not the Cartesian *Cogito ergo sum*, it is: 'You suffer therefore I am!' Or to formulate it in another way: Becoming a subject in history and society means being responsible for the other. Being responsible means becoming aware of the non-identity of the other and the non-identity of the object of knowledge – facing an unintentional truth.[30]

Only anamnestic reason enables enlightenment to re-enlighten itself concerning the harm it has caused. The memory of suffering evokes responsibility – a responsibility which binds knowledge inevitably to the victims.[31] A culture which is rooted in such a remembrance opposes any development which creates a history coloured by evolutionary theory that presupposes that what is past is past and that no longer considers such a development as a challenge which must be interrupted.[32]

In order to develop a concept of an anamnestic ethic as a foundation of a theology after Auschwitz we have to realize the following:

Biblical memory is connected with epoch-making events (Fackenheim) which are generally both incomprehensible and not comparable. Biblical memory makes us aware that uniqueness could not be defined in discursive language because facing uniqueness means to tell a story and narrative expression is able to speak of uniqueness without rationalizing it. As such telling a story is a guarantor not to forget, because it is a never ending process which provides for praxis. Thus remembering Auschwitz would require us to remember Auschwitz practically.

By facing Auschwitz we see indeed that the question of how to remember Auschwitz is a question of a morality after Auschwitz and vice versa. Remembering Auschwitz from a biblical perspective means to remember for the sake of the victims. It is an expression of calling into being a responsibility that is grounded in an asymmetrical relationship and challenged by the other, the victim, whose otherness is rooted in his experience, in his suffering.

A theology after Auschwitz must promote the transformation of oppressive social structures and thought patterns. Based on the *memoria passionis* it provokes a just society to transform itself into a more just society. Thus we become aware that we have to distinguish between two kinds of responsibility: justice and care.[33] These are different because justice, located on the cognitive level, is the symmetrical principle of responsibility with rights and duties towards everyone. At this level the other has the role of the generalized other. At the other level, the affective level, responsibility is the result of compassion and not of a procedural process and thus it comes from an asymmetrical responsibility. This responsibility is the basis for the existence of moral sensitivity, basic because it refers to a generalized non-representative individual for whom I am responsible. Thus Emmanuel Lévinas emphasizes: 'Morality arises not from equality, it arises through the infinite demands which converge in the universe in one point, that you serve the poor, the stranger, the widow, and the orphan.'[34]

The memory of suffering does not allow a restriction of our responsibility as some authors are preaching today. The Catholic Church came late, maybe too late, to awareness of the danger of immunizing ourselves against the harm of others. The document 'Unsere Hoffnung' (1975) published by the West German bishopric says:

> Our country's recent political history is darkened by the systematic attempt to wipe out the Jewish people. Apart from some admirable efforts by individuals and groups, most of us during the time of National Socialism formed a church community preoccupied with the threat to our own institutions. We turned our backs to the persecuted Jewish people and were silent about the crimes perpetrated on Jews and Judaism. Some have been guilty out of pure anxiety for their lives.'

Memory of suffering resists acts of instrumentalization because it is the other who demands that we remember his suffering. As such it carries a responsibility which is indeed a response. Its responsibility provokes an emotional response. Due to its one-sidedness memory of suffering is a radical form of responsibility. Its motion could be compared with burying someone because to bury someone is to act without expectation of any tangible reward.[35] With regard to the dead of Auschwitz memory might also be a kind of 'substitute' because the dead have no graves, they lie deep in our memory. A religion defined as an anamnestic culture is grounded in an anamnestic ethic which fights against the powers that put millions of suffering, oppressed people in a faceless mass. Anamnestic ethic bears an anamnestic solidarity which tries to reverse the Nazis destruction of individual identity. In order to underline this solidarity one might keep in mind the following event:

> Adolf Eichmann was talking to several SS officers of equal rank as himself. One of them asked how many Jews had been killed. Eichmann answered: 'about five million'. Then another SS leader, who had no illusions any more about the coming end of war and its outcome, asked: 'What will happen when the world asks about these millions of dead?' Eichmann apparently snapped back: 'One hundred dead are a catastrophe, one million dead are nothing but a statistic.'[36]

Anamnestic solidarity is aware of what Walter Benjamin has stated: '...even the dead will not be safe from the enemy if he wins. And this enemy has not ceased to be victorious.'[37] We have to fight for an alliance of the historian and the theologian because there is no understanding of a catastrophe without the soul-searching stories and poems of those who experienced them. Or to put it into other words: We have to argue for an alliance of the Chronicler with Job, as a way of approaching the problems of Auschwitz.[38] Of course so-called objectivity is essential but as generally understood it is lethal.[39]

WHAT NEEDS TO BE SAID FROM THE VANTAGE POINT OF
POLITICAL THEOLOGY ABOUT THE CATHOLIC CHURCH AND THE
RELATIONSHIP BETWEEN CHRISTIANS AND JEWS

Documents of the Catholic Church about National Socialism after 1945.[40] Only recently the
Catholic Church published a document about Auschwitz – but documents going further
in gestures toward Jews and with much more emphasis on the guilt of the Catholic
church had already been published: for example, in 1995 by the German bishops and in
1997 by the French bishops. Other documents just deal with the relationship between
Christianity and Judaism. Let me summarize very briefly the most important insights of
the documents of the Catholic Church from a political-theological perspective:

First, probably no accusation against the Jews by the church is responsible for more
Jewish suffering throughout history than the deicide charge. Thus we could formulate
the first insight of a theology after Auschwitz: The conciliar decree *Nostra aetate* of
Vatican Council II emphasizes clearly that any collective accusation against the Jews,
then or now, for the death of Jesus is contrary to Christian teaching.[41]

Second: To speak of persecutions in a general way is a cover-up of injustice and
suffering. What needs to be done is to face the catastrophe in its uniqueness. A first
attempt could be seen in the last document on the Shoah.

Third: A world wherein forgiveness becomes omnipotent becomes inhuman.

Fourth: I want to call attention to the fact that our Christian identity has to be
established, not in the face of Judaism, but in the face of the Jews. And to speak about
the horrors of the past means not only facing the Jews who were murdered and who
survived, but taking into account the problems of present Jews, too. This very important
insight was first declared by the French bishops in 1973. It seems to me that Christians
in Germany have failed to do so. The Gulf War was a watershed in the so-called dialogue
between Jews and Christians in Germany. Christians in Germany demonstrated against
the engagement of the USA in Kuwait without realizing that Iraq was a threat to Israel.
With a kind of moral imperialism, Christians defined Iraq as a victim because it belongs
to so-called third world countries whereas Israel was viewed as a perpetrator.[42] The state
of Israel has to be regarded, as Fackenheim said, as a house against death. Without the
existence of this state Jews were unable to live in contemporary Germany. This does not
mean that we are not allowed to criticize Israel. We have to criticize violence everywhere.
Not criticizing Israel is an expression of philo-Semitism and philo-Semitism is another
kind of anti-Semitism.

Fifth: We could speak of God after Auschwitz because people prayed to God in
Auschwitz. This means today's Christians owe their faith to the Jews who suffered in
Auschwitz.[43]

Sixth: Not every Catholic and Christian was a Nazi, but every Nazi was a baptized
Christian; whether a bad Christian or not. This raises in a most fundamental way the
question of the credibility of Christianity.[44]

Seventh: The God-question should not be kept open out of false modesty. We
owe Jews a christology after Auschwitz because christology is the centre of Christian
theology. It is true that Christian theologians have attempted to confront their various
christological concepts with the catastrophe of the Holocaust. But – as Baird asked –
did they formulate christology in light of the experience and testimony of death
camp survivors themselves?[45] Did they realize that survival is often not seen as
a triumph? Being required to face the non-redemptive nature of suffering we
must avoid making the death of Jesus conform with the suffering in the death
camps. The survivors do not claim that they have chosen their fate. We have to be

very careful to reject a new Christian supersessionism.[46] Instead of this we have to raise questions honestly, for example: 'Whether one must not decide that it were better that Jesus had not come, rather than that such scenes be enacted six million times over – and more?'[47]

And we Christians should ask ourselves: 'What is one crucifixion beside a whole people crucified through centuries?' Could we maintain the one crucified was god, whereas the untold millions of Jewish men, women, and children were only human beings – as if the murder of an innocent human being were a lesser crime than the killing of god.[48] Berkovits states: 'Had Christianity, instead of being preoccupied with what it believed to have been a deicide, concentrated its educative attention on the human crime of homicide, mankind would have been spared much horror and tragedy.' Instead of this, teaching of deicide became an excuse and often a licence.[49]

I am afraid of creating too quickly a totally new form of christology because if this 'new' christology becomes anti-Judaic again then it will be much more dangerous than the older ones. Perhaps at this moment it might be sufficient to take up the ethically responsible task of dismantling ecclesial, theological and, especially, christological Christian anti-Judaism.[50] Such a critique would be based on remembrance.

As we all know anti-Judaism is a function of Christian triumphalism. Christianity should 'work out' salvation as a hope which is threatened. From this perspective redemptive suffering arguments are in danger of becoming anti-Semitic. Furthermore they are problematic concerning its impact on sustained liberation activity because, on some level, they embrace the injustice that the oppressed claim to fight.[51] At least 'the redemptive nature of suffering must be in absolute tension with the dialectical reality that must be fought, cut down, eliminated.'[52]

A christology that could emerge out of Christianity as an anamnestic culture requires not the mentality of Easter but of Good Saturday[53] – which means living between hopelessness and hope. In such an eschatological situation theology has to formulate hope, not at first for the bourgeois Christians, but for the hopeless.

Eighth: Auschwitz is not only a question of theodicy, but also a very dramatic question of anthropodicy.

What is at stake in Christian–Jewish Dialogue? After the publication of the document about the Shoah we have to recognize the disappointment within the Jewish community at the document. For example, David Blumenthal points out:

> The document claims that 'many' churches aided Jews during the Holocaust, though 'others' did not. This . . . seems to Jews to be inaccurate. Although there were some very courageous souls – clergy and laity alike – who risked their lives to save Jews, the overwhelming majority of Catholics were passive bystanders, and a sizable percentage were active perpetrators. Further, the document, in attempting to assess the 'guilt' of Catholics during the Shoah, indicates that this can only be done 'case by case.' To be sure, there is no such thing as collective guilt. But must justice wait while . . . a million Catholics are examined? Can there be no confession of sin, no admission of guilt – at least for the sin of omission, of not having done enough, as Catholic individuals and as the church?'[54]

MEMORY OF SUFFERING: A THEOLOGICAL CONTRIBUTION TO A WORLD AFTER AUSCHWITZ

According to Darrell Fasching, human beings are not just storytellers, they are story dwellers. Only by living in the story do we become human. From this anthropological foundation we must regard the project of modernity. As important as this project might be, we must recognize that modernity without stories will become inhuman. Stories are the best way to communicate ethical values and lessons. If modernity is the story to end all stories, if modernity tells us that we need no longer stories – only universal human reason – then the post-traditional character of modernity becomes violent.[55] But how could we decide which story is true? According to Stanley Hauerwas the central criterion is that a true story shapes actual lives and actual communities and results in truthful lives and lives open to the foreign – 'the strangers and their stories, which we should make our own stories.'[56] Could this story-concept be of some help in the Christian–Jewish Dialogue?

I, for example, as a Catholic and a German should never make the stories of the victims my own story. Instead of being allowed to make other's stories my own I should make the true interests of others my own. My story is first and foremost the story of the perpetrators and the bystanders but this does not mean I do not remember the stories of the victims. Through the memory of the stories of the victims we should observe our own story. And then we will see if our story is indeed able to face the stories of the others. Therefore, according to Fasching, we have to realize that the first test of each story remains its openness to questions and questioning. And the 'second requirement is that the story must permit one to follow the questions wherever they lead, even if that takes one beyond the story one is in'[57] – even if it entails the risk of damaging the faith one seeks to secure. The danger of the stories of the victims of Auschwitz is indicated by the following statement of Elie Wiesel: 'The thoughtful Christian knows that the Jewish People did not die in Auschwitz but Christianity.'

Our own story has to call us into question. Fasching writes: 'A master story that does not permit itself to be called into question is ultimately demonic.'[58] Listening to the stories of the others leads to questions. But if we make in our theology the answers more important than the questions, then we make the finite more important than the infinite and we end in idolatry – according to Fasching: 'we make an idol of our answers'.[59]

If the remembrance of foreign suffering is the core of theology then this theology is not a theodicy but a theology which expresses the hidden face of God. Such a theology indicates a way to speak about the trace of God in the god-loneliness of the face of the victim. The absence of God in the horror on the face of the other unconditionally demands that I must help him in the situation.[60] The biblical religions could not for their own sake be divorced from praxis. Thus we have to recognize the connection between our responsibility and the presence of God. We theologians often know more about God than about our neighbour, but one cannot serve God without serving the other. God is not above history. According to Dietrich Bonhoeffer, the transcendence we are talking about reveals itself in being for the other.

From here we should work out an understanding of politics which is rooted in the memory of suffering. But the 'politics of memory'[61] is a risk if it is not centred in the memory of suffering of the other. Religions could play an important role in this situation as resources for such a memory. For my church, the task would be to become an institution of memory, but of dangerous memory calling the church into question because this memory demands a remembrance of the most radical protest against Christianity – Auschwitz. The church is obliged not to abandon the memory of the God of Abraham, Isaac and Jacob for the sake of the hopeless because this God reminds the church that the hope He is promising is one for the others. Thus, the church would not have its interest in self-preservation but only in the victims of the world. It must remember a messianic future which does not extend our future but interrupts it.[62] It cannot confirm our 'habits of heart' as the theorists of democracy intend; it would demand that we change our hearts.

But will there be a chance to remember this God in our present situation in Europe which could be described as a 'God in crisis' (_Gotteskrise_)[63] – of God's death in the realm of the public?

Different kinds of concepts of political theologies have been discussed during our century. After the First World War the political theology of Carl Schmitt was the subject of controversies; after the Second World War the new political theology of Johann Baptist Metz. The first concept focused on the Catholic Church as an institution of pure sovereignty influenced by catholic counter-revolutionaries, for example Joesph de Maistre, whereas the second took a positive view of liberation and enlightenment, influenced by the critical theory of the Frankfurt School and grounded in a concept of an eschatological reservation with regard to all stages of progress and emancipation in history.

In our present situation the influence of the old political theology seems to become stronger.[64] To Nietzsche's proclamation of God's death Hitler's Crown Jurist, the Catholic and political theologian Carl Schmitt, responded with his own concept of a political theology. But instead of the belief in God he installed a belief in the Catholic Church as a form of power or, as he calls it, a '_katholische Verschärfung_' (catholic intensification).

To resist this in our time we need a passion for God which means a passion for God and a passion unto God so that Europe will never be again the graveyard of those who 'invented' this God – the Jews. Finally, we have reason to assume that the fascists did not hate Jews because they had murdered God, as the Christians maintained, but because the Jews had invented Him.

And last but not least, a theology after Auschwitz in the context of the Christian–Jewish Dialogue must focus its thinking on pedagogical problems. If we fail to educate children and students we fail to give an answer to Auschwitz because this answer must be a response grounded in responsibility. Furthermore we have to realize that the way we teach about Auschwitz is an expression of how we really think about Auschwitz and what we have learned, not from but about, Auschwitz. One of the first steps might be to speak of responsibility. Jewish victims continue to tell young Germans not to talk about collective guilt but to talk about collective responsibility. To tell students that they are guilty for something they didn't do creates hate – but being responsible means becoming a subject. It is interesting to realize that mostly anti-Semitic politicians use the phrase 'collective guilt' in order to create hate among young people against Jews. The pedagogy of our theology should be guided by the words of Israeli historian Yehuda Bauer: 'Do not be a perpetrator. Do not be a victim. Do not be a bystander.'

NOTES

1 J.B. Metz, 'Im Angesichte der Juden. Christliche Theologie nach Auschwitz', in _Concilium: Internationale Zeitschrift für Theologie_ 5 (1984): 76–92, 76.

2 See J.B. Metz, 'Kirche nach Auschwitz', in _Kirche und Israel. Neukirchener Theologische Zeitschrift_ 5 (1990): 99–108.

3 See J.B. Metz, 'Im Angesichte', _op.cit._, 76–92.

4 See J.B. Metz, 'Theologie als Theodizee?', in W. Oelmüller (ed.), _Theodizee: Gott vor Gericht?_ (München: Fink-Verlag, 1990), pp.103–118.

5 See A. Camus, _Der Mensch in der Revolte_ (Reinbek: Rowohlt-Verlag, 1964), pp.39–40.

6 See J.B. Metz, 'Unterwegs zu einer nachidealistischen Theologie', in J.B. Bauer (ed.), _Entwürfe der Theologie_ (Graz, Wien, Köln: Grünewald-Verlag, 1985), pp.209–235, 215.

7 M. Horkheimer and T.W. Adorno, _Dialektik der Aufklärung: Philosophische Fragemente_ (Frankfurt: Fischer Taschenbuch-Verlag, 1986), p.161.

8 See J.B. Metz, *Jenseits bürgerlicher Religion: Reden über die Zukunft des Christentums* (München Mainz: Grünewald-Verlag, 1980), pp.29–50.

9 Y. Bauer, *The Holocaust in Historical Perspective* (New York/Seattle:, 1980), p.46.

10 See J. Manemann, 'Die Katholische Kirche nach Auschwitz. Zur Auseinandersetzung mit dem Nationalsozialismus nach 1945', in *Trumah. Zeitschrift der Hochschule für Jüdische Studien* 5 (1996): 69–92.

11 See J. Manemann, 'Weil es nicht nur Geschichte ist' in *Die Begründung der Notwendigkeit einer fragmentarischen Historiographie des Nationalsozialismus aus politisch–theologischer Sicht* (Hamburg, Münster: Lit-Verlag, 1995).

12 Elie Wiesel, Foreword, in A.J. Peck (ed.), *Jews and Christians after the Holocaust* (Philadelphia: Fortress Press, 1982), p.x.

13 See Emil Fackenheim, in: Harry James Cargas (ed.), *Voices from the Holocaust* (Louisville: The University Press of Kentucky, 1993), pp.131–156; here p.132.

14 *ibid.*, p.133.

15 *ibid.*, p.135.

16 *ibid.*, p.137. 'Hannah Arendt has an easy time saying Eichmann is banal. Arendt was a philosopher, so I followed her idea through in her writings – but she never followed it through to its logical end herself, because to my knowledge she never said Hitler was banal, never. So it comes to the old thing, only Hitler runs everybody, and everybody else is banal. As for Hitler, he's crazy. So how come a crazy man practically runs the world? We run around in circles' (p.139).

17 Steven T. Katz, 'Auschwitz and the Gulag: Discontinuities and Dissimilarities', in S.T. Katz, *Historicism, The Holocaust, and Zionism: Critical Studies in Modern Jewish Thought and History* (New York London, 1992), pp.138–161, 142.

18 See J. Manemann, 'Wider das Vergessen. Entwurf einer Kritischen Theorie des Eingedenkens aus politisch–theologischer Sicht', in R. Boschki and F.-M. Konrad (eds.), *Ist die Vergangenheit noch ein Argument? Aspekte einer Erziehung nach Auschwitz* (Tübingen: Attempto-Verlag, 1997), pp.88–118.

19 See J. Manemann, 'Weil es nicht nur Geschichte ist', *op.cit.*

20 *ibid.*

21 E. Fackenheim, *To Mend the World: Foundations of Post-Holocaust Jewish Thought* (New York, 1989), p.10.

22 *ibid.*

23 See J.B. Metz, 'Jenseits bürgerlicher Religion', pp.29–50.

24 Theodor W. Adorno, *Minima Moralia. Reflexionen aus dem beschädigten Leben* (Frankfurt: Suhrkamp-Verlag, 1987), p.65.

25 See C. West, *Prophetic Thought in Postmodern Times: Beyond Eurocentrism and Multiculturalism*, vol.1 (Monroe: Common Courage Press, 1993), pp.2–6.

26 This notion is also to be found in C. West, *op.cit.*

27 See J.B. Metz, 'Für eine anamnetische Kultur', in H. Loewy (ed.), *Holocaust: Die Grenzen des Verstehens: Eine Debatte über die Besetzung der Geschichte* (Reinbek: Rowohlt-Verlag 1992), pp.35–41.

28 See J.B. Metz, 'Anamnetische Vernunft. Anmerkungen eines Theologen zur Krise der Geisteswissenschaften', in A. Honneth, T. McCarthy, C. Offe and A. Welmer (eds.), *Zwischenbetrachtungen im Proze der Aufklärung. Jürgen Habermas zum 60. Geburtstag* (Frankfurt: Suhrkamp-Verlag, 1989), pp.733–738.

29 See J.B. Metz, *Glaube in Geschichte und Gesellschaft: Studien zu einer praktischen Fundnamentaltheologie* (Mainz: Grünewald-Verlag, 1984).

30 See J. Manemann, 'Wider das Vergessen', *op.cit.*, pp.88–118.

31 *ibid.*, pp.88–118.

32 See J.B. Metz, 'Anamnetische Vernunft', *op.cit.* pp.733–738.

33 See J. Manemann, 'Liberal Democracy – The End of History or Carl Schmitt Redivivus? The Need for an Anamnestic Culture for Germany After Auschwitz', in G.J. Colijn and M.S. Littell (eds.), *Confronting the Holocaust: A Mandate for the 21st Century* (Lanham/New York/Oxford: American University Press, 1997), pp.81–91, pp.85–86.

34 E. Lévinas, *Totalität und Unendlichkeit. Versuch über die Exteriorität* (Freiburg and München: Alber-Verlag, 1987), p.361.
35 See D.R. Blumenthal, *The Place of Faith and Grace in Judaism* (Ohio, 1985), p.18.
36 S. Wiesenthal, *Every Day Remembrance Day: A Chronicle of Jewish Martyrdom* (New York, 1987), pp.28–29.
37 W. Benjamin, 'Über den Begriff der Geschichte', in W. Benjamin, *Illuminationen: Ausgewählte Schriften* (Frankfurt: Suhrkamp Verlag, 1977), pp.251–261, 253.
38 See, for example, Y. Bauer, *The Holocaust in Historical Perspective, op.cit.*, p.49.
39 J. Manemann, 'Die Gottesfrage – eine Anfrage an ein Projekt historischer Sinnbildung?', in J. Rüsen and K. Müller (eds.), *Historische Sinnbildung* (Reinbek: Rowohlt-Verlag, 1997), pp.373–387. See also J. Manemann, *'Weil es nicht nur Geschichte ist': Die Begründung der Notwendigkeit einer fragmentarischen Historiographie des Nationalsozialismus aus politisch-theologischer Sicht* (Hamburg Münster: Lit-Verlag, 1995).
40 For the above-mentioned decrees and documents see J. Manemann, 'Die Katholische Kirche nach Auschwitz', 69–92.
41 See the very informative overview by J.T. Pawlikowski, *What are they saying about Christian–Jewish relations?* (New York, 1980).
42 See: E. Brocke, 'Seit Auschwitz mu jeder wissen, da Schlimmeres als Krieg möglich ist', in *Kirche und Israel. Neukrchener Theologische Zeitschrift* 1 (1991): 61–74.
43 See J.B. Metz, 'Jenseits bürgerlicher Religion', *op.cit.*, pp.29–50.
44 See F. Littell, *The Crucifixion of the Jews. The Failure of Christians to Understand the Jewish Experience* (Macon: Mercer University Press, 1996), p.3.
45 See M. Baird, 'Jesus at Auschwitz? An (Ongoing) Critique of Post-Holocaust Christologies', paper presented at the Conference on the Holocaust and the Churches in Seattle, 1998.
46 *ibid.*
47 I. Greenberg, 'Cloud of Smoke, Pillar of Fire: Judaism, Christianity, and Modernity after the Holocaust', in: E. Fleischner (ed.), *Auschwitz: Beginning of a New Era? Reflections on the Holocaust* (New York, 1977), pp.7–56, 13.
48 E. Berkovits, *Faith after the Holocaust*, (New York, 1973), p.126.
49 *ibid.*, p.127.
50 See Marie Baird, 'Jesus at Auschwitz?', *op.cit.*
51 A.B. Pinn, *Why Lord? Suffering and Evil in Black Theology* (New York: Continuum Publishing Company, 1995).
52 I. Greenberg, 'Cloud of Smoke', *op.cit*, pp.7–56, 39.
53 See J.B. Metz, in E. Schuster and R. Boschert-Kimmig (eds.), *Trotzdem Hoffen: Mit Johann Baptist Metz und Elie Wiesel im Gespräch* (Mainz: Grünewald-Verlag, 1993), p.51.
54 David Blumenthal, 'A time to embrace. Catholics must go further in gesture toward Jews'.
55 See D.J. Fasching, *Narrative Theology after Auschwitz: From Alienation to Ethics* (Minneapolis: Fortress Press, 1992).
56 Concerning this interpretation of Hauerwas see Fasching, *op.cit.*
57 *ibid.*, p.118.
58 *ibid.*, p.120.
59 *ibid.*, p.123.
60 D. Polleyfeyt, 'Facing the Other. The Philosophy of Emmanuel Lévinas as a Philosophy against Idolatry as a Jewish Answer to the Holocaust', paper presented at the Faculty of Catholic Theology at the University of Münster, December 1997.
61 See H. Hirsch, *Genocide and the Politics of Memory. Studying Death to Preserve Life. Why Genocide occurs and a vision of how it can be prevented* (Durham, NC: University of North Carolina Press, 1994).
62 See J.B. Metz, 'Jenseits bürgerlicher Religion', *op.cit.*, pp.9–29.
63 See: J.B. Metz, 'Gotteskrise: Versuch zur "geistigen Situation der Zeit"', in *Diagnosen zur Zeit: Mit Beiträgen von Johann Baptist Metz, Günther Bernd Ginzel, Peter Glotz, Jürgen Habermas, Dorothee Sölle* (Düsseldorf: Patmos-Verlag, 1994), pp.76–92.
64 See J. Manemann, 'Liberal Democracy', *op.cit.*, pp.81–91.

JOHN 8:31–59 FROM A JEWISH PERSPECTIVE

Adele Reinhartz

R ARELY A week goes by that I do not face the question, 'How *did* you end up in New Testament studies?' Behind this query often lies the assumption that there is a contradiction between my area of study and my Jewish identity. Interestingly enough, this query comes more often from Jews than from non-Jews. The notion that being Jewish is incompatible with a professional interest in the New Testament reflects two profound and rarely articulated views held by many Jews. One is the perceived theological gulf between Judaism and Christianity. Related to this perception is a suspicion of the New Testament itself, perhaps fuelled by the fear, or the suspicion, that reading this set of texts may cause Jews to question or even to reject their Jewish identities. A second is the view that the New Testament is inimical not only to Jewish faith but also to the Jews as a people. Many Jews believe that the New Testament is in some way implicated in the roots and development of anti-Semitism and therefore helped to lay the groundwork for genocide.

For many years I ignored these issues completely and simply did not consider the possibility that my Jewish identity had any bearing at all on my academic pursuits. Strongly committed to scholarly objectivity, I argued (to myself) that my preoccupation with the New Testament was no different from my brother's dedication to the field of medicine, my cousin's academic achievements in the area of English literature, or my daughter's blossoming interest in autism and child development. As a New Testament scholar I had imbibed the values and methods of my field. That is, I saw my main task as the effort to understand how the New Testament, and, in particular, the Gospel of John, was read and understood by its earliest audience. I was much taken by the advice of J.L Martyn, who urged Johannine scholars

> to make every effort to take up temporary residence in the Johannine community. We must
> see with the eyes and hear with the ears of that community. We must sense at least some of
> the crises that helped to shape the lives of its members. And we must listen carefully to the
> kind of conversations in which all of its members found themselves engaged. Only in the
> midst of this endeavour will we be able to hear the Fourth Evangelist speak *in his own terms*,
> rather than merely in words which we moderns want to hear from his mouth.[1]

What this approach required, I thought, was complete disengagement between my personal identity and scholarly interests; the fact that I was Jewish, with all the particular meanings that that label had for me, was irrelevant to what I studied or how I studied it.

In recent years, however, I have begun to question my complacency. In this process I have been spurred on by new streams of academic discourse, in particular, feminist and postmodern criticism which assert rather emphatically that scholarly objectivity is impossible and indeed, undesirable. I began to consider that it may be no accident that I, a child of holocaust survivors, would be drawn to the Gospel of John in which the Jews play the role of Jesus' quintessential enemies and are on the receiving end of some very harsh language. The changing norms of my field, including the growing interest in the ethical dimensions of biblical texts,[2] encouraged me to look seriously at two questions: first; is the Fourth Gospel itself anti-Jewish, in the sense of expressing and fostering negative attitudes towards Jews and Judaism? Or has it simply been subjected to later anti-Jewish interpretations as it made its way into the Christian canon?[3] Second, is there a way to read the Gospel that takes the questions raised by one's Jewish identity seriously and yet does not compromise the scholarly integrity of the enterprise?

A passage that raises these questions most acutely is John 8:31–59. John 8:31–59 is a dialogue or, more accurately, an acrimonious argument between Jesus and an unspecified number of Jews. It begins with Jesus promising the Jews: 'If you continue in my word, you are truly my disciples' (8:31).[4] At its conclusion, the Jews, far from continuing in Jesus' word, pick up stones to throw at him, so that he must hide himself and leave the temple where their discussion had taken place (8:59). The accusations and counter-accusations fly back and forth rapidly and viciously. The most memorable of these occurs in 8:44 in which Jesus accuses the Jews of being liars and murderers and declares: 'You are of your father the devil, and your will is to do your father's desires.' This image of the Jews as children of the devil has echoed through the centuries in theology, art, literature and anti-Semitic invective, including its latest manifestations in the website materials of neo-Nazi groups.[5]

In analysing this text we must recognize that the Gospel of John, like the other Gospels, is not a biography; it does not recount the factual history of a historical figure in Palestine in the early decades of the first century. Rather, it provides a fictionalized narrative of Jesus that reflects the traditions, theological perspective and the life experience of a particular community – generally referred to as the Johannine community – at the end of the first century in Asia Minor. Thus John 8:31–59 does not provide us with the transcript of an exchange between Jesus and the Jews that actually occurred. On the contrary, the roles of both Jesus and the Jews are scripted in order to serve the interests and agendas of the narrator and may have little – if anything – in common with the views and relationships of Jesus and the Jews as historical figures. Knowing all this, however, does not diminish the emotional impact of this dialogue. A Jew who reads this passage cannot help being aware of the pain and hostility that permeates the dialogue. Acknowledging the gap in distance, time and place that separates us from this text does not prevent us from identifying with the characters referred to as 'Jews'; the very label 'Jew' binds us to them and to a common ethnic and religious identity.

One option for a Jewish reader is to close the book, never to open it again. But for a Jewish reader who also happens to be a Johannine scholar closing the book is not a viable option. Such a reader can take one of two paths. One is to turn away from John 8 and to focus on passages that are less painful: this was the choice I made for many years. A second option, however, is to focus precisely on the Johannine representation of the Jews. This possibility will be explored in the pages that follow. That is, I will attempt to read from a perspective first developed in the area of feminist literary criticism that explicitly focuses on those labelled as 'the other' within and by the text one is reading. In her book *The Resisting Reader: A Feminist Approach to American Fiction*',[6] Judith Fetterley argues that the classics of American literature which attempt to come to grips with, or to explain, American identity, do so in terms only of male characters. These works, contends Fetterley, create a serious dilemma for women readers:

What is a woman to do with 'Rip Van Winkle'? How is she to read our 'first and most famous' story in which the American imagination is born if the defining act of that imagination is to identify the real American Revolution with the avoidance of adulthood, which means the avoidance of women, which means the avoidance of one's wife? What is the impact of this American dream on her? The answer is obvious: disastrous. What is essentially a simple act of identification when the reader of the story is male becomes a tangle of contradictions when the reader is female. Where in this story is the female reader to locate herself? Certainly she is not Rip, for the fantasy he embodies is thoroughly male and is defined precisely by its opposition to woman. Nor is she Dame Van Winkle, for Dame is not a person: she is a scapegoat, the enemy, the OTHER.[7]

The Jewish reader of the Gospel of John is in precisely the same position as the female reader of 'Rip Van Winkle'. If she identifies with Jesus, the hero of the Gospel narrative, she must accede to a set of beliefs that are inimical to Jewish identity; if she locates herself alongside the Jews, the villains of the piece, she must endure the onslaught of Jesus' invective, feel herself accused of persecution and murder and take on the role of the vilified 'other' of Johannine narrative.

A resistant reading allows a way out of this impasse. It explicitly reads against the grain of the text; that is, it identifies the ideological perspective of the text and the rhetorical strategies that guide a reader to identify with one character over against another and then attempts to construct an alternative perspective that is filtered, not through the story's protagonist, but through the individual or group identified as the 'other'. A resistant reading of John 8:31–59 will therefore move beyond recognizing the pain of the discourse that is evident upon a first reading, in order to explore the passage through the lens provided by the Jewish characters within the text.

My resistant reading will therefore have two focal points. First, I will look at the narrative role assigned to the Jews in John 8:31–59. I will argue that, while the Johannine Jesus is presented as the innocent victim of a Jewish murder plot, it is the Jews themselves who are victimized by both the structure and the content of this discourse. Second, I will look at the basis of the Jews' own resistance to Jesus' message: why, from their perspective, were they unable or unwilling to continue in Jesus' word and truly become his disciples (8:31)? Considering this question may illuminate some of the issues at stake in one corner of the ancient Jewish–Christian debate.

A resistant reading will not resolve the question of whether or to what extent this passage, or the Gospel of John as a whole, contributed to the ideological framework that justified anti-Semitic attitudes and behaviour through the centuries and that ultimately allowed for genocide in the 20th century. But it may provide a test case for observing and analysing religious polemic. In doing so, it will underscore the importance of exposing and disarming potentially dangerous texts wherever we should find them.

I. THE RHETORICAL VICTIMIZATION OF THE JEWS
That Jesus is an innocent victim of a Jewish murder plot is a pervasive and unambiguous theme in this Gospel. As God's only son (1:18 and passim) Jesus takes away the sin of the world (1:29) and provides salvation. Moreover, Jesus is tried and found innocent by Pilate, who represents the Roman legal system; the crucifixion occurs only through the insistence of the Jewish leadership (19:12, 15). Thus from the Gospel's point of view, Jesus is a victim of a brutal Jewish leadership and, by implication, of all Jews who refuse to accept his message.

But this relationship is reversed, persuasively though subtly, by the rhetoric of 8:31–59. This occurs in three ways. First, the Jews enter into this discourse burdened by the negative representation to which they have been subject in the previous chapters. From the prologue on, the Jews are both implicitly and explicitly characterized as the ones who do not accept Jesus. From chapter five onward the conflict becomes more explicit and escalates to its climax in the passion narrative. By chapter 8 the Jews are firmly established as Jesus' enemies, as being hostile to his teachings and as attempting to kill him.[8]

Second, within this passage, as elsewhere in the Gospel, the Jews are given relatively little 'air-time' in which to state their case. The Jews speak in seven verses (8:33, 39a, 41, 48, 52, 53 and 57); Jesus speaks in twenty-two verses. His speeches are consistently longer than those of the Jews and, as in all Johannine discourses, Jesus has the last word. The implication is that Jesus' word is decisive within the Gospel narrative and therefore should be normative for its readers.

Finally, and most seriously, Jesus robs the Jews of their identity. In this discourse the Jews define themselves in three ways: they are the children of Abraham (8:33, 39), they have never served, or been enslaved to, anyone or anything (8:33) and they are children of God (8:41). Jesus denies them all three claims. The Jews are not children of Abraham, he says, because they do not do what their father did (8:39). The child of Abraham welcomes Jesus, perhaps as the biblical Abraham welcomed his three heavenly visitors and believed their prophecies concerning his future son, Isaac, and the destruction of Sodom and Gomorrah (Genesis 18–19). Though the Jews claim not to have served anyone or anything, in fact they are slaves to sin, and as slaves shall not remain in the father's house (8:34–35). Only the one who continues in Jesus' word and accepts him as the truth can be truly free (8:43; 8:31). Far from being children of God the Jews' behaviour as murderers and liars reveals that the devil is their true father (8:44). A child of God loves Jesus and knows that he has been sent by the Father (8:42).

Jesus not only denies the Jews' entitlement to these identity markers but he also usurps or appropriates them for himself. Jesus is not a mere child of Abraham, but existed before and was celebrated by Abraham (8:56, 58); Jesus not only achieves freedom but provides freedom for others (8:32, 36); Jesus is not only a child of God but is the (only) Son of God, the one who has full and legitimate access to God's house (8:36).

In 8:31–59, therefore, the narrator strips the Jews of their voice and Jesus denies them those features which are central to their own self-understanding as articulated in this passage. By silencing the Jews, undermining their self-identification and transferring their identifying characteristics to Jesus and, by extension, to those who believe in him, this passage contributes to the complete delegitimization of the Jews as a community in a covenantal relationship with God. Whereas Jesus as a character within the narrative is a victim of the machinations of the Jewish authorities, the Jews within this discourse are a victim of the rhetorical violence of the narrator and his leading man.

2. THE JEWS' CHARGES AGAINST JESUS

Jesus has no doubt 'won' the verbal bout in 8:31–59. The sheer quantity of Jesus' words compared with those afforded the Jews allows the spotlight to linger upon him, leaving the Jews largely in the dark. The Jews appear unable to respond to Jesus' accusations or to reclaim their identities as the children of God and of Abraham. Jesus has the last word, to which the Jews can respond only inarticulately, by throwing stones (8:59).

Jesus' 'victory' of course accords with the truth as the Gospel perceives and portrays it. For the narrator, Jesus is truly the pre-existent Son of God (1:1–2), who uniquely reveals the Father (1:18) and shows the path to the Father's house (14:2, 6). Given this negative attitude towards the Jews and the fact that the presentation of the Jews is tightly controlled by the narrator for whom they are the 'other', one might think that John 8:31–59 is a poor source of information about the Jews and has little potential for helping readers understand the Jews' rather different perspective vis à vis Jesus.

One-sided though it is, this discourse nevertheless provides the raw materials from which to construct the Jews' objections to Jesus. A resistant reading allows us to consider why it is that the Jews reject the path offered by Jesus and fail to continue in his word (8:31). Again, the keys are to be found in the three statements that the Jews make about themselves: that Abraham is their father, that they have never served or been enslaved to anyone or anything and that they are children of God. Together these claims express a commitment to the foundational tenet of second temple Judaism, namely, monotheism.[9] The centrality of monotheism – the belief in one God – and monolatry – the worship of one God – is axiomatic in Jewish texts from the biblical period to the present day. Two biblical texts may be singled out: the Shema and the opening verses of the Decalogue (Exod 20:2–17, Deuteronomy 5:6–21). The Shema begins with the famous declaration of faith in the one God: 'Hear, O Israel: The Lord is our God, the Lord alone' (Deut 6:4). The opening section of the Decalogue similarly declares God's uniqueness and singularity: 'I am the Lord your God, who brought you out of the land of Egypt, out of the house of slavery; you shall have no other gods before me. You shall not make for yourself an idol, whether in the form of anything that is in heaven above, or that is on the earth beneath, or that is in the water under the earth. You shall not bow down to them or worship them ...' Both these texts assert the absolute uniqueness of YHWH as the one and only God and as the only one whom Israel should worship.[10]

Of the three identity claims made by the Jews in John 8, two have an obvious connection to the theme of monotheism. Abraham's status as the patriarch of the Jewish people – father of the Jews – is based entirely on his role as the first monotheist.[11] According to post-biblical Jewish sources, Abraham's father was not only an idolator but also an idol-maker. Abraham came to realize the futility and wrongheadedness of idolatry through awareness of the powerlessness of his father's idols and, by contrast, a sense of a supreme being to whom the natural world, in its beauty and intricacy, was to be attributed (Apocalypse of Abraham 1:1–8:6; Jubilees 12:12–14).[12] As a result of this faith Abraham had a special relationship with God as God's beloved friend (Testament of Abraham 1:6).[13] According to Josephus (Antiquities 1,155), '[Abraham] was a man of ready intelligence on all matters, persuasive with his hearers, and not mistaken in his inferences. Hence he began to have more lofty conceptions of virtue than the rest of mankind, and determined to reform and change the ideas universally current concerning God. He was thus the first boldly to declare that God, the creator of the universe, is one, and that, if any other being contributed aught to man's welfare, each did so by His command and not in virtue of its own inherent power.'[14] Philo describes Abraham in a similar fashion, as a Chaldean reared in the worship of numerous gods, but whose soul's eye was opened 'as though after profound sleep' and he then discerned what he had not beheld before, namely, a single guiding force, 'a charioteer and pilot presiding o'er the world and directing in safety his own work' (On Abraham 69–71).[15]

Filial language is also used as a metaphor for the covenantal relationship between God and Israel and appears in passages in which the concepts of election and monotheism are central. In Exodus 4:22–23 God instructs Moses to tell Pharaoh, 'Thus says the LORD: Israel is my firstborn son. I said to you, "Let my son go that he may worship me." But you refused to let him go; now I will kill your firstborn son.' In Deuteronomy 14:1 Moses instructs Israel to avoid the rituals associated with idolatry: 'You are children of the LORD your God. You must not lacerate yourselves or shave your forelocks for the dead.' The prophet Malachi laments, 'Have we not all one father? Has not one God created us? Why then are we faithless to one another, profaning the covenant of our ancestors?' (Malachi 2:10). Filial language also appears in post-biblical Jewish sources. According to Josephus (Ant 5:93), Joshua's farewell address began by evoking 'God, the Father and Lord of the Hebrew race'.[16] In Jubilees 1:24–28 God tells Moses: 'And their souls will cleave to me and to all my commandments. And they will do my commands. And I shall be a father to them, and they will be sons to me . . . and I shall love them . . . And everyone will know that I am the God of Israel and the father of all the children of Jacob and king upon Mount Zion forever and ever.' In Jubilees 2:20, the language of God's fatherhood is connected explicitly with Israel's election: 'And I have chosen the seed of Jacob from among all that I have seen. And I have recorded him as my firstborn son, and have sanctified him for myself forever and ever.' In Jubilees 19:29–29 Isaac blesses Jacob and prays that 'the spirit of *Mastema* not rule over you or over your seed in order to remove you from following the Lord who is your God henceforth and forever and may the Lord God be for you and for the people a father always and may you be a firstborn son.' This last passage is significant, for it implies that the falling away from God, and hence from sonship is the work of *Mastema*, that is, the devil.[17]

The Jews' claim that they have never served or been enslaved to anyone[18] (οὐδενὶ δεδουλεύκαμεν πώποτε) is more ambiguous. Commentators view this statement as yet another example of the typical Johannine device of misunderstanding,[19] as a sign of the Jews' inordinate and unrealistic pride and as evidence that the Jews really are liars, as Jesus has declared them to be in 8:44.[20] Typical is R.E. Brown who explains:

> 'The Jews' seem to misunderstand Jesus' words about freedom and take them in a political sense. Even on this level, however, their boast is ill founded, for Egypt, Babylonia, and Rome had enslaved them. Perhaps they mean that, being the privileged heirs to the promise to Abraham, they cannot be truly enslaved, although occasionally God has allowed them to be chastised through temporary subjection . . .'[21]

Schnackenburg comments: 'Whatever the religious inspiration of the Jewish sense of freedom, it is far removed from freedom as Jesus understands it. The Jews' pride and complacency are clean contrary to the attitude which would make them receptive to Jesus' message of freedom.'[22]

These interpretations read the Greek verb δουλεύω as 'to be enslaved'. This reading coheres with the context of the Jews' claim in 8:33 which is preceded by Jesus' promise that the truth will make them free (8:32) and followed by Jesus' contrast between the slave who has only temporary access to the house and the son, who remains in the house forever (8:35). But the verb has another well-established meaning, namely, 'to serve', and, specifically, 'to worship.' This usage appears frequently in the Septuagint, particularly in portions of the historical books, the prophetic literature and the Psalms. In 1 Samuel 7:3, the prophet Samuel enjoins Israel to 'prepare your hearts to serve the Lord, and to serve [δουλεύσατε] him only'. Jeremiah prophesies that when Israel seeks the cause of her misfortunes she will be told: 'because you served (ἐδουλεύσατε] strange gods in your land, so shall you serve [δουλεύσετε] strangers in a land that is not yours' (Jer 5:19). Psalm 105(106):36 refers to the period in the wilderness when the Israelites served (ἐδούλευσαν) idols. In Galatians 4:9 Paul uses this verb in a way that implies both worship and slavery (as in Jer 5:19). He chastises the Galatians, who are of gentile background, by asking, 'Now, however, that you have come to know God, or rather to be known by God, how can you turn back again to the weak and beggarly elemental spirits? How can you want to be enslaved [δουλεύειν] to them again?'

Perhaps the Jews' claim in 8:33 that they have never 'served' anyone or anything, can be taken on two levels. From the Johannine Jesus' point of view the Jews' declaration reveals their complete ignorance of and blindness to their own spiritual state, from which they can be set free only by continuing in Jesus' word. For the Jews, however, this declaration expresses their unshakeable commitment to monotheism: they have never served any being other than God; indeed, to serve another 'divine' being would be tantamount to slavery. Read in this way, the Jews are neither lying nor boasting but simply explaining why they cannot believe in Jesus or continue in his word: to do so would be to violate the foundation of their faith and self-understanding as Jews.

These claims – that the Jews are in a filial relationship to both Abraham and God and that they have never served or been enslaved (religiously) to anyone or anything, therefore suggest that Jesus violates or transgresses the boundaries of monotheism as they understood it.[23] This conclusion is bolstered by the two direct accusations that the Jews hurl at Jesus in 8:48: that he is a Samaritan and has a demon. This verse may simply be an ancient version of name-calling devoid of specific content. Nevertheless it is worth noting that both insults are associated with heresy in other ancient sources. Psalm 105 (106):36–37, for example, draws a parallel between the Israelites' worship of idols and the sacrificing of their sons and daughters to demons. In his first Apology addressed to the Emperor of Rome Justin describes how

> . . . after the ascension of Christ in Heaven, the demons produced certain men who claimed to be gods, who were not only not molested by you, but even showered with honors. There was a certain Simon, a Samaritan, from the village called Gitta, who, in the time of Emperor Claudius, through the force of the demons working in him, performed mighty acts of magic in your royal city of Rome, and was reputed to be a god. And as a god he was honoured by you with a statue. . . . Almost every Samaritan, and even a few from other regions, worship him and call him the first God (First Apology, 26).[24]

This passage attributes Simon's wonder-working ability to demons and views the Samaritans' worship of a magician as an idolatrous act. Similarly, as we saw earlier, the hand of *Mastema*, or the devil, is considered by Jubilees to be at work in those who worship other gods. Therefore in calling Jesus a Samaritan and claiming that he is possessed by a demon the Jews are accusing him of straying from the one true God.

To discern the basis for these accusations we turn to the claims that Jesus makes for himself. These emerge not only from Jesus' own words, but from the words assigned to his Jewish accusers. Jesus claims to provide eternal life for others, a statement that the Jews regard as evidence of demonic possession: 'Now we know that you have a demon. Abraham died, and so did the prophets; yet you say, "Whoever keeps my word will never taste death" (8:52).' Jesus also claims eternal life for himself, as implied in the Jews' challenge: 'Are you greater than our father Abraham, who died? The prophets also died. Who do you claim to be? (8:53).' Even more shocking, it seems, is Jesus' claim for his own pre-existence: 'Your ancestor Abraham rejoiced that he would see my day; he saw it and was glad' (8:56). The Jews exclaim: 'You are not yet fifty years old, and have you seen Abraham?' Jesus reasserts his claim: 'Very truly, I tell you, before Abraham was, I am [ἐλὼ εἰμί]' (8:58).

This last claim itself asserts Jesus' divine status in the absolute use of the words 'I was' (literally, 'I am,' ἐλὼ εἰμί), a divine self-designation.[25] Eternal life, the providing of eternal life to others and pre-existence are explicitly labelled as divine characteristics in the context of the Fourth Gospel itself. God existed before the creation of the world (1:1) and will presumably exist for all time; God 'raises the dead and gives them life' (5:21).

Therefore in describing himself in this manner Jesus is assigning divine attributes to himself. That the Jews are deeply troubled by this is made explicit elsewhere in the Gospel. In 5:18 the narrator informs us that the Jews aimed to kill Jesus because he 'called God his own Father, making himself equal to [or like] God'. In 10:33 the Jews themselves tell us that 'it is not for a good work that we are going to stone you, but for blasphemy, because you, though only a human being, make yourself God.' From the Gospel's point of view these statements are ironic; for Jesus is the Son of God and is equal to, or resembles, God. Jesus is not calling for the worship of a god other than the God of Israel. Rather, he is proclaiming himself to be the Messiah, the Son of God (20:31) and the one through whom God reveals himself to the world (1:18).

But the Jews' accusations show that they are not convinced. Rather, their ultimate response – of throwing stones – implies not only their firm rejection of Jesus but also their conviction that he is guilty of a capital crime. This response therefore implies that, in claiming to be the Son of God who shares in God's attributes, Jesus is setting himself up as a god in his own right. From the Jewish perspective belief in Jesus is not the path to the God of Israel but away from God to idolatry. No flesh and blood person can be equal or similar to God or share in the attributes that are uniquely and singularly divine.

From the point of view of a strict monotheism these claims are truly offensive and support the Jewish charge against Jesus of blasphemy (10:33). But I would argue that even more problematic than Jesus' claim to have divine attributes is his proselytizing activity. The purpose of John 8:31–59, as of the Fourth Gospel as a whole, is not merely to assert Jesus' identity as Christ and Son of God but to persuade others to believe in Jesus (3:18), follow him (10:4), accept his word (3:33) and, most provocatively, to eat his body and drink his blood (6:53). That the purpose of the Gospel is to persuade its readers of a particular understanding of Jesus is made explicit in the Gospel's statement of purpose: 'Now Jesus did many other signs in the presence of his disciples that are not written in his book. But these are written so that you may come to believe that Jesus is the Messiah, the Son of God, and that through believing you may have life in his name.'[26] If Jesus is setting himself up as God and if this act transgresses the boundaries of monotheism, as the Johannine Jews, in my reading, believe, then Jesus' offence is not simply blasphemy or idolatry but rather the fact that he urges others to believe in him and thereby to stray from their service to and worship of the one true God of Israel.

Deuteronomy 13 prescribes death by stoning (Deut 13:10) for the one who seeks to lead Israel astray and provides guidance for identifying such a person:

> If prophets ... appear among you and promise you omens or portents, and the omens or the portents declared by them take place, and they say, 'Let us follow other gods' (whom you have not known) 'and let us serve them,' you must not heed the words of those prophets or those who divine by dreams; for the LORD your God is testing you, to know whether you indeed love the LORD your God with all your heart and soul. The LORD your God you shall follow, him alone you shall fear, his commandments you shall keep, his voice you shall obey, him you shall serve, and to him you shall hold fast. But those prophets ... shall be put to death for having spoken treason against the LORD your God. ... (13:1–5).

From a Jewish perspective the Johannine Jesus bears a striking resemblance to the deceitful prophet described in this passage. He has appeared among them (1:26), has promised portents (for example 1:51), at least some of his portents have taken place (for example 4:50) and he has urged others to follow him (as in 1:43; 8:31).

Talmudic sources identify Jesus' crime in precisely these terms. In the tractate Sanhedrin of the Babylonian Talmud (107b) the following story is told:

One day [when] R. Jehoshua ben Perahjah was reciting the Shema, he [Jesus] came before him. He [R. Jehoshua] was minded to receive him, and made a sign to him. He [Jesus] thought that he repelled him. He [Jesus] went and hung up a tile and worshipped it. He (R. Jehoshua] said to him, "Return." He [Jesus] replied, "Thus I have received from you, that every one who sins and causes the multitude to sin, they give him not the chance to repent. And a teacher has said, "Jesus the Nazarene practised magic and led astray and deceived Israel.'

Sanhedrin 43a describes Jesus' death:

On the eve of Pesach they hung Jesus. And the crier went forth before him forty days (saying), 'Jesus the Nazarene goes forth to be stone, because he has practised magic and deceived and led astray Israel... He was a deceiver and the Merciful has said: 'If prophets ... appear among you... (Deut 13:8)'.[27]

These talmudic passages postdate the Fourth Gospel by several centuries and therefore cannot corroborate my reading of the Johannine Jews' objections to Jesus. But some evidence that Jesus was viewed as leading the populace astray may be found in the Gospel itself. In 7:12 the crowds debate whether Jesus is a good person or one who intends to lead them astray. After the raising of Lazarus, 'the chief priests planned to put Lazarus to death as well, since it was on account of him that many of the Jews were deserting and were believing in Jesus' (12:10–11). These passages imply that the Johannine Jews were concerned about Jesus' ability to gather followers and that the Jews viewed such followers as deserters from Judaism and, by extension, from its monotheistic understanding of God.

CONCLUSION

Recovering the Jewish voice in John 8:31–59 raises to the fore the issue of monotheism and suggests that the fundamental issue at stake in the Jewish–Christian debate within this text is whether or not Jesus and the claims made for him are an enhancement of monotheism, that is, a 'new and improved' but fundamentally recognizable revelation, or, conversely, a radical infringement of this basic Jewish belief. It is not too far-fetched to speculate that monotheism may have been an issue not only in early Christian texts but also in the relationship between real Jews and Christians in the first century.[28]

This attempt at a resistant reading of John 8:31–59 also raises issues that extend beyond the scope of the passage, and concern the early Christian movement itself. As we saw, the rhetoric of the passage silences the Jews in this text and strips them of their identity. In the first century context this rhetorical move expresses both the hostile relationship between Jews and Christians as experienced by the Johannine community and also the understandable need for early Christians to define themselves and defend their own legitimacy over against Judaism, which was far better established than the Christian movement within the Roman Empire at that time. Although the powerful and hostile emotions that fuel the discourse are apparent to any reader, the political situation of the Christian community in the late first century did not create the possibilities within which their animosity could be acted upon. On the contrary, they felt themselves to be the victims of Jewish power in this regard (consider, for example, 9:22). A shift in the balance of power, however, could have created the conditions in which the hostility of the text towards the Johannine Jews would come to fruition in hostile acts against real Jews. Furthermore, such acts could have been justified on the basis of the rhetoric and language of the text itself. A resistant reading, that is, reading from the point of view of those oppressed by the text itself, can help us to recognize that some texts can be dangerous. It also points up the issue of evaluation: rhetoric in which one group is valorized and another group vilified needs to be recognized as mere rhetoric. It need not be taken as an accurate reflection of reality even when we readers might naturally identify with the valorized group. Finally, a resistant reading points out that in texts as in real life there are always at least two sides to every dispute, and can help us to tease out the 'other side' of a one-sided polemical text.

One does not have to be a Jew to engage in a resistant reading of John 8, just as one does not have to be a woman to do a resistant reading of 'Rip Van Winkle'. Indeed, the success of inter-religious dialogue, feminism and the quest for human justice may well depend precisely on our ability to read from the point of view of the 'other,' whether that other is like or unlike ourselves.

NOTES

1 J.L. Martyn, *History and Theology in the Fourth Gospel* (New York: Harper and Row, 1968), p.xviii. This statement appears also in the second edition of this book (Nashville: Abingdon, 1979), p.18.

2 See, for example, Danna Nolan Fewell and Gary A. Phillips, *Bible and the Ethics of Reading (Semeia* 77; Atlanta: Scholars Press, 1997).

3 These issues were the subject of an interdisciplinary academic seminar, 'Anti-Judaism in the Fourth Gospel and Jewish–Christian Dialogue', Leuven, 17 and 18 January 2000.

4 Unless otherwise noted English translations of biblical texts are from the New Revised Standard Version, © 1989 by the Division of Christian Education of the National Council of the Churches of Christ in the USA.

5 For a study written in the middle of the Second World War of the medieval afterlife of the description of the Jews as children of the devil, see Joshua Trachtenberg, *The Devil and the Jews: The Medieval Conception of the Jew and its Relation to Modern Anti-Semitism* (New Haven: Yale University Press, 1943).

6 Judith Fetterley, *The Resisting Reader: A Feminist Approach to American Fiction* (Bloomington: Indiana University Press, 1978).

7 *ibid.*, p.9. Emphasis hers.

8 See R. Alan Culpepper, *The Anatomy of the Fourth Gospel* (Philadelphia: Fortress, 1983), pp.89–98.

9 Richard Bauckham, *God Crucified: Monotheism and Christology in the New Testament* (Grand Rapids, MI: Eerdmans, 1999), p.6.

10 *ibid.*

11 Sigfred Pedersen, in 'Anti-Judaism in John's Gospel: John 8', in *New Readings in John: Literary and Theological Perspectives from the Scandinavian Conference on the Fourth Gospel; Århus 1997*, eds. Johannes Nissen and Sigfred Pedersen (JSOTSup 182; Sheffield: Sheffield Academic Press, 1999), p.186, suggests that the reference to Abraham may also allude to God as creator and in this way bring the creation language of the Johannine prologue to bear on our reading of John 8.

12 'Apocalypse of Abraham', ed. R. Rubinkiewicz in *The Old Testament Pseudepigrapha*, vol.1, ed. J.H. Charlesworth (Garden City, New York: Doubleday, 1983), pp.689–693; 'Jubilees', ed. O.S. Wintermute in *The Old Testament Pseudepigrapha*, vol.2, ed. J.H. Charlesworth (Garden City, New York: Doubleday, 1985), p.80.

13 '*Testament of Abraham*', (ed.) E.P. Sanders in *The Old Testament Pseudepigrapha*, vol.2, p.882.

14 *Josephus in Nine Volumes*, vol.4, tr. and ed. H.St.J. Thackeray (Loeb Classical Library; Cambridge: Harvard University Press, 1978), p.77.

15 *Philo*, vol.6, tr. and ed. F.H. Colson (Loeb Classical Library; Cambridge: Harvard University Press, 1966), p.41.

16 *Josephus in Nine Volumes*, vol.5, tr. and ed. H.St.J. Thackeray and Ralph Marcus (Loeb Classical Library; Cambridge: Harvard University Press, 1935), p.45.

17 '*Jubilees*', *The Old Testament Pseudepigrapha, op. cit.* pp.47–48.

18 οὐδενὶ can mean 'to anything' or 'to anyone'.

19 See Culpepper, *Anatomy*, pp.152–165.

20 John Ashton in *Understanding the Fourth Gospel* (Oxford: Clarendon Press, 1991), p.423 sees this statement as the Gospel's effort to show that the Jews are liars.

21 R.A. Brown, *The Gospel According to John: I–XII* (AB 29; Garden City, New York: Doubleday, 1966), p.355.

22 Rudolf Schnackenburg, *The Gospel According to St. John*, vol.2 (New York: Crossroad, 1982), p.207.

23 For an introduction to the scholarly debate regarding the nature of first century Jewish monotheism, see Bauckham, *God Crucified* and James D.G. Dunn, 'Was Christianity a Monotheistic Faith from the Beginning?' *Scottish Journal of Theology* 35 (1982): 303–336.

24 *Writings of Saint Justin Martyr*, tr. T.B. Falls (New York: Christian Heritage, 1948), pp.61–62.

25 For a detailed discussion of the Johannine use of ἐγὼ εἰμί as a divine name see Brown, *Gospel*, pp.533–538.

26 For a discussion of the question of whether the Fourth Gospel is a missionary text or not see Adele Reinhartz, 'Historical Critics and Narrative Texts: A Look at the Missionary Position in Johannine Scholarship', in *The Making of Proselytes: Jewish Missionary Activity in the Hellenistic World*, ed. by Amy-Jill Levine (Atlanta: Scholars Press, 2000 [forthcoming]).

27 As cited with some minor modifications in R. Travers Herford, *Christianity in Talmud and Midrash* (New York: Ktav, 1903), pp.51, 83, 403, 406.

28 See G.N. Stanton, 'Aspects of Early Christian–Jewish Polemic and Apologetic', *New Testament Studies* 31 (1985): 377–92.

TURNING AND WANDERING:
THE JOURNEY FROM DEATH TO LIFE AT NES AMMIM

Kathleen J. Rusnak

IMAGINE THAT you have joined a group of Christians for a tour of Israel. Your guide tells you about an international ecumenical Christian settlement in the Galilee called Nes Ammim, which means 'a sign to the nations', from Isaiah 11:10. Founded in 1963, it is a community with a post-Holocaust Christian outlook towards Jews and the State of Israel. Your group decides to visit. When you arrive at Nes Ammim your guide arranges for you to receive a lecture about Nes Ammim and a tour of the village.

As you walk between the Village Centre and Floriculture, where Nes Ammim grows roses for export, you are taken to a building you cannot clearly identify. Its architecture is beautiful. Except for a few missing items, it could be a church or a synagogue. You are told that this is indeed the House of Prayer and Study, the church at Nes Ammim, and that its basilica–style structure is modelled after 1st-century CE Galilean churches and synagogues.[1] It has no bomb shelter and faces Jerusalem. It also has no steeple and no cross, and does not stand out among the other buildings in the village, except for its beauty.

Someone in your group voices your own question, 'Why is there no cross?' You are told that the church, without a cross embellishing it, reveals Nes Ammim's sensitivity to the cross's symbolic meaning for Jews. The cross was turned into a sword which has meant persecution, crusades, pogroms, and death to Jews for centuries. Its absence from the church is also a daily reminder to Christians of their anti-Jewish past. The questioner is taken aback, not so much by the consequences of the cross for Jews, but because he is focused on defending the central symbol of his Christian identity. This is apparent in the tone and choice of words in his next question, expressing the anti-Judaism latent in every Christian mind, 'So, you are hiding your identity for the Jews?'

No, comes the response, we are not hiding our identity. The cross symbolizes for many, especially for Jews, the long-standing Christian attitude of triumphalism. Nes Ammim is a place where we try to learn from the past, questioning and rediscovering our Christian tradition in light of the Holocaust. The absence of the cross is for us the absence of triumphalism. When Nes Ammim's church was first built, someone from the regional council called to ask where our church was. She had been in the village the day before and couldn't find 'a church'.[2] Also, long after the church was built in 1990, two Israeli engineers came to Nes Ammim asking when the church would be built. In both cases these Jews expected a church to be a triumphal building with a high tower. When the committee discussing the building of the church met in 1986, it was a serious concern that the church building not be 'impressive', and that people who worshipped there should feel humble. The resulting decision was that the building should be a symbolic fifty centimetres shorter than the Village Centre so as not to be the tallest building in the village.[3]

Christine Pilon, the wife of the founder of Nes Ammim, was a strong advocate that the church should have no cross and be symbolically shorter than the tallest building. She said at that time, 'A building is a representation of what you are.'[4] The House of Study and Prayer at Nes Ammim is indeed a representation of who its inhabitants are and raises the question with which they continually grapple: 'What is our Christian identity and how will we represent ourselves as Christians after the Holocaust?' The community of Nes Ammim is like its church: its identity is not easily recognizable.

NES AMMIM'S FOUNDERS

As seen in the above scenario, when Nes Ammim's inhabitants enter the church building, they are exposed to many of the core issues that brought Nes Ammim into existence.

Nes Ammim's founders, Dr. Johan Pilon, a Dutch Christian physician serving in a hospital in Tiberias in the 1950s, and Shlomo Bezek, a Dutch Jew living in kibbutz Ayel-et Ha Shachar, met in Tiberias when Dr. Pilon assisted in the delivery of Bezek's baby. Influenced by Bezek, the encounter with other Jewish colleagues in Tiberias, the recent memory of the Second World War, and the writings of Martin Luther, Pilon struggled to understand the relationship between the Holocaust and Christianity, painfully aware that Dutch Christians allowed seventy percent of Amsterdam's Jews to be deported. He was greatly distressed by Luther's 1543 treatise *On the Jews and their Lies*[5] and wondered what there was in Christianity that contributed to the Holocaust. Pilon and Bezek discussed with each other how something so horrific as the Holocaust could have happened in Christian Europe, and together conceived the idea of a unique Christian settlement in Israel. The new community would be committed to dialogue with Jews, reject mission to Jews, and promote reconciliation between Christians and Jews.

The 1960 Memorandum[6] of Nes Ammim speaks of the abyss between Christians and Jews, the need for personal contact between them, and the necessity of working together to accomplish reconciliation:

> Considering the depth of the abyss between the two groups and the extent of Christianity's moral failure, the initiators of the [Nes Ammim] project believe that an attitude of moral distant co-existence without genuine human contact and co-operation in practical constructive tasks, would be unworthy of the moral and religious traditions of the two groups.[7]

At the first Nes Ammim Board of Directors meeting in Nahariya in 1964, Dr. Pilon gave two reasons why a settlement like Nes Ammim was necessary: 'Nes Ammim is our visible confession of guilt. I don't have to go deeper into this because we all know. The second reason [why we are here] is to help improve the relationship between Jews and Christians because Israel is our brother.' Nes Ammim was to be a Christian settlement 'serving Israel by investment, economic initiative and technical know-how'. It was to be a kibbutz-like settlement, a village based on a cooperative economy. Its Memorandum states that by working the land, the new settlement would express its lived solidarity with Israel. Nes Ammim began with the rose industry, introducing hothouses to Israelis, and in time added avocado plantations and built a hotel. It wasn't long, however, before Dr. Pilon realized more was needed than work. His wife, Christine, recalls:

> He began to realise how little the average Christian knows about Judaism and Jewish tradition and of what vital importance this knowledge is to our own Christian identity. 'Nes Ammim must become a "house of study" too', he used to say.[8]

Nes Ammim has become all of these things: a place of work (avocados, roses, and hotel) and a place of study with a full curriculum that accompanies work. In its life, work, and study, Nes Ammim remains a place of repentance. It seeks to eliminate anti-Judaism from its thinking and behaviour, and to turn away from attitudes which paved the way for the Holocaust.

PREPARATION FOR THE NES AMMIM JOURNEY

Turning. Repentance is not a concept, at least not in the Christian tradition, which evokes excitement and energy. More often than not, repentance evokes fear in the more conservative camps and disinterest in the more liberal camps. In the Christian tradition we are assured that forgiveness is a free, unmerited gift accomplished for us through the death and resurrection of Christ. If we ask God for forgiveness through Jesus Christ, we are assured of receiving it. We are focused on what has been done for us through Christ. Christians are not often focused on a detailed process of repentance, as are Jews, on how not to repeat patterns of offence or destruction in our lives.

But Nes Ammim is not about seeking forgiveness. It does not ask Jews for forgiveness. The quest for forgiveness is not a subject discussed in any official Nes Ammim document. While Christians may be assured of God's mercy and forgiveness for their contrite hearts in the aftermath of Holocaust atrocities, the founders of Nes Ammim knew that that isn't enough. The dead victims cannot absolve us; we must face the survivors, the Jewish world, and we must discover how not to repeat the Holocaust again for their sake and for ours. In its confession of complicity in the Holocaust, Nes Ammim plunges itself into an identity crisis. It seeks not to repeat its offences to Jews by investigating the very roots of Christianity, not only its anti-Jewishness, but also its non-Jewishness.

Without intending to, perhaps, Nes Ammim is acting out the Jewish notion of repentance. In the story known in Christian tradition as the Prodigal Son (Luke 15), the interpretive emphasis is usually placed upon God as the Father whose delinquent son is now journeying home after a dissolute life. According to the text, the son 'came to himself' only after he hit rock bottom, was broke and hungry. Most Christians reading this text do not see the son as repentant in his desire to return home, but simply destitute and with no where else to turn. The young man rehearses the plea he will make to his father on arriving home, but while he is still at a distance, his father sees him and runs to him. The son starts to recite his plea, but before he can get the words out of his mouth, the father embraces him and organises a feast in celebration of his son's return.

Christian exegesis of this parable has usually focused on the nature of God as unconditionally forgiving. However, other interpretations are possible. At a Jewish-Christian dialogue I recently attended, discussion of this text from a Jewish perspective helped shed light on my understanding of Nes Ammim's situation.[9] According to a Jewish understanding of repentance, all that is required is a desire to repent; first, step in the right direction, and God will be there with open arms:

> Open to me. R. Jassa said: The Holy One, blessed be He, said to Israel: 'My sons, present to me an opening of repentance no bigger than the eye of a needle, and I will widen it into openings through which wagons and carriages can pass.'[10]

There is also a Midrash about a king's son who 'was far away from his father'. When his friends encouraged him to return to his father he responded, 'I just can't!' His father sent word to him saying, 'Go as far as your strength allows and I will be with you the rest of the way.'[11] In both these texts we see that the son must only take a first step in the right direction. He does not know the way back. He does not know how his life will change on the journey home. He does not even know the way home.

In all three texts, we are assured of one thing *only*, and that is God's compassion and forgiveness for the sinner. What is not assured or even foreseen for the one returning home is what will happen on the journey home, how one will be transformed by the decision to return, made possible first only by the desire. There is no clear vision of what one's new identity will be once one has expunged from one's essence the old habits and set patterns that dominate and cause harm.

From Judaism we learn that repentance entails an elimination of sin and a renewal of the person. It is a process and not an event. It means acknowledging one's sin, confessing it, compensating for it, and not repeating it. This last stage involves an elimination of a way of being, an old pattern of seeing and acting. It involves a turning around. It is this elimination process in which Nes Ammim is engaged. At the same time, it experiences renewal through discovery of a new focus which slowly emerges from new experiences and impressions which fill the vacuum. A new identity is not yet foreseeable or predictable. That is the uncertainty. That is the way of faith.

Because traditional Christology is the centre of Christian identity which Nes Ammim seeks to leave behind, Nes Ammim works to eliminate from its teaching, preaching, and liturgy anything that ignores the fact that Jesus was a Jew, portrays Jesus as anti-Jewish, or claims that Jesus and Christianity have replaced Judaism. This elimination is an important part of the process of repentance.

Repentance becomes a life-giving dynamic when we realize it offers the possibility of new life when facing our death. For example, when some persons are given a terminal diagnosis, a new consciousness arises in them and their entire lives flash before them like a movie being replayed in slow motion. This is called *life review*.[12] Every facet of their lives is reviewed with fresh eyes, and without ego involvement. There is no longer anyone to impress and no one and nothing to lose. Death is imminent and a new feeling of freedom emerges such as they have never experienced before. A facade falls away and an authentic person emerges. It is amazing to witness the transformation that can take place in people's lives when they are willing to risk letting go of the past, turning in a new direction, and living authentically in the present. Life review gives the dying the opportunity to see the whole picture, an opportunity to *choose* and initiate that 'turning.'

A similar experience took place for some Christians (and Jews) affected by the Holocaust and the founding of the State of Israel. If life review is triggered in an individual by the awareness of imminent death (called a near-death awareness), then a 'collective life review' (creating what is called Holocaust theology), is triggered within the collective conscience of Judaism and Christianity, characterized by a thorough looking back. Christianity's very credibility, and therefore existence (extinction?), is called into question as a result of its own complicity, theologically and ethically, in the Holocaust. For these Christians, Christianity is in imminent danger of dying.

The Holocaust and the founding of the State of Israel are thus viewed as crises that trigger an automatic and collective life review of Christian theology. For Jews the Holocaust has been a 'near extinction experience' (comparable to the 'nearing death awareness' in the dying). As with the dying, the content of that life review of Christianity is brought forward without ego involvement. Perhaps for the first time in history that review is not selective. It is not how the church wishes it were remembered, but instead, the whole picture appears, and with fresh eyes and without fear the church can see itself and choose to initiate a 'turning'.

Every tenet and doctrine, every thought, word, and deed is reviewed (I liken it to the search in a Jewish home during Passover for every crumb of leaven that may be hidden). One critic of such a search by Christian Holocaust theologians into the past has called them 'theological bloodhounds'.[13] I use the analogy with the dying to permit a more compassionate perspective on such a search, for as with any dying patient, time is running out.

Nes Ammim does not deny the 'near extinction experience' which resulted from its credibility crisis during the Holocaust. It does not deny that Christianity is in a crisis. Nes Ammim is therefore involved in a non-selective life review that results practically and theologically in a 'turning around.' For Christians, Christology is the natural focus of the collective life review, because Christology, the question of Jesus, 'Who do you say that I am?' gives the Christian his/her Christian identity. Nes Ammim insists that to claim that Jesus came to save the Jews, that Jesus is the Messiah of the Jews, that Jesus rejected Jews and replaced their covenant with God with a new covenant, is the source and foundation of anti-Judaism and antisemitism in Christian tradition.

Wandering. To repent is to move from death to life. This is the paradigm of Easter for Christians and Passover for Jews. Christians move from death to resurrection at Easter and Jews move from slavery to liberation at Passover. Repentance is a movement, a process toward renewal from death. It is not the renewal itself. In between is the journey of changing, the discovery of what it means not to repeat, to let go of fixed ideas, and to receive new things. In the wandering itself we discover our mistake as Christians, our desire to return to the possession of a fixed theology and a solid dwelling place of absolutes. We discover that our dwelling place, Nes Ammim, is a kind of *sukkah* (fragile temporary huts used by the Israelites in the desert during the forty years of wandering after the Exodus from Egypt). The spiritual symbolism of the *sukkah*, built every year by Jews at Sukkot,[14] reminds Jews of the necessity of letting go whatever is fixed and nailed down permanently in their lives, thoughts and behaviour. According to Rabbi Irving Greenberg, Sukkot asks the questions, 'What is the nature of protection?' and 'What is the nature of true security?' The construction of the *sukkah* itself, says Greenberg, can answer these questions. It is built to be fragile, open, and not too solid so that it can be destroyed by a strong storm. The roof must be loosely spread and cannot be nailed down permanently. According to Greenberg, the *sukkah* teaches us that the desire for solid security is a trap:

> Human beings instinctively strive to build solid walls of security. People heap up treasures and power and status symbols in the hope of excluding death and disaster and even the unexpected. This search for 'solid' security all too often leads to idolatry, to worship things that give security. People end up sacrificing values and even loved ones to obtain the tangible sources of security. The *sukkah* urges people to give up this pseudo-safety.[15]

Nes Ammim experiences fragility and exposure. Secure symbols and fixed statements of faith have been relinquished.

THE JOURNEY BEGINS

Who are the people who come to live, work, and study at Nes Ammim? In what ways do they live out the aim and purpose of Nes Ammim?

Nes Ammim's current population is about ninety people, twenty of whom are children. They come as 'short-stayers' (mostly single, between the ages of 18 and 25, who stay for less than two years), and as 'long-stayers' (mostly married, between 25 and 40, some of them parents with children, who stay up to five years). Seventy-five percent come from Holland and twenty percent from Germany. The remaining five percent are from other countries. Most are therefore Europeans whose parents or grandparents experienced the Second World War. They all have their family stories. They are mostly between the ages of eighteen and thirty-five, with a few of them older, and several pensioners who come for three months of the year to work and live.

Nes Ammim is not a permanent home for its residents. Of the two hundred and eighty kibbutzim in Israel, not only is it the only Christian kibbutz, it is the only one without permanent members, except for Christine Pilon. Nes Ammimers are to return to their home churches as ambassadors of Nes Ammim.

Those individuals or families who decide to come to live and work at Nes Ammim have learned about Nes Ammim from their churches or from advertisements in their home countries. In their application and interview process, they will learn that Nes Ammim's founders acknowledged that Christian theology helped pave the way for the Holocaust, and that Nes Ammim therefore exists to renew a relationship between Christians and Jews after the Holocaust and to be in solidarity with the State of Israel. They will be told that Nes Ammim is a place of repentance, which recognises that Christianity was *wrong* to insist that with the coming of Jesus Judaism was replaced and therefore rejected by God. Because Nes Ammim rejects missionary activity to Jews, applicants are required to sign a statement that they will not participate in missionary activities at Nes Ammim.

People apply to Nes Ammim for many reasons. They would like to live, work, and study in Israel for a year or two, and to meet and dialogue with Jews, since after the Holocaust there are few Jews left in Germany and Holland and they may never have even met one. They want to see the land of the bible, and learn about Judaism and Israeli culture. They want to experience eating kosher for a year, since Nes Ammim's kitchen is kosher in order to attract Israeli Orthodox clientele to the hotel. They look forward to an ecumenical church service and the experience of meeting Christians of different denominations. Most applicants can agree with everything on an intellectual level. Repentance is far from their minds. They will not see the church building nor be confronted with its symbolism until they live here. What they learn about Nes Ammim before arriving will be on an *informational* level, not a *symbolic* level.

Church life.   When newcomers arrive at Nes Ammim, they will come to the church service in the House of Study and Prayer held on Saturday evening. Since the evening is considered the following day in Jewish time, it is already Sunday. The service is held Saturday evening, at the end of the Sabbath, because Sunday is a regular work and school day in Israel. Nes Ammim inhabitants also work on Sunday and their children go to school at the neighbouring Jewish kibbutz in Regba. Some newcomers notice immediately that there is no cross in the church. The service itself and the atmosphere surrounding worship are very different from what they have been used to at home. Some hymns are unfamiliar, or the texts to familiar tunes have been changed. The hymns are sung in at least three languages, Dutch, German, and English, to reflect the population. There is no creed and the Old Testament reading is replaced by the Torah Portion of the Week, the Parashat Hashavua, which is a text from one of the five books of Moses read that week in synagogues everywhere. The pastor mentions in the sermon that she disagrees with how church Fathers have interpreted the day's text. It is an unexpectedly open atmosphere for many.

In the church building, through symbol, and in the church service, through liturgy, the inhabitants of Nes Ammim are introduced to and confronted with the official theological criteria which are foundational for all education and worship at Nes Ammim. These criteria include: 1) 'Israel remains God's Chosen People and elder partner in His covenant.' 2) 'Jesus of Nazareth lived and died as a Jew. This fact is central to the Christian belief. The disdain for Jews has deeply wounded the Christian faith.' 3) 'The Jewish interpretation of the Holy Scriptures is recognised as a tradition of equal value with the Christian one.'[16] Nes Ammim's founders insisted that if contempt for Jews and Judaism was expressed in traditional Christian liturgy, then sensitivity to Jews and Judaism could also be expressed in the liturgy and hymns. Like all symbol and ritual, liturgy teaches on a feeling level as well as a rational level; a fact even the Nazis knew and employed.[17]

A newcomer first experiences *what is missing*, what has been taken away, from traditional Christian worship: the cross, the creed, and the reading from the bible called the Old Testament reading. At a Congregational meeting in 1985, an 'order of service' was proposed which omitted the use of any creed. While no discussion were recorded concerning this decision, the second criterion for deciding theological decisions at Nes Ammim, the recognition of the Jewishness of Jesus, appears to be at work here since traditional Christian creeds do not acknowledge either the Jewishness of Jesus or Jesus' relationship to the God of Israel. Omitting any creed reflects the 'in-between' status of Christology after the Holocaust at Nes Ammim, and can be seen as a consequence of repentance by refusing to allow Jesus to be summarised in a non-Jewish way. As with the cross, the creed is taken away and not replaced. It is hoped that in the empty space, what is missing in symbol and liturgy will give way to respect for Jesus the Jew and the Judaism to which he was faithful.

Another liturgical change in Nes Ammim's worship service is the replacement of the Christian lectionary's 'Old Testament' reading with the Torah portion of the week read in synagogues. The Old Testament lesson is often chosen in order to present the *promise* of what is then *fulfilled* through Jesus in the Gospel lesson. Replacing the Old Testament text with the Torah portion of the week reflects Nes Ammim's wish to avoid *suggesting* such a 'fulfilment' theology, acknowledging the 'in between' status of Christology. It also satisfies the first and third criteria of Nes Ammim's theological principles, that the covenant between God and Israel is valid and not replaced by Christianity, and that, according to the official Nes Ammim brochure, the Jewish interpretation of the Holy Scriptures is recognised as a tradition of equal value with the Christian one. Through the addition of the Torah portion of the week and the elimination of the creed from its worship service, Nes Ammim repents by 'turning' its Christology away from anti-Judaism.[18]

The newcomer at Nes Ammim is thus confronted with Nes Ammim's theological foundations, foundations upon which a fully developed Christology has not been developed, not at Nes Ammim, and not within the Christian church. To say that the covenant between God and Israel is valid and to reject mission to Jews prompts an often unanticipated entrance by Nes Ammimers into the theological realm of Christology. Many Nes Ammim inhabitants are not prepared for the Christological implications they experience in the church building and church service. They had no idea what no mission to Jews meant for their Christian identity, for Christology, only that it takes something away, that they have to withhold something of their true selves. Others arrive at Nes Ammim already convinced that mission to Jews can no longer to be part of the Christian endeavour, but must then face the difficult Christological consequences of that conviction.

Study life. The symbol and liturgy of Nes Ammim's church life touch the feeling dimension of Nes Ammim's inhabitants. They see what is missing. However, the absence of cross, creed, and traditional Christian anti- or non-Jewish expressions does not mean that intellectual or spiritual life at Nes Ammim is barren. Nes Ammim has a full educational programme on Judaism, Israeli society, Holocaust, and Christology, with an emphasis in all areas on encounter with Jews. Nes Ammim is founded on the premise that the Holocaust and the founding of the State of Israel are two major events that affect Christian identity. Therefore, the study programme is geared toward studying these areas in depth in order to inform, confront, and provoke discussion of Christian identity. The programme is presented through study evenings, lectures, excursions, and seminars.

A major event in the study year and in Israeli society is Yom HaShoah, Holocaust Remembrance Day. In this event several study areas come together: the Holocaust, Israeli society, Jewish/Christian encounter, and Christian identity. An examination of this experience can illuminate its significance for Nes Ammim inhabitants:

It is after work, and small groups of Nes Ammimers begin to slowly leave for the two-kilometre walk on the dirt road that joins Nes Ammim and Beit Lohamei Hagetaot, the Ghetto Fighters' Museum and kibbutz. Survivors of the ghetto uprisings in Poland and Lithuania founded the kibbutz in 1949.[19] Several months before this night, most of the newcomers walked this road home in the dark at the end of the two-day Holocaust seminar especially designed for them. For every inhabitant the seminar has an unexpected content. All of the inhabitants have had Holocaust education in their respective countries. Most think they have had enough, but they have not learned about the Holocaust in Israel or been to a Holocaust museum that focuses on Jewish resistance in the ghettos and that emphasizes life and not death. Here they hear about the Holocaust from a Jewish perspective, where the Jewish victims have faces, names, and personal stories of resistance and are not just numbers and statistics. For the first time in their lives they hear about Jews fighting back during the war and they meet survivors who give testimonies. It is a different side of the Holocaust. This is not the sheep-to-the-slaughter image of the Jew. It is life fighting for life, and for dignity. Most participants are moved to silence. They have never heard this story, much less heard Jews tell it.

Now they walk again on the familiar dirt road to the kibbutz and the museum where Miriam Novich was curator until her death. In the seminars before 1986 she always emphasized to the Nes Ammim participants the lack of Christian help for their Jewish neighbours when 'we were taken by trains to the gas chambers.'[20] She underscored that 'together with the Jewish children thrown alive into the burning pits in Auschwitz were thrown also the Christian ethics on which modern civilisation is still based.'[21] She added that she could speak to the Nes Ammim participants this way 'knowing that my accusations will find an echo in their hearts...and that the founders of Nes Ammim... somehow want to expiate, consciously or unconsciously, all the wrong that was done by the church.'[22]

Today, such words are not spoken directly to the Nes Ammimers attending the museum, but segments of the seminar itself now provoke such thoughts, as discussions that follow find them sharing thoughts about their parents' or grandparents' experiences and part in the war, and how they are affected by it. Some, however, are far too affected to speak at all, especially in a large group. Not far from their minds is the issue of the bystander that is raised at the Kristallnacht commemoration of November 9, held at Nes Ammim on that date, in which Christians, Jews, and Muslims participate.

Since their initial seminar, many Nes Ammimers have gone back to Beit Lohamei Hagetaot in their spare time to take another look or to ask another question, or simply to be there. It becomes a pilgrimage, part of their wandering and pondering. But today they walk the road to the museum to join thousands of Israelis who will gather from throughout Israel for the annual commemoration of Yom HaShoah, or Holocaust Remembrance Day. The commemoration takes place in two parts of the country. The first ceremony takes place at Yad Vashem, the world renowned Holocaust Museum in Jerusalem, the night before. Remembrance Day ends the next evening at Beit Lohamei Hagetaot.

The expectation from the Nes Ammimer is that such a commemoration will focus on the concentration camps, on the destroyed communities, and on death. That is true of the first ceremony held at Yad Vashem. But the ceremony that ends Yom HaShoah at Beit Lohamei Hagetaot focuses on the ghetto uprisings and heroes of the Holocaust. It focuses on military strength and power. 'Never Again' is self-evident. One feels the motto of the museum: 'Fight for this place Israel; there is no other place in the world where a Jew will be defended.'[23] Israeli flags proudly surround the stage outside the museum, which is the site for the evening programme. The next hours are filled with units of soldiers marching across the stage, speeches, a choir singing ghetto songs, a skit involving a burning ghetto, poetry, ballet, quotations from diaries, and the arrival by helicopter of the Prime Minister or another government official.

Nes Ammimers wait expectantly for their unique part in the ceremony. Every year Beit Lohamei Hagetaot asks Nes Ammim to participate in the ceremony by making and presenting seven wreaths of roses, six wreaths for the six million who perished and one wreath for the Righteous Gentiles who rescued Jews. The ceremony begins with the lighting of six candles for the six million, the reading of a text, and then the laying of the wreaths by a representative of Nes Ammim before the symbol of the six million. At the end of the evening everyone stands to sing the Israeli national anthem, Hatikvah, the Hope. This request for Nes Ammim's participation shows how well accepted it has become by Beit Lohamei Hagetaot as well as by other kibbutzim in the neighbourhood, so much so that in 1975, Beit Lohamei Hagetaot presented Nes Ammim with a remembrance medal, 'for being a sign of recognition and blessing for our neighbours'.[24]

At the end of the ceremony, Nes Ammimers embark on their journey home on the dark dirt road leading back to Nes Ammim, flashlights the only source of light. After thirty minutes of walking home, the residents notice the village slowly coming into view. They can see the trees and bushes that hide its interior. The only building in view is a beautiful white structure with a red tiled roof. It is the church, the church without a steeple, the church without a cross. A question arises as they stand between Beit Lohamei Hagetaot and Nes Ammim village, and their own Christian history flashes before them and becomes vivid. How can they put an end to the way they have historically avoided dealing with all aspects of their Christian identity?

THE SPIRITUAL DILEMMA

Inhabitants respond to Nes Ammim church and study life in psychologically recognisable ways: denial, flight, or openness. All three are spiritual responses that the founders of Nes Ammim did not anticipate would affect community life as much or more than the *conscious theological task* and purpose of Nes Ammim to be 'a sign to the nations' and to live in solidarity with the State of Israel.

The spiritual dilemma begins when inhabitants realize through *experience* that Nes Ammim is a place of repentance, that it exists to make reparation for Christianity's contribution to the Holocaust, and that the things now missing from the church building and the church service are the first fruits of that repentance.

The spiritual dilemma quickens and becomes defined with the gut level realization that what is missing is not being replaced. Dealing with grief over the loss of comforting symbols, hymns, and liturgical expressions is difficult enough, but Nes Ammim's inhabitants experience loss with no guarantee of replacement. Normally one expects a loss to be resolved when there is a reinvestment of energy and interest into something new. Jewish thinker Richard Rubenstein has said concerning this Christian dilemma, 'It is very difficult for a people to surrender a myth that has infused its existence with meaning for over two thousand years until a way is found to incorporate the newer, demythologized *Weltanschauung* into its religious and institutional structure.'[25]

At Nes Ammim there is no promise that what is missing will be replaced. How long are the inhabitants expected to live with absence? How long can they surrender a myth and remain 'in between' without the comfort of an alternate theology? This is the dilemma that confronts Nes Ammim as it walks the path of repentance, which induces a 'paradigm shift' of the Christian essence. Nes Ammim becomes a 'threshold community', a place of 'liminality', and a place of uncertainty.[26]

Nes Ammim has put its hand to the plow and has begun to till new ground. It cannot look back, cannot return to the old ways of an anti-Jewish paradigm.[27] It has taken a first step towards repentance without knowing how to take the second step, without knowing where its steps will ultimately lead. It has stepped off the solid ground of anti-Judaism, and consequently off the seemingly solid Christological ground upon which Christian identity has been built. Upon what new ground does it build?

In preparing my dissertation on Holocaust theology at Nes Ammim,[28] I became aware of my own need for an alternate Christian theology. Episcopal priest and theologian Paul van Buren has espoused an alternative Christology after the Holocaust. My first reading of his three-volume *Theology of the Jewish-Christian Reality* was sceptical. It appeared to me that his motive for discovering such an alternative theology might be his need to salvage Christianity and make it credible again because he could not face its possible demise. I reread his theology after hearing his lecture on Christology at Nes Ammim and was able to claim in the summary pages of my dissertation that van Buren had found a way through the grief that accompanies the loss of one's traditional Christian paradigm, a grief that leads to a *spiritual resolution* (italics mine)[29].

One of my professors asked why I had not chosen to align myself with Heinz Kremers, a founder of Nes Ammim, who advocated in his lecture on Christology an open Christology and advised Christians not to resolve the question of Christology. That professor, Michael Ryan, expressed his concern that if the christian church found a new definitive Christology and settled in again with a new firm foundation, it would once again have an *answer*, be tempted once again toward self-righteousness and pride, and would once again be dangerous to other people.

My own need was to find theological comfort, to have an answer, to get off the uncomfortable seat of uncertainty, to find a landing strip. Similarly, some Nes Ammimers, respond to the idea that Jews may not need Jesus because they are already with the Father by commenting, 'Well if Jews don't need Jesus, and you can get to heaven without Jesus, why should I believe in Jesus?' In other words, if I don't have the *only way*, the only answer, my answer is not valid. Irving Greenberg has said of definitive answers, or solidified alternate theologies after Auschwitz, 'After the Holocaust, there should be no final solutions, not even theological ones.'[30] This is the dilemma for Christians after the Holocaust, Christians who have basked in the comfort of absolutes and fixed dogmas.

Flight: Going Back One reaction to the experiences at Nes Ammim is flight. This reaction has created enormous crises in Nes Ammim's 36-year history. The open question of Christian identity has resulted in both social and theological crises for some Nes Ammimers. Results of such crises have included clandestine bible studies, proselytising other Christians within the Nes Ammim community, rebaptisms, and associating with Jews who converted to Christianity (Messianic Jews) and with Christian groups in Israel whose theology was anti-Jewish.

Nes Ammim historians give reasons for these involvements: the need or desire to cling to the same triumphalistic Christology that paved the way for the Holocaust in the first place, and the lack of a strong Christian identity:[31]

Of triumphalism at Nes Ammim, one theologian said:

> Now, related to Nes Ammim: there are groups that do Bible study, each in its own circle. That is not forbidden, but when a group closes itself off, it is not prepared to [risk its interpretation of the Bible] for the upbuilding of the village. [The group] becomes sectarian. Sectarian means that you [enforce] your notion of the truth. Execution of a theological truth is always deadly. You have only to look in church history, the Crusades, the Huguenots killing in Paris, the thirty-year war and the persecution of the Jews unto the Holocaust, the burning of heretics and witches. That is execution of a theological truth. We Christians are very susceptible to this [behaviour].[32]

Of the need for a clear Christian identity, one inhabitant said:

> What should we expect to find? Two thousand years of anti-Jewish prejudice cannot be erased or forgotten overnight. A new idea cannot be integrated into a self-contained, historic tradition without changes being made in the traditional outlook...The Nes Ammim idea and certain traditional Christian views cannot be integrated with each other without the 'most determined moral and spiritual effort.'[33]

These crises resulted negatively in the expulsion of individuals from the Nes Ammim community, and positively in the creation of the European-based 'International Theological and Church Committee' to advise Nes Ammim in theological matters.[34]

Living in a Contradiction: the Struggle.   When confronted with crisis, individuals either react or respond. To react is to go back to what is comfortable and secure. At Nes Ammim some inhabitants reacted negatively to the crisis of loss and chose the path of secret bible studies as a means of concretising the tradition and feeling secure. To respond is to stay with the struggle and to live within the contradictions open to the future. It means to be willing to go on the journey.

How can we put an end to the way we have historically avoided dealing with our Christian identity? This was the question asked upon the return to Nes Ammim at the end of the Yom HaShoah ceremony. But what is involved in the struggle and search for a new Christian identity? Protestant theologian F.W. Marquardt gives us a hint when he describes a Christian hermeneutic for theology after the Holocaust, one that Nes Ammim seems to have taken upon itself. He argues that

> Auschwitz confronts us as a call to repentance. Not only our behaviour but our faith itself should change. Auschwitz should bring forth not only ethical consequences but also consequences for faith. Auschwitz cries out for us to hear the Word of God today radically otherwise than as we heard it before Auschwitz....[35]

Marquardt argues for a new way that begins with repentance and leads to theological and practical changes that cannot stand side by side with pre-Auschwitz theology.

We have witnessed Nes Ammim's entrance into this framework of struggle. It has repented in the face of Auschwitz and eliminated what it deems to be either anti-Jewish or non-Jewish from its symbols and liturgy. It has entered into study that 'looks back' into Judaism to discover what for nineteen centuries was thought to be dead, replaced by a new covenant. It studies this because Jesus was Jewish and cannot be understood for Christian identity until he is no longer a stranger to Christians. It studies Israel, the context of Jesus, and therefore the context of the Church. It studies its own anti-Jewish past, its contempt for Jews and what that hatred ultimately led to. But where does the journey end? When will the uncertainty be resolved? When will Nes Ammim and the Church arrive at home?

Heinz Kremers has advocated what he called an 'open Christology'. In 1984 he gave a lecture to the inhabitants of Nes Ammim on Christology in which he explained[36] that the Holocaust created a crisis within the Christian Church because it was the end result of centuries of Christian anti-Judaism. As the heart of Christian belief, Kremers claims that Christology has been used as a weapon against Jews throughout history. As the key to defining the relationship between Christians and Jews, he insists Christology is in need of heart surgery: 'We must risk a heart operation for the sake of Israel.'[37] Kremers entered into a 'collective life review' of Christianity as a German and as a New Testament scholar, a review that broadened his vision and opened a Christological scope that he claims cannot be settled. He advocates leaving 'open' the identity of Christ, and asks Christians to live without certainty.

The use of the term 'open' Christology indicates how painful it is to even think of Christian identity without a definitive Christology. To keep Christology 'open' is to somehow retain it without holding on to it. It means no more absolutes. Once we can admit this it is possible to begin the process of turning, wandering, and letting go.

ACCOMPLISHING OUR TASKS

The Particular.   Some visitors have asked me if we are not being too narrow in our goal of focusing on Christian-Jewish relations at Nes Ammim when many religious and ethnic groups in the world do not get along with each other. I responded that one cannot make a contribution to solving bad relationships between groups of people in the world until one has dealt with one's own. Nes Ammim is dealing with its own history with the Jewish people. This does not mean that we are not interested in how other groups of people are relating to each other, but until we can take the log from our own eye, we are in no position to take the speak from our neighbour's. To focus on the global, or universal, before focusing on the particular, is to escape one's own pain. Perhaps Nes Ammim can be a model for others.

When we read in the news the week following Yom Kippur in 1999 that the Southern Baptists in the United States had chosen the Days of Awe, the ten holiest days of the Jewish faith, the days of repentance between Rosh Hashanah and Yom Kippur (the Day of Atonement), to target Jews for conversion, a heaviness overtakes us at Nes Ammim, and we know that our work is far from complete.[38] This raises the question of how influential Nes Ammim is within the Christian Church.

The official influence of Nes Ammim on the Church is evident in both Germany and Holland. Nes Ammim influenced the Evangelical Church in the Rhineland, Germany, concerning the relationship between Jews and Christians, in its 1980 document, 'Towards Renovation of the Relationship of Christians and Jews.'[39] Heinz Kremers, a member of the Rhineland Synod, along with other members of the German board of Nes Ammim, greatly influenced the Rhineland decision. The statement renounces mission to

Jews, and at the same time affirms Jewish survival by the return of the Jewish people to Israel, a sign of God's faithfulness. Nes Ammim also influenced a recent 1997 'Church Order statement of the United Protestant Church in the Netherlands'. Article 7 of the statement speaks of 'a connection that cannot be broken' (*onopgeefbare verbondenheid*)[40] between the Church and the people of Israel. This word *onopgeefbare* entered the Dutch language after it was coined at Nes Ammim.[41]

Another important though less measurable influence of Nes Ammim occurs when Nes Ammimers leave Israel and return home. Many take with them their new questions about their Christian identity and no longer feel comfortable attending a church that is uncritical of its traditional anti-Judaism in teaching, preaching, and liturgy. There is a growing concern among the supporting churches and boards of Nes Ammim (from Germany, Holland, and Switzerland) for hundreds of returned Nes Ammim inhabitants who have no real home church. Some do return to their churches, because they experience some significant changes there and hope to contribute towards those efforts. Some return to churches already influenced by Nes Ammimers. On occasion whole groups of returned Nes Ammimers meet with each other for support. The question remains open as to just how they can be ambassadors of Nes Ammim.

Nes Ammim is very well respected in Israel. I was introduced to Nes Ammim in 1989 when I was participating in a course at Yad Vashem. We took an excursion to Nes Ammim because our educational director, a Jew, expressed pride in 'these different Christians.' Nes Ammim has been successful as a sign of goodwill towards Israelis. When Israelis come on a lecture tour of Nes Ammim they are greatly impressed with the aim and purpose of Nes Ammim, with the friendliness of the inhabitants, and with the commitment they witness. When they visit the church they are impressed with the absence of the cross and with our sensitivity in removing it. Israelis who stay in the hotel, who are official guides who bring visiting groups to Nes Ammim, or who simply wander in by themselves to buy roses, remark that we should be better known to Israelis in the country. For these Israelis Nes Ammim is a sign of a new way after the Holocaust. Through every war since the 1967 Six-Day War, Nes Ammimers have stayed in the country and, when needed, helped with agricultural responsibilities in its neighbours' kibbutzim when inhabitants were called to fight.

Nes Ammim fulfills its name, to be 'a sign to the nations', not only to Christians, but simultaneously to Jews, signaling that a new leaf has been turned in Christianity, and that 'never again' will Christians not stand by them in time of need.

Nes Ammim's Contributions.   Is Nes Ammim an experimental model that can be adapted to other countries? This is a question that many a visitor asks and we ask ourselves. The answer is twofold.

First, Nes Ammim is unique. Being in Israel as Nes Ammim Christians means living as a Christian minority among Jews in a Jewish/Israeli context, adapting our life rhythm to the Israeli life rhythm, e.g., working Sunday through Thursday, understanding Judaism in this rhythm, and discovering the Jewish festivals that are not observed in one's home country. No amount of planned interaction between synagogue and church can duplicate this incredible experience for Christians. In Germany, for instance, there are only 60 thousand Jews in a population of 80 million. Most Germans who come to Nes Ammim have never before met a Jew. Israel is very important in this regard. Holland has a small population of Jews, but most Dutch people who come to Nes Ammim have never met one of them. In America, in areas where there are Jews, churches and synagogues might build a common community center for study and exposure to each other.

Jews living outside of Israel do not know what it is to live in an Israeli context. American Jews, for example, are different from the sabra, the Israeli Jew born in Israel. Jews can simply be people here in Israel; they can collect garbage for a living and drive buses.

How is the Nes Ammim experience adapted? Nes Ammim inhabitants experience first hand the impact on Israeli culture of the Holocaust and five wars in Israel's short history. This experience cannot be duplicated elsewhere or understood outside of the Israeli context. Theologically, one could say that if one believes that the covenant between God and Israel is a living covenant, then Israel is an important context to experience as Israel's story continues to unfold.

Second, Nes Ammim can inspire Christianity to face other people it has diminished, persecuted, and hurt. Christianity has still to deal with the fact that its theology also paved the way for its non-intervention on behalf of the rest of Hitler's victims – homosexuals, gypsies, and individuals considered mentally or physically defective. In America, Christianity condoned racism and the inferior status of women.

One must begin with a repentant mind, a change of mind and heart – one must make amends by removing the spirit of triumphalism and domination, and rejecting ideologies of 'one way' thinking. In America, one must be willing to live within the environment of the other in order to learn who the other is, to live in Jewish, gay or black neighbour-hoods as guests there to learn, or to participate in all women's groups as guests there to learn. In Holland and Germany, the Dutch and German Christians must be willing to live within the environment of the Turks, Moroccans, and other immigrants.

This returns us to our *sukkah* image, the image of an open connectedness to each other and to something larger. In this image, our own truth coexists side by side with the truth of another. The goal is not to integrate, but to be enriched by each other, to take each other in, to discover ourselves more fully in the other, and to accept and respect the other and ourselves – to live in peace with each other. If Nes Ammim, as a Christian model of repentance and wandering, can inspire Christianity to continue its identity search, much can be accomplished.

The process of entering a new way begins with repentance. Being on the way is the process of being open. Both processes take us back to our image of Nes Ammim as a *sukkah*. The *sukkah* is vulnerable and open. In its openness and vulnerability it is part of and related to something larger than itself. It symbolizes that we are all wanderers along with each other, searching for answers on the way, finding moments of truth and then moving on.[42] The *sukkah* reminds us that our only ground, our only certainty, is the God who waits for us with open arms. This God was always Jesus' certainty as a Jew, and should be no less a certainty for us as Christians.

NOTES

1 Minutes of the Congregational Meeting, 5 March 1989, 2.
2 Klaus Dürsch, 'The House of Prayer and Study', *Nes Ammim News* (English ed.), Winter, 1990:12.
3 Kathleen Rusnak, *Post-Holocaust Theology on a Christian Kibbutz in Israel: Nes Ammim* (Ann Arbor: UMI Dissertation Services, 1998), 371.
4 Congregational Meeting, 5 March 1989, 3.
5 Martin Luther, *On the Jews and Their Lies*, 1543 tr. Martin H. Bertram, in vol.47 of *Luther's Works* (Philadelphia: Fortress, 1972), 121–306.
6 In 1960, a 'Memorandum to the Government of Israel' was drafted that explained the settlements principle, project, and motivation for seeking government approval.
7 The Memoradum.
8 Christine Pilon, 'The Beginning', Nes Ammim News (English ed), February 1984:2.

9　Nes Ammim is a member of the Interreligious Coordinating Council in Israel (ICCI) and was invited to participate with other ICCI members in a day of dialogue about the issue of repentance in Christian and Jewish texts. This was apropos timing because the conference took place during the Days of Awe (days of repentance) on the Jewish calendar, falling between Rosh Hashanah and Yom Kippur. I introduced the Christian perspective, using Luke 15, asking our Jewish participants to illuminate the Jewish ideas in the text that we Christians have missed due to our lack of knowledge about Judaism. I asked them to inform us what sources or understanding from Jesus as a Jew was incorporated into this parable.

10　Song of Songs Rabah V.2, 2.

11　Pesikta Rabati, *Shuvah*.

12　Robert N. Butler, 'The Life Review: An Interpretation of Reminiscence in the Aged', *Psychiatry*, 26 (1963), 66. For a full discussion of the relation of life review to Holocaust theology, see Kathleen Rusnak, *Post-Holocaust Theology on a Christian Kibbutz in Israel: Nes Ammim*, 361–367.

13　Stephen Haynes, 'Christian Holocaust Theology: A Critical Assessment', *Journal of the American Academy of Religion* LXII/2.

14　Sukkot is a major Jewish festival observed two weeks after Rosh Hashanah. Sukkot, the Festival of Booths, lasts seven days and is a reminder of the forty-year journey in the desert to the Promised Land (Leviticus 23:42–43).

15　Irving Greenberg, *The Jewish Way: Living the Holidays* (New York: Simon & Schuster, 1988), 100.

16　Nes Ammim brochure.

17　Catholic theologian, John Pawlikowski, claims that the Nazis recognised that symbols bind people together in ways those ideas alone cannot and used them to implement their Nazi plans. See John T. Pawlikowski, 'Worship after the Holocaust: An Ethician's Reflections', in *Living No Longer for Ourselves: Liturgy and Justice in the Nineties*, eds. Kathleen Hughes and Mark. Francis (Minnesota: The Liturgical Press, 1991).

18　Rusnak, *Christian Kibbutz in Israel*, 374.

19　These survivors made it their task in 1951 to build a Museum and Resistance Centre to remember and teach about the resistance. The kibbutz and museum are a daily reminder to Nes Ammimers as to why it is there. Initially the kibbutz rejected the idea that European Christians should move into their backyard. They feared a repeat of the age-old missionary activities. Even after the settlement was approved they initially rejected the idea that Germans should live in the village. In the beginning of Nes Ammim in 1963, the first settlers came to a barren piece of land. A small abandoned bus from Nazareth was hauled in for residents to live in. There was no electricity or running water. Lohamei Hagetaot supplied a water line to the bus Nes Ammim. Over the years trust was built up between the two communities as Nes Ammim proved itself a good and trustworthy ally.

20　Miriam Novich, 'My Relations with Nes Ammim', *Nes Ammim News* (English ed.), September 1976.

21　*ibid.*

22　*ibid.*

23　'Remembrance Days and the Ceremony at Kibbutz Lochamei HaGettaot.' Undated Nes Ammim document outlining and summarizing the Yom HaShoah program

24　Simon Schoon and Heinz Kremers, *Nes Ammim: Ein Christliches Experiment in Israel*, (Neukirchen-Vluyn: Neukirchener Verlag, 1978).

25　Richard L. Rubenstein, *After Auschwitz: History, Theology, and Contemporary Judaism* (Baltimore and London: The Johns Hopkins University Press, 1992), 20.

26　Rusnak, *Christian Kibbutz in Israel*, 51.

27　This refers to Luke 9: 62, in which Jesus says, 'No one who puts his hand to the plow and looks back is fit for the kingdom of God' NRSV.

28　Rusnak, *Christian Kibbutz in Israel*.

29　ibid., see pages 449–455.

30　Irving Greenberg, 'Cloud of Smoke, Pillar of Fire: Judaism, Christianity, and Modernity after the Holocaust', in *Auschwitz: Beginning of a New Era?* ed. Eva Fleischer (New York: KTAV, 1977), 26.

31　Spoken at a Congregational meeting at Nes Ammim in 1987 by Dr. Friedrich Hasselhoff, a theological advisor to Nes Ammim from Germany.

32 Minutes of the Congregational Meeting with the I.T.C.C., Nes Ammim, Israel, 14 November 1987, 5.

33 Jim Winfield, 'Some Aspects of the Ideological Crisis Affecting Nes Ammim' undated document, Nes Ammim, Israel.

34 The International Theological and Church Committee, Nes Ammim', *Nes Ammim News* (English ed.), March 1982: 2. Because of these internal problems, the International Theological and Church Committee was founded in cooperation with the home associations in 1982. The committee is made up of both German and Dutch home board members, the theologians of the German home board and the representatives of the 'Contact Committee, Churches, Nes Ammim' in Holland.

35 As cited by Paul M. van Buren in *Christ in Context*, Part 3 of *A Theology of the Jewish–Christian Reality* (San Francisco: Harper & Row, 1988), 159. F.W. Marquardt and Albert Friedlander, *Das Schweigen der Christen und die Menschlichkeit Gottes*, (Munich: Chr. Kaiser Verlag, 1980), 10.

36 Heinz Kremers, 'Christology', lecture at Nes Ammim on 14 November 1984, no. 196. Kremers composed the 1970 theological basis of Nes Ammim called 'Grundsatzerlarung'. In this document Kremers affirms that the Jewish tradition is a living tradition. Based on this, Christians should build a relationship with Jews and Judaism. Kremers was involved with the Nes Ammim movement since 1961. He died on 26 May 1988.

37 ibid., 3–4.

38 Jane Lampman, 'Jews Troubled by Baptist Push for Converts', *Christian Science Monitor*, electronic edition, 23 September, 1999.

39 Nikolaus Becker and Gerda E.H. Koch, ed., *Bewahren und Erneuern: Die Christliche Siedlung NES AMMM in Israel*, Germany: Neukirchener Verlag, 1993.

40 Enlish paraphrase from the Dutch by Jowien van der Zaag, pastor of Nes Ammim.

41 Jowien van der Zaag, 'Gaandeweg Leren in Nes Ammim', *Gesprekken in Israël*, No. 3, (Amersfoort: Stichting Nes Ammim, Nederland, 1998), 15. Van der Zaag is the pastor of Nes Ammim, and in this article makes the connection between Nes Ammim and the sukkah, and the openness of the sukkah that invites all humankind to join a common journey.

CHRISTIAN DOCTRINE AND THE 'FINAL SOLUTION':
THE STATE OF THE QUESTION

Marc Saperstein

The German extermination of Jews can be interpreted broadly as a logical extension of a two-thousand year anti-Jewish tradition initiated and nourished by the Christian Church, or as a drastic new departure from centuries of familiar persecution, pogroms and forcible expulsions.[1]

A MONG THE unresolved issues and unanswered questions pertaining to Holocaust, this fundamental problem of its relationship to the past remains one of the most tantalizing.[2] Unlike the issue of intentionalism versus functionalism, it is not a matter merely of the interpretation of past events, but one that has significant implications for the religious self-conception of millions of believers. It is not my intention to try to resolve this issue in the present paper. I do hope, from my perspective as a historian of the Jewish experience in the Middle Ages, to review and assess the state of the question, on which little progress appears to have been made. Indeed, there seems to be no consensus even on the kind of research or argumentation that might lead to a clarification.

The nature of my review will require abundant reference to and citation of writers on the Holocaust. It will soon be clear that my approach to this material is eclectic. I do not limit my selection to professional historians, although many of them are represented. I include as well other communities of discourse, including those identified with religious groups, and more popular works by authors without any special standing or credentials. Some of the passages cited were written in a style of academic detachment, some with deep remorse, some in white-hot passion. My purpose is to demonstrate that the same kinds of assertions, formulations, metaphors, arguments recur in many different kinds of literature with an impact on contemporary culture considerably wider than the writing of most professional scholars would have.

THE CONTINUITY MODEL ('NOT MUCH NEW', OR 'IT NATURALLY LED THERE')

The continuity model has two basic components. First there is the claim that there is no fundamental difference between Hitler's Final Solution and events inspired by Christian anti-Judaism in the past. The policies taken by the Nazi regime were based on precedents already established by the Church. The numbers of those killed, the dimensions of the calamity were greater, to be sure, but that is a matter of demographics, not essence. Second is the claim that the annihilation of the Jewish people is the natural consequence of doctrines about Judaism and the Jewish people embedded in the heart of Christianity. If they were not implemented before, it was because of limits imposed by logistics and technology, not because the doctrine itself pointed to a different solution.

We find expressions of this interpretative model from the very first years following the war. Perhaps most dramatic and influential was the French historian Jules Isaac, who was to play an important role in the Vatican decision to include a positive statement on the relationship of the Church with the Jewish people among the documents issued by Vatican Council II. In his *Jésus et Israël*, published in 1948, Isaac began the final and largest section of his book with a powerful rhetorical passage:

> Murderer of Jesus, of the Christ-Messiah, murderer of the Man-God, **Deicide**! Such is the accusation leveled against the entire Jewish people, without exceptions, without distinctions of any kind, the blind violence of the ignorant masses relying closely upon the cold science of the theologians.
>
> A capital offense to which is linked the theme of capital punishment, of the terrifying curse weighing upon the shoulders of Israel, explaining (and justifying beforehand) its miserable destiny, its most cruel ordeals, the worst acts of violence committed against it, the streams of blood that escape from its wounds constantly reopened and not allowed to heal.
>
> Thus, by an ingenious mechanism, alternatively of learned pronouncements and popular passions, there is projected upon God's account that which, seen from the early perspective, is certainly the act of incurable human vileness, of this perversity variously but cleverly exploited from century to century, from generation, which culminates in Auschwitz, in the gas chambers and the crematoria of Nazi Germany.[3]

There follows a discussion of the charge of Jewish responsibility for the crucifixion that lasts for more than 200 pages. In this exhaustive study of the crucifixion as historical event and theological doctrine, of the persistence of rhetoric linking the Jews with the destruction of the most holy, there is never an attempt to demonstrate a connection with Nazi antisemitic discourse. One hundred and fifty pages later, Isaac returns and repeats what is no more than a highly-charged rhetorical assertion of continuity: the tradition that the Jewish people as a whole is responsible for the death of Christ is a 'living tradition, infinitely harmful, a murderous tradition, of which I have said and now repeat that it leads to Auschwitz'. Here, however, he takes a further step and explains the connection: 'For, without the centuries of Christian catechism, preaching and vitupera-tion, the Hitlerian catechism, propaganda and vituperation would have been impossible' (p.508). It is unclear whether the claim is that Hitler himself would never have said what he did about the Jews, or that Hitler's antisemitism would not have been accepted by the German population. No support is provided for either possible reading. As we shall see, the claim that the Christian 'teaching of contempt' was a necessary precondition for the Holocaust would have powerful influence even among those who did not follow Isaac in his claim that Christian doctrine leads to Auschwitz.

About the same time that Isaac was writing, a distinguished Christian historian, James Parkes, was making a similar point in language that is rhetorically quite distant from the highly-charged indictment of the French work. He did not come to this conclusion overnight. His doctoral dissertation at Oxford was published in 1934 as *The Conflict of the Church and the Synagogue*. In this solid, rigorous, academic study of the relationship between Jews and Christians in the world of antiquity and the early Middle Ages, Parkes focuses on the past, not on the present. Only in a brief final chapter does he maintain that it is in the religious conflict of the distant past that 'modern antisemitism finds its root'.[4] The book concludes invoking the ongoing power of the belief that '"the Jews" killed God, that they are a people rejected by their God, that all the beauty of their Bible belongs to the Christian Church,' and continues, 'if on this ground, so carefully prepared, modern antisemites have reared a structure of racial and economic propaganda, the final responsibility still rests with those who prepared the soil, created the deformation of the people, and so made these ineptitudes credible' (p.376).

Parkes made the assertion of continuity more forcefully in a book based on a series of lectures delivered at New York's Jewish Institute of Religion in 1946 and 1947.

> In our own day and within our own civilisation, more than six million deliberate murders are the consequence of teaching about Jews for which the Christian Church is ultimately responsible, and of an attitude to Judaism which is not only maintained by all the Christian Churches, but has its ultimate resting place in the teaching of the New Testament itself.[5]

This anchoring of lethal anti-Judaism in the New Testament goes beyond Isaac, who argued that the charge of deicide was the creation of post-Scriptural Christian thinkers who distorted the assertions of the Gospels.[6] Almost two decades later, in a survey of antisemitism focusing more on the 20th century, Parkes returned to this theme, asserting that 'there is no break in the line which leads from the beginning of the denigration of Judaism in the formative period of Christian history, from the exclusion of Jews from civil equality in the period of the Church's first triumph in the fourth century, through the horrors of the Middle Ages to the Death Camps of Hitler in our own day.'[7]

The model of continuity was given additional *gravitas* with the publication in 1961 of Raul Hilberg's classic study of the Nazi mechanism of genocide. *The Destruction of the European Jews*. To be sure, in his introductory chapter, Hilberg paid due respect to the novelty of the Nazi 'Final Solution': 'The destruction of the European Jews between 1933 and 1945 appears to us now as an unprecedented event in history. Indeed, in its dimensions and total configuration, nothing like it had every happened before.' But the force of this passage is to emphasize not the break from the past but the continuity with it. In words that would be cited so frequently by later writers that they would seem to have the status of a medieval author's citation of an 'Authority,' Hilberg continues,

> Yet, if we analyze this singularly massive upheaval, we discover that most of what happened in those twelve years had already happened before. The Nazi destruction process did not come out of a void; it was the culmination of a cyclical trend.... The missionaries of Christianity had said in effect: You have no right to live among us as Jews. The secular rulers who followed had proclaimed: You have no right to live among us. The German Nazis at last decreed: You have no right to live. These progressively more drastic goals brought in their wake a slow and steady growth of anti-Jewish action and anti-Jewish thinking. The process began with the attempt to drive the Jews into Christianity. The development was continued in order to force the victims into exile. It was finished when the Jews were driven to their deaths. The German Nazis, then, did not discard the past; they built upon it. They did not begin a development; they completed it.[8]

The assertion that 'most of what happened in those twelve years had already happened before' is buttressed by the frequently reproduced first Table of the book, setting out in parallel columns 'Canonical and Nazi Anti-Jewish Measures'. Twenty-two canonical laws are presented in chronological order, each one juxtaposed by an analogous Nazi ordinance dating from 1933 to 1942.[9] The impression is of organic development, a process naturally developing from the past to an ineluctable conclusion unprecedented 'in its dimensions and total configuration'. A few pages later, Hilberg does mention the limits and restraints on Christian destructiveness (p.8), but this seems trivial in comparison with the long list of parallels. Whether or not this was the intent of the author, the implication of this treatment seems to be that continuity can be established by a quantitative measure of similarities: 'most of what happened in those twelve years had already happened before.' The differences between Church doctrine or canon law and Nazi policy – pre-eminently, the doctrine re-affirmed by Popes and councils throughout the Middle Ages that Jews were not to be killed by Christians, juxtaposed with the Nazi policy of annihilation of all those included in their racial definition of 'Jew' – seem totally outweighed by the long list of 'parallels'.[10]

A significant and consistent academic argument for the continuity has been made over the past two decades by Hyam Maccoby, a British Jewish historian specializing in the period of Christian origins. Maccoby's central thesis appears to hark back to Jules Isaac. 'In Christendom, however, the Jews were diabolized,' he wrote, and 'this arises not from Jewish rejection of Jesus, but from the Jewish mythic role as the murderers, or deicides, of Jesus.'[11] The Jew thus becomes, in the title of one his works, the 'Sacred Executioner', the 'acolyte of Satan, the evil god'.

> Out of this came the cry, 'Who killed Christ?' This is the cry that was heard at the time of Hitler's Holocaust and at every other massacre of Jews in Christendom: this is the reason that Hitler's massacre of the Jews met with silent acquiescence from the vast majority of his subjects. Though public outcry and protests from the people brought a quick end to Hitler's program for the extermination of the insane and unfit, no such outcry or protest was forthcoming about the Jews. For it is endemic in Christendom that the Jews, the murderers of God, deserve all possible sufferings.[12]

This despite the fact that in the same essay (p.13), Maccoby concedes that 'Post-Christian anti-Semitism can thus be more dangerous to the Jews than Christian anti-Semitism itself, for in post-Christian anti-Semitism, the moral restraints of Christianity have disappeared,' an argument important to the discontinuity model.[13] He does not seem to consider whether the disappearance of the 'moral restraints of Christianity' might be at least as significant for Hitler's massacre of the Jews as the Christian myth he outlines. Elsewhere, Maccoby articulates what we have designated the 'nothing really new' aspect of the continuity model: 'As a result of the Gospel story, the Jews were made into an outcast, accursed nation in Christendom and were persecuted in all Christian lands. The massacre of 6 million Jews in Nazi Europe was only the most recent and worst of these persecutions.'[14]

Let us turn for the moment from professional academic studies to three popular works based on a model of continuity. In 1968, Dagobert D. Runes published a book entitled *The War Against the Jews*. While this appears to be an apt title for a book on the Holocaust – indeed, Lucy Dawidowicz chose the same title, with the clarifying dates 1933–1945, for her survey published seven years later – Runes's work turns out to be about 'The War of the Christian Churches against the Jews.' Responding to the innovations of Vatican II, which Runes considered to be totally inadequate, this is an openly polemical work, written in white-hot anger. The indictment is set out in the introduction:

> However, need I remind anyone that the supreme holocaust took place only a few decades ago under the very eyes of Christian Europe; that the bishops of Austria and Germany blessed the arms of the killers, and the Vicar of Christ looked out of his window in Rome while Jewish children and women were dragged to extermination camps?
>
> But the churches are not only guilty of ignoring the doom of a million Jewish children, choked to death along with their parents and grandparents.
>
> The churches are guilty of directly inciting this massacre by their persistent religious teaching based on this thesis: '*The* Jews killed God, therefore *all Jews* are damned.'[15]

Here we have the Isaac thesis that the doctrine of deicide leads directly to Auschwitz sharpened into an indictment of guilt through direct incitement to murder. The leap between the theological assertion '*all Jews* are damned' and the policy directive that all Jews must be killed is ignored, as is the fact that classical Christian doctrine consigned to damnation *all* those who did not accept the Christ through the Church for reasons that had nothing to do with the crucifixion, and certainly did not suggest that those who were destined to be damned had to be killed. Further on in the book, Runes suggests the link by associating Hitler himself with the deicide charge. 'Yet such is the nature of Christian "reasoning" that their theologians, like Hitler, hold all Jews responsible for what one or a few of them might have done thousands of years ago' (p.98).

This indictment is substantiated by an argument and a quotation that we encounter frequently in the literature. The argument has to do with the ability of Hitler to win mass support for his 'Final Solution': 'It was all the easier for Hitler to sway the Christian Germans and Austrians and much of the rest of Catholic Europe to his anti-Semitic philosophy because the Christians of Europe had for thousands of years been Church-trained to hold all Jews guilty of the failings of even one' (p.98). The quotation expresses Hitler's claim to be acting in continuity with the Christian past: 'Church anti-Semitism fitted Nazi anti-Semitism hand in glove' as Hitler said, "I am only continuing the work of the Catholic Church in my fight against the Jews"' (p.98).[16]

Runes continues in his introduction with a passage that echoes the words of Raul Hilberg cited above:

> The German Christians had centuries of preparation for Jew slaughter, first by the Catholic Church and then by the renegade monk Martin Luther ... ' (p.xvi).

> Indeed, everything Hitler did to the Jews, all the horrible, unspeakable misdeeds, had already been done to the smitten people before by the Christian churches, especially the Catholic Church (p.xvii).

The core of this book is in the form of a dictionary, with key terms and personalities presented in alphabetical order. Some examples of the entries will be analysed in the final section, below.

If Runes's book presents itself as a dictionary of antisemitism and persecution of Jews, a more recent book by Simon Wiesenthal sets forth a similar theme organized as a calendar. This too is a tribute to, and an embodiment of, what S.W. Baron famously called the 'lachrymose conception of Jewish history'. Continuity is suggested by the very structure of the book: beginning with 1 January and ending with 31 December, examples of persecution are listed chronologically day after day. One instance would be 25 August, for which the first date is '1255 – A Jew in Lincoln, England, is victim of a blood libel.' The second date is '1941 – During a night raid, several thousand Jews are taken from the ghetto of Minsk, Belorussian S.S.R, and murdered,' as well as other atrocities committed in the wake of the Germany invasion of the USSR, followed by other Holocaust-related events of 1942, 1943, and 1944 (p.191). No connection between the blood libel and the murder of Minsk Jews is explicitly claimed, but the very juxtaposition on the page implies the continuity. Yet the author goes beyond mere implication to assert, in the introduction, 'As this calendar shows, the story of the persecution of the Jews has always been directed by Christians: first of all by the Roman Catholic Church, then by the Orthodox Church' (p.9). How the *calendar* shows this is never explained. But the claim made later in the introduction brings us back to the motif of 'nothing new,' as in Runes without Hilberg's qualification about '*most* of what happened. ... ' In Wiesenthal's words, 'To sum up: The National Socialists did not invent anything new in the measures they took against the Jews; they simply took over existing models, such as the proof of Aryan ancestry, the stigmatization of the Jews, and the burning of their books, borrowing them from the Church' (p.17).[17]

A third popular example of the influence of the Hilberg passage is perhaps less expected: *The Road to Holocaust* by the enormously influential Protestant Evangelical writer Hal Lindsey. The author cites Hilberg's formulation extensively at the beginning of his book,[18] and then continues to mobilize the Holocaust as a powerful weapon in an internal theological debate within contemporary Evangelicals between premillennial and 'Dominion' theology. In a rapid survey of Christian history, which Lindsey calls 'The Trial from Origen to Auschwitz', the 3rd-century Greek Father is said to have provided the key to Christian anti-Semitism through his allegorical interpretation of Scripture that substitutes Christians for Jews as the 'true Israel,' shifting the Biblical prophecies of redemption to the Church. What follows is a familiar litany of Christian persecution: Constantine, the Crusades, Blood Libel, Desecration of the Host, Black Death, Martin Luther.

Lindsey's conclusion is that 'good Christian leaders with erroneous prophetic views laid the theological groundwork for evil men, often masquerading as Christians, to justify the extermination of the Jewish race. And sadly, it also influenced true Christians to join in with the prevailing anti-Semitism' (p.7). This legacy, he maintains, is still affirmed by 'Dominion' theology, which, by removing the Scriptural promises of restoration from the historical Jewish people opens the possible conclusion that continued Jewish existence has no real purpose. By contrast, Lindsey's own premillenialist theology, which provides an eschatological role for the Jews, safeguards against the murderous implications of the Christian doctrine, holding that even though God may discipline the Jewish people, 'woe to the man or nation that mistreats them' (p.24). Asserting, like Isaac, that the 'road to Holocaust' begins with the Church Fathers, Lindsey bypasses the theme of 'decide' and picks a theme more relevant to his own theological agenda – the claim of the Church to be the 'New Israel' – as crucial to the teaching of contempt. What he does not explain is why the premise that the Jewish people has lost its eschatological role would necessarily lead to the conclusion that it must be annihilated, or why Christian leaders who were saddled with this theology never drew the radical conclusion that the Nazis did.[19]

To conclude this quick survey with a recent publication, the central thesis in the highly controversial book by Daniel Goldhagen is not directly related to our topic, and his emphasis on the distinctiveness of German 'exterminationist antisemitism' might appear as a rejection of the continuity model. Yet the first two chapters situate it clearly within the continuity model, indeed make it perhaps the most important expression of this model written in the 1990s. 'European antisemitism is a corollary of Christianity.'[20] For the 'underlying need to think ill of Jews, to hate them' is 'woven into the fabric of Christianity itself' (p.42). Why? First, Christians in each generation felt the psychological need to condemn Jews in order in order to justify their own theological beliefs. In addition, Christians thought their religion superseded Judaism. 'Therefore, Jews as Jews ought to disappear from the earth' (p.49). Finally, all Jews at all times were 'Christ-killers' (p.50). Consequently, 'the very definition of what it meant to be a Christian entailed a thoroughgoing and visceral hostility to Jews, just as it did to evil, and to the devil' (p.51). The fact that 'the Church wanted not to kill the Jews...but to convert them' is presented as if it were a trivial detail compared with the immensity of medieval European hatred of the Jew (p.53).

Thus, at least from the late 11th century, antisemitism has been a 'permanent feature of Christian civilization' (p.39). At times it may not be manifest, at times it may appear in different garbs, but it is always present, an underlying reality that is always the same (pp. 39, 40, 43): 'the enduring and bitter hatred of Jews by the Church, the Christian clergy, and the people of Europe' (p.52), a 'ubiquitous and profound hatred of the ghettoized

Jews that was integral to German culture as Germany emerged from the middle ages and early modern times' (p.55). In the 19th century, 'antisemitism shed much of its religious medieval garb and adopted new, secular clothing' (p.43) – again the apparent differences are only an external cloak that conceals the reified essence beneath. This is the background that explains 'why the German people so easily accepted the tenets of Nazi antisemitism and supported the Nazis' anti-Jewish policies' (p.47). Before this stunning example of groundless, generalized assertion – maintaining pervasiveness without data, ubiquity without manifestations, sameness despite the appearance of change – conventional historical argumentation falls mute. Although the book appears to be of a different genre, and Goldhagen would not argue that there was nothing new in the Nazi mass murder, these first two chapters suggest affinities with the works of Runes and Wiesenthal described above.

THE DISCONTINUITY MODEL ('FUNDAMENTALLY NOVEL')

The alternative position to the continuity model does not, of course, sever all connection between Nazi anti-Jewish doctrine or policy and the past. Rather, in assessing the factors that led to the 'Final Solution' – whether the content of Hitler's worldview, the rhetoric of Nazi antisemitic propaganda, the support of the German people for the Nazi regime, the conception and implementation of a programme to annihilate physically all Jews in Europe under German control, and the behaviour of the bystanders – considerably more weight is given to 20th-century dynamics than to the legacy from the New Testament, the Church Fathers, and the Middle Ages.

This position was outlined at an early stage by the French historian Marcel Simon, who specialized not in the 20th century but in early Christianity. Following his *Verus Israel*, a 1948 book that was to become classic, Simon wrote reviews of Jules Isaac's *Jésus et Israël* (1948) and *Genèse de l'antisémitisme* (1956) contesting the continuity that Isaac claimed. A Postscript added to a 1964 reprinting of *Verus Israel* provided a measured response to Isaac's assertions:

> The more general influence of the teaching of the various Christian churches and the part it played in spreading anti-Semitic ideas cannot of course be disputed. . . . But to argue from this that the Church must bear the essential responsibility, even though it be an indirect responsibility, for the Nazi atrocities, or *to see the gas chambers of Auschwitz as the natural result of the Church's teaching* – this is to take a step that the historian will hesitate to regard as legitimate. It seems hardly likely, on a priori grounds, that in an age as secularized as ours, and even more so, under a regime as utterly hostile to Christian ideas as that of the Nazis, it should be the theological components of anti-Semitism that are the determining factors in it. . . . [21]

This is merely an argument from plausibility about the relative importance religious and non-religious influences in a 'secularized' age. Simon then continues to sketch – in general terms, as to be expected from a non-specialist in a book that focuses on an entirely different period – the alternative, secular components of Nazi ideology that he considers more significant:

> If Hitler's Germany execrated and massacred Jews, it was, first, because Nazism saw in them, by means of gross generalizations and simplifications, the principal subscribers to contemptible ideologies, democracy, political and economic liberalism, cosmopolitanism, and Marxism. Second, it was because they were categorized by a pseudoscientific racism as representatives of a biological stock that was distinct and unassimilable. It must not be forgotten, when the attempt is made to connect the Nazis' anti-Jewish persecutions too closely with Christian teaching, that the Jewish massacre was not the only example of genocide engaged in by the Third Reich [. . . the Gypsies, for example] (p. 397).

Finally, he highlights the fundamental difference between Christian doctrine and Nazi ideology:

> From the Church's point of view, at any period, a Jew was characterized by his religion. If he was converted, he ceased to be a Jew, and the ultimate aim was just that, the conversion of Israel. The anti-Semitism of the Church was, if one may so express it, provisional and conditional. For Hitler's anti-Semites, a Jew turned Christian was still a Jew, because a Jew was characterized by his race, and it was neither desirable nor possible to change his ethnic characteristics. Total extermination was the only solution. This, in my opinion, marks a fundamental difference that forbids us to establish any very definite or close connecting link or continuity between the two (p.398).

The implication is that the racial definition of the Jew and the commitment to total extermination far outweigh all the similarities that can be listed.

Subsequent writers, many of whom, like Simon, were historians who specialized in the pre-modern period, picked up and developed these elements in greater detail. An especially noteworthy example was the presentation by Yosef Yerushalmi, a historian then at Harvard, later at Columbia, at a pioneering International Symposium on the Holocaust held at New York's Cathedral of Saint John the Divine in 1974. Formally, this paper was a response to the presentation of Rosemary Radford Ruether, whose *Faith and Fratricide*, published in the same year, was a searing indictment of Christian anti-Semitism in the New Testament and the Church Fathers, which she described theologically as 'the left hand of Christology'. Neither in the conference paper nor in the book did Ruether make the case for direct continuity between Christian doctrine and the death camps; she did argue that modern antisemitism 'takes its chief mythology directly from the Christian legacy,' which it both continues and transforms.[22]

Yerushalmi's response is actually to the continuity model that is not explicit in Ruether, but was held by others, as noted above. Without defending the tradition of Christian anti-Judaism or minimizing its significance, he picks up Ruether's passing comment that 'preservation' as well as 'reprobation' was part of the church's doctrine of the Jewish people, and argues that this aspect of Christian tradition, translated into a continuous legal tradition that tolerated Jews and protected them from physical harm, was by no means self-evident and was unquestionably crucial for Jewish survival. That aspect of traditional church doctrine and law reveals that modernity brought a rupture from the past.

> The crucial problem in the shift from medieval to modern anti-Semitism is that while the Christian tradition of 'reprobation' continued into the modern era, the Christian tradition of 'preservation' fell by the wayside and was no longer operative.... Surely there must be some significance in the fact that the Holocaust took place in our secular century, and *not* in the Middle Ages.... The climactic anti-Jewish measure of which the medieval Christian state was capable was always expulsion and, on rare occasions, forced conversion. The Holocaust was the work of a thoroughly modern, neopagan state.[23]

In addition to the substantive references to medieval Jewish history revealing a policy quite different from that of the 'Final Solution,' Yerushalmi's argument presents a methodological challenge to the continuity model. Those who hold it need to explain why genocide, though conceivable and feasible, was never sanctioned by Christian leaders in the Middle Ages. Furthermore, an assessment of the relationship between the Holocaust and the past must weigh and evaluate not only similarities, but differences. The presentation of the Nazi regime not as Christianity in a new disguise but as something fundamentally different, an eruption of paganism, would be taken up by many subsequent writers in this camp.

About the same time, the theologian Richard Rubenstein was making a similar argument. 'Before the twentieth century, the Christian religious tradition was both the source of much traditional anti-Jewish hostility and an effective barrier against the final murderous step. Something changed in the twentieth century ... The methods proposed were no longer limited by traditional religious or moral restraints.'[24] This was a different way of formulating the point by emphasizing not just the Christian doctrine of 'preservation', but the role of Christianity, and religion in general, in fostering restraints that safeguarded against mass murder in the past. The Holocaust therefore needs to be explained primarily by recourse to 20th-century phenomena.

Perhaps the most extensive effort to assess the relationship between the Holocaust and the past is Steven Katz's projected three-volume *The Holocaust in Historical Context*. Katz by no means minimizes the virulence of Christian anti-Jewish teachings, citing Chrysostom in support of the generalization that 'to hate Jews is for the church fathers a Christian *mitzvah*' (p.259). Yet despite his assertion, as we shall see below, that this legacy of hatred was a necessary precondition for the Nazi programme, he insists on a rupture model, repudiating any suggestion that the death camps were the logical conclusion or the natural consequence of the older teaching of contempt. 'Auschwitz is emblematic of the revolutionary overthrow of Christian dogma rather than a sign of its fulfillment' (p.234). Perhaps in a wry allusion to Emil Fackenheim's famous '614th commandment' (not to hand Hitler another, posthumous victory),[25] Katz entitles a section of his book 'The Eleventh Christian Commandment,' not – as might be predicted from the quotation above – 'Thou shalt hate Jews,' but rather, 'Thou shalt Not Annihilate the Jews.' Yet this passage continues with an echo not of Fackenheim but of Yerushalmi (who surprisingly, despite Katz's exhaustive annotation, is not referenced here):

> Though Christendom possessed the power, over the course of nearly fifteen hundred years, to destroy that segment of the Jewish people it dominated, it chose not to do so. Though many, many, Jews were killed by Christians, most Jews resident in Christian states were not murdered. And they were not murdered because the physical extirpation of Jewry was never, at any time, the official policy of any church or of any Christian state. Rather than actively seeking to eliminate Jewry, the ultimate luminescent irony, coincident with the accession of the church to wordly power, is that Christian dogmatics entailed protecting Jews and Judaism from extinction.[26]

This is followed by close to a hundred pages reviewing the history of Christian persecution from the First Crusade through Luther in support of his insistence on discontinuity from Nazi policies, concluding:

> Christianity can be fairly and accurately described, for all the voluminous violence it legitimated and unloosed, as an ambivalent, cautious, mediating, moral, nongenocidal program, whereas Nazism, in sharp contrast, must be described as a resolute, unhesitating, nonmediating, immoral, genocidal project ... [I]t is modernity's adaptation and transformation of the Christian legacy, by virtue of categories and conceptions that are unique to it, that is decisive. Christian anti-Judaism and Nazi antisemitism are related, but they are not alike.[27]

The passages cited above indicate two different impulses that might serve as the 'decisive' influence on the murderous character of Nazi antisemitism: pagan amorality and modern secularism. Both of these have been emphasized in statements of the Catholic Church, which clearly advance a discontinuity model of the Holocaust's relationship to Christianity. In August 1987, Pope John Paul II stated that 'Reflection upon the *Shoah* shows us to what terrible consequences the lack of faith in God and a contempt for man created in his image can lead.'[28] Ten years later, the Pope affirmed that there was indeed a legacy of Christian anti-Judaism, in that 'the wrong and unjust interpretations of the New Testament relating to the Jewish people' had contributed to feelings of 'hostility' on the part of Christians toward the Jews. But this was quite different from Nazi doctrine: 'a pagan anti-Semitism – which in its essence was equal to anti-Christianity'.[29] The 1998 Vatican document entitled 'We Remember: A Reflection on the Shoah,' makes a similar point: 'The Shoah was the work of a thoroughly modern neo-pagan regime...Its anti-Semitism had its roots outside of Christianity, and in pursuing its aims, it did not hesitate to oppose the Church and persecute her members also.'[30] Especially among the more conservative Catholic writers, we find this theme of Nazism as eruption of paganism, or 'neo-paganism', into heart of Christian Europe.[31]

In addition to the claim that Christian anti-Judaism had no influence on the Nazi worldview, we find many supporters of the discontinuity model making the argument reflected in the 1998 Vatican Statement: that Nazi antisemitism could not have been the result of the Christian legacy, as Hitler and the Nazi regime were fundamentally anti-Christian as well as profoundly anti-Jewish. The number of priests killed by the Nazis is frequently invoked, although generally without any suggestion that this was in the same category as the systematic murder of all European Jews. Secondly, the record of Christian clergy and institutions saving Jews from probable death by concealing them is regularly cited as support for the claim that Christian doctrine did not support genocide. This data is used to counterbalance claims made in support of the continuity model about Christian collaboration with, or passive acquiescence in, the Nazi regime even while the Jews were being murdered.

A MIDDLE GROUND ('IMPOSSIBLE WITHOUT', 'NECESSARY PRECONDITION')

An intermediate position between the continuity and discontinuity models is represented by those who assert that, although the Holocaust was in some fundamental way different from persecution of Jews in the past, and that factors other than the Christian past were crucial in conceiving, articulating and executing the Nazi genocide, the tradition of Christian anti-Judaism was necessary for the Holocaust to have taken place. The fundamental difference between this and the continuity model is the insistence that the Christian background alone would not have led to genocide had it not been for other intellectual, social, and political factors deriving from the historical experience of the 19th and 20th centuries. Frequently, this assertion is simply made as if it were self-evident; sometimes it is expressed through various metaphors that we shall note below. Where further explanation is given, it may be that Hitler's antisemitism would never have received the support it did in German society, or that the German or Polish populations would not have looked on with indifference as Jews were rounded up, deported and killed, had they not been heirs to the Christian teaching of contempt. Sometimes the behaviour of church leaders is invoked as evidence. In most cases, it should be noted, the argument pertains to the behaviour not of the perpetrators but of the bystanders, although this distinction is frequently not made explicit.

Our survey of representative statements of this position will begin with the formulations of several historians. Here is Nora Levin, in her 1968 survey:

> [T]he Christian view of the Jew throughout European history *formed the basis* of the anti-Jewish propaganda worked up by Nazi minds and accepted as a program of action by large

numbers of Germans. The minds may have been sick and the German people too susceptible to old myths about Jews because of their extreme fears, hatreds and envies, but the key
formulation had had a long history. *The destruction of European Jewry could not have happened
without this historic preparation.*[32]

In his paper given at the 1974 Saint John the Divine Symposium on the Holocaust, Yosef
Yerushalmi maintains a similar position, though in the context of emphasizing the break
between the Christian past and the Holocaust. 'There is no question but that Christian
anti-Semitism through the ages helped create the climate and mentality in which
genocide, once conceived, could be achieved with little or no opposition,' he wrote.
'But even if we grant that Christian teaching was a *necessary cause* leading to the
Holocaust, it was surely not a *sufficient* one.'[33] Significantly, the burden of Yerushalmi's
argument is to establish that the Christian legacy was not sufficient to explain the Final
Solution. That it was a 'necessary cause' is conceded virtually without argument.

A few years later, Byron Sherwin, writing on 'The Ideological Antecedents of the
Holocaust', provides a similar formulation in an entirely different context. His purpose is
to show the similarities between the Christian past and the Final Solution. After
reviewing many examples of discrimination culminating with Martin Luther, he concludes that 'it should be apparent that Christian anti-Semitism was a contributing factor
to Nazi anti-Semitism, Christian teachings were a *necessary precondition* for the Holocaust.'[34] He then quotes James Parkes's statement of continuity that the 'six million
deliberate murders are the consequence of the teachings about the Jews for which the
Christian Church is ultimately responsible' (see above at n.5). It is only the continuation
of his discussion, treating the importance of modern developments, that removes him
from an unambiguous stance within the continuity model.

Like Yerushalmi, Steven Katz defends a position that we have identified with the
discontinuity model, emphasizing the innovation of the Nazi programme. Nevertheless,
he too asserts the necessary if not sufficient role of the Christian anti-Jewish legacy.
Negative Christian teachings about the Jews were 'the *absolute precondition*' for Nazi
antisemitism, a phrase that Katz explains to mean that 'the Sho'ah would never have
occurred had there been no classical Christian tradition of antisemitism.' Shifting to the
level of responsibility for the mass murder, Katz reiterates this formulation: 'The earliest
Christian teachers bear no direct responsibility for the Sho'ah, but they bear a heavy
responsibility for transforming "the Jews" into a principle of contrariness and evil that
has become an abiding legacy in Christian and post-Christian ideology, without which
the Sho'ah would have been impossible.'[35]

To broaden the selection of evidence beyond the professional historian, we shall
consider several examples of figures identified not primarily as academics but as religious
thinkers. On the Jewish side, quite striking is the formulation by one of the most highly
respected rabbinic authorities of the past generation, Rabbi Joseph Soloveitchik. According to a recently published anthology of passages from his oral discourses, in a lecture
delivered in Boston on Hanukkah of 1971, Soloveitchik reported to his audience what he
told to 'a member of the Catholic hierarchy from Rome'. Addressing the problem of the
passivity of millions of Christians who would have tried to help a wounded dog yet
'witnessed the slaughter of six million Jews, among them little babies and infants,' Rabbi
Soloveitchik reviewed the anti-Jewish doctrines of the Church, stating, "the idea that the
Jew is a subhuman is a Catholic idea"' (2:162). His conclusion:

> Yes, Hitler was not a Catholic.[36] If not for your doctrine of the eternal wandering Jew,
> however, Hitler could not have succeeded. If not for your constant and continued preaching

that the Jew blocks the arrival of your Messiah, the Holocaust could not have taken place. Perhaps you are not directly responsible. But indirectly you are responsible. You are the culprit! If not for your teachings, such cruelty *could not have taken place*.[37]

In this reading, it is not Hitler himself (perhaps along with all the most virulently antisemitic Nazi leaders) who reveals the decisive influence of negative Christian doctrines,[38] but those millions who, by their support of Hitler or passive indifference, allowed the Holocaust to happen. The noted Jewish theologian Emil Fackenheim, in somewhat more dispassionate language, articulates a similar position: 'Indeed, the Christian failure vis-à-vis Nazi Jew-hatred *would have been impossible* without a history of Jew-hatred on the part of Christian saints, among them St. Chrysostom, St. Augustine, St. Thomas, and Martin Luther.'[39]

Many Christian thinkers have also found this formulation compelling. Invoking the classic formulation of Jules Isaac, the Presbyterian Church USA, in a 1987 statement on Jewish–Christian relations, acknowledged 'in repentance the church's long and deep complicity in the proliferation of anti-Jewish attitudes and actions through its "teaching of contempt" for the Jews'. In its explication of this passage, it affirmed that this teaching was a 'major ingredient that *made possible* the monstrous policy of annihilation of Jews by Nazi Germany.'[40]

As we have seen, the main thrust of official Catholic discourse has been within the discontinuity model, expressing remorse for negative Christian teachings about the Jews and Judaism but insisting that the Nazi antisemitism leading to the Holocaust was not connected with this tradition. By contrast, the controversial German Catholic theologian Hans Küng, in a massive work on Judaism published in English in 1992, maintained an intermediate position. After reproducing Raul Hilberg's list of parallels between canonical and Nazi anti-Jewish acts, Küng continues:

> There was never any convincing resistance against the persecution of the Jews on a broad front by the official churches either. Why not? The basic answer can already be given here – in the light of the story which I told in the first part of this book. It is connected with the deeply-rooted religious, Christian anti-Judaism which even for a Catholic like Joseph Goebbels was the basis of his commitment to National Socialism – along with the Führer cult. Bitter though this recognition may be, it cannot be passed over in silence. The racist antisemitism which reached its climax of terrorism in the Holocaust *would not have been possible without* the prehistory of the religious anti-Judaism of the Christian church extending over almost two thousand years.[41]

The last sentence of this statement was cited as authoritative in an article published just this past year by a Jewish historian from Chicago: 'The prominent German theologian Hans Küng pointed out a fact now widely accepted among Christian scholars of the Holocaust: "The racist antisemitism . . . two thousand years."' The assertion of the necessary role played by Christian doctrine has become a 'fact' representing the consensus of Christian scholars.[42]

Thus those who stake out a position in this middle ground tend to do so by use of terminology drawn from logic: 'a necessary precondition', 'impossible without'. But they also frequently resort to an array of metaphors intended to illustrate the connection between the two phenomena. Some examples of this trope will be instructive.

The metaphor of roots had already been used as the subtitle of the English edition of Jules Isaac's classic study, *The Teaching of Contempt: Christian Roots of Anti-Semitism*; this has been echoed by such authors as Rosemary Ruether in her *Faith and Fratricide: The Theological Roots of Anti-Semitism*, and Leonore Siegel-Wenschkewitz in her 1984 article, 'Christian Anti-Judaism as the Root of Anti-Semitism'.[43] The roots metaphor implies that the new phenomenon was indeed dependent upon its predecessor, as a plant cannot grow without roots, and organically connected to it, even though it is both in appearance and substance something different. The liberal Protestant theologian Paul van Buren has made an even stronger claim, linking Christian doctrine not just with modern antisemitism but with the death camps, by asserting that 'the roots of Hitler's final solution are to be found . . . in the proclamation of the very *kerygma* ['message'] of the early Christians.'[44]

Similarly organic, but implying a somewhat less direct relationship is the statement by the Catholic theologian John Pawlikowski, 'There is no question that Christian anti-Semitism provided an *indispensable seedbed* for Nazis.'[45] While the metaphor of 'roots' implies something about the origins of Nazi doctrine, the 'indispensable seedbed' or 'fertile field' metaphor suggests something about the environment in which the Nazi doctrine could be accepted and thrive. Quite close to this is the 1982 statement of the World Council of Churches, 'Teachings of contempt for Jews and Judaism in certain Christian traditions proved a *spawning ground* for the evil of the Nazi Holocaust.'[46] Or the assertion by Steven Katz that 'the millennia of Christian violence, both conceptual and physical, were crucial to creating the *matrix* for the rise of Naz-ism.'[47]

Still other metaphors apply something about the process of development from the old to the new. The scientific language of 'evolution' suggests a natural development, if one that leaves open the possibility of mutation, as in the statement, 'In the *evolution* of modern anti-Semitism from medieval anti-Semitism, there were continuities and there were discontinuities.'[48] Still a natural development but suggesting a process that is rather unexpected and obviously unwelcome is the language of cancer employed in a statement by the United Church of Christ in 1987: 'The Church's frequent portrayal of the Jews as blind, recalcitrant, evil, and rejected by God . . . has been a factor in the shaping of anti-Jewish attitudes of societies and the policies of governments. The most devastating *lethal metastasis* of this process occurred in our own century during the Holocaust.'[49] One of the most complex metaphors, attempting to express both forceful rupture from and connectedness with the past is in Arthur Cohen's formulation that the Holocaust was 'a historical explosion whose detonation leads by subtle conductors back into the theological matrix of Christianity itself where the igniting spark had its origin'.[50]

Such metaphors may have been intended as nothing more than colourful language. But as the discourse of antisemitism teaches us, metaphors – the blood-sucking parasite, the infectious micro-organism, the gangrenous appendix – can be powerful indeed. The choice of figurative language implies something about the assertion being made, whether or not the author intends it. In addition, those subjected to vivid metaphorical discourse not infrequently tend to start thinking in terms of the image rather than of the under-lying reality. How would one *prove* (or disprove) that the 'roots' of Hitler's antisemitism are in traditional Christian doctrine – through a rigorous history of ideas approach, or a biographical study of the works he read and the people who influenced him? How would one *prove* (or disprove) that Christian tradition provided an 'indispensable seedbed' or 'spawning ground' for Nazi antisemitism? By attempting to correlate the support for anti-Jewish legislation and deportation with the level of religious affiliation within different circles of German society? One often has the impression that the use of metaphors to express a relationship seems to substitute for an actual historical argument based on evidence, as if mere picturesque assertion is enough.

EVIDENCE AND ARGUMENTATION

This leads us to an analysis of some of the evidence and argumentation used in defending the various models. To begin with the previous section, assertions that the legacy of Christian anti-Judaism was the necessary precondition for the Holocaust, which would have been impossible without it, or the various metaphors that imply this assertion, need more careful analysis than they are usually given.[51] Often, such claims are simply made without argument as if they were self-evident. But what does it actually mean to assert that one historical event would have been impossible without a prior event? Is the claim about Christian anti-Judaism analogous to the assertion that the Holocaust would have been impossible without World War I, or the German defeat in World War I, or the conditions imposed upon Germany in the Treaty of Versailles, for without these Hitler would never have come to power? Or that it would have been impossible without the invention of the machine gun, or of the steam engine to power the trains that moved millions of Jews to the death camps? While such propositions are indeed defensible, we ordinarily do not include the architects of the Treaty of Versailles or the inventor of the steam engine among those who share responsibility for the Holocaust. Yet in most cases, assertions about the indispensability of the legacy of Christian anti-Judaism are made precisely in order to affirm some measure of Christian responsibility. How do we determine which of a number of theoretically necessary preconditions is the most significant?[52]

Furthermore, how strong is the argument that the Christian legacy was actually indispensable for the Holocaust? Concerning the behaviour of the perpetrators, there is an ongoing debate about the role of antisemitic hatred in comparison with other factors such as obedience to authority and peer pressure in motivating Germans to take part in the actual killing. But even accepting for the sake of argument the decisive importance of antisemitism, the question remains whether receptivity to an antisemitic ideology needed to be grounded in a centuries-old tradition. Is it inconceivable that this totalitarian regime could have sufficiently indoctrinated the German population in the eight years between 1933 and 1941 to produce both acquiescence in deportation and participation in killing without any legacy from the past? Other regimes have carried out mass murder of parts of their own population without an ancient tradition of hostility. The massacres in Pol Pot's Cambodia, which rapidly followed after a fierce ideological onslaught that targeted members of specific social strata or classes, seem a particularly dramatic example, but other communist regimes as well have demonstrated the power of propaganda, combining ideology and dehumanizing rhetoric, to expose new groups of opponents to annihilation.[53] This is not, of course, to equate communist mass murder with Nazi genocide, but simply to question whether it is self-evident that the destruction of European Jewry would have been inconceivable without the Christian legacy of opprobrium.

But why were the Jews selected as the scapegoat, the enemy, the embodiment of evil by Hitler and the Nazis? Surely, as has been frequently argued, this can be explained only on the basis of the Christian demonization of the Jews in late antiquity and the Middle Ages.[54] Yet there are questions on both sides of this argument. First, the presentation of the Jew as the Enemy, the Antichrist, the paradigmatic ally of the devil, is an oversimplification of Christian thought. There was, of course, a tradition identifying the Antichrist with the Jew, but there were other traditions identifying Christians (including the Pope), or the Turk, in this role.[55] In some ways, Jews were understood to have the right to a more protected position in Christian society than were others, especially Christian heretics. In the 1060s, Pope Alexander II wrote to the bishops of

Spain to assert that while it was legitimate to go to war against Muslims in the *Reconquista*, it was a sin 'to bring about the slaughter of those whom divine charity has perhaps predestined for salvation,' namely, the Jews.[56]

In explaining the Nazi selection of the Jews, might not the dynamics of defining national identity by the vehement exclusion of a group deemed 'outside' be as significant as the specific identity of that outsider? What other group in Germany could have served this purpose? To raise a hypothetical, if there had been a significant minority of black Africans living in Germany in 1933, can we say with certainty that they would not have been targeted for annihilation alongside the Jews – without the legacy of Christian teaching of contempt?[57] All of this is to suggest that the assertion of the necessity of Christian anti-Judaism to explain the Holocaust is much more complicated, and considerably more argument is needed to prove it, than is usually assumed.

To move to the continuity model, many of the arguments and evidence evinced in its support seem to me to be especially problematic. One of the most common characteristics of such argumentation is selectivity: taking the most negative anti-Jewish statements scattered throughout Christian literature and the most devastating acts performed by Christians and gathering them as a presentation of the Christian tradition, without any effort to place them in a proper historical context, assess their representative character, evaluate their influence, or balance them with more positive expressions (a polemical style familiar from the work of such Christian writers as Johannes Eisenmenger, who used it in his *Entdektes Judentums* to present a devastating portrait of Talmudic Judaism).

Dagobert Runes's *War Against the Jews*, a fierce anti-Christian polemic, is a good example of this. As noted above, it is in the form of a dictionary. His entry on Bernard of Clairvaux, for example, reads as follows, 'Of the Jews, the saintly philosopher said: They are no better than beasts, in fact 'More than bestial...They are of the Devil.' Julius Streicher urged the killing of all Jews as the 'offspring of the Devil' (p.19). One would never know from this of Bernard's explicit warning in his call for the Second Crusade that the Jews are under divine protection, not to be killed, not to mention his travel to the Rhineland to intervene personally and put an end to anti-Jewish violence when it erupted, an action recorded gratefully in Jewish sources. The line is drawn directly from Bernard to Streicher to genocide, when all that the material shows is the ongoing influence of a verse from the Gospel of John (8:44).[58] As indicated above, Simon Weisenthal's book, by its very nature, exemplifies this same kind of selectivity by including only acts of anti-Jewish persecution. A recent book by Daniel Cohn-Sherbok called *The Crucified Jew: Twenty Centuries of Christian Antisemitism*, uses the same approach, perhaps more surprisingly in that it purports to be a historical survey.

Another characteristic of argumentation is the removal of medieval policies from their proper historical context, presenting them together with modern phenomena that are actually quite different. This point can be made about Raul Hilberg's table juxtaposing canonical and Nazi anti-Jewish measures, the enormous influence of which we have noted above. In many cases, especially pertaining to the 1930s, the Nazi were indeed attempting to reinstate the older pre-Emancipation status of Jews. But in some cases, Hilberg's juxtaposition is patently forced. For example, 'Construction of new synagogues prohibited', attributed to the 'Council of Oxford, 1222' (theoretically in effect since a 423 Edict of Theodosius II, though rarely enforced) is juxtaposed with 'Destruction of synagogues in the entire Reich' on Kristallnacht. Even where the parallels are more convincing, the difference in context makes the Nazi measures more than just a repetition of their medieval 'precedents'. The principle that Jews (as well as Muslims) should be identifiable by their clothing, introduced in Christendom in the Fourth Lateran Council of 1215, meant one thing in medieval Christian society where *every* social group was identifiable by conventions of dress; it meant something quite different in occupied Poland of 1939, where marking was for the sole purpose of opprobrium and persecution. The Jewish quarters of the Middle Ages were entirely different from the Nazi ghettos of occupied Poland.[59]

Disregard for historical context is illustrated also by Byron Sherwin's 1979 essay on 'Ideological Antecedents of the Holocaust.' Clearly drawing from Hilberg's parallel tables, he asserts that 'The canonical measures taken in the Middle Ages began to clearly foreshadow legal measures taken against the Jews in Nazi Germany.' He then continues with specifics:

> In medieval Christian Europe, Jewish rights were legislated out of existence and Jewish degradation became the legally, socially, and theologically accepted norm...For example, concrete legal and social measures helped to insure Jewish degradation and serfdom. Medieval legal codes depicted Jews as a species unto themselves. Compared to deer and other animals in the royal forest, they became the *property* of Kings. For example, the penalty in a number of kingdoms for killing a Jew was a fine for having destroyed the King's property (p.29).[60]

Even the casual reader might note the contradiction between 'Jewish rights were legislated out of existence' – the quickest look at the charter literature or a code such as the *Siete Partidas* reveals how mistaken this is – and the legislation cited imposing a fine for killing Jews. The comparison between Jews and deer in the royal forest, in its medieval context, was clearly intended to communicate royal *protection*, but here it is implied to be akin to the German signs 'No dogs or Jews allowed'. Perhaps on a more subtle level, the concept of Jewish 'serfdom', which in its medieval context was not at all the same as the status of the actual serfs, seems invoked to suggest that Christianity reduced the Jews to property akin to black slaves in the American South. All of this exemplifies the distortions and inaccuracies of the 'precursorism' of presenting earlier material in light of events that occurred considerably later and suggesting that they share something of the character of the later manifestation.[61]

A third characteristic of this argumentation is the use of broad, simplistic generalizations that simply cannot be documented (or, in some cases, even plausibly defended). Consider the following passage from Sherwin:

> By the fifth century, the Jew was no longer described as a human being. He was a demonic monster, a theological abstraction, a useless obsolescence, a subhuman creature. The scene for the future was already set before the Middle Ages. The 'moral' and theological basis for persecuting and even for murdering Jews had been established. Jews might be killed because they killed Christ; Jews might be oppressed because it is the will of God; Jews must be subdued because otherwise their demonic power will contaminate or will destroy mankind. Thus the struggle against the Jews was portrayed as a self-defensive battle for God against the Devil.[62]

No note is provided for these statements. The consistent use of the passive tense ('was no longer described,' 'was already set,' 'had been established,' 'was portrayed') camouflages the statements by removing any need for informing the reader precisely who among the Church Fathers is doing this describing and portraying, and whether this rhetoric (some of which but not all can indeed be found in Chrysostom) was universal, prevalent, or relatively anomalous. To be sure, Patristic literature is filled with anti-Jewish formulations, but the dominant themes, as presented in the classic (and by no means apologetic) treatment by Rosemary Ruether, are quite different from those stated here. 'Demonic monster'? A 'subhuman creature'? A ' "moral" and theological basis for ... murdering Jews'? 'Their demonic power will contaminate or will destroy mankind'? A 'self-defensive battle for God'? All of this sounds like a well-known passage from *Mein Kampf* projected back upon the Church Fathers, not like the Church Fathers themselves. To claim a warrant for genocide in the patristic literature when Augustine forcefully argued precisely the opposite – that it was a sin, against God's will, to kill Jews – is puzzling indeed.

In our first section, we noted how Dagobert D. Runes recapitulates Hilberg's claim that most of the Nazi anti-Jewish measures had already happened before, but in a more extreme form ('*everything* that Hitler did to the Jews'). The culmination of this passage connects even the gas chambers and crematoria with alleged Christian precedents. In a series of grotesque generalizations nowhere anchored in specific realities, Runes paints a picture of Jewish life under Christian Europe:

> from one end of Europe to the other the almighty Catholic Church put the Jews to the pyre and sword. No child, no woman, no invalid was spared. . . . Wild agitators of hate against the Jews, armed with supreme powers by the Church, were sent through all Christian lands. Wherever they passed, the pyres were built up, with whimpering flesh dying an agonized death at the hands of executioners with the big silver cross dangling from their necks' (p.xvi).

He then makes the most extraordinary claim for the absolute lack of Nazi originality I have seen in print:

> The isolation of Jews in ghetto camps, the wearing of the yellow spot, the burning of Jewish books, and finally the burning of the people – Hitler learned it all from the Catholic Church. However, the Church burned the Jewish women and children alive, while Hitler granted them a quicker death, choking them first with gas (p.xvii).

In this daredevil rhetorical cartwheel, Hitler becomes merciful in comparison with his medieval Christian predecessors. It would be difficult to find a more blatant example of mythos parading as historical reality.

We have already cited Raul Hilberg's now celebrated formulation: 'The missionaries of Christianity had said in effect: You have no right to live among us as Jews. The secular rulers who followed had proclaimed: You have no right to live among us. The German Nazis at last decreed: You have no right to live. These progressively more drastic goals brought in their wake a slow and steady growth of anti-Jewish action and anti-Jewish thinking.' In moving from rhetoric to historical reality, one might be permitted to wonder about the basis for the first two generalizations? Of course there were Christians who tried to convert Jews, as they tried to convert pagans and Muslims. But who said (even 'in effect') 'You have no right to live among us as Jews'? The official doctrine of the Church – not always observed in practice to be sure, but consistently maintained by the leadership – was that conversion could not be coerced, it had to come from conviction resulting from persuasion. Even those preachers who addressed Jewish audiences forced by the authorities to attend knew that Jews had the 'right' to ignore their blandishments and remain, obstinately, in their 'blindness'. And while there were indeed some 'secular rulers' who expelled the Jews from their domains, many of them did not, and those who did invariably gave the Jews an option to remain by converting. So the more accurate quotation would be to attribute to *some* secular rulers (not to the 'missionaries'), 'You have no right to live among us *as Jews*.' Put that way, the natural progression suggested by Hilberg from conditional expulsion to genocide, the 'slow and steady growth of anti-Jewish action and anti-Jewish thinking' seems far less obvious than

Hilberg would make it, less an organic development from the past than a revolutionary break.

Apparently following Hilberg's lead, Nora Levin states, 'Historic Christianity would not tolerate the Jew in his (sic) midst – the Jew who stubbornly refused to accept Christian truth and who would not convert' (p.10). Her evidence for this statement is the expulsions of late middle ages. But do these expulsions – all of them decisions by secular rulers, not Church officials – justify the generalization about 'historic Christianity'? What about the Jewish communities that were indeed tolerated in Christian Europe, including the Papal States? What about Poland, from which there was never a universal expulsion? How can one reconcile this statement with the classical doctrine of Augustine explaining how the continued presence of Jews living under Christian rule is desired by God and serves a positive Christian purpose? Levin's formulation suggests a direct continuity with Nazi policy; the historical reality is far more ambiguous.

We have frequently heard that the legacy of Christian anti-Judaism can be seen in the support for Hitler within Germany and in the passive acquiescence to genocide in the European population under German domination. Such assertions are generally made not as hypotheses that need to be proven, but as propositions that are self-evident facts. With regard to the German support of Nazism, the introductory film 'Antisemitism' in the U.S. Holocaust Memorial Museum, after reviewing the history of Christian persecution, continues, 'Enter Adolph Hitler, Austrian-born and baptized a Catholic.' It soon shows him addressing a massive Nuremberg rally in German, with a voiceover saying, ' "In defending myself against the Jews I am acting for the Lord," Hitler said. "The difference between the church and me is that I am finishing the job." ' The impression is certainly that the adoring German masses are enthusiastically endorsing Hitler's anti-Jewish battle in the name of traditional religion.[63]

But this impression is misleading: the German of Hitler's speech has nothing to do with the quotations, or anything Jewish, and the quotations (to which I shall return below), were not used at Nuremberg. Recent scholarship has established that a majority of those who joined the Nazi Party at an early stage were not motivated to do so by a pre-existent antisemitism, that Germans had other apparently compelling reasons to vote for the Nazis in 1932, that – as one recent study put it, 'Hitler was astute enough as a politician to realize that his rabid anti-Semitism lacked drawing power among the German masses,'[64] and that the German population became more antisemitic because of the Nazi regime. I know of no data that would establish a clear correlation between degree of traditional Christian commitment and support for Nazi anti-Jewish policies. Why then is the connection repeated so frequently as axiomatic?

As for the behaviour of the bystanders, their passive acquiescence, their failure to speak out and protest about the persecution, deportation and murder of European Jews, is the influence of Christian prejudice indeed the only, or even primary, explanation? In a powerful essay, Irving Greenberg maintained that 'In general, there is an inverse ratio between the presence of a fundamentalist Christianity and the survival of Jews during the Holocaust period.'[65] Do we really have the data to establish this claim? As is well known, 85% of Italian Jews survived while 75% of Dutch Jews perished. Can that be correlated with the 'presence of a fundamentalist Christianity' three times as strong in Holland as it was in Italy? Was it the religious beliefs of the Ukrainian population that impelled many to welcome the Nazi invasion, or their nationalist sentiment and bitter resentment against the Stalinist regime? Do we really believe that if the Ukrainians had been less religious, the Jews would not have been murdered in Babi Yar?

Traditional Christian antisemitism in Poland has been invoked as an explanation for why the Nazis built the death camps there. Again, Greenberg states that although there were other factors (which he enumerates), 'it is clear that anti-Semitism played a role in the decision not to shield Jews – or to actually turn them in' (p.12). But is not 'played a role in the decision' far too nebulous for the searing indictment that Greenberg makes? Under the Nazi occupation, Poles knew that sheltering a Jew meant summary execution; do we need to appeal to religious factors to explain why most decided not to defy the occupying authorities? Would anyone contend that if the Poles in Warsaw had been less religious, they could have stopped the deportation of Jews to Treblinka? In the absence of firm demographic evidence for various locations, what justifies invoking the religious background as the most significant explanation for passivity?

Even where some support is evinced to justify the statements made, frequently, the 'evidence' simply does not sustain the proposition to which it is attached. I have cited the passage from the U.S. Holocaust Memorial Museum film, 'In defending myself against the Jews I am acting for the Lord,' Hitler said. 'The difference between the church and me is that I am finishing the job,' as a voiceover for a speech to a Nuremberg rally. As these sentences are undoubtedly the most frequently-cited evidence from Hitler himself (alongside the fact that he was baptized a Catholic and never excommunicated by the Church) to buttress the continuity model, they are worth identifying. The two sentences come from two totally different contexts. The first is a rhetorical climax from a passage in *Mein Kampf* explaining how he became an antisemite. In context, it is clear that it has nothing at all to do with the God of Christian Scripture or tradition. The 'Lord' invoked by Hitler here is the creator of the Darwinian world in which the strong rightfully prevail over the weak; the battle is against the egalitarian, levelling worldview of 'Jewish Bolshevism'. There is nothing in this statement to help the case for a Christian influence on Hitler's antisemitism.[66] As for the second, one form of it is attributed to Hitler when three bishops visited him in 1933 to protest against Nazi anti-Jewish legislation. In that context, it is clearly a debater's ploy to put the Catholic prelates on the defensive. He did not say 'finishing the job', which might imply the 'Final Solution', but something like 'I am only putting into practice what the Church has been teaching.'[67] In the 1933 context, this referred to legislation limiting the social and economic status of Jews; there is no ground to think that anyone would have interpreted this as a religious precedent or justification for genocide. The quotations simply do mean what they have been used to imply.[68]

Consider also, for example, the statement by Daniel Cohn-Sherbok: 'Within Germany itself the Nazis believed they were performing their Christian duty in advancing Hitler's anti-Jewish policies. Thus Heinrich Himmler declared that 'by and large ... we can say that we have performed this task in love of our people, and we have suffered no damage from it, in our inner self, in our soul, in our character.'[69] The first sentence is another example of broad generalization; the 'evidence' raises the additional methodological problems of generalizing about 'the Nazis' from one text, and of drawing conclusions about what people 'believed' from what one of them said.

But the most serious problem is that Himmler's statement about 'love of our people' has absolutely nothing to do with Christian duty; it is about responsibility to the German nation. Nor is there anything in his discussion of Jews in this address that even hints of traditional Christian anti-Judaism. Note the preceding sentences. 'We had the moral right, we had the duty toward our people, to kill this people which wanted to kill us. But we do not have the right to enrich ourselves with so much as a fur, a watch, a mark, or a cigarette or anything else. Having exterminated a germ, we do not want, in the end, to be infected by the germ, and die of it. I will not stand by and let even a small rotten spot develop or take hold.'[70] Himmler's 1943 address to the SS officers is actually one of the strongest pieces of evidence *against* the continuity model that Cohn-Sherbok favours, in that it reveals a system of 'moral' reasoning justifying the annihilation of the Jewish people that has absolutely no apparent connection to Christian tradition. Its use as evidence in this context is, to put it mildly, baffling.

We have seen a number of examples of assertions that 'Christian doctrine', especially the charge of 'deicide,' led to the conclusion that Jews deserved to be killed, that the Nazi Final Solution was therefore a logical continuation of the Christian tradition, and that Christian leaders as well as the Christian masses therefore passively acquiesced in, or even actively supported, the annihilation of the Jewish people. In almost all cases, these assertions are made without substantiating evidence. The one author I have found who does try to substantiate this accusation is Irving Greenberg. Let us be quite clear on what the issue is. We are not speaking of Christian leaders who defended (or refused to condemn) discriminatory legislation against the Jews on traditional religious grounds. This would not be surprising, as such legislation appeared to be consistent with the traditional doctrine that Jews should live in a Christian domain under conditions that demonstrate their reprobate status. The question is whether we have evidence of Christian leaders justifying the *murder* of Jews by the Nazis as an appropriate sentence for the crime of deicide. It is in this context that Greenberg cites Archbishop Kametko of Nietra, the papal nuncio in Slovakia, and a pastoral letter by Archbishop Konrad Gröber of Meissen (pp.11–12). If all of this were true, and if these statements were representative, not anomalous, it would indeed be strong support for the continuity model. It would not prove that the Nazi ideologues came to their antisemitic worldview or that perpetrators were motivated to kill Jews from their Christian training, but it would demonstrate that leaders among the bystanders acquiesced in the Final Solution as consistent with their religious commitments.

There are two points to be made. First, the statements attributed to the Archbishop of Nietra and the papal nuncio in Slovakia, even though they appear in direct quotes, are not taken from documents linked with the speakers themselves. In both cases, the source is Rabbi Dov Weissmandl, reporting in his own words, in a book written after the war, what he heard from the Nietra Rebbe about the Archbishop and what he himself claims to have heard from the nuncio. In the latter case, Greenberg concedes that this statement conflicts with what the nuncio is known to have done in Slovakia – namely, try to convince the head of state to put an end to the deportations (p.442, n.7). Weissmandl is one of the tragic and heroic figures of the Holocaust, but he is not the most reliable source for such statements. As for the statement of Gröber, the context is important. Greenberg admits that its date, March 1941, puts it 'before the full destruction was unleashed;' a better formulation might have been, before any policy of systematic mass murder was in effect. And the statement itself, 'the self-imposed curse of the Jews, "His blood be upon us and upon our children," has come true terribly until the present time, until today,' would appear to be not an endorsement of persecution, certainly not of genocide, but rather the stumbling effort of a theologian, who was undoubtedly a Nazi sympathizer with racist and antisemitic attitudes, to make sense of Jewish suffering.[71]

But Greenberg insists that 'this judgement that the Jews deserved their fate as punishment for deicide or rejecting Christ is a strong and recurrent phenomenon' (p.442), and that 'there are literally hundreds of similar anti-Semitic statements...'. Here the distinction made above is crucial. If 'the Jews deserved their fate' and 'similar anti-Semitic statements,' applies to discriminatory legislation, or even ghettoization, then perhaps 'hundreds' of such statements could be identified. But if 'deserved their fate' refers to physical annihilation, why have hundreds or even dozens of such statements by Christian leaders never been identified even by those who condemn the Church most vociferously?

And what about the statements by Christian leaders that assert precisely the opposite, many of them not based on hearsay but appearing in authentic documents. In some cases, they come from traditionalists who accept the classical doctrine of the Jews as a reprobate people yet insist that punishment must be left to God and not administered by a human regime.[72] In other cases, they are statements from east-European, French, even German prelates, who speak of Jews as their brothers, fellow human beings, who deserve compassion and protection from harm.[73] Is it appropriate to buttress a continuity model, and consequently a condemnation of Christianity, by citing only the first category of statement and ignoring the second?

This not to suggest that all of the problematic argumentation is on the side of those who support the continuity model. There are legitimate questions to be raised about arguments employed by the other side as well. The claim that the Holocaust must be seen as fundamentally different from the Christian tradition because the Nazis persecuted Christians as well as Jews, and because many Christians sheltered and saved Jews from the Nazis, strikes me as largely irrelevant to the central point. After all, Christians persecuted other Christians and some Christians tried to shelter and protect Jews in the Middle Ages as well.

The tendency to draw an absolute line of demarcation between Christian anti-Judaism and Nazi antisemitism by characterizing Nazism as a 'pagan' or 'neo-pagan' revolt against Christianity oversimplifies a complex issue. As has been frequently noted, paganism was characteristically tolerant of religious and ethnic diversity; Nazi intolerance toward Jews cannot be explained by leaping over the centuries back to the pagan worldview.

While the dominant metaphors of Nazi antisemitism – the dehumanized, microbial, pestilential imagery – are quite different from traditional Christian doctrine with its emphasis on Christ-killing and deicide, reprobate character and rejection by God, carnality, decadence, and blindness to the truth, there are motifs in (unofficial) Christian sources that suggest continuity and are often overlooked in the discontinuity model. Perhaps most significant is the idea of the world Jewish conspiracy to harm Christians, attested in the twelfth-century *Life and Miracles of St. William of Norwich*.[74] Some of the language of late medieval Christian preachers (not to mention Martin Luther) transcends the traditional doctrine and sounds quite 'modern'. Here is the fifteenth-century Italian bishop of Foligno, Antonio Bettini, in 1471: 'The Jews of this city and diocese open their famished jams like slavering dogs, not just to gobble up the possessions of the poor, but actually to drink their blood, sucking it from their veins,' or his contemporary Andrea da Faenza in Spoleto, in 1491: the Jews are 'treacherous, rabid and mercenary, usurping the Christians' goods and sucking their blood'.[75] Connections with this past cannot be casually dismissed.

As noted from the outset, my purpose in this review is not to make a definitive case for one side of the debate, although my own preference – emphasizing the novelty of Nazi conceptions, discourse and ultimate policy – will probably be clear from what is written above.[76] But this is a matter more of conceptualization and emphasis than of demonstrable right or wrong. I do hope to have helped in articulating the positions and the issues of disagreement, to have suggested what kind of argumentation and evidence may be relevant in reaching greater clarity on this question, and to have urged that even what might seem to be the most obvious claims on this deeply-felt issue be soberly tested by a careful use of the evidence pertaining both to the distant and the more recent past.

N O T E

1 Nora Levin, *The Holocaust* (New York: Schocken, 1973; original edition New York: T.Y. Crowell, 1968), p.10.

2 This question has internal significance within the context of Jewish historical experience, but in this context it has largely been resolved in favour of discontinuity and uniqueness. There was a tendency among traditionalist religious thinkers to argue that there is no fundamental difference between the Holocaust and other disasters of the Jewish past, and some Zionist historians sought to present it as the inevitable culmination of Jewish life in the Diaspora. But the decision to designate a separate day and new rituals for the tragedy of the Holocaust, rather than incorporate it into the traditional day of mourning on the Ninth of Av, reflects a consensus that this was something significantly different. It is noteworthy that many Jewish writers who insist on the absolute uniqueness of the Holocaust nevertheless maintain the position that it is a natural continuation of Christian teaching and behaviour in the past.

3 Jules Isaac, *Jésus et Israël* (Paris, Éditions Albin Michel, 1948), p.351–52.

4 James Parkes, *The Conflict of the Church and the Synagogue: A Study in the Origins of anti-Semitism* (London: Soncino Press, 1934), p.374.

5 James Parkes, *Judaism and Christianity* (Chicago: University of Chicago Press, 1948), p.167.

6 On the whole, however, Parkes sympathized with the work of Isaac, whose Sorbonne lecture of 15 December 1959 he translated, together with his wife, under the title, 'Has Anti-Semitism Roots in Christianity?' See the introduction by Claire Huchet Bishop to Isaac, *The Teaching of Contempt* (New York: Holt, Rinehart and Winston, 1964), p.12.

7 James Parkes, *Antisemitism* (Chicago: Quadrangle Books, 1964), p.60. Here, however, Parkes goes on to modify his claim in a manner that might appear to undermine the assertion of continuity: 'Other causes indeed came in during the passage through the centuries; *the motives and climate of the Nazi period owed nothing to Christian teaching*; individual Christians risked and forfeited their lives in rescuing [Hitler's] victims' (italics added). These clauses might be used by other writers to build a case for a different model, emphasizing discontinuity. He then continues, 'But so far as the Churches are concerned the line is still unbroken by any adequate recognition of the sin, by any corporate act of amendment or repentance.' This seems to shift the 'unbroken line' from the plane of historical causality to one of moral or theological responsibility.

8 Raul Hilberg, *The Destruction of the European Jews* (New York: Quadrangle Books, 1961), pp.3–4, repeated in the revised and definitive edition (New York: Holmes & Meier), 1985. On the level of ideology and discourse rather than action, a similar continuity is suggested: 'When Hitler spoke about the Jew, he could speak to the Germans in familiar language. When he reviled his victim, he resurrected a medieval conception... The picture of the Jew we encounter in Nazi propaganda and Nazi correspondence had been drawn several hundred years before. Martin Luther had already sketched the main outlines of that portrait, and the Nazis, in their time, had little to add' (p.8)

9 Hilberg, pp.5–6. See the discussion of this table in the final section, below.

10 Nora Levin apparently followed this in writing, 'The Hitler era added new intensities of degradation, new scales of horror and stripped away all earlier limits, but the main precedents had already been established' (*The Holocaust*, p.11). The 'earlier limits' presumably include limits against mass murder and total annihilation, but this is presented here as if it were relatively trivial in comparison with the long list of 'the main precedents' for the Holocaust.

11 Hyam Maccoby, 'The Origins of Anti-Semitism', in *The Origins of the Holocaust: Christian Anti-Semitism*, ed. Randolph L. Braham (New York: Columbia University Press, 1986), p.3; the title of this volume expresses the continuity model succinctly. Note the response of Eugene Fisher in this volume, p.24, that "Deicide," while popularly held – even among bishops and theologians [he may be thinking here of Chrysostom: see Rosemary Ruether, *Faith and Fratricide* (New York: Seabury Press, 1979), p.130] – has never been an official Catholic teaching, since it represents a denial of the Incarnation, a form of Docetism early condemned as heresy and bitterly fought by the Church.'

12 Maccoby, 'Origins', p.26. This formulation is filled with the kinds of problems (including simplistic generalizations and unsubstantiated claims) that I will discuss in the final section of my paper. Steven Katz cites this passage (with similar reservations) in *The Holocaust in Historical Context*, Volume 1 (New York: Oxford University Press, 1994), pp.232–33.

13 Maccoby, 'Origins', p.13. In *The Sacred Executioner* (New York: Thames and Hudson, 1982), p.163, Maccoby also concedes that Nazi antisemitism was 'in some important respects different from the theologically derived medieval theory. This is shown by the very fact that the Nazis embarked on a plan of complete extermination, for, as we have seen, Christendom did not want the Jews to disappear from the world.' Nevertheless, he insists on 'the continuity between Nazi anti-Semitism and its Christian background, without which the former would never have come into existence' (p.163), that 'the choice of the Jews as the target arose directly out of centuries of Christian teaching, which had singled out the Jews as a demonic people dedicated to evil' (p.175), and that 'even the Final Solution of the extermination of the Jews had strong Christian antecedents' (p.175). Despite some apparent ambivalence and qualification, therefore, these and the following quotation justify placing Maccoby in the 'continuity' paradigm. His assertions cited by Ron Rosenbaum in *Explaining Hitler* (New York: Random House, 1999) seem less equivocal: The Holocaust is 'the evil of Christendom' (p.320). Cf. also his 'Theologian of the Holocaust' in *Commentary* 74 (December 1982), and below, n.38.

14 *New Society*, 6 January 1983.

15 Dagobert D. Runes, *The War Against the Jew* (New York, Philosophical Library, 1968), pp.xi–xii.

16 Runes actually conflates two statements by Hitler here; see below at notes 66 and 67.

17 Simon Wiesenthal, *Every Day Remembrance Day: A Chronicle of Jewish Martyrdom* (New York: Henry Holt, 1986). On this theme of 'nothing [much] new', compare the formulation by Leo Kuper in his comparative study of genocide: 'It is startling to find within Christian practice in the period of the Crusades, the Inquisition and the religious wars, all the elements in the major genocide of our day, that of the Nazis against the Jews. There were the laws corresponding to the Nuremberg laws, there were the distinguishing badges, the theory of a Jewish conspiracy, appointed centres of annihilation corresponding to Auschwitz, and some systematic organization, with the Dominican friars for example providing the professional expertise and the bureaucratic cadres in the Inquisition.' Leo Kuper, *Genocide: Its Political Use in the Twentieth Century* (New Haven: Yale University Press, 1982), pp.13–14.
      Another book by a Jewish author bearing a message similar to that of Runes and Wiesenthal, though written in a more conventional format is Dan Cohn-Sherbok, *The Crucified Jew: Twenty Centuries of Christian Anti-Semitism* (London: HarperCollinsPublishers, 1992). The sub-title indicates clearly the author's stance on the matter of continuity with the Holocaust, which is clearly affirmed in the introduction: 'for twenty centuries Christian anti-Semitism has generated hostility toward the Jewish faith and the people of Israel' (p.xiv). As in the two other books, only the negatives are collected, without any attempt to balance or distinction. When he comes to Hitler, we are informed (without evidence) that his 'vitriolic denunciation of Jewry echoed the sentiments of Christian writers down the centuries' (p.xix). As for the Holocaust period, most Christians, including their leaders, 'refused to help' the Jews (pp.xix, 208), or 'remained aloof from the horrors of the Holocaust' (p.239), thereby indicating that they remain very much a part of the 'twenty centuries of Christian anti-Semitism.' Precision, nuance, even elemental fairness, are difficult to discover in such a presentation.

18 Hal Lindsey, *The Road to Holocaust* (New York: Bantam Books, 1989), pp.6–7.

19 Cf. Franklin Littell, *The Crucifixion of the Jews* (New York: Harper and Row, 1975), p.2: 'The cornerstone of Christian Antisemitism is the superseding or displacement myth, which already rings with the genocidal note.... To teach that a people's mission in God's providence is finished, that they have been related to the limbo of history, has murderous implications which murderers will in time spell out'; cited also by A. Roy and Alice L. Eckardt, *Long Night's Journey Into Day* (Detroit: Wayne State University Press, 1982), p.61.

20 Daniel Goldhagen: *Hitler's Willing Executioners* (New York: Alfred A. Knopf, 1996), p.49.

21 Marcel Simon, *Verus Israel: A Study of the Relations between Christians and Jews in the Roman Empire (AD 135–425)* (London: Littman Library, 1986), p.397, my italics. This passage was cited with approval by Edward Flannery, *The Anguish of the Jews* (New York: Macmillan, 1964), p.274.

22 *Auschwitz: Beginning of a New Era? Reflections on the Holocaust*, ed. Eva Fleischner (New York: KTAV, 1977), p.90. In her book, she also noted the new elements in racial antisemitism, and the novelty of massacres coming from the state, which previously had been 'the protector of Jewish continued existence' (*Faith and Fratricide*), p.224.

23 Hayim Yerushalmi, response to Ruether in *Auschwitz: Beginning of a New Era?*, p.103. The medievalist Gavin Langmuir, despite his claim of continuity between medieval (12th-cent) antisemitism and the Nazis, similarly emphasizes that 'the Nazi solution to the Jewish problem differed fundamentally from that of Christians, and the problem that remains is why the Aryan myth inspired an effort to extirpate Jews physically. Although medieval Christians had made "the Jews" the incarnate symbol of disbelief and persecuted Jews severely, medieval authorities almost never condoned the slaughter of Jews.' *History, Religion, and Antisemitism* (Berkeley: University of California Press, 1990), p.342.

24 Rubenstein, *The Cunning of History: Mass Death and the American Future* (New York Harper & Row, 1975), p.6.

25 See his early formulation of this in the Symposium on 'Jewish Values in the Post-Holocaust Future', *Judaism* 16 (Summer 1967): 272.

26 Steven T. Katz, *The Holocaust in Historical Context*, Volume 1, p.317; the quotation about hating Jews as a 'Christian *mitzvah*' is from p.259.

27 Katz, pp.399–400.

28 Quoted in *The New York Times*, 20 August 1987, A9.

29 *The New York Times*, 1 November, 1997, A6.

30 While unwilling to concede any connection between Christian anti-Judaism and Nazi ideology, both this and the 1997 papal statement do affirm that the legacy of Christian teachings about the Jews may have undermined the capacity of some Christian bystanders for spiritual resistance to Nazism.

31 See, for example, the recent statement by Hannes Stein, 'Return of the Gods', *First Things*, November 1999, p.37, describing Nazism as an eruption of paganism into heart of early 20th-century Christian Europe. The author provides a long, prophetic citation from Heine's *History of Religion and Philosophy in Germany* (1834) – 'Thor with his giant hammer will jump up and smash the Gothic cathedrals' – juxtaposed with a quotation from Hitler insisting that the tablets of the Ten Command-ments must be smashed. For a Jewish writer, in a highly critical response to the 1998 Vatican statement, see Leon Wieseltier in *The New Republic*, 9 February 1998, p.10: 'It is true that the Nazi ideology was hostile to Christianity, that it preached a new paganism.'

32 Levin, *The Holocaust*, p.10, my italics.

33 Yosef Hayim Yerushalmi, 'Response to Rosemary Ruether', in *Auschwitz: Beginning of a New Era?*, p.103, my italics. In an article published in *America*, September 11, 1999, Eugene Fisher, associated director of the Secretariat for Ecumenical and Inter-Religious Affairs of the U.S. Bishops' Conference, cited Yerushalmi and endorses his conclusion. Despite the important distinctions between the anti-Judaism of the Church fathers and modern anti-Semitism, 'it is unlikely that the Jews of the 20th century could have been so easily pinpointed and scapegoated by Nazi theory were it not for the traditions of Christian anti-Judaism and anti-Jewishness that preceded the 19th-century invention of racial anti-Semitism. A Christian tradition of negative teaching about Jews and Judaism is thus a necessary cause for the Holocaust, Yerushalmi argued. But it is not a sufficient cause . . . ' (p.14).

34 *Encountering the Holocaust: An Interdisciplinary Survey*, ed. Sherwin and Ament (Chicago: Impact Press, 1979), p.34; my italics.

35 Steven T. Katz, *The Holocaust in Historical Context*, Volume 1 (New York: Oxford University Press, 1994), pp.263 and note 109 (italics in original), 264. Elsewhere, Katz argues that the major impact of the Christian legacy on the Nazi worldview was in the choice of the Jew to play a major role in the cosmic Manichean antithesis: pp.170, 234, 257, an argument used often in connection with the continuity model.

36 This assertion is meant in a substantive, not a formal sense. A few moments earlier, Soloveitchik had said, 'Of course, Hitler was not a Christian. He was a pagan, even worse than a pagan. None of Hitler's friends were pious Christians.'

37 Aaron Rakeffet-Rothkoff, *The Rav: The World of Rabbi Joseph B. Soloveitchik*, 2 vols. (KTAV, 1999), 2:162–63, my italics. Note the repeated assertion without any pretence of argumentation or appeal to

evidence. Was it indeed a 'Catholic idea' in any significant sense that 'the Jew is subhuman'? Were Jews indeed blamed for the delay in the Second Coming? What is the connection between the 'eternal wandering Jew' and policy of annihilation of Jewish people? The general question of what the Polish bystanders might have been expected to do to prevent the deportations of Jews to death camps had they not been infused with Christian anti-Jewish teaching is, of course, not even considered.

38 Though there are some writers who maintain this. For example, 'Hitler's fixation on the Jews could hardly have developed without his Catholic upbringing; his obsession manifestly stems from an otherwise forgotten Catholicism. He was an extreme case of a renegade who has retained the negative elements of what he has abandoned...', Joel Carmichael, *The Satanizing of the Jews: Origin and Development of Mystical Anti-Semitism* (New York: Fromm, 1992), p.152. The continuation of this passage contains no reference to anything in Catholic doctrine that alone could explain this 'obsession'. A similar assertion, also without a shred of evidence, is made by Hyam Maccoby, quoted by Ron Rosenbaum in *Explaining Hitler*, p.326: '"Hitler was brought up to hate the Jews, *particularly* to hate the Jews as the people of the Devil," he [Maccoby] insists. "He lost his Christian faith, but he retained the hatred of the Jews as the people of the Devil."'

39 Fackenheim, *To Mend the World* (New York: Schocken Books, 1989), p.284. His note for this assertion is: 'see Ruether, *Faith and Fratricide*, esp. chap 3)' which indeed discusses the anti-Jewish doctrines of the Church Fathers, but does not attempt to make the case that Nazi antisemitism would have been 'impossible' without it. On the issue of continuity/discontinuity, Fackenheim writes, 'Without doubt an abyss yawns between Christian supersessionism and Auschwitz.... Even so, the terrible fact is that there is a thread that spans the abyss... the idea that, strictly speaking, Jews – and no one but Jews – should not exist at all' (pp.282–83). An even stronger statement of this position is made by Yeshayahu Leibowitz, who maintains that Pope Pius XII 'could not help but see the finger of the divine agency in the appearance of Hitler, proponent of the "final solution" of the Jewish problem, a solution which concurrently achieves a goal of Christianity since its inception,' and he therefore 'could not pay attention to those few among his priests who... wanted to protect the Jews against the will of the Christian god and against the interest of the Church': *Judaism, Human Values, and the Jewish State* (Cambridge: Harvard University Press, 1992), p.254. No evidence is cited for any of these assertions.

40 'A Theological Understanding of the Relationship Between Christians and Jews', adopted 'for study and reflection' by the 199th General Assembly of the Presbyterian Church (USA), pp.8–9, my italics.

41 *Judaism: Between Yesterday and Tomorrow* (New York: Crossroad, 1992), pp.235–36; my italics. See notes p.675; not surprisingly, there is no argument to sustain this: not that Goebbels' Christian education led him to Nazism, and certainly not that Nazi antisemitism would have been impossible without the Christian background.

42 Leon Stein, 'Christians as Holocaust Scholars', in Harry James Cargas (ed.), *Problems Unique to the Holocaust* (Lexington: University Press of Kentucky, 1999), p.137.

43 Elizabeth Schussler Fiorenza and David Tracy (eds.), *The Holocaust as Interruption* (Edinburgh: T.T. Clark Ltd., 1984), p.60.

44 Paul van Buren, 'The Status and Prospects for Theology', *CCI Notebook* 24 (November 1975), p.3, quoted in A. Roy Eckardt and Alice Eckardt, *Long Night's Journey Into Day: Life and Faith After the Holocaust* (Detroit: Wayne State University Press, 1982), p.62.

45 John Pawlikowski, 'The Holocaust and Contemporary Christology', in Fiorenza and Tracy (eds.), *The Holocaust as Interruption*, p.44.

46 'Ecumenical Considerations on Dialogue', in Helga Croner (ed.), *More Stepping Stones to Jewish–Christian Relations* (New York: Paulist Press, 1985), p.173.

47 Katz, p.234; cf. p.264, where he repeats this image, continuing, 'to reduce Nazism to this matrix would be a serious error. For this matrix was not genocidal; Nazism was.'

48 Leon Wieseltier in *The New Republic*, 9 February 1998, p.42.

49 'The Relationship Between the United Church of Christ and the Jewish Community', passed as a resolution in the 1987 'Sixteenth General Synod' of the UCC; my italics.

50 Arthur Cohen in Otto Dov Kulka and Paul Mendes-Flohr (eds.), *Judaism and Christianity Under the Impact of National Socialism* (Jerusalem: Zalman Shazar Center for Jewish History, 1987), p.475.

51 For an exception, see Katz, *The Holocaust in Historical* Context, vol.1, p.235.

52 See, for example, Yehuda Bauer's widely-used survey, *A History of the Holocaust* (New York: Franklin Watts, 1982). Bauer begins with a chapter that includes anti-Jewish Christian teachings, yet he ends that chapter with a paragraph emphasizing 'long years of relative peace' between persecutions, 'social contacts and much fruitful interchange'. 'A different Christian approach to Jews seemed possible, one that would . . . view the Jews not as demons, but as humans, as representatives of one of the most ancient civilizations on earth, as a people who had the right to be different' (p.25). In his second chapter, he discusses World War I, concluding, 'The killing, mutilation and gas poisoning of millions of soldiers on both sides had broken taboos and decisively blunted moral sensitivities. Auschwitz cannot be explained without reference to World War I' (pp. 58–59). This seems to suggest that for Bauer, the legacy of the 'Great War' was at least as important as, and perhaps even more important than, that of the Christian past.

53 This has recently been documented, in exhaustive detail and thoroughness, in Stéphane Courtois et al., *The Black Book of Communism: Crimes, Terror, Repression* (Cambridge: Harvard University Press, 1999). It is striking that the very same language of 'precondition' has been used by Nolte and others in the *Historikerstreit:* 'Was not "class murder" by the Bolsheviks the logical and real precondition of "race murder" by the Nazis?' (cited in Richard Evans, *In Hitler's Shadow* [New York: Pantheon Books, 1989], p.28.)

54 See, for example, Maccoby, *The Sacred Executioner*, p.175 (cited above, n.13), and Carmichael, *The Satanizing of the Jews* (cited above, n.38).

55 Despite his rabid antisemitism, Martin Luther identified the Antichrist with the office of the papacy and emphasized the role of Antichrist, especially the Turks, as its most important allies. See Bernard McGinn, *Antichrist* (New York: Harper Collins, 1994), pp.201–208.

56 The document is published in Robert Chazan, *Church, State, and Jew in the Middle Ages* (New York: Behrman House, 1980), pp.99–100.

57 German policy toward the native Herero population in colonial South-West Africa (modern Namibia) under Wilhelm II reached genocidal dimensions in 1904. For Hitler's attitude toward the black as subhuman, see the quotation from *Mein Kampf*, below, n.66.

58 Runes, *The War Against the Jews*, p.19; for Bernard see Chazan, *Church, State, and Jew*, pp.104–107. Compare the formulation by a Jewish writer some ten years later: 'When Julius Streicher, in 1941, recommended "the extermination of that people whose father is the Devil," he was reiterating a tradition long established by the Church' (Byron Sherwin, 'Ideological Antecedents of the Holocaust,' in *Encountering the Holocaust: An Interdisciplinary Survey* (Chicago: Impact Press, 1979), p.30). Note the rhetorical sleight of hand: the phrase 'whose father is the devil' is of course from the Gospel of John; but there was no 'long established' Church tradition recommending 'the extermination of that people.'

For another example of Runes's selectivity, see the entry on Augustine: 'In the judgment of this fountain of Christian love, the Jew must forever spend his life as a slave' (p.10). This suggests actual slavery, where what Augustine meant was theological servitude, which, as shown by S.W. Baron, was often used by rulers to protect the Jews from harm. But more important is the failure to mention that Augustine was responsible for formulating the doctrine prohibiting murder of Jews, a doctrine invoked by Christian leaders (including Bernard) consistently throughout the Middle Ages. There are no notes in Runes's book, no identification of the source for any quotation, no way of assessing the broad generalizations that are ubiquitous.

59 Hilberg juxtaposes 'compulsory ghettos, Synod of Breslau, 1267' with Heydrich's order of September 21, 1939. The Breslau provincial Council, by no means the first to call for segregated housing, had no authority to legislate or make anything compulsory, and of course the term 'ghetto' was not used until 1516 in Venice. The Breslau canon ends, 'the Jewish quarter be separated from the common habitation of the Christians by a fence, a wall or a ditch' (see S.W. Baron, *A Social and Religious History of the Jews*, vol.9 (New York: Columbia University Press, 1965), pp.32–33. The difference between this and the hermetically sealed Nazi-imposed ghettos is obvious, and was clear to the Nazis themselves. See also the important general critique of Hilberg's composite list in Katz, *The Holocaust in Historical Context*, p.233 n.20, 298 n.195.

60 Sherwin, p.29.

61 For another example, see Wiesenthal, in *Every Day Rembrance Day*, Wiesenthal, 'When the Inquisi-
    tion was set up in Spain – and it was the Dominican order that ran this instrument of the Church –
    the institution took on characteristics that are very similar to those of the SS in the Nazi state much
    later on' (p.5). While others have made the rhetorical comparison between the Dominicans and the
    SS (e.g., Rolf Hochhuth, *The Deputy* [New York: Grove Press, 1964], p.248: 'We are the Dominicans
    of the technological age'), so dramatic are the differences between the Spanish Inquisition – which for
    all of its capacity to persecute was a court that operated according to a rule of law and provided an
    option of confession and penitence to save the life of the accused – and the SS as it operated in Nazi
    concentration camps and Einsatzgruppen that the claim of 'similarity' seems totally misguided.
    Wiesenthal then continues, 'The Spanish blood laws served as a model for the Nazis' "Aryan
    certificate" centuries later; the Spanish "blood purity certificate" affected seven generations and
    the first draft of the Nazi law pertaining to the Aryan certificate also demanded proof of seven
    generations. But that proved impractical in Germany . . . [so] the Nazis gave in and restricted the
    'blood hunting' to three generations' (p.7). While the Spanish *limpieza de sangre* laws were indeed a
    revolutionary attempt to discriminate against Jews who had converted to Christianity and their
    descendants, and thus suggests an ethnic definition of the 'Jew' independent of religious identity, I
    am aware of no evidence that the Nazis ever invoked the Spanish legislation as a 'model' for their own
    (which is not accurately described here). They apparently felt they did not need any precedent. More
    important, the Spanish legislation was not legislation by the Church, which opposed it as a denial of
    the efficacy of baptism. So it cannot help in the argument for continuity between 'Christian doctrine'
    and the Holocaust.
        The most blatant, sustained attempt to characterize the Spanish legislation in a precursorist
    manner in light of Nazi racist doctrine is in B.Z. Netanyahu's *The Origins of the Spanish Inquisition*
    (New York: Random House, 1995).

62 Sherwin, p.29.

63 Compare the statement by Leon Wieseltier: 'The anti-Semitism of the Nazi satraps and the Nazi
    ideologues was certainly not Christian anti-Semitism, but it owed its rapturous reception in Germany
    and elsewhere to centuries and centuries of Christian anti-Semitism. All this is elementary and
    incontrovertible' (*The New Republic*, April 6, 1998, p.7).

64 Brustein, *The Logic of Evil: The Social Origins of the Nazi Party, 1925–1933* (New Haven: Yale
    University Press, 1996), p.58; see also Sarah Gordon, *Hitler Germans, and the 'Jewish Question'*,
    pp.68–70.

65 Irving Greenberg, in *Auschwitz: Beginning of a New Era?*, p.12. Cf. Maccoby, *The Sacred Executioner*,
    p.163: 'It was in those countries where the medieval picture of the Jew was strongest that the [Nazi]
    policy could be implemented with the tacit and, in some cases, active support of the populace.'

66 *Mein Kampf* (New York: Reynal and Hitchcock, 1940), pp.83–84. A similar invocation of God as
    Creator of a natural order based on racial hierarchy is revealed in the following passage about
    the training of individual Negroes for the professions: 'it is a criminal absurdity to train a born
    half-ape until one believes a lawyer has been made of him, while millions of members of the highest
    culture race have to remain in entirely unworthy positions; it is a sin against the will of the eternal
    Creator to lets hundreds and hundreds of thousands of His most talented beings degenerate in the
    proletarian swamp of today, while Hottentots and Zulu Kafirs are trained for intellectual vocations'
    (p.640).

67 See Ruether, *Faith and Fratricide*, p.224. As in the case of the quotation about the Armenians,
    tracking down the actual source for this frequently-quoted statement is considerably more difficult
    than it might seem.

68 Compare Joel Carmichael, *The Satanizing of the Jews* (New York: Fromm, 1992), p.152: 'Hitler's
    interest in religion was marginal, indeed minimal. His occasional remarks to Church leaders that in
    fighting the Jews he was "doing God's work" [a fusing of the two passages cited above] were merely
    opportunistic.' Yet he continues, in the passage cited above in n.38, to insist that Hitler's obsession
    with the Jews 'manifestly stems from an otherwise forgotten Catholicism.'

69 Cohn-Sherbok, p.209.

70 For the context of this statement in Himmler's Address, see Lucy Dawidowicz, *A Holocaust Reader* (New York: Behrman House, 1976), p.133.

71 Greenberg took the quotation from Guenter Lewy, *The Catholic Church and Nazi Germany* (New York: McGraw-Hill, 1964), p.294, where evidence of his racist and antisemitic views in abundant (e.g., p.277).

72 See the examples from Bonhoeffer, Niemöller, and the Metropolitan Stefan of Sofia cited in my *Moments of Crisis in Jewish–Christians Relations* (Philadelphia: Trinity Press International, 1989), pp.41–42.

73 Perhaps the best-known example of consistent and courageous opposition to Nazi persecution of Jews by East European prelate is the Ukrainian Metropolitan Andreas Sheptitsky in Lwów, on whom see Philip Friedman, *Roads to Extinction* (Philadelphia: JPS, 1980), pp.191–92, 247, 416; his pastroal letter of fall 1942 was entitled 'Thou Shalt Not Murder'; for the text, see David Kahane, *Lvov Ghetto Diary* (Amherst: University of Massachusetts Press, 1990), pp.158–62. For statements by the French Archbishop Saliège of Toulouse and Bishop Théas of Montauban, see Michael Marrus and Robert Paxton, *Vichy France and the Jews* (New York: Basic Books, 1981), p.271. See also the pastoral letters of German bishops from December 1942 and 1943 cited by Friedman, *Roads to Extinction*, p.431; and the statement of the Protestant Theofil Wrum, regional bishop of Wuttemberg: 'From the depths of my religious and moral feelings, and in agreement with the thoughts of all true Christians in Germany, I must declare that we Christians consider the policy of extermination of Jews to be a grave wrong . . . Our nation widely regards the suffering wrought by enemy fliers as a just retribution for what has been done to the Jews' (p.437).

74 See the text in Jacob Marcus, *The Jew in the Medieval World* (Cincinnati: HUC Press, 1990), p.125, and see also the early-16th-century forgery cited in Norman Cohn, *Warrant for Genocide* (Chico, Calif.: Scholars Press), pp.45–46.

75 Both passages cited in Ariel Toaff, *Love, Death, and Work* (London: Littman Library, 1998), p.119.

76 A statement of my own view can be found in my 'Christian Doctrine and the Death Camps: The Ambiguities of Influence' (The Rabbi Robert P. Jacobs Lecture, 7 October 1998) published by The St. Louis Interfaith Dialogue, 1998.

THE SEARCH FOR JUSTICE

The Holocaust and genocide tip the scales of justice in ways that can never be balanced. Yet these disasters make the search for justice all the more important, for the alternative is that gross theft and mass murder win victories that should never be theirs. The search for justice has brought the Holocaust and genocide into courts of law in ways that were scarcely imaginable a few years ago. These legal preceedings provide one important means by which ethical decisions can be effected in society. As this set of articles testifies, when Remembering for the Future 2000 took place, cases about the restitution of stolen property occupied centre stage. These studies expand the Holocaust's immensity. They also show how important it is to prevent genocide so that such wrenching searches for justice do not have to be repeated again and again.

HOLOCAUST RESTITUTION IN THE UNITED STATES:
THE SEARCH FOR JUSTICE

Michael J. Bazyler

HIS PAPER examines one of the most important developments of the post-Holocaust era: the legal efforts in the United States by survivors of the Holocaust and their heirs to obtain restitution from European and American corporations[1] for their nefarious activities during World War II.

The filing of such lawsuits now – over one-half century after the events took place – is astounding. In the history of American litigation, a class of cases has never appeared in which so much time had passed between the wrongful act and the filing of a lawsuit. Most surprisingly, the recent spate of lawsuits, for the most part, have been successful. This is in contrast to Holocaust-era suits filed between 1945 and 1995, when only ten lawsuits were filed in American courts seeking compensation for World War II-era wrongs, with most of these being summarily dismissed.[2]

The Holocaust did not occur in the United States, but in Europe. Most Holocaust survivors reside also outside of the United States. It is the United States legal system, however, that has taken the lead in delivering some measure of long-overdue justice to aging Holocaust survivors.

Why the United States? As with all transnational litigation today, the highly developed and expansive system of American justice makes the United States the best – and, in most instances, the only – legal forum for the disposition of such claims. American courts have a long history of recognizing jurisdiction over defendants where courts of other countries would find jurisdiction lacking. American-style discovery, mostly unknown in Europe, allows the plaintiffs' lawyer to develop the case through production of documents requests, requests for admission, and depositions of adverse parties and witnesses during the pre-trial process, rather than having all the evidence available at the outset of the litigation. Guarantee of jury trials in civil cases – and a culture where juries are acclimated to granting awards in the millions of dollars, both as compensation and as punitive damages – makes the filing of a Holocaust-era lawsuit in the United States more likely of financial success. The existence of the concept of a 'class action', where representative plaintiffs can file suit not only on their behalf, but also on behalf of all others similarly situated, creates a more efficient system of filing suits and raises the prospect of large awards against the wrongdoers.[3]

Moreover, American attorneys are greater risk-takers than their European counterparts, and, unlike in most other countries, can take a case on a 'contingency basis' – where the client does not pay if the case is unsuccessful, but must share a percentage of the award if the case succeeds. Moreover, in the United States, a losing party, except in unusual cases, does not pay the attorneys' fees of the successful litigant. As a result, an American lawyer has less to lose if the case fails, and, therefore, is more likely to file suit.[4]

The recognition of American courts as the most desirable forum for transnational litigation was recognized by Lord Denning, when he wryly observed in an English court opinion: 'As a moth is drawn to light, so is a litigant drawn to the United States. If he can only get his case into their courts, he stands to win a fortune.'[5]

The stark reality, however, is that until recently, a Holocaust-era lawsuit would have been summarily dismissed if brought in the United States.[6] What made these lawsuits possible is the development of human rights law by courts in the United States over the last two decades. An American court today is more likely to allow a human rights case to be litigated even if (1) the acts complained of did not occur in the United States and (2) are brought by a foreign plaintiff.

The recognition of such suits began with the seminal opinion of *Filartiga v. Pena*, 630 F.2d 876 (2d. Cir. 1980), where the Second Circuit of the Court of Appeals held that the Paraguayan father and sister of a victim of state-sanctioned torture and killing committed in Paraguay can sue the perpetrator, a government official, if the perpetrator is found in the United States.[7] Thereafter, a number of other human rights victims injured abroad have been able to successfully bring suit in the United States.[8] In 1992, Congress confirmed the right of victims of foreign torture to sue in American courts by enacting the Torture Victims Protection Act ('TVPA'), Publ. L. No. 102–256, 106 Stat. 73 (1992) (codified as an amendment to the ATCA at 28 U.S.C. §. 1350).

Without the groundwork laid out by *Filartiga*, the cases that followed it, and the TVPA, the recently filed Holocaust-era cases would have been summarily dismissed.

I. CASES AGAINST EUROPEAN BANKS

A. SWISS BANKS LITIGATION

The modern era of Holocaust asset litigation began in October 1996 with the filing of a class action lawsuit against the three largest private Swiss banks – Credit Suisse, Union Bank of Switzerland ('UBS') and Swiss Bank Corporation – in federal district court in Brooklyn, New York. Thereafter, two other lawsuits were filed against the same banks, with all three actions consolidated in April 1997 as *In re Holocaust Victim Assets Litigation*, and heard by Judge Edward R. Korman, one of the heroes of this litigation.

The consolidated lawsuits made three types of accusations against the Swiss banks: (1) that the banks failed to return moneys deposited with them by Jews seeking a safe haven for their assets in the face of persecution by the Nazis – since such moneys are alleged to have been lain dormant in Swiss banks for the last half-century, these claims became known as the 'dormant account' claims; (2) that the banks traded in assets looted from the Jews by the Nazis – these became known as the 'looted assets' claims; and (3) that the banks traded in assets made by slave labour which were then sold, and the sale proceeds deposited with the banks – these became known as the 'slave labour' claims.

The lawsuits alleged that the banks, for the dormant account claims, set up specious requirements, such as the necessity by heirs to produce death certificates for Holocaust victims, as a reason for failing to return funds deposited with them for safekeeping, and for the latter two categories, accepted deposits from the Nazis knowing that the funds deposited were either looted from Jews or came from sale of goods made by Jewish slave labour.

The Swiss banks, in response to the suits, filed voluminous motions to dismiss, setting out numerous reasons why the lawsuits could not proceed. In addition to arguing that

American courts lacked jurisdiction over these claims and that the claims were time-barred, the banks contended that they were already dealing with the problem; specifically, by publishing a list of dormant accounts and by creating the so-called Independent Committee of Eminent Persons ('ICEP'), chaired by Paul Volcker, the former head of the U.S. Federal Reserve Board, to both process claims made against them by Holocaust survivors or heirs and to reexamine their actions during the war. According to the banks, 'Plaintiffs were not required to come to a court of law to seek redress... [Superior, cooperative mechanisms are available, and those alternatives become more attractive every day.]'[9] In June 1998, while Judge Korman was considering their motions, the banks made what they called their first and last offer to settle the claims: $600 million.

In the meantime, a number of political factors came into the picture. First, the Senate Banking Committee, headed by Senator Alfonse D'Amato, began holding hearings on the issue. Second, a number of state and local governments threatened to stop doing business with the Swiss banks unless they settled the claims. Third, the United States government issued a report, written by Stuart Eizenstat, then Undersecretary of State (now Deputy Treasury Secretary and Special Representative of the President and the Secretary of State for Holocaust Issues), sharply criticizing the Swiss for their World War II dealings with the Nazis. Finally, UBS, now undergoing a merger with co-defendant Swiss Bank Corporation, was caught attempting to shred World War II-era financial documents, in contravention of a newly enacted Swiss law forbidding such actions.[10]

In August 1998, the banks doubled their offer and, under Judge Korman's guidance, settled the case for $1.25 billion. Rather than a lump-sum payment, the banks would pay the $1.25 billion in four installments over three years, with the final payment to be made in November 2001.

The settlement agreement sets out five classes of claimants eligible to receive payments from the $1.25 billion fund:

(1) the 'Deposited Assets Class,' consisting of 'Victims or Targets of Nazi Persecution' ('VTNP') claimants and their heirs seeking to recover World War II-era assets deposited in a Swiss bank prior to 9 May 1945;

(2) the 'Looted Assets Class,' consisting of VTNP claimants and their heirs seeking to recover compensation for assets belonging to them and stolen by the Nazis, which made their way to the Swiss banks;

(3) 'Slave Labour Class I,' consisting of VTNP claimants who performed slave labour for companies that deposited assets derived from that slave labour in Switzerland;

(4) 'Slave Labour Class II,' consisting of individuals who performed slave labour at a facility or business or business concern headquartered, organized, or based in Switzerland; and

(5) the 'Refugee Class,' consisting of VTNP claimants, and their heirs, who sought entry into Switzerland to escape the Nazis and were either denied entry, or, after gaining entry, were either sent back or mistreated by the Swiss.

A close analysis of these five categories reveals, however, that they make little sense. First, the claimants in the middle three categories are required to prove that the Swiss government or private Swiss industry did business with the Nazis. For example, a claimant who worked as a slave labourer for the Nazis does not fall under the 'Slave Labour I' class unless the company for whom the slave labourer worked 'deposited the revenues or proceeds of that labour with, or transacted such revenues or proceeds through [Switzerland.]' (Settlement Agreement, para. 8.2(c)).

Of course, a now-elderly Holocaust survivor, whose only goal was to stay alive, would almost never be able to offer proof that the benefits of his or her labour for the Nazis were eventually sent to Switzerland. It appears, however, that this nexus to Switzerland will never have to be made, since a mere allegation of such a charge by a claimant seems to be sufficient for the claimant to come within the class.[11]

Second, the term VTNP, appearing in four of the five class categories, does not comport with reality. It was not utilized in the Nuremberg trials, nor has it been used by any Holocaust scholar. Rather, the term was unveiled for the first time in the Settlement Agreement document.

Most striking is that VTNPs are not limited to Jews. Rather, the Swiss settlement also contemplates that, in addition to Jewish victims, the following four groups persecuted by the Nazis are also VTNPs and, therefore, will receive a part of the $1.25 billion settlement: (1) homosexuals; (2) physically or mentally disabled or handicapped persons; (3) the Romani (Gypsy) peoples; and (4) Jehovah's Witnesses. These non-Jewish victims groups included in the settlement, however, are small, and exclude the entire category of Slavic peoples – primarily Poles and Russians – forced to work as slave labourers for the Nazis. These victims of Nazi persecution will not receive anything from the Swiss settlement, but must await recovery from the slave labour settlement now being finalized with Germany (see discussion below).

In return for $1.25 billion, plaintiffs agreed to drop all lawsuits against the Swiss banks being sued. In addition, the settlement released not only the defendant banks but also 'the government of Switzerland, the Swiss National Bank, all other Swiss banks, and all other members of Swiss industry, except for the three Swiss insurers who are defendants in the [federal class action insurance litigation]' (see discussion below).[12] Finally, as a condition of settlement, all sanctions and threats of sanctions against Switzerland and any of its businesses were dropped.

In effect, the settlement agreement obtained by the two private Swiss banks insulates the entire nation of Switzerland and all its businesses from any kind of litigation – anywhere in the world – having any connection to World War II.

The case, nevertheless, marks a milestone in American litigation as the largest settlement of a human rights case in United States history. Asked to explain the banks' sudden reversal of their position, Rabbi Marvin Heir, head of the Simon Wiesenthal Center, commented: 'It was for only one reason: they were pressured into it. Without the pressure, without Sen. D'Amato's banking committee, without the threat of sanctions, the Holocaust survivors would have gotten nothing.'[13] The *Financial Times* came to the same conclusion:

> The clearest lesson from the Swiss banks' $1.25bn settlement with holocaust survivors is this: threatening to impose sanctions can work. Every important breakthrough in the negotiations came soon after threats from US local government officials to impose sanctions (banning, for example, Swiss banks from certain kinds of business in New York). The settlement itself came two weeks before a threat to start the sanctions and a week after Moody's, the rating agency, published a report saying that UBS, Switzerland's (and Europe's) biggest bank, might lose its triple-A rating if sanctions were imposed.[14]

In accordance with American federal class action rules, Judge Korman held a hearing in November 1999 to confirm the fairness of the settlement, and in July 2000, finalized the settlement. Additionally, Judge Korman appointed a special master to propose a distribution plan for the $1.25 billion.

While the U.S. justice system produced results, they were not necessarily speedy. It took nearly two years after the initial agreement was reached, in August, 1998, to finalize the settlement, and longer to have the funds distributed to the victims. The current status of the Swiss banks settlement is available at <www.swissbankclaims.com>.

B. GERMAN AND AUSTRIAN BANKS LITIGATION

German and Austrian banks maintained close business relationships with the Nazis, and profited handsomely from such dealings. Deutsche Bank, Germany's largest bank, helped to finance the building of Auschwitz.[15] A historical report of Dresdner Bank found that in Nazi-occupied lands the saying went, 'Right after the first German tank comes Dr. Rasche from the Dresdner Bank.'[16]

In June 1998, three Holocaust survivors, all American citizens, filed a class action lawsuit against the two German banks, charging them with profiteering from the looting of gold and personal property of Jews. Thereafter, other lawsuits were filed against these two banks and other German and Austrian banks for their World War II-era activities.

In March 1999, the lawsuits were consolidated as *In re Austrian and German Bank Holocaust Litigation* (No. 98 Civ. 3938), in the Southern District of New York before Judge Shirley Wohl Kram. That same month, Bank Austria and its recently-purchased subsidiary, Creditanstalt, settled the lawsuits against them for $40 million. A fairness hearing was held on 1 November 1999, and Judge Kram approved the settlement on 10 January 2000.

As of August 2000, no moneys had yet been distributed from the settlement. The current status of the Austrian banks' settlement is available at <www.austrianbankclaims.com>.

Litigation against the German banks continued. However, the 'rough justice' settlement reached with the German government and industry in December 1999, and finalized in July 2000 (see discussion below), also included the settlement of the claims made against the German banks.

C. FRENCH BANKS LITIGATION

After the Nazis conquered France, French banks began to confiscate the accounts of their Jewish depositors in a process known as 'Aryanization' of the accounts.

In late 1997 and early 1998 two class actions were filed against one-half dozen French banks in federal court in New York, followed by another action in California state court in San Francisco.[17] The defendant French banks all do business in the United States, and plaintiffs were both American nationals and foreigners. The lawsuits also named the British bank, Barclays Bank, and two U.S. financial institutions, Chase Manhattan Bank and J.P. Morgan & Co. These banks had branches in France during the war, and are alleged also to have participated in the confiscation of the assets of their Jewish depositors.

In July, 1999, Barclays settled for $3.6 million, to be paid to the families of its Jewish customers in France who lost their assets during the Nazi occupation. The other banks declined to settle, and litigation against them continues.

II. CASES AGAINST EUROPEAN INSURANCE COMPANIES

In the time before the two world wars, insurance policies and annuities were popular investment vehicles in Europe. Jews in pre-war Europe often purchased insurance, and an insurance policy was known as a 'poor man's Swiss bank account'.

The European insurance company with the most notoriety in the field of Holocaust-era restitution is Assicurazioni Generali S.p.A., the largest insurance company in Italy, and owner of Israel's largest insurer, Migdal. Generali, as the company is commonly known, was founded in 1831 by a group of Jewish merchants, and, until recently, its chairman was a Jewish survivor of Auschwitz. In pre-war Europe, Generali was known as a 'Jewish company, whose agents saturated the major Jewish population centers before the war.'[18] In a situation akin to the failure by the Swiss banks to return moneys deposited with them prior to the war, Generali, along with other European insurers, has been accused of failing to honour policies purchased from them by Holocaust victims in pre-war Europe.[19]

The other insurance company with a large stake in the pre-war European market is Allianz of Germany, presently the second largest insurance concern in the world. Allianz's CEO, Kurt Schmidt, was Hitler's Minister of Economy. Allianz also insured a number of concentration camps, including Auschwitz and Dachau.

Upon coming to power in Germany, the Nazis' persecution of Jews included confiscation of insurance policies from its Jewish citizenry. A particularly poignant example of the theft of insurance proceeds by the Nazis, and German insurers' collusion in such theft, occurred in the aftermath of *Kristallnacht*, in November 1938. Since many of the Jewish merchants, whose shops and other properties were damaged or looted during the campaign, held casualty insurance to cover such losses, the Nazis ordered the insurance companies to pay all such claims to the state rather than to the injured parties. In a deal made with the insurers, the companies were allowed to expunge the claims of their Jewish policyholders by paying only a fraction of the claims' value to the German state.[20]

Beginning in 1997, two class action lawsuits were filed against more than one-dozen European insurers in federal court in New York, followed by six individual actions in California state court. The claims were brought either by Holocaust survivors or heirs, with the insurance companies sued doing business in the United States.

As with the Swiss bank litigation, political pressure has been an important component in either settlement, or, at the least, in bringing the European insurers to the bargaining table.

In 1997, the National Association of Insurance Commissioners, composed of the insurance regulators in all fifty states, created a working group on Holocaust and insurance issues. Some of the regulators began holding hearings, inviting the companies to explain their reasons for non-payment of these pre-war policies. Since insurance companies in America are regulated at the state level, and receive their licences to operate from the state, the commissioners began threatening to revoke the licences of the European insurers for failure to honour these claims.

Prodded by the commissioners from California, New York and Florida, which contain the largest concentration of Holocaust survivors in the United States, five of the insurers sued – including Generali and Allianz[21] – formed (and funded) the International Commission on Holocaust Era Insurance Claims, commonly known as ICHEIC, headed by former U.S. Secretary of State Lawrence Eagleburger.[22]

Following the model of the ICEP, created by the Swiss banks, ICHEIC, likewise, is intended to be a non-adversarial alternative to the American litigation brought against the insurance companies. In February 2000, after numerous delays, ICHEIC announced that it would begin a two-year claim process to locate and pay unpaid Holocaust-era insurance policies. That same month, ICHEIC began placing adverts in newspapers and journals world-wide soliciting Holocaust survivors and heirs to submit claims.

As of August 2000, ICHEIC had processed and actually paid out a small number of claims presented to it. An unfortunate development, as reported by the London-based *Jewish Chronicle*, is that, to date, 'three out of every four insurance policy claims submitted by Holocaust-survivors or by heirs of victims are being rejected by the European insurers [participating in ICHEIC]...The 75-per-cent rejection rate – which is based on the commission's internal documents – is particularly startling since the claims involved were considered to be the strongest ones, and were to be processed on a fast-track basis, requiring only minimum back-up proof.'[23]

The current status of the ICHEIC claims settlement process is available at <www.icheic.org.>. Since ICHEIC is a voluntary process, it legally has no effect on the ongoing litigation. The class actions in federal court, therefore, continue. Of the six individual actions filed in California, four of the suits, all against Generali, have settled.[24] While the settlement terms remain confidential, the *New York Times* reported that one of the cases settled for $1.25 million, substantially less than the $10 million in insurance claims and $125 million in punitive damages sought by the plaintiffs.[25]

III. CASES STEMMING FROM THE USE OF SLAVE LABOUR

Between eight and ten million people were forced to work as labourers in factories and camps in Germany and throughout occupied Europe during World War II. Approximately 700,000 of these labourers – now elderly – are alive today, with some estimates placing the number as high as 2.3 million.[26]

The reparations programme to Jewish victims of Nazi persecution promulgated by West Germany specifically excluded payment for slave labour. Former German slave labourers found themselves in a 'Catch-22' situation: the German government claimed that it was not obligated to make payments to them because the labourers worked during the war for private German firms; German industry, on the other hand, argued that any payments should come from government coffers, since, German firms claimed, they were forced to use the slave labourers to support the Nazi war effort.[27]

In October 1998, the then-newly elected Chancellor Gerhard Schroeder reversed German government policy by announcing the creation of a fund to compensate the former slave labourers. By that time, however, American plaintiffs' lawyers, emboldened by their success with the Swiss bank litigation, had already begun filing suits in American courts against various German – and even American – companies on behalf of the slave labourers, living both in the United States and abroad.

Eventually, close to forty separate lawsuits were filed in various courts throughout the United States against numerous German companies which used slave labour during World War II. These slave labour lawsuits constituted the largest category of cases filed in the United States stemming from the Holocaust.

On 13 September 1999, the claimants suffered a serious setback in the litigation. That day, two federal judges sitting in New Jersey issued separate opinions dismissing five of the lawsuits. Judge Joseph Greenaway, Jr. dismissed the lawsuit against Ford Motor Company and its German subsidiary Ford Werke, filed by a Belgian national who was deported by the Nazis from the Soviet Union and forced to work at the Ford Werke plant in Cologne. (*Iwanowa v. Ford Motor Co.*, 67 F.Supp.2d 424 (D.N.J. 1999)). Judge Dickinson R. Debevoise dismissed four separate lawsuits against German companies Degussa and Siemens (*Burger-Fischer v. Degussa A.G.*, 65 F. Supp.2d 248 (D.N.J. 1999)).

Both judges held that the suits were non-justiciable, specifically that they were precluded by the treaties entered into by Germany and the Allied powers after the war. Judge Greenaway also found some claims against Ford to be time-barred.

Both dismissals were appealed, but eventually became moot when German government and industry, in December 1999, entered into a preliminary settlement with the plaintiffs' lawyers and representatives of Jewish organizations to resolve all slave labour and related claims[28] for DM 10 billion (approximately $5 billion). While the total amount may seem significant, it appears that each survivor will receive a lump sum payment of only between $2,500 and $7,500.[29]

Under the contemplated scheme for distribution, those forced by the Nazis to work to death – slave labourers, and primarily Jews – who survived the war and are still living will receive payments up to $7,500. Former forced labourers –primarily non-Jews – will be awarded $2,500 each.[30]

In return for the settlement, the attorneys agreed to drop all the pending slave labour suits. To block future litigation, the United States government, as part of the deal, agreed to intervene on behalf of German defendants in any future lawsuit for wartime slave labour filed in the United States. As with the Swiss banks' $1.25 billion settlement, Germany and its entire private industry, for DM10 billion, have bought for themselves complete legal peace from bothersome American litigation.

The Germans have conceded that, after a half-century of failing to recognize the claims of the slave labourers, the fear of American litigation is what finally brought them to the bargaining table.

Chancellor Schroeder, announcing in February 1999 the establishment of a fund for slave labourers (then set at $1.7 billion), explicitly stated that the fund was being established 'to counter lawsuits, particularly class action suits, and to remove the basis of the campaign being led against German industry and our country.'[31] German industry, in a website devoted to charting the progress of the settlement fund, stated: 'For the Foundation to be established and for the funds to be made available, it is an indispensable prerequisite that the enterprises have full and lasting legal certainty, in other words, that they are safe from legal action in the future.'[32]

The *Economist*, in its analysis of the slave labour negotiations, came to the same conclusion: 'Why now? Partly because of the claims now being made against German firms by lawyers, particularly in America, acting on behalf of former slave labourers under the Nazis.'[33]

The settlement was finalized in a ceremony in Berlin on 17 July 2000, and distribution of the funds is contemplated to begin in 2001.

IV. NAZI-STOLEN ART CASES

The disposition of art found to be looted by the Nazis during World War II is complex because so much art is at stake.[34] According to the Nuremberg trial records, it took almost 30,000 railroad cars to transport to Germany all the art stolen by the Nazis. After the war, the art was dispersed throughout the world, finding its way into the most unlikely places.

For instance, in early 2000, the Israel Museum in Jerusalem returned to its rightful owners an impressionist Pisarro stolen by the Nazis. The painting made its way after the war to the United States, and then was donated to the Israeli Museum by American benefactors who purchased the painting years earlier on the New York art market.

In August 1998, a lawsuit in federal court in Chicago brought over a Degas artwork was settled. The lawsuit was brought by the grandchildren of the owner of the Degas, who was murdered by the Nazis, against a Chicago pharmaceutical magnate who bought the work and donated it to the Chicago Art Museum (*Goodman v. Searle*, Case No. 96-C-6459 (N.D. Illinois, filed 24 September 1996). On the eve of trial, the parties agreed to have the museum keep the painting and pay the grandchildren one-half its value.

In June 1999, a case brought against the Seattle Art Museum for a Nazi-stolen Matisse also settled. The museum, after researching the history of the painting, agreed that it was indeed stolen by the Nazis from the plaintiffs' relatives (*Rosenberg v. Seattle Art Museum*, Case No. C99–5462 (W.D. Washington, filed 31 July 1998)).

A third case, brought by Manhattan District Attorney Robert Morgenthau against the New York Museum of Modern Art ('MOMA') still continues, albeit in another forum. The case involved two paintings by the Austrian painter Egon Schiele, which were on loan to MOMA for an exhibition. On the eve of the painting's return to Austria, Morgenthau issued a criminal subpoena seizing the paintings as stolen property (*New York v. MOMA*, Case No.28012–98 (N.Y. Supreme Court, filed 7 Jan. 1998). In September 1998, the New York Court of Appeals, the highest court in New York State, reversed the intermediate appellate court decision and upheld the trial court's quashing of the subpoena as being in violation of Section 12.03 of the New York State Arts and Cultural Affairs Law.[35]

The dismissal, however, did not end the litigation. While one of the two Schiele paintings was allowed to leave for Austria, the other painting, *Portrait of Wally*, remains in the United States. On the same day that the New York Court of Appeals issued its decision, the federal government, through the U.S. Attorney for the Southern District of New York (having federal jurisdiction over New York City), filed a federal civil action seeking the forfeiture of the painting under federal law (*United States v. Portrait of Wally*, Case No. 99CV 9940 (S.D.N.Y, filed 21 September 1999). A few days later, with the painting still with MOMA for safekeeping, the U.S. heirs to the European pre-war owner of the painting filed suit seeking a declaratory judgment that *Portrait of Wally* belongs to them.

As of this writing, the Schiele saga continues.

CONCLUSION

Much has been made of the fact that American lawyers will be taking fees for prosecuting Holocaust-era restitution lawsuits.[36] However, the lawyers have played a critical role in the European companies finally admitting responsibility for their activities during World War II. Until the class action lawsuits were filed in the United States, the companies were able, for over half a century, to ignore the restitution claims of Holocaust survivors.

Rabbi Abraham Cooper, Associate Dean of the Simon Wiesenthal Center, one of the Jewish organizations intimately involved with the Holocaust restitution issues, applauds the role of the lawyers:

> The only reason the Swiss were at the table, the only reason these guys are quaking is because lawyers came in and things moved forward.
>
> I'm not giving them all the credit, but there's no question without [lawyers getting involved in] these issues, there wouldn't be a heck of a lot to be talking about in the year 1999.[37]

An editorial in the *Washington Post* puts it more bluntly:

Yes, there is something unseemly about a bunch of lawyers trolling Eastern Europe for the few remaining Holocaust survivors on whose behalf they can – with near absolute justification – sue everyone in sight.

... But this is the way of the world – not just of Jews and Holocaust settlements ...

Who, then, are better suited to taking on European insurance companies and banks which, smiling and always cordial, insisted on death certificates for the poor souls who went into the atmosphere as ash from the Nazi crematoriums? Who better to demand an accounting from companies whose management in the 1930s and '40s did business as the Nazis wanted? No one is suggesting the present management of these companies is antisemitic, but I am suggesting they would never own up – open their files, never mind their wallets, if those awful contingency lawyers had not surrounded them and run up the Jolly Roger.[38]

The same author also accurately answers criticism that seeking compensation and making the wrongdoers pay demeans the memory of the Holocaust.

An immense calamity was committed in Europe, a moral calamity that left a black hole in the middle of the 20th century. Money is the least of it. But money is part of it. Holocaust victims paid once for being Jewish. Now, in a way, they or their heirs are being asked to pay again – a virtual Jewish tax which obliges them not to act as others would in the same situation. But in avoiding one stereotype, they adopt a worse one – perpetual victim.[39]

Besides obtaining long-overdue restitution, the litigation in America has produced other beneficial effects.

The litigation has forced European governments to create various historical commissions[40], which have unearthed new and valuable information about the financial wrongs committed against European Jewry during the war. Private companies, against whom similar accusations have been made, are likewise putting Holocaust historians on retainer and, for the first time ever, opening up their wartime files for inspection.[41]

This trend by governments and corporations finally to 'come clean' about their activities during World War II would not be occurring without the spotlight being shined on their activities through the lawsuits in the United States. The suits for Holocaust restitution have also led to claims being filed against Japanese corporations for their use of captured soldiers and civilians as slaves during World War II.[42] Without a doubt, the claims against the Japanese multinationals are a direct result of the earlier litigation brought against their European counterparts. Ageing victims of Japan's wartime atrocities began filing their lawsuits in American courts only after seeing the successes achieved by their counterparts in the Holocaust litigation.

The hope is that the Holocaust restitution cases can serve as a template for a new era of relief to victims of war crimes and crimes against humanity – but, this time, without the 50-year wait for justice. As a result of the victories achieved by victims of the Holocaust in courts of the United States, individuals and corporations presently engaged in human rights abuses are being put on notice: eventually you will be held responsible for your misdeeds.

NOTES

1 Almost all of the lawsuits filed in the United States to-date stemming from the Holocaust have beenagainst private entities rather than against governments, since litigation against foreign governments would, most likely, be barred by the Foreign Sovereign Immunities Act of 1976, 28 U.S.C. § 1330 *et. seq.* For examples of unsuccessful litigation against foreign governments *see Princz v. Federal Rep. of Germany*, 26 F.3d 1166 (D.C. Cir. 1994) (suit against present-day Germany by Jewish-American sent to concentration camp by the Nazis dismissed; Germany subsequently settles with Princz and ten other Holocaust survivors who were American citizens during the war for $2.1

million); *Haven v. Rep. of Poland*, Case No. 99 C 1727, filed on 25 June 1999 in the U.S. District Court for the Northern District of Illinois, and dismissed on 29 Sept. 1999 (suit dismissed against Poland for failure to return properties to Holocaust survivors from Poland living abroad; case is now on appeal).

This paper uses, for the judicial opinions cited from the courts of the United States, the American legal style of citations. Thus, for example, for the citations in this endnote:

   (a) for statutes: 28 U.S.C. §1330 signifies that the Foreign Sovereign Immunities Act, a federal law, can be located in volume 28 of the United States Code, at section 1330;

   (b) for court opinions: *Princz v. Federal Rep. of Germany* signifies the parties to the action (Princz being the plaintiff and Germany being the lead defendant); 26 F.3d 1166 signifies that the opinion can be found in volume 26 of the 3rd edition of the Federal Reporter (being a reporter of published cases from the federal intermediate appellate courts of the United States) at page 1166; (D.C. Cir. 1994) signifies that the court issuing the opinion was the United States Court of Appeals for the District of Columbia, and that the opinion was published in 1994.

An 'F. Supp.' citation (for example, endnote 8) signifies that the opinion comes from the federal trial court (titled 'federal district court'), and is published in the volumes of the Federal Supplement Reporter, being a reporter of published opinion issued by federal trial courts.

These reporters are found in every law library in the United States, and can also be accessed through two American on-line legal services: Westlaw (www.westlaw.com) and Lexis (www.lexis. com).

For unpublished cases (for example, the *Haven* case in this endnote) the name of the case, its case number, and the date of filing is given.

2 In contrast to less than a dozen lawsuits filed in the first fifty years after the end of World War II, since 1996 over 75 lawsuits have been filed in the United States by various World War II survivors or their heirs seeking damages for wartime wrongs. As I describe in another article, 'the floodgates of litigation have opened [in the United States]. . . .' Michael J. Bazyler, 'Nuremberg in America: Litigating the Holocaust in United States Courts', *Univ. of Richmond Law Review*, March 2000: 6. Appendix A of this article (at pp.265–271) lists every lawsuit filed in the United States since October, 1996, by Holocaust survivors or heirs.

3 In Germany, for instance, every former slave labourer had to file a separate lawsuit against his or her former German corporate master, making slave labour litigation both inefficient and expensive. In the United States, rather than repeating the same claims in hundreds of individual lawsuits, the cases were filed – and settled – as class actions and could all be consolidated before one judge.

4 David Irving learned the bitter lesson of filing an unsuccessful defamation lawsuit in the UK against Deborah Lipstadt, the American Holocaust scholar, and being forced to pay Lipstadt's legal fees. In the United States, Irving would only be assessed court costs.

5 *Smith Kline & French Labs. v. Bloch* [1983] 2 All E.R. 72, 74 (Denning, MR).

6 For examples of earlier lawsuits brought by Holocaust survivors against private parties which were dismissed by American courts *see Kelberine v. Societe Internationale*, 363 F.2d 989 (D.C. Cir. 1966) (slave labor class action lawsuit brought by Holocaust survivor against European corporation dismissed as non-justiciable); *Handel v. Artukovic*, 601 F.Supp. 1421 (C.D. Cal. 1985) (class action lawsuit brought by Holocaust survivors from Yugoslavia against former pro-Nazi Croatian official living in the United States dismissed for lack of jurisdiction and also as being time-barred). See also *Princz, ibid.*, note 1.

7 The Second Circuit found jurisdiction based upon a long-forgotten law, passed by the first U.S. Congress in 1789, entitled the Alien Torts Claims Act, 28 U.S.C. §1350 ('ATCA'), which declares that federal district courts shall have jurisdiction over 'any civil action by an alien for a tort only, committed in violation of the law of nations or a treaty of the United States.'

The *Filartiga* court found that state-sanctioned torture is a clear violation of the law of nations, or (using modern terminology) international law, and since the plaintiffs were Paraguayan nationals, as aliens, their claims fell within the ambit of the ATCA.

For a treatise discussing the *Filartiga* case and its aftermath, *see* Ralph Steinhardt and Anthony D'Amato (eds.), *The Alien Torts Claim Act: An Analytical Anthology* (New York: Transnational Pubs. 1999).

Many of the Holocaust-era lawsuits have relied on the ATCA to establish jurisdiction in United States courts. *See e.g. Sonabend v. Union Bank of Switzerland*, Case No. CV-97–0461 (E.D.N.Y., filed 29 Jan. 1997) (class action against Swiss banks; alien plaintiffs assert jurisdiction under the ATCA); *Snopczyk v. Volkswagen AG*, Case No. 99–C–0472 (E.D. Wis., filed May 5, 1999) (slave labour lawsuit against VW; alien plaintiffs asset jurisdiction under the ATCA).

8 *See e.g. Kadic v. Karadzic*, 70 F.3d 232 (2d Cir. 1995) (lawsuit against Bosnian Serb warlord Rodovan Karadzic brought by victims of Serb atrocities in Bosnia; in August 2000, jury awards $745 million to plaintiffs); *Marcos Estate II*, 25 F.3d 1467 (9th Cir. 1994) (lawsuit against estate of former Philippine dictator Ferdinand Marcos brought by victims of human rights abuses in the Philippines); *Siderman de Blake v. Republic of Argentina*, 965 F.2d 699 (*9th Cir. 1992*) (lawsuit against Argentina for human rights abuses during military rule brought by Argentine Jew and his family); *Doe v. Unocal Corp.*, 963 F. Supp. 880 (C.D. Cal. 1997) (lawsuit against American oil company by Burmese nationals forced to resettle due to building of oil pipeline in Burma).

9 Defendants' Overview Reply Memorandum at 1 (filed 9 July 1997), *In re Holocaust Victims Assets*, *ibid.*

10 In January, 1997, Christoph Meili, a night security guard working at the UBS offices in Zurich, discovered such documents in the UBS shredding room, and publicly disclosed the bank's shredding activities.

11 In a letter to Class Members, Professor Burt Neuborne, Court-appointed Settlement Counsel, confirmed the actual irrelevancy of this nexus between slave labour-produced assets or looted assets and their proceeds being sent to Switzerland. In encouraging all former slave labourers to complete and remit the initial settlement questionnaire, and thereby registering the applicant to possibly receive funds, Professor Neuborne advised:

> Even if you are unsure of whether you have a claim against a Swiss entity, you should complete the enclosed Initial Questionnaire, and follow the procedures described in the enclosed Notice to preserve your rights. For example, if you performed slave labor, you may not know whether revenue or proceeds of that slave labor were deposited with Swiss banks. Or, you may have had assets looted by the Nazi regime, but you may not know whether those assets were disposed of through a Swiss bank. In both instances, you may still be entitled to share in the Settlement Fund. Although there is no guarantee that you will recover any money, you should complete the enclosed Initial Questionnaire.
>
> (Letter from Professor Burt Neuborne to Class Members, 9 June 1999:2, available at <www.swissbankclaims.com>.)

12 Settlement Agreement, paragraph 13, available at <www.swissbankclaims.com>.

13 Lisa Anderson, 'Jewish Leaders Hail Decision by Swiss on Stolen War Assets', *Chicago Tribune*, 13 August 1998: A3.

14 John Authers and Richard Wolfe, 'When Sanctions Work', *Financial Times*, 9 September 1998: 1.

15 'Deutsche Bank disclosed that officials discovered documents showing a branch of the bank in Nazi-occupied Katowice, Poland, had provided loans to construction companies with contracts for facilities at Auschwitz, as well as an adjacent IG Farben chemical plant.' Brian Milner, 'Auschwitz Role May Derail Bank Deal – German Institution's Revelation of Activities during War Adds Firepower to Holocaust Suits', *Globe & Mail*, 6 February 1999, at A16.

   This information came to light through an independent historical commission created by Deutsche Bank after it was sued. The same commission found that Deutsche Bank 'had bought more than 4.4 tons of gold from the Reichsbank, the onetime central bank. "This gold business was normal business during the war," [stated a Deutsche Bank spokesperson]. . . . Of purchases totaling 4,446 kilograms of gold, the [historical] report concluded, 744 kilograms were dental gold taken from Jews' teeth, wedding bands and personal jewelry amassed in Berlin by an SS officer known as Bruno Melmer. . . . [In a statement, Deutsche Bank] "fully acknowledged its moral and ethical responsibility for the darkest chapter of its history" ': Alan Cowell, 'Biggest German Bank Admits and Regrets Dealing in Gold', *The New York Times*, 1 August 1998, at A2.

16 Holman W. Jenkins, Jr., 'Once More into the Dock with "Nazi" Companies', *Wall Street Journal*, 24 March 1999, at A27.

17 *Bodner v. Banque Paribas*, Case No. CV 97–7443 (E.D.N.Y. filed 17 December 1997); *Benisti v. Banque Paribas, Case No. CV 98–7851* (E.D.N.Y. filed December 23, 1998); *Mayer v. Banque Paribas*, Case No. BC 302225 (Cal. Superior Court, San Fran., filed 24 March 1999).

18 Marilyn Henry, 'A Holocaust Paper Trail to Nowhere?', *Jerusalem Post*, 12 May 1999: 11.

19 Generali originally maintained that it had no records of policies it issued before the war. In late 1997, however, it revealed that a warehouse at its headquarters in Trieste, Italy, was found to contain partial records (called 'water copies,' akin to carbon copies) of such policies. Originally, said to contain records of between 330,000 and 384,000 pre-war policyholders, Generali culled the list down to approximately 100,000 policies, which it transferred to a CD-ROM disc. In mid-1998, it turned over the disc to Yad Vashem to match the names of Holocaust victims found in Yad Vashem's archives with its list. To date, Yad Vashem is still working on this project.

20 For a discussion of the scheme concocted in the aftermath of *Kristalnacht*, as well as a general discussion of the Holocaust-era restitution claims, *see* Deborah Senn, Private Insurers and Unpaid Holocaust Era Insurance Claims (Olympia, Wash: Washington State Insurance Commission, 1999), available at <http://www.insurance.wa.gov>.

21 The other three insurers participating in ICHEIC are France's AXA, and Swiss insurers Winterhur Lieben (owned by Credit Suisse Bank), and Zurich. Eagleburger has attempted to have the other European insurers sued join the Commission, but, so far, without success.

22 In addition to the participating insurance companies and the insurance commissioners of the three states, the World Jewish Congress, the Claims Conference, and the World Jewish Restitution Organization (all related NGOs), as well as the State of Israel, have a seat on the ICHEIC board.

23 Tom Tugend, 'Holocaust claims are rejected', *Jewish Chronicle*, 12 May 2000: 4.

24 A substantial reason for settlement of these individual suits in California has been the aggressive stance taken by California against the insurers accused of failing to honor Holocaust-era insurance claims. California led the way in enacting new laws threatening suspension of licenses of such insurers (California Insurance Code Sections 790–790. 15, enacted in 1998), requiring the insurers to open their pre-war insurance records (California Insurance Code Section 13800, enacted in 1999), and extending the limitations period for filing suits for such claims until 31 December 2010 (California code of Civil Procedure section 354.5, enacted in 1998). The states of Washington and Florida have followed suit by enacting similar statutes. *See* Holocaust Victim Insurance Act, Fla. Statutes, chapter 626.9543 (1999); Holocaust Victims Insurance Relief Act, Wash. Revised Code Section 48.104.060 (1999) and Holocaust victims Insurance Act, Wash. Revised Code Section 48.104.040 (1999).

25 'Holocaust Insurance Settlement Reported,' *The New York Times*, 25 November 1999: A4, reporting settlement of Stern v. Generali, a case filed by Holocaust survivor, Adolf Stern, 82 years old, and his family for policies purchased from Generali by his father Moshe 'Mor' Stern, a wealthy wine and spirits merchant from Uzghorod, Hungary, who perished at Auschwitz. In June, 1945, Adolf, who survived Buchenwald and was then 28 years old, presented himself to Generali's offices in Prague seeking payment on the policies. At his deposition, Adolf testified that the Generali officials demanded that he produce a death certificate for Mor. When Adolf explained that the Nazis did not issue death certificates, he was forcibly ejected from Generali's offices. Deposition of Adolf Stern, pp.26–27.

26 In August, 1999, Nathan & Associates, an American economic consulting firm based in Virginia, issued a report estimating that about 2.3 million people who survived the enslavement or forced labour by the Nazis are still alive today. The report was solicited by attorneys representing claimants in the slave labour litigation.

27 As stated by Bernard Graef, head of the Volkswagen historical archives, 'From a legal position the crimes of the Nazis were a state crime, and the issue of slave labour compensation must be addressed to the [German] government.' Adam Lebor, 'Holocaust Slaves Set to Gain Compensation', *Independent* (London), 22 August 1998: 15 (quoting Mr. Graef).

28 In addition to claims for slave labour, the settlement would also include: (1) claims by mothers shipped to Germany whose infants were taken away from them and placed in a *kinderheim*, a children's home, where infants often died; and (2) claims by survivors of horrible medical experiments conducted by the Nazis, allegedly for the benefit of German private pharmaceutical concerns.

29 Count Otto Lambsdorf, the German government representative to the slave labour negotiations, testifying before the U.S. Congress, defended the settlement figure as follows: 'Believe me, I wish I had greater funds available for distribution. But 10 billion marks is what we got and what was agreed upon all the participating parties after long and arduous negotiations.' U.S. House of Representatives, 106th Congress, Hearing of the Committee on Banking and Financial Services 6 (9 February 2000).

30 INTERNATIONAL MONITOR, August 2000, p.1, available at <*www.comptroller.nyc.gov*> (website of the Office the New York City Comptroller Alan G. Hevesi, head of the U.S.-based Executive Monitoring Committee, 'a panel of [U.S. state and local] public and regulatory officials who monitor worldwide progress in Holocaust-era asset restitution efforts.'

31 Roger Cohen, 'German Companies set up Fund for Slave Laborers under Nazis', *The New York Times*, 17 February 1999: A1.

32 See <www.stiftungsinitiave.de> (preamble of the German Economy Foundation Initiative Steering Group).

33 'Germany: Can it be normal? The more the Germans try to look to the future, the more their past seems to return to haunt them', *The Economist*, 12 December 1998:51.

34 For a partial list of Nazi-stolen art see <www.theartnewspaper.com>. In March 2000, British museums, in an attempt to ferret out from their collections art stolen by the Nazis, published a list of artworks with a checkered provenance during the war years. The list can be found at <www.nationalmuseums.org.uk/spoilation>. German museums also launched a list, which can be found at <www.beutekunst.de>. American museums, at first reluctant, are now planning to follow the British and German examples and post such lists on the web.

35 Section 12.03 aims to protect artworks on loan to New York museums from seizure. The law exists to encourage out-of-state fine art to be loaned to New York museums for exhibitions. Morgenthau argued that the law only applies to civil seizures by creditors, and excludes seizures by governmental authorities of potentially stolen art brought into New York. While the New York intermediate appellate court agreed with Morgenthau's reasoning, the New York Court Appeals found that Section 12.03 permits no exceptions to the seizure ban.

36 For the Swiss banks settlement, most attorneys worked *pro bono*, charging only their out-of-pocket expenses. For the Holocaust-era cases, attorneys have applied for fees, which must be approved by the court as reasonable. For instance, in the Swiss banks litigation, Judge Korman approved the maximum amount of fees for attorneys not working *pro bono*, allocating $25 million, or 2 percent of the $1.25 billion, for fees and costs. It is expected, however, that the actual fees awarded would be substantially less that $25 million.

37 Elli Wohlgelernter, 'Lawyers and the Holocaust', *Jerusalem Post*, 2 July 1999: 4B.

38 Richard Cohen, '*The Money Matters*', *Washington Post*, 8 December 1998: A21.

39 *ibid.*

40 For example, Switzerland created a historical commission headed by Swiss historian Francois Bergier, to examine its role during World War II. *See* Independent Commission of Experts, *Second World War, Switzerland and Refugees in the Nazi Era* (1999) (report of Bergier Commission on wartime treatment of refugees by Switzerland). France created a historical commission under former Cabinet minister and Resistance hero Jean Matteoli to examine the looting of assets of Jews in wartime France. *See* The Prime Minister's Office, *Extracts From the Second Report of the Study Mission Into the Looting of Jewish Assets in France* (1999).

Even the United States has gotten into the act, by creating the Presidential Commission on Holocaust Assets, chaired by Edgar Bronfman, financier and head of the World Jewish Congress, to determine the scope of Nazi-stolen assets still present in the United States and also to investigate American companies' wartime complicity with the Nazis. For current information on the Presidential Commission see <www.pcha.gov>. Already, the Presidential Commission has issued one report: a preliminary study of the plunder by American troops of a train loaded with gold, artworks, and other valuables stolen from the Hungarian Jews by the Nazis. The train was captured by the Allies on 16 May 1945, eight days after V-E Day. According to the report, in a notable exception to the generally good effort of American troops to restore property to its rightful owners, both high-ranking U.S. Army officers and lower-level personnel may have helped themselves to these valuables, rather than returning them to the Hungarian Holocaust survivors or the postwar Hungarian Jewish community. For a copy of the report, see <www.pcha.gov/pr99317.htm>.

41 For example, the Swiss Bankers Association created the Volcker Committee to determine the Swiss banks' dealing with the Nazis. *See* Independent Committee of Eminent Persons, Report on *Dormant Accounts of Victims of Nazi Persecution* (1999). Deutsche Bank also hired a team of historians to examine its wartime activities. *See* Jonathan Steinberg, *The Deutsche Bank and its Gold Transactions During the Second World War (30 July 1998)*. Other German companies have followed suit. As reported by *The New York Times*, 'the lawsuits have also created a mini-boom for...[World War II-era] historians and research [scholars].' Barry Meier, 'Chronicles of Collaboration: Historians Are in Demand to Study Corporate Ties to Nazis', *The New York Times*, 18 February 1999: C1.

42 For news articles describing the ongoing claims made against both Japan and Japanese corporations, *see* Michael Dobbs, 'Lawyers Target Japanese Abuses', *Washington Post*, 5 March 2000: A1; Mike Tharp, 'Past-Due Bills for Japan', *U.S. News & World Report*, 7 February 2000: 30; Sonni Efron, 'U.S. Rabbi Presses Japan To Investigate Its War Crimes', *L.A. Times*, 19 February 2000: A6; Shirley Leung, 'Suit Will Test State Law on War Labor', *Wall Street Journal*, 27 October 1999; CA1; Teresa Watanable, 'Japan's War Victims in New Battle', *L.A. Times*, 16 August 1999: A1. For a list of lawsuits filed to-date in the United States against Japanese companies (maintained by the author) see <www.law.whittier.edu/sypo/final/lawsuit.htm>.

In the UK, the government is considering compensation for British soldiers captured by the Japanese during the war. See 'Japanese POWs "in line for £10,000 pay-out"', *The Daily Telegraph*, 4 May 2000: 2.

THE HOLOCAUST GOES TO COURT: A VIEW FROM THE CANADIAN COURTROOM

Ruth Bettina Birn[*]

T HE 20TH-CENTURY event with the greatest moral impact is the Holocaust. It changed and continues to influence western moral thinking in many significant ways: immediately after the war, there were changes to international criminal law to prosecute the Nazi leadership for their role in the Holocaust; laws and policies were developed to ban racism, the evil tool used by the Nazi government; the international community became more conscious of its responsibilities to humankind following the failure to prevent the Holocaust. On the individual level, the Holocaust caused individuals to develop their own moral standards, to question blind acceptance of authority, to search for truth, even if it hurt.

The Holocaust has become a legacy. But all legacies are open to interpretation, increasingly influenced by present-day views, attitudes and political agendas. The transformation of the Holocaust has been subtle but marked. The Holocaust has been removed from our own and historical reality and moved into a virtual reality. The delinking of the Holocaust from the past and present is problematic and subject to misuse and abuse. One recent striking example is the transformation of the meaning of the word 'survivor'. It used to be a special term reserved for those who had escaped the unprecedented horrors of ghettos and camps; in present usage a word signifying the essence of human suffering has become mere rhetoric.[1]

As a Nazi-period historian, I have observed this transformation and its impact on cases involving alleged Nazi war criminals. From this vantage point, past events relevant to the involvement of the alleged Nazi war criminal must be, to the extent they can, reconstructed and proven and given meaning in the present having regard to all their interpretations and distortions. In these cases, the Holocaust is both far away from and close to the Canadian court room; far away from because the events occurred more than fifty-five years ago and were not a part of Canadian experience and close to because the historical events are central to and have a real and direct impact on the decision-making process. It makes a difference, whether there is an acquittal or conviction. The judges deciding these cases define reality based on proven facts, and not on memory and remembrance.

THE HOLOCAUST GOES TO COURT

Historical evidence is essential to proving cases against alleged Nazi war criminals because their role and involvement in the crimes can only be understood and properly

[*] The author is employed as Chief Historian, War Crimes Section, Department of Justice of Canada. It should be noted that the views expressed in this paper are entirely those of the author. Nothing in this paper should be interpreted or construed as reflecting, in any way, the views of the Department of Justice or the Government of Canada.

evaluated within a full historical framework. There are several basic challenges caused by the fact that the realities of Eastern Europe at the time of German occupation are distant from Canada in the 90's. Many Canadians are unaware of where, for instance, Belarus is exactly located. The public remembrance of the war in Canada is largely based on the recollections of Canadian war veterans, who saw action only on the Western Front. Generally, the Canadian public perception of German occupation is at the level of France (the impact of the 'French resistance theme' on Anglo-Saxon popular culture is remarkable) and Western Europe where conditions were worlds apart from the harsh realities of the German occupation of the East.

In Canada, the overwhelming majority of allegations concern Eastern Europe, mainly the former Soviet Union. Until a specialized unit was set up in 1987, the gap in understanding the realities between the German occupation of the East impacted on attempts to investigate Nazi crimes or to estimate the numbers of perpetrators who might have found their way to Canada.[2] Canadian 'common sense' was not sufficient to detect that a person who carried arms in occupied Ukraine could not have been a mere peaceful citizen.[3] The first task of an historian involved in the litigation of World War II cases is to reconstruct historical realities as a backdrop for the evaluation of evidence. However, what for the professional historian requires a flash of recognition when dealing within the same framework of reference, can in assembling this evidence for a court proceeding become difficult and labour intensive.

The task is made more difficult when one superimposes the problems arising from the distrust of evidence and information emanating from the former Soviet Union. Images of KGB conspiracies and forgeries loom large, which is hardly surprising considering how large a part this theme plays in popular culture. Preconceived notions are as much a problem as ignorance. Although the Soviet Union used the Nazi period information for propaganda purposes, through the critical evaluation of sources – in particular now, when access to the former Soviet Archives is possible – it is possible to determine the provenance, genuineness and creditworthiness of this documentation. Apart from the post-war political considerations which kept Canada from taking action against alleged Nazi perpetrators, it is well accepted by war crimes investigators that meaningful investigations could only be conducted after the break-up of the Soviet Union and the negotiated direct access to materials in the archives – that is to say, at a time, which was too late, according to Canadian interest groups. Even under the present conditions, a general suspicion about Soviet evidence remains.

Contrast the court's approach in the only case not involving allegations from Eastern Europe, a case of a Dutch collaborator, who had been sentenced *in absentia* by a Dutch criminal court after the war. This was the first Nazi war criminal denaturalization case heard by the Federal Court of Canada and based on the recent decisions, it was an untypical case because the court accepted as evidence without reservation the verdict by a Dutch court, the expert opinion of Dutch historians and historical documents from Dutch archives.[4] Although these evidentiary rulings did not guarantee success in this case, in future cases, the Canadian government has not been in such a favourable position in presenting historical evidence.[5]

How history is written depends on several factors. The histories by scholars associated with an ethnic community present one challenge. Partisanship can significantly influence their accounts, especially of the war period. Ethnic communities in Canada and the United States depict the war years in a way compatible to their self-image and collective memory, which is not always consistent with reality. Another factor is that historiography is subject to historical developments allowing each generation to define its own focus on the past. With the Holocaust, it is increasingly noticeable that the images of the past are being manipulated to accommodate present-day notions. In North America, the Nazi period and the Holocaust is often depicted as a counter-image to our own society and values. The recent flood of novels, books and movies about the Holocaust and the Nazi period do not present mirror-images of the past, on the contrary, they reflect present-day society mirrored in the past. The Holocaust and the Nazis have been pressed into the service of almost any political and public concern, from abortion clinics to animal rights.[6] Finally, there is the sensationalizing of the Holocaust. The frequent depictions of acts of violence and stacks of corpses raise concerns in a society where cruelty plays such a large part in the entertainment culture. The Holocaust has taken on a life of its own in North America, unconnected with the past or the present, existing in a virtual reality. It is in the courtroom where the virtual reality of the Holocaust inevitably clashes with the Holocaust of reality.

THE SEARCH FOR REALITY

The clash between the two realities is illustrated in the case of Antanas Kenstavicius, which dealt with the Holocaust in Lithuania and the involvement and collaboration of Lithuanians. Kenstavicius was alleged to have been the chief of police of Svencionys, a smaller town in Lithuania, where in early October 1941 approximately 6000 Jews were murdered.[7] The depiction of the relationship between Jewish Lithuanians and Christian Lithuanians vary greatly in the available secondary sources. According to Milda Danys, a Lithuanian-Canadian, Lithuanians were opposed to the persecution of Jews, would not get involved in the actions taken by the Germans, because they saw the victims as 'neighbours, classmates, respected professionals and personal friends'.[8] On the opposite side, Sol Littman, the Canadian Representative of the Simon Wiesenthal Center, draws a different picture in describing 'one of the most vicious pogroms in history' in Kaunas, where 'The indiscriminate slaughter was conducted by so-called Lithuanian freedom fighters, at the urging of the Nazis, in the name of Lithuanian independence.' This is of little surprise to him, as 'anti-Semitism was endemic in Lithuania'.[9]

The documents found in the Lithuanian State Archive on Svencionys – which are uncommonly detailed – show a much more complex picture. The Lithuanian police, who had been set up on a voluntary basis following the occupation by Germany, presents itself as a law-abiding body. In the daily event reports by the chief of police of Svencionys, much is made about orderliness, proper uniforms and record keeping. Policemen are dismissed from service for 'dishonouring the police', or disciplined for black-market activities or harassment of the population. After all, 'all police actions must be supported by law.'[10] The first hint about the police's engagement in not so lawful activities is found in the curriculum for training of the indigenous police in the Baltic States, in which Adolf Hitler's struggle against World Jewry takes a prominent place.[11] The persecution of the Jewish population is well documented (yellow star, ghettoization, forced labour, miserable working and living conditions), but less so the implementations of these measures. This results in the lower level perpetrators being out of focus. The murder of the majority of the Jews of Svencionys can only be inferred because they are not there any more, their property has been seized and their houses have been confiscated. The order to put chlorinated lime on 'the site where the Jews were liquidated' is the strongest worded proof to be found.[12] (In comparison, the involvement of the indigenous police in the murder of Gypsies is better documented.) The reasons for the paucity of information on the murder of the Jews lies in the systematic destruction of incriminating documents at the end of the war and the use of sanitized language in contemporary documents. For instance, the only reference to the 'Special Unit', which came from Vilnius to conduct the mass shooting in early October, has been preserved by chance. The leader was a Lithuanian and as such, the unit must have been comprised of Lithuanians. During 'celebrations' after the mass-murder, members of the 'Special Unit' opened fire at the band playing killing several Polish men, then tried to cover up by attempting to hide their bodies. This caused considerable upset in the population resulting in a police investigation in which these references were discovered.

While this material is sufficient for the historian to draw the inference that the Lithuanian police must have been involved in actions against Jews, is this material sufficient to support an inference by a judge in a legal proceeding?[13] From this fragmented record what can be determined about the attitude of the Lithuanian police, officials and ordinary citizens? The documents cover a wide range of events: a Lithuanian mayor is alleged to have stolen property of the murdered Jews, but the allegation is made by a group of Lithuanian partisans, who had concerns about this type of behaviour.[14] The clearest indication of an anti-Jewish animus can be found in those reports where Lithuanians claim or take possession of Jewish property; but what can we conclude about the attitude of the carpenter who received payment for boarding up the windows of the synagogue? Did he do it gleefully or mournfully? How does one interpret the report of the German gendarme, who accompanies two Jewish women to confront a Lithuanian woman, with whom they had left their valuables that the Lithuanian woman does not want to return? According to the report, the Lithuanians were clearly scandalized by the behaviour of the gendarme and appealed to the authorities: 'please intervene quickly, the Jewesses are threatening to have us shot!'[15] With such contradictory and fragmented primary sources, are the aforementioned secondary sources helpful to a court in evaluating and weighing the primary documentary evidence? The answer is obvious.

Overcoming the adaptation of history to conform to present-day notions is the second problem. An interesting example is the remarkable story of Oswald Rufeisen, a young Jewish man, who fled from Poland proper to Byelorussia, and who, because of his excellent command of the German language, managed to become the interpreter for the German Gendarmerie post in the town of Mir. In this capacity, he was able to assist the Jewish ghetto. A number of court cases in Britain and Canada concern the Holocaust in Byelorussia and this specific region. Rufeisen has made a number of statements that were used in German investigations in the 1960s.[16] (After the archives in Byelorussia became available to Western researchers, Rufeisen's statements were corroborated by documents.[17]) Based on the prior statements and in close cooperation with Rufeisen, Nechama Tec wrote a biography of Rufeisen's life that provides many interesting insights on the German and non-German perpetrators.[18] Only somebody in Rufeisen's unique position could make the detailed observations illuminating the motives, conduct and degree of involvement of the perpetrators. While his account is very differentiated and portrays the perpetrators as human beings, Rufeisen is never blind to the fact that they were conducting mass-murder at the time he knew them nor does he make excuses for them.

On the other hand, a recent Israeli publication on the 'Jews of Byelorussia',[19] while being based partly on the same sources, provides a different picture. Although the history of the Jews of Byelorussia during World War II is overwhelmingly a history of persecution and mass-murder, a significant part of this book addresses Jewish heroism and resistance. Cholawski's portrait of the perpetrators is one-dimensional and facts like the denunciation of Rufeisen to the Germans by a Jewish inmate of the ghetto are left out. His focus is understandable in light of the demands of present-day society on the presentation of the past (helplessness in the face of evil is very frightening), but it results in his not providing a tool for our understanding of perpetrators as Rufeisen and Tec do. Rufeisen, by recounting the facts as he lived and observed them, no doubt assisted the judge hearing the case against Serafimowicz, the chief of Mir Rayon Police, in assessing Serafimowicz's character and motivation. What assistance can be gained from Cholawski?[20]

To illustrate how the steady stream of sensationalist representations and images of Nazis and Holocaust plays out in court; the recent Canadian case of Eduard Podins is useful. In this case, the central problem was terminology: How to refer to a specific place of incarceration in Valmiera, Latvia? While, in the sense of the contemporary German terminology, it was not a 'concentration camp',[21] it belonged to the camp system that the Security Police and SD set up in 1941 in occupied Latvia. (These camps were called *'Ersatzgefaengnis'* [EG]). 'The case against the defendant with respect to alleged collaboration' turned 'to a significant degree on the nature of Valmiera EG'. After reviewing the evidence, the judge decided that notwithstanding evidence of 'forced labour, inadequate food and beatings', and 'evidence of an execution', the conditions at Valmiera would not 'suggest the systematic brutality of an concentration camp.' In the end, the judge decided in favour of the defendant. Inundated by images of barking German shepherds, sadists in black boots, gas ovens and crematoria, can the present-day observer recognize a place of incarceration as it really existed?[22]

THE IMMIGRATION SYSTEM GOES TO COURT

Denaturalization cases in Canada and the United States are based on immigration regulations prohibiting Nazi perpetrators or collaborators from entry into the country after World War II. In Canada, criminal cases were initially brought forward until the decision by the Supreme Court of Canada in *R.v. Finta* closed this option. The alternative legal remedy of denaturalization was also available, as Nazi perpetrators found in Canada must have gained citizenship by fraud. In every Nazi related case, the government has to set out its argument supported by the relevant documents on immigration policy and the mechanisms of screening out undesirable immigrants.[23] The proof of the immigration policy and screening mechanisms is complicated by the vigorous attacks by certain authors positing that there was a consistent policy to keep Jews out of Canada, stretching from the pre-war to the post-war years;[24] and that Canada was notoriously lenient towards Nazi perpetrators, and sloppy at best in its attempts to keep them out.[25] In the media, this culminated in statements like 'Nazis were virtually welcomed into Canada'; or, as one historian put it, showing a SS-tattoo under the arm was enough to get a visa to Canada over the counter.[26] Indeed, another historian's findings on Canadian post-war immigration and screening policy,[27] were praised for revealing 'Ottawa's dirty little secrets'.[28] According to her, lack of concern for the Jewish victims of Nazism, overt or hidden sympathy for the perpetrators, and a political agenda entirely driven by anti-Communist concerns, are the root causes why Nazi perpetrators could escape punishment and successfully migrate to Canada.[29] This alleged chain of evil intentions stretches from international organizations, like UNRRA or IRO to Canadian bureaucracy. Indeed, she speaks of 'Canada's complicity in crimes against humanity.'[30]

There is no indication that the proponents of these arguments realize how anathema their views are to their stated aim of bringing Nazis found in Canada to justice. Indeed, one of the proponents, Canadian historian Irving Abella promotes this position as the

Canadian Jewish Congress's representative on war crimes matters. Ironically, defense counsel in denaturalization cases have seized on the contradiction and used the above argumentation against Canada's position. They argue that their clients did not resort to fraud to gain entry into Canada because they were welcome. Defense counsel in a recent World War II related case subpoenaed Dr. Rodal, the other historian quoted above. Following a review of her expertise and research methods, the judge concluded that she could not be a 'properly qualified expert on citizenship matters'[31] making a detailed discussion of the correctness of her opinion superfluous.[32]

A discussion of Canadian security screening is of little interest in the context of this paper, however some historical background to the allegations of official callousness and leniency towards Nazis is relevant. Canada had been practically closed to immigration from the early 1930's on. Its doors were gradually re-opened as a part of the international attempts to provide relief for the millions of Displaced Persons (DP's) found in Central Europe after the war. After an initial phase of repatriations, resettlement was attempted through the UN-sponsored International Refugee Organization (IRO)[33], whose intended beneficiaries were the victims of Nazism. Perpetrators and collaborators were explicitly excluded from the IRO mandate. The IRO established procedures designed to screen out Nazi-affiliated people from those seeking admission into their relief and resettlement programmes. Canada and other western countries involved in this effort also established screening programmes to the same purpose.[34] Accepting the 'evil intentions' theory would mean that major international organizations and the Canadian and other western governments were motivated by racism or pro-Nazi sympathies. In view of the fact that Canada and its Allies had just fought a long and bitter war against the Nazis and the Western media were reverberating with discoveries of Nazi atrocities, this theory is difficult to sustain. Alti Rodal is alone in arguing that, in the first weeks after Germany's surrender, a 'serious effort would have succeeded in finding war criminals'.[35] Even a superficial knowledge of the real conditions in Central Europe in these months must lead to a different conclusion.

One does not need a detailed knowledge of the history of postwar Europe to understand this type of situation; a comparison with present-day events is sufficient. Recall recent events such as the aftermath of the genocide in Rwanda, when international relief organizations continued to supply goods to refugee camps notwithstanding warnings that they were supporting the perpetrators. Are we to infer that this relief was a disguised support of the 'genocidaires' or is it one of the fallacies to which well-meaning relief organizations can fall prey? Indeed, experienced relief-workers will recognize strategies such as falsifying life histories, forging documents, and obtaining access to relief fraudulently – which we know, must have happened frequently in post-war DP camps – as common occurrences in every refugee camp. The post-war IRO screening information was more sophisticated and detailed than what is available in many present-day refugee-screening situations. It was unable to prevent fraud, but it was not because of any evil intentions.[36]

Looking at post-war immigration in its own historical framework, politicians and bureaucrats managed risk, made trade-offs between humanitarian relief and immigration security. The same trade-offs would be made today. Indeed, Canada's harshest critics of post-war immigration screening programmes subscribe to such views when addressing present-day events. David Matas, in his book on *Nazi War Criminals in Canada* writes that 'one is too many', as 'even one perpetrator at large threatens the integrity of Canadian justice.'[37] Yet, in response to a Canadian Security and Intelligence Service (CSIS) report about the activities of political terrorist groups in Canada, Mr. Matas, an immigration lawyer, admitted 'terrorists do slip through, but it's the price to be paid living in a democratic society. You can't expect a system that is admitting 600,000 visitors and 200,000 immigrants a year to be error free.'[38] A sentiment those immigration officials in the 1940's would have applauded! (Actually, it was a sentiment they occasionally expressed.)

These examples show that two different yardsticks are being used: one for the Nazi period and another for the present. While reactions of outrage in the face of the appalling fact that Nazi perpetrators could find safe havens are understandable, an ahistorical tunnel vision linking less than desirable outcomes with evil intentions impairs our ability to learn from the past. It is more important to realize that even the best of intentions can lead to poor results, to identify the common factors permitting abuses, to change the mechanisms within international organizations to reduce error and to apply the lessons of the past to the present.

THE LEGAL FOUNDATION AND ITS CRACKS

The Nuremberg trials are generally regarded as the genesis of the international community's commitment to deal with perpetrators of war crimes and crimes against humanity. In light of this fundamental perception, the surprise of the audience was palpable when several law professors on a panel discussing 'Transitional Justice and the History of the GDR' at the 1998 conference of the *German Studies' Association* argued that the Nuremberg trials were also the end. One panelist, Peter E. Quint, author of *The Imperfect Union*[39] dealt with the question of retroactivity and whether political crimes committed in the GDR, which at the time might have been in accordance with the law, could be prosecuted in a unified Germany. According to Quint, 'the relevance of Nuremberg' is that these crimes cannot be prosecuted – even if they violated general principles of international law – because the acts committed by the GDR were not comparable to those punished in Nuremberg.[40] In essence, he argues that only crimes of the order of magnitude of the Holocaust can retroactively be rendered criminal offences.

This is a most uncomfortable consequence for the concept of the 'uniqueness' of the Holocaust. Initially introduced to combat attempts at minimizing the horrors of the mass-murder of the Jews of Europe by comparison with other political crimes, 'uniqueness' has led to some rather problematical uses in recent years,[41] but the argument that uniqueness justifies the immunity of every political criminal after 1945 amounts to a travesty of the lessons of Nuremberg.

Professor Inga Markovits, another panelist, took the argument one step further. For her, even the attempt to right the wrongs done by the Communist regime in East Germany is dubious. Again, her yardstick is the Nazi past. The Germans did not want to prosecute Nazis, so the logic goes, now they are scapegoating the communists to distract attention from this failure, and it all is motivated by continuous but disguised German right-wing tendencies.[42] Dr. Markovits's arguments are highly unfair to the German prosecutors engaged in this work – among them several formerly dedicated to prosecuting of Nazi crimes.

Learning from the past is a major goal of these prosecutions, in the hope that the collective conscience is sharpened against political crimes, regardless who commits them. Professor Markovits's book, *Imperfect Justice*, reveals a strong bias in favour of the former GDR. As the subtitle, 'a diary', indicates, it is mainly a collection of conversations with East German lawyers (in universities and in courts).[43] These people are depicted as vulnerable following the disappearance of their power-base and their state. (Their former victims do not appear.) Their patterns of self-explanation and strategies of exoneration have a familiar ring to those of their Nazi counterparts. Without doubt, one cannot compare the crimes committed by the GDR in magnitude to the Nazi's crimes. However, on an individual level, the reprehensible acts in which the lawyers described by Markovits participated can easily be compared to some of their Nazi counterparts. This illustrates one of the main problems connected to 'uniqueness': if one only looks at the Holocaust in its entirety, one is incapacitated from properly evaluating the conduct of individuals, particularly at the lower level. This distorts our understanding of state-sponsored crime. Markovits' book reveals how attempts at self-exoneration, which were discredited when used by Nazis and should be discredited for anybody else, become credible when former GDR functionaries decline individual responsibility, blame the party and claim to have been taken in by propaganda, etc.[44] Is not the participation in oppressive regimes universally unacceptable, and not just limited to the Nazis?

There has been extensive criticism of the less than satisfactory results of investigations and trials against Nazi perpetrators. Given the continuity of personnel in the German legal system before and after 1945, Nazi sympathies may very well have been an issue. Indeed, about 30 years ago accusations of this kind had an explosive effect in the Federal Republic of Germany. Interestingly, notwithstanding the passage of time, allegations about the hidden complicity of law enforcement bodies, foot-dragging and delaying tactics persist today. A review published by one such harsh critic – under the title: 'Acquittal for the murder battalion' – reveals its author to have very little knowledge of the investigative and legal problems of such cases.[45] By way of illustration, the author criticizes the prosecutors for not having tried harder to find witnesses from among the former victims. Common sense and the record of everyone who has investigated mobile killing units establishes that victims are rarely of assistance in identifying individual perpetrators because the units came from another place. One is lucky if they can recall the colours of the uniforms the members of the killing unit wore.[46] The author, though full of righteous indignation, is clearly unaware of such difficulties.

What is the impact of these types of critical remarks? They do not contribute to any meaningful discussion about the ability of the domestic or international legal systems to deal with political crimes, particularly genocide. Recent events have shown that high hopes are pinned on diplomatic and legal solutions to the atrocities everybody watches on TV, but which nobody can stop. What is needed is a sober assessment of the effective legal tools within which the world community will operate,[47] not denunciations of the unpalatable results of prosecutions. The latter serve to demonstrate the moral sensibilities of the outraged observer, but have no positive effect if the legal realities are ignored.

A recent deportation case in Toronto illustrates this. Konrad Kalejs, an Australian citizen living in the United States was ordered deported to Australia following a finding by the US Court of Appeals that he had been a member of the 'Arajs-Kommando', a Latvian mobile killing unit attached to the German Security Police in the Baltics. It conducted large-scale mass-killing actions of Jews, guarded concentration camps, etc. Kalejs came to Canada as a visitor and although he had no official immigration status, he wanted to visit and live in Canada. In order to prevent him from entering Canada, a deportation hearing was started. The hearing before the Immigration and Refugee Board lasted for most of 1996. Observers of these proceedings have questioned whether the latitude given to the defendant Kalejs and the legal and evidentiary burdens placed on the government were appropriate. For example, Kalejs was allowed to dismiss the substantial documentary evidence of his membership in the Arajs-Kommando off-hand as 'KGB forgeries', thus requiring the Government to prove them in spite of the fact the US Court of Appeals had relied on the same documents and had rejected the same argument on this point. Some observers have commented that the fact that this hearing took place at all showed that the Canadian government does not care about Nazi crimes.[48] But the reason for these hearings lies not in anyone's ill will but in the decision of the Supreme Court of Canada[49] which gave a person without status the right to a 'full, fair and impartial hearing' before deportation. The basis for this and similar decisions find their roots in the humanitarian concern for the rights of refugees and migrants which are founded, in part, on the lessons of history from the Nazi period. Supreme Court Justice Bertha Wilson, who wrote the Singh decision, is highly revered among human rights advocates, including some of the harshest critics of the Canadian war crimes programme.[50] To my knowledge, the media has not made the connection between cause and effect. Public perception is entirely split. This split is so manifest and so far from reality that one can only assume it serves a social function. Would it not be very disturbing to realize that our good enlightened liberal values might in fact incapacitate our legal systems from effectively dealing with the horrors of genocide or ethnic cleansing? As the critics know, it is much easier to doubt the good intentions of the individuals who do the work (the standard line in Canada is about prosecutors who have 'no fire in their belly') than to doubt the legal systems' ability to deal with evil in the world.

THE DEFENDANT AND DEFENCE STRATEGIES
The defendant is the tangible link between the present and the past. The judge must assess the evidence brought forward against him by the government, but must also consider his testimony. In short, he has to associate the defendant in the courtroom with the events that happened long ago in Europe. Inevitably, the defendants are now rather old, a fact which has an obvious impact.[51] In addition, the media have created an image of alleged Nazi war criminals, which no doubt influences the judge in assessing the evidence against the defendant. In the Canadian context, the standard reference is to the 'world's most heinous murderers of all time'.[52] While this might apply to Hitler or Himmler or when speaking of the perpetrators of the Holocaust as an entity, it is unlikely that a judge will associate a real-life defendant with this label. Due to the restrictions in post-war immigration and security screening, Nazi masterminds never made it to Canada. None of the Canadian defendants held policy-making positions; the vast majority are not Germans. The defendants commonly claim they acted out of fear of German oppression, pointing to their low level in the hierarchy, and in some cases, their young age during the war. Countering these defences requires a detailed and painstaking reconstruction of the real situation in order to show that even these low-level perpetrators had an impact on the fate of the victims in their locality. The available direct evidence is very limited. Media statements like 'We are dealing with men who committed horrendous crimes: mass-murder; torture; theft and intimidation. They killed men, women, babies, not just once but repeatedly'[53] can hardly be substantiated by the evidence available in real cases.

The incongruity between a statement like: 'There is no one in the United States who has more blood on this hands than John Demjanjuk'[54] and an old man in the courtroom is so glaring that it becomes counter-productive. Just how counter-productive became apparent in the reactions in the media to the recent determination in the case of Johann Dueck. The media reported the judge's finding that Dueck was not 'a war criminal', but 'a simple man compelled under threat of death to act as translator to Nazi thugs', referring to the proceedings as 'a Nazi war-crimes circus', the letters to the editor as to a witch-hunt, and the defence lawyer description of his client's ordeal as years of 'vilification'.[55]

In historiography, demonization of the perpetrators of the Holocaust is a highly popular image as shown by the unprecedented support Daniel Goldhagen's book: 'Hitler's Willing Executioners'[56] received in North America and subsequently in Germany. Goldhagen sees the causes for the Holocaust in a centuries old, demonological hallucinatory hatred of Jews, particular to Germans. According to him, this is what motivated the perpetrators, including those on the lower levels. Goldhagen's perpetrator is a sadistic, enthusiastic killer, motivated by ideological convictions. And he is German.

Small wonder that counsel for two Ukrainian defendants in Canadian cases realized the similarity of Goldhagen's argument to their own. Goldhagen writes 'The Germans had defeated, repressed and dehumanized Ukrainians' and that the 'German's conduct towards their eastern European minions... was generally draconian.'[57] This mirrored the claims of defence counsel that their clients were intimidated and oppressed by the Germans and acted out of fear.[58]

Goldhagen's image of the perpetrator has them unlike 'us', in fact, has them outside of the range of normal human behaviour. This image is comforting to the reader – as shown by the reception of his book on both sides of the Atlantic. It was not surprising that this reassuring view gained ground at the present stage of Holocaust interpretation, where perpetrators (and survivors) are less and less a real part of the picture; World War II related cases being one of the few exceptions. But, as the experience in Canadian courts has shown, the Goldhagen image of the perpetrator is entirely inadequate, indeed is counterproductive in the real world.

THE CHOICE OF LEGACIES – REALITY OR VIRTUAL REALITY

The trends discussed above are not unique to Canada, they can be generally observed. The same allegations about clandestine sympathies with the Nazis have been made against other countries, the short circuit conclusions were drawn about evil intentions leading to evil results. The greater the role the Holocaust and its legacy plays in the public discourse, the more pronounced is the transformation from reality to virtual reality. (And occasions like court hearings, which sharply illuminate the clash between the two, are rare.) In fact, one has to ask oneself what appeal a certain depiction of history has to our present society? Again, Goldhagen's success story may provide a clue.

To the uninformed reader, the most attractive feature of Goldhagen's book is the split between 'them' – the perpetrators of the Holocaust, the Nazis, the Germans – and 'us', our society, our state. Goldhagen's depiction of Nazi Germany and its racist policies is so stark, so black in black, that it forecloses any comparisons to our own political systems or values. In fact, the political dimension is almost non-existent in the book. The Nazis are not referred to as a right wing political force with the foremost political goal to eliminate the left. This follows a common trend in North America that avoids reference to any tradition lines of the Nazi right wing political movement to contemporary right wing politics and political philosophy in general. It also assuages any nagging doubts about anything troublesome in our own political culture.

One reason for the increasing popularity Holocaust related topics enjoy in North America may be that in the Second World War, 'we' were on the right side, and, as nothing can ever be compared to the horrors of the Holocaust ('the *world's* most heinous murderers *of all time*), 'our' place is forever on the right side. Goldhagen himself demonstrated the political implications of this type of logic. In an article on the Kosovo crisis, he sees any moral doubts about NATO bombing Serbia 'answered by the undeniable rightness and success' of World War II.[59] NATO should start a ground war, occupy Serbia, and extend to the Serbian population the benefits of the re-education, which had entirely changed post-war Germany and Japan in the course of a few years. It is not surprising that a speaker at the 29th Scholars' Conference on the Holocaust and the Churches would remark that in the USA, the Holocaust is only evoked with respect to Rwanda or Bosnia, but not Guatemala. And an observer of the tragedy in East Timor will probably wait in vain for an appeal to occupy and re-educate Indonesia given the involvement of the US.[60] This point brings us to one of the most fundamental questions. The Holocaust is the history of the persecution and murder of defenceless people by a powerful state. Given the above comments, one must ask, how closely a connection can Holocaust organizations have with state powers without putting their message at risk?

Other observations give one pause about the future moral guidance of the lessons of the past. Some of the moral standards drawn from the Holocaust are so high, that it seems unlikely they can be considered as yardsticks for present-day behaviour.[61] For example, the term 'bystander community' is being used more and more for the Polish community during World War II. 'By-standers' has a connotation of complicity. Other statements are more explicit: 'Statistics show that the more co-operative the occupied country, the greater was the loss in life. In Poland, 3,000,000 Jews were killed out of a population of 3,300,00, or ninety percent.'[62] While statements like this might reflect strong animosities between the Jewish and Polish communities in pre-war Poland,[63] in respect to the war situation, they are untenable. Poland is the prime example that the Holocaust could happen without or with minimal assistance of non-Germans. Whatever their sentiments towards Jews may have been, the basic fact is that the Polish population lived at a time and in a place where the mass-murder happened and they were not allowed any political input by their German occupiers. Is this complicity? Could we as citizens of one of the Western powers live up to such high moral standards? Moreover, Goldhagen has added new meaning to the term 'by-stander' by his assertion that it is impossible to be an 'indifferent' observer or by-stander of criminal acts, that even silence more likely indicates 'tacit approval'.[64] By this definition, are we all not by-standers to whatever happens in our own society or in the world? Or, have we developed two moral yardsticks, one for the past and one for the present?

And, what of the individual? Should the lessons of the Holocaust not influence every individual's moral choices and commitments? How much real choice exists, however, is doubtful as is illustrated by the controversy over John Roth's nomination as Director of the Institute for Advanced Holocaust Studies at the Holocaust Museum in Washington. Initially, Roth was attacked for having drawn comparisons between Israel and the Nazis in his earlier writings. Then, Republican politicians joined the attack on the basis that Roth had asked critical questions about Ronald Reagan and US politics.[65] In recent years, comparing the Holocaust to any other event in history has become taboo (though comparing German chancellors, including the present incumbent, to Hitler seems still permissible).[66] However, the Roth controversy took matters a step further. Not only is comparing two historical events considered reprehensible, but so is using the guidance of past events to inform one's present and future political and moral decisions. This is important. There is a difference between equating, let's say, Reagan to Hitler, and opposing certain American policies on the basis of the lessons one has learned from the history of the Nazis. A ban of the latter means preventing any student of the Holocaust from forming his own decisions of conscience.

History can only have an impact through the conscience of individuals; whether or not their conclusions seem acceptable or absurd. If the lessons of the past can be limited and prescribed, then they will become mere rhetoric. 'Remembering for the future' demands real insights connecting the Holocaust to the present, and demands honesty and courage, not meaningless virtual images and hollow words.[67]

N O T E S

1 After the war, very rough estimates had 50,000 survivors, maybe as high as 100,000. Recent growing popular interest in the Holocaust has seen a broadening of meaning of 'survivor' to include people who were not liberated from the camps. Thus, an Israeli committee recently estimated roughly 900,000 living survivors in 1997 – several times more than after the war. In 1999, 'millions of other Holocaust survivors, who emerged from concentration camps' is reported on the jacket of one of the latest Holocaust related books. See Timothy W. Ryback, *The Last Survivor. In search of Martin Zaidenstadt* (New York: Pantheon Books, 1999).

2 Immediately after the war, a War Crimes Investigations Unit dealt with crimes committed against Canadian army personnel. In 1985, a Commission of Inquiry on War Criminals was appointed under Judge Jules Deschênes. Deschênes published his findings in a report on 30 December 1986. Following his recommendations, a War Crimes Section was set up within the Department of Justice of Canada. After the Office of Special Investigation in Washington, the Canadian unit was the second unit set up outside of Europe. Units in Australia, Britain and Scotland followed, but they have been closed down.

3 The problem of a lack of background information continues to arise, in an even stronger form, in respect of people coming to Canada from the scenes of recent political catastrophes. While lack of knowledge on the side of Canadian officials in the post-war period is customarily depicted by Canadian Jewish groups as ill-will, no such allegations are raised in respect of the present-day situation.

4 A number of other factors were also different. The person in question had immigrated to Paraguay immediately after the war, and came to Canada only comparatively late. This was of importance as one of the major obstacles in Canadian cases is the loss of all post-war immigration records, which were routinely destroyed. Therefore, with a later date of entry, the evidence on the immigration part of a case is greatly improved. See *Canada (Secretary of State) v. Luitjens*, [1991] F.T.R. 267, 15 Imm. L.R. (2d) 40 (F.C.T.D.).

5 While this case is widely referred to in the media and in publications, no one mentions the particular circumstances.

6 An interesting example of how wrong the invocations of the past can be is acted out almost daily in Ottawa. At noontime, demonstrations take place in front of an abortion clinic, which is called the 'Auschwitz on Sparks Street'. Historically, the anti-abortionists got it wrong, because the Nazis cracked down on abortions – but, of course, only, if the woman in question possessed 'good, Aryan blood'. If not, the authorities could encourage abortions, or have them even forcibly performed. The wishes of the pregnant women, in any case, did not carry any weight. Historically, the pro–choice direction is the one which is contrary to the Nazi position, and not the other way around. As it happens, the doctor who started the clinic in Ottawa, and others in other provinces of Canada, did that with the explicit intention of taking a stand for women's right to self-determination, this means, against the Nazi position. He himself was an inmate of Auschwitz. How he must feel when reading the demonstrators' signs?

7 Kenstavicius died during the hearing, so no decision on the veracity of the allegations against him was made.

8 Danys, Milda: *DP. Lithuanian Immigration to Canada after the Second World War* (Toronto, Multicultural History Society of Ontario, 1986), p.11. According to Danys, 'once Nazi power was established over Europe', resettlement, slave labour and destruction would await the Lithuanians as well. Latvian-American historian Andrew Ezergailis argues that the same fate would have awaited the Latvian nation, Ezergailis, Andrew: *The Holocaust in Latvia. 1941–1944*, (Washington/Riga: The Historical Institute of Latvia and the US Holocaust Museum, 1996, p.50). In his book Ezergailis uses an argument, which was widely used in Germany in the forties and fifties: only a small group of hardcore perpetrators are guilty – in the Latvian context, the Arajs command, – while everybody else was

victim of circumstances. As expert historian for the defence of a Latvian police officer in Toronto, Ezergailis considered the deportations of 'able-bodied' children to labour camps in the course of a major anti-partisan action as 'an act of mercy' because it took them away from burning buildings. *The Minister of Citizenship and Immigration v. Peteris Vitols*, Transcript of Proceedings of 25 February 1998 at p.2301. Ezergailis' book was co-published by the Holocaust Museum in Washington. The defence won their case.

9 Sol Littman, *War Criminal on Trial. Rauca of Kaunas* (Toronto, Key Porter Books, 1998), p.55, p.59. Littman also stresses the 'failure of any responsible Lithuanian element to speak out' ibid, p.59. In the latter part of his book, Littman turns to the present Canadian effort to investigate Nazi crimes. Accuracy does not seem to be his strong suit; in his account, he mixes up the information on three of the present cases, ibid., p.219. He also presents unfounded theories, such as that the, then conservative Canadian government would have wanted war crimes cases to fail. Other examples are as egregious.

10 Order, 5 March 1942, Lithuanian State Archives, R 721/3/5. The relevant information is contained in holdings R 613, R 659, R 683, R 685, R 721, R 1216, R 1399, R 1548, all at the same archive.

11 Lithuania, Latvia, Estonia and Western Byelorussia (till 1944) formed under German occupation 'Reichskommissariat Ostland'.

12 25 April 1942, R 685/5/10.

13 The obvious solution would be to augment documentary evidence with witness statements. Many eyewitnesses have died, however, and the Canadian evidence rules preclude the use of previous statements, even if they were sworn statements from other trials. This applies not only to KGB interrogations and Soviet trials, but also to West German investigations and trials as well.

14 The term 'partisan' in this context refers to Lithuanian nationalist irregular units, which formed themselves as soon as Soviet power was weakening in 1941.

15 'Ich bitte um schnelles Eingreifen, denn die Juedinnen bedrohen uns mit dem Erschiessen!' This request was sent to the Criminal Police, which in Svencionys contained Lithuanian officers, 2 January 1942, R 613/1/62.

16 For instance in the investigation against Eibner, Zentrale Stelle, Ludwigsburg, 202 AR-Z 16/67, vol.1.

17 See: Brest Oblast Archive, F 995/1/7.

18 Nechama Tec, *In the Lion's Den. The Life of Oswald Rufeisen* (New York: Oxford University Press, 1990).

19 Shalom Cholawski, *The Jews of Bielorussia during World War II* (Amsterdam: Harwood Academic Publ., 1998); with an introduction by Jehuda Bauer, one of the world's leading authorities on the Holocaust.

20 Serafimovicz was indicted in a criminal court in London. The case had to be discontinued due to defendant's ill health; he died shortly thereafter. Serafimovicz, and his family, figure largely in Tec's book. Oswald Rufeisen gave testimony in the English court.

21 Concentration Camps were camps and were under the administration of the *Inspektion der Konzentrationslager* or the *WVHA*.

22 All quotes from the decision of McKeown, J. in *The Minister of Citizenship and Immigration v. Eduard Podins* released on 9 July 1999, T-1093-97, pp.18, 98.

23 As mentioned above, one big obstacle is that the original immigration records of individuals are not available in Canadian cases, as they have been destroyed on a routine basis. In the US, these records are available.

24 See: Irving Abella and Harold Trooper, *None is too many. Canada and the Jews of Europe 1933–1948*, Toronto, Lester and Orpen Dennys, 1982. Whenever this theory, or a similar one, is promoted in the literature, the reference is Abella and Trooper.

25 See: David Matas with Susan Charendoff, *Justice Delayed. War Criminals in Canada*, Toronto, Summerhill Press, 1987; James E. McKenzie, *War Criminals in Canada*, Calgary, Detselig Enterprises, 1995; Sol Littman, op. cit.

26 Ellie Tesher, 'How Nazi War Criminal got into Canada', *The Toronto Star*, 12 November 1997. The historian quoted is Irving Abella.

27 Dr. Alti Rodal's report for the Deschênes Commission.

28 This is the title of one chapter in James E. McKenzie, op. cit. McKenzie calls Deschênes' final report a 'Massive Volume Covering Up War Crimes Secrets', p.119; an official document of this nature is certainly not an easy read. See also David Matas, Justice Delayed, op. cit., p.38. The government's decision not to release Dr. Rodal's report fuelled suspicions that it had something to hide, however, for anybody familiar with the workings of governments, this indicates a reflex reaction rather than sinister intentions.

29 See: Alti Rodal, Nazi *War Criminals in Canada: The historical and policy setting from the 1940s to the present*, Prepared for the Commission of Inquiry on War Criminals, September 1986, in particular p.117.

30 Ellie Tesher, op. cit.

31 *The Minister of Citizenship and Immigration v. Peteris Vitols*, Transcript of Proceedings, vol.XII, 6 February 1998, p.1455. The defence won their case.

32 For a balanced account of Canadian post-war immigration screening, see: Howard Margolian, *Unauthorized Entry. The Truth about Nazi War Criminals in Canada, 1946–56* (Toronto: University of Toronto Press, 2000).

33 See: Louise W. Holborn, The *International Refugee Organisation. A specialized agency of the United Nations. Its history and work 1946–1952* (London: Oxford University Press, 1956).

34 Immigrants who were not IRO sponsored still had to undergo Canadian security screening.

35 Alti Rodal, op. cit., p.32.

36 One major problem was the sources that were available to IRO and Canadian screening officials. The overwhelming majority of Canadian allegations concern persons from the former Soviet Union (Germans were barred from immigration until 1950) Information in Soviet or Communist bloc archives concerning persons from Eastern Europe, however, was inaccessible.

37 David Matas, op. cit., p.158–159.

38 *Ottawa Citizen*, 'CSIS fanning terrorist hysteria, critics say', 17 October 1998. A comparison of the language Mr. Matas uses is quite instructive. On Nazi perpetrators: 'A single Nazi criminal symbolizes the atrocity of the Holocaust. By ignoring even one perpetrator Canada disregards the murder of millions of innocents.' David Matas, op. cit., p.159. In respect of abusers of the refugee process, who might be war criminals, he says 'If we admit abusers, all we have done is admit an immigrant who does not meet the criteria', David Matas with Ilona Simon, *Closing the Doors. The Failure of Refugee Protection*, Toronto 1989, p.103.

39 Peter E. Quint, *The Imperfect Union, Constitutional Structures of German Unification* (Princeton: Princeton University Press, 1997).

40 Peter E. Quint, op. cit., p.203–204.

41 Such as that the suffering of victims of other genocides or criminal regimes was not so terrible, in comparison. A few stark examples can be found in Daniel Goldhagen, *Hitler's Willing Executioners. Ordinary Germans and the Holocaust* (New York: Alfred Knopf, 1996), p.587 n91, p.412 n86.

42 It has to be mentioned that Dr. Markovits is not alone with this opinion. The same argument was made repeatedly after 1990 by North American observers.

43 Inga Markovits, *Imperfect Justice. An East-West German Diary* (Oxford, Clarendon Press, 1995). The bias shows in particular in the terminology she uses, which is close to the former Communist usage.

44 How the issue has been clouded becomes apparent when one 'translates' Markovits' account from GDR to Nazi: The story of a former judge, now awaiting political vetting and in danger of losing her job, while 'former West German occupants have raised ownership claims to both her flat and her allotment garden' is met by Markowits with a sympathetic response. She writes: 'I stare at her, aghast. Where does she find the strength each morning to face the day?' Inga Markovits, op. cit., p.161. If we were to exchange 'former West German occupants' to 'former Jewish occupants' the response would be one of outrage. Former Nazi judges talked exactly that way after 1945, but we found this self-pity from former shareholders of the oppressive Nazi regime unacceptable.

45 Stefan Klemp, *Freispruch fuer das 'Mord-Bataillon'. Die NS-Ordnungspolizei und die Nachkriegsjustiz* (Muenster: LIT Verlag, 1998).

46   Cases concerning camps or ghettos, where victims and perpetrators were facing each other over
     longer time periods, are different in this respect.
47   The section on murder in the German Penal Code is an unwieldy tool for the prosecution of
     politically motivated murder. Equally cumbersome are certain legal tests that are applicable, which
     are the results of long-standing traditions in German legal thinking. Surprisingly enough, one does
     not hear anybody calling for a reform of the murder section, including those politicians who are
     constantly scape-goating individual prosecutors.
48   See: *Toronto Star*, February 29, 1996, 4 May 1996, 28 May 1996; *Toronto Sun*, 2 May 1996, 3 May
     1996, 25 September 1996; *Canadian Jewish News*, 9 May 1996, 23 May 1996, 25 September 1996.
49   *The Minister of Citizenship and Immigration v. Singh.*
50   See David Matas, *Closing the Doors*, op. cit.
51   The age of the defendants is often used as an argument in favour of not pursuing these cases any
     further. However, while the Baltic communities call for closure of Nazi related crimes in Canada,
     prosecution of Soviet officials who committed crimes even before the German invasion are taking
     place in Latvia and Estonia. As for Canada itself, most Canadians do not seem to have a problem
     punishing old men for crimes committed long ago – if the nature of the crime offends popular
     opinion, for example, sexual assaults on children.
52   Rick Mofina, 'Pursuit of suspected war criminals too slow, critics say', *National Post*, 29 July 1999
     quoting Irving Abella.
53   Stephan Bindman, 'Re-opening war-crimes wounds', *The Edmonton Journal*, 1 February 1998 quoting
     Sol Littman.
54   Andrew Cohen, 'Settling the Score with John Demjanjuk', *Globe and Mail*, 21 June 1999 quoting
     Neal Sher. At this point, Demjanjuk had been extradited to Israel under the allegation of having
     personally committed atrocious acts in Treblinka as the so-called 'Ivan the Terrible'. He was
     sentenced to death, but the sentence was overturned by the Supreme Court of Israel, after some
     doubts were raised as to the real identity of 'Ivan the Terrible'. At the time Mr. Sher made this
     statement, the evidence which is publicly available only shows that John Denjanjuk was in a training
     camp for death-camp guards, and was transferred to one of them (not Treblinka) afterwards.
55   Kirk Makin, 'Witch Hunt. For Crimes not Committed', *Globe and Mail*, 20 February 1999. The
     front-page notice read: 'In 1995, a Nazi war-crimes circus came to St. Catherines, Ont., for a long
     engagement. Two months ago, federal prosecutors folded their tents after a Federal Court judge
     concluded that Johann Dueck was exactly what he said he was (. . .)'. Letters to the editor following
     this article came under the heading: 'Inside the Johann Dueck file. Kirk Makin, Federal Court throws
     out case against Nazi suspect', *Globe and Mail*, 22. December 1998; Court thwarts gov't Nazi
     deportation, The *Vancouver Sun*, 2 December 1998; 'Four-year nightmare is over: Johann Dueck
     and his family can celebrate holidays with end of trial ordeal and threat of deportation', *The Standard*,
     23 December 1998;
56   Daniel Goldhagen, op. cit. It should be noted that this writer reviewed Goldhagen's use of historical
     sources critically. See: Ruth Bettina Birn, 'Revising the Holocaust', *The Historical Journal*, 40/1
     (1997): 195–215. In my review, I set out a number of sources that contradict Goldhagen's finding;
     interestingly enough, one constantly encounters potential new ones. In the context of this paper,
     Oswald Rufeisen's account of the two major perpetrators in Mir (Hein and Serafimowicz) that he
     could observe in close detail, is another example, which entirely contradicts Goldhagen's assertions.
57   Daniel Goldhagen, op. cit., p.408–409.
58   In these two cases, defence counsel used Goldhagen's book to cross-examine the Canadian govern-
     ment's expert historians. Their arguments were: '. . . that the indigenous (population) were, if any-
     thing, usually at the wrong place at the wrong time', that the Holocaust 'was a German initiative,
     German performance, and the assistance was barely nil'. . . *The Minister of Citizenship and Immigration
     v. Vladimir Katriuk*, Transcripts of Proceedings, 2 December 1997; pp.81; 4 December, p.102.
     Defence added: 'now, I had understood him to say that the Germans were somehow genetically
     programmed to be anti-Semites.'. Attempts to discredit the government's experts using Goldhagen
     culminated in the cross-examination of Christopher Browning. Browning had used the same docu-
     ments in a publication before Goldhagen, but came to different conclusions. Goldhagen attacked him

repeatedly in his book, in a manner, which many observers have deplored. It is little surprising that the defence challenged his expert opinion using Goldhagen. *The Minister of Citizenship and Immigration v. Serge Kislyuk*, Transcript of Proceedings, 4 February 1998, p.720.

59 Daniel Goldhagen, 'A New Serbia', in *The New Republic*, 17 May 1999.

60 An article in the *Canadian Jewish News* commented on 'the irony' of the United States' opposition to a permanent International Criminal Court, given it 'has done more to bring Nazi war criminals to justice than any other democracy. Paul Lungen, 'Jewish groups welcome international court', in: *The Canadian Jewish News*, 2 July 1998. This is hardly surprising, considering that Nazis have no lobby in the United States and that an International Criminal Court would be a restraint to the power politics of any country.

61 Some contributions to the field of 'Holocaust Studies' make one wonder how much reality there is at all. Author Daniel Levy, in an effort to interpret what the controversy about Goldhagen tells us about German identity, considers the accuracy of Goldhagen's thesis negligible. Indeed, that equates a 'this is not the truth' to 'I do not want to hear the truth'. Daniel Levy: 'The future of the past: Historiographical disputes and competing memories in Germany and Israel', in: *History and Theory*, vol.38, (1) 1999, Wesleyan University, p.51–66.

62 David Matas, *Justice Delayed*, op. cit., p.19; Alti Rodal, op. cit., p.3, writes the same.

63 It is somewhat disturbing to see that stereotypes about Poles being born anti-Semites are repeated today by Canadians, who – self-admittedly – have no contact to present-day Poles. See Leonard Stern, 'Hatred that outlives its victims. In Poland, the graveyard of European Jewry, it's still not easy to be Jewish', *The Ottawa Citizen*, 18. October 1998. Obviously, ethnic prejudices are compatible with Holocaust education.

64 Daniel Goldhagen, op. cit., p.439–441. Goldhagen draws this conclusion about the Germans who watched the events of Kristallnacht.

65 Roth finally withdrew his candidacy. Ira Stoll, 'Museum Nominee once compared Israel to German Nazis', *Forward*, 5 June 1998; Ira Stoll, 'Roth will retreat to California, Friend says', *Forward*, 19 June 1998; Robin Friedman, 'Comparing Israelis to Nazi leaders called wrong for a museum leader', *NJJN–MetroWest*, 9 July 1998; Jonathan Mahler, 'Museum of Woe', *The Wall Street Journal*, 31 July 1998; Michael P. Forbes, Jon D. Fox, Congress of the United States, open letter to Miles Lerman, Chairman, US Holocaust Memorial Council, Washington, 10 June 1998. For Forbes and Fox, 'troubling remarks about our own country' are: criticism of Ronald Reagan's American Dream, suggesting a moral equivalence between the US and the Soviet Union, and questioning US policies in Latin America.

66 See, for instance, Gregg Rickman, 'Real Justice Denied', *Canadian Jewish News*, 9 April 1999.

67 As a postscript: At the same time this article was finished, reports appeared in Canadian newspapers about allegations of a massacre US troops had committed against civilians in the Korean War. 'When families of the victims sought redress, they met only rejection and denial from the U.S. Military and their own government' US 'Korea veterans admit to slaughter of civilian's, *National Post*, 30 September 1999. 'War-crimes prosecution so many years later is a practical impossibility, experts say.' 'Memories of war', *Globe and Mail*, 30 September 1999. The alleged events would have taken place in 1950.

THE HOLOCAUST-ERA ASSETS DEBATE AND BEYOND:
A SWISS PERSPECTIVE

Thomas Borer-Fielding and Hanspeter Mock

'We have heard survivors and witnesses speak. Paradoxically, they advocate hope, not despair, solidarity instead of anger. They all insisted on the importance of memory: it may well be our only answer, our human hope to save our children.'

– Elie Wiesel

TOWARDS THE end of 1996, a heated discussion began on Switzerland's role during the Second World War[1]. Admittedly, at the beginning, the Swiss did not take this criticism seriously enough[2]. Why did Switzerland underestimate the problem? It is probably fair to say that for us – as for many throughout the world – the tragedy of the Holocaust was history, was bygone. As to the financial issues, we considered that our ancestors had dealt with them after the war. Today, some of us may find comfort in the fact that other countries – some of which are much more concerned by the issue than Switzerland – have similarly underestimated the problem, in spite of the Swiss precedent.

Abroad, the hesitant Swiss reaction led to the impression that Switzerland was willing to deal with its past and to bear the consequences only under pressure. Switzerland was – and still is – often portrayed in the U.S. media as a country 'dragging its feet', stone-walling and deferring any concrete steps to resolve the problems of the past. Clearly, this perception is wrong. There is hardly a country that has taken such far-reaching measures and investigations concerning the issue of Holocaust-era assets as Switzerland[3]. Switzerland has been lauded for these steps by many countries and interested organizations, and is now often cited as a model.

THE SWISS RESPONSE TO THE RESURGENCE OF THE PAST
Admittedly, it took a while for Switzerland to realize the magnitude of the problem, which had been concealed by the Cold War. However, once it became clear that the darker sides of the recent past had to be revisited, unprecedented steps were initiated and acted upon along the principles of truth, justice and solidarity:

First, an Independent Commission of Experts was established in autumn 1996. It is examining historical and legal aspects of Switzerland's role before, during, and after World War II. Members include internationally recognized experts, several of them of Jewish faith. The Commission's mandate is broad, compared to historical commissions recently set up in other countries. It will deliver its final reports in 2001.

Second, a Committee of Eminent Persons headed by Paul Volcker, former Chairman of the U.S. Federal Reserve, conducted a thorough forensic investigation of Swiss banks with a view to identifying all unclaimed assets left behind in Swiss banks by Nazi victims. The Committee's final report was released last December[4]. The cost of this, worldwide unmatched, auditing process amounted to hundreds of millions of Swiss Francs. On 31 March 2000, The Swiss Federal Banking Commission (SFBC) decided to follow the recommendations made by the ICEP in its final report. The ICEP recommended that approximately 3000 open dormant accounts and 23,000 closed accounts be published, which they deemed to have a probability of being related to victims of the Holocaust. In addition, the SFBC has authorized the creation of a central database containing details of approximately 46,000 accounts that the ICEP considers having a 'probable or possible' relationship with victims of the Holocaust[5]. In implementing the ICEP's broadly formulated recommendations on the central data base, the SFBC has discussed the categories of accounts to be included in the database for a solution that is appropriate, expeditious and fair. The SFBC has decided to limit the central database to the approximately 46,000 accounts, which in the view of the ICEP are probably or possibly related to Holocaust victims[6].

Third, a Swiss Fund for Needy Victims of the Holocaust was set up in February 1997, as a gesture of solidarity and with contributions from Swiss banks, private-sector companies and the Swiss National Bank. The Fund was endowed with SFr 273 million. The distribution is undertaken by major victims' organizations and was due to be completed in the course of the year 2000.

Fourth, two major Swiss insurance companies are participating in the efforts of an international commission chaired by former Secretary of State L. Eagleburger with a view to solving the problem of unpaid insurance policies dating from the World War II period.

Finally, the Swiss government published a list of account holders whose assets remained unclaimed in the 1960s and 1970s, in the context of the Federal Decree of 1962 on assets owned by foreigners or stateless persons persecuted for racial, religious or political reasons. Rightful claimants are entitled to get compensation.

Parallel to their efforts to return heirless assets to their legitimate owners, the Swiss banks concluded a settlement agreement with the World Jewish Restitution Organization and class action lawyers in August 1998. The banks committed themselves to setting up a so-called 'Class Action Fund' of US$1.25 billion. In return, the plaintiffs release all Swiss banks, Swiss industry, the Swiss National Bank, and the Swiss government from all claims in connection with World War II and the Holocaust. The only exceptions are three Swiss insurance companies that have been sued in the U.S. along with other European insurance companies. Hence, the agreement provides a closure for virtually all the financial claims related to World War II raised against Switzerland. The final adoption and implementation of the Settlement Agreement is expected to take place in the coming months.

Following the example of Switzerland, many countries have established historical commissions with the mandate to review their role during World War II and to re-examine restitution and reparation policies pursued after the war. However, both the scope and the results of these historical investigations vary widely from one country to the other.

The agreement recently reached in Berlin under the leadership of the US and German governments on how to allocate a DM 10 billion German 'slave labour' fund is worth mentioning in this context. Under the terms of the agreement, some 240,000 people – about half of them Jews – will be eligible for payments of up to DM 15,000 for the time they spent working for German industry during World War II. Perhaps one million more, primarily in Central and Eastern Europe, will get smaller payments for their Nazi-era forced labour. The DM 10 billion will be paid in equal parts by the German government and industry. Other countries, like France or the Netherlands have recently established compensation procedures.

The debate has also been taken to the international level. Two international conferences held in London and in Washington addressed the problem of Holocaust-era assets,[7] whilst this year's Stockholm International Forum on the Holocaust put the emphasis on the moral and pedagogic aspects of this tragedy.[8] This is definitely a development to be welcomed: First, because obviously, the unfinished business of the Holocaust-Era assets is, by far, not exclusively a 'Swiss' issue and second, because beyond material and moral compensation, we should always keep our eyes and minds open to the lessons that this unspeakable tragedy can, and should, teach us.

THE INTERNATIONAL DEBATE ABOUT HOLOCAUST-ERA ASSETS: A MISSED OPPORTUNITY?

In March 1999, a panel discussion was held at Harvard Law School. It focused on the issue 'Litigating the Holocaust: the role of private law and litigation in international calamities'. Discussed were questions such as: How is it that demands for compensation for damage and losses arising from the Holocaust are given validity through class actions in U.S. courts, half a century later? Are these class actions before U.S. courts the fairest and most effective means of achieving the as yet, unfinished business of compensating victims of the Holocaust? Do settlements have the power to make amends in a moral sense, bring financial closure and convince the world that justice has been achieved?[9]

Of course, the participants were not able to agree on clear and exhaustive answers to all those questions. However, the event was a success merely because of the fact that it enabled an open, factual, non-adversarial dialogue between European and American experts. Complex and sensitive issues could be discussed without resorting to emotional argumentation or political hot air. Some participants considered that despite its shortcomings, litigation was a useful means of enforcing Holocaust-related claims, particularly if it was supported by actors outside the court, such as politicians, NGOs and government agencies. Others had strong reservations against some of the methods applied in the U.S. (particularly outside the courts), questioned some aspects of the U.S. legal system and had serious doubts whether the wave of World War II-related litigation that takes place almost exclusively in the U.S. is a fair and efficient way to deal with material claims dating from that period, as compared to politically agreed solutions that had prevailed after the war. After all, even U.S. court jurisdiction has its limits.

Now that the heat and acrimony that too often surrounded the debate on Holocaust-Era assets – and, particularly on Switzerland's past – have died down, these appear to be important aspects that deserve to be dealt with. In particular, one should be permitted to ask if the confrontational path chosen by some in dealing with the painful issues left open after World War II did not, at least to some extent, prove to be counterproductive in many ways.

First, at the political level, the traditional and long lasting close Swiss – U.S. bilateral relations[10] were, deliberately or not, put under considerable strains.[11] To take but one example, many in Switzerland will not easily forget that in May 1997, the U.S. government formally entered into the controversy about Switzerland's role in World War II, by publishing a highly critical report.[12] From a Swiss perspective, the authors of this report – while criticizing Switzerland's neutrality in this war as inherently immoral – were anything but neutral in their judgment of Switzerland's situation and behaviour.[13] While acknowledging that Switzerland – like many other nations – had made mistakes during the wartime period, the Swiss government firmly rejected these unfounded allegations.

Meanwhile, emotions have calmed down on both sides. In January 1999, the then President of the Swiss Confederation, Ruth Dreifuss, and U.S. Vice President Al Gore expressed their satisfaction that this issue had been brought to a satisfactory conclusion as it relates to Swiss-American bilateral relations. They expressed their commitment to strengthening and deepening the ties between the two countries in the political, economic and cultural spheres. At this year's Davos meeting, a Joint Economic Commission was established. If needed, it will address problems related to ongoing U.S. State initiatives and threats of sanctions against Swiss insurers.

These recent events mark a milestone in this long debate, often characterized by misunderstandings, polemics and confrontation. The Swiss government sincerely hopes that we will enter into a new era of cooperation and mutual understanding.

Nevertheless, on a more general, and probably more important level, one can't avoid the question whether, by putting the 'Holocaust-Era Assets' in the centre of the debate, the main actors in this 'restitution campaign' didn't, consciously or not, run the risk of reducing this unspeakable tragedy to a material controversy. Certainly, individuals who had bank accounts, insurance policies or works of art that were stolen have a right to pursue their claims. Switzerland recognized this and was the first country to establish comprehensive measures to deal with such claims, to locate and restitute any belongings that may have been looted from Holocaust victims and then stored within the country. But, as Abe Foxman, National Director of the Anti-Defamation League pointed out in 1998: 'when these legitimate claims become the main focus of activity regarding the Holocaust, rather than the unique horror of six million Jews, including 1.5 million children, being murdered simply because they were Jewish, then something has gone wrong.'[14] Or, to put it in the words of Charles Krauthammer: 'The Holocaust commands the preservation of memory. It is not an instrument for the generation of money. The dead are honored by learning the truth and never letting the world forget it, not by entering into rancorous negotiations with corporate leaders who represent a generation entirely innocent of these crimes.'[15]

Again, the mentioning of these issues and risks must not be understood as implying that material restitution should not be pursued wherever and whenever possible. The point is much more that, as everyone will agree,[16] the tragedy of the Holocaust should never be treated as a merely financial affair. Now that the financial issues are in the process of being settled, it is high time to focus on moral aspects and to turn towards the much more difficult task of remembrance, education and prevention.

REMEMBERING – AND ACTING – FOR THE FUTURE

As Federal Councilor Ruth Dreifuss, Head of the Swiss Federal Department of Home Affairs, recently stated in Stockholm, 'The horrors of the Shoah, the atrocities suffered and inflicted and the fate of the victims must live on in our memories. This essential process of remembering goes hand in hand with the equally essential one of asking questions.'

In dealing with the past, this questioning is of the utmost importance, because it serves to shape our future. To do this, each country must be willing to scrutinize its history in depth – a process which involves its citizens, shedding light on their own actions and reactions. This exercise in coming to terms with the past has to be part of a wider debate worthy of the democratic principles in the name of which history has to be known, vigilance intensified and lessons learnt.

That is what Switzerland wanted when it gave a very broad mandate to its Independent Commission of Experts on the Second World War, headed by Professor Jean-François Bergier, which has already produced two important reports[17] and is due to publish its final report in 2001. Similar efforts in each country are necessary, so we can join forces to put a determined stop to racism, intolerance and discrimination against whole groups in our societies and prevent the resurgence of deliberate, organized violence.

In the process of remembering – and acting – for the future, education plays a key role. Through international cooperation and exchange, countries must focus on how best to link teaching of history to awareness of the fight against intolerance and racism. Responsibility for this lies just as much with governments as with teachers. Young people should not complete their schooling without learning why and how exclusion and racism undermine democracy and, in the long run, destroy society.

International exchanges of experience in education and comparison of the results achieved help to improve and develop teaching resources. In Switzerland for example, the feedback obtained shows that anti-Semitism and the Shoah must not be taught in isolation but explained in the light of topical events and linked to modern-day xenophobia and racism. The objective is to promote tolerance and the respect for human dignity – topics which must be addressed in parallel in several disciplines, such as history, literature or philosophy.

These are important tasks. They are imperative though, since the mere fact that the Holocaust was possible in the middle of the so-called 'civilized' world shows that we can never take for granted an enlightened, free and peaceful, tolerant society. On the contrary, we have to fight, together, for our freedom and the future of our children.

NOTES

1　J. Rossier, 'Switzerland, Gold and the Banks: Analysis of a Crisis', Speech at the Harvard Faculty Club, 26 May 1999.

2　H.J. Bär, 'Switzerland revisited – a case of managerial incompetence?', Remarks on the occasion of the 1998 Global Forum on Management Education, Chicago, 13 June 1998.

3　For a detailed overview, see the Task Force 'Switzerland World War II' website: www.switzerland.taskforce.ch.

4　Independent Committee of Eminent Persons (ICEP): 'Report on Dormant Accounts of Victims of Nazi Persecution in Swiss Banks', December 1999.

5　The body to be set up in Switzerland that will in future deal with the claims of Holocaust victims pursuant to the New York Settlement Agreement between banks, class action plaintiffs and Jewish organizations, will have access to this data base

6　The creation of a central data base for all the 4.1 million accounts that existed in Swiss banks in the period prior to 1945, is viewed by the SFBC as neither necessary nor meaningful, as for these accounts the ICEP itself had, after a very thorough investigation, no reason to believe that these accounts were in any way related to victims of Holocaust.

7　See *Nazi Gold, The London Conference* (London: Foreign & Commonwealth Office, 1998) and J.-D. Bindenagel (ed.), *Washington Conference on Holocaust-Era Assets, Proceeding*, (Washington, D.C.: US Department of State, 1999).

8　See the Program and the Proceedings of the Stockholm International Forum on the Holocaust at www.holocaustforum.gov.se.

9　On these questions see D. Vagts, J. Drolshammer and P.J. Murray, 'Mit prozessieren den Holocaust bewältigen? Die Rolle des Zivilrechts und Zivilprozesses beim Versuch der Wiedergutmachung internationaler Katastrophen' in *Zeitschrift für Schweizerisches Recht (ZSR)*, 1999, p.511ff.

10　J.H. Huston, *The Sister Republics – Switzerland and the United States from 1776 to the Present* (Washington, D.C.: Library of Congress, 1991).

11 F.S. Whittlesey, 'U.S. – Swiss Friendship Tested 1996–1999', *Selected Essays by Ambassador Faith Whittlesey*, Chairman and President American Swiss Foundation (New York, Summer 1999).

12 'U.S. and Allied Efforts to Recover and Restore Gold and other Assets Stolen or Hidden by Germany during World War II, Preliminary Study', U.S. Department of State, May 1997.

13 For a recent review in English of Switzerland's situation during the war years see S.P. Halbrook, *Target Switzerland – Swiss Armed Neutrality in World War II*, Rockville Centre, NY: Sarpedon, 1998).

14 A. Foxman, 'The Dangers of Holocaust Restitution', *Wall Street Journal*, 4 December 1998. For a radical critique, see N. Finkelstein, *The Holocaust Industry – an Essay on the Exploitation of Jewish Suffering* (New York: **Verso**, 2000).

15 C. Krauthammer, 'The Holocaust Scandal', *Washington Post*, 4 December 1998.

16 See the Program and the Proceedings of the 'Stockholm International Forum on the Holocaust' at www.holocaustforum.gov.se.

17 Independent Commission of Experts (ICE), 'Switzerland and Refugees in the Nazi Era', (December 1999) and 'Switzerland and Gold Transactions in World War II' (May 1998). For a critical review of the ICE report on Refugees, see J.-C. Lambelet, 'Evaluation critique du Rapport Bergier sur la Suisse et les réfugiés à l'époque du national-socialisme et nouvelle analyse de la question', *Cahiers de recherches économiques*, no. 00.04 (Université de Lausanne, Département d'économétrie et d'économie politique, HEC, March 2000).

THE MACHINERY OF NAZI ART LOOTING:
THE NAZI LAW ON THE CONFISCATION OF
CULTURAL PROPERTY IN POLAND

Wojciech W. Kowalski

WORLD WAR II is commonly associated first of all with tremendous human losses and demolished towns, which were often left in almost complete ruin. In view of millions of victims, tragic memories from the death camps, or photographs of the sea of ruins, the plunder of works of art, even though effected on a massive scale, seems to make no impression.[1] In fact, it is often treated as less important, especially since a considerable part of the plundered cultural property was restored after the war. This 'second position' on the list of war misfortunes should not, however, overshadow the extent of the losses that resulted from thoroughly planned and meticulously organized confiscation of works of art, books and archives. As in many other fields of activity, the Nazi machine generally operated with no failures, and the goals that it was supposed to achieve were often diversified, depending, for example, on the nationality of the people subjected to expropriation, or on the occupied country in which it functioned.

If we were to make an attempt at systematizing this phenomenon from the geographical point of view, we could observe certain tendencies. The territory of France, where the public museums and galleries had remained intact, suffered relatively small losses, and it is primarily the Jewish collections that were plundered there.[2] But further to the east of Europe, more plunder and losses were carried out on both public and private possessions. It was in Eastern Europe, and particularly in Russia, that the Nazi plunder had the most criminal character, as the local cultures of these lands were considered to have little or no value and were often completely destroyed.[3]

Poland has been chosen for this case study for two reasons. First of all, its central geographic location in occupied Europe coincided with a specific role in the context discussed. It was in Poland that the Nazi activity was executed in the two utterly different manners described above.[4] Although on the one hand, a few cases were noted of a certain limited respect for the cultural heritage, which was much more common towards the West European culture, yet on the other hand, unprecedented plunder on large scale and demolition of whole towns were common, as in other eastern lands. The cases of respect were reserved exclusively to the places that the Nazis considered as purely 'German'. Such was the case of Cracow, which was saved only because it had been regarded as 'wahr deutsche Stadt', although even this 'label' did not prevent the removal of the most valuable works of art from its churches, museums and private collections. Warsaw, the capital of Poland, serves as an example of planned destruction – about 80% of the city was left in ruins, together with the Royal Castle, the Jewish quarter and most historic buildings, including the cultural property they were endowed with.[5]

The example of Poland is also interesting in the context discussed because it was the occupied country for which the Nazis prepared and then implemented the most fully developed 'legal grounds' for their activity, unsurpassed in any other occupied territory. In Poland these legal foundations were thoroughly prepared in the form of standard acts with the force of law, mainly regulations and executive orders published in official promulgation agencies of the Third Reich or of the authorities responsible for the occupied territories. It should be emphasized that all citizens of occupied Poland were subject to these 'laws'; in this particular context there was no difference between citizens of Polish origin and, for example, citizens of Jewish origin. Thus it should be remembered that writing about these laws is also writing about the Holocaust.

Should one ask why these developments happened in Poland, the answer is probably that the Nazis had been well prepared for the occupation of September 1939. Such fully developed legal grounds were not needed in other countries (or there was no time to prepare them), and acts of plunder or demolition were often committed simply pursuant to orders issued directly to the commanders of the military units operating in a given area.

In view of these circumstances, the example of the occupied Poland provides exceptional background for the analysis of the 'legal basis' of the Nazi mechanism for the plunder of works of art. The outline of the response of the Allied Forces to such plunder – adopted later in the form of the Allied restitution law – will be of a more general nature, as this law was not established for one particular country but for the entire anti-Nazi coalition.[6]

In the analysis of the law established by the Nazi occupants concerning the issue under discussion, it should be emphasized that this law was made up of numerous different types of regulations, from provisions of more general nature, which could also constitute the basis for the seizure of works of art, to special regulations concerning only a narrow category of cultural property.

The first provisions were issued by the German military authorities as early as 14 September 1939,[7] in the city of Poznań (Posen), while the military operations were still in progress, exactly two weeks after they had been started. These provisions referred to 'cash turnover' (*Geldverkehr*) and prohibited the possession of cash in any amount exceeding the sum that could be spent within the period of two weeks. Such excessive amounts of cash were to be deposited in a bank. But the provisions were not restricted to cash: all gold and foreign currency were also subject of obligatory bank deposit within ten days. The supervision over property matters referred to all citizens of Poland whatever their nationality, and sometimes were imposed with retroactive force as well. Pursuant to the regulation issued two weeks after the first provisions, the supervision also included all 'legal transactions concerning property' made in the period between 1 September 1918 and 31 December 1938. These transactions were subject to specially adopted scrutiny and could be annulled. Moreover, all transactions concluded between 1 January 1939 and 31 September 1939 were proclaimed without legal effect (*schwebend unwirksam*), and could be considered as valid only on the basis of a proper permission issued by the occupation authorities *ex post*, after a relevant application had been submitted. Furthermore, from 1 October 1939 all legal transactions concerning property were forbidden.

This outline of the legal regulations[8] clearly indicates that immediately after the outbreak of the war, the Occupation authorities managed to establish absolute control over property matters, which, as will be discussed later, provided grounds for the consequent confiscation of property. Such preparatory activities were not universal for the entire occupied territory of Poland. For example, in the neighbouring district of Pomorze (Pommern-Westpreussen), confiscation of property was executed directly without any earlier preparatory provisions. The first provision concerning this matter was the regulation on the seizure of property in Pomorze dated 27 September 1939,[9] pursuant to which the property of the Polish state, Polish state institutions, communes and all legal and physical persons could be seized and confiscated. A specially appointed State Commissioner was responsible for any decisions concerning property matters, acting at his own discretion.[10]

The above-mentioned provisions had a temporary character and served either to secure property in view of its pending confiscation, or provided the first but not perfect legal basis for it. The situation changed on 26 October 1939, when the invaded territory of the Republic of Poland was formally divided into the so-called 'incorporated Eastern Territories' (*eingegliederte Ostgebiete*),[11] that is Poland's western territory, which from that day on became an integral part of the Third Reich, and other lands referred to as 'General Government' (*Generalgouvernement*).[12] This territory did not entail the eastern part of Poland, invaded by the Red Army after 17 September 1939 and later incorporated to the Soviet Union pursuant to the Ribbentrop–Molotov Treaty. After this division, the control over particular parts of the former Polish Republic was taken over by separate authorities. The lands incorporated into the Third Reich were managed directly from Berlin, but for the General Government its own authorities were established with the seat in Cracow. Accordingly, the authorities had separate legislative powers. It should be stressed that after the temporary provisions had been enforced, the Nazi authorities exercised their powers with 'due diligence'.[13]

'INCORPORATED EASTERN TERRITORIES'

Regarding the incorporated Eastern Territories, the proclamation of two regulations was of crucial importance for the fate of cultural heritage; although of general nature, they provided grounds for the confiscation of cultural property as well. The regulations, dated 15 January 1940[14] and 17 September 1940,[15] concerned the seizure of the Polish state property and modes of dealing with the property of the former Polish subjects respectively.

Pursuant to the first of these laws, practically all the movable and immovable property of the Polish state was seized. All persons, including legal and physical persons, who held any property on the basis of any legal relation, were obliged to report it to the appropriate administrative authorities (district president or town commissioner) within one month, unless it had already been subjected to the supervision of any supreme authority of the Third Reich.

The second law concerned all movable and immovable property in possession of physical persons who did not acquire German citizenship after the lands had been incorporated to the Third Reich. This property was subject to sequestration, trustee administration or confiscation, but the establishment of trustee administration equalled confiscation. There were two types of seizure: obligatory and optional. Obligatory seizure concerned the property of Jews and persons who had fled or were permanently absent.[16] However, the latter category entailed the majority of Poles, as they had been subjected to compulsory displacement to the General Government with the right to take no more than 25 to 30 kg of personal belongings, including the portion of food sufficient for 14 days. Optional seizure involved the necessity of defending the Third Reich, 'strengthening Germanism', or might be ordered in respect of the property of the persons who had immigrated to the German Reich after 1 September 1918. Upon seizure, former estate owners lost the right to dispose of their property, and likely holders were allowed to manage it only until relevant orders were issued. Only 'movable objects serving exclusively for personal needs' as well as money and bank deposits up to the value of 1000

Reichsmarks were excluded from seizure. Acts of disobedience to the provisions of the two laws were severely punished.[17]

Even a general presentation of these legal acts makes it possible to conclude that pursuant to these laws the Nazis could dispose of practically all the estate of the Polish subjects in the lands incorporated to the Third Reich; and, the confiscation was always obligatory in respect of the Jews, refugees or displaced persons. Clearly, it entailed all works of art and other cultural objects. In the case of optional seizure, the decisive argument was the 'strengthening of Germanism'.

Another point in our discussion is the technical side of such organization of plunder and management of the property seized in this way. This task was the responsibility of a special agency called High Trustee Office East (*Haupttreuhandstelle Ost*, further referred to as 'HTO'), which had been established by Hermann Goering's regulation issued especially for this purpose.[18] The official powers of this agency included seizure of the property pursuant to the above mentioned laws, and their consequent administration until their respective takeover by a new German owner. Several main branches and special depots were created by HTO in the incorporated territories to accomplish the seizure and management of property. Despite its extensive administrative machinery and far-reaching powers, HTO was not the only organization entitled to perform confiscation. For example, similar powers were vested upon the office of the Reich Commissioner for the Strengthening of Germanism (*Reichskommissar für die Festigung deutschen Volkstums*), established by Führer's secret order dated 7 October 1939.[19] Nevertheless, it was HTO that was endowed with the widest range of tasks and the major responsibility. It was responsible for the confiscation and management of all possible property. However, as we are interested in cultural objects only, it is enough to quote a fragment of one of the executive orders issued by its headquarter to illustrate the scope and scale of the robbery in this field. Acting as Reich Commissioner for the Strengthening of Germanism, and also as Reichsführer SS and a chief of the German Police (*Chef der deutschen Polizei*), Heinrich Himmler ordered the police *(Staatpolizei)* in the incorporated Eastern Territories to fulfil immediately the following instruction prepared by HTO:

'(. . .). I. In order to fortify Germanism and the defence of the Reich confiscation is ordered (. . .) of all objects mentioned in point II of this order on confiscation found in the territories which have (. . .) become a component part of the Reich, as well as those found in the Gouvernementship General (. . .) providing that these objects do not belong to the Reichsdeutsch or the Volksdeutsch,[20] or that the Reichsdeutsch and Volksdeutsch do not own more than 75% of the rights to the property in question. Most particularly, subject to confiscation are all objects mentioned in point II found in archives, museums, public collections and in Polish or Jewish possession, but whose security and appropriate treatment lies in German interest.

II. 1. Objects of historical and prehistoric provenience, records, books, documents important for research on the history of civilisation and public life, and those particularly relevant to the question of German contribution to the historic, cultural and economic development of the country as well as documents of importance to current history.

2. Objects of artistic, cultural and historic value, such as paintings, sculptures, furniture, rugs, crystal pieces, books, etc.

3. Objects of interior decoration and objects of precious metals. (. . .)

4. All objects and especially the apparatus and parts designed for the maintenance (and repair), for the development and improvement as well as preservation of materials and collections in the context of research. They also include objects of strictly educational, medical, technical and agricultural character and those applied to the natural sciences,

hence also scientific in nature.

5. Weapons, costumes, musical instruments, coins, postage stamps and similar collections.

6. All objects listed above under points 1 to 5 as well as all found in schools, particularly in schools of higher education and trade schools.[21]

The confiscated cultural property was handed over for administration to the special General Trustee for Securing German Cultural Material in the Incorporated Eastern Territories. Following his decision, the works of art regarded as valuable from the Nazi point of view were directed to be sent to supply certain museums and other institutes in Germany, whereas other works of art were subject to sale. This attitude was expressed in the letter dated 9 July 1940 forwarded to HTO's headquarters:

(. . .). Basically, I agree that the term 'cultural good' should not be defined too broadly. But we must be careful to avoid the situation, that objects of folk art and historical value be excluded only because they bring no profit from their sale. We have learned from experience that the following two points must be considered:

1. Identified as cultural goods must be objects that, regardless of their commercial value, have a cultural and historical importance that constitute a historical document and that have some relation to historical events.

2. Of concern also is appropriate care of objects that bring a profit when sold. That is why it has been resolved that, regardless of whether they are of artistic quality and whether they do or do not possess a cultural and historical value, all objects of gold and silver should be delivered to the General trustee so they could be quickly turned into cash.

As to dealing with other objects, such as paintings of no artistic value, furniture and generally objects that should be regarded as objects of daily use, HTO or its depots shall sell them on site.[22]

It should also be mentioned that for the HTO experts, Polish and Jewish art held no artistic value in principle. This point of view was clearly expressed in a memorandum dated 17 February 1941 addressed to the director of a museum in Silesia after the seizure of the transport of the Polish paintings which had been sent to an exhibition in Paris immediately before the outbreak of war. Referring to the information on this seizure, SS-Obersturmführer Kraut explains that:

It is planned to collect particularly blatant examples of Polish artistic junk (*Kulturkitsch*) for future use as propaganda materials (in a form of a book or exhibition). For this reason I am asking you to let me know about any examples of the Polish or Jewish artistic junk among the above mentioned materials. If so, please secure these objects against damage, to enable their future disposal for serving the above mentioned purpose.[23]

Enjoying such broad powers, HTO was an incredibly successful organization. The extent of effected confiscation may be inferred from abundant documents providing evidence of its operation, many of which were published after the war. Let me quote a passage from one of the reports of the General Trustee for Securing German Cultural Material in the Incorporated Eastern Territories. This report relates to his activity concerning the period up to early 1941:

(. . .) 5. Results already achieved:

● Cultural goods were found in: 74 castles, 96 mansion-houses and major number of flats. There were in total 500 castles, mansion-houses and flats searched.

● There were chosen and secured: 102 libraries, 15 museums, 3 galleries of paintings, 8 collections of weapon, 10 collections of coins, 1 collection of Egyptian antiquities, 1 collection of antique vases, 1 ethnographic collection, 21 various private collections (folk art, porcelain, horns, etc.), 1100 paintings and watercolours, some hundreds of prints, 25 statues, 500 pieces of furniture, 33 chests with religious objects (not yet opened), some hundred of rugs and carpets, of which only 3 to 5 are of museum value and can be recognized as cultural goods, 25 major shipments of precious metals, which have arrived separately or in groups. Apart from jewellery, there was 1 particular object noted as cultural good – Irish golden box of 1760.

● There were also chosen and secured numerous other objects of artistic craftsmanship, porcelain, glass, weapon, and alike. The exact numbers will be reported after cultural goods are separated from other objects.[24]

Apart from detailed enumeration, another interesting aspect of this document is the personal particulars of the people involved in the confiscations. They include artists, for example the sculptor Max Schmidt, and university professors. According to point 4 of the report, Einsatzkommado C was dismissed on 28 February 1941: 'because Prof. Clasen and SS-Untersturmführer Dr Thaerigen, due to their return to research activity at the university and at the prehistoric institute, shall be now working only on pre-history'.[25]

The activity of HTO was organized in a very detailed, often bureaucratic manner, as evidenced, among other data, by prolific correspondence forwarded from local agencies to Berlin. This correspondence perfectly illustrates the character of HTO. The letters ask for guidelines on how to act in various cases, often very particular cases. Sometimes, the main objective was to achieve the best economic result, at other times difficulties in establishing the nationality of potential victims of confiscation were reported. For example, in a letter directed to HTO's headquarters dated 9 April 1941 the following doubt was expressed:

> Recently we have seized a considerable number of silver candleholders, which, although of no artistic value in accordance with the SS-Reichsführer's (...) circular of 16 December 1939, should, in my opinion, be sorted out before sale. To the best of my knowledge, silver objects (...) are to be melted. But the said candleholders do not weigh much, so after melting they will bring only insignificant income; yet, on the antique dealer market they may fetch a price in the range of 60–100 RM. Therefore, I think that silver candleholders should not be melted, instead, they should be stored and next turned into cash in the best, most profitable manner. Please let me know your instruction in this matter.[26]

In another letter dated 9 July 1940 SS-Obersturmführer Kraut asked his staff to take 'special care while liquidating Polish private libraries and disposing them to scrap paper stores, and not to act with too much routine, as among private book collections, particularly in Poznań and Łódź, valuable books could be found, especially among those belonging to university professors, writers and members of similar professions'.[27] Accordingly, so many books had been confiscated that it was impossible for HTO to store and sort them in an appropriate manner. This information is confirmed by a quote from another report, dated 27 February 1941:

> (...) 2 or 3 ml books had been gathered at random on the premises of a former church. The books were arranged in a pile 50 m long, 6 m wide and reaching the height of 4 m. Another similar pile was placed on the lower floor of the church (...). In general, the Polish books were stacked together, whereas the other ones were laid down one by one without any concept; yet old books, especially first editions and incunabula were placed separately. After 3 quarters of the year, huge bookshelves placed along the walls were packed with non-Polish books, piled in indiscriminate chaos, including German, English, French and other ones. So, next to Savigny and other classics, one may find the books by Courths-Mahler. As I have

heard, the building police are to prohibit any additional increase in the store, as, due to continued gathering of confiscated books the roof and the dome have become overloaded.[28]

In yet another letter, Berlin was faced to settle the problem of 'determining the nationality in doubtful cases'. The letter asked for prompt reply to the issue 'how we should treat cultural property whose owners are German citizens married to Jews or Poles'.[29]

THE GENERAL GOUVERNMENT

As far as the General Government is concerned, the laws established by the occupying authorities were not essentially different from those finally introduced in the territories incorporated to the Third Reich.

Beside the adoption of slightly different organizational solutions, another interesting fact is that these laws had been proclaimed and put into force much earlier. But, as in the situation already discussed, there were really two acts of crucial importance. The first was issued as early as 15 October 1939[30] and was concerned with state property. The act is very concise, containing only two paragraphs. Pursuant to §1.1, 'All movable and immovable property of the former Polish state and its appurtenances, (...) in the territory of the General Government shall be confiscated to secure all valuable instances of public utility'. Pursuant to clause 2, 'Registration, administration and disposal of the confiscated property shall be the responsibility of the Trustee for the General Government'.

The second regulation was issued on 16 December 1939[31] and was devoted specially to the confiscation of cultural property. The main objective of the Nazi policy was openly declared in its para 1:

> Public possession of the works of art in the General Gouvernement is hereby confiscated for the sake of public benefit and use, provided the property in question does not fall under the regulation dated 15 November 1939 (...) concerning the confiscation of the State property of the former Polish State which is now located in the General Gouvernement.

Although already quoted provision referred only to 'public possession', one should not be misled with this term. As the next paragraph made clear, the term covered a very wide range of objects including:

1. Private collections of works of art, (...);
2. The works of art in the exclusive possession of the Church, except for the property needed for everyday liturgy.

All such defined 'publicly possessed' works of art were 'subject to registration and security procedures undertaken by the appointed commissioner to protect their cultural and historical value'. They all had to be declared specifying their number, type and condition. According to The First Executive Order issued on 15 January 1940[32] to execute the above regulation, these declarations had to be completed before 15 February 1940 at the Office of the Special Commissioner for Registering and Securing Artistic and Cultural Property in Cracow. As this order specified, all artistic, cultural and historical property made before 1850 had to be declared; certain categories of cultural property, however, were subject to obligatory declaration. They were precisely enumerated and included, in particular: (a) works of art, (b) paintings, (c) craft and handiwork (antique furniture, china, glass, gold and silver articles, carpets, tapestry, embroidery and lace works, liturgical vessels, etc.), (d) drawings, wood engravings, copperplate engravings, etc., (e) rare manuscripts, music note scripts, autographs, miniatures, prints, frames, etc., (f) weapons, armoury, etc., (g) coins, medals, rings, etc.[33]

The obligation to make such declarations was imposed upon every person in possession of described objects since 15 March 1939 or entitled to dispose them. Every person was also obliged to reveal the true information concerning the possession of the said works of art at the request of the relevant authorities. Any disputable cases were to be settled by the Special Commissioner for Registering and Securing Artistic and Cultural Property. He was also the only and final authority to decide which works of art or which collections felt into the category of the public possession, as well as to allow for any exemptions.

All persons who failed to fulfil these obligations were subject to imprisonment. Those treated as offenders were those who attempted 'to hide, dispose of or export from Generalgouvernement the said works of art' and those who, being obliged to reveal information, refused to do so, or related the information which was false or insufficient.

The responsibility for enforcement of these regulations lay with the Special Commissioner who in their practical execution was assisted by Security Police (*Sicherheitspolizei*), acting in this case, on the basis of the already quoted Himmler's order of 16 December 1939. This order, originally issued for Incorporated Eastern Territories, was also sent to Security Police Commanders (*Kommandeure der Sicherheitpolizei und des SD*) in Cracow, Radom, Warsaw and Lublin,[34] and therefore decided that the HTO instruction on the confiscation of cultural property was also implemented in the General Gouvernement.[35]

As can be seen from the above description of the Nazi 'law-making' activity in occupied Poland, all essential regulations and law-enforcement provisions on confiscation of cultural property were issued within a few months after the outbreak of war. They regulated the obligation of reporting precisely defined categories of works of art and other objects of cultural significance, stipulated punishment for instances of disobedience and suppression, etc. In practical terms, this 'legal framework' paved the way to confiscation of the whole cultural heritage located on the territory of occupied Poland. As one of the members of the underground resistance movement concluded his everyday observations in the report sent to London in 1940: 'theoretically the whole of Poland's artistic, cultural and historic heritage was subject to confiscation to the benefit of the occupant.'[36] This statement referred particularly to the rich heritage of Polish Jews, who had been living in this country for around 1000 years. They simply lost not only their collections but the whole Jewish heritage was methodically erased from the earth. Just to illustrate the scale of this loss it is enough to say that no single example of hundreds of unique old wooden synagogues is left from the occupation. Finally it must be added, that none of the discussed regulations obliged the Office of the Special Commissioner for Registering and Securing Artistic and Cultural Property to produce a certificate or any other document giving evidence of what had been confiscated. So all confiscated objects if not later found and given back were lost for ever without trace.[37]

LATER PROBLEMS

In the light of the above, it was really not easy to find an answer to the question, how the consequences of the confiscation could be reversed after the war. As the present author has written in his book, the restitution of works of art looted during World War II constituted an extremely complex and difficult task. Apart from the necessity of solving purely technical problems in relation to the search for looted cultural material, the identification and recovery of such a huge number of high value objects required a legal basis with an international scope.[38] Certain early concepts and projects in this matter discussed within the framework of the Conference of Allied Ministers of Education were found rather unrealistic and consequently were not applied in practice.[39] The first successful international step towards construction of this basis was the Declaration of the Allied Nations against Acts of Dispossession Committed in Territories under Enemy Occupation or Control of 5 January 1943.[40] States-signatories of the declaration warned those who could be concerned, in particular persons in neutral countries, that they 'intended to do their utmost to defeat the methods of dispossession practised by the governments with which they were at war against countries and peoples who have been so wantonly assaulted and despoiled.' To achieve this effect they reserved 'all their rights to declare invalid any transfers of, or dealing with, property, rights and interests situated in the territories which have come under the occupation or control, direct or indirect,' of the enemy, 'or belonged, or have belonged, to persons, including juridical persons, residents in such territories'. The Declaration referred to every form of transfer of property irrespective of 'whether such transfers or dealings have taken the form of open looting or plunder, or of transactions apparently legal in form, even when they purport to be voluntarily effected.'

After the war Allied Nations tried to introduce declared objectives which in practice proved to be quite complicated as they had to be reconciled with various other interests. Accomplishment of this task led them to the adoption of sophisticated restitution laws, which recognised the claims for cultural property *sui generis*, requiring special legislation.[41] As a result two different bodies of laws were adopted. On the one hand, there were laws regulating external restitution allowing Allied countries to get back their property removed to Germany during the occupation, on the other hand there were special laws dealing with internal restitution, aimed at the restitution of property to persons who lost it in Germany itself. The external restitution was based on the Definition of the Term Restitution agreed by the Allied Control Council for Germany on 21 January 1946.[42] This regulation formulated certain principles which had to serve as foundations for laws to be adopted by Military Governments responsible for all zones of occupation. It decided, for example, that restitution had to be limited, in the first instance, to identifiable goods which existed at the time of occupation of the country concerned and which had been taken by the enemy by force from the territory of this country. It also stated in respect to goods of unique character, restitution of which was impossible, that 'a special instruction will fix the categories of goods which will be subject to replacement, the nature of these replacements, and the conditions under which such goods could be replaced by equivalent objects.' Undoubtedly, this paragraph referred to works of art which by definition are of unique character. For various reasons however, mainly political, such an instruction has never been issued, and formally announced restitution in kind could not help to make good cultural losses sustained during this war.[43] As already mentioned, the internal restitution was based on laws adopted by respective Military Governments for their zones of occupation. The purpose of these laws was 'to effect to the largest extent possible the speedy restitution of identifiable property (...) to persons who were wrongfully deprived of such property within the period from 30 January 1933 to 8 May 1945 for reasons of race, religion, nationality, ideology or political opposition to National Socialism'.[44] Although objectives were once again clearly established, it was not easy to introduce them in practice. As it could be learned from the quoted Nazi documents, many of the objects were sold on the market, others, for example those made of silver, were often melted down. The main problem that emerged just after the war and still remains is the lack of proper documentation. Acting in 1991–1994 as a Government of Poland Commissioner for Cultural Property Abroad, the author of this paper tried again, and possibly for the last time, to collect information on losses sustained during the war and Nazi occupation of Poland by various institutions, museums, etc., as well as private collectors. Due to the facts mentioned above, the results of these efforts were not very promising. The only outcome was a chance to elaborate new versions of catalogues of lost works of art which were published some years after the war. Their content certainly still does not match more the scale of real losses.[45]

This reflection is surely particularly appropriate in the context of Jewish cultural losses. Even institutions specializing in the study of the history of Polish Jewry such as the Jewish Historical Institute in Warsaw or Jagiellonian University in Cracow were not able to produce any further precise data in this respect. Details of only approximately 500 lost objects have been collected to date. Information on other objects, if available, is incomplete. For example, it is known that Jewish communities from southern Poland (region called formerly Galicia) were forced by the occupiers to send their religious objects to Prague. So certain traces led to the Central Jewish Museum in that city, but the museum's documentation was not sufficiently precise to give full information on the origin of the objects in its possession. The main problem, exactly the same as in the case of Polish museums and collections, lies in the lack of adequate documentation. It very seldom happens that one finds an object in a museum with a letter stating that the object was given as a deposit conditionally and should be given back to the descendants of the family X if they had happened to survive and might come to collect their property one day.

NOTES

1 For decades historians as well as public opinion have been interested mainly in human fates and losses. Common knowledge recognizes also the cultural losses, however we still do not know enough about how systematic and well organized this robbery was, although the relevant sources are available but not sufficiently explored and brought to light. It can even be argued that various efforts recently undertaken in many countries (e.g. in the United Kingdom, USA, France, or Austria) to redress these losses will not be fully effective without learning more about the nature and scope of their initial cause. The 1998 Washington Conference on Holocaust-Era Assets clearly showed great interest in making good losses but did not shed much light on the Nazi machinery which produced them.

2 As an official French report noted: 'Différentes méthodes furent employées par les Allemands en vue d'accaparer des objets d'art ou précieux. La méthode officielle incombait à l'Organisation Rosenberg, que présidait Goering; elle consistait à profiter de l'occupation pour enlever toutes les collections juives, (. . .) Le contenu des Musées nationaux, évacué dès le début de la guerre vers les châteaux de la Loire et du Sud-Ouest, est resté en France. Le Traité de Paix devait s'en occuper. Par contre, près de 2.000 piéces du Musée de l'Armée furent emmenées en Allemagne. La plupart ont été retrouvées d'ailleurs. (. . .) En province, les "déménagements" des musées n'ont été ni nombreux ni importants :. . .'. Spoliations et restitutions des biens culturels publics et privés. (Objets d'art ou précieux). La Documentation Française. Notes et Études Documentaires. No. 1. 109, Paris, 14 Avril 1949, pp.3–4. For more details on the relevant Nazi policy towards France see also: Ch. de Jaeger, *The Linz File. Hitler's Plunder of Europe's Art.* (Exeter, Webb & Bower, 1981), p.64 et seq.; L.H. Nicholas, *The Rape of Europe. The Fate of Europe' Treasures in the Third Reich and the Second World War* (New York: Alfred A. Knopf, 1994), p.115 et seq.; J. Cassou, *Le pillage par les Allemands des ouvres d'art et des bibliothèques appartenant à des Juifs en France. Recueil des Documents* (Paris 1949); C. Lorentz, *La France et les réstitutions allemandes au lendemain de la seconde guerre mondiale (1943–1945)*, (Paris, 1998); and two works of the Mission d'étude sur la spoliation des Juifs de France: *Rapport Général* (Paris, 2000) and I. le Masne de Chermont and D. Schulmann (eds.), *Le pillage de l'art en France*

pendant l'occupation et la situation des 2000 oeuvres confiées aux musées nationaux (Paris: La documentation Française, 2000).

3 'Far to the east of Paris, in the vast lands which Hitler had conquered in the Soviet Union, the intricate legalistic quadrille justifying the confiscations and trading would be far less subtle and 'correct'. In these Slavic wastelands the National Socialist fanatics did not bother with velvet gloves.' L.H. Nicholas, *op.cit.*, p.185.

4 Ch. de Jaeger, *op.cit.*, p.57 et seq., L.H. Nicholas, *op.cit.*, p.57.

5 Tentative List of Jewish Cultural Treasures in Axis-Occupied Countries. By the Research Staff of the Commission on European Jewish Cultural Reconstruction. *Jewish Social Studies*, 1946, Vol.8, No.1, Supplement. Ch. Estreicher (ed.), *Cultural Losses of Poland. Index of Polish Cultural Losses during German Occupation 1939–1943.* (London HMSO, 1943), W. Tomkiewicz, *Catalogue of Paintings Removed from Poland by the German Occupation Authorities during the years 1939–1945.* Vol. I. *Foreign Paintings.* (Warsaw, Ministry of Culture and Art., 1950), Vol. II. *Polish Paintings.* (Warsaw, Ministry of Culture and Art., 1953), B. Bieńkowska, *Losses of Polish Libraries during World War II.* (Warsaw, Ministry of Culture and Art. 1994).

6 For more details see: W. Kowalski, *Art Treasures and War. A Study on the Restitution of Looted Cultural Property, pursuant to Public International Law.* (Leicester, Institute of Art and Law, 1998).

7 Verordnung über den Geldverkehr, 14 September 1939, *Verordnungsblatt des Chefs der Zivilverwaltung beim Militärbefehlshaber Posen*, No.1.

8 For the review of all military regulations concerning property matters see: Deutsches Recht, Wochenausgabe 1941, pp.828 et seq. They are commented in: K.M. Pospieszalski, *Polska pod niemieckim prawem 1939–1945 (Ziemie Zachodnie). [Poland under the German Law 1939–1945 (Western Lands)].* (Poznań, Instytut Zachodni, 1946), pp.73 et seq., see also by the same author: *Hitlerowskie 'prawo' okupacyjne w Polsce. Wybór dokumentów. Część I. Ziemie 'wcielone'. [Hitler's occupational 'law' in Poland. A Selection of Documents. Part I. Incorporated Territories]. (Poznań, Instytut Zachodni, 1952).*

9 Verordnung über die Beschlagnahme polnischen Vermögens in Westpreussen, 27 September 1939, *Verordnungsblatt des Militärbefehlshabers Danzig–Westpresussen, 1939, 61.*

10 K.M. Pospieszalski, *op.cit.*, p.74.

11 Erste Verordnung zur Durchführung des Erlasses des Führers und Reichskanzlers über Gliederung und Vervaltung der Ostgebiete, 26 October 1939, *Reichsgesetzblatt, 1939, I*, p.2108, for more information see, in particular, H.J. Klee, *Bürgerliche Rechtspflege in den eingegliederten Ostgebieten u. Behandlung polnischen Vermögens.* (Berlin, Deckers Verlag G. Schenck, 1941), pp.13 et seq.

12 K.M. Pospieszalski, *Hitlerowskie 'prawo' okupacyjne w Polsce. .Część II. Generalna Gubernia. Wybór dokumentów i próba syntezy. [Hitler's occupational 'law' in Poland. Part II. General Gouvernement. A Selection of Documents and the First Synthesis. (Poznań, Instytut Zachodni, 1958),* W. Röhr, E. Heckert, B. Gottberg, J. Wenzel, H.M. Grünthal (eds), *Die faschistische Okkupationspolitik in Polen (1939–1945).* (Berlin, VEB Deutscher Verlag der Wissenschaften, 1989).

13 The first account of this policy is given in: *The Nazi Kultur in Poland by Several Authors of Necessity Temporarily Anonymous.* (London, HMSO, 1945).

14 Verordnung über die Sicherstellung des Vermögens des ehemaligen polnishen Staates, 15 January 1940, *Reichsgesetzblatt 1940, I*, p.174.

15 Verordnung über die Behandlung von Vermögen der Angehörigen des ehemaligen polnishen Staates, 17 September 1940, *Reichsgesetzblatt 1940, I*, p.1270, English text of this regulation see: R. Lemkin, *Axis Rule in Occupied Europe*, (Washington, 1944), p.511, (Decree concerning the Treatment of the Property of Citizens of the Former Polish State, September 17, 1940).

16 Section 2. (1) 'Sequestration shall be ordered in connection with the property of: (a) Jews; (b) Persons who have fled or are not merely temporarily absent.' R. Lemkin, *op. cit.*, p.511.

17 Section 21. (1) 'Imprisonment and a fine or either of these penalties shall be imposed on anyone who, intentionally or through negligence, fails to carry out, or carries out incorrectly or incompletely, the obligation imposed by the present decree, an executive order issued in connection therewith, or an order, under Sec. 18 and 19, to register property or give information'. R. Lemkin, *op. cit.*, pp.515–516.

18 Bekanntmachung des Ministerpräsidenten Generalfeldmarschal Goering über die Errichtung einer Haupttreuhandstelle Ost, 19 November 1939, *Deuscher Reichsanzeiger Nr 260, Neuordn.* p.100.

19 Erlass des Führers und Reichskanzlers zur Festigung deutschen Volkstums, 7 October 1939, Haupttreuchandstelle Ost. *Materialsammlung zum inneren Dienstgebrauch.* (Secret collection of documents regulating the activity of HTO for its exclusive use), also published by K.M. Pospieszalski, *op. cit.*, Part.I, pp.176 et seq.

20 Categories of the Third Reich citizenship.

21 Document dated Berlin, 16 December 1939, including HTO instructions of 1 and 5 December 1939, N. Szuman, Grabież dóbr Kultury polskiej w ramach działalności Generalnego Powiernika dla Zabezpieczenia Niemieckich Dóbr Kultury na Wschodnich Ziemiach Przyłączonych [Plunder of Polish Cultural Goods within the Activity of the General Trustee for Securing German Cultural Material in the Incorporated Eastern Territories]. *Bulletin of the Central Commission on the Investigation of Nazi Crimes in Poland*, Vol.4, 1948, pp.185–186.

22 Document dated Berlin, 9 July 1940. It was issued when the HTO branch in Poznań asked for permission to define „cultural goods' more narrowly because they had problems with the management of too many objects already confiscated. N. Szuman, *op. cit.*, p.188.

23 T. Kułakowski, Dokumenty dotyczące eksterminacji kultury polskiej [Documents Related to the Extermination of Polish Culture], *Najnowsze dzieje Polski. Materiały i Studia [Modern History of Poland. Materials and Studies]*, Vol.1, (Warszawa: Państwowe Wydawnictwo Naukowe, 1957), p.242. It is worth adding, that according to the information available to the author of this paper, these plans were not accomplished and no books or exhibitions were ever compiled. Nevertheless, because the collection had been secured, the paintings mentioned in the letter were saved form destruction and today they are a pride of the art gallery in the Museum of Silesia in Katowice.

24 T. Kułakowski, *op. cit.*, p.222, also W. Röhr and others, *op. cit.*, p.197.

25 T. Kułakowski, *op. cit.*, p.221.

26 N. Szuman, *op. cit.*, p.202.

27 N. Szuman, *op. cit.*, p.196.

28 T. Kułakowski, *op. cit.*, p.227.

29 N. Szuman, *op. cit.*, p.199.

30 Verordnung über die Beschlagnahme des Vermögens des früheren polnischen Staates innerhalb des Generalgouvernements, 15 November 1939, *Verordnungsblatt für die besetzten Gebiete in Polen* 1939, No.6, p.37.

31 Verordnung über die Beschlagnahme von Kunstgegenständen im Generalgouvernement, 16 December 1939, *Verordnungsblatt für die besetzten Gebiete in Polen* 1939, No.12, p.209, for English text see: W. Kowalski, *Art Treasures*, p.91.

32 Erste Durchführung Vorschrift zur Verordnung vom 16. December 1939 über die Beschlagnahme von Kunstgegenständen im Generalgouvernement. *Verordnungsblatt für die besetzten Gebiete in Polen*, 1940, No.6, pp.61–62, for English text see: W. Kowalski, *Art Treasures*, p.92.

33 According to para 2. 3 of The First Executive Order. declarations of all these objects had to contain 'the information about the origin, master, theme presented, dimensions and materials (e.g. wood, brass, canvas) (. . .)'.

34 These towns served during the Nazi occupation of Poland as administrative centres of specially created districts in the General Gouvernement.

35 See notes 21 and 22.

36 For more details see: W. Kowalski, *Liquidation of the Effects of World War II in the Area of Culture*, (Warsaw: Institute of Culture, 1994), p.21.

37 Such effect is clearly reflected, among other things, by not very successful result of works undertaken secretly even during the war, and officially after its end on the catalogues of losses. See note 5.

38 W. Kowalski, *Art Treasures*. p.37.

39 Conference of Allied Ministers of Education was active in London from 1942 to 1945. Representatives of 14 governments and other bodies produced 3 important documents: Scheme for the Restitution of Objects d'Art, Books and Archives, Memorandum upon the Measures to be Taken

Immediately upon the Occupation of Germany, and, Recommendation as to the Methods of Arranging and Pooling Information. For the analysis of these documents see: W. Kowalski, *Liquidation*, p.54 et seq.

40 For the text of the Declaration see: W. Kowalski, *Art Treasures*, p.93, for comments, also pp.40–41.

41 Background of these legislative works is shown by L. Wooley in *A Record of the Work done by the Military Authorities for the Protection of the Treasures of Art and History in War Areas* (London, HMSO, 1947), p.5.

42 For the full text of the Definition of the Term Restitution see: W. Kowalski, *Art Treasures*, p.106.

43 More details on the restitution in kind in: W. Kowalski, *Art Treasures*, p.70 et seq.

44 Art. 1 of the Law No. 59 – Restitution of Identifiable Property (U. S. Zone). Laws adopted in other zones were similar to the quoted one. The full text of this law in English and German is published in W. Kowalski, *Art Treasures...*, p.115.

45 The 1998 catalogue of lost Polish painting gives more precise data referring only to 442 pictures, while the office responsible for the work on this catalogue gathered more general and often only fragmentary information on about 4 600 lost paintings. It is generally acknowledged that the second number also does not reflect real losses. A. Tyczyńska, K. Znojewska, *Wartime Losses. Polish Painting. Oil Paintings, Pastels, Watercolours lost between 1939 and 1945 within the post–1945 Borders of Poland* (Poznań, Ministerstwo Kultury i Sztuki: Biuro Pełnomocnika Rządu do Spraw Polskiego Dziedzictwa Kulturalnego za Granicą, 1998).

RESEARCH FINDINGS WITH RESPECT TO HOLOCAUST-ERA ART IN GERMAN AND CZECH PUBLIC COLLECTIONS

Eva Kurz

THE ART Loss Register, a private company established in 1990 by the art and insurance industries, maintains the world's largest database of stolen and looted works of art. The objectives of the Art Loss Register are to identify and recover stolen art, deter theft and reduce the trade in stolen art as well as to mould the practices of all those engaged in the buying, selling and exhibiting of art objects to ensure that establishing provenance and providing assurance of good title becomes a routine research proceedure. Over the ten years since the establishment of the Register, $100 million's worth of stolen or missing art was identified through the systematic screening of art-works on offer on the international art market (via auction houses or by individual art dealers) by trained art historians operating out of London, New York and Cologne. 1998 saw the foundation of a special *pro bono* project to identify the location of works of art looted or subjected to forced sales between 1933 and 1945 with particular, though not exclusive, emphasis on Holocaust era losses. Specialist art historians are engaged full time in assisting Holocaust survivors and heirs worldwide to trace the thousands of looted or forcibly sold objects that have been registered on the claims database. All art claims are registered at no cost to the claimant and research and recovery fees are waived. To comply with the calls for co-operation that were made at the December 1998 Washington Conference on Holocaust Era Assets, unique information bridges have been built with the Commission for Art Recovery of the World Jewish Congress and the Holocaust Claims Processing Office, both engaged in claimant orientated research, to ensure that information on art losses is disseminated as widely as possible.

In the course of my research for the looted art project at the Art Loss Register, I have come across archives and information which raise doubts about the German Government's and the German museums' apparent determination 'to locate and return works of art taken or purchased under duress, in particular items of Jewish ownership'.[1] I would like to demonstrate how the refusal to open so-called 'tax' archives and the reluctance to search the museums' inventories for provenance actively and systematically contradict the Government's and the museums' apparent adherence to principle 2 of the Washington Conference Principles with Respect to Nazi-Confiscated Art.[2] These principles were reiterated by the German delegates during the recent Stockholm Forum,[3] and even though they are not legally binding they represent a moral imperative.

I am not suggesting that if all the archives were opened, objects could easily be identified as belonging to specific individuals and returned to the original owners or their heirs. Even though the Nazis kept precise records of confiscations from Jews, some records were destroyed by Allied bombing and others do not provide sufficient information to identify the original owner. This applies in particular to the art objects taken from

Jews from the occupied territories (during the so-called Möbelaktion or M-Aktion). However if all tax archives were opened and if the museums made resources and personnel available to facilitate the identification and restitution of Nazi-looted objects, the chances of Holocaust survivors being reunited with their artworks would be greatly increased. Museums have explained their inactivity by stating that they have insufficient funds to use existing or employ new staff to search their collections for provenance. However, the example of Cologne demonstrates that it is not necessarily a case of lack of funds but rather a question of will coupled with spending priorities.

I have concentrated in this essay on archives located in tax ministries and museums in Cologne for three reasons. First, having grown up in Cologne I have close contacts with the Jewish community and good access to the Ministry of Culture and museum authorities for the Cologne region. Second, Cologne is one of the most important centres for art in Germany and the Art Loss Register runs an office there.[4] Thirdly, Cologne is considered to be the home of the first Jewish community in northern Europe[5]. The idea of a Jewish museum to house the impressive collection of Judaica has to date been unsuccessful because of the city's apparent lack of public funds. Considering that presently three new museums are under construction, including a new building for the Wallraf-Richartz-Museum, it is disappointing that no funds are being made available for the construction of a long-overdue Jewish museum. A group of sponsors, mostly non-Jewish Germans, is presently trying to raise funds for the establishment of a Haus und Museum der jüdischen Kultur.

In the late 1940s and 1950s the West German Government returned to their original owners several hundred thousand artworks found on its territory after the end of World War II.[6] The Communist Government of East Germany rejected all responsibility for the common German past and no research was seemingly done on the provenance of artworks in museum collections. East German and East Berlin museums held countless pieces of art owned by Jewish collectors before the Holocaust and only years after German reunification and the efforts of individual researchers like Anja Heuss, formerly an employee of the Claims Conference, are East German museums facing up to the legacy of Nazi looting.

There are now some positive signs that change is on the way:

(1)   On 10 April 2000, thanks to the initiative of Michael Naumann, the Federal Minister for Culture, the Koordinierungsstelle der Länder für die Rückführung von Kulturgütern published an internet listing of the entire inventory of remaining objects from Hitler's planned museum of World Art in Linz, Austria. The inventory includes 2242 works of art described as of 'uncertain' origin and in need of a legitimate owner. There are high expectations that many of these items will be returned to their true owners. However, it has been suggested that the majority of paintings included in the list are objects sold voluntarily in order to stock Hitler's intended museum rather than works of art confiscated from Jews. Furthermore, the listing is erroneous in some cases. For example, the regional gallery in Kassel disputes the inclusion of Tintoretto's *Lot and his Daughters* on the list as the provenance is not in dispute.

(2)   At federal and municipal levels, initiatives are underway to research the efforts undertaken by museums in respect of checking their collections' provenance. According to Frau Marie Hüllenkremer, the Departmental Head of Culture for the Cologne region, a report on Cologne museums should be completed in late 2001. To date only the Kölner Stadt Museum and the Wallraf-Richartz-Museum

(WRM) have made staff available to research the museums' transactions during the Nazi era. And only the Kölner Stadt Museum is openly giving information about its research and asking for assistance in piecing together the missing provenance of artworks acquired between 1933 and 1945. In view of this, unless resources are devoted to this research, the above-mentioned report is unlikely to shed much new light on the museums' holdings of works of questionable provenance.

(3)   Since 1998 several German museums have returned art works tainted by the Nazi era to the original owners. In 1998 the Prussian Cultural Heritage Foundation returned Vincent van Gogh's drawing *L'Olivette* to the heirs of Max Silberberg. The drawing had been purchased by the Berlin National Gallery at a 'Jewish Auction' held by the Berlin auction house, Paul Graupe, in 1935. More recently, the Director General of the Bavarian State Collection of Paintings handed the triptych *The Three Stages of Life* by Count Leopold von Kalchkreuth recently on exhibit at *1900: Art at the Crossroads* at the Royal Academy in London to the heirs of Elizabeth Glanville, a Viennese collector. In Cologne, the Ludwig Museum returned two paintings, Otto Müller's *Pair of Female Nudes* to Ruth Haller, the daughter of the Breslau art collector Ismar Littman, and *The Grape* by the French-Polish painter Louis Marcoussis to the son of the Russian painter El Lissitzky. Until the late 1990s German museums had refused to return confiscated art on the grounds that the deadline for restitution had expired in 1959. Museums now waive this legal impediment, and base the decision to return the confiscated paintings on moral grounds. Frau Hüllenkremer said after the return of the Marcoussis painting that restitutions were 'self-evident'.[7]

Even the museums that make an effort to identify Nazi-looted art often refuse to publicly disseminate their research thus preventing researchers, claimants and the public from filling in the gaps of paintings with questionable or unclear provenance. For example, the WRM published a report of its entire collection in 1986, which since 1996 has been available on CD-Rom.[8] Of the listed paintings, 26 had been acquired between 1939 and 1945. All these paintings have a missing or an incomplete provenance. However, some provide the name and place of residence of previous owners, among whom were prominent Jewish collectors.

The WRM is reluctant to share information with researchers regarding these paintings. The museum now employs a full-time research assistant to investigate the museum's collection and a report should be finalized in two years. Whilst welcoming this rather belated initiative, the museum's unwillingness to share information on paintings of unclear provenance via the Internet for example slows down the identification process. Public dissemination does not guarantee a positive identification of every picture, but it vastly increases the chances of identifying a confiscated painting and returning it to the original owner or his/her descendants. Also, information may be forthcoming that removes the shadow of suspicion from a museum piece which can only be to the museum's benefit. Furthermore, the publication of paintings of unclear provenance as demonstrated by the National Museums Directors Conference in the UK,[9] reinforces the museums' commitment to dealing with this issue in an open and transparent way.

In keeping with its increased commitment to museums, the Art Loss Register has undertaken to develop and maintain a single Internet site of standardized information, that will incorporate information from all participating museums in both Europe and the

United States. This will be known as the Museum Provenance Database. It is the intention that the Museum Provenance Database be held separate from the central 'stolen' database and will be accessible to claimants, researchers and others having a legitimate interest. The database will be systematically checked as new Holocaust-era claims are registered.

While some museums in the Cologne region have published information about acquisitions made during the Nazi era, little has been published about the implication of museum officials in this process or the enrichment of the museums' collections due to the confiscation of Jewish-owned paintings. For example, the current Director of the WRM, Dr Rainer Budde, comments in an essay written in 1985 on the acquisition of 87 paintings and sculptures during the years 1941/42, among them famous works by Cézanne, Renoir, Manet and Rodin.[10] Dr. Budde stresses that the then acting director made the purchases in good faith on the basis that they had an untainted provenance. But an explanation of how the purchases were made and their previous owner details are conspicuously lacking. Rather, the essay describes the museum's failure to receive compensation for 39 paintings and five sculptures it was obliged to return to the countries of origin after the War. Without disputing that this may be a valid grievance, it is obvious that museums prefer to dwell on an injustice they suffered rather than uncovering any misdeeds or failings committed by their senior staff during the Nazi era.

Frau Beatrix Alexander, a researcher at the Kölner Stadt Museum has written a report about documents which she accidentally discovered in Cologne's Historic Archives. The report has not yet been published but has been passed to the Art Loss Register.[11] The documents refer to the City of Cologne's acquisitions from occupied France. They show how senior museum officials sold items in their collections to dealers and private persons, and how after the war they tried to conceal their involvement. Furthermore, the disappearance of paintings from the museum's inventory is designated in the documents as 'war-losses'. Alexander demonstrates the difficulty of identifying confiscated objects due to the accidental or intentional disappearance of a large number of important files and correspondence, which implicated senior officials in positions at the time. Her attempt to publish the report was twice rejected and she was told that she might be able to present it at a conference in the autumn 2000. It is rather surprising that a report which throws light on the museum's dealings during the Nazi era is met with so little interest by the museum community.

In blatant contradiction of the Government's apparent determination to open archives is the Federal Finance ministry's refusal to open all files stored in local tax offices. These list in painstaking detail the expropriation and plunder of property (including works of art) from German Jews and Jews from the occupied territories. Professor Wolfgang Dressen, a social science professor at the University of Düsseldorf managed to gain access to 4000 out of 25,000 files stored in the Cologne tax office after years of frustrated efforts. He published his findings in the book *Betriffi Aktion 3*[12] and showed the material in an exhibition in Düsseldorf, Cologne and a number of other German venues.

The files he discovered give a complete record of how the regions' Jews were robbed and what happened to the loot. The records include court records, bailiffs' orders, removal firms' invoices, auctioneers' listings and the signed property declarations all Jews, including children, were required to submit before surrendering their goods and being sent to concentration camps.

The Nazis put the Finance Ministry in charge of the expropriation and after the War, the files remained a secret. They are to stay closed for a further seventy years under 1988 legislation by the parliament barring disclosure of tax information even though these records contain no tax information. Paradoxically the storage period for these records ran out on 31 December 1999 and had it not been for the intervention of Professor Dressen and the support of the Nordrhein-Westfalen finance ministry, the records would have been shredded. Similar records were unearthed by Jim Tobias, a journalist in Nuremberg who gained access to files in the city tax office.[13] Bavaria is the first state in Germany that has opened its archives to researchers.

The book reveals also how ordinary German citizens profited from property taken from German Jews, including their former neighbours:

> In villages and cities individual auctions took place. The former Jewish owners were known as they had been deported only a few days earlier. Following official notification, tax officers appeared and offered all the household goods for sale. Everything from furniture to preserving jars full of onions was included. Only family photographs of the deported Jews found no takers and were destroyed [my translation].[14]

Other documents in the book demonstrate how Germans acquired objects shipped to Germany from the occupied territories in the 'Möbelaktionen'. These goods were often of better quality than the items from German Jews since Jews in the occupied territories were targeted later than their already-impoverished German counterparts. The most valuable items were given to highly decorated officers, the Ritterkreuzträger.

There is also proof of how looted works of art were sold off at auctions which had been organized especially for this purpose. One of the documents discovered shows how the Lord Mayor of Cologne purchased a gobelin-style tapestry from the finance ministry at an auction in Cologne on the 3 January 1944 for the sum of 2000 Reichsmarks.[15] When Beatrix Alexander asked me to investigate the provenance of two gobelins which are presently in the Lord Mayor's office in Cologne and which she suspected might have been dubiously acquired during the Nazi period, I was hopeful that one could be identified as that purchased by the Lord Mayor in 1944. Unfortunately the scant information available has not led to a positive identification. However, if all museums took similar proactive steps to identify paintings or art objects of questionable provenance, the identification and restitution process would be much more advanced than it is.

Professor Dressen also publishes a list of paintings which were taken from the occupied territories and were auctioned at in the Café Nutt in Cologne on 9 February 1944.[16] The Nazis marked property emanating from the 'M-Aktionen' as 'Vermögen von verschiedenen Juden' ('property belonging to various Jews'). The property of German Jews is accompanied with a description of the person's name and other personal details. This differentiation between property of German Jews and property from Jews from the occupied territories is significant, since even if an item emanating from a M-Aktion was found, one would have great difficulties in finding the rightful owner. The catalogue of the auction gives details of the name of the painter, date of the painting, auction price as well as the name and address of the purchaser. It has to be assumed that some of the purchasers or their heirs could be traced given the information available. This would open a new and much more controversial discussion than the present situation, which is restricted to the restitution of Nazi-looted property from public museums.

It is not surprising that the German Government does not want to open the archives since they may expose by name various prominent art shipping firms, such as Kühne & Nagel, who are still in business today, and banks, such as Dresdner Bank or Commerzbank who profited from the 'Entjudungsgewinne' (seizure of Jewish profits).

Professor Dressen has had great difficulty in finding venues willing to show this material. Recently, the Humbold Universität in Berlin declined to stage the exhibition on the grounds that 'the material exhibited showed too little understanding for the Germans'. When a member of the Green party asked about the files in Parliament, the Government told her that the information contained in these files was 'unimportant'. However, the existence of these files can no longer be kept hidden and according to Professor Dreßen, the Government is considering limited access to certain files under the condition that names are kept anonymous.

The Art Loss Register has brought this issue to the attention of the Federal Finance Ministry. We have pointed out the extent to which the refusal to open the archives is in contradiction with the Government's utterances for transparency and how it may impede the chances of Holocaust survivors to be reunited with their works of art.

Considering all this, the overall picture is a mixed one. Undoubtedly since the posting of the Washington Principles, both the Government and some museums have taken a number of initiatives to facilitate the identification and restitution of Nazi-looted assets. However, in Cologne only two museums have made personnel available for this purpose. According to Dr. Jochen Pötter, the outgoing director of the Ludwig Museum, which houses a most impressive collection of 20th-century art, the museum lacked the resources to employ or use existing staff for searching the museum's collection for looted works of art. Whereas generally the museums are now prepared to hand over objects when approached by claimants who have the necessary proof of ownership, hardly any of the museums take steps to publicize art that may have been confiscated so that claimants could come forward. When I mentioned that paintings with questionable provenance could be listed on the Internet, the general response was positive, but technical and financial problems were proposed as to why this has not yet been done. I was told that it would be wrong of me to assume that these were delaying actions. Whether or not this may be true, if there was a genuine will to reunite Holocaust survivors with their works of art, both the Government and museums could do more and could do it faster.

Since one of the Conference's aims is to assess the impact of new material and research, particularly in the post-Communist era, I would like to elaborate on the handling of the restitution process in the Czech Republic. It will become clear that the Government and the museums are ambivalent about facilitating the identification of Nazi-looted paintings and are reluctant to restitute the confiscated items to the true owners or their heirs once they come forward. I will also illustrate how thanks to the tremendous efforts and persistence of certain individuals, notably Michaela Hajkova of the Jewish Museum in Prague,[17] the names of some of the original owners could be matched with certain objects confiscated from them. Some of these works of art are presently in Prague's National Gallery, whereas the whereabouts of others still needs to be ascertained.

Before elaborating on these issues, I would like to show how the legal framework disadvantaged claimants whose property was liable to 'double confiscation', and how the present lack of valid restitution laws prevents individuals from recovering their property. In the past four years, the return of an object to a claimant merely depended on the goodwill of the present owner. After increased international pressure, on 24 May 2000, the Czech Parliament voted in favour of a new restitution law (Law 212/2000) which specifically applies to property taken by the Nazis between 29 September 1938 and 8 May 1945. The law has been ratified by the Senate and the President. It is impossible to say yet whether it will rectify the injustices produced by the application of the previous laws. However, like the past legislation the law only applies to the return of State-owned property.[18]

Nowhere in the last century had Jews suffered as much as in Central and Eastern Europe. In the former Czechoslovakia, first the Nazis (who killed 300,000 of 357,000 Czechoslovak Jews) and then the Communists robbed the previously affluent Czech Jews of their assets, including their art collections. After the 1989 'Velvet Revolution' and President's Havel's stated support for Israel and Jews, Czech Jews finally believed that they would recover their property.[19]

Between 1992 and 1996, restitution laws were in force that allowed for the return of property, including works of art, under certain conditions. However these laws supposedly intended to help individual Jewish owners whose properties were confiscated by the Nazis and then nationalised by the Communists have proven to be anomalous. Claimants were given a scant five months in which to procure all the complicated documentation needed to file a claim. For claimants living abroad this period was extended to one year (end April 1995). More discriminatory yet, unlike the laws regulating claims for Communist-confiscated property, the 'Jewish law' disallowed any claim for the return of property whose title had been acquired by a third non-state party after 1 October 1991 or on properties the Government had simply decided to privatize (though financial compensation might be available for these).

The laws also excluded from restitution and/or compensation any agricultural land and property confiscated from Jews by the Nazis and then taken over by the Communist Czech state after 1948. A very large amount of property has been subject to this 'double confiscation', considering that there was only a period of barely three years to recover Nazi-confiscated property between the end of the war and the Communist coup. Moreover only a small percentage of Czech Jews, who had not managed to escape in time, survived the war.[20] The majority of those left the country before 1948. Many Czech Jews who survived the war in exile often did not manage to get their property back before the coup of February 1948.

For example, I received documents (in Czech) from the Jewish Museum in Prague regarding the attempts of the two surviving sisters of the Czech art collector, Emil Freund, to recover their brother's important and confiscated art collection at the end of the war. Emil Freund died in Lodz, Poland in 1942. His two sisters, Berta Sieben and Olga Hoppe emigrated to Chicago in the United States in the 1920s. The documents reveal how the sisters' request for the return of their brother's art collection was dismissed by the Czech Communist Government. A letter to Berta Sieben dated 15 April 1948 from the 'National Fund for Property' lists the whereabouts of specific items of Freund's collection, including four paintings at the renowned Strahov Monastery,[21] and asks for additional information. In contrast, the next item in the correspondence was a letter dated 7 November 1949 from the 'National Council of Jewish Elders' (by then under state control) to the Ministry of Labour and Social Affairs. While the Council agreed with the valuation of Freund's art collection (500,000 Czechoslovak crowns), it refused to return these art works to Freund's sisters on the ground that they were no longer resident in Czechoslovakia, and that taking such valuable objects out of the country would be against the interests of Czechoslovak culture. The sisters' appeal to the District Court for financial compensation was finally rejected on 23 March 1950. It is disturbing that fifty years later those individuals who have succeeded in reclaiming some of their works of art are still prevented from taking them to their country of current residence because of export legislation.

Export licences have been refused with respect to the majority of valuable artworks and collectibles which were returned to the heirs of Jindrich Waldes and Richard Morawetz. According to the Action Sale and Export of Works of Art, No 71/1994, any individual who wants to export a work of art requires a certificate to the effect that the object is not a 'listed cultural monument' (Law 71/1994, clause2). Since the Ministry does not employ specialists to decide on this matter, the decision whether or not to grant a licence is left to state museums and galleries that are listed in the law. Considering that many of the restituted works came from these institutions, one has to question the impartiality of the parties taking the decision. If the museum or gallery declares that the work may qualify as a 'cultural monument', then the Ministry of Culture has four months to decide whether or not to grant the licence. When a licence is refused, the families have no option other than selling the objects (below the market value) in the Czech Republic. One might argue that the whole purpose of restitution is defeated if owners are prevented from taking their works out of the Czech Republic to the country of their residence.

In 1997, after six years of wrangling with the Government, the heirs of Jindrich Waldes, finally secured the restitution of twenty major paintings from the Czech National Gallery. Waldes was the most important supporter of Czech modern art in Prague before the war; the works concerned were all by the Czech abstract pioneer Frantisek Kupka (1871–1957) and had been confiscated by the Nazis and later nationalized by the Communists. As with other claimants, the paintings were returned on condition that the National Gallery was allowed to keep some other valuable items of his collection. The same method was used in Austria in the late 1940s with respect to the famous collections of Alphonse and Louis de Rothschild, Ferdinand Bloch-Bauer and the Lederer family. In addition, the Waldes heirs, who are now living in the United States, were not granted an export licence for any of the paintings and were therefore obliged to sell the paintings in the Czech Republic. In fact, the National Gallery used a Czech law to buy back the works from the Waldes family. During that process the nation's resolve to clear its record on looted art was called into question.[22]

Although museum officials were eager to get back the prized paintings, they were dragging their feet to pay the full market price (three million US dollars). In the end the National Gallery bought the paintings for the set price. The Art Loss Register has been advised that the National Gallery together with the State (the Gallery is officially a state institution) were only prepared to pay the actual market price because Kupka was Czechoslovakia's most famous modernist. When I spoke to Jiri Waldes, Jindrich's son about the restitution of these works, he mentioned that his father's whole collection included 14,000 items. Among these was a huge collection of books, which had been taken from Waldes' villa and which is now in Prague's central library. Unfortunately Mr Waldes has given up hope of identifying the confiscated books as the library holds a total of six million books.

Furthermore, the Waldes heirs discovered that part of their collection, including their gold and coins collection, is now held in a museum in Jablonec, which belongs to a factory. When they contacted the director of the museum, they were told that they could 'take a look at the paintings', but that they would not get them back. The factory owners do not dispute the heirs' title to the collection (they have even produced affidavits to this effect), but refuse to give it back on the ground that legally they are not obliged to do so. This situation has arisen in respect of property which was transferred in 1991 by the state to the municipalities. The restitution laws have never applied to the municipalities and they are therefore legally not obliged to return any property. It must be hoped that the new draft law redresses this unsatisfactory state of affairs.

There are some signs that the Czech Government has started to address the issue. In the beginning of 1999 a joint commission containing members of Government, the

Jewish community and the B'nai Brith Lodge was set up by the Government. The commission functions as an umbrella for different restitution claims, including claims for looted art. Since September 1999, an expert term has been doing its basic research in the Czech archives, mainly the Central State Archives in Prague, in the archives in Brno and Ostrava. It intends to do some basic research in the Bundesarchiv in Berlin, in the Archives of the Ministry of Foreign Affairs, Ministry of the Interior, Ministry of Finance, in the Municipal Archives in Prague and in selected family archives. Outside the Czech Republic, research was carried out in archives in Munich and Vienna. The commission hopes that after this research, it will be able to explain at least the mechanisms through which the confiscation of Jewish property was possible and the fate of these confiscated works of art. The expert team is supposed to present the final report of its research by the end of September 2000.

Dr Michaela Hajkova, curator of the Jewish Museum in Prague and one of the experts on the 'Provenance' Commission, is sceptical about the Government's and the museum's approach to checking archives. Hajkova says that the employees in the museums lack any training in order to be able to identify 'looted works of art', nor do they have the time to do any special archive research. Therefore, they do not know what to look for. Furthermore, the Government only required of museums that they check their own entries in their museum catalogues. According to Hajkova, this allows museums to argue that since most of their records date only from the 1948 putsch, they are incapable of ascertaining the ownership of a large number of works in their museums.

Nevertheless, the Czech Ministry of Culture has already announced that the 'first stage' of this so called 'investigation' in the Czech public collections has been accomplished and that, as a result of these efforts, it will publish an internet listing of the objects which the Czech public museums and galleries have identified as having been 'looted'. According to Michaela Hajkova the list is in the least 'very incomplete' but apparently it includes the paintings, drawings and graphic art that were transferred in 1950 from the Jewish Museum in Prague to the National Gallery.

The following example demonstrates that, in spite of what the museums assert, provenance can be traced indirectly by searching through the relevant state archives. In 1996, Hajkova discovered a batch of transport numbers referring to paintings looted from Emil Freund. Researchers at the Jewish Museum in Prague have been able to identify the people to whom the numbers relate thanks to the records in the Museum's 'German' catalogues. These are the entries which have been established by the Jewish scholars working between 1942 and 1945 in the so-called 'Central Jewish Museum'. The paintings were confiscated from their owners during the Nazi occupation and the majority went to the 'Treuhandstelle' which was part of the 'Auswanderungsfonds', the organization that financed the deportations to the death camps. From the 'Treuhandstelle', many some of the paintings were taken to the Jewish Museum, but the whereabouts of the majority is unknown. On certain cards it is possible to find also the transport numbers, under which the former owners were registered and deported from Prague to the Ghetto of Lodz, Poland (October 1941) and then to the Terezin Ghetto (from December 1941 onwards). For example, Dr. Emil Freund had the transport number: B126 and had been transported to Lodz on 21 October 1941. Hajkova then traced the numbers to paintings in the National Gallery – including works by Paul Signac, Renoir and Utrillo. She then drew up a list of 84 items, which were transferred to the Gallery due to the 'double confiscation' in 1950. Another set of around 100 paintings from the museum holdings were also seized by the Communists in 1950 and were sold through the Antikva Auction House, which was by then nationalized and under Communist supervision.

Until recently the National Gallery held 63 of the 84 paintings. The Jewish Museum first asked for their return in 1996, which was denied. In October 2000, 63 paintings were transferred back from the National Gallery to the Jewish Museum. Among these are paintings by Emil Freund, and the Jewish museum is now trying to trace any surviving family of his sisters, Olga Hoppe and Berta Sieben, using all possible contacts in the area.

At the request of the Jewish Museum in Prague, the Art Loss Register will place on its Internet site the above mentioned sixty six paintings in the hope the heirs of the original pre-Holocaust owners can be traced. This listing will be maintained separately from the ALR's claims database and the Museum Provenance Database.

Since the collapse of the Iron Curtain, the hopes of Holocaust survivors and their heirs to be reunited finally with their works of art have been dashed for the following reasons. (1) Restitution laws have proven to be discriminatory in the past; the impact of the new law cannot yet be assessed. Furthermore, judgements favouring the restitution of artworks to the original owners or their heirs have often been simply ignored by the museums. For example, Mrs Marie Grunwald, formerly of the Czech Republic, and now resident in Australia secured a ruling from the Czech Constitutional Court for the return of a painting by Courbet from the National Gallery in Prague. The gallery is refusing to return the painting since they allege that legally they are not obliged to do so. Another claimant had to go back to Court, when the first ruling to return a painting was simply ignored by the defendant museum. (2) Failing valid legislation, few museums and galleries in the Czech Republic, have chosen to return confiscated works of art on 'moral grounds', as has been the case in Germany. (3) Even when objects have been restituted, the owners are unable to take them out of the country and are thus prevented from passing them on to their descendants. An article in the *Frankfurter Allgemeine Zeitung* asks whether 'Nazi laws are still valid in the Czech Republic', referring to the great number of families who had to fight so hard to get back some of their collections.[23] The State should consider waiving the application of the export law with respect to restituted property so that Holocaust survivors and their heirs have a choice to keep the returned art objects if they wish to do so.

Dr. Tomas Kraus, President of the Federation of Jewish communities in the Czech Republic, told me that the Jewish community has requested from the Government that all identified looted artworks are returned to their original owners and that all heirless works to be given to the Jewish museum in Prague. Both, Kraus and Hajkova are sceptical about the Government's willingness to grant this request. However, the progress made in the identification of confiscated paintings, and the decision to return 63 paintings to the Jewish Museum, are encouraging signs that as expressed by Michaela Hajkova 'things are slowly getting better'.

NOTES

1 In December 1999, Michael Naumann, the first Federal Minister of Culture since 1949, issued together with the 16 state governments and the association of German municipalities a joint 'declaration on *locating and restituting* (author's italics) art and cultural objects taken or purchased under duress because of Nazi persecution, in particular items of Jewish ownership'.

2 See Appendix.

3 The Stockholm International Forum on the Holocaust, A Conference on Education, Remembrance and Research, 26–28 January 2000.

4   I am grateful to Ulli Segers and Bernd Fesel in the Art Loss Register's Cologne office for having assisted me with acquiring information and for Ulli's introduction to Beatrix Alexander of the Kölner Stadtmuseum.

5   Jews were mentioned in a letter by the Emperor Constantine the Great (321–331 A.D.). These documents will be exhibited in the museum.

6   There is no consensus as to how many artworks were returned after World War II; some suggest the number is over one million, e.g. John Dornberg, 'Germany's Last Ghost', *Art & Auction*, January 2000, p.96.

7   *Der Spiegel*, Raubkunst-Moralische Selbstverständlichkeit (Issue 5, 2000).

8   Wallraf-Richartz Museum Köln, *Gemälde- und Skulpturenbestand*, CD-Rom, 1996, available in English and German, DM.-98, under ISBN 3-598-40309-7.

9   The National Museums' Directors Conference Holocaust spoliation discussion and preliminary research findings can be found on the internet at www.nationalmuseums.org.uk/spoliation.

10   Dr Rainer Budde, Anmerkungen zu den Erwerbungen des Wallraf-Richartz-Museums in den Jahren 1941–1945, Wallraf-Richartz-Jahrbuch, Bd.XLVI/XLVII (1985–86).

11   Beatrix Alexander, *Im eigenen Interesse-Nachforschungen über den Verbleib von Kunstgut im Dritten Reich*, Kölnisches Stadt Museum, Zeughausstrasse1–3, 50667 Köln.

12   Wolfgang Dressen, *Betrifft: 'Aktion 3' – Deutsche verwerten jüdische Nachbarn, Dokumente zur Arisierung*, (Berlin: Aufbau-Verlag Gmbh, 1998).

13   Jim Tobias, 'Dokumente über Arisierung fallen nicht unter Steuergeheimnis-Forscher erhalten Einblick in NS-Akten', *Süddeutsche Zeitung*, 6 September 1999, and 'Eigentum ermorderter jüdischer Bürger vereinnahmt und verwertet-Akten belegen Raubzüge der NS-Finanzverwaltung', Süddeutsche Zeitung, 27 January 2000.

14   'Auf den Dörfern und teilweise in den Städten fanden Einzelversteigerungen statt. Die ehemaligen jüdischen Nachbarn waren bekannt, sie waren erst vor einigen Tagen deportiert waren. Nach der öffentlichen Ankündigen erschienen die Finanzbeamten und boten den Hausrat an, von den Möbeln bis zu den Einmachgläsern mit Inhalt oder den Zwiebeln, nur die Familienfotos der deportierten Juden fanden keine Abnehmer und wurden vernichtet.'

15   *Betrifft: 'Aktion 3'*, p.169.

16   *ibid.*, pp.186–87.

17   On behalf of the Art Loss Register, I am grateful to Michaela Hajkova for being an invaluable source of information, and for having given the permission to the ALR to publish her list of confiscated paintings on the internet.

18   Rainer Koch, 'Tschechien beschloss Rückgabe an Juden', *Der Standard*, 26 May 2000.

19   A good summary of the plunder of Czech Jews can be found in Richard Z. Chesnoff, *Pack of Thieves – How Hitler and Europe plundered the Jews and committed the greatest Theft in History*, (New York: Doubleday, New York, 1999), pp.44–77.

20   Of the 50,000 Czechoslovak Jews who survived the Holocaust, more than half were in Slovakia.

21   The Strahov Monastery was the central archive where the Nazis recorded 'the bureaucracy of death – the nuts and bolts of genocide and, most painfully, the shame of Czech complicity, betrayal and theft', *Pack of Thieves*, p.64. Even now there is only limited, access, if any, to the files kept there.

22   Robert Rigney, 'Keeping the Kupkas – How a collection of art restituted by the Czech National Gallery ended up back in the museum', *Art News*, January 2000.

23   Stephan Templ, Bock als Gärtner, Frankfurter Allgemeine Zeitung, Feuilleton, 17. December 1999, Nr.294/p.47

APPENDIX

WASHINGTON CONFERENCE PRINCIPLES WITH RESPECT TO NAZI-
CONFISCATED ART
(Released at the Washington Conference on Holocaust-Era Assets, Washington, D.C., December 3, 1998)

In developing a consensus on non-binding principles to assist revolving issues relating to Nazi confiscated art, the Conference recognizes that among participating nations there are differing legal systems and that countries act within the contact of their own laws.

1 Art that had been confiscated by the Nazis and not subsequently restituted should be identified.
2 Relevant records and archives should be open and accessible to researchers, in acordance with the guidelines of the International Council on Archives.
3 Resources and personnel should be made available to facilitate the identification of all art that had been confiscated by the Nazis and not subsequently restituted.
4 In establishing that a work of art had been confiscated by the Nazis and not subsequently restituted, consideration should be given to unavoidable gaps or ambiguities in the provenance in light of the passage of time and the circumstances of the Holocaust era.
5 Every effort should be made to publicize art that is found to have been confiscated by the Nazis and not subsequently restituted in order to locate its pre-War owners or their heirs.
6 Efforts should be made to establish a central registry of such information.
7 Pre-War owners and their heirs should be encouraged to come forward and make known their claims to art that was confiscated by the Nazis and not subsequently restituted.
8 If the pre-War owners of art that is found to have been confiscated by the Nazis and not subsequently restituted, or their heirs, can be identified, steps should be taken expeditiously to achieve a just and fair solution, recognizing this may vary according to the facts and circumstances surrounding a specific case.
9 If the pre-War owners of art that is found to have been confiscated by the Nazis, or their heirs, can not be identified, steps should be taken expeditiously to achieve a just and fair solution.
10 Commissions or other bodies established to identify art that was confiscated by the Nazis and to assist in addressing ownership issues should have a balanced membership.
11 Nations are encouraged to develop national processes to implement these principles, particularly as they relate to alternative dispute resolution mechanisms for resolving ownership issues.

SWISS VICTIMS OF NATIONAL SOCIALISM:
AN EXAMPLE OF HOW SWITZERLAND CAME TO TERMS WITH THE PAST

Regula Ludi and Anton-Andreas Speck

THE TOPIC of our essay is the Swiss government's treatment of Swiss victims of National Socialist persecution.[1] This may initially appear surprising, since one might assume that Swiss, as citizens of a neutral country, survived the National Socialist period unharmed. And indeed, historiography has long presented this picture. Until now, Swiss historiography assessed the consequences of the Nazi period from the chronologically limited perspective of the war years and concentrated primarily on economic relations.[2] With the exception of refugee policy, which has caused a number of controversies since the 1950s, the fate of victims of National Socialism has largely been ignored.[3] This pronounced historiographical blindness reflects to a large extent the policies of the time regarding people whose lives, personalities, freedom and physical existence were directly threatened by National Socialism. It is an expression of the fact that Switzerland denies its past involvement with National Socialism or has reinterpreted it as a myth of national self-assertion. Recent research has made clear to what extent Swiss Jews became victims of National Socialist race policy[4], and in the context of the current debate on heirless assets, the new research has also rescued from oblivion the history of Nazi victims in Switzerland.[5]

In reality, the number of Swiss victims of persecution is not inconsiderable. At the end of the 1950s, the government estimated that there were about 1,100 Swiss citizens alone who were not eligible for restitution from the Federal Republic of Germany.[6] The survey included above all relatives of persons who had been deported and murdered in extermination camps, as well as people who had suffered severe physical and psychological damage through loss of freedom, mistreatment and imprisonment in concentration camps, while addressing material losses only on a rudimentary level. Thus, if one includes the number of people who suffered losses through seizure of property, special taxes, roundups and other actions, boycotts and employment bans in the National Socialist sphere of domination between 1933 and 1945, the actual number of Swiss victims is likely to have numbered several thousand.

In 1962, Switzerland signed an agreement with the FRG in which Germany pledged to pay DM 10 million as global restitution for violations of international law committed by the Third Reich against citizens of Switzerland.[7] The Swiss negotiating team was rightly proud of this result, since it had been able to obtain much more than the European nations that had been occupied by the Third Reich. The average Swiss individual restitution payment of more than DM 9,000 was more than twice as much as the amount paid to France (DM 4,000 per person) and was about four times the amount received by Dutch victims of National Socialism.[8]

THE DEPORTATION OF FAMILY R. FROM FRANCE TO AUSCHWITZ
In order to reconstruct the memory of Swiss victims, we preface our further discussion with a case study. The story of the Jewish R. family illustrates the difficulties of persecuted Swiss who lived abroad and has paradigmatic significance for subsequent history.[9]

On the night of 15–16 July 1942, the Gestapo arrested Selma R., a Swiss Jewish woman living in the occupied part of France, with her children Jula and Frédéric and imprisoned them in Angers. The following day – 16 July 1942 – friends of the family informed the Swiss consulate in Paris of the imprisonment of the R. family. Five days after their arrest, on 20 July 1942, Selma, Jula and Frédéric R. were deported to Auschwitz and murdered there shortly after their arrival. The arrest of the family took place at a time when Swiss authorities had not yet begun to recommend that their Jewish citizens return home and they intervened with German officials only in special cases.[10] In light of the roundups of Jews that began in 1941 and repeatedly included Swiss Jews, the officials of the Swiss consulate in Paris did not see the arrest of the R. family as special. Thus in this case, the consul contacted the German security police in Paris through the usual diplomatic channels asking for information regarding the place of residence, reason for imprisonment and requesting the release of the arrested persons. When, after several requests, the German police responded in December 1942 with a report stating that Selma R. and her children had 'voluntarily reported for a work assignment'[11] in Germany, the Swiss consulate in Paris considered the case closed. Without further comment, the unbelievable report was passed on to Selma R.'s oldest son, Jean R., who lived in Switzerland. That this was not the end of the 'R. case' is due primarily to his persistent requests for information to the Swiss Political Department (EDP). The EDP could not avoid acknowledging that Jean R.'s exposure of the German police statement as an obvious lie contained 'a certain portion of truth'[12] and it requested that the Swiss Embassy in Berlin continue to intervene on behalf of the R. family. The EDP indicated to the diplomatic mission in Germany that the matter would be of some significance, should it come to light that the R. family had not gone to Germany voluntarily. Despite this, the embassy's efforts remained restricted to the usual and unsuccessful methods of requesting information on the whereabouts of the missing Swiss citizens from German authorities. It was not until December 1943, when the arrest of the R. family and other Swiss Jews threatened to cause a public uproar in Switzerland, that the EDP tried to intensify its previous half-hearted attempts to obtain information. But even at this point, the Swiss embassy continued to send friendly notes to the Foreign Ministry of the German Reich. After an unmistakable statement by the German Foreign Ministry in July 1944 that persons affected by a 'Judenaktion' could not possibly be found before the end of the war,[13] Swiss authorities concluded their efforts on behalf of the R. family.

The example of the R. family shows that even in individual cases where the rights of Jewish citizens had obviously been violated, Switzerland reacted only under pressure from outside. Although the Swiss government was informed about what took place in the extermination camps of the east, the arrest of Swiss Jews did not really become a problem until relatives or other interested parties intervened on behalf of the persecuted individuals.[14]

Swiss officials were not able simply to close the 'R. case' at the end of the war. Jean R. accused the consulate in Paris of neglecting to take immediate action to obtain the release of his family and thus of bearing a part of the blame for their deaths. Claiming that Switzerland had failed to provide his relatives with diplomatic protection, he demanded restitution from German assets in Switzerland for the loss of his relatives. The EDP for its part vehemently rejected any responsibility on the part of Swiss authorities. In the question of reparations, Jean R. was referred to the future German government, since, according to the EPD, international law offered no possibility of compensating him out of the German assets held in Switzerland. Although the EPD appeared cool and collected towards the claimant, it was only a mask for the high level of anxiety that gripped the ministry. It desperately collected arguments against shared responsibility by the consulate for the deportation of the R. family. As its main argument, it asserted that the excessive workload and the lack of personnel at the consulate had made it impossible for officials to intervene directly in Angers. Still, the consulate had not ceased to protect its citizens, the EDP argued. Officials concerned themselves once again with Jean R.'s accusations at the end of the 1950s, when a commission examined restitution claims by Swiss victims of National Socialism and made advance compensation payments against the global restitution expected from the FRG. The commission followed the line of argument put forth by the EPD and gave the National Socialist perpetrators full responsibility for the deportation of the R. family. It did not respond explicitly to the question of shared Swiss guilt, since examining the activities of Swiss foreign missions to protect persecuted Swiss citizens lay outside its purview. Still, the steadily increasing amount of restitution Jean R. received during the course of the inquiry suggests that the commission was aware of reprehensible behaviour by Swiss diplomatic offices and wished to address it indirectly without admitting to any specific mistakes by Switzerland.

LACK OF DIPLOMATIC PROTECTION AND ABDICATION OF STATE RESPONSIBILITY

Beginning in 1933, the persecution of Jews in Nazi Germany forced the Swiss government to make fundamental decisions on how the rights of Swiss Jewish citizens abroad were to be protected. An official statement by the Swiss Federal Council revealing its policy was not issued until 1941 in reaction to parliamentary criticism of discrimination against Swiss Jews in France.[15] In September 1941, the Federal Council outlined the significance anti-Jewish legislation in France would have for Swiss Jews. It explained that not only Jews in France, but also those in other states were subject to special legal conditions that were part of public policy ('*ordre public*') and thus also applied to citizens of foreign nations. The Federal Council took the position that Jews with Swiss nationality could not claim privileged status above those in their host country and chose not to demand equal treatment for all Swiss citizens living in France. This choice confirmed and strengthened the policy followed since the 1930s by Swiss foreign missions in Germany, which did not protest when Swiss Jews were subjected to anti-Semitic measures. Although Swiss Jews were repeatedly subjected to persecution, Swiss officials initially could not decide on an official recall of their Jewish citizens. Only after the German Foreign Ministry announced in early 1943 that in future Jews from neutral states would be subject to the same laws and regulations as Jews in Germany and the occupied areas, without exception, did Swiss officials decide to repatriate Swiss Jewish citizens living abroad.

The Federal Council's failure to insist upon equal treatment for all Swiss citizens in France was judged by the Union of Swiss Jewish Communities (SIG) to be a betrayal of the equality before the law guaranteed in the constitution. A legal expert opinion of the SIG written by Paul Guggenheim, a professor of international law, stated that the position of the Federal Council stood in contradiction to the Swiss legal tradition. The reciprocal right-of-residence treaties had been based since 1878 on the equality of all male Swiss citizens and in such state treaties it is understood that equality takes priority to national laws. The Federal Council's reference to foreign domestic regulations thus contradicts Swiss legal concepts, he declared. SIG accused the Federal Council of accepting unequal treatment of Jewish and non-Jewish Swiss citizens without protest. It concluded from this that Jews could not claim the same diplomatic protection afforded all other Swiss.[16] There was never any official response to SIG's petition, but within the government, officials felt that the mandate of equality was upheld if Swiss Jews were given the same treatment as French Jews.

Did the decision of the Federal Council cause Swiss foreign missions to fail to provide diplomatic protection for Jews? Lawyer Veit Wyler posed this question when he applied to SIG in 1950 for 'a legal expert opinion on the issue of protection by the Swiss Federation for actions or lack of same by its diplomatic representatives abroad.' Wyler implied that his client Jean R. might be a case in which the state bore responsibility for the failure to provide diplomatic protection. He based this on the following: 'It seems clear to me that people died as a result of a failure to act when action was necessary. The Swiss diplomatic mission in Paris had the duty to appeal to Swiss citizens in France to return home if they could not guarantee diplomatic protection.' The consulate in Paris obviously carried out this duty 'so slowly and ineffectually' that the R. family could no longer be saved. Veit Wyler also felt it was the responsibility of SIG to approach the authorities on behalf of Swiss victims of the Nazis and demand compensation, for he considered his client's restitution claim 'a basic issue that affects all of us.'[17] SIG rejected Veit Wyler's suggested approach and did not refer back to the petition it had submitted nine years earlier on the protection of Swiss Jews in France. A legal expert opinion concluded that a lawsuit to force the Federation to recognize its responsibility had no chance of success. SIG also chose not to intervene with the authorities on behalf of Swiss Nazi victims.[18]

It is difficult to judge whether this undertaking would have proven successful. A Swiss Jew, who was deported from France to Auschwitz in the summer of 1942 and who survived the concentration camp, applied to the Federation for compensation in August 1945 and encountered a lack of understanding or even a willingness to listen.[19] In the years that followed, the government took the position over and over again that Swiss citizens living abroad had no claim to legal protection outside of Switzerland and thus no claim to restitution. The Federal Council rejected the introduction of legislation that would have provided such a claim to protection. In 1948, the government stated that citizens could not derive a claim to compensation from violations of law by foreign powers, although the Federation could demand compensation for violations of international laws regarding foreigners by third states.[20] The legal position of Nazi victims, thus, was and remained a shaky one, especially since older international law was exclusively between states; it did not recognize any individual claim for safeguarding rights.[21] Finally, federal authorities did all they could to avoid giving the impression to the outside world that they would assume liability for failures to provide diplomatic protection. The draft of a letter expressing a hint of doubt about the zeal of Swiss diplomats in intervening on behalf of persecuted citizens during the 1940's never left the offices of the administration.[22] Within the administration, however, there were officials who tended to the view 'that it was a weakness of our diplomatic offices, not to free every single Swiss from the concentration camps.' More energetic efforts could have achieved more for those who were arrested and deported, they felt.[23]

Apart from these critical comments, which were not intended for the public, there are sufficient indications that the Federal Council did not use all the means at its disposal to save persecuted Swiss citizens during the National Socialist era. The story of the R. family described above is only one example. In 1942, the Federal Council rejected an exchange of prisoners suggested by Germany that would have freed many Swiss citizens from concentration camps.[24] Hans Frölicher, Swiss ambassador in Berlin beginning in 1938, misjudged the character of the Nazi regime. In the view of the historian Edgar Bonjour, 'he simply believed the reassuring, misleading explanations offered by the Foreign Ministry.' Bonjour also says that Frölicher's reports to the Federal Council played down National Socialism and prevented the Federal Council from correctly assessing the dangers posed by the Nazis.[25] The extent to which this judgement can be expanded to the safeguarding of the interests of Swiss living in the National Socialist area of power is difficult to estimate, given the paucity of systematic research. There are certainly some indications that allow the conclusion that Swiss diplomats in Berlin were much too quick to believe statements by the German Foreign Ministry on the whereabouts of missing Swiss citizens. In the case of a Swiss Jewish woman who was arrested in Warsaw at the end of 1943 and died in the Ravensbrück concentration camp in the summer of 1944, the Swiss embassy in Berlin simply passed on to Bern without comment a report from the German Foreign Ministry stating that the woman had died of 'old age'. This report, however, did cause federal officials to wonder about the credibility of the supposed cause of death. A high-ranking official of the Swiss Foreign Ministry informed the embassy in Berlin that 'we cannot dismiss a feeling of unease and therefore must probably remember that Frau B.'s conditions of imprisonment could have accelerated her death.'[26] The federal authorities also occasionally received complaints from relatives of Swiss citizens missing in the Nazi-occupied areas. The son of a Swiss Jewish woman imprisoned in the ghetto of Lwow complained that the Swiss ambassador had made too little effort to contact his mother and receive some indication that she was still alive.[27] The federal authorities in Bern had also paid little attention to the fate of persecuted Swiss who were long considered 'missing' and who it was assumed had been deported. It was not until the danger arose that 'the cases could easily attract extremely undesirable attention in Switzerland,' because prominent persons and parliamentarians also inquired into the whereabouts of arrested persons, that the possibility of intervening with greater vehemence with the German authorities was considered.[28]

These fragmentary examples show that there were already indications during the National Socialist period that Swiss officials had done too little for endangered citizens abroad and had abandoned them to their fate. In the mid-1950s, the government tried its best to prevent the subject of Swiss Nazi victims from becoming public.[29] There were a number of reasons for this. First, even after 1945, the federal administration neglected the Nazi victims for a long time. Therefore, one could easily see 'what a scandal it would cause if it were to become public knowledge that nothing has yet been done to obtain compensation from Germany for this Nazi horror,' a high-ranking official warned the employees of the Foreign Ministry and continued: 'In order to instruct the gentlemen in the correct attitude toward this matter, I have advised them urgently to read one of these horrendous reports and pretend it concerned their brother or their parents! I added that I had received the impression that in all these matter the Political Department was lacking in human warmth.'[30] The fear of publicity can also be explained by the fact that officials were aware that the diplomatic missions and the federal authorities had failed their citizens and deliberately sought to conceal it, especially since Switzerland's shared responsibility in the discriminatory marking of passports of German Jews had come to light in 1954 and had provoked vehement criticism of anti-Jewish refugee policy. The authorities wanted to avoid the possibility of having the charge of anti-Semitism levelled against policies concerning their own citizens.[31]

For the time being, victims of the Nazis could not expect restitution from federal coffers. As a consequence, Swiss citizens who had suffered persecutory measures were referred to German restitution offices. It was quickly discovered, however, that the claims of many Swiss citizens had no chance of success due to the principle of territoriality in the restitution laws in the occupation zones and later because of restrictions in the 1953 German restitution law.[32] Needy victims of persecution remained dependent on welfare, and those who sought compensation for imprisonment in concentration camps or for the loss of murdered relatives were disappointed. In Switzerland, victims of the Nazis had to wait at the end of a long queue of claimants. Their claims competed with the demands of creditors, Swiss from abroad who had incurred losses through the war and returnees. As a small, extremely heterogeneous and politically weak group, the victims of Nazi persecution had neither an organization to represent their interests nor prominent representatives in parliament and in associations.

POLICY CONCERNING THE CONSEQUENCES OF NATIONAL
SOCIALISM IN THE 1940S AND 1950S

Overcoming the problems that arose through Switzerland's economic and political relations with National Socialist Germany dominated Swiss politics of the postwar period until far into the 1950s. Switzerland's international reputation had suffered greatly as a result of its close economic ties to the Third Reich. With the slogan 'neutrality and solidarity' and with reconstruction aid to war-damaged Europe, the government attempted to cleanse its strongly discredited policy of neutrality of the stains left by economic cooperation with Nazi Germany, the acceptance of looted valuables and the suspicion that Switzerland as a financial centre had aided in the escape of former National Socialists.[33] Switzerland thus expected that the conference on reparations convened by the Allies in Washington in March 1946 might lead to normalization of its financial and trade relations with the victorious powers.[34] Although the government rejected the Allied reparations policy – liquidation of German assets abroad as repayment for restitution – it could not afford to refuse to participate, if it wished to achieve the deblocking of Swiss accounts in the U.S. and the removal of Swiss firms from the blacklist.

The results of the conference were extremely positive for Switzerland. The Washington Agreement gave Switzerland a way out of its foreign policy isolation and provided access to the European economic area controlled by the United States. True, in the face of economic and moral pressure by the U.S., Switzerland was not able to maintain its refusal to liquidate German accounts and turn them over to the Allies. But it did obtain agreement that the German owners of the liquidated assets would be compensated. This regulation preserved both the interests and the reputation of Switzerland as a financial centre. Moreover, the foundation for future economic cooperation with Germany had been laid. The Allies, for their part, deblocked Swiss accounts in the U.S. and removed Swiss firms from their blacklists. The economic circles that had been heavily involved with German industry during the war were declared 'clean'. Additionally, Switzerland was promised to receive half of the revenue from the liquidated German accounts, which was supposed to go to Swiss war victims.

But the claims of victims of war and persecution were increasingly marginalized in international postwar negotiations. The London Debt Agreement of 1953 sealed the discrimination of the victims vis-à-vis financial interests. It passed over reparation demands and restitution for those who had been persecuted and gave priority to satisfying the claims of creditors against Germany. This regulation allowed the FRG to exclude foreign victims of persecution from any reparations whatsoever for many years.[35] In accordance with international developments, Swiss negotiators sacrificed the restitution claims of their compatriots to economic interests and sought a regulation that greatly favoured the Federation and private Swiss creditors. While Swiss diplomats after 1945 dealt only peripherally with the concerns of victims of persecution and war, in domestic politics officials were very much confronted with the problems of those citizens who had suffered in past years and were returning to Switzerland in growing numbers. Once there, they frequently encountered considerable difficulties in starting a new life. Several months after the cease-fire, the federal authorities estimated the number of returnees at about 50,000.[36] The lives of those Swiss who remained abroad were also often marked by war damages, requisitions and losses through looting. The war-related losses of Swiss nationals abroad was calculated in the early 1950s at about 2.5 billion Swiss francs.

For the authorities, Swiss nationals abroad were a social problem. For one thing, the government feared that the economy of the last war years could quickly slide into a postwar depression and lead to increased competition on the labour market. Also, many of the returnees were dependent on public support and were a burden to the social service budgets.[37] Associations that cared for the returnees and knew how to approach the authorities as interest groups, created additional pressure to take action. This led the Federal Council to expand the aid available to Swiss nationals living abroad that had been first introduced in the period between the wars. They hoped that giving aid to the compatriots who still lived abroad would motivate them to stay where they were.[38] Thus, the government promised in 1946 that the funds Switzerland expected to receive from the liquidation of the blocked German accounts would be used for aid payments to Swiss citizens who had suffered losses during the war. Organizations of Swiss living abroad read this as a right to claim compensation.

It was not until 1953 that the government presented parliament with draft legislation for support of Swiss abroad who had suffered war-related losses. It projected a credit of 121.5 million Swiss francs, the same amount that Switzerland received from the proceeds of the liquidation of German assets, but explicitly refrained from including a right to compensation in the law. The payments were conceived of as startup help in the sense of 'high-level welfare', not as replacement for lost property.[39] In reality, the purpose of the Federal Aid for War-Related Damages for Swiss Citizens Abroad was to relieve the strain upon the cantonal and municipal social services offices. The law was approved by parliament but failed to pass a popular referendum in 1954, not least due to the opposition of a number of organizations of Swiss abroad, for whom the lack of any reparation payments made the legislation unacceptable. They argued that Swiss foreign policy during the Nazi period had sacrificed the needs of Swiss abroad to economic interests. Thus the questions arises 'whether the Federation, in light of its abandonment of the legitimate rights of Swiss abroad to benefit trade policy considerations, has not assumed a special obligation to compensate Swiss victims of the war for a part of their losses from public funds [...] and to do this not as welfare, but as just recompense.'[40] Supporters of the Swiss abroad accused the Federal Council of safeguarding the interests of financial circles, above all, while the war-damaged returnees were forced into humiliating petitions to the social services agencies.[41]

VERGANGENHEITSBEWÄLTIGUNG AND THE INVISIBLE VICTIMS

'Even if {the economy} really takes precedence before {politics}, we repeatedly gained the impression from the statements of some federal councilors as well as talks with members of parliament that those in high places perhaps do not have a sufficient understanding of the extent and the nature of Nazi injustice,' was the frustrated conclusion of a diplomat in 1955 who was responsible for the files of restitution claims of Nazi victims during the time.[42] Like few others he expresses where Switzerland placed its focus during the first postwar decade regarding the confrontation with the Nazi period and its consequences. While the interests of victims of persecution in international postwar negotiations generally came after debt and reparation claims, influential Swiss politicians paid attention above all to foreign policy matters and ignored the rights of the victims of persecution.

Overcoming the past – *Vergangenheitsbewältigung* as a specific German term – has become synonymous with the suppression of a history whose effect upon the present and the future can be recognized only through painful and critical recall. During the late 1940s and the 1950s in Switzerland, it was the victims of National Socialist persecution, whose history and claims nobody wanted to hear, who paid the price for Swiss *Vergangenheitsbewältigung*. They were simply not present in the debates of the 1940s and 1950s. At most, they were identified with those who had suffered losses through war, as, for example, in the 1953 draft legislation, which says that support may be given to those 'who were adversely affected by economic and political conditions related to the war in the pre-war and post-war period.'[43] This formulation demonstrates a singular blindness toward the consequences of National Socialist race policy. It reflects the division into epochs common in Switzerland, which places the chronological turning point at the beginning of the war and thus blends out, or fails to recognize, the systematic National Socialist persecution of 'non-Aryans' and those who held different beliefs, failing to recognize as well that the exclusion of Jews from economic and public life, and the confiscation of their property, began long before the beginning of the war and had no direct connection to it.[44] This narrow perception, which focuses on the war as the actual damage-causing event of the epoch, also explains why the victims of National Socialist persecution were not defined as a separate category for a long time. The perception of their history would have meant recalling the denied and suppressed aspects of the past and acknowledging that Switzerland was much more deeply involved with National Socialism than the myth of the hard-pressed but stubbornly resistant little country would have allowed.

THE PATH TO RESTITUTION FOR VICTIMS OF NATIONAL SOCIALISM

Still, the authorities were faced with restitution claims by victims of National Socialism beginning in 1945. During the 1940's, however, the federation was not in the least inclined to do anything for Swiss victims of National Socialism, be it on the level of diplomatic intervention, or even simply through legal aid to Swiss who had made restitution claims in the German occupation zones.[45] In the early 1950s, the EPD saw an alternative to individual restitution procedures in Germany in the call for global restitution. There was a legal justification for approaching the German federal government with this claim, since the actionable violations of international foreign law provided a basis for compensation by the FRG as the successor state to the Third Reich.[46] Additionally, the Adenauer government had acknowledged to Israel in 1952 that it had a moral obligation to make restitution payments for the Shoah. The Luxembourg agreements also contained the clause stating that the FRG would further expand the inner-German restitution legislation.[47] Still, a number of categories of victims of persecution continued to fall through the loopholes in the law.[48] After the London Debt Conference, the legal situation for most foreign victims of persecution remained hopeless, since the agreement postponed all German obligations arising through the war until such a time when a peace treaty should be concluded. In negotiations between Switzerland and Germany, the German delegation always referred to this clause in order to reject Swiss demands for global restitution. Still, the federal administration carried out initial surveys of Swiss victims of National Socialism in 1951, not least for the purposes of having documentation at hand for negotiations. This research brought to light that at least 108 Swiss citizens had been murdered by German agents of the state or had died in concentration camps. Initial calculations arrived at a global restitution claim of over 42 million Swiss francs.[49] In the meantime, Swiss officials had come to recognize the possible political dangers of continuing to ignore the claims of Nazi victims. They quite openly feared claims for compensation for damages if demands for restitution from the FRG were not made with sufficient vehemence.[50] Moreover, the officials of the Swiss Foreign Ministry now also found the situation of the Nazi victims disturbing. 'Swiss victims of National Socialist injustice, therefore, are risking continuing to receive inadequate restitution. They will perceive this all the more (until) the demands of the federation and individual categories of financial creditors can be satisfied at least to an acceptable degree,' reads an internal memorandum from 1953.[51]

It was not until 1954, however, that political pressure to take action arose. The government had long hoped to include the victims of persecution in the projected aid for Swiss living abroad, and thus solve the political problem temporarily. 'An especially liberal distribution of welfare,' said Federal Councilor Max Petitpierre '[...] would allow us, with relatively little effort, to take care of a the relatively large number of smaller cases that cause us the greatest concern.'[52] The rejection of the draft legislation for aid for those damaged by the war in the summer of 1954 confronted the authorities with an impasse. The possibility of closing a dark chapter of the past without arousing a public outcry was not longer available. Thus, the need arose for an independent solution for restitution for Nazi victims. At the same time, the 1954 public scandal surrounding the revelation of Swiss involvement in the anti-Semitic measures of the National Socialists had awakened a need for critical assessment of Swiss refugee policy during the Nazi period. The responsible authorities in the Political Department sensed that they too could suddenly find themselves in the position of having to answer questions about diplomatic protection during the Nazi period.[53] Out of fear that the media might uncover their neglect of Nazi victims and accuse the federation of 'cover-ups and neglect', the authorities decided that gentler treatment of individual victims of persecution was appropriate.[54] But they decided against a public appeal to Nazi victims to register, partly because they did not wish to awaken hopes they had no intention of fulfilling and partly because the administration feared the additional work caused by the 'avalanche of claims' they feared would follow such an appeal.[55] In other words: the government's primary interest was to pacify those victims of Nazi crimes who persistently renewed their claims for restitution and to keep them from initiating a press campaign against federal agencies.

Under these conditions the idea first arose in 1954 to try to provide federal funds for advance compensation instead of continuing to wait for the success of the negotiations with the FRG, which at this point seemed hopeless. 'We see the justification for making advance payments [...] in the circumstances that the victims hardest hit by fate [...]

apparently will have to wait much longer for direct restitution and possibly will no longer be able to receive it personally. Nor can consideration in the context of welfare now and possibly in the future even begin to correspond to the nature of damages incurred through violation of international law. [...] Thus, primarily moral considerations make such advance payments appear desirable.'[56] After the German Foreign Ministry in the summer of 1954 accepted the files on violations of international law committed by the Third Reich against Swiss citizens, and thus indicated its willingness to respond to restitution claims, the officials in the Swiss Foreign Ministry drew sighs of relief, since they now had a kind of guarantee that the planned advance payment of restitution would be reimbursed by the FRG at some point. Also, the danger that the victims of persecution might sue the federation was finally banished. There is now the possibility, of 'concluding the painful affair of the damage wrought by National Socialist injustice. No one will be able to accuse the federation that it cared only for the bankers and for its own accounts [...] while ignoring the victims of violence.'[57] On 18 February 1956, agreement was finally reached on the so-called pre-war cases – those Swiss citizens who had fallen victim to National Socialist persecution before 1939 – for whom the FRG paid a first global restitution. Out of consideration for the German negotiating partners, who feared that the agreement could set a precedent for the demands of other states and also in their own interests, Switzerland refrained once again from issuing a public appeal that could attract further claimants not known to the administration. Their rights were sacrificed to the need to carry out the matter through the channels of secret diplomacy, especially since the Swiss diplomats hoped that doing so would be more likely to net them compensation for the violations of law committed during the war. 'It is appropriate that these cases, which are part of a painful past, should be settled in total secrecy,' reads a commentary to this act of Swiss overcoming of the past.[58]

Still, the idea of advance payment needed more public pressure before it took on concrete form. In 1956, critical reports on German restitution appeared in a number of Swiss daily newspapers. They also touched on the question of Swiss victims of National Socialism, who up to that point had received nothing. On 6 July 1956 the Federal Council made the decision to draw up 'Special Draft Legislation for Advance Payment of Restitution for Swiss Nazi Victims'.[59] The government had by that time distanced itself from the notion of providing welfare payments instead of compensation. On 1 February 1957 the Federal Council made public draft legislation providing for advance payment of restitution. The council wrote in an accompanying statement: 'This is an unusual action and does not set a precedent. Its justification can be found in the particular circumstances arising from the situation created by the London Debt Conference and through the specific character of the injustice that has been done to our compatriots. [...] By paying the suggested restitution the federation does not act in compliance with any legal obligation, rather, it carries out a voluntary act.'[60] What is striking about the justification of the projected decree is not only the insistence that it is a one-time act that does not set a precedent. It is also revealing that the government had come to recognize that the injustice suffered by the Nazi victims represented a special category of suffering that was not comparable with war-related damages.

The draft legislation was presented to parliament in June of 1957. Debate was marked by the obvious wish to rid Switzerland of the unpleasant consequences of National Socialism. In a number of statements one senses a clear resistance against having to concern oneself, twelve years after the end of the war, with a past that one would prefer to see forgotten and buried. 'In the main we are faced today with matters that recall a dark chapter of history. Evoking these memories is not a pleasant task, but in light of the persecution that Swiss citizens had to endure through the National Socialist system, it is necessary in order for the victims of this system to receive justice.'[61] In the perception of many parliamentarians, the Nazi victims were burdensome disturbances in a view of the past whose dark stains they preferred to ignore. Paradoxically, opposition to the legislation came primarily from the groups that since the early 1950s had fought for appropriate restitution for Swiss abroad and returnees who had suffered during the war. The representatives of the Swiss abroad were disturbed by what they saw as the privileged legal position given Nazi victims, as opposed to those who had suffered damages during the war or had been victims of Communist persecution. The objections of Gottlieb Duttweiler, the most persistent representative of the interests of Swiss abroad, were clearly tinged with anti-Semitism. 'It used to be that the Jews were discriminated by a "J" in their passports; today the non-Jews are being discriminated, since four-fifths of the victims of National Socialism are surely Jews. [...] I am not anti-Semitic, but it is also not right for the Jews to be privileged.'[62] Instead of pointing to the fact that among Swiss Nazi victims the Jews were often those who had suffered the worst injustices, Federal Councilor Max Petitpierre responded to this assertion by saying that only a fifth, if that, of those eligible to file claims were Jewish. The demand of some parliamentarians that victims of persecution and victims of war were to be treated equally trivialized National Socialism and failed to recognize the historic significance of the Holocaust, just as a number of counsellors ignored the long-term psychological consequences suffered by the survivors, people who had been deemed unworthy of life and dignity by National Socialism. Thus, one parliamentarian claimed that the physical and emotional damages of many victims of persecution 'were long since healed and no longer discernible.'[63]

While the government's announcement presented the advance compensation payments to Nazi victims as a voluntary decision by the Federation and not a state obligation in the name of justice, the parliament weakened the position of the claimants in the compensation process even further. The law of 1957 does not contain an actual legal right to compensation and the regulation under which income level and assets were to determine the amount of compensation turned the compensatory character into a farce. The concept of restitution was sacrificed to a welfare payment. The perception of the individual victims of persecution was marked by welfare-like categories. In the view of the administrative clerks, the ideal type of restitution claimant was elderly, helpless and poverty-stricken.[64] The 'moral' situation of applicants was also supposed to have an influence on the level of compensation.[65] This regulation placed the Nazi victims in the humiliating situation of having to prove that their lifestyle before, during and after the persecution they suffered made them worthy of compensation.

A commission was established in the spring of 1958 and given the task of formulating the law in detail. The commission consisted primarily of employees of the federal administration and it had a great deal of leeway in its work, being empowered to render a decision based on the evidence it considered. The applicants had only one appeals instance, to an internal administrative committee, and there was no possibility of appealing to an independent court. Finally, the commission could also decide that payments were used 'for specific purposes', meaning that the money was not paid to the claimant himself or herself but to a social services agency or guardian institution.[66] The weakening of the law and the worsening of the legal position of the victims of persecution did not go unremarked. A Swiss diplomat renounced the welfare character of the law in particular and noted: 'The size of the victim's bank account should not be the decisive factor when compensating for moral crimes.' The regulation that the victim's degree of guilt had an influence on the amount of compensation also ran contrary to his notion of justice. 'The man who dared to call Hitler an idiot in public [. . .], the Swiss man who refused to hang anti-Jewish banners in his store window, are they not all partially responsible for the fact that they came into conflict with Nazi laws? Should these courageous compatriots, who in other places would be praised for their positions, now be punished retroactively by not allowing them to share in or share only partially in the advance payments for the victims of National Socialism?'[67] He made clear that the examination of the level of guilt could turn into retroactive approval of the National Socialist system, a second punishment for people who as opponents of the system of injustice had demonstrated civil courage and defended the rule of law and human dignity, thus lending legitimization to National Socialist persecution.

In the final analysis, the payments were less compensation for injustice suffered than aid for victims determined according to each individual's circumstances. An array of non-economic reasons also led to adjustments in individual compensation claims. Criminal records, statements by guardians and the assessment of the character and lifestyle of the individual victims were the decisive factors for the commission in deciding whether it found statements made by applicants credible or not. The applicants, for their part, were obligated to give very detailed information about their personal circumstances and to sign a power of attorney granting private and public agencies the right to provide the authorities with all the information they wanted. Above and beyond proof that it had not been their own fault that they became victims of persecution, the applicants also had to demonstrate purity of character in order to receive full payment.[68]

On the one hand, the criteria for judging the amount of payment illuminate the view the commission responsible for the advance payments had formed of National Socialist policies of persecution and extermination. On the other hand, they also demonstrate how the authorities perceived victims. Thus, the advance payments were a part of official historical policy where the commission transformed its interpretation of a past marked by National Socialism into specific political action toward the victims of persecution. Examining this in detail will be the focus of our continuing research.

BETRAYING THE VICTIMS

Switzerland's stability as a financial centre and the interests of Swiss foreign creditors, normalizing relations to the Allied powers and the establishment of economic relationships to the dollar economy dominated foreign policy in the immediate aftermath of the war. These priorities were reflected in the Washington agreement that rehabilitated Switzerland as a financial centre and normalized relations to the U.S.; they were reaffirmed in the London Debt Agreement, which gave preference to financial creditors over the needs of the victims of persecution. Absorbed in domestic politics into the larger group of Swiss living abroad who had suffered damages during the war, the victims of Nazi persecution were not perceived as a separate category for a long time. Their claims reminded Switzerland of the dark stains in its history during the Nazi period and recognition of their right to compensation would have implied an admission of the failure of Swiss foreign policy during the Nazi period, at least as long as the FRG hid behind the London Debt Agreement.

The willingness after 1954 to seek a domestic policy solution to the issue of compensation for National Socialist injustice depended essentially on two factors. The failure of the first draft legislation for federal aid to Swiss abroad who had suffered damages through the war meant that the possibility of also providing welfare aid to Nazi victims was out of reach for the foreseeable future. The public controversy surrounding anti-Jewish refugee policy made clear that the question of diplomatic protection during the Nazi period could also become the focus of critical assessment, whereby federal authorities' neglect of victims of persecution since 1945 could come to light. The 1957 law and especially the procedures adopted for advance payment of restitution in effect constituted a further betrayal of the victims. Instead of accepting the fact of persecution alone to justify claims for payment, the applicants were forced to endure a humiliating examination of their material circumstances and personal situations; they were forced to provide evidence that they had financial need of the payments and that their flawless personal character, both at the time the persecution took place and afterwards, proved that they were worthy of receiving compensation. Furthermore, the commission considered the degree to which the victims of persecution had been 'at fault' and thus, in the eyes of the applicants, again retroactively legitimated the injustice that had been done them.

NOTES

Translation by Susan M. Steiner

1   The following text is the preliminary result of our continuing research. It is based primarily on source materials in the Swiss Federal Archives in Bern (in the following FA) and in the Archiv for Contemporary History in Zurich (Archiv für Zeitgeschichte, in following AfZ). We thank the Saly Mayer Memorial Foundation for financial support and Sybil Milton, Jacques Picard, Res Zimmermann and Jan Brönnimann for their comments and suggestions.

2   For an overview of more recent historiography, see Hans Ulrich Jost, *Politik und Wirtschaft im Krieg. Die Schweiz 1938–1948* (Zurich: Chronos 1998) and the contributions in the special issue: *Die Schweiz und der zweite Weltkrieg* of *Schweizerische Zeitschrift für Geschichte*, 1997/4. See also: Peter Hug, Martin Kloter (eds.), *Aufstieg und Niedergang des Bilateralismus. Schweizerische Aussen-und Aussenwirtschaftspolitik 1930–1960* (Zurich: Chronos, 1999)

3   On this, see the report commissioned by the government, Carl Ludwig, *Die Flüchtlingspolitik der Schweiz seit 1933 bis zur Gegenwart* (Bern 1957). For an overview see also Alfred A. Häsler, *Das Boot ist voll* (Zurich: Limmat 1992); André Lasserre, *Frontières et camps. Le refuge en Suisse de 1933 à 1945* (Lausanne: Payot, 1995).

4   Jacques Picard, *Die Schweiz und die Juden 1933–1945* (Zurich: Chronos 1994); Beat Balzli, *Treuhänder des Reichs. Die Schweiz und die Vermögen der Naziopfer: Eine Spurensuche* (Zurich: Werd 1997), pp.65ff.

5   Jacques Picard, 'Die Vermögen rassisch, religiös und politisch Verfolgter in der Schweiz und ihre Ablösung von 1946 bis 1973,' *Studien und Quellen*, 22/1996, pp.233–269; Peter Hug, Marc Perrenoud, *In der Schweiz liegende Vermögenswerte von Nazi-Opfern und Entschädigungsabkommen mit Oststaaten*, (Bern: Swiss Federal Archives 1997); Peter Hug, 'Die nachrichtenlosen Guthaben von Nazi-Opfern in der Schweiz,' *Schweizerische Zeitschrift für Geschichte*, 1997/4, pp.532–551.

6   FA E 2001–08 (-) 1978/107, Vol.7: Swiss victims of National Socialist persecution: list of 6 May 1959. On German restitution laws: Constantin Goschler, *Wiedergutmachung und die Verfolgten des Nationalsozialismus (1945–1954)* (Munich: R. Oldenburg 1992).

7   FA E 2001–08 (-) 1978/107, Vol.8: Treaty between the Swiss Federation and the Federal Republic of Germany on payments for Swiss citizens who were affected by National Socialist persecution, 29 June 1962.

8   Cornelius Pawlita, *Wiedergutmachung als Rechtsfrage? Die politische und juristische Auseinandersetzung um Entschädigung für die Opfer nationalsozialistischer Verfolgung (1945–1990)*, (Frankfurt a.M.: Peter Lang Verlag 1993), pp.322ff.

9   All following information on the R. family from: FA E 2001–08 (-) 1978/107, Vol.118.

10   See Paul Widmer, *Die Schweizer Gesandtschaft in Berlin. Geschichte eines schwierigen diplomatischen Postens* (Zurich: Verlag Neue Zürcher Zeitung 1997), pp.171–186, Jacques Picard, *Die Schweiz und die Juden 1933–1945* (Zurich: Chronos 1994), pp.163ff.

11 FA E 2001–08 (-) 1978/107, Vol.118: Letter from the Swiss consulate to the Swiss Political Department (EPD), 21 December 1942.

12 FA E 2001–08 (-) 1978/107, Vol.118: Letter from the EPD to the Swiss Embassy in Germany, 28 January 1943.

13 FA E 2001–08 (-) 1978/107, Vol.118: Letter from the Swiss ambassador in Germany to the Swiss Justice and Police Department, informing it of a conversation with an employee of the German Foreign Ministry, 17 July 1944.

14 On the Swiss government's knowledge of the Holocaust: Gaston Haas, *'Wenn man damals gewusst hätte, was sich drüben im Reich abspielte...' Was man in der Schweiz von der Judenvernichtung wusste* (Basel: Helbing & Lichtenhahn, 1994).

15 On the following see Jacques Picard, *Die Schweiz und die Juden 1933–1945* (Zurich: Chronos 1994), pp.194–208.

16 The relevant files can be found in AfZ JUNA Archives II, 213 (file 'Ordre public II').

17 AfZ SIG Archives: Interventions, demarches, resolutions 1947–1951 (not initialed): Dr. Veit Wyler to the President of the Union of Swiss Jewish Communities, 18 December 1950.

18 AfZ SIG Archives: SIG transcripts (not initialed) 19 December 1950, 24 January 1951, 21 February 1951.

19 FA E 2001–08 (-) 1978/107, Vol.1: Memo on a conversation with W. by Felix Schnyder, 3 August 1945.

20 'Botschaft des Bundesrates an die Bundesversammlung betreffend einen Handelsvertrag [...] und ein Nationalisierungsabkommen zwischen der Schweiz und Jugoslawien,' 29 October 1948, *Bundesblatt*, 1948/III, p.69. In 1965, the Federal Council rejected the guarantee of diplomatic protection with the justification that it could come into conflict with foreign policy measures to preserve the national interests of the federation. 'Botschaft des Bundesrates an die Bundesbversammlung über die Ergänzung der Bundesverfassung durch einen Artikel 45 bis betreffend die Schweizer im Ausland,' 2 July 1965, *Bundesblatt*, 1965/II, pp.434f.

21 Albrecht Randelzhofer, Oliver Dörr, *Entschädigung für Zwangsarbeit? Zum Problem individueller Entschädigungsansprüche von ausländischen Zwangsarbeitern während des Zweiten Weltkrieges gegen die Bundesrepublik Deutschland*, (Berlin: Duncker und Humblot, 1994), pp.22ff; pp.32f.

22 FA E 2001–08 (-) 1978/107, Vol.1: Draft of a letter to the Swiss Embassy in Germany, 5 April 1951.

23 FA E 2001–08 (-) 1978/107, Vol.3: Heinrich Rothmund, head of the Police Division of the Swiss Justice and Police Department to the General Secretary of the EDP, 3 September 1954. At this point, Rothmund had come under public fire after publication of German files discovered by the Allies in Berlin revealing in 1954 that the introduction of the 'J' stamp in the passports of Jews of the Third Reich in October 1938 had had its roots in an initiative by the Swiss. In this context, Rothmund's judgement must also be interpreted as an attempt to reduce his share of blame for anti-Semitic refugee policy by pointing to the failure of Swiss diplomatic offices to protect Swiss victims of persecution. On criticism of refugee policy in 1954, see Jürg Stadelmann, *Umgang mit Fremden in bedrängter Zeit. Schweizerische Flüchtlingspolitik 1940–1945 und ihre Bedeutung bis heute*, (Zurich: Orell Fuessli, 1998).

24 FA E 2001–08 (-) 1978/107, Vol.1: Letter from Walter Stucki, head of the Division of Foreign Affairs, 22 March 1945.

25 Edgar Bonjour, *Geschichte der schweizerischen Neutralität IV* (Basel: Helbing & Lichtenhahn 1970), p.246. On Frölicher's perception of German anti-Semitism and the Holocaust see also: Paul Widmer, *Die Schweizer Gesandtschaft in Berlin. Geschichte eines schwierigen diplomatischen Postens* (Zurich: Verlag Neue Zürcher Zeitung 1997), S. 248–263.

26 FA E 2001–08 (-) 1978/107, Vol.42: The EPD to the Swiss ambassador in Germany, 20 November 1944.

27 FA E 2001 (D) 3, Vol.457: Letter of 12 October 1943.

28 FA E 2001 (D) 3, Vol.457: Internal memo by Felix Schnyder, 23 November 1943.

29 FA E 2001–08 (-) 1978/107, Vol.3: Memo on a confidential meeting on 16 March concerning restitution for Nazi injustice, 29 March 1954.

30 FA E 4800.1 (-) 1967/111, file 95: Internal memo by Heinrich Rothmund, 24 March 1953.

31 See Jacques Picard, *Die Schweiz und die Juden 1933–1945* (Zurich: Chronos, 1994), pp.145–157.

32 See Ulrich Herbert, 'Nicht entschädigungsfähig? Die Wiedergutmachungsansprüche der Ausländer' in Ludolf Herbst, Constantin Goschler (eds.), *Wiedergutmachung in der Bundesrepublik Deutschland* (Munich: R. Oldenburg Verlag, 1989), pp.273–302.

33 See Hans Ulrich Jost, *Politik und Wirtschaft im Krieg. Die Schweiz 1938–1948* (Zurich: Chronos, 1998).

34 On the Washington agreement see Linus von Castelmur, *Schweizerisch-allierte Finanzbeziehungen im Uebergang vom zweiten Weltkrieg zum Kalten Krieg. Die deutschen Guthaben in der Schweiz zwischen Zwangsliquidierung und Freigabe (1945–1952)* (Zurich: Chronos 1992) and Marco Durrer, *Die schweizerisch-amerikanischen Finanzbeziehungen im Zweiten Weltkrieg. Von der Blockierung der schweizerischen Guthaben über die 'Safehaven'-Politik zum Washingtoner Abkommen 1941–1946* (Bern: Paul Haupt 1984).

35 Ulrich Herbert, 'Nicht entschädigungsfähig? Die Wiedergutmachungsansprüche der Ausländer' in Ludolf Herbst, Constantin Goschler (eds.), *Wiedergutmachung in der Bundesrepublik Deutschland* (Munich: R. Oldenburg Verlag, 1989), pp.273–302; Jörg Fisch, *Reparationen nach dem Zweiten Weltkrieg* (Munich: C.H. Beck, 1992), pp.117ff.

36 Minutes of the Federal Council session of 10 November 1945, database DoDis-1322 (*www.bar.admin.ch/dds/e dds1.htm*; FA E 1004.1 (-) -/1, Vol.463). Jürg Stadelmann, *Umgang mit Fremden in bedrängter Zeit. Schweizerische Flüchtlingspolitik 1940–1945 und ihre Bedeutung bis heute* (Zurich: Orell Fuessli, 1998), pp.63ff., calculates that 80,000 Swiss who had been living abroad returned between 1939 and 1948.

37 Social Services in Switzerland are regulated at the canton and municipal level. The expansion of obligatory social security did not begin in Switzerland until the 1940's.

38 Database DoDis-5480 (*www.bar.admin.ch/dds/e dds1.htm*; FA E 4001 (C) -1, Vol.13): Suggestions for the solution of the issue of Swiss living abroad by Ernst Scheim, 15 December 1945.

39 Debate in the National Council of 17 September 1953, *Amtliches Stenographisches Bulletin der Bundesversammlung*, 1953, pp.632–675. See also: Database DoDis-5481 (*www.bar.admin.ch/dds/e dds1.htm*; FA E 4001 (C) -1, Vol.13): Exposé by Federal Councilor Max Petitpierre, 15. April 1948. 'Botschaft des Bundesrates an die Bundesversammlung über ausserordentliche Leistungen an Auslandschweizer', 10 May 1946, *Bundesblatt*, 1946/II, S. 125.

40 Speech by Dr. jur. Jakob Maag, undated, Swiss National Library, Berne, V Schweiz 252.

41 National Councilor Gottlieb Duttweiler in the parliamentary debate on 13 March 1957, *Amtliches Stenographisches Bulletin der Bundesversammlung*, 1957, pp.138ff.

42 FA E 2001 -08 (-) 1978/107, Vol.4: Internal memo, 3 March 1955.

43 'Botschaft des Bundesrates an die Bundesversammlung zum Entwurf eines Bundesbeschlusses über ausserordentliche Zuwendungen an kriegsgeschädigte Auslandschweizer', 27 March 1953, *Bundesblatt*, 1953/I, p.740

44 See Saul Friedländer, *Nazi Germany and the Jews. Vol.I: The Years of Persecution, 1933–1939* (New York: Harper Collins Publishers 1997); Daniel Wildmann, 'Wo liegt Auschwitz? Geographie Geschichte und Neutralität', in Arbeitskreis Armenien (ed.), *Völkermord und Verdrängung* (Zürich: Chronos, 1998), pp.163–168.

45 FA E 2001–08 (-) 1978/107, Vol.1: Internal memo, 9 December 1946.

46 FA E 2001–08 (-) 1978/107, Vol.2: Internal legal expert reports, February 1953.

47 See the contributions by Yeshayahu A. Jelinek, Rudolf Huhn, Michael Wolffsohn and Schlomo Shafir in Ludolf Herbst, Constantin Goscher (eds.), *Wiedergutmachung in der Bundesrepublik Deutschland* (Munich: R. Oldenburg Verlag, 1989), pp.119–203.

48 See Ulrich Herbert, Nicht entschädigungsfähig? Die Wiedergutmachungsansprnche der Ausländer' in Ludolf Herbst, Constantin Goscher (eds.), *Wiedergutmachung in der Bundesrepublik Deutschland* (Munich: R. Oldenburg Verlag 1989), pp.273–302.

49 FA E 2001–08 (-) 1978/107, Vol.2: Internal memo, 3 May 1952.

50 FA E 2001–08 (-) 1978/107, Vol.2: Alfred Zehnder, head of the Division for Political Affairs at the EPD to Heinrich Rothmund, head of the Police Division of the Swiss Justice and Police Department, 7 April 1953.

51   FA E 2001–08 (-) 1978/107, Vol.2: Memo of 17 February 1953.
52   FA E 2001–08 (-) 1978/107, Vol.3: Federal Councilor Max Petitpierre to Federal Councilor Markus
     Feldmann, 10 June 1954.
53   On 30 January 1958, National Councilor Gottlieb Duttweiler called in parliament for an examination
     of the activities of foreign missions regarding diplomatic protection anologous to that of refugee
     policy, *Amtliches Stenographisches Bulletin der Bundesversammlung*, 1958, p.30.
54   FA E 2001–08 (-) 1978/107, Vol.3: Highly confidential memo, 4 August 1954; FA E 2001–08 (-)
     1978/107, Vol.4: minutes of a confidential meeting, 18 April 1955.
55   FA E 2001–08 (-) 1978/107, Vol.4: Internal memo of 18 October 1955.
56   FA E 2001–08 (-) 1978/107, Vol.3: Petition by Federal Councilor Max Petitpierre, Chairman of the
     EPD, 12 April 1954.
57   FA E 2001–08 (-) 1978/107, Vol.3: Internal memo by Maurice Jaccard, 5 July 1954.
58   FA E 2001–08 (-) 1978/107, Vol.5: Letter by Federal Councilor Max Petitpierre, 2 March 1956.
59   FA E 2001–08 (-) 1978/107, Vol.5: Excerpt from the minutes of the Federal Council, 6 July 1956.
60   'Botschaft des Bundesrates an die Bundesversammlung zum Entwurf eines Bundesbeschlusses
     über die Gewährung von Vorschussleistungen an schweizerische Opfer der nationalsozialistischen
     Verfolgung', 1 February 1957, *Bundesblatt*, 1957/II, p.305.
61   National council debate of 14 June 1957, *Amtliches Stenographisches Bulletin der Bundesversammlung*,
     1957, p.418.
62   FA E 2001–08 (-) 1978/107, Vol.6: Minutes of the meeting of the commission of national councilors
     of 21 and 22 February 1957.
63   National council debate of 14 June 1957, *Amtliches Stenographisches Bulletin der Bundesversammlung*
     1957, p.423.
64   FA E 2001–08 (-) 1978/107, Vol.4: minutes of a confidential meeting on 18 April 1955.
65   'Bundesbschluss über die Gewährung von Vorauszahlungen an schweizerische Opfer nationalsozial-
     istischer Verfolgung', 27 September 1957, *Sammlung eidgenössischer Gesetze*, 13/1958, pp.199–201.
66   FA E 2001–08 (-) 1978/107, Vol.7: 'Ordinance concerning the Commission for Advance Payment to
     Swiss Victims of National Socialist Persecution,' undated.
67   FA 2001–08 (-) 1978/107, Vol.7: Hans Müller, ambassador in Great Britain, to the commission for
     advance payment to Swiss victims of National Socialist persecution, 20 September 1958.
68   The following examples are cited here as illustrations: FA E 2001–08 (-) 1978/107, Vol.49: The
     commission chose not to believe a Jewish woman's statement concerning her torture at the hands of
     the Gestapo after it discovered that she might have gained Swiss citizenship before the war through a
     fake marriage. FA E 2001–08 (-) 1978/107, Vol.43: The commission refused payment to another
     applicant, whose husband and father-in-law had been murdered by the National Socialists, because
     the woman became an alcoholic after the war.

THE STRUGGLE FOR JUSTICE:
A SURVEY OF CHILD HOLOCAUST SURVIVORS' EXPERIENCES WITH RESTITUTION

Sarah Moskovitz and Robert Krell with Itzik Moskovitz and Ariella Askren

ONE AND a half million children and adolescents were murdered during the Holocaust. Throughout Europe, thousands of children were hidden. They had the best chance of surviving. Very few children survived concentration camps. From 1938 to 1945, children fled (as in the *Kindertransport* from Germany and Austria), others hid in cellars, forests, orphanages, convents and with Christian families. By the war's end, the majority of child survivors under age 16 had been orphaned. Many were entirely alone.[1]

The youngest, within the crucial developmental years to age six, had no recall of birthplace, family or even their first language, They had endured separation from parents, hunger, unremitting persecution and terror throughout their formative years.[2] The oldest of the child survivors were born approximately 1929 and turned 16 or 17 in the year of liberation. Preoccupied with finding family, emigrating, returning to school or finding work, the children themselves – and their helpers – bypassed critical opportunities for emotional healing and support. They tried hard to make life work, with considerable success in some cases, but not mindful of life long impairments[3] or the resurfacing, in later years, of traumatic memory. Therefore, no one thought of the children when issues of compensation and restitution first surfaced. Now, over fifty years later, these children seek justice through acknowledgement of their suffering.

Over the past fifteen years child survivors have shattered a number of taboos. They have overcome the taboo of silence about their past. They have connected and learned to talk more openly with each other about themselves in the past as well as the present. They have come forward to give testimonies and speak to school children and organize into groups.

But the last taboo to crack has been the silence around their experience with restitution, which began to break only within the past three years. Strong emotions that surround this topic have kept it so off limits. Some of these emotions are: shame over ever considering applying for anything and shame over needing it; discomfort that accepting a small pension or even a small one-time payment in some way meant having sold out to the Germans; 'blood money'; anger at the frustrations encountered in the process; worry that others will disapprove of their accepting restitution and, lastly, resistance to experiencing the sadness and pain that accompanies re-examination of one's traumatic losses in order to fill out a form.

It has taken fifty years to become aware and vocal about justice and restitution for child survivors. Why has it taken so long? People who survived as children were inculcated with denial of their own survivor status. Those adults closely responsible for them, as well as social agencies and governments, preferred not to recognize the survivor status of children. Since the majority of children were hidden and not in concentration camps, it was incorrectly assumed that despite their uprooted lives, the loss of parents, the loss of security and the persecutions they experienced in their childhoods, they were not affected life long.

It was common as recently as five years ago for people who were totally orphaned and had been hidden in many places to say 'I'm not a child survivor; I was *only* in hiding'. There was resistance on the part of adults and older camp survivors to understand and acknowledge how painful it was for a child to have experiences of sudden parent loss and hiding in wartime. The general view was that children were too young to understand what was happening and so did not suffer and remember trauma – and if they did, it was best not to encourage children to speak about it, best to encourage them to forget.

Denial by others and consequently personal denial of the child's own survivor status compromised the opportunity to talk, to mourn and to cope with the reality of losses. It also closed off the possibilities of petitioning for justice and restitution, even for those old enough to do so. If you do not consider yourself a survivor because others have told you that you are not and that you did not suffer, you cannot advocate for yourself as a survivor.

We decided in 1998 to develop a survey focusing on four areas: *1. How child survivors now view themselves to have been affected by their Holocaust experiences. 2. What were their experiences in trying to get restitution. 3. What have been the roadblocks to restitution for them. 4. How they think restitution funds should be distributed.* The questionnaire was disseminated by Child Survivor Associations and the ADL-sponsored Hidden Child Foundation. Approximately 5200 surveys went out and 664 were returned from people in the United States, Canada, Israel, Australia, France, Belgium, Greece and Sweden etc. The largest number of respondents, more than 27%, were born in Poland, followed by 14% born in France, 14% in Belgium, 10% each in Hungary and the Netherlands, 5% in Czechoslovakia, 4% in Austria, 2% in Romania and less than 1% each in Italy and Yugoslavia.

The information presented by the 664 who responded is presented in two parts. Part I provides information as to who our respondents are, what they experienced, and how they report themselves as having been affected. Part II answers questions about applying for restitution, and the survivors' experience, of the Roadblocks in that process as well as results. Part two also registers our respondents' vote on how and to whom restitution should be given, i.e. through agencies, or directly to the survivor.

PART I: WHO ARE OUR PARTICIPANTS?

Female survivors in our survey outnumber men over two to one. 65.3% of respondents were female, 29.2% were male; 5.5% did not identify their gender. We speculate that it was harder to hide male children especially if the males were circumcised. Our figures may manifest the fact that far fewer male children than female children survived.

WARTIME EXPERIENCES

We learned that the overwhelming majority of children, 54%, are survivors of hiding. Another 16.9% were in ghettos and hiding and 9% in hiding and in camps. Those who were in camps alone (5.2%) or ghettos and camps (4.8%) are a small percentage of child survivors in this study.

We must keep in mind that when we look at the numbers on hiding that rarely was a person hidden with a parent all of the time and that most children hidden alone experienced at least three or four hiding places.[5] Some were moved as many as 22 times, as was Dr. Yehudi Lindeman of Montreal.[6] As one survivor, Maya Schwartz, summed it up looking back at her hidden childhood, 'After a while you feel like a suitcase', ready to be picked up and dumped someplace else.

Of crucial importance to vulnerable young children is the presence, guidance, love and secure anchoring provided by their parents, or a parent substitute in *life-long, continuous,* caring commitment. The figures below summarize the loss of parents, which varied from separation for one year to six years and longer if the parent was not found right after the war. For too many the losses became permanent.

Losses of Mothers and Fathers. Figures 1, 2 and 3 reveal staggering disruption and tragic loss among respondents. We see that few were not separated from at least one parent during the Holocaust. In Figure 1 we see that 81% of our respondents were separated from their mothers during the war, that 33% of those mothers did return, but 66% did not return, meaning that two thirds of the wartime separations resulted in a permanent loss of mother.

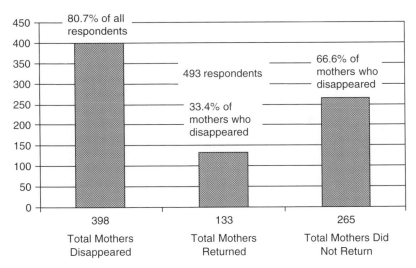

Fig. 1 Loss of Mother

When we look at Figure 2 to learn about separations and loss of fathers, we see that *nearly every* one of our respondents (97%) was separated from fathers during the Holocaust. Less than 25% of the fathers returned, leaving 75% of these child survivors fatherless. Our data show that more fathers were taken away from their children than mothers, and many fewer fathers than mothers survived to return.

We learned from Figure 3 that 77.7 percent (more than three fourths) were separated from *both* parents. Only 19.3 percent (about one-fifth) were fortunate enough to have both parents return. In 58 percent of the cases, neither parent returned. Of the remaining 22.7 percent where one parent returned, it was twice as likely to be the mother than the father.

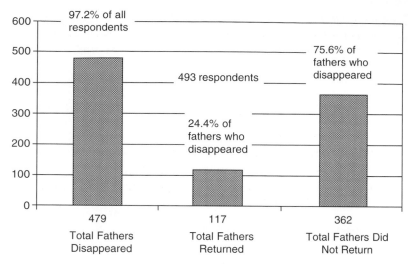

Fig. 2   Loss of Fathers

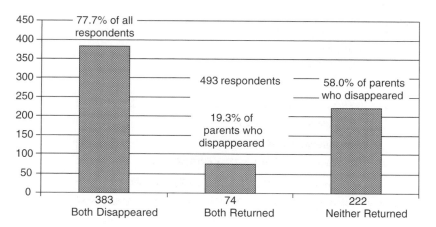

Fig. 3   Loss of Both Parents

In the next section we asked people to consider if they think they have been affected by their Holocaust experiences and if so to describe 'How you were affected' in their own words, their replies on a five point scale: 1 Not at all; 2. Very little; 3. Moderately; 4. Seriously; 5. Severely and Permanently. The areas investigated were Physical, Social, Emotional, Educational, and Economic.

Physical.   Over one-half (53%) report serious to severe and permanent physical harm as a result of their Holocaust experiences. A wide array of physical complaints affect respondents. Most frequently mentioned are headaches, early loss of teeth, gastro-intestinal problems and chronic problems resulting from malnutrition, and medical neglect such as unattended scoliosis and ear infections. The following are illustrative responses: '*I have a nervous stomach and a sense of foreboding all the time.*' '*I am easily agitated and have many ticks and nervous problems.*' '*Back problems and spinal stenosis.*' '*Due to starvation and TB, I had numerous sores on my back and stomach problems.' 'I am sick ever since...' 'Sexual problems – I was abused in hiding.' 'Health was always fragile.' 'Pulmonary disease stemming from untreated Kyphos Colesis during the war years.' 'I have chronic bronchitis.'*

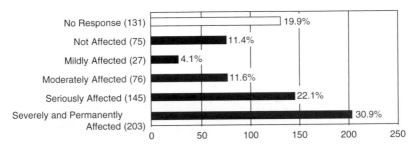

Fig. 4 Physical Effects of the Holocaust on Child Survivors

Social. Socially, almost 55 percent of the respondents report themselves to be in the most affected categories (Figure 5). Only 9 percent report no effect or mildly affected. People in the most affected categories say the following: *'I'm still afraid to let people know my origins.' 'I'm a lonely person.' 'I try to be friendly but I am always suspicious.' 'I fear rejection.' 'Who can I trust?' 'I still continue to hide – I only feel safe behind the locked door of my apartment.' 'I'm always shy.' 'I never married.' 'I have no feeling of belonging anywhere.' 'I always feel alone.' 'My whole life I'm an outsider.'*

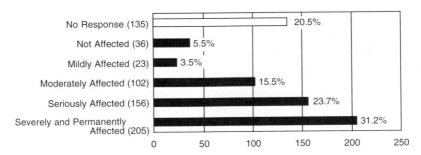

Fig. 5 Social Effects of the Holocaust on Child Survivors

Emotional. Life-long emotional suffering over loss of family and parents is the single most outstanding finding of this study. The highest number of reported negative effects of Holocaust experience is in this category of emotional consequences. Three fourths (75%) of the respondents clearly recognise the devastation of their losses conveyed in the following typical comments: *'All ruins, in my heart.' 'I cannot get over the loss of my wonderful family.' 'I live in sadness.' 'I was a little girl who had everything and suddenly was thrown out alone in a wild world.' 'I think of my father everyday; I am half a person without him.' 'On the surface I look pretty normal – I'm a wreck. Guilt, grief, rage, distrust and no stability.' 'I couldn't cry for many years.' 'I am sure bad things will happen, I'm always anxious.' 'I still don't trust anyone who is "nice" to me.' 'I'm depressed most of the time.' 'I'm a mess but not suicidal anymore.' 'I'm afraid to leave my house.' 'I have anxiety attacks.' 'I fear abandonment.'*

It is clear that survivors looking back on their emotional lives from the vantage point of maturity, fifty five years later, report themselves as suffering serious and life-long effects emotionally.

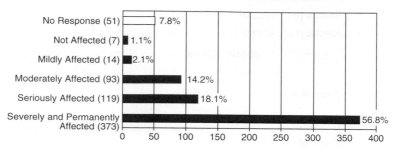

Fig. 6   Emotional Effects of the Holocaust on Child Survivors

Educational.   Responses in this area are related not only to the years of disruption of schooling but to the inability to focus on schooling when it finally became available after the war. Figure 7 shows that more than 55 percent of the respondents report serious and permanent effects. These are the representative comments: *'I have poor concentration.'* *'No helping hand for high school or college.'* *'I've had no guidance or support.'* *'I've moved to different countries and am not fluent in any one language, therefore I'm always behind.'* *'I never had a chance to finish my education.'* *'I married too early.'* *'My adoptive parents didn't encourage education – they wanted me to bring money into the house.'*

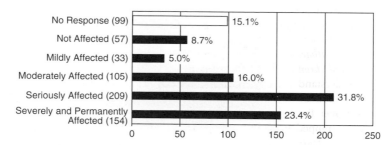

Fig. 7   Educational Effects of the Holocaust on Child Survivors

Economic.   The data of Figure 8. very nearly duplicate the pattern of responses in Figure 7. (Educational Effects of the Holocaust on Child Survivors). This appears to confirm a relationship between Education and Economics. People who had both educational opportunity with or without encouragement and the ability to concentrate in school despite their anxieties, nightmares, insecurities would be better equipped educationally to compete economically. *'I am doing poorly at my age (58) with no chance for advancement.'* *'I never had a home, always rent for a short time.'* *'I was disadvantaged as an orphan, had to take vocational training at fourteen and was never able to work.'* *'No education, lost childhood, hard to cope, now I am widowed and worried if I can manage finances until the end of my life.'* *'I lost everything, didn't attend school for five years, was liberated at age fourteen all alone.'* *'I never had a very good job, I am presently living on very little.'* *'I couldn't work and was unable to keep jobs.'*

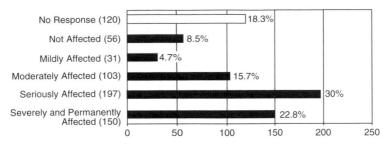

Fig. 8   Economic Effects of the Holocaust on Child Survivors

Summary of Part I.   An overview of all of the above data and comments reveals that in each and every sphere of life in this study, more than half of the respondents view themselves to have been affected seriously and severely life long. In the area of *emotional* harm, their self assessment of being affected negatively takes a dramatic upsurge to 74.9 percent. For about three fourths of the respondents, the losses of parents and the deprivations and disruptions in childhood under threat of German genocide depressed their innate childhood capacity for resilience and their capacity to experience social ease, a sense of trust and belonging, emotional security, and interfered with their educational and economic achievement.

Recent biologic research has demonstrated the impact of trauma at different stages of early human development and how it affects subsequent maturation. Van der Kolk and Pelcovitz[7] emphasize that *'the literature suggests that the impact of trauma on self-regulation, self-concept and interpersonal functioning is most profound in younger victims, and when the source of trauma is personal as opposed to natural disasters such as earthquakes and hurricanes'*. They call attention to the diagnostic category (in the ICD10) reflecting *'lasting personality changes following catastrophic stress which comprised impairment in interpersonal, social withdrawal, feelings of emptiness and hopelessness, a chronic feeling of being on the edge and chronic sense of estrangement.'*

If we are to understand the consequences of severe psychologic trauma on children, the time and duration of exposure need not be very long. Terr[8] demonstrated that children held prisoner for two days had lasting post-traumatic consequences. Herman[9] describes children trapped in abuse and/or neglect as follows: *'The child is faced with formidable tasks of adaptation. She must find a way to preserve a sense of trust in people who are untrustworthy, safety in a situation that is unsafe, control in a situation that is terrifyingly unpredictable, power in a situation of helplessness. Unable to care for or protect herself, she must compensate for the failures of adult care and protection with the only means at her disposal, an immature system of psychological defense.'*

Both current research and our survey support the conclusion that child survivors of the Holocaust were deeply harmed by their profound losses and experiences of mortal threat.

PART II: EXPERIENCE WITH RESTITUTION

We believe that the data in Part I supports the case for child survivors to receive meaningful restitution and apology. What has been the reality of restitution for child survivors? The reality has been grim. 54% or our respondents have received no restitution at all or restitution so minimal as not to be meaningful (lump sum, one time and less than $700US). Only 11% have received any kind of a pension.

Figure 9 shows that 22% of the respondents have never applied for any restitution. When asked why, their responses fall into the following categories:

(1) They were discouraged from applying: *'I was told it was useless.' 'I had no documentation.' 'I had no witnesses.'* (2) They were not informed: *'I didn't know where to go to apply.' 'I didn't know how to apply.' 'I believed you had to be in a camp.' 'I believed the French official who said "You didn't lose work when you were a child so that there is nothing to compensate for."'* (3) They were fearful: *'I was raised as a Christian.' 'I was afraid of being on anyone's list.' 'I was afraid of having to remember things I am afraid of remembering.' 'I was afraid I wouldn't know how to prove my suffering.' 'I was afraid of getting nervous.' 'I was afraid of dealing with Germans.' 'I was afraid of being humiliated.'* (4) Some wanted to avoid *'taking blood money'*. (5) Timing: *'When I was young, I was trying to forget and make a life – later it was too late (to apply).'*

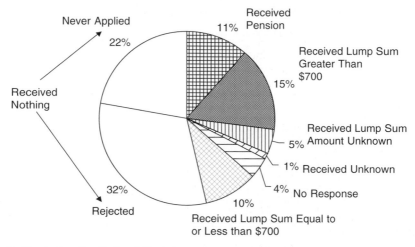

Fig. 9   Restitution Received and Denied

Another 32% percent did apply but were rejected and never received anything. Ten percent who received a one-time lump sum of seven hundred US dollars or less had to sign an agreement stating that receipt of this grant would prohibit any future applications. Therefore, almost two thirds (64%) of all Child Survivors in this survey received either *no* restitution or no meaningful restitution. Of the remaining thirty six percent, eleven percent are receiving a pension and another fifteen percent have received a one time lump sum of more than seven hundred US dollars.

Why have these vulnerable persons of tender age during the Holocaust not received the most attention and appropriate restitution? Because they were faced with the following roadblocks.

Roadblock 1: Missed Deadlines
Children who were placed in adoptive or foster homes were not in touch with the adult survivors nor the institutions and organizations that could have helped them to apply. As we have seen, child survivors were taught not to think of themselves as survivors. They were discouraged from talking about their losses. So by the time some of these younger people came out of their second hiding (after the war) and realized they were entitled to

restitution, various deadlines had passed. For others, the maze of application forms and procedures via the URO, the Claims Conference, and individual governments were too overwhelming and confusing to engage with in time.

Older survivors had organizations and friendship networks which disseminated information about what help was available, where and how and by when to apply. Young survivors were generally isolated having only begun to be in touch with each other in recent years. By then they had long ago missed various deadlines including the 1969 deadlines for the German Federal Indemnification Law (BEG)[10] which made pensions possible.

Roadblock 2 – Documentation Requirements
'*First they killed my family and now they want proof that they existed.' 'I have no proof of origin, no papers, I was too young to remember the name of my hiders in Poland.' 'I was too young to know my address.'* Applications typically required proof of the country of origin, birth certificates, death certificates of parents and names and locations of witnesses. In most instances these do not exist or are beyond the Child Survivor's ability to remember or to obtain. It is very difficult and often impossible for a person who was a child to prove location. They were too young to know where they were. Some had been adopted by parents who changed their names and refused to tell them about their past, often for reasons of safety and security, and they did not know who they were or where exactly they had been.

Unlike adults, children had no way to stay in touch with those who witnessed their suffering as most were taken far away to new locations after the war. It is with great pain that now in later adulthood these hidden children are struggling to remember the forgotten pieces and to find the places where they once lived. It is common for those who can to go to great lengths to find the nuns who took care of them or the villages where they were hidden. They yearn for someone who could remember and tell them about themselves to erase the vacuum they feel inside. They yearn for someone who had a picture of their parents.

Some suffer amnesia from extraordinarily traumatic events complicated by the constant disruption of frequent moves. Being handed from person to person and organization to organization prevented them from knowing and following an accurate history of themselves. In most cases, the persons who might have been able to help them reconstruct their history did not survive or are no longer alive.

It is not unusual for a person to learn, at this late stage in life, at the bedside of a dying parent, that those who raised him were not his birth parents, that indeed he or she was a child handed to Polish peasants or to others in a variety of desperate circumstances. This discovery opens a new arena of loss, conflict and doubt. It is sad that most in need of legal help for obtaining documentation and assisting them with agencies are least able financially and emotionally to get that help. Some fifty years later a few have taken great pains to overcome the fear of returning to the sites of their parents' murder and have retrieved valuable documentation. But not everyone is emotionally or financially capable of this, and some documentation is non-existent.

Road Block 3 – Time Requirements: 18 months for those in Hiding or in Ghettos
Where young children are concerned, the length of time in hiding required to qualify for compensation, eighteen months is far too long. Also required was 'closed hiding' which meant to be hidden under one's own name. This implies that Jewish children in 'open' hiding with a false identity did not suffer enough to warrant restitution, discounting their

having been suddenly taken from their parents, discounting the loss of security of home and family, and discounting the life long toll for many of having been forced to assume a false identity and another religion, leaving them with feelings of abandonment, unworthiness, identity confusion and loyalty conflicts for the remainder of their lives.

There exists a mistaken assumption that children hidden in convents, monasteries, or in homes were emotionally safe, well cared for and not abused. However, a conservative estimate based on a 1987 study of child survivors hidden in such circumstances revealed that over half were harshly treated and beaten, including one in six who were sexually abused. Half lived with threats of being turned over to the Nazis.[5] The requirement to prove 'inhumane' conditions, begs the question as to whether there were humane circumstances of hiding since discovery meant instant death or deportation to a killing site.

It was common that the children whose lives were saved by nuns in convents but whose trauma was expressed in losing bladder control at night were made every morning to announce their nightly failure by parading around in their wet sheets and being humiliated by the other children. A religious Jewish child in hiding was expected to become a devout Catholic and consequently heard his parents and family condemned to burn in hell for not accepting Jesus Christ.

Consider also the requirement of confinement in a ghetto for eighteen months for a young child. Confinement in a Ghetto meant experiencing the contagion of parental and adult fears of being taken away, to live in starvation, in crowded living conditions with rampant disease, to be deprived of secure adult role models who could take charge, protect and provide. Often the children had to be used to smuggle food into the ghetto and messages out. It meant deprivation of schooling. It meant being expected to behave beyond the ability of one's age in conditions of trauma. A child in the Ghetto lived in fear of personal annihilation based on realistic threats and the observation of beatings and shootings. Seldom did a child live as long as eighteen months in Ghetto captivity before dying of starvation or illness, or being deported and murdered. Is less than eighteen months in these conditions for a child harmless or unworthy of acknowledgment through restitution?

Road Block 4 – Time Requirements of Six Months in Concentration Camps
In Treblinka and Majdanek, young children were unlikely to live more than a few days. In Auschwitz, the majority of adults who were not murdered upon arrival lived less than three months. The few children who miraculously survived concentration camps often have no documents or certificates to verify their incarceration. Why is a child required to have survived six months in a concentration camp? Were two weeks in Ravensbriick, Bergen-Belsen or Buchenwald not sufficiently traumatic to provide nightmares to last a lifetime?

Even where there are records, such as those on the twins subjected to cruel experimentation by Mengele, some twins have been unable to get pensions despite the existence of blood drawing records. The Bayer company, which recently celebrated the 100th anniversary of the discovery of aspirin, had supplied Mengele with unidentified drugs for his brutal studies.[11] Many surviving twins of those studies still do not know why or with what they were injected, do not know what health risks they face personally, nor what may have caused a twin's postwar premature death.

Road Block 5 – The Means Test
It appears that if the above conditions are met (a virtual impossibility for most young child survivors) then a final means of exclusion comes into play. One's economic status

must be at the poverty level, $16,000 US for a single person, $21,000 US for a couple. It is precisely this group of survivors who are struggling, who cannot afford legal representation and do not have the emotional stamina to pursue their rightful compensation. Survivors report that having to convince bureaucrats and social workers who were never 'over there' of their suffering and need is a demeaning experience that is for the survivor a continuation of Holocaust trauma.

We believe the application of a means test changes the focus of restitution to economic issues when that focus should remain on the crimes of murderous perpetrators and on the victim's grievous injuries. In fact, representatives of the perpetrating nations sit in judgment and will not assess the physical, social, and emotional damage done unless the victim lives below the poverty level. This approach confuses restitution with charity. Restitution requires that wrongs committed during the Holocaust years be recognized regardless of a person's means. Living above the poverty level provides no immunity to traumatic memories, nightmares and lifelong vulnerability to depression.

When the United States compensated its Japanese-Americans for wrongly having interned them in camps during World War II (Camps that were neither slave labour or death camps) it did so outright, without requiring a means test. Japanese internees in Canada similarly were paid $26,000 each, unconditionally.

Road Block 6 – Requirement to be Interviewed by a German-appointed Psychiatrist
There are certain circumstances in which a survivor must submit to an interview (for example for a continuation or increase of pension) with a German psychiatrist. This requirement cannot be justified. There is no reason why the evaluation of a competent, accredited Board certified psychiatrist other than a German one appointed by the German government cannot be arranged to save the survivor needless traumatization.

Eissler[12] exposed many years ago the outrageous decisions made by three psychiatrists, members of a panel of twelve licensed physicians employed by the German Consulate in New York as psychiatric experts. One example is a woman whose parents, brother, three sisters with their children, husband and eight-year old daughter, had been killed during the course of the persecutions; she herself spent years in a Ghetto and in several concentration camps and had frequently been beaten to unconsciousness. Of her anxiety and depressive symptoms Dr. A. wrote in his report: '*Despite such grave experiences, of which no one is spared, most people continue their lives and have no chronic depressions.*'

So while the West German Republic may have made an effort to indemnify Nazi victims, the methods by which it was carried out, were highly questionable. But that was in the 1960s.

Let us fast forward to the 1990s and offer two accounts of child survivors presently seeking restitution for their grievous experiences.

EXAMPLES OF THE PERSONAL STRUGGLE FOR RESTITUTION
Charles. Born in Skarzysko in 1930, Charles was in a Ghetto at age 10, worked in a munitions factory at age 11, dug anti-tank ditches at age 12 and was aged 14 on arrival at Buchenwald and aged 15 at liberation. Here is his testimony in an application for compensation:

> *In Skarzysko I worked in the ammunition factory. I stamped the words 'FES' on both sides of anti-aircraft shells. I had to do 3,200 everyday. I was very young and very frightened Both my older brother and I contracted typhoid fever. We became very ill, weak and could not work. My brother Abraham, was taken out on a truck into the woods and murdered. I was lucky and survived.*

I lost four older brothers, my mother and father, aunts, uncles, cousins, my entire family. Only my sister and I survived. From Skarzysko we were transported to Przetbosz – I was there all summer digging anti tank ditches. Life was very hard – many people died! Then I was shipped to Chestochowa where I almost died in an explosion in the ammunition factory. Finally I went to Buchenwald where I was liberated by the American army on April 11, 1945.

In support of his application, his wife added:

Three times he was loaded onto a truck with many others – to be shot. At the last moment he was miraculously spared. The others were not. While he was a slave labourer in an ammunition factory, there was an explosion close to him. He suffered scarring to his face. He also suffered several illnesses, including typhoid fever.

One of the worst traumas he suffered was the death of his parents and four brothers. Until this day, he mourns their loss.

As an adult he is plagued by the ghosts of the past. He suffers eczema, ulcers and chronic depression. He has had several surgeries – which resulted from a build up of severe stress. This stress finally took a toll on his body. He received a one-time lump sum payment of approximately $2,900. It was compensation for three years hard labour while in German camps. He also applied to the German government for a claim on the basis of 'suffering and damage to health'.

Their requirement was that Charles must get a physical examination given by the German doctor of their choice. His report was as follows: '*Due to the fact that Charles has low blood pressure, he will probably live longer than the average person.*' On this basis he concluded that Charles had no ill effects from his war experiences and therefore was not deserving of a claim.

Charles's advisors handling his case said it was futile, he should give it up. He finally abandoned his efforts. Charles was not in the Ghetto for eighteen months nor in Buchenwald for the required six months, and he had received a one-time payment. Therefore, according to these bizarre rules, Charles cannot receive an appropriate pension in his later years to ease financial stress and the continuing struggle with physical and emotional conditions, whereas the SS have no problem collecting their pensions.

Marta. She was born in 1931 in Ukraine. When the Germans approached their village in 1941, she and her mother fled. Her father was already somewhere in Russia. They returned home but were caught and sent to the town centre, where she witnessed the men separated from the women and children and taken to a nearby forest. All day she heard the shooting and the cries. They tried to kill everyone in one day but couldn't, so Marta and her mother were sent home where they hid, undetected, in a cellar for three days. They subsequently were caught, released (miraculously) and wandered from village to village, finally hiding for ten months in a haystack, cared for by a Ukrainian family.

Marta came to Canada in 1970 and some years later her hiders provided a written statement that she and her mother were tortured and barely escaped being murdered. She applied for restitution primarily for arthritis stemming from her many months of hiding in freezing cellars on frozen ground and in damp hay. Marta's completed 1985 application to Germany was rejected with a note she had missed the 1974 deadline. They suggested another organization with a 1978 deadline. A claim to the German Consulate of Canada in 1985 was forwarded to the URO (United Restitution Organization) because claims to the Consulate are only for property or business, not personal losses or suffering.

Marta was then told to write to Frankfurt for a 'Hardship' claim. She was asked to sign over power of attorney to be represented by someone unknown to her. *'Should we not receive the Power of Attorney from you within three weeks, we shall inform our office in Germany that you do not wish to be represented by us.'*

An inquiry to the Paris URO resulted in a suggestion to write to the Soviet Red Cross *'to get a certificate about your story in June 1941 and during the war'.* And so, a Jewish-Ukrainian child, on the run and hiding in many places, foraging for food for her and her mother at age ten, with life-long emotional and physical consequences, now financially destitute, is blocked at every turn in her attempt to receive a modest pension. Without money for lawyers, and with limited command of English, she soldiers on to achieve compensation. She is typical of many.

OBSERVATIONS ON ROADBLOCKS CRITERIA

The criteria used to determine compensation and restitution remind us of the barbed wire surrounding the doomed Ghetto. Within those confined quarters, a set of rules evolved which determined life and justice on a day to day basis, forcing people to interact with one another and blame each other for the problems, thereby forgetting those who enclosed them with barbed wire in the first place. Unaware of the bizarre restrictions and regulations of their seeking compensation, even today, survivors may turn on their social workers representing various Jewish family services, or even the physicians and lawyers who try to represent them (mostly unsuccessfully) because once again those who set the boundaries within which professionals can operate are themselves not challenged over the new perversity of justice that has been created.

When the child survivor is caught in the complex pursuit of restitution where all roads lead to failure, memories are rekindled of the madness of running from place to place in the struggle to survive. Safety and security remain beyond one's grasp. There is no end in sight. Each news item offers hope, each renewed attempt is soon dashed leaving the person discouraged and emotionally spent and angry.

What do people say about the process of applying and their interactions with (1) government representatives of Germany, France, Holland, and other formerly occupied countries, etc.; (2) interactions with Jewish Agencies including the Conference of Jewish Material Claims, (3) interactions with lawyers?

Their responses are overwhelmingly negative in all three areas. We learn about being retraumatized by government bureaucrats who want you to prove your suffering with documents, tell you you're too late that you don't qualify; or do not respond. We learn about French officials who tell child survivors that since they were young children and too young to work, there is nothing to compensate the for, since they lost no work. We learn about Jewish Agencies who treat you like a beggar and stall and delay for years 'just like the Germans'. And we learn about lawyers, some of whom have pocketed most of the survivor's claim. Applying for restitution, a process in which the survivor seeks acknowledgement of perpetrator responsibility and apology for harm done proves to be a continuation of war trauma for most child survivors.

A great deal of frustration, hurt and anger can be seen in the overwhelming 88% rating of Child Survivor experiences as *negative* with the Jewish Conference on Material claims. It comes as no surprise therefore that, when asked 'How should future restitution awards be distributed? 1) Direct to agencies (to give to the survivors) or 2) Direct to the Survivors? We see in figure 10 that 93% chose 'Direct to the survivors'.

This adds up to more than 100% because some of the survivors said 'both', but that any monies for agencies such as Amcha or Jewish Social Services, should be for survivor services only. In comments justifying their preference for Direct to the Survivor, the reasons given include *'We are the ones who lost our childhoods, we suffered, we are the ones who should be recipients.'* *'They should not use that money to build big museums, educational institutions, memorials, or social service agencies as long as there are any survivors alive.'* *'Let me make the decision for what to do with restitution that goes to me because I suffered; let me make the choice to donate it if I don't need it.'*

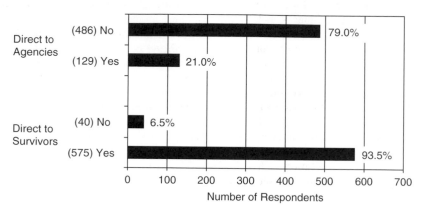

Fig. 10   Where Restitution Funds Should Go

SUMMARY AND RECOMMENDATIONS

In recent years there has been growing evidence that severe stress in early life has long-term effects on the brain and glandular systems that govern stress responses and create persistent vulnerability to depression and post-traumatic stress disorder, not only in childhood but in later life. Heit, Graham and Nemeroff[13] state 'There is now experimental and clinical evidence that early experiences can also cause prolonged hypersensitivity to acute stress. People who suffer childhood trauma may suffer from persistent hyperactivity in the brain region that contains CRF (corticotrophin releasing factor) receptors.'

These recent findings and the self-reports of child survivors summarized in our survey support each other. Furthermore, they lead us to question what further harm has been done to child survivors over the past fifty-five years and continuing to this day, by governments, and agencies that persistently deny the survivors' suffering, deny the survivors' claim to restitution for years and years, and treat them as beggars or con artists.

The information gathered from 664 child survivors plus recent work on the lifelong effects of early trauma mandate the revision of the criteria for restitution awards. After all, how many days in Auschwitz were required to emotionally traumatize a child inmate, how many weeks of hiding in a cupboard, closet or hole in the ground, make an impact on a hidden child, how many months without a mother, a father? How many months of malnutrition did a child need to endure to sustain physical change to growth and stature and damage to internal organs?

No wonder the child survivors find even the process of application demeaning and prejudicial. The demands for proof of duration of suffering is insulting. The costs incurred by existing bureaucracies in screening could be better put to use in seeking out the destitute child survivors who are too proud or too intimidated, too discouraged or depressed to seek redress.

Every Jewish child who survived the Holocaust in hiding, ghettos and concentration camps, and was torn from home and family by the Nazi occupation, is entitled to monetary compensation and freedom from degrading and unnecessary evaluations. Any child salvaged from that inferno is entitled to apology and compensation without question.

A concerted effort toward compassionate understanding of child survivors must take place in every bureaucracy that controls the purse whether it is Jewish Agencies, the Claims Conference offices, governmental agencies of Germany, France, Belgium and the Netherlands, Hungary, Poland, Lithuania, etc.

The concept of apology on the part of the perpetrators needs to be introduced into the process. Authorization for restitution could come with an official note of apology from the relevant government. Regaining a sense of justice done would greatly aid the healing process with which we have seen so many child survivors still struggle, fifty five years later.

The last surviving victims of the Holocaust will be those who were young children during the genocide. They are the ones who lost their normal childhoods, their parents and families and extended families, all who could care for them with family intimacy. They are the ones who were too young to know if their parents had insurance etc. Their needs for security and well being must not continue to be ignored, postponed, neglected and betrayed by governments and Jewish organizations. They must not once again be allowed to suffer abandonment, loneliness and hardship in old age as they did in childhood.

NOTES

 1 Robert Krell (ed.), *Child Survivors of the Holocaust: 40 Years Later.* Special Section, *Journal of the American Academy of Child Psychiatry* 24 (1985): 377–412.
 2 Sarah Moskovitz, *Love Despite Hate: Child Survivors of the Holocaust and Their Adult Lives* (New York: Shocken Books, 1983).
 3 Sarah Moskovitz and Robert Krell, 'Child Survivors of the Holocaust: Psychological Adaptations to Survival', *Israel Journal of Psychiatry and Other Related Sciences* 17/2 (1990): 81ff.
 4 Leon Stabinsky, then chair of the Los Angeles Child Survivors Association, was instrumental in our initial understanding of the roadblocks. His help in the distribution of the survey is hereby also acknowledged.
 5 Sarah Moskovitz, 'Barriers to Gratitude', *Remembering for the Future*, ed. Yehuda Bauer (Oxford: Pergamon Press, 1988), Vol.I, pp.494–505.
 6 Personal communication Dr. Yehudi Lindeman, October 1998.
 7 Bessel van der Kolk and David Pelcovitz, 'Clinical applications of the structured interviews for disorders of extreme stress (SIDES)' National Centre for Post-Traumatic Stress Studies, *Clinical Quarterly* 8/2 (1999): 1.
 8 Lenore Terr, 'Children Revisited: The Effects of Psychic Trauma after a School Bus Kidnapping', *American Journal of Psychiatry* 140 (1983): 1543–1550.
 9 Judith Herman, *Trauma and Recovery* (New York: Basic Books, 1992).
10 Roman Kent, 'The Claims Conference as I see it', in *Together*, a publication of the American Gathering of Jewish Holocaust Survivors (New York: 1999). Christian Pross, Wiedergutmachung. *Der Kleinkrieg gegen die Opfer* [Compensation: The Small War Against the Victim]. (Frankfurt am Main: Athenaum, 1988), p.384. English translation as *Paying for the Past* (Baltimore: The Johns Hopkins University Press, 1998).
11 Civil action initiated by Eva Kor against Bayer AC, 17 February 1999. In brief, the suit alleges that a Bayer representative, Dr. Koenig, accompanied Mengele on experiments performed using Bayer products and recorded the results.
12 Kurt Eissler, 'Perverted psychiatry?' *American Journal of Psychiatry* 123/11 (1967): 1352–1358
13 S. Heit, Y. Graham, C. Nemeroff, Neurobiological effects of early trauma. *The Harvard Mental Health Letter*, 16/4 (October 1999): 4–6.

THE SECOND PERSECUTION:
LEGAL DISCOURSE AND THE CONSTRUCTION OF HISTORY IN SWITZERLAND

Daniel Wildmann

H OW CAN a state legally come to terms with its own history? Places where this question is pressing include Switzerland. At the time of writing, the highest Swiss court, the Bundesgericht in Lausanne, is considering two cases shedding light on the question. Charles Sonabend and Joseph Spring are former Jewish refugees who were denied entry at the Swiss border in 1942 and 1943. They are suing the state on account of this treatment. I will examine the arguments of the plaintiffs and defendants below. My purpose is not to present a legal assessment of the arguments, but to discuss certain trends of thought in the legal argumentation, including ideas relating to Swiss history and possible ties between Switzerland and Nazi Germany. This gives rise to the following questions: To what extent does pronouncing judgment mean formulating an official answer to the question of the ties between Switzerland and the Third Reich? To what extent does it mean constructing history?

I. TWO STORIES

On the night of 12 August 1942, the Sonabend family from Brussels illegally crossed the Swiss border in the region of Le Sentier in the Vallée de Joux, hoping to thus reach safety from persecution under the Third Reich.[1] In Brussels, the family's daughter was on the official list of Belgian Jews to be deported to the east in the summer of 1942. Two days after they crossed the border, business friends of the father took the family into their home in Biel and reported their arrival to the police in order to regularize their stay. They were unaware that the previous day (13 August 1942), the Swiss Federal Department of Justice and Police (the EJPD) had ordered the *de facto* closing of the borders to Jews through a confidential circular to the police directorates and detachments of the various cantons. The circular was entitled 'Containment of the Inflow of Foreign Civil and Military Refugees' and specified those categories of refugees who could be accepted. Among the 'civil refugees', only 'political refugees' were to be accepted. Jews did not fall into this category *a priori*; the appended directive explained that 'refugees who are such on strictly racial grounds, e.g. Jews, do not qualify as political refugees.'[2] Refugees not fulfilling the acceptance-criteria were to be sent back.

14 August 1942 was a Saturday, i.e. the Jewish sabbath. Shortly after the Sonabends' friend made his telephone call a policeman from the canton arrested Simon and Laja Sonabend. The children, 11-year-old Charles and 15-year-old Sabine, were sent to a local cloister. Three days later (17 August), the Swiss cantonal police expelled the Sonabend family across the border into occupied France. The expulsion took place after a consultation with Heinrich Rothmund, director of the EJPD's police division. The Sonabend parents paid in cash both for their taxi to the Swiss border and their

Swiss-police escort. In their expulsion-report the cantonal police confirmed that 'the border crossing proceeded smoothly.'[3]

The same night, a German patrol arrested the family. A week later, on August 24, the parents were deported to Auschwitz. The mother was gassed on arrival; the father was murdered later. Probably because the transport capacities of the train system were exhausted, the children escaped deportation. The Union Général des Israélites de France was able to place Charles and Sabine with a Jewish married couple, and they survived the German occupation together.

Joseph Spring illegally crossed the Swiss border in 1943; together with his cousins Henri and Sylver Henenberg, he arrived at La Cure in the Waadt canton on 12–13 November.[4] Spring was 16 years old, Sylver 14, and Henry 21. They asked for help from a local farmer, who handed them to Swiss custom officers. The three refugees carried false papers designating them as 'Aryans', but they also carried their proper passes with their correct names so as to be able to apply for asylum in Switzerland as Jews. The authorities sent them back to occupied France, warning that next time they would be delivered directly to the Germans. This procedure corresponded precisely to the 29 December 1942 directive of the EJPD's police division, 'Directions for the expulsion or acceptance of illegally entering foreigners'. It once more reinforced the principle that 'refugees who are such on strictly racial grounds' were not to be considered political refugees and were to be expelled. The directive specified that 'With every expulsion a threat is to be issued of delivery to the foreign border-authorities in the case of an additional illicit entry.'[5]

Spring and the Henenbergs crossed the border a second time. The border guard discovered them and handed them directly to the German authorities, as threatened. Furthermore, the Swiss border officials informed their German colleagues of the three refugees' real identities. A month after being handed over, the three were sent to Auschwitz; the Henenbergs were gassed the day of their arrival. Joseph Spring survived.

In 1998, 55 and 56 years later, respectively, Joseph Spring and Charles Sonabend filed a lawsuit against the Swiss government with the Bundesgericht in Lausanne.

II. THE LEGAL ARGUMENT

If a plaintiff wishes to have the Swiss government found legally responsible for its officials' actions, and this involves a demand for financial compensation, he must apply to the Federal Department of Finance (the EFD). First, he submits a 'request' directed toward the Bundesrat (i.e. the Swiss executive). If the Bundesrat rejects the 'request', the plaintiff then initiates a legal proceeding, filing a 'complaint' with the Bundesgericht. Both parties, plaintiff and defendant, i.e. the government, represented by the EFD, now submit documents detailing their arguments to the Bundesgericht. In a further step, the Bundesgericht offers both parties a hearing, after which it delivers its decision.[6]

The law regulating the state's responsibility for actions of its officials is the 'law of responsibility'. Only actions that are classified as 'illegal' can here be considered. Article 3, par. 1 of this law specifies that the government is responsible for damage that officials illegally inflict on third parties.

The central legal questions in the Sonabend and Spring proceedings are 'illegality', the connection between the actions of Swiss officials and the Nazi anti-Jewish policies, and superannuation (*Verjährung*) or 'forfeiture' (*Verwirkung*), i.e. the question of whether after more than fifty years claims are still valid. Where the questions of illegality and 'adequate causal connection' are central to the plaintiff's argumentation, the EFD, representing the government, focuses on the question of 'forfeiture'.[7]

Sonabend's lawyer, Marc Richter, has made the officials' knowledge of the consequences of the expulsion of Jewish refugees one of his chief arguments. In July 1942, Heinrich Rothmund's adjunct Robert Jetzler wrote a 'Report on the Refugee Problem' for Eduard von Steiger, head of the EJPD. The report described the situation of Jews living under the Third Reich. It noted that:

> The concurrent, reliable reports concerning the manner the deportations are being carried out and over circumstances in the Jewish districts in the east are so horrible that it is necessary to understand desperate efforts by the refugees to escape such a fate; expulsion can thus hardly any longer be justified.
>
> The situation of Jews seems especially grim in the occupied regions [former Poland], the Protectorate [Bohemia and Moravia], Holland, Belgium, and northern France. The Jews living there do not know one hour if they will be deported the next hour, arrested as hostages, or executed on one excuse or another.[8]

Despite the 'grim situation', the above-cited circular of 13 August 1942 was sent out, with its statement that 'refugees who are such on strictly racial grounds, e.g. Jews, do not qualify as political refugees'.

When the Sonabends were arrested on 15 August, they resisted the threat of expulsion. Friends of the family also attempted to intervene with the cantonal police. In consultation with Rothmund, the responsible officials finally opted for expulsion.

Marc Richter links this official act with what occurred once it had been carried out: capture by a German border patrol, deportation of the parents to Auschwitz, their gassing in the death camp. This linkage, the legal argument goes, had produced damages for Charles Sonabend justifying financial compensation.[9] Richter thus formulates a connection between Swiss refugee policy and Nazi *Judenpolitik* in the summer of 1942 – a set of policies that had already shifted into the 'final solution' phase, i.e. the physical extinction of the European Jews. In juridical parlance, Richter defines this connection as an 'adequate causal connection' between the actions at issue and the damage.

Richter maintains that this 'causal connection' means that the circular and the expulsion were in conflict with basic rights that both the Swiss constitution and international law guaranteed everyone in the country, including foreigners. Richter interprets this connection as involvement in 'crimes against humanity'. For just this reason, he argues for adopting a new legal orientation through the use of 'Radbruch's formula' – a legal principle not previously introduced in Switzerland.

The German jurist Gustav Radbruch first formulated the principle in 1946, in the context of the ongoing political and legal-theoretical debates over both coming to terms with Nazi law and the significance of the Nuremberg trials.[10] According to 'Radbruch's formula', 'legal injustice' can be present and a law can lose its legal status when

> the conflict between the positive law and justice reaches such an unbearable degree that justice must prevail over the law, as an 'incorrect law' ... [W]hen justice is not even aimed at, when in the establishment of positive law equality, the core of justice, is consciously denied, then the law is not merely something like an 'incorrect law'; rather, it altogether lacks legal status.[11]

For Radbruch, a law thus loses its legality when it conflicts with justice – with, as he puts it, 'super-legal law'. Radbruch thus postulates a law preceding positive law and oriented toward universal ethical norms.[12] For Richter, just such norms were violated in the Sonabend case.[13]

Richter characterizes the implications of the circular and expulsion as particularly grave because the officials acted in knowledge of the consequences, in knowledge that the

Sonabend family's deportation was to be expected. With this knowledge, he argues, the expulsion can be legally classified as 'premeditated,' premeditated action involving awareness of at least a decent possibility of damage.[14] By way of this category of knowledge, Richter ties both the actions of the Swiss officials and the legal basis of their actions to Nazi antisemitic norms and practices. And implicitly, this poses the question of possible ideological complicity: such remaining the case even – as Richter stressed – if the actions in no way meant approval in principle of the ideology and practice of Nazi *Judenpolitik*.[15]

In the Spring case, Paul Rechsteiner likewise postulates a linkage between the expulsion, the party who was expelled, and Nazi *Judenpolitik*. He classifies the 'Final Solution' as 'genocide' and legally defines the connection between the expulsion and its consequences as 'complicity in genocide'. Rechsteiner traces this complicity back to the above-cited state directive, approved by the Bundesrat, of 29 December 1942.[16] He judges the directive itself as illegal, since it conflicts with both the Swiss constitution and international law, placing in question the constitutional guarantee of inviolable physical integrity.[17]

Now an attempt could be made to justify a limitation on basic rights through then prevailing emergency law. On 30 August 1939, the parliament issued a decree of discretionary power authorizing the Bundesrat to proclaim emergency law. Emergency law can annul basic constitutional rights. But this is precisely the basis for Rechsteiner's challenge to the legality of the emergency law justifying the directive.[18]

Rechsteiner maintains that international law was violated by the 29 December 1942 directive, since such law forbids the forced return of political refugees to states that are persecuting them.[19] By May 1943, the Swiss Federal Political Department was aware of the existence of various death camps including Belzec, Sobibor, Treblinka, and Auschwitz-Birkenau. It was aware, for example, of the incinerating capacity of the crematoria operational since March in Auschwitz-Birkenau.[20]

Rechsteiner takes issue with the substance of the Swiss state's official definition of 'political refugee'. In his report, Adjunct Jetzler indicates that Nazi Germany considers being Jewish *per se* as a potential crime ('The Jew *qua* Jew is already viewed as suspicious'), concluding that the Third Reich has in effect criminalized the mere attempt by Jews to flee.[21] Jetzler here points to the political nature of the persecution. The significance of the EJPD's interpretation of the concept of the 'political refugee' in 1943 thus lies in a refusal, nevertheless, to ascribe a political character to the *Judenpolitik* of the Third Reich.

Interestingly, this legal non-recognition was accompanied by detailed knowledge of the Jews' everyday life under the Nazis, as well as that reality's political dimension. For Rechsteiner, as for Richter, this knowledge closely ties the responsible agents in Switzerland to Nazi German *Judenpolitik*. Rechsteiner also classifies their action as premeditated. In this context, the approach of the government agents, the Swiss border officials, to their own up-to-date and highly specific knowledge of the refugees' Jewish origins takes on particular importance: they informed the Germans that Spring and the Henenbergs, his cousins, were Jews. This was a form of collaboration not referred to in any circular or directive. Rechsteiner characterizes it as denunciation.[22]

The expulsion had personal consequences for Spring that have lasted until this day. Like Richter in the Sonabend case, Rechsteiner here introduces the concept of traumatization. This traumatization, in other words the intimate consequences of the expulsion for Spring's physical and psychic health, demonstrates the illegality of the state's action. The expulsion, Rechsteiner maintains, violates the individual's constitutional protection against physical and personal trespass.[23]

The Sonabend and Spring cases are not identical or interchangeable. The Sonabends were sent back across the border, Spring and the Henenbergs delivered directly to the German authorities. In the Spring case, the Swiss informed the Germans of the refugees' Jewish status. Spring was deported to Auschwitz; Sonabend was fortunate and escaped the planned deportation. In any event one thing does hold for both cases: Swiss law had a not inessential and not haphazard impact on the personal fate of Spring and Sonabend and that of their family members in the Third Reich. The family members were gassed in Auschwitz.

In their basic arguments, the EFD's negative responses to Richter and Rechsteiner correspond. And in both cases, the response to the complaint culminates in the following requests to the Bundesgericht:

1. that the complaint be rejected;
2. that the remaining proceedings be limited to the question of the punctuality of the claim-presentation, or the question of 'forfeiture' [*Verwirkung*].[24]

The EFD's choice of the legal concept of 'forfeiture', *Verwirkung*, rather than 'super-annuation', *Verjährung*, is deliberate. The argument being offered is that on formal legal grounds a 'forfeiture' rather than a case of superannuation is present. The EFD explains that in contrast to *Verjährung*, a 'forfeiture' can never be overridden – even through a complaint regarding complicity in genocide or crimes against humanity. To this extent, should a 'forfeiture' actually be present in the Sonabend and Spring cases, no further legal demands could be submitted. In proper legal language: 'The forfeiture leads to a complete extinguishment of the law.'[25]

In a legal context, the 'question of forfeiture' is a formal and not a material question. From this strictly formal vantage, the question of a possible material involvement in a crime against humanity vanishes. The EFD's desire to limit the proceedings to a formal question, as confirmed in the second request of both complaint-responses, thus has one meaning: that the EFD, as representative of the Swiss government, wishes to exclude a substantive legal evaluation of the cases, e.g. the question of whether the state is or is not guilty of complicity in genocide. The proceedings are meant to be carried on as if this question were not at issue.

Nevertheless, the EFD does proceed to argue that the complaints are also 'unfounded in terms of material law.'[26] It here takes issue with several points: first, it considers the circulars and directives as legal, since the points of international law now conflicting with them and rendering them void were then not internationally binding. They had only become so 'after World War II', something holding true even for 'the principle of equality of all human beings, namely admitting no distinctions based on race, skin-colour, sex, religion, origin, or other factors'.[27]

The EFD then argues that now-prevailing international law cannot be applied retro-actively.[28] In addition, it maintains that the disputed actions by the Swiss officials do not constitute crimes against humanity or complicity in genocide. Repeatedly, the Federal Department of Finance grounds this assessment in the absence of Swiss participation in World War II.[29]

Along with the above-mentioned points, three additional arguments of the EFD are illuminating in the present context:

• In regard to the Spring case, the ministry's jurists take up the concept of 'political refugee'. Concerning the year 1943, they observe that 'the fact of the plaintiff's Jewish origin did not represent a political offence according to then-prevailing law.'[30] Implicitly, then, they maintain that the flight of a Jew *qua* Jew from territory controlled by Nazi Germany did not legally constitute action 'of a primarily political nature'. They assert that Spring could thus not have been a political refugee.[31]

- In contrast to the plaintiffs, the EFD does not discuss the Swiss officials' knowledge; rather, the knowledge it discusses is that of the plaintiffs, the Jewish refugees. The EFD thus stresses that the plaintiffs knew what happened to them after it happened. They consequently disposed of enough knowledge to file a complaint in timely fashion, the 'forfeiture' thus being partly their own responsibility.[32]

- Finally, the EFD suggests that Spring's memory is not accurate. It calls into question Spring's remarks regarding the direct delivery to the Germans and the 'denunciation'. It here relies on its own witnesses, who assert that they cannot remember 'that in La Cure a delivery to the German authorities had ever taken place'. In this manner, the EFD disputes that such a delivery ever occurred. The witnesses it cites remain anonymous in the complaint-response.[33]

III. LAW AND POLITICS

To what extent do the arguments of the accused parties described above comprise a construction and interpretation of history? The following analysis focuses on three themes that are important for this question: the continuity of law; the approach to knowledge; and temporal perspectivization.

In its complaint-response to Rechsteiner, the EFD asserts that even if the delivery it disputes had actually occurred it would have been legal, since in the Third Reich Spring had not committed any political offence.[34] Now the Third Reich considered Jews *a priori* as opponents in a struggle, as enemies; and as is well known, on a legal level it placed them progressively outside the normal legal order, valid for 'Aryan' citizens. Jews were subject, for instance, to a 'special law' applicable to them strictly on the basis of their being Jewish.[35] The 'Nuremberg Laws' can be understood as an early expression of such a specific locus for Jews inside the Nazi legal system.[36] After 1945, the Allied occupation authorities in Germany tried to break the continuity between the Nazi legal order and the law now prevailing. A central procedure here was annulment of laws at the core of the Third Reich. For example, the 'enabling law' of 23 March 1933, the 'Reich-citizenship law' of 15 September 1935 with its various implementing regulations, and the special criminal law, along with the 'decree regarding criminal law for Poles and Jews', were all annulled.[37] The 'enabling law' had made it possible to revoke the principle of universal equality before the law. The Nuremberg Laws of 1935 and other special laws for 'non-Aryans' gave legal status to politically required, antisemitically or racially determined inequality.[38]

On the jurisdictional level, the political and legal break with the Third Reich was meant to be executed through Allied Control Law 10, 20 December 1945. This law was meant to prevent legal continuity in the case of legal injustice, thus declaring 'crimes against humanity' as liable to punishment. 'Persecution on political, racial, or religious grounds' was included in this category. Radbruch viewed the law as a locus for the shifting of super-legal law into positive law.[39]

In its response, the EFD does not acknowledge these legal-historical contextual factors. It does not question the legal denial of the legal-political reality of Nazi *Judenpolitik*, the elision of the persecution of the Jews from the concept of the political, as expressed in the disputed circulars and directives of 1942 and 1943. At the same time, the Federal Department of Finance denies that the officials' actions violated the Swiss constitution. By so doing, the EFD can understand the circulars and directives as legally valid. In this manner, the EFD's argument postulates a specific continuity of law: one that only exists through an exclusion of any juridical linkage to the 'Final Solution' – of the 'adequate causal connection' between action and injury and the 'illegality' of the action – thereby deleting Nazi *Judenpolitik*, as demonstrated in the response to Spring's complaint. We can thus read the insistence of the EFD upon the legal validity of the Swiss directives as the insistence on a past untrammelled by Nazi policies of persecution and extinction.

Three forms of knowledge can be distinguished in both the Spring and Sonabend legal contests: the knowledge of the officials at the time of the expulsions; the knowledge of the plaintiffs directly after 1945; and the knowledge of the plaintiffs at present. The EFD correctly designates the last form of knowledge as memory. The plaintiffs raise the subject of the officials' knowledge of Nazi anti-Jewish policies in order to legally link these policies to the question of responsibility. The EFD reacts by not addressing that knowledge in its response; instead, it raises questions regarding the knowledge or memory of the plaintiffs.

The EFD judges Spring's memory as imprecise and that of its own witnesses, most likely former officials, as accurate – as correct memory. It argues that imprecise memory is usual in the case of long-term witnesses. But it does not explain why this general observation applies to the Jewish witness Spring and not to the witnesses for the EFD.[40] For the EFD's jurists, when it comes to the question of memory the perspective of officaldom has objectively valid status, while the perspective of those who were persecuted is called into question. In addition, the jurists reproach the former refugees (now plaintiffs) with being *at fault* in not having submitted a timely suit despite their knowledge.

In its approach to the category of knowledge, the EFD avoids the question of premeditation, hence the possible linkages between Swiss refugee policy and Nazi *Judenpolitik*. Instead, it attempts to cast doubt on the integrity of the plaintiff's testimony, steering the debate toward the question of punctuality, or the 'forfeiture' of the lawsuit.[41]

In its two responses, the EFD substantiates its position that the officials' actions do not comprise 'crimes against humanity' by essentially asserting that Switzerland did not participate in World War II.[42]

It is self-evident that without the violent territorial expansion of the Third Reich, without its brutal occupation policies in Eastern Europe, and without the war, the extensive annihilation of the European Jews (the 'Final Solution') could never have been realized. But by the same token, the policy of extermination is not conceivable without the preceding persecution of German and Austrian Jewry, and without multi-faceted, sometimes conflicting developments inside the Nazi power-apparatus. For this reason alone, the 'Final Solution' cannot be understood solely in relation to World War II; rather it is to be understood in relation to both the war and other factors.[43]

In a 1971 article, Heinz Artzt, then the West German Chief Prosecutor and acting director of the Central Bureau for the Judical Authority of the German Länder for the Investigation of Nazi Crimes in Ludwigsburg, clarified the differences between 'war crimes' and the 'crimes against humanity' committed in the context of the Third Reich, which he refers to collectively as 'Nazi crimes.' As a first, basic distinction, he indicates that 'a state of war is not a premise for Nazi crime. The war simply offered an opportunity for its most gruesome form; its execution was simply favoured by the wartime circumstances.'[44] And again: at issue here are 'crimes having no inner connection with the war, touching even in peacetime on the substance of human value itself.'[45] And the interior context within which such crimes stands is exemplified precisely by Nazi *Judenpolitik*.[46]

The EFD's argumentation is oriented around the concept 'World War II' and a 1939–1945 periodization. But a 'crime against humanity' is not defined by a linkage of the deed to a period of war.[47] For this reason, the impression emerges that ideas at play in Switzerland's present public debate on the entire thematic complex – dormant accounts, Swiss relations with Nazi Germany, etc. – have made their way into that argumentation. A striking feature of the debate is, in fact, the unquestioned, repetitive evocation of 'World War II'.[48] The Bergier Commission thus bears the official title 'Independent Commission of Experts: Switzerland – Second World War' and the recently published collection of articles on the theme published by the Swiss General Society of Historians is titled 'Switzerland and World War II'.[49] Likewise, the series of pieces treating the matter In the *Neue Zürcher Zeitung* has the general heading 'Shadows of World War II', and a diplomats' 'task force' recently established by the Swiss Federal Department of Foreign Affairs to confront it has the title 'Task Force Switzerland – Second World War.'[50]

With its onset in 1995, the debate over 'dormant' Jewish accounts is generally seen as the catalyst of the present heated discussion.[51] But the orientation toward 1939–1945 does not correspond to the time in which the accounts now considered dormant were established. This process frequently took place before the war, to great extent certainly between 1933 and 1939. The assets only became a problem of dormant assets in the postwar period.[52] Jews were already trying to escape the Third Reich for Switzerland before 1939. And in the same period, Swiss concerns were involved in the violent process of forcing the Jews out of Germany's business and economy.

What is the source of this Swiss linguistic convention, steering the public debate toward the years 1939–45 or 'World War II' – and not, say, toward the years 1933–45?[53] If we follow Luc van Dongen, the convention – a periodization whose direct reference points are the six years of war but not the 12 years of the Third Reich – emerged between 1945 and 1948.[54] It is tied to a much older Swiss tradition connecting Swiss identity to neutrality: a successful connection, first formulated, described, and propagated in the 1890s, whose impact can be felt in contemporary plebiscite-results.[55] It is important to note that within Swiss foreign policy, the interpretation and elaboration of the international-legal concept of 'neutrality' has remained inconsistent. A number of questions are in fact at play here: the manner in which 'neutrality' has become inscribed in the Swiss collective memory; the mutation it has undergone in relation to the original international-legal concept; and whether the mutation has changed over the course of time.

Debates over neutrality have resonated in Swiss historical research on Switzerland's role in World War II.[56] Ideas about the notion of neutrality codified in the 1907 Hague Convention have also often been manifest in the recent public discussion. Within that international-legal context, neutrality regulates the conduct between states engaged in war and states that are not. It thus connects neutral states to politics and, in the end, to history. But it is quite clear that in the present public debate, the conceptual figure of a 'neutrality' periodized between 1939 and 1945 is being used to convey a substantively different meaning. What is in fact being presented is a metaphoric neutrality,[57] tied to notions of balance and non-involvement and implying, in the end, an *absence* from historical entanglement.

This raises the question of whether the EFD responses are informed by the premises of metaphorical neutrality, premises circulating in the public discussion that by their very nature exclude any link with the 'Final Solution'. Situated beyond the conceivable, the potential linkage *vanishes* as an idea.

While the EFD does address material questions, its main argument is formal: the argument of 'forfeiture'. In his answer to the complaint-response, Marc Richter suggests that such a line of argument is the same as a refusal to legally qualify state actions.[58] Within such a refusal, basically the same phenomenon is evident, stamping and organizing the material arguments: an effort to avoid having to confront a possible connection between state actions and the 'Final Solution'.

The question of continuity can also be formulated from another perspective, that of the persecuted. At the end of the 1970s, the Dutch psychoanalyst Hans Keilson proposed a concept of trauma resulting from Nazi persecution that distinguishes between three 'traumatic sequences'. The third such sequence starts with liberation from Nazi rule. This idea of a third sequence modifies the temporal structure for traumatization at work in the widespread legal and medical term 'latent injury'. For Keilson, the years following 1945 are no longer the period in which the 'latent injury' of the preceding traumatic events becomes visible. Rather, this period itself inflicts additional trauma. In light of Keilson's theory, viewing the 'third traumatic sequence' as a separate, second persecution would seem well grounded. Keilson indicates that the course of the 'third traumatic sequence' essentially depends on the manner the victim's social environment comes to terms with the first persecution: whether that persecution is acknowledged or negated. The 'third sequence' can thus either break or carry forward the chain of traumatization.[59]

Applying this theoretical conception of trauma to the EDF's juridical argumentation in its responses to Sonabend and Spring suggests the following: The EFD's approach to the events associated with the persecution, events in which Switzerland was involved, signifies non-recognition of the involvement; beyond this, it signifies a repetition of the expulsion on both a legal and a discursive level. From this vantage, the rejection of the lawsuits demanded by the EFD can be situated within a specifically Jewish periodization as part of the 'third traumatic sequence.' In both the Sonabend and Spring cases, the legal continuity generated by the EFD's line of argument is linked to a continuity of ostracization.

That traumatic memory of events linked to the persecution does not diminish with time, but rather intensifies, and that simultaneously another traumatic sequence can begin, stands opposed to the temporal concept at the base of 'forfeiture' within the EFD's interpretation. For hovering within that temporal concept is the postulate that a clean break with the past has long-since been realized: a break that means, in the cases of Spring and Sonabend, not so much terminating a dispute as simply not allowing it in.

Through a consideration of the categories of knowledge, temporal perspectivization, and continuity, we have seen how ideas and premises concerning possible Swiss complicity with the Third Reich make their way into legal arguments. It is no coincidence that a core of official policy regarding the disputed past reveals itself in the legal arguments. What is at stake is avoiding a financially comprehensible acknowledgment of guilt.[60]

The arguments of the plaintiffs reflect an effort to formulate a legal juncture between Swiss refugee policies, Nazi *Judenpolitik*, and damages incurred by Jewish refugees. Richter and Rechsteiner are themselves requesting demarcation of a specific sort of break with the past through legal judgment. The break is symbolized by financial payment as a consequence of the legal acknowledgment of guilt: 'state liability'. The legal debate thus represents a conflict over legally valid norms. Whose claim will be taken into the law's continuum: that of the foreign Jewish refugee, or that of the EFD, itself based on a continuum within the law, antisemitic directives and Bundesrat decrees?

What would be the results of Spring and Sonabend winning their cases before the Bundesgericht? Such a victory could only mean the court's recognition of a legal and causal connection between Swiss refugee policies and Nazi *Judenpolitik*, and of the damage incurred by the refugees who were affected.[61]

What remains, however, is the striking discrepancy between an often-cited remark of Federal Councillor (and, for a time, Federal President) Kaspar Villiger offered in 1995, and the refusal in 1998 of Villiger, his ministry, and the entire Bundesrat to pay two Jewish refugees 100,000 Swiss francs each as an acknowledgment of guilt. 'I have no doubt whatsoever that through our policies toward the persecuted Jews, we have a weight of guilt on our shoulders,' declared President Villiger at the United Federal Assembly's memorial ceremonies for the fiftieth anniversary of the end of the war in Europe on 7 May 1995. He thus confirmed that the state, as an active agent, had incurred guilt. Villiger continued: 'Fear of Germany, of being overrun by foreigners through mass immigration, and of political impetus for an antisemitism that also existed here at home often carried more weight . . . than our humanitarian ideals.'[62]

These remarks define the expulsions as a reaction to a German threat and as a preventive measure in face of antisemitism. They are a denial of independent, intentionally culpable action. Villiger's talk thus speaks of guilt while not recognizing its incurrence. This denial is to be found again in the arguments of his ministry, the EFD. A discrepancy thus emerges between an abstract acknowledgment of guilt and a non-acknowledgment of guilty action when concrete cases are at issue.

Even if the Bundesgericht ends up finding in favour of the lawsuits filed by Sonabend and Spring, one question will consequently remain open: how the legal judgment can make its way into the political arena, locus of public debate and clashing historical perspectives. For when all is said and done, this is the locus where how (if at all) to carry forward the confrontation with guilt and debt will be decided.

On 21 January 2000, the Federal Court in Lausanne struck down Spring's claim. In essence, it followed the arguments of the Federal Ministry of Finance. The Federal Court awarded Spring 'party damages' in the amount of 100,000 Swiss francs. In May 2000, the Sonabends came to an out-of-court settlement with the Federal Ministry of Finance. The Sonabends withdrew their claim, and were awarded damages in the amount of 200,000 Swiss francs. As Daniel Eckmann, spokesman for the Federal Ministry of Finance, explained, this solution had been arrived at by following the guidelines of the Federal Court's decision of 21 January 2000. He stated expressly that the damages did not represent the recognition of a legal claim. The damages – as had been the case with the 'party damages' in Spring's case – were not to be understood as damages for the harm as formulated in the claim, but rather as damages for the costs to the claimant associated with the trial.[63]

NOTES

 1 This case has examined in detail in Stefan Mächler, 'Ein Abgrund zwischen zwei Welten. Zwei Rückweisungen jüdischer Flüchtlinge im Jahre 1942', *Zeitschrift des Schweizerischen Bundesarchivs. Studien und Quellen* 22 (Bern 1996): 137–232, here: 140–164. Cf. Mächler's and Kaspar Kasics's 1999 documentary film on Sonabend, entitled *Closed Country*.

 2 Schweizerisches Bundesarchiv Bern (BAR), E 6351 (F) 1, 251/58 (1942), EJPD (Rothmund), 13 August 1942, vertrauliches Kreisschreiben Nr. 296 an die Polizeidirektionen der Kantone und an die kantonalen Polizeikommandos ('Eindämmung des Zustroms ausländischer Zivil-und Militärflüch-

tlinge'). On the genesis of this circular see Guido Koller, 'Entscheidung über Leben und Tod. Die behördliche Praxis in der Schweizerischen Flüchtlingspolitik während des Zweiten Weltkrieges', in: *Zeitschrift des Schweizerischen Bundesarchivs. Studien und Quellen*, 22, Bern 1996, 17–106, here: 30–38. Independent Commission of Experts, *Switzerland – Second World War, Switzerland and Refugees in the Nazi Era* (Bern, 1999), 85–99.

3 ('Le passage de la frontière s'est effectué dans de bonnes conditions.') BAR, E 4264 1985/196, Bd. 193, N 3757. Choffat to Mr. le Commandant de la Police cantonal, Porrentruy, 18. Aug. 1942. Cf. Mächler, 161f. Independent Commission 85 – 99.

4 At the time Joseph Spring was named Joseph Sprung. His story has been detailed in Stefan Keller, 'Was wird der Bundesrat diesmal sagen?', *Wochen Zeitung* 11, 12 February 1998, 5 as well as Stefan Keller, 'Ein Glück, trotz Schweiz zu leben', *Wochen Zeitung* 15, 9 April 1998, 26f.

5 'Weisungen über die Rückweisung oder Aufnahme illegal einreisender Ausländer', in *Documents Diplomatiques Suisses* (DDS), préparé par Antoine Fleury, Mauro Cerutti, Marc Perrenoud, vol.14, (Bern: Benteli, 1997), pp.952–954, here: 952. Cf. Koller, 36f. Independent Commission, 85–99.

6 The Sonabend case was near the hearing stage when, in March 1999, it was adjourned by the Bundesgericht at the EFD's request until November 1999. The reason given was the settlement that had been arrived at between the major Swiss banks United Bank of Switzerland and Credit Suisse Group, the World Jewish Restitution Organisation, and the lawyers in the 'dormant accounts' case. Charles Sonabend is one of the class-action plaintiffs – which in any event has nothing to do with his and his family's expulsion. In the Spring case, the Bundesgericht rejected the EFD request to adjourn the proceedings, since Spring was not a participant in any class-action suit.

7 Charles Sonabend is represented by Marc Richter, Joseph Spring by Paul Rechsteiner. Both lawyers, as well as Stefan Keller, have generously offered me access to the relevant files.

8 BAR, 4800 (A) 1967/111 Dossier 412. Robert Jetzler: 'Bericht der Polizeiabteilung zum Flüchtlingsproblem vom 30. Juli 1942', 14. The report is classified as 'strictly confidential'.

9 According to art. 6, par. 1 of the 'law of responsibility', the damaged party can be offered a sum of money as 'compensation.'

10 Clea Laage, 'Die Auseinandersetzung um den Begriff des gesetzlichen Unrechts nach 1945', *Kritische Justiz* 22 (1989): 409–432; Norbert Frei, *Vergangenheitspolitik. Die Anfänge der Bundesrepublik und die NS-Vergangenheit*, (Munich: Beck, 1996), pp.154f.

11 Gustav Radbruch 'Gesetzliches Unrecht und übergesetzliches Recht', *Süddeutsche Juristen Zeitung* (1946): 107, reprinted in his *Gesamtausgabe*, vol.3, *Rechtsphilosophie III*, ed. Arthur Kaufmann (Heidelberg: Muller, 1990), pp.83–93, here 89.

12 On the connection between ethics, universalism, and particularism see Raphael Gross and Werner Konitzer, 'Geschichte und Ethik. Zum Fortwirken der nationalsozialistischen Moral', *Mittelweg. Zeitschrift des Hamburger Instituts für Sozialforschung*, 4 (1999), 44–67. On the relation between 'super-legal' law and natural law in Radbruch cf. Laage, as well as Arthur Kaufmann, 'Die Radbruchsche Formel vom gesetzlichen Unrecht und vom übergesetzlichen Recht in der Diskussion um das im Namen der DDR begangene Unrecht', *Neue Juristische Wochenschrift* 2 (1995): 81–86.

13 Marc Richter: *Klage in Sachen Charles Sonabend gegen Schweizerische Eidgnossenschaft*, Zürich, 6 March 1998, 16, 19f.

14 *ibid.*, 24f.

15 Marc Richter, *Replik für Charles Sonabend gegen Schweizerische Eidgenossenschaft*, Zurich, 14 August 1998, 15. Cf. Paul Rechsteiner, *Klage für Joseph Spring gegen Schweizerische Eidgnossenschaft*, St. Gallen 13 July 1998, 16f.

16 Rechsteiner, *Klage*, 10–12, 15–17. Legally and historically, the directive can be placed in the broader context of the Swiss law on the 'residence and settlement of foreigners' of 16 March 1931, Bundesratdecrees of 17 October 1939 and 4 August 1942, and the circular of 13 August 1942. See Uriel Gast, *Von der Kontrolle zur Abwehr. Die Eidgenössische Fremdenpolizei im Spannungsfeld von Politik und Wirtschaft 1915–1933* (Zurich: Chronos, 1997); Koller, *Entscheidung*; and Jacques Picard, *Die Schweiz und die Juden 1933–1945. Schweizerischer Antisemitismus, jüdische Abwehr und internationale Migrationsund Flüchtlingspolitik* (Zurich: Chronos, 1994).

17 Rechsteiner, *Klage*, 25–27, 29. See also Richter, *Klage*, 22. Richter argues that in the Sonabend case the constitutional right to equality before the law was violated. On the one hand, he indicates, this right applies in Switzerland not only to the Swiss but to foreigners; on the other, a directive cannot treat different foreigners differently, merely on the basis, say, of one being Jewish, the other not.

18 Rechsteiner, *Klage*, 28. See also Rechsteiner, *Replik für Joseph Spring gegen Schweizerische Eidgenossenschaft*, St. Gallen 17 December 1998, 6–9.

19 Rechsteiner, *Klage*, 21f, 24f.

20 Gaston Haas: '*Wenn man gewusst hätte, was sich drüben im Reich abspielte . . .*'. *1941–1943 Was man in der Schweiz von der Judenvernichtung wusste* (Basel: Helbing & Lichtenhahn, 1994), 99f.

21 Jetzler, 14. Jetzler writes that the Third Reich would 'direct the most grave suspicion of activities dangerous to the state' against fleeing Jews. Ibid.

22 Rechsteiner, *Klage*, 10.

23 Rechsteiner, *Klage*, 25–27, 29.

24 EFD, *Klageantwort für die Schweizerische Eidgenossenschaft gegen Charles Sonabend*, Bern 26 Mai 1998, 2. The corresponding formulation to point 2 in the Spring case is as follows: 'Additional proceedings are to be limited to the question of the punctuality of the claim-presentation (forfeiture).' EFD, *Klageantwort für die Schweizerische Eidgenossenschaft gegen Joseph Spring*, Bern 15 October 1998, 2.

25 EFD *Klageantwort Sonabend*, 8–10, 15. EFD, *Klageantwort Spring*, 15f. Cited from: EFD, *Klageantwort Sonabend*, 9. EFD, *Klageantwort Spring*, 11.

26 EFD, *Klageantwort Sonabend*, 2. EFD *Klageantwort Spring*, 2.

27 EFD, *Klageantwort Sonabend*, 29. EFD, *Klageantwort Spring*, 30.

28 *ibid.* I cannot here examine at length the EFD argument that present international law cannot be applied retroactively. Any such discussion would need to take account of the following: The EFD cites the legal principle of nulla poena sine lege, no punishment without a law. But this principle is narrowly tied to liberal bourgeois engagement on behalf of the legal state; its purpose is to protect the individual citizen against arbitrary exercise of state power. The question thus arises of whether in the context of Nazism this purpose is not rendered into its precise opposite when the principle is used to impede prosecution of arbitrary state power such as crimes against humanity. Cf. Laage, 426–429.

29 EFD, *Klageantwort Sonabend*, 18. EFD, *Klageantwort Spring*, 26f. See also the legal opinion produced by the Swiss Directorate for International Law for the EFD. Direction du droit international public (M.Krafft): Action en responsabilité de la Confédération. Joseph Spring c. Confédération Suisse, Bern 1998, 8. The response makes the additional point that since 1945, the legal definition of genocide and crimes against humanity has varied. *Ibid.*, as well as Direction 5–8.

30 EFD, *Klageantwort Spring*, 29.

31 EFD, *Klageantwort Spring*, 28f. Cit. from *ibid.*, 28.

32 To be sure, as the EFD explains the law upon which the complaint and response are based was only passed in 1959. And according to the limitation statutes, the complaint would have already been 'forfeited' in 1959. Cf. EFD, *Klageantwort Sonabend*, 13f. EFD, *Klageantwort Spring*, 10.

33 EFD, *Klageantwort Spring*, 5f. Cit. from: *ibid.*, 6.

34 EFD, *Klageantwort Spring*, 28f.

35 Diemut *Majer Grundlagen des nationalsozialistischen Rechtssystems. Führerprinzip, Sonderrecht, Einheitspartei*, Stuttgart 1987, 121–131, 156–182. On the progressive nature of the development see Saul Friedländer, *Nazi Germany and the Jews*, vol.I: *The Years of Persecution, 1933–1939* (New York: HarperCollins, 1997); Diemut Majer: 'Fremdvölkische' im Dritten Reich. Ein Beitrag zur nationalsozialistischen Rechtssetzung und Rechtspraxis' in *Verwaltung und Justiz unter besonderer Berücksichtigung der eingegliederten Ostgebiete und des Generalgouvernements*, (Boppard: Kohlhammer, 1981). Bernd Rüthers, *Die unbegrenzte Auslegung. Zum Wandel der Privatrechtsordnung im Nationalsozialismus* (Tübingen: Muller, 1968). Michael Stolleis, *Recht im Unrecht. Studien zur Rechtsgeschichte des Nationalsozialismus* (Frankfurt a.M.: Suhrkamp, 1994), 7–35. See also Ulrich Herbert, *Best. Biographische Studien über Radikalismus, Weltanschauung und Vernunft 1903–1989* (Bonn: Dietz, 1996), 170–180.

36 Norbert Frei, *Der Führerstaat. Nationalsozialistische Herrschaft 1933–1945* (Munich: DTV, 1989), 59. Majer, *Grundlagen*, 185–187. Cf. Dirk Blasius, 'Zwischen Rechtsvertrauen und Rechtszerstörung.

Deutsche Juden 1933–1935', Dirk Blasius and Dan Diner (eds.): *Zerbrochene Geschichte. Leben und Selbstverständnis der Juden in Deutschland* (Frankfurt a.M.: Fischer, 1991), 121–137.

37 Laage, 413.

38 Majer, *Grundlagen*, 121–131, 149, 156–182. Frei, *Führerstaat*, 59.

39 Laage, 414–416. Adalbert Rückerl: NS-Verbrechen vor Gericht. Versuch einer Vergangenheitsbewältigung, Heidelberg 1982, 107f. See also Michael Stolleis, 'Rechtsordnung und Justizpolitik 1945–1949', in Norbert Horn (ed.), *Europäisches Rechtsdenken in Geschichte und Gegenwart. Festschrift für Helmut Coing zum 70. Geburtstag*, vol.I (Munich: Beck, 1982), 383–407.

40 EFD, *Klageantwort Spring*, 5f.

41 Let us in any case note that Stefan Keller has established the dubious nature of the EFD's witness-testimony and the accuracy of Spring's memory. Stefan Keller, 'Wer ist den hier vergesslich? Joseph Spring und das eidg. Finanzdepartement', *WochenZeitung*, 24 December 1998, 3f.

42 EFD, *Klageantwort Sonabend*, 18. EFD, *Klageantwort Spring*, 26f.

43 Cf. Norbert Frei and Hermann Kling (eds.), *Der nationalsozialistische Krieg* (Frankfurt a.M.: Campus, 1990). Götz Aly, 'Endlösung', *Völkerverschiebung und der Mord an den europäischen Juden* (Frankfurt a.M.: Fischer, 1995). Christopher R. Browning: *Der Weg zur 'Endlösung'. Entscheidungen und Täter* (Bonn: Dietz, 1998). Ulrich Herbert: 'Vernichtungspolitik. Neue Antworten und Fragen zur Geschichte des "Holocaust"', in Ulrich Herbert (ed.) *Nationalsozialistische Vernichtungspolitik 1939–1945. Neue Forschungen und Kontroversen*, (Frankfurt a.M.: Fischer, 1998), 9–66. Friedländer, *Nazi Germany and the Jews*. See also Dan Diner, *Das Jahrhundert verstehen. Eine universalhistorische Deutung* (Munich: Luchterhand, 1999), 209–227.

44 Heinz Artzt, 'Zur Abgrenzung von Kriegsverbrechen und NS-Verbrechen', in Adalbert Rückerl (ed.), *NS-Prozesse. Nach 25 Jahren Strafverfolgung: Möglichkeiten-Grenzen-Ergebnisse*, (Karlsruhe: Muller, 1971), 163–194, here: 185.

45 *ibid.*, 190.

46 Ibid, 178f. See also Herbert Jäger: Verbrechen unter totalitärer Herrschaft. Studien zur nationalsozialistischen Gewaltkriminalität, Olten and Freiburg i.Br. 1967, 352–368; and Eric David: Principes de droit des conflits armés, Bruxelles 1994, 603–606.

47 On the theoretical and practical evolution of the notion of 'crimes against humanity' in connection with the Nuremberg Trials see Gerd Hankel and Gerhard Stuby (eds.): Strafgerichte gegen Menschheitsverbrechen. Zum Völkerstrafrecht 50 Jahre nach den Nürnberger Prozessen, Hamburg 1995. M. Cherif Bassiouni: Crimes against Humanity in International Criminal Law, Dordrecht, Boston, London 1992.

48 The concept also stamps the historical perception of other countries – to be sure with different premises. See, for instance, the exploration of the presumptions and substantive consequences of this periodization in English historiography in Dan Diner's 'Ereignis und Erinnerung. Über Variationen historischen Gedächtnisses', in: Nicolas Berg, Jess Jochimsen, and Bernd Stiegler (eds.): *Shoah. Formen der Erinnerung*. Geschichte, Philosophie, Literatur, Kunst (Munich 1996), 13–30.

49 Georg Kreis and Bertrand Müller (eds.), *Die Schweiz und der Zweite Weltkrieg* (Basel: Schwabe, 1997).

50 Also worth noting: publication by the Federal Office for Cultural Affairs of a bibliography on the same theme entitled *The Role of Switzerland in World War II*, and the Swiss Federal Archive's overview of the relevant scholarly research entitled *Switzerland and World War II*. Bundesamt für Kultur: Die Rolle der Schweiz im Zweiten Weltkrieg. Auswahlbibliographie, Bern 1997; Schweizerisches Bundesarchiv: Die Schweiz und der Zweite Weltkrieg: Forschungsstand und offene Fragen. Bericht für die Bundesverwaltung, Bern 1997.

51 On 1995 as the controversy's starting-point, see Thomas Maissen 'Die Schweiz und die nationalsozialistische Hinterlassenschaft. Anlass, Phasen und Analyse einer neu entflammten Debatte', in: Kenneth Angst (ed.), *Der Zweite Weltkrieg und die Schweiz. Reden und Analysen* (Zürich: NZZ, 1997), 119–142, esp.131.

52 See Jacques Picard, 'Die Schweiz und die Vermögen verschwundener Nazi-Opfer. Die Vermögen rassisch, religiös und politisch Verfolgter in der Schweiz und ihre Ablösung von 1946–1973', in *Zeitschrift des Schweizerischen Bundesarchivs. Studien und Quellen*, 22 (Bern 1996), 271–324. Peter Hug,

'Das Verschwindenmachen der nachrichtenlosen Guthaben in der Schweiz', in Philipp Sarasin and Regina Wecker (eds.), *Raubgold, Reduit, Flüchtlinge. Zur Geschichte der Schweiz im Zweiten Weltkrieg* (Zürich: Chronos, 1998), 13–31.

53 For a critique of this periodization see Daniel Wildmann, 'Wo liegt Auschwitz? Geographie, Geschichte und Neutralität', in *Völkermord und Verdrängung. Der Genozid an den Armeniern – Die Schweiz und die Shoah*, ed. Arbeitskreis Armenien (Zurich: Chronos, 1998), 163–168. The subject is not addressed in the most recent overviews of the debate in Swiss scholarship, politics and the public sector. Cf. Georg Kreis: 'Vier Debatten und wenig Dissens', in Georg Kreis and Bertrand Müller (eds.), *Die Schweiz und der Zweite Weltkrieg* (Basel: Schwabe, 1997), 451–476; Hans Ulrich Jost, *Politik und Wirtschaft im Krieg. Die Schweiz 1938–1948* (Zurich: Chronos, 1998), 213–230.

54 Luc van Dongen, *La Suisse face à la Seconde Guerre Mondial. 1945–1948. Emergence et construction d'une mémoire publique* (Geneva, 1998). Van Dongen himself does not question 1939 as the starting point for a valid periodization.

55 On the origins of this linkage see Andreas Suter, 'Neutralität. Prinzip, Praxis und Geschichtsbewusstsein', in Manfred Hettling, Mario König et. al., *Eine kleine Geschichte der Schweiz. Der Bundesstaat und seine Traditionen* (Frankfurt a.M.: Suhrkamp, 1998), 133–188, here: 134–140 und 163–170. Borrowing from Eric Hobsbawn and Terence Ranger, Suter refers to an 'invention of tradition'.

56 See e.g. Georg Kreis: Die schweizerische Neutralität während des Zweiten Weltkrieges in der historischen Forschung, in: Louis-Eduard Roulet (ed., with the collaboration of Roland Blättler), *Les états neutres européens et la seconde guerre mondiale* (Neuchâtel: Baconnière, 1985), 29–53.

57 Wildmann, Auschwitz, 167.

58 Richter, Replik, 13.

59 Hans Keilson (with the collaboration of Herman R. Sarphatie), *Sequentielle Traumatisierung bei Kindern. Deskriptiv-klinische und quantifizierend-statistische follow-up Untersuchung zum Schicksal der jüdischen Kriegswaisen in den Niederlanden* (Stuttgart: Enke, 1979), 69–71, 430.

60 This policy-core also emerges in the debate concerning the 'Solidarity Fund'. The crux of the debate is less the question of financing the trust as that of whether and – if so – how it is to be linked to the past in a Swiss law. See *Bericht über die Ergebnisse der Vernehmlassung zum Entwurf eines Bundesgesetzes über die Stiftung solidarische Schweiz* (Bern: EFD, 1998). On the origins of the Trust see Maissen, 134–136.

61 The possible implications of such a decision for present-day Swiss refugee-policy cannot be discussed in these pages.

62 Kaspar Villiger, 'Auch die Schweiz hat Schuld auf sich geladen. 50 Jahre danach – Dankbarkeit, Respekt, Nachdenklichkeit' ['Even Switzerland has Incurred Guilt. Fifty Years Later – Appreciation, Respect, Reflection'], in: Kenneth Angst (ed.), *Der Zweite Weltkrieg und die Schweiz. Reden und Analysen* (Zürich: NZZ, 1997), 15–22, here: 19. This collection was published by the press of the *Neue Zürcher Zeitung*. When the talk was first published in that newspaper in 1995, its title was '50 Jahre Frieden' ('Fifty Years of Peace'): *Neue Zürcher Zeitung*, nr.105, 8 May 1995, 17.

63 Markus Felber, 'Keine Genugtuung für Joseph Spring', *Neue Zürcher Zeitung* no.18, 22/23 January 2000, 15. Daniel Suter, 'Bund entschädigt die Geschwister Sonabend', *Tages Anzeiger* no. 117, 20 May 2000, 8. Urteil des Schweizerischen Bundesgerichts 2A.373/1998, 21 January 2000.

THE RETURN OF NAZI-LOOTED ART:
CHOICE OF LAW ISSUES

Geri J. Yonover

I N T H E late 1990s extraordinary attention, too long delayed, has been given to the return to Holocaust survivors and/or their descendants of art works that were taken from them during the Holocaust years. Other owners, under duress from Nazi persecution, simply fled and were unable to bring along their art collections. While sporadic attempts were made in the years following World War II to regain ownership of some of this art,[1] with varying results, these efforts took place in relative isolation. Today, in contrast, a week seldom passes when a newspaper somewhere in the world does not report stories of families who seek to recover Nazi-looted art or who seek to be compensated by various governments such as Switzerland, Germany and Austria for Holocaust-related injuries[2].

In late 1998, the State Department and the United States Holocaust Museum sponsored a four-day conference on Holocaust-Era Assets, drawing delegates from 45 nations with considerable attendant publicity. The conference adopted eleven non-binding principles concerning Nazi-confiscated art.[3] In the summer of 1998, the American Association of Museums issued a report by its task force on the 'Spoilation of Art during the Nazi/World War II Era'. The report contained a statement of principles and guidelines to assist museums in resolving claims.[4] Austria agreed to return 250 Nazi-taken art objects to the Rothschild family, including three paintings by Franz Hals; this announcement followed the passage of a 1998 law which furnishes the basis for such return.[5] The head of France's State Museum network recently announced that a 1914 cubist painting by Fernand Léger, worth around $2 million, which had been exhibited at the Georges Pompidou Centre, in fact belonged to a family whose ancestor had fled France when the Nazis invaded.[6] Additionally, there are many web pages devoted to the field of World War II/Holocaust art restitution, including a site posted by the Commission for Art Recovery in affiliation with the World Jewish Congress.[7]

It is not clear what triggered this long overdue attention. In the years following World War II there were a number of international efforts, including the 1970 UNESCO Convention on the Means of Prohibiting and Preventing the Illicit Import, Export and Transfer of Ownership of Cultural Property, implemented by the United States in 1983.[8] But it has taken more than fifty years for these efforts to reach critical mass. The opening and subsequent substantial attendance figures of the Holocaust Museum in Washington, D.C., the events surrounding the fiftieth anniversary of the end of World War II, and perhaps even the phenomenal worldwide success of Spielberg's *Schindler's List* and his ongoing Shoah projects may have helped pave the way.[9]

A recent case, *Goodman v. Searle*, involving the heirs of a Holocaust family, a Degas landscape, the Chicago Art Institute and a scion of the G.D. Searle Company, who is also a current trustee of the Art Institute, illustrates the complicated web surrounding art ownership disputes.[10] The following discussion will focus on the background of the *Goodman v. Searle* lawsuit and its resolution – a resolution praised as a 'model' by Stuart Eisenstat, State Department Under Secretary for Economic and Business Affairs, at the December 1998 Holocaust Conference in Washington.[11] At one point the parties had reached an agreement to settle the dispute. The settlement provided that Searle would give a fifty percent share of the pastel to the Gutmann heirs; he would then donate the remaining half to the Art Institute. The Museum, in turn, would pay the Holocaust heirs for their half of the Degas. However, disputes over the value of the painting initially placed the settlement in jeopardy,[12] illustrating the difficult legal, economic and human costs involved in resolving the disposition of the 'last prisoners of war' – a term used to describe Nazi-looted art objects.[13] Friedrich Gutmann's (Goodman) grandsons have also tried to recover a Renoir and a Botticelli, two paintings out of fourteen missing from a significant collection of old masters and impressionists. The Botticelli, the subject of a Sotheby's sale, was returned after a meeting between the seller and the Goodmans. The Renoir is being stored in London by its current owner and its return is disputed.[14]

The delicate balancing required to assess the interests of (1) the Nazi-era survivors and heirs, (2) the current owners who may not have been aware of the actual provenance of the art work at the time of purchase, (3) a Museum's interest in keeping its collection intact, and (4) the public interest in access to certain art works is a daunting task. The task becomes even more complicated when the applicable law may be in dispute. Complex choice of law issues inevitably arise in cases involving the return of Nazi-looted art because the law of two or more jurisdictions could apply. This paper concludes with the hope that the tentative resolution initially achieved in the *Goodman v. Searle* dispute will prevail and that the case will serve as a benchmark for resolution of similar disputes, wherever they may arise. *Vita brevis est, ars longa.*

The return of Nazi-looted art to rightful owners or their heirs has a certain urgency: those who survived the Holocaust are elderly. Further, artistic property, while classified as personal, rather than real property, has particular qualities which other personal property, such as a car, a piece of furniture, or clothing, or real property, land, does not.[15] A painting or sculpture reflects the personality of its author;[16] as John Ruskin noted, 'all great art is the work of the whole living creature, body and soul, and chiefly of the soul.'[17] Additionally, the owner too shares a special bond with the art work. Art speaks to us, the viewer or owner, in special, intimate ways. Thus, in addition to a sense of urgency surrounding the problem of Nazi-looted art, there is a poignancy about the cultural atrocity which shapes our current attitudes toward the return of such art.

I. 'THE DISMAL SWAMP': CHOICE OF LAW

Virtually every case about the return of Nazi-looted art will involve intricate choice of law issues; that is, a judge will have to decide the law applicable to several disputes which are common to art recovery cases. These include issues of statutes of limitation (has too much time elapsed so that plaintiff's suit is barred);[18] acquiring good title to stolen goods (does the art belong to the current owner, who may have obtained it in good faith or to the original owner from whom the art was taken or by whom it was abandoned when the owner fled the Nazi invasion); and, most important perhaps, whether United States law or the civil law of Germany or some other European country applies. Even if the court decides that United States law does indeed apply, the court may then have to determine which state's law governs the disputed issue of ownership. In short, art recovery cases are not easy to resolve, nor is their resolution predictable and uniform. Dean William Prosser may well have been prescient when he declared: 'The realm of conflict of laws is a dismal swamp, filled with quaking quagmires, and inhabited by learned but eccentric professors who theorize about mysterious matters in a strange and incomprehensible jargon. The ordinary court, or lawyer is quite lost when engulfed and entangled in it.'[19]

As the discussion of the complex choice of law issues in art recovery cases will show, the best result, obtained in the shortest amount of time and with the least cost to the litigants, is the type finally achieved (although with some difficulty) by the Goodman and Searle parties' settlement. However, if an art recovery case with multistate or multi-national connections does proceed to trial, choice of law questions inevitably arise. The next sections will explore three areas of potential conflict of laws problems: (1) whether United States or European law apply; (2) which state's law of the United States will govern if the judge finds United States law to be applicable; and (3) whether laws governing title and statutes of limitations, common issues in art recovery disputes, may differ among the states. The discussion will focus on the impact of these choice of law problems on art recovery cases such as *Goodman v. Searle*.

A. UNITED STATES OR EUROPEAN LAW

1. *The Act of State Doctrine.*   In an *ordinary* United States conflict of laws case (this might well be oxymoronic) a court may be free to choose or apply the law of one or another jurisdiction that is connected to the parties and the facts of the case.[20] But when a case has international connections, a court may confront the Act of State Doctrine. This doctrine is implicated when a foreign sovereign government confiscates property and can in certain circumstances preclude legislative jurisdiction in a United States court; that is, the court cannot apply United States law to resolve the disputed issues involving that property.[21] Application of United States law is precluded if: (1) the United States recognizes the foreign government at the time of the suit; and (2) the foreign sovereign has taken the disputed property within its own territorial boundaries.[22]

Menzel v. List, one of the earliest cases dealing with the return of Nazi-looted art, presented an Act of State issue. In 1941 the Menzels had left a Marc Chagall painting in their Brussels apartment which they were unable to take with them as they fled the Nazi onslaught. The Einsatzstab Reichsleiter Rosenberg soon seized the painting, treating it as 'decadent Jewish art'.[23] This painting was just one of the vast numbers taken by the Nazis. As Lynn Nicholas notes, 'Never had works of art been so important to a political movement and never had they been moved about on such a vast scale, pawns in the cynical and desperate game of ideology, greed, and survival.'[24]

After settling in the United States, the Menzels searched for the painting but were unable to locate it until 1962, when they discovered that Albert A. List, a well-known art collector, had purchased the Chagall from a gallery. When Menzel asked List to return the painting, List refused and Menzel sued to recover the painting or to be compensated for its value.[25]

One of the defences raised was based on the Act of State Doctrine: that the New York court should not apply its law, but rather must defer to the law of Nazi Germany under which 'law' the initial confiscation was legal. Since this was so, the defendant argued, then anyone purchasing through that chain, whether the gallery or List, could obtain good title to the Chagall. However, the New York court rejected the Act of State defence. The doctrine was inapplicable because (1) the Einsatzstab Rosenberg seizure was done under the aegis of the Nazi party, not a foreign sovereign government; (2) the painting was confiscated in Brussels, outside Germany's territorial limits; (3) the Third

Reich no longer existed at the time of suit; and (4) the taking violated the Hague Convention of 1907,[26] to which the United States was a signatory. Thus, the court concluded that under New York law Menzel could recover the Chagall or its value.[27] Had the court held the Act of State Doctrine to be applicable the Menzels would not have been able to prove the illegality of the confiscation.[28]

2. *Choosing United States or Foreign Law.* In art restitution cases, as in other cases involving choice of law issues, the difference between winning and losing often depends on the law determined to be applicable. To resolve a dispute between the original owner and an alleged good-faith purchaser of stolen or looted art, much depends on whether the court chooses to apply United States law or the civil law of a European country. Under United States common law, a thief or an illegal taker cannot acquire good title to personal property; thus whoever purchases art via the chain of title that flows from the original illegal taker cannot obtain good title.[29] In contrast, European civil law generally allows a good faith purchaser, even though he or she traces title through the thief, to obtain good title, even against the rightful owner.[30] For example, in Switzerland, a good faith purchaser acquires title superior to the owner after five years from the theft. In France the period is a mere three years and in Italy a good faith purchaser obtains good title, superior to the owner, immediately.[31]

A 1981 New York case addresses the good title issue. In *Kunstsammlungen Zu Weimar v. Elicofon*[32] the Federal Republic of Germany sought return of two Albrecht Dürer paintings which a German museum had safeguarded in Schwarzberg Castle in 1943. When American forces occupied the castle in 1945, the paintings disappeared and were reported stolen by the museum director. In 1946 Edward Elicofon purchased the paintings in New York from a returning American soldier.

In seeking to retain possession of the Dürers, Elicofon claimed that since the transfer of the painting occurred in Germany, German law applied and thus, as a good faith purchaser (even if from a thief), he should prevail. The court rejected the argument holding that since the transfer to Elicofon occurred in New York, New York choice of law governs questions concerning the validity of transfers of personal property. New York choice of law pointed to New York law under which a thief neither acquires nor can transfer good title to a good faith purchaser.[33]

As *Elicofon* shows, if a court, through application of choice of law principles, chooses to apply the law of Germany (or Switzerland, France or Italy) to a title to art dispute, the original owner may not prevail. However, since the *Elicofon* court viewed the unlawful transfer as having taken place in New York, rather than in Germany as the defendant had urged, New York choice of law led to application of New York law and the return of the Dürers to the Federal Republic of Germany.[34]

B. WHICH STATE'S LAW APPLIES

Even if a court decides that the law of the United States applies,[35] or tacitly so assumes, there may remain issues as to which state's law is to be applied. *Goodman v. Searle* raises such a problem, even though neither the New York federal court nor the Illinois federal court had occasion to consider it.

1. *Transfer and its Effect on Choice of Law.* Defendant Searle's first response to the Goodmans' New York complaint was to move to transfer the case to the Northern District of Illinois, which motion the New York court granted by a Consent Order.[36] However, the New York court did not make clear the basis upon which transfer was granted. Section 1404(a) of the Federal Rules of Civil Procedure permits a federal court

to transfer a case to another federal district if it can be justified in terms of 'convenience of parties and witnesses, and in the interest of justice'.[37] Alternatively, section 1406 allows a court to dismiss or transfer a case brought in an improper venue to another district that has proper jurisdiction.[38] Whether a plaintiff or defendant seeks 1404(a) transfer, the law to be applied is that of the transferor forum (or, more accurately, the law to which the transferor forum choice of law would point).[39] In *Goodman v. Searle* the transferor forum is New York. If, however, the transfer to Illinois was based on section 1406(a) – improper venue in New York – then it is generally held that the transferee forum law applies (or any law that the transferee forum – here Illinois – thinks applicable).[40] Thus, a section 1406(a) transfer would require the transferee federal court – Illinois – to use Illinois choice of law, which may point to Illinois rather than to New York law.

2. *Differing Laws.*   Though both New York and Illinois law typify the general rule in the United States that a thief cannot obtain or convey good title, there are some differences which could be significant enough to affect the outcome of the case; for example, New York treats its demand rule as substantive, while Illinois' discovery rule is tied to the running of its statute of limitations and is treated as procedural.[41]

Since *Menzel v. List*, New York has adhered to the demand and refusal rule there articulated. Under this rule an original owner's cause of action for recovery of property does not accrue for statute of limitations purposes until that owner demands that the possessor return the property and the possessor refuses to do so.[42] New York has recently reaffirmed this position in *Solomon R. Guggenheim Foundation v. Lubell* and noted that the 'demand and refusal' rule does not require a showing of reasonable diligence to defeat a statute of limitations problem.[43]

In contrast, several other states voice concerns about an owner who might have 'sle[pt] on his rights'.[44] Under this approach the statute of limitations clock starts to tick only when the rightful owner knows 'or reasonably should have known of his cause of action and the identity of the possessor of the chattels'.[45] For example, the Illinois federal appellate court adopted a similar analysis in examining whether the Republic of Cyprus and the Church of Cyprus had satisfied the due diligence requirement of the discovery rule in their search for stolen mosaics.[46] California, Illinois, Indiana, New Jersey, Ohio and Oklahoma are among the states which apply a discovery/due diligence approach in dealing with the statute of limitations problem.[47] Although at one time the Second Circuit thought New York law required due diligence,[48] subsequent New York state court decisions have rejected that interpretation of New York law.[49]

Without getting bogged down into the intricacies of the complicated choice of law analyses that might have been required in the *Goodman* case if the settlement had not been achieved, it should be clear to the reader that it is never a simple matter for a court to choose applicable law, especially where a transfer has been effected.

However, even if the case had remained in New York federal court or was filed in and remained in an Illinois federal court, complex choice of law decisions are still implicated and outcomes may differ depending on which law the court finds applicable.[50] First, Illinois and New York have adopted different choice of law approaches. New York's choice of law approach is a somewhat murky amalgam of 'interest analysis'[51] and fixed rules[52] based on the doctrine of *lex locus delictus* (place of wrong or injury).[53] Illinois, on the other hand, adheres to the Second Restatement,[54] under which the law to be applied is the law of the place with the most significant relation to the case.[55] While it is certainly possible that the outcome of a case may not vary depending on the choice of law method employed by the court, certainty of outcome is reduced. Experience even within the same jurisdiction suggests that modern choice of methods have sufficient room for manoeuvre to make predictions of outcomes somewhat foolhardy when conflicting laws are present.[56]

For example, should Illinois choice of law lead to the application of the Illinois due diligence approach, defendant Searle might have argued that the Goodmans failed to meet this requirement. Searle bought the Degas in 1987, some nine years before the Goodmans filed their complaint in New York.[57] Emile Wolf, who owned the Degas prior to Searle, had purchased it from Hans Fankhauser, a Swiss art dealer, in 1951 and had exhibited the painting in 1965 at Finch College, New York and in 1968 at the Fogg Museum, Boston. Thus, it is possible that Searle would argue that Wolf's exhibitions in 1965 and 1968 should have led the Goodmans, if they had acted with due diligence, to discover their missing Degas. Building on this, Searle might claim that the long delay in filing the complaint is unreasonable and prejudicial because he may not be able to recover against the prior purchaser should he be liable to the Goodmans.

In contrast, if either Illinois choice of law or New York choice of law points to New York's law – no due diligence required/demand and refusal approach – then the Goodmans are timely. They demanded the return of the painting in December 1995, which demand Searle refused, and filed their complaint in July 1996.

In any event, the litigation finally has ended. Settlement has been reached even though the case, according to the Goodmans, almost depleted their funds. They say that if the then current appraisals of the work stand their one-half share (per the initial failed settlement) would put them $100,000 in out-of-pocket expenses.[58]

Given the choice of law complexities of private art-recovery cases and their attendant cost, it may well be that judicial resolution of claims such as the Goodmans' is not the best way to proceed. The next section will describe some of the attempts of the international community, including the United States, to deal with the burgeoning problem of the return of Nazi-looted art.

II. ATTEMPTS TO FACILITATE RECOVERY OF NAZI-LOOTED ART

Several international provisions are available to assist *nations*, rather than *individuals* such as the Goodmans, in recovering their cultural property. For example, in 1970 the United Nations Educational Scientific and Cultural Organization adopted the convention on Cultural Property (UNESCO), which is intended to protect a nation's 'cultural patrimony' from 'pillage' and does so by providing import restrictions for art objects.[59] Although the United States is a member of this convention, many countries are not. That prompted the International Institute for the Unification of Private Law to prepare a new treaty, Unidroit, which extends similar protection.[60]

Like the UNESCO Convention, Unidroit focuses on the return of cultural property to a nation and permits a nation that has a law proscribing illegal excavation or the illegal keeping of found objects to bring a claim. An individual may bring a claim under Unidroit, but there is a fifty year time limit for such claims; thus, Unidroit is of no use to individuals who seek return of Nazi-looted art because more than fifty years have elapsed since World War II's end.[61]

Potentially more helpful to an individual who tries to recover art taken by the Nazis is the United States Holocaust Assets Commission Act of 1998.[62] With this Act, Congress recognized the necessity for all governments to facilitate the return of Nazi-looted artworks to the rightful owners.[63] To that end, Congress established a commission made up of twenty-one members, including representatives of the Executive and Legislative branches as well as eight qualified private citizens.[64]

The Commission, funded by up to $3,500,000 for 1998–2000, is to 'conduct a thorough study and develop a historical record of the collection and disposition' of certain assets, including works of art, should those assets have come into the possession of the federal government after 30 January 1933. Further, the Commission is empowered to review other research of assets that came into the control of individuals or other non-federal governmental entities after the same date provided that any relevant individual or entity grants permission. Finally, the Commission will issue a report to the President before 31 December 1999 with recommendations of action, be it legislative, administrative or other, that Commission members believe to be necessary.[65]

This Act clearly has the potential to help rightful owners recover their art treasures. Not only has Congress placed its imprimatur on the seriousness of the problem, but it now may be possible for private individuals to seek federal assistance in research designed to unearth the details of the whereabouts of their art, including, perhaps, research about provenance. Though but a small step and one that offers no monetary assistance to the rightful owners or heirs (as was proposed in the Holocaust Victims Redress Act by several members of the House of Representatives and a New York senator[66]), it seems likely that the Holocaust Assets Commission will have access to information which may have heretofore been unavailable to private individuals. The light of Congress will shine on the tragic and twisted tales of the dispossession of untold numbers of art works and, hopefully, will facilitate return of these Nazi-looted art works to their rightful owners or their heirs. This assistance, however, will not obviate the possibility of complex choice of law issues arising in a typical art recovery case. Nevertheless, it may aid the dispossessed owners or their heirs[67] in developing certain crucial facts, such as the provenance and location of the art, which goes a long way toward accomplishing the desired result.

The issue of Nazi-looted art has also come to the attention of state prosecutors in New York. In 1997, the Museum of Modern Art held an exhibit of three expressionist paintings by Egon Schiele on loan from the Leopold Foundation in Vienna. Just before the paintings were to be returned to Austria, the family claiming ownership of the paintings objected. Subsequently, the Manhattan District Attorney's office issued a subpoena for the Museum to surrender the paintings as part of an inquiry into whether the paintings were stolen from Jewish owners during World War II.[68] In March, a New York appellate court held that even though a New York statute exempted works of fine art owned by non-residents 'from any kind of seizure' during exhibitions, the statute was inapplicable to a subpoena issued as part of a criminal investigation.[69] The Museum appealed and on 21 September 1999, the New York Court of Appeals reversed and quashed the subpoena, holding that New York's anti-seizure statute applied.[70]

CONCLUSION

The accumulated weight of international attention, media reportage, prior United States case law,[71] the writings of legal and other scholars[72] and state and congressional recognition of the extensiveness and urgency of the problem[73] should make the task of art recovery less daunting despite labyrinthine choice of law issues. Rather than turning its back, the world is watching.

Tragically, many of the original owners may never be reunited with their art – so many were murdered in the Nazi death camps. But now that more than fifty years have passed since the end of World War II and the Nazi regime, it is time for 'the last prisoners of war' – looted art – to be returned to their rightful owners or their families whether that art is currently possessed by private individuals, museums or governments. The return of such art will not bring back the dead nor can it assuage the horror of the Holocaust. It will, however, offer a measure of justice and recognition that inaction will no longer be tolerated:

Memory is moral; what we consciously remember is what our conscience remembers.[74]

ACKNOWLEDGMENTS
The author gratefully acknowledges the fine work of her Art Law Seminar students Amy Blumberg, J.D. Valparaiso University School of Law, 1997, and Cynthia Martindale, J.D. Valparaiso University School of Law, 1999. Both Ms. Blumberg and Ms. Martindale wrote papers addressing some of the issues involved in Nazi-plundered art. I thank the team of Donna Cuckovich, Makedonka Papuckoski and Jeff Kljajich (all J.D. Valparaiso University School of Law, 2000) for their cite-checking assistance and Nancy Young for her able and enthusiastic secretarial support. I appreciate, too, the generous sharing of information by Rita McCarthy, Director of the Brauer Museum of Art, Valparaiso University.

I dedicate this article to the memory of my father, Irving Schinder, 1914–1993, who worked in the art reproduction and picture-framing field. He provided the stimulus for my life-long interest in art and issues surrounding its ownership.

NOTES
1 See, e.g., *Menzel v. List*, 267 N.Y.S. 2d 804 (1966) (holding that plaintiffs could recover a painting by Marc Chagall from the art collector-current owner which they had left in their Brussels apartment in March, 1941, just before the Nazi invasion).
2 See 'Austria to return art taken by Nazis', *Chicago Tribune*,. 12 February 1999 at 18, § 1; Regina Hackett, 'Sam sues gallery in dispute over Matisse work', *Seattle Post-Intelligencer*, 26 August 1998 at El; Jeffrey Kastner, 'Schiele case has wide-ranging impact', *Artnews*, 1 March 1998 at 61. Several authors have described meticulously 'the greatest displacement of art in history' that occurred during the Nazi era. See Lawrence M. Kaye, 'Looted Art: What can and should be done', 20 *Cardozo Law Review*. 657 (1998), citing Lynn H. Nicholas, *The Rape of Europa* (New York: Vintage Books 1995). See also Hector Feliciano, *The Lost Museum*, trans. Hector Feliciano and Tim Brent (New York: Harper Collins Publishers, Inc., 1997); another analysis of the subject scheduled for April 2000 publication is: Peter Harclerode and Brendan Pittaway, *The Lost Masters, the Looting of Europe's Treasurehouses* (London: Victor Gollancz, forthcoming). For claims against Swiss and Austrian banks, see, e.g., Henry Weinstein, 'Simon Wiesenthal to Head Holocaust Reparations Panel Victims: Famed Nazi hunter is appointed to help oversee distribution of $40 million settlement stemming from claims against two Austrian banks', *Los Angeles Times*, 5 August 1999, at A15; Elise Labott, 'German companies oppose Nazi slaves' compensation suit', *Agence France-Presse*, 12 July 1999 (1999 WL 2637079); Barry Meier, 'Swiss banks and victims of the Nazis nearing pact', *New York Times Abstracts*, 23 January 1999, at A6.
3 U.S. Department of State, Washington Conference on Holocaust-Era Assets (30 November–3 December 1998). The principles recognize the sovereignty of nations acting under their own laws and suggest:
I   Art that had been confiscated by the Nazis and not subsequently restituted should be identified.
II   Relevant records and archives should be open and accessible to researchers, in accordance with the guidelines of the International Conference on Archives.
III   Resources and personnel should be made available to facilitate the identification of all art that had been confiscated by the Nazis and not subsequently restituted.
IV   In establishing that a work of art had been confiscated by the Nazis and not subsequently restituted, consideration should be made for unavoidable gaps or ambiguities in the provenance in light of the passage of time and the circumstances of the Holocaust era.
V   Every effort should be made to publicize art that is found to have been confiscated by the Nazis and not subsequently restituted in order to locate its pre-War owners or their heirs.
VI   Efforts should be made to establish a central registry of such information.

VII Pre-War owners and their heirs should be encouraged to come forward and make known their claims to art that was confiscated by the Nazis and not subsequently restituted.

VIII If the pre-War owners of art that is found to have been confiscated by the Nazis and not subsequently restituted, or their heirs, can be identified, steps should be taken expeditiously to achieve a just and fair solution, recognizing this may vary according to the facts and circumstances surrounding a specific case.

IX If the pre-War owners of art that is found to have been confiscated by the Nazis, or their heirs, can not be identified, steps should be taken expeditiously to achieve a just and fair solution.

X Commissions or other bodies established to identify art that was confiscated by the Nazis and to assist in addressing ownership issues should have a balanced membership.

XI Nations are encouraged to develop national processes to implement these principles, particularly as they relate to alternative dispute resolution mechanisms for resolving ownership.

See: *www.state.gov/www*regions/eur/981203_heac_art_princ.html.

Responding, perhaps, to the Goodman claim, as well as one made by another Holocaust heir seeking recovery of a Gustave Courbet in its collection, the Art Institute of Chicago became the first major United States museum to publish a list of art works in its collection with questionable ownership during the Nazi years. See Kirsten Scharnwerg, 'Art Institute takes initiative on works looted in Nazi era', *Chicago Tribune*, 10 March 2000, at 1.

4 The Report of the AAMD Task Force on the Spoliation of Art during the Nazi/World War II Era (1933–1945) can be found at www.aamd.org/guideln.shtml. The report consists of a statement of five principles and seven guidelines with respect to research regarding existing collections, future gifts, bequests and purchases, access to museum records, discovery of unlawfully confiscated works of art, response to claims against museums, incoming loans and database recommendations.

5 See *Chicago Tribune* 12 February 1999, *op.cit.*, note 2.

6 See 'Paris museum has proof cubist painting looted by Nazis from Jewish collector', www.museum-security.org/reports/001999.html#5 (17 February 1999).

7 See, e.g., WWII/Holocaust (Stolen Art Resources), www.museum-security.org/reports/002199.html#2 (17 February 1999).

8 823 *United Nations Treaty Series*, reprinted in 10 *International Legal Materials* 289 (1971). The Convention on Cultural Property Implementation Act of 1983, Pub. L. No. 97–446, 96 Stat. 2350, codified at 19 U.S.C. §2601 *et seq.* (1984).

9 In Geri J. Yonover, 'Anti-Semitism and Holocaust Denial in the Academy: A Tort Remedy', 101 *Dickinson Law Review* 71 (1996), I allude to some of these events in discussing the ironic juxtaposition of increased Holocaust awareness with increased Holocaust denial within and without the academic setting.

10 *Goodman v. Searle*, originally filed in New York, No. 96–CIV–5310 C. (S.D.N.Y. filed 17 July 1996), was transferred by consent to the federal district court in Illinois (No. 96–C–6459 (N.D. Ill.)).

11 See Lee Rosenbaum, 'Nazi loot claims: art with a history', *Wall Street Journal*, 14 January 1999, at A18.

12 The parties finally achieved an out-of-court settlement and on 11 June 1999 the Art Institute of Chicago displayed the Degas in Gallery 202A, near its Degas collection: see Della de Lafuente, 'Degas to be shown here as part of settlement', *Chicago Sun-Times*, 11 June 1999, at 22. The credit line for the Degas indicates that it was purchased from the collection of Fritz and Louise Gutmann and a gift of Daniel C. Searle (telephone interview with Dorothy Pesch, Secretary, Museum Registration, Art Institute of Chicago, 31 August 1999).

13 Ms. Rosenbaum, a contributing editor of the magazine *Art in America*, attributed this phrase to the head of a major Jewish organization. *See also* Margaret M. Mastrobernardino, 'The Last Prisoners of World War II', 9 *Pace International Law Review* 315 (1997).

14 See ABC News, 'Hunt for a looted legacy: the profits of plunder – art ownership under review', www.museum-security.org/wwz/diversen.html (7 July 1999).

15 Several treatises explain the difference between real and personal property, which are often accorded different treatment for such disparate purposes as interstate succession and choice of applicable law. See e.g., *Restatement (Third) of Property* §2.1 (1998 Main Volume) (U.S.); *Restatement (Second) of*

Conflict of Laws §278 (1971) (U.S.) ('the validity of a trust of an interest in land is determined by the law that would be applied by courts of the situs'); *Restatement (Second) of Conflict of Laws* §244 (1971) (U.S.) (the local law of the state with 'the most significant relationship to the parties, the chattel and the conveyance' determines 'the validity and effect of an interest in a chattel as between the parties to the conveyance').

16　The European concept of an author's personal, moral rights ('*droit moral*') of integrity and attribution has been adopted in the United States, see 17 U.S.C. §106A (1999), and in other countries as well. See generally, Geri J. Yonover, 'The "Dissing" of Da Vinci: The Imaginary Case of Leonardo v. Duchamp: Moral Rights, Parody, and Fair Use', 29 *Valparaiso University. Law Review* 935 (1995); Roberta Rosenthal Kwall, 'Copyright and the Moral Right: Is an American Marriage Possible', 38 *Vanderbilt Law Review* 1 (1985).

17　John Ruskin, *The States of Venice* (New York: Peter Fenelon Collier & Son, 1900), 180.

18　One commentator notes that '[s]tatutes of limitations are likely the biggest single cause of forum-shopping under present [United States] law'. See Michael H. Gottesman, 'Draining the Dismal Swamp: The Case for Federal Choice of Law Statutes', 80 *Georgetown Law Journal*, 1, 48 (1991).

19　William Prosser, 'Interstate Publication', 51 *Michigan Law Review*, 959, 971 (1953). Cf. William L. Reynolds, 'Legal Process and Choice of Law', 56 *Maryland Law Review*, 1371 & n. 2 (1997) (noting that '[c]hoice of Law today, both the theory and the practice of it, is universally said to be a disaster'.)

20　Thousands of conflict of laws cases indicate that a 'simple' conflicts case rarely presents itself. Even the relatively straightforward guest statute cases which were at one point the darling of conflict of laws scholars, see Friedrich K. Juenger, 'American Conflicts Scholarship and the New Law Merchant', 28 *Vanderbilt Journal of Transnational Law*, 487, 500 & n.78 (1995), were often unpredictable and tortuous in their reasoning as the New York experience demonstrates. See, e.g., *Neumeier v. Kuehner*, 286 N.E. 2d 454 (New York, 1972); *Tooker v. Lopez*, 249, N.E.2d 394 (New York, 1969); *Dym v. Gordon*, 209 N.E.2d 792 (New York, 1965); *Babcock v. Jackson*, 191 N.E.2d 279 (New York, 1963). See generally Friedrich K. Juenger, 'Babcock v. Jackson Revisited: Judge Fuld's Contribution to American Conflicts Law', 56 *Albany Law Review*, 727, 739 (1993). See also Geri J. Yonover, 'The Golden Anniversary of the Choice of Law Revolution: Indiana Fired the First Shot', 29 *Indiana Law Review*, 1201, 1202 n.8 (1996) (noting that one observer of New York's conflict of laws history describes its courts as 'hopp[ing] frenetically from one theory to another like an overheated Mexican jumping bean'.)

　　The Due Process clause of the Fourteenth Amendment, U.S. Constitution amend. XIV, §1 and the Full Faith and Credit clause, U.S. Constitution art. 4, §1, impose constitutional restraints on a court's ability to choose freely among the conflicting laws of two or more jurisdictions. See *Phillips Petroleum Co. v. Shutts*, 472 U.S. 797 (1985); *Allstate Insurance Co. v. Hague*, 449 U.S. 302 (1981). '[T]o ensure that the choice of law is neither arbitrary nor fundamentally unfair [a state must have a] significant contact or significant aggregation of contacts, creating state interests, with the parties and the occurrence or transaction' (*Allstate*, 472 U.S. at 308).

21　Legislative jurisdiction, the ability of a court to apply its law, is to be distinguished from judicial jurisdiction. The latter speaks to the ability of a court to entertain the case in the first instance. Legislative jurisdiction has been described as focusing on sovereignty interests, whereas judicial jurisdiction emphasizes fairness. See John R. Leathers, 62 *Washington Law Review*, 631, 668 (1987). The doctrine is also somewhat related to the court's decision about the extraterritorial reach of United States laws, such as antitrust. See, e.g., *Hartford Insurance Co. v. California*, 509 U.S. 764 (1993). As Justice Harlan noted in *Sabbatino*, 376 U.S. at 438, '[t]he act of state doctrine ... although it shares with [sovereign] immunity a respect for sovereign states, concerns the limits for determining the validity of an otherwise applicable rule of law'. *See also* Michael Gruson, 'The Act of State Doctrine in Contract Cases as a Conflict-of- Laws Rule', 703 *PLI/Comm* 225 (October 1994). See, e.g., *Banco Nacional de Cuba v. Sabbatino*, 376 U.S. 398 (1964).

22　See John Henry Merryman and Albert E. Elsen, *Law, Ethics and the Visual Arts* 26 (Philadelphia: University of Pennsylvania Press 2nd edn., 1987).

23　In 1940, Hitler named Alfred Rosenberg as head of the Centre for National Socialist Ideological and Educational Research which soon developed into a project for the seizure of cultural property. The magnitude of the project is indicated by the following: from March 1941 until July 1944 over 4,000 cases of art works were brought into Nazi Germany. See *Merryman, supra* note 22 at 22.

In Munich, 1937, Hitler had exhibited a collection of art, taken from museums throughout Germany, which he intended to serve as examples of decadence, waste, low morals and un-art. After the exhibition, much of this art was purchased for a song or by sham transactions by the Nazi high command including Goering, who was an art collector for some time. The 'degenerate art' included paintings by Cezanne, Munch, Van Gogh, Klee and Kandinsky. See Lynn H. Nicholas, *The Rape of Europa*, pp.18–25.

24 Nicholas, *The Rape of Europa*, p.444.

25 *Menzel v. List*, 267 N.Y.S. 2d 804 (1966). The suit based on replevin (return of goods taken unlawfully) was successful.

26 Convention (IV) Respecting the Law and Customs of War on Land, 36 Stat. 2277 (1907). The Convention's purpose was to prevent looting and destruction during war.

27 *Menzel*, 267 N.Y.S. 2d at 813–15.

28 Compare the contrary result reached by another New York court in *Stroganoff-Scherbatoff v. Weldon*, 420 F. Supp. 18 (S.D.N.Y. 1976), where the court employed the Act of State Doctrine to works of art nationalized by the Soviet Union in the 1920s. The doctrine precluded the descendant of the original owner from recovering the art works.

Note that the Act of State Doctrine, if found applicable, would require courts to enforce foreign laws (i.e. upholding the validity of Nazi confiscation of art) even if those laws 'are repugnant to forum policy' (Roger C. Cramton, David P. Currie, Herma Hill Kay and Larry Kramer, *Conflict of Laws, Cases-Comments-Questions*) 705 (St. Paul, Minnesota: West Publishing, 5th edn., 1993). Probably the lowest point reached in the (non) use of forum public policy to avoid repugnant but otherwise applicable non-forum law is the 1938 decision of the New York Court of Appeals in *Holzer v. Deutsche Reichsbahn-Gesellschaft*, 14 N.E.2d 798 (NY, 1938) (*per curiam*). In *Holzer*, a Jewish German national claimed that in 1933 defendant discharged him solely because he was a Jew and sought damages for breach of contract. Sadly, the court upheld the company's defence that it did not breach, but rather was forced by operation of German non-Aryan laws to discharge Holzer.

29 See, e.g., *Kunstsammlungen zu Weimar v. Elicofon*, 678 F.2d 1150, 1161 (2d Cir. 1982); Uniform Commercial Code §§ 1–201 (32), (33), 2–403(1)(1998).

30 Robin Morris Collin, 'The Law and Stolen Art, Artifacts and Antiquities', 36 *Howard Law Journal* 17 (1993).

31 Alexandre A. Montagu, 'Recent Cases on the Recovery of Stolen Art: The Tug of War Between Owners and Purchasers Continues', 18 *Columbia–VLA Journal of Law & Arts* 75, 79 n.20 (1993).

32 536 F. Supp. 829 (E.D.N.Y. 1981), *aff'd*, 678 F.2d 1150 (2d Cir. 1982).

33 *Elicofon*, 678 F.2d at 1160, 1164.

34 The court also barred under the Act of State Doctrine the cross-claim of a descendant of the original owner seeking return of the painting or payment. *Elicofon*, 678 F.2d at 1160.

35 See *Elifocon*, 536 F. Supp. 829 (E.D.N.Y. 1981), *aff'd*, 678 F.2d 1150 (2d Cir. 1982).

36 No. 96-CIV-530 (S.D.N.Y. filed 17 July 1996). After transfer to Illinois: No. 96-C-6359. Many of the facts are reported in Amy J. Blumberg, '*Goodman v. Searle*: How ownership rights should be decided' (1997; unpublished manuscript on file with the present author), p.7 & n.35.

37 28 U.S.C. § 1404(a) (West 1994).

38 *Goldlawr v. Heiman*, 269 U.S. 463 (1962).

39 See *Ferens v. John Deere Co.*, 494 U.S. 516 (1990) (plaintiff sought 1404(a) transfer); *Van Dusen v. Barrack*, 376 U.S. 612 (1964) (defendant sought 1404(a) transfer).

40 See 15 Charles Alan Wright, Arthur R. Miller and Edward H. Cooper, *Federal Practice & Procedure Jurisdiction* ch. 8 §3827 (Minnesota: West Publishing, 2nd ed, 1986); 19 'Wright, Miller and Cooper', *Federal Practice & Procedure Jurisdiction* ch. 14, § 4506 (Minnesota: West Publishing, 2nd ed., 1996).

41 See *Solomon R. Guggenheim Foundation v. Lubell*, 569 N.E. 2d 426, 430–31 (NY 1991); cf. *Mucha v. King*, 792 F.2d 602 (7th Cir. 1986) (applying Illinois law).

42 *Elicofon*, 536 F. Supp. at 848.

43 See *Guggenheim*, 569 N.E. 2d 426, 431 (NY 1991).

44 See, e.g., *O'Keefe v. Snyder*, 416 A. 2d 862, 875 (New Jersey 1980).

45 *ibid*. at 874.

46 See *Autocephalous Greek Orthodox Church of Cyprus v. Goldberg and Feldman Fine Arts, Inc.*, 917 F.3d
878 (7th Cir., 1990) (applying Indiana law).

47 See California Civil Procedure Code § 338(c) (West Supp., 1994); Ashton Hawkins, Richard A.
Rothman and David B. Goldstein, 'A Tale of Two Innocents: Creating an Equitable Balance Between
the Rights of Former Owners and Good Faith Purchasers', 64 *Fordham Law Review* 49, 79 & n.68
(1995). See also: *Mucha v. King*, 792 F.2d 602, 611–12 (7th Cir., 1986) (applying Indiana law); *Ohio
Review Code Ann.* §2305.09 (Page 1991) (amended 1994); *O'Keefe*, 416 A.2d 862; *In re 1973 John
Deere Tractor*, 816 P.2d 1126, 1132–33 (Oklahoma 1991).

See generally Patty Gerstenblith, 'The Adverse Possession of Personal Property', 37 *Buffalo Law
Review* 119 (1989). Prof. Gerstenblith's other contributions to the field include Patty Gerstenblith,
'Cultural Property and World War II: Some Implications for American Museums, A Legal Back-
ground', SC 40 *ALI-ABA* 17 (26 March 1998). Two authors have proposed suspending statutes of
limitation for victims of art theft. See Stephanie Cuba, Note, 'Stop the Clock: The Case to Suspend
the Statute of Limitations on Claims for Nazi-looted Art', 17 *Cardozo Arts & Entertainment Law
Journal*, 447 (1999); Steven A. Bibas, Note, 'The Case Against Statutes of Limitations for Stolen
Art', 103 *Yale Law Journal*, 2437 (1994).

48 See *DeWeerth v. Baldinger*, 836 F2d 103, 111–12 (2d Cir. 1987), *cert. denied*, 486 U.S. 1056 (1988).

49 See *Guggenheim*, 569 N.E.2d 426.

50 Under the *Erie* doctrine, a federal court asserting diversity jurisdiction must apply the substantive law
of the forum state to questions of a substantive character, *Erie R.R. Co. v. Tompkins*, 304 U.S. 64, 78–
80 (1938), as well as the forum state's conflicts of law methods. See *Klaxon Co. v. Stentor Elec. Mfg.
Co.*, 313 U.S. 487 (1941).

51 Brainerd Currie, the father of interest analysis, was one of the first to reject the rigid rules of the 1934
First Restatement of Conflicts of Laws. See Brainerd Currie, 'Married Women's Contracts: A Study in
Conflict-of-Laws Method', 25 *University of Chicago Law Review*, 227 (1958). Currie employed a pure
policy analysis of conflicting laws to determine if the case posed a true or false conflict. Although his
approach has been adopted by very few states, his influence has been enormous in that most modern
courts examine the purpose underlying the conflicting laws to ascertain the interest the respective
jurisdictions might have in having their law applied. See, e.g., *Bryant v. Silverman*, 703 P.2d 1190
(Arizona, 1985); *Schultz v. Boy Scouts of America*, Inc. 480 N.E.2d 679 (New York, 1985); *Bernhard v.
Harrah's Club*, 546 P.2d 719 (California, 1976); *Erwin v. Thomas*, 506 P.2d 494 (Oregon, 1973).

Even courts that adhere arguably to the Second Restatement of Conflict of Laws (1971) (most
significant relationship approach), the most widely adopted choice of law method, see Geri J. Yonover,
'The Golden Anniversary of the Choice of Law Revolution: Indiana Fired the First Shot', 29 *Indiana
Law Review*, 1201, 1211 & n. 91 (1996), apply its multifactor final check list (section 6) 'in a way
indistinguishable from straightforward interest analysis'. See *Cramton, supra* note 28 at 151.

52 The so-called 'Neumeier' rules are set out in *Neumeier v. Kuehner*, 286 N.E.2d 454 (NY 1972), and
employ essentially a territorialist view which focuses on the place of domicile, conduct and, by
default, place of injury.

53 See *Cooney v. Osgood Mach., Inc.*, 612 N.E.2d 277 (NY 1993). *Lex locus*, the focus on the law of the
place of injury (for torts) or the place of contracting or performance (for contract disputes) is, for all
intents, a single factor inquiry. See *Restatement of Conflict of Laws* (1934) (The First Conflict of Laws
Restatement).

54 *Restatement (Second) of Conflict of Laws* (1971). The Second Restatement claims the most adherents
among the states and is the most widely used alternative to the First Restatement. This is perhaps
due to its multifactor approach which gives a judge increased flexibility in choosing the applicable
law.

55 See *id*. at §145.

56 See, e.g., Yonover, *The Golden Anniversary, supra* note 51 at 1210–1212 & Appendix (describing
the inconsistent results reached by Indiana courts after adoption of a version of the Second Restatement).

57 This and the following facts are discussed in *60 Minutes Profile: The Search* (CBS television broadcast, 19 January 1997). On 26 July 1998 CBS ran another *60 Minutes* programme on the *Goodman v. Searle* dispute.

58 The appraisals' average is $437,500, far less than the $850,000 Searle paid for the Degas in 1987. Lee Rosenbaum, 'Nazi Loot Claims: Art With a History', *Wall Street Journal of Europe*, 29 January 1999, at 14. The Goodmans placed an ad in the Jewish *Forward* requesting financial contributions to pursue their claim for the recovery of the Degas. See Kevin M. Williams, 'Plaintiffs Place Ad in Fight for Degas', *Chicago Sun-Times*, 28 February 1998 at 44.

59 1970 UNESCO Convention on the *Means of Prohibiting and Preventing the Illicit Import, Export and Transfer of Ownership of Cultural Property*, (14 November 1970), 823 U.N.T.S. § 231, 10 I.L.M. 289 (1971). The United States ratified this convention in 1983. Pub. L. No.97–446, 96 Stat.2352 (codified at 19 U.S.C. § 2602 (1999)).

60 Unidroit Convention on the *International Return of Stolen or Illegally Exported Cultural Objects*, (24 June 1995), 34 I.L.M. 1322–1332.

61 See Brian Bengs, 'Dead on Arrival? A Comparison of the Unidroit Convention of Stolen or Illegally Exported Cultural Objects and U.S. Property Law', 6 *Transnational & Contemporary Probs.* 503, 530–32 (1996).

62 Pub. L. No.105–186, 112 Stat. 611 (codified at 22 U.S.C. § 1621 (1998)).

63 See Beverly Schreiber Jacoby, 'The Nazi Legacy in the Art World, Effect on Value is One of Many Issues', 219 *New York Law Journal*, at S2, col.3 (30 March 1998).

64 Holocaust Assets Commission Act of 1998, *supra* note 62 at §§(2a)–(b).

65 *ibid*, at §§9, 3(a)(1), 3(a)(2)(G), 3(a)(1), 3(b), 3(d)(1). Under the U.S. Holocaust Assets Commission Extension Act of 1999, the date may be extended to December 2000. See 145 Cong. Rec., S10375–01 (5 August 1999) (statement of Sen. Smith).

66 Reps. Jim Leach and Ben Gilman and Senator D'Amato proposed a bill that would provide funding for Jewish organizations that assist persons in tracing Nazi loot. See 'Holocaust Victims Redress Act', 143 Cong. Rec. H10943–01 (13 November 1997) (statement of Rep. Leach); 144 Cong. Rec. S63–01 (27 Jan. 1998) (statement of Sen. D'Amato). The bill would authorize a United States contribution of up to $25 million to organizations which serve survivors of the Holocaust residing in this country as well as a donation of an additional $5 million to the United States Holocaust Museum to assist in the restitution of assets looted or extorted from Holocaust victims. 143 Cong. Rec. H10943–01.

The Senate is also considering the Holocaust Era Assets Tax Exclusion Act amendment to the Taxpayer Relief Act of 1999. The Tax Exclusion bill would exempt from income tax imposition 'any settlement payments, received by Holocaust survivors of their families resulting from a Holocaust claim'. See 145 *Cong. Rec.* S10069–02 (3 August 1999) (statement by Sen. Abraham).

67 There remain questions about what to do with other Nazi-looted art, once its whereabouts are discovered, when the rightful owner is dead and no heirs can be found. In the similar issue of restitution by Swiss banks in Holocaust-related claims, one author suggests that unclaimed, but proven damages be used to help all 'whose lives have been shattered by genocide and ethnic slaughter', not only Jewish people and Jewish causes. This would be an act, he says, 'of tremendous moral beauty'. Jeff Jacoby, 'Spoils of War Swiss Banks Paid Up; Now, What About the Money?', *Tulsa World* (13 December 1998), at 2.

68 See Tracey Tully, 'Lawyer: Don't hang up paintings in court fight', *New York Daily News*, 25 August 1999, at 14.

69 In re Application to Quash Grand Jury Subpoena Duces Tecum, 688 N.Y.S. 2d 3 (NY App. Div., 1999).

70 719 N.E.2d 897 (N.Y. 1999).

71 See, e.g., *Menzel v. List*, 267 N.Y.S.2d 804 (New York, 1966). In a more recent case, *Rosenberg v. Seattle Art Museum*, 42 F. Supp. 2d 1029 (W.D. Washington, 1999), heirs of an art dealer who had owned *L'Odalisque* by Matisse sued the museum for its return. The museum had acquired the painting through a bequest. The plaintiffs claimed that the Matisse rightfully belonged to their father (and father-in-law) and was looted by the Nazis; thus the museum did not have good title to the work. On 14 June 1999, the Museum agreed to return the painting to the heirs in a decision unanimously

approved by the Museum's board. Regina Hackett, 'Seattle's Matisse will go back to owners', *Seattle Post-Intelligencer* 15 June 1999, at A1.

72 In Fall 1988, the Whittier Law Review published a symposium, 'Nazi Gold and Other Assets of the Holocaust: The Search for Justice', 20 *Whittier Law Review*, 3 (1998). Nick Goodman, one of the plaintiffs in the *Goodman v. Searle* case, tells his family's story in Hector Feliciano, Owen Pell and Nick Goodman, 'Nazi-Stolen Art', 20 *Whittier Law Review*, 67, 86–90 (1998). In December 1998, Yeshiva University, New York published a symposium, 'The Holocaust, Moral and Legal Issues Resolved', 20 *Cardozo Law Review*, 415 (1998). In October 1999, DePaul College of Law, DePaul-LCA Journal of Art Entertainment Law, presented a symposium, *Theft of Art During World War II: Its Legal and Ethical Consequences.*

73 For example, New York City, California and New Jersey have enacted sanction laws against Swiss banks that have held assets stolen from Holocaust victims by Nazi Germany. See 144 Cong. Rec. H7262-02, H7279 (5 August 1998), 1998 WL 441501 (Cong. Rec.).

74 Anne Michaels, *Fugitive Pieces* (New York: Knopf, 1997), quoted in W.S. Di Piero, 'Fossil Remains', *New York Times Book Review*, 20 April 1997, at 10.